PERRINE'S

*L*ITERATURE

Structure, Sound, and Sense

SEVENTH EDITION

PERRINE'S
$\mathscr{L}$ITERATURE
Structure, Sound, and Sense

THOMAS R. ARP
Southern Methodist University

HARCOURT BRACE COLLEGE PUBLISHERS

Fort Worth   Philadelphia   San Diego   New York   Orlando   Austin   San Antonio
Toronto   Montreal   London   Sydney   Tokyo

Publisher	Christopher P. Klein
Executive Editor	Michael Rosenberg
Acquisitions Editor	John Meyers
Product Manager	Ilse Wolfe West
Senior Project Editor	Charles J. Dierker
Production Manager	Serena Barnett Manning
Art Director	Carol Kincaid

ISBN: 0-03-064421-6

Library of Congress Catalog Card Number: 97-72035

Copyright © 1998, 1993, 1988, 1987, 1983, 1982, 1978, 1974, 1973, 1970, 1969, 1966, 1963, 1959, 1956 by Harcourt Brace & Company
Copyright renewed 1991, 1987, 1984 by Laurence Perrine

Some material in this work was previously published in SOUND AND SENSE: AN INTRODUCTION TO POETRY, Ninth Edition, copyright © 1997, 1992, 1987, 1977, 1973, 1969, 1963, 1956 by Harcourt Brace & Company, copyright renewed 1991, 1984, by Laurence Perrine and STORY AND STRUCTURE, Ninth Edition, copyright © 1998, 1993, 1988, 1983, 1978, 1974, 1970, 1966, 1959 by Harcourt Brace & Company, copyright renewed 1994, 1987 by Laurence Perrine. All rights reserved.

Address for Editorial Correspondence: Harcourt Brace College Publishers, 301 Commerce Street, Suite 3700, Fort Worth, TX 76102.

Address for Orders: Harcourt Brace & Company, 6277 Sea Harbor Drive, Orlando, FL 32887-6777. 1-800-782-4479.

Website address: http://www.hbcollege.com

Harcourt Brace College Publishers may provide complimentary instructional aids and supplements or supplement packages to those adopters qualified under our adoption policy. Please contact your sales representative for more information. If as an adopter or potential user you receive supplements you do not need, please return them to your sales representative or send them to: Attn: Returns Department, Troy Warehouse, 465 South Lincoln Drive, Troy, MO 63379.

Copyright acknowledgments appear on page 1497 and constitute a continuation of this page.

Printed in the United States of America

9   0   1   2   3   4   5   6   071   10   9   8   7   6

Preface

In the previous six editions of this book, the preface has contained a brief introduction to the plan of the book and some expressions of gratitude. The seventh edition requires an expanded and more personal preface.

Most of the loyal users of this book and its predecessors will know that Laurence Perrine died in April 1995 after a protracted battle with Parkinson's disease. His death was a sad occasion for me, for his family, and I am sure for many who since 1970 have regarded *Literature: Structure, Sound, and Sense* with high respect and esteem.

In 1977, a few years after I arrived at Southern Methodist University, I received a brief note from Laurence Perrine asking me to name a convenient day to join him for lunch off campus. I naturally panicked: What had I done that my senior colleague needed to move to neutral turf to counsel or chide me? We met at a cafeteria, filled our trays, and sat down, and instead of detailing my manifold shortcomings, Larry asked me if I would join him in revising his series of textbooks. My delight was even greater than my relief, and I accepted on the spot. From that point we worked together in producing the fourth and fifth editions of *Literature,* and I graduated from being "with the assistance of" to coauthor for the sixth, with chief responsibility for selecting stories and plays and revising the text.

Because of his health, Larry was not able to be as fully involved in the two latest revisions of the book, although as late as February 1995 he was still making suggestions that he thought were worth considering for the new edition. Over the years that we worked together, he expressed his confidence in my knowing how the book works, and how individual selections function in the book. I hope that his confidence will be justified by the decisions I have made in this edition.

Literature: Structure, Sound, and Sense is designed for the student who is beginning a serious study of imaginative literature. It provides a comprehensive introduction to the principal forms of fiction, poetry, and drama. Each section begins with a simple discussion of the elements of the form and is illustrated, throughout, by carefully selected stories, poems, or plays. Each section also includes a compact anthology of additional selections for further reading. In this book we seek to give the student a sufficient grasp of the nature and variety of literary works, some reasonable means for reading them with appreciative understanding, and some basic principles for making literary judgments. Our objective is to help the student understand, enjoy, and prefer good works of literature.

The seventh edition of *Literature* maintains the balance between "classic" and contemporary writers, and continues to offer a wide sampling of vicarious experiences through the work of women as well as men, ethnic minorities as well as other American and European authors. One innovation in the fiction section is the inclusion of a group of three novellas, where students may exercise their knowledge and skill on longer and more complex fictional forms. In the poetry section, Chapter 12 on "Rhythm and Meter" has been extensively revised to take into account the increasing interest in nonmetrical verse. (And I have felt free to do what Larry never did—I have included three examples of his own limericks, a verse form of which he was a master.) In the drama section, at the request of readers, I have restored Molière's *The Misanthrope* and have added six contemporary playwrights, all of them represented by one-act plays. This addition affords both the opportunity to sample more fully the kinds of drama being written in our time, and to broaden the representation of women and ethnic minorities in the book.

A book of such enduring usefulness grows through time and advice, and the debts to the helpful attention of others are now innumerable. With Larry, I wish to thank especially his wife, Catherine. I have also been given valued assistance by Ann Hayes of Carnegie Mellon University and Robert Wallace of Case Western Reserve University, and by my two editors at Harcourt Brace, Helen Triller and John Meyers. But as the sole signatory, I must of course reserve most of my gratitude for Laurence Perrine.

T. R. A.

Professional Acknowledgments

The following instructors have offered helpful reactions and suggestions for this seventh edition of *Literature: Structure, Sound, and Sense.*

Alice Adams
Glendale Community College

Donald W. Adams
Chipola Junior College

Frank J. Albert
Community College of Beaver County

B. J. Alexander
Tarleton State University

Carolyn Allison
Essex Community College (Baltimore County Community Colleges)

Warren Almand
Chipola Junior College

Lillian H. Andon-Milligan
North Idaho College

Martha Atkins
Dyersburg State Community College

Diane S. Baird
Palm Beach Community College, Central

Donna Bauerly
Loras College

Frank Beesley
Dalton College

Louise D. Bentley
Union University

Don Blankenship
West Valley College

Paul Bodmer
Bismarck State College

Richard R. Bollenbacher
Edison State Community College

Arnold J. Bradford
Northern Virginia Community College, Manassas

Steve Brahlek
Palm Beach Community College, Central

Elaine Brookshire
Northeast Alabama State Community College

Richard G. Brown
Ball State University

Annie L. Burns
Meridian Community College

Robert A. Burns
Southern Missouri State University

Susan McCann Butler
Thomas Nelson Community College

Randall Calhoun
Ball State University

Catherine Calloway
Arkansas State University, Jonesboro

Norman E. Carlson
Western Michigan University

Sophie Cashdollar
Dyersburg State Community College

Susan Catalano
Samford University, Birmingham

Nathan Anthony Cervo
Franklin Pierce College

Jan M. Chalupnik
Moorehead State University

Betty Cochran
Beaufort County Community College

Michael Colonnese
Methodist College, Fayetteville

Charlotte C. Crittenden
Georgia Southern University

Charles R. Croghan, Jr.
Indian River Community College

Brenda Crowe
Gadsden State Community College

Sharon Cupples
Stanly Community College

Michael J. Daly
Glendale Community College

Elizabeth H. Davis
Southern Arkansas University, Magnolia

Wayne G. Deahl
Eastern Wyoming College

Margaret DeHart
Trinity Valley Community College

Charles DeMatteo
Sage Junior College of Albany

Marvin Diogenes
University of Arizona

David C. Downing
Elizabethtown College

Richard Downing
Pasco-Hernando Community College

Kirby L. Duncan
Stephen F. Austin State University

Robert Dunkle
Chipola Junior College

John Early
Moorehead State University

Will Farrell
Mt. San Jacinto College

Marilyn Fontane
St. Louis College of Pharmacy

Barbara J. Frieling
Bainbridge College

Dick Frontain
Pima Community College, Downtown

Geneva Frost
University of Maine, Machias

Kevin J. Gardner
Mount Vernon Nazarene College

C. Herbert Gilliland
U. S. Naval Academy

Rachel Hadas
Rutgers University, Newark

W. M. Hagen
Oklahoma Baptist University

John D. Hain
Tennessee Temple University

John K. Hanes
Duquesne University

Carol Hansen
City College of San Francisco

Ruth M. Harrison
Arkansas Tech University

Anne M. Haselkorn
New York City Technical College,
CUNY

Wayne E. Haskin
North Carolina State University

Donald Heidt
College of the Canyons

Jeff Henderson
University of Central Arkansas

Kathryn Henkins
Mt. San Antonio College

Timothy K. Hobert, Sr.
San Joaquin Delta College

Jean Hodgin
North Shore Community College

Roderick Hofer
Indian River Community College

James Hoggard
Midwestern State University

Robert M. Hogge
Weber State University

Wayne P. Hubert
Chaffey Community College

Pamela Hudson
Hawaii Community College

John B. Humma
Georgia Southern University

O. Glade Hunsaker
Brigham Young University

Jodi Wood Jewell
Utah Valley State College

Carole Johnson
Shelton State Community College

Mellania Johnson
Wallace State Community College

Ruby T. Johnson
Wallace State Community College

James L. Jolly, Jr.
Shelton State Community College

Joyce Jolly
Shelton State Community College

Mary Jordan
Illinois Central College, East Peoria

Harvey Kassebaum
Cuyahoga Community College,
Western Campus

David Kelly
Dyersburg State Community College

George M. Kelly
Hinds Community College

Dolores Keranen
University of Illinois, Chicago

Charlotte H. Kern
Northwestern Oklahoma State
University

Sue Kimball
Methodist College

Patricia C. Knight
Amarillo College

Albert E. Krahn
Milwaukee Area Technical College

William Lawlor
University of Wisconsin, Stevens Point

William G. Leftwich III
U.S. Naval Academy

Kenneth P. Leisch
Danville Area Community College

Roy Lynn Lewis
Brazosport College

John Lightfoot
Brazosport College

Gary W. Longrie
Milwaukee Area Technical College

Vincent Lopresti
University of Wisconsin, Oshkosh

Gerald F. Luboff
County College of Morris

Eleanor Lyons
Indiana University, South Bend

Robert L. McBroom
Midwestern State University

Kelly J. McCaffrey
Palm Beach Community College

Adelio F. Maccentelli
Essex Community College

Carole McClanahan
Danville Community College

Alexander J. Maxwell
Shoreline Community College

Thomas Carl Merriman
University of Texas–Pan American

Terry Miller
Indian River Community College

Al Mitchell
Meridian Community College

Virginia Ramey Mollenkott
William Paterson College

Nancy Newell Moore
University of Wisconsin, Stevens Point

Phil Murdock
Ricks College

Caroline C. Nakamura
Kapiolani Community College

Vivian B. Naylor
Meridian Community College

Elizabeth Nelson
St. Peter's College

John D. Nesbitt
Eastern Wyoming College

Jane Neuburger
Cazenovia College

Alice O'Melia
Essex Community College

Sherry Balthrop Organ
Arkansas State University, Beebe

David M. Packard
John A. Logan College

John S. Pappas
San Joaquin Delta College

Kathleen Parks
Antelope Valley College

Art Petersen
University of Alaska Southeast

Daniel Peterson
Southern University, Baton Rouge

Lynn Pfannkuche
Lincoln Land Community College

Helmuth C. Poggemiller
Liberty University

Gloria Dibble Pond
Naugatuck Valley Community
Technical College

Neil B. Porterfield
San Joaquin Delta Community College

Norman Prinsky
Augusta College

Barbara Read
Kilgore College

Carol Robbins
Meridian Community College

Mary Roberti
Monroe County Community College

Horace S. Rockwood III
California University of Pennsylvania

Gordon K. W. Roeder
North Dakota State University,
Bottineau

Mary Rosa
University of St. Thomas

Mardee M. Rose
University of Wisconsin, Stevens Point

Daniel W. Ross
Columbus College

Paula J. Ross
Gadsden State Community College

Alan Sandy
Sonoma State University

Karen Saupe
Calvin College

J. R. Scrutchins
Oklahoma Baptist University

Philip Duhan Segal
Queensborough Community College,
CUNY

Linda R. Selman
Southern Arkansas University

Sharon Shapiro
Naugatuck Valley Community
Technical College

Bill Shaw
Brazosport College

Kathleen A. Sherfick
Albion College

Craig L. Shurtleff
Illinois Central College

Lynne M. Shuster
Erie Community College,
North Campus

Keith Slocum
Montclair State University

Roxanne Solomon
Palm Beach Community College

Diane Vanner Steinberg
University of St. Thomas

William Stephenson
Northland College

William Studebaker
College of Southern Idaho

Lou Suarez
Lorain County Community College

Mitchell E. Summerlin
John C. Calhoun Community College

S. Gregory Tiernan
Mission College, Santa Clara

Edwina Trentham
Asnuntuck Community Technical
College

Guy Turcotte
Mount Wachusett Community College

Ann Tyler
Crowley High School

Mikel Vause
Weber State University

Kathryn A. Walterscheid
St. Louis College of Pharmacy

Gene Washington
Utah State University

Cathy Webb
Meridian Community College

Stan Webb
Bainbridge College

John P. Weber
Cypress College

Michael White
Odessa College

Glenn Whitesides
Newberry College

Richard Wilcher
Brazosport College

Marcella Willson
Wilmington College, New Castle

Cheryl Wotring
Middlesex Community College,
City Campus

CONTENTS

Stories for Further Reading   377

Three Novellas   449

POETRY   The Elements of Poetry   559

Chapter One   What Is Poetry?   561

Chapter Five   Figurative Language 1

Simile, Metaphor, Personification, Apostrophe, Metonymy   619

Chapter Six   Figurative Language 2

Symbol, Allegory   638

Chapter Seven   Figurative Language 3

Paradox, Overstatement, Understatement, Irony   659

Chapter Eight   Allusion   680

Chapter Nine   Meaning and Idea   691

Chapter Ten   Tone   704

Chapter Fifteen   Bad Poetry and Good   795

Chapter Sixteen   Good Poetry and Great   809

Poems for Further Reading   827

DRAMA   The Elements of Drama   907

Chapter One   The Nature of Drama   909

Chapter Two   Realistic and Nonrealistic Drama   955

Chapter Three   Tragedy and Comedy   1079

Plays for Further Reading   1277

SEVENTH EDITION

PERRINE'S
LITERATURE
Structure, Sound, and Sense

FICTION

The Elements of Fiction

Escape and Interpretation

The first question to ask about fiction is, Why bother to read it? With life as short as it is, with so many pressing demands on our time, with books of information, instruction, and discussion waiting to be read, why should we spend precious time on works of imagination? The eternal answers to this question are two: enjoyment and understanding.

Since the invention of language, people have taken pleasure in following and participating in the imaginary adventures and imaginary experiences of imaginary men and women. Whatever—without causing harm—serves to make life less tedious, to make the hours pass more quickly and pleasurably, surely needs nothing else to recommend it. Enjoyment—and ever more enjoyment—is the first aim and justification of reading fiction.

But, unless fiction gives something more than pleasure, it hardly justifies itself as a subject of serious study. Unless it expands or refines our minds or quickens our sense of life, its value is not appreciably greater than that of video games, bridge, or Ping-Pong. To have a compelling claim on our attention, it must yield not only enjoyment but also understanding.

The experience of humankind through the ages is that literature may furnish such understanding and do so effectively—that the depiction of imagined experiences can provide authentic insights. "The truest history," said Diderot of the novels of Samuel Richardson, "is full of falsehoods, and your romance is full of truths." But the bulk of fiction does not present such insights. Only some does. Initially, therefore, fiction may be classified into two broad categories: literature of escape and literature of interpretation.

Escape literature is that written purely for entertainment—to help us pass the time agreeably. **Interpretive literature** is written to broaden and deepen and sharpen our awareness of life. Escape literature takes us *away* from the real world: it enables us temporarily to forget our troubles. Interpretive literature takes us, through the imagination, deeper *into* the real world: it enables us to understand our troubles. Escape literature has pleasure as its only object. Interpretive literature has as its object pleasure *plus* understanding.

Having established a distinction, however, we must not exaggerate or oversimplify it. Escape and interpretation are not two great bins, into one or the other of which we can toss any given story. Rather, they are opposite ends of a scale—the two poles between which the world of fiction spins. The difference between them does not lie in the absence or presence of a "moral." The story that in all of its incidents and characters is shallow may have an unimpeachable moral, while the interpretive story may have no moral at all in any conventional sense. The difference does not lie in the absence or presence of "facts." The historical romance may be full of historical information and yet be pure escape in its depiction of human behavior. The difference does not lie in the presence or absence of an element of fantasy. The escape story may have a surface appearance of everyday reality, while the tale of seeming wildest fancy may press home on us some sudden truth. The difference between the two kinds of literature is deeper and more subtle than any of these distinctions. A story is interpretive to the extent that it truly illuminates some aspect of human life or behavior. An interpretive story presents an insight—large or small—into the nature and conditions of our existence. It gives us a keener awareness of what it is to be a human being in a universe sometimes friendly, sometimes hostile. It helps us to understand our world, our neighbors, and ourselves.

Perhaps we can clarify the difference by suggestion. Escape writers are like inventors who devise a contrivance for our diversion. When we push the button, lights flash, bells ring, and cardboard figures move jerkily across a painted horizon. Interpretive writers are discoverers: they take us out into the midst of life and say, "Look, here is the world!" Escape writers are full of tricks and surprises: they pull rabbits out of hats, saw beautiful women in two, and snatch brightly colored balls out of the air. Interpretive writers take us behind the scenes, where they show us the props and mirrors and seek to make clear the illusions. This is not to say that interpretive writers are merely reporters. More surely than escape writers they shape and give form to their materials. But they shape and form them always with the intent that we may see, feel, and understand them better, not for the primary purpose of furnishing entertainment.

Now just as there are two opposite extremes of fiction, there are also two poles between which different kinds of readers move. At one extreme are readers who find their demands gratified by escape fiction.

Even when they suppose that they are reading for interpretation, they expect that what they read will return them always some pleasant or exciting image of the world or some flattering image of themselves. Our early reading experiences are likely to be with stories such as that of Cinderella, whose fairy godmother transforms a pumpkin and some mice into a coach-and-four, whose slim foot is the only one that fits the crystal slipper, who rises superior to her cruel stepmother and taunting stepsisters to marry and "live happily ever after" with the charming prince, and who—never for a moment anything but sweet and virtuous—forgives her former tormenters.

Though most people move on from fairy tales into a seemingly more adult kind of reading, if they find themselves wholly satisfied with escape literature they may not have progressed as much as they suppose. The element of unreality in fiction does not lie primarily in magic wands and fairy godmothers but in a superficial treatment of life. The story of a poor but honest, hardworking shopgirl who is lifted from the painful conditions of her work and home life by a handsome young suitor from the upper classes may be as truly a Cinderella story as the one we read in childhood, though its setting is Memphis rather than a kingdom by the sea. Unfortunately, some readers never accept the challenges of interpretive literature and remain contented with escapist fairy tales, however transformed their settings and actions.

Those who prefer escape literature often make fixed demands of every story and feel frustrated and disappointed unless those demands are satisfied. Often they stick to one type of subject matter. Instead of being receptive to any story that puts human beings in human situations, they read only crime stories, or love stories, or science fiction. If they are willing to explore a wider range of experience, they may still unconsciously want every story to conform to certain formulated expectations. Among the most common of these expectations are (a) a sympathetic hero or heroine—one with whom the reader can identify and whose adventures and triumphs the reader can share; (b) a plot in which something exciting is always happening and in which there is a strong element of suspense; (c) a happy outcome that sends the reader away undisturbed and optimistic about the world; (d) a theme—if the story has a theme—that confirms the reader's already-held opinions of the world.

There is nothing intrinsically wrong with any of these characteristics as story elements. Significant fiction has been written having all of them. But if they become a rigid set of requirements and form the basis for deciding the value of a story, they drastically reduce the opportunity for expanding one's experience or broadening one's insights. They reduce one's demands on literature to a formula.*

Readers whose tastes run to escape literature want the essentially familiar combined with superficial novelty. Each story must have a slightly new setting or twist or "gimmick," though the fundamental features of the characters and situations remain pretty much the same. These readers evaluate a story not by its truth but by its twists, turns, and surprises, by its suspense or its love interest or its exciting action. They want stories to be mainly pleasant: evil, danger, and misery may occur, but not in such a way as to be taken seriously or be oppressive or permanent. Readers at this extreme end of the spectrum prefer reading that slips easily and smoothly through the mind, requiring little mental effort. Most of all, they want something that helps sustain their dreams, providing ready-made experiences in which they overcome their limitations, thwart their enemies, and win success or fame or the desired mate.

Readers who seek out interpretive literature, in contrast, take deeper pleasure in fiction that deals significantly with life than in fiction based on the formulations of escape. They do not totally dismiss escape literature, for escape literature need not be cheap or trite. It may be original, witty, absorbing, beautifully written, and artistically constructed. Some of literature's most enduring masterpieces are essentially escape—Barrie's *Peter Pan*, Stevenson's *Treasure Island*, even Dickens's *A Christmas Carol*, for instance. Such reading may be

---

*Fiction is sometimes roughly divided into **commercial** fiction—that written for wide popular consumption—and **quality** fiction—that written with a more serious artistic intent. In commercial fiction, the most general formula has a sympathetic hero faced with obstacles that he finally overcomes to achieve his goal. Most frequently, the hero's goal is to win the hand of the heroine; therefore, the most common subtype of the formula is boy meets girl, boy loses girl, boy wins girl. The hero is usually ruggedly handsome, and the heroine is beautiful or at least winsomely attractive. Even when the hero's primary objective is something other than love, commercial writers usually toss in a beautiful girl in order to supply their stories with some element of "love interest." The cheaper types of commercial fiction are generally characterized by a good deal of physical conflict—fistfights and gunfights—and by crude contrasts between good and evil. Although its more sophisticated forms use less obvious contrasts between good and evil and put less emphasis on physical conflict, they still cling to the happy ending. These forms are often concerned with marital problems that find a happy solution or with sentimental treatments of children or old people, in which the "innocent wisdom" of childhood or the "mellow wisdom" of old age is shown to be superior to the "practical wisdom" of the years between. In contrast, quality fiction does not rely upon tested formulas. It is more original—sometimes experimental—and seeks to be interpretive. All of the classifications made in this chapter are meant to be suggestive rather than rigid: absolute distinctions between commercial and quality fiction or between escape and interpretation cannot be made. Each blends into the other.

a refreshment for the mind and spirit. For a steady diet, however, discriminating readers prefer interpretive literature. They know, moreover, that an exclusive diet of escape, especially of the cruder sorts, has two dangers: (a) it may leave us with merely superficial attitudes toward life; (b) it may actually distort our view of reality and give us false concepts and false expectations.

Fiction, like food, is of different nutritive values. Some is rich in protein and vitamins; it builds bone and sinew. Some is highly agreeable to the taste but not permanently sustaining. Some may be adulterated and actually harmful to our health. Escape fiction is of the latter two sorts. The harmless kind bears frankly on the face of it what it is. It pretends to be nothing other than pleasant diversion and never asks to be taken seriously. The second kind masquerades under the appearance of interpretation. It pretends to give a faithful treatment of life as it is—perhaps even thinks that it does so—but through its shallowness it subtly falsifies life in every line. Such fiction, taken seriously and without corrective, may give us false notions of reality and lead us to expect from experience what experience does not provide.

When we enter a library and glance at the books on the shelves, we are at first likely to be bewildered by their variety and profusion. Thousands of books sit there, each making its claim on us, each seeming to cry out "Read me! Read me! Read me!" or "No, read *me!*" We have time to read only a fraction of them. If we are wise, we shall read as many as we can without neglecting the other claims of life. Our problem is how to get the most out of what time we have. To make the richest use of our portion, we need to know two things: (a) how to get the most out of any book we read and (b) how to choose the books that will best repay the time and attention we devote to them. The assumption of this book is that a proper selection will include both fiction and nonfiction—nonfiction as an indispensable fund of information and ideas, of one kind of knowledge of the world; fiction as an equally indispensable source of a different kind of knowledge, a knowledge of experience, felt in the emotions as well as apprehended by the mind. The aim of this book is to aid in the growth of understanding and judgment.

Richard Connell

The Most Dangerous Game

"Off there to the right—somewhere—is a large island," said Whitney. "It's rather a mystery—"

"What island is it?" Rainsford asked.

"The old charts call it 'Ship-Trap Island,'" Whitney replied. "A suggestive name, isn't it? Sailors have a curious dread of the place. I don't know why. Some superstition—"

"Can't see it," remarked Rainsford, trying to peer through the dank tropical night that was palpable as it pressed its thick warm blackness in upon the yacht.

5   "You've good eyes," said Whitney, with a laugh, "and I've seen you pick off a moose moving in the brown fall bush at four hundred yards, but even you can't see four miles or so through a moonless Caribbean night."

"Nor four yards," admitted Rainsford. "Ugh! It's like moist black velvet."

"It will be light in Rio," promised Whitney. "We should make it in a few days. I hope the jaguar guns have come from Purdey's. We should have some good hunting up the Amazon. Great sport, hunting."

"The best sport in the world," agreed Rainsford.

"For the hunter," amended Whitney. "Not for the jaguar."

10   "Don't talk rot, Whitney," said Rainsford. "You're a big-game hunter, not a philosopher. Who cares how a jaguar feels?"

"Perhaps the jaguar does," observed Whitney.

"Bah! They've no understanding."

"Even so, I rather think they understand one thing—fear. The fear of pain and the fear of death."

"Nonsense," laughed Rainsford. "This hot weather is making you soft, Whitney. Be a realist. The world is made up of two classes—the hunters and the huntees. Luckily, you and I are the hunters. Do you think we've passed that island yet?"

15   "I can't tell in the dark. I hope so."

"Why?" asked Rainsford.

"The place has a reputation—a bad one."

"Cannibals?" suggested Rainsford.

"Hardly. Even cannibals wouldn't live in such a God-forsaken place. But it's gotten into sailor lore, somehow. Didn't you notice that the crew's nerves seemed a bit jumpy today?"

THE MOST DANGEROUS GAME   First published in 1924. Richard Connell (1893–1949) was a native of New York state, graduated from Harvard, and served a year in France with the United States Army during World War I.

"They were a bit strange, now you mention it. Even Captain Nielsen—" 20

"Yes, even that tough-minded old Swede, who'd go up to the devil himself and ask him for a light. Those fishy blue eyes held a look I never saw there before. All I could get out of him was: 'This place has an evil name among seafaring men, sir.' Then he said to me, very gravely: 'Don't you feel anything?'—as if the air about us was actually poisonous. Now, you mustn't laugh when I tell you this—I did feel something like a sudden chill.

"There was no breeze. The sea was as flat as a plate-glass window. We were drawing near the island then. What I felt was a—a mental chill; a sort of sudden dread."

"Pure imagination," said Rainsford. "One superstitious sailor can taint the whole ship's company with his fear."

"Maybe. But sometimes I think sailors have an extra sense that tells them when they are in danger. Sometimes I think evil is a tangible thing—with wave lengths, just as sound and light have. An evil place can, so to speak, broadcast vibrations of evil. Anyhow, I'm glad we're getting out of this zone. Well, I think I'll turn in now, Rainsford."

"I'm not sleepy," said Rainsford. "I'm going to smoke another pipe on 25 the after deck."

"Good night, then, Rainsford. See you at breakfast."

"Right. Good night, Whitney."

There was no sound in the night as Rainsford sat there, but the muffled throb of the engine that drove the yacht swiftly through the darkness, and the swish and ripple of the wash of the propeller.

Rainsford, reclining in a steamer chair, indolently puffed on his favorite brier. The sensuous drowsiness of the night was on him. "It's so dark," he thought, "that I could sleep without closing my eyes; the night would be my eyelids—"

An abrupt sound startled him. Off to the right he heard it, and his ears, 30 expert in such matters, could not be mistaken. Again he heard the sound, and again. Somewhere, off in the blackness, some one had fired a gun three times.

Rainsford sprang up and moved quickly to the rail, mystified. He strained his eyes in the direction from which the reports had come, but it was like trying to see through a blanket. He leaped upon the rail and balanced himself there, to get greater elevation; his pipe, striking a rope, was knocked from his mouth. He lunged for it; a short, hoarse cry came from his lips as he realized he had reached too far and had lost his balance. The cry was pinched off short as the blood-warm waters of the Caribbean Sea closed over his head.

He struggled up to the surface and tried to cry out, but the wash from the speeding yacht slapped him in the face and the salt water in his open mouth made him gag and strangle. Desperately he struck out with strong strokes after the receding lights of the yacht, but he stopped before he had swum

fifty feet. A certain cool-headedness had come to him; it was not the first time
he had been in a tight place. There was a chance that his cries could be heard
by some one aboard the yacht, but that chance was slender, and grew more
slender as the yacht raced on. He wrestled himself out of his clothes, and
shouted with all his power. The lights of the yacht became faint and ever-
vanishing fireflies; then they were blotted out entirely by the night.

Rainsford remembered the shots. They had come from the right, and
doggedly he swam in that direction, swimming with slow, deliberate strokes,
conserving his strength. For a seemingly endless time he fought the sea. He
began to count his strokes; he could do possibly a hundred more and then—

Rainsford heard a sound. It came out of the darkness, a high screaming
sound, the sound of an animal in an extremity of anguish and terror.

35   He did not recognize the animal that made the sound; he did not try to;
with fresh vitality he swam toward the sound. He heard it again; then it was
cut short by another noise, crisp, staccato.

"Pistol shot," muttered Rainsford, swimming on.

Ten minutes of determined effort brought another sound to his ears—
the most welcome he had ever heard—the muttering and growling of the sea
breaking on a rocky shore. He was almost on the rocks before he saw them;
on a night less calm he would have been shattered against them. With his
remaining strength he dragged himself from the swirling waters. Jagged
crags appeared to jut into the opaqueness; he forced himself upward, hand
over hand. Gasping, his hands raw, he reached a flat place at the top. Dense
jungle came down to the very edge of the cliffs. What perils that tangle of
trees and underbrush might hold for him did not concern Rainsford just
then. All he knew was that he was safe from his enemy, the sea, and that utter
weariness was on him. He flung himself down at the jungle edge and tumbled headlong into the deepest sleep of his life.

When he opened his eyes he knew from the position of the sun that it was
late in the afternoon. Sleep had given him new vigor; a sharp hunger was
picking at him. He looked about him, almost cheerfully.

"Where there are pistol shots, there are men. Where there are men, there
is food," he thought. But what kind of men, he wondered, in so forbidding a
place? An unbroken front of snarled and ragged jungle fringed the shore.

40   He saw no sign of a trail through the closely knit web of weeds and trees;
it was easier to go along the shore, and Rainsford floundered along by the
water. Not far from where he had landed, he stopped.

Some wounded thing, by the evidence a large animal, had thrashed
about in the underbrush; the jungle weeds were crushed down and the moss
was lacerated; one patch of weeds was stained crimson. A small, glittering
object not far away caught Rainsford's eye and he picked it up. It was an
empty cartridge.

"A twenty-two," he remarked. "That's odd. It must have been a fairly
large animal too. The hunter had his nerve with him to tackle it with a light

gun. It's clear that the brute put up a fight. I suppose the first three shots I heard was when the hunter flushed his quarry and wounded it. The last shot was when he trailed it here and finished it."

He examined the ground closely and found what he had hoped to find—the print of hunting boots. They pointed along the cliff in the direction he had been going. Eagerly he hurried along, now slipping on a rotten log or a loose stone, but making headway; night was beginning to settle down on the island.

Bleak darkness was blacking out the sea and jungle when Rainsford sighted the lights. He came upon them as he turned a crook in the coast line, and his first thought was that he had come upon a village, for there were many lights. But as he forged along he saw to his great astonishment that all the lights were in one enormous building—a lofty structure with pointed towers plunging upward into the gloom. His eyes made out the shadowy outlines of a palatial château; it was set on a high bluff, and on three sides of it cliffs dived down to where the sea licked greedy lips in the shadows.

"Mirage," thought Rainsford. But it was no mirage, he found, when he   45
opened the tall spiked iron gate. The stone steps were real enough; the massive door with a leering gargoyle for a knocker was real enough; yet about it all hung an air of unreality.

He lifted the knocker, and it creaked up stiffly, as if it had never before been used. He let it fall, and it startled him with its booming loudness. He thought he heard steps within; the door remained closed. Again Rainsford lifted the heavy knocker, and let it fall. The door opened then, opened as suddenly as if it were on a spring, and Rainsford stood blinking in the river of glaring gold light that poured out. The first thing Rainsford's eyes discerned was the largest man Rainsford had ever seen—a gigantic creature, solidly made and black-bearded to the waist. In his hand the man held a long-barreled revolver, and he was pointing it straight at Rainsford's heart.

Out of the snarl of beard two small eyes regarded Rainsford.

"Don't be alarmed," said Rainsford, with a smile which he hoped was disarming. "I'm no robber. I fell off a yacht. My name is Sanger Rainsford of New York City."

The menacing look in the eyes did not change. The revolver pointed as rigidly as if the giant were a statue. He gave no sign that he understood Rainsford's words, or that he had even heard them. He was dressed in uniform, a black uniform trimmed with gray astrakhan.

"I'm Sanger Rainsford of New York," Rainsford began again. "I fell off a   50
yacht. I am hungry."

The man's only answer was to raise with his thumb the hammer of his revolver. Then Rainsford saw the man's free hand go to his forehead in a military salute, and he saw him click his heels together and stand at attention. Another man was coming down the broad marble steps, an erect, slender man in evening clothes. He advanced to Rainsford and held out his hand.

In a cultivated voice marked by a slight accent that gave it added precision and deliberateness, he said: "It is a very great pleasure and honor to welcome Mr. Sanger Rainsford, the celebrated hunter, to my home."

Automatically Rainsford shook the man's hand.

"I've read your book about hunting snow leopards in Tibet, you see," explained the man. "I am General Zaroff."

55   Rainsford's first impression was that the man was singularly handsome; his second was that there was an original, almost bizarre quality about the general's face. He was a tall man past middle age, for his hair was a vivid white; but his thick eyebrows and pointed military mustache were as black as the night from which Rainsford had come. His eyes, too, were black and very bright. He had high cheek bones, a sharp-cut nose, a spare, dark face, the face of a man used to giving orders, the face of an aristocrat. Turning to the giant in uniform, the general made a sign. The giant put away his pistol, saluted, withdrew.

"Ivan is an incredibly strong fellow," remarked the general, "but he has the misfortune to be deaf and dumb. A simple fellow, but, I'm afraid, like all his race, a bit of a savage."

"Is he Russian?"

"He is a Cossack," said the general, and his smile showed red lips and pointed teeth. "So am I.

"Come," he said, "we shouldn't be chatting here. We can talk later. Now you want clothes, food, rest. You shall have them. This is a most restful spot."

60   Ivan had reappeared, and the general spoke to him with lips that moved but gave forth no sound.

"Follow Ivan, if you please, Mr. Rainsford," said the general. "I was about to have my dinner when you came. I'll wait for you. You'll find that my clothes will fit you, I think."

It was to a huge, beam-ceilinged bedroom with a canopied bed big enough for six men that Rainsford followed the silent giant. Ivan laid out an evening suit, and Rainsford, as he put it on, noticed that it came from a London tailor who ordinarily cut and sewed for none below the rank of duke.

The dining room to which Ivan conducted him was in many ways remarkable. There was a medieval magnificence about it; it suggested a baronial hall of feudal times with its oaken panels, its high ceiling, its vast refectory table where twoscore men could sit down to eat. About the hall were the mounted heads of many animals—lions, tigers, elephants, moose, bears; larger or more perfect specimens Rainsford had never seen. At the great table the general was sitting, alone.

"You'll have a cocktail, Mr. Rainsford," he suggested. The cocktail was surpassingly good; and, Rainsford noted, the table appointments were of the finest—the linen, the crystal, the silver, the china.

They were eating *borsch*, the rich, red soup with whipped cream so dear   65
to Russian palates. Half apologetically General Zaroff said: "We do our best
to preserve the amenities of civilization here. Please forgive any lapses. We
are well off the beaten track, you know. Do you think the champagne has
suffered from its long ocean trip?"

"Not in the least," declared Rainsford. He was finding the general a most
thoughtful and affable host, a true cosmopolite. But there was one small trait
of the general's that made Rainsford uncomfortable. Whenever he looked up
from his plate he found the general studying him, appraising him narrowly.

"Perhaps," said General Zaroff, "you were surprised that I recognized
your name. You see, I read all books on hunting published in English,
French, and Russian. I have but one passion in my life, Mr. Rainsford, and it
is the hunt."

"You have some wonderful heads here," said Rainsford as he ate a particularly well cooked filet mignon. "That Cape buffalo is the largest I ever saw."

"Oh, that fellow. Yes, he was a monster."

"Did he charge you?"   70

"Hurled me against a tree," said the general. "Fractured my skull. But
I got the brute."

"I've always thought," said Rainsford, "that the Cape buffalo is the most
dangerous of all big game."

For a moment the general did not reply; he was smiling his curious red-
lipped smile. Then he said slowly: "No. You are wrong, sir. The Cape buffalo is not the most dangerous big game." He sipped his wine. "Here in my
preserve on this island," he said in the same slow tone, "I hunt more dangerous game."

Rainsford expressed his surprise. "Is there big game on this island?"
The general nodded. "The biggest."   75

"Really?"

"Oh, it isn't here naturally, of course. I have to stock the island."

"What have you imported, general?" Rainsford asked. "Tigers?"

The general smiled. "No," he said. "Hunting tigers ceased to interest me
some years ago. I exhausted their possibilities, you see. No thrill left in tigers, no real danger. I live for danger, Mr. Rainsford."

The general took from his pocket a gold cigaret case and offered his guest   80
a long black cigaret with a silver tip; it was perfumed and gave off a smell like
incense.

"We will have some capital hunting, you and I," said the general. "I shall
be most glad to have your society."

"But what game——" began Rainsford.

"I'll tell you," said the general. "You will be amused, I know. I think I
may say, in all modesty, that I have done a rare thing. I have invented a new
sensation. May I pour you another glass of port, Mr. Rainsford?"

"Thank you, general."

85   The general filled both glasses, and said: "God makes some men poets.
Some He makes kings, some beggars. Me He made a hunter. My hand was
made for the trigger, my father said. He was a very rich man with a quarter of
a million acres in the Crimea, and he was an ardent sportsman. When I was
only five years old he gave me a little gun, specially made in Moscow for me,
to shoot sparrows with. When I shot some of his prize turkeys with it, he did
not punish me; he complimented me on my marksmanship. I killed my first
bear in the Caucasus when I was ten. My whole life has been one prolonged
hunt. I went into the army—it was expected of noblemen's sons—and for a
time commanded a division of Cossack cavalry, but my real interest was
always the hunt. I have hunted every kind of game in every land. It would be
impossible for me to tell you how many animals I have killed."
        The general puffed at his cigaret.
        "After the debacle in Russia I left the country, for it was imprudent for
an officer of the Czar to stay there. Many noble Russians lost everything. I,
luckily, had invested heavily in American securities, so I shall never have to
open a tea room in Monte Carlo or drive a taxi in Paris. Naturally, I continued to hunt—grizzlies in your Rockies, crocodiles in the Ganges, rhinoc-
eroses in East Africa. It was in Africa that the Cape buffalo hit me and laid
me up for six months. As soon as I recovered I started for the Amazon to
hunt jaguars, for I had heard they were unusually cunning. They weren't."
The Cossack sighed. "They were no match at all for a hunter with his wits
about him, and a high-powered rifle. I was bitterly disappointed. I was lying
in my tent with a splitting headache one night when a terrible thought
pushed its way into my mind. Hunting was beginning to bore me! And hunting, remember, had been my life. I have heard that in America business men
often go to pieces when they give up the business that has been their life."
        "Yes, that's so," said Rainsford.
        The general smiled. "I had no wish to go to pieces," he said. "I must do
something. Now, mine is an analytical mind, Mr. Rainsford. Doubtless that
is why I enjoy the problems of the chase."
90   "No doubt, General Zaroff."
        "So," continued the general, "I asked myself why the hunt no longer
fascinated me. You are much younger than I am, Mr. Rainsford, and have
not hunted as much, but you perhaps can guess the answer."
        "What was it?"
        "Simply this: hunting had ceased to be what you call 'a sporting proposi-
tion.' It had become too easy. I always got my quarry. Always. There is no
greater bore than perfection."
        The general lit a fresh cigaret.
95   "No animal had a chance with me any more. That is no boast; it is a
mathematical certainty. The animal had nothing but his legs and his instinct.
Instinct is no match for reason. When I thought of this it was a tragic moment for me, I can tell you."
        Rainsford leaned across the table, absorbed in what his host was saying.

"It came to me as an inspiration what I must do," the general went on.

"And that was?"

The general smiled the quiet smile of one who has faced an obstacle and surmounted it with success. "I had to invent a new animal to hunt," he said.

"A new animal? You're joking."   100

"Not at all," said the general. "I never joke about hunting. I needed a new animal. I found one. So I bought this island, built this house, and here I do my hunting. The island is perfect for my purposes—there are jungles with a maze of trails in them, hills, swamps—"

"But the animal, General Zaroff?"

"Oh," said the general, "it supplies me with the most exciting hunting in the world. No other hunting compares with it for an instant. Every day I hunt, and I never grow bored now, for I have a quarry with which I can match my wits."

Rainsford's bewilderment showed in his face.

"I wanted the ideal animal to hunt," explained the general. "So I said: 105
'What are the attributes of an ideal quarry?' And the answer was, of course: 'it must have courage, cunning, and, above all, it must be able to reason.'"

"But no animal can reason," objected Rainsford.

"My dear fellow," said the general, "there is one that can."

"But you can't mean—" gasped Rainsford.

"And why not?"

"I can't believe you are serious, General Zaroff. This is a grisly joke."   110

"Why should I not be serious? I am speaking of hunting."

"Hunting? Good God, General Zaroff, what you speak of is murder."

The general laughed with entire good nature. He regarded Rainsford quizzically. "I refuse to believe that so modern and civilized a young man as you seem to be harbors romantic ideas about the value of human life. Surely your experiences in the war—"

"Did not make me condone cold-blooded murder," finished Rainsford stiffly.

Laughter shook the general. "How extraordinarily droll you are!" he   115
said. "One does not expect nowadays to find a young man of the educated class, even in America, with such a naive, and, if I may say so, mid-Victorian point of view. It's like finding a snuff-box in a limousine. Ah, well, doubtless you had Puritan ancestors. So many Americans appear to have had. I'll wager you'll forget your notions when you go hunting with me. You've a genuine new thrill in store for you, Mr. Rainsford."

"Thank you, I'm a hunter, not a murderer."

"Dear me," said the general, quite unruffled, "again that unpleasant word. But I think I can show you that your scruples are quite ill founded."

"Yes?"

"Life is for the strong, to be lived by the strong, and, if need be, taken by the strong. The weak of the world were put here to give the strong pleasure. I am strong. Why should I not use my gift? If I wish to hunt, why should I not? I hunt the scum of the earth—sailors from tramp ships—lascars, blacks, Chinese, whites, mongrels—a thoroughbred horse or hound is worth more than a score of them."

120   "But they are men," said Rainsford hotly.

"Precisely," said the general. "That is why I use them. It gives me pleasure. They can reason, after a fashion. So they are dangerous."

"But where do you get them?"

The general's left eyelid fluttered down in a wink. "This island is called Ship-Trap," he answered. "Sometimes an angry god of the high seas sends them to me. Sometimes, when Providence is not so kind, I help Providence a bit. Come to the window with me."

Rainsford went to the window and looked out toward the sea.

125   "Watch! Out there!" exclaimed the general, pointing into the night. Rainsford's eyes saw only blackness, and then, as the general pressed a button, far out to sea Rainsford saw the flash of lights.

The general chuckled. "They indicate a channel," he said, "where there's none: giant rocks with razor edges crouch like a sea monster with wide-open jaws. They can crush a ship as easily as I crush this nut." He dropped a walnut on the hardwood floor and brought his heel grinding down on it. "Oh, yes," he said, casually, as if in answer to a question, "I have electricity. We try to be civilized here."

"Civilized? And you shoot down men?"

A trace of anger was in the general's black eyes, but it was there for but a second, and he said, in his most pleasant manner: "Dear me, what a righteous young man you are! I assure you I do not do the thing you suggest. That would be barbarous. I treat these visitors with every consideration. They get plenty of good food and exercise. They get into splendid physical condition. You shall see for yourself tomorrow."

"What do you mean?"

130   "We'll visit my training school," smiled the general. "It's in the cellar. I have about a dozen pupils down there now. They're from the Spanish bark San Lucar that had the bad luck to go on the rocks out there. A very inferior lot, I regret to say. Poor specimens and more accustomed to the deck than to the jungle."

He raised his hand, and Ivan, who served as waiter, brought thick Turkish coffee. Rainsford, with an effort, held his tongue in check.

"It's a game, you see," pursued the general blandly. "I suggest to one of them that we go hunting. I give him a supply of food and an excellent hunting knife. I give him three hours' start. I am to follow, armed only with a pistol of the smallest caliber and range. If my quarry eludes me for three whole days, he wins the game. If I find him"—the general smiled—"he loses."

"Suppose he refuses to be hunted?"

"Oh," said the general, "I give him his option, of course. He need not play that game if he doesn't wish to. If he does not wish to hunt, I turn him over to Ivan. Ivan once had the honor of serving as official knouter to the Great White Czar, and he has his own ideas of sport. Invariably, Mr. Rainsford, invariably they choose the hunt."

"And if they win?"   135

The smile on the general's face widened. "To date I have not lost," he said.

Then he added, hastily: "I don't wish you to think me a braggart, Mr. Rainsford. Many of them afford only the most elementary sort of problem. Occasionally I strike a tartar. One almost did win. I eventually had to use the dogs."

"The dogs?"

"This way, please. I'll show you."

The general steered Rainsford to a window. The lights from the windows   140
sent a flickering illumination that made grotesque patterns on the courtyard below, and Rainsford could see moving about there a dozen or so huge black shapes; as they turned toward him, their eyes glittered greenly.

"A rather good lot, I think," observed the general. "They are let out at seven every night. If anyone should try to get into my house—or out of it— something extremely regrettable would occur to him." He hummed a snatch of song from the Folies Bergère.

"And now," said the general, "I want to show you my new collection of heads. Will you come with me to the library?"

"I hope," said Rainsford, "that you will excuse me tonight, General Zaroff. I'm really not feeling at all well."

"Ah, indeed?" the general inquired solicitously. "Well, I suppose that's only natural, after your long swim. You need a good, restful night's sleep. Tomorrow you'll feel like a new man, I'll wager. Then we'll hunt, eh? I've one rather promising prospect—"

Rainsford was hurrying from the room.   145

"Sorry you can't go with me tonight," called the general. "I expect rather fair sport—a big, strong black. He looks resourceful—Well, good night, Mr. Rainsford; I hope you have a good night's rest."

The bed was good, and the pajamas of the softest silk, and he was tired in every fiber of his being, but nevertheless Rainsford could not quiet his brain with the opiate of sleep. He lay, eyes wide open. Once he thought he heard stealthy steps in the corridor outside his room. He sought to throw open the door; it would not open. He went to the window and looked out. His room was high up in one of the towers. The lights of the château were out now, and it was dark and silent, but there was a fragment of sallow moon, and by its wan light he could see, dimly, the courtyard; there, weaving in and out in the pattern of shadow, were black, noiseless forms; the hounds heard him at the window and looked up, expectantly, with their green eyes. Rainsford went back to the bed and lay down. By many methods he tried to put himself to sleep. He had achieved a doze when, just as morning began to come, he heard, far off in the jungle, the faint report of a pistol.

General Zaroff did not appear until luncheon. He was dressed faultlessly in the tweeds of a country squire. He was solicitous about the state of Rainsford's health.

"As for me," sighed the general, "I do not feel so well. I am worried, Mr. Rainsford. Last night I detected traces of my old complaint."

150   To Rainsford's questioning glance the general said: "Ennui. Boredom."

Then, taking a second helping of Crêpes Suzette, the general explained: "The hunting was not good last night. The fellow lost his head. He made a straight trail that offered no problems at all. That's the trouble with these sailors; they have dull brains to begin with, and they do not know how to get about in the woods. They do excessively stupid and obvious things. It's most annoying. Will you have another glass of Chablis, Mr. Rainsford?"

"General," said Rainsford firmly, "I wish to leave this island at once."

The general raised his thickets of eyebrows; he seemed hurt. "But, my dear fellow," the general protested, "you've only just come. You've had no hunting—"

"I wish to go today," said Rainsford. He saw the dead black eyes of the general on him, studying him. General Zaroff's face suddenly brightened.

155   He filled Rainsford's glass with venerable Chablis from a dusty bottle.

"Tonight," said the general, "we will hunt—you and I."

Rainsford shook his head. "No, general," he said. "I will not hunt."

The general shrugged his shoulders and delicately ate a hothouse grape. "As you wish, my friend," he said. "The choice rests entirely with you. But may I not venture to suggest that you will find my idea of sport more diverting than Ivan's?"

He nodded toward the corner to where the giant stood, scowling, his thick arms crossed on his hogshead of chest.

160   "You don't mean—" cried Rainsford.

"My dear fellow," said the general, "have I not told you I always mean what I say about hunting? This is really an inspiration. I drink to a foeman worthy of my steel—at last."

The general raised his glass, but Rainsford sat staring at him.

"You'll find this game worth playing," the general said enthusiastically. "Your brain against mine. Your woodcraft against mine. Your strength and stamina against mine. Outdoor chess! And the stake is not without value, eh?"

"And if I win—" began Rainsford huskily.

165   "I'll cheerfully acknowledge myself defeated if I do not find you by midnight of the third day," said General Zaroff. "My sloop will place you on the mainland near a town."

The general read what Rainsford was thinking.

"Oh, you can trust me," said the Cossack. "I will give you my word as a gentleman and a sportsman. Of course you, in turn, must agree to say nothing of your visit here."

"I'll agree to nothing of the kind," said Rainsford.

"Oh," said the general, "in that case— But why discuss that now? Three days hence we can discuss it over a bottle of Veuve Cliquot, unless—"

The general sipped his wine.

Then a businesslike air animated him. "Ivan," he said to Rainsford, "will supply you with hunting clothes, food, a knife. I suggest you wear moccasins; they leave a poorer trail. I suggest too that you avoid the big swamp in the southeast corner of the island. We call it Death Swamp. There's quicksand there. One foolish fellow tried it. The deplorable part of it was that Lazarus followed him. You can imagine my feelings, Mr. Rainsford. I loved Lazarus; he was the finest hound in my pack. Well, I must beg you to excuse me now. I always take a siesta after lunch. You'll hardly have time for a nap, I fear. You'll want to start, no doubt. I shall not follow till dusk. Hunting at night is so much more exciting than by day, don't you think? Au revoir, Mr. Rainsford, au revoir."

General Zaroff, with a deep, courtly bow, strolled from the room.

From another door came Ivan. Under one arm he carried khaki hunting clothes, a haversack of food, a leather sheath containing a long-bladed hunting knife; his right hand rested on a cocked revolver thrust in the crimson sash about his waist. . . .

Rainsford had fought his way through the bush for two hours. "I must keep my nerve. I must keep my nerve," he said through tight teeth.

He had not been entirely clear-headed when the château gates snapped shut behind him. His whole idea at first was to put distance between himself and General Zaroff, and, to this end, he had plunged along, spurred on by the sharp rowels of something very like panic. Now he had got a grip on himself, had stopped, and was taking stock of himself and the situation.

He saw that straight flight was futile; inevitably it would bring him face to face with the sea. He was in a picture with a frame of water, and his operations, clearly, must take place within that frame.

"I'll give him a trail to follow," muttered Rainsford, and he struck off from the rude paths he had been following into the trackless wilderness. He executed a series of intricate loops; he doubled on his trail again and again, recalling all the lore of the fox hunt, and all the dodges of the fox. Night found him leg-weary, with hands and face lashed by the branches, on a thickly wooded ridge. He knew it would be insane to blunder on through the dark, even if he had the strength. His need for rest was imperative and he thought: "I have played the fox, now I must play the cat of the fable." A big tree with a thick trunk and outspread branches was nearby, and, taking care to leave not the slightest mark, he climbed up into the crotch, and stretching

170

175

out on one of the broad limbs, after a fashion, rested. Rest brought him new confidence and almost a feeling of security. Even so zealous a hunter as General Zaroff could not trace him there, he told himself; only the devil himself could follow that complicated trail through the jungle after dark. But, perhaps, the general was a devil—

An apprehensive night crawled slowly by like a wounded snake, and sleep did not visit Rainsford, although the silence of a dead world was on the jungle. Toward morning when a dingy gray was varnishing the sky, the cry of some startled bird focused Rainsford's attention in that direction. Something was coming through the bush, coming slowly, carefully, coming by the same winding way Rainsford had come. He flattened himself down on the limb, and through a screen of leaves almost as thick as tapestry, he watched. The thing that was approaching was a man.

It was General Zaroff. He made his way along with his eyes fixed in utmost concentration on the ground before him. He paused, almost beneath the tree, dropped to his knees and studied the ground. Rainsford's impulse was to hurl himself down like a panther, but he saw the general's right hand held something metallic—a small automatic pistol.

180   The hunter shook his head several times, as if he were puzzled. Then he straightened up and took from his case one of his black cigarets; its pungent incense-like smoke floated up to Rainsford's nostrils.

Rainsford held his breath. The general's eyes had left the ground and were traveling inch by inch up the tree. Rainsford froze there, every muscle tensed for a spring. But the sharp eyes of the hunter stopped before they reached the limb where Rainsford lay; a smile spread over his brown face. Very deliberately he blew a smoke ring into the air; then he turned his back on the tree and walked carelessly away, back along the trail he had come. The swish of the underbrush against his hunting boots grew fainter and fainter.

The pent-up air burst hotly from Rainsford's lungs. His first thought made him feel sick and numb. The general could follow a trail through the woods at night; he could follow an extremely difficult trail; he must have uncanny powers; only by the merest chance had the Cossack failed to see his quarry.

Rainsford's second thought was even more terrible. It sent a shudder of cold horror through his whole being. Why had the general smiled? Why had he turned back?

Rainsford did not want to believe what his reason told him was true, but the truth was as evident as the sun that had by now pushed through the morning mists. The general was playing with him! The general was saving him for another day's sport! The Cossack was the cat; he was the mouse. Then it was that Rainsford knew the full meaning of terror.

185   "I will not lose my nerve. I will not."

He slid down from the tree, and struck off again into the woods. His face was set and he forced the machinery of his mind to function. Three hundred yards from his hiding place he stopped where a huge dead tree leaned precariously on a smaller, living one. Throwing off his sack of food, Rainsford took his knife from its sheath and began to work with all his energy.

The job was finished at last, and he threw himself down behind a fallen log a hundred feet away. He did not have to wait long. The cat was coming again to play with the mouse.

Following the trail with the sureness of a bloodhound, came General Zaroff. Nothing escaped those searching black eyes, no crushed blade of grass, no bent twig, no mark, no matter how faint, in the moss. So intent was the Cossack on his stalking that he was upon the thing Rainsford had made before he saw it. His foot touched the protruding bough that was the trigger. Even as he touched it, the general sensed his danger and leaped back with the agility of an ape. But he was not quick enough; the dead tree, delicately adjusted to rest on the cut living one, crashed down and struck the general a glancing blow on the shoulder as it fell; but for his alertness, he must have been smashed beneath it. He staggered, but he did not fall; nor did he drop his revolver. He stood there, rubbing his injured shoulder, and Rainsford, with fear again gripping his heart, heard the general's mocking laugh ring through the jungle.

"Rainsford," called the general, "if you are within the sound of my voice, as I suppose you are, let me congratulate you. Not many men know how to make a Malay man-catcher. Luckily, for me, I too have hunted in Malacca. You are proving interesting, Mr. Rainsford. I am going now to have my wound dressed; it's only a slight one. But I shall be back. I shall be back."

When the general, nursing his bruised shoulder, had gone, Rainsford   190
took up his flight again. It was flight now, a desperate, hopeless flight, that carried him on for some hours. Dusk came, then darkness, and still he pressed on. The ground grew softer under his moccasins; the vegetation grew ranker, denser; insects bit him savagely. Then, as he stepped forward, his foot sank in the ooze. He tried to wrench it back, but the muck sucked viciously at his foot as if it were a giant leech. With a violent effort, he tore loose. He knew where he was now. Death Swamp and its quicksand.

His hands were tight closed as if his nerve were something tangible that some one in the darkness was trying to tear from his grip. The softness of the earth had given him an idea. He stepped back from the quicksand a dozen feet or so, and, like some huge prehistoric beaver, he began to dig.

Rainsford had dug himself in in France when a second's delay meant death. That had been a placid pastime compared to his digging now. The pit grew deeper; when it was above his shoulders, he climbed out and from some hard saplings cut stakes and sharpened them to a fine point. These stakes he planted at the bottom of the pit with the points sticking up. With flying fingers he wove a rough carpet of weeds and branches and with it he covered the mouth of the pit. Then, wet with sweat and aching with tiredness, he crouched behind the stump of a lightning-charred tree.

He knew his pursuer was coming; he heard the padding sound of feet on the soft earth, and the night breeze brought him the perfume of the general's cigaret. It seemed to Rainsford that the general was coming with unusual swiftness; he was not feeling his way along, foot by foot. Rainsford, crouching there, could not see the general, nor could he see the pit. He lived a year in a minute. Then he felt an impulse to cry aloud with joy, for he heard the sharp crackle of the breaking branches as the cover of the pit gave way; he heard the sharp scream of pain as the pointed stakes found their mark. He leaped up from his place of concealment. Then he cowered back. Three feet from the pit a man was standing, with an electric torch in his hand.

"You've done well, Rainsford," the voice of the general called. "Your Burmese tiger pit has claimed one of my best dogs. Again you score. I think, Mr. Rainsford, I'll see what you can do against my whole pack. I'm going home for a rest now. Thank you for a most amusing evening."

195   At daybreak Rainsford, lying near the swamp, was awakened by the sound that made him know that he had new things to learn about fear. It was a distant sound, faint and wavering, but he knew it. It was the baying of a pack of hounds.

Rainsford knew he could do one of two things. He could stay where he was and wait. That was suicide. He could flee. That was postponing the inevitable. For a moment he stood there, thinking. An idea that held a wild chance came to him, and, tightening his belt, he headed away from the swamp.

The baying of the hounds drew nearer, then still nearer, nearer, ever nearer. On a ridge Rainsford climbed a tree. Down a watercourse, not a quarter of a mile away, he could see the bush moving. Straining his eyes, he saw the lean figure of General Zaroff; just ahead of him Rainsford made out another figure whose wide shoulders surged through the tall jungle weeds; it was the giant Ivan, and he seemed pulled forward by some unseen force; Rainsford knew that Ivan must be holding the pack in leash.

They would be on him any minute now. His mind worked frantically. He thought of a native trick he had learned in Uganda. He slid down the tree. He caught hold of a springy young sapling and to it he fastened his hunting knife, with the blade pointing down the trail; with a bit of wild grapevine he tied back the sapling. Then he ran for his life. The hounds raised their voices as they hit the fresh scent. Rainsford knew now how an animal at bay feels.

He had to stop to get his breath. The baying of the hounds stopped abruptly, and Rainsford's heart stopped too. They must have reached the knife.

200   He shinnied excitedly up a tree and looked back. His pursuers had stopped. But the hope that was in Rainsford's brain when he climbed died, for he saw in the shallow valley that General Zaroff was still on his feet. But Ivan was not. The knife, driven by the recoil of the springing tree, had not wholly failed.

"Nerve, nerve, nerve!" he panted, as he dashed along. A blue gap showed between the trees dead ahead. Ever nearer drew the hounds. Rainsford forced himself on toward that gap. He reached it. It was the shore of the sea. Across a cove he could see the gloomy gray stone of the château. Twenty feet below him the sea rumbled and hissed. Rainsford hesitated. He heard the hounds. Then he leaped far out into the sea. . . .

When the general and his pack reached the place by the sea, the Cossack stopped. For some minutes he stood regarding the blue-green expanse of water. He shrugged his shoulders. Then he sat down, took a drink of brandy from a silver flask, lit a perfumed cigaret, and hummed a bit from *Madame Butterfly.*

General Zaroff had an exceedingly good dinner in his great paneled dining hall that evening. With it he had a bottle of Pol Roger and half a bottle of Chambertin. Two slight annoyances kept him from perfect enjoyment. One was the thought that it would be difficult to replace Ivan; the other was that his quarry had escaped him; of course the American hadn't played the game—so thought the general as he tasted his after-dinner liqueur. In his library he read, to soothe himself, from the works of Marcus Aurelius. At ten he went up to his bedroom. He was deliciously tired, he said to himself, as he locked himself in. There was a little moonlight, so, before turning on his light, he went to the window and looked down at the courtyard. He could see the great hounds, and he called: "Better luck another time," to them. Then he switched on the light.

A man, who had been hiding in the curtains of the bed, was standing there.

"Rainsford!" screamed the general. "How in God's name did you get here?"   205

"Swam," said Rainsford. "I found it quicker than walking through the jungle."

The general sucked in his breath and smiled. "I congratulate you," he said. "You have won the game."

Rainsford did not smile. "I am still a beast at bay," he said, in a low, hoarse voice. "Get ready, General Zaroff."

The general made one of his deepest bows. "I see," he said. "Splendid! One of us is to furnish a repast for the hounds. The other will sleep in this very excellent bed. On guard, Rainsford. . . ."

He had never slept in a better bed, Rainsford decided.   210

QUESTIONS

1. On what simple ironic reversal is the plot of the story based? What two meanings has the title?
2. How important is suspense in the story? In what ways is it aroused and sustained? What part do chance and coincidence play in the story?

3. Discuss the characterizations of Rainsford and General Zaroff. Which one is more fully characterized? Are both characters plausible?
4. What purpose is served by the "philosophical" discussion between Whitney and Rainsford at the beginning of the story (paragraphs 7–24)? What limitation does it show Rainsford to have? To what extent is his character illuminated during the course of the story? Does he change his ideas?
5. In what ways is the discussion between Whitney and Rainsford paralleled by the after-dinner discussion between Rainsford and Zaroff (paragraphs 68–145)? In these discussions, is Rainsford more like Whitney or Zaroff? How does he differ from Zaroff? Does the end of the story resolve that difference?
6. Is the principal emphasis of the story on plot, character, or theme? On escape or interpretation? Support your answer.

Thomas Wolfe

The Child by Tiger

> Tiger, tiger, burning bright
> In the forests of the night,
> What immortal hand or eye
> Could frame thy fearful symmetry?

One day after school, twenty-five years ago, several of us were playing with a football in the yard at Randy Shepperton's. Randy was calling signals and handling the ball. Nebraska Crane was kicking it. Augustus Potterham was too clumsy to run or kick or pass, so we put him at center, where all he'd have to do would be to pass the ball back to Randy when he got the signal.

It was late in October and there was a smell of smoke, of leaves, of burning in the air. Nebraska had just kicked to us. It was a good kick, too—a high, soaring punt that spiraled out above my head, behind me. I ran back and tried to get it, but it was far and away "over the goal line"—that is to say, out in the street. It hit the street and bounded back and forth with that peculiarly erratic bounce a football has.

The ball rolled away from me down toward the corner. I was running out to get it when Dick Prosser, Shepperton's new Negro man, came along, gathered it up neatly in his great black paw and tossed it to me. He turned in then, and came on down the alleyway, greeting us as he did. He called all of us "Mister" except Randy, and Randy was always "Cap'n"—"Cap'n Shepperton." This formal address—"Mr." Crane, "Mr." Potterham, "Mr." Spangler, "Cap'n" Shepperton—pleased us immensely, gave us a feeling of mature importance and authority.

THE CHILD BY TIGER   First published in 1937. Thomas Wolfe (1900–1938) was born and grew up in Asheville, North Carolina. An altered, expanded version of this story was included in Chapter 8 of his novel *The Web and the Rock* (1939).

"Cap'n Shepperton" was splendid! It had a delightful military association, particularly when Dick Prosser said it. Dick had served a long enlistment in the United States Army. He had been a member of a regiment of crack Negro troops upon the Texas border, and the stamp of the military man was evident in everything he did. It was a joy, for example, just to watch him split up kindling. He did it with a power, a kind of military order, that was astounding. Every stick he cut seemed to be exactly the same length and shape as every other one. He had all of them neatly stacked against the walls of the Shepperton basement with such regimented faultlessness that it almost seemed a pity to disturb their symmetry for the use for which they were intended.

It was the same with everything else he did. His little whitewashed base-   5
ment room was as spotless as a barracks room. The bare board floor was always cleanly swept, a plain bare table and a plain straight chair were stationed exactly in the center of the room. On the table there was always just one object: an old Bible almost worn out by constant use, for Dick was a deeply religious man. There was a little cast-iron stove and a little wooden box with a few lumps of coal and a neat stack of kindling in it. And against the wall, to the left, there was an iron cot, always precisely made and covered cleanly with a coarse gray blanket.

The Sheppertons were delighted with him. He had come there looking for work just a month or two before, and modestly presented his qualifications. He had, he said, only recently received his discharge from the Army and was eager to get employment, at no matter what wage. He could cook, he could tend the furnace, he knew how to drive a car—in fact, it seemed to us boys that there was very little that Dick Prosser could not do. He could certainly shoot. He gave a modest demonstration of his prowess one afternoon, with Randy's .22, that left us gasping. He just lifted that little rifle in his powerful black hands as if it were a toy, without seeming to take aim, pointed it toward a strip of tin on which we had crudely marked out some bull's-eye circles, and he simply peppered the center of the bull's-eye, putting twelve holes through a space one inch square, so fast we could not even count the shots.

He knew how to box too. I think he had been a regimental champion. At any rate, he was as cunning and crafty as a cat. He never boxed with us, of course, but Randy had two sets of gloves, and Dick used to coach us while we sparred. There was something amazingly tender and watchful about him. He taught us many things—how to lead, to hook, to counter and to block— but he was careful to see that we did not hurt each other.

He knew about football, too, and today he paused, a powerful, respectable-looking Negro man of thirty years or more, and watched us for a moment as we played.

Randy took the ball and went up to him. "How do you hold it, Dick?" he said. "Is this right?"

Dick watched him attentively as he gripped the ball, and held it back   10
above his shoulder. The Negro nodded approvingly and said, "That's right,

Cap'n Shepperton. You've got it. Only," he said gently, and now took the ball in his own powerful hand, "when you gits a little oldah yo' handses gits biggah and you gits a bettah grip."

His own great hand, in fact, seemed to hold the ball as easily as if it were an apple. And, holding it so a moment, he brought it back, aimed over his outstretched left hand as if he were pointing a gun, and rifled it in a beautiful, whizzing spiral thirty yards or more to Gus. He then showed us how to kick, how to get the ball off of the toe in such a way that it would rise and spiral cleanly. He knew how to do this too. He must have got off kicks there, in the yard at Shepperton's, that traveled fifty yards.

He showed us how to make a fire, how to pile the kindling so that the flames shot up cone-wise, cleanly, without smoke or waste. He showed us how to strike a match with the thumbnail of one hand and keep and hold the flame in the strongest wind. He showed us how to lift a weight, how to tote a burden on our shoulders in the easiest way. There was nothing that he did not know. We were all so proud of him. Mr. Shepperton himself declared that Dick was the best man he'd ever had, the smartest darky that he'd ever known.

And yet? He went too softly, at too swift a pace. He was there upon you sometimes like a cat. Looking before us, sometimes, seeing nothing but the world before us, suddenly we felt a shadow at our backs and, looking up, would find that Dick was there. And there was something moving in the night. We never saw him come or go. Sometimes we would waken, startled, and feel that we had heard a board creak, and the soft clicking of a latch, a shadow passing swiftly. All was still.

"Young white fokes, oh, young white gent'mun,"—his soft voice ending in a moan, a kind of rhythm in his hips—"oh, young white fokes, Ise tellin' *you*"—that soft low moan again—"you gotta love each othah like a brothah." He was deeply religious and went to church three times a week. He read his Bible every night. It was the only object on his square board table.

15   Sometimes Dick would come out of his little basement room, and his eyes would be red, as if he had been weeping. We would know, then, that he had been reading his Bible. There would be times when he would almost moan when he talked to us, a kind of hymnal chant that came from some deep and fathomless intoxication of the spirit, and that transported him. For us, it was a troubling and bewildering experience. We tried to laugh it off and make jokes about it. But there was something in it so dark and strange and full of a feeling that we could not fathom that our jokes were hollow, and the trouble in our minds and in our hearts remained.

Sometimes on these occasions his speech would be made up of some weird jargon of Biblical phrases, of which he seemed to have hundreds, and which he wove together in this strange pattern of his emotion in a sequence that was meaningless to us, but to which he himself had the coherent clue. "Oh, young white fokes," he would begin, moaning gently, "de dry bones in de valley. I tell you, white fokes, de day is comin' when He's comin' on dis earth again to sit in judgment. He'll put de sheep upon de right hand and de goats upon de left. Oh, white fokes, white fokes, de Armageddon day's a-comin', white fokes, an' de dry bones in de valley."

Or again, we could hear him singing as he went about his work, in his deep rich voice, so full of warmth and strength, so full of Africa, singing hymns that were not only of his own race but familiar to us all. I don't know where he learned them. Perhaps they were remembered from his Army days. Perhaps he had learned them in the service of former masters. He drove the Sheppertons to church on Sunday morning, and would wait for them throughout the morning service. He would come up to the side door of the church while the service was going on, neatly dressed in his good dark suit, holding his chauffeur's hat respectfully in his hand, and stand there humbly and listen during the course of the entire sermon.

And then, when the hymns were sung and the great rich sound would swell and roll out into the quiet air of Sunday, Dick would stand and listen, and sometimes he would join in quietly in the song. A number of these favorite Presbyterian hymns we heard him singing many times in a low rich voice as he went about his work around the house. He would sing Who Follows in His Train? or Alexander's Glory Song, or Rock of Ages, or Onward, Christian Soldiers!

And yet? Well, nothing happened—there was just "a flying hint from here and there," and the sense of something passing in the night. Turning into the square one day as Dick was driving Mr. Shepperton to town, Lon Everett skidded murderously around the corner, sideswiped Dick and took the fender off. The Negro was out of the car like a cat and got his master out. Shepperton was unhurt. Lon Everett climbed out and reeled across the street, drunk as a sot at three o'clock. He swung viciously, clumsily, at the Negro, smashed him in the face. Blood trickled from the flat black nostrils and from the thick liver-colored lips. Dick did not move. But suddenly the whites of his eyes were shot with red, his bleeding lips bared for a moment over the white ivory of his teeth. Lon smashed at him again. The Negro took it full in the face again; his hands twitched slightly, but he did not move. They collared the drunken sot and hauled him off and locked him up. Dick stood there for a moment, then he wiped his face and turned to see what damage had been done to the car. No more now, but there were those who saw it who remembered later how the eyes went red.

Another thing: Sheppertons had a cook named Pansy Harris. She was a comely Negro wench, young, plump, black as the ace of spades, a good-hearted girl with a deep dimple in her cheeks and faultless teeth, bared in the most engaging smile. No one ever saw Dick speak to her. No one ever saw her glance at him, or him at her, and yet that smilingly good-natured wench became as mournful-silent and as silent-sullen as midnight pitch. She went about her work as mournfully as if she were going to a funeral. The gloom deepened all about her. She answered sullenly now when spoken to.

One night toward Christmas she announced that she was leaving. In response to all entreaties, all efforts to find the reason for her sudden and

20

unreasonable decision, she had no answer except a sullen repetition of the assertion that she had to leave. Repeated questionings did finally wring from her a sullen statement that her husband needed her at home. More than this she would not say, and even this excuse was highly suspect, because her husband was a Pullman porter, only home two days a week and well accustomed to do himself such housekeeping tasks as she might do for him.

The Sheppertons were fond of her. They tried again to find the reason for her leaving. Was she dissatisfied? "No'm"—an implacable monosyllable, mournful, unrevealing as the night. Had she been offered a better job elsewhere? "No'm"—as untelling as before. If they offered her more wages, would she stay with them? "No'm," again and again, sullen and unyielding, until finally the exasperated mistress threw her hands up in a gesture of defeat and said, "All right then, Pansy. Have it your own way, if that's the way you feel. Only for heaven's sake don't leave us in the lurch until we get another cook."

This, at length, with obvious reluctance, the girl agreed to. Then, putting on her hat and coat and taking the paper bag of "leavings" she was allowed to take home with her at night, she went out the kitchen door and made her sullen and morose departure.

This was on Saturday night, a little after eight o'clock. That afternoon Randy and I had been fooling around the basement and, seeing that Dick's door was slightly ajar, we looked in to see if he was there. The little room was empty, swept and spotless, as it had always been.

25 But we did not notice that! We saw it! At the same moment, our breaths caught sharply in a gasp of startled wonderment. Randy was the first to speak. "Look!" he whispered. "Do you see it?"

See it! My eyes were glued upon it. Squarely across the bare board table, blue-dull, deadly in its murderous efficiency, lay a modern repeating rifle. Beside it was a box containing one hundred rounds of ammunition, and behind it, squarely in the center, face downward on the table, was the familiar cover of Dick's worn old Bible.

Then he was on us like a cat. He was there like a great dark shadow before we knew it. We turned, terrified. He was there above us, his thick lips bared above his gums, his eyes gone small and red as rodents'.

"Dick!" Randy gasped, and moistened his dry lips. "Dick!" he fairly cried now.

It was all over like a flash. Dick's mouth closed. We could see the whites of his eyes again. He smiled and said softly, affably, "Yes, suh, Cap'n Shepperton. Yes, suh! You gent'mun lookin' at my rifle?" he said, and moved into the room.

30 I gulped and nodded my head and couldn't say a word, and Randy whispered, "Yes." And both of us still stared at him, with an expression of appalled and fascinated interest.

Dick shook his head and chuckled. "Can't do without my rifle, white fokes. No, suh!" he shook his head good-naturedly again. "Ole Dick, he's—

he's—he's an ole Ahmy man, you know. If they take his rifle away from him, why, that's jest lak takin' candy from a little baby. Yes, suh!" he chuckled, and picked the weapon up affectionately. "Ole Dick felt Christmas comin' on—he-he—I reckon he must have felt it in his bones"—he chuckled—"so I been savin' up my money. I just thought I'd hide this heah and keep it as a big surprise fo' the young white fokes untwil Christmas morning. Then I was gonna take the young white fokes out and show 'em how to shoot."

We had begun to breathe more easily now and, almost as if we had been under the spell of the Pied Piper of Hamelin, we had followed him, step by step, into the room.

"Yes, suh," Dick chuckled, "I was just fixin' to hide this gun away twill Christmas Day, but Cap'n Shepperton—hee!" He chuckled heartily and slapped his thigh. "You can't fool ole Cap'n Shepperton. He just must've smelled this ole gun right out. He comes right in and sees it befo' I has a chance to tu'n around. . . . Now, white fokes"—Dick's voice fell to a tone of low and winning confidence—"now that you's found out, I'll tell you what I'll do. If you'll just keep it a surprise from the other white fokes twill Christmas Day, I'll take all you gent'mun out and let you shoot it. Now, cose," he went on quietly, with a shade of resignation, "if you want to tell on me, you can, but"—here his voice fell again, with just the faintest, yet most eloquent shade of sorrowful regret—"old Dick was looking fahwad to this; hopin' to give all the white fokes a surprise Christmas Day."

We promised earnestly that we would keep his secret as if it were our own. We fairly whispered our solemn vow. We tiptoed away out of the little basement room as if we were afraid our very footsteps might betray the partner of our confidence.

This was four o'clock on Saturday afternoon. Already, there was a somber moaning of the wind, gray storm clouds sweeping over. The threat of snow was in the air.

35

Snow fell that night. It came howling down across the hills. It swept in on us from the Smokies. By seven o'clock the air was blind with sweeping snow, the earth was carpeted, the streets were numb. The storm howled on, around houses warm with crackling fires and shaded light. All life seemed to have withdrawn into thrilling isolation. A horse went by upon the streets with muffled hoofs. Storm shook the houses. The world was numb. I went to sleep upon this mystery, lying in the darkness, listening to that exultancy of storm, to that dumb wonder, that enormous and attentive quietness of snow, with something dark and jubilant in my soul I could not utter.

A little after one o'clock that morning I was awakened by the ringing of a bell. It was the fire bell of the city hall, and it was beating an alarm—a hard fast stroke that I had never heard before. Bronze with peril, clangorous through the snow-numbed silence of the air, it had a quality of instancy and menace I had never known before. I leaped up and ran to the window to look for the telltale glow against the sky. But almost before I looked, those deadly strokes beat in upon my brain the message that this was no alarm for fire. It was a savage clangorous alarm to the whole town, a brazen tongue to warn mankind against the menace of some peril, secret, dark, unknown, greater than fire or flood could ever be.

I got instantly, in the most overwhelming and electric way, the sense that the whole town had come to life. All up and down the street the houses were beginning to light up. Next door, the Shepperton house was ablaze with light from top to bottom. Even as I looked, Mr. Shepperton, wearing an overcoat over his pajamas, ran down the snow-covered steps and padded out across the snow-covered walk toward the street.

People were beginning to run out of doors. I heard excited shouts and questions everywhere. I saw Nebraska Crane come pounding down the middle of the street. I knew that he was coming for me and Randy. As he ran by Shepperton's, he put his fingers to his mouth and whistled piercingly. It was a signal we all knew.

40   I was all ready by the time he came running down the alley toward our cottage. He hammered at the door; I was already there.

"Come on!" he said, panting with excitement, his black eyes burning with an intensity I'd never seen before. "Come on!" he cried. We were halfway out across the yard by now. "It's that nigger. He's gone crazy and is running wild."

"Wh-wh-what nigger?" I gasped, pounding at his heels.

Even before he spoke, I had the answer. Mr. Crane had already come out of his house, buttoning his heavy policeman's overcoat as he came. He had paused to speak for a moment to Mr. Shepperton, and I heard Shepperton say quickly, in a low voice, "Which way did he go?"

Then I heard somebody cry, "It's that nigger of Shepperton's!"

45   Mr. Shepperton turned and went quickly back across his yard toward the house. His wife and two girls stood huddled in the open doorway, white, trembling, holding themselves together, their arms thrust into the wide sleeves of their kimonos.

The telephone in Shepperton's house was ringing like mad, but no one was paying any attention to it. I heard Mrs. Shepperton say quickly, as he ran up the steps, "Is it Dick?" He nodded and passed her brusquely, going toward the phone.

At this moment, Nebraska whistled piercingly again upon his fingers and Randy Shepperton ran past his mother and down the steps. She called sharply to him. He paid no attention to her. When he came up, I saw that his fine thin face was white as a sheet. He looked at me and whispered, "It's—it's Dick!" And in a moment, "They say he's killed four people."

"With—" I couldn't finish.

Randy nodded dumbly, and we both stared there for a minute, aware now of the murderous significance of the secret we had kept, with a sudden sense of guilt and fear, as if somehow the crime lay on our shoulders.

50   Across the street a window banged up in the parlor of Sugg's house, and Old Man Suggs appeared in the window, clad only in his nightgown, his

brutal old face inflamed with excitement, his shock of silvery white hair awry, his powerful shoulders, and his thick hands gripping his crutches.

"He's coming this way!" he bawled to the world in general. "They say he lit out across the square! He's heading out in this direction!"

Mr. Crane paused to yell back impatiently over his shoulder, "No, he went down South Dean Street! He's heading for Wilton and the river! I've already heard from headquarters!"

Automobiles were beginning to roar and sputter all along the street. Across the street I could hear Mr. Potterham sweating over his. He would whirl the crank a dozen times or more; the engine would catch for a moment, cough and sputter, and then die again. Gus ran out-of-doors with a kettle of boiling water and began to pour it feverishly down the radiator spout.

Mr. Shepperton was already dressed. We saw him run down the back steps toward the carriage house. All three of us, Randy, Nebraska, and myself, streaked down the alleyway to help him. We got the old wooden doors open. He went in and cranked the car. It was a new one, and started up at once. Mr. Shepperton backed out into the snowy drive. We all clambered up on the running board. He spoke absently, saying, "You boys stay here. . . . Randy, your mother's calling you," but we all tumbled in and he didn't say a word.

He came backing down the alleyway at top speed. We turned into the   55 street and picked up Mr. Crane at the corner. We lit out for town, going at top speed. Cars were coming out of alleys everywhere. We could hear people shouting questions and replies at one another. I heard one man shout, "He's killed six men!"

I don't think it took us over five minutes to reach the square, but when we got there, it seemed as if the whole town was there ahead of us. Mr. Shepperton pulled the car up and parked in front of the city hall. Mr. Crane leaped out and went pounding away across the square without another word to us.

From every corner, every street that led into the square, people were streaking in. One could see the dark figures of running men across the white carpet of the square. They were all rushing in to one focal point.

The southwest corner of the square where South Dean Street came into it was like a dog fight. Those running figures streaking toward that dense crowd gathered there made me think of nothing else so much as a fight between two boys upon the playgrounds of the school at recess time. The way the crowd was swarming in was just the same.

But then I *heard* a difference. From that crowd came a low and growing mutter, an ugly and insistent growl, of a tone and quality I had never heard before. But I knew instantly what it meant. There was no mistaking the blood note in that foggy growl. And we looked at one another with the same question in the eyes of all.

Only Nebraska's coal-black eyes were shining now with a savage sparkle   60 even they had never had before. "Come on," he said in a low tone, exultantly.

"They mean business this time, sure. Let's go." And he darted away toward the dense and sinister darkness of the crowd.

Even as we followed him we heard coming toward us now, growing, swelling at every instant, one of the most savagely mournful and terrifying sounds that night can know. It was the baying of the hounds as they came up upon the leash from Niggertown. Full-throated, howling deep, the savagery of blood was in it, and the savagery of man's guilty doom was in it too.

They came up swiftly, fairly baying at our heels as we sped across the snow-white darkness of the square. As we got up to the crowd, we saw that it had gathered at the corner where my uncle's hardware store stood. Cash Eager had not yet arrived, but, facing the crowd which pressed in on them so close and menacing that they were almost flattened out against the glass, three or four men were standing with arms stretched out in a kind of chain, as if trying to protect with the last resistance of their strength and eloquence the sanctity of private property.

Will Hendershot was mayor at that time, and he was standing there, arm to arm with Hugh McNair. I could see Hugh, taller by half a foot than anyone around him, his long gaunt figure, the gaunt passion of his face, even the attitude of his outstretched bony arms, strangely, movingly Lincoln-esque, his one good eye blazing in the cold glare of the corner lamp with a kind of cold inspired Scotch passion.

"Wait a minute! You men wait a minute!" he cried. His words cut out above the clamor of the mob like an electric spark. "You'll gain nothing, you'll help nothing if you do this thing!"

65   They tried to drown him out with an angry and derisive roar. He shot his big fist up into the air and shouted at them, blazed at them with that cold single eye, until they had to hear. "Listen to me!" he cried. "This is no time for mob law! This is no case for lynch law! This is a time for law and order! Wait till the sheriff swears you in! Wait until Cash Eager comes! Wait—"

He got no farther. "Wait, hell!" cried someone. "We've waited long enough! We're going to get that nigger!"

The mob took up the cry. The whole crowd was writhing angrily now, like a tormented snake. Suddenly there was a flurry in the crowd, a scattering. Somebody yelled a warning at Hugh McNair. He ducked quickly, just in time. A brick whizzed past him, smashing the plate-glass window into fragments.

And instantly a bloody roar went up. The crowd surged forward, kicked the fragments of jagged glass away. In a moment the whole mob was storming into the dark store. Cash Eager got there just too late. He arrived in time to take out his keys and open the front doors, but as he grimly remarked it was like closing the barn doors after the horse had been stolen.

The mob was in and helped themselves to every rifle they could find. They smashed open cartridge boxes and filled their pockets with the loose cartridges. Within ten minutes they had looted the store of every rifle, every cartridge in the stock. The whole place looked as if a hurricane had hit it. The mob was streaming out into the street, was already gathering round the dogs a hundred feet or so away, who were picking up the scent at that point, the place where Dick had halted last before he had turned and headed south, downhill along South Dean Street toward the river.

The hounds were scampering about, tugging at the leash, moaning softly   70 with their noses pointed to the snow, their long ears flattened down. But in that light and in that snow it almost seemed no hounds were needed to follow Dick. Straight as a string right down the center of the sheeted car tracks, the Negro's footsteps led away until they vanished downhill in the darkness.

But now, although the snow had stopped, the wind was swirling through the street and making drifts and eddies in the snow. The footprints were fading rapidly. Soon they would be gone.

The dogs were given their head. They went straining on softly, sniffing at the snow; behind them the dark masses of the mob closed in and followed. We stood there watching while they went. We saw them go on down the street and vanish. But from below, over the snow-numbed stillness of the air, the vast low mutter of the mob came back to us.

Men were clustered now in groups. Cash Eager stood before his shattered window, ruefully surveying the ruin. Other men were gathered around the big telephone pole at the corner, pointing out two bullet holes that had been drilled cleanly through it.

And swiftly, like a flash, running from group to group, like a powder train of fire, the full detail of that bloody chronicle of night was pieced together.

This was what had happened. Somewhere between nine and ten o'clock   75 that night, Dick Prosser had gone to Pansy Harris's shack in Niggertown. Some said he had been drinking when he went there. At any rate, the police had later found the remnants of a gallon jug of raw corn whisky in the room. What happened, what passed between them, was never known. And, besides, no one was greatly interested. It was a crazy nigger with "another nigger's woman."

Shortly after ten o'clock that night, the woman's husband appeared upon the scene. The fight did not start then. According to the woman, the real trouble did not come until an hour or more after his return.

The men drank together. Each was in an ugly temper. Shortly before midnight, they got into a fight. Harris slashed at Dick with a razor. In a second they were locked together, rolling about and fighting like two madmen on the floor. Pansy Harris went screaming out-of-doors and across the street into a dingy little grocery store.

A riot call was telephoned at once to police headquarters on the public square. The news came in that a crazy nigger had broken loose on Gulley Street in Niggertown, and to send help at once. Pansy Harris ran back across the street toward her little shack.

As she got there, her husband, with blood streaming from his face, staggered out into the street, with his hands held up protectively behind his head in a gesture of instinctive terror. At the same moment, Dick Prosser appeared in the doorway of the shack, deliberately took aim with his rifle and shot the fleeing Negro squarely through the back of the head. Harris dropped forward on his face into the snow. He was dead before he hit the ground. A huge dark stain of blood-soaked snow widened out around him. Dick Prosser seized the terrified Negress by the arm, hurled her into the shack, bolted the door, pulled down the shades, blew out the lamp and waited.

80   A few minutes later, two policemen arrived from town. They were a young constable named Willis, and John Grady, a lieutenant of police. The policemen took one look at the bloody figure in the snow, questioned the frightened keeper of the grocery store and, after consulting briefly, produced their weapons and walked out into the street.

Young Willis stepped softly down on to the snow-covered porch of the shack, flattened himself against the wall between the window and the door, and waited. Grady went around to the side and flashed his light through the window, which, on this side, was shadeless. Grady said in a loud tone: "Come out of there!"

Dick's answer was to shoot him cleanly through the wrist. At the same moment Willis kicked the door in and, without waiting, started in with pointed revolver. Dick shot him just above the eyes. The policeman fell forward on his face.

Grady came running out around the house, rushed into the grocery store, pulled the receiver of the old-fashioned telephone off the hook, rang frantically for headquarters and yelled out across the wire that a crazy nigger had killed Sam Willis and a Negro man, and to send help.

At this moment Dick stepped out across the porch into the street, aimed swiftly through the dirty window of the little store and shot John Grady as he stood there at the phone. Grady fell dead with a bullet that entered just below his left temple and went out on the other side.

85   Dick, now moving in a long, unhurried stride that covered the ground with catlike speed, turned up the long snow-covered slope of Gulley Street and began his march toward town. He moved right up the center of the street, shooting cleanly from left to right as he went. Halfway up the hill, the second-story window of a two-story Negro tenement flew open. An old Negro man stuck out his ancient head of cotton wool. Dick swiveled and shot casually from his hip. The shot tore the top of the old Negro's head off.

By the time Dick reached the head of Gulley Street, they knew he was coming. He moved steadily along, leaving his big tread cleanly in the middle of the sheeted street, shifting a little as he walked, swinging his gun crosswise before him. This was the Negro Broadway of the town, but where those poolrooms, barbershops, drugstores and fried-fish places had been loud with dusky life ten minutes before, they were now silent as the ruins of Egypt. The word was flaming through the town that a crazy nigger was on the way. No one showed his head.

Dick moved on steadily, always in the middle of the street, reached the end of Gulley Street and turned into South Dean—turned right, uphill, in the middle of the car tracks, and started toward the square. As he passed the lunchroom on the left, he took a swift shot through the window at the counter man. The fellow ducked behind the counter. The bullet crashed into the wall above his head.

Meanwhile, at police headquarters, the sergeant had sent John Chapman out across the square to head Dick off. Mr. Chapman was perhaps the best-liked man upon the force. He was a pleasant florid-faced man of forty-five, with curling brown mustaches, congenial and good-humored, devoted to his family, courageous, but perhaps too kindly and too gentle for a good policeman.

John Chapman heard the shots and ran. He came up to the corner by Eager's hardware store just as Dick's last shot went crashing through the lunchroom window. Mr. Chapman took up his post there at the corner behind the telephone post that stood there at that time. Mr. Chapman, from his vantage point behind this post, took out his revolver and shot directly at Dick Prosser as he came up the street.

By this time Dick was not more than thirty yards away. He dropped   90
quietly upon one knee and aimed. Mr. Chapman shot again and missed. Dick fired. The high-velocity bullet bored through the post a little to one side. It grazed the shoulder of John Chapman's uniform and knocked a chip out of the monument sixty yards or more behind him in the center of the square.

Mr. Chapman fired again and missed. And Dick, still coolly poised upon his knee, as calm and steady as if he were engaging in a rifle practice, fired again, drilled squarely through the center of the post and shot John Chapman through the heart. Then Dick rose, pivoted like a soldier in his tracks and started down the street, straight as a string, right out of town.

This was the story as we got it, pieced together like a train of fire among the excited groups of men that clustered there in trampled snow before the shattered glass of Eager's store.

But now, save for these groups of talking men, the town again was silent. Far off in the direction of the river, we could hear the mournful baying of the hounds. There was nothing more to see or do. Cash Eager stopped, picked up some fragments of the shattered glass and threw them in the window. A policeman was left on guard, and presently all five of us—Mr. Shepperton, Cash Eager and we three boys—walked back across the square and got into the car and drove home again.

But there was no more sleep, I think, for anyone that night. Black Dick had murdered sleep. Toward daybreak, snow began to fall again. The snow continued through the morning. It was piled deep in gusting drifts by noon. All footprints were obliterated; the town waited, eager, tense, wondering if the man could get away.

They did not capture him that day, but they were on his trail. From time   95
to time throughout the day, news would drift back to us. Dick had turned east along the river and gone out for some miles along the Fairchilds road.

There, a mile or two from Fairchilds, he crossed the river at the Rocky Shallows.

Shortly after daybreak, a farmer from the Fairchilds section had seen him cross a field. They picked the trail up there again and followed it across the field and through a wood. He had come out on the other side and got down into the Cane Creek section, and there, for several hours, they lost him. Dick had gone right down into the icy water of the creek and walked upstream a mile or so. They brought the dogs down to the creek, to where he broke the trail, took them over to the other side and scented up and down.

Toward five o'clock that afternoon they picked the trail up on the other side, a mile or more upstream. From that point on, they began to close in on him. The dogs followed him across the fields, across the Lester road, into a wood. One arm of the posse swept around the wood to head him off. They knew they had him. Dick, freezing, hungry and unsheltered, was hiding in that wood. They knew he couldn't get away. The posse ringed the wood and waited until morning.

At 7:30 the next morning he made a break for it. He got through the line without being seen, crossed the Lester road and headed back across the field in the direction of Cane Creek. And there they caught him. They saw him plunging through the snowdrift of a field. A cry went up. The posse started after him.

Part of the posse were on horseback. The men rode in across the field. Dick halted at the edge of the wood, dropped deliberately upon one knee and for some minutes held them off with rapid fire. At two hundred yards he dropped Doc Lavender, a deputy, with a bullet through the throat.

The posse came in slowly, in an encircling, flankwise movement. Dick got two more of them as they closed in, and then, as deliberately as a trained soldier retreating in good order, still firing as he went, he fell back through the wood. At the other side he turned and ran down through a sloping field that bordered on Cane Creek. At the creek edge, he turned again, knelt once more in the snow and aimed.

It was Dick's last shot. He didn't miss. The bullet struck Wayne Foraker, a deputy, dead center in the forehead and killed him in his saddle. Then the posse saw the Negro aim again, and nothing happened. Dick snapped the breech open savagely, then hurled the gun away. A cheer went up. The posse came charging forward. Dick turned, stumblingly, and ran the few remaining yards that separated him from the cold and rock-bright waters of the creek.

And here he did a curious thing—a thing that no one ever wholly understood. It was thought that he would make one final break for freedom, that he would wade the creek and try to get away before they got to him. Instead, he sat down calmly on the bank and, as quietly as if he were seated on his cot in an Army barracks, he unlaced his shoes, took them off, placed them together neatly at his side, and then stood up like a soldier, erect, in his bare bleeding feet, and faced the mob.

The men on horseback reached him first. They rode up around him and discharged their guns into him. He fell forward in the snow, riddled with bullets. The men dismounted, turned him over on his back, and all the other men came in and riddled him. They took his lifeless body, put a rope around his neck and hung him to a tree. Then the mob exhausted all their ammunition on the riddled carcass.

By nine o'clock that morning the news had reached town. Around eleven o'clock, the mob came back along the river road. A good crowd had gone out to meet it at the Wilton Bottoms. The sheriff rode ahead. Dick's body had been thrown like a sack and tied across the saddle of the horse of one of the deputies he had killed.

It was in this way, bullet-riddled, shot to pieces, open to the vengeful and   105
the morbid gaze of all, that Dick came back to town. The mob came back right to its starting point in South Dean Street. They halted there before an undertaking parlor, not twenty yards away from where Dick knelt to kill John Chapman. They took that ghastly mutilated thing and hung it in the window of the undertaker's place, for every woman, man, and child in town to see.

And it was so we saw him last. We said we wouldn't look. But in the end we went. And I think it has always been the same with people. They protest. They shudder. And they say they will not go. But in the end they always have their look.

At length we went. We saw it, tried wretchedly to make ourselves believe that once this thing had spoken to us gently, had been partner to our confidence, object of our affection and respect. And we were sick with nausea and fear, for something had come into our lives we could not understand.

We looked and whitened to the lips, craned our necks and looked away, and brought unwilling, fascinated eyes back to the horror once again, and craned and turned again, and shuffled in the slush uneasily, but could not go. And we looked up at the leaden reek of day, the dreary vapor of the sky, and, bleakly, at these forms and faces all around us—the people come to gape and stare, the poolroom loafers, the town toughs, the mongrel conquerors of earth—and yet, familiar to our lives and to the body of our whole experience, all known to our landscape, all living men.

And something had come into life—into our lives—that we had never known about before. It was a kind of shadow, a poisonous blackness filled with bewildered loathing. The snow would go, we knew; the reeking vapors of the sky would clear away. The leaf, the blade, the bud, the bird, then April, would come back again, and all of this would be as it had ever been. The homely light of day would shine again familiarly. And all of this would vanish as an evil dream. And yet not wholly so. For we would still remember the old dark doubt and loathing of our kind, of something hateful and unspeakable in the souls of men. We knew that we should not forget.

Beside us, a man was telling the story of his own heroic accomplishments   110
to a little group of fascinated listeners. I turned and looked at him. It was

Ben Pounders of the ferret face, the furtive and uneasy eye, Ben Pounders of the mongrel mouth, the wiry muscles of the jaw, Ben Pounders, the collector of usurious lendings to the blacks, the nigger hunter. And now Ben Pounders boasted of another triumph. He was the proud possessor of another scalp.

"I was the first one to git in a shot," he said. "You see that hole there?" He pointed with a dirty finger. "That big hole right above the eye?" They turned and goggled with a drugged and feeding stare.

"That's mine," the hero said, turned briefly to the side and spat tobacco juice into the slush. "That's where I got him. Hell, after that he didn't know what hit him. He was dead before he hit the ground. We all shot him full of holes then. We sure did fill him full of lead. Why, hell, yes," he declared, with a decisive movement of his head, "we counted up to two hundred and eighty-seven. We must have put three hundred holes in him."

And Nebraska, fearless, blunt, outspoken as he always was, turned abruptly, put two fingers to his lips and spat between them, widely and contemptuously.

"Yeah—*we!*" he grunted. "*We* killed a big one! We—we killed a b'ar, we did! . . . Come on, boys," he said gruffly. "Let's be on our way!"

And, fearless and unshaken, untouched by any terror or any doubt, he moved away. And two white-faced, nauseated boys went with him.

A day or two went by before anyone could go into Dick's room again. I went in with Randy and his father. The little room was spotless, bare and tidy as it had always been. But even the very austerity of that little room now seemed terribly alive with the presence of its black tenant. It was Dick's room. We all knew that. And somehow we all knew that no one else could ever live there again.

Mr. Shepperton went over to the table, picked up Dick's old Bible that still lay there, open and face downward, held it up to the light and looked at it, at the place that Dick had marked when he last read in it. And in a moment, without speaking to us, he began to read in a quiet voice:

"The Lord is my shepherd; I shall not want.

"2. He maketh me to lie down in green pastures: he leadeth me beside the still waters.

"3. He restoreth my soul: he leadeth me in the paths of righteousness for his name's sake.

"4. Yea, though I walk through the valley of the shadow of death, I will fear no evil: for thou art with me—"

Then Mr. Shepperton closed the book and put it down upon the table, the place where Dick had left it. And we went out the door, he locked it, and we went back into that room no more forever.

side of man's dark soul, a symbol of those things that pass by darkness and that still remain, a symbol of man's evil innocence, and the token of his mystery, a projection of his own unfathomed quality, a friend, a brother and a mortal enemy, an unknown demon, two worlds together—a tiger and a child.

QUESTIONS

1. Discuss the setting of the story (assuming for the purpose that the action takes place roughly twenty-five years before the first publication in 1937, as suggested by the first sentence). How important are time and place to the events and attitudes of various characters? How much do we learn about the town and its people? On what implicit premise are the black-white relationships in this town based? How does the use of offensive language contribute to your understanding of the characters?

2. The story begins and ends with stanzas from William Blake's poem, "The Tiger." How does this poem relate to the theme of the story? If you are not familiar with it, look it up and read the whole poem. How is it related to the passage in the Bible to which Dick's Bible was left open (paragraphs 118–21)?

3. The second sentence in "The Most Dangerous Game" is, "It's rather a mystery." Are there any "mysteries" in this story? With what kind of mystery is each story concerned? To what extent is the mystery in each resolved?

4. Dick Prosser's character, like that of General Zaroff, consists of many contradictions. Discuss. In his contradictions, is Dick completely unlike the people of the white community? Why does he "go crazy"? Is his character more or less plausible than General Zaroff's?

5. Compare the manhunt in this story with that in "The Most Dangerous Game." How is it similar? How is it different?

6. What feelings and considerations motivate the whites in tracking Dick down? What meaning has Dick's final gesture of removing his shoes and awaiting the posse (paragraph 102)? How does this action contrast with the way his body is treated by the whites?

7. "The Most Dangerous Game" ends with General Zaroff's death. "The Child by Tiger" continues for several pages after Dick Prosser's death. Why? In what element of the story is each author most interested?

8. The narrator tells this story twenty-five years after its events took place. What importance does this removal in time have for the meaning of the story? Should we identify the author with the attitudes of the narrator as a boy? As a man?

9. Discuss the conflict of good and evil as it is presented in this story and in "The Most Dangerous Game." Which story has greater moral significance? Why?

The years passed, and all of us were given unto time. We went our ways. But often they would turn and come again, these faces and these voices of the past, and burn there in my memory again, upon the muted and immortal geography of time.

And all would come again—the shout of the young voices, the hard thud of the kicked ball, and Dick moving, moving steadily, Dick moving, moving silently, a storm-white world and silence, and something moving, moving in the night. Then I would hear the furious bell, the crowd a-clamor and the baying of the dogs, and feel the shadow coming that would never disappear. Then I would see again the little room that we would see no more, the table and the book. And the pastoral holiness of that old psalm came back to me and my heart would wonder with perplexity and doubt.

For I had heard another song since then, and one that Dick, I know, had   12
never heard, and one perhaps he might not have understood, but one whose phrases and whose imagery it seemed to me would suit him better:

> What the hammer? What the chain?
> In what furnace was thy brain?
> What the anvil? What dread grasp
> Dare its deadly terrors clasp?
>
> When the stars threw down their spears,
> And water'd heaven with their tears,
> Did He smile His work to see?
> Did He who made the lamb make thee?

"*What* the hammer? *What* the chain?" No one ever knew. It was a mystery and a wonder. There were a dozen stories, a hundred clues and rumors; all came to nothing in the end. Some said that Dick had come from Texas, others that his home had been in Georgia. Some said that it was true that he had been enlisted in the Army, but that he had killed a man while there and served a term at Leavenworth. Some said he had served in the Army and had received an honorable discharge, but had later killed a man and had served a term in a state prison in Louisiana. Others said that he had been an Army man, but that he had gone crazy, that he had served a period in an asylum, that he had escaped from prison, that he was a fugitive from justice at the time he came to us.

But all these stories came to nothing. Nothing was ever proved. Men debated and discussed these things a thousand times—who and what he had been, what he had done, where he had come from—and all of it came to nothing. No one knew the answer. But I think that I have found the answer. I think I know from where he came.

He came from darkness. He came out of the heart of darkness, from the dark heart of the secret and undiscovered South. He came by night, just as he passed by night. He was night's child and partner, a token of the other

CHAPTER TWO

Plot

Plot is the sequence of incidents or events of which a story is composed, presented in a significant order. When recounted by itself, it bears about the same relationship to a story that a map does to a journey. Just as a map may be drawn on a finer or grosser scale, so may a plot be recounted with lesser or greater detail. It may include what characters say or think, as well as what they do, but it leaves out description and analysis and concentrates ordinarily on major happenings.

Because plot is the easiest element in fiction to comprehend and put into words, less experienced readers tend to equate it with the content of the work. When asked what a story is about, they may say that it is about a person who does certain things, or to whom certain things happen—not that it is about a certain kind of person or that it presents a particular insight into life. Less experienced readers read chiefly for plot; experienced readers read for whatever revelations of character or life may be presented by means of plot. Those who read chiefly for plot may put a high valuation on intricacy of plot or on violent physical action. On the one hand, they may want schemes and intrigues, mixed identities, disguises, secret letters, hidden passages, and similar paraphernalia. On the other, they may demand fights by land and sea, dangerous missions, hazardous journeys, hair-breadth escapes. There is nothing improper in liking such things, of course, and sometimes the greatest fiction provides them. But if readers can be satisfied *only* with stories having these elements, they are like persons who can enjoy only highly spiced foods. Physical action by itself, after all, is meaningless. In a good story a minimum of physical action may be used to yield a maximum of insight. Every story has *some* action, but in an interpretive story it is *significant* action. For a superior writer there may be as much significant action in the way a man greets a friend as in how he handles a sword.

Conceivably a plot might consist merely of a sequence of related actions. Ordinarily, however, both the excitement craved by less experienced readers and the meaningfulness demanded by experienced readers arise out of some sort of **conflict**—a clash of actions, ideas, desires, or wills. Characters may be pitted against some other person or group of persons (conflict of person against person); they may be in conflict with some external force—physical nature, society, or "fate" (conflict of person against environment); or they may be in conflict with some elements in their own natures (conflict of person against himself or herself). The conflict may be physical, mental, emotional, or moral. There is conflict in a chess game, where the competitors sit quite still for hours, as surely as in a wrestling match; emotional conflict may be raging within a person sitting quietly in an empty room.

The central characters in a conflict, whether sympathetic or unsympathetic as persons, are referred to as **protagonists***; the forces arrayed against them, whether persons, things, conventions of society, or traits of their own characters, are the **antagonists.** In some stories the conflict is single, clear-cut, and easily identifiable. In others it is multiple, various, and subtle. A person may be in conflict with other persons, with social norms or nature, and with herself or himself all at the same time, and sometimes may be involved in conflict without being aware of it.

"The Most Dangerous Game" illustrates most of these kinds of conflict. Rainsford, the protagonist, is pitted first against other men— against Whitney and General Zaroff in the discussions preceding the manhunt and against Zaroff and Ivan during the manhunt. Early in the story he is pitted against nature when he falls into the sea and is unable to get back to the yacht. At the beginning of the manhunt, he is in conflict with himself when he tries to fight off his panic by saying to himself, over and over, "I must keep my nerve. I must keep my nerve." The various conflicts illuminated in this story are physical (Rainsford against the sea and Zaroff), mental (Rainsford's initial conflict of ideas with Whitney and his battle of wits with Zaroff during the manhunt, which Zaroff refers to as "outdoor chess"), emotional (Rainsford's efforts to control his terror), and moral (Rainsford's refusal to "condone cold-blooded murder" in contrast with Zaroff's contempt for "romantic ideas about the value of human life").

Excellent interpretive fiction has been written utilizing all four of these major kinds of conflict. The weaker varieties of commercial

---

*The technical term **protagonist** is preferable to the popular terms "hero" or "heroine" because it is less ambiguous. The protagonist is simply the central character, the one whose struggles we follow with interest, whether he or she be good or bad, sympathetic or repulsive. A "hero" or "heroine" may be *either* a person of heroic qualities *or* simply the main character, heroic or unheroic.

fiction, however, emphasize the conflict between man and man, depending on the element of physical conflict to supply the main part of their excitement. It is hard to conceive of a western story without a fistfight or a gunfight. Even in the crudest kinds of fiction, however, something more will be found than mere physical combat. Good people will be arrayed against bad ones, and thus the conflict will also be between moral values. In escape fiction this conflict is usually clearly defined in terms of moral absolutes, hero versus villain. In interpretive fiction, the contrasts are likely to be less marked. Good may be opposed to good or half-truth to half-truth. There may be difficulty in determining what *is* the good, and internal conflict tends therefore to be more frequent than physical conflict. In the world in which we live, significant moral issues are seldom sharply defined—judgments are difficult, and choices are complex rather than simple. Interpretive writers are aware of this complexity and are more concerned with displaying its various shadings of moral values than with presenting glaring contrasts of good and evil, right and wrong.

Suspense is the quality in a story that makes readers ask "What's going to happen next?" or "How will this turn out?" and impels them to read on to find the answers to these questions. Suspense is greatest when the readers' curiosity is combined with anxiety about the fate of some sympathetic character. Thus in the old serial movies—often appropriately called "cliffhangers"—a strong element of suspense was created at the end of each episode by leaving the hero hanging from the edge of a cliff or the heroine tied to the railroad tracks with the express train rapidly approaching. In murder mysteries—often called "whodunits"—suspense is created by the question of who committed the murder. In love stories it is created by the question "Will the boy win the girl?" or "Will the lovers be reunited, and how?" In more interpretive forms of fiction the suspense often involves not so much the question *what* as the question *why*—not "What will happen next?" but "How is the protagonist's behavior to be explained in terms of human personality and character?" The forms of suspense range from crude to subtle and may concern not only actions but psychological considerations and moral issues. Two common devices for achieving suspense are to introduce an element of **mystery** (an unusual set of circumstances for which the readers crave an explanation), or to place the protagonist in a **dilemma** (a position in which he or she must choose between two courses of action, both undesirable). But suspense can be readily created for most readers by placing *anybody* on a seventeenth-story window ledge or simply by bringing together two physically attractive young people.

In "The Most Dangerous Game," suspense is initiated in the opening sentences with Whitney's account of the mystery of "Ship-Trap Island," of which sailors "have a curious dread"—a place that seems to emanate evil. The mystery grows when, in this out-of-the-way spot, Rainsford discovers an enormous château with a leering gargoyle knocker on its massive door and is confronted by a bearded giant pointing a long-barreled revolver straight at his heart. A second mystery is introduced when General Zaroff tells Rainsford that he hunts "more dangerous game" on this island than the Cape buffalo. He then puts off Rainsford's (and the reader's) curiosity for some thirty-six paragraphs before revealing what the game is. Meanwhile, by placing the hero in physical danger, a second kind of suspense is introduced. Initiated by Rainsford's fall into the sea and his confrontation with Ivan, this kind of suspense becomes the principal suspense device in the second half of the story. Whether Rainsford will escape and how are the questions that keep the reader going. The manhunt itself begins with a dilemma. Rainsford must choose between three undesirable courses of action: he can hunt men with Zaroff; he can let himself be hunted; or he can submit to being tortured by Ivan. During the hunt, he is faced with other lesser dilemmas. For instance, on the third day, pursued by Zaroff's hounds, "Rainsford knew he could do one of two things. He could stay where he was and wait. That was suicide. He could flee. That was postponing the inevitable."

Suspense is usually the first quality mentioned by less experienced readers when asked what makes a good story—and, indeed, unless a story makes us eager to keep on reading it, it can have little merit at all. Nevertheless, the importance of suspense is often overrated. After all, we don't listen to a Beethoven symphony to discover how it will turn out. A good story, like a good dinner, should furnish its pleasure as it goes, because it is amusing or well written or morally penetrating or because the characters are interesting to live with. One test of a story is whether it creates a desire to read it again. Like a Beethoven symphony, a good story should be as good or better on a second or third encounter—when we already know what is going to happen—as on the first. Discriminating readers, therefore, while they do not *disvalue* suspense, may be suspicious of stories in which suspense is artificially created—by the simple withholding of vital information, for instance—or in which suspense is all there is. They will ask whether the author's purpose has been merely to keep them guessing what will happen next or to reveal something about experience. They will be less interested in whether the man on the seventeenth-story window ledge will jump than in the reasons for his being on the ledge. When the readers' primary interest is shifted from "What happens next?" to "*Why* do things happen as they do?" or "What is the significance of this series of events?" they have taken their most important step forward.

Closely connected with the element of suspense in a short story is the element of **surprise.** If we know ahead of time exactly what is going to happen in a story and why, there can be no suspense; as long as we do not know, whatever happens comes with an element of surprise. The surprise is proportional to the unexpectedness of what happens; it becomes pronounced when the story departs radically from our expectation. In the short story such radical departure is most often found in a **surprise ending:** one that reveals a sudden new turn or twist.

As with physical action and suspense, less experienced readers make a heavier demand for surprise than do experienced readers. The escape story supplies a surprise ending more frequently than does the interpretive. There are two ways by which the legitimacy and value of a surprise ending may be judged: (a) by the fairness with which it is achieved and (b) by the purpose that it serves. If the surprise is brought about as a result of an improbable coincidence or an unlikely series of small coincidences, or by the planting of false clues (details whose only purpose is to mislead the reader), or through the withholding of information that the readers ought to have been given earlier in the story, or by manipulation of the point of view (see Chapter 5), then we may well dismiss it as a cheap trick. If, on the other hand, the ending that comes at first as a surprise seems perfectly logical and natural as we look back over the story, we may grant it as fairly achieved. Again, a surprise ending may be judged as trivial if it exists simply for its own sake—to shock or to titillate the reader. We may judge it as a fraud if it serves, as it does in much routine commercial fiction, to conceal earlier weaknesses in the story by giving the readers a shiny bauble at the end to absorb and concentrate their attention. Its justification comes when it serves to open up or to reinforce the meaning of the story. The worthwhile surprise is one that furnishes illumination, not just a reversal of expectation.

Whether or not a story has a surprise ending, readers who prefer escape fiction often demand that it have a **happy ending:** the protagonist must solve his problems, defeat the villain, win the girl, "live happily ever after." A common obstacle confronting readers who are making their first attempts to enjoy interpretive fiction is that such fiction often, though by no means always, ends unhappily. They are likely to label such stories as "depressing" and to complain that "real life has troubles enough of its own" or, conversely, that "real life is seldom as unhappy as all that."

Two justifications may be made for the **unhappy ending.** First, many situations in real life have unhappy endings; therefore, if fiction is to illuminate life, it must present defeat as well as triumph. Commercial sports-story writers usually write of how an individual or a team achieves victory against odds. Yet, if one team wins the pennant, thirteen others must lose it, and if a golfer wins a tournament, fifty or a hundred others must fail to win it. In situations like these, at least, success is much less frequent than failure. Sometimes sports writers, for a variant, will tell how an individual lost the game but learned some important moral lesson—good sportsmanship, perhaps, or the importance of fair play. But here again, in real life, such compensations are gained only occasionally. Defeat, in fact, sometimes embitters people and makes them less able to cope with life than before. Thus we need to understand and perhaps expect defeat as well as victory.

Second, the unhappy ending has a peculiar value for writers who wish us to ponder life. The story with a happy ending has been "wrapped up" for us: readers are sent away feeling pleasantly if vaguely satisfied with the world and cease to think about the story searchingly. The unhappy ending, on the other hand, may cause them to brood over the results, to go over the story in their minds, and thus by searching out its implications to get more from it. Just as we can judge individuals better when we see how they behave in times of trouble, so we can see deeper into life when it is pried open for inspection. The unhappy endings are more likely to raise significant issues. Shakespeare's tragedies reverberate longer and more resonantly than his comedies. The ending of "The Most Dangerous Game" is designed to resolve all our anxieties. The ending of "The Child by Tiger" is designed to make us brood over the mysteries and contradictions of human nature—that is, of our own natures.

Discriminating readers evaluate an ending not by whether it is happy or unhappy but by whether it is logical in terms of what precedes it* and by the fullness of revelation it affords. They have learned

---

*The movies or television sometimes make a book with an unhappy ending into a film with a happy ending. Such an operation, if the book was artistically successful, sets aside the laws of logic and the expectations we naturally build on them.

that an ending that meets these tests can be profoundly satisfying, whether happy or unhappy. They have learned also that a story, to be artistically satisfying, need have no ending at all in the sense that its central conflict is resolved in favor of protagonist or antagonist. In real life some problems are never solved and some contests never permanently won. A story, therefore, may have an **indeterminate ending,** one in which no definitive conclusion is reached. Conclusion of some kind there must of course be: the story, if it is to be an artistic unit, cannot simply stop. But the conclusion need not be in terms of a resolved conflict. We cannot be sure whether Miss Brill in Mansfield's story (page 97) consciously realizes that she has created a fantasy life for herself, nor whether such a realization (if it occurs) will permanently change her life. But the story is more effective without a resolution, for it leaves us pondering the question: is it always better to face reality, or may a life based on fantasy be preferable?

Artistic unity is essential to a good plot. There must be nothing in the story that is irrelevant, that does not contribute to the total meaning, nothing that is there only for its own sake or its own excitement. Good writers exercise rigorous selection: they include nothing that does not advance the central intention of the story. But they not only select; they also arrange. The incidents and episodes are placed in the most effective order, which is not necessarily the chronological order, and when rearranged in chronological order by the reader, make a logical progression. In a highly unified story each event grows out of the preceding one in time and leads logically to the next. The various stages of the story are linked together in a chain of cause and effect. With such a story one seldom feels that events might as easily have taken one turn as another. One feels not that the author is managing the plot but rather that the plot has a quality of inevitability, given a certain set of characters and an initial situation.

An author who gives a story a turn unjustified by the situation or the characters involved is guilty of **plot manipulation.** Any unmotivated action furnishes an instance of plot manipulation. We suspect authors of plot manipulation also if they rely too heavily on chance or on coincidence to bring about a solution to a story. In Poe's famous story "The Pit and the Pendulum," when the victim of the Spanish Inquisition is rescued by the outstretched arm of the commanding general of the invading French army just at the moment when the converging fiery walls of his torture chamber have caused him to fall fainting into the abyss, we have a notorious example of such a contrived or manipulated ending.*

Chance cannot be barred from fiction, of course, any more than it can be barred from life. But if an author uses an improbable chance to effect a resolution to a story, the story loses its sense of conviction and inevitability. The objections to such a use of coincidence† are even more forcible, for coincidence is chance compounded. Coincidence may be justifiably used to initiate a story, and occasionally to complicate it, but not to resolve it. It is objectionable in proportion to its improbability, its importance to the story, and its nearness to the end. If two characters in a story both start talking of the same topic at once, it may be a coincidence but hardly an objectionable one. If they both decide suddenly to kill their mothers at the same time, we may find the coincidence less acceptable. But the use of even a highly improbable coincidence may be perfectly appropriate at the start of a story. Just as a chemist may wonder what will happen if certain chemical elements are placed together in a test tube, an author may wonder what will happen if two former lovers accidentally meet in Majorca, where they longed as young lovers to go, long after they have each married someone else. The improbable initial situation is justified because it offers a chance to observe human nature in conditions that may be particularly revealing, and experienced readers demand only that the author develop a story logically from that initial situation. But the writer who uses a similar coincidence to resolve a story is avoiding the logic of life rather than revealing it. It is often said that fact is stranger than fiction: it *should* be stranger than fiction. In life almost any concatenation of events is possible; in a story the sequence of events should be probable.

There are various approaches to the analysis of plot. We may, if we wish, draw diagrams of different kinds of plots or trace the development of **rising action, climax,** and **falling action.** Such procedures, how-

---

*This kind of coincidental resolution is sometimes referred to as *deus ex machina* ("god from the machine") after the practice of some ancient Greek dramatists in having a god descend from heaven at the last minute (in the theater by means of a stage machine) to rescue the protagonist from some impossible situation. The general in Poe's story is clearly the modern counterpart of such a supernatural deliverer.

† **Chance** is the occurrence of an event that has no apparent cause in antecedent events or in predisposition of character. In an automobile accident in which a drunk, coming home from a party, crashes into a sober driver from behind, we say that the accident was a chance event in the life of the sober driver but that it was a logical consequence in the life of the drunk. **Coincidence** is the chance concurrence of *two* events that have a peculiar correspondence. If the two drivers involved in the accident had been brothers and were coming from different places, it would be coincidence.

ever, if they are concerned with the examination of plot per se, are not likely to take us far into the story. Better questions will concern themselves with the *function* of plot—with the relationship of each incident to the total meaning of the story. Plot is important, in interpretive fiction, for what it reveals. The analysis of a story through its central conflict is likely to be especially fruitful, for it rapidly takes us to what is truly at issue in the story. In testing a story for quality, it is useful to examine how the incidents and episodes are connected, for such an examination is a test of the story's probability and unity. We can never get very far, however, by analysis of plot alone. In any good story, plot is inextricable from character and total meaning. Plot by itself gives little more indication of the total story than a map gives of the quality of a journey.

Graham Greene

The Destructors

1

It was the eve of August Bank Holiday that the latest recruit became the leader of the Wormsley Common Gang. No one was surprised except Mike, but Mike at the age of nine was surprised by everything. "If you don't shut your mouth," somebody once said to him, "you'll get a frog down it." After that Mike had kept his teeth tightly clamped except when the surprise was too great.

The new recruit had been with the gang since the beginning of the summer holidays, and there were possibilities about his brooding silence that all recognized. He never wasted a word even to tell his name until that was required of him by the rules. When he said "Trevor" it was a statement of fact, not as it would have been with the others a statement of shame or defiance. Nor did anyone laugh except Mike, who finding himself without support and meeting the dark gaze of the newcomer opened his mouth and was quiet again. There was every reason why T., as he was afterwards referred to, should have been an object of mockery—there was his name (and they substituted the initial because otherwise they had no excuse not to laugh at it), the fact that his father, a former architect and present clerk, had "come

---

THE DESTRUCTORS   First published in 1954. The setting is London nine years after the conclusion of World War II (1939–1945). During the first sustained bombing attacks on London ("the first blitz") from September 1940 to May 1941, many families slept in the Underground (i.e., subway) stations, which were used as bomb shelters. "Trevor" was typically an upper-class English name. Sir Christopher Wren (1632–1723), England's most famous architect, designed St. Paul's Cathedral and many other late seventeenth- and early eighteenth-century buildings. Graham Greene (1904–1991), who was born just outside London, lived in that city at various stages of his life.

down in the world" and that his mother considered herself better than the neighbors. What but an odd quality of danger, of the unpredictable, established him in the gang without any ignoble ceremony of initiation?

The gang met every morning in an impromptu car-park, the site of the last bomb of the first blitz. The leader, who was known as Blackie, claimed to have heard it fall, and no one was precise enough in his dates to point out that he would have been one year old and fast asleep on the down platform of Wormsley Common Underground Station. On one side of the car-park leant the first occupied house, No. 3, of the shattered Northwood Terrace— literally leant, for it had suffered from the blast of the bomb and the side walls were supported on wooden struts. A smaller bomb and some incendiaries had fallen beyond, so that the house stuck up like a jagged tooth and carried on the further wall relics of its neighbor, a dado, the remains of a fireplace. T., whose words were almost confined to voting "Yes" or "No" to the plan of operations proposed each day by Blackie, once startled the whole gang by saying broodingly, "Wren built that house, father says."

5   "Who's Wren?"

"The man who built St. Paul's."

"Who cares?" Blackie said. "It's only Old Misery's."

Old Misery—whose real name was Thomas—had once been a builder and decorator. He lived alone in the crippled house, doing for himself: once a week you could see him coming back across the common with bread and vegetables, and once as the boys played in the car-park he put his head over the smashed wall of his garden and looked at them.

"Been to the lav," one of the boys said, for it was common knowledge that since the bombs fell something had gone wrong with the pipes of the house and Old Misery was too mean to spend money on the property. He could do the redecorating himself at cost price, but he had never learnt plumbing. The lav was a wooden shed at the bottom of the narrow garden with a star-shaped hole in the door: it had escaped the blast which had smashed the house next door and sucked out the window-frames of No. 3.

The next time the gang became aware of Mr. Thomas was more surprising. Blackie, Mike and a thin yellow boy, who for some reason was called by his surname Summers, met him on the common coming back from the market. Mr. Thomas stopped them. He said glumly, "You belong to the lot that play in the car-park?"

10   Mike was about to answer when Blackie stopped him. As the leader he had responsibilities. "Suppose we are?" he said ambiguously.

"I got some chocolates," Mr. Thomas said. "Don't like 'em myself. Here you are. Not enough to go round, I don't suppose. There never is," he added with somber conviction. He handed over three packets of Smarties.

The gang were puzzled and perturbed by this action and tried to explain it away. "Bet someone dropped them and he picked 'em up," somebody suggested.

"Pinched 'em and then got in a bleeding funk," another thought aloud.

"It's a bribe," Summers said. "He wants us to stop bouncing balls on his wall."

"We'll show him we don't take bribes," Blackie said, and they sacrificed   15
the whole morning to the game of bouncing that only Mike was young enough to enjoy. There was no sign from Mr. Thomas.

Next day T. astonished them all. He was late at the rendezvous, and the voting for the day's exploit took place without him. At Blackie's suggestion the gang was to disperse in pairs, take buses at random and see how many free rides could be snatched from unwary conductors (the operation was to be carried out in pairs to avoid cheating). They were drawing lots for their companions when T. arrived.

"Where you been, T.?" Blackie asked. "You can't vote now. You know the rules."

"I've been *there*," T. said. He looked at the ground, as though he had thoughts to hide.

"Where?"

"At Old Misery's." Mike's mouth opened and then hurriedly closed   20
again with a click. He had remembered the frog.

"At Old Misery's?" Blackie said. There was nothing in the rules against it, but he had a sensation that T. was treading on dangerous ground. He asked hopefully, "Did you break in?"

"No. I rang the bell."

"And what did you say?"

"I said I wanted to see his house."

"What did he do?"   25

"He showed it to me."

"Pinch anything?"

"No."

"What did you do it for then?"

The gang had gathered round: it was as though an impromptu court were   30
about to form and to try some case of deviation. T. said, "It's a beautiful house," and still watching the ground, meeting no one's eyes, he licked his lips first one way, then the other.

"What do you mean, a beautiful house?" Blackie asked with scorn.

"It's got a staircase two hundred years old like a corkscrew. Nothing holds it up."

"What do you mean, nothing holds it up. Does it float?"

"It's to do with opposite forces, Old Misery said."

"What else?"   35

"There's paneling."

"Like in the Blue Boar?"

"Two hundred years old."

"Is Old Misery two hundred years old?"

40   Mike laughed suddenly and then was quiet again. The meeting was in a serious mood. For the first time since T. had strolled into the car-park on the first day of the holidays his position was in danger. It only needed a single use of his real name and the gang would be at his heels.

"What did you do it for?" Blackie asked. He was just, he had no jealousy, he was anxious to retain T. in the gang if he could. It was the word "beautiful" that worried him—that belonged to a class world that you could still see parodied at the Wormsley Common Empire° by a man wearing a top hat and a monocle, with a haw-haw accent. He was tempted to say, "My dear Trevor, old chap," and unleash his hell hounds. "If you'd broken in," he said sadly—that indeed would have been an exploit worthy of the gang.

"This was better," T. said. "I found out things." He continued to stare at his feet, not meeting anybody's eye, as though he were absorbed in some dream he was unwilling—or ashamed—to share.

"What things?"

"Old Misery's going to be away all tomorrow and Bank Holiday."

45   Blackie said with relief, "You mean we could break in?"

"And pinch things?" somebody asked.

Blackie said, "Nobody's going to pinch things. Breaking in—that's good enough, isn't it? We don't want any court stuff."

"I don't want to pinch anything," T. said. "I've got a better idea."

"What is it?"

50   T. raised his eyes, as grey and disturbed as the drab August day. "We'll pull it down," he said. "We'll destroy it."

Blackie gave a single hoot of laughter and then, like Mike, fell quiet, daunted by the serious implacable gaze. "What'd the police be doing all the time?" he asked.

"They'd never know. We'd do it from inside. I've found a way in." He said with a sort of intensity, "We'd be like worms, don't you see, in an apple. When we came out again there'd be nothing there, no staircase, no panels, nothing but just walls, and then we'd make the walls fall down—somehow."

"We'd go to jug," Blackie said.

"Who's to prove? And anyway we wouldn't have pinched anything." He added without the smallest flicker of glee, "There wouldn't be anything to pinch after we'd finished."

55   "I've never heard of going to prison for breaking things," Summers said.

"There wouldn't be time," Blackie said. "I've seen housebreakers at work."

"There are twelve of us," T. said. "We'd organize."

"None of us know how . . ."

"I know," T. said. He looked across at Blackie, "Have you got a better plan?"

Wormsley Common Empire: a music hall for revues and popular entertainments

"Today," Mike said tactlessly, "we're pinching free rides . . ."   60

"Free rides," T. said. "You can stand down, Blackie, if you'd rather . . ."

"The gang's got to vote."

"Put it up then."

Blackie said uneasily, "It's proposed that tomorrow and Monday we destroy Old Misery's house."

"Here, here," said a fat boy called Joe.   65

"Who's in favor?"

T. said, "It's carried."

"How do we start?" Summers asked.

"He'll tell you," Blackie said. It was the end of his leadership. He went away to the back of the car-park and began to kick a stone, dribbling it this way and that. There was only one old Morris in the park, for few cars were left there except lorries: without an attendant there was no safety. He took a flying kick at the car and scraped a little paint off the rear mudguard. Beyond, paying no more attention to him than to a stranger, the gang had gathered round T.; Blackie was dimly aware of the fickleness of favor. He thought of going home, of never returning, of letting them all discover the hollowness of T.'s leadership, but suppose after all what T. proposed was possible—nothing like it had ever been done before. The fame of the Wormsley Common car-park gang would surely reach around London. There would be headlines in the papers. Even the grown-up gangs who ran the betting at the all-in wrestling and the barrow-boys would hear with respect of how Old Misery's house had been destroyed. Driven by the pure, simple and altruistic ambition of fame for the gang, Blackie came back to where T. stood in the shadow of Misery's wall.

T. was giving his orders with decision: it was as though this plan had   70
been with him all his life, pondered through the seasons, now in his fifteenth year crystallized with the pain of puberty. "You," he said to Mike, "bring some big nails, the biggest you can find, and a hammer. Anyone else who can better bring a hammer and a screwdriver. We'll need plenty of them. Chisels too. We can't have too many chisels. Can anybody bring a saw?"

"I can," Mike said.

"Not a child's saw," T. said. "A real saw."

Blackie realized he had raised his hand like any ordinary member of the gang.

"Right, you bring one, Blackie. But now there's a difficulty. We want a hacksaw."

"What's a hacksaw?" someone asked.   75

"You can get 'em at Woolworth's," Summers said.

The fat boy called Joe said gloomily, "I knew it would end in a collection."

"I'll get one myself," T. said. "I don't want your money. But I can't buy a sledge-hammer."

Blackie said, "They are working on No. 15. I know where they'll leave their stuff for Bank Holiday."

80   "Then that's all," T. said. "We meet here at nine sharp."

"I've got to go to church," Mike said.

"Come over the wall and whistle. We'll let you in."

2

On Sunday morning all were punctual except Blackie, even Mike. Mike had had a stroke of luck. His mother felt ill, his father was tired after Saturday night, and he was told to go to church alone with many warnings of what would happen if he strayed. Blackie had had difficulty in smuggling out the saw, and then in finding the sledge-hammer at the back of No. 15. He approached the house from a lane at the rear of the garden, for fear of the policeman's beat along the main road. The tired evergreens kept off a stormy sun: another wet Bank Holiday was being prepared over the Atlantic, beginning in swirls of dust under the trees. Blackie climbed the wall into Misery's garden.

There was no sign of anybody anywhere. The lav stood like a tomb in a neglected graveyard. The curtains were drawn. The house slept. Blackie lumbered nearer with the saw and the sledge-hammer. Perhaps after all nobody had turned up: the plan had been a wild invention: they had woken wiser. But when he came close to the back door he could hear a confusion of sound hardly louder than a hive in swarm: a clickety-clack, a bang bang, a scraping, a creaking, a sudden painful crack. He thought: it's true, and whistled.

85   They opened the back door to him and he came in. He had at once the impression of organization, very different from the old happy-go-lucky ways under his leadership. For a while he wandered up and down stairs looking for T. Nobody addressed him: he had a sense of great urgency, and already he could begin to see the plan. The interior of the house was being carefully demolished without touching the outer walls. Summers with hammer and chisel was ripping out the skirting-boards in the ground floor dining-room: he had already smashed the panels of the door. In the same room Joe was heaving up the parquet blocks, exposing the soft wood floor-boards over the cellar. Coils of wire came out of the damaged skirting and Mike sat happily on the floor clipping the wires.

On the curved stairs two of the gang were working hard with an inadequate child's saw on the banisters—when they saw Blackie's big saw they signaled for it wordlessly. When he next saw them a quarter of the banisters had been dropped into the hall. He found T. at last in the bathroom—he sat moodily in the least cared-for room in the house, listening to the sounds coming up from below.

"You've really done it," Blackie said with awe. "What's going to happen?"

"We've only just begun," T. said. He looked at the sledge-hammer and gave his instructions. "You stay here and break the bath and the wash-basin. Don't bother about the pipes. They come later."

Mike appeared at the door. "I've finished the wires, T.," he said.

"Good. You've just got to go wandering round now. The kitchen's in the basement. Smash all the china and glass and bottles you can lay hold of. Don't turn on the taps—we don't want a flood—yet. Then go into all the rooms and turn out drawers. If they are locked get one of the others to break them open. Tear up any papers you find and smash all the ornaments. Better take a carving-knife with you from the kitchen. The bedroom's opposite here. Open the pillows and tear up the sheets. That's enough for the moment. And you, Blackie, when you've finished in here crack the plaster in the passage up with your sledge-hammer."

"What are you going to do?" Blackie asked.

"I'm looking for something special," T. said.

It was nearly lunch-time before Blackie had finished and went in search of T. Chaos had advanced. The kitchen was a shambles of broken glass and china. The dining-room was stripped of parquet, the skirting was up, the door had been taken off its hinges, and the destroyers had moved up a floor. Streaks of light came in through the closed shutters where they worked with the seriousness of creators—and destruction after all is a form of creation. A kind of imagination had seen this house as it had now become.

Mike said, "I've got to go home for dinner."

"Who else?" T. asked, but all the others on one excuse or another had brought provisions with them.

They squatted in the ruins of the room and swapped unwanted sandwiches. Half an hour for lunch and they were at work again. By the time Mike returned, they were on the top floor, and by six the superficial damage was completed. The doors were all off, all the skirtings raised, the furniture pillaged and ripped and smashed—no one could have slept in the house except on a bed of broken plaster. T. gave his orders—eight o'clock next morning, and to escape notice they climbed singly over the garden wall, into the car-park. Only Blackie and T. were left: the light had nearly gone, and when they touched a switch, nothing worked—Mike had done his job thoroughly.

"Did you find anything special?" Blackie asked.

T. nodded. "Come over here," he said, "and look." Out of both pockets he drew bundles of pound notes. "Old Misery's savings," he said. "Mike ripped out the mattress, but he missed them."

"What are you going to do? Share them?"

"We aren't thieves," T. said. "Nobody's going to steal anything from this house. I kept these for you and me—a celebration." He knelt down on the floor and counted them out—there were seventy in all. "We'll burn them," he said, "one by one," and taking it in turns they held a note upwards and lit the top corner, so that the flame burnt slowly towards their fingers. The grey

90

95

100

ash floated above them and fell on their heads like age. "I'd like to see Old Misery's face when we are through," T. said.

"You hate him a lot?" Blackie asked.

"Of course I don't hate him," T. said. "There'd be no fun if I hated him." The last burning note illuminated his brooding face. "All this hate and love," he said, "it's soft, it's hooey. There's only things, Blackie," and he looked round the room crowded with the unfamiliar shadows of half things, broken things, former things. "I'll race you home, Blackie," he said.

3

Next morning the serious destruction started. Two were missing—Mike and another boy whose parents were off to Southend and Brighton in spite of the slow warm drops that had begun to fall and the rumble of thunder in the estuary like the first guns of the old blitz. "We've got to hurry," T. said.

Summers was restive. "Haven't we done enough?" he said. "I've been given a bob for slot machines. This is like work."

105   "We've hardly started," T. said. "Why, there's all the floor left, and the stairs. We haven't taken out a single window. You voted like the others. We are going to *destroy* this house. There won't be anything left when we've finished."

They began again on the first floor picking up the top floor-boards next to the outer wall, leaving the joists exposed. Then they sawed through the joists and retreated into the hall, as what was left of the floor heeled and sank. They had learnt with practice, and the second floor collapsed more easily. By the evening an odd exhilaration seized them as they looked down the great hollow of the house. They ran risks and made mistakes: when they thought of the windows it was too late to reach them. "Cor," Joe said, and dropped a penny down in the dry rubble-filled well. It cracked and span among the broken glass.

"Why did we start this?" Summers asked with astonishment; T. was already on the ground, digging at the rubble, clearing a space along the outer wall. "Turn on the taps," he said. "It's too dark for anyone to see now, and in the morning it won't matter." The water overtook them on the stairs and fell through the floorless rooms.

It was then they heard Mike's whistle at the back. "Something's wrong," Blackie said. They could hear his urgent breathing as they unlocked the door.

"The bogies?"° Summers asked.

110   "Old Misery," Mike said. "He's on his way." He put his head between his knees and retched. "Ran all the way," he said with pride.

"But why?" T. said. "He told me . . ." He protested with the fury of the child he had never been, "It isn't fair."

bogies: police

"He was down at Southend," Mike said, "and he was on the train coming back. Said it was too cold and wet." He paused and gazed at the water. "My, you've had a storm here. Is the roof leaking?"

"How long will he be?"

"Five minutes. I gave Ma the slip and ran."

"We better clear," Summers said. "We've done enough, anyway."   115

"Oh, no, we haven't. Anybody could do this—" "This" was the shattered hollowed house with nothing left but the walls. Yet the walls could be preserved. Façades were valuable. They could build inside again more beautifully than before. This could again be a home. He said angrily, "We've got to finish. Don't move. Let me think."

"There's no time," a boy said.

"There's got to be a way," T. said. "We couldn't have got this far . . ."

"We've done a lot," Blackie said.

"No. No, we haven't. Somebody watch the front."   120

"We can't do any more."

"He may come in at the back."

"Watch the back too." T. began to plead. "Just give me a minute and I'll fix it. I swear I'll fix it." But his authority had gone with his ambiguity. He was only one of the gang. "Please," he said.

"Please," Summers mimicked him, and then suddenly struck home with the fatal name. "Run along home, Trevor."

T. stood with his back to the rubble like a boxer knocked groggy against   125 the ropes. He had no words as his dreams shook and slid. Then Blackie acted before the gang had time to laugh, pushing Summers backward. "I'll watch the front, T.," he said, and cautiously he opened the shutters of the hall. The grey wet common stretched ahead, and the lamps gleamed in the puddles. "Someone's coming, T. No, it's not him. What's your plan, T.?"

"Tell Mike to go out to the lav and hide close beside it. When he hears me whistle he's got to count ten and start to shout."

"Shout what?"

"Oh, 'Help,' anything."

"You hear, Mike," Blackie said. He was the leader again. He took a quick look between the shutters. "He's coming, T."

"Quick, Mike. The lav. Stay here, Blackie, all of you till I yell."   130

"Where are you going, T.?"

"Don't worry. I'll see to this. I said I would, didn't I?"

Old Misery came limping off the common. He had mud on his shoes and he stopped to scrape them on the pavement's edge. He didn't want to soil his house, which stood jagged and dark between the bomb-sites, saved so narrowly, as he believed, from destruction. Even the fanlight had been left unbroken by the bomb's blast. Somewhere somebody whistled. Old Misery looked sharply round. He didn't trust whistles. A child was shouting: it seemed to come from his own garden. Then a boy ran into the road from the car-park. "Mr. Thomas," he called. "Mr. Thomas."

"What is it?"

135   "I'm terribly sorry, Mr. Thomas. One of us got taken short, and we thought you wouldn't mind, and now he can't get out."

"What do you mean, boy?"

"He's got stuck in your lav."

"He'd no business . . . Haven't I seen you before?"

"You showed me your house."

140   "So I did. So I did. That doesn't give you the right to . . ."

"Do hurry, Mr. Thomas. He'll suffocate."

"Nonsense. He can't suffocate. Wait till I put my bag in."

"I'll carry your bag."

"Oh no, you don't. I carry my own."

145   "This way, Mr. Thomas."

"I can't get in the garden that way. I've got to go through the house."

"But you *can* get in the garden this way, Mr. Thomas. We often do."

"You often do?" He followed the boy with a scandalized fascination. "When? What right? . . ."

"Do you see . . . ? The wall's low."

150   "I'm not going to climb walls into my own garden. It's absurd."

"This is how we do it. One foot here, one foot there, and over." The boy's face peered down, an arm shot out, and Mr. Thomas found his bag taken and deposited on the other side of the wall.

"Give me back my bag," Mr. Thomas said. From the loo° a boy yelled and yelled. "I'll call the police."

"Your bag's all right, Mr. Thomas. Look. One foot there. On your right. Now just above. To your left." Mr. Thomas climbed over his own garden wall. "Here's your bag, Mr. Thomas."

"I'll have the wall built up," Mr. Thomas said. "I'll not have you boys coming over here, using my loo." He stumbled on the path, but the boy caught his elbow and supported him. "Thank you, thank you, my boy," he murmured automatically. Somebody shouted again through the dark. "I'm coming, I'm coming," Mr. Thomas called. He said to the boy beside him, "I'm not unreasonable. Been a boy myself. As long as things are done regular. I don't mind you playing round the place Saturday mornings. Sometimes I like company. Only it's got to be regular. One of you asks leave and I say Yes. Sometimes I'll say No. Won't feel like it. And you come in at the front door and out at the back. No garden walls."

155   "Do get him out, Mr. Thomas."

"He won't come to any harm in my loo," Mr. Thomas said, stumbling slowly down the garden. "Oh, my rheumatics," he said. "Always get 'em on Bank Holiday. I've got to go careful. There's loose stones here. Give me your hand. Do you know what my horoscope said yesterday? 'Abstain from any dealings in first half of week. Danger of serious crash.' That might be on this path," Mr. Thomas said. "They speak in parables and double meanings." He

loo: outdoor toilet (an older term for "lav")

paused at the door of the loo. "What's the matter in there?" he called. There was no reply.

"Perhaps he's fainted," the boy said.

"Not in my loo. Here, you come out," Mr. Thomas said, and giving a great jerk at the door he nearly fell on his back when it swung easily open. A hand first supported him and then pushed him hard. His head hit the opposite wall and he sat heavily down. His bag hit his feet. A hand whipped the key out of the lock and the door slammed. "Let me out," he called, and heard the key turn in the lock. "A serious crash," he thought, and felt dithery and confused and old.

A voice spoke to him softly through the star-shaped hole in the door. "Don't worry, Mr. Thomas," it said, "we won't hurt you, not if you stay quiet."

Mr. Thomas put his head between his hands and pondered. He had   160
noticed that there was only one lorry in the car-park, and he felt certain that the driver would not come for it before the morning. Nobody could hear him from the road in front, and the lane at the back was seldom used. Anyone who passed there would be hurrying home and would not pause for what they would certainly take to be drunken cries. And if he did call "Help," who, on a lonely Bank Holiday evening, would have the courage to investigate? Mr. Thomas sat on the loo and pondered with the wisdom of age.

After a while it seemed to him that there were sounds in the silence—they were faint and came from the direction of his house. He stood up and peered through the ventilation-hole—between the cracks in one of the shutters he saw a light, not the light of a lamp, but the wavering light that a candle might give. Then he thought he heard the sound of hammering and scraping and chipping. He thought of burglars—perhaps they had employed the boy as a scout, but why should burglars engage in what sounded more and more like a stealthy form of carpentry? Mr. Thomas let out an experimental yell, but nobody answered. The noise could not even have reached his enemies.

4

Mike had gone home to bed, but the rest stayed. The question of leadership no longer concerned the gang. With nails, chisels, screwdrivers, anything that was sharp and penetrating, they moved around the inner walls worrying at the mortar between the bricks. They started too high, and it was Blackie who hit on the damp course and realized the work could be halved if they weakened the joints immediately above. It was a long, tiring, unamusing job, but at last it was finished. The gutted house stood there balanced on a few inches of mortar between the damp course and the bricks.

There remained the most dangerous task of all, out in the open at the edge of the bomb-site. Summers was sent to watch the road for passers-by, and Mr. Thomas, sitting on the loo, heard clearly now the sound of sawing.

It no longer came from his house, and that a little reassured him. He felt less concerned. Perhaps the other noises too had no significance.

A voice spoke to him through the hole. "Mr. Thomas."

165   "Let me out," Mr. Thomas said sternly.

"Here's a blanket," the voice said, and a long grey sausage was worked through the hole and fell in swathes over Mr. Thomas's head.

"There's nothing personal," the voice said. "We want you to be comfortable tonight."

"Tonight," Mr. Thomas repeated incredulously.

"Catch," the voice said. "Penny buns—we've buttered them, and sausage-rolls. We don't want you to starve, Mr. Thomas."

170   Mr. Thomas pleaded desperately. "A joke's a joke, boy. Let me out and I won't say a thing. I've got rheumatics. I got to sleep comfortable."

"You wouldn't be comfortable, not in your house, you wouldn't. Not now."

"What do you mean, boy?" but the footsteps receded. There was only the silence of night: no sound of sawing. Mr. Thomas tried one more yell, but he was daunted and rebuked by the silence—a long way off an owl hooted and made away again on its muffled flight through the soundless world.

At seven next morning the driver came to fetch his lorry. He climbed into the seat and tried to start the engine. He was vaguely aware of a voice shouting, but it didn't concern him. At last the engine responded and he backed the lorry until it touched the great wooden shore that supported Mr. Thomas's house. That way he could drive right out and down the street without reversing. The lorry moved forward, was momentarily checked as though something were pulling it from behind, and then went on to the sound of a long rumbling crash. The driver was astonished to see bricks bouncing ahead of him, while stones hit the roof of his cab. He put on his brakes. When he climbed out the whole landscape had suddenly altered. There was no house beside the car-park, only a hill of rubble. He went round and examined the back of his car for damage, and found a rope tied there that was still twisted at the other end round part of a wooden strut.

The driver again became aware of somebody shouting. It came from the wooden erection which was the nearest thing to a house in that desolation of broken brick. The driver climbed the smashed wall and unlocked the door. Mr. Thomas came out of the loo. He was wearing a grey blanket to which flakes of pastry adhered. He gave a sobbing cry. "My house," he said. "Where's my house?"

175   "Search me," the driver said. His eye lit on the remains of a bath and what had once been a dresser and he began to laugh. There wasn't anything left anywhere.

"How dare you laugh," Mr. Thomas said. "It was my house. My house."

"I'm sorry," the driver said, making heroic efforts, but when he remembered the sudden check to his lorry, the crash of bricks falling, he became convulsed again. One moment the house had stood there with such dignity between the bomb-sites like a man in a top hat, and then, bang, crash, there wasn't anything left—not anything. He said, "I'm sorry. I can't help it, Mr. Thomas. There's nothing personal, but you got to admit it's funny."

QUESTIONS

1. Who is the protagonist in this story—Trevor, Blackie, or the gang? Who or what is the antagonist? Identify the conflicts of the story.
2. How is suspense created?
3. This story uses the most common basic formula of commercial fiction: protagonist aims at a goal, is confronted with various obstacles between himself and his goal, overcomes the obstacles, and achieves his goal. How does this story differ from commercial fiction in its use of this formula? Does the story have a happy ending?
4. Discuss the gang's motivations, taking into account (a) the age and beauty of the house, (b) Blackie's reasons for not going home after losing his position of leadership, (c) the seriousness with which the boys work at their task, and their loss of concern over their leadership, (d) the burning of the banknotes, (e) their consideration for Old Misery, (f) the lorry driver's reaction. What characteristics do the gang's two named exploits—pinching free rides and destroying the house—have in common?
5. Of what significance, if any, is the setting of this story in blitzed London? Does the story have anything to say about the consequences of war? About the causes of war?
6. Explain as fully as you can the causes of the gang's delinquency, taking into account (a) their reaction to the name Trevor, (b) their reaction to Old Misery's gift of chocolates, (c) Blackie's reaction to the word "beautiful," (d) Trevor's comments on "hate and love," (e) Summers's reaction to the word "Please," (f) the setting.
7. What good qualities do the delinquents in this story have? Do they differ as a group from other delinquent gangs you have read or know about? If so, account for the differences.
8. On the surface this is a story of action, suspense, and adventure. At a deeper level it is about delinquency, war, and human nature. Try to sum up what the story says about human nature in general.

Edith Wharton

Roman Fever

1

From the table at which they had been lunching two American ladies of ripe but well-cared-for middle age moved across the lofty terrace of the Roman restaurant and, leaning on its parapet, looked first at each other, and then down on the outspread glories of the Palatine and the Forum, with the same expression of vague but benevolent approval.

As they leaned there a girlish voice echoed up gaily from the stairs leading to the court below. "Well, come along, then," it cried, not to them but to an invisible companion, "and let's leave the young things to their knitting"; and a voice as fresh laughed back: "Oh, look here, Babs, not actually *knitting*—" "Well, I mean figuratively," rejoined the first. "After all, we haven't left our poor parents much else to do. . . ." and at that point the turn of the stairs engulfed the dialogue.

The two ladies looked at each other again, this time with a tinge of smiling embarrassment, and the smaller and paler one shook her head and colored slightly.

"Barbara!" she murmured, sending an unheard rebuke after the mocking voice in the stairway.

5   The other lady, who was fuller, and higher in color, with a small determined nose supported by vigorous black eyebrows, gave a good-humored laugh. "That's what our daughters think of us!"

Her companion replied by a deprecating gesture. "Not of us individually. We must remember that. It's just the collective modern idea of Mothers. And you see—" Half-guiltily she drew from her handsomely mounted black handbag a twist of crimson silk run through by two fine knitting needles. "One never knows," she murmured. "The new system has certainly given us a good deal of time to kill; and sometimes I get tired just looking—even at this." Her gesture was now addressed to the stupendous scene at their feet.

The dark lady laughed again, and they both relapsed upon the view, contemplating it in silence, with a sort of diffused serenity which might have been borrowed from the spring effulgence of the Roman skies. The luncheon hour was long past, and the two had their end of the vast terrace to themselves. At its opposite extremity a few groups, detained by a lingering look at the outspread city, were gathering up guide-

ROMAN FEVER   First published in 1934. Edith Wharton (1862–1937) was born into a socially prominent New York family and was privately educated by governesses and tutors. She married in 1885 and began a financially and critically successful writing career in 1890. After frequent visits to Europe beginning in her childhood, she took up permanent residence in France. Both she and her husband had a history of adulterous affairs, and she divorced him in 1913; she had no children. "Roman fever" was the name given to a type of malaria prevalent in Rome in the nineteenth century.

books and fumbling for tips. The last of them scattered, and the two ladies were alone on the air-washed height.

"Well, I don't see why we shouldn't just stay here," said Mrs. Slade, the lady of the high color and energetic brows. Two derelict basket chairs stood near, and she pushed them into the angle of the parapet, and settled herself in one, her gaze upon the Palatine. "After all, it's still the most beautiful view in the world."

"It always will be, to me," assented her friend Mrs. Ansley, with so slight a stress on the "me" that Mrs. Slade, though she noticed it, wondered if it were not merely accidental, like the random underlinings of old-fashioned letter writers.

"Grace Ansley was always old-fashioned," she thought; and added   10
aloud, with a retrospective smile: "It's a view we've both been familiar with for a good many years. When we first met here we were younger than our girls are now. You remember?"

"Oh, yes, I remember," murmured Mrs. Ansley, with the same undefinable stress. "There's that headwaiter wondering," she interpolated. She was evidently far less sure than her companion of herself and of her rights in the world.

"I'll cure him of wondering," said Mrs. Slade, stretching her hand toward a bag as discreetly opulent-looking as Mrs. Ansley's. Signing to the headwaiter, she explained that she and her friend were old lovers of Rome, and would like to spend the end of the afternoon looking down on the view—that is, if it did not disturb the service? The headwaiter, bowing over her gratuity, assured her that the ladies were most welcome, and would be still more so if they would condescend to remain for dinner. A full-moon night, they would remember. . . .

Mrs. Slade's black brows drew together, as though references to the moon were out of place and even unwelcome. But she smiled away her frown as the headwaiter retreated. "Well, why not? We might do worse. There's no knowing, I suppose, when the girls will be back. Do you even know back from *where?* I don't!"

Mrs. Ansley again colored slightly. "I think those young Italian aviators we met at the Embassy invited them to fly to Tarquinia for tea. I suppose they'll want to wait and fly back by moonlight."

"Moonlight—moonlight! What a part it still plays. Do you suppose   15
they're as sentimental as we were?"

"I've come to the conclusion that I don't in the least know what they are," said Mrs. Ansley. "And perhaps we didn't know much more about each other."

"No; perhaps we didn't."

Her friend gave her a shy glance. "I never should have supposed you were sentimental, Alida."

"Well, perhaps I wasn't." Mrs. Slade drew her lids together in retrospect; and for a few moments the two ladies, who had been intimate since childhood, reflected how little they knew each other. Each one, of course,

had a label ready to attach to the other's name; Mrs. Delphin Slade, for
instance, would have told herself, or anyone who asked her, that Mrs.
Horace Ansley, twenty-five years ago, had been exquisitely lovely—no,
you wouldn't believe it, would you? . . . though, of course, still charming,
distinguished. . . . Well, as a girl she had been exquisite; far more beautiful
than her daughter Barbara, though certainly Babs, according to the new
standards at any rate, was more effective—had more *edge,* as they say.
Funny where she got it, with those two nullities as parents. Yes; Horace
Ansley was—well, just the duplicate of his wife. Museum specimens of
old New York. Good-looking, irreproachable, exemplary. Mrs. Slade and
Mrs. Ansley had lived opposite each other—actually as well as figuratively—for years. When the drawing-room curtains in No. 20 East 73rd
Street were renewed, No. 23, across the way, was always aware of it.
And of all the movings, buyings, travels, anniversaries, illnesses—the
tame chronicle of an estimable pair. Little of it escaped Mrs. Slade. But
she had grown bored with it by the time her husband made his big *coup*
in Wall Street, and when they bought in upper Park Avenue had already
begun to think: "I'd rather live opposite a speakeasy for a change; at
least one might see it raided." The idea of seeing Grace raided was so
amusing that (before the move) she launched it at a woman's lunch. It
made a hit, and went the rounds—she sometimes wondered if it had
crossed the street, and reached Mrs. Ansley. She hoped not, but didn't
much mind. Those were the days when respectability was at a discount,
and it did the irreproachable no harm to laugh at them a little.

20   A few years later, and not many months apart, both ladies lost their
husbands. There was an appropriate exchange of wreaths and con-
dolences, and a brief renewal of intimacy in the half-shadow of their
mourning; and now, after another interval, they had run across each
other in Rome, at the same hotel, each of them the modest appendage of
a salient daughter. The similarity of their lot had again drawn them
together, lending itself to mild jokes, and the mutual confession that, if in
old days it must have been tiring to "keep up" with daughters, it was
now, at times, a little dull not to.

No doubt, Mrs. Slade reflected, she felt her unemployment more
than poor Grace ever would. It was a big drop from being the wife of
Delphin Slade to being his widow. She had always regarded herself (with
a certain conjugal pride) as his equal in social gifts, as contributing her
full share to the making of the exceptional couple they were: but the
difference after his death was irremediable. As the wife of the famous
corporation lawyer, always with an international case or two on hand,
every day brought its exciting and unexpected obligation: the impromptu
entertaining of eminent colleagues from abroad, the hurried dashes on
legal business to London, Paris or Rome, where the entertaining was so
handsomely reciprocated; the amusement of hearing in her wake: "What,
that handsome woman with the good clothes and the eyes is Mrs. Slade—

the Slade's wife? Really? Generally the wives of celebrities are such frumps."

Yes; being *the* Slade's widow was a dullish business after that. In living up to such a husband all her faculties had been engaged; now she had only her daughter to live up to, for the son who seemed to have inherited his father's gifts had died suddenly in boyhood. She had fought through that agony because her husband was there, to be helped and to help; now, after the father's death, the thought of the boy had become unbearable. There was nothing left but to mother her daughter; and dear Jenny was such a perfect daughter that she needed no excessive mothering. "Now with Babs Ansley I don't know that I *should* be so quiet," Mrs. Slade sometimes half-enviously reflected; but Jenny, who was younger than her brilliant friend, was that rare accident, an extremely pretty girl who somehow made youth and prettiness seem as safe as their absence. It was all perplexing—and to Mrs. Slade a little boring. She wished that Jenny would fall in love—with the wrong man, even; that she might have to be watched, out-maneuvered, rescued. And instead, it was Jenny who watched her mother, kept her out of drafts, made sure that she had taken her tonic. . . .

Mrs. Ansley was much less articulate than her friend, and her mental portrait of Mrs. Slade was slighter, and drawn with fainter touches. "Alida Slade's awfully brilliant; but not as brilliant as she thinks," would have summed it up; though she would have added, for the enlightenment of strangers, that Mrs. Slade had been an extremely dashing girl; much more so than her daughter, who was pretty, of course, and clever in a way, but had none of her mother's—well, "vividness," someone had once called it. Mrs. Ansley would take up current words like this, and cite them in quotation marks, as unheard-of audacities. No; Jenny was not like her mother. Sometimes Mrs. Ansley thought Alida Slade was disappointed; on the whole she had had a sad life. Full of failures and mistakes; Mrs. Ansley had always been rather sorry for her. . . .

So these two ladies visualized each other, each through the wrong end of her little telescope.

2

For a long time they continued to sit side by side without speaking. It seemed as though, to both, there was a relief in laying down their somewhat futile activities in the presence of the vast Memento Mori° which faced them. Mrs. Slade sat quite still, her eyes fixed on the golden slope of the Palace of the Caesars, and after a while Mrs. Ansley ceased to fidget with her bag, and she too sank into meditation. Like many intimate

25

Memento Mori: reminder of mortality (Latin: literally, "remember that you must die").

friends, the two ladies had never before had occasion to be silent together, and Mrs. Ansley was slightly embarrassed by what seemed, after
so many years, a new stage in their intimacy, and one with which she did
not yet know how to deal.

Suddenly the air was full of that deep clangor of bells which periodically covers Rome with a roof of silver. Mrs. Slade glanced at her
wristwatch. "Five o'clock already," she said, as though surprised.

Mrs. Ansley suggested interrogatively: "There's bridge at the Embassy at five." For a long time Mrs. Slade did not answer. She appeared
to be lost in contemplation, and Mrs. Ansley thought the remark had
escaped her. But after a while she said, as if speaking out of a dream:
"Bridge, did you say? Not unless you want to. . . . But I don't think I will,
you know."

"Oh, no," Mrs. Ansley hastened to assure her. "I don't care to at
all. It's so lovely here; and so full of old memories, as you say." She
settled herself in her chair, and almost furtively drew forth her knitting.
Mrs. Slade took sideway note of this activity, but her own beautifully
cared-for hands remained motionless on her knee.

"I was just thinking," she said slowly, "what different things Rome
stands for to each generation of travelers. To our grandmothers, Roman
fever; to our mothers, sentimental dangers—how we used to be guarded!
—to our daughters, no more dangers than the middle of Main Street.
They don't know it—but how much they're missing!"

30   The long golden light was beginning to pale, and Mrs. Ansley lifted
her knitting a little closer to her eyes. "Yes; how we were guarded!"

"I always used to think," Mrs. Slade continued, "that our mothers
had a much more difficult job than our grandmothers. When Roman
fever stalked the streets it must have been comparatively easy to gather in
the girls at the danger hour; but when you and I were young, with such
beauty calling us, and the spice of disobedience thrown in, and no worse
risk than catching cold during the cool hour after sunset, the mothers
used to be put to it to keep us in—didn't they?"

She turned again toward Mrs. Ansley, but the latter had reached a
delicate point in her knitting. "One, two, three—slip two; yes, they must
have been," she assented, without looking up.

Mrs. Slade's eyes rested on her with a deepened attention. "She can
knit—in the face of *this!* How like her. . . ."

Mrs. Slade leaned back, brooding, her eyes ranging from the ruins
which faced her to the long green hollow of the Forum, the fading glow
of the church fronts beyond it, and the outlying immensity of the Colosseum. Suddenly she thought: "It's all very well to say that our girls have
done away with sentiment and moonlight. But if Babs Ansley isn't out to
catch that young aviator—the one who's a Marchese—then I don't know
anything. And Jenny has no chance beside her. I know that too. I wonder
if that's why Grace Ansley likes the two girls to go everywhere together?

My poor Jenny as a foil—!" Mrs. Slade gave a hardly audible laugh, and at the sound Mrs. Ansley dropped her knitting.

"Yes—?"   35

"I—oh, nothing. I was only thinking how your Babs carries everything before her. That Campolieri boy is one of the best matches in Rome. Don't look so innocent, my dear—you know he is. And I was wondering, ever so respectfully, you understand . . . wondering how two such exemplary characters as you and Horace had managed to produce anything quite so dynamic." Mrs. Slade laughed again, with a touch of asperity.

Mrs. Ansley's hands lay inert across her needles. She looked straight out at the great accumulated wreckage of passion and splendor at her feet. But her small profile was almost expressionless. At length she said: "I think you overrate Babs, my dear."

Mrs. Slade's tone grew easier. "No; I don't. I appreciate her. And perhaps envy you. Oh, my girl's perfect; if I were a chronic invalid I'd—well, I think I'd rather be in Jenny's hands. There must be times . . . but there! I always wanted a brilliant daughter . . . and never quite understood why I got an angel instead."

Mrs. Ansley echoed her laugh in a faint murmur. "Babs is an angel too."

"Of course—of course! But she's got rainbow wings. Well, they're   40 wandering by the sea with their young men; and here we sit . . . and it all brings back the past a little too acutely."

Mrs. Ansley had resumed her knitting. One might almost have imagined (if one had known her less well, Mrs. Slade reflected) that, for her also, too many memories rose from the lengthening shadows of those august ruins. But no; she was simply absorbed in her work. What was there for her to worry about? She knew that Babs would almost certainly come back engaged to the extremely eligible Campolieri. "And she'll sell the New York house, and settle down near them in Rome, and never be in their way . . . she's much too tactful. But she'll have an excellent cook, and just the right people in for bridge and cocktails . . . and a perfectly peaceful old age among her grandchildren."

Mrs. Slade broke off this prophetic flight with a recoil of self-disgust. There was no one of whom she had less right to think unkindly than of Grace Ansley. Would she never cure herself of envying her? Perhaps she had begun too long ago.

She stood up and leaned against the parapet, filling her troubled eyes with the tranquilizing magic of the hour. But instead of tranquilizing her the sight seemed to increase her exasperation. Her gaze turned toward the Colosseum. Already its golden flank was drowned in purple shadow, and above it the sky curved crystal clear, without light or color. It was the moment when afternoon and evening hang balanced in midheaven.

Mrs. Slade turned back and laid her hand on her friend's arm. The gesture was so abrupt that Mrs. Ansley looked up, startled.

45   "The sun's set. You're not afraid, my dear?"

"Afraid—?"

"Of Roman fever or pneumonia? I remember how ill you were that winter. As a girl you had a very delicate throat, hadn't you?"

"Oh, we're all right up here. Down below, in the Forum, it does get deathly cold, all of a sudden . . . but not here."

"Ah, of course you know because you had to be so careful." Mrs. Slade turned back to the parapet. She thought: "I must make one more effort not to hate her." Aloud she said: "Whenever I look at the Forum from up here, I remember that story about a great-aunt of yours, wasn't she? A dreadfully wicked great-aunt?"

50   "Oh, yes; great-aunt Harriet. The one who was supposed to have sent her young sister out to the Forum after sunset to gather a night-blooming flower for her album. All our great-aunts and grandmothers used to have albums of dried flowers."

Mrs. Slade nodded. "But she really sent her because they were in love with the same man—"

"Well, that was the family tradition. They said Aunt Harriet confessed it years afterward. At any rate, the poor little sister caught the fever and died. Mother used to frighten us with the story when we were children."

"And you frightened *me* with it, that winter when you and I were here as girls. The winter I was engaged to Delphin."

Mrs. Ansley gave a faint laugh. "Oh, did I? Really frightened you? I don't believe you're easily frightened."

55   "Not often; but I was then. I was easily frightened because I was too happy. I wonder if you know what that means?"

"I—yes . . ." Mrs. Ansley faltered.

"Well, I suppose that was why the story of your wicked aunt made such an impression on me. And I thought: 'There's no more Roman fever, but the Forum is deathly cold after sunset—especially after a hot day. And the Colosseum's even colder and damper.'"

"The Colosseum—?"

"Yes. It wasn't easy to get in, after the gates were locked for the night. Far from easy. Still, in those days it could be managed; it *was* managed, often. Lovers met there who couldn't meet elsewhere. You knew that?"

60   "I—I dare say. I don't remember."

"You don't remember? You don't remember going to visit some ruins or other one evening, just after dark, and catching a bad chill? You were supposed to have gone to see the moon rise. People always said that expedition was what caused your illness."

There was a moment's silence; then Mrs. Ansley rejoined: "Did they? It was all so long ago."

"Yes. And you got well again—so it didn't matter. But I suppose it struck your friends—the reason given for your illness, I mean—because everybody knew you were so prudent on account of your throat, and your mother took such care of you. . . . You *had* been out late sight-seeing, hadn't you, that night?"

"Perhaps I had. The most prudent girls aren't always prudent. What made you think of it now?"

Mrs. Slade seemed to have no answer ready. But after a moment she   65
broke out: "Because I simply can't bear it any longer—!"

Mrs. Ansley lifted her head quickly. Her eyes were wide and very pale. "Can't bear what?"

"Why—your not knowing that I've always known why you went."

"Why I went—?"

"Yes. You think I'm bluffing, don't you? Well, you went to meet the man I was engaged to—and I can repeat every word of the letter that took you there."

While Mrs. Slade spoke Mrs. Ansley had risen unsteadily to her   70
feet. Her bag, her knitting and gloves, slid in a panic-stricken heap to the ground. She looked at Mrs. Slade as though she were looking at a ghost.

"No, no—don't," she faltered out.

"Why not? Listen, if you don't believe me. 'My one darling, things can't go on like this. I must see you alone. Come to the Colosseum immediately after dark tomorrow. There will be somebody to let you in. No one whom you need fear will suspect'—but perhaps you've forgotten what the letter said?"

Mrs. Ansley met the challenge with an unexpected composure. Steadying herself against the chair she looked at her friend, and replied: "No; I know it by heart too."

"And the signature? 'Only *your* D.S.' Was that it? I'm right, am I? That was the letter that took you out that evening after dark?"

Mrs. Ansley was still looking at her. It seemed to Mrs. Slade that a   75
slow struggle was going on behind the voluntarily controlled mask of her small quiet face. "I shouldn't have thought she had herself so well in hand," Mrs. Slade reflected, almost resentfully. But at this moment Mrs. Ansley spoke. "I don't know how you knew. I burnt that letter at once."

"Yes; you would, naturally—you're so prudent!" The sneer was open now. "And if you burnt the letter you're wondering how on earth I know what was in it. That's it, isn't it?"

Mrs. Slade waited, but Mrs. Ansley did not speak.

"Well, my dear, I know what was in that letter because I wrote it!"

"You wrote it?"

80   "Yes."

The two women stood for a minute staring at each other in the last golden light. Then Mrs. Ansley dropped back into her chair. "Oh," she murmured, and covered her face with her hands.

Mrs. Slade waited nervously for another word or movement. None came, and at length she broke out: "I horrify you."

Mrs. Ansley's hands dropped to her knee. The face they uncovered was streaked with tears. "I wasn't thinking of you. I was thinking—it was the only letter I ever had from him!"

"And I wrote it. Yes; I wrote it! But I was the girl he was engaged to. Did you happen to remember that?"

85   Mrs. Ansley's head drooped again. "I'm not trying to excuse myself . . . I remembered. . . ."

"And still you went?"

"Still I went."

Mrs. Slade stood looking down on the small bowed figure at her side. The flame of her wrath had already sunk, and she wondered why she had ever thought there would be any satisfaction in inflicting so purposeless a wound on her friend. But she had to justify herself.

"You do understand? I'd found out—and I hated you, hated you. I knew you were in love with Delphin—and I was afraid; afraid of you, of your quiet ways, your sweetness . . . your . . . well, I wanted you out of the way, that's all. Just for a few weeks; just till I was sure of him. So in a blind fury I wrote that letter. . . I don't know why I'm telling you now."

90   "I suppose," said Mrs. Ansley slowly, "it's because you've always gone on hating me."

"Perhaps. Or because I wanted to get the whole thing off my mind." She paused. "I'm glad you destroyed the letter. Of course I never thought you'd die."

Mrs. Ansley relapsed into silence, and Mrs. Slade, leaning above her, was conscious of a strange sense of isolation, of being cut off from the warm current of human communion. "You think me a monster!"

"I don't know. . . . It was the only letter I had, and you say he didn't write it?"

"Ah, how you care for him still!"

95   "I cared for that memory," said Mrs. Ansley.

Mrs. Slade continued to look down on her. She seemed physically reduced by the blow—as if, when she got up, the wind might scatter her like a puff of dust. Mrs. Slade's jealousy suddenly leapt up again at the sight. All these years the woman had been living on that letter. How she must have loved him, to treasure the mere memory of its ashes! The letter of the man her friend was engaged to. Wasn't it she who was the monster?

"You tried your best to get him away from me, didn't you? But you failed; and I kept him. That's all."

"Yes. That's all."

"I wish now I hadn't told you. I'd no idea you'd feel about it as you do; I thought you'd be amused. It all happened so long ago, as you say; and you must do me the justice to remember that I had no reason to think you'd ever taken it seriously. How could I, when you were married to Horace Ansley two months afterward? As soon as you could get out of bed your mother rushed you off to Florence and married you. People were rather surprised—they wondered at its being done so quickly; but I thought I knew. I had an idea you did it out of *pique*—to be able to say you'd got ahead of Delphin and me. Girls have such silly reasons for doing the most serious things. And your marrying so soon convinced me that you'd never really cared."

"Yes. I suppose it would," Mrs. Ansley assented.   100

The clear heaven overhead was emptied of all its gold. Dusk spread over it, abruptly darkening the Seven Hills. Here and there lights began to twinkle through the foliage at their feet. Steps were coming and going on the deserted terrace—waiters looking out of the doorway at the head of the stairs, then reappearing with trays and napkins and flasks of wine. Tables were moved, chairs straightened. A feeble string of electric lights flickered out. Some vases of faded flowers were carried away, and brought back replenished. A stout lady in a dust coat suddenly appeared, asking in broken Italian if anyone had seen the elastic band which held together her tattered Baedeker.° She poked with her stick under the table at which she had lunched, the waiters assisting.

The corner where Mrs. Slade and Mrs. Ansley sat was still shadowy and deserted. For a long time neither of them spoke. At length Mrs. Slade began again: "I suppose I did it as a sort of joke—"

"A joke?"

"Well, girls are ferocious sometimes, you know. Girls in love especially. And I remember laughing to myself all that evening at the idea that you were waiting around there in the dark, dodging out of sight, listening for every sound, trying to get in— Of course I was upset when I heard you were so ill afterward."

Mrs. Ansley had not moved for a long time. But now she turned   105
slowly toward her companion. "But I didn't wait. He'd arranged everything. He was there. We were let in at once," she said.

Mrs. Slade sprang up from her leaning position. "Delphin there? They let you in?— Ah, now you're lying!" she burst out with violence.

Mrs. Ansley's voice grew clearer, and full of surprise. "But of course he was there. Naturally he came—"

Baedeker: tourist guidebook (one of a series issued by the German publisher Karl Baedeker)

"Came? How did he know he'd find you there? You must be raving!"

Mrs. Ansley hesitated, as though reflecting. "But I answered the letter. I told him I'd be there. So he came."

110   Mrs. Slade flung her hands up to her face. "Oh, God—you answered! I never thought of your answering. . . ."

"It's odd you never thought of it, if you wrote the letter."

"Yes. I was blind with rage."

Mrs. Ansley rose, and drew her fur scarf about her. "It is cold here. We'd better go . . . I'm sorry for you," she said, as she clasped the fur about her throat.

The unexpected words sent a pang through Mrs. Slade. "Yes; we'd better go." She gathered up her bag and cloak. "I don't know why you should be sorry for me," she muttered.

115   Mrs. Ansley stood looking away from her toward the dusky secret mass of the Colosseum. "Well—because I didn't have to wait that night."

Mrs. Slade gave an unquiet laugh. "Yes; I was beaten there. But I oughtn't to begrudge it to you, I suppose. At the end of all these years. After all, I had everything; I had him for twenty-five years. And you had nothing but that one letter that he didn't write."

Mrs. Ansley was again silent. At length she turned toward the door of the terrace. She took a step, and turned back, facing her companion.

"I had Barbara," she said, and began to move ahead of Mrs. Slade toward the stairway.

QUESTIONS

1. Characterize Grace Ansley and Alida Slade as fully as you can. By what characterizing devices does the author imply the superiority of Mrs. Slade (what gestures, what statements, what unspoken thoughts)? At what point does Mrs. Ansley begin to seem the superior person?

2. What does the author mean by her comment about "the wrong end of [the] little telescope" (paragraph 24)? How is that comment a suitable conclusion for the first part of the story?

3. What purpose is served by the discussion of the different meanings of Rome to mothers and daughters of different generations (paragraphs 29–31)? How does it expand the meaning of the title of the story?

4. Trace the revelation of the animosity that Mrs. Slade feels for Mrs. Ansley. Is Mrs. Ansley doing anything on this evening to provoke her envy? Why has Mrs. Slade always harbored negative feelings about her friend?

5. The story has a double plot, one occurring in the present at a restaurant in Rome, the other sequence of events in the past that is gradually revealed. How do the two plots contrast, and how do they resemble each other? What is the purpose of the contrasts drawn between the two daughters, Babs and Jenny?

6. Is the coincidence that brings these women together probable or improbable? What is your judgment about the surprise ending of this story? How does it compare to the surprise ending of "The Most Dangerous Game"?

John Galsworthy

The Japanese Quince

As Mr. Nilson, well known in the City, opened the window of his dressing room on Campden Hill, he experienced a peculiar sweetish sensation in the back of his throat, and a feeling of emptiness just under his fifth rib. Hooking the window back, he noticed that a little tree in the Square Gardens had come out in blossom, and that the thermometer stood at sixty. "Perfect morning," he thought; "spring at last!"

Resuming some meditations on the price of Tintos, he took up an ivory-backed handglass and scrutinized his face. His firm, well-colored cheeks, with their neat brown mustaches, and his round, well-opened, clear grey eyes, wore a reassuring appearance of good health. Putting on his black frock coat, he went downstairs.

In the dining room his morning paper was laid out on the sideboard. Mr. Nilson had scarcely taken it in his hand when he again became aware of that queer feeling. Somewhat concerned, he went to the French window and descended the scrolled iron steps into the fresh air. A cuckoo clock struck eight.

"Half an hour to breakfast," he thought; "I'll take a turn in the Gardens."

He had them to himself, and proceeded to pace the circular path with   5 his morning paper clasped behind him. He had scarcely made two revolutions, however, when it was borne in on him that, instead of going away in the fresh air, the feeling had increased. He drew several deep breaths, having heard deep breathing recommended by his wife's doctor; but they augmented rather than diminished the sensation—as of some sweetish liquor in course within him, together with a faint aching just above his heart. Running over what he had eaten the night before, he could recollect no unusual dish, and it occurred to him that it might possibly be some smell affecting him. But he could detect nothing except a faint sweet lemony scent, rather agreeable than otherwise, which evidently emanated from the bushes budding in the sunshine. He was on the point of resuming his promenade, when a blackbird close by burst into song, and, looking up, Mr. Nilson saw at a distance of perhaps five yards a little tree, in the heart of whose branches the bird was perched. He stood staring curiously at this tree, recognizing it for that which he had noticed from his window. It was covered with young blossoms, pink and white, and little bright green leaves both round and spiky; and on all this blossom and these leaves the sunlight

THE JAPANESE QUINCE   First published in 1910. "The City" is the financial and commercial center of London: the term has roughly the meaning for the British that "Wall Street" has for Americans. "Tintos" are stock shares, probably in the Rio Tinto Mining Company. John Galsworthy (1867–1933) was born in London, educated at Harrow and Oxford, and graduated with honors in law, but, after a period of travel, turned to writing as a career.

glistened. Mr. Nilson smiled; the little tree was so alive and pretty! And instead of passing on, he stayed there smiling at the tree.

"Morning like this!" he thought; "and here I am the only person in the Square who has the—to come out and—!" But he had no sooner conceived this thought than he saw quite near him a man with his hands behind him, who was also staring up and smiling at the little tree. Rather taken aback, Mr. Nilson ceased to smile, and looked furtively at the stranger. It was his next-door neighbor, Mr. Tandram, well known in the City, who had occupied the adjoining house for some five years. Mr. Nilson perceived at once the awkwardness of his position, for, being married, they had not yet had occasion to speak to one another. Doubtful as to his proper conduct, he decided at last to murmur: "Fine morning!" and was passing on, when Mr. Tandram answered: "Beautiful, for the time of year!" Detecting a slight nervousness in his neighbor's voice, Mr. Nilson was emboldened to regard him openly. He was of about Mr. Nilson's own height, with firm, well-colored cheeks, neat brown mustaches, and round, well-opened, clear grey eyes; and he was wearing a black frock coat. Mr. Nilson noticed that he had his morning paper clasped behind him as he looked up at the little tree. And, visited somehow by the feeling that he had been caught out, he said abruptly:

"Er—can you give me the name of that tree?"

Mr. Tandram answered:

"I was about to ask you that," and stepped towards it. Mr. Nilson also approached the tree.

10   "Sure to have its name on, I should think," he said.

Mr. Tandram was the first to see the little label, close to where the blackbird had been sitting. He read it out.

"Japanese quince!"

"Ah!" said Mr. Nilson, "thought so. Early flowerers."

"Very," assented Mr. Tandram, and added: "Quite a feelin' in the air today."

15   Mr. Nilson nodded.

"It was a blackbird singin'," he said.

"Blackbirds," answered Mr. Tandram. "I prefer them to thrushes myself; more body in the note." And he looked at Mr. Nilson in an almost friendly way.

"Quite," murmured Mr. Nilson. "These exotics, they don't bear fruit. Pretty blossoms!" and he again glanced up at the blossom, thinking: "Nice fellow, this, I rather like him."

Mr. Tandram also gazed at the blossom. And the little tree, as if appreciating their attention, quivered and glowed. From a distance the blackbird gave a loud, clear call. Mr. Nilson dropped his eyes. It struck him suddenly that Mr. Tandram looked a little foolish; and, as if he had seen himself, he said: "I must be going in. Good morning!"

20   A shade passed over Mr. Tandram's face, as if he, too, had suddenly noticed something about Mr. Nilson.

"Good morning," he replied, and clasping their journals to their backs they separated.

Mr. Nilson retraced his steps toward his garden window, walking slowly so as to avoid arriving at the same time as his neighbor. Having seen Mr. Tandram mount his scrolled iron steps, he ascended his own in turn. On the top step he paused.

With the slanting spring sunlight darting and quivering into it, the Japanese quince seemed more living than a tree. The blackbird had returned to it, and was chanting out his heart.

Mr. Nilson sighed; again he felt that queer sensation, that choky feeling in his throat.

The sound of a cough or sigh attracted his attention. There, in the shadow of his French window, stood Mr. Tandram, also looking forth across the Gardens at the little quince tree. 25

Unaccountably upset, Mr. Nilson turned abruptly into the house, and opened his morning paper.

QUESTIONS

1. Although we are given only a brief glimpse of Mr. Nilson's life, there are many clues as to what the whole of his life is like. What kind of house and district does he live in? To what social class does he belong? What kind of existence does he lead? What clues enable us to answer these questions?
2. Mr. Nilson at first thinks something is wrong with his health. What really is troubling him? How do the terms in which his symptoms are described (paragraphs 1 and 5) help to define his "ailment"?
3. In what ways might Mr. Nilson's fragmentary sentence at the beginning of paragraph 6 be completed? Why doesn't Mr. Nilson complete it?
4. How are Mr. Nilson and Mr. Tandram alike in appearance, manner, and situation? Of what significance are these similarities?
5. Mr. Nilson's meeting of Mr. Tandram at the tree might be described as a coincidence. Is it pure coincidence or does it have antecedent causes? Is it a legitimate device in terms of the story? Why or why not?
6. The quince tree is what we shall later refer to as a *symbol* (see Chapter 6). What qualities or abstractions does it seem to you to represent?
7. Although this story contains little action, it dramatizes a significant conflict. What are the opposed forces? How can the conflict be stated in terms of protagonist and antagonist? Is the conflict external or internal? How is it resolved—that is, which force wins?
8. This story demonstrates how a very slight plot may be used to provide a considerable illumination of life. How would you describe, in a sentence, the purpose of the story?

CHAPTER THREE

Character

In the preceding chapter plot was considered apart from character, as if the two were separable. Actually, like the ends of a seesaw, the two are one substance; there can be no movement at one end without movement at the other. The two ends of the seesaw may be talked about separately, however, and we can determine which element in any story is being emphasized—which end is up and which is down. As fiction passes from escape to interpretive, the character end is likely to go up. Experienced readers are less interested in actions done by characters than in characters doing actions.

Reading for character is more difficult than reading for plot, for character is much more complex, variable, and ambiguous. Anyone can repeat what a person has done in a story, but considerable skill may be needed to describe what a person *is*. Even the puzzles posed by the detective story are less complex and put less strain on comprehension than does human nature. Hence, escape fiction tends to emphasize plot and to present characters that are relatively simple and easy to understand. Less experienced readers demand that the characters be easily identifiable and clearly labeled as good or bad; they must not be so complex as to tax the readers' understanding.

These readers may also demand that the main character always be an attractive one. If the main character is male, he need not be perfect, but he must ordinarily be fundamentally decent—honest, good-hearted, and preferably good looking. If he is not virtuous, he must have strong compensatory qualities—he must be daring, dashing, or gallant. He may defy law and order only if he has a tender heart, a great love, or a gentleman's code. Readers who make these demands do so because for them the story is not a vehicle for understanding but material for a daydream. Identifying with the main character as they read, they vicariously share that character's adventures, escapes, and triumphs. The main character must therefore return them a pleasing image of self, must be someone such as they imagine themselves to be or such as they would like to be. In this way the story subtly flatters its readers, who forget their own inadequacies and satisfy their egos. If the hero or heroine has vices, these vices must be such as the readers themselves would not mind or would enjoy having. Some escape fiction has been about the man or woman who is appealing but sexually promiscuous. Readers have thus been able to indulge imaginatively in forbidden pleasures without losing a flattering self-image.

Interpretive fiction does not necessarily renounce the attractive central character. It simply furnishes a greater variety of central characters, characters that are less easily labeled and pigeonholed, characters that are sometimes unsympathetic. Human nature is not often entirely bad or perfectly good, and interpretive fiction deals usually with characters that are neither.

Once we get past the desire for a mechanical opposition between hero and villain, we discover that fiction offers an unparalleled opportunity to observe human nature in all its complexity and multiplicity. It enables us to know people, to understand them, and to learn compassion for them, as we might not otherwise do. In some respects we can know fictional characters even better than we know real people. For one thing, we observe them in situations that are always significant and that serve to bring forth their character as the ordinary situations of life only occasionally do. For another, we can view their inner life in a way that is impossible to us in ordinary life. Authors can tell us, if they wish, exactly what is going on in a character's mind and exactly what the character feels. In real life we can only guess at these inner thoughts and feelings from a person's external behavior, which may be designed to conceal what is going on inside. In limited ways, therefore, we can know people in fiction more thoroughly than we can know them in real life. And by knowing fictional characters we can also understand people in real life better than we otherwise could.

Authors present their characters either directly or indirectly. In **direct presentation** they tell us straight out, by exposition or analysis, what the characters are like, or have someone else in the story tell us what they are like. In **indirect presentation** the authors *show* us the characters in action; we infer what they are like from what they think or say or do. Graham Greene uses direct presentation when he tells us about Blackie: "He was just, he had no jealousy." He uses indirect presentation when he shows Blackie allowing the gang to vote on Trevor's project, accepting the end of his leadership fairly calmly, taking orders from Trevor without resentment, burning banknotes with Trevor, and racing him home. In this story, of course, the word "just" has a slight ironic twist—it applies only to behavior within the gang—and Greene presents this indirectly. John Galsworthy (page 73) relies entirely on indirect presentation to show that Mr. Nilson is a man of regulated habit who lives a life that is ordered and convention-bound.

The method of direct presentation has the advantages of being clear and economical, but it is scarcely ever used alone. The characters must act if there is to be a story; when they do not act, the story approaches the condition of an essay. The direct method, moreover, unless supported by the indirect, may not be emotionally convincing. It will give us not a character but an explanation. Readers want to be shown as well as told. They need to see and hear and overhear. In a successful story the characters are **dramatized**—shown speaking and acting, as in a drama. If we are really to believe in the selfishness of a character, we must see the character acting selfishly. Successful writers therefore rely mainly on indirect presentation and may use it entirely.

When most convincing, characterization also observes three other principles. First, the characters are consistent in their behavior: they do not behave one way on one occasion and a different way on another unless there is clearly a sufficient reason for the change. Second, the characters are motivated in whatever they do, especially when there is any change in their behavior: we must be able to understand the reasons for what they do, if not immediately, at least by the end of the story. Third, the characters are plausible or lifelike. They are neither paragons of virtue nor monsters of evil nor an impossible combination of contradictory traits. Whether we have observed anyone like them in our own experience or not, we must feel that they have come from the author's experience—that they could appear somewhere in the normal course of events.

In proportion to the fullness of their development, the characters in a story are relatively flat or round.* **Flat characters** are characterized by one or two traits; they can be summed up in a sentence. **Round characters** are complex and many sided; they might require an essay for full analysis. Both types of character can have the vitality that good fiction demands. Round characters live by their very roundness, by the many points at which they touch life. Huck Finn, in all respects an individual, lives vigorously in the imagination of the reader, while scholars and critics debate his moral development. Flat characters, though they touch life at only one or two points, may be made memorable in the hands of an expert author through some individualizing detail of appearance, gesture, or speech. Ebenezer Scrooge, in

---

*These terms were originated by the novelist E. M. Forster, who discussed them in *Aspects of the Novel* (New York: Harcourt, 1927), 103–18.

Dickens's *A Christmas Carol,* can be summed up and fully expressed in the two words "miserly misanthropy," but his "Bah! Humbug!" makes him live vividly in every reader's memory.

In good fiction all characters are characterized fully enough to justify their roles in the story and make them convincing. Most short stories will hardly have room for more than one or two round characters. Minor characters must necessarily remain flat. If the primary intention of a story is something other than the exhibition of character, none of the characters may be fully developed. Inferior fiction, however, is often built around characters who are insufficiently characterized to justify their roles. The essential nature and motivations of the protagonist may be so vaguely indicated that we are neither shocked nor convinced by any unusual action he performs or change of nature he undergoes. If a thief suddenly reforms and becomes an honest man, we must obviously know a great deal about him if the change is to be truly convincing. It is easier, of course, for writers to leave the characterization shadowy and hope that this weakness will slip by their readers unnoticed—as with less experienced readers it very well may.

A special kind of flat character is the **stock character**—stereotyped figures who have occurred so often in fiction that their nature is immediately known: the strong silent sheriff, the brilliant detective of eccentric habits, the mad scientist who performs fiendish experiments on living human beings, the beautiful international spy of mysterious background, the comic Englishman with a monocle and an exaggerated Oxford accent, the handsome brave hero, the beautiful modest heroine, the cruel stepmother, the sinister villain with a waxed black mustache. Such stock characters are found very often in inferior fiction since they require neither imagination nor observation on the part of the writer and are instantly recognizable to the reader. Like interchangeable parts, they might be transferred from one story to another with little loss of efficacy. Really good writers, however, may take a conventional type and by individualizing touches create a new and memorable figure. Conan Doyle's Sherlock Holmes is constructed on a pattern often imitated since, but he outlives the imitations and remains in our imaginations long after we have forgotten the details of his adventures. To the degree that characters have such individualizing touches, they become less flat and accordingly less stock.

All fictional characters may be classified as static or developing. The **static character** is the same sort of person at the end of the story as at the beginning. The **developing** (or dynamic) **character** undergoes a permanent change in some aspect of character, personality, or

outlook. The change may be a large or a small one; it may be for better or for worse; but it is something important and basic: it is more
than a change in condition or a minor change in opinion. Cinderella
is a static character, though she rises from cinder girl to princess. Dick
Prosser in "The Child by Tiger" is a dynamic character, for he changes
from a gentle, "amazingly tender," "deeply religious" man (who tells
the white boys, "you gotta love each othah like a brothah") into a
"crazy" killer. Paul in "Paul's Case" (page 154) is likewise dynamic, for
his need to escape from everyday reality grows progressively stronger.

Obviously, we must not expect many developing characters in *any*
piece of fiction: in a short story there is not usually room for more
than one. A not-infrequent basic plan of short stories is to show
change in the protagonist as the result of a crucial situation in his or
her life. When this is done in an interpretive story, the change is likely
to be the surest clue to the story's meaning. To state and explain the
change will be the best way to get at the point of the story. In escape
fiction, changes in character are likely to be more superficial, intended
merely to ensure a happy ending. Such changes are necessarily less
believable. A convincing change usually meets three conditions: (a) it
is within the possibilities of the character who makes it, (b) it is sufficiently motivated by the circumstances in which the character is
placed, and (c) it is allowed sufficient time for a change of its magnitude believably to take place. Basic changes in human character seldom occur suddenly. Interpretive writers do not present bad people
who suddenly reform at the end of the story and become good, or
drunkards who jump on the wagon at a moment's notice. They are
satisfied with smaller changes that are carefully prepared.

Human life began, we are told, when God breathed life into a
handful of dust and created Adam. Fictional life begins when an author breathes life into characters and convinces us of their reality.
Though fullness of characterization need not be the ultimate aim,
soundness of characterization is a test by which an author stands or
falls. The reader of good fiction lives in a world where the initial act of
creation is repeated again and again by the miracle of imagination.

Sherwood Anderson

I'm a Fool

It was a hard jolt for me, one of the most bitterest I ever had to face. And it all came about through my own foolishness, too. Even yet sometimes, when I think of it, I want to cry or swear or kick myself. Perhaps, even now, after all this time, there will be a kind of satisfaction in making myself look cheap by telling of it.

It began at three o'clock one October afternoon as I sat in the grandstand at the fall trotting and pacing meet at Sandusky, Ohio.

To tell the truth, I felt a little foolish that I should be sitting in the grandstand at all. During the summer before, I had left my hometown with Harry Whitehead and, with a nigger named Burt, had taken a job as swipe with one of the two horses Harry was campaigning through the fall race meets that year. Mother cried and my sister Mildred, who wanted to get a job as a schoolteacher in our town that fall, stormed and scolded about the house all during the week before I left. They both thought it something disgraceful that one of our family should take a place as a swipe with race horses. I've an idea Mildred thought my taking the place would stand in the way of her getting the job she'd been working so long for.

But after all I had to work, and there was no other work to be got. A big lumbering fellow of nineteen couldn't just hang around the house and I had got too big to mow people's lawns and sell newspapers. Little chaps who could get next to people's sympathies by their sizes were always getting jobs away from me. There was one fellow who kept saying to everyone who wanted a lawn mowed or a cistern cleaned that he was saving money to work his way through college, and I used to lay awake nights thinking up ways to injure him without being found out. I kept thinking of wagons running over him and bricks falling on his head as he walked along the street. But never mind him.

I got the place with Harry and I liked Burt fine. We got along splendid together. He was a big nigger with a lazy sprawling body and soft, kind eyes, and when it came to a fight he could hit like Jack Johnson.° He had Bucephalus, a big black pacing stallion that could do 2.09 or 2.10 if he had to, and I had a little gelding named Doctor Fritz that never lost a race all fall when Harry wanted him to win.

We set out from home late in July, in a box car with the two horses and after that, until late November, we kept moving along to the race meets and

I'M A FOOL   First published in 1922. The time of the story ("before prohibition") is probably well before 1919, when the Eighteenth Amendment was passed. The racing in the story is harness racing, in which the horse draws a light two-wheeled vehicle seating the driver. *Swipe* is a slang term for one who rubs down horses. Sherwood Anderson (1876–1941) grew up in northern Ohio near Sandusky.

Jack Johnson: world heavyweight boxing champion, 1908–1915, black

the fairs. It was a peachy time for me, I'll say that. Sometimes now I think that boys who are raised regular in houses, and never have a fine nigger like Burt for best friend, and go to high schools and college, and never steal anything, or get drunk a little, or learn to swear from fellows who know how, or come walking up in front of a grandstand in their shirt sleeves and with dirty horsy pants on when the races are going on and the grandstand is full of people all dressed up—What's the use of talking about it? Such fellows don't know nothing at all. They've never had no opportunity.

But I did. Burt taught me how to rub down a horse and put the bandages on after a race and steam a horse out and a lot of valuable things for any man to know. He could wrap a bandage on a horse's leg so smooth that if it had been the same color you would think it was his skin, and I guess he'd have been a big driver, too, and got to the top like Murphy and Walter Cox and the others if he hadn't been black.

Gee whizz! it was fun. You got to a county-seat town, maybe say on a Saturday or Sunday, and the fair began the next Tuesday and lasted until Friday afternoon. Doctor Fritz would be, say, in the 2.25 trot on Tuesday afternoon and on Thursday afternoon Bucephalus would knock 'em cold in the "free-for-all" pace. It left you a lot of time to hang around and listen to horse talk, and see Burt knock some yap cold that got too gay, and you'd find out about horses and men and pick up a lot of stuff you could use all the rest of your life, if you had some sense and salted down what you heard and felt and saw.

And then at the end of the week when the race meet was over, and Harry had run home to tend up to his livery-stable business, you and Burt hitched the two horses to carts and drove slow and steady across country, to the place for the next meeting, so as to not overheat the horses, etc., etc., you know.

10   Gee whizz! Gosh amighty! the nice hickory-nut and beechnut and oaks and other kinds of trees along the roads, all brown and red, and the good smells, and Burt singing a song called "Deep River," and the country girls at the windows of houses and everything. You can stick your colleges up your nose for all me. I guess I know where I got my education.

Why, one of those little burgs of towns you came to on the way, say now on a Saturday afternoon, and Burt says, "Let's lay up here." And you did.

And you took the horses to a livery stable and fed them, and you got your good clothes out of a box and put them on.

And the town was full of farmers gaping, because they could see you were racehorse people, and the kids maybe never see a nigger before and was afraid and run away when the two of us walked down their main street.

And that was before prohibition and all that foolishness, and so you went into a saloon, the two of you, and all the yaps come and stood around, and there was always some one pretended he was horsy and knew things and spoke up and began asking questions, and all you did was to lie and lie all you could about what horses you had, and I said I owned them, and then some fellow said, "Will you have a drink of whiskey?" and Burt knocked his eye out the way he could say, offhand like, "Oh, well, all right, I'm agreeable to a little nip. I'll split a quart with you." Gee whizz!

But that isn't what I want to tell my story about. We got home late in November and I promised mother I'd quit the race horses for good. There's a lot of things you've got to promise a mother because she don't know any better.

And so, there not being any work in our town any more than when I left there to go to the races, I went off to Sandusky and got a pretty good place taking care of horses for a man who owned a teaming and delivery and storage and coal and real-estate business there. It was a pretty good place with good eats, and a day off each week, and sleeping on a cot in a big barn, and mostly just shoveling in hay and oats to a lot of big good-enough skates of horses that couldn't have trotted a race with a toad. I wasn't dissatisfied and I could send money home.

And then, as I started to tell you, the fall races come to Sandusky and I got the day off and I went. I left the job at noon and had on my good clothes and my new brown derby hat I'd bought the Saturday before, and a stand-up collar.

First of all I went downtown and walked about with the dudes. I've always thought to myself, "Put up a good front," and so I did it. I had forty dollars in my pockets and so I went into the West House, a big hotel, and walked up to the cigar stand. "Give me three twenty-five cent cigars," I said. There was a lot of horsemen and strangers and dressed-up people from other towns standing around in the lobby and in the bar, and I mingled amongst them. In the bar there was a fellow with a cane and a Windsor tie° on, that it made me sick to look at him. I like a man to be a man and dressed up, but not to go put on that kind of airs. So I pushed him aside, kind of rough, and had me a drink of whiskey. And then he looked at me, as though he thought maybe he'd get gay, but he changed his mind and didn't say anything. And then I had another drink of whiskey, just to show him something, and went out and had a hack out to the races, all to myself, and when I got there I bought myself the best seat I could get up in the grandstand, but didn't go in for any of these boxes. That's putting on too many airs.

And so there I was, sitting up in the grandstand as gay as you please and looking down on the swipes coming out with their horses, and with their dirty horsy pants on and the horseblankets swung over their shoulders, same as I had been doing all the year before. I liked one thing about the same as the other, sitting up there and feeling grand and being down there and looking up at the yaps and feeling grander and more important, too.

One thing's about as good as another, if you take it just right. I've often said that.

15

20

Windsor tie: a wide black silk necktie tied in a loose bow

Well, right in front of me, in the grandstand that day, there was a fellow with a couple of girls and they was about my age. The young fellow was a nice guy, all right. He was the kind maybe that goes to college and then comes to be a lawyer or maybe a newspaper editor or something like that, but he wasn't stuck on himself. There are some of that kind are all right and he was one of the ones.

He had his sister with him and another girl and the sister looked around over his shoulder, accidental at first, not intending to start anything—she wasn't that kind—and her eyes and mine happened to meet.

You know how it is. Gee, she was a peach! She had on a soft dress, kind of a blue stuff and it looked carelessly made, but was well sewed and made and everything. I knew that much. I blushed when she looked right at me and so did she. She was the nicest girl I've ever seen in my life. She wasn't stuck on herself and she could talk proper grammar without being like a schoolteacher or something like that. What I mean is, she was O.K. I think maybe her father was well-to-do, but not rich to make her chesty because she was his daughter, as some are. Maybe he owned a drug store or a dry-goods store in their home town, or something like that. She never told me and I never asked.

My own people are all O.K. too, when you come to that. My grandfather was Welsh and over in the old country, in Wales he was—But never mind that.

25   The first heat of the first race come off and the young fellow setting there with the two girls left them and went down to make a bet. I knew what he was up to, but he didn't talk big and noisy and let everyone around know he was a sport, as some do. He wasn't that kind. Well, he come back and I heard him tell the two girls what horse he'd bet on, and when the heat trotted they all half got to their feet and acted in the excited, sweaty way people do when they've got money down on a race, and the horse they bet on is up there pretty close at the end, and they think maybe he'll come on with a rush, but he never does because he hasn't got the old juice in him, come right down to it.

And then, pretty soon, the horses came out for the 2.18 pace and there was a horse in it I knew. He was a horse Bob French had in his string but Bob didn't own him. He was a horse owned by a Mr. Mathers down at Marietta, Ohio.

This Mr. Mathers had a lot of money and owned some coal mines or something and he had a swell place out in the country, and he was stuck on race horses, but was a Presbyterian or something, and I think more than likely his wife was one, too, maybe a stiffer one than himself. So he never raced his horses hisself, and the story round the Ohio race tracks was that when one of his horses got ready to go to the races he turned him over to Bob French and pretended to his wife he was sold.

So Bob had the horses and he did pretty much as he pleased and you can't blame Bob, at least, I never did. Sometimes he was out to win and sometimes he wasn't. I never cared much about that when I was swiping a horse. What I did want to know was that my horse had the speed and could go out in front, if you wanted him to.

And, as I'm telling you, there was Bob in this race with one of Mr. Mathers's horses, was named "About Ben Ahem"° or something like that, and was fast as a streak. He was a gelding and had a mark of 2.21, but could step in .08 or .09.

Because when Burt and I were out, as I've told you, the year before, there   30
was a nigger Burt knew, worked for Mr. Mathers and we went out there one day when we didn't have no race on at the Marietta Fair and our boss Harry was gone home.

And so everyone was gone to the fair but just this one nigger and he took us all through Mr. Mathers's swell house and he and Burt tapped a bottle of wine Mr. Mathers had hid in his bedroom, back in a closet, without his wife knowing, and he showed us this Ahem horse. Burt was always stuck on being a driver but didn't have much chance to get to the top, being a nigger, and he and the other nigger gulped the whole bottle of wine and Burt got a little lit up.

So the nigger let Burt take this About Ben Ahem and step him a mile in a track Mr. Mathers had all to himself, right there on the farm. And Mr. Mathers had one child, a daughter, kinda sick and not very good looking, and she came home and we had to hustle to get About Ben Ahem stuck back in the barn.

I'm only telling you to get everything straight. At Sandusky, that afternoon I was at the fair, this young fellow with the two girls was fussed, being with the girls and losing his bet. You know how a fellow is that way. One of them was his girl and the other his sister. I had figured that out.

"Gee whizz," I says to myself, "I'm going to give him the dope."

He was mighty nice when I touched him on the shoulder. He and the   35
girls were nice to me right from the start and clear to the end. I'm not blaming them.

And so he leaned back and I give him the dope on About Ben Ahem. "Don't bet a cent on this first heat because he'll go like an oxen hitched to a plow, but when the first heat is over go right down and lay on your pile." That's what I told him.

Well, I never saw a fellow treat any one sweller. There was a fat man sitting beside the little girl, that had looked at me twice by this time, and I at her, and both blushing, and what did he do but have the nerve to turn and ask the fat man to get up and change places with me so I could set with his crowd.

Gee whizz, craps amighty. There I was. What a chump I was to go and get gay up there in the West House bar, and just because that dude was standing there with a cane and that kind of a necktie on, to go and get all balled up and drink that whiskey, just to show off.

"About Ben Ahem": Abou Ben Adhem is the title character of a well-known poem by Leigh Hunt.

Of course she would know, me setting right beside her and letting her smell of my breath. I could have kicked myself right down out of that grand-stand and all around that racetrack and made a faster record than most of the skates of horses they had there that year.

40   Because that girl wasn't any mutt of a girl. What wouldn't I have give right then for a stick of chewing gum to chew, or a lozenger, or some licorice, or most anything. I was glad I had those twenty-five cent cigars in my pocket and right away I gave that fellow one and lit one myself. Then that fat man got up and we changed places and there I was, plunked right down beside her.

They introduced themselves and the fellow's best girl, he had with him, was named Miss Elinor Woodbury, and her father was a manufacturer of barrels from a place called Tiffin, Ohio. And the fellow himself was named Wilbur Wessen and his sister was Miss Lucy Wessen.

I suppose it was their having such swell names that got me off my trolley. A fellow, just because he has been a swipe with a race horse, and works tak-ing care of horses for a man in the teaming, delivery, and storage business isn't any better or worse than any one else. I've often thought that, and said it too.

But you know how a fellow is. There's something in that kind of nice clothes, and the kind of nice eyes she had, and the way she had looked at me, awhile before, over her brother's shoulder, and me looking back at her, and both of us blushing.

I couldn't show her up for a boob, could I?

45   I made a fool of myself, that's what I did. I said my name was Walter Mathers from Marietta, Ohio, and then I told all three of them the smash-ingest lie you ever heard. What I said was that my father owned the horse About Ben Ahem and that he had let him out to this Bob French for racing purposes, because our family was proud and had never gone into racing that way, in our own name, I mean, and Miss Lucy Wessen's eyes were shining, and I went the whole hog.

I told her about our place down at Marietta, and about the big stables and the grand brick house we had on a hill, up above the Ohio River, but I knew enough not to do it in no bragging way. What I did was to start things and then let them drag the rest out of me. I acted just as reluctant to tell as I could. Our family hasn't got any barrel factory, and since I've known us, we've always been pretty poor, but not asking anything of anyone at that, and my grandfather, over in Wales—but never mind that.

We sat there talking like we had known each other for years and years, and I went and told them that my father had been expecting maybe this Bob French wasn't on the square, and had sent me up to Sandusky on the sly to find out what I could.

And I bluffed it through I had found out all about the 2.18 pace, in which About Ben Ahem was to start.

I said he would lose the first heat by pacing like a lame cow and then he would come back and skin 'em alive after that. And to back up what I said I took thirty dollars out of my pocket and handed it to Mr. Wilbur Wessen and asked him, would he mind, after the first heat, to go down and place it on

About Ben Ahem for whatever odds he could get. What I said was that I didn't want Bob French to see me and none of the swipes.

Sure enough the first heat come off and About Ben Ahem went off his stride, up the back stretch, and looked like a wooden horse or a sick one, and come in to be last. Then this Wilbur Wessen went down to the betting place under the grandstand and there I was with the two girls, and when that Miss Woodbury was looking the other way once, Lucy Wessen kinda, with her shoulder you know, kinda touched me. Not just tucking down, I don't mean. You know how a woman can do. They get close, but not getting gay either. You know what they do. Gee whizz. 50

And then they give me a jolt. What they had done, when I didn't know, was to get together, and they had decided Wilbur Wessen would bet fifty dollars, and the two girls had gone and put in ten dollars each, of their own money, too. I was sick then, but I was sicker later.

About the gelding, About Ben Ahem, and their winning their money, I wasn't worried a lot about that. It came out O.K. Ahem stepped the next three heats like a bushel of spoiled eggs going to market before they could be found out, and Wilbur Wessen had got nine to two for the money. There was something else eating at me.

Because Wilbur come back, after he had bet the money, and after that he spent most of his time talking to that Miss Woodbury, and Lucy Wessen and I was left alone together like on a desert island. Gee, if I'd only been on the square or if there had been any way of getting myself on the square. There ain't any Walter Mathers, like I said to her and them, and there hasn't ever been one, but if there was, I bet I'd go to Marietta, Ohio, and shoot him tomorrow.

There I was, big boob that I am. Pretty soon the race was over, and Wilbur had gone down and collected our money, and we had a hack downtown, and he stood us a swell supper at the West House, and a bottle of champagne beside.

And I was with the girl and she wasn't saying much, and I wasn't saying much either. One thing I know. She wasn't stuck on me because of the lie about my father being rich and all that. There's a way you know . . . Craps amighty. There's a kind of girl you see just once in your life, and if you don't get busy and make hay, then you're gone for good and all, and might as well go jump off a bridge. They give you a look from inside of them somewhere, and it ain't no vamping, and what it means is—you want that girl to be your wife, and you want nice things around her like flowers and swell clothes, and you want her to have the kids you're going to have, and you want good music played and no ragtime. Gee whizz. 55

There's a place over near Sandusky, across a kind of bay, and it's called Cedar Point. And after we had supper we went over to it in a launch, all by ourselves. Wilbur and Miss Lucy and that Miss Woodbury had to catch a ten o'clock train back to Tiffin, Ohio, because, when you're out with girls like that you can't get careless and miss any trains and stay out all night, like you can with some kinds of Janes.

And Wilbur blowed himself to the launch and it cost him fifteen cold plunks, but I wouldn't never have knew if I hadn't listened. He wasn't no tin horn kind of a sport.

Over at the Cedar Point place, we didn't stay around where there was a gang of common kind of cattle at all.

There was big dance halls and dining places for yaps, and there was a beach you could walk along and get where it was dark, and we went there.

60   She didn't talk hardly at all and neither did I, and I was thinking how glad I was my mother was all right, and always made us kids learn to eat with a fork at the table, and not swill soup, and not be noisy and rough like a gang you see around a racetrack that way.

Then Wilbur and his girl went away up the beach and Lucy and I sat down in a dark place, where there was some roots of old trees the water had washed up, and after that the time, till we had to go back in the launch and they had to catch their trains, wasn't nothing at all. It went like winking your eye.

Here's how it was. The place we were setting in was dark, like I said, and there was the roots from that old stump sticking up like arms, and there was a watery smell, and the night was like—as if you could put your hand out and feel it—so warm and soft and dark and sweet like an orange.

I most cried and I most swore and I most jumped up and danced, I was so mad and happy and sad.

When Wilbur come back from being alone with his girl, and she saw him coming, Lucy she says, "We got to go to the train now," and she was most crying too, but she never knew nothing I knew, and she couldn't be so all busted up. And then, before Wilbur and Miss Woodbury got up to where we was, she put her face up and kissed me quick and put her head up against me and she was all quivering and—Gee whizz.

65   Sometimes I hope I have cancer and die. I guess you know what I mean. We went in the launch across the bay to the train like that, and it was dark, too. She whispered and said it was like she and I could get out of the boat and walk on water, and it sounded foolish, but I knew what she meant.

And then quick we were right at the depot, and there was a big gang of yaps, the kind that goes to the fairs, and crowded and milling around like cattle, and how could I tell her? "It won't be long because you'll write and I'll write to you." That's all she said.

I got a chance like a hay barn afire. A swell chance I got.

And maybe she would write me, down at Marietta that way, and the letter would come back, and stamped on the front of it by the U.S.A. "there ain't any such guy," or something like that, whatever they stamp on a letter that way.

And me trying to pass myself off for a big-bug and a swell—to her, as decent a little body as God ever made. Craps amighty—swell chance I got!

70   And then the train come in, and she got on it, and Wilbur Wessen, he come and shook hands with me, and that Miss Woodbury was nice too and bowed to me, and I at her, and the train went and I busted out and cried like a kid.

Gee, I could have run after the train and made Dan Patch° look like a freight train after a wreck but, socks amighty, what was the use? Did you ever see such a fool?

I'll bet you what—if I had an arm broke right now or a train had run over my foot—I wouldn't go to no doctor at all. I'd go set down and let her hurt and hurt—that's what I'd do.

I'll bet you what—if I hadn't a drunk that booze I'd never been such a boob as to go tell such a lie—that couldn't never be made straight to a lady like her.

I wish I had that fellow right here that had on a Windsor tie and carried a cane. I'd smash him for fair. Gosh darn his eyes. He's a big fool—that's what he is.

And if I'm not another you just go find me one and I'll quit working and   75
be a bum and give him my job. I don't care nothing for working, and earning money, and saving it for no such boob as myself.

QUESTIONS

1. This story is told by an uneducated man who is handicapped in the telling by bad grammar, an inadequate vocabulary, ignorance, and a digressive storytelling method. Find a clear example of each. Why do these handicaps advance rather than hinder the story? What is the story's main purpose?

2. What kind of moral standards does the narrator have? Is he mean? What standards of behavior has he learned from his racetrack experiences?

3. What is the narrator's attitude toward education? Can you reconcile "You can stick your colleges up your nose for all me" (paragraph 10) with "The young fellow was a nice guy, all right. He was the kind maybe that goes to college and then comes to be a lawyer . . ." (paragraph 21)? What is an *ambivalent* attitude? What is *rationalization*? How are these terms appropriate for the narrator?

4. One main tenet of the narrator's rather rudimentary philosophy is "Put up a good front" (paragraph 18). On what occasions in the story does he put up a good front? What is the difference between "putting up a good front" and "putting on . . . airs" (paragraph 18)?

5. Another tenet of the narrator's philosophy is that "A fellow, just because he has been a swipe with a race horse, and works taking care of horses for a man in the teaming, delivery, and storage business isn't any better or worse than any one else" (paragraph 42). If that is so, why is he so impressed by the "swell names" and good clothes of the Wessens and Miss Woodbury? What does he like about the two jobs he has had?

6. Why does the narrator resent the man in the Windsor tie? What does he like about Burt? What does he like about the Wessens and Miss Woodbury? Why does he refer to other young women as "Janes" (paragraph 56), to blacks as "niggers" (paragraph 3 and elsewhere), and to most people as "yaps" (paragraph 19 and elsewhere)?

Dan Patch: one of the fastest harness horses in history

7. Evaluate the narrator's emotional maturity in the light of (a) his reactions to the little chap who got jobs away from him (paragraph 4); (b) his behavior toward the man in the Windsor tie (paragraph 18); (c) what he would do to the real Walter Mathers if there were one (paragraph 53); and (d) what he would like to happen to himself at the end of the story. How old is he?
8. The narrator blames his whopper at the racetrack on the whiskey, and he blames the whiskey on the man in the Windsor tie. What is the real reason for his behavior?
9. How is your attitude toward the narrator affected by the fact that you hear his story from himself? How would it be different if you had heard it from, say, an analyst?

Alice Walker

Everyday Use

for your grandmama

I will wait for her in the yard that Maggie and I made so clean and wavy yesterday afternoon. A yard like this is more comfortable than most people know. It is not just a yard. It is like an extended living room. When the hard clay is swept clean as a floor and the fine sand around the edges lined with tiny, irregular grooves, anyone can come and sit and look up into the elm tree and wait for the breezes that never come inside the house.

Maggie will be nervous until after her sister goes: she will stand hopelessly in corners, homely and ashamed of the burn scars down her arms and legs, eying her sister with a mixture of envy and awe. She thinks her sister has held life always in the palm of one hand, that "no" is a word the world never learned to say to her.

You've no doubt seen those TV shows where the child who has "made it" is confronted, as a surprise, by her own mother and father, tottering in weakly from backstage. (A pleasant surprise, of course: What would they do if parent and child came on the show only to curse out and insult each other?) On TV mother and child embrace and smile into each other's faces. Sometimes the mother and father weep, the child wraps them in her arms and leans across the table to tell how she would not have made it without their help. I have seen these programs.

EVERYDAY USE   First published in 1973. Alice Walker was born in Georgia in 1944, attended Spelman College for two years, earned her B.A. from Sarah Lawrence, and was active in the civil rights movement. She has taught and been writer-in-residence at various colleges including Jackson State, Tougaloo, Wellesley, the University of California at Berkeley, and Brandeis. The names adopted by two of the characters in the story reflect the practice among some members of the black community of rejecting names inherited from the period of slavery and selecting others more in keeping with their African heritage. The greetings used by Hakim and Wangero ("Asalamalakim" and "Wa-su-zo-Tean-o") are apparently adaptations of Arabic and African languages.

Sometimes I dream a dream in which Dee and I are suddenly brought together on a TV program of this sort. Out of a dark and soft-seated limousine I am ushered into a bright room filled with many people. There I meet a smiling, gray, sporty man like Johnny Carson who shakes my hand and tells me what a fine girl I have. Then we are on the stage and Dee is embracing me with tears in her eyes. She pins on my dress a large orchid, even though she had told me once that she thinks orchids are tacky flowers.

In real life I am a large, big-boned woman with rough, man-working hands. In the winter I wear flannel nightgowns to bed and overalls during the day. I can kill and clean a hog as mercilessly as a man. My fat keeps me hot in zero weather. I can work outside all day, breaking ice to get water for washing; I can eat pork liver cooked over the open fire minutes after it comes steaming from the hog. One winter I knocked a bull calf straight in the brain between the eyes with a sledge hammer and had the meat hung up to chill before nightfall. But of course all this does not show on television. I am the way my daughter would want me to be: a hundred pounds lighter, my skin like an uncooked barley pancake. My hair glistens in the hot bright lights. Johnny Carson has much to do to keep up with my quick and witty tongue.   5

But that is a mistake. I know even before I wake up. Who ever knew a Johnson with a quick tongue? Who can even imagine me looking a strange white man in the eye? It seems to me I have talked to them always with one foot raised in flight, with my head turned in whichever way is farthest from them. Dee, though. She would always look anyone in the eye. Hesitation was no part of her nature.

"How do I look, Mama?" Maggie says, showing just enough of her thin body enveloped in pink skirt and red blouse for me to know she's there, almost hidden by the door.

"Come out into the yard," I say.

Have you ever seen a lame animal, perhaps a dog run over by some careless person rich enough to own a car, sidle up to someone who is ignorant enough to be kind to him? That is the way my Maggie walks. She has been like this, chin on chest, eyes on ground, feet in shuffle, ever since the fire that burned the other house to the ground.

Dee is lighter than Maggie, with nicer hair and a fuller figure. She's a   10 woman now, though sometimes I forget. How long ago was it that the other house burned? Ten, twelve years? Sometimes I can still hear the flames and feel Maggie's arms sticking to me, her hair smoking and her dress falling off her in little black papery flakes. Her eyes seemed stretched open, blazed open by the flames reflected in them. And Dee. I see her standing off under the sweet gum tree she used to dig gum out of; a look of concentration on her face as she watched the last dingy gray board of the house fall in toward the red-hot brick chimney. Why don't you do a dance around the ashes? I'd wanted to ask her. She had hated the house that much.

I used to think she hated Maggie, too. But that was before we raised the money, the church and me, to send her to Augusta to school. She used to read to us without pity; forcing words, lies, other folks' habits, whole lives upon us two, sitting trapped and ignorant underneath her voice. She washed us in a river of make-believe, burned us with a lot of knowledge we didn't necessarily need to know. Pressed us to her with the serious way she read, to shove us away at just the moment, like dimwits, we seemed about to understand.

Dee wanted nice things. A yellow organdy dress to wear to her graduation from high school; black pumps to match a green suit she'd made from an old suit somebody gave me. She was determined to stare down any disaster in her efforts. Her eyelids would not flicker for minutes at a time. Often I fought off the temptation to shake her. At sixteen she had a style of her own: and knew what style was.

I never had an education myself. After second grade the school was closed down. Don't ask me why: in 1927 colored asked fewer questions than they do now. Sometimes Maggie reads to me. She stumbles along good-naturedly but can't see well. She knows she is not bright. Like good looks and money, quickness passed her by. She will marry John Thomas (who has mossy teeth in an earnest face) and then I'll be free to sit here and I guess just sing church songs to myself. Although I never was a good singer. Never could carry a tune. I was always better at a man's job. I used to love to milk till I was hooked in the side in '49. Cows are soothing and slow and don't bother you, unless you try to milk them the wrong way.

I have deliberately turned my back on the house. It is three rooms, just like the one that burned, except the roof is tin; they don't make shingle roofs any more. There are no real windows, just some holes cut in the sides, like the portholes in a ship, but not round and not square, with rawhide holding the shutters up on the outside. This house is in a pasture, too, like the other one. No doubt when Dee sees it she will want to tear it down. She wrote me once that no matter where we "choose" to live, she will manage to come see us. But she will never bring her friends. Maggie and I thought about this and Maggie asked me, "Mama, when did Dee ever *have* any friends?"

15   She had a few. Furtive boys in pink shirts hanging about on washday after school. Nervous girls who never laughed. Impressed with her, they worshipped the well-turned phrase, the cute shape, the scalding humor that erupted like bubbles in lye. She read to them.

When she was courting Jimmy T she didn't have much time to pay to us, but turned all her faultfinding power on him. He *flew* to marry a cheap city girl from a family of ignorant flashy people. She hardly had time to recompose herself.

When she comes I will meet—but there they are!

Maggie attempts to make a dash for the house, in her shuffling way, but I stay her with my hand. "Come back here," I say. And she stops and tries to dig a well in the sand with her toe.

It is hard to see them clearly through the strong sun. But even the first glimpse of leg out of the car tells me it is Dee. Her feet were always neat-looking, as if God himself had shaped them with a certain style. From the other side of the car comes a short, stocky man. Hair is all over his head a foot long and hanging from his chin like a kinky mule tail. I hear Maggie suck in her breath. "Uhnnnh," is what it sounds like. Like when you see the wriggling end of a snake just in front of your foot on the road. "Uhnnnh."

Dee next. A dress down to the ground, in this hot weather. A dress so   20
loud it hurts my eyes. There are yellows and oranges enough to throw back the light of the sun. I feel my whole face warming from the heat waves it throws out. Earrings gold, too, and hanging down to her shoulders. Bracelets dangling and making noises when she moves her arm up to shake the folds of the dress out of her armpits. The dress is loose and flows, and as she walks closer, I like it. I hear Maggie go "Uhnnnh" again. It is her sister's hair. It stands straight up like the wool on a sheep. It is black as night and around the edges are two long pigtails that rope about like small lizards disappearing behind her ears.

"Wa-su-zo-Tean-o!" she says, coming on in that gliding way the dress makes her move. The short stocky fellow with the hair to his navel is all grinning and he follows up with "Asalamalakim, my mother and sister!" He moves to hug Maggie but she falls back, right up against the back of my chair. I feel her trembling there and when I look up I see the perspiration falling off her chin.

"Don't get up," says Dee. Since I am stout it takes something of a push. You can see me trying to move a second or two before I make it. She turns, showing white heels through her sandals, and goes back to the car. Out she peeks next with a Polaroid. She stoops down quickly and lines up picture after picture of me sitting there in front of the house with Maggie cowering behind me. She never takes a shot without making sure the house is included. When a cow comes nibbling around the edge of the yard she snaps it and me and Maggie *and* the house. Then she puts the Polaroid in the back seat of the car, and comes up and kisses me on the forehead.

Meanwhile Asalamalakim is going through motions with Maggie's hand. Maggie's hand is as limp as a fish, and probably as cold, despite the sweat, and she keeps trying to pull it back. It looks like Asalamalakim wants to shake hands but wants to do it fancy. Or maybe he don't know how people shake hands. Anyhow, he soon gives up on Maggie.

"Well," I say. "Dee."

"No, Mama," she says. "Not 'Dee,' Wangero Leewanika Kemanjo!"   25

"What happened to 'Dee'?" I wanted to know.

"She's dead," Wangero said. "I couldn't bear it any longer, being named after the people who oppress me."

"You know as well as me you was named after your aunt Dicie," I said. Dicie is my sister. She named Dee. We called her "Big Dee" after Dee was born.

"But who was *she* named after?" asked Wangero.

30   "I guess after Grandma Dee," I said.

"And who was she named after?" asked Wangero.

"Her mother," I said, and saw Wangero was getting tired. "That's about as far back as I can trace it," I said. Though, in fact, I probably could have carried it back beyond the Civil War through the branches.

"Well," said Asalamalakim, "there you are."

"Uhnnnh," I heard Maggie say.

35   "There I was not," I said, "before 'Dicie' cropped up in our family, so why should I try to trace it that far back?"

He just stood there grinning, looking down on me like somebody inspecting a Model A car. Every once in a while he and Wangero sent eye signals over my head.

"How do you pronounce this name?" I asked.

"You don't have to call me by it if you don't want to," said Wangero.

"Why shouldn't I?" I asked. "If that's what you want us to call you, we'll call you."

40   "I know it might sound awkward at first," said Wangero.

"I'll get used to it," I said. "Ream it out again."

Well, soon we got the name out of the way. Asalamalakim had a name twice as long and three times as hard. After I tripped over it two or three times he told me to just call him Hakim-a-barber. I wanted to ask him was he a barber, but I didn't really think he was, so I didn't ask.

"You must belong to those beef-cattle peoples down the road," I said. They said "Asalamalakim" when they met you, too, but they didn't shake hands. Always too busy: feeding the cattle, fixing the fences, putting up salt-lick shelters, throwing down hay. When the white folks poisoned some of the herd the men stayed up all night with rifles in their hands. I walked a mile and a half just to see the sight.

Hakim-a-barber said, "I accept some of their doctrines, but farming and raising cattle is not my style." (They didn't tell me, and I didn't ask, whether Wangero [Dee] had really gone and married him.)

45   We sat down to eat and right away he said he didn't eat collards and pork was unclean. Wangero, though, went on through the chitlins and corn bread, the greens and everything else. She talked a blue streak over the sweet potatoes. Everything delighted her. Even the fact that we still used the benches her daddy made for the table when we couldn't afford to buy chairs.

"Oh, Mama!" she cried. Then turned to Hakim-a-barber. "I never knew how lovely these benches are. You can feel the rump prints," she said, running her hands underneath her and along the bench. Then she gave a sigh and her hand closed over Grandma Dee's butter dish. "That's it!" she said. "I knew there was something I wanted to ask you if I could have." She jumped up from the table and went over in the corner where the churn stood, the milk in it clabber by now. She looked at the churn and looked at it.

"This churn top is what I need," she said. "Didn't Uncle Buddy whittle it out of a tree you all used to have?"

"Yes," I said.

"Uh huh," she said happily. "And I want the dasher, too."

"Uncle Buddy whittle that, too?" asked the barber.   50

Dee (Wangero) looked up at me.

"Aunt Dee's first husband whittled the dash," said Maggie so low you almost couldn't hear her. "His name was Henry, but they called him Stash."

"Maggie's brain is like an elephant's," Wangero said, laughing. "I can use the churn top as a centerpiece for the alcove table," she said, sliding a plate over the churn, "and I'll think of something artistic to do with the dasher."

When she finished wrapping the dasher the handle stuck out. I took it for a moment in my hands. You didn't even have to look close to see where hands pushing the dasher up and down to make butter had left a kind of sink in the wood. In fact, there were a lot of small sinks; you could see where thumbs and fingers had sunk into the wood. It was beautiful light yellow wood, from a tree that grew in the yard where Big Dee and Stash had lived.

After dinner Dee (Wangero) went to the trunk at the foot of my bed and   55
started rifling through it. Maggie hung back in the kitchen over the dishpan. Out came Wangero with two quilts. They had been pieced by Grandma Dee and then Big Dee and me had hung them on the quilt frames on the front porch and quilted them. One was in the Lone Star pattern. The other was Walk Around the Mountain. In both of them were scraps of dresses Grandma Dee had worn fifty and more years ago. Bits and pieces of Grandpa Jarrell's Paisley shirts. And one teeny faded blue piece, about the size of a penny matchbox, that was from Great Grandpa Ezra's uniform that he wore in the Civil War.

"Mama," Wangero said sweet as a bird. "Can I have these old quilts?"

I heard something fall in the kitchen, and a minute later the kitchen door slammed.

"Why don't you take one or two of the others?" I asked. "These old things was just done by me and Big Dee from some tops your grandma pieced before she died."

"No," said Wangero. "I don't want those. They are stitched around the borders by machine."

"That'll make them last better," I said.   60

"That's not the point," said Wangero. "These are all pieces of dresses Grandma used to wear. She did all this stitching by hand. Imagine!" She held the quilts securely in her arms, stroking them.

"Some of the pieces, like those lavender ones, come from old clothes her mother handed down to her," I said, moving up to touch the quilts. Dee (Wangero) moved back just enough so that I couldn't reach the quilts. They already belonged to her.

"Imagine!" she breathed again, clutching them closely to her bosom.

"The truth is," I said, "I promised to give them quilts to Maggie, for when she marries John Thomas."

65   She gasped like a bee had stung her.

"Maggie can't appreciate these quilts!" she said. "She'd probably be backward enough to put them to everyday use."

"I reckon she would," I said. "God knows I been saving 'em for long enough with nobody using 'em. I hope she will!" I didn't want to bring up how I had offered Dee (Wangero) a quilt when she went away to college. Then she had told me they were old-fashioned, out of style.

"But they're *priceless!*" she was saying now, furiously; for she has a temper. "Maggie would put them on the bed and in five years they'd be in rags. Less than that!"

"She can always make some more," I said. "Maggie knows how to quilt."

70   Dee (Wangero) looked at me with hatred. "You just will not understand. The point is these quilts, *these* quilts!"

"Well," I said, stumped. "What would *you* do with them?"

"Hang them," she said. As if that was the only thing you *could* do with quilts.

Maggie by now was standing in the door. I could almost hear the sound her feet made as they scraped over each other.

"She can have them, Mama," she said, like somebody used to never winning anything, or having anything reserved for her. "I can 'member Grandma Dee without the quilts."

75   I looked at her hard. She had filled her bottom lip with checkerberry snuff and it gave her face a kind of dopey, hangdog look. It was Grandma Dee and Big Dee who taught her how to quilt herself. She stood there with her scarred hands hidden in the folds of her skirt. She looked at her sister with something like fear but she wasn't mad at her. This was Maggie's portion. This was the way she knew God to work.

When I looked at her like that something hit me in the top of my head and ran down to the soles of my feet. Just like when I'm in church and the spirit of God touches me and I get happy and shout. I did something I never had done before: hugged Maggie to me, then dragged her on into the room, snatched the quilts out of Miss Wangero's hands and dumped them into Maggie's lap. Maggie just sat there on my bed with her mouth open.

"Take one or two of the others," I said to Dee.

But she turned without a word and went out to Hakim-a-barber.

"You just don't understand," she said, as Maggie and I came out to the car.

80   "What don't I understand?" I wanted to know.

"Your heritage," she said. And then she turned to Maggie, kissed her, and said, "You ought to try to make something of yourself, too, Maggie. It's really a new day for us. But from the way you and Mama still live you'd never know it."

She put on some sunglasses that hid everything above the tip of her nose and her chin.

Maggie smiled; maybe at the sunglasses. But a real smile, not scared. After we watched the car dust settle I asked Maggie to bring me a dip of snuff. And then the two of us sat there just enjoying, until it was time to go in the house and go to bed.

QUESTIONS

1. Characterize the speaker and evaluate her reliability as a reporter and interpreter of events. Where does she refrain from making judgments? Where does she present less than the full truth? Do these examples of reticence undercut her reliability?

2. Describe as fully as possible the lives of the mother, Dee, and Maggie prior to the events of the story. How are the following incidents from the past also reflected in the present actions: (a) Dee's hatred of the old house; (b) Dee's ability "to stare down any disaster"; (c) Maggie's burns from the fire; (d) the mother's having been "hooked in the side while milking a cow"; (e) Dee's refusal to accept a quilt when she went away to college?

3. As evidence of current social movements and as innovations that the mother responds to, what do the following have in common: (a) Dee's new name and costume; (b) Hakim's behavior and attitudes; (c) the "beef-cattle peoples down the road"; (d) Dee's concern for her "heritage"?

4. Does the mother's refusal to let Dee have the quilts indicate a permanent or temporary change of character? Why has she never done anything like it before? Why does she do it now? What details in the story prepare for and foreshadow that refusal?

5. How does the physical setting give support to the contrasting attitudes of both the mother and Dee? Does the author indicate that one or the other of them is entirely correct in her feelings about the house and yard?

6. Is Dee wholly unsympathetic? Is the mother's victory over her altogether positive? What emotional ambivalence is there in the final scene between Maggie and her mother in the yard?

Katherine Mansfield

Miss Brill

Although it was so brilliantly fine—the blue sky powdered with gold and great spots of light like white wine splashed over the Jardins Publiques—Miss Brill was glad that she had decided on her fur. The air was motionless, but when you opened your mouth there was just a faint chill, like a chill from a glass of iced water before you sip, and now and again a leaf came drifting—

MISS BRILL   Written in 1921; first published in 1922. "Jardins Publiques" is French for Public Gardens. Katherine Mansfield (1888–1923) was born and grew up in New Zealand, but lived her adult life in London with various sojourns on the Continent.

from nowhere, from the sky. Miss Brill put up her hand and touched her fur. Dear little thing! It was nice to feel it again. She had taken it out of its box that afternoon, shaken out the moth powder, given it a good brush, and rubbed the life back into the dim little eyes. "What has been happening to me?" said the sad little eyes. Oh, how sweet it was to see them snap at her again from the red eiderdown! . . . But the nose, which was of some black composition, wasn't at all firm. It must have had a knock, somehow. Never mind—a little dab of black sealing-wax when the time came—when it was absolutely necessary . . . Little rogue! Yes, she really felt like that about it. Little rogue biting its tail just by her left ear. She could have taken it off and laid it on her lap and stroked it. She felt a tingling in her hands and arms, but that came from walking, she supposed. And when she breathed, something light and sad—no, not sad, exactly—something gentle seemed to move in her bosom.

There were a number of people out this afternoon, far more than last Sunday. And the band sounded louder and gayer. That was because the Season had begun. For although the band played all the year round on Sundays, out of season it was never the same. It was like some one playing with only the family to listen; it didn't care how it played if there weren't any strangers present. Wasn't the conductor wearing a new coat, too? She was sure it was new. He scraped with his foot and flapped his arms like a rooster about to crow, and the bandsmen sitting in the green rotunda blew out their cheeks and glared at the music. Now there came a little "flutey" bit—very pretty!—a little chain of bright drops. She was sure it would be repeated. It was; she lifted her head and smiled.

Only two people shared her "special" seat: a fine old man in a velvet coat, his hands clasped over a huge carved walking-stick, and a big old woman, sitting upright, with a roll of knitting on her embroidered apron. They did not speak. This was disappointing, for Miss Brill always looked forward to the conversation. She had become really quite expert, she thought, at listening as though she didn't listen, at sitting in other people's lives just for a minute while they talked round her.

She glanced, sideways, at the old couple. Perhaps they would go soon. Last Sunday, too, hadn't been as interesting as usual. An Englishman and his wife, he wearing a dreadful Panama hat and she button boots. And she'd gone on the whole time about how she ought to wear spectacles; she knew she needed them; but that it was no good getting any; they'd be sure to break and they'd never keep on. And he'd been so patient. He'd suggested everything—gold rims, the kind that curve round your ears, little pads inside the bridge. No, nothing would please her. "They'll always be sliding down my nose!" Miss Brill had wanted to shake her.

5   The old people sat on the bench, still as statues. Never mind, there was always the crowd to watch. To and fro, in front of the flower beds and the band rotunda, the couples and groups paraded, stopped to talk, to greet, to buy a handful of flowers from the old beggar who had his tray fixed to the

railings. Little children ran among them, swooping and laughing; little boys with big white silk bows under their chins, little girls, little French dolls, dressed up in velvet and lace. And sometimes a tiny staggerer came suddenly rocking into the open from under the trees, stopped, stared, as suddenly sat down "flop," until its small high-stepping mother, like a young hen, rushed scolding to its rescue. Other people sat on the benches and green chairs, but they were nearly always the same, Sunday after Sunday, and—Miss Brill had often noticed—there was something funny about nearly all of them. They were odd, silent, nearly all old, and from the way they stared they looked as though they'd just come from dark little rooms or even—even cupboards!

Behind the rotunda the slender trees with yellow leaves down drooping, and through them just a line of sea, and beyond the blue sky with gold-veined clouds.

Tum-tum-tum tiddle-um! tiddle-um! tum tiddley-um tum ta! blew the band.

Two young girls in red came by and two young soldiers in blue met them, and they laughed and paired and went off arm-in-arm. Two peasant women with funny straw hats passed, gravely, leading beautiful smoke-colored donkeys. A cold, pale nun hurried by. A beautiful woman came along and dropped her bunch of violets, and a little boy ran after to hand them to her, and she took them and threw them away as if they'd been poisoned. Dear me! Miss Brill didn't know whether to admire that or not! And now an ermine toque and a gentleman in gray met just in front of her. He was tall, stiff, dignified, and she was wearing the ermine toque she'd bought when her hair was yellow. Now everything, her hair, her face, even her eyes, was the same color as the shabby ermine, and her hand, in its cleaned glove, lifted to dab her lips, was a tiny yellowish paw. Oh, she was so pleased to see him— delighted! She rather thought they were going to meet that afternoon. She described where she'd been—everywhere, here, there, along by the sea. The day was so charming—didn't he agree? And wouldn't he, perhaps? . . . But he shook his head, lighted a cigarette, slowly breathed a great deep puff into her face, and, even while she was still talking and laughing, flicked the match away and walked on. The ermine toque was alone; she smiled more brightly than ever. But even the band seemed to know what she was feeling and played more softly, played tenderly, and the drum beat, "The Brute! The Brute!" over and over. What would she do? What was going to happen now? But as Miss Brill wondered, the ermine toque turned, raised her hand as though she'd seen some one else, much nicer, just over there, and pattered away. And the band changed again and played more quickly, more gayly than ever, and the old couple on Miss Brill's seat got up and marched away, and such a funny old man with long whiskers hobbled along in time to the music and was nearly knocked over by four girls walking abreast.

Oh, how fascinating it was! How she enjoyed it! How she loved sitting here, watching it all! It was like a play. It was exactly like a play. Who could believe the sky at the back wasn't painted? But it wasn't till a little brown dog trotted on solemn and then slowly trotted off, like a little "theater" dog, a little dog that had been drugged, that Miss Brill discovered what it was that made it so exciting. They were all on stage. They weren't only the audience, not only looking on; they were acting. Even she had a part and came every Sunday. No doubt somebody would have noticed if she hadn't been there; she was part of the performance after all. How strange she'd never thought of it like that before! And yet it explained why she made such a point of start-ing from home at just the same time each week—so as not to be late for the performance—and it also explained why she had quite a queer, shy feeling at telling her English pupils how she spent her Sunday afternoons. No wonder! Miss Brill nearly laughed out loud. She was on the stage. She thought of the old invalid gentleman to whom she read the newspaper four afternoons a week while he slept in the garden. She had got quite used to the frail head on the cotton pillow, the hollowed eyes, the open mouth and the high pinched nose. If he'd been dead she mightn't have noticed for weeks; she wouldn't have minded. But suddenly he knew he was having the paper read to him by an actress! "An actress!" The old head lifted; two points of light quivered in the old eyes. "An actress—are ye?" And Miss Brill smoothed the newspaper as though it were the manuscript of her part and said gently: "Yes, I have been an actress for a long time."

10   The band had been having a rest. Now they started again. And what they played was warm, sunny, yet there was just a faint chill—a something, what was it?—not sadness—no, not sadness—a something that made you want to sing. The tune lifted, lifted, the light shone; and it seemed to Miss Brill that in another moment all of them, all the whole company, would begin singing. The young ones, the laughing ones who were moving together, they would begin, and the men's voices, very resolute and brave, would join them. And then she too, she too, and the others on the benches—they would come in with a kind of accompaniment—something low, that scarcely rose or fell, something so beautiful—moving . . . And Miss Brill's eyes filled with tears and she looked smiling at all the other members of the company. Yes, we understand, we understand, she thought—though what they understood she didn't know.

Just at that moment a boy and girl came and sat down where the old couple had been. They were beautifully dressed; they were in love. The hero and heroine, of course, just arrived from his father's yacht. And still sound-lessly singing, still with that trembling smile, Miss Brill prepared to listen.

"No, not now," said the girl. "Not here, I can't."

"But why? Because of that stupid old thing at the end there?" asked the boy. "Why does she come here at all—who wants her? Why doesn't she keep her silly old mug at home?"

"It's her fu-fur which is so funny," giggled the girl. "It's exactly like a fried whiting."

15   "Ah, be off with you!" said the boy in an angry whisper. Then: "Tell me, ma petite chère—"

"No, not here," said the girl. "Not *yet.*"

On her way home she usually bought a slice of honeycake at the baker's. It was her Sunday treat. Sometimes there was an almond in her slice, sometimes not. It made a great difference. If there was an almond it was like carrying home a tiny present—a surprise—something that might very well not have been there. She hurried on the almond Sundays and struck the match for the kettle in quite a dashing way.

But today she passed the baker's by, climbed the stairs, went into the little dark room—her room like a cupboard—and sat down on the red eiderdown. She sat there for a long time. The box that the fur came out of was on the bed. She unclasped the necklet quickly; quickly, without looking, laid it inside. But when she put the lid on she thought she heard something crying.

QUESTIONS

1. We view the people and events of this story almost entirely through the eyes and feelings of its protagonist. The author relies upon indirect presentation for her characterization of Miss Brill. After answering the following questions, write as full an account as you can of the nature and temperament of the story's main character.
2. What nationality is Miss Brill? What is the story's setting? Why is it important?
3. How old is Miss Brill? What are her circumstances? Why does she listen in on conversations?
4. Why does Miss Brill enjoy her Sundays in the park? Why especially this Sunday?
5. Of what importance to the story is the woman in the ermine toque?
6. What is Miss Brill's mood at the beginning of the story? What is it at the end? Why? Is she a static or a developing character?
7. What function does Miss Brill's fur serve in the story? What is the meaning of the final sentence?

CHAPTER FOUR

Theme

"Daddy, the man next door kisses his wife every morning when he leaves for work. Why don't you do that?"
"Are you kidding? I don't even know the woman."

"Daughter, your young man stays until a very late hour. Hasn't your mother said anything to you about this habit of his?"
"Yes, father. Mother says men haven't altered a bit."

For readers who contemplate the two jokes above, a significant difference emerges between them. The first joke depends only upon a reversal of expectation. We expect the man to explain why he doesn't kiss his wife; instead he explains why he doesn't kiss his neighbor's wife. The second joke, though it contains a reversal of expectation, depends as much or more for its effectiveness on a truth about human life, namely, that *people tend to grow more conservative as they grow older* or that *parents often scold their children for doing exactly what they did themselves when young.* This truth, which might be stated in different ways, is the *theme* of the joke.

The **theme** of a piece of fiction is its controlling idea or its central insight. It is the unifying generalization about life stated or implied by the story. To derive the theme of a story, we must determine what its central *purpose* is: what view of life it supports or what insight into life it reveals.

Not all stories have theme. The purpose of a horror story may be simply to scare readers, to give them gooseflesh. The purpose of an adventure story may be simply to carry readers through a series of exciting escapades. The purpose of a murder mystery may be simply to pose a problem for readers to try to solve (and to prevent them from solving it, if possible, until the last paragraph). The purpose of some stories may be simply to provide suspense or to make readers laugh or to surprise them with a sudden twist at the end. Theme exists only (a) when an author has seriously attempted to record life accurately or to reveal some truth about it or (b) when an author has deliberately introduced as a unifying element some concept or theory of life that the story illuminates. Theme exists in all interpretive fiction but only in some escape fiction. In interpretive fiction it is the purpose of the story; in escape fiction, when it exists, it is usually an excuse, a peg to hang the story from.

In many stories the theme may be equivalent to the revelation of human character. If a story has as its central purpose to exhibit a certain kind of human being, our statement of theme may be no more than a concentrated description of the person revealed, with the addition, "Some people are like this." Frequently, however, a story through its portrayal of specific persons in specific situations will have something to say about the nature of all human beings or about their relationship to each other or to the universe. Whatever central generalization about life arises from the specifics of the story constitutes theme.

The theme of a story, like its plot, may be stated very briefly or at greater length. With a simple or very brief story, we may be satisfied to sum up the theme in a single sentence. With a more complex story, if it is successfully unified, we can still state the theme in a single sentence, but we may feel that a paragraph—or occasionally even an essay—is needed to state it adequately. A rich story will give us many and complex insights into life. In stating the theme in a sentence, we must pick the *central* insight, the one that explains the greatest number of elements in the story and relates them to each other. For theme is what gives a story its unity. In any story at all complex, however, we are likely to feel that a one-sentence statement of theme leaves out a great part of the story's meaning. Though the theme of *Othello* may be expressed as "Jealousy exacts a terrible cost," such a statement does not begin to suggest the range and depth of Shakespeare's play. Any successful story is a good deal more and means a good deal more than any one-sentence statement of theme that we may extract from it, for the story will modify and expand this statement in various and subtle ways.

We must never think, once we have stated the theme of a story, that the whole purpose of the story has been to yield up this abstract statement. If this were so, there would be no reason for the story: we could stop with the abstract statement. The function of interpretive writers is not to state a theme but to vivify it. They wish to deliver it not simply to our intellects but to our emotions, our senses, and our imaginations. The theme of a story may be little or nothing except as it is embodied and vitalized by the story. Unembodied, it is a dry backbone, without flesh or life.

Sometimes the theme of a story is explicitly stated somewhere in the story, either by the author or by one of the characters. More often, however, the theme is implied. Story writers, after all, are story writers, not essayists or philosophers. Their first business is to reveal life, not to comment on it. They may well feel that unless the story somehow expresses its own meaning, without their having to point it out, they have not told the story well. Or they may feel that if the story is to have its maximum emotional effect, they must refrain from interrupting it or making remarks about it. They are also wary of spoiling a story for perceptive readers by "explaining" it as some people ruin jokes by explaining them. For these reasons theme is more often left implicit than stated explicitly. Good writers do not ordinarily write a story for the sole purpose of "illustrating" a theme, as do the writers of parables or fables. They write stories to bring alive some segment of human existence. When they do so searchingly and coherently, theme arises naturally out of what they have written. Good readers may state the generalizations for themselves.

Some readers—especially inexperienced readers—look for a "moral" in everything they read—some rule of conduct that they regard as applicable to their lives. They consider the words "theme" and "moral" to be interchangeable. Sometimes the words are interchangeable. Occasionally the theme of a story may be expressed as a moral principle without doing violence to the story. More frequently, however, the word "moral" is too narrow to fit the kind of illumination provided by a first-rate story. It is hardly suitable, for instance, for the kind of story that simply displays human character. Such nouns as "moral" and "lesson" and "message" are therefore best avoided in the discussion of fiction. The critical term **theme** is preferable for several reasons. First, it is less likely to obscure the fact that a story is not a preachment or a sermon: a story's *first* object is enjoyment. Second, it should keep us from trying to wring from every story a didactic pronouncement about life. The person who seeks a moral in every story is likely to oversimplify and conventionalize it—to reduce it to some dusty platitude like "Be kind to animals" or "Look before you leap" or "Crime does not pay." The purpose of interpretive story writers is to give us a greater awareness and a greater understanding of life, not to inculcate a code of moral rules for regulating daily conduct. In getting at the theme of the story it is better to ask not *What does this story teach?* but *What does this story reveal?* Readers who interpret Anderson's "I'm a Fool" as being merely a warning against lying have missed nine-tenths of the story. It is really a marvelously penetrating exploration of a complex personality. The theme is *not* "Honesty is the best policy" but something more like this: "A young man of decent background who fails in various enterprises may develop ambivalent or contradictory values as well as feelings of inferiority. Consciously or unconsciously he will adopt various stratagems to compensate for these feelings by magnifying his importance both in his own eyes and in the eyes of others. If these stratagems backfire, he may recognize his folly but not the underlying reasons for it." Obviously, this dry statement is a poor thing beside the living reality of the story. But it is a more faithful abstracting of the content of the story than any "moral."

The revelation offered by a good story may be something fresh or something old. The story may bring us some insight into life that we had not had before, and thus expand our horizons, or it may make us *feel* or *feel again* some truth of which we have long been merely intellectually aware. We may know in our minds, for instance, that "War is horrible" or that "Old age is often pathetic and in need of understanding," but these are insights that need to be periodically renewed. *Emotionally* we may forget them, and if we do, we are less alive and complete as human beings. Story writers perform a service for us— interpret life for us—whether they give us new insights or refresh and extend old ones.

The themes of commercial and quality stories may be identical, but frequently they are different. Commercial stories, for the most part, confirm their readers' prejudices, endorse their opinions, ratify their feelings, and satisfy their wishes. Usually, therefore, the themes of such stories are widely accepted platitudes of experience that may or may not be supported by the life around us. They represent life as we would like it to be, not always as it is. We should certainly like to believe, for instance, that "Motherhood is sacred," that "True love always wins through," that "Virtue and hard work are rewarded in the end," that "Cheaters never win," that "Old age brings a mellow wisdom that compensates for its infirmity," and that "Every human being has a soft spot in him somewhere." Interpretive writers, however, being thoughtful observers of life, are likely to question these beliefs and often to challenge them. Their ideas about life are not simply taken over ready-made from what they were taught in Sunday school or from the books they read as children; they are the formulations of sensitive and independent observers who have collated all that they have read and been taught with life itself. The themes of their stories therefore do not often correspond to the pretty little sentiments we find inscribed in greeting cards. They may sometimes represent rather somber truths. Much of the process of maturing as a reader lies in the discovery that there may be more nourishment and deeper enjoyment in these somber truths than in the warm and fuzzy optimism of "Love is . . ." cartoons.

We do not, however, have to accept the theme of an interpretive story any more than we do that of a commercial story. Though we should never summarily dismiss it without reflection, we may find that the theme of a story represents a judgment on life with which, on examination, we cannot agree. If it is the reasoned view of a seasoned and serious artist, nevertheless, it cannot be without value to us. There is value in knowing what the world looks like to others, and we can thus use a judgment to expand our knowledge of human experience even though we cannot ourselves accept it. Genuine artists and thoughtful observers, moreover, can hardly fail to present us with partial insights along the way although we disagree with the total view. Good readers, therefore, will not reject a story because they reject its theme. They can enjoy any story that arises from sufficient depth of observation and reflection and is artistically composed, though they disagree with its theme; and they will prefer it to a shallower, less thoughtful, or less successfully integrated story that presents a theme they endorse.

Discovering and stating the theme of a story is often a delicate task. Sometimes we will *feel* what the story is about strongly enough and yet find it difficult to put this feeling into words. If we are skilled readers, it is perhaps unnecessary that we do so. The bare statement of the theme, so lifeless and impoverished when abstracted from the story, may seem to diminish the story to something less than it is. Often, however, the attempt to state a theme will reveal to us aspects of a story that we should otherwise not have noticed and will thereby lead to more thorough understanding. The ability to state theme, moreover, is a test of our understanding of a story. Inexperienced readers often think they understand a story when in actuality they have misunderstood it. They understand the events but not what the events add up to. Or, in adding up the events, they arrive at an erroneous total. People sometimes miss the point of a joke. It is not surprising that they should occasionally miss the point of a good piece of fiction, which is many times more complex than a joke.

There is no prescribed method for discovering theme. Sometimes we can best get at it by asking in what way the main character has changed in the course of the story and what, if anything, the character has learned before its end. Sometimes the best approach is to explore the nature of the central conflict and its outcome. Sometimes the title will provide an important clue. At all times we should keep in mind the following principles:

1. Theme should be expressible in the form of a statement with a subject and a predicate. It is insufficient to say that the theme of a story is motherhood or loyalty to country. Motherhood and loyalty are simply subjects. Theme must be a statement *about* the subject. For instance, "Motherhood sometimes has more frustrations than rewards" or "Loyalty to country often inspires heroic self-sacrifice." If we express the theme in the form of a phrase, the phrase must be convertible to sentence form. A phrase such as "the futility of envy," for instance, may be converted to the statement "Envy is futile": it may therefore serve as a statement of theme.

2. The theme should be stated as a *generalization* about life. In stating theme we do not use the names of the characters or refer to precise places or events, for to do so is to make a specific rather than a general statement. The theme of "The Destructors" is not that "The Wormsley Common Gang of London, in the aftermath of World War II, found a creative outlet in destroying a beautiful two-hundred-year-old house designed by Sir Christopher Wren." Rather, it is something like this: "The dislocations caused by a devastating war may produce among the young a conscious or unconscious rebellion against all the values of the reigning society—a rebellion in which the creative instincts are channeled into destructive enterprises."

3. We must be careful not to make the generalization larger than is justified by the terms of the story. Terms like *every, all, always* should be used very cautiously; terms like *some, sometimes, may* are often more accurate. The theme of "Everyday Use" is not that "Habitually compliant and tolerant mothers will eventually stand up to their bullying children," for we have only one instance of such behavior in the story. But the story does sufficiently present this event as a climactic change in a developing character. Because the story's narrator recalls precise details of her previous behavior that she brings to bear on her present decision, we can safely infer that this decision will be meaningful and lasting, and should feel we can generalize beyond the specific situation. The theme might be expressed thus: "A person whose honesty and tolerance have long made her susceptible to the strong will of another may reach a point where she will exert her own will for the sake of justice," or more generally, "Ingrained habits can be given up if justice makes a greater demand." Notice that we have said *may* and *can,* not *will* and *must.* Only occasionally will the theme of a story be

expressible as a universal generalization. In "The Child by Tiger" we know from Wolfe's use of Blake's poem and from his concluding paragraphs that the author considers Dick Prosser not as a special case but as a symbol of something present in us all. The soul of every man (so the story seems to say) is mysterious in its origins and contains unfathomed possibilities for evil and violence as well as for innocence and love.

4. Theme is the *central* and *unifying* concept of a story. Therefore (a) it accounts for all the major details of the story. If we cannot explain the bearing of an important incident or character on the theme, either in exemplifying it or modifying it in some way, it is probable that our interpretation is partial and incomplete, that at best we have got hold only of a subtheme. Another alternative, though it must be used with caution, is that the story itself is imperfectly constructed and lacks entire unity. (b) The theme is not contradicted by any detail of the story. If we have to overlook or blink at or "force" the meaning of some significant detail in order to frame our statement, we may be sure that our statement is defective. (c) The theme cannot rely upon supposed facts—facts not actually stated or clearly implied by the story. The theme exists *inside,* not *outside,* the story. The statement of it must be based on the data of the story itself, not on assumptions supplied from our own experience.

5. There is no *one* way of stating the theme of a story. The story is not a guessing game or an acrostic that is supposed to yield some magic verbal formula that won't work if a syllable is changed. It merely presents a view of life, and, as long as the above conditions are fulfilled, that view may surely be stated in more than one way. Here, for instance, are three possible ways of stating the theme of "Miss Brill": (a) A person living alone may create a protective fantasy life by dramatizing insignificant activities, but such a life can be jeopardized when she is forced to see herself as others see her. (b) Isolated elderly people, unsupported by a network of family and friends, may make a satisfying adjustment through a pleasant fantasy life, but when their fantasy is punctured by the cold claw of reality, the effect can be devastating. (c) Loneliness is a pitiable emotional state that may be avoided by refusing to acknowledge that one feels lonely, though such an avoidance may also require one to create unrealistic fantasies about oneself.

6. We should avoid any statement that reduces the theme to some familiar saying that we have heard all our lives, such as "You can't judge a book by its cover" or "A stitch in time saves nine." Although

such a statement *may* express the theme accurately, too often it is simply a lazy shortcut that impoverishes the essential meaning of the story in order to save mental effort. When readers force every new experience into an old formula, they lose the chance for a fresh perception. Instead of letting the story expand their knowledge and awareness of the world, they fall back dully on a cliché. To come out with "Honesty is the best policy" as the theme of "I'm a Fool" is almost to lose the whole value of the story. If the impulse arises to express the meaning of a story in a ready-made phrase, it should be suppressed.

Toni Cade Bambara

The Lesson

Back in the days when everyone was old and stupid or young and foolish and me and Sugar were the only ones just right, this lady moved on our block with nappy hair and proper speech and no makeup. And quite naturally we laughed at her, laughed the way we did at the junk man who went about his business like he was some big-time president and his sorry-ass horse his secretary. And we kinda hated her too, hated the way we did the winos who cluttered up our parks and pissed on our handball walls and stank up our hallways and stairs so you couldn't halfway play hide-and-seek without a goddamn gas mask. Miss Moore was her name. The only woman on the block with no first name. And she was black as hell, cept for her feet, which were fish-white and spooky. And she was always planning these boring-ass things for us to do, us being my cousin, mostly, who lived on the block cause we all moved North the same time and to the same apartment then spread out gradual to breathe. And our parents would yank our heads into some kinda shape and crisp up our clothes so we'd be presentable for travel with Miss Moore, who always looked like she was going to church, though she never did. Which is just one of the things the grownups talked about when they talked behind her back like a dog. But when she came calling with some sachet she'd sewed up or some gingerbread she'd made or some book, why then they'd all be too embarrassed to turn her down and we'd get handed over all spruced

THE LESSON   First published in her collection *Gorilla, My Love* in 1972. Toni Cade Bambara (1939–1995) was born in New York City, the site of the various place-names in the story, and was raised in Harlem and Bedford-Stuyvesant. She earned a B.A. at Queens College and an M.A. at the City College of New York. She began publishing her fiction in 1960 and earned distinction as an advocate of civil rights and as an anthologist of black literature. F. A. O. Schwarz (named in paragraph 45) is a toy store located on fashionable Fifth Avenue in Manhattan.

up. She'd been to college and said it was only right that she should take responsibility for the young ones' education, and she not even related by marriage or blood. So they'd go for it. Specially Aunt Gretchen. She was the main gofer in the family. You got some ole dumb shit foolishness you want somebody to go for, you send for Aunt Gretchen. She been screwed into the go-along for so long, it's a blood-deep natural thing with her. Which is how she got saddled with me and Sugar and Junior in the first place while our mothers were in a la-de-da apartment up the block having a good ole time.

So this one day Miss Moore rounds us all up at the mailbox and it's puredee hot and she's knockin herself out about arithmetic. And school suppose to let up in summer I heard, but she don't never let up. And the starch in my pinafore scratching the shit outta me and I'm really hating this nappy-head bitch and her goddamn college degree. I'd much rather go to the pool or to the show where it's cool. So me and Sugar leaning on the mailbox being surly, which is a Miss Moore word. And Flyboy checking out what everybody brought for lunch. And Fat Butt already wasting his peanut-butter-and-jelly sandwich like the pig he is. And Junebug punchin on Q.T.'s arm for potato chips. And Rosie Giraffe shifting from one hip to the other waiting for somebody to step on her foot or ask her if she from Georgia so she can kick ass, preferably Mercedes'. And Miss Moore asking us do we know what money is, like we a bunch of retards. I mean real money, she say, like it's only poker chips or monopoly papers we lay on the grocer. So right away I'm tired of this and say so. And would much rather snatch Sugar and go to the Sunset and terrorize the West Indian kids and take their hair ribbons and their money too. And Miss Moore files that remark away for next week's lesson on brotherhood, I can tell. And finally I say we oughta get to the subway cause it's cooler and besides we might meet some cute boys. Sugar done swiped her mama's lipstick, so we ready.

So we heading down the street and she's boring us silly about what things cost and what our parents make and how much goes for rent and how money ain't divided up right in this country. And then she gets to the part about we all poor and live in the slums, which I don't feature. And I'm ready to speak on that, but she steps out in the street and hails two cabs just like that. Then she hustles half the crew in with her and hands me a five-dollar bill and tells me to calculate 10 percent tip for the driver. And we're off. Me and Sugar and Junebug and Flyboy hangin out the window and hollering to everybody, putting lipstick on each other cause Flyboy a faggot anyway, and making farts with our sweaty armpits. But I'm mostly trying to figure how to spend this money. But they all fascinated with the meter ticking and Junebug starts laying bets as to how much it'll read when Flyboy can't hold his breath no more. Then Sugar lays bets as to how much it'll be when we get there. So I'm stuck. Don't nobody want to go for my plan, which is to jump out at the next light and run off to the first bar-b-que we can find. Then the driver tells us to get the hell out cause we there already. And the meter reads eighty-five cents. And I'm stalling to figure out the tip and Sugar say give him a dime. And I decide he don't need it bad as I do, so later for him. But then he tries to take off with Junebug foot still in the door so we talk about his mama something ferocious. Then we check out that we on Fifth Avenue and everybody dressed up in stockings. One lady in a fur coat, hot as it is. White folks crazy.

"This is the place," Miss Moore say, presenting it to us in the voice she uses at the museum. "Let's look in the windows before we go in."

"Can we steal?" Sugar asks very serious like she's getting the ground   5
rules squared away before she plays. "I beg your pardon," say Miss Moore, and we fall out. So she leads us around the windows of the toy store and me and Sugar screamin, "This is mine, that's mine, I gotta have that, that was made for me, I was born for that," till Big Butt drowns us out.

"Hey, I'm goin to buy that there."

"That there? You don't even know what it is, stupid."

"I do so," he say punchin on Rosie Giraffe. "It's a microscope."

"Whatcha gonna do with a microscope, fool?"

"Look at things."   10

"Like what, Ronald?" ask Miss Moore. And Big Butt ain't got the first notion. So here go Miss Moore gabbing about the thousands of bacteria in a drop of water and the somethinorother in a speck of blood and the million and one living things in the air around us is invisible to the naked eye. And what she say that for? Junebug go to town on that "naked" and we rolling. Then Miss Moore ask what it cost. So we all jam into the window smudgin it up and the price tag say $300. So then she ask how long'd take for Big Butt and Junebug to save up their allowances. "Too long," I say. "Yeh," adds Sugar, "outgrown it by that time." And Miss Moore say no, you never outgrow learning instruments. "Why, even medical students and interns and," blah, blah, blah. And we ready to choke Big Butt for bringing it up in the first damn place.

"This here costs four hundred eighty dollars," say Rosie Giraffe. So we pile up all over her to see what she pointin out. My eyes tell me it's a chunk of glass cracked with something heavy, and different-color inks dripped into the splits, then the whole thing put into a oven or something. But for $480 it don't make sense.

"That's a paperweight made of semi-precious stones fused together under tremendous pressure," she explains slowly, with her hands doing the mining and all the factory work.

"So what's a paperweight?" asks Rosie Giraffe.

"To weigh paper with, dumbbell," say Flyboy, the wise man from   15
the East.

"Not exactly," say Miss Moore, which is what she say when you warm or way off too. "It's to weigh paper down so it won't scatter and make your desk untidy." So right away me and Sugar curtsy to each other and then to Mercedes who is more the tidy type.

"We don't keep paper on top of the desk in my class," say Junebug, figuring Miss Moore crazy or lyin one.

"At home, then," she say. "Don't you have a calendar and a pencil case and a blotter and a letter-opener on your desk at home where you do your homework?" And she know damn well what our homes look like cause she nosys around in them every chance she gets.

"I don't even have a desk," say Junebug. "Do we?"

20   "No. And I don't get no homework neither," says Big Butt.

"And I don't even have a home," say Flyboy like he do at school to keep the white folks off his back and sorry for him. Send this poor kid to camp posters, is his specialty.

"I do," says Mercedes. "I have a box of stationery on my desk and a picture of my cat. My godmother bought the stationery and the desk. There's a big rose on each sheet and the envelopes smell like roses."

"Who wants to know about your smelly-ass stationery," say Rosie Giraffe fore I can get my two cents in.

"It's important to have a work area all your own so that . . ."

25   "Will you look at this sailboat, please," say Flyboy, cuttin her off and pointin to the thing like it was his. So once again we tumble all over each other to gaze at this magnificent thing in the toy store which is just big enough to maybe sail two kittens across the pond if you strap them to the posts tight. We all start reciting the price tag like we in assembly. "Hand-crafted sailboat of fiberglass at one thousand one hundred ninety-five dollars."

"Unbelievable," I hear myself say and am really stunned. I read it again for myself just in case the group recitation put me in a trance. Same thing. For some reason this pisses me off. We look at Miss Moore and she lookin at us, waiting for I dunno what.

"Who'd pay all that when you can buy a sailboat set for a quarter at Pop's, a tube of glue for a dime, and a ball of string for eight cents? It must have a motor and a whole lot else besides," I say. "My sailboat cost me about fifty cents."

"But will it take water?" say Mercedes with her smart ass.

"Took mine to Alley Pond Park once," say Flyboy. "String broke. Lost it. Pity."

30   "Sailed mine in Central Park and it keeled over and sank. Had to ask my father for another dollar."

"And you got the strap," laugh Big Butt. "The jerk didn't even have a string on it. My old man wailed on his behind."

Little Q.T. was staring hard at the sailboat and you could see he wanted it bad. But he too little and somebody'd just take it from him. So what the hell. "This boat for kids, Miss Moore?"

"Parents silly to buy something like that just to get all broke up," say Rosie Giraffe.

"That much money it should last forever," I figure.

"My father'd buy it for me if I wanted it." 35

"Your father, my ass," say Rosie Giraffe getting a chance to finally push Mercedes.

"Must be rich people shop here," say Q.T.

"You are a very bright boy," say Flyboy. "What was your first clue?" And he rap him on the head with the back of his knuckles, since Q.T. the only one he could get away with. Though Q.T. liable to come up behind you years later and get his licks in when you half expect it.

"What I want to know is," I says to Miss Moore though I never talk to her, I wouldn't give the bitch that satisfaction, "is how much a real boat costs? I figure a thousand'd get you a yacht any day."

"Why don't you check that out," she says, "and report back to the 40 group?" Which really pains my ass. If you gonna mess up a perfectly good swim day least you could do is have some answers. "Let's go in," she say like she got something up her sleeve. Only she don't lead the way. So me and Sugar turn the corner to where the entrance is, but when we get there I kinda hang back. Not that I'm scared, what's there to be afraid of, just a toy store. But I feel funny, shame. But what I got to be shamed about? Got as much right to go in as anybody. But somehow I can't seem to get hold of the door, so I step away from Sugar to lead. But she hangs back too. And I look at her and she looks at me and this is ridiculous. I mean, damn, I have never ever been shy about doing nothing or going nowhere. But then Mercedes steps up and then Rosie Giraffe and Big Butt crowd in behind and shove, and next thing we all stuffed into the doorway with only Mercedes squeezing past us, smoothing out her jumper and walking right down the aisle. Then the rest of us tumble in like a glued-together jigsaw done all wrong. And people lookin at us. And it's like the time me and Sugar crashed into the Catholic church on a dare. But once we got in there and everything so hushed and holy and the candles and the bowin and the handkerchiefs on all the drooping heads, I just couldn't go through with the plan. Which was for me to run up to the altar and do a tap dance while Sugar played the nose flute and messed around in the holy water. And Sugar kept givin me the elbow. Then later teased me so bad I tied her up in the shower and turned it on and locked her in. And she'd be there till this day if Aunt Gretchen hadn't finally figured I was lyin about the boarder takin a shower.

Same thing in the store. We all walkin on tiptoe and hardly touchin the games and puzzles and things. And I watched Miss Moore who is steady watchin us like she waitin for a sign. Like Mama Drewery watches the sky and sniffs the air and takes note of just how much slant is in the bird formation. Then me and Sugar bump smack into each other, so busy gazing at the toys, 'specially the sailboat. But we don't laugh and go into our fat-lady bump-stomach routine. We just stare at that price tag. Then Sugar run a finger over the whole boat. And I'm jealous and want to hit her. Maybe not her, but I sure want to punch somebody in the mouth.

"Watcha bring us here for, Miss Moore?"

"You sound angry, Sylvia. Are you mad about something?" Givin me one of them grins like she tellin a grown-up joke that never turns out to be funny. And she's lookin very closely at me like maybe she plannin to do my portrait from memory. I'm mad, but I won't give her that satisfaction. So I slouch around the store bein very bored and say, "Let's go."

Me and Sugar at the back of the train watchin the tracks whizzin by large then small then gettin gobbled up in the dark. I'm thinkin about this tricky toy I saw in the store. A clown that somersaults on a bar then does chin-ups just cause you yank lightly at his leg. Cost $35. I could see me askin my mother for a $35 birthday clown. "You wanna who that costs what?" she'd say, cocking her head to the side to get a better view of the hole in my head. Thirty-five dollars could buy new bunk beds for Junior and Gretchen's boy. Thirty-five dollars and the whole household could go visit Granddaddy Nelson in the country. Thirty-five dollars would pay for the rent and the piano bill too. Who are these people that spend that much for performing clowns and $1000 for toy sailboats? What kinda work they do and how they live and how come we ain't in on it? Where we are is who we are, Miss Moore always pointin out. But it don't necessarily have to be that way, she always adds then waits for somebody to say that poor people have to wake up and demand their share of the pie and don't none of us know what kind of pie she talking about in the first damn place. But she ain't so smart cause I still got her four dollars from the taxi and she sure ain't gettin it. Messin up my day with this shit. Sugar nudges me in my pocket and winks.

45   Miss Moore lines us up in front of the mailbox where we started from, seem like years ago, and I got a headache for thinkin so hard. And we lean all over each other so we can hold up under the draggy-ass lecture she always finishes us off with at the end before we thank her for borin us to tears. But she just looks at us like she readin tea leaves. Finally she say, "Well, what did you think of F. A. O. Schwarz?"

Rosie Giraffe mumbles, "White folks crazy."

"I'd like to go there again when I get my birthday money," says Mercedes, and we shove her out the pack so she has to lean on the mailbox by herself.

"I'd like a shower. Tiring day," say Flyboy.

Then Sugar surprises me by sayin, "You know, Miss Moore, I don't think all of us here put together eat in a year what that sailboat costs." And Miss Moore lights up like somebody goosed her. "And?" she say, urging Sugar on. Only I'm standin on her foot so she don't continue.

"Imagine for a minute what kind of society it is in which some people   50
can spend on a toy what it would cost to feed a family of six or seven.
What do you think?"

"I think," say Sugar pushing me off her feet like she never done before, cause I whip her ass in a minute, "that this is not much of a democracy if you ask me. Equal chance to pursue happiness means an equal
crack at the dough, don't it?" Miss Moore is besides herself and I am disgusted with Sugar's treachery. So I stand on her foot one more time to see
if she'll shove me. She shuts up, and Miss Moore looks at me, sorrowfully
I'm thinkin. And somethin weird is goin on, I can feel it in my chest.

"Anybody else learn anything today?" lookin dead at me. I walk away
and Sugar has to run to catch up and don't even seem to notice when I
shrug her arm off my shoulder.

"Well, we got four dollars anyway," she says.

"Uh hunh."

"We could go to Hascombs and get half a chocolate layer and then go   55
to the Sunset and still have plenty money for potato chips and ice cream
sodas."

"Uh hunh."

"Race you to Hascombs," she say.

We start down the block and she gets ahead which is O.K. by me
cause I'm going to the West End and then over to the Drive to think this
day through. She can run if she want to and even run faster. But ain't nobody gonna beat me at nuthin.

QUESTIONS

1. Define the nature of the conflict between the narrator Sylvia and Miss
   Moore. What are the differences between that conflict and how the other
   children respond to Miss Moore? What conflicts exist among the children
   themselves?
2. What strengths and weaknesses in Sylvia's character are illuminated by her
   being the narrator? How is her language evidence of both strengths and
   weaknesses? In particular, what extremes of character are displayed in paragraph 58 when Sylvia says to herself that she will have "to think this day
   through" yet is determined that "nobody [is] gonna beat [her] at nuthin"?
   Is she a developing character?
3. What is the relationship between Sylvia and her cousin Sugar? How are
   they contrasted?
4. Sugar states the lesson that she has learned in paragraph 51. How does the
   sorrowful look that Miss Moore gives Sylvia in that paragraph suggest that
   there is more to the lesson? What more? Explain the effect of Sugar's definition of happiness as "an equal crack at the dough" on Miss Moore and
   on Sylvia?
5. State the theme of the story.

Philip Roth

Defender of the Faith

In May of 1945, only a few weeks after the fighting had ended in Europe, I was rotated back to the States, where I spent the remainder of the war with a training company at Camp Crowder, Missouri. Along with the rest of the Ninth Army, I had been racing across Germany so swiftly during the late winter and spring that when I boarded the plane, I couldn't believe its destination lay to the west. My mind might inform me otherwise, but there was an inertia of the spirit that told me we were flying to a new front, where we would disembark and continue our push eastward—eastward until we'd circled the globe, marching through villages along whose twisting, cobbled streets crowds of the enemy would watch us take possession of what, up till then, they'd considered their own. I had changed enough in two years not to mind the trembling of old people, the crying of the very young, the uncertainty and fear in the eyes of the once arrogant. I had been fortunate enough to develop an infantryman's heart, which, like his feet, at first aches and swells but finally grows horny enough for him to travel the weirdest paths without feeling a thing.

Captain Paul Barrett was my C.O. in Camp Crowder. The day I reported for duty, he came out of his office to shake my hand. He was short, gruff, and fiery, and—indoors or out—he wore his polished helmet liner pulled down to his little eyes. In Europe, he had received a battlefield commission and a serious chest wound, and he'd been returned to the States only a few months before. He spoke easily to me, and at the evening formation he introduced me to the troops. "Gentlemen," he said. "Sergeant Thurston, as you know, is no longer with this company. Your new first sergeant is Sergeant Nathan Marx, here. He is a veteran of the European theater, and consequently will expect to find a company of soldiers here, and not a company of *boys.*"

I sat up late in the orderly room that evening, trying half-heartedly to solve the riddle of duty rosters, personnel forms, and morning reports. The Charge of Quarters slept with his mouth open on a mattress on the floor. A trainee stood reading the next day's duty roster, which was posted on the bulletin board just inside the screen door. It was a warm evening, and I could hear radios playing dance music over in the barracks. The trainee, who had been staring at me whenever he thought I wouldn't notice, finally took a step in my direction.

DEFENDER OF THE FAITH   First published in 1959. World War II officially ended in Europe with the surrender of Germany on May 7, 1945; it ended in the Pacific with the surrender of Japan on September 2, 1945. The action of the story occurs within that interval. Philip Roth, of Jewish parentage, was born (1933) and grew up in Newark, New Jersey, and was educated at Rutgers, Bucknell, and the University of Chicago. He enlisted in the army in 1955 after receiving his M.A. in English but was discharged within a year due to a back injury suffered during basic training.

"Hey, Sarge—we having a G.I. party tomorrow night?" he asked. A G.I. party is a barracks cleaning.

"You usually have them on Friday nights?" I asked him.   5

"Yes," he said, and then he added, mysteriously, "that's the whole thing."

"Then you'll have a G.I. party."

He turned away, and I heard him mumbling. His shoulders were moving and I wondered if he was crying.

"What's your name, soldier?" I asked.

He turned, not crying at all. Instead, his green-speckled eyes, long and   10 narrow, flashed like fish in the sun. He walked over to me and sat on the edge of my desk. He reached out a hand. "Sheldon," he said.

"Stand on your feet, Sheldon."

Getting off the desk, he said, "Sheldon Grossbart." He smiled at the familiarity into which he'd led me.

"You against cleaning the barracks Friday night, Grossbart?" I said. "Maybe we shouldn't have G.I. parties. Maybe we should get a maid." My tone startled me. I felt I sounded like every top sergeant I had ever known.

"No, Sergeant." He grew serious, but with a seriousness that seemed to be only the stifling of a smile. "It's just—G.I. parties on Friday night, of all nights."

He slipped up onto the corner of the desk again—not quite sitting, but   15 not quite standing, either. He looked at me with those speckled eyes flashing, and then made a gesture with his hands. It was very slight—no more than a movement back and forth of the wrist—and yet it managed to exclude from our affairs everything else in the orderly room, to make the two of us the center of the world. It seemed, in fact, to exclude everything even about the two of us except our hearts.

"Sergeant Thurston was one thing," he whispered, glancing at the sleeping C.Q., "but we thought that with you here things might be a little different."

"We?"

"The Jewish personnel."

"Why?" I asked, harshly. "What's on your mind?" Whether I was still angry at the "Sheldon" business, or now at something else, I hadn't time to tell, but clearly I was angry.

"We thought you—Marx, you know, like Karl Marx. The Marx   20 Brothers. Those guys are all—M-a-r-x. Isn't that how *you* spell it, Sergeant?"

"M-a-r-x."

"Fishbein said—" He stopped. "What I mean to say, Sergeant—" His face and neck were red, and his mouth moved but no words came out. In a moment, he raised himself to attention, gazing down at me. It was as though he had suddenly decided he could expect no more sympathy from me than from Thurston, the reason being that I was of Thurston's faith, and not his. The young man had managed to confuse himself as to what my faith really was, but I felt no desire to straighten him out. Very simply, I didn't like him.

When I did nothing but return his gaze, he spoke, in an altered tone. "You see, Sergeant," he explained to me, "Friday nights, Jews are supposed to go to services."

"Did Sergeant Thurston tell you you couldn't go to them when there was a G.I. party?"

25   "No."

"Did he say you had to stay and scrub the floors?"

"No, Sergeant."

"Did the Captain say you had to stay and scrub the floors?"

"That isn't it, Sergeant. It's the other guys in the barracks." He leaned toward me. "They think we're goofing off. But we're not. That's when Jews go to services, Friday night. We have to."

30   "Then go."

"But the other guys make accusations. They have no right."

"That's not the Army's problem, Grossbart. It's a personal problem you'll have to work out yourself."

"But it's un*fair.*"

I got up to leave. "There's nothing I can do about it," I said.

35   Grossbart stiffened and stood in front of me. "But this is a matter of *religion,* sir."

"Sergeant," I said.

"I mean 'Sergeant,'" he said, almost snarling.

"Look, go see the chaplain. You want to see Captain Barrett, I'll arrange an appointment."

"No, no. I don't want to make trouble, Sergeant. That's the first thing they throw up to you. I just want my rights!"

40   "Damn it, Grossbart, stop whining. You have your rights. You can stay and scrub floors or you can go to shul—"°

The smile swam in again. Spittle gleamed at the corners of his mouth. "You mean church, Sergeant."

"I mean shul, Grossbart!"

I walked past him and went outside. Near me, I heard the scrunching of the guard's boots on gravel. Beyond the lighted windows of the barracks, young men in T shirts and fatigue pants were sitting on their bunks, polishing their rifles. Suddenly there was a light rustling behind me. I turned and saw Grossbart's dark frame fleeing back to the barracks, racing to tell his Jewish friends that they were right—that, like Karl and Harpo, I was one of them.

The next morning, while chatting with Captain Barrett, I recounted the incident of the previous evening. Somehow, in the telling, it must have

shul: synagogue

seemed to the Captain that I was not so much explaining Grossbart's position as defending it. "Marx, I'd fight side by side with a nigger if the fella proved to me he was a man. I pride myself," he said, looking out the window, "that I've got an open mind. Consequently, Sergeant, nobody gets special treatment here, for the good *or* the bad. All a man's got to do is prove himself. A man fires well on the range, I give him a weekend pass. He scores high in P.T., he gets a weekend pass. He *earns* it." He turned from the window and pointed a finger at me. "You're a Jewish fella, am I right, Marx?"

"Yes, sir."   45

"And I admire you. I admire you because of the ribbons on your chest. I judge a man by what he shows me on the field of battle, Sergeant. It's what he's got *here*," he said, and then, though I expected he would point to his chest, he jerked a thumb toward the buttons straining to hold his blouse across his belly. "Guts," he said.

"O.K., sir. I only wanted to pass on to you how the men felt."

"Mr. Marx, you're going to be old before your time if you worry about how the men feel. Leave that stuff to the chaplain—that's his business, not yours. Let's us train these fellas to shoot straight. If the Jewish personnel feels the other men are accusing them of goldbricking—well, I just don't know. Seems awful funny that suddenly the Lord is calling so loud in Private Grossman's ear he's just got to run to church."

"Synagogue," I said.

"Synagogue is right, Sergeant. I'll write that down for handy reference.   50
Thank you for stopping by."

That evening, a few minutes before the company gathered outside the orderly room for the chow formation, I called the C.Q., Corporal Robert LaHill, in to see me. LaHill was a dark, burly fellow whose hair curled out of his clothes wherever it could. He had a glaze in his eyes that made one think of caves and dinosaurs. "LaHill," I said, "when you take the formation, remind the men that they're free to attend church services *whenever* they are held, provided they report to the orderly room before they leave the area."

LaHill scratched his wrist, but gave no indication that he'd heard or understood.

"LaHill," I said, "*church*. You remember? Church, priest, Mass, confession."

He curled one lip into a kind of smile; I took it for a signal that for a second he had flickered back up into the human race.

"Jewish personnel who want to attend services this evening are to fall out   55
in front of the orderly room at 1900," I said. Then, as an afterthought, I added, "By order of Captain Barrett."

A little while later, as the day's last light—softer than any I had seen that year—began to drop over Camp Crowder, I heard LaHill's thick, inflectionless voice outside my window: "Give me your ears, troopers. Toppie says for me to tell you that at 1900 hours all Jewish personnel is to fall out in front, here, if they want to attend the Jewish Mass."

At seven o'clock, I looked out the orderly-room window and saw three soldiers in starched khakis standing on the dusty quadrangle. They looked at their watches and fidgeted while they whispered back and forth. It was getting dimmer, and, alone on the otherwise deserted field, they looked tiny. When I opened the door, I heard the noises of the G.I. party coming from the surrounding barracks—bunks being pushed to the walls, faucets pounding water into buckets, brooms whisking at the wooden floors, cleaning the dirt away for Saturday's inspection. Big puffs of cloth moved round and round on the windowpanes. I walked outside, and the moment my foot hit the ground I thought I heard Grossbart call to the others "'Ten-*hut!*'" Or maybe, when they all three jumped to attention, I imagined I heard the command.

Grossbart stepped forward, "Thank you, sir," he said.

"'Sergeant,' Grossbart," I reminded him. "You call officers 'sir.' I'm not an officer. You've been in the Army three weeks—you know that."

60 He turned his palms out at his sides to indicate that, in truth, he and I lived beyond convention. "Thank you anyway," he said.

"Yes," a tall boy behind him said. "Thanks a lot."

And the third boy whispered, "Thank you," but his mouth barely fluttered, so that he did not alter by more than a lip's movement his posture of attention.

"For what?" I asked.

Grossbart snorted happily. "For the announcement. The Corporal's announcement. It helped. It made it—"

65 "Fancier." The tall boy finished Grossbart's sentence.

Grossbart smiled. "He means formal, sir. Public," he said to me. "Now it won't seem as though we're just taking off—goldbricking because the work has begun."

"It was by order of Captain Barrett," I said.

"Aaah, but you pull a little weight," Grossbart said. "So we thank you." Then he turned to his companions. "Sergeant Marx, I want you to meet Larry Fishbein."

The tall boy stepped forward and extended his hand. I shook it. "You from New York?" he asked.

70 "Yes."

"Me too." He had a cadaverous face that collapsed inward from his cheekbone to his jaw, and when he smiled—as he did at the news of our communal attachment—revealed a mouthful of bad teeth. He was blinking his eyes a good deal, as though he were fighting back tears. "What borough?" he asked.

I turned to Grossbart. "It's five after seven. What time are services?"

"Shul," he said, smiling, "is in ten minutes. I want you to meet Mickey Halpern. This is Nathan Marx, our sergeant."

The third boy hopped forward. "Private Michael Halpern." He saluted.

75 "Salute officers, Halpern," I said. The boy dropped his hand, and, on its way down, in his nervousness, checked to see if his shirt pockets were buttoned.

"Shall I march them over, sir?" Grossbart asked. "Or are you coming along?"

From behind Grossbart, Fishbein piped up. "Afterward, they're having refreshments. A ladies auxiliary from St. Louis, the rabbi told us last week."

"The chaplain," Halpern whispered.

"You're welcome to come along," Grossbart said.

To avoid his plea, I looked away, and saw, in the windows of the bar- 80
racks, a cloud of faces staring out at the four of us. "Hurry along, Grossbart," I said.

"O.K., then," he said. He turned to the others. "Double time, *march!*"

They started off, but ten feet away Grossbart spun around and, running backward, called to me "Good *shabbus*,° sir!" And then the three of them were swallowed into the alien Missouri dusk.

Even after they had disappeared over the parade ground, whose green was now a deep blue, I could hear Grossbart singing the double-time cadence, and as it grew dimmer and dimmer, it suddenly touched a deep memory—as did the slant of the light—and I was remembering the shrill sounds of a Bronx playground where, years ago, beside the Grand Con- course, I had played on long spring evenings such as this. It was a pleasant memory for a young man so far from peace and home, and it brought so many recollections with it that I began to grow exceedingly tender about myself. In fact, I indulged myself in a reverie so strong that I felt as though a hand were reaching down inside me. It had to reach so very far to touch me! It had to reach past those days in the forests of Belgium, and past the dying I'd refused to weep over; past the nights in German farmhouses whose books we'd burned to warm us; past endless stretches when I had shut off all soft- ness I might feel for my fellows, and had managed even to deny myself the posture of a conqueror—the swagger that I, as a Jew, might well have worn as my boots whacked against the rubble of Wesel, Münster, and Braunschweig.

But now one night noise, one rumor of home and time past, and memory plunged down through all I had anesthetized, and came to what I suddenly remembered was myself. So it was not altogether curious that, in search of more of me, I found myself following Grossbart's tracks to Chapel No. 3, where the Jewish services were being held.

I took a seat in the last row, which was empty. Two rows in front of me sat 85
Grossbart, Fishbein, and Halpern, holding little white Dixie cups. Each row of seats was raised higher than the one in front of it, and I could see clearly what was going on. Fishbein was pouring the contents of his cup into Grossbart's, and Grossbart looked mirthful as the liquid made a purple arc between Fishbein's hand and his. In the glaring yellow light, I saw the chap- lain standing on the platform at the front; he was chanting the first line of the responsive reading. Grossbart's prayer book remained closed on his lap; he was swishing the cup around. Only Halpern responded to the chant by

shabbus: Sabbath

praying. The fingers of his right hand were spread wide across the cover of his open book. His cap was pulled down low onto his brow, which made it round, like a yarmulke.° From time to time, Grossbart wet his lips at the cup's edge; Fishbein, his long yellow face a dying light bulb, looked from here to there, craning forward to catch sight of the faces down the row, then of those in front of him, then behind. He saw me, and his eyelids beat a tattoo. His elbow slid into Grossbart's side, his neck inclined toward his friend, he whispered something, and then, when the congregation next responded to the chant, Grossbart's voice was among the others. Fishbein looked into his book now, too; his lips, however, didn't move.

Finally, it was time to drink the wine. The chaplain smiled down at them as Grossbart swigged his in one long gulp, Halpern sipped, meditating, and Fishbein faked devotion with an empty cup. "As I look down amongst the congregation"—the chaplain grinned at the word—"this night, I see many new faces, and I want to welcome you to Friday-night services here at Camp Crowder. I am Major Leo Ben Ezra, your chaplain." Though an American, the chaplain spoke deliberately—syllable by syllable, almost—as though to communicate, above all, with the lip readers in his audience. "I have only a few words to say before we adjourn to the refreshment room, where the kind ladies of the Temple Sinai, St. Louis, Missouri, have a nice setting for you."

Applause and whistling broke out. After another momentary grin, the chaplain raised his hands, palms out, his eyes flicking upward a moment, as if to remind the troops where they were and Who Else might be in attendance. In the sudden silence that followed, I thought I heard Grossbart cackle, "Let the goyim° clean the floors!" Were those the words? I wasn't sure, but Fishbein, grinning, nudged Halpern. Halpern looked dumbly at him, then went back to his prayer book, which had been occupying him all through the rabbi's talk. One hand tugged at the black kinky hair that stuck out under his cap. His lips moved.

The rabbi continued. "It is about the food that I want to speak to you for a moment. I know, I know, I know," he intoned, wearily, "how in the mouths of most of you the *trafe*° food tastes like ashes. I know how you gag, some of you, and how your parents suffer to think of their children eating foods unclean and offensive to the palate. What can I tell you? I can only say, close your eyes and swallow as best you can. Eat what you must to live, and throw away the rest. I wish I could help more. For those of you who find this impossible, may I ask that you try and try, but then come to see me in private. If your revulsion is so great, we will have to seek aid from those higher up."

A round of chatter rose and subsided. Then everyone sang "Ain Kelohainu"°; after all those years, I discovered I still knew the words. Then,

yarmulke: skull cap   **goyim:** gentiles   *trafe*: nonkosher
"Ain Kelohainu": "There's no God like our God"

suddenly, the service over, Grossbart was upon me. "Higher up? He means the General?"

"Hey, Shelly," Fishbein said, "he means God." He smacked his face and looked at Halpern. "How high can you go!"

"Sh-h-h!" Grossbart said. "What do you think, Sergeant?"

"I don't know," I said. "You better ask the chaplain."

"I'm going to. I'm making an appointment to see him in private. So is Mickey."

Halpern shook his head. "No, no, Sheldon—"

"You have rights, Mickey," Grossbart said. "They can't push us around."

"It's O.K.," said Halpern. "It bothers my mother, not me."

Grossbart looked at me. "Yesterday he threw up. From the hash. It was all ham and God knows what else."

"I have a cold—that was why," Halpern said. He pushed his yarmulke back into a cap.

"What about you, Fishbein?" I asked. "You kosher, too?"

He flushed. "A little. But I'll let it ride. I have a very strong stomach, and I don't eat a lot anyway." I continued to look at him, and he held up his wrist to reinforce what he'd just said; his watch strap was tightened to the last hole, and he pointed that out to me.

"But services are important to you?" I asked him.

He looked at Grossbart. "Sure, sir."

" 'Sergeant.' "

"Not so much at home," said Grossbart, stepping between us, "but away from home it gives one a sense of his Jewishness."

"We have to stick together," Fishbein said.

I started to walk toward the door; Halpern stepped back to make way for me.

"That's what happened in Germany," Grossbart was saying, loud enough for me to hear. "They didn't stick together. They let themselves get pushed around."

I turned. "Look, Grossbart. This is the Army, not summer camp."

He smiled. "So?"

Halpern tried to sneak off, but Grossbart held his arm.

"Grossbart, how old are you?" I asked.

"Nineteen."

"And you?" I said to Fishbein.

"The same. The same month, even."

"And what about him?" I pointed to Halpern, who had by now made it safely to the door.

"Eighteen," Grossbart whispered. "But like he can't tie his shoes or brush his teeth himself. I feel sorry for him."

"I feel sorry for all of us, Grossbart," I said, "but just act like a man. Just don't overdo it."

"Overdo what, sir?"

"The 'sir' business, for one thing. Don't overdo that," I said.

120   I left him standing there. I passed by Halpern, but he did not look at me. Then I was outside, but, behind, I heard Grossbart call, "Hey, Mickey, my *leben*,° come on back. Refreshments!"

"*Leben!*" My grandmother's word for me!

One morning a week later, while I was working at my desk, Captain Barrett shouted for me to come into his office. When I entered, he had his helmet liner squashed down so far on his head that I couldn't even see his eyes. He was on the phone, and when he spoke to me, he cupped one hand over the mouthpiece. "Who the hell is Grossbart?"

"Third platoon, Captain," I said. "A trainee."

"What's all this stink about food? His mother called a goddam congressman about the food." He uncovered the mouthpiece and slid his helmet up until I could see his bottom eyelashes. "Yes, sir," he said into the phone. "Yes, sir. I'm still here, sir. I'm asking Marx, here, right now—"

125   He covered the mouthpiece again and turned his head back toward me. "Lightfoot Harry's on the phone," he said, between his teeth. "This congressman calls General Lyman, who calls Colonel Sousa, who calls the Major, who calls me. They're just dying to stick this thing on me. Whatsa matter?" He shook the phone at me. "I don't feed the troops? What is this?"

"Sir, Grossbart is strange—" Barrett greeted that with a mockingly indulgent smile. I altered my approach. "Captain, he's a very orthodox Jew, and so he's only allowed to eat certain foods."

"He throws up, the congressman said. Every time he eats something, his mother says, he throws up!"

"He's accustomed to observing the dietary laws, Captain."

"So why's his old lady have to call the White House?"

130   "Jewish parents, sir—they're apt to be more protective than you expect. I mean, Jews have a very close family life. A boy goes away from home, sometimes the mother is liable to get very upset. Probably the boy mentioned something in a letter, and his mother misinterpreted."

"I'd like to punch him one right in the mouth," the Captain said. "There's a war on, and he wants a silver platter!"

"I don't think the boy's to blame, sir. I'm sure we can straighten it out by just asking him. Jewish parents worry—"

"*All* parents worry, for Christ's sake. But they don't get on their high horse and start pulling strings—"

I interrupted, my voice higher, tighter than before. "The home life, Captain, is very important—but you're right, it may sometimes get out of hand.

leben: darling

It's a very wonderful thing, Captain, but because it's so close, this kind of thing . . ."

He didn't listen any longer to my attempt to present both myself and   135
Lightfoot Harry with an explanation for the letter. He turned back to the phone. "Sir?" he said. "Sir—Marx, here, tells me Jews have a tendency to be pushy. He says he thinks we can settle it right here in the company . . . Yes, sir . . . I *will* call back, sir, soon as I can." He hung up. "Where are the men, Sergeant?"

"On the range."

With a whack on the top of his helmet, he crushed it down over his eyes again, and charged out of his chair. "We're going for a ride," he said.

The Captain drove, and I sat beside him. It was a hot spring day, and under my newly starched fatigues I felt as though my armpits were melting down into my sides and chest. The roads were dry, and by the time we reached the firing range, my teeth felt gritty with dust, though my mouth had been shut the whole trip. The Captain slammed the brakes on and told me to get the hell out and find Grossbart.

I found him on his belly, firing wildly at the five-hundred-feet target. Waiting their turns behind him were Halpern and Fishbein. Fishbein, wearing a pair of steel-rimmed G.I. glasses I hadn't seen on him before, had the appearance of an old peddler who would gladly have sold you his rifle and the cartridges that were slung all over him. I stood back by the ammo boxes, waiting for Grossbart to finish spraying the distant target. Fishbein straggled back to stand near me.

"Hello, Sergeant Marx," he said.   140

"How are you?" I mumbled.

"Fine, thank you. Sheldon's really a good shot."

"I didn't notice."

"I'm not so good, but I think I'm getting the hang of it now. Sergeant, I don't mean to, you know, ask what I shouldn't—" The boy stopped. He was trying to speak intimately, but the noise of the shooting forced him to shout at me.

"What is it?" I asked. Down the range, I saw Captain Barrett standing   145
up in the jeep, scanning the line for me and Grossbart.

"My parents keep asking and asking where we're going," Fishbein said. "Everybody says the Pacific. I don't care, but my parents—if I could relieve their minds, I think I could concentrate more on my shooting."

"I don't know where, Fishbein. Try to concentrate anyway."

"Sheldon says you might be able to find out."

"I don't know a thing, Fishbein. You just take it easy, and don't let Sheldon—"

"*I'm* taking it easy, Sergeant. It's at home—"   150

Grossbart had finished on the line, and was dusting his fatigues with one hand. I called to him. "Grossbart, the Captain wants to see you."

He came toward us. His eyes blazed and twinkled. "Hi!"

"Don't point that rifle!" I said.

"I wouldn't shoot you, Sarge." He gave me a smile as wide as a pumpkin, and turned the barrel aside.

155　"Damn you, Grossbart, this is no joke! Follow me."

I walked ahead of him, and had the awful suspicion that, behind me, Grossbart was *marching*, his rifle on his shoulder as though he were a one-man detachment. At the jeep, he gave the Captain a rifle salute. "Private Sheldon Grossbart, sir."

"At ease, Grossman." The Captain sat down, slid over into the empty seat, and, crooking a finger, inviting Grossbart closer.

"Bart, sir. Sheldon Gross*bart*. It's a common error." Grossbart nodded at me; *I* understood, he indicated. I looked away just as the mess truck pulled up to the range, disgorging a half-dozen K.P.s with rolled-up sleeves. The mess sergeant screamed at them while they set up the chow line equipment.

"Grossbart, your mama wrote some congressman that we don't feed you right. Do you know that?" the Captain said.

160　"It was my father, sir. He wrote to Representative Franconi that my religion forbids me to eat certain foods."

"What religion is that, Grossbart?"

"Jewish."

"'Jewish, *sir*,'" I said to Grossbart.

"Excuse me, sir, Jewish, sir."

165　"What have you been living on?" the Captain asked. "You've been in the Army a month already. You don't look to me like you're falling to pieces."

"I eat because I have to, sir. But Sergeant Marx will testify to the fact that I don't eat one mouthful more than I need to in order to survive."

"Is that so, Marx?" Barrett asked.

"I've never seen Grossbart eat, sir," I said.

"But you heard the rabbi," Grossbart said. "He told us what to do, and I listened."

170　The Captain looked at me. "Well, Marx?"

"I still don't know what he eats and doesn't eat, sir."

Grossbart raised his arms to plead with me, and it looked for a moment as though he were going to hand me his weapon to hold. "But, Sergeant—"

"Look, Grossbart, just answer the Captain's questions," I said sharply.

Barrett smiled at me, and I resented it. "All right, Grossbart," he said. "What is it you want? The little piece of paper? You want out?"

175　"No, sir. Only to be allowed to live as a Jew. And for the others, too."

"What others?"

"Fishbein, sir, and Halpern."

"They don't like the way we serve, either?"

"Halpern throws up, sir. I've seen it."

180　"I thought *you* throw up."

"Just once, sir. I didn't know the sausage was sausage."

"We'll give menus, Grossbart. We'll show training films about the food, so you can identify when we're trying to poison you."

Grossbart did not answer. The men had been organized into two long chow lines. At the tail end of one, I spotted Fishbein—or, rather, his glasses spotted me. They winked sunlight back at me. Halpern stood next to him, patting the inside of his collar with a khaki handkerchief. They moved with the line as it began to edge up toward the food. The mess sergeant was still screaming at the K.P.s. For a moment, I was actually terrified by the thought that somehow the mess sergeant was going to become involved in Grossbart's problem.

"Marx," the Captain said, "you're a Jewish fella—am I right?"

I played straight man. "Yes, sir."   185

"How long you been in the Army? Tell this boy."

"Three years and two months."

"A year in combat, Grossbart. Twelve goddam months in combat all through Europe. I admire this man." The Captain snapped a wrist against my chest. "Do you hear him peeping about the food? Do you? I want an answer, Grossbart. Yes or no."

"No, sir."

"And why not? He's a Jewish fella."   190

"Some things are more important to some Jews than other things to other Jews."

Barrett blew up. "Look, Grossbart. Marx, here, is a good man—a goddam hero. When you were in high school, Sergeant Marx was killing Germans. Who does more for the Jews—you, by throwing up over a lousy piece of sausage, a piece of first-cut meat, or Marx, by killing those Nazi bastards? If I was a Jew, Grossbart, I'd kiss this man's feet. He's a goddam hero, and *he* eats what we give him. Why do you have to cause trouble is what I want to know! What is it you're buckin' for—a discharge?"

"No, sir."

"I'm talking to a wall! Sergeant, get him out of my way." Barrett swung himself back into the driver's seat. "I'm going to see the chaplain." The engine roared, the jeep spun around in a whirl of dust, and the Captain was headed back to camp.

For a moment, Grossbart and I stood side by side, watching the jeep.   195
Then he looked at me and said, "I don't want to start trouble. That's the first thing they toss up to us."

When he spoke, I saw that his teeth were white and straight, and the sight of them suddenly made me understand that Grossbart actually did have parents—that once upon a time someone had taken little Sheldon to the dentist. He was their son. Despite all the talk about his parents, it was hard to believe in Grossbart as a child, an heir—as related by blood to anyone, mother, father, or, above all, to me. This realization led me to another.

"What does your father do, Grossbart?" I asked as we started to walk back toward the chow line.

"He's a tailor."

"An American?"

200   "Now, yes. A son in the Army," he said, jokingly.

"And your mother?" I asked.

He winked. "A *ballabusta*.° She practically sleeps with a dustcloth in her hand."

"She's also an immigrant?"

"All she talks is Yiddish, still."

205   "And your father, too?"

"A little English. 'Clean,' 'Press,' 'Take the pants in.' That's the extent of it. But they're good to me."

"Then, Grossbart—" I reached out and stopped him. He turned toward me, and when our eyes met, his seemed to jump back, to shiver in their sockets. "Grossbart—you were the one who wrote that letter, weren't you?"

It took only a second or two for his eyes to flash happy again. "Yes." He walked on, and I kept pace. "It's what my father *would* have written if he had known how. It was his name, though. *He* signed it. He even mailed it. I sent it home. For the New York postmark."

I was astonished, and he saw it. With complete seriousness, he thrust his right arm in front of me. "Blood is blood, Sergeant," he said, pinching the blue vein in his wrist.

210   "What the hell *are* you trying to do, Grossbart?" I asked. "I've seen you eat. Do you know that? I told the Captain I don't know what you eat, but I've seen you eat like a hound at chow."

"We work hard, Sergeant. We're in training. For a furnace to work, you've got to feed it coal."

"Why did you say in the letter that you threw up all the time?"

"I was really talking about Mickey there. I was talking *for* him. He would never write, Sergeant, though I pleaded with him. He'll waste away to nothing if I don't help. Sergeant, I used my name—my father's name—but it's Mickey, and Fishbein, too, I'm watching out for."

"You're a regular Messiah, aren't you?"

215   We were at the chow line now.

"That's a good one, Sergeant," he said, smiling. "But who knows? Who can tell? Maybe you're the Messiah—a little bit. What Mickey says is the Messiah is a collective idea. He went to Yeshiva,° Mickey, for a while. He says *together* we're the Messiah. Me a little bit, you a little bit. You should hear that kid talk, Sergeant, when he gets going."

"Me a little bit, you a little bit," I said. "You'd like to believe that, wouldn't you, Grossbart? That would make everything so clean for you."

"It doesn't seem too bad a thing to believe, Sergeant. It only means we should all *give* a little, is all."

I walked off to eat my rations with the other noncoms.

ballabusta: housewife   **Yeshiva:** seminary

Two days later, a letter addressed to Captain Barrett passed over my   220
desk. It had come through the chain of command—from the office of Congressman Franconi, where it had been received, to General Lyman, to Colonel Sousa, to Major Lamont, now to Captain Barrett. I read it over twice. It
was dated May 14, the day Barrett had spoken with Grossbart on the rifle
range.

Dear Congressman:

    *First let me thank you for your interest in behalf of my son, Private Sheldon
Grossbart. Fortunately, I was able to speak with Sheldon on the phone the other
night, and I think I've been able to solve our problem. He is, as I mentioned in my
last letter, a very religious boy, and it was only with the greatest difficulty that I
could persuade him that the religious thing to do—what God Himself would want
Sheldon to do—would be to suffer the pangs of religious remorse for the good of his
country and all mankind. It took some doing, Congressman, but finally he saw the
light. In fact, what he said (and I wrote down the words on a scratch pad so as
never to forget), what he said was "I guess you're right, Dad. So many millions of
my fellow-Jews gave up their lives to the enemy, the least I can do is live for a
while minus a bit of my heritage so as to help end this struggle and regain for all the
children of God dignity and humanity." That, Congressman, would make any
father proud.*

    *By the way, Sheldon wanted me to know—and to pass on to you—the name
of a soldier who helped him reach this decision: SERGEANT NATHAN
MARX. Sergeant Marx is a combat veteran who is Sheldon's first sergeant. This
man has helped Sheldon over some of the first hurdles he's had to face in the Army,
and is in part responsible for Sheldon's changing his mind about the dietary laws. I
know Sheldon would appreciate any recognition Marx could receive.*

    *Thank you and good luck. I look forward to seeing your name on the next
election ballot.*

Respectfully,
Samuel E. Grossbart

Attached to the Grossbart communiqué was another, addressed to Gen-   225
eral Marshall Lyman, the post commander, and signed by Representative
Charles E. Franconi, of the House of Representatives. The communiqué
informed General Lyman that Sergeant Nathan Marx was a credit to the
U.S. Army and the Jewish people.

    What was Grossbart's motive in recanting? Did he feel he'd gone too far?
Was the letter a strategic retreat—a crafty attempt to strengthen what he
considered our alliance? Or had he actually changed his mind, via an imaginary dialogue between Grossbart *père* and Grossbart *fils?* I was puzzled, but
only for a few days—that is, only until I realized that, whatever his reasons,
he had actually decided to disappear from my life; he was going to allow
himself to become just another trainee. I saw him at inspection, but he never
winked; at chow formations, but he never flashed me a sign. On Sunday,

with the other trainees, he would sit around watching the noncoms' softball team, for which I pitched, but not once did he speak an unnecessary word to me. Fishbein and Halpern retreated, too—at Grossbart's command, I was sure. Apparently he had seen that wisdom lay in turning back before he plunged over into the ugliness of privilege undeserved. Our separation allowed me to forgive him our past encounters, and finally, to admire him for his good sense.

Meanwhile, free of Grossbart, I grew used to my job and my administrative tasks. I stepped on a scale one day, and discovered I had truly become a noncombatant; I had gained seven pounds. I found patience to get past the first three pages of a book. I thought about the future more and more, and wrote letters to girls I'd known before the war. I even got a few answers. I sent away to Columbia for a Law School catalogue. I continued to follow the war in the Pacific, but it was not my war. I thought I could see the end, and sometimes, at night, I dreamed that I was walking on the streets of Manhattan—Broadway, Third Avenue, 116th Street, where I had lived the three years I attended Columbia. I curled myself around these dreams and I began to be happy.

And then, one Sunday, when everybody was away and I was alone in the orderly room reading a month-old copy of the *Sporting News,* Grossbart reappeared.

"You a baseball fan, Sergeant?"

230   I looked up. "How are you?"

"Fine," Grossbart said. "They're making a soldier out of me."

"How are Fishbein and Halpern?"

"Coming along," he said. "We've got no training this afternoon. They're at the movies."

"How come you're not with them?"

235   "I wanted to come over and say hello."

He smiled—a shy, regular-guy smile, as though he and I well knew that our friendship drew its sustenance from unexpected visits, remembered birthdays, and borrowed lawnmowers. At first it offended me, and then the feeling was swallowed by the general uneasiness I felt at the thought that everyone on the post was locked away in a dark movie theater and I was here alone with Grossbart. I folded up my paper.

"Sergeant," he said, "I'd like to ask a favor. It is a favor, and I'm making no bones about it."

He stopped, allowing me to refuse him a hearing—which, of course, forced me into a courtesy I did not intend. "Go ahead."

"Well, actually, it's two favors."

240   I said nothing.

"The first one's about these rumors. Everybody says we're going to the Pacific."

"As I told your friend Fishbein, I don't know," I said. "You'll just have to wait to find out. Like everybody else."

"You think there's a chance of any of us going East?"

"Germany?" I said. "Maybe."

"I meant New York."

"I don't think so, Grossbart. Offhand."

"Thanks for the information, Sergeant," he said.

"It's not information, Grossbart. Just what I surmise."

"It certainly would be good to be near home. My parents—you know." He took a step toward the door and then turned back. "Oh, the other thing. May I ask the other?"

"What is it?"

"The other thing is—I've got relatives in St. Louis, and they say they'll give me a whole Passover dinner if I can get down there. God, Sergeant, that'd mean an awful lot to me."

I stood up. "No passes during basic, Grossbart."

"But we're off from now till Monday morning, Sergeant. I could leave the post and no one would even know."

"I'd know. You'd know."

"But that's all. Just the two of us. Last night, I called my aunt, and you should have heard her. 'Come—come,' she said. 'I got gefilte fish, *chrain*°— the works!' Just a day, Sergeant. I'd take the blame if anything happened."

"The Captain isn't here to sign a pass."

"You could sign."

"Look, Grossbart—"

"Sergeant, for two months, practically, I've been eating *trafe* till I want to die."

"I thought you'd made up your mind to live with it. To be minus a little bit of heritage."

He pointed a finger at me. "You!" he said. "That wasn't for you to read."

"I read it. So what?"

"The letter was addressed to a congressman."

"Grossbart, don't feed me any baloney. You *wanted* me to read it."

"Why are you persecuting me, Sergeant?"

"Are you kidding!"

"I've run into this before," he said, "but never from my own!"

"Get out of here, Grossbart! Get the hell out of my sight!"

He did not move. "Ashamed, that's what you are," he said. "So you take it out on the rest of us. They say Hitler himself was half a Jew. Hearing you, I wouldn't doubt it."

"What are you trying to do with me, Grossbart?" I asked him. "What are

245

250

255

260

265

270

chrain: horseradish

you after? You want me to give you special privileges, to change the food, to find out about your orders, to give you weekend passes."

"You even talk like a goy!"° Grossbart shook his fist. "Is this just a weekend pass I'm asking for? Is a Seder° sacred, or not?"

Seder! It suddenly occurred to me that Passover had been celebrated weeks before. I said so.

"That's right," he replied. "Who says no? A month ago—and I was in the field eating hash! And now all I ask is a simple favor. A Jewish boy I thought would understand. My aunt's willing to go out of her way—to make a Seder a month later . . ." He turned to go, mumbling.

"Come back here!" I called. He stopped and looked at me. "Grossbart, why can't you be like the rest? Why do you have to stick out like a sore thumb?"

275 "Because I'm a Jew, Sergeant. I *am* different. Better, maybe not. But different."

"This is a war, Grossbart. For the time being *be* the same."

"I refuse."

"What?"

"I refuse. I can't stop being me, that's all there is to it." Tears came to his eyes. "It's a hard thing to be a Jew. But now I understand what Mickey says—it's a harder thing to stay one." He raised a hand sadly toward me. "Look at *you.*"

280 "Stop crying!"

"Stop this, stop that, stop the other thing! *You* stop, Sergeant. Stop closing your heart to your own!" And, wiping his face with his sleeve, he ran out the door. "The least we can do for one another—the least . . ."

An hour later, looking out of the window, I saw Grossbart headed across the field. He wore a pair of starched khakis and carried a little leather ditty bag. I went out into the heat of the day. It was quiet; not a soul was in sight except, over by the mess hall, four K.P.s sitting around a pan, sloped forward from their waists, gabbing and peeling potatoes in the sun.

"Grossbart!" I called.

He looked toward me and continued walking.

285 "Grossbart, get over here!"

He turned and came across the field. Finally, he stood before me.

"Where are you going?" I asked.

"St. Louis. I don't care."

"You'll get caught without a pass."

290 "So I'll get caught without a pass."

"You'll go to the stockade."

"I'm *in* the stockade." He made an about-face and headed off.

I let him go only a step or two. "Come back here," I said, and he followed

goy: gentile   **Seder:** ceremonial dinner on first day of Passover

me into the office, where I typed out a pass and signed the Captain's name, and my own initials after it.

He took the pass and then, a moment later, reached out and grabbed my hand. "Sergeant, you don't know how much this means to me."

"O.K.," I said. "Don't get in any trouble."   295

"I wish I could show you how much this means to me."

"Don't do me any favors. Don't write any more congressmen for citations."

He smiled. "You're right. I won't. But let me do something."

"Bring me a piece of that gefilte fish. Just get out of here."

"I will!" he said. "With a slice of carrot and a little horseradish. I won't   300
forget."

"All right. Just show your pass at the gate. And don't tell *anybody*."

"I won't. It's a month late, but a good Yom Tov° to you."

"Good Yom Tov, Grossbart," I said.

"You're a good Jew, Sergeant. You like to think you have a hard heart, but underneath you're a fine, decent man. I mean that."

Those last three words touched me more than any words from   305
Grossbart's mouth had the right to. "All right, Grossbart," I said. "Now call me 'sir,' and get the hell out of here."

He ran out the door and was gone. I felt very pleased with myself; it was a great relief to stop fighting Grossbart, and it had cost me nothing. Barrett would never find out, and if he did, I could manage to invent some excuse. For a while, I sat at my desk, comfortable in my decision. Then the screen door flew back and Grossbart burst in again. "Sergeant!" he said. Behind him I saw Fishbein and Halpern, both in starched khakis, both carrying ditty bags like Grossbart's.

"Sergeant, I caught Mickey and Larry coming out of the movies. I almost missed them."

"Grossbart—did I say to tell no one?" I said.

"But my aunt said I could bring friends. That I should, in fact."

"*I'm* the Sergeant, Grossbart—not your aunt!"   310

Grossbart looked at me in disbelief. He pulled Halpern up by his sleeve. "Mickey, tell the Sergeant what this would mean to you."

Halpern looked at me and, shrugging, said. "A lot."

Fishbein stepped forward without prompting. "This would mean a great deal to me and my parents, Sergeant Marx."

"No!" I shouted.

Grossbart was shaking his head. "Sergeant, I could see you denying me,   315
but how can you deny Mickey, a Yeshiva boy—that's beyond me."

"I'm not denying Mickey anything," I said. "You just pushed a little too hard, Grossbart. *You* denied him."

Yom Tov: holiday (literally, good day)

"I'll give him my pass, then," Grossbart said. "I'll give him my aunt's address and a little note. At least let him go."

In a second, he had crammed the pass into Halpern's pants pocket. Halpern looked at me, and so did Fishbein. Grossbart was at the door, pushing it open. "Mickey, bring me a piece of gefilte fish, at least," he said, and then he was outside again.

The three of us looked at one another, and then I said, "Halpern, hand that pass over."

320   He took it from his pocket and gave it to me. Fishbein had now moved to the doorway, where he lingered. He stood there for a moment with his mouth slightly open, and then he pointed to himself. "And me?" he asked.

His utter ridiculousness exhausted me. I slumped down in my seat and felt pulses knocking at the back of my eyes. "Fishbein," I said, "you understand I'm not trying to deny you anything, don't you? If it was my Army, I'd serve gefilte fish in the mess hall. I'd sell *kugel*° in the PX, honest to God."

Halpern smiled.

"You understand, don't you, Halpern?"

"Yes, Sergeant."

325   "And you, Fishbein? I don't want enemies. I'm just like you—I want to serve my time and go home. I miss the same things you miss."

"Then, Sergeant," Fishbein said, "why don't you come, too?"

"Where?"

"To St. Louis. To Shelly's aunt. We'll have a regular Seder. Play hide-the-matzoh."° He gave me a broad, black-toothed smile.

I saw Grossbart again, on the other side of the screen.

330   "Psst!" He waved a piece of paper. "Mickey, here's the address. Tell her I couldn't get away."

Halpern did not move. He looked at me, and I saw the shrug moving up his arms into his shoulders again. I took the cover off my typewriter and made out passes for him and Fishbein. "Go," I said. "The three of you."

I thought Halpern was going to kiss my hand.

That afternoon, in a bar in Joplin, I drank beer and listened with half an ear to the Cardinal game. I tried to look squarely at what I'd become involved in, and began to wonder if perhaps the struggle with Grossbart wasn't as much my fault as his. What was I that I had to *muster* generous feelings? Who was I to have been feeling so grudging, so tight-hearted? After all, I wasn't being asked to move the world. Had I a right, then, or a reason, to clamp down on Grossbart, when that meant clamping down on Halpern, too? And Fishbein—that ugly, agreeable soul? Out of the many recollections of my childhood that had tumbled over me these past few days I heard my grandmother's voice: "What are you making a *tsimmes?*"° It was what she would

kugel: noodle pudding   **matzoh:** unleavened bread eaten at Passover
tsimmes: a to-do

ask my mother when, say, I had cut myself while doing something I shouldn't have done, and her daughter was busy bawling me out. I needed a hug and a kiss, and my mother would moralize. But my grandmother knew—mercy overrides justice. I should have known it, too. Who was Nathan Marx to be such a penny pincher with kindness? Surely, I thought, the Messiah himself—if He should ever come—won't niggle over nickels and dimes. God willing, he'll hug and kiss.

The next day, while I was playing softball over on the parade ground, I decided to ask Bob Wright, who was noncom in charge of Classification and Assignment, where he thought our trainees would be sent when their cycle ended, in two weeks. I asked casually, between innings, and he said, "They're pushing them all into the Pacific. Shulman cut the orders on your boys the other day."

The news shocked me, as though I were the father of Halpern, Fishbein, and Grossbart.   335

That night, I was just sliding into sleep when someone tapped on my door. "Who is it?" I asked.

"Sheldon."

He opened the door and came in. For a moment, I felt his presence without being able to see him. "How was it?" I asked.

He popped into sight in the near-darkness before me. "Great, Sergeant." Then he was sitting on the edge of the bed. I sat up.

"How about you?" he asked. "Have a nice weekend?"   340

"Yes."

"The others went to sleep." He took a deep, paternal breath. We sat silent for a while, and a homey feeling invaded my ugly little cubicle; the door was locked, the cat was out, the children were safely in bed.

"Sergeant, can I tell you something? Personal?"

I did not answer, and he seemed to know why. "Not about me. About Mickey. Sergeant, I never felt for anybody like I feel for him. Last night I heard Mickey in the bed next to me. He was crying so, it could have broken your heart. Real sobs."

"I'm sorry to hear that."   345

"I had to talk to him to stop him. He held my hand, Sergeant—he wouldn't let it go. He was almost hysterical. He kept saying if he only knew where we were going. Even if he knew it *was* the Pacific, that would be better than nothing. Just to know."

Long ago, someone had taught Grossbart the sad rule that only lies can get the truth. Not that I couldn't believe in the fact of Halpern's crying; his eyes *always* seemed red-rimmed. But, fact or not, it became a lie when Grossbart uttered it. He was entirely strategic. But then—it came with the force of indictment—so was I! There are strategies of aggression, but there are strategies of retreat as well. And so, recognizing that I myself had not been without craft and guile, I told him what I knew. "It is the Pacific."

He let out a small gasp, which was not a lie. "I'll tell him. I wish it was otherwise."

"So do I."

350   He jumped on my words. "You mean you think you could do something? A change, maybe?"

"No, I couldn't do a thing."

"Don't you know anybody over at C. and A.?"

"Grossbart, there's nothing I can do," I said. "If your orders are for the Pacific, then it's the Pacific."

"But Mickey—"

355   "Mickey, you, me—everybody, Grossbart. There's nothing to be done. Maybe the war'll end before you go. Pray for a miracle."

"But—"

"Good night, Grossbart." I settled back, and was relieved to feel the springs unbend as Grossbart rose to leave. I could see him clearly now; his jaw had dropped, and he looked like a dazed prizefighter. I noticed for the first time a little paper bag in his hand.

"Grossbart." I smiled. "My gift?"

"Oh, yes, Sergeant. Here—from all of us." He handed me the bag. "It's egg roll."

360   "Egg roll?" I accepted the bag and felt a damp grease spot on the bottom. I opened it, sure that Grossbart was joking.

"We thought you'd probably like it. You know—Chinese egg roll. We thought you'd probably have a taste for—"

"Your aunt served egg roll?"

"She wasn't home."

"Grossbart, she invited you. You told me she invited you and your friends."

365   "I know," he said. "I just reread the letter. *Next* week."

I got out of bed and walked to the window. "Grossbart," I said. But I was not calling to him.

"What?"

"What are you, Grossbart? Honest to God, what are you?"

I think it was the first time I'd asked him a question for which he didn't have an immediate answer.

370   "How can you do this to people?" I went on.

"Sergeant, the day away did us all a world of good. Fishbein, you should see him, he *loves* Chinese food."

"But the Seder," I said.

"We took second best, Sergeant."

Rage came charging at me. I didn't sidestep. "Grossbart, you're a liar!" I said. "You're a schemer and a crook. You've got no respect for anything. Nothing at all. Not for me, the truth—not even for poor Halpern! You use us all—"

375   "Sergeant, Sergeant, I feel for Mickey. Honest to God, I do. I *love* Mickey. I try—"

"You try! You feel!" I lurched toward him and grabbed his shirt front. I shook him furiously. "Grossbart, get out! Get out and stay the hell away from me. Because if I see you, I'll make your life miserable. *You understand that?*"

"Yes."

I let him free, and when he walked from the room, I wanted to spit on the floor where he had stood. I couldn't stop the fury. It engulfed me, owned me, till it seemed I could only rid myself of it with tears or an act of violence. I snatched from the bed the bag Grossbart had given me and, with all my strength, threw it out the window. And the next morning, as the men policed the area around the barracks, I heard a great cry go up from one of the trainees, who had been anticipating only his morning handful of cigarette butts and candy wrappers. "Egg roll!" he shouted. "Holy Christ, Chinese goddam egg roll!"

A week later, when I read the orders that had come down from C. and A., I couldn't believe my eyes. Every single trainee was to be shipped to Camp Stoneman, California, and from there to the Pacific—every trainee but one. Private Sheldon Grossbart. He was to be sent to Fort Monmouth, New Jersey. I read the mimeographed sheet several times. Dee, Farrell, Fishbein, Fuselli, Fylypowycz, Glinicki, Gromke, Gucwa, Halpern, Hardy, Helebrandt, right down to Anton Zygadlo—all were to be headed West before the month was out. All except Grossbart. He had pulled a string, and I wasn't it.

I lifted the phone and called C. and A.   380

The voice on the other end said smartly, "Corporal Shulman, sir."

"Let me speak to Sergeant Wright."

"Who is this calling, sir?"

"Sergeant Marx."

And, to my surprise, the voice said, "*Oh!*" Then, "Just a minute,   385
Sergeant."

Shulman's "*Oh!*" stayed with me while I waited for Wright to come to the phone. Why "*Oh!*"? Who was Shulman? And then, so simply, I knew I'd discovered the string that Grossbart had pulled. In fact, I could hear Grossbart the day he'd discovered Shulman in the PX, or in the bowling alley, or maybe even at services. "Glad to meet you. Where you from? Bronx? Me, too. Do you know So-and-So? And So-and-So? Me, too! You work at C. and A.? Really? Hey, how's chances of getting East? Could you do something? Change something? Swindle, cheat, lie? We gotta help each other, you know. If the Jews in Germany . . ."

Bob Wright answered the phone. "How are you, Nate? How's the pitching arm?"

"Good. Bob, I wonder if you could do me a favor." I heard clearly my own words, and they so reminded me of Grossbart that I dropped more easily than I could have imagined into what I had planned. "This may sound crazy, Bob, but I got a kid here on orders to Monmouth who wants them changed.

He had a brother killed in Europe, and he's hot to go to the Pacific. Says he'd feel like a coward if he wound up Stateside. I don't know, Bob—can anything be done? Put somebody else in the Monmouth slot?"

"Who?" he asked cagily.

390   "Anybody. First guy in the alphabet. I don't care. The kid just asked if something could be done."

"What's his name?"

"Grossbart, Sheldon."

Wright didn't answer.

"Yeah," I said. "He's a Jewish kid, so he thought I could help him out. You know."

395   "I guess I can do something," he finally said. "The Major hasn't been around for weeks. Temporary duty to the golf course. I'll try, Nate, that's all I can say."

"I'd appreciate it, Bob. See you Sunday." And I hung up, perspiring.

The following day, the corrected orders appeared: Fishbein, Fuselli, Fylypowycz, Glinicki, Gromke, Grossbart, Gucwa, Halpern, Hardy . . . Lucky Private Harley Alton was to go to Fort Monmouth, New Jersey, where, for some reason or other, they wanted an enlisted man with infantry training.

After chow that night, I stopped back at the orderly room to straighten out the guard-duty roster. Grossbart was waiting for me. He spoke first.

"You son of a bitch!"

400   I sat down at my desk, and while he glared at me, I began to make the necessary alterations in the duty roster.

"What do you have against me?" he cried. "Against my family? Would it kill you for me to be near my father, God knows how many months he has left to him?"

"Why so?"

"His heart," Grossbart said. "He hasn't had enough troubles in a lifetime, you've got to add to them. I curse the day I ever met you, Marx! Shulman told me what happened over there. There's no limit to your anti-Semitism, is there? The damage you've done here isn't enough. You have to make a special phone call! You really want me dead!"

I made the last notations in the duty roster and got up to leave. "Good night, Grossbart."

405   "You owe me an explanation!" He stood in my path.

"Sheldon, you're the one who owes explanations."

He scowled. "To *you?*"

"To me, I think so—yes. Mostly to Fishbein and Halpern."

"That's right, twist things around. I owe nobody nothing. I've done all I could for them. Now I think I've got the right to watch out for myself."

410   "For each other we have to learn to watch out, Sheldon. You told me yourself."

"You call this watching out for me—what you did?"

"No. For all of us."

I pushed him aside and started for the door. I heard his furious breathing behind me, and it sounded like steam rushing from an engine of terrible strength.

"*You'll* be all right," I said from the door. And, I thought, so would Fishbein and Halpern be all right, even in the Pacific, if only Grossbart continued to see—in the obsequiousness of the one, the soft spirituality of the other—some profit for himself.

I stood outside the orderly room, and I heard Grossbart weeping behind   415
me. Over in the barracks, in the lighted windows, I could see the boys in their T shirts sitting on their bunks talking about their orders, as they'd been doing for the past two days. With a kind of quiet nervousness, they polished shoes, shined belt buckles, squared away underwear, trying as best they could to accept their fate. Behind me, Grossbart swallowed hard, accepting his. And then, resisting with all my will an impulse to turn and seek pardon for my vindictiveness, I accepted my own.

QUESTIONS

1. More use of dilemma is made in this story than in any other in this text. Identify some of the dilemmas the protagonist finds himself in. Are they used primarily to create suspense, to reveal character, or to illuminate theme? Might all of these dilemmas be classified as specific applications of one general dilemma? If so, how might this general dilemma be described? (One suggestion for an answer is contained in the wisdom shown by Nathan Marx's grandmother in paragraph 333.)

2. Sergeant Marx finds himself in many dilemmas because he is trying to reconcile three roles—top sergeant, Jew, and human being. To what extent do these roles conflict? Point out places where Marx is thinking or acting primarily as a sergeant, as a Jew, as a human being.

3. The plot has four major episodes, centering in conflicts over (a) attendance at Friday night services, (b) company food, (c) pass to St. Louis, (d) shipping orders. Insofar as these involve conflict between Sergeant Marx and Grossbart, which is the victor in each?

4. "What are you, Grossbart? Honest to God, what are you?" asks Sergeant Marx. Answer this question as precisely as possible. What is Grossbart's philosophy? Catalogue the various methods he uses to achieve his goals.

5. Even more important to Sergeant Marx is the question, Who is Sergeant Marx? What does the fact that he asks this question (paragraph 333) tell us about him? By what principles does he try to govern his conduct? In paragraph 347, Marx speaks of "strategies of aggression" and "strategies of retreat"; on what occasions does *he* use strategies similar to Grossbart's?

6. What are Sergeant Marx's motivations in his final decision? In which of his roles—sergeant, Jew, human being—is he acting at this point? Is his decision right?

7. What is meant by Sergeant Marx's final statement that he accepted his fate? What *is* his fate?

8. Describe as precisely as possible Captain Barrett's attitude toward Jews.
9. Differentiate Grossbart, Fishbein, and Halpern. How would you rank these three, Captain Barrett, and Sergeant Marx on a scale of human worth?
10. To what character (or characters) does the title refer? Is it used straight-forwardly or ironically?
11. This story—by a Jewish author about Jewish characters—has a complex theme. Does the theme at its most general level necessarily involve the idea of Jewishness? Is it more crucial to the story that Nathan Marx is a Jew or a top sergeant? Try stating the theme without mentioning the idea of Jewishness. Now expand it to include the idea of Jewishness. Can it be stated without mentioning the idea of responsibility for command and judgment?

Anton Chekhov

In Exile

Old Semyon, whose nickname was Preacher, and a young Tartar, whose name no one knew, were sitting by a campfire on the bank of the river; the other three ferrymen were inside the hut. Semyon, a gaunt, toothless old man of sixty, broad-shouldered and still healthy-looking, was drunk; he would have gone to bed long ago, but he had a bottle in his pocket and was afraid his comrades in the hut would ask him for a drink of vodka. The Tartar was worn out and ill, and, wrapping himself in his rags, he talked about how good it was in the province of Simbirsk, and what a beautiful and clever wife he had left at home. He was not more than twenty-five, and in the firelight his pale, sickly face and woebegone expression made him seem like a boy.

"Well, this is no paradise, of course," said Preacher. "You can see for yourself: water, bare banks, nothing but clay wherever you look. . . . It's long past Easter and there's still ice on the river . . . and this morning there was snow."

"Bad! Bad!" said the Tartar, surveying the landscape with dismay.

A few yards away the dark, cold river flowed, growling and sluicing against the pitted clay banks as it sped on to the distant sea. At the edge of the

IN EXILE   First published in 1892. Translated from the Russian by Ann Dunnigan. Although old Semyon in the story comes from Kursk, about three hundred miles south of Moscow, and the young Tartar from Simbirsk, only about five hundred miles to the east, the Tartar, whose native tongue is Turkish-related, can talk to Semyon only in bro-ken Russian. Siberia, under the czars (as under the Soviets), was a place for sending ex-iles and criminals. Anton Chekhov (1860–1904), though he earned a medical degree from the University of Moscow, pursued writing as his main career. In 1890 he made a hazardous ten-thousand mile trip by river boat and carriage across Siberia to the Pacific, writing about his experiences for a newspaper. Near Omsk he was forced to spend one night at a ferry shelter when the boatmen would not take him across the flooded river because of dangerous winds. For information on Russian names, see the note on page 515.

bank loomed a capacious barge, which ferrymen call a *karbas*. Far away on the opposite bank crawling snakes of fire were dying down then reappearing—last year's grass being burned. Beyond the snakes there was darkness again. Little blocks of ice could be heard knocking against the barge. It was cold and damp. . . .

The Tartar glanced at the sky. There were as many stars as there were at home, the same blackness, but something was lacking. At home, in the province of Simbirsk, the stars and the sky seemed altogether different.

"Bad! Bad!" he repeated.

"You'll get used to it!" said Preacher with a laugh. "You're still young and foolish—the milk's hardly dry on your lips—and in your foolishness you think there's no one more unfortunate than you, but the time will come when you'll say to yourself: may God give everyone such a life. Just look at me. In a week's time the floods will be over and we'll launch the ferry; you'll all go gadding about Siberia, while I stay here, going back and forth, from one bank to the other. For twenty-two years now that's what I've been doing. Day and night. The pike and the salmon under the water and me on it. That's all I want. God give everyone such a life."

The Tartar threw some brushwood onto the fire, lay down closer to it, and said, "My father is sick man. When he dies, my mother, my wife, will come here. Have promised."

"And what do you want a mother and a wife for?" asked Preacher. "Just foolishness, brother. It's the devil stirring you up, blast his soul! Don't listen to him, the Evil One! Don't give in to him. When he goes on about women, spite him: I don't want them! When he talks to you about freedom, you stand up to him: I don't want it! I want nothing! No father, no mother, no wife, no freedom, no house nor home! I want nothing, damn their souls!"

Preacher took a swig at the bottle and went on, "I'm no simple peasant, brother; I don't come from the servile class; I'm a deacon's son, and when I was free I lived in Kursk, and used to go around in a frock coat; but now I've brought myself to such a point that I can sleep naked on the ground and eat grass. And God give everyone such a life. I don't want anything. I'm not afraid of anyone, and the way I see it, there's no man richer or freer than I am. When they sent me here from Russia, from the very first day I jibbed: I want nothing! The devil was at me about my wife, about my kin, about freedom, but I told him: I want nothing! And I stuck to it; and here, you see, I live well, I don't complain. But if anyone humors the devil and listens to him even once, he's lost, no salvation for him. He'll be stuck fast in the bog, up to his ears, and he'll never get out.

"It's not only the likes of you, foolish peasants, that are lost, but even the well-born and educated. Fifteen years ago they sent a gentleman here from Russia. He forged a will or something—wouldn't share with his brothers. It was said he was a prince or a baron, but maybe he was only an official, who knows? Well, the gentleman came here, and the first thing, he bought himself a house and land in Mukhortinskoe. 'I want to live by my own labor,' says he, 'in the sweat of my brow, because I'm no longer a gentleman, but an exile.' . . . 'Well,' says I, 'may God help you, that's the right thing.' He was a young man then, a hustler, always on the move; he used to do the mowing himself, catch fish, ride sixty versts on horseback. But here was the trouble: from the very first year he began riding to Gyrino to the post office. He used to stand on my ferry and sigh, 'Ah, Semyon, for a long time now they haven't sent me any money from home.' . . . 'You don't need money, Vasily Sergeich. What good is it? Throw off the past, forget it as if it had never happened, as if it was only a dream, and start life afresh. Don't listen to the devil,' I tell him, 'he'll bring you to no good; he'll tighten the noose. Now you want money,' says I, 'and in a little while, before you know it, you'll want something else, and then more and more. But,' says I, 'if you want to be happy, the very first thing is not to want anything.' Yes. . . . 'And if fate has cruelly wronged you and me,' says I, 'it's no good going down on your knees to her and asking her favor; you have to spurn her and laugh at her, otherwise she'll laugh at you.' That's what I said to him. . . .

"Two years later I ferried him over to this side, and he was rubbing his hands together and laughing. 'I'm going to Gyrino,' says he, 'to meet my wife. She has taken pity on me and come here. She's so kind and good!' He was panting with joy. Next day he comes with his wife. A young, beautiful lady in a hat, carrying a baby girl in her arms. And plenty of baggage of all sorts. My Vasily Sergeich was spinning around her; couldn't take his eyes off her; couldn't praise her enough. 'Yes, brother Semyon, even in Siberia people can live!' . . . 'Well,' thinks I, 'just you wait; better not rejoice too soon.' . . . And from that time on, almost every week he went to Gyrino to find out if money had been sent from Russia. As for money—it took plenty! 'It's for my sake that her youth and beauty are going to ruin here in Siberia,' he says, 'sharing with me my bitter fate, and for this,' he says, 'I ought to provide her with every diversion.' To make it more cheerful for his lady he took up with the officials and with all sorts of riff-raff. And there had to be food and drink for this crowd, of course, and they must have a piano, and a fuzzy little lap dog on the sofa—may it croak! . . . Luxury, in short, indulgence. The lady did not stay with him long. How could she? Clay, water, cold, no vegetables for you, no fruit; uneducated and drunken people all around, no manners at all, and she a pampered lady from the capital. . . . Naturally, she grew tired of it. Besides, her husband, say what you like, was no longer a gentleman, but an exile—not exactly an honor.

"Three years later, I remember, on the eve of the Assumption, someone shouted from the other side. I went over in the ferry, and what do I see but the lady—all muffled up, and with her a young gentleman, an official. There was a troika. . . . And after I ferried them across, they got in it and vanished into thin air! That was the last that was seen of them. Toward morning Vasily Sergeich galloped up to the ferry. 'Didn't my wife pass this way, Semyon, with a gentleman in spectacles?' . . . 'She did,' says I. 'Seek the wind in the fields!' He galloped off in pursuit of them, and didn't stop for five days and five nights. Afterwards, when I took him over to the other side, he threw himself down on the ferry, beat his head against the planks, and howled. 'So that's how it is,' says I. . . . I laughed and recalled to him: 'Even in Siberia people can live!' And he beat his head all the more.

"After that he began to long for freedom. His wife had slipped away to Russia, so, naturally, he was drawn there, both to see her and to rescue her from her lover. And, my friend, he took to galloping off every day, either to the post office or the authorities; he kept sending in petitions, and presenting them personally, asking to be pardoned so he could go back home; and he used to tell how he had spent some two hundred rubles on telegrams alone. He sold his land, and mortgaged his house to the Jews. He grew gray, stooped, and yellow in the face, as if he was consumptive. He'd talk to you and go: khe-khe-khe . . . and there would be tears in his eyes. He struggled with those petitions for eight years, but now he has recovered his spirits and is more cheerful: he's thought up a new indulgence. His daughter, you see, has grown up. He keeps an eye on her, dotes on her. And, to tell the truth, she's all right, a pretty little thing, black-browed, and with a lively disposition. Every Sunday he goes to church with her in Gyrino. Side by side they stand on the ferry, she laughing and he not taking his eyes off her. 'Yes, Semyon,' says he, 'even in Siberia people can live. Even in Siberia there is happiness. Look,' says he, 'see what a daughter I've got! I suppose you wouldn't find another like her if you went a thousand versts.' . . . 'Your daughter,' says I, 'is a fine young lady, that's true, certainly. . . .' But I think to myself: Wait a while. . . . The girl is young, her blood is dancing, she wants to live, and what life is there here? And, my friend, she did begin to fret. . . . She withered and withered, wasted away, fell ill; and now she's completely worn out. Consumption.

"That's your Siberian happiness for you, the pestilence take it! That's 15
how people can live in Siberia! . . . He's taken to running after doctors and taking them home with him. As soon as he hears that there's a doctor or quack two or three hundred versts away, he goes to fetch him. A terrible lot of money has been spent on doctors; to my way of thinking, it would have been better to spend it on drink. . . . She'll die anyway. She's certain to die, and then he'll be completely lost. He'll hang himself from grief, or run away to Russia—that's sure. He'll run away, they'll catch him, there'll be a trial, and then hard labor; they'll give him a taste of the lash. . . ."

"Good, good," muttered the Tartar, shivering with cold.

"What's good?" asked Preacher.

"Wife and daughter. . . . Let hard labor, let suffer; he saw his wife and daughter. . . . You say: want nothing. But nothing is bad! Wife was with him three years—God gave him that. Nothing is bad; three years is good. How you not understand?"

Shivering and stuttering, straining to pick out the Russian words, of which he knew so few, the Tartar said God forbid one should fall sick and die in a strange land, and be buried in the cold, sodden earth; that if his wife came to him even for one day, even for one hour, he would be willing to accept any torture whatsoever, and thank God for it. Better one day of happiness than nothing.

20   After that he again described the beautiful and clever wife he had left at home; then, clutching his head with both hands, he began crying and assuring Semyon that he was innocent and had been falsely accused. His two brothers and his uncle stole some horses from a peasant, and beat the old man till he was half dead, and the commune had not judged fairly, but had contrived a sentence by which all three brothers were sent to Siberia, while the uncle, a rich man, remained at home.

"You'll get u-u-used to it!" said Semyon.

The Tartar relapsed into silence and fixed his tearful eyes on the fire; his face expressed bewilderment and fright, as though he still did not understand why he was here in the dark, in the damp, among strangers, instead of in the province of Simbirsk. Preacher lay down near the fire, chuckled at something, and began singing in an undertone.

"What joy has she with her father?" he said a little later. "He loves her, she's a consolation to him, it's true; but you have to mind your p's and q's with him, brother: he's a strict old man, a severe old man. And strictness is not what young girls want. . . . They want petting and ha-ha-ha and ho-ho-ho, scents and pomades! Yes. . . . Ekh, life, life!" sighed Semyon, getting up with difficulty. "The vodka's all gone, so it's time to sleep. Eh? I'm going, my boy."

Left alone, the Tartar put more brushwood onto the fire, lay down, and, looking into the blaze, began thinking of his native village, and of his wife: if she would come only for a month, even for a day, then, if she liked, she might go back again. Better a month or even a day than nothing. But if she kept her promise and came, how could he provide for her? Where could she live?

25   "If not something to eat, how you live?" the Tartar asked aloud.

He was paid only ten kopecks for working at the oars a day and a night; the passengers gave him tips, it was true, but the ferrymen shared everything among themselves, giving nothing to the Tartar, but only making fun of him. And he was hungry, cold, and frightened from want. . . . Now, when his whole body was shivering and aching, he ought to go into the hut and lie down to sleep, but he had nothing there to cover himself with, and it was colder there than on the river bank; here, too, he had nothing to put over him, but at least he could make a fire. . . .

In another week, when the floods had subsided and the ferry could sail, none of the ferrymen except Semyon would be needed, and the Tartar would begin going from village to village, looking for work and begging alms. His wife was only seventeen years old; beautiful, pampered, shy—could she possibly go from village to village, her face unveiled, begging? No, even to think of it was dreadful. . . .

It was already growing light; the barge, the bushes of rose-willow, and the ripples on the water were clearly distinguishable, and looking back there was the steep clay precipice, below it the little hut thatched with brown straw, and above clung the huts of the villagers. The cocks were already crowing in the village.

The red clay precipice, the barge, the river, the strange, unkind people, hunger, cold, illness—perhaps all this did not exist in reality. Probably it was all a dream, thought the Tartar. He felt that he was asleep, and hearing his own snoring. . . . Of course, he was at home in the province of Simbirsk, and he had only to call his wife by name for her to answer, and in the next room his mother. . . . However, what awful dreams there are! Why? The Tartar smiled and opened his eyes. What river was this? The Volga?

"Bo-o-at!" someone shouted from the other side. "Kar-ba-a-s!" 30

The Tartar woke up and went to wake his comrades, to row over to the other side. Putting on their torn sheepskins as they came, the ferrymen appeared on the bank, swearing in hoarse, sleepy voices, and shivering from the cold. After their sleep, the river, from which there came a piercing gust of cold air, evidently struck them as revolting and sinister. They were not quick to jump into the barge. The Tartar and the three ferrymen took up the long, broad-bladed oars, which looked like crabs' claws in the darkness. Semyon leaned his belly against the long tiller. The shouting from the other side continued, and two shots were fired from a revolver; the man probably thought that the ferrymen were asleep or had gone off to the village tavern.

"All right, plenty of time!" said Preacher in the tone of a man who is convinced that there is no need to hurry in this world—that it makes no difference, really, and nothing will come of it.

The heavy, clumsy barge drew away from the bank and floated between the rose-willows; and only because the willows slowly receded was it possible to see that the barge was not standing still but moving. The ferrymen plied the oars evenly, in unison; Preacher hung over the tiller on his belly, and, describing an arc in the air, flew from one side of the boat to the other. In the darkness it looked as if the men were sitting on some antediluvian animal with long paws, and sailing to a cold, bleak land, the very one of which we sometimes dream in nightmares.

They passed beyond the willows and floated out into the open. The rhythmic thump and splash of the oars were now audible on the further shore, and someone shouted, "Hurry! Hurry!" Another ten minutes passed and the barge bumped heavily against the landing stage.

"And it keeps coming down, and coming down!" muttered Semyon, wiping the snow from his face. "Where it comes from, God only knows!" 35

On the other side stood a thin old man of medium height wearing a jacket lined with fox fur and a white lambskin cap. He was standing at a little distance from his horses and not moving; he had a concentrated, morose expression, as if, trying to remember something, he had grown angry with his unyielding memory. When Semyon went up to him with a smile and took off his cap, he said, "I'm hastening to Anastasyevka. My daughter is worse again, and they say there's a new doctor at Anastasyevka."

They dragged the tarantass° onto the barge and rowed back. The man, whom Semyon called Vasily Sergeich, stood motionless all the way back, his thick lips tightly compressed, his eyes fixed on one spot; when the coachman asked permission to smoke in his presence, he made no reply, as if he had not heard. And Semyon, hanging over the tiller on his belly, glanced mockingly at him and said, "Even in Siberia people can live. Li-i-ve!"

There was a triumphant expression on Preacher's face, as if he had proved something and was rejoicing that it had turned out exactly as he had surmised. The helpless, unhappy look of the man in the fox-lined jacket evidently afforded him great satisfaction.

"It's muddy driving now, Vasily Sergeich," he said when the horses were harnessed on the bank. "You'd better have waited a week or two till it gets drier. . . . Or else not have gone at all. . . . If there were any sense in going, but, as you yourself know, people have been driving about for ever and ever, by day and by night, and there's never any sense in it. That's the truth!"

40   Vasily Sergeich tipped him without a word, got into the tarantass, and drove off.

"See there, he's gone galloping off for a doctor!" said Semyon, shrinking with cold. "Yes, looking for a real doctor is like chasing the wind in the fields, or catching the devil by the tail, damn your soul! What freaks! Lord forgive me, a sinner!"

The Tartar went up to Preacher and, looking at him with hatred and abhorrence, trembling, mixing Tartar words with his broken Russian, said, "He is good—good. You bad! You bad! Gentleman is good soul, excellent, and you beast, you bad! Gentleman alive and you dead. . . . God created man to be live, be joyful, be sad and sorrow, but you want nothing. . . . You not live, you stone, clay! Stone want nothing and you want nothing. . . . You stone—and God not love you, love gentleman!"

Everyone laughed; the Tartar frowned scornfully and, with a gesture of despair, wrapped himself in his rags and went to the fire. Semyon and the ferrymen trailed off to the hut.

"It's cold," said one of the ferrymen hoarsely as he stretched out on the straw that covered the damp floor.

45   "Well, it's not warm!" one of the others agreed. "It's a hard life!"

They all lay down. The door was blown open by the wind, and snow drifted into the hut. No one felt like getting up and closing the door; it was cold and they were lazy.

"I'm all right!" said Semyon, falling asleep. "God give everyone such a life."

"You're a hard case, we know that. Even the devils won't take you!"

---

tarantass: a heavy four-wheeled carriage

From outside there came sounds like the howling of a dog.

"What's that? Who's there?"   50

"It's the Tartar crying."

"He'll get u-u-used to it!" said Semyon, and instantly fell asleep.

Soon the others fell asleep too. And the door remained unclosed.

QUESTIONS

1. Who is the protagonist of the story? Does the central conflict involve man against man, man against environment, man against himself—or elements of all three?
2. How is the physical environment represented? What details are especially vivid, and what emotional connotations do they have? Is there a difference between the initial presentation of the landscape during the night and the appearance of it after dawn?
3. Characterize Semyon, considering (a) his physical appearance, (b) his actions, and (c) his speech. Is there anything about him that might be called admirable?
4. How is the story Semyon tells about Vasily Sergeich relevant to the situation of the young Tartar? How do Vasily's appearance and behavior when he appears in person measure up to the expectations about him created by Semyon's story?
5. What dilemma does the Tartar face? How do the histories of Semyon and Vasily define that dilemma?
6. Does the ending resolve the conflicts that have been presented? Formulate the theme of the story, being sure to include the idea of "exile" in your statement.

CHAPTER FIVE

Point of View

Primitive storytellers, unbothered by considerations of form, simply spun their tales. "Once upon a time," they began, and proceeded to narrate the story to their listeners, describing the characters when necessary, telling what the characters thought and felt as well as what they did, and interjecting comments and ideas of their own. Modern fiction writers are artistically more self-conscious. They realize that there are many ways of telling a story; they decide upon a method before they begin, or discover one while in the act of writing, and may even set up rules for themselves. Instead of telling the story themselves, they may let one of the characters tell it; they may tell it by means of letters or diaries; they may confine themselves to recording the thoughts of one of the characters. With the growth of artistic consciousness, the question of **point of view**—of who tells the story, and, therefore, of how it gets told—has assumed especial importance.*

To determine the point of view of a story we ask, "Who tells the story?" and "How much is this person allowed to know?" and, especially, "To what extent does the narrator look inside the characters and report their thoughts and feelings?"

Though many variations and combinations are possible, the basic points of view are four, as follows:

1. Omniscient

2. Limited omniscient   { (a) Major character
                           { (b) Minor character

3. First person   { (a) Major character
                           { (b) Minor character

4. Objective

---

*When analyzing fiction, it is important to reserve the term "point of view" for its technical meaning as defined in this chapter. Using it also in its nontechnical meaning of "opinion" or "attitude" may lead to confusion.

1. In the **omniscient point of view,** the story is told in the third person by a narrator whose knowledge and prerogatives are unlimited. Such narrators are free to go wherever they wish, to peer inside the minds and hearts of characters at will and tell us what they are thinking or feeling. These narrators can interpret behavior and can comment, if they wish, on the significance of their stories. They know all. They can tell us as much or as little as they please.

The following version of Aesop's fable "The Ant and the Grasshopper" is told from the omniscient point of view. Notice that in it we are told not only what both characters do and say, but also what they think and feel; notice also that the narrator comments at the end on the significance of the story. (The phrases in which the narrator enters into the thoughts or feelings of the ant and the grasshopper have been italicized; the comment by the author is printed in small capitals.)

> *Weary in every limb,* the ant tugged over the snow a piece of corn he had stored up last summer. *It would taste mighty good at dinner tonight.*
>
> A grasshopper, *cold and hungry,* looked on. *Finally he could bear it no longer.* "Please, friend ant, may I have a bite of corn?"
>
> "What were you doing all last summer?" asked the ant. He looked the grasshopper up and down. *He knew its kind.*
>
> "I sang from dawn till dark," replied the grasshopper, *happily unaware of what was coming next.*
>
> "Well," said the ant, *hardly bothering to conceal his contempt,* "since you sang all summer, you can dance all winter."
>
> HE WHO IDLES WHEN HE'S YOUNG
> WILL HAVE NOTHING WHEN HE'S OLD

Stories told from the omniscient point of view may differ widely in the amount of omniscience the narrator is allowed. In "In Exile," we enter the mind of the Tartar, particularly when he is left alone by the fire, but most of the time the narrator either quotes old Semyon or directly reports actions and appearances. In "The Destructors," though we are taken into the minds of Blackie, Mike, the gang as a group, Old Misery, and the lorry driver, we are not taken into the mind of Trevor—the most important character. In "The Most Dangerous Game," we are confined to the thoughts and feelings of Rainsford, except for the brief passage between Rainsford's leap into the sea and his waking in Zaroff's bed, during which the point of view shifts to General Zaroff.

The omniscient is the most flexible point of view and permits the widest scope. It is also the most subject to abuse. It offers constant danger that the narrator may come between the readers and the story, or that the continual shifting of viewpoint from character to character may cause a breakdown in coherence or unity. Used skillfully it enables the author to achieve simultaneous breadth and depth. Unskillfully used, it can destroy the illusion of reality that the story attempts to create.

2. In the **limited omniscient point of view,** the story is told in the third person, but from the viewpoint of one character in the story. Such point-of-view characters are filters through whose eyes and minds writers look at the events. Authors employing this perspective may move both inside and outside these characters but never leave their sides. They tell us what these characters see and hear and what they think and feel; they possibly interpret the characters' thoughts and behavior. They know everything about their point-of-view characters— often more than the characters know about themselves. But they limit themselves to these characters' perceptions and show no direct knowledge of what *other* characters are thinking or feeling or doing, except for what the point-of-view character knows or can infer about them. The chosen character may be either a major or a minor character, a participant or an observer, and this choice also will be a very important one for the story. "The Japanese Quince," "Roman Fever," and "Miss Brill" are told from the limited omniscient point of view, from the perspective of the main character. The use of this viewpoint with a minor character is rare in the short story, and is not illustrated in this book.

Here is "The Ant and the Grasshopper" told, in the third person, from the point of view of the ant. Notice that this time we are told nothing of what the grasshopper thinks or feels. We see and hear and know of him only what the ant sees and hears and knows.

> *Weary in every limb,* the ant tugged over the snow a piece of corn he had stored up last summer. *It would taste mighty good at dinner tonight. It was then that he noticed the grasshopper, looking cold and pinched.*
>
> "Please, friend ant, may I have a bite of your corn?" asked the grasshopper.
>
> He looked the grasshopper up and down. "What were you doing all last summer?" he asked. *He knew its kind.*
>
> "I sang from dawn till dark," replied the grasshopper.
>
> "Well," said the ant, *hardly bothering to conceal his contempt,* "since you sang all summer, you can dance all winter."

The limited omniscient point of view, since it acquaints us with the world through the mind and senses of only one person, approximates more closely than the omniscient the conditions of real life; it also offers a ready-made unifying element, since all details of the story are the experience of one person. And it affords an additional device of characterization, since what a point-of-view character does or does not find noteworthy, and the inferences that such a character draws about other characters' actions and motives, may reveal biases or limitations in the observer. At the same time it offers a limited field of observation, for the readers can go nowhere except where the chosen character goes, and there may be difficulty in having the character naturally cognizant of all important events. Clumsy writers will constantly have the focal character listening at keyholes, accidentally overhearing important conversations, or coincidentally being present when important events occur.

3. In the **first-person point of view**, the author disappears into one of the characters, who tells the story in the first person. This character, again, may be either a major or minor character, protagonist or observer, and it will make considerable difference whether the protagonist tells the story or someone else tells it. In "I'm a Fool," "The Lesson," and "Defender of the Faith," the protagonist tells the story in the first person. In "The Child by Tiger" and "Spotted Horses" (page 350), the story is told by an observer.

Our fable is retold below in the first person from the point of view of the grasshopper. (The whole story is italicized because it all comes out of the grasshopper's mind.)

> *Cold and hungry, I watched the ant tugging over the snow a piece of corn he had stored up last summer. My feelers twitched, and I was conscious of a tic in my left hind leg. Finally I could bear it no longer. "Please, friend ant," I asked, "may I have a bite of your corn?"*
>
> *He looked me up and down. "What were you doing all last summer?" he asked, rather too smugly it seemed to me.*
>
> *"I sang from dawn till dark," I said innocently, remembering the happy times.*
>
> *"Well," he said, with a priggish sneer, "since you sang all summer, you can dance all winter."*

The first-person point of view shares the virtues and limitations of the limited omniscient. It offers, sometimes, a gain in immediacy and reality, since we get the story directly from a participant, the author as intermediary being eliminated. It offers no opportunity, however, for *direct* interpretation by the author, and there is constant danger that narrators may be made to transcend their own sensitivity, their knowledge, or their powers of language in telling a story. Good authors, however, can make tremendous literary capital out of the very limitations of their narrators. The first-person point of view offers excellent opportunities for dramatic irony and for studies in limited or blunted human perceptivity. Often, as in "I'm a Fool," the very heart of the story may lie in the difference between what the narrator perceives and what the reader perceives. In such stories authors offer interpretations of the material *indirectly,* through the use of irony. They may also indicate their own judgment, more straightforwardly though still indirectly, by expressing it through the lips of a discerning and sympathetic narrator. In "Defender of the Faith" the reader is disposed to accept Sergeant Marx's interpretation of characters and events as being largely the author's own. Such identifications of a narrator's attitude with the author's, however, must always be undertaken with extreme caution; they are justified only if the total material of the story supports them. In "Defender of the Faith" the moral sensitivity and intelligence of the narrator reflects the author's own; nevertheless, much of the interest of the story arises from Marx's own uncertainty about his judgments—the nagging apprehension that he may be mistaken.

4. In the **objective point of view,** the narrator disappears into a kind of roving sound camera. This camera can go anywhere but can record only what is seen and heard. It cannot comment, interpret, or enter a character's mind. With this point of view (sometimes called also the **dramatic point of view**) readers are placed in the position of spectators at a movie or play. They see what the characters do and hear what they say but must infer what they think or feel and what they are like. Authors are not there to explain. The purest example of a story told from the objective point of view would be one written entirely in dialogue, for as soon as authors add words of their own, they begin to interpret through their very choice of words. Actually, few stories using this point of view are antiseptically pure, for the limitations it imposes on the author are severe. "Hills Like White Elephants" (page 170) is an excellent example, however, and "The Father" (page 391) and "The Lottery" (page 421) are essentially objective in their narration.

The following version of "The Ant and the Grasshopper" is also told from the objective point of view. (Since we are nowhere taken into the thoughts or feelings of the characters, none of this version is printed in italics.)

The ant tugged over the snow a piece of corn he had stored up last summer, perspiring in spite of the cold.

A grasshopper, his feelers twitching and with a tic in his left hind leg, looked on for some time. Finally he asked, "Please, friend ant, may I have a bite of your corn?"

The ant looked the grasshopper up and down. "What were you doing all last summer?" he snapped.

"I sang from dawn till dark," replied the grasshopper, not changing his tone.

"Well," said the ant, and a faint smile crept into his face, "since you sang all summer, you can dance all winter."

The objective point of view has the most speed and the most action; also, it requires readers to draw their own inferences. But it must rely heavily on external action and dialogue, and it offers no opportunities for direct interpretation by the author.

Each of the points of view has its advantages, its limitations, and its peculiar uses. Ideally the choice of the author will depend upon the materials and the purpose of a story. Authors choose the point of view that enables them to present their particular materials most effectively in terms of their purposes. Writers of murder mysteries with suspense and thrills as the purpose will ordinarily avoid using the point of view of the murderer or the brilliant detective: otherwise they would have to reveal at the beginning the secrets they wish to conceal till the end. On the other hand, if they are interested in exploring criminal psychology, the murderer's point of view might be by far the most effective. In the Sherlock Holmes stories, A. Conan Doyle effectively uses the somewhat imperceptive Dr. Watson as his narrator, so that the reader may be kept in the dark as long as possible and then be as amazed as Watson is by Holmes's deductive powers. In Dostoevsky's *Crime and Punishment,* however, the author is interested not in mystifying and surprising but in illuminating the moral and psychological operations of the human soul in the act of taking life; he therefore tells the story from the viewpoint of a sensitive and intelligent murderer.

For readers, the examination of point of view may be important both for understanding and for evaluating the story. First, they should know whether the events of the story are being interpreted by a narrator or by one of the characters. If the latter, they must ask how this character's mind and personality affect the interpretation, whether the character is perceptive or imperceptive, and whether the interpretation can be accepted at face value or must be discounted because of ignorance, stupidity, or self-deception. Often, as in "I'm a Fool," an author achieves striking and significant effects by using a narrator not aware of the full import of the events he is reporting.

Next, readers should ask whether the writer has chosen the point of view for maximum revelation of the material or for another reason. The author may choose the point of view mainly to conceal certain information till the end of the story and thus maintain suspense and create surprise. The author may even deliberately mislead readers by presenting the events through a character who puts a false interpretation on them. Such a false interpretation may be justified if it leads eventually to more effective revelation of character and theme. If it is there merely to trick readers, it is obviously less justifiable.

Finally, readers should ask whether the author has used the selected point of view fairly and consistently. Even in escape literature, we have a right to demand fair treatment. If the person to whose thoughts and feelings we are admitted has pertinent information that is not revealed, we legitimately feel cheated. To have a chance to solve a murder mystery, we must know what the detective learns. A writer also should be consistent in the point of view; if it shifts, it should do so for a just artistic reason. Serious interpretive writers choose and use point of view so as to yield ultimately the greatest possible insight, either in fullness or in intensity.

Willa Cather

Paul's Case

It was Paul's afternoon to appear before the faculty of the Pittsburgh High School to account for his various misdemeanors. He had been suspended a week ago, and his father had called at the Principal's office and confessed his perplexity about his son. Paul entered the faculty room suave and smiling. His clothes were a trifle outgrown, and the tan velvet on the collar of his open overcoat was frayed and worn; but for all that there was something of a dandy about him, and he wore an opal pin in his neatly knotted black four-in-hand, and a red carnation in his buttonhole. This latter adornment the faculty somehow felt was not properly significant of the contrite spirit befitting a boy under the ban of suspension.

Paul was tall for his age and very thin, with high, cramped shoulders and a narrow chest. His eyes were remarkable for a certain hysterical brilliancy, and he continually used them in a conscious, theatrical sort of way, peculiarly offensive in a boy. The pupils were abnormally large, as though he

PAUL'S CASE   Written in 1904, first published in 1905. Willa Cather (1873–1947) was born in Virginia and grew up and was educated in Nebraska. From 1895 to 1905 she lived and worked in Pittsburgh, first as a journalist, writing drama and music criticism, later as a teacher of English and Latin in two Pittsburgh high schools. In 1902 she traveled in Europe.

were addicted to belladonna, but there was a glassy glitter about them which that drug does not produce.

When questioned by the Principal as to why he was there, Paul stated, politely enough, that he wanted to come back to school. This was a lie, but Paul was quite accustomed to lying; found it, indeed, indispensable for overcoming friction. His teachers were asked to state their respective charges against him, which they did with such a rancor and aggrievedness as evinced that this was not a usual case. Disorder and impertinence were among the offences named, yet each of his instructors felt that it was scarcely possible to put into words the real cause of the trouble, which lay in a sort of hysterically defiant manner of the boy's; in the contempt which they all knew he felt for them, and which he seemingly made not the least effort to conceal. Once, when he had been making a synopsis of a paragraph at the blackboard, his English teacher had stepped to his side and attempted to guide his hand. Paul had started back with a shudder and thrust his hands violently behind him. The astonished woman could scarcely have been more hurt and embarrassed had he struck at her. The insult was so involuntary and definitely personal as to be unforgettable. In one way and another, he had made all his teachers, men and women alike, conscious of the same feeling of physical aversion. In one class he habitually sat with his hand shading his eyes; in another he always looked out of the window during the recitation; in another he made a running commentary on the lecture, with humorous intent.

His teachers felt this afternoon that his whole attitude was symbolized by his shrug and his flippantly red carnation flower, and they fell upon him without mercy, his English teacher leading the pack. He stood through it smiling, his pale lips parted over his white teeth. (His lips were continually twitching, and he had a habit of raising his eyebrows that was contemptuous and irritating to the last degree.) Older boys than Paul had broken down and shed tears under that ordeal, but his set smile did not once desert him, and his only sign of discomfort was the nervous trembling of the fingers that toyed with the buttons of his overcoat, and an occasional jerking of the other hand which held his hat. Paul was always smiling, always glancing about him, seeming to feel that people might be watching him and trying to detect something. This conscious expression, since it was as far as possible from boyish mirthfulness, was usually attributed to insolence or "smartness."

As the inquisition proceeded, one of his instructors repeated an impertinent remark of the boy's, and the Principal asked him whether he thought that a courteous speech to make to a woman. Paul shrugged his shoulders slightly and his eyebrows twitched.

"I don't know," he replied. "I didn't mean to be polite or impolite, either. I guess it's a sort of way I have, of saying things regardless."

The Principal asked him whether he didn't think that a way it would be well to get rid of. Paul grinned and said he guessed so. When he was told that he could go, he bowed gracefully and went out. His bow was like a repetition of the scandalous red carnation.

5

His teachers were in despair, and his drawing-master voiced the feeling of them all when he declared there was something about the boy which none of them understood. He added: "I don't really believe that smile of his comes altogether from insolence; there's something sort of haunted about it. The boy is not strong for one thing. There is something wrong about the fellow."

The drawing-master had come to realize that, in looking at Paul, one saw only his white teeth and the forced animation of his eyes. One warm afternoon the boy had gone to sleep at his drawing-board, and his master had noted with amazement what a white, blue-veined face it was; drawn and wrinkled like an old man's about the eyes, the lips twitching even in his sleep.

10   His teachers left the building dissatisfied and unhappy; humiliated to have felt so vindictive toward a mere boy, to have uttered this feeling in cutting terms, and to have set each other on, as it were, in the gruesome game of intemperate reproach. One of them remembered having seen a miserable street cat set at bay by a ring of tormentors.

As for Paul, he ran down the hill whistling the Soldiers' Chorus from *Faust,* looking behind him now and then to see whether some of his teachers were not there to witness his light-heartedness. As it was now late in the afternoon and Paul was on duty that evening as usher at Carnegie Hall, he decided that he would not go home to supper.

When he reached the concert hall, the doors were not yet open. It was chilly outside, and he decided to go up into the picture gallery—always deserted at this hour—where there were some of Raffelli's gay studies of Paris streets and an airy blue Venetian scene or two that always exhilarated him. He was delighted to find no one in the gallery but the old guard, who sat in the corner, a newspaper on his knee, a black patch over one eye and the other closed. Paul possessed himself of the place and walked confidently up and down, whistling under his breath. After a while he sat down before a blue Rico and lost himself. When he bethought him to look at his watch, it was after seven o'clock and he rose with a start and ran downstairs, making a face at Augustus Caesar, peering out from the cast-room, and an evil gesture at the Venus of Milo as he passed her on the stairway.

When Paul reached the ushers' dressing-room, half a dozen boys were there already, and he began excitedly to tumble into his uniform. It was one of the few that at all approached fitting, and Paul thought it very becoming— though he knew the tight, straight coat accentuated his narrow chest, about which he was exceedingly sensitive. He was always excited while he dressed, twanging all over to the tuning of the strings and the preliminary flourishes of the horns in the music-room; but tonight he seemed quite beside himself, and he teased and plagued the boys until, telling him that he was crazy, they put him down on the floor and sat on him.

Somewhat calmed by his suppression, Paul dashed out to the front of the house to seat the early comers. He was a model usher. Gracious and smiling he ran up and down the aisles. Nothing was too much trouble for him; he carried messages and brought programs as though it were his greatest pleasure in life, and all the people in his section thought him a charming boy, feeling that he remembered and admired them. As the house filled, he grew more and more vivacious and animated, and the color came to his cheeks and lips. It was very much as though this were a great reception and Paul were the host. Just as the musicians came out to take their places, his English teacher arrived with checks for the seats which a prominent manufacturer had taken for the season. She betrayed some embarrassment when she handed Paul the tickets, and a *hauteur* which subsequently made her feel very foolish. Paul was startled for a moment, and had the feeling of wanting to put her out; what business had she here among all these fine people and gay colors? He looked her over and decided that she was not appropriately dressed and must be a fool to sit downstairs in such togs. The tickets had probably been sent her out of kindness, he reflected, as he put down a seat for her, and she had about as much right to sit there as he had.

When the symphony began, Paul sank into one of the rear seats with a   15 long sigh of relief, and lost himself as he had done before the Rico. It was not that symphonies, as such, meant anything in particular to Paul, but the first sight of the instruments seemed to free some hilarious spirit within him; something that struggled there like the Genius in the bottle found by the Arab fisherman. He felt a sudden zest of life; the lights danced before his eyes and the concert hall blazed into unimaginable splendor. When the soprano soloist came on, Paul forgot even the nastiness of his teacher's being there, and gave himself up to the peculiar intoxication such personages always had for him. The soloist chanced to be a German woman, by no means in her first youth, and the mother of many children; but she wore a satin gown and a tiara, and she had that indefinable air of achievement, that worldshine upon her, which always blinded Paul to any possible defects.

After a concert was over, Paul was often irritable and wretched until he got to sleep—and tonight he was even more than usually restless. He had the feeling of not being able to let down; of its being impossible to give up his delicious excitement which was the only thing that could be called living at all. During the last number he withdrew and, after hastily changing his clothes in the dressing-room, slipped out to the side door where the singer's carriage stood. Here he began pacing rapidly up and down the walk, waiting to see her come out.

Over yonder the Schenley, in its vacant stretch, loomed big and square through the fine rain, the windows of its twelve stories glowing like those of a lighted cardboard house under a Christmas tree. All the actors and singers of any importance stayed there when they were in Pittsburgh, and a number of the big manufacturers of the place lived there in the winter. Paul had often hung about the hotel, watching the people go in and out, longing to enter and leave schoolmasters and dull care behind him forever.

At last the singer came out, accompanied by the conductor, who helped her into her carriage and closed the door with a cordial *auf wiedersehen*— which set Paul to wondering whether she were not an old sweetheart of his. Paul followed the carriage over to the hotel, walking so rapidly as not to be far from the entrance when the singer alighted and disappeared behind the swinging glass doors which were opened by a Negro in a tall hat and a long coat. In the moment that the door was ajar, it seemed to Paul that he, too, entered. He seemed to feel himself go after her up the steps, into the warm, lighted building, into an exotic, a tropical world of shiny, glistening surfaces and basking ease. He reflected upon the mysterious dishes that were brought into the dining-room, the green bottles in buckets of ice, as he had seen them in the supper-party pictures of the Sunday supplement. A quick gust of wind brought the rain down with sudden vehemence, and Paul was startled to find that he was still outside in the slush of the gravel driveway; that his boots were letting in the water and his scanty overcoat was clinging wet about him; that the lights in front of the concert hall were out, and that the rain was driving in sheets between him and the orange glow of the windows above him. There it was, what he wanted—tangibly before him, like the fairy world of a Christmas pantomime; as the rain beat in his face, Paul wondered whether he were destined always to shiver in the black night outside, looking up at it.

He turned and walked reluctantly toward the car tracks. The end had to come sometime; his father in his night-clothes at the top of the stairs, explanations that did not explain, hastily improvised fictions that were forever tripping him up, his upstairs room and its horrible yellow wallpaper, the creaking bureau with the greasy plush collar-box, and over his painted wooden bed the pictures of George Washington and John Calvin, and the framed motto, "Feed my Lambs," which had been worked in red worsted by his mother, whom Paul could not remember.

20   Half an hour later, Paul alighted from the Negley Avenue car and went slowly down one of the side streets off the main thoroughfare. It was a highly respectable street, where all the houses were exactly alike, and where business men of moderate means begot and reared large families of children, all of whom went to Sabbath School and learned the shorter catechism, and were interested in arithmetic; all of whom were as exactly alike as their homes, and of a piece with the monotony in which they lived. Paul never went up Cordelia Street without a shudder of loathing. His home was next to the house of the Cumberland minister. He approached it tonight with the nerveless sense of defeat, the hopeless feeling of sinking back forever into ugliness and commonness that he had always had when he came home. The moment he turned into Cordelia Street he felt the waters close above his head. After each of these orgies of living, he experienced all the physical depression which follows a debauch; the loathing of respectable beds, of common food, of a house permeated by kitchen odors; a shuddering repulsion for the flavorless, colorless mass of everyday existence; a morbid desire for cool things and soft lights and fresh flowers.

The nearer he approached the house, the more absolutely unequal Paul felt to the sight of it all: his ugly sleeping chamber; the old bathroom with the grimy zinc tub, the cracked mirror, the dripping spigots; his father, at the top of the stairs, his hairy legs sticking out from his nightshirt, his feet thrust into carpet slippers. He was so much later than usual that there would certainly be enquiries and reproaches. Paul stopped short before the door. He felt that he could not be accosted by his father tonight; that he could not toss again on that miserable bed. He would not go in. He would tell his father that he had no carfare, and it was raining so hard he had gone home with one of the boys and stayed all night.

Meanwhile, he was wet and cold. He went around to the back of the house and tried one of the basement windows, found it open, and raised it cautiously, and scrambled down the cellar wall to the floor. There he stood, holding his breath, terrified by the noise he had made; but the floor above him was silent, and there was no creak on the stairs. He found a soap-box, and carried it over to the soft ring of light that streamed from the furnace door, and sat down. He was horribly afraid of rats, so he did not try to sleep, but sat looking distrustfully at the dark, still terrified lest he might have awakened his father.

In such reactions, after one of the experiences which made days and nights out of the dreary blanks of the calendar, when his senses were deadened, Paul's head was always singularly clear. Suppose his father had heard him getting in at the window and had come down and shot him for a burglar? Then, again, suppose his father had come down, pistol in hand, and he had cried out in time to save himself, and his father had been horrified to think how nearly he had killed him? Then again, suppose a day should come when his father would remember that night, and wish there had been no warning cry to stay his hand? With this last supposition Paul entertained himself until daybreak.

The following Sunday was fine; the sodden November chill was broken by the last flash of autumnal summer. In the morning Paul had to go to church and Sabbath School, as always. On seasonable Sunday afternoons the burghers of Cordelia Street usually sat out on their front "stoops," and talked to their neighbors on the next stoop, or called to those across the street in neighborly fashion. The men sat placidly on gay cushions placed upon the steps that led down to the sidewalk, while the women, in their Sunday "waists," sat in rockers on the cramped porches, pretending to be greatly at their ease. The children played in the streets; there were so many of them that the place resembled the recreation grounds of a kindergarten. The men on the steps, all in their shirt-sleeves, their vests unbuttoned, sat with their legs well apart, their stomachs comfortably protruding, and talked of the prices of things, or told anecdotes of the sagacity of their various chiefs and overlords. They occasionally looked over the multitude of squabbling children, listened affectionately to their high-pitched, nasal voices, smiling to see their own proclivities reproduced in their offspring, and interspersed their legends of the iron kings with remarks about their sons' progress at school, their grades in arithmetic, and the amounts they had saved in their toy banks.

25   On this last Sunday of November, Paul sat all afternoon on the lowest step of his "stoop," staring into the street, while his sisters, in their rockers, were talking to the minister's daughters next door about how many shirt-waists they had made in the last week, and how many waffles someone had eaten at the last church supper. When the weather was warm, and his father was in a particularly jovial frame of mind, the girls made lemonade, which was always brought out in a red-glass pitcher, ornamented with forget-me-nots in blue enamel. This the girls thought very fine, and the neighbors joked about the suspicious color of the pitcher.

Today Paul's father, on the top step, was talking to a young man who shifted a restless baby from knee to knee. He happened to be the young man who was daily held up to Paul as a model, and after whom it was his father's dearest hope that he would pattern. This young man was of a ruddy com-plexion, with a compressed, red mouth, and faded, nearsighted eyes, over which he wore thick spectacles, with gold bows that curved about his ears. He was clerk to one of the magnates of a great steel corporation, and was looked upon in Cordelia Street as a young man with a future. There was a story that, some five years ago—he was now barely twenty-six—he had been a trifle "dissipated," but in order to curb his appetites and save the loss of time and strength that a sowing of wild oats might have entailed, he had taken his chief's advice, oft reiterated to his employees, and at twenty-one had married the first woman whom he could persuade to share his fortunes. She happened to be an angular schoolmistress, much older than he, who also wore thick glasses, and who had now borne him four children, all near-sighted like herself.

The young man was relating how his chief, now cruising in the Mediter-ranean, kept in touch with all the details of the business, arranging his office hours on his yacht just as though he were at home, and "knocking off work enough to keep two stenographers busy." His father told, in turn, the plan his corporation was considering, of putting in an electric railway plant at Cairo. Paul snapped his teeth; he had an awful apprehension that they might spoil it all before he got there. Yet he rather liked to hear these legends of the iron kings, that were told and retold on Sundays and holidays; these stories of palaces in Venice, yachts on the Mediterranean, and high play at Monte Carlo appealed to his fancy, and he was interested in the triumphs of cash-boys who had become famous, though he had no mind for the cash-boy stage.

After supper was over, and he had helped to dry the dishes, Paul ner-vously asked his father whether he could go to George's to get some help in his geometry, and still more nervously asked for carfare. This latter request he had to repeat, as his father, on principle, did not like to hear requests for money, whether much or little. He asked Paul whether he could not go to some boy who lived nearer, and told him that he ought not to leave his school work until Sunday; but he gave him the dime. He was not a poor man, but he had a worthy ambition to come up in the world. His only reason for allowing Paul to usher was that he thought a boy ought to be earning a little.

Paul bounded upstairs, scrubbed the greasy odor of the dishwater from his hands with the ill-smelling soap he hated, and then shook over his fingers a few drops of violet water from the bottle he kept hidden in his drawer. He left the house with his geometry conspicuously under his arm, and the moment he got out of Cordelia Street and boarded a downtown car, he shook off the lethargy of two deadening days, and began to live again.

The leading juvenile of the permanent stock company which played at   30
one of the downtown theaters was an acquaintance of Paul's, and the boy had been invited to drop in at the Sunday-night rehearsals whenever he could. For more than a year Paul had spent every available moment loitering about Charley Edwards's dressing-room. He had won a place among Edwards's following not only because the young actor, who could not afford to employ a dresser, often found him useful, but because he recognized in Paul something akin to what churchmen term "vocation."

It was at the theater and at Carnegie Hall that Paul really lived; the rest was but a sleep and a forgetting. This was Paul's fairy tale, and it had for him all the allurement of a secret love. The moment he inhaled the gassy, painty, dusty odor behind the scenes, he breathed like a prisoner set free, and felt within him the possibility of doing or saying splendid, brilliant things. The moment the cracked orchestra beat out the overture from *Martha*, or jerked at the serenade from *Rigoletto,* all stupid and ugly things slid from him, and his senses were deliciously, yet delicately fired.

Perhaps it was because, in Paul's world, the natural nearly always wore the guise of ugliness, that a certain element of artificiality seemed to him necessary in beauty. Perhaps it was because his experience of life elsewhere was so full of Sabbath-School picnics, petty economies, wholesome advice as to how to succeed in life, and the unescapable odors of cooking, that he found this existence so alluring, these smartly clad men and women so attractive, that he was so moved by these starry apple orchards that bloomed perennially under the limelight. It would be difficult to put it strongly enough how convincingly the stage entrance of the theater was for Paul the actual portal of Romance. Certainly none of the company ever suspected it, least of all Charley Edwards. It was very like the old stories that used to float about London of fabulously rich Jews, who had subterranean halls, with palms, and fountains, and soft lamps and richly appareled women who never saw the disenchanting light of London day. So, in the midst of that smoke-palled city, enamored of figures and grimy toil, Paul had his secret temple, his wishing-carpet, his bit of blue-and-white Mediterranean shore bathed in perpetual sunshine.

Several of Paul's teachers had a theory that his imagination had been perverted by garish fiction; but the truth was he scarcely ever read at all. The books at home were not such as would either tempt or corrupt a youthful mind, and as for reading the novels that some of his friends urged upon him—well, he got what he wanted much more quickly from music; any sort of music, from an orchestra to a barrel-organ. He needed only the spark, the indescribable thrill that made his imagination master of his senses, and he could make plots and pictures enough of his own. It was equally true that he was not stage-struck—not, at any rate, in the usual acceptation of the expression. He had no desire to become an actor, any more than he had to become a musician. He felt no necessity to do any of these things; what he wanted was to see, to be in the atmosphere, float on the wave of it, to be carried out, blue league after league, away from everything.

After a night behind the scenes, Paul found the schoolroom more than ever repulsive; the bare floors and naked walls; the prosy men who never wore frock coats, or violets in their buttonholes; the women with their dull gowns, shrill voices, and pitiful seriousness about prepositions that govern the dative. He could not bear to have the other pupils think, for a moment, that he took these people seriously; he must convey to them that he considered it all trivial, and was there only by the way of a joke, anyway. He had autographed pictures of all the members of the stock company which he showed his classmates, telling them the most incredible stories of his familiarity with these people, of his acquaintance with the soloists who came to Carnegie Hall, his suppers with them and the flowers he sent them. When these stories lost their effect, and his audience grew listless, he would bid all the boys goodbye, announcing that he was going to travel for a while; going to Naples, to California, to Egypt. Then, next Monday, he would slip back, conscious and nervously smiling; his sister was ill, and he would have to defer his voyage until spring.

35   Matters went steadily worse with Paul at school. In the itch to let his instructors know how heartily he despised them, and how thoroughly he was appreciated elsewhere, he mentioned once or twice that he had no time to fool with theorems; adding—with a twitch of the eyebrows and a touch of that nervous bravado which so perplexed them—that he was helping the people down at the stock company; they were old friends of his.

The upshot of the matter was that the Principal went to Paul's father, and Paul was taken out of school and put to work. The manager at Carnegie Hall was told to get another usher in his stead; the doorkeeper at the theater was warned not to admit him to the house; and Charley Edwards remorsefully promised the boy's father not to see him again.

The members of the stock company were vastly amused when some of Paul's stories reached them—especially the women. They were hard-working women, most of them supporting indolent husbands or brothers, and they laughed rather bitterly at having stirred the boy to such fervid and florid inventions. They agreed with the faculty and with his father, that Paul's was a bad case.

The east-bound train was plowing through a January snowstorm; the dull dawn was beginning to show grey when the engine whistled a mile out of Newark. Paul started up from the seat where he had lain curled in uneasy slumber, rubbed the breath-misted window-glass with his hand, and peered out. The snow was whirling in curling eddies above the white bottom lands, and the drifts lay already deep in the fields and along the fences, while here and there the tall dead grass and dried weed stalks protruded black above it. Lights shone from the scattered houses, and a gang of laborers who stood beside the track waved their lanterns.

Paul had slept very little, and he felt grimy and uncomfortable. He had made the all-night journey in a day coach because he was afraid if he took a Pullman he might be seen by some Pittsburgh business man who had noticed him in Denny and Carson's office. When the whistle woke him, he clutched quickly at his breast pocket, glancing about him with an uncertain smile. But the little, clay-bespattered Italians were still sleeping, the slatternly women across the aisle were in open-mouthed oblivion, and even the crumby, crying babies were for the time stilled. Paul settled back to struggle with his impatience as best he could.

When he arrived at the Jersey City station, he hurried through his break-   40
fast, manifestly ill at ease and keeping a sharp eye about him. After he reached the Twenty-Third Street station, he consulted a cabman, and had himself driven to a men's furnishing establishment which was just opening for the day. He spent upward of two hours there, buying with endless reconsidering and great care. His new street suit he put on in the fitting-room; the frock coat and dress clothes he had bundled into the cab with his new shirts. Then he drove to a hatter's and a shoe house. His next errand was at Tiffany's, where he selected silver-mounted brushes and a scarf-pin. He would not wait to have his silver marked, he said. Lastly, he stopped at a trunk shop on Broadway, and had his purchases packed into various traveling-bags.

It was a little after one o'clock when he drove up to the Waldorf, and, after settling with the cabman, went into the office. He registered from Washington; said his mother and father had been abroad, and that he had come down to await the arrival of their steamer. He told his story plausibly and had no trouble, since he offered to pay for them in advance, in engaging his rooms; a sleeping-room, sitting-room, and bath.

Not once, but a hundred times Paul had planned this entry into New York. He had gone over every detail of it with Charley Edwards, and in his scrapbook at home there were pages of description about New York hotels, cut from the Sunday papers.

When he was shown to his sitting-room on the eighth floor, he saw at a glance that everything was as it should be; there was but one detail in his mental picture that the place did not realize, so he rang for the bell-boy and sent him down for flowers. He moved about nervously until the boy returned, putting away his new linen and fingering it delightedly as he did so. When the flowers came, he put them hastily into water, and then tumbled into a hot bath. Presently he came out of his white bathroom, resplendent in his new silk underwear, and playing with the tassels of his red robe. The snow was whirling so fiercely outside his windows that he could scarcely see across the street; but within, the air was deliciously soft and fragrant. He put the violets and jonquils on the taboret beside the couch, and threw himself down with a long sigh, covering himself with a Roman blanket. He was thoroughly tired; he had been in such haste, he had stood up to such a strain, covered so much ground in the last twenty-four hours, that he wanted to think how it had all come about. Lulled by the sound of the wind, the warm air, and the cool fragrance of the flowers, he sank into deep, drowsy retrospection.

It had been wonderfully simple; when they had shut him out of the theater and concert hall, when they had taken away his bone, the whole thing was virtually determined. The rest was a mere matter of opportunity. The only thing that at all surprised him was his own courage—for he realized well enough that he had always been tormented by fear, a sort of apprehensive dread which, of late years, as the meshes of the lies he had told closed about him, had been pulling the muscles of his body tighter and tighter. Until now, he could not remember a time when he had not been dreading something. Even when he was a little boy, it was always there—behind him, or before, or on either side. There had always been the shadowed corner, the dark place into which he dared not look, but from which something seemed always to be watching him—and Paul had done things that were not pretty to watch, he knew.

45   But now he had a curious sense of relief, as though he had at last thrown down the gauntlet to the thing in the corner.

Yet it was but a day since he had been sulking in the traces; but yesterday afternoon that he had been sent to the bank with Denny and Carson's deposit, as usual—but this time he was instructed to leave the book to be balanced. There was above two thousand dollars in checks, and nearly a thousand in the banknotes which he had taken from the book and quietly transferred to his pocket. At the bank he had made out a new deposit slip. His nerves had been steady enough to permit of his returning to the office, where he had finished his work and asked for a full day's holiday tomorrow, Saturday, giving a perfectly reasonable pretext. The bank book, he knew, would not be returned before Monday or Tuesday, and his father would be out of town for the next week. From the time he slipped the banknotes into his pocket until he boarded the night train for New York, he had not known a moment's hesitation.

How astonishingly easy it had all been; here he was, the thing done; and this time there would be no awakening, no figure at the top of the stairs. He watched the snowflakes whirling by his window until he fell asleep.

When he awoke, it was four o'clock in the afternoon. He bounded up with a start; one of his precious days gone already! He spent nearly an hour in dressing, watching every stage of his toilet carefully in the mirror. Everything was quite perfect; he was exactly the kind of boy he had always wanted to be.

When he went downstairs, Paul took a carriage and drove up Fifth Avenue toward the Park. The snow had somewhat abated; carriages and tradesmen's wagons were hurrying soundlessly to and fro in the winter twilight;

boys in woolen mufflers were shoveling off the doorsteps; the Avenue stages made fine spots of color against the white street. Here and there on the corners whole flower gardens blooming behind glass windows, against which the snowflakes stuck and melted; violets, roses, carnations, lilies-of-the-valley—somehow vastly more lovely and alluring that they blossomed thus unnaturally in the snow. The Park itself was a wonderful stage winter-piece.

When he returned, the pause of the twilight had ceased, and the tune of the streets had changed. The snow was falling faster, lights streamed from the hotels that reared their many stories fearlessly up into the storm, defying the raging Atlantic winds. A long, black stream of carriages poured down the Avenue, intersected here and there by other streams, tending horizontally. There were a score of cabs about the entrance of his hotel, and his driver had to wait. Boys in livery were running in and out of the awning stretched across the sidewalk, up and down the red velvet carpet laid from the door to the street. Above, about, within it all, was the rumble and roar, the hurry and toss of thousands of human beings as hot for pleasure as himself, and on every side of him towered the glaring affirmation of the omnipotence of wealth.

The boy set his teeth and drew his shoulders together in a spasm of realization; the plot of all dramas, the text of all romances, the nerve-stuff of all sensations was whirling about him like the snowflakes. He burnt like a fagot in a tempest.

When Paul came down to dinner, the music of the orchestra floated up the elevator shaft to greet him. As he stepped into the thronged corridor, he sank back into one of the chairs against the wall to get his breath. The lights, the chatter, the perfumes, the bewildering medley of color—he had, for a moment, the feeling of not being able to stand it. But only for a moment; these were his own people, he told himself. He went slowly about the corridors, through the writing-rooms, smoking-rooms, reception-rooms, as though he were exploring the chambers of an enchanted palace, built and peopled for him alone.

When he reached the dining-room he sat down at a table near a window. The flowers, the white linen, the many-colored wine-glasses, the gay toilettes of the women, the low popping of corks, the undulating repetitions of the "Blue Danube" from the orchestra, all flooded Paul's dream with bewildering radiance. When the roseate tinge of his champagne was added—that cold, precious, bubbling stuff that creamed and foamed in his glass—Paul wondered that there were honest men in the world at all. This was what all the world was fighting for, he reflected; this was what all the struggle was about. He doubted the reality of his past. Had he ever known a place called Cordelia Street, a place where fagged-looking business men boarded the early car? Mere rivets in a machine they seemed to Paul—sickening men, with combings of children's hair always hanging to their coats, and the smell of cooking in their clothes. Cordelia Street— Ah, that belonged to another time and country! Had he not always been thus, had he not sat here night after night, from as far back as he could remember, looking pensively over

50

just such shimmering textures, and slowly twirling the stem of a glass like this one between his thumb and middle finger? He rather thought he had.

He was not in the least abashed or lonely. He had no especial desire to meet or to know any of these people; all he demanded was the right to look on and conjecture, to watch the pageant. The mere stage properties were all he contended for. Nor was he lonely later in the evening, in his loge at the Opera. He was entirely rid of his nervous misgivings, of his forced aggressiveness, of the imperative desire to show himself different from his surroundings. He felt now that his surroundings explained him. Nobody questioned the purple; he had only to wear it passively. He had only to glance down at his dress coat to reassure himself that here it would be impossible for anyone to humiliate him.

55   He found it hard to leave his beautiful sitting-room to go to bed that night, and sat long watching the raging storm from his turret window. When he went to sleep, it was with the lights turned on in his bedroom; partly because of his old timidity, and partly so that, if he should wake in the night, there would be no wretched moment of doubt, no horrible suspicion of yellow wallpaper, or of Washington and Calvin above his bed.

On Sunday morning the city was practically snowbound. Paul breakfasted late, and in the afternoon he fell in with a wild San Francisco boy, a freshman at Yale, who said he had run down for a "little flyer" over Sunday. The young man offered to show Paul the night side of the town, and the two boys went off together after dinner, not returning to the hotel until seven o'clock the next morning. They had started out in the confiding warmth of a champagne friendship, but their parting in the elevator was singularly cool. The freshman pulled himself together to make his train, and Paul went to bed. He awoke at two o'clock in the afternoon, very thirsty and dizzy, and rang for ice-water, coffee, and the Pittsburgh papers.

On the part of the hotel management, Paul excited no suspicion. There was this to be said for him, that he wore his spoils with dignity and in no way made himself conspicuous. His chief greediness lay in his ears and eyes, and his excesses were not offensive ones. His dearest pleasures were the grey winter twilights in his sitting-room; his quiet enjoyment of his flowers, his clothes, his wide divan, his cigarette, and his sense of power. He could not remember a time when he had felt so at peace with himself. The mere release from the necessity of petty lying, lying every day and every day, restored his self-respect. He had never lied for pleasure, even at school; but to make himself noticed and admired, to assert his difference from other Cordelia Street boys; and he felt a good deal more manly, more honest, even, now that he had no need for boastful pretensions, now that he could, as his actor friends used to say, "dress the part." It was characteristic that remorse did not occur to him. His golden days went by without a shadow, and he made each as perfect as he could.

On the eighth day after his arrival in New York, he found the whole affair exploited in the Pittsburgh papers, exploited with a wealth of detail which indicated that local news of a sensational nature was at a low ebb. The firm of

Denny and Carson announced that the boy's father had refunded the full amount of his theft, and that they had no intention of prosecuting. The Cumberland minister had been interviewed, and expressed his hope of yet reclaiming the motherless lad, and Paul's Sabbath-School teacher declared that she would spare no effort to that end. The rumor had reached Pittsburgh that the boy had been seen in a New York hotel, and his father had gone East to find him and bring him home.

Paul had just come in to dress for dinner; he sank into the chair, weak in the knees, and clasped his head in his hands. It was to be worse than jail, even; the tepid waters of Cordelia Street were to close over him finally and forever. The grey monotony stretched before him in hopeless, unrelieved years;—Sabbath School, Young People's Meeting, the yellow-papered room, the damp dish-towels; it all rushed back upon him with sickening vividness. He had the old feeling that the orchestra had suddenly stopped, the sinking sensation that the play was over. The sweat broke out on his face, and he sprang to his feet, looked about him with his white, conscious smile, and winked at himself in the mirror. With something of the childish belief in miracles with which he had so often gone to class, all his lessons unlearned, Paul dressed and dashed whistling down the corridor to the elevator.

He had no sooner entered the dining-room and caught the measure of the music than his remembrance was lightened by his old elastic power of claiming the moment, mounting with it, and finding it all-sufficient. The glare and glitter about him, the mere scenic accessories had again, and for the last time, their old potency. He would show himself that he was game, he would finish the thing splendidly. He doubted, more than ever, the existence of Cordelia Street, and for the first time he drank his wine recklessly. Was he not, after all, one of these fortunate beings? Was he not still himself, and in his own place? He drummed a nervous accompaniment to the music and looked about him, telling himself over and over that it had paid.

He reflected drowsily, to the swell of the violin and the chill sweetness of his wine, that he might have done it more wisely. He might have caught an outbound steamer and been well out of their clutches before now. But the other side of the world had seemed too far away and too uncertain then; he could not have waited for it; his need had been too sharp. If he had to choose over again, he would do the same thing tomorrow. He looked affectionately about the dining-room, now gilded with a soft mist. Ah, it had paid indeed!

Paul was awakened next morning by a painful throbbing in his head and feet. He had thrown himself across the bed without undressing, and had slept with his shoes on. His limbs and hands were lead-heavy, and his tongue and throat were parched. There came upon him one of those fateful attacks of clear-headedness that never occurred except when he was physically exhausted and his nerves hung loose. He lay still and closed his eyes and let the tide of realities wash over him.

His father was in New York; "stopping at some joint or other," he told himself. The memory of successive summers on the front stoop fell upon him like a weight of black water. He had not a hundred dollars left; and he

60

knew now, more than ever, that money was everything, the wall that stood between all he loathed and all he wanted. The thing was winding itself up; he had thought of that on his first glorious day in New York, and had even provided a way to snap the thread. It lay on his dressing-table now; he had got it out last night when he came blindly up from dinner—but the shiny metal hurt his eyes, and he disliked the look of it, anyway.

He rose and moved about with a painful effort, succumbing now and again to attacks of nausea. It was the old depression exaggerated; all the world had become Cordelia Street. Yet somehow he was not afraid of anything, was absolutely calm; perhaps because he had looked into the dark corner at last, and knew. It was bad enough, what he saw there; but somehow not so bad as his long fear of it had been. He saw everything clearly now. He had a feeling that he had made the best of it, that he had lived the sort of life he was meant to live, and for half an hour he sat staring at the revolver. But he told himself that was not the way, so he went downstairs and took a cab to the ferry.

65   When Paul arrived at Newark, he got off the train and took another cab, directing the driver to follow the Pennsylvania tracks out of town. The snow lay heavy on the roadways and had drifted deep in the open fields. Only here and there the dead grass or dried weed stalks projected, singularly black, above it.

Once well into the country, Paul dismissed the carriage and walked, floundering along the tracks, his mind a medley of irrelevant things. He seemed to hold in his brain an actual picture of everything he had seen that morning. He remembered every feature of both his drivers, the toothless old woman from whom he had bought the red flowers in his coat, the agent from whom he had got his ticket, and all of his fellow-passengers on the ferry. His mind, unable to cope with vital matters near at hand, worked feverishly and deftly at sorting and grouping these images. They made for him a part of the ugliness of the world, of the ache in his head, and the bitter burning on his tongue. He stooped and put a handful of snow into his mouth as he walked, but that, too, seemed hot. When he reached a little hillside, where the tracks ran through a cut some twenty feet below him, he stopped and sat down.

The carnations in his coat were drooping with cold, he noticed; all their red glory over. It occurred to him that all the flowers he had seen in the show windows that first night must have gone the same way, long before this. It was only one splendid breath they had, in spite of their brave mockery at the winter outside the glass. It was a losing game in the end, it seemed, this revolt against the homilies by which the world is run. Paul took one of the blossoms carefully from his coat and scooped a little hole in the snow, where he covered it up. Then he dozed awhile, from his weak condition, seeming insensible to the cold.

The sound of an approaching train woke him and he started to his feet, remembering only his resolution, and afraid lest he should be too late. He stood watching the approaching locomotive, his teeth chattering, his lips drawn away from them in a frightened smile; once or twice he glanced nervously sidewise, as though he were being watched. When the right moment came, he jumped. As he fell, the folly of his haste occurred to him with merciless clearness, the vastness of what he had left undone. There flashed through his brain, clearer than ever before, the blue of Adriatic water, the yellow of Algerian sands.

He felt something strike his chest—his body being thrown swiftly through the air, on and on, immeasurably far and fast, while his limbs gently relaxed. Then, because the picture-making mechanism was crushed, the disturbing visions flashed into black, and Paul dropped back into the immense design of things.

QUESTIONS

1. Technically we should classify the author's point of view as omniscient, for she enters into the minds of characters at will. Nevertheless early in the story the focus changes rather abruptly. Locate the point where the change occurs. Through whose eyes do we see Paul prior to this point? Through whose eyes do we see him afterward? What is the purpose of this shift? Does it offer any clue to the purpose of the story?

2. What details of Paul's appearance and behavior, as his teachers see him, indicate that he is abnormal?

3. Explain Paul's behavior. Why does he lie? What does he hate? What does he want? Contrast the world of Cordelia Street with the worlds that Paul finds at Carnegie Hall, at the Schenley, at the stock theater, and in New York.

4. Is Paul artistic? Describe his reactions to music, to painting, to literature, and to the theater. What value does he find in the arts?

5. Is Paul a static or a developing character? If the latter, at what points does he change? Why?

6. What do Paul's clandestine trips to the stock theater, his trip to New York, and his suicide have in common?

7. Compare Paul and the college boy he meets in New York (paragraph 56). Are they two of a kind? If not, how do they differ?

8. What are the implications of the title? What does the last sentence of the story do to the reader's focus of vision?

9. Are there any clues to the causes of Paul's abnormality? How many? In what is the author chiefly interested?

10. In what two cities is the story set? Does this choice of setting have any symbolic value? Could the story have been set as validly in Cleveland and Detroit? In San Francisco and Los Angeles? In New Orleans and Birmingham?

Ernest Hemingway

Hills Like White Elephants

The hills across the valley of the Ebro were long and white. On this side there was no shade and no trees and the station was between two lines of rails in the sun. Close against the side of the station there was the warm shadow of the building and a curtain, made of strings of bamboo beads, hung across the open door into the bar, to keep out flies. The American and the girl with him sat at a table in the shade, outside the building. It was very hot and the express from Barcelona would come in forty minutes. It stopped at this junction for two minutes and went on to Madrid.

"What should we drink?" the girl asked. She had taken off her hat and put in on the table.

"It's pretty hot," the man said.

"Let's drink beer."

5   "Dos cervezas," the man said into the curtain.

"Big ones?" a woman asked from the doorway.

"Yes. Two big ones."

The woman brought two glasses of beer and two felt pads. She put the felt pads and the beer glasses on the table and looked at the man and the girl. The girl was looking off at the line of hills. They were white in the sun and the country was brown and dry.

"They look like white elephants," she said.

10   "I've never seen one," the man drank his beer.

"No, you wouldn't have."

"I might have," the man said. "Just because you say I wouldn't have doesn't prove anything."

The girl looked at the bead curtain. "They've painted something on it," she said. "What does it say?"

"Anis del Toro. It's a drink."

15   "Could we try it?"

The man called "Listen" through the curtain. The woman came out from the bar.

"Four reales."

"We want two Anis del Toro."

"With water?"

20   "Do you want it with water?"

"I don't know," the girl said. "Is it good with water?"

"It's all right."

HILLS LIKE WHITE ELEPHANTS   First published in 1927. Ernest Hemingway (1899–1961) was born and grew up in Oak Park, Illinois, with summer vacations in northern Michigan. By the time he wrote this story he had been wounded in Italy during World War I; had traveled extensively in Europe as a newspaper correspondent and writer; had married, fathered a son, been divorced, and remarried.

"You want them with water?" asked the woman.

"Yes, with water."

"It tastes like licorice," the girl said and put the glass down.   25

"That's the way with everything."

"Yes," said the girl. "Everything tastes of licorice. Especially all the things you've waited so long for, like absinthe."

"Oh, cut it out."

"You started it," the girl said. "I was being amused. I was having a fine time."

"Well, let's try to have a fine time."   30

"All right. I was trying. I said the mountains looked like white elephants. Wasn't that bright?"

"That was bright."

"I wanted to try this new drink. That's all we do, isn't it—look at things and try new drinks."

"I guess so."

The girl looked across at the hills.   35

"They're lovely hills," she said. "They don't really look like white elephants. I just meant the coloring of their skin through the trees."

"Should we have another drink?"

"All right."

The warm wind blew the bead curtain against the table.

"The beer's nice and cool," the man said.   40

"It's lovely," the girl said.

"It's really an awfully simple operation, Jig," the man said. "It's not really an operation at all."

The girl looked at the ground the table legs rested on.

"I know you wouldn't mind it, Jig. It's really not anything. It's just to let the air in."

The girl did not say anything.   45

"I'll go with you and I'll stay with you all the time. They just let the air in and then it's all perfectly natural."

"Then what will we do afterward?"

"We'll be fine afterward. Just like we were before."

"What makes you think so?"

"That's the only thing that bothers us. It's the only thing that's made us   50 unhappy."

The girl looked at the bead curtain, put her hand out and took hold of two of the strings of beads.

"And you think then we'll be all right and be happy."

"I know we will. You don't have to be afraid. I've known lots of people that have done it."

"So have I," said the girl. "And afterward they were all so happy."

"Well," the man said, "if you don't want to you don't have to. I wouldn't   55 have you do it if you didn't want to. But I know it's perfectly simple."

"And you really want to?"

"I think it's the best thing to do. But I don't want you to do it if you don't really want to."

"And if I do it you'll be happy and things will be like they were and you'll love me?"

"I love you now. You know I love you."

"I know. But if I do it, then it will be nice again if I say things are like white elephants, and you'll like it?"

"I'll love it. I love it now but I just can't think about it. You know how I get when I worry."

"If I do it you won't ever worry."

"I won't worry about that because it's perfectly simple."

"Then I'll do it. Because I don't care about me."

"What do you mean?"

"I don't care about me."

"Well, I care about you."

"Oh, yes. But I don't care about me. And I'll do it and then everything will be fine."

"I don't want you to do it if you feel that way."

The girl stood up and walked to the end of the station. Across, on the other side, were fields of grain and trees along the banks of the Ebro. Far away, beyond the river, were mountains. The shadow of a cloud moved across the field of grain and she saw the river through the trees.

"And we could have all this," she said. "And we could have everything and every day we make it more impossible."

"What did you say?"

"I said we could have everything."

"We can have everything."

"No, we can't."

"We can have the whole world."

"No, we can't."

"We can go everywhere."

"No, we can't. It isn't ours any more."

"It's ours."

"No, it isn't. And once they take it away, you never get it back."

"But they haven't taken it away."

"We'll wait and see."

"Come on back in the shade," he said. "You mustn't feel that way."

"I don't feel any way," the girl said. "I just know things."

"I don't want you to do anything that you don't want to do—"

"Nor that isn't good for me," she said. "I know. Could we have another beer."

"All right. But you've got to realize—"

"I realize," the girl said. "Can't we stop talking?"

They sat down at the table and the girl looked across at the hills on the dry side of the valley and the man looked at her and at the table.

"You've got to realize," he said, "that I don't want you to do it if you don't want to. I'm perfectly willing to go through with it if it means anything to you."

"Doesn't it mean anything to you? We could get along."

"Of course it does. But I don't want anybody but you. I don't want any one else. And I know it's perfectly simple."

"Yes, you know it's perfectly simple."

"It's all right for you to say that, but I do know it."   95

"Would you do something for me now?"

"I'd do anything for you."

"Would you please please please please please please please stop talking?"

He did not say anything but looked at the bags against the wall of the station. There were labels on them from all the hotels where they had spent nights.

"But I don't want you to," he said. "I don't care anything about it."   100

"I'll scream," said the girl.

The woman came out through the curtains with two glasses of beer and put them down on the damp felt pads. "The train comes in five minutes," she said.

"What did she say?" asked the girl.

"That the train is coming in five minutes."

The girl smiled brightly at the woman, to thank her.   105

"I'd better take the bags over to the other side of the station," the man said. She smiled at him.

"All right. Then come back and we'll finish the beer."

He picked up the two heavy bags and carried them around the station to the other tracks. He looked up the tracks but could not see the train. Coming back, he walked through the barroom, where people waiting for the train were drinking. He drank an Anis at the bar and looked at the people. They were all waiting reasonably for the train. He went out through the bead curtain. She was sitting at the table and smiled at him.

"Do you feel better?" he asked.

"I feel fine," she said. "There's nothing wrong with me. I feel fine."   110

QUESTIONS

1. The main topic of discussion between the man and the girl is never named. What is the "awfully simple operation"? Why is it not named? What different attitudes are taken toward it by the man and the girl? Why?

2. What is indicated about the past life of the man and the girl? How? What has happened to the quality of their relationship? Why? How do we know? How accurate is the man's judgment about their future?

3. Though the story consists mostly of dialogue, and though it contains strong emotional conflict, it is entirely without adverbs indicating the tone of the remarks. How does Hemingway indicate tone? At what points are the characters insincere? Self-deceived? Ironic or sarcastic? To what extent

do they give open expression to their feelings? Does either want an open conflict? Why or why not? Trace the various phases of emotion in the girl.

4. How sincere is the man in his insistence that he would not have the girl undergo the operation if she does not want to and that he is "perfectly willing to go through with it" if it means anything to the girl? What is "it"? How many times does he repeat these ideas? What significance has the man's drinking an Anis by himself before rejoining the girl at the end of the story?

5. Much of the conversation seems to be about trivial things (ordering drinks, the weather, and so on). What purposes does this conversation serve? What relevance has the girl's remark about absinthe?

6. What is the point of the girl's comparison of the hills to white elephants? Does the remark assume any significance for the reader beyond its significance for the characters? Why does the author use it for his title?

7. What purpose does the setting serve—the hills across the valley, the treeless railroad tracks and station? What is contributed by the precise information about time at the end of the first paragraph?

8. Which of the two characters is more "reasonable"? Which "wins" the conflict between them? The point of view is objective. Does this mean that we cannot tell whether the sympathy of the author lies more with one character than with the other? Explain your answer.

Katherine Anne Porter

The Jilting of Granny Weatherall

She flicked her wrist neatly out of Doctor Harry's pudgy careful fingers and pulled the sheet up to her chin. The brat ought to be in knee breeches. Doctoring around the country with spectacles on his nose! "Get along now, take your schoolbooks and go. There's nothing wrong with me."

Doctor Harry spread a warm paw like a cushion on her forehead where the forked green vein danced and made her eyelids twitch. "Now, now, be a good girl, and we'll have you up in no time."

"That's no way to speak to a woman nearly eighty years old just because she's down. I'd have you respect your elders, young man."

"Well, Missy, excuse me." Doctor Harry patted her cheek. "But I've got to warn you, haven't I? You're a marvel, but you must be careful or you're going to be good and sorry."

5   "Don't tell me what I'm going to be. I'm on my feet now, morally speaking. It's Cornelia. I had to go to bed to get rid of her."

Her bones felt loose, and floated around in her skin, and Doctor Harry floated like a balloon around the foot of the bed. He floated and pulled down his waistcoat and swung his glasses on a cord. "Well, stay where you are, it certainly can't hurt you."

THE JILTING OF GRANNY WEATHERALL   First published in 1930. Katherine Anne Porter (1890–1980) was born and grew up in Texas, was educated at convent schools in New Orleans, and lived in Chicago, Fort Worth, Mexico, and New York City before writing this story.

"Get along and doctor your sick," said Granny Weatherall. "Leave a well woman alone. I'll call for you when I want you. . . . Where were you forty years ago when I pulled through milk-leg and double pneumonia? You weren't even born. Don't let Cornelia lead you on," she shouted, because Doctor Harry appeared to float up to the ceiling and out. "I pay my own bills, and I don't throw my money away on nonsense!"

She meant to wave good-by, but it was too much trouble. Her eyes closed of themselves, it was like a dark curtain drawn around the bed. The pillow rose and floated under her, pleasant as a hammock in a light wind. She listened to the leaves rustling outside the window. No, somebody was swishing newspapers: no, Cornelia and Doctor Harry were whispering together. She leaped broad awake, thinking they whispered in her ear.

"She was never like this, *never* like this!" "Well, what can we expect?" "Yes, eighty years old. . . ."

Well, and what if she was? She still had ears. It was like Cornelia to   10
whisper around doors. She always kept things secret in such a public way. She was always being tactful and kind. Cornelia was dutiful; that was the trouble with her. Dutiful and good: "So good and dutiful," said Granny, "that I'd like to spank her." She saw herself spanking Cornelia and making a fine job of it.

"What'd you say, Mother?"

Granny felt her face tying up in hard knots.

"Can't a body think, I'd like to know?"

"I thought you might want something."

"I do. I want a lot of things. First off, go away and don't whisper."   15

She lay and drowsed, hoping in her sleep that the children would keep out and let her rest a minute. It had been a long day. Not that she was tired. It was always pleasant to snatch a minute now and then. There was always so much to be done, let me see: tomorrow.

Tomorrow was far away and there was nothing to trouble about. Things were finished somehow when the time came; thank God there was always a little margin over for peace: then a person could spread out the plan of life and tuck in the edges orderly. It was good to have everything clean and folded away, with the hair brushes and tonic bottles sitting straight on the white embroidered linen: the day started without fuss and the pantry shelves laid out with rows of jelly glasses and brown jugs and white stone-china jars with blue whirligigs and words painted on them: coffee, tea, sugar, ginger, cinnamon, allspice: and the bronze clock with the lion on top nicely dusted off. The dust that lion could collect in twenty-four hours! The box in the attic with all those letters tied up, well, she'd have to go through that tomorrow. All those letters—George's letters and John's letters and her letters to them both—lying around for the children to find afterwards made her uneasy. Yes, that would be tomorrow's business. No use to let them know how silly she had been once.

While she was rummaging around she found death in her mind and it felt clammy and unfamiliar. She had spent so much time preparing for death there was no need for bringing it up again. Let it take care of itself now. When she was sixty she had felt very old, finished, and went around making farewell trips to see her children and grandchildren, with a secret in her mind: This is the very last of your mother, children! Then she made her will and came down with a long fever. That was all just a notion like a lot of other things, but it was lucky too, for she had once for all got over the idea of dying for a long time. Now she couldn't be worried. She hoped she had better sense now. Her father had lived to be one hundred and two years old and had drunk a noggin of strong hot toddy on his last birthday. He told the reporters it was his daily habit, and he owed his long life to that. He had made quite a scandal and was very pleased about it. She believed she'd just plague Cornelia a little.

"Cornelia! Cornelia!" No footsteps, but a sudden hand on her cheek. "Bless you, where have you been?"

20   "Here, Mother."

"Well, Cornelia, I want a noggin of hot toddy."

"Are you cold, darling?"

"I'm chilly, Cornelia. Lying in bed stops the circulation. I must have told you that a thousand times."

Well, she could just hear Cornelia telling her husband that Mother was getting a little childish and they'd have to humor her. The thing that most annoyed her was that Cornelia thought she was deaf, dumb, and blind. Little hasty glances and tiny gestures tossed around her and over her head saying, "Don't cross her, let her have her way, she's eighty years old," and she sitting there as if she lived in a thin glass cage. Sometimes Granny almost made up her mind to pack up and move back to her own house where nobody could remind her every minute that she was old. Wait, wait, Cornelia, till your own children whisper behind your back!

25   In her day she had kept a better house and had got more work done. She wasn't too old yet for Lydia to be driving eighty miles for advice when one of the children jumped the track, and Jimmy still dropped in and talked things over: "Now, Mammy, you've a good business head, I want to know what you think of this? . . ." Old. Cornelia couldn't change the furniture around without asking. Little things, little things! They had been so sweet when they were little. Granny wished the old days were back again with the children young and everything to be done over. It had been a hard pull, but not too much for her. When she thought of all the food she had cooked, and all the clothes she had cut and sewed, and all the gardens she had made—well, the children showed it. There they were, made out of her, and they couldn't get away from that. Sometimes she wanted to see John again and point to them and say, Well, I didn't do so badly, did I? But that would have to wait. That was for tomorrow. She used to think of him as a man, but now all the children were older than their father, and he would be a child beside her if she saw him now. It seemed strange and there was something wrong in the idea. Why, he couldn't possibly recognize her. She had fenced in a hundred acres once, digging the post holes herself and clamping the wires with

just a negro boy to help. That changed a woman. John would be looking for a young woman with the peaked Spanish comb in her hair and the painted fan. Digging post holes changed a woman. Riding country roads in the winter when women had their babies was another thing: sitting up nights with sick horses and sick negroes and sick children and hardly ever losing one. John, I hardly ever lost one of them! John would see that in a minute, that would be something he could understand, she wouldn't have to explain anything!

It made her feel like rolling up her sleeves and putting the whole place to rights again. No matter if Cornelia was determined to be everywhere at once, there were a great many things left undone on this place. She would start tomorrow and do them. It was good to be strong enough for everything, even if all you made melted and changed and slipped under your hands, so that by the time you finished you almost forgot what you were working for. What was it I set out to do? she asked herself intently, but she could not remember. A fog rose over the valley, she saw it marching across the creek swallowing the trees and moving up the hill like an army of ghosts. Soon it would be at the near edge of the orchard, and then it was time to go in and light the lamps. Come in, children, don't stay out in the night air.

Lighting the lamps had been beautiful. The children huddled up to her and breathed like little calves waiting at the bars in the twilight. Their eyes followed the match and watched the flame rise and settle in a blue curve, then they moved away from her. The lamp was lit, they didn't have to be scared and hang on to mother any more. Never, never, never more. God, for all my life I thank Thee. Without Thee, my God, I could never have done it. Hail, Mary, full of grace.

I want you to pick all the fruit this year and see that nothing is wasted. There's always someone who can use it. Don't let good things rot for want of using. You waste life when you waste good food. Don't let things get lost. It's bitter to lose things. Now, don't let me get to thinking, not when I am tired and taking a little nap before supper. . . .

The pillow rose about her shoulders and pressed against her heart and the memory was being squeezed out of it: oh, push down the pillow, somebody: it would smother her if she tried to hold it. Such a fresh breeze blowing and such a green day with no threats in it. But he had not come, just the same. What does a woman do when she has put on the white veil and set out the white cake for a man and he doesn't come? She tried to remember. No, I swear he never harmed me but in that. He never harmed me but in that . . . and what if he did? There was the day, the day, but a whirl of dark smoke rose and covered it, crept up and over into the bright field where everything was planted so carefully in orderly rows. That was hell, she knew hell when she saw it. For sixty years she had prayed against remembering him and against losing her soul in the deep pit of hell, and now the two things were mingled in one and the thought of him was a smoky cloud from hell that moved and crept in her head when she had just got rid of Doctor Harry and was trying to rest a minute. Wounded vanity, Ellen, said a sharp voice in the top of her mind. Don't let your wounded vanity get the upper hand of you. Plenty of girls get jilted. You were jilted, weren't you? Then stand up to it. Her eyelids wavered and let in streamers of blue-gray light like tissue paper over her eyes. She must get up and pull the shades down or she'd never sleep. She was in bed again and the shades were not down. How could that happen? Better turn over, hide from the light, sleeping in the light gave you nightmares. "Mother, how do you feel now?" and a stinging wetness on her forehead. But I don't like having my face washed in cold water!

30   Hapsy? George? Lydia? Jimmy? No, Cornelia, and her features were swollen and full of little puddles. "They're coming, darling, they'll all be here soon." Go wash your face, child, you look funny.

Instead of obeying, Cornelia knelt down and put her head on the pillow. She seemed to be talking but there was no sound. "Well, are you tongue-tied? Whose birthday is it? Are you going to give a party?"

Cornelia's mouth moved urgently in strange shapes. "Don't do that, you bother me, daughter."

"Oh, no, Mother. Oh, no. . . ."

Nonsense. It was strange about children. They disputed your every word. "No what, Cornelia?"

35   "Here's Doctor Harry."

"I won't see that boy again. He just left five minutes ago."

"That was this morning, Mother. It's night now. Here's the nurse."

"This is Doctor Harry, Mrs. Weatherall. I never saw you look so young and happy!"

"Ah, I'll never be young again—but I'd be happy if they'd let me lie in peace and get rested."

40   She thought she spoke up loudly, but no one answered. A warm weight on her forehead, a warm bracelet on her wrist, and a breeze went on whispering, trying to tell her something. A shuffle of leaves in the everlasting hand of God, He blew on them and they danced and rattled. "Mother, don't mind, we're going to give you a little hypodermic." "Look here, daughter, how do ants get in this bed? I saw sugar ants yesterday." Did you send for Hapsy too?

It was Hapsy she really wanted. She had to go a long way back through a great many rooms to find Hapsy standing with a baby on her arm. She seemed to herself to be Hapsy also, and the baby on Hapsy's arm was Hapsy and himself and herself, all at once, and there was no surprise in the meeting. Then Hapsy melted from within and turned flimsy as gray gauze and the baby was a gauzy shadow, and Hapsy came up close and said, "I thought you'd never come," and looked at her very searchingly and said, "You haven't changed a bit!" They leaned forward to kiss, when Cornelia began whispering from a long way off, "Oh, is there anything you want to tell me? Is there anything I can do for you?"

Yes, she had changed her mind after sixty years and she would like to see George. I want you to find George. Find him and be sure to tell him I forgot him. I want him to know I had my husband just the same and my children and my house like any other woman. A good house too and a good husband that I loved and fine children out of him. Better than I hoped for even. Tell him I was given back everything he took away and more. Oh, no, oh, God, no, there was something else besides the house and the man and the children. Oh, surely they were not all? What was it? Something not given back. . . . Her breath crowded down under her ribs and grew into a monstrous frightening shape with cutting edges; it bored up into her head, and the agony was unbelievable: Yes, John, get the Doctor now, no more talk, my time has come.

When this one was born it should be the last. The last. It should have been born first, for it was the one she had truly wanted. Everything came in good time. Nothing left out, left over. She was strong, in three days she would be as well as ever. Better. A woman needed milk in her to have her full health.

"Mother, do you hear me?"

"I've been telling you—"   45

"Mother, Father Connolly's here."

"I went to Holy Communion only last week. Tell him I'm not so sinful as all that."

"Father just wants to speak to you."

He could speak as much as he pleased. It was like him to drop in and inquire about her soul as if it were a teething baby, and then stay on for a cup of tea and a round of cards and gossip. He always had a funny story of some sort, usually about an Irishman who made his little mistakes and confessed them, and the point lay in some absurd thing he would blurt out in the confessional showing his struggles between native piety and original sin. Granny felt easy about her soul. Cornelia, where are your manners? Give Father Connolly a chair. She had her secret comfortable understanding with a few favorite saints who cleared a straight road to God for her. All as surely signed and sealed as the papers for the new Forty Acres. Forever . . . heirs and assigns forever. Since the day the wedding cake was not cut, but thrown out and wasted. The whole bottom dropped out of the world, and there she was blind and sweating with nothing under her feet and the walls falling away. His hand had caught her under the breast, she had not fallen, there was the freshly polished floor with the green rug on it, just as before. He had cursed like a sailor's parrot and said, "I'll kill him for you." Don't lay a hand on him, for my sake leave something to God. "Now, Ellen, you must believe what I tell you. . . ."

So there was nothing, nothing to worry about any more, except some-   50
times in the night one of the children screamed in a nightmare, and they both hustled out shaking and hunting for the matches and calling, "There, wait a minute, here we are!" John, get the doctor now, Hapsy's time has come. But there was Hapsy standing by the bed in a white cap. "Cornelia, tell Hapsy to take off her cap. I can't see her plain."

Her eyes opened very wide and the room stood out like a picture she had seen somewhere. Dark colors with the shadows rising towards the ceiling in long angles. The tall black dresser gleamed with nothing on it but John's picture, enlarged from a little one, with John's eyes very black when they should have been blue. You never saw him, so how do you know how he looked? But the man insisted the copy was perfect, it was very rich and handsome. For a picture, yes, but it's not my husband. The table by the bed had a linen cover and a candle and a crucifix. The light was blue from Cornelia's silk lampshades. No sort of light at all, just frippery. You had to live forty years with kerosene lamps to appreciate honest electricity. She felt very strong and she saw Doctor Harry with a rosy nimbus around him.

"You look like a saint, Doctor Harry, and I vow that's as near as you'll ever come to it."

"She's saying something."

"I heard you, Cornelia. What's all this carrying-on?"

55   "Father Connolly's saying—"

Cornelia's voice staggered and bumped like a cart in a bad road. It rounded corners and turned back again and arrived nowhere. Granny stepped up in the cart very lightly and reached for the reins, but a man sat beside her and she knew him by his hands, driving the cart. She did not look in his face, for she knew without seeing, but looked instead down the road where the trees leaned over and bowed to each other and a thousand birds were singing a Mass. She felt like singing too, but she put her hand in the bosom of her dress and pulled out a rosary, and Father Connolly murmured Latin in a very solemn voice and tickled her feet. My God, will you stop that nonsense? I'm a married woman. What if he did run away and leave me to face the priest by myself? I found another a whole world better. I wouldn't have exchanged my husband for anybody except St. Michael himself, and you may tell him that for me with a thank you in the bargain.

Light flashed on her closed eyelids, and a deep roaring shook her. Cornelia, is that lightning? I hear thunder. There's going to be a storm. Close all the windows. Call the children in. . . . "Mother, here we are, all of us." "Is that you, Hapsy?" "Oh, no, I'm Lydia. We drove as fast as we could." Their faces drifted above her, drifted away. The rosary fell out of her hands and Lydia put it back. Jimmy tried to help, their hands fumbled together, and Granny closed two fingers around Jimmy's thumb. Beads wouldn't do, it must be something alive. She was so amazed her thoughts ran round and round. So, my dear Lord, this is my death and I wasn't even thinking about it. My children have come to see me die. But I can't, it's not time. Oh, I always hated surprises. I wanted to give Cornelia the amethyst set—Cornelia, you're to have the amethyst set, but Hapsy's to wear it when she wants, and, Doctor Harry, do shut up. Nobody sent for you. Oh, my dear Lord, do wait a minute. I meant to do something about the Forty Acres, Jimmy doesn't need it and Lydia will later on, with that worthless husband of hers. I meant to finish the altar cloth and send six bottles of wine to Sister Borgia for her dyspepsia. I want to send six bottles of wine to Sister Borgia, Father Connolly, now don't let me forget.

Cornelia's voice made short turns and tilted over and crashed. "Oh, Mother, oh, Mother, oh, Mother. . . ."

"I'm not going, Cornelia. I'm taken by surprise. I can't go."

You'll see Hapsy again. What about her? "I thought you'd never come."   60
Granny made a long journey outward, looking for Hapsy. What if I don't
find her? What then? Her heart sank down and down, there was no bottom
to death, she couldn't come to the end of it. The blue light from Cornelia's
lampshade drew into a tiny point in the center of her brain, it flickered and
winked like an eye, quietly it fluttered and dwindled. Granny lay curled
down within herself, amazed and watchful, staring at the point of light that
was herself; her body was now only a deeper mass of shadow in an endless
darkness and this darkness would curl around the light and swallow it up.
God, give a sign!

For the second time there was no sign. Again no bridegroom and the
priest in the house. She could not remember any other sorrow because this
grief wiped them all away. Oh, no, there's nothing more cruel than this—I'll
never forgive it. She stretched herself with a deep breath and blew out the
light.

QUESTIONS

1. The narrative technique of this story is called **stream of consciousness,**
   a subspecies of the limited omniscient point of view. Stream of consciousness presents the apparently random thoughts going through a person's
   head within a certain interval of time, in which memory and present experience are mingled, and in which the transitional links are psychological
   rather than logical. What characteristics of Ellen Weatherall's condition does
   this narrative technique represent? How effectively does it reveal events of
   the past? How clearly does it reflect the present? What is gained by the lack
   of clarity?

2. The protagonist reveals herself to be in conflict with other persons, and
   with her physical environment, both in the past and in the present. Identify
   her antagonists. To what extent has she experienced conflicts within herself? To what extent is she now experiencing such conflicts?

3. What does her memory present as the major turning points in her life? Is it
   more than a coincidence that one of them occurs every twenty years? Considering the many major events in a woman's life that *might* have been climactic (her marriage, the birth of her first child, and so forth), how do the
   ones she recalls so vividly define her character?

4. What kind of life has Granny Weatherall made for herself? What have been
   her characteristic activities and attitudes? Can her "jilting" be seen as a partial cause for these activities and attitudes?

5. What is the significance of Hapsy? What religious symbolism is attached to
   the vision of her and her infant son (paragraph 41)?

6. Most critics understand the title to refer to two "jiltings," the one by her
   fiancé sixty years earlier, the other by God at the moment of her death.
   Can you justify this interpretation? Does the story have a determinate or
   indeterminate ending?

CHAPTER SIX

Symbol and Irony

Most successful stories are characterized by compression. The writer's aim is to say as much as possible as briefly as possible. This does not mean that most good stories are brief. It means only that nothing is wasted and that each word and detail is chosen for maximum effectiveness. The force of an explosion is proportionate to the strength and amount of powder used and the smallness of the space it is confined in.

Good writers achieve compression by exercising a rigid selectivity. They choose the details and incidents that contribute most to the meaning they are after; they omit those whose usefulness is minimal. As far as possible they choose details that are multivalued—that serve a variety of purposes at once. A detail that expresses character at the same time that it advances plot is more useful than a detail that does only one or the other.

This chapter will discuss two contributory resources of the writer for gaining compression: symbol and irony. Both of them may increase the explosive force of a story, but both demand awareness and maturity on the part of the reader.

A literary **symbol*** is something that means *more* than what it is. It is an object, a person, a situation, an action, or some other item that has a literal meaning in the story but suggests or represents other meanings as well. A very simple illustration is to be found in name symbolism. Most names are simply labels. Seldom does a name tell anything about the person to whom it is attached, except possibly the individual's nationality. In a story, however, authors may choose names for their characters that serve not only to label them but also to suggest something about them. The name of the young civil rights activist in "Just Like a Tree" (page 219), Emmanuel, is derived from the Hebrew for "God with us" and is identified with the Messiah in

---

*Literary symbols are to be distinguished from *arbitrary* symbols, like letters of the alphabet, numbers, and algebraic signs, which have no meaning in and of themselves but which mean only something *else*, not something *more* than what they are.

Isaiah 7:14. When in parting from him, Aunt Fe blesses him, "God be with you," the symbolism is made overt. In "Everyday Use," Dee's rejection of her name and her adoption of the alternative "Wangero" symbolizes for her a changed perspective on her heritage. The name of General Zaroff in "The Most Dangerous Game" is fitting for a former "officer of the Czar" who now behaves like a czar himself. Trevor's name in Greene's "The Destructors" suggests his upper-class origins. Equally meaningful in that story is the name of the Wormsley Common Gang. First, the word "Common," here designating a small public park or green, also suggests the "common people" or the lower middle and laboring classes as opposed to the upper class. More significant, when Trevor advocates his plan for gutting the old house— "We'd do it from inside. . . . We'd be like worms, don't you see, in an apple" (paragraph 52), we see that Greene's choice of the name Wormsley was quite deliberate and that it is appropriate also (as well as perfectly natural) that Wormsley Common should have an Underground Station. (The word "apple," in Trevor's speech, also has symbolic resonances. Though it is often a mistake to push symbolism too hard, the reader may well ask whether anything would be lost if Trevor had compared the gang's activities to those of worms in a peach or a pear.)

More important than name symbolism is the symbolic use of objects and actions. In some stories these symbols will fit so naturally into the literal context that their symbolic value will not at first be apparent except to the most perceptive reader. In other stories—usually stories with a less realistic surface—they will be so central and so obvious that they will demand symbolical interpretation if the story is to yield significant meaning. In the first kind of story the symbols *reinforce* and *add* to the meaning. In the second kind of story they *carry* the meaning.

In "Hills Like White Elephants" a man and a girl sit waiting for the train to Madrid, where the girl is to have an abortion. But the girl is not fully persuaded that she wants an abortion (at the deepest levels of her being, she does not). The man is aware of this and seeks to reassure her: "It's really an awfully simple operation. . . . It's not really an operation at all. . . . But I don't want you to do it if you don't really want to." The man *does* want her to do it even if she doesn't really want to; nevertheless, the decision is not irrevocable. They are at a railroad junction, a place where one can change directions. Symbolically it represents a juncture where they can change the direction of their lives. Their bags, with "labels on them from all the hotels where they had spent nights," indicate the kind of rootless, pleasure-seeking existence without responsibility they have hitherto lived. The man wants the girl to have the abortion so that they can go on living as they have before.

The railway station is situated in a river valley between two mountain ranges. On one side of the valley there is no shade and no trees and the country is "brown and dry." It is on this side, "the dry side," that the station sits in the heat, "between two lines of rails." It is also this side which the couple see from their table and which prompts the girl's remark that the hills look "like white elephants." On the other side of the valley, which the girl can see when she walks to the end of the station, lies the river, with "fields of grain and trees" along its banks, the "shadow of a cloud" moving across a field of grain, and another range of mountains in the distance. Looking in this direction, the girl remarks, "And we could have all this." The two landscapes, on opposite sides of the valley, have symbolic meaning in relation to the decision that the girl is being asked to reconfirm. The hot arid side of the valley represents sterility; the other side, with water in the river and the cloud, a hint of coolness in the cloud's moving shadow, and growing things along the river banks, represents fertility. The girl's remark about this other side shows a conscious recognition of its symbolism.

But what does the girl mean by her remark that the mountains on the dry side of the valley look "like white elephants"? Perhaps nothing at all. It is intended as a "bright" remark, a clever if far-fetched comparison made to amuse the man, as it would have in their earlier days together. But whether or not the girl means anything by it, almost certainly Hemingway means something. Or perhaps several things. Clearly the child begun in the girl's womb is a "white elephant" for the man, who says, "I don't want anybody but you. I don't want any one else." For the girl, on the other hand, the abortion itself, the decision to continue living as they have been living, without responsibility, may be considered a "white elephant." We already know that this life has lost its savor for her. When she remarks that the Anis del Toro "tastes like licorice," the man's response—"That's the way with everything"—is probably meant to apply only to the drinks and food in this section of the country, but the girl's confirmation of his observation seems to enlarge its meaning to the whole life they have been living together, which consists, she says, only of looking at things and trying new drinks. Thus the licorice flavor, suggesting tedium and disillusion, joins the "hills like white elephants," the opposed sides of the river valley, and the railroad junction in a network of symbols that intensify the meaning and impact of the story.*

The ability to recognize and identify symbols requires perception and tact. The great danger facing readers when they first become aware of symbolic values is a tendency to run wild—to find symbols everywhere and to read into the details of a story all sorts of fanciful meanings not legitimately supported by it. But we need to remember that most stories operate almost wholly at the literal level and that, even in highly symbolic stories, the majority of the details are purely literal. A story is not an excuse for an exercise in ingenuity. It is better, indeed, to miss the symbolic meanings of a story than to pervert its meaning by discovering symbols that are nonexistent. Better to miss the boat than to jump wildly for it and drown.

The ability to interpret symbols is nevertheless essential for a full understanding of literature. Readers should always be alert for symbolic meanings but should observe the following cautions:

1. The story itself must furnish a clue that a detail is to be taken symbolically. In Mansfield's story, Miss Brill's fur is given prominence at the beginning of the story, when it is taken out of its box; at the climax of the story, when the girl on the bench compares it to "a fried whiting"; and at the end of the story, when Miss Brill puts it back in the box and thinks she hears it crying. The fur is clearly a symbol for Miss Brill herself. It comes out of a box like a dark little room or a cupboard, it is old and in need of repair, it is ridiculed by the boy and the girl on the park bench, and it is returned to its box at the end of the story. Symbolically, it is herself whom Miss Brill hears crying. In Hemingway's story, the comparison of the hills to white elephants is used for the title of the story and is mentioned four times within the story, while the opposed sides of the river valley are rather pointedly described in a story that otherwise has very little description in it. Both items are given emphasis, yet neither has any part in the action. Even greater emphasis is given to the quilts in the story by Walker. Symbols nearly always signal their existence by *emphasis, repetition,* or *position.* In the absence of such signals, we should be reluctant to identify an item as symbolic.

2. The meaning of a literary symbol must be established and supported by the entire context of the story. The symbol has its meaning

---

*Some critics have found symbolism also in the bead curtain that separates the bar from the table where the man and girl are sitting. But there is not space here, nor need, to discuss all symbolic implications of the story.

in the story, not *outside* it. Our meaning, for instance, in "Hills Like White Elephants" for the "shadow of a cloud" moving over the field of grain, is supported by and dependent on its relation to other elements in the story: the river, the field of grain, the stifling heat at the station, the brown, dry country on the near side of the valley, and so on. In another work of literature, in another context, a shadow or a cloud might have an almost opposite meaning, or no symbolic meaning at all. The cloud in the ancient saying "Every cloud has a silver lining" and the shadow in the Twenty-third Psalm—"though I walk through the valley of the shadow of death"—have entirely different meanings than they have here. Here, by suggesting the possibility of rain, a spot of shade from the sun, and the existence of a breeze, the moving cloud shadow extends the meaning of the fertility symbol of which it is a part.

3. To be called a symbol, an item must suggest a meaning different in *kind* from its literal meaning; a symbol is something more than the representative of a class or type. Miss Brill, for instance, is an old, odd, silent, friendless person, set in her ways, who does not realize (until the climax of the story) that she herself is old, odd, and set in her ways—like other elderly people she observes in the park each Sunday. But to say this is to say no more than that the story has a theme. Every interpretive story suggests a generalization about life, is more than an accounting of the specific fortunes of specific individuals. There is no point, therefore, in calling Miss Brill a *symbol* of odd, self-deluded elderly people; she *is* an odd, self-deluded elderly person: a member of the class of odd, self-deluded elderly persons. Her fur is a symbol, but she is not. We ought not to use the phrase *is a symbol of* when we can easily use *is,* or *is an example of,* or *is an evidence of.* Dick Prosser, in "The Child by Tiger," through his association with the tiger in Blake's poem, and by the way he is spoken of in the story's concluding paragraphs, is clearly meant to be something more than an *example* of any class of men, or of mankind in general; he is a symbol of something *in* man, of hidden possibilities that are latent in us all.

In "Hills Like White Elephants" the railroad junction is neither an example nor an evidence of a point in time in the characters' lives when a crucial decision must be made, nor are the opposed sides of the valley examples or evidences of the two kinds of future that might result from their choice. The meanings these things suggest are different from what they are. The label-covered suitcases of the traveling couple, on the other hand, are an *evidence* or sign of their past and should not properly be called a symbol of their past.

4. A symbol may have more than one meaning. It may suggest a cluster of meanings. At its most effective a symbol is like a many-faceted jewel: it flashes different colors when turned in the light. This is not to say that it can mean anything we want it to: the area of possible meanings is always controlled by the context. Nevertheless, this possibility of complex meaning, plus concreteness and emotional power, gives the symbol its peculiar compressive value. We have identified the far side of the valley in "Hills Like White Elephants" with fertility, but it suggests also pleasantness, growth, beauty, fulfill-ment—everything that the girl vaguely includes in her statement, "And we could have all this." The Japanese quince in Galsworthy's story symbolizes life, growth, beauty, freedom, joy—all qualities op-posed to convention and habit and "foreign" to the proper and "re-spectable" English upper-middle-class environment in which it is found. The quilts in Walker's story have an equally wide range of meaning—inherited values, family attachments, independence and self-reliance, the beauty of useful objects, the virtue of craftsman-ship—all in contrast to the shallow, monetary meaning expressed in Dee's acquisitive demand for them. When she says, "But they're *price-less!*" she means that they are worth a great deal of money, but in the truer sense their symbolic values cannot be reckoned at any price. The meaning is not confined to any one of these qualities: it is all of them, and therein lies the symbol's value.

Irony is a term with a range of meanings, all of them involving some sort of discrepancy or incongruity. It is a contrast in which one term of the contrast in some ways mocks the other term. It is not to be confused with sarcasm, however, which is simply language designed to cause pain. The story writer uses irony to suggest the complexity of experience, to furnish indirectly an evaluation of the material, and at the same time to achieve compression.

Three kinds of irony may be distinguished here. **Verbal irony,** the simplest and, for the story writer, the least important kind, is a figure of speech in which the opposite is said from what is intended. The discrepancy is between what is said and what is meant. In "The Child by Tiger," when the narrator tells us that the man who fired the first shot into Dick Prosser was "telling the story of his own heroic ac-complishments" and refers to him as "the hero," he is using the words "heroic" and "hero" ironically, for it is clear that he feels only con-tempt for both the man and his actions. In "Defender of the Faith," when Sergeant Marx says to Grossbart, "You're a regular Messiah, aren't you?" he is speaking ironically—and sarcastically—for he thinks Grossbart's motives are self-interested rather than Messianic. Another use of irony for sarcastic purposes is made by the girl in "Hills Like White Elephants." The man has been assuring her that, after the operation, they will be "just like" they were before, for her pregnancy has been the only thing making them unhappy:

> "And you think then we'll be all right and be happy."
> "I know we will. You don't have to be afraid. I've known lots of people that have done it."
> "So have I," said the girl. "And afterward they were all so happy."

Abortions, the girl means, make couples anything but "all so happy" afterward. She also speaks ironically at the very end of the story, when she says: "I feel fine. . . . There's nothing wrong with me. I feel fine."

In **dramatic irony** the contrast is between what a character says and what the reader knows to be true. The value of this kind of irony lies in the comment it implies on the speaker or the speaker's expectations. Miss Brill, sitting in the park, thinks about others doing the same as she:

> Other people sat on the benches and green chairs, but they were nearly always the same, Sunday after Sunday, and—Miss Brill had often noticed—there was something funny about nearly all of them. . . . from the way they stared they looked as though they'd just come from dark little rooms or even—even cupboards!

It is ironic that the judgment she makes of them is what the story makes of her—even including the word "funny," which the young girl later uses about her beloved fur. She is unaware that her phrase "nearly always the same, Sunday after Sunday" describes her own behavior, which she unwittingly reveals when she thinks that she "had *often* noticed" them. And of course the irony of the statement about the "cupboards" they must have come from is made overt when she returns at the end of the story to "her room like a cupboard." Perhaps the most poignant of the dramatic ironies surrounding Miss Brill is contained in her boastful thought, "'Yes, I have been an actress for a long time,'" for she has indeed created a fictitious role that she lives in—not that of a glamorous stage actress in a romantic musical play, but that of a perceptive, happy, and self-sufficient woman. Another effective example occurs in "I'm a Fool" when the swipe blames his lie at the racetrack on the whiskey he had drunk and on the man in the

Windsor tie. The reader sees, as the swipe does not, that *these are simply additional symptoms of his plight, not its cause.*

In **irony of situation,** usually the most important kind for the story writer, the discrepancy is between appearance and reality, or between expectation and fulfillment, or between what is and what would seem appropriate. In "The Most Dangerous Game," it is ironic that Rainsford, "the celebrated hunter," should become the hunted, for this is a reversal of his expected and appropriate role. In "The Destructors," it is ironic that Old Misery's horoscope should read, "Abstain from any dealings in first half of week. Danger of serious crash," for the horoscope is valid in a sense that is quite different from that which the words seem to indicate. In "Roman Fever," it is ironic that Barbara, the daughter of the "smaller and paler" Mrs. Ansley, should be the more "dynamic" of the two girls, and of course even more ironic that Barbara should be the daughter of Mr. Slade. In "The Japanese Quince" it is ironic that the beauty and joy of springtime symbolized by the quince tree should seem to Mr. Nilson the symptoms of illness.

As a final example, the title of "Defender of the Faith" points to a complex irony, partly verbal, partly situational. The phrase "defender of the faith" ordinarily suggests a staunch religious champion and partisan, but, insofar as Sergeant Marx fills this role, he does so against his will, even against his intention, for his motivation is to give fair and equal treatment to all his men—he does not want to be partial to Jews. Unwillingly, he is trapped into being a "defender of the faith" by Private Grossbart.

> The next morning, while chatting with Captain Barrett, I recounted the incident of the previous evening. Somehow, in the telling, it must have seemed to the Captain that I was not so much explaining Grossbart's position as defending it.

At the end of the story, however, when Marx has Grossbart's orders changed to the Pacific, the irony is that he becomes most truly a defender of his faith when he seems to be turning against it. "You call this watching out for me—what you did?" asks Grossbart. "No," answers Marx. "For all of us." The cause of the whole Jewish faith is set back when Jews like Grossbart get special favors for themselves, for other people will mistakenly attribute Grossbart's objectionable qualities to the Jewish people as a whole. Thus Marx is unwillingly a "defender of the faith" when he helps his coreligionist and becomes truly a defender of the faith when he turns against him. These ironies underscore the difficulties involved in being at the same time a good Jew and a good person in a world where Jews are so often the objects of prejudice and persecution.

In all these examples, irony enables the author to gain power with economy. Like symbolism, irony makes it possible to suggest meanings without stating them. Simply by juxtaposing two discordant facts in the right contextual mix, the writer can start a current of meaning flowing between them, as between the two poles of an electric battery. We do not *need* to be told how difficult it is for an aging, solitary woman to cope with being alone; we see it. We do not need to be told that the racetrack swipe is lacking in self-knowledge; we see it. We do not need to be told how difficult it is for a Jewish sergeant to balance justice and mercy in a position of command; we feel it. The ironic contrast generates meaning.

Albert Camus

The Guest

The schoolmaster was watching the two men climb toward him. One was on horseback, the other on foot. They had not yet tackled the abrupt rise leading to the schoolhouse built on the hillside. They were toiling onward, making slow progress in the snow, among the stones, on the vast expanse of the high, deserted plateau. From time to time the horse stumbled. He could not be heard yet but the breath issuing from his nostrils could be seen. The schoolmaster calculated that it would take them a half hour to get onto the hill. It was cold; he went back into the school to get a sweater.

He crossed the empty, frigid classroom. On the blackboard the four rivers of France, drawn with four different colored chalks, had been flowing toward their estuaries for the past three days. Snow had suddenly fallen in mid-October after eight months of drought without the transition of rain, and the twenty pupils, more or less, who lived in the villages scattered over the plateau had stopped coming. With fair weather they would return. Daru

THE GUEST   First published in 1957. Translated into English by Justin O'Brien. Algeria, now a republic, was until midcentury a French territory with a population about 88 percent Moslem (either Arab or Berber). Daru and Balducci, in the story, are French civil servants. Algeria gained its independence as a result of the Algerian War, 1954–1962, a Moslem revolt against French rule. Albert Camus (1913–1960), though a Frenchman, was born in northeastern Algeria, was educated in Algiers, and did not see France until 1939. In 1940, with the fall of France to Germany, he returned to Algiers and taught for two years in a private school in Oran, on the seacoast. In 1942 he returned to Paris and engaged actively in the resistance movement by writing for the underground press. He continued his residence in Paris after World War II.

now heated only the single room that was his lodging, adjoining the class-room. One of the windows faced, like the classroom windows, the south. On that side the school was a few kilometers from the point where the plateau began to slope toward the south. In clear weather the purple mass of the mountain range where the gap opened onto the desert could be seen.

Somewhat warmed, Daru returned to the window from which he had first noticed the two men. They were no longer visible. Hence they must have tackled the rise. The sky was not so dark, for the snow had stopped falling during the night. The morning had dawned with a dirty light which had scarcely become brighter as the ceiling of clouds lifted. At two in the afternoon it seemed as if the day were merely beginning. But still this was better than those three days when the thick snow was falling amidst unbroken darkness with little gusts of wind that rattled the double door of the classroom. Then Daru had spent long hours in his room, leaving it only to go to the shed and feed the chickens or get some coal. Fortunately the delivery truck from Tadjid, the nearest village to the north, had brought his supplies two days before the blizzard. It would return in forty-eight hours.

Besides, he had enough to resist a seige, for the little room was cluttered with bags of wheat that the administration had left as a supply to distribute to those of his pupils whose families had suffered from the drought. Actually they had all been victims because they were all poor. Every day Daru would distribute a ration to the children. They had missed it, he knew, during these bad days. Possibly one of the fathers or big brothers would come this after-noon and he could supply them with grain. It was just a matter of carrying them over to the next harvest. Now shiploads of wheat were arriving from France and the worst was over. But it would be hard to forget that poverty, that army of ragged ghosts wandering in the sunlight, the plateaus burned to a cinder month after month, the earth shriveled up little by little, literally scorched, every stone bursting into dust under one's foot. The sheep had died then by thousands, and even a few men, here and there, sometimes without anyone's knowing.

In contrast with such poverty, he who lived almost like a monk, in his   5
remote schoolhouse, had felt like a lord with his whitewashed walls, his narrow couch, his unpainted shelves, his well, and his weekly provisioning with water and food. And suddenly this snow, without warning, without the foretaste of rain. This is the way the region was, cruel to live in, even without men, who didn't help matters either. But Daru had been born here. Every-where else, he felt exiled.

He went out and stepped forward on the terrace in front of the school-house. The two men were now halfway up the slope. He recognized the horse-man to be Balducci, the old gendarme he had known for a long time. Bald-ucci was holding at the end of a rope an Arab walking behind him with hands bound and head lowered. The gendarme waved a greeting to which Daru did not reply, lost as he was in contemplation of the Arab dressed in a faded blue *jellaba*, his feet in sandals but covered with socks of heavy raw wool, his head crowned with a narrow, short *chèche*. Balducci was holding back his horse in order not to hurt the Arab, and the group was advancing slowly.

Within earshot, Balducci shouted, "One hour to do the three kilometers from El Ameur!" Daru did not answer. Short and square in his thick sweater, he watched them climb. Not once had the Arab raised his head. "Hello," said Daru when they got up onto the terrace. "Come in and warm up." Balducci painfully got down from his horse without letting go of the rope. He smiled at the schoolmaster from under his bristling mustache. His little dark eyes, deepset under a tanned forehead, and his mouth surrounded with wrinkles made him look attentive and studious. Daru took the bridle, led the horse to the shed, and came back to the two men who were now waiting for him in the school. He led them into his room. "I am going to heat up the classroom," he said. "We'll be more comfortable there."

When he entered the room again, Balducci was on the couch. He had undone the rope tying him to the Arab, who had squatted near the stove. His hands still bound, the *chèche* pushed back on his head, the Arab was looking toward the window. At first Daru noticed only his huge lips, fat, smooth, almost Negroid; yet his nose was straight, his eyes dark and full of fever. The *chèche* uncovered an obstinate forehead and, under the weathered skin now rather discolored by the cold, the whole face had a restless and rebellious look. "Go into the outer room," said the schoolmaster, "and I'll make you some mint tea." "Thanks," Balducci said. "What a chore! How I long for retirement." And addressing his prisoner in Arabic, he said, "Come on, you." The Arab got up and, slowly, holding his bound wrists in front of him, went into the classroom.

With the tea, Daru brought a chair. But Balducci was already sitting in state at the nearest pupil's desk, and the Arab had squatted against the teacher's platform facing the stove, which stood between the desk and the window. When he held out the glass of tea to the prisoner, Daru hesitated at the sight of his bound hands. "He might perhaps be untied." "Sure," said Balducci. "That was for the trip." He started to get to his feet. But Daru, setting the glass on the floor, had knelt beside the Arab. Without saying anything, the Arab watched him with his feverish eyes. Once his hands were free, he rubbed his swollen wrists against each other, took the glass of tea and sucked up the burning liquid in swift little sips.

10   "Good," said Daru. "And where are you headed?"

Balducci withdrew his mustache from the tea. "Here, son."

"Odd pupils! And you're spending the night?"

"No. I'm going back to El Ameur. And you will deliver this fellow to Tinguit. He is expected at police headquarters."

Balducci was looking at Daru with a friendly little smile.

15   "What's this story?" asked the schoolmaster. "Are you pulling my leg?"

"No, son. Those are the orders."

"The orders? I'm not . . ." Daru hesitated, not wanting to hurt the old Corsican. "I mean, that's not my job."

"What! What's the meaning of that? In wartime people do all kinds of jobs."

"Then I'll wait for the declaration of war!"

Balducci nodded. "O.K. But the orders exist and they concern you too. Things are bubbling, it appears. There is talk of a forthcoming revolt. We are mobilized in a way."   20

Daru still had his obstinate look.

"Listen, son," Balducci said. "I like you and you've got to understand. There's only a dozen of us at El Ameur to patrol the whole territory of a small department and I must be back in a hurry. He couldn't be kept there. His village was beginning to stir; they wanted to take him back. You must take him to Tinguit tomorrow before the day is over. Twenty kilometers shouldn't faze a husky fellow like you. After that, all will be over. You'll come back to your pupils and your comfortable life."

Behind the wall the horse could be heard snorting and pawing the earth. Daru was looking out the window. Decidedly the weather was clearing and the light was increasing over the snowy plateau. When all the snow was melted, the sun would take over again and once more would burn the fields of stone. For days still, the unchanging sky would shed its dry light on the solitary expanse where nothing had any connection with man.

"After all," he said, turning around toward Balducci, "what did he do?" And, before the gendarme had opened his mouth, he asked, "Does he speak French?"

"No, not a word. We had been looking for him for a month, but they   25 were hiding him. He killed his cousin."

"Is he against us?"

"I don't think so. But you can never be sure."

"Why did he kill?"

"A family squabble, I think. One owed grain to the other, it seems. It's not at all clear. In short, he killed his cousin with a billhook. You know, like a sheep, *kreezk!*"

Balducci made the gesture of drawing a blade across his throat, and the   30 Arab, his attention attracted, watched him with a sort of anxiety. Daru felt a sudden wrath against the man, against all men with their rotten spite, their tireless hates, their blood lust.

But the kettle was singing on the stove. He served Balducci more tea, hesitated, then served the Arab again, who drank avidly a second time. His raised arms made the *jellaba* fall open, and the schoolmaster saw his thin, muscular chest.

"Thanks, son," Balducci said. "And now I'm off."

He got up and went toward the Arab, taking a small rope from his pocket.

"What are you doing?" Daru asked dryly.

Balducci, disconcerted, showed him the rope.   35

"Don't bother."

The old gendarme hesitated. "It's up to you. Of course, you are armed?"

"I have my shotgun."

"Where?"

40   "In the trunk."

"You ought to have it near your bed."

"Why? I have nothing to fear."

"You're crazy, son. If there's an uprising, no one is safe; we're all in the same boat."

"I'll defend myself. I'll have time to see them coming."

45   Balducci began to laugh, then suddenly the mustache covered the white teeth. "You'll have time? O.K. That's just what I was saying. You always have been a little cracked. That's why I like you; my son was like that."

At the same time he took out his revolver and put it on the desk. "Keep it; I don't need two weapons from here to El Ameur."

The revolver shone against the black paint of the table. When the gendarme turned toward him, the schoolmaster caught his smell of leather and horseflesh.

"Listen, Balducci," Daru said suddenly, "all this disgusts me, beginning with your fellow here. But I won't hand him over. Fight, yes, if I have to. But not that."

The old gendarme stood in front of him and looked at him severely.

50   "You're being a fool," he said slowly. "I don't like it either. You don't get used to putting a rope on a man even after years of it, and you're even ashamed—yes, ashamed. But you can't let them have their way."

"I won't hand him over," Daru said again.

"It's an order, son, and I repeat it."

"That's right. Repeat to them what I've said to you: I won't hand him over."

Balducci made a visible effort to reflect. He looked at the Arab and at Daru. At last he decided.

55   "No, I won't tell them anything. If you want to drop us, go ahead; I'll not denounce you. I have an order to deliver the prisoner and I'm doing so. And now you'll just sign this paper for me."

"There's no need. I'll not deny that you left him with me."

"Don't be mean with me. I know you'll tell the truth. You're from around these parts and you are a man. But you must sign; that's the rule."

Daru opened his drawer, took out a little square bottle of purple ink, the red wooden penholder with the "sergeant-major" pen he used for models of handwriting, and signed. The gendarme carefully folded the paper and put it into his wallet. Then he moved toward the door.

"I'll see you off," Daru said.

60   "No," said Balducci. "There's no use being polite. You insulted me."

He looked at the Arab, motionless in the same spot, sniffed peevishly, and turned away toward the door. "Good-bye, son," he said. The door slammed behind him. His footsteps were muffled by the snow. The horse stirred on the other side of the wall and several chickens fluttered in fright. A moment later Balducci reappeared outside the window leading the horse by the bridle. He walked toward the little rise without turning around and disappeared from sight with the horse following him.

Daru walked back toward the prisoner, who, without stirring, never took his eyes off him. "Wait," the schoolmaster said in Arabic and went toward the bedroom. As he was going through the door, he had a second thought, went to the desk, took the revolver, and stuck it in his pocket. Then, without looking back, he went into his room.

For some time he lay on his couch watching the sky gradually close over, listening to the silence. It was this silence that had seemed painful to him during the first days here, after the war. He had requested a post in the little town at the base of the foothills separating the upper plateaus from the desert. There rocky walls, green and black to the north, pink and lavender to the south, marked the frontier of eternal summer. He had been named to a post farther north, on the plateau itself. In the beginning, the solitude and the silence had been hard for him on these wastelands peopled only by stones. Occasionally, furrows suggested cultivation, but they had been dug to uncover a certain kind of stone good for building. The only plowing here was to harvest rocks. Elsewhere a thin layer of soil accumulated in the hollows would be scraped out to enrich paltry village gardens. This is the way it was: bare rock covered three quarters of the region. Towns sprang up, flourished, then disappeared; men came by, loved one another or fought bitterly, then died. No one in this desert, neither he nor his guest, mattered. And yet, outside this desert neither of them, Daru knew, could have really lived.

When he got up, no noise came from the classroom. He was amazed at the unmixed joy he derived from the mere thought that the Arab might have fled and that he would be alone with no decision to make. But the prisoner was there. He had merely stretched out between the stove and the desk and he was staring at the ceiling. In that position, his thick lips were particularly noticeable, giving him a pouting look. "Come," said Daru. The Arab got up and followed him. In the bedroom the schoolmaster pointed to a chair near the table under the window. The Arab sat down without ceasing to watch Daru.

"Are you hungry?"

"Yes," the prisoner said.

Daru set the table for two. He took flour and oil, shaped a cake in a frying pan, and lighted the little stove that functioned on bottled gas. While the cake was cooking, he went out to the shed to get cheese, eggs, dates, and condensed milk. When the cake was done he set it on the window sill to cool, heated some condensed milk diluted with water, and beat up the eggs into an omelette. In one of his motions he bumped into the revolver stuck in his right pocket. He set the bowl down, went into the classroom, and put the revolver in his desk drawer. When he came back to the room, night was falling. He put on the light and served the Arab. "Eat," he said. The Arab took a piece of the cake, lifted it eagerly to his mouth, and stopped short.

65

"And you?" he asked.

"After you. I'll eat too."

70   The thick lips opened slightly. The Arab hesitated, then bit into the cake determinedly.

The meal over, the Arab looked at the schoolmaster. "Are you the judge?"

"No, I'm simply keeping you until tomorrow."

"Why do you eat with me?"

"I'm hungry."

75   The Arab fell silent. Daru got up and went out. He brought back a camp cot from the shed and set it up between the table and the stove, at right angles to his own bed. From a large suitcase which, upright in a corner, served as a shelf for papers, he took two blankets and arranged them on the cot. Then he stopped, felt useless, and sat down on his bed. There was nothing more to do or to get ready. He had to look at this man. He looked at him therefore, trying to imagine his face bursting with rage. He couldn't do so. He could see nothing but the dark yet shining eyes and the animal mouth.

"Why did you kill him?" he asked in a voice whose hostile tone surprised him.

The Arab looked away. "He ran away. I ran after him."

He raised his eyes to Daru again and they were full of a sort of woeful interrogation. "Now what will they do to me?"

"Are you afraid?"

80   The Arab stiffened, turning his eyes away.

"Are you sorry?"

The Arab stared at him openmouthed. Obviously he did not understand. Daru's annoyance was growing. At the same time he felt awkward and self-conscious with his big body wedged between the two beds.

"Lie down there," he said impatiently. "That's your bed."

The Arab didn't move. He cried out, "Tell me!"

85   The schoolmaster looked at him.

"Is the gendarme coming back tomorrow?"

"I don't know."

"Are you coming with us?"

"I don't know. Why?"

90   The prisoner got up and stretched out on top of the blankets, his feet toward the window. The light from the electric bulb shone straight into his eyes and he closed them at once.

"Why?" Daru repeated, standing beside the bed.

The Arab opened his eyes under the blinding light and looked at him, trying not to blink. "Come with us," he said.

In the middle of the night, Daru was still not asleep. He had gone to bed after undressing completely; he generally slept naked. But when he suddenly realized that he had nothing on, he wondered. He felt vulnerable and the temptation came to him to put his clothes back on. Then he shrugged his shoulders; after all, he wasn't a child and, if it came to that, he could break his adversary in two. From his bed, he could observe him lying on his back, still motionless, his eyes closed under the harsh light. When Daru turned out the light, the darkness seemed to congeal all of a sudden. Little by little, the night came back to life in the window where the starless sky was stirring gently. The schoolmaster soon made out the body lying at his feet. The Arab was still motionless but his eyes seemed open. A faint wind was prowling about the schoolhouse. Perhaps it would drive away the clouds and the sun would reappear.

During the night the wind increased. The hens fluttered a little and then were silent. The Arab turned over on his side with his back to Daru, who thought he heard him moan. Then he listened for his guest's breathing, which had become heavier and more regular. He listened to that breathing so close to him and mused without being able to go to sleep. In the room where he had been sleeping alone for a year, this presence bothered him. But it bothered him also because it imposed on him a sort of brotherhood he re-fused to accept in the present circumstances; yet he was familiar with it. Men who share the same rooms, soldiers or prisoners, develop a strange alliance as if, having cast off their armor with their clothing, they fraternized every evening, over and above their differences, in the ancient community of dream and fatigue. But Daru shook himself; he didn't like such musings, and it was essential for him to sleep.

A little later, however, when the Arab stirred slightly, the schoolmaster was still not asleep. When the prisoner made a second move, he stiffened, on the alert. The Arab was lifting himself slowly on his arms with almost the motion of a sleepwalker. Seated upright in bed, he waited motionless with-out turning his head toward Daru, as if he were listening attentively. Daru did not stir; it had just occurred to him that the revolver was still in the drawer of his desk. It was better to act at once. Yet he continued to observe the prisoner, who, with the same slithery motion, put his feet on the ground, waited again, then stood up slowly. Daru was about to call out to him when the Arab began to walk, in a quite natural but extraordinarily silent way. He was heading toward the door at the end of the room that opened into the shed. He lifted the latch with precaution and went out, pushing the door behind him but without shutting it. 95

Daru had not stirred. "He is running away," he merely thought. "Good riddance!" Yet he listened attentively. The hens were not fluttering; the guest must be on the plateau. A faint sound of water reached him, and he didn't know what it was until the Arab again stood framed in the doorway, closed the door carefully, and came back to bed without a sound. Then Daru turned his back on him and fell asleep. Still later he seemed from the depths of his sleep, to hear furtive steps around the schoolhouse. "I'm dreaming! I'm dreaming!" he repeated to himself. And he went on sleeping.

When he awoke, the sky was clear; the loose window let in a cold, pure air. The Arab was asleep, hunched up under the blankets now, his mouth open, utterly relaxed. But when Daru shook him he started dreadfully, staring at Daru with wild eyes as if he had never seen him and with such a frightened expression that the schoolmaster stepped back. "Don't be afraid. It is I. You must eat." The Arab nodded his head and said yes. Calm had returned to his face, but his expression was vacant and listless.

The coffee was ready. They drank it seated together on the cot as they munched their pieces of the cake. Then Daru led the Arab under the shed and showed him the faucet where he washed. He went back into the room, folded the blankets on the cot, made his own bed, and put the room in order. Then he went through the classroom and out onto the terrace. The sun was already riding in the blue sky; a soft, bright light enveloped the deserted plateau. On the ridge the snow was melting in spots. The stones were about to reappear. Crouched on the edge of the plateau, the schoolmaster looked at the deserted expanse. He thought of Balducci. He had hurt him, for he had sent him off as though he didn't want to be associated with him. He could still hear the gendarme's farewell and, without knowing why, he felt strangely empty and vulnerable.

At that moment, from the other side of the schoolhouse, the prisoner coughed. Daru listened to him almost despite himself and then, furious, threw a pebble that whistled through the air before sinking into the snow. That man's stupid crime revolted him, but to hand him over was contrary to honor; just thinking of it made him boil with humiliation. He simultaneously cursed his own people who had sent him this Arab and the Arab who had dared to kill and not managed to get away. Daru got up, walked in a circle on the terrace, waited motionless, and then went back into the schoolhouse.

100   The Arab, leaning over the cement floor of the shed, was washing his teeth with two fingers. Daru looked at him and said, "Come." He went back into the room ahead of the prisoner. He slipped a hunting jacket on over his sweater and put on walking shoes. Standing, he waited until the Arab had put on his *chèche* and sandals. They went into the classroom, and the schoolmaster pointed to the exit saying, "Go ahead." The fellow didn't budge. "I'm coming," said Daru. The Arab went out. Daru went back into the room and made a package with pieces of rusk, dates, and sugar in it. In the classroom, before going out, he hesitated a second in front of his desk, then crossed the threshold and locked the door. "That's the way," he said. He started toward the east, followed by the prisoner. But a short distance from the schoolhouse he thought he heard a slight sound behind him. He retraced his steps and examined the surroundings of the house; there was no one there. The Arab watched him without seeming to understand. "Come on," said Daru.

They walked for an hour and rested beside a sharp needle of limestone. The snow was melting faster and faster and the sun was drinking up the puddles just as quickly, rapidly cleaning the plateau, which gradually dried and vibrated like the air itself. When they resumed walking, the ground rang under their feet. From time to time a bird rent the space in front of them with a joyful cry. Daru felt a sort of rapture before the vast familiar expanse, now almost entirely yellow under its dome of blue sky. They walked an hour more, descending toward the south. They reached a sort of flattened elevation made up of crumbly rocks. From there on, the plateau sloped down—eastward toward a low plain on which could be made out a few spindly trees, and to the south toward outcroppings of rock that gave the landscape a chaotic look.

Daru surveyed the two directions. Not a man could be seen. He turned toward the Arab, who was looking at him blankly. Daru offered the package to him. "Take it," he said. "There are dates, bread, sugar. You can hold out for two days. Here are a thousand francs too."

The Arab took the package and the money but kept his full hands at chest level as if he didn't know what to do with what was being given him.

"Now look," the schoolmaster said as he pointed in the direction of the east, "there's the way to Tinguit. You have a two-hour walk. At Tinguit are the administration and the police. They are expecting you."

The Arab looked toward the east, still holding the package and the   105
money against his chest. Daru took his elbow and turned him rather roughly toward the south. At the foot of the elevation on which they stood could be seen a faint path. "That's the trail across the plateau. In a day's walk from here you'll find pasturelands and the first nomads. They'll take you in and shelter you according to their law."

The Arab had now turned toward Daru, and a sort of panic was visible in his expression. "Listen," he said.

Daru shook his head. "No, be quiet. Now I'm leaving you." He turned his back on him, took two long steps in the direction of the school, looked hesitantly at the motionless Arab, and started off again. For a few minutes he heard nothing but his own step resounding on the cold ground, and he did not turn his head. A moment later, however, he turned around. The Arab was still there on the edge of the hill, his arms hanging now, and he was looking at the schoolmaster. Daru felt something rise in his throat. But he swore with impatience, waved vaguely, and started off again. He had already gone a distance when he again stopped and looked. There was no longer anyone on the hill.

Daru hesitated. The sun was now rather high in the sky and beginning to beat down on his head. The schoolmaster retraced his steps, at first somewhat uncertainly, then with decision. When he reached the little hill, he was bathed in sweat. He climbed it as fast as he could and stopped, out of breath, on the top. The rock fields to the south stood out sharply against the blue sky, but on the plain to the east a steamy heat was rising. And in that slight haze, Daru, with heavy heart, made out the Arab walking slowly on the road to prison.

A little later, standing before the window of the classroom, the schoolmaster was watching the clear light bathing the whole surface of the plateau. Behind him on the blackboard, among the winding French rivers, sprawled the clumsily chalked up words he had just read: "You handed over our brother. You will pay for this." Daru looked at the sky, the plateau, and beyond, the invisible lands stretching all the way to the sea. In this vast landscape he had loved so much, he was alone.

QUESTIONS

1. What is the central conflict of the story? Is it external or internal? Can it be defined in terms of dilemma?
2. Compare and contrast the attitudes of Daru and Balducci toward the prisoner and the situation. What is their attitude toward each other? Is either a bad or a cruel man? How does the conflict between Daru and Balducci intensify the central conflict?
3. Why does Daru give the prisoner his freedom? What reasons are there for not giving him his freedom?
4. In what respect is the title ironic? Why does "The Guest" make a better title than "The Prisoner"? And why does the French title "L'Hôte" (which can mean either "The Guest" or "The Host") make an even better title than its English translation?
5. This story contains the materials of explosive action—a revolver, a murderer, a state of undeclared war, an incipient uprising, a revenge note—but no violence occurs in the story. In what aspect of the situation is Camus principally interested?
6. This story has as its background a specific political situation—the French Algerian crisis in the years following World War II. How does Daru reflect France's plight? Is the story's meaning limited to this situation? What does the story tell us about good and evil and the nature of moral choice? How does the story differ in its treatment of these things from the typical Western story or the patriotic editorial?
7. In what respect is the ending of the story ironic? What kind of irony is this? What does it contribute to the meaning of the story?
8. Besides the ironies of the title and the ending, there are other ironies in the story. Find and explain them. Daru uses verbal irony in paragraph 12 when he exclaims, "Odd pupils!" Is verbal irony the same thing as sarcasm?
9. Comment on the following: (a) Daru's behavior toward firearms and how it helps reveal him; (b) Camus's reason for making the Arab a murderer; (c) the Arab's reason for taking the road to prison.

Flannery O'Connor

Greenleaf

Mrs. May's bedroom window was low and faced on the east and the bull, silvered in the moonlight, stood under it, his head raised as if he listened—like some patient god come down to woo her—for a stir inside the room. The window was dark and the sound of her breathing too light to be carried outside. Clouds crossing the moon blackened him and in the dark he began to tear at the hedge. Presently they passed and he appeared again in the same spot, chewing steadily, with a hedge-wreath that he had ripped loose for himself caught in the tips of his horns. When the moon drifted into retirement again, there was nothing to mark his place but the sound of steady chewing. Then abruptly a pink glow filled the window. Bars of light slid across him as the venetian blind was slit. He took a step backward and lowered his head as if to show the wreath across his horns.

For almost a minute there was no sound from inside, then as he raised his crowned head again, a woman's voice, guttural as if addressed to a dog, said, "Get away from here, Sir!" and in a second muttered, "Some nigger's scrub bull."

The animal pawed the ground and Mrs. May, standing bent forward behind the blind, closed it quickly lest the light make him charge into the shrubbery. For a second she waited, still bent forward, her nightgown hanging loosely from her narrow shoulders. Green rubber curlers sprouted neatly over her forehead and her face beneath them was smooth as concrete with an egg-white paste that drew the wrinkles out while she slept.

She had been conscious in her sleep of a steady rhythmic chewing as if something were eating one wall of the house. She had been aware that whatever it was had been eating as long as she had the place and had eaten everything from the beginning of her fence line up to the house and now was eating the house and calmly with the same steady rhythm would continue through the house, eating her and the boys, and then on, eating everything but the Greenleafs, on and on, eating everything until nothing was left but the Greenleafs on a little island all their own in the middle of what had been her place. When the munching reached her elbow, she jumped up and found herself, fully awake, standing in the middle of her room. She identified the sound at once: a cow was tearing at the shrubbery under the window. Mr. Greenleaf had left the lane gate open and she didn't doubt that the entire

GREENLEAF   First published in 1956. Flannery O'Connor (1925–1964), Roman Catholic by birth and belief, was born in Savannah and lived, from 1938 until 1945, in Milledgeville, Georgia. After five years spent writing in Iowa, New York, and Connecticut, she was stricken with an incurable disease (which had already killed her father) and spent several months in an Atlanta hospital. In the summer of 1951, with the disease only partially checked, she and her mother moved to a dairy farm a few miles outside of Milledgeville, which her mother managed, while she continued to write.

herd was on her lawn. She turned on the dim pink table lamp and then went to the window and slit the blind. The bull, gaunt and long-legged, was standing about four feet from her, chewing calmly like an uncouth country suitor.

5   For fifteen years, she thought as she squinted at him fiercely, she had been having shiftless people's hogs root up her oats, their mules wallow on her lawn, their scrub bulls breed her cows. If this one was not put up now, he would be over the fence, ruining her herd before morning—and Mr. Greenleaf was soundly sleeping a half mile down the road in the tenant house. There was no way to get him unless she dressed and got in her car and rode down there and woke him up. He would come but his expression, his whole figure, his every pause, would say: "Hit looks to me like one or both of them boys would not make their maw ride out in the middle of the night thisaway. If hit was my boys, they would have got the bull up theirself."

The bull lowered his head and shook it and the wreath slipped down to the base of his horns where it looked like a menacing prickly crown. She had closed the blind then; in a few seconds she heard him move off heavily.

Mr. Greenleaf would say, "If hit was my boys they would never have allowed their maw to go after the hired help in the middle of the night. They would have did it theirself."

Weighing it, she decided not to bother Mr. Greenleaf. She returned to bed thinking that if the Greenleaf boys had risen in the world it was because she had given their father employment when no one else would have him. She had had Mr. Greenleaf fifteen years but no one else would have had him five minutes. Just the way he approached an object was enough to tell anybody with eyes what kind of a worker he was. He walked with a high-shouldered creep and he never appeared to come directly forward. He walked on the perimeter of some invisible circle and if you wanted to look him in the face, you had to move and get in front of him. She had not fired him because she had always doubted she could do better. He was too shiftless to go out and look for another job; he didn't have the initiative to steal, and after she had told him three or four times to do a thing, he did it; but he never told her about a sick cow until it was too late to call the veterinarian and if her barn had caught fire, he would have called his wife to see the flames before he began to put them out. And of the wife, she didn't even like to think. Beside the wife, Mr. Greenleaf was an aristocrat.

"If hit had been my boys," he would have said, "they would have cut off their right arm before they would have allowed their maw to . . ."

10   "If your boys had any pride, Mr. Greenleaf," she would like to say to him some day, "there are many things that they would not *allow* their mother to do."

The next morning as soon as Mr. Greenleaf came to the back door, she told him there was a stray bull on the place and that she wanted him penned up at once.

"Done already been here three days," he said, addressing his right foot which he held forward, turned slightly as if he were trying to look at the sole. He was standing at the bottom of the three back steps while she leaned out the kitchen door, a small woman with pale near-sighted eyes and grey hair that rose on top like the crest of some disturbed bird.

"Three days!" she said in the restrained screech that had become habitual with her.

Mr. Greenleaf, looking into the distance over the near pasture, removed a package of cigarets from his shirt pocket and let one fall into his hand. He put the package back and stood for a while looking at the cigaret. "I put him in the bull pen but he torn out of there," he said presently. "I didn't see him none after that." He bent over the cigaret and lit it and then turned his head briefly in her direction. The upper part of his face sloped gradually into the lower which was long and narrow, shaped like a rough chalice. He had deep-set fox-colored eyes shadowed under a grey felt hat that he wore slanted forward following the line of his nose. His build was insignificant.

"Mr. Greenleaf," she said, "get the bull up this morning before you do   15
anything else. You know he'll ruin the breeding schedule. Get him up and keep him up and the next time there's a stray bull on this place, tell me at once. Do you understand?"

"Where do you want him put at?" Mr. Greenleaf asked.

"I don't care where you put him," she said. "You are supposed to have some sense. Put him where he can't get out. Whose bull is he?"

For a moment Mr. Greenleaf seemed to hesitate between silence and speech. He studied the air to the left of him. "He must be somebody's bull," he said after a while.

"Yes, he must!" she said and shut the door with a precise little slam.

She went into the dining room where the two boys were eating breakfast   20
and sat down on the edge of her chair at the head of the table. She never ate breakfast but she sat with them to see that they had what they wanted. "Honestly!" she said, and began to tell about the bull, aping Mr. Greenleaf saying, "It must be *somebody's* bull."

Wesley continued to read the newspaper folded beside his plate but Scofield interrupted his eating from time to time to look at her and laugh. The two boys never had the same reaction to anything. They were as different, she said, as night and day. The only thing they did have in common was neither of them cared what happened on the place. Scofield was a business type and Wesley was an intellectual.

Wesley, the younger child, had had rheumatic fever when he was seven and Mrs. May thought that this was what had caused him to be an intellectual. Scofield, who had never had a day's sickness in his life, was an insurance salesman. She would not have minded his selling insurance if he had sold a nicer kind but he sold the kind that only Negroes buy. He was what Negroes call a "policy man." He said there was more money in nigger-insurance than any other kind, and before company, he was very loud about it. He would shout, "Mama don't like to hear me say it but I'm the best nigger-insurance salesman in this county!"

Scofield was thirty-six and he had a broad pleasant face but he was not married. "Yes," Mrs. May would say, "and if you sold decent insurance, some *nice* girl would be willing to marry you. What nice girl wants to marry a nigger-insurance man? You'll wake up some day and it'll be too late."

And at this Scofield would yodel and say, "Why Mamma, I'm not going to marry until you're dead and gone and then I'm going to marry me some nice fat girl that can take over this place!" And once he had added, "—some nice lady like Mrs. Greenleaf." When he had said this Mrs. May had risen from her chair, her back stiff as a rake handle, and had gone to her room. There she had sat down on the edge of her bed for some time with her small face drawn. Finally she had whispered, "I work and slave, I struggle and sweat to keep this place for them and as soon as I'm dead, they'll marry trash and bring it in here and ruin everything. They'll marry trash and ruin everything I've done," and she had made up her mind at that moment to change her will. The next day she had gone to her lawyer and had had the property entailed so that if they married, they could not leave it to their wives.

25   The idea that one of them might marry a woman even remotely like Mrs. Greenleaf was enough to make her ill. She had put up with Mr. Greenleaf for fifteen years, but the only way she had endured his wife had been by keeping entirely out of her sight. Mrs. Greenleaf was large and loose. The yard around her house looked like a dump and her five girls were always filthy; even the youngest one dipped snuff. Instead of making a garden or washing their clothes, her preoccupation was what she called "prayer healing."

Every day she cut all the morbid stories out of the newspaper—the accounts of women who had been raped and criminals who had escaped and children who had been burned and of train wrecks and plane crashes and the divorces of movie stars. She took these to the woods and dug a hole and buried them and then she fell on the ground over them and mumbled and groaned for an hour or so, moving her huge arms back and forth under her and out again and finally just lying down flat and, Mrs. May suspected, going to sleep in the dirt.

She had not found out about this until the Greenleafs had been with her a few months. One morning she had been out to inspect a field that she wanted planted in rye but that had come up in clover because Mr. Greenleaf had used the wrong seeds in the grain drill. She was returning through a wooded path that separated two pastures, muttering to herself and hitting the ground methodically with a long stick she carried in case she saw a snake. "Mr. Greenleaf," she was saying in a low voice, "I cannot afford to pay for your mistakes. I am a poor woman and this place is all I have. I have two boys to educate. I cannot . . ."

Out of nowhere a guttural agonized voice groaned, "Jesus! Jesus!" In a second it came again with a terrible urgency. "Jesus! Jesus!"

Mrs. May stopped still, one hand lifted to her throat. The sound was so piercing that she felt as if some violent unleashed force had broken out of the ground and was charging toward her. Her second thought was more reasonable: somebody had been hurt on the place and would sue her for everything she had. She had no insurance. She rushed forward and turning a bend in the path, she saw Mrs. Greenleaf sprawled on her hands and knees off the side of the road, her head down.

"Mrs. Greenleaf!" she shrilled, "what's happened?"   30

Mrs. Greenleaf raised her head. Her face was a patchwork of dirt and tears and her small eyes, the color of two field peas, were red-rimmed and swollen, but her expression was as composed as a bulldog's. She swayed back and forth on her hands and knees and groaned, "Jesus, Jesus."

Mrs. May winced. She thought the word, Jesus, should be kept inside the church building like other words inside the bedroom. She was a good Christian woman with a large respect for religion, though she did not, of course, believe any of it was true. "What is the matter with you?" she asked sharply.

"You broke my healing," Mrs. Greenleaf said, waving her aside. "I can't talk to you until I finish."

Mrs. May stood, bent forward, her mouth open and her stick raised off the ground as if she were not sure what she wanted to strike with it.

"Oh, Jesus, stab me in the heart!" Mrs. Greenleaf shrieked. "Jesus, stab   35 me in the heart!" and she fell back flat in the dirt, a huge human mound, her legs and arms spread out as if she were trying to wrap them around the earth.

Mrs. May felt as furious and helpless as if she had been insulted by a child. "Jesus," she said, drawing herself back, "would be *ashamed* of you. He would tell you to get up from there this instant and go wash your children's clothes!" and she had turned and walked off as fast as she could.

Whenever she thought of how the Greenleaf boys had advanced in the world, she had only to think of Mrs. Greenleaf sprawled obscenely on the ground, and say to herself, "Well, no matter how far they go, they *came* from that."

She would like to have been able to put in her will that when she died, Wesley and Scofield were not to continue to employ Mr. Greenleaf. She was capable of handling Mr. Greenleaf; they were not. Mr. Greenleaf had pointed out to her once that her boys didn't know hay from silage. She had pointed out to him that they had other talents, that Scofield was a successful businessman and Wesley a successful intellectual. Mr. Greenleaf did not comment, but he never lost an opportunity of letting her see, by his expression or some simple gesture, that he held the two of them in infinite contempt. As scrub-human as the Greenleafs were, he never hesitated to let her know that in any like circumstance in which his own boys might have been involved, they—O. T. and E. T. Greenleaf—would have acted to better advantage.

The Greenleaf boys were two or three years younger than the May boys. They were twins and you never knew when you spoke to one of them

whether you were speaking to O. T. or E. T., and they never had the politeness to enlighten you. They were long-legged and raw-boned and red-
skinned, with bright grasping fox-colored eyes like their father's. Mr. Greenleaf's pride in them began with the fact that they were twins. He acted,
Mrs. May said, as if this were something smart they had thought of themselves. They were energetic and hard-working and she would admit to anyone that they had come a long way—and that the Second World War was
responsible for it.

40   They had both joined the service and, disguised in their uniforms,
they could not be told from other people's children. You could tell, of course,
when they opened their mouths but they did that seldom. The smartest thing
they had done was to get sent overseas and there to marry French wives.
They hadn't married French trash either. They had married nice girls who
naturally couldn't tell that they murdered the king's English or that the
Greenleafs were who they were.

She Wesley's heart condition had not permitted him to serve his country but
Scofield had been in the army for two years. He had not cared for it and at the
end of his military service, he was only a Private First Class. The Greenleaf
boys were both some kind of sergeants, and Mr. Greenleaf, in those days,
had never lost an opportunity of referring to them by their rank. They had
both managed to get wounded and now they both had pensions. Further, as
soon as they were released from the army, they took advantage of all the
benefits and went to the school of agriculture at the university—the tax-
payers meanwhile supporting their French wives. The two of them were
living now about two miles down the highway on a piece of land that the government had helped them to buy and in a brick duplex bungalow that the
government had helped to build and pay for. If the war had made anyone,
Mrs. May said, it had made the Greenleaf boys. They each had three little
children apiece, who spoke Greenleaf English and French, and who, on account of their mothers' background, would be sent to the convent school and
brought up with manners. "And in twenty years," Mrs. May asked Scofield
and Wesley, "do you know what those people will be?"

"*Society,*" she said blackly.

She had spent fifteen years coping with Mr. Greenleaf and, by now, handling him had become second nature with her. His disposition on any particular day was as much a factor in what she could and couldn't do as the
weather was, and she had learned to read his face the way real country people
read the sunrise and sunset.

She was a country woman only by persuasion. The late Mr. May, a businessman, had bought the place when land was down, and when he died it
was all he had to leave her. The boys had not been happy to move to the
country to a broken-down farm, but there was nothing else for her to do. She
had the timber on the place cut and with the proceeds had set herself up in
the dairy business after Mr. Greenleaf had answered her ad. "i seen yor add
and i will come have 2 boys," was all his letter said, but he arrived the next

day in a pieced-together truck, his wife and five daughters sitting on the floor in the back, himself and the two boys in the cab.

Over the years they had been on her place, Mr. and Mrs. Greenleaf had 45 aged hardly at all. They had no worries, no responsibilities. They lived like the lilies of the field, off the fat that she struggled to put into the land. When she was dead and gone from overwork and worry, the Greenleafs, healthy and thriving, would be just ready to begin draining Scofield and Wesley.

Wesley said the reason Mrs. Greenleaf had not aged was because she released all her emotions in prayer healing. "You ought to start praying, Sweetheart," he had said in the voice that, poor boy, he could not help making deliberately nasty.

Scofield only exasperated her beyond endurance but Wesley caused her real anxiety. He was thin and nervous and bald and being an intellectual was a terrible strain on his disposition. She doubted if he would marry until she died but she was certain that then the wrong woman would get him. Nice girls didn't like Scofield but Wesley didn't like nice girls. He didn't like anything. He drove twenty miles every day to the university where he taught and twenty miles back every night, but he said he hated the twenty-mile drive and he hated the second-rate university and he hated the morons who attended it. He hated the country and he hated the life he lived; he hated living with his mother and his idiot brother and he hated hearing about the damn dairy and the damn help and the damn broken machinery. But in spite of all he said, he never made any move to leave. He talked about Paris and Rome but he never went even to Atlanta.

"You'd go to those places and you'd get sick," Mrs. May would say. "Who in Paris is going to see that you get a salt-free diet? And do you think if you married one of those odd numbers you take out that *she* would cook a salt-free diet for you? No indeed, she would not!" When she took this line, Wesley would turn himself roughly around in his chair and ignore her. Once when she had kept it up too long, he had snarled, "Well, why don't you do something practical, Woman? Why don't you pray for me like Mrs. Greenleaf would?"

"I don't like to hear you boys make jokes about religion," she had said. "If you would go to church, you would meet some nice girls."

But it was impossible to tell them anything. When she looked at the two 50 of them now, sitting on either side of the table, neither one caring the least if a stray bull ruined her herd—which was their herd, their future—when she looked at the two of them, one hunched over a paper and the other teetering back in his chair, grinning at her like an idiot, she wanted to jump up and beat her fist on the table and shout, "You'll find out one of these days, you'll find out what *Reality* is when it's too late!"

"Mamma," Scofield said, "don't you get excited now but I'll tell you whose bull that is." He was looking at her wickedly. He let his chair drop forward and he got up. Then with his shoulders bent and his hands held up to cover his head, he tiptoed to the door. He backed into the hall and pulled the door almost to so that it hid all of him but his face. "You want to know, Sugar-pie?" he asked.

Mrs. May sat looking at him coldly.

"That's O. T. and E. T.'s bull," he said. "I collected from their nigger yesterday and he told me they were missing it," and he showed her an exaggerated expanse of teeth and disappeared silently.

Wesley looked up and laughed.

55   Mrs. May turned her head forward again, her expression unaltered. "I am the only *adult* on this place," she said. She leaned across the table and pulled the paper from the side of his plate. "Do you see how it's going to be when I die and you boys have to handle him?" she began. "Do you see why he didn't know whose bull that was? Because it was theirs. Do you see what I have to put up with? Do you see that if I hadn't kept my foot on his neck all these years, you boys might be milking cows every morning at four o'clock?"

Wesley pulled the paper back toward his plate and staring at her full in the face, he murmured, "I wouldn't milk a cow to save your soul from hell."

"I know you wouldn't," she said in a brittle voice. She sat back and began rapidly turning her knife over at the side of her plate. "O. T. and E. T. are fine boys," she said. "They ought to have been my sons." The thought of this was so horrible that her vision of Wesley was blurred at once by a wall of tears. All she saw was his dark shape, rising quickly from the table. "And you two," she cried, "you two should have belonged to that woman!"

He was heading for the door.

"When I die," she said in a thin voice, "I don't know what's going to become of you."

60   "You're always yapping about when-you-die," he growled as he rushed out, "but you look pretty healthy to me."

For some time she sat where she was, looking straight ahead through the window across the room into a scene of indistinct grays and greens. She stretched her face and her neck muscles and drew in a long breath but the scene in front of her flowed together anyway into a watery gray mass. "They needn't think I'm going to die any time soon," she muttered, and some more defiant voice in her added: I'll die when I get good and ready.

She wiped her eyes with the table napkin and got up and went to the window and gazed at the scene in front of her. The cows were grazing on two pale green pastures across the road and behind them, fencing them in, was a black wall of trees with a sharp sawtooth edge that held off the indifferent sky. The pastures were enough to calm her. When she looked out any window in her house, she saw the reflection of her own character. Her city friends said she was the most remarkable woman they knew, to go, practically penniless and with no experience, out to a rundown farm and make a success of it. "Everything is against you," she would say, "the weather is against you and the dirt is against you and the help is against you. They're all in league against you. There's nothing for it but an iron hand!"

"Look at Mamma's iron hand!" Scofield would yell and grab her arm and hold it up so that her delicate blue-veined little hand would dangle from her wrist like the head of a broken lily. The company always laughed.

The sun, moving over the black and white grazing cows, was just a little brighter than the rest of the sky. Looking down, she saw a darker shape that might have been its shadow cast at an angle, moving among them. She uttered a sharp cry and turned and marched out of the house.

Mr. Greenleaf was in the trench silo, filling a wheelbarrow. She stood on   65
the edge and looked down at him. "I told you to get up that bull. Now he's in with the milk herd."

"You can't do two thangs at oncet," Mr. Greenleaf remarked.

"I told you to do that first."

He wheeled the barrow out of the open end of the trench toward the barn and she followed close behind him. "And you needn't think, Mr. Greenleaf," she said, "that I don't know exactly whose bull that is or why you haven't been in any hurry to notify me he was here. I might as well feed O. T. and E. T.'s bull as long as I'm going to have him here ruining my herd."

Mr. Greenleaf paused with the wheelbarrow and looked behind him "Is that them boys' bull?" he asked in an incredulous tone.

She did not say a word. She merely looked away with her mouth taut.   70

"They told me their bull was out but I never known that was him," he said.

"I want that bull put up now," she said, "and I'm going to drive over to O. T. and E. T.'s and tell them they'll have to come get him today. I ought to charge for the time he's been here—then it wouldn't happen again."

"They didn't pay but seventy-five dollars for him," Mr. Greenleaf offered.

"I wouldn't have had him as a gift," she said.

"They was just going to beef him," Mr. Greenleaf went on, "but he got   75
loose and run his head into their pickup truck. He don't like cars and trucks. They had a time getting his horn out the fender and when they finally got him loose, he took off and they was too tired to run after him—but I never known that was him there."

"It wouldn't have paid you to know, Mr. Greenleaf," she said. "But you know now. Get a horse and get him."

In a half hour, from her front window she saw the bull, squirrel-colored, with jutting hips and long light horns, ambling down the dirt road that ran in front of the house. Mr. Greenleaf was behind him on the horse. "That's a Greenleaf bull if I ever saw one," she muttered. She went out on the porch and called, "Put him where he can't get out."

"He likes to bust loose," Mr. Greenleaf said, looking with approval at the bull's rump. "This gentleman is a sport."

"If those boys don't come for him, he's going to be a dead sport," she said. "I'm just warning you."

80   He heard her but he didn't answer.
"That's the awfullest looking bull I ever saw," she called but he was too far down the road to hear.

It was mid-morning when she turned into O. T. and E. T.'s driveway. The house, a new red-brick, low-to-the-ground building that looked like a warehouse with windows, was on top of a treeless hill. The sun was beating down directly on the white roof of it. It was the kind of house that everybody built now and nothing marked it as belonging to Greenleafs except three dogs, part hound and part spitz, that rushed out from behind it as soon as she stopped her car. She reminded herself that you could always tell the class of people by the class of dog, and honked her horn. While she sat waiting for someone to come, she continued to study the house. All the windows were down and she wondered if the government could have air-conditioned the thing. No one came and she honked again. Presently a door opened and several children appeared in it and stood looking at her, making no move to come forward. She recognized this as a true Greenleaf trait—they could hang in the door, looking at you for hours.
"Can't one of you children come here?" she called.
After a minute they all began to move forward, slowly. They had on overalls and were barefooted but they were not as dirty as she might have expected. There were two or three that looked distinctly like Greenleafs; the others not so much so. The smallest child was a girl with untidy black hair. They stopped about six feet from the automobile and stood looking at her.

85   "You're mighty pretty," Mrs. May said, addressing herself to the smallest girl.
There was no answer. They appeared to share one dispassionate expression between them.
"Where's your Mamma?" she asked.
There was no answer to this for some time. Then one of them said something in French. Mrs. May did not speak French.
"Where's your daddy?" she asked.

90   After a while, one of the boys said, "He ain't hyar neither."
"Ahhhh," Mrs. May said as if something had been proven. "Where's the colored man?"
She waited and decided no one was going to answer. "The cat has six little tongues," she said. "How would you like to come home with me and let me teach you how to talk?" She laughed and her laugh died on the silent air. She felt as if she were on trial for her life, facing a jury of Greenleafs. "I'll go down and see if I can find the colored man," she said.
"You can go if you want to," one of the boys said.
"Well, thank you," she murmured and drove off.

95   The barn was down the lane from the house. She had not seen it before

but Mr. Greenleaf had described it in detail for it had been built according to the latest specifications. It was a milking parlor arrangement where the cows are milked from below. The milk ran in pipes from the machines to the milk house and was never carried in no bucket, Mr. Greenleaf said, by no human hand. "When you gonter get you one?" he had asked.

"Mr. Greenleaf," she had said, "I have to do for myself. I am not assisted hand and foot by the government. It would cost me $20,000 to install a milking parlor. I barely make ends meet as it is."

"My boys done it," Mr. Greenleaf had murmured and then—"but all boys ain't alike."

"No indeed!" she had said. "I thank God for that!"

"I thank Gawd for ever-thang," Mr. Greenleaf had drawled.

You might as well, she had thought in the fierce silence that followed;   100
you've never done anything for yourself.

She stopped by the side of the barn and honked but no one appeared. For several minutes she sat in the car, observing the various machines parked around, wondering how many of them were paid for. They had a forage harvester and a rotary hay baler. She had those too. She decided that since no one was here, she would get out and have a look at the milking parlor and see if they kept it clean.

She opened the milking room door and stuck her head in and for the first second she felt as if she were going to lose her breath. The spotless white concrete room was filled with sunlight that came from a row of windows head-high along both walls. The metal stanchions gleamed ferociously and she had to squint to be able to look at all. She drew her head out the room quickly and closed the door and leaned against it, frowning. The light outside was not so bright but she was conscious that the sun was directly on top of her head, like a silver bullet ready to drop into her brain.

A Negro carrying a yellow calf-feed bucket appeared from around the corner of the machine shed and came toward her. He was a light yellow boy dressed in the cast-off army clothes of the Greenleaf twins. He stopped at a respectable distance and set the bucket on the ground.

"Where's Mr. O. T. and Mr. E. T.?" she asked.

"Mist O. T. he in town, Mist E. T. he off yonder in the field," the Negro   105
said, pointing first to the left and then to the right as if he were naming the position of two planets.

"Can you remember a message?" she asked, looking as if she thought this doubtful.

"I'll remember it if I don't forget it," he said with a touch of sullenness.

"Well, I'll write it down then," she said. She got in her car and took a stub of pencil from her pocket book and began to write on the back of an empty envelope. The Negro came and stood at the window. "I'm Mrs. May," she said as she wrote. "Their bull is on my place and I want him off *today*. You can tell them I'm furious about it."

"That bull lef here Sareday," the Negro said, "and none of us ain't seen him since. We ain't knowed where he was."

110   "Well, you know now," she said, "and you can tell Mr. O. T. and Mr. E. T. that if they don't come get him today, I'm going to have their daddy shoot him the first thing in the morning. I can't have that bull ruining my herd." She handed him the note.

"If I knows Mist O. T. and Mist E. T.," he said, taking it, "they goin to say go ahead on and shoot him. He done busted up one of our trucks already and we be glad to see the last of him."

She pulled her head back and gave him a look from slightly bleared eyes. "Do they expect me to take my time and my worker to shoot their bull?" she asked. "They don't want him so they just let him loose and expect somebody else to kill him? He's eating my oats and ruining my herd and I'm expected to shoot him too?"

"I speck you is," he said softly. "He done busted up . . ."

She gave him a very sharp look and said, "Well, I'm not surprised. That's just the way some people are," and after a second she asked, "Which is boss, Mr. O. T. or Mr. E. T.?" She had always suspected that they fought between themselves secretly.

115   "They never quarls," the boy said. "They like one man in two skins."

"Hmp. I expect you just never heard them quarrel."

"Nor nobody else heard them neither," he said, looking away as if this insolence were addressed to someone else.

"Well," she said, "I haven't put up with their father for fifteen years not to know a few things about Greenleafs."

The Negro looked at her suddenly with a gleam of recognition. "Is you my policy man's mother?" he asked.

120   "I don't know who your policy man is," she said sharply. "You give them that note and tell them if they don't come for that bull today, they'll be making their father shoot it tomorrow," and she drove off.

She stayed at home all afternoon waiting for the Greenleaf twins to come for the bull. They did not come. I might as well be working for them, she thought furiously. They are simply going to use me to the limit. At the supper table, she went over it again for the boys' benefit because she wanted them to see exactly what O. T. and E. T. would do. "They don't want that bull," she said, "—pass the butter—so they simply turn him loose and let somebody else worry about getting rid of him for them. How do you like that? I'm the victim. I've always been the victim."

"Pass the butter to the victim," Wesley said. He was in a worse humor than usual because he had had a flat tire on the way home from the university.

Scofield handed her the butter and said, "Why, Mamma, ain't you ashamed to shoot an old bull that ain't done nothing but give you a little scrub strain in your herd? I declare," he said, "with the Mamma I got it's a wonder I turned out to be such a nice boy!"

"You ain't her boy, Son," Wesley said.

She eased back in her chair, her fingertips on the edge of the table.   125

"All I know is," Scofield said, "I done mighty well to be as nice as I am seeing what I come from."

When they teased her they spoke Greenleaf English but Wesley made his own particular tone come through it like a knife edge. "Well lemme tell you one thang, Brother," he said, leaning over the table, "that if you had half a mind you would already know."

"What's that, Brother?" Scofield asked, his broad face grinning into the thin constricted one across from him.

"That is," Wesley said, "that neither you nor me is her boy. . . . ," but he stopped abruptly as she gave a kind of hoarse wheeze like an old horse lashed unexpectedly. She reared up and ran from the room.

"Oh, for God's sake," Wesley growled, "what did you start her off for?"   130

"I never started her off," Scofield said. "You started her off."

"Hah."

"She's not as young as she used to be and she can't take it."

"She can only give it out," Wesley said. "I'm the one that takes it."

His brother's pleasant face had changed so that an ugly family resem-   135
blance showed between them. "Nobody feels sorry for a lousy bastard like you," he said and grabbed across the table for the other's shirtfront.

From her room she heard a crash of dishes and she rushed back through the kitchen into the dining room. The hall door was open and Scofield was going out of it. Wesley was lying like a large bug on his back with the edge of the over-turned table cutting him across the middle and broken dishes scattered on top of him. She pulled the table off him and caught his arm to help him rise but he scrambled up and pushed her off with a furious charge of energy and flung himself out the door after his brother.

She would have collapsed but a knock on the door stiffened her and she swung around. Across the kitchen and back porch, she could see Mr. Greenleaf peering eagerly through the screenwire. All her resources returned in full strength as if she had only needed to be challenged by the devil himself to regain them. "I heard a thump," he called, "and I thought the plastering might have fell on you."

If he had been wanted someone would have had to go on a horse to find him. She crossed the kitchen and the porch and stood inside the screen and said, "No, nothing happened but the table turned over. One of the legs was weak," and without pausing, "the boys didn't come for the bull so tomorrow you'll have to shoot him."

The sky was crossed with thin red and purple bars and behind them the sun was moving down slowly as if it were descending a ladder. Mr. Greenleaf squatted down on the step, his back to her, the top of his hat on a level with her feet. "Tomorrow I'll drive him home for you," he said.

"Oh no, Mr. Greenleaf," she said in a mocking voice, "you drive him   140
home tomorrow and next week he'll be back here. I know better than that."

Then in a mournful tone, she said, "I'm surprised at O. T. and E. T. to treat me this way. I thought they'd have more gratitude. Those boys spent some mighty happy days on this place, didn't they, Mr. Greenleaf?"

Mr. Greenleaf didn't say anything.

"I think they did," she said. "I think they did. But they've forgotten all the nice little things I did for them now. If I recall, they wore my boys' old clothes and played with my boys' old toys and hunted with my boys' old guns. They swam in my pond and shot my birds and fished in my stream and I never forgot their birthday and Christmas seemed to roll around very often if I remember it right. And do they think of any of those things now?" she asked. "NOOOOO," she said.

For a few seconds she looked at the disappearing sun and Mr. Greenleaf examined the palms of his hands. Presently as if it had just occurred to her, she asked, "Do you know the real reason they didn't come for that bull?"

"Naw I don't," Mr. Greenleaf said in a surly voice.

145   "They didn't come because I'm a woman," she said. "You can get away with anything when you're dealing with a woman. If there were a man running this place . . ."

Quick as a snake striking Mr. Greenleaf said, "You got two boys. They know you got two men on the place."

The sun had disappeared behind the tree line. She looked down at the dark crafty face, upturned now, and at the wary eyes, bright under the shadow of the hatbrim. She waited long enough for him to see that she was hurt and then she said, "Some people learn gratitude too late, Mr. Greenleaf, and some never learn it at all," and she turned and left him sitting on the steps.

Half the night in her sleep she heard a sound as if some large stone were grinding a hole on the outside wall of her brain. She was walking on the inside, over a succession of beautiful rolling hills, planting her stick in front of each step. She became aware after a time that the noise was the sun trying to burn through the tree line and she stopped to watch, safe in the knowledge that it couldn't, that it had to sink the way it always did outside of her property. When she first stopped it was a swollen red ball, but as she stood watching it began to narrow and pale until it looked like a bullet. Then suddenly it burst through the tree line and raced down the hill toward her. She woke up with her hand over her mouth and the same noise, diminished but distinct, in her ear. It was the bull munching under her window. Mr. Greenleaf had let him out.

She got up and made her way to the window in the dark and looked out through the slit blind, but the bull had moved away from the hedge and at first she didn't see him. Then she saw a heavy form some distance away, paused as if observing her. This is the last night I am going to put up with this, she said, and watched until the iron shadow moved away in the darkness.

150   The next morning she waited until exactly eleven o'clock. Then she got in her car and drove to the barn. Mr. Greenleaf was cleaning milk cans. He

had seven of them standing up outside the milk room to get the sun. She had been telling him to do this for two weeks. "All right, Mr. Greenleaf," she said, "go get your gun. We're going to shoot that bull."

"I thought you wanted theseyer cans . . ."

"Go get your gun, Mr. Greenleaf," she said. Her voice and face were expressionless.

"That gentleman torn out of there last night," he murmured in a tone of regret and bent again to the can he had his arm in.

"Go get your gun, Mr. Greenleaf," she said in the same triumphant tone-less voice. "The bull is in the pasture with the dry cows. I saw him from my upstairs window. I'm going to drive you up to the field and you can run him into the empty pasture and shoot him there."

He detached himself from the can slowly. "Ain't nobody ever ast me to   155
shoot my boys' own bull!" he said in a high rasping voice. He removed a rag from his back pocket and began to wipe his hands violently, then his nose.

She turned as if she had not heard this and said, "I'll wait for you in the car. Go get your gun."

She sat in the car and watched him stalk off toward the harness room where he kept a gun. After he had entered the room, there was a crash as if he had kicked something out of his way. Presently he emerged again with the gun, circled behind the car, opened the door violently and threw himself onto the seat beside her. He held the gun between his knees and looked straight ahead. He'd like to shoot me instead of the bull, she thought, and turned her face away so that he could not see her smile.

The morning was dry and clear. She drove through the woods for a quar-ter of a mile and then out into the open where there were fields on either side of the narrow road. The exhilaration of carrying her point had sharpened her senses. Birds were screaming everywhere, the grass was almost too bright to look at, the sky was an even piercing blue. "Spring is here!" she said gaily. Mr. Greenleaf lifted one muscle somewhere near his mouth as if he found this the most asinine remark ever made. When she stopped at the second pasture gate, he flung himself out of the car door and slammed it behind him. Then he opened the gate and she drove through. He closed it and flung himself back in, silently, and she drove around the rim of the pasture until she spotted the bull, almost in the center of it, grazing peacefully among the cows.

"The gentleman is waiting on you," she said and gave Mr. Greenleaf's furious profile a sly look. "Run him into that next pasture and when you get him in, I'll drive in behind you and shut the gate myself."

He flung himself out again, this time deliberately leaving the car door   160
open so that she had to lean across the seat and close it. She sat smiling as she watched him make his way across the pasture toward the opposite gate. He seemed to throw himself forward at each step and then pull back as if he were calling on some power to witness that he was being forced. "Well," she said aloud as if he were still in the car, "it's your own boys who are making you do this, Mr. Greenleaf." O. T. and E. T. were probably splitting their sides

laughing at him now. She could hear their identical nasal voices saying, "Made Daddy shoot our bull for us. Daddy don't know no better than to think that's a fine bull he's shooting. Gonna kill Daddy to shoot that bull!"

"If those boys cared a thing about you, Mr. Greenleaf," she said, "they would have come for that bull. I'm surprised at them."

He was circling around to open the gate first. The bull, dark among the spotted cows, had not moved. He kept his head down, eating constantly. Mr. Greenleaf opened the gate and then began circling back to approach him from the rear. When he was about ten feet behind him, he flapped his arms at his sides. The bull lifted his head indolently and then lowered it again and continued to eat. Mr. Greenleaf stooped again and picked up something and threw it at him with a vicious swing. She decided it was a sharp rock for the bull leapt and then began to gallop until he disappeared over the rim of the hill. Mr. Greenleaf followed at his leisure.

"You needn't think you're going to lose him!" she cried and started the car straight across the pasture. She had to drive slowly over the terraces and when she reached the gate, Mr. Greenleaf and the bull were nowhere in sight. This pasture was smaller than the last, a green arena, encircled almost entirely by woods. She got out and closed the gate and stood looking for some sign of Mr. Greenleaf but he had disappeared completely. She knew at once that his plan was to lose the bull in the woods. Eventually, she would see him emerge somewhere from the circle of trees and come limping toward her and when he finally reached her, he would say, "If you can find that gentleman in them woods, you're better than me."

She was going to say, "Mr. Greenleaf, if I have to walk into those woods with you and stay all afternoon, we are going to find that bull and shoot him. You are going to shoot him if I have to pull the trigger for you." When he saw she meant business, he would return and shoot the bull quickly himself.

165 She got back into the car and drove to the center of the pasture where he would not have so far to walk to reach her when he came out of the woods. At this moment she could picture him sitting on a stump, making lines in the ground with a stick. She decided she would wait exactly ten minutes by her watch. Then she would begin to honk. She got out of the car and walked around a little and then sat down on the front bumper to wait and rest. She was very tired and she lay her head back against the hood and closed her eyes. She did not understand why she should be so tired when it was only mid-morning. Through her closed eyes, she could feel the sun, red-hot overhead. She opened her eyes slightly but the white light forced her to close them again.

For some time she lay back against the hood, wondering drowsily why she was so tired. With her eyes closed, she didn't think of time as divided into days and nights but into past and future. She decided she was tired because she had been working continuously for fifteen years. She decided she had every right to be tired, and to rest for a few minutes before she began working again. Before any kind of judgment seat, she would be able to say:

I've worked, I have not wallowed. At this very instant while she was recalling a lifetime of work, Mr. Greenleaf was loitering in the woods and Mrs. Greenleaf was probably flat on the ground, asleep over her holeful of clippings. The woman had got worse over the years and Mrs. May believed that now she was actually demented. "I'm afraid your wife has let religion warp her," she said once tactfully to Mr. Greenleaf. "Everything in moderation, you know."

"She cured a man oncet that half his gut was eat out with worms," Mr. Greenleaf said, and she had turned away, half-sickened. Poor souls, she thought now, so simple. For a few seconds she dozed.

When she sat up and looked at her watch, more than ten minutes had passed. She had not heard any shot. A new thought occurred to her; suppose Mr. Greenleaf had aroused the bull chunking stones at him and the animal had turned on him and run him up against a tree and gored him? The irony of it deepened: O. T. and E. T. would then get a shyster lawyer and sue her. It would be the fitting end to her fifteen years with the Greenleafs. She thought of it almost with pleasure as if she had hit on the perfect ending for a story she was telling her friends. Then she dropped it, for Mr. Greenleaf had a gun with him and she had insurance.

She decided to honk. She got up and reached inside the car window and gave three sustained honks and two or three shorter ones to let him know she was getting impatient. Then she went back and sat down on the bumper again.

In a few minutes something emerged from the tree line, a black heavy shadow that tossed its head several times and then bounded forward. After a second she saw it was the bull. He was crossing the pasture toward her at a slow gallop, a gay almost rocking gait as if he were overjoyed to find her again. She looked beyond him to see if Mr. Greenleaf was coming out of the woods too but he was not. "Here he is, Mr. Greenleaf!" she called and looked on the other side of the pasture to see if he could be coming out there but he was not in sight. She looked back and saw that the bull, his head lowered, was racing toward her. She remained perfectly still, not in fright, but in a freezing disbelief. She stared at the violent black streak bounding toward her as if she had no sense of distance, as if she could not decide at once what his intention was, and the bull had buried his head in her lap, like a wild tormented lover, before her expression changed. One of his horns sank until it pierced her heart and the other curved around her side and held her in an unbreakable grip. She continued to stare straight ahead but the entire scene in front of her had changed—the tree line was a dark wound in a world that was nothing but sky—and she had the look of a person whose sight has been suddenly restored but who finds the light unbearable.

Mr. Greenleaf was running toward her from the side with his gun raised and she saw him coming though she was not looking in his direction. She saw him approaching on the outside of some invisible circle, the tree line gaping behind him and nothing under his feet. He shot the bull four times through

170

the eye. She did not hear the shots but she felt the quake in the huge body as it sank, pulling her forward on its head, so that she seemed, when Mr. Greenleaf reached her, to be bent over whispering some last discovery into the animal's ear.

QUESTIONS

1. The characters and events of the story are almost entirely reflected through Mrs. May's mind. How objective are her evaluations? How far are they reliable testimony and how far only an index of her own mind?

2. What is Mrs. May's mental image of herself? How does it compare with the image her sons have of her? How does it compare with the reader's image?

3. What is Mrs. May's dominant emotion? What is the consuming preoccupation of her mind? Are there any occasions on which she feels joy? What are they?

4. Describe the behavior of Mrs. May and Greenleaf toward each other. Why does Mrs. May keep Greenleaf on when she despises him so?

5. The two families—the Mays and the Greenleafs—are obviously contrasted. Describe this contrast as fully as possible, considering especially the following: (a) their social and economic status—past, present, and future; (b) their religious attitudes; (c) the attitudes of Mrs. May and Greenleaf respectively toward their children; (d) Wesley and Scofield versus O. T. and E. T. What are the reasons for Mrs. May's feelings toward the Greenleafs?

6. The turning point of the story comes when Mrs. May commands Greenleaf to get his gun. What emotional reversal takes place at this point? What are Mrs. May's motivations in having the bull shot?

7. "Suppose [thinks Mrs. May in paragraph 168] Mr. Greenleaf had aroused the bull chunking stones at him and the animal had turned on him and run him up against a tree and gored him? . . . She thought of it almost with pleasure as if she had hit on the perfect ending for a story she was telling her friends." From what perspective is the actual ending of the story a perfect ending? Is the ending of the story purely chance, or is there a sense in which Mrs. May has brought this on herself?

8. What symbolic implications, if any, have the following: (a) the name Greenleaf; (b) the bull; (c) the sun; (d) Mrs. May's two dreams (paragraphs 4 and 148); and (e) the name May? How important is symbolism to the final effect of the story?

9. What kinds of irony predominate in the story? Identify examples of each of the three kinds of irony. How important is irony to the final effect of the story?

Ernest J. Gaines

Just Like a Tree

I shall not;
    I shall not be moved.
I shall not;
    I shall not be moved.
Just like a tree that's
planted 'side the water.
    Oh, I shall not be moved.

I made my home in glory;
    I shall not be moved.
Made my home in glory;
    I shall not be moved.
Just like a tree that's
planted 'side the water.
    Oh, I shall not be moved.

(from an old Negro spiritual)

Chuckkie

Pa hit him on the back and he jeck in them chains like he pulling, but ever'body in the wagon knew he ain't, and Pa hit him on the back again. He jeck again like he pulling, but even Big Red know he ain't doing a thing.

"That's why I'm go'n get a horse," Pa say. "He'll kill that other mule. Get up there, Mr. Bascom."

"Oh, let him alone," Gran'mon say. "How would you like it if you was pulling a wagon in all that mud?"

Pa don't answer Gran'mon; he just hit Mr. Bascom on the back again.

"That's right, kill him," Gran'mon say. "See where you get mo' money to 5 buy another one."

"Get up there, Mr. Bascom," Pa say.

"You hear me talking to you, Emile?" Gran'mon say. "You want me hit you with something?"

"Ma, he ain't pulling," Pa say.

"Leave him alone," Gran'mon say.

Pa shake the lines little bit, but Mr. Bascom don't even feel it, and you 10 can see he letting Big Red do all the pulling again. Pa say something kind o' low to hisself, and I can't make out what it is.

JUST LIKE A TREE   First published in 1968. The quoted spiritual became an anthem of the civil rights movement. Ernest J. Gaines was born in 1933 in rural southern Louisiana, an area that remains central to his fiction, although he was educated at San Francisco State College and Stanford University.

I low' my head little bit, 'cause that wind and fine rain was hitting me in the face, and I can feel Mama pressing close to me to keep me warm. She sitting on one side o' me and Pa sitting on the other side o' me, and Gran'mon in the back o'me in her setting chair. Pa didn't want bring the setting chair, telling Gran'mon there was two boards in that wagon already and she could sit on one of 'em all by herself if she wanted to, but Gran'mon say she was taking her setting chair with her if Pa liked it or not. She say she didn't ride in no wagon on nobody board, and if Pa liked it or not, that setting chair was going.

"Let her take her setting chair," Mama say. "What's wrong with taking her setting chair?"

"Ehhh, Lord," Pa say, and picked up the setting chair and took it out to the wagon. "I guess I'll have to bring it back in the house, too, when we come back from there."

Gran'mon went and clambed in the wagon and moved her setting chair back little bit and sat down and folded her arms, waiting for us to get in, too. I got in and knelt down 'side her and Pa so I could stay warm. Soon 's I sat down, Pa hit Mr. Bascom on the back, saying what a trifling thing Mr. Bascom was, and soon 's he got some mo' money he was getting rid o' Mr. Bascom and getting him a horse.

15   I raise my head to look see how far we is.

"That's it, yonder," I say.

"Stop pointing," Mama say, "and keep your hand in your pocket."

"Where?" Gran'mon say, back there in her setting chair.

" 'Cross the ditch, yonder," I say.

20   "Can't see a thing for this rain," Gran'mon say.

"Can't hardly see it," I say. "But you can see the light little bit. That chinaball tree standing in the way."

"Poor soul," Gran'mon say. "Poor soul."

I know Gran'mon was go'n say "poor soul, poor soul," 'cause she had been saying "poor soul, poor soul," ever since she heard Aunt Fe was go'n leave from back there.

Emile

Darn cane crop to finish getting in and only a mule and a half to do it. If I had my way I'd take that shotgun and a load o' buckshots and—but what's the use.

25   "Get up, Mr. Bascom—please," I say to that little dried-up, long-eared, tobacco-color thing. "Please, come up. Do your share for God sake—if you don't mind. I know it's hard pulling in all that mud, but if you don't do your share, then Big Red'll have to do his and yours, too. So, please, if it ain't asking you too much to—"

"Oh, Emile, shut up," Leola say.

"I can't hit him," I say, "or Mama back there'll hit me. So I have to talk to him. Please, Mr. Bascom, if you don't mind it. For my sake. No, not for mine; for God sake. No, not even for His'n; for Big Red sake. A fellow mule just like yourself is. Please, come up."

"Now, you hear that boy blaspheming God right in front o' me there," Mama say. "Ehhh, Lord—just keep it up. All this bad weather there like this whole world coming apart—a clap o' thunder come there and knock the fool out you. Just keep it up."

Maybe she right, and I stop. I look at Mr. Bascom there doing nothing, and I just give up. That mule know long 's Mama's alive he go'n do just what he want to do. He know when Papa was dying he told Mama to look after him, and he know no matter what he do, no matter what he don't do, Mama ain't go'n never let me do him anything. Sometimes I even feel Mama care mo' for Mr. Bascom 'an she care for me her own son.

We come up to the gate and I pull back on the lines.   30

"Whoa up, Big Red," I say. "You don't have to stop, Mr. Bascom. You never started."

I can feel Mama looking at me back there in that setting chair, but she don't say nothing.

"Here," I say to Chuckkie.

He take the lines and I jump down on the ground to open the old beat-up gate. I see Etienne's horse in the yard, and I see Chris new red tractor 'side the house, shining in the rain. When Mama die, I say to myself, Mr. Bascom, you going. Ever'body getting tractors and horses and I'm still stuck with you. You going, brother.

"Can you make it through?" I ask Chuckkie. "That gate ain't too wide."   35

"I can do it," he say

"Be sure to make Mr. Bascom pull," I say.

"Emile, you better get back up here and drive 'em through," Leola say. "Chuckkie might break up that wagon."

"No, let him stay down there and give orders," Mama say, back there in that setting chair.

"He can do it," I say. "Come on, Chuckkie boy."   40

"Come up here, mule," Chuckkie say.

And soon 's he say that, Big Red make a lunge for the yard, and Mr. Bascom don't even move, and 'fore I can bat my eyes I hear *pow-wow; sagg-sagg; pow-wow*. But above all that noise, Leola up there screaming her head off. And Mama—not a word; just sitting in that chair, looking at me with her arms still folded.

"Pull Big Red," I say. "Pull Big Red, Chuckkie."

Poor little Chuckkie up there pulling so hard till one of his little arms straight out in back; and Big Red throwing his shoulders and ever'thing else in it, and Mr. Bascom just walking there just 's loose and free, like he's suppose to be there just for his good looks. I move out the way just in time to let the wagon go by me, pulling half o' the fence in the yard behind it. I glance up again, and there's Leola still hollering and trying to jump out, but

Mama not saying a word—just sitting there in that setting chair with her arms still folded.

45   "Whoa," I hear little Chuckkie saying. "Whoa up, now."

Somebody open the door and a bunch o' people come out on the gallery.

"What the world—?" Etienne say. "Thought the whole place was coming to pieces there."

"Chuckkie had a little trouble coming in the yard," I say.

"Goodness," Etienne say. "Anybody hurt?"

50   Mama just sit there about ten seconds, then she say something to herself and start clambing out the wagon.

"Let me help you there, Aunt Lou," Etienne say, coming down the steps.

"I can make it," Mama say. When she get on the ground she look up at Chuckkie. "Hand me my chair there, boy."

Poor little Chuckkie, up there with the lines in one hand, get the chair and hold it to the side, and Etienne catch it just 'fore it hit the ground. Mama start looking at me again, and it look like for at least a' hour she stand there looking at nobody but me. Then she say, "Ehhh, Lord," like that again, and go inside with Leola and the rest o' the people.

I look back at half o' the fence laying there in the yard, and I jump back on the wagon and guide the mules to the side o' the house. After unhitching 'em and tying 'em to the wheels, I look at Chris pretty red tractor again, and me and Chuckkie go inside: I make sure he kick all that mud off his shoes 'fore he go in the house.

Leola

55   Sitting over there by that fireplace, trying to look joyful when ever'body there know she ain't. But she trying, you know; smiling and bowing when people say something to her. How can she be joyful, I ask you; how can she be? Poor thing, she been here all her life—or the most of it, let's say. 'Fore they moved in this house, they lived in one back in the woods 'bout a mile from here. But for the past twenty-five or thirty years, she been right in this one house. I know ever since I been big enough to know people I been seeing her right here.

Aunt Fe, Aunt Fe, Aunt Fe, Aunt Fe; the name's been 'mongst us just like us own family name. Just like the name o' God. Like the name of town— the city. Aunt Fe, Aunt Fe, Aunt Fe, Aunt Fe.

Poor old thing; how many times I done come here and washed clothes for her when she couldn't do it herself. How many times I done hoed in that garden, ironed her clothes, wrung a chicken neck for her. You count the days in the year and you'll be pretty close. And I didn't mind it a bit. No, I didn't mind it a bit. She there trying to pay me. Proud—Lord, talking 'bout pride. "Here." "No, Aunt Fe; no." "Here, here; you got a child there, you can use it." "No, Aunt Fe. No. No. What would Mama think if she knowed I took money from you? Aunt Fe, Mama would never forgive me. No. I love doing these thing for you. I just wish I could do more."

And there, now, trying to make 'tend she don't mind leaving. Ehhh, Lord.

I hear a bunch o' rattling round in the kitchen and I go back there. I see Louise stirring this big pot o' eggnog.

"Louise," I say.   60

"Leola," she say.

We look at each other and she stir the eggnog again. She know what I'm go'n say next, and she can't even look in my face.

"Louise, I wish there was some other way."

"There's no other way," she say.

"Louise, moving her from here's like moving a tree you been used to in   65
your front yard all your life."

"What else can I do?"

"Oh, Louise, Louise."

"Nothing else but that."

"Louise, what people go'n do without her here?"

She stir the eggnog and don't answer.   70

"Louise, us'll take her in with us."

"You all no kin to Auntie. She go with me."

"And us'll never see her again."

She stir the eggnog. Her husband come back in the kitchen and kiss her on the back o' the neck and then look at me and grin. Right from the start I can see I ain't go'n like that nigger.

"Almost ready, honey?" he say.   75

"Almost."

He go to the safe and get one o' them bottles of whiskey he got in there and come back to the stove.

"No," Louise say. "Everybody don't like whiskey in it. Add the whiskey after you've poured it up."

"Okay, hon."

He kiss her on the back o' the neck again. Still don't like that nigger.   80
Something 'bout him ain't right.

"You one o' the family?" he say.

"Same as one," I say. "And you?"

He don't like the way I say it, and I don't care if he like it or not. He look at me there a second, and then he kiss her on the ear.

"Un-unnn," she say, stirring the pot.

"I love your ear, baby," he say.   85

"Go in the front room and talk with the people," she say.

He kiss her on the other ear. A nigger do all that front o' public got something to hide. He leave the kitchen. I look at Louise.

"Ain't nothing else I can do," she say.

"You sure, Louise? You positive?"

90   "I'm positive," she say.

The front door open and Emile and Chuckkie come in. A minute later Washington and Adrieu come in, too. Adrieu come back in the kitchen, and I can see she been crying. Aunt Fe is her godmother, you know.

"How you feel, Adrieu?"

"That weather out there," she say.

"Y'all walked?"

95   "Yes."

"Us here in the wagon. Y'all can go back with us."

"Y'all the one tore the fence down?" she ask.

"Yes, I guess so. That brother-in-law o' yours in there letting Chuckkie drive that wagon."

"Well, I don't guess it'll matter too much. Nobody go'n be here, anyhow."

100   And she start crying again. I take her in my arms and pat her on the shoulder, and I look at Louise stirring the eggnog.

"What I'm go'n do and my nan-nane gone? I love her so much."

"Ever'body love her."

"Since my mama died, she been like my mama."

"Shhh," I say. "Don't let her hear you. Make her grieve. You don't want her grieving, now, do you?"

105   She sniffs there 'gainst my dress few times.

"Oh, Lord," she say. "Lord, have mercy."

"Shhh," I say. "Shhh. That's what life's 'bout."

"That ain't what life's 'bout," she say. "It ain't fair. This been her home all her life. These the people she know. She don't know them people she going to. It ain't fair."

"Shhh, Adrieu," I say. "Now, you saying things that ain't your business."

110   She cry there some mo'.

"Oh, Lord, Lord," she say.

Louise turn from the stove.

"About ready now," she say, going to the middle door. "James, tell ev'rybody to come back and get some."

James

Let me go on back here and show these country niggers how to have a good time. All they know is talk, talk, talk. Talk so much they make me buggy round here. Damn this weather—wind, rain. Must be a million cracks in this old house.

115   I go to that old beat-up safe in that corner and get that fifth of Mr. Harper (in the South now; got to say Mister), give the seal one swipe, the stopper one jerk, and head back to that old wood stove. (Man, like, these cats are primitive—goodness. You know what I mean? I mean like wood stoves. Don't

mention TV, man, these cats here never heard of that.) I start to dump Mr. Harper in the pot and Baby catches my hand again and say not all of them like it. You ever heard of anything like that? I mean a stud's going to drink eggnog, and he's not going to put whiskey in it. I mean he's going to drink it straight. I mean, you ever heard anything like that? Well, I wasn't pressing none of them on Mr. Harper. I mean, me and Mr. Harper get along too well together for me to go around there pressing.

I hold my cup there and let Baby put a few drops of this egg stuff in it; then I jerk my cup back and let Mr. Harper run a while. Couple of these cats come over (some of them aren't so lame) and set their cups, and I let Mr. Harper run for them. Then this cat says he's got 'nough. I let Mr. Harper run for this other stud, and pretty soon he says, "Hold it. Good." Country cat, you know. "Hold it. Good." Real country cat. So I raise the cup to see what Mr. Harper's doing. He's just right. I raise the cup again. Just right, Mr. Harper; just right.

I go to the door with Mr. Harper under my arm and the cup in my hand and I look into the front room where they all are. I mean, there's about ninety-nine of them in there. Old ones, young ones, little ones, big ones, yellow ones, black ones, brown ones—you name them, brother, and they were there. And what for? Brother, I'll tell you what for. Just because me and Baby are taking this old chick out of these sticks. Well, I'll tell you where I'd be at this moment if I was one of them. With that weather out there like it is, I'd be under about five blankets with some little warm belly pressing against mine. Brother, you can bet your hat I wouldn't be here. Man, listen to that thing out there. You can hear that rain beating on that old house like grains of rice; and that wind coming through them cracks like it does in those old Charlie Chaplin movies. Man, like you know—like *whooo-ee; whooo-ee.* Man, you talking about some weird cats.

I can feel Mr. Harper starting to massage my wig and I bat my eyes twice and look at the old girl over there. She's still sitting in that funny-looking little old rocking chair, and not saying a word to anybody. Just sitting there looking into the fireplace at them two pieces of wood that aren't giving out enough heat to warm a baby, let alone ninety-nine grown people. I mean, you know, like that sleet's falling out there like all get-up-and-go, and them two pieces of wood are lying there just as dead as the rest of these way-out cats.

One of the old cats—I don't know which one he is—Mose, Sam, or something like that—leans over and pokes in the fire a minute; then a little blaze shoots up, and he raises up, too, looking as satisfied as if he'd just sent a rocket into orbit. I mean, these cats are like that. They do these little bitty things, and they feel like they've really done something. Well, back in these sticks, I guess there just isn't nothing big to do.

I feel Mr. Harper touching my skull now—and I notice this little chick passing by me with these two cups of eggnog. She goes over to the fireplace and gives one to each of these old chicks. The one sitting in that setting chair

120

she brought with her from God knows where, and the other cup to the old chick that Baby and I are going to haul from here sometime tomorrow morning. Wait, man, I mean like, you ever heard of anybody going to somebody else's house with a chair? I mean, wouldn't you call that an insult at the basest point? I mean, now, like tell me what you think of that? I mean—dig—here I am at my pad, and in you come with your own stool. I mean, now, like man, you know. I mean that's an insult at the basest point. I mean, you know . . . you know, like way out. . . .

Mr. Harper, what you trying to do, boy?—I mean, *sir.* (Got to watch myself, I'm in the South. Got to keep watching myself.)

This stud touches me on the shoulder and raise his cup and say, "How 'bout a taste?" I know what the stud's talking about, so I let Mr. Harper run for him. But soon 's I let a drop get in, the stud say, "'Nough." I mean I let about two drops get in, and already the stud's got enough. Man, I mean, like you know. I mean these studs are 'way out. I mean like 'way back there.

This stud takes a swig of his eggnog and say, "Ahhh." I mean this real down-home way of saying "Ahhhh." I mean, man, like these studs—I notice this little chick passing by me again, and this time she's crying. I mean weeping, you know. And just because this old ninety-nine-year-old chick's packing up and leaving. I mean, you ever heard of anything like that? I mean, here she is pretty as the day is long and crying because Baby and I are hauling this old chick away. Well, I'd like to make her cry. And I can assure you, brother, it wouldn't be from leaving her.

I turn and look at Baby over there by the stove, pouring eggnog in all these cups. I mean, there're about twenty of these cats lined up there. And I bet you not half of them will take Mr. Harper along. Some way-out cats, man. Some way-out cats.

125   I go up to Baby and kiss her on the back of the neck and give her a little pat where she likes for me to pat her when we're in the bed. She say, "Uh-uh," but I know she likes it anyhow.

Ben O

I back under the bed and touch the slop jar, and I pull back my leg and back somewhere else, and then I get me a good sight on it. I spin my aggie couple times and sight again and then I shoot. I hit it right square in the middle and it go flying over the fireplace. I crawl over there to get it and I see 'em all over there drinking they eggnog and they didn't even offer me and Chuckkie none. I find my marble on the bricks, and I go back and tell Chuckkie they over there drinking eggnog.

"You want some?" I say.

"I want shoot marble," Chuckkie say. "Yo' shot. Shoot up."

"I want some eggnog," I say.

130   "Shoot up, Ben O," he say. "I'm getting cold staying in one place so long. You feel that draft?"

"Coming from that crack under that bed," I say.

"Where?" Chuckkie say, looking for the crack.

"Over by that bedpost over there," I say.

"This sure's a beat-up old house," Chuckkie say.

"I want me some eggnog," I say.   135

"Well, you ain't getting none," Gran'mon say, from the fireplace. "It ain't good for you."

"I can drink eggnog," I say. "How come it ain't good for me? It ain't nothing but eggs and milk. I eat chicken, don't I? I eat beef, don't I?"

Gran'mon don't say nothing.

"I want me some eggnog," I say.

Gran'mon still don't say no more. Nobody else don't say nothing,   140
neither.

"I want me some eggnog," I say.

"You go'n get a eggnog," Gran'mon say. "Just keep that noise up."

"I want me some eggnog," I say; "and I 'tend to get me some eggnog tonight."

Next thing I know, Gran'mon done picked up a chip out o' that corner and done sailed it back there where me and Chuckkie is. I duck just in time, and the chip catch old Chuckkie side the head.

"Hey, who that hitting me?" Chuckkie say.   145

"Move, and you won't get hit," Gran'mon say.

I laugh at old Chuckkie over there holding his head, and next thing I know here's Chuckkie done haul back there and hit me in my side. I jump up from there and give him two just to show him how it feel, and he jump up and hit me again. Then we grab each other and start tussling on the floor.

"You, Ben O," I hear Gran'mon saying. "You, Ben O, cut that out. Y'all cut that out."

But we don't stop, 'cause neither one o' us want be first. Then I feel somebody pulling us apart.

"What I ought to do is whip both o' you," Mrs. Leola say. "Is that what   150
y'all want?"

"No'm," I say.

"Then shake hand."

Me and Chuckkie shake hand.

"Kiss," Mrs. Leola say.

"No, ma'am," I say. "I ain't kissing no boy. I ain't that crazy."   155

"Kiss him, Chuckkie," she say.

Old Chuckkie kiss me on the jaw.

"Now, kiss him, Ben O."

"I ain't kissing no Chuckkie," I say. "No'm. Uh-uh. You kiss girls."

And the next thing I know, Mama done tipped up back o' me and done   160
whop me on the leg with Daddy belt.

"Kiss Chuckkie," she say.

Chuckkie turn his jaw to me and I kiss him. I almost wipe my mouth. I even feel like spitting.

"Now, come back here and get you some eggnog," Mama say.

"That's right, spoil 'em," Gran'mon say. "Next thing you know, they be drinking from bottles."

165   "Little eggnog won't hurt 'em, Mama," Mama say.

"That's right, never listen," Gran'mon say. "It's you go'n suffer for it. I be dead and gone, me."

Aunt Clo

Be just like wrapping a chain round a tree and jecking and jecking, and then shifting the chain little bit and jecking and jecking some in that direction, and then shifting it some mo' and jecking and jecking in that direction. Jecking and jecking till you get it loose, and then pulling with all your might. Still it might not be loose enough and you have to back the tractor up some and fix the chain round the tree again and start jecking all over. Jeck, jeck, jeck. Then you hear the roots crying, and then you keep on jecking, and then it give, and you jeck some mo', and then it falls. And not till then that you see what you done done. Not till then you see the big hole in the ground and piece of the taproot still way down in it—a piece you won't never get out no matter if you dig till doomsday. Yes, you got the tree—least got it down on the ground, but did you get the taproot? No. No, sir, you didn't get the taproot. You stand there and look down in this hole at it and you grab yo' axe and jump down in it and start chopping at the taproot, but do you get the taproot? No. You don't get the taproot, sir. You never get the taproot. But, sir, I tell you what you do get. You get a big hole in the ground, sir; and you get another big hole in the air where the lovely branches been all these years. Yes, sir, that's what you get. The holes, sir, the holes. Two holes, sir, you can't never fill no matter how hard you try.

So you wrap yo' chain round yo' tree again, sir, and you start dragging it. But the dragging ain't so easy, sir, 'cause she's a heavy old tree—been there a long time, you know—heavy. And you make yo' tractor strain, sir, and the elements work 'gainst you, too, sir, 'cause the elements, they on her side, too, 'cause she part o' the elements, and the elements, they part o' her. So the elements, they do they little share to discourage you—yes, sir, they does. But you will not let the elements stop you. No, sir, you show the elements that they just elements, and man is stronger than elements, and you jeck and jeck on the chain, and soon she start to moving with you, sir, but if you look over yo' shoulder one second you see her leaving a trail—a trail, sir, that can be seen from miles and miles away. You see her trying to hook her little fine branches in different little cracks, in between pickets, round hills o' grass, round anything they might brush 'gainst. But you is a determined man, sir, and you jeck and you jeck, and she keep on grabbing and trying to hold, but you stronger, sir—course you the strongest—and you finally get her out on the pave road. But what you don't notice, sir, is just 'fore she get on the pave road she leave couple her little branches to remind the people that it ain't her that want leave, but you, sir, that think she ought to. So you just drag her and drag her, sir, and the folks that live in the houses 'side the pave road, they come out on they gallery and look at her go by, and then they go back in they house and sit by the fire and forget her. So you just go on, sir, and you just go and you go—and for how many days? I don't know. I don't have the least idea. The North to me, sir, is like the elements. It mystify me. But never mind, you finally get there, and then you try to find a place to set her. You look in this corner and you look in that corner, but no corner is good. She kind o' stand in the way no matter where you set her. So finally, sir, you say, "I just stand her up here a little while and see, and if it don't work out, if she keep getting in the way, I guess we'll just have to take her to the dump."

Chris

Just like him, though, standing up there telling them lies when everybody else feeling sad. I don't know what you do without people like him. And, yet, you see him there, he sad just like the rest. But he just got to be funny. Crying on the inside, but still got to be funny.

He didn't steal it, though; didn't steal it a bit. His grandpa was just like him. Mat? Mat Jefferson? Just like that. Mat could make you die laughing. 'Member once at a wake. Who was dead? Yes—Robert Lewis. Robert Lewis laying up in his coffin dead as a door nail. Everybody sad and droopy. Mat look at that and start his lying. Soon, half o' the place laughing. Funniest wake I ever went to, and yet— 170

Just like now. Look at 'em. Look at 'em laughing. Ten minutes ago you would 'a' thought you was at a funeral. But look at 'em now. Look at her there in that little old chair. How long she had it? Fifty years—a hundred? It ain't a chair no mo', it's little bit o' her. Just like her arm, just like her leg.

You know, I couldn't believe it. I couldn't. Emile passed the house there the other day, right after the bombing, and I was in my yard digging a water drain to let the water run out in the ditch. Emile, he stopped the wagon there 'fore the door. Little Chuckkie, he in there with him with that little rain cap buckled up over his head. I go out to the gate and I say, "Emile, it's the truth?"

"The truth," he say. And just like that he say it. "The truth."

I look at him there, and he looking up the road to keep from looking back at me. You know, they been pretty close to Aunt Fe ever since they was children coming up. His own mon, Aunt Lou, and Aunt Fe, they been like sisters, there, together.

Me and him, we talk there little while 'bout the cane cutting, then he say he got to get on to the back. He shake the lines and drive on. 175

Inside me, my heart feel like it done swole up ten times the size it ought to be. Water come in my eyes, and I got to 'mit I cried right there. Yes sir, I cried right there by that front gate.

Louise come in the room and whisper something to Leola, and they go back in the kitchen. I can hear 'em moving things round back there, still getting things together they go'n be taking along. If they offer me anything, I'd like that big iron pot out there in the back yard. Good for boiling water when you killing hog, you know.

You can feel the sadness in the room again. Louise brought it in when she come in and whispered to Leola. Only, she didn't take it out when her and Leola left. Every pan they move, every pot they unhook keep telling you she leaving, she leaving.

Etienne turn over one o' them logs to make the fire pick up some, and I see that boy, Lionel, spreading out his hands over the fire. Watch out, I think to myself, here come another lie. People, he just getting started.

Anne-Marie Duvall

180   "You're not going?"

"I'm not going," he says, turning over the log with the poker. "And if you were in your right mind, you wouldn't go, either."

"You just don't understand, do you?"

"Oh, I understand. She cooked for your daddy. She nursed you when your mama died."

"And I'm trying to pay her back with a seventy-nine-cents scarf. Is that too much?"

185   He is silent, leaning against the mantel, looking down at the fire. The fire throws strange shadows across the big, old room. Father looks down at me from against the wall. His eyes do not say go nor stay. But I know what he would do.

"Please go with me, Edward."

"You're wasting your breath."

I look at him a long time, then I get the small package from the coffee table.

"You're still going?"

190   "I am going."

"Don't call for me if you get bogged down anywhere back there."

I look at him and go out to the garage. The sky is black. The clouds are moving fast and low. A fine drizzle is falling, and the wind coming from the swamps blows in my face. I cannot recall a worse night in all my life.

I hurry into the car and drive out of the yard. The house stands big and black in back of me. Am I angry with Edward? No, I'm not angry with Edward. He's right. I should not go out into this kind of weather. But what he does not understand is I must. Father definitely would have gone if he were alive. Grandfather definitely would have gone, also. And, therefore, I must. Why? I cannot answer why. Only, I must go.

As soon as I turn down that old muddy road, I begin to pray. Don't let me go into that ditch, I pray. Don't let me go into that ditch. Please, don't let me go into that ditch.

The lights play on the big old trees along the road. Here and there the   195
lights hit a sagging picket fence. But I know I haven't even started yet. She
lives far back into the fields. Why? God, why does she have to live so far
back? Why couldn't she have lived closer to the front? But the answer to that
is as hard for me as is the answer to everything else. It was ordained before
I—before father—was born—that she should live back there. So why
should I try to understand it now?

The car slides towards the ditch, and I stop it dead and turn the wheel,
and then come back into the road again. Thanks, father. I know you're with
me. Because it was you who said that I must look after her, didn't you? No,
you did not say it directly, father. You said it only with a glance. As grandfather must have said it to you, and as his father must have said it to him.

But now that she's gone, father, now what? I know. I know. Aunt Lou,
Aunt Clo, and the rest.

The lights shine on the dead, wet grass along the road. There's an old
pecan tree, looking dead and all alone. I wish I was a little nigger gal so I
could pick pecans and eat them under the big old dead tree.

The car hits a rut, but bounces right out of it. I am frightened for a
moment, but then I feel better. The windshield wipers are working well,
slapping the water away as fast as it hits the glass. If I make the next half mile
all right, the rest of the way will be good. It's not much over a mile now.

That was too bad about that bombing—killing that woman and her two   200
children. That poor woman; poor children. What is the answer? What will
happen? What do they want? Do they know what they want? Do they really
know what they want? Are they positively sure? Have they any idea? Money
to buy a car, is that it? If that is all, I pity them. Oh, how I pity them.

Not much farther. Just around that bend and—there's a water hole. Now
what?

I stop the car and just stare out at the water a minute; then I get out to see
how deep it is. The cold wind shoots through my body like needles. Lightning comes from towards the swamps and lights up the place. For a split
second the night is as bright as day. The next second it is blacker than it has
ever been.

I look at the water, and I can see that it's too deep for the car to pass
through. I must turn back or I must walk the rest of the way. I stand there a
while wondering what to do. Is it worth it all? Can't I simply send the gift by
someone tomorrow morning? But will there be someone tomorrow morning? Suppose she leaves without getting it, then what? What then? Father
would never forgive me. Neither would grandfather or great-grandfather,
either. No, they wouldn't.

The lightning flashes again and I look across the field, and I can see the
tree in the yard a quarter of a mile away. I have but one choice: I must walk. I
get the package out of the car and stuff it in my coat and start out.

I don't make any progress at first, but then I become a little warmer and I   205
find I like walking. The lightning flashes just in time to show up a puddle of
water, and I go around it. But there's no light to show up the second puddle,

and I fall flat on my face. For a moment I'm completely blind, then I get slowly to my feet and check the package. It's dry, not harmed. I wash the mud off my raincoat, wash my hands, and I start out again.

The house appears in front of me, and as I come into the yard, I can hear the people laughing and talking. Sometimes I think niggers can laugh and joke even if they see somebody beaten to death. I go up on the porch and knock and an old one opens the door for me. I swear, when he sees me he looks as if he's seen a ghost. His mouth drops open, his eyes bulge—I swear.

I go into the old crowded and smelly room, and every one of them looks at me the same way the first one did. All the joking and laughing has ceased. You would think I was the devil in person.

"Done, Lord," I hear her saying over by the fireplace. They move to the side and I can see her sitting in that little rocking chair I bet you she's had since the beginning of time. "Done, Master," she says. "Child, what you doing in weather like this? Y'all move; let her get to that fire. Y'all move. Move, now. Let her warm herself."

They start scattering everywhere.

210   "I'm not cold, Aunt Fe," I say. "I just brought you something—something small—because you're leaving us. I'm going right back."

"Done, Master," she says. Fussing over me just like she's done all her life. "Done, Master. Child, you ain't got no business in a place like this. Get close to this fire. Get here. Done, Master."

I move closer, and the fire does feel warm and good.

"Done, Lord," she says.

I take out the package and pass it to her. The other niggers gather around with all kinds of smiles on their faces. Just think of it—a white lady coming through all of this for one old darky. It is all right for them to come from all over the plantation, from all over the area, in all kinds of weather: this is to be expected of them. But a white lady, a white lady. They must think we white people don't have their kind of feelings.

215   She unwraps the package, her bony little fingers working slowly and deliberately. When she sees the scarf—the seventy-nine-cents scarf—she brings it to her mouth and kisses it.

"Y'all look," she says. "Y'all look. Ain't it the prettiest little scarf y'all ever did see? Y'all look."

They move around her and look at the scarf. Some of them touch it.

"I go'n put it on right now," she says. "I go'n put it on right now, my lady."

She unfolds it and ties it round her head and looks up at everybody and smiles.

220   "Thank you, my lady," she says. "Thank you, ma'am, from the bottom of my heart."

"Oh, Aunt Fe," I say, kneeling down beside her. "Oh, Aunt Fe."

But I think about the other niggers there looking down at me, and I get up. But I look into that wrinkled old face again, and I must go back down again. And I lay my head in that bony old lap, and I cry and I cry—I don't know how long. And I feel those old fingers, like death itself, passing over my hair and my neck. I don't know how long I kneel there crying, and when I stop, I get out of there as fast as I can.

Etienne

The boy come in, and soon, right off, they get quiet, blaming the boy. If people could look little farther than the tip of they nose— No, they blame the boy. Not that they ain't behind the boy, what he doing, but they blame him for what she must do. What they don't know is that the boy didn't start it, and the people that bombed the house didn't start it, neither. It started a million years ago. It started when one man envied another man for having a penny mo' 'an he had, and then the man married a woman to help him work the field so he could get much 's the other man, but when the other man saw the man had married a woman to get much 's him, he, himself, he married a woman, too, so he could still have mo'. Then they start having children—not from love; but so the children could help 'em work so they could have mo'. But even with the children one man still had a penny mo' 'an the other, so the other man went and bought him a ox, and the other man did the same—to keep ahead of the other man. And soon the other man had bought him a slave to work the ox so he could get ahead of the other man. But the other man went out and bought him two slaves so he could stay ahead of the other man, and the other man went out and bought him three slaves. And soon they had a thousand slaves apiece, but they still wasn't satisfied. And one day the slaves all rose and kill the masters, but the masters (knowing slaves was men just like they was, and kind o' expected they might do this) organized theyself a good police force, and the police force, they come out and killed the two thousand slaves.

So it's not this boy you see standing here 'fore you, 'cause it happened a million years ago. And this boy here's just doing something the slaves done a million years ago. Just that this boy here ain't doing it they way. 'Stead of raising arms 'gainst the masters, he bow his head.

No, I say; don't blame the boy 'cause she must go. 'Cause when she's dead, and that won't be long after they get her up there, this boy's work will still be going on. She's not the only one that's go'n die from this boy's work. Many mo' of 'em go'n die 'fore it's over with. The whole place—everything. A big wind is rising, and when a big wind rise, the sea stirs, and the drop o' water you see laying on top the sea this day won't be there tomorrow. 'Cause that's what wind do, and that's what life is. She ain't nothing but one little drop o' water laying on top the sea, and what this boy's doing is called the wind . . . and she must be moved. No, don't blame the boy. Go out and blame the wind. No, don't blame him, 'cause tomorrow, what he's doing today, somebody go'n say he ain't done a thing. 'Cause tomorrow will be his time to be turned over just like it's hers today. And after that, be somebody

225

else time to turn over. And it keep going like that till it ain't nothing left to turn—and nobody left to turn it.

"Sure, they bombed the house," he say; "because they want us to stop. But if we stopped today, then what good would we have done? What good? Those who have already died for the cause would have just died in vain."

"Maybe if they had bombed your house you wouldn't be so set on keeping this up."

"If they had killed my mother and my brothers and sisters, I'd press just that much harder. I can see you all point. I can see it very well. But I can't agree with you. You blame me for their being bombed. You blame me for Aunt Fe's leaving. They died for you and for your children. And I love Aunt Fe as much as anybody in here does. Nobody in here loves her more than I do. Not one of you." He looks at her. "Don't you believe me, Aunt Fe?"

She nods—that little white scarf still tied round her head.

230   "How many times have I eaten in your kitchen, Aunt Fe? A thousand times? How many times have I eaten tea cakes and drank milk on the back steps, Aunt Fe? A thousand times? How many times have I sat at this same fireplace with you, just the two of us, Aunt Fe? Another thousand times— two thousand times? How many times have I chopped wood for you, chopped grass for you, ran to the store for you? Five thousand times? How many times have we walked to church together, Aunt Fe? Gone fishing at the river together—how how many times? I've spent as much time in this house as I've spent in my own. I know every crack in the wall. I know every corner. With my eyes shut, I can go anywhere in here without bumping into anything. How many of you can do that? Not many of you." He looks at her. "Aunt Fe?"

She looks at him.

"Do you think I love you, Aunt Fe?"

She nods.

"I love you, Aunt Fe, much as I do my own parents. I'm going to miss you much as I'd miss my own mother if she were to leave me now. I'm going to miss you, Aunt Fe, but I'm not going to stop what I've started. You told me a story once, Aunt Fe, about my great-grandpa. Remember? Remember how he died?"

235   She looks in the fire and nods.

"Remember how they lynched him—chopped him into pieces?"
She nods.

"Just the two of us were sitting here beside the fire when you told me that. I was so angry I felt like killing. But it was you who told me get killing out of my mind. It was you who told me I would only bring harm to myself and sadness to the others if I killed. Do you remember that, Aunt Fe?"

She nods, still looking in the fire.

240   "You were right. We cannot raise our arms. Because it would mean death for ourselves, as well as for the others. But we will do something else—and that's what we will do." He looks at the people standing round him. "And if they were to bomb my own mother's house tomorrow, I would still go on."

"I'm not saying for you not to go on," Louise says. "That's up to you. I'm just taking Auntie from here before hers is the next house they bomb."

The boy look at Louise, and then at Aunt Fe. He go up to the chair where she sitting.

"Good-bye, Aunt Fe," he say, picking up her hand. The hand done shriveled up to almost nothing. Look like nothing but loose skin's covering the bones. "I'll miss you," he say.

"Good-bye, Emmanuel," she say. She look at him a long time. "God be with you."

He stand there holding the hand a while longer, then he nods his head,   245
and leaves the house. The people stir round little bit, but nobody say anything.

Aunt Lou

They tell her good-bye, and half of 'em leave the house crying, or want cry, but she just sit there 'side the fireplace like she don't mind going at all. When Leola ask me if I'm ready to go, I tell her I'm staying right there till Fe leave that house. I tell her I ain't moving one step till she go out that door. I been knowing her for the past fifty some years now, and I ain't 'bout to leave her on her last night here.

That boy, Chuckkie, want stay with me, but I make him go. He follow his mon and paw out the house and soon I hear that wagon turning round. I hear Emile saying something to Mr. Bascom even 'fore that wagon get out the yard. I tell myself, well, Mr. Bascom, you sure go'n catch it, and me not there to take up for you—and I get up from my chair and go to the door.

"Emile?" I call.

"Whoa," he say.

"You leave that mule 'lone, you hear me?"   250

"I ain't done Mr. Bascom a thing, Mama," he say.

"Well, you just mind you don't," I say. "I'll sure find out."

"Yes'm," he say. "Come up here, Mr. Bascom."

"Now, you hear that boy. Emile?" I say.

"I'm sorry, Mama," he say. "I didn't mean no harm."   255

They go out in the road, and I go back to the fireplace and sit down again. Louise stir round in the kitchen a few minutes, then she come in the front where we at. Everybody else gone. That husband o' hers, there, got drunk long 'fore midnight, and Emile and them had to put him to bed in the other room.

She come there and stand by the fire.

"I'm dead on my feet," she say.

"Why don't you go to bed," I say. "I'm go'n be here."

"You all won't need anything?"   260

"They got wood in that corner?"

"Plenty."

"Then we won't need a thing."

She stand there and warm, and then she say good night and go round the other side.

265   "Well, Fe?" I say.

"I ain't leaving here tomorrow, Lou," she say.

"'Course you is," I say. "Up there ain't that bad."

She shake her head. "No, I ain't going nowhere."

I look at her over in her chair, but I don't say nothing. The fire pops in the fireplace, and I look at the fire again. It's a good little fire—not too big, not too little. Just 'nough there to keep the place warm.

270   "You want sing, Lou?" she say, after a while. "I feel like singing my 'termination song."

"Sure," I say.

She start singing in that little light voice she got there, and I join with her. We sing two choruses, and then she stop.

"My 'termination for Heaven," she say. "Now—now—"

"What's the matter, Fe?" I say.

275   "Nothing," she say. "I want get in my bed. My gown hanging over there."

I get the gown for her and bring it back to the firehalf. She get out of her dress slowly, like she don't even have 'nough strength to do it. I help her on with her gown, and she kneel down there 'side the bed and say her prayers. I sit in my chair and look at the fire again.

She pray there a long time—half out loud, half to herself. I look at her kneeling down there, little like a little old girl. I see her making some kind o' jecking motion there, but I feel she crying 'cause this her last night here, and 'cause she got to go and leave ever'thing behind. I look at the fire.

She pray there ever so long, and then she start to get up. But she can't make it by herself. I go to help her, and when I put my hand on her shoulder, she say, "Lou? Lou?"

I say, "What's the matter, Fe?"

280   "Lou?" she say. "Lou?"

I feel her shaking in my hand with all her might. Shaking, shaking, shaking—like a person with the chill. Then I hear her take a long breath, longest I ever heard anybody take before. Then she ease back on the bed—calm, calm, calm.

"Sleep on, Fe," I tell her. "When you get up there, tell 'em all I ain't far behind."

QUESTIONS

1. Define the types of conflict in this story and locate their causes.
2. The narrative method here may cause some initial difficulties. It resembles the dramatic point of view in that each section of the story simply reports the thoughts of the named characters, without direct commentary or interpretation by the author; it resembles stream of consciousness (see

page 181) in that it presents *unspoken* monologues of the characters rather than speeches addressed to others. While this technique may at first present obstacles, it should be possible to infer motives and past histories for most of the narrators in the story. Can you also infer them for characters who do not narrate—in particular, for Aunt Fe, Louise, and Emmanuel? Why doesn't the author give monologues to these characters?

3. All of the narrators but two are blacks from the local area. Which two are not? What do the perspectives of these "outsiders" contribute to the story?

4. What is the import of the story's haziness about blood- and marriage-links between the characters? Does your inability to chart all the relationships have a positive value for the story's theme?

5. Given the emotional effects of the story, is it possible to say whether Emmanuel's actions are right? Whether Louise's are right?

6. What happens to Aunt Fe? What does she mean by repeating "Done, Lord" and "Done, Master" when Anne-Marie arrives? Supposing that the song quoted at the beginning of the story is Aunt Fe's "'termination song" (paragraph 270), what meanings does the author imply for the word *'termination?*

7. What does the "Tree" (title, Aunt Clo's monologue) symbolize? Is Anne-Marie Duvall's "seventy-nine-cents scarf" symbolic?

CHAPTER SEVEN

Emotion and Humor

Interpretive fiction presents the reader with significant and therefore durable insights into life. But these insights represent something more than mere intellectual comprehension; otherwise, the story does nothing that cannot be done as well or better by psychology, history, or philosophy. Fiction derives its unique value from its power to give *felt* insights. Its truths take a deeper hold on our minds because they are conveyed through our feelings. Its effectiveness in awakening a sensuous and emotional apprehension of experience that enriches understanding is what distinguishes imaginative literature from other forms of discourse.

All successful stories arouse emotions in the reader. The adventure thriller causes fear, excitement, suspense, anxiety, exultation, surprise. Some stories make us laugh; some cause us to thrill with horror; some make us cry. We value all the arts precisely because they enrich and diversify our emotional life.

A truly significant story pursues emotion indirectly, not directly. Emotion accompanying and producing insight, not emotion for itself, is the aim of the interpretive story. It presents a sample of experience truthfully; the emotions it arouses flow naturally from the experience presented.

Over a century and a half ago, in a review of Hawthorne's *Tales*, Edgar Allan Poe made a famous but misleading pronouncement about the short story:

> A skilful literary artist has constructed a tale. If wise, he has not fashioned his thoughts to accommodate his incidents; but having conceived with deliberate care, a certain unique or single *effect* to be brought out, he then invents such incidents—he then combines such events as may best aid him in establishing this preconceived effect. If his very initial sentence tend not to the outbringing of this effect, then he has failed in his first step. In the whole composition there should be no word written, of which the tendency, direct or indirect, is not to the one preestablished design.

Poe's formulation has been enormously influential, for both good and bad. Historically it is important as one of the first discussions of the short story as a unique form. Critically it is important because Poe so clearly enunciates here the basic critical principle of all art—the principle of artistic unity, requiring all details and elements of a piece to contribute harmoniously to the total design. Its influence has been deleterious because of the emphasis Poe put on a "unique" and "preconceived" *effect.*

The serious writer is an interpreter, not an inventor. Like a good actor, the writer is an intermediary between a segment of experience and an audience. The actor must pay some consideration to the audience—being careful, for instance, to face *toward* it, not away from it. But the great actor is the one who is wrapped up in the thoughts and feelings of a role, not the one who is continually stealing glances at the audience to determine the effect of a gesture or bit of business. The actor who begins taking cues from the audience rather than from the script soon becomes a "ham," exaggerating and falsifying for the sake of effects. The writer, too, though paying some consideration to the reader, focuses primarily on the subject. The writer who begins to think primarily of the effect of the tale on the reader begins to manipulate the material, to heighten reality, to contrive and falsify for the sake of effects. The serious writer selects and arranges material in order to convey most effectively the feeling or truth of a human situation. The commercial writer selects and arranges the material so as to stimulate a response in the reader.

Discriminating readers, then, will distinguish between contrived emotion and that which springs naturally from a human story truly told. They will mark a difference between the story that attempts to "play upon" the feelings directly, as if readers were pianos, and one that draws emotion forth as naturally as a plucked string draws forth sympathetic vibrations from another instrument in a room. The difference between the two types of story is the difference between escape and interpretation. In interpretive fiction, emotion is the by-product, not the goal.

No doubt there is pleasure in having our emotions directly stimulated, and in some forms such pleasure is both delightful and innocent. We all enjoy the laugh that follows a good joke, and the story that attempts no more than to provoke laughter may be both pleasant and harmless. There is a difference, nevertheless, between the story written for humor's sake and that in which humor springs from a way of viewing experience. Humor may be as idle as the wisecrack or as vicious as the practical joke; it becomes of significant value when it flows from a comic perception of life.

Most of us enjoy the gooseflesh and the tingle along the spine produced by the successful ghost story. There is something agreeable in letting our blood be chilled by bats in the moonlight, guttering candles, creaking doors, eerie shadows, piercing screams, inexplicable bloodstains, and weird noises. But the terror aroused by tricks and external "machinery" is a far cry from the terror evoked by some terrifying treatment of the human situation. The horror we experience in watching the Werewolf or Dracula or the Frankenstein monster is far less significant than that we get from watching the bloody ambition of Macbeth or the jealousy of Othello. In the first, terror is the end-product; in the second, it is the natural accompaniment of a powerful revelation of life. In the first, we are always aware of a basic unreality; in the second, reality is terrifying.

The story designed merely to provoke laughter or to arouse terror may be an enjoyable and innocent pleasure. The story directed at stimulating tears belongs to a less innocent category. The difference is that the humor story and the terror story seldom ask to be taken for more than what they are: pleasant diversions to help us pass the time agreeably. We enjoy the custard pie in the face and the ghost in the moonlight without taking them seriously. The fiction that depends on such ingredients is pure escape. The tear-jerker, however, asks to be taken seriously. Like the fraudulent street beggar who artfully disposes his rags, puts on dark glasses over perfectly good eyes, holds out a tin cup, and wails about his seven starving children (there are really only two, and he doesn't know what has become of them), the tear-jerker cheats us. It is escape literature posing as its opposite; it is counterfeit interpretation. It cheats us by exaggerating and falsifying reality by asking for compassion that is not deserved.

The quality in a story that aims at drawing forth unmerited tender feeling is known as **sentimentality.** Sentimentality is not the same as genuine emotion. Sentimentality is contrived or excessive or faked emotion. A story contains genuine emotion when it treats life faithfully and perceptively. The sentimentalized story oversimplifies and sweetens life to get its feeling. It exaggerates, manipulates, and prettifies. It mixes tears with sugar.

Genuine emotion, like character, is presented indirectly—it is dramatized. It cannot be produced by words that identify emotions, like *angry, sad, pathetic, heart-breaking,* or *passionate.* A writer draws forth genuine emotion by producing a character in a situation that deserves our sympathy and showing us enough about the character and the situation to make them real and convincing.

Sentimental writers are recognizable by a number of characteristics. First, they often try to make words do what the situation faithfully presented by itself will not do. They **editorialize**—that is, comment on the story and, in a manner, instruct us how to feel. Or they overwrite and **poeticize**—use an immoderately heightened and distended language to accomplish their effects. Second, they make an excessively selective use of detail. All artists, of course, must be selective in their use of detail, but good writers use representative details while sentimentalists use details that all point one way—toward producing emotion rather than conveying truth. The little child that dies will be shown as always uncomplaining and cheerful under adversity, never as naughty, querulous, or ungrateful. It will possibly be an orphan or the only child of a mother who loves it dearly; in addition, it may be lame, hungry, ragged, and possessed of one toy, from which it cannot be parted. The villain will be *all* villain, with a cruel laugh and a sharp whip, though he may reform at the end, for sentimentalists are firm believers in the heart of gold beneath the rough exterior. In short, reality will be unduly heightened and drastically oversimplified. Third, sentimentalists rely heavily on the stock response—an emotion that has its source outside the facts established by the story. In some readers certain situations and objects—babies, mothers, grandmothers, young love, patriotism, worship—produce an almost automatic response, whether the immediate situation warrants it or not. Sentimental writers, to affect such readers, have only to draw out certain stops, as on an organ, to produce an easily anticipated effect. They depend on stock materials to produce a stock response. They thus need not go to the trouble of picturing the situation in realistic and convincing detail. Finally, sentimental writers present, nearly always, a fundamentally "sweet" picture of life. They rely not only on stock characters and situations but also on stock themes. For them every cloud has its silver lining, every bad event its good side, every storm its rainbow. If the little child dies, it goes to heaven or makes some life better by its death. Virtue is characteristically triumphant: the villain is defeated, the ne'er-do-well redeemed. True love is rewarded in some fashion; it is love—never hate—that makes the world go round. In short, sentimental writers specialize in the sad but sweet. The tears called for are warm tears, never bitter. There is always sugar at the bottom of the cup.

For experienced readers, emotion is a highly valued but not easily achieved component of a story. It is a by-product, not the end-product. It is gained by honestly portrayed characters in honestly drawn situations that reflect the complexity, the ambiguity, and the endless variety of life. It is produced by a carefully exercised restraint on the part of the writer rather than by "pulling out all the stops." It is one of the chief rewards of art.

EXERCISES

The six stories that follow are paired. In the first pair, both stories depict terror, but one of them is more purely interpretive than the other. In the second pair, both stories are humorous, but again one of them is interpretive, the other escapist. In the third pair, both stories contain sentiment, but one of them is guilty of sentimentality. For each pair, decide which story is more authentic or significant and give reasons for your choice.

McKnight Malmar

The Storm

She inserted her key in the lock and turned the knob. The March wind snatched the door out of her hand and slammed it against the wall. It took strength to close it against the pressure of the gale, and she had no sooner closed it than the rain came in a pounding downpour, beating noisily against the windows as if trying to follow her in. She could not hear the taxi as it started up and went back down the road.

She breathed a sigh of thankfulness at being home again and in time. In rain like this, the crossroads always were flooded. Half an hour later her cab could not have got through the rising water, and there was no alternative route.

There was no light anywhere in the house. Ben was not home, then. As she turned on the lamp by the sofa she had a sense of anticlimax. All the way home—she had been visiting her sister—she had seen herself going into a lighted house, to Ben, who would be sitting by the fire with his paper. She had taken delight in picturing his happy surprise at seeing her, home a week earlier than he had expected her. She had known just how his round face would light up, how his eyes would twinkle behind his glasses, how he would catch her by the shoulders and look down into her face to see the changes a month had made in her, and then kiss her resoundingly on both cheeks, like a French general bestowing a decoration. Then she would make coffee and find a piece of cake, and they would sit together by the fire and talk.

THE STORM   First published in 1944. McKnight Malmar (1903–1985) was born in Albany, New York, grew up in suburban New York City, and spent the rest of her life in Virginia.

But Ben wasn't here. She looked at the clock on the mantel and saw it was nearly ten. Perhaps he had not planned to come home tonight, as he was not expecting her; even before she had left he frequently was in the city all night because business kept him too late to catch the last train. If he did not come soon, he would not be able to make it at all.

She did not like the thought. The storm was growing worse. She could   5
hear the wild lash of the trees, the whistle of the wind around the corners of the little house. For the first time she regretted this move to the far suburbs. There had been neighbors at first, a quarter-mile down the road; but they moved away several months ago, and now their house stood empty.

She had thought nothing of the lonesomeness. It was perfect here—for two. She had taken such pleasure in fixing up her house—her very own house—and caring for it that she had not missed company other than Ben. But now, alone and with the storm trying to batter its way in, she found it frightening to be so far away from other people. There was no one this side of the crossroads; the road that passed the house wandered past farmland into nothingness in the thick woods a mile farther on.

She hung her hat and her coat in the closet and went to stand before the hall mirror to pin up the soft strands of hair that the wind had loosened. She did not really see the pale face with its blunt nose, the slender, almost childish figure in its grown-up black dress, or the big brown eyes that looked back at her.

She fastened the last strands into the pompadour and turned away from the mirror. Her shoulders drooped a little. There was something childlike about her, like a small girl craving protection, something immature and yet appealing, in spite of her plainness. She was thirty-one and had been married for fifteen months. The fact that she had married at all still seemed a miracle to her.

Now she began to walk through the house, turning on lights as she went. Ben had left it in fairly good order. There was very little trace of an untidy masculine presence; but then, he was a tidy man. She began to realize that the house was cold. Of course, Ben would have lowered the thermostat. He was very careful about things like that. He would not tolerate waste.

No wonder it was cold; the thermostat was set at fifty-eight. She pushed   10
the little needle up to seventy, and the motor in the cellar started so suddenly and noisily that it frightened her for a moment.

She went into the kitchen and made some coffee. While she waited for it to drip she began to prowl around the lower floor. She was curiously restless and could not relax. Yet it was good to be back again among her own things, in her own home. She studied the living-room with fresh eyes. Yes, it was a pleasant room even though it was small. The bright, flowered chintzes on the furniture and at the windows were cheerful and pretty, and the lowboy she had bought three months ago was just right for the middle of the long wall. But her plants, set so bravely along the window sill, had died. Ben had forgotten to water them, in spite of all her admonitions, and now they drooped, shrunken and pale, in whitened, powdery soil. The sight of them added to the depression that was beginning to blot out all the pleasure of homecoming.

She returned to the kitchen and poured herself a cup of coffee, wishing that Ben would come home to share it with her. She carried her cup into the living-room and set it on the small, round table beside Ben's special big chair. The furnace was still mumbling busily, sending up heat, but she was colder than ever. She shivered and got an old jacket of Ben's from the closet and wrapped it around her before she sat down.

The wind hammered at the door and the windows, and the air was full of the sound of water, racing in the gutters, pouring from the leaders, thudding on the roof. Listening, she wished for Ben almost feverishly. She never had felt so alone. And he was such a comfort. He had been so good about her going for this long visit, made because her sister was ill. He had seen to everything and had put her on the train with her arms loaded with books and candy and fruit. She knew those farewell gifts had meant a lot to him—he didn't spend money easily. To be quite honest, he was a little close.

But he was a good husband. She sighed unconsciously, not knowing it was because of youth and romance missed. She repeated it to herself, firmly, as she sipped her coffee. He was a good husband. Suppose he was ten years older than she, and a little set in his ways; a little—perhaps—dictatorial at times, and moody. He had given her what she thought she wanted, security and a home of her own; if security were not enough, she could not blame him for it.

15   Her eye caught a shred of white protruding under a magazine on the table beside her. She put out a hand toward it, yet her fingers were almost reluctant to grasp it. She pulled it out nevertheless and saw that it was, as she had known instinctively, another of the white envelopes. It was empty, and it bore, as usual, the neat, typewritten address: *Benj. T. Willsom, Esq., Wildwood Road, Fairport, Conn.* The postmark was *New York City.* It never varied.

She felt the familiar constriction about the heart as she held it in her hands. What these envelopes contained she never had known. What she did know was their effect on Ben. After receiving one—one came every month or two—he was irritable, at times almost ugly. Their peaceful life together fell apart. At first she had questioned him, had striven to soothe and comfort him; but she soon had learned that this only made him angry, and of late she had avoided any mention of them. For a week after one came they shared the same room and the same table like two strangers, in a silence that was morose on his part and a little frightened on hers.

This one was postmarked three days before. If Ben got home tonight he would probably be cross, and the storm would not help his mood. Just the same she wished he would come.

She tore the envelope into tiny pieces and tossed them into the fireplace. The wind shook the house in its giant grip, and a branch crashed on the roof. As she straightened, a movement at the window caught her eye.

She froze there, not breathing, still half-bent toward the cold fireplace, her hand still extended. The glimmer of white at the window behind the sheeting blur of rain had been—she was sure of it—a human face. There had been eyes. She was certain there had been eyes staring in at her.

The wind's shout took on a personal, threatening note. She was rigid for 20
a long time, never taking her eyes from the window. But nothing moved there now except the water on the windowpane; beyond it there was blackness, and that was all. The only sounds were the thrashing of the trees, the roar of water, and the ominous howl of the wind.

She began to breathe again, at last found courage to turn out the light and go to the window. The darkness was a wall, impenetrable and secret, and the blackness within the house made the storm close in, as if it were a pack of wolves besieging the house. She hastened to put on the light again.

She must have imagined those staring eyes. Nobody could be out on a night like this. Nobody. Yet she found herself terribly shaken.

If only Ben would come home. If only she were not so alone.

She shivered and pulled Ben's coat tighter about her and told herself she was becoming a morbid fool. Nevertheless, she found the aloneness intolerable. Her ears strained to hear prowling footsteps outside the windows. She became convinced that she did hear them, slow and heavy.

Perhaps Ben could be reached at the hotel where he sometimes stayed. 25
She no longer cared whether her homecoming was a surprise to him. She wanted to hear his voice. She went to the telephone and lifted the receiver.

The line was quite dead.

The wires were down, of course.

She fought panic. The face at the window had been an illusion, a trick of the light reflected on the sluicing pane; and the sound of footsteps was an illusion, too. Actual ones would be inaudible in the noise made by the wild storm. Nobody would be out tonight. Nothing threatened her, really. The storm was held at bay beyond these walls, and in the morning the sun would shine again.

The thing to do was to make herself as comfortable as possible and settle down with a book. There was no use going to bed—she couldn't possibly sleep. She would only lie there wide awake and think of that face at the window, hear the footsteps.

She would get some wood for a fire in the fireplace. She hesitated at the 30
top of the cellar stairs. The light, as she switched it on, seemed insufficient; the concrete wall at the foot of the stairs was dank with moisture and somehow gruesome. And wind was chilling her ankles. Rain was beating in through the outside door to the cellar, because that door was standing open.

The inner bolt sometimes did not hold, she knew very well. If it had not been carefully closed, the wind could have loosened it. Yet the open door increased her panic. It seemed to argue the presence of something less impersonal than the gale. It took her a long minute to nerve herself to go down the steps and reach out into the darkness for the doorknob.

In just that instant she was soaked; but her darting eyes could find nothing outdoors but the black, wavering shapes of the maples at the side of the house. The wind helped her and slammed the door resoundingly. She jammed the bolt home with all her strength and then tested it to make sure it would hold. She almost sobbed with the relief of knowing it to be firm against any intruder.

She stood with her wet clothes clinging to her while the thought came that turned her bones to water. Suppose—suppose the face at the window had been real, after all. Suppose its owner had found shelter in the only shelter to be had within a quarter-mile—this cellar.

She almost flew up the stairs again, but then she took herself firmly in hand. She must not let herself go. There had been many storms before; just because she was alone in this one, she must not let morbid fancy run away with her. But she could not throw off the reasonless fear that oppressed her, although she forced it back a little. She began to hear again the tread of the prowler outside the house. Although she knew it to be imagination, it was fearfully real—the crunch of feet on gravel, slow, persistent, heavy, like the patrol of a sentinel.

35   She had only to get an armful of wood. Then she could have a fire, she would have light and warmth and comfort. She would forget these terrors.

The cellar smelled of dust and old moisture. The beams were fuzzed with cobwebs. There was only one light, a dim one in the corner. A little rivulet was running darkly down the wall and already had formed a foot-square pool on the floor.

The woodpile was in the far corner away from the light. She stopped and peered around. Nobody could hide here. The cellar was too open, the supporting stanchions too slender to hide a man.

The oil burner went off with a sharp click. Its mutter, she suddenly realized, had had something human and companionable about it. Nothing was down here with her now but the snarl of the storm.

She almost ran to the woodpile. Then something made her pause and turn before she bent to gather the logs.

40   What was it? Not a noise. Something she had seen as she hurried across that dusty floor. Something odd.

She searched with her eyes. It was a spark of light she had seen, where no spark should be.

An inexplicable dread clutched at her heart. Her eyes widened, round and dark as a frightened deer's. Her old trunk that stood against the wall was open just a crack; from the crack came this tiny pinpoint of reflected light to prick the cellar's gloom.

She went toward it like a woman hypnotized. It was only one more insignificant thing, like the envelope on the table, the vision of the face at the window, the open door. There was no reason for her to feel smothered in terror.

Yet she was sure she had not only closed, but clamped the lid on the trunk; she was sure because she kept two or three old coats in it, wrapped in newspapers and tightly shut away from moths.

Now the lid was raised perhaps an inch. And the twinkle of light was still   45
there.

She threw back the lid.

For a long moment she stood looking down into the trunk, while each
detail of its contents imprinted itself on her brain like an image on a film.
Each tiny detail was indelibly clear and never to be forgotten.

She could not have stirred a muscle in that moment. Horror was a black
cloak thrown around her, stopping her breath, hobbling her limbs.

Then her face dissolved into formlessness. She slammed down the lid
and ran up the stairs like a mad thing. She was breathing again, in deep,
sobbing breaths that tore at her lungs. She shut the door at the top of the
stairs with a crash that shook the house; then she turned the key. Gasping she
clutched one of the sturdy maple chairs by the kitchen table and wedged it
under the knob with hands she could barely control.

The wind took the house in its teeth and shook it as a dog shakes a rat.   50

Her first impulse was to get out of the house. But in the time it took to get
to the front door she remembered the face at the window.

Perhaps she had not imagined it. Perhaps it was the face of a murderer—
a murderer waiting for her out there in the storm; ready to spring on her out
of the dark.

She fell into the big chair, her huddled body shaken by great tremors.
She could not stay here—not with that thing in her trunk. Yet she dared not
leave. Her whole being cried out for Ben. He would know what to do. She
closed her eyes, opened them again, rubbed them hard. The picture still
burned into her brain as if it had been etched with acid. Her hair, loosened,
fell in soft straight wisps about her forehead, and her mouth was slack with
terror.

Her old trunk had held the curled-up body of a woman.

She had not seen the face; the head had been tucked down into the hol-   55
low of the shoulder, and a shower of fair hair had fallen over it. The woman
had worn a red dress. One hand had rested near the edge of the trunk, and on
its third finger there had been a man's ring, a signet bearing the raised figure
of a rampant lion with a small diamond between its paws. It had been the
diamond that caught the light. The little bulb in the corner of the cellar had
picked out this ring from the semidarkness and made it stand out like a
beacon.

She never would be able to forget it. Never forget how the woman
looked: the pale, luminous flesh of her arms; her doubled-up knees against
the side of the trunk, with their silken covering shining softly in the gloom;
the strands of hair that covered her face . . .

Shudders continued to shake her. She bit her tongue and pressed her
hand against her jaw to stop the chattering of her teeth. The salty taste of
blood in her mouth steadied her. She tried to force herself to be rational, to
plan; yet all the time the knowledge that she was imprisoned with the body of
a murdered woman kept beating at her nerves like a flail.

She drew the coat closer about her, trying to dispel the mortal cold that held her. Slowly something beyond the mere fact of murder, of death, began to penetrate her mind. Slowly she realized that beyond this fact there would be consequences. That body in the cellar was not an isolated phenomenon; some train of events had led to its being there and would follow its discovery there.

There would be policemen.

60   At first the thought of policemen was a comforting one; big, brawny men in blue, who would take the thing out of her cellar, take it away so she never need think of it again.

Then she realized it was *her* cellar—hers and Ben's; and policemen are suspicious and prying. Would they think *she* killed the woman? Could they be made to believe she never had seen her before?

Or would they think Ben had done it? Would they take the letters in the white envelopes, and Ben's absences on business, and her own visit to her sister, about which Ben was so helpful, and out of them build a double life for him? Would they insist that the woman had been a discarded mistress, who had hounded him with letters until out of desperation he had killed her? That was a fantastic theory, really; but the police might do that.

They might.

Now a sudden new panic invaded her. The dead woman must be taken out of the cellar, must be hidden. The police must never connect her with this house.

65   Yet the dead woman was bigger than she herself was; she could never move her.

Her craving for Ben became a frantic need. If only he would come home! Come home and take that body away, hide it somewhere so the police could not connect it with this house. He was strong enough to do it.

Even with the strength to move the body by herself she would not dare do it, because there was the prowler—real or imaginary—outside the house. Perhaps the cellar door had not been open by chance. Or perhaps it had been, and the murderer, seeing it so welcoming, had seized the opportunity to plant the evidence of his crime upon the Willsoms' innocent shoulders.

She crouched there, shaking. It was as if the jaws of a great trap had closed on her: on one side the storm and the silence of the telephone, on the other the presence of the prowler and of that still, cramped figure in her trunk. She was caught between them, helpless.

As if to accent her helplessness, the wind stepped up its shriek and a tree crashed thunderously out in the road. She heard glass shatter.

70   Her quivering body stiffened like a drawn bow. Was it the prowler attempting to get in? She forced herself to her feet and made a round of the windows on the first floor and the one above. All the glass was intact, staunchly resisting the pounding of the rain.

Nothing could have made her go into the cellar to see if anything had happened there.

The voice of the storm drowned out all other sounds, yet she could not rid herself of the fancy that she heard footsteps going round and round the house, that eyes sought an opening and spied upon her.

She pulled the shades down over the shiny black windows. It helped a little to make her feel more secure, more sheltered; but only a very little. She told herself sternly that the crash of glass had been nothing more than a branch blown through a cellar window.

The thought brought her no comfort—just the knowledge that it would not disturb that other woman. Nothing could comfort her now but Ben's plump shoulder and his arms around her and his neat, capable mind planning to remove the dead woman from this house.

A kind of numbness began to come over her, as if her capacity for fear were exhausted. She went back to the chair and curled up in it. She prayed mutely for Ben and for daylight. 75

The clock said half-past twelve.

She huddled there, not moving and not thinking, not even afraid, only numb for another hour. Then the storm held its breath for a moment, and in the brief space of silence she heard footsteps on the walk—actual footsteps, firm and quick and loud. A key turned in the lock. The door opened and Ben came in.

He was dripping, dirty, and white with exhaustion. But it was Ben. Once she was sure of it she flung herself on him, babbling incoherently of what she had found.

He kissed her lightly on the cheek and took her arms down from around his neck. "Here, here, my dear. You'll get soaked. I'm drenched to the skin." He removed his glasses and handed them to her, and she began to dry them for him. His eyes squinted at the light. "I had to walk in from the crossroads. What a night!" He began to strip off rubbers and coat and shoes. "You'll never know what a difference it made, finding the place lighted. Lord, but it's good to be home."

She tried again to tell him of the past hours, but again he cut her short. "Now, wait a minute, my dear. I can see you're bothered about something. Just wait until I get into some dry things; then I'll come down and we'll straighten it out. Suppose you rustle up some coffee and toast. I'm done up—the whole trip out was a nightmare, and I didn't know if I'd ever make it from the crossing. I've been hours." 80

He did look tired, she thought with concern. Now that he was back, she could wait. The past hours had taken on the quality of a nightmare, horrifying but curiously unreal. With Ben here, so solid and commonplace and cheerful, she began to wonder if the hours *were* nightmare. She even began to doubt the reality of the woman in the trunk, although she could see her as vividly as ever. Perhaps only the storm was real.

She went to the kitchen and began to make fresh coffee. The chair, still wedged against the kitchen door, was a reminder of her terror. Now that Ben was home it seemed silly, and she put it back in its place by the table.

He came down very soon, before the coffee was ready. How good it was to see him in that old gray bathrobe of his, his hands thrust into its pockets. How normal and wholesome he looked with his round face rubbed pink by a rough towel and his hair standing up in damp little spikes around his bald spot. She was almost shamefaced when she told him of the face at the window, the open door, and finally of the body in the trunk. None of it, she saw quite clearly now, could possibly have happened.

Ben said so, without hesitation. But he came to put an arm around her. "You poor child. The storm scared you to death, and I don't wonder. It's given you the horrors."

85   She smiled dubiously. "Yes. I'm almost beginning to think so. Now that you're back, it seems so safe. But—but you will *look* in the trunk, Ben? I've got to *know*. I can see her so plainly. How could I imagine a thing like that?"

He said indulgently, "Of course I'll look, if it will make you feel better. I'll do it now. Then I can have my coffee in peace."

He went to the cellar door and opened it and snapped on the light. Her heart began to pound once more, a deafening roar in her ears. The opening of the cellar door opened, again, the whole vista of fear: the body, the police, the suspicions that would cluster about her and Ben. The need to hide this evidence of somebody's crime.

She could not have imagined it; it was incredible that she could have believed, for a minute, that her mind had played such tricks on her. In another moment Ben would know it, too.

She heard the thud as he threw back the lid of the trunk. She clutched at the back of a chair, waiting for his voice. It came in an instant.

90   She could not believe it. It was as cheerful and reassuring as before. He said, "There's nothing here but a couple of bundles. Come take a look."

Nothing!

Her knees were weak as she went down the stairs, down into the cellar again.

It was still musty and damp and draped with cobwebs. The rivulet was still running down the wall, but the pool was larger now. The light was still dim.

It was just as she remembered it except that the wind was whistling through a broken window and rain was splattering in on the bits of shattered glass on the floor. The branch lying across the sill had removed every scrap of glass from the frame and left not a single jagged edge.

95   Ben was standing by the open trunk, waiting for her. His stocky body was a bulwark. "See," he said, "there's nothing. Just some old clothes of yours, I guess."

She went to stand beside him. Was she losing her mind? Would she, now, see that crushed figure in there, see the red dress and the smooth shining knees, when Ben could not? And the ring with the diamond between the lion's paws?

Her eyes looked, almost reluctantly, into the trunk. "It *is* empty!"

There were the neat, newspaper-wrapped packages she had put away so carefully, just as she had left them deep in the bottom of the trunk. And nothing else.

She must have imagined the body. She was light with the relief the knowledge brought her, and yet confused and frightened, too. If her mind could play such tricks, if she could imagine anything so gruesome in the complete detail with which she had seen the dead woman in the trunk, the thought of the future was terrifying. When might she not have another such hallucination?

The actual, physical danger did not exist, however, and never existed. 100
The threat of the law hanging over Ben had been based on a dream.

"I—dreamed it all, I must have," she admitted. "Yet it was so horribly clear and I wasn't asleep." Her voice broke. "I thought—oh, Ben, I thought—"

"What did you think, my dear?" His voice was odd, not like Ben's at all. It had a cold cutting edge to it.

He stood looking down at her with an immobility that chilled her more than the cold wind that swept in through the broken window. She tried to read his face, but the light from the little bulb was too weak. It left his features shadowed in broad, dark planes that made him look like a stranger, and somehow sinister.

She said, "I—" and faltered.

He still did not move, but his voice hardened. "What was it you 105
thought?"

She backed away from him.

He moved, then. It was only to take his hands from his pockets to stretch his arms toward her; but she stood for an instant staring at the thing that left her stricken, with a voiceless scream forming in her throat.

She was never to know whether his arms had been outstretched to take her within their shelter or to clutch at her white neck. For she turned and fled, stumbling up the stairs in a mad panic of escape.

He shouted, "Janet! Janet!" His steps were heavy behind her. He tripped on the bottom step and fell on one knee and cursed.

Terror lent her strength and speed. She could not be mistaken. Although 110
she had seen it only once, she knew that on the little finger of his left hand there had been the same, the unmistakable ring the dead woman had worn.

The blessed wind snatched the front door from her and flung it wide, and she was out in the safe, dark shelter of the storm.

QUESTIONS

1. By what means does this story create and build suspense? What uses does it make of mystery? At what points does it employ surprise?
2. Is the ending of the story determinate or indeterminate?
3. From what point of view is the story told? What advantages has this point of view for this story? Are there any places where the contents of Janet's consciousness are suppressed, at least temporarily? For what purpose?

4. Put together an account of Ben's activities that will explain as many as possible of the phenomena that Janet observes—or thinks she observes—during the course of the evening. Are any left unexplained? Is any motivation provided for the murder of the woman in the trunk? How?
5. What are the chief features of Ben's characterization? Why is he characterized as he is? Has the characterization been fashioned to serve the story or the story to serve the characterization?
6. To what extent does the story depend on coincidence?
7. What is the main purpose of the story? Does it have a theme? If so, what?
8. What do you find most effective in the story?

Nadine Gordimer

Once Upon a Time

Someone has written to ask me to contribute to an anthology of stories for children. I reply that I don't write children's stories; and he writes back that at a recent congress/book fair/seminar a certain novelist said every writer ought to write at least one story for children. I think of sending a postcard saying I don't accept that I "ought" to write anything.

And then last night I woke up—or rather was awakened without knowing what had roused me.

A voice in the echo-chamber of the subconscious?

A sound.

5   A creaking of the kind made by the weight carried by one foot after another along a wooden floor. I listened. I felt the apertures of my ears distend with concentration. Again: the creaking. I was waiting for it; waiting to hear if it indicated that feet were moving from room to room, coming up the passage—to my door. I have no burglar bars, no gun under the pillow, but I have the same fears as people who do take these precautions, and my windowpanes are thin as rime, could shatter like a wineglass. A woman was murdered (how do they put it) in broad daylight in a house two blocks away, last year, and the fierce dogs who guarded an old widower and his collection of antique clocks were strangled before he was knifed by a casual laborer he had dismissed without pay.

I was staring at the door, making it out in my mind rather than seeing it, in the dark. I lay quite still—a victim already—the arrhythmia of my heart was fleeing, knocking this way and that against its body-cage. How finely tuned the senses are, just out of rest, sleep! I could never listen intently as

ONCE UPON A TIME   First published in 1989. Nadine Gordimer was born in 1923 in a small town near Johannesburg, South Africa, and graduated from the University of Witwatersrand. She has taught at several American universities, but continues to reside in her native country. A prolific writer, Gordimer has published more than twenty books of fiction (novels and short story collections). In addition to England's prestigious Booker Prize for Fiction, she received the Nobel Prize for Literature in 1991.

that in the distractions of the day; I was reading every faintest sound, identifying and classifying its possible threat.

But I learned that I was to be neither threatened nor spared. There was
no human weight pressing on the boards, the creaking was a buckling, an
epicenter of stress. I was in it. The house that surrounds me while I sleep is
built on undermined ground; far beneath my bed, the floor, the house's
foundations, the stopes and passages of gold mines have hollowed the rock,
and when some face trembles, detaches and falls, three thousand feet below,
the whole house shifts slightly, bringing uneasy strain to the balance and
counterbalance of brick, cement, wood and glass that hold it as a structure
around me. The misbeats of my heart tailed off like the last muffled flourishes on one of the wooden xylophones made by the Chopi and Tsonga°
migrant miners who might have been down there, under me in the earth at
that moment. The stope where the fall was could have been disused, dripping water from its ruptured veins; or men might now be interred there in
the most profound of tombs.

I couldn't find a position in which my mind would let go of my body—
release me to sleep again. So I began to tell myself a story; a bedtime story.

In a house, in a suburb, in a city, there were a man and his wife who loved
each other very much and were living happily ever after. They had a little
boy, and they loved him very much. They had a cat and a dog that the little
boy loved very much. They had a car and a caravan trailer for holidays, and a
swimming-pool which was fenced so that the little boy and his playmates
would not fall in and drown. They had a housemaid who was absolutely
trustworthy and an itinerant gardener who was highly recommended by the
neighbors. For when they began to live happily ever after they were warned,
by that wise old witch, the husband's mother, not to take on anyone off the
street. They were inscribed in a medical benefit society, their pet dog was
licensed, they were insured against fire, flood damage and theft, and sub-
scribed to the local Neighborhood Watch, which supplied them with a
plaque for their gates lettered YOU HAVE BEEN WARNED over the silhouette of a would-be intruder. He was masked; it could not be said if he was
black or white, and therefore proved the property owner was no racist.

It was not possible to insure the house, the swimming pool or the car   10
against riot damage. There were riots, but these were outside the city, where
people of another color were quartered. These people were not allowed into
the suburb except as reliable housemaids and gardeners, so there was nothing to fear, the husband told the wife. Yet she was afraid that some day such
people might come up the street and tear off the plaque YOU HAVE BEEN
WARNED and open the gates and stream in . . . Nonsense, my dear, said the
husband, there are police and soldiers and tear-gas and guns to keep them
away. But to please her—for he loved her very much and buses were being

Chopi and Tsonga: two peoples from Mozambique, northeast of South Africa

burned, cars stoned, and schoolchildren shot by the police in those quarters out of sight and hearing of the suburb—he had electronically controlled gates fitted. Anyone who pulled off the sign YOU HAVE BEEN WARNED and tried to open the gates would have to announce his intentions by pressing a button and speaking into a receiver relayed to the house. The little boy was fascinated by the device and used it as a walkie-talkie in cops and robbers play with his small friends.

The riots were suppressed, but there were many burglaries in the suburb and somebody's trusted housemaid was tied up and shut in a cupboard by thieves while she was in charge of her employers' house. The trusted housemaid of the man and wife and little boy was so upset by this misfortune befalling a friend left, as she herself often was, with responsibility for the possessions of the man and his wife and the little boy that she implored her employers to have burglar bars attached to the doors and windows of the house, and an alarm system installed. The wife said, She is right, let us take heed of her advice. So from every window and door in the house where they were living happily ever after they now saw the trees and sky through bars, and when the little boy's pet cat tried to climb in by the fanlight to keep him company in his little bed at night, as it customarily had done, it set off the alarm keening through the house.

The alarm was often answered—it seemed—by other burglar alarms, in other houses, that had been triggered by pet cats or nibbling mice. The alarms called to one another across the gardens in shrills and bleats and wails that everyone soon became accustomed to, so that the din roused the inhabitants of the suburb no more than the croak of frogs and musical grating of cicadas' legs. Under cover of the electronic harpies' discourse intruders sawed the iron bars and broke into homes, taking away hi-fi equipment, television sets, cassette players, cameras and radios, jewelry and clothing, and sometimes were hungry enough to devour everything in the refrigerator or paused audaciously to drink the whiskey in the cabinets or patio bars. Insurance companies paid no compensation for single malt,° a loss made keener by the property owner's knowledge that the thieves wouldn't even have been able to appreciate what it was they were drinking.

Then the time came when many of the people who were not trusted housemaids and gardeners hung about the suburb because they were unemployed. Some importuned for a job: weeding or painting a roof; anything, baas,° madam. But the man and his wife remembered the warning about taking on anyone off the street. Some drank liquor and fouled the street with discarded bottles. Some begged, waiting for the man or his wife to drive the car out of the electronically operated gates. They sat about with their feet in the gutters, under the jacaranda trees that made a green tunnel of the street—for it was a beautiful suburb, spoilt only by their presence—and sometimes they fell asleep lying right before the gates in the midday sun.

single malt: an expensive Scotch whiskey   ***baas:*** boss

The wife could never see anyone go hungry. She sent the trusted housemaid out with bread and tea, but the trusted housemaid said these were loafers and *tsotsis,*° who would come and tie her and shut her in a cupboard. The husband said, She's right. Take heed of her advice. You only encourage them with your bread and tea. They are looking for their chance . . . And he brought the little boy's tricycle from the garden into the house every night, because if the house was surely secure, once locked and with the alarm set, someone might still be able to climb over the wall or the electronically closed gates into the garden.

You are right, said the wife, then the wall should be higher. And the wise old witch, the husband's mother, paid for the extra bricks as her Christmas present to her son and his wife—the little boy got a Space Man outfit and a book of fairy tales.

But every week there were more reports of intrusion: in broad daylight   15 and the dead of night, in the early hours of the morning, and even in the lovely summer twilight—a certain family was at dinner while the bedrooms were being ransacked upstairs. The man and his wife, talking of the latest armed robbery in the suburb, were distracted by the sight of the little boy's pet cat effortlessly arriving over the seven-foot wall, descending first with a rapid bracing of extended forepaws down on the sheer vertical surface, and then a graceful launch, landing with swishing tail within the property. The whitewashed wall was marked with the cat's comings and goings; and on the street side of the wall there were larger red-earth smudges that could have been made by the kind of broken running shoes, seen on the feet of unemployed loiterers, that had no innocent destination.

When the man and wife and little boy took the pet dog for its walk round the neighborhood streets they no longer paused to admire this show of roses or that perfect lawn; these were hidden behind an array of different varieties of security fences, walls and devices. The man, wife, little boy and dog passed a remarkable choice: there was the low-cost option of pieces of broken glass embedded in cement along the top of walls, there were iron grilles ending in lance-points, there were attempts at reconciling the aesthetics of prison architecture with the Spanish Villa style (spikes painted pink) and with the plaster urns of neoclassical façades (twelve-inch pikes finned like zigzags of lightning and painted pure white). Some walls had a small board affixed, giving the name and telephone number of the firm responsible for the installation of the devices. While the little boy and the pet dog raced ahead, the husband and wife found themselves comparing the possible effectiveness of each style against its appearance; and after several weeks when they paused before this barricade or that without needing to speak, both came out with the conclusion that only one was worth considering. It was the ugliest but the most honest in its suggestion of the pure concentration-camp style, no frills, all evident efficacy. Placed the length of walls, it consisted of a

tsotsis: hooligans

continuous coil of stiff and shining metal serrated into jagged blades, so that there would be no way of climbing over it and no way through its tunnel without getting entangled in its fangs. There would be no way out, only a struggle getting bloodier and bloodier, a deeper and sharper hooking and tearing of flesh. The wife shuddered to look at it. You're right, said the husband, anyone would think twice . . . And they took heed of the advice on a small board fixed to the wall: Consult DRAGON'S TEETH The People For Total Security.

Next day a gang of workmen came and stretched the razor-bladed coils all round the walls of the house where the husband and wife and little boy and pet dog and cat were living happily ever after. The sunlight flashed and slashed, off the serrations, the cornice of razor thorns encircled the home, shining. The husband said, Never mind. It will weather. The wife said, You're wrong. They guarantee it's rust-proof. And she waited until the little boy had run off to play before she said, I hope the cat will take heed . . . The husband said, Don't worry, my dear, cats always look before they leap. And it was true that from that day on the cat slept in the little boy's bed and kept to the garden, never risking a try at breaching security.

One evening, the mother read the little boy to sleep with a fairy story from the book the wise old witch had given him at Christmas. Next day he pretended to be the Prince who braves the terrible thicket of thorns to enter the palace and kiss the Sleeping Beauty back to life: he dragged a ladder to the wall, the shining coiled tunnel was just wide enough for his little body to creep in, and with the first fixing of its razor-teeth in his knees and hands and head he screamed and struggled deeper into its tangle. The trusted house-maid and the itinerant gardener, whose "day" it was, came running, the first to see and to scream with him, and the itinerant gardener tore his hands trying to get at the little boy. Then the man and his wife burst wildly into the garden and for some reason (the cat, probably) the alarm set up wailing against the screams while the bleeding mass of the little boy was hacked out of the security coil with saws, wire-cutters, choppers, and they carried it— the man, the wife, the hysterical trusted housemaid and the weeping gar-dener—into the house.

QUESTIONS

1. The opening section of the story is told by a writer who is awakened by a frightening sound in the night. What two causes for the sound does she consider? Ultimately, which is the more significant cause for fear? How do these together create an emotional background for the "children's story" that she tells?
2. What stylistic devices does the writer use to create the atmosphere of chil-dren's stories?
3. To what extent does the story explore the motives for the behavior of the wife and husband, the husband's mother, the servants, and the people who surround the suburb and the house? What motives can you infer for these people? What ironies do they display in their actions?

4. Why do the wife and husband keep increasing the security devices of their home? What is ironic about the conclusion of the story?
5. Can you fix the blame for the calamity that befalls the child? What are the possible meanings for the repeated phrase "YOU HAVE BEEN WARNED"?
6. What details in the introductory section and in the children's story imply the nature of the social order in which both occur?
7. Compare this story with "The Storm" as a study in fear. What are the most significant differences? What are the themes of the two stories?

James Thurber

The Catbird Seat

Mr. Martin bought the pack of Camels on Monday night in the most crowded cigar store on Broadway. It was theater time and seven or eight men were buying cigarettes. The clerk didn't even glance at Mr. Martin, who put the pack in his overcoat pocket and went out. If any of the staff at F & S had seen him buy the cigarettes, they would have been astonished, for it was generally known that Mr. Martin did not smoke, and never had. No one saw him.

It was just a week to the day since Mr. Martin had decided to rub out Mrs. Ulgine Barrows. The term "rub out" pleased him because it suggested nothing more than the correction of an error—in this case an error of Mr. Fitweiler. Mr. Martin had spent each night of the past week working out his plan and examining it. As he walked home now he went over it again. For the hundredth time he resented the element of imprecision, the margin of guess-work that entered into the business. The project as he had worked it out was casual and bold, the risks were considerable. Something might go wrong anywhere along the line. And therein lay the cunning of his scheme. No one would ever see in it the cautious, painstaking hand of Erwin Martin, head of the filing department at F & S of whom Mr. Fitweiler had once said, "Man is fallible but Martin isn't." No one would see his hand, that is, unless it were caught in the act.

Sitting in his apartment, drinking a glass of milk, Mr. Martin reviewed his case against Mrs. Ulgine Barrows, as he had every night for seven nights. He began at the beginning. Her quacking voice and braying laugh had first profaned the halls of F & S on March 7, 1941 (Mr. Martin had a head for dates). Old Roberts, the personnel chief, had introduced her as the newly appointed special adviser to the president of the firm, Mr. Fitweiler. The

THE CATBIRD SEAT   First published in 1942 in *The New Yorker*. At that time the Dodgers were located in Brooklyn, and Red Barber, originally from Mississippi, was the beloved radio announcer for all the Dodgers' games. James Thurber (1894–1961), cartoonist and writer, was born and grew up in Columbus, Ohio. In 1925, after a year's sojourn in France, he joined the staff of *The New Yorker,* with which he was associated until his death.

woman had appalled Mr. Martin instantly, but he hadn't shown it. He had given her his dry hand, a look of studious concentration, and a faint smile. "Well," she had said, looking at the papers on his desk, "are you lifting the oxcart out of the ditch?" As Mr. Martin recalled the moment, over his milk, he squirmed slightly. He must keep his mind on her crimes as a special adviser, not on her peccadillos as a personality. This he found difficult to do, in spite of entering an objection and sustaining it. The faults of the woman as a woman kept chattering on in his mind like an unruly witness. She had, for almost two years now, baited him. In the halls, in the elevator, even in his own office, into which she romped now and then like a circus horse, she was constantly shouting these silly questions at him. "Are you lifting the oxcart out of the ditch? Are you tearing up the pea patch? Are you hollering down the rain barrel? Are you scraping around the bottom of the pickle barrel? Are you sitting in the catbird seat?"

It was Joey Hart, one of Mr. Martin's two assistants, who had explained what the gibberish meant. "She must be a Dodger fan," he had said. "Red Barber announces the Dodger games over the radio and he uses those expressions—picked 'em up down South." Joey had gone on to explain one or two. "Tearing up the pea patch" meant going on a rampage; "sitting in the catbird seat" meant sitting pretty, like a batter with three balls and no strikes on him. Mr. Martin dismissed all this with an effort. It had been annoying, it had driven him near to distraction, but he was too solid a man to be moved to murder by anything so childish. It was fortunate, he reflected as he passed on to the important charges against Mrs. Barrows, that he had stood up under it so well. He had maintained always an outward appearance of polite tolerance. "Why, I even believe you like the woman," Miss Paird, his other assistant, had once said to him. He had simply smiled.

5   A gavel rapped in Mr. Martin's mind and the case was resumed. Mrs. Ulgine Barrows stood charged with willful, blatant, and persistent attempts to destroy the efficiency and system of F & S. It was competent, material, and relevant to review her advent and rise to power. Mr. Martin had got the story from Miss Paird, who seemed always able to find things out. According to her, Mrs. Barrows had met Mr. Fitweiler at a party, where she had rescued him from the embraces of a powerfully built drunken man who had mistaken the president of F & S for a famous retired Middle Western football coach. She had led him to a sofa and somehow worked upon him a monstrous magic. The aging gentleman had jumped to the conclusion there and then that this was a woman of singular attainments, equipped to bring out the best in him and the firm. A week later he had introduced her into F & S as his special adviser. On that day confusion got its foot in the door. After Miss Tyson, Mr. Brundage and Mr. Bartlett had been fired and Mr. Munson had taken his hat and stalked out, mailing in his resignation later, old Roberts had been emboldened to speak to Mr. Fitweiler. He mentioned that Mr. Munson's department had been "a little disrupted" and hadn't they perhaps better resume the old system there? Mr. Fitweiler had said certainly not. He had the greatest faith in Mrs. Barrows's

ideas. "They require a little seasoning, a little seasoning, is all," he had added. Mr. Roberts had given it up. Mr. Martin reviewed in detail all the changes wrought by Mrs. Barrows. She had begun chipping at the cornices of the firm's edifice and now she was swinging at the foundation with a pickaxe.

Mr. Martin came now, in his summing up, to the afternoon of Monday, November 2, 1942—just one week ago. On that day, at 3 P.M., Mrs. Barrows had bounced into his office. "Boo!" she had yelled. "Are you scraping around the bottom of the pickle barrel?" Mr. Martin had looked at her from under his green eyeshade, saying nothing. She had begun to wander about the office, taking it in with her great, popping eyes. "Do you really need *all* these filing cabinets?" she had demanded suddenly. Mr. Martin's heart had jumped. "Each of these files," he had said, keeping his voice even, "plays an indispensable part in the system of F & S." She had brayed at him, "Well, don't tear up the pea patch!" and gone to the door. From there she had bawled, "But you sure have got a lot of fine scrap in here!" Mr. Martin could no longer doubt that the finger was on his beloved department. Her pickaxe was on the upswing, poised for the first blow. It had not come yet; he had received no blue memo from the enchanted Mr. Fitweiler bearing nonsensical instructions deriving from the obscene woman. But there was no doubt in Mr. Martin's mind that one would be forthcoming. He must act quickly. Already a precious week had gone by. Mr. Martin stood up in his living room, still holding his milk glass. "Gentlemen of the jury," he said to himself, "I demand the death penalty for this horrible person."

The next day Mr. Martin followed his routine, as usual. He polished his glasses more often and once sharpened an already sharp pencil, but not even Miss Paird noticed. Only once did he catch sight of his victim; she swept past him in the hall with a patronizing "Hi!" At five-thirty he walked home, as usual, and had a glass of milk, as usual. He had never drunk anything stronger in his life—unless you could count ginger ale. The late Sam Schlosser, the S of F & S, had praised Mr. Martin at a staff meeting several years before for his temperate habits. "Our most efficient worker neither drinks nor smokes," he had said. "The results speak for themselves." Mr. Fitweiler had sat by, nodding approval.

Mr. Martin was still thinking about that red-letter day as he walked over to the Schrafft's on Fifth Avenue near Forty-sixth Street. He got there, as he always did, at eight o'clock. He finished his dinner and the financial page of the *Sun* at a quarter to nine, as he always did. It was his custom after dinner to take a walk. This time he walked down Fifth Avenue at a casual pace. His gloved hands felt moist and warm, his forehead cold. He transferred the Camels from his overcoat to a jacket pocket. He wondered, as he did so, if they did not represent an unnecessary note of strain. Mrs. Barrows smoked only Luckies. It was his idea to puff a few puffs on a Camel (after the rubbing-out), stub it out in the ashtray holding her lipstick-stained Luckies, and thus drag a small red herring across the trail. Perhaps it was not a good idea. It would take time. He might even choke, too loudly.

Mr. Martin had never seen the house on West Twelfth Street where Mrs. Barrows lived, but he had a clear enough picture of it. Fortunately, she had bragged to everybody about her ducky first-floor apartment in the perfectly darling three-story red-brick. There would be no doorman or other attendants; just the tenants of the second and third floors. As he walked along, Mr. Martin realized that he would get there before nine-thirty. He had considered walking north on Fifth Avenue from Schrafft's to a point from which it would take him until ten o'clock to reach the house. At that hour people were less likely to be coming in or going out. But the procedure would have made an awkward loop in the straight thread of his casualness, and he had abandoned it. It was impossible to figure when people would be entering or leaving the house, anyway. There was a great risk at any hour. If he ran into anybody, he would simply have to place the rubbing-out of Ulgine Barrows in the inactive file forever. The same thing would hold true if there were someone in her apartment. In that case he would just say that he had been passing by, recognized her charming house, and thought to drop in.

10   It was eighteen minutes after nine when Mr. Martin turned into Twelfth Street. A man passed him, and a man and a woman, talking. There was no one within fifty paces when he came to the house, halfway down the block. He was up the steps and in the small vestibule in no time, pressing the bell under the card that said "Mrs. Ulgine Barrows." When the clicking in the lock started he jumped forward against the door. He got inside fast, closing the door behind him. A bulb in a lantern hung from the hall ceiling on a chain seemed to give a monstrously bright light. There was nobody on the stair, which went up ahead of him along the left wall. A door opened down the hall in the wall on the right. He went toward it swiftly, on tiptoe.

"Well, for God's sake, look who's here!" bawled Mrs. Barrows, and her braying laugh rang out like the report of a shotgun. He rushed past her like a football tackle, bumping her. "Hey, quit shoving!" she said, closing the door behind them. They were in her living room, which seemed to Mr. Martin to be lighted by a hundred lamps. "What's after you?" she said. "You're as jumpy as a goat." He found he was unable to speak. His heart was wheezing in his throat. "I—yes," he finally brought out. She was jabbering and laughing as she started to help him off with his coat. "No, no," he said. "I'll put it here." He took it off and put it on a chair near the door. "Your hat and gloves, too," she said. "You're in a lady's house." He put his hat on top of the coat. Mrs. Barrows seemed larger than he had thought. He kept his gloves on. "I was passing by," he said. "I recognized—is there anyone here?" She laughed louder than ever. "No," she said, "we're all alone. You're as white as a sheet, you funny man. Whatever *has* come over you? I'll mix you a toddy." She started toward a door across the room. "Scotch-and-soda be all right? But say, you don't drink, do you?" She turned and gave him her amused look. Mr. Martin pulled himself together. "Scotch-and-soda will be all right," he heard himself say. He could hear her laughing in the kitchen.

Mr. Martin looked quickly around the living room for the weapon. He had counted on finding one there. There were andirons and a poker and something in a corner that looked like an Indian club. None of them would do. It couldn't be that way. He began to pace around. He came to a desk. On it lay a metal paper knife with an ornate handle. Would it be sharp enough? He reached for it and knocked over a small brass jar. Stamps spilled out of it and it fell to the floor with a clatter. "Hey," Mrs. Barrows yelled from the kitchen, "are you tearing up the pea patch?" Mr. Martin gave a strange laugh. Picking up the knife, he tried its point against his left wrist. It was blunt. It wouldn't do.

When Mrs. Barrows reappeared, carrying two highballs, Mr. Martin, standing there with his gloves on, became acutely conscious of the fantasy he had wrought. Cigarettes in his pocket, a drink prepared for him—it was all too grossly improbable. It was more than that; it was impossible. Somewhere in the back of his mind a vague idea stirred, sprouted. "For heaven's sake, take off those gloves," said Mrs. Barrows. "I always wear them in the house," said Mr. Martin. The idea began to bloom, strange and wonderful. She put the glasses on a coffee table in front of a sofa and sat on the sofa. "Come over here, you odd little man," she said. Mr. Martin went over and sat beside her. It was difficult getting a cigarette out of the pack of Camels, but he managed it. She held a match for him, laughing. "Well," she said, handing him his drink, "this is perfectly marvelous. You with a drink and a cigarette."

Mr. Martin puffed, not too awkwardly, and took a gulp of the highball. "I drink and smoke all the time," he said. He clinked his glass against hers. "Here's nuts to that old windbag, Fitweiler," he said, and gulped again. The stuff tasted awful, but he made no grimace. "Really, Mr. Martin," she said, her voice and posture changing, "you are insulting our employer." Mrs. Barrows was now all special adviser to the president. "I am preparing a bomb," said Mr. Martin, "which will blow the old goat higher than hell." He had only had a little of the drink, which was not strong. It couldn't be that. "Do you take dope or something?" Mrs. Barrows asked coldly. "Heroin," said Mr. Martin. "I'll be coked to the gills when I bump the old buzzard off." "Mr. Martin!" she shouted, getting to her feet. "That will be all of that. You must go at once." Mr. Martin took another swallow of his drink. He tapped his cigarette out in the ashtray and put the pack of Camels on the coffee table. Then he got up. She stood glaring at him. He walked over and put on his hat and coat. "Not a word about this," he said, and laid an index finger against his lips. All Mrs. Barrows could bring out was "Really!" Mr. Martin put his hand on the doorknob. "I'm sitting in the catbird seat," he said. He stuck his tongue out at her and left. Nobody saw him go.

Mr. Martin got to his apartment, walking, well before eleven. No one saw him go in. He had two glasses of milk after brushing his teeth, and he felt elated. It wasn't tipsiness, because he hadn't been tipsy. Anyway, the walk had worn off all effects of the whiskey. He got in bed and read a magazine for a while. He was asleep before midnight.

Mr. Martin got to the office at eight-thirty the next morning, as usual. At a quarter to nine, Ulgine Barrows, who had never before arrived at work before ten, swept into his office. "I'm reporting to Mr. Fitweiler now!" she

15

shouted. "If he turns you over to the police, it's no more than you deserve!" Mr. Martin gave her a look of shocked surprise. "I beg your pardon?" he said. Mrs. Barrows snorted and bounced out of the room, leaving Miss Paird and Joey Hart staring after her. "What's the matter with that old devil now?" asked Miss Paird. "I have no idea," said Mr. Martin, resuming his work. The other two looked at him and then at each other. Miss Paird got up and went out. She walked slowly past the closed door of Mr. Fitweiler's office. Mrs. Barrows was yelling inside, but she was not braying. Miss Paird could not hear what the woman was saying. She went back to her desk.

Forty-five minutes later, Mrs. Barrows left the president's office and went into her own, shutting the door. It wasn't until half an hour later that Mr. Fitweiler sent for Mr. Martin. The head of the filing department, neat, quiet, attentive, stood in front of the old man's desk. Mr. Fitweiler was pale and nervous. He took his glasses off and twiddled them. He made a small, bruffing sound in his throat. "Martin," he said, "you have been with us more than twenty years." "Twenty-two, sir," said Mr. Martin. "In that time," pursued the president, "your work and your—uh—manner have been exemplary." "I trust so, sir," said Mr. Martin. "I have understood, Martin," said Mr. Fitweiler, "that you have never taken a drink or smoked." "That is correct, sir," said Mr. Martin. "Ah, yes," Mr. Fitweiler polished his glasses. "You may describe what you did after leaving the office yesterday, Martin," he said. Mr. Martin allowed less than a second for his bewildered pause. "Certainly, sir," he said. "I walked home. Then went to Schrafft's for dinner. Afterward I walked home again. I went to bed early, sir, and read a magazine for a while. I was asleep before eleven." "Ah, yes," said Mr. Fitweiler again. He was silent for a moment, searching for the proper words to say to the head of the filing department. "Mrs. Barrows," he said finally, "Mrs. Barrows has worked hard, Martin, very hard. It grieves me to report that she has suffered a severe breakdown. It has taken the form of a persecution complex accompanied by distressing hallucinations." "I am very sorry, sir," said Mr. Martin. "Mrs. Barrows is under the delusion," continued Mr. Fitweiler, "that you visited her last evening and behaved yourself in an—uh—unseemly manner." He raised his hand to silence Mr. Martin's little pained outcry. "It is the nature of these psychological diseases," Mr. Fitweiler said, "to fix upon the least likely and most innocent party as the—uh—source of persecution. These matters are not for the lay mind to grasp, Martin. I've just had my psychiatrist, Dr. Fitch, on the phone. He would not, of course, commit himself, but he made enough generalizations to substantiate my suspicions. I suggested to Mrs. Barrows, when she had completed her—uh—story to me this morning, that she visit Dr. Fitch, for I suspected a condition at once. She flew, I regret to say, into a rage, and demanded—uh—requested that I call you on the carpet. You may not know, Martin, but Mrs. Barrows had planned a reorganization of your department—subject to my approval, of course, subject to my approval. This brought you, rather than anyone else, to her mind—but again that is a phenomenon for Dr. Fitch and not for us.

So, Martin, I am afraid Mrs. Barrows's usefulness here is at an end." "I am dreadfully sorry, sir," said Mr. Martin.

It was at this point that the door to the office blew open with the suddenness of a gas-main explosion and Mrs. Barrows catapulted through it. "Is the little rat denying it?" she screamed. "He can't get away with that!" Mr. Martin got up and moved discreetly to a point beside Mr. Fitweiler's chair. "You drank and smoked at my apartment," she bawled at Mr. Martin, "and you know it! You called Mr. Fitweiler an old windbag and said you were going to blow him up when you got coked to the gills on your heroin!" She stopped yelling to catch her breath and a new glint came into her popping eyes. "If you weren't such a drab, ordinary little man," she said, "I'd think you'd planned it all. Sticking your tongue out, saying you were sitting in the catbird seat, because you thought no one would believe me when I told it! My God, it's really too perfect!" She brayed loudly and hysterically, and the fury was on her again. She glared at Mr. Fitweiler. "Can't you see how he has tricked us, you old fool? Can't you see his little game?" But Mr. Fitweiler had been surreptitiously pressing all the buttons under the top of his desk and employees of F & S began pouring into the room. "Stockton," said Mr. Fitweiler, "you and Fishbein will take Mrs. Barrows to her home. Mrs. Powell, you will go with them." Stockton, who had played a little football in high school, blocked Mrs. Barrows as she made for Mr. Martin. It took him and Fishbein together to force her out of the door into the hall, crowded with stenographers and office boys. She was still screaming imprecations at Mr. Martin, tangled and contradictory imprecations. The hubbub finally died out down the corridor.

"I regret that this has happened," said Mr. Fitweiler. "I shall ask you to dismiss it from your mind, Martin." "Yes sir," said Mr. Martin, anticipating his chief's "That will be all" by moving to the door. "I will dismiss it." He went out and shut the door, and his step was light and quick in the hall. When he entered his department he had slowed down to his customary gait, and he walked quietly across the room to the W20 file, wearing a look of studious concentration.

QUESTIONS

1. How is suspense aroused and maintained in the story? What is the story's principal surprise?
2. Through whose consciousness are the events of the story chiefly seen? Are there any departures from this strictly limited point of view? Where in the story are we taken most fully into Mr. Martin's mind? For what purpose?
3. At what point in the story do Mr. Martin's plans change? What happens to the point of view at this point? What does Thurber's handling of the point of view here tell us about the seriousness of the story's purpose?
4. Characterize Mr. Martin and Mrs. Barrows respectively. In what ways are they character foils?

5. Analyze the story in terms of its conflicts. What kinds of conflict are in-volved? Is there any internal conflict? What kind of conflict that *might* be expected in a murder story is missing?
6. Evaluate the surprise ending of the story by the criteria suggested on page 45.
7. What insights into the life of a business office does the story provide? What kind of insight does the story not provide? What is the story's greatest improbability?
8. What are the main sources of the story's humor?
9. Why does Thurber choose this particular expression of Mrs. Barrows's for his title rather than one of her others?

Frank O'Connor

The Drunkard

It was a terrible blow to Father when Mr. Dooley on the terrace died. Mr. Dooley was a commercial traveler with two sons in the Dominicans and a car of his own, so socially he was miles ahead of us, but he had no false pride. Mr. Dooley was an intellectual, and, like all intellectuals, the thing he loved best was conversation, and in his own limited way Father was a well-read man and could appreciate an intelligent talker. Mr. Dooley was remarkably intelligent. Between business acquaintances and clerical contacts, there was very little he didn't know about what went on in town, and evening after evening he crossed the road to our gate to explain to Father the news behind the news. He had a low, palavering voice and a knowing smile, and Father would listen in astonishment, giving him a conversational lead now and again, and then stump triumphantly in to Mother with his face aglow and ask: "Do you know what Mr. Dooley is after telling me?" Ever since, when somebody has given me some bit of information off the record I have found myself on the point of asking: "Was it Mr. Dooley told you that?"

Till I actually saw him laid out in his brown shroud with the rosary beads entwined between his waxy fingers I did not take the report of his death seriously. Even then I felt there must be a catch and that some summer evening Mr. Dooley must reappear at our gate to give us the lowdown on the next world. But Father was very upset, partly because Mr. Dooley was about one age with himself, a thing that always gives a distinctly personal turn to another man's demise; partly because now he would have no one to tell him what dirty work was behind the latest scene at the Corporation.° You could

THE DRUNKARD   First published in 1948. Frank O'Connor (1903–1966) was born Michael O'Donovan, the only child of very poor, Roman Catholic parents in Cork, Ire-land. He used his mother's maiden name as a pseudonym when he began to publish. "The Drunkard" is based on an incident from his boyhood in Cork, as revealed in the first two chapters of his autobiographical volume, *An Only Son* (1961).
Corporation: the officials of the city (mayor, aldermen, councillors)

count on your fingers the number of men in Blarney Lane who read the papers as Mr. Dooley did, and none of these would have overlooked the fact that Father was only a laboring man. Even Sullivan, the carpenter, a mere nobody, thought he was a cut above Father. It was certainly a solemn event.

"Half past two to the Curragh," Father said meditatively, putting down the paper.

"But you're not thinking of going to the funeral?" Mother asked in alarm.

"'Twould be expected," Father said, scenting opposition. "I wouldn't give it to say to them."   5

"I think," said Mother with suppressed emotion, "it will be as much as anyone will expect if you go to the chapel with him."

("Going to the chapel," of course, was one thing, because the body was removed after work, but going to a funeral meant the loss of a half-day's pay.)

"The people hardly know us," she added.

"God between us and all harm," Father replied with dignity, "we'd be glad if it was our own turn."

To give Father his due, he was always ready to lose a half day for the sake   10 of an old neighbor. It wasn't so much that he liked funerals as that he was a conscientious man who did as he would be done by, and nothing could have consoled him so much for the prospect of his own death as the assurance of a worthy funeral. And, to give Mother her due, it wasn't the half-day's pay she begrudged, badly as we could afford it.

Drink, you see, was Father's great weakness. He could keep steady for months, even for years, at a stretch, and while he did he was as good as gold. He was first up in the morning and brought the mother a cup of tea in bed, stayed home in the evenings and read the paper; saved money and bought himself a new blue serge suit and bowler hat. He laughed at the folly of men who, week in, week out, left their hard-earned money with the publicans; and sometimes, to pass an idle hour, he took pencil and paper and calculated precisely how much he saved each week through being a teetotaller. Being a natural optimist he sometimes continued this calculation through the whole span of his prospective existence and the total was breathtaking. He would die worth hundreds.

If I had only known it, this was a bad sign; a sign he was becoming stuffed up with spiritual pride and imagining himself better than his neighbors. Sooner or later, the spiritual pride grew till it called for some form of celebration. Then he took a drink—not whiskey, of course; nothing like that—just a glass of some harmless drink like lager beer. That was the end of Father. By the time he had taken the first he already realized that he had made a fool of himself, took a second to forget it and a third to forget that he couldn't forget, and at last came home reeling drunk. From this on it was "The Drunkard's Progress," as in the moral prints. Next day he stayed in from work with a sick head while Mother went off to make his excuses at the works, and inside a fortnight he was poor and savage and despondent again.

Once he began he drank steadily through everything down to the kitchen clock. Mother and I knew all the phases and dreaded all the dangers. Funerals were one.

"I have to go to Dunphy's to do a half-day's work," said Mother in distress. "Who's to look after Larry?"

"I'll look after Larry," Father said graciously. "The little walk will do him good."

15   There was no more to be said, though we all knew I didn't need anyone to look after me, and that I could quite well have stayed home and looked after Sonny, but I was being attached to the party to act as a brake on Father. As a brake I had never achieved anything, but Mother still had great faith in me.

Next day, when I got home from school, Father was there before me and made a cup of tea for both of us. He was very good at tea, but too heavy in the hand for anything else; the way he cut bread was shocking. Afterwards, we went down the hill to the church, Father wearing his best blue serge and a bowler cocked to one side of his head with the least suggestion of the masher. To his great joy he discovered Peter Crowley among the mourners. Peter was another danger signal, as I knew well from certain experiences after Mass on Sunday morning: a mean man, as Mother said, who only went to funerals for the free drinks he could get at them. It turned out that he hadn't even known Mr. Dooley! But Father had a sort of contemptuous regard for him as one of the foolish people who wasted their good money in public-houses when they could be saving it. Very little of his own money Peter Crowley wasted!

It was an excellent funeral from Father's point of view. He had it all well studied before we set off after the hearse in the afternoon sunlight.

"Five carriages!" he exclaimed. "Five carriages and sixteen covered cars! There's one alderman, two councillors and 'tis unknown how many priests. I didn't see a funeral like this from the road since Willie Mack, the publican, died."

"Ah, he was well liked," said Crowley in his husky voice.

20   "My goodness, don't I know that?" snapped Father. "Wasn't the man my best friend? Two nights before he died—only two nights—he was over telling me the goings-on about the housing contract. Them fellows in the Corporation are night and day robbers. But even I never imagined he was as well connected as that."

Father was stepping out like a boy, pleased with everything: the other mourners, and the fine houses along Sunday's Well. I knew danger signals were there in full force: a sunny day, a fine funeral and a distinguished company of clerics and public men were bringing out all the natural vanity and flightiness of Father's character. It was with something like genuine pleasure that he saw his old friend lowered into the grave; with the sense of having performed a duty and the pleasant awareness that however much he would miss poor Mr. Dooley in the long summer evenings, it was he and not poor Mr. Dooley who would do the missing.

"We'll be making tracks before they break up," he whispered to Crowley as the gravediggers tossed in the first shovelfuls of clay, and away he went, hopping like a goat from grassy hump to hump. The drivers, who were probably in the same state as himself, though without months of abstinence to put an edge on it, looked up hopefully.

"Are they nearly finished, Mick?" bawled one.

"All over now bar the last prayers," trumpeted Father in the tone of one who brings news of great rejoicing.

The carriages passed us in a lather of dust several hundred yards from the   25
public-house, and Father, whose feet gave him trouble in hot weather, quickened his pace, looking nervously over his shoulder for any sign of the main body of mourners crossing the hill. In a crowd like that a man might be kept waiting.

When we did reach the pub the carriages were drawn up outside, and solemn men in black ties were cautiously bringing out consolation to mysterious females whose hands reached out modestly from behind the drawn blinds of the coaches. Inside the pub there were only the drivers and a couple of shawly women. I felt if I was to act as a brake at all, this was the time, so I pulled Father by the coattails.

"Dadda, can't we go home now?" I asked.

"Two minutes now," he said, beaming affectionately. "Just a bottle of lemonade and we'll go home."

This was a bribe, and I knew it, but I was always a child of weak character. Father ordered lemonade and two pints. I was thirsty and swallowed my drink at once. But that wasn't Father's way. He had long months of abstinence behind him and an eternity of pleasure before. He took out his pipe, blew through it, filled it, and then lit it with loud pops, his eyes bulging above it. After that he deliberately turned his back on the pint, leaned one elbow on the counter in the attitude of a man who did not know there was a pint behind him, and deliberately brushed the tobacco from his palms. He had settled down for the evening. He was steadily working through all the important funerals he had ever attended. The carriages departed and the minor mourners drifted in till the pub was half full.

"Dadda," I said, pulling his coat again, "can't we go home now?"   30

"Ah, your mother won't be in for a long time yet," he said benevolently enough. "Run out in the road and play, can't you."

It struck me very cool, the way grown-ups assumed that you could play all by yourself on a strange road. I began to get bored as I had so often been bored before. I knew Father was quite capable of lingering there till nightfall. I knew I might have to bring him home, blind drunk, down Blarney Lane, with all the old women at their doors, saying: "Mick Delaney is on it again." I knew that my mother would be half crazy with anxiety; that next day Father wouldn't go out to work; and before the end of the week she would be running down to the pawn with the clock under her shawl. I could never get over the lonesomeness of the kitchen without a clock.

I was still thirsty. I found if I stood on tiptoe I could just reach Father's glass, and the idea occurred to me that it would be interesting to know what the contents were like. He had his back to it and wouldn't notice. I took down the glass and sipped cautiously. It was a terrible disappointment. I was astonished that he could even drink such stuff. It looked as if he had never tried lemonade.

I should have advised him about lemonade but he was holding forth himself in great style. I heard him say that bands were a great addition to a funeral. He put his arms in the position of someone holding a rifle in reverse and hummed a few bars of Chopin's Funeral March. Crowley nodded reverently. I took a longer drink and began to see that porter might have its advantages. I felt pleasantly elevated and philosophic. Father hummed a few bars of the Dead March in *Saul*. It was a nice pub and a very fine funeral, and I felt sure that poor Mr. Dooley in Heaven must be highly gratified. At the same time I thought they might have given him a band. As Father said, bands were a great addition.

35   But the wonderful thing about porter was the way it made you stand aside, or rather float aloft like a cherub rolling on a cloud, and watch yourself with your legs crossed, leaning against a bar counter, not worrying about trifles but thinking deep, serious, grown-up thoughts about life and death. Looking at yourself like that, you couldn't help thinking after a while how funny you looked, and suddenly you got embarrassed and wanted to giggle. But by the time I had finished the pint, that phase too had passed; I found it hard to put back the glass, the counter seemed to have grown so high. Melancholia was supervening again.

"Well," Father said reverently, reaching behind him for his drink, "God rest the poor man's soul, wherever he is!" He stopped, looked first at the glass, and then at the people around him. "Hello," he said in a fairly good-humored tone, as if he were just prepared to consider it a joke, even if it was in bad taste, "who was at this?"

There was silence for a moment while the publican and the old women looked first at Father and then at his glass.

"There was no one at it, my good man," one of the women said with an offended air. "Is it robbers you think we are?"

"Ah, there's no one here would do a thing like that, Mick," said the publican in a shocked tone.

40   "Well, someone did it," said Father, his smile beginning to wear off.

"If they did, they were them that were nearer it," said the woman darkly, giving me a dirty look; and at the same moment the truth began to dawn on Father. I suppose I must have looked a bit starry-eyed. He bent and shook me.

"Are you all right, Larry?" he asked in alarm.

Peter Crowley looked down at me and grinned.

"Could you beat that?" he exclaimed in a husky voice.

45   I could and without difficulty. I started to get sick. Father jumped back in holy terror that I might spoil his good suit, and hastily opened the back door.

"Run! run! run!" he shouted.

I saw the sunlit wall outside with the ivy overhanging it, and ran. The intention was good but the performance was exaggerated, because I lurched right into the wall, hurting it badly, as it seemed to me. Being always very polite, I said "Pardon" before the second bout came on me. Father, still concerned for his suit, came up behind and cautiously held me while I got sick.

"That's a good boy!" he said encouragingly. "You'll be grand when you get that up."

Begor, I was not grand! Grand was the last thing I was. I gave one unmerciful wail out of me as he steered me back to the pub and put me sitting on the bench near the shawlies. They drew themselves up with an offended air, still sore at the suggestion that they had drunk his pint.

"God help us!" moaned one, looking pityingly at me. "Isn't it the likes of   50 them would be fathers?"

"Mick," said the publican in alarm, spraying sawdust on my tracks, "that child isn't supposed to be in here at all. You'd better take him home quick in case a bobby would see him."

"Merciful God!" whimpered Father, raising his eyes to heaven and clapping his hands silently as he only did when distraught. "What misfortune was on me? Or what will his mother say? . . . If women might stop at home and look after their children themselves!" he added in a snarl for the benefit of the shawlies. "Are them carriages all gone, Bill?"

"The carriages are finished long ago, Mick," replied the publican.

"I'll take him home," Father said despairingly. . . . "I'll never bring you out again," he threatened me. "Here," he added, giving me the clean handkerchief from his breast pocket, "put that over your eye."

The blood on the handkerchief was the first indication I got that I was   55 cut, and instantly my temple began to throb and I set up another howl. "Whisht, whisht, whisht!" Father said testily, steering me out the door. "One'd think you were killed. That's nothing. We'll wash it when we get home."

"Steady now, old scout!" Crowley said, taking the other side of me. "You'll be all right in a minute."

I never met two men who knew less about the effects of drink. The first breath of fresh air and the warmth of the sun made me groggier than ever and I pitched and rolled between wind and tide till Father started to whimper again.

"God Almighty, and the whole road out! What misfortune was on me didn't stop at my work! Can't you walk straight?"

I couldn't. I saw plain enough that, coaxed by the sunlight, every woman old and young in Blarney Lane was leaning over her half-door or sitting on her doorstep. They all stopped gabbling to gape at the strange spectacle of two sober, middle-aged men bringing home a drunken small boy with a cut over his eye. Father, torn between the shamefast desire to get me home as quick as he could, and the neighborly need to explain that it wasn't his fault, finally halted outside Mrs. Roche's. There was a gang of old women outside a door at the opposite side of the road. I didn't like the look of them from the first. They seemed altogether too interested in me. I leaned against the wall of Mrs. Roche's cottage with my hands in my trousers pockets, thinking mournfully of poor Mr. Dooley in his cold grave on the Curragh, who would never walk down the road again, and, with great feeling, I began to sing a favorite song of Father's.

> Though lost to Mononia and cold in the grave
> He returns to Kincora no more.

60   "Wisha, the poor child!" Mrs. Roche said, "Haven't he a lovely voice, God bless him!"

That was what I thought myself, so I was the more surprised when Father said "Whisht!" and raised a threatening finger at me. He didn't seem to realize the appropriateness of the song, so I sang louder than ever.

"Whisht, I tell you!" he snapped, and then tried to work up a smile for Mrs. Roche's benefit. "We're nearly home now. I'll carry you the rest of the way."

But, drunk and all as I was, I knew better than to be carried home ignominiously like that.

"Now," I said severely, "can't you leave me alone? I can walk all right. 'Tis only my head. All I want is a rest."

65   "But you can rest at home in bed," he said viciously, trying to pick me up, and I knew by the flush on his face that he was very vexed.

"Ah, Jasus," I said crossly, "what do I want to go home for? Why the hell can't you leave me alone?"

For some reason the gang of old women at the other side of the road thought this was very funny. They nearly split their sides over it. A gassy fury began to expand in me at the thought that a fellow couldn't have a drop taken without the whole neighborhood coming out to make game of him.

"Who are ye laughing at?" I shouted, clenching my fists at them. "I'll make ye laugh at the other side of yeer faces if ye don't let me pass."

They seemed to think this funnier still; I had never seen such ill-mannered people.

70   "Go away, ye bloody bitches!" I said.

"Whisht, whisht, whisht, I tell you!" snarled Father, abandoning all pretence of amusement and dragging me along behind him by the hand. I was maddened by the women's shrieks of laughter. I was maddened by Father's bullying. I tried to dig in my heels but he was too powerful for me, and I could only see the women by looking back over my shoulder.

"Take care or I'll come back and show ye!" I shouted. "I'll teach ye to let decent people pass. Fitter for ye to stop at home an wash yeer dirty faces."

"'Twill be all over the road," whimpered Father. "Never again, never again, not if I live to be a thousand!"

To this day I don't know whether he was forswearing me or the drink. By way of a song suitable to my heroic mood I bawled "The Boys of Wexford," as he dragged me in home. Crowley, knowing he was not safe, made off and Father undressed me and put me to bed. I couldn't sleep because of the whirling in my head. It was very unpleasant, and I got sick again. Father came in with a wet cloth and mopped up after me. I lay in a fever, listening to him chopping sticks to start a fire. After that I heard him lay the table.

Suddenly the front door banged open and Mother stormed in with Sonny in her arms, not her usual gentle, timid self, but a wild, raging woman. It was clear that she had heard it all from the neighbors.

"Mick Delaney," she cried hysterically, "what did you do to my son?"

"Whisht, woman, whisht, whisht!" he hissed, dancing from one foot to the other. "Do you want the whole road to hear?"

"Ah," she said with a horrifying laugh, "the road knows all about it by this time. The road knows the way you filled your unfortunate innocent child with drink to make sport for you and that other rotten, filthy brute."

"But I gave him no drink," he shouted, aghast at the horrifying interpretation the neighbors had chosen to give his misfortune. "He took it while my back was turned. What the hell do you think I am?"

"Ah," she replied bitterly, "everyone knows what you are now. God forgive you, wasting our hard-earned few ha'pence on drink, and bringing up your child to be a drunken corner-boy like yourself."

Then she swept into the bedroom and threw herself on her knees by the bed. She moaned when she saw the gash over my eye. In the kitchen Sonny set up a loud bawl on his own, and a moment later Father appeared in the bedroom door with his cap over his eyes, wearing an expression of the most intense self-pity.

"That's a nice way to talk to me after all I went through," he whined. "That's a nice accusation, that I was drinking. Not one drop of drink crossed my lips the whole day. How could it when he drank it all? I'm the one that ought to be pitied, with my day ruined on me, and I after being made a show for the whole road."

But the next morning, when he got up and went out quietly to work with his dinner-basket, Mother threw herself on me in the bed and kissed me. It seemed it was all my doing, and I was being given a holiday till my eye got better.

"My brave little man!" she said with her eyes shining. "It was God did it you were there. You were his guardian angel."

QUESTIONS

1. What are the sources of humor in this story? Does the humor arise from observation of life or from distortion of life? What elements of the story seem to you funniest?
2. Is this a purely humorous story, or are there undertones of pathos in it? If the latter, from what does the pathos arise?
3. List what seem to you the chief insights into life and character presented by the story.

4. Is the title seriously meant? To whom does it refer?
5. The boy's drunkenness is seen from four perspectives. What are they, and how do they differ?
6. What is the principal irony in the story?
7. The story is told in retrospect by a man recalling an incident from his boyhood. What does this removal in time do to the treatment of the material?
8. Which story—this one or "The Catbird Seat"—is more purely an interpretive story? Discuss.
9. *Did* Larry's father forswear liquor? Support your answer with evidence from the story.

Truman Capote

A Christmas Memory

Imagine a morning in late November. A coming of winter morning more than twenty years ago. Consider the kitchen of a spreading old house in a country town. A great black stove is its main feature; but there is also a big round table and a fireplace with two rocking chairs placed in front of it. Just today the fireplace commenced its seasonal roar.

A woman with shorn white hair is standing at the kitchen window. She is wearing tennis shoes and a shapeless gray sweater over a summery calico dress. She is small and sprightly, like a bantam hen; but, due to a long youthful illness, her shoulders are pitifully hunched. Her face is remarkable—not unlike Lincoln's, craggy like that, and tinted by sun and wind; but it is delicate too, finely boned, and her eyes are sherry-colored and timid. "Oh my," she exclaims, her breath smoking the windowpane, "it's fruitcake weather!"

The person to whom she is speaking is myself. I am seven; she is sixty-something. We are cousins, very distant ones, and we have lived together— well, as long as I can remember. Other people inhabit the house, relatives; and though they have power over us, and frequently make us cry, we are not, on the whole, too much aware of them. We are each other's best friend. She calls me Buddy, in memory of a boy who was formerly her best friend. The other Buddy died in the 1880's, when she was still a child. She is still a child.

"I knew it before I got out of bed," she says, turning away from the window with a purposeful excitement in her eyes. "The courthouse bell sounded so cold and clear. And there were no birds singing; they've gone to warmer country, yes indeed. Oh, Buddy, stop stuffing biscuit and fetch our buggy. Help me find my hat. We've thirty cakes to bake."

A CHRISTMAS MEMORY   First published in 1956. Truman Capote (1924–1984) was born in New Orleans. His parents divorced when he was four, and Capote lived until he was nine or ten with a family of distant and elderly cousins in the small town of Monroeville, Alabama. Miss Sook Faulk, the real-life distant cousin on whom this story is based, died in 1938 while Capote was a student in a military academy in New York State.

It's always the same: a morning arrives in November, and my friend, as   5
though officially inaugurating the Christmas time of year that exhilarates her
imagination and fuels the blaze of her heart, announces: "It's fruitcake
weather! Fetch our buggy. Help me find my hat."

The hat is found, a straw cartwheel corsaged with velvet roses out-of-
doors has faded: it once belonged to a more fashionable relative. Together,
we guide our buggy, a dilapidated baby carriage, out to the garden and into a
grove of pecan trees. The buggy is mine; that is, it was bought for me when I
was born. It is made of wicker, rather unraveled, and the wheels wobble like
a drunkard's legs. But it is a faithful object; springtimes, we take it to the
woods and fill it with flowers, herbs, wild fern for our porch pots; in the
summer, we pile it with picnic paraphernalia and sugar-cane fishing poles
and roll it down to the edge of a creek; it has its winter uses, too: as a truck
for hauling firewood from the yard to the kitchen, as a warm bed for
Queenie, our tough little orange and white rat terrier who has survived dis-
temper and two rattlesnake bites. Queenie is trotting beside it now.

Three hours later we are back in the kitchen hulling a heaping buggyload
of windfall pecans. Our backs hurt from gathering them: how hard they were
to find (the main crop having been shaken off the trees and sold by the
orchard's owners, who are not us) among the concealing leaves, the frosted,
deceiving grass. Caarackle! A cheery crunch, scraps of miniature thunder
sound as the shells collapse and the golden mound of sweet oily ivory meat
mounts in the milk-glass bowl. Queenie begs to taste, and now and again my
friend sneaks her a mite, though insisting we deprive ourselves. "We
mustn't, Buddy. If we start, we won't stop. And there's scarcely enough as
there is. For thirty cakes." The kitchen is growing dark. Dusk turns the
window into a mirror: our reflections mingle with the rising moon as we
work by the fireside in the firelight. At last, when the moon is quite high, we
toss the final hull into the fire and, with joined sighs, watch it catch flame.
The buggy is empty, the bowl is brimful.

We eat our supper (cold biscuits, bacon, blackberry jam) and discuss
tomorrow. Tomorrow the kind of work I like best begins: buying. Cherries
and citron, ginger and vanilla and canned Hawaiian pineapple, rinds and
raisins and walnuts and whiskey and oh, so much flour, butter, so many eggs,
spices, flavoring: why we'll need a pony to pull the buggy home.

But before these purchases can be made, there is the question of money.
Neither of us has any. Except for skinflint sums persons in the house occasionally provide (a dime is considered very big money); or what we earn
ourselves from various activities: holding rummage sales, selling buckets of
hand-picked blackberries, jars of homemade jam and apple jelly and peach
preserves, rounding up flowers for funerals and weddings. Once we won
seventy-ninth prize, five dollars, in a national football contest. Not that we
know a fool thing about football. It's just that we enter any contest we hear
about: at the moment our hopes are centered on the fifty-thousand-dollar
Grand Prize being offered to name a new brand of coffee (we suggest "A.M.";

and, after some hesitation, for my friend thought it perhaps sacrilegious, the slogan "A.M.! Amen!"). To tell the truth, our only *really* profitable enterprise was the Fun and Freak Museum we conducted in a backyard woodshed two summers ago. The Fun was a stereopticon with slide views of Washington and New York lent us by a relative who had been to those places (she was furious when she discovered why we'd borrowed it); the Freak was a three-legged biddy chicken hatched by one of our hens. Everyone hereabouts wanted to see that biddy: we charged grownups a nickel, kids two cents. And took in a good twenty dollars before the museum shut down due to the decease of the main attraction.

10   But one way and another we do each year accumulate Christmas savings, a Fruitcake Fund. These moneys we keep hidden in an ancient bead purse under a loose board under the floor under a chamber pot under my friend's bed. The purse is seldom removed from this safe location except to make a deposit, or, as happens every Saturday, a withdrawal; for on Saturdays I am allowed ten cents to go to the picture show. My friend has never been to a picture show, nor does she intend to: "I'd rather hear you tell the story, Buddy. That way I can imagine it more. Besides, a person my age shouldn't squander their eyes. When the Lord comes, let me see him clear." In addition to never having seen a movie, she has never: eaten in a restaurant, traveled more than five miles from home, received or sent a telegram, read anything except funny papers and the Bible, worn cosmetics, cursed, wished someone harm, told a lie on purpose, let a hungry dog go hungry. Here are a few things she has done, does do: killed with a hoe the biggest rattlesnake ever seen in this county (sixteen rattles), dip snuff (secretly), tame hummingbirds (just try it) till they balance on her finger, tell ghost stories (we both believe in ghosts) so tingling they chill you in July, talk to herself, take walks in the rain, grow the prettiest japonicas in town, know the recipe for every sort of old-time Indian cure, including a magical wart remover.

Now, with supper finished, we retire to the room in a faraway part of the house where my friend sleeps in a scrap-quilt-covered iron bed painted rose pink, her favorite color. Silently, wallowing in the pleasures of conspiracy, we take the bead purse from its secret place and spill its contents on the scrap quilt. Dollar bills, tightly rolled and green as May buds. Somber fifty-cent pieces, heavy enough to weight a dead man's eyes. Lovely dimes, the liveliest coin, the one that really jingles. Nickels and quarters, worn smooth as creek pebbles. But mostly a hateful heap of bitter-odored pennies. Last summer others in the house contracted to pay us a penny for every twenty-five flies we killed. Oh, the carnage of August: the flies that flew to heaven! Yet it was not work in which we took pride. And, as we sit counting pennies, it is as though we were back tabulating dead flies. Neither of us has a head for figures; we count slowly, lose track, start again. According to her calculation, we have $12.73. According to mine, exactly $13. "I do hope you're wrong, Buddy. We can't mess around with thirteen. The cakes will fall. Or put somebody in the cemetery. Why, I wouldn't dream of getting out of bed on the thirteenth." This is true: she always spends thirteenths in bed. So, to be on the safe side, we subtract a penny and toss it out the window.

Of the ingredients that go into our fruitcakes, whiskey is the most expensive, as well as the hardest to obtain: State laws forbid its sale. But everybody knows you can buy a bottle from Mr. Haha Jones. And the next day, having completed our more prosaic shopping, we set out for Mr. Haha's business address, a "sinful" (to quote public opinion) fish-fry and dancing café down by the river. We've been there before, and on the same errand; but in previous years our dealings have been with Haha's wife, an iodine-dark Indian woman with brazzy peroxided hair and a dead-tired disposition. Actually, we've never laid eyes on her husband, though we've heard that he's an Indian too. A giant with razor scars across his cheeks. They call him Haha because he's so gloomy, a man who never laughs. As we approach his café (a large log cabin festooned inside and out with chains of garish-gay naked lightbulbs and standing by the river's muddy edge under the shade of river trees where moss drifts through the branches like gray mist) our steps slow down. Even Queenie stops prancing and sticks close by. People have been murdered in Haha's café. Cut to pieces. Hit on the head. There's a case coming up in court next month. Naturally these goings-on happen at night when the colored lights cast crazy patterns and the victrola wails. In the daytime Haha's is shabby and deserted. I knock at the door, Queenie barks, my friend calls: "Mrs. Haha, ma'am? Anyone to home?"

Footsteps. The door opens. Our hearts overturn. It's Mr. Haha Jones himself! And he *is* a giant; he *does* have scars; he *doesn't* smile. No, he glowers at us through Satan-tilted eyes and demands to know: "What you want with Haha?"

For a moment we are too paralyzed to tell. Presently my friend half-finds her voice, a whispery voice at best: "If you please, Mr. Haha, we'd like a quart of your finest whiskey."

His eyes tilt more. Would you believe it? Haha is smiling! Laughing, too.   15 "Which one of you is a drinkin' man?"

"It's for making fruitcakes, Mr. Haha. Cooking."

This sobers him. He frowns. "That's no way to waste good whiskey." Nevertheless, he retreats into the shadowed café and seconds later appears carrying a bottle of daisy yellow unlabeled liquor. He demonstrates its sparkle in the sunlight and says: "Two dollars."

We pay him with nickels and dimes and pennies. Suddenly, jangling the coins in his hands like a fistful of dice, his face softens. "Tell you what," he proposes, pouring the money back into our bead purse, "just send me one of them fruitcakes instead."

"Well," my friend remarks on our way home, "there's a lovely man. We'll put an extra cup of raisins in *his* cake."

The black stove, stoked with coal and firewood, glows like a lighted   20 pumpkin. Eggbeaters whirl, spoons spin round in bowls of butter and sugar, vanilla sweetens the air, ginger spices it; melting, nose-tingling odors saturate the kitchen, suffuse the house, drift out to the world on puffs of chimney smoke. In four days our work is done. Thirty-one cakes, dampened with whiskey, bask on window sills and shelves.

Who are they for?

Friends. Not necessarily neighbor friends: indeed, the larger share are intended for persons we've met maybe once, perhaps not at all. People who've struck our fancy. Like President Roosevelt. Like the Reverend and Mrs. J. C. Lucey, Baptist missionaries to Borneo who lectured here last winter. Or the little knife grinder who comes through town twice a year. Or Abner Packer, the driver of the six o'clock bus from Mobile, who exchanges waves with us every day as he passes in a dust-cloud whoosh. Or the young Wistons, a California couple whose car one afternoon broke down outside the house and who spent a pleasant hour chatting with us on the porch (young Mr. Wiston snapped our picture, the only one we've ever had taken). Is it because my friend is shy with everyone *except* strangers that these strangers, and merest acquaintances, seem to us our truest friends? I think yes. Also, the scrapbooks we keep of thank-you's on White House station-ery, time-to-time communications from California and Borneo, the knife grinder's penny post cards, make us feel connected to eventful worlds be-yond the kitchen with its view of a sky that stops.

Now a nude December fig branch grates against the window. The kitchen is empty, the cakes are gone; yesterday we carted the last of them to the post office, where the cost of stamps turned our purse inside out. We're broke. That rather depresses me, but my friend insists on celebrating—with two inches of whiskey left in Haha's bottle. Queenie has a spoonful in a bowl of coffee (she likes her coffee chicory-flavored and strong). The rest we di-vide between a pair of jelly glasses. We're both quite awed at the prospect of drinking straight whiskey; the taste of it brings screwed-up expressions and sour shudders. But by and by we begin to sing, the two of us singing differ-ent songs simultaneously. I don't know the words to mine, just: *Come on along, come on along, to the dark-town strutters' ball.* But I can dance: that's what I mean to be, a tap dancer in the movies. My dancing shadow rollicks on the walls; our voices rock the chinaware; we giggle: as if unseen hands were tickling us. Queenie rolls on her back, her paws plow the air, something like a grin stretches her black lips. Inside myself, I feel warm and sparky as those crumbling logs, carefree as the wind in the chimney. My friend waltzes round the stove, the hem of her poor calico skirt pinched between her fingers as though it were a party dress: *Show me the way to go home,* she sings, her tennis shoes squeaking on the floor. *Show me the way to go home.*

Enter: two relatives. Very angry. Potent with eyes that scold, tongues that scald. Listen to what they have to say, the words tumbling together into a wrathful tune: "A child of seven! whiskey on his breath! are you out of your mind? feeding a child of seven! must be loony! road to ruination! remember Cousin Kate? Uncle Charlie? Uncle Charlie's brother-in-law? shame! scan-dal! humiliation! kneel, pray, beg the Lord!"

Queenie sneaks under the stove. My friend gazes at her shoes, her chin   25
quivers, she lifts her skirt and blows her nose and runs to her room. Long
after the town has gone to sleep and the house is silent except for the chim-
ings of clocks and the sputter of fading fires, she is weeping into a pillow
already as wet as a widow's handkerchief.

"Don't cry," I say, sitting at the bottom of her bed and shivering despite
my flannel nightgown that smells of last winter's cough syrup, "Don't cry," I
beg, teasing her toes, tickling her feet, "you're too old for that."

"It's because," she hiccups, "I *am* too old. Old and funny."

"Not funny. Fun. More fun than anybody. Listen. If you don't stop
crying you'll be so tired tomorrow we can't go cut a tree."

She straightens up. Queenie jumps on the bed (where Queenie is not
allowed) to lick her cheeks. "I know where we'll find pretty trees, Buddy.
And holly, too. With berries big as your eyes. It's way off in the woods.
Farther than we've ever been. Papa used to bring us Christmas trees from
there: carry them on his shoulder. That's fifty years ago. Well now: I can't
wait for morning."

Morning. Frozen rime lusters the grass; the sun, round as an orange and   30
orange as hot-weather moons, balances on the horizon, burnishes the silvered winter woods. A wild turkey calls. A renegade hog grunts in the undergrowth. Soon, by the edge of knee-deep, rapid-running water, we have to
abandon the buggy. Queenie wades the stream first, paddles across barking
complaints at the swiftness of the current, the pneumonia-making coldness
of it. We follow, holding our shoes and equipment (a hatchet, a burlap sack)
above our heads. A mile more: of chastising thorns, burs and briers that
catch at our clothes; of rusty pine needles brilliant with gaudy fungus and
molted feathers. Here, there, a flash, a flutter, an ecstasy of shrillings remind
us that not all the birds have flown south. Always, the path unwinds through
lemony sun pools and pitch vine tunnels. Another creek to cross: a disturbed
armada of speckled trout froths the water round us, and frogs the size of
plates practice belly flops; beaver workmen are building a dam. On the farther shore, Queenie shakes herself and trembles. My friend shivers, too: not
with cold but enthusiasm. One of her hat's ragged roses sheds a petal as she
lifts her head and inhales the pine-heavy air. "We're almost there; can you
smell it, Buddy?" she says, as though we were approaching an ocean.

And, indeed, it is a kind of ocean. Scented acres of holiday trees, prickly-
leafed holly. Red berries shiny as Chinese bells: black crows swoop upon
them screaming. Having stuffed our burlap sacks with enough greenery and
crimson to garland a dozen windows, we set about choosing a tree. "It
should be," muses my friend, "twice as tall as a boy. So a boy can't steal the
star." The one we pick is twice as tall as me. A brave handsome brute that
survives thirty hatchet strokes before it keels with a creaking rending cry.
Lugging it like a kill, we commence the long trek out. Every few yards we
abandon the struggle, sit down and pant. But we have the strength of triumphant huntsmen; that and the tree's virile, icy perfume revive us, goad us on.

Many compliments accompany our sunset return along the red clay road to town; but my friend is sly and noncommital when passers-by praise the treasure perched on our buggy: what a fine tree and where did it come from? "Yonderways," she murmurs vaguely. Once a car stops and the rich mill owner's lazy wife leans out and whines: "Giveya two-bits cash for that ol tree." Ordinarily my friend is afraid of saying no; but on this occasion she promptly shakes her head: "We wouldn't take a dollar." The mill owner's wife persists. "A dollar, my foot! Fifty cents. That's my last offer. Goodness, woman, you can get another one." In answer, my friend gently reflects: "I doubt it. There's never two of anything."

Home: Queenie slumps by the fire and sleeps till tomorrow, snoring loud as a human.

A trunk in the attic contains: a shoebox of ermine tails (off the opera cape of a curious lady who once rented a room in the house), coils of frazzled tinsel gone gold with age, one silver star, a brief rope of dilapidated, undoubtedly dangerous candy-like bulbs. Excellent decorations, as far as they go, which isn't far enough: my friend wants our tree to blaze "like a Baptist window," droop with weighty snows of ornament. But we can't afford the made-in-Japan splendors at the five-and-dime. So we do what we've always done: sit for days at the kitchen table with scissors and crayons and stacks of colored paper. I make sketches and my friend cuts them out: lots of cats, fish too (because they're easy to draw), some apples, some watermelons, a few winged angels devised from saved-up sheets of Hershey-bar tin foil. We use safety pins to attach these creations to the tree; as a final touch, we sprinkle the branches with shredded cotton (picked in August for this purpose). My friend, surveying the effects, clasps her hands together. "Now honest, Buddy. Doesn't it look good enough to eat?" Queenie tries to eat an angel.

After weaving and ribboning holly wreaths for all the front windows, our next project is the fashioning of family gifts. Tie-dye scarves for the ladies, for the men a home-brewed lemon and licorice and aspirin syrup to be taken "at the first Symptoms of a Cold and after Hunting." But when it comes time for making each other's gift, my friend and I separate to work secretly. I would like to buy her a pearl-handled knife, a radio, a whole pound of chocolate-covered cherries (we tasted some once, and she always swears: "I could live on them, Buddy, Lord yes I could—and that's not taking His name in vain"). Instead, I am building her a kite. She would like to give me a bicycle (she's said so on several million occasions: "If only I could, Buddy. It's bad enough in life to do without something *you* want; but confound it, what gets my goat is not being able to give somebody something you want *them* to have. Only one of these days I will, Buddy. Locate you a bike. Don't ask how. Steal it, maybe"). Instead, I'm fairly certain that she is building me a kite—the same as last year, and the year before: the year before that we exchanged slingshots. All of which is fine by me. For we are champion kite-fliers who study the wind like sailors; my friend, more accomplished than I, can get a kite aloft when there isn't enough breeze to carry clouds.

Christmas Eve afternoon we scrape together a nickel and go to the   35
butcher's to buy Queenie's traditional gift, a good gnawable beef bone. The
bone, wrapped in funny paper, is placed high in the tree near the silver star.
Queenie knows it's there. She squats at the foot of the tree staring up in a
trance of greed: when bedtime arrives she refuses to budge. Her excitement
is equaled by my own. I kick the covers and turn my pillow as though it were
a scorching summer's night. Somewhere a rooster crows: falsely, for the sun
is still on the other side of the world.

"Buddy, are you awake?" It is my friend, calling from her room, which is
next to mine; and an instant later she is sitting on my bed holding a candle.
"Well, I can't sleep a hoot," she declares. "My mind's jumping like a jack
rabbit. Buddy, do you think Mrs. Roosevelt will serve our cake at dinner?"
We huddle in the bed, and she squeezes my hand I-love-you. "Seems like
your hand used to be so much smaller. I guess I hate to see you grow up.
When you're grown up, will we still be friends?" I say always. "But I feel so
bad, Buddy. I wanted so bad to give you a bike. I tried to sell my cameo Papa
gave me. Buddy"—she hesitates, as though embarrassed—"I made you another kite." Then I confess that I made her one, too; and we laugh. The
candle burns too short to hold. Out it goes, exposing the starlight, the stars
spinning at the window like a visible caroling that slowly, slowly daybreak
silences. Possibly we doze; but the beginnings of dawn splash us like cold
water: we're up, wide-eyed and wandering while we wait for others to waken.
Quite deliberately my friend drops a kettle on the kitchen floor. I tap-dance
in front of closed doors. One by one the household emerges, looking as
though they'd like to kill us both; but it's Christmas, so they can't. First, a
gorgeous breakfast: just everything you can imagine—from flapjacks and
fried squirrel to hominy grits and honey-in-the-comb. Which puts everyone
in a good humor except my friend and I. Frankly, we're so impatient to get at
the presents we can't eat a mouthful.

Well, I'm disappointed. Who wouldn't be? With socks, a Sunday school
shirt, some handkerchiefs, a hand-me-down sweater and a year's subscription to a religious magazine for children. *The Little Shepherd.* It makes me
boil. It really does.

My friend has a better haul. A sack of Satsumas, that's her best present.
She is proudest, however, of a white wool shawl knitted by her married
sister. But she *says* her favorite gift is the kite I built her. And it *is* very
beautiful; though not as beautiful as the one she made me, which is blue
and scattered with gold and green Good Conduct stars; moreover, my name is
painted on it, "Buddy."

"Buddy, the wind is blowing."

The wind is blowing, and nothing will do till we've run to a pasture below   40
the house where Queenie has scooted to bury her bone (and where, a winter
hence, Queenie will be buried, too). There, plunging through the healthy
waist-high grass, we unreel our kites, feel them twitching at the string like
sky fish as they swim into the wind. Satisfied, sun-warmed, we sprawl in the
grass and peel Satsumas and watch our kites cavort. Soon I forget the socks

and hand-me-down sweater. I'm as happy as if we'd already won the fifty-thousand-dollar Grand Prize in that coffee-naming contest.

"My, how foolish I am!" my friend cries, suddenly alert, like a woman remembering too late she has biscuits in the oven. "You know what I've always thought?" she asks in a tone of discovery, and not smiling at me but a point beyond. "I've always thought a body would have to be sick and dying before they saw the Lord. And I imagined that when He came it would be like looking at the Baptist window: pretty as colored glass with the sun pouring through, such a shine you don't know it's getting dark. And it's been a comfort: to think of that shine taking away all the spooky feeling. But I'll wager it never happens. I'll wager at the very end a body realizes the Lord has already shown Himself. That things as they are"—her hand circles in a gesture that gathers clouds and kites and grass and Queenie pawing earth over her bone—"just what they've always seen, was seeing Him. As for me, I could leave the world with today in my eyes."

This is our last Christmas together.

Life separates us. Those who Know Best decide that I belong in a military school. And so follows a miserable succession of bugle-blowing prisons, grim reveille-ridden summer camps. I have a new home too. But it doesn't count. Home is where my friend is, and there I never go.

And there she remains, puttering around the kitchen. Alone with Queenie. Then alone. ("Buddy dear," she writes in her wild hard-to-read script, "yesterday Jim Macy's horse kicked Queenie bad. Be thankful she didn't feel much. I wrapped her in a Fine Linen sheet and rode her in the buggy down to Simpson's pasture where she can be with all her Bones . . ."). For a few Novembers she continues to bake her fruitcakes single-handed; not as many, but some: and, of course, she always sends me "the best of the batch." Also, in every letter she encloses a dime wadded in toilet paper: "See a picture show and write me the story." But gradually in her letters she tends to confuse me with her other friend, the Buddy who died in the 1880's; more and more thirteenths are not the only days she stays in bed: a morning arrives in November, a leafless birdless coming of winter morning, when she cannot rouse herself to exclaim: "Oh my, it's fruitcake weather!"

45   And when that happens, I know it. A message saying so merely confirms a piece of news some secret vein had already received, severing from me an irreplaceable part of myself, letting it loose like a kite on a broken string. That is why, walking across a school campus on this particular December morning, I keep searching the sky. As if I expected to see, rather like hearts, a lost pair of kites hurrying toward heaven.

QUESTIONS

1. Although the Christmas memory of the title is more than twenty years old, it is recollected in the present tense. How is this managed? What advantages has it for the story?

2. What does the narrator mean by saying that his more than sixty-year-old friend "is still a child"? Is she like a child in more than one sense? Cite instances of behavior to support different meanings. What does she herself mean when she says that she is "old and funny" (paragraph 27)? What are her chief sources of pleasure? Why does she make a perfect companion for the narrator? Are there places where she exhibits a superior wisdom to that of the adults in the story? Is she in any sense a developing character?

3. If the narrator and his friend—and Queenie—be taken as the protagonists of the story, who are the antagonists? At what points do they enter the story, and with what results? What are the sources of conflict? What people ultimately have the upper hand?

4. Where does the primary interest of the story lie? What are the principal sources of its appeal? Does it illuminate human character?

5. Can you formulate a theme for the story?

Benjamin Capps

The Night Old Santa Claus Came

Imagine a white schoolhouse sitting on a hill. It had two large rooms. The one on the north was full of desks, blackboards, a bookshelf, a teacher's desk, a pedal organ, and everything needed for the seventeen pupils who attended Mama's school. It smelled like chalk dust and ink and glue.

The other room in the schoolhouse was ours. It was the only place at Anarene for us to live, but it was a good home. It had a kitchen and closet curtained off at one end, with a kerosene cook stove and linoleum on the floor; the rest of our room had a lumber floor and two beds, one for me and Bill, one for Mama and Roy, and in between our wood-burning heater stove.

Roy was five years old. I was going on eight. Bill was nine. Mama was ancient, at least thirty, maybe even thirty-one. The pupils who came were different ages, two in highschool, two in the first grade, the rest scattered in between. They walked in across the prairie and through the mesquite brush from every direction each school morning. From schoolhouse hill you could only see where four other families lived; the other kids had long walks, and one rode horseback.

At one end of the white painted schoolhouse rose a flagpole, where we flew the U.S. flag on good days; at the other end stood the cistern with its squeaky pully and fuzzy rope to draw drinking water. Out on the flat ground we had three swings and a see-saw, a baseball field to play scrub, a garage for Mama's Model-T, and the woodpile and toilets. From schoolhouse hill you

THE NIGHT OLD SANTA CLAUS CAME   First published in 1981. Benjamin Capps was born in 1922 in Dundee near Wichita Falls, Texas, and from the age of eight was raised on a ranch nearby. He attended Texas Tech, and in 1944 was commissioned a second lieutenant in the Air Corps and flew forty bombing missions in the Pacific. After the war he completed his education at the University of Texas. He is the author of eight novels and has been honored by the Western Writers of America and by the Cowboy Hall of Fame and Western Heritage Center. He lives in Grand Prairie, Texas.

could see a long way, and it looked lonely out there—not much happening, except a few white-face cattle grazing.

5   That winter Mama said she hoped it would snow at the right time so we would have a white Christmas, but we would take whatever God sent. He did not often send the best snow to West Texas, but usually north wind and blowing sleet.

Mama was rich. Since she was the principal as well as the teacher and also mopped the schoolhouse floor, she got paid a hundred dollars a month. They had said when we first came there that you could not be a teacher at Anarene unless you could whip the biggest boy in school. They did not know her; she had fierce eyes. She was beautiful, but she could look at a big boy and say, "I thought you were older and more responsible than that," and he would start blushing and stammering.

But usually she gave rewards. If a big girl made ninety on spelling, Mama would let her sit in one of the long desks and teach a smaller kid his reading lesson. Or if a big boy did good in Geography, Mama would let him bring in wood or stoke the fire or draw water for the water keg.

We had been thinking about Christmas and one Saturday Mama gave me and Bill and Roy each fifty cents for gift money. We could spend it any way we wanted to, but Mama said, "Remember, it's better to give than to receive." Even more exciting, we were going shopping that day to the great city of Wichita Falls. She needed to buy some bright crepe paper and things for decorations. She did not ask the school trustees about such things, but used her own money because she made such a big salary.

Mama knew how to get to Wichita Falls and all the streets and stores, for she went up there sometimes to junior college. She had got her certificate that showed she was smart enough to teach school a long time ago by taking a test at the capital of Archer County. But she said that in her spare time she might as well further her education. So she got assignments from Wichita Falls and did them at night after us kids went to bed and sent them in through the mail. Anyway, me and Bill and Roy found ourselves in the biggest nickel and dime store in the world with fifty cents in our pockets.

10   Everything looked bright and colorful and shiny, hundreds of things in trays and hanging up wherever you looked. And the store smelled good. I could have walked around in there for weeks just looking.

Roy was dumb. He could not see past his own nose. We were not supposed to spy on what each other bought, but I could not take care of him and not let him get lost without seeing what he did. And here's exactly what he did. He bought himself a thirty-five-cent wind-up caterpillar tractor made out of tin with rubber tracks. Then he lost a dime and never could find it. The last nickel he spent for a sack of yellow candy corn, which he stuffed down before he even got back to the car. Me and Bill told him how dumb he was and said, "Boy, you're going to be sorry when it comes time to put gifts on the Christmas tree." It didn't seem to bother him, but we said, "You wait and see!"

I got Mama a new spatula to turn pancakes and Bill got her a hand-kerchief with flowers embroidered in the corner. I got the other two kids a pewter whistle with a bird on top; you could put a little water in it and it would make a tweeting sound. But I didn't know whether I wanted to give Roy a present or not; a kid of five ought to be more responsible than that.

The school days got long during the week before Christmas, but we all had to work decorating the room for the tree and program the night all the parents would come. Mama said that our studies must not stop, so each pupil must show each day that he learned some lessons before he could help deco-rate. By the time for the last recess each day we had all earned the right to work on green and red pasted chains or twisted crepe-paper chains or Christmas posters for the walls or little cut-out figures for the tree. A big girl named Myrtle Farmer made a star and put silver tinfoil on it. A boy named Tots, who could draw real good, made beautiful scenes on the blackboards with colored chalk. Some girls got to string popcorn which Mama popped, and we all teased them and accused them of eating some.

During those days Mama changed our breakfast Bible reading too. Each morning in our room when we washed our hands and sat down to eat, she would read a few verses, then say a short prayer. Usually she read straight through the Bible, including somebody begat somebody and they begat somebody else. Then we would eat our oatmeal with canned milk and maybe have hot chocolate. Now she skipped over to Isaiah and explained that it meant that Jesus was coming. Three days before Christmas she started read-ing about the Christ in the New Testament.

The last school day before the holiday was the day to get the tree. Two big boys, Auzy Brown and Garland Andrews, went to hunt it on a creek a long way off. They had got their Algebra and other lessons caught up, so they left early. The only trees with leaves were chaparral bushes, but Mama said leaves didn't matter, except we had to have a tree that could come in the door and would not be too high for the ceiling. The smaller boys could not go, because the big boys were taking an axe. We watched from the school-house hill and when we saw them dragging the tree over the prairie, we ran to help bring it. We struggled and pushed from every side to get it in the door and stood up. Later in the day some boys went to get mistletoe.   15

Mama had a habit of going with a coal oil lamp into the schoolroom to work on her college after us kids went to bed. Bill said part of the time she prayed in there and asked God to make her know how to be a good father as well as a mother and to be a good teacher of young minds. Bill could have been wrong; a boy of nine is not so smart, but it could be true. Anyway, before the holidays Mama practiced on the organ at night in her spare time. She could play good enough for us to sing in school, but she was afraid Mrs. Meaders, the lady who usually played for community programs, would not get over her flu before Christmas, so she had to be ready. We would lay in bed nearly asleep and listen to her away over there in the other half of the school-house, softly playing, "Oh, Little Town of Bethlehem" and "Silent Night."

On Christmas Eve morning before breakfast Mama said we would read a little more than usual. She read: "And there were in the same country shepherds abiding in the field, keeping watch over their flock by night. And, lo, the angel of the Lord came upon them, and the glory of the Lord shone round about them; and they were sore afraid. And the angel said unto them, Fear not: for, behold, I bring you good tidings of great joy, which shall be to all people." And she read all of it about the shepherds coming to visit the new baby Jesus.

After breakfast we started wrapping presents, each one working in a different place, me on one bed, Mama on one, and Bill behind the kitchen curtain, to keep the presents a surprise. Roy tried to play with his caterpillar tractor, which now had the spring broken and one track lost. Then he played with the stove wood some. Finally he stood out in the middle of the room and started bawling.

After a minute Mama went over to him and asked, "What's the matter, honey? Don't cry."

20   He didn't want to say. She knelt down and petted him and kept saying, "Don't cry. What's the matter?"

Finally he said, "I love you, Mama."

"I know you do, honey. Don't cry."

"I would give you my tractor, but you already seen it and it wouldn't be a surprise."

She got the whole story out of him and said, "I ought to spank you good." But she smiled a little and went to her purse hanging on the nail. She got out a nickel for him to buy her a present and asked me if I would go down to the store with him.

25   We put on our coats. Roy no sooner got out the door than he started running. It was about a minute run to the store. Before we got there he was laughing and talking just like he'd never done anything wrong in his life. He bought Mama a Peanut Pattie candy bar about the size of a pancake, only thicker, with peanuts sticking out of the top and wrapped in clear paper.

On the way back up the hill he began to open the sack and I said, "What are you doing?"

"Nothing, I'm just going to look at it."

I said, "Leave it in the sack. What are you doing?" I had thought at first that it was useless for me to go with him, since there are no rattlesnakes in winter and you won't get on a cactus if you stay in the road; but it was a good thing I went—to protect Mama's present.

He said, "I just want to smell of it."

30   "Roy," I told him, "don't you unwrap that! What do you think you're doing?"

"I'm just going to take a little bite. Mama won't care."

"Don't you dare! Haven't you got a lick of sense?" I got tough with him. "You put that back in that sack and don't you touch it! I'll knock you right on the seat of your pants!"

He knew I meant it. I watched him all the way home and until he got it wrapped in red paper and tied with a string and had put Mama's name on it.

God did not send us a white Christmas that day, but the air was still and cold and clear, like you could see a hundred miles. Later, when dark came, the sky was like purple velvet and the stars were like diamonds, and you could imagine looking up there that you could hear the tune of "Silent Night."

Mama had pumped up and lighted the two gasoline lanterns in the   35
schoolroom, and the schoolhouse hill seemed the most wonderful place a person could possibly be when the people started coming in across the prairie from every direction, driving and walking, most of them laughing. There must have been a hundred, or at least forty. They brought presents to put on the tree for each other. Everyone said how great the schoolroom looked with all our decoration.

It looked as good as a five and ten cent store, not so shiny, but happier. Our chains and ribbons, mostly red and green, looped around on the walls, and the popcorn looked like snow. It was a whole roomful of people, all smiling, and everyone talking at once, until the program started. The lady with the flu was well, so she played the pedal organ and Mama announced. We all sang "Jingle Bells" and other songs. Then the kids who had practiced up gave readings. Two girls and a boy, who could sing good together, sang "Hark, the Herald Angels Sing." Bill, who was good at memory, said, " 'Twas the Night Before Christmas."

When Santa Claus came in, dressed in red and white, saying "Ho! Ho! Ho! Have all you boys and girls been good this year?" it was thrilling, but us big kids knew it was Mr. Charlie Graham dressed up that way. The dumb little kids like Roy thought he had just got in on his sled from the North Pole. I had learned about Santa Claus a long time ago, before our daddy died. I even knew where Mama kept the red suit and beard, in a box on top of the green metal bookcase.

The program lasted real late, at least till ten o'clock. All the grown people told Mama thank you before they left. You could hear their voices and laughter going away into the clear, cold night. When we got in our room, after we had looked at our gifts a minute, Roy began talking about hanging up stockings; he'd been talking to the other kids about it.

Mama said, "Boys, we've had a big Christmas. I don't think we need to hang up our stockings this year. We will have some goodies to eat in the next few days."

Roy said, "Well, I want to hang mine up."   40

"We've had a big Christmas," she said. "Don't you think we should just go to bed and have a good, lazy night's sleep?"

He didn't know what she meant about getting a night's sleep; she meant she didn't have to practice the organ or do any college lessons tonight and she didn't want any other duties in her spare time. See, she had several things to do all the time, being principal, like getting the trustees to haul firewood and getting all the right textbooks and getting chalk and stuff, then keeping up with all the lessons with two in highschool, and making state reports, and getting the broken window fixed, and entertaining the community, and practicing the organ, and furthering her education, and doing all the things mamas like to do such as wash clothes and cook oatmeal and make stew and put patches on your overalls. So she said to us, like it was the last word, "Well, I'm going to bed. Tomorrow I'm going to bake chicken and make dressing." Me and Bill sniggered.

Roy, that dumb kid, took his socks up to the curtain which marked off the kitchen, got two clothes pins, stood on a chair, and hung his socks to the top of the curtain. I could read his dumb mind; this was between him and Santa Claus. After Mama blew out the lamp, me and Bill lay there laughing. Boy, was that kid going to learn something! If your mama says Old Santa Claus ain't coming, then he sure ain't coming anymore tonight! I would have laughed forever if I hadn't been so sleepy.

We nearly always waked up when Mama was building the fire in the morning, because the stove clanked. When she saw us sitting up in bed, she said, "Christmas gift!" It was a joke meaning you had to give them a gift if they said it first, but nobody really did it. Suddenly Roy hopped out of bed and ran toward his socks. I and Bill got to sniggering again.

45   About that time Roy squealed. His socks were so full he had to take them down one at a time. He ran and started spilling goodies out onto the bed.

Me and Bill looked at Mama. Why in the world had she done that? How could she be such a traitor? It wasn't fair. We liked candy and things as much as him, and he was the one who hadn't acted grown up, but he got a reward for being dumb.

"Jump up, lazy bones," Mama said to me and Bill. How could she be so cheerful when she had acted like a traitor to us? "It's a nice day," she said. "Get your clothes on."

I didn't even want to speak to her as I walked over the cold floor to the chair where I left my clothes. A crazy thought was going through my mind: Could it be possible that there really is a Santa Claus who fills up the stockings of dumb little kids? I got my shoes and socks out from under the chair. I couldn't get my socks on. Something was the matter with them. Lumpy. I nearly cried as old as I was because my mind was still going over the idea if there is really a Santa Claus for dumb little kids.

In my socks was one orange, one apple, fourteen pecans, nine little pieces of hard candy, one big piece of wavy ribbon candy, eleven English walnuts, four Brazil nuts, twelve almonds, and a third of a Peanut Pattie.

50   We all offered Mama a piece of our candy, and she said she would take a small piece of peppermint, because she didn't care for anything that was too sweet. When she got a chance, she winked at me and Bill. I believe it was a year before Roy ever figured out how come Old Santa Claus put a third of a Peanut Pattie in his sock that night.

QUESTIONS

1. Who is the protagonist of this story—the narrator, the mother, or little Roy? Characterize each of them. How does the story judge any failings or weaknesses that they display?
2. What period in time is the narrator remembering? (What date is implied by "Mama's Model-T" in paragraph 4?) What details of the story give a sense of the quality of life that the narrator is recalling? How are we expected to feel about the family's deprivations?
3. Explore the ironic contrasts between the narrator's present evaluation of himself as a child and the child's self-evaluations. Is there any blame attached to the child's?
4. What was the narrator's evaluation of Roy's behavior? What does he feel about it now?
5. What are the similarities between this story and Truman Capote's "A Christmas Memory"? Consider character (including stock characters), plot, point of view, and theme.
6. Which of these two stories is designed to leave us with a happy glow? Which takes us into a deeper understanding of life?

CHAPTER EIGHT

Fantasy

Truth in fiction is not the same as fidelity to fact. Fiction, after all, is the opposite of fact. It is a game of make-believe—though, at its best, a serious game—in which the author imaginatively conceives characters and situations and sets them down on paper. And yet these characters and situations, if deeply imagined, may embody truths of human life and behavior more fully and significantly than any number of the miscellaneous facts reported on the front pages of our morning papers. The purpose of the interpretive artist is to communicate truths by means of imagined facts.

The story writer begins, then, by saying "Let's suppose. . . ." "Let's suppose," for instance, "that a fair-minded, conscientious, but not cold-hearted Jewish top sergeant, during World War II, is placed in charge of a training company in which a Jewish recruit tries to play on their common Jewishness to obtain special favors for himself and his friends." From this initial assumption the author goes on to develop a story ("Defender of the Faith") which, though entirely imaginary in the sense that it never happened, nevertheless reveals convincingly to us some truths of human behavior.

But now, what if the author goes a step further and supposes not just something that might very well have happened (though it didn't) but something highly improbable—something that could happen, say, only as the result of a very surprising coincidence? What if he begins, "Let's suppose that a misogynist and a charming woman find themselves alone on a desert island"? This initial supposition causes us to stretch our imaginations a bit further, but is not this situation just as capable of revealing human truths as the former? The psychologist puts a rat in a maze (certainly an improbable situation for a rat), observes its reactions to the maze, and discovers some truth of rat nature. The author may put imaginary characters on an imagined desert island, imaginatively study their reactions, and reveal some truth of human nature. The improbable initial situation may yield as much truth as the probable one.

From the improbable it is but one step further to the impossible (as we know it in this life). Why should not our author begin "Let's suppose that a miser and his termagant wife find themselves in hell" or "Let's suppose that a timid but ambitious man discovers how to make himself invisible" or "Let's suppose that in the course of an afternoon a man experiences the next year of his life" or "Let's suppose that a primitive scapegoat ritual still survives in contemporary America." Could not these situations also be used to exhibit human truth?

The nonrealistic story, or **fantasy,** is one that transcends the bounds of known reality. Commonly, it conjures up a strange and marvelous world, which one enters by falling down a rabbit hole or climbing up a beanstalk or getting shipwrecked in an unfamiliar ocean or dreaming a dream; or else it introduces strange powers and occult forces into the world of ordinary reality, allowing one to foretell the future or communicate with the dead or separate the mind from the body or turn into a monster. It introduces human beings into a world where the ordinary laws of nature are suspended or superseded and where the landscape and its creatures are unfamiliar, or it introduces ghosts or fairies or dragons or werewolves or talking animals or invaders from Mars or miraculous occurrences into the normal world of human beings. Fables, ghost stories, science fiction—all are types of fantasy.

Fantasy may be escapist or interpretive, true or false. The space ship on its way to a distant planet may be filled with stock characters or with human beings. The story may be designed chiefly to exhibit mechanical marvels or to provide thrills or adventures, or it may be a means of creating exacting circumstances in which human behavior may be sharply observed and studied. Fantasy, like other elements of fiction, may be employed sheerly for its own sake or as a means of communicating an important insight. The appeal may be to our taste for the strange or to our need for the true. The important point to remember is that truth in fiction is not to be identified with realism in method. Stories that never depart from the three dimensions of actuality—like "The Catbird Seat" or "The Storm"—may distort and falsify life. Stories that fly on the wings of fantasy may be vehicles for truth. Fantasy may convey truth through symbolism or allegory or simply by providing an unusual setting for the observation of human beings. Some of the world's greatest works of literature have been partly or wholly fantasy: *The Odyssey, The Book of Job, The Divine Comedy, The Tempest, Pilgrim's Progress, Gulliver's Travels, Faust, Alice in*

Wonderland. All these have had important things to say about the human condition.

We must not judge a story, then, by whether or not it stays within the limits of the possible. Rather, we begin by granting every story a "Let's suppose"—an initial assumption. The initial assumption may be plausible or implausible. The writer may begin with an ordinary, everyday situation or with a far-fetched, improbable coincidence. Or the writer may be allowed to suspend a law of nature or to create a marvelous being or machine or place. But once we have granted the impossibility, we have a right to demand probability in the treatment of it. The realm of fantasy is not a realm in which *all* laws of logic are suspended. We need to ask, too, for what reason the story employs the element of fantasy. Is it used simply for its own strangeness or for thrills or surprises or laughs? Or is it used to illumine the more normal world of our experience? What is the purpose of the author's invention? Is it, like a roller coaster, simply a machine for producing thrills? Or does it, like an observation balloon, provide a vantage point from which we may view the world?

D. H. Lawrence

The Rocking-Horse Winner

There was a woman who was beautiful, who started with all the advantages, yet she had no luck. She married for love, and the love turned to dust. She had bonny children, yet she felt they had been thrust upon her, and she could not love them. They looked at her coldly, as if they were finding fault with her. And hurriedly she felt she must cover up some fault in herself. Yet what it was that she must cover up she never knew. Nevertheless, when her children were present, she always felt the center of her heart go hard. This troubled her, and in her manner she was all the more gentle and anxious for her children, as if she loved them very much. Only she herself knew that at the center of her heart was a hard little place that could not feel love, no, not for anybody. Everybody else said of her: "She is such a good mother. She adores her children." Only she herself, and her children themselves, knew it was not so. They read it in each other's eyes.

There were a boy and two little girls. They lived in a pleasant house, with a garden, and they had discreet servants, and felt themselves superior to anyone in the neighborhood.

THE ROCKING-HORSE WINNER   First published in 1933. D. H. Lawrence (1885–1930), son of a coal miner and a school teacher, was born and grew up in Nottinghamshire, England, was rejected for military service in World War I because of lung trouble, and lived most of his adult life abroad, including parts of three years in New Mexico.

Although they lived in style, they felt always an anxiety in the house. There was never enough money. The mother had a small income, and the father had a small income, but not nearly enough for the social position which they had to keep up. The father went into town to some office. But though he had good prospects, these prospects never materialized. There was always the grinding sense of the shortage of money, though the style was always kept up.

At last the mother said: "I will see if I can't make something." But she did not know where to begin. She racked her brains, and tried this thing and the other, but could not find anything successful. The failure made deep lines come into her face. Her children were growing up, they would have to go to school. There must be more money, there must be more money. The father, who was always very handsome and expensive in his tastes, seemed as if he never would be able to do anything worth doing. And the mother, who had a great belief in herself, did not succeed any better, and her tastes were just as expensive.

And so the house came to be haunted by the unspoken phrase: There   5
must be more money! There must be more money! The children could hear it all the time, though nobody said it aloud. They heard it at Christmas, when the expensive and splendid toys filled the nursery. Behind the shining modern rocking horse, behind the smart doll's-house, a voice would start whispering: "There must be more money! There must be more money!" And the children would stop playing, to listen for a moment. They would look into each other's eyes, to see if they had all heard. And each one saw in the eyes of the other two that they too had heard. "There must be more money! There must be more money!"

It came whispering from the springs of the still-swaying rocking horse, and even the horse, bending his wooden, champing head, heard it. The big doll, sitting so pink and smirking in her new pram, could hear it quite plainly, and seemed to be smirking all the more self-consciously because of it. The foolish puppy, too, that took the place of the Teddy bear, he was looking so extraordinarily foolish for no other reason but that he heard the secret whisper all over the house: "There must be more money!"

Yet nobody ever said it aloud. The whisper was everywhere, and therefore no one spoke it. Just as no one ever says: "We are breathing!" in spite of the fact that breath is coming and going all the time.

"Mother," said the boy Paul one day, "why don't we keep a car of our own? Why do we always use uncle's, or else a taxi?"

"Because we're the poor members of the family," said the mother.

"But why are we, mother?"   10

"Well—I suppose," she said slowly and bitterly, "it's because your father has no luck."

The boy was silent for some time.

"Is luck money, mother?" he asked, rather timidly.

"No, Paul. Not quite. It's what causes you to have money."

15   "Oh!" said Paul vaguely. "I thought when Uncle Oscar said filthy lucker, it meant money."

"Filthy lucre° does mean money," said the mother. "But it's lucre, not luck."

"Oh!" said the boy. "Then what is luck, mother?"

"It's what causes you to have money. If you're lucky you have money. That's why it's better to be born lucky than rich. If you're rich, you may lose your money. But if you're lucky, you will always get more money."

"Oh! Will you? And is father not lucky?"

20   "Very unlucky, I should say," she said bitterly.

The boy watched her with unsure eyes.

"Why?" he asked.

"I don't know. Nobody ever knows why one person is lucky and another unlucky."

"Don't they? Nobody at all? Does nobody know?"

25   "Perhaps God. But He never tells."

"He ought to, then. And aren't you lucky either, mother?"

"I can't be, if I married an unlucky husband."

"But by yourself, aren't you?"

"I used to think I was, before I married. Now I think I am very unlucky indeed."

30   "Why?"

"Well—never mind! Perhaps I'm not really," she said.

The child looked at her, to see if she meant it. But he saw, by the lines of her mouth, that she was only trying to hide something from him.

"Well, anyhow," he said stoutly, "I'm a lucky person."

"Why?" said his mother, with a sudden laugh.

35   He stared at her. He didn't even know why he had said it.

"God told me," he asserted, brazening it out.

"I hope He did, dear!" she said, again with a laugh, but rather bitter.

"He did, mother!"

"Excellent!" said the mother, using one of her husband's exclamations.

40   The boy saw she did not believe him; or, rather, that she paid no attention to his assertion. This angered him somewhat, and made him want to compel her attention.

He went off by himself, vaguely, in a childish way, seeking for the clue to "luck." Absorbed, taking no heed of other people, he went about with a sort of stealth, seeking inwardly for luck. He wanted luck, he wanted it, he wanted it. When the two girls were playing dolls in the nursery, he would sit on his big rocking horse, charging madly into space, with a frenzy that made the little girls peer at him uneasily. Wildly the horse careered, the waving dark hair of the boy tossed, his eyes had a strange glare in them. The little girls dared not speak to him.

filthy lucre: see New Testament, I Timothy 3:3

When he had ridden to the end of his mad little journey, he climbed down and stood in front of his rocking horse, staring fixedly into its lowered face. Its red mouth was slightly open, its big eye was wide and glassy-bright.

"Now!" he would silently command the snorting steed. "Now, take me to where there is luck! Now take me!"

And he would slash the horse on the neck with the little whip he had asked Uncle Oscar for. He knew the horse could take him to where there was luck, if only he forced it. So he would mount again, and start on his furious ride, hoping at last to get there. He knew he could get there.

"You'll break your horse, Paul!" said the nurse.   45

"He's always riding like that! I wish he'd leave off!" said his elder sister Joan.

But he only glared down on them in silence. Nurse gave him up. She could make nothing of him. Anyhow he was growing beyond her.

One day his mother and his Uncle Oscar came in when he was on one of his furious rides. He did not speak to them.

"Hallo, you young jockey! Riding a winner?" said his uncle.

"Aren't you growing too big for a rocking horse? You're not a very little   50
boy any longer, you know," said his mother.

But Paul only gave a blue glare from his big, rather close-set eyes. He would speak to nobody when he was in full tilt. His mother watched him with an anxious expression on her face.

At last he suddenly stopped forcing his horse into the mechanical gallop, and slid down.

"Well, I got there!" he announced fiercely, his blue eyes still flaring, and his sturdy long legs straddling apart.

"Where did you get to?" asked his mother.

"Where I wanted to go," he flared back at her.   55

"That's right, son!" said Uncle Oscar. "Don't you stop till you get there. What's the horse's name?"

"He doesn't have a name," said the boy.

"Gets on without all right?" asked the uncle.

"Well, he has different names. He was called Sansovino last week."

"Sansovino, eh? Won the Ascot. How did you know his name?"   60

"He always talks about horse races with Bassett," said Joan.

The uncle was delighted to find that his small nephew was posted with all the racing news. Bassett, the young gardener, who had been wounded in the left foot in the war and got his present job through Oscar Cresswell, whose batman he had been, was a perfect blade of the "turf." He lived in the racing events, and the small boy lived with him.

Oscar Cresswell got it all from Bassett.

"Master Paul comes and asks me, so I can't do more than tell him, sir," said Bassett, his face terribly serious, as if he were speaking of religious matters.

"And does he ever put anything on a horse he fancies?"   65

"Well—I don't want to give him away—he's a young sport, a fine sport, sir. Would you mind asking him yourself? He sort of takes a pleasure in it, and perhaps he'd feel I was giving him away, sir, if you don't mind."

Bassett was serious as a church.

The uncle went back to his nephew, and took him off for a ride in the car.

"Say, Paul, old man, do you ever put anything on a horse?" the uncle asked.

70   The boy watched the handsome man closely.

"Why, do you think I oughtn't to?" he parried.

"Not a bit of it! I thought perhaps you might give me a tip for the Lincoln."

The car sped on into the country, going down to Uncle Oscar's place in Hampshire.

"Honor bright?" said the nephew.

75   "Honor bright, son!" said the uncle.

"Well, then, Daffodil."

"Daffodil! I doubt it, sonny. What about Mirza?"

"I only know the winner," said the boy. "That's Daffodil."

"Daffodil, eh?"

80   There was a pause. Daffodil was an obscure horse comparatively.

"Uncle!"

"Yes, son?"

"You won't let it go any further, will you? I promised Bassett."

"Bassett be damned, old man! What's he got to do with it?"

85   "We're partners. We've been partners from the first. Uncle, he lent me my first five shillings, which I lost. I promised him, honor bright, it was only between me and him; only you gave me that ten-shilling note I started winning with, so I thought you were lucky. You won't let it go any further, will you?"

The boy gazed at his uncle from those big, hot, blue eyes, set rather close together. The uncle stirred and laughed uneasily.

"Right you are, son! I'll keep your tip private. Daffodil, eh? How much are you putting on him?"

"All except twenty pounds," said the boy. "I keep that in reserve."

The uncle thought it a good joke.

90   "You keep twenty pounds in reserve, do you, you young romancer? What are you betting, then?"

"I'm betting three hundred," said the boy gravely. "But it's between you and me, Uncle Oscar! Honor bright?"

The uncle burst into a roar of laughter.

"It's between you and me all right, you young Nat Gould,"° he said, laughing. "But where's your three hundred?"

Nat Gould: a journalist and novelist (1857–1919) who wrote about horse racing

"Bassett keeps it for me. We're partners."

"You are, are you! And what is Bassett putting on Daffodil?"   95

"He won't go quite as high as I do, I expect. Perhaps he'll go a hundred and fifty."

"What, pennies?" laughed the uncle.

"Pounds," said the child, with a surprised look at his uncle. "Bassett keeps a bigger reserve than I do."

Between wonder and amusement Uncle Oscar was silent. He pursued the matter no further, but he determined to take his nephew with him to the Lincoln races.

"Now, son," he said, "I'm putting twenty on Mirza, and I'll put five for   100 you on any horse you fancy. What's your pick?"

"Daffodil, uncle."

"No, not the fiver on Daffodil!"

"I should if it was my own fiver," said the child.

"Good! Good! Right you are! A fiver for me and a fiver for you on Daffodil."

The child had never been to a race meeting before, and his eyes were blue   105 fire. He pursed his mouth tight, and watched. A Frenchman just in front had put his money on Lancelot. Wild with excitement, he flayed his arms up and down, yelling "Lancelot! Lancelot!" in his French accent.

Daffodil came in first, Lancelot second, Mirza third. The child, flushed and with eyes blazing, was curiously serene. His uncle brought him four five-pound notes, four to one.

"What am I to do with these?" he cried, waving them before the boy's eyes.

"I suppose we'll talk to Bassett," said the boy. "I expect I have fifteen hundred now; and twenty in reserve; and this twenty."

His uncle studied him for some moments.

"Look here, son!" he said. "You're not serious about Bassett and that   110 fifteen hundred, are you?"

"Yes, I am. But it's between you and me, uncle. Honor bright!"

"Honor bright all right, son! But I must talk to Bassett."

"If you'd like to be a partner, uncle, with Bassett and me, we could all be partners. Only, you'd have to promise, honor bright, uncle, not to let it go beyond us three. Bassett and I are lucky, and you must be lucky, because it was your ten shillings I started winning with . . ."

Uncle Oscar took both Bassett and Paul into Richmond Park for an afternoon, and there they talked.

"It's like this, you see, sir," Bassett said. "Master Paul would get me   115 talking about racing events, spinning yarns, you know, sir. And he was always keen on knowing if I'd made or if I'd lost. It's about a year since, now, that I put five shillings on Blush of Dawn for him—and we lost. Then the luck turned, with that ten shillings he had from you, that we put on

Singhalese. And since that time, it's been pretty steady, all things considering. What do you say, Master Paul?"

"We're all right when we're sure," said Paul. "It's when we're not quite
sure that we go down."

"Oh, but we're careful then," said Bassett.

"But when are you sure?" smiled Uncle Oscar.

"It's Master Paul, sir," said Bassett, in a secret, religious voice. "It's as if
he had it from heaven. Like Daffodil, now, for the Lincoln. That was as sure
as eggs."

120   "Did you put anything on Daffodil?" asked Oscar Cresswell.

"Yes, sir, I made my bit."

"And my nephew?"

Bassett was obstinately silent, looking at Paul.

"I made twelve hundred, didn't I, Bassett? I told uncle I was putting
three hundred on Daffodil."

125   "That's right," said Bassett, nodding.

"But where's the money?" asked the uncle.

"I keep it safe locked up, sir. Master Paul he can have it any minute he
likes to ask for it."

"What, fifteen hundred pounds?"

"And twenty! and forty, that is, with the twenty he made on the course."

130   "It's amazing!" said the uncle.

"If Master Paul offers you to be partners, sir, I would, if I were you; if
you'll excuse me," said Bassett.

Oscar Cresswell thought about it.

"I'll see the money," he said.

They drove home again, and sure enough, Bassett came round to the
garden-house with fifteen hundred pounds in notes. The twenty pounds
reserve was left with Joe Glee, in the Turf Commission deposit.

135   "You see, it's all right, uncle, when I'm sure! Then we go strong, for all
we're worth. Don't we Bassett?"

"We do that, Master Paul."

"And when are you sure?" said the uncle, laughing.

"Oh, well, sometimes I'm absolutely sure, like about Daffodil," said the
boy; "and sometimes I have an idea; and sometimes I haven't even an idea,
have I, Bassett? Then we're careful, because we mostly go down."

"You do, do you! And when you're sure, like about Daffodil, what
makes you sure, sonny?"

140   "Oh, well, I don't know," said the boy uneasily. "I'm sure, you know,
uncle; that's all."

"It's as if he had it from heaven, sir," Bassett reiterated.

"I should say so!" said the uncle.

But he became a partner. And when the Leger was coming on, Paul was
"sure" about Lively Spark, which was a quite inconsiderable horse. The boy

insisted on putting a thousand on the horse, Bassett went for five hundred, and Oscar Cresswell two hundred. Lively Spark came in first, and the betting had been ten to one against him. Paul had made ten thousand.

"You see," he said, "I was absolutely sure of him."

Even Oscar Cresswell had cleared two thousand.   145

"Look here son," he said, "this sort of thing makes me nervous."

"It needn't, uncle! Perhaps I shan't be sure again for a long time."

"But what are you going to do with your money?" asked the uncle.

"Of course," said the boy, "I started it for mother. She said she had no luck, because father is unlucky, so I thought if I was lucky, it might stop whispering."

"What might stop whispering?"   150

"Our house. I hate our house for whispering."

"What does it whisper?"

"Why—why"—the boy fidgeted—"why, I don't know. But it's always short of money, you know, uncle."

"I know it, son, I know it."

"You know people send mother writs, don't you, uncle?"   155

"I'm afraid I do," said the uncle.

"And then the house whispers, like people laughing at you behind your back. It's awful, that is! I thought if I was lucky . . ."

"You might stop it," added the uncle.

The boy watched him with big blue eyes that had an uncanny cold fire in them, and he said never a word.

"Well, then!" said the uncle. "What are we doing?"   160

"I shouldn't like mother to know I was lucky," said the boy.

"Why not, son?"

"She'd stop me."

"I don't think she would."

"Oh!"—and the boy writhed in an odd way—"I don't want her to know,   165 uncle."

"All right, son! We'll manage it without her knowing."

They managed it very easily. Paul, at the other's suggestion, handed over five thousand pounds to his uncle, who deposited it with the family lawyer, who was then to inform Paul's mother that a relative had put five thousand pounds into his hands, which sum was to be paid out a thousand pounds at a time, on the mother's birthday, for the next five years.

"So she'll have a birthday present of a thousand pounds for five successive years," said Uncle Oscar. "I hope it won't make it all the harder for her later."

Paul's mother had her birthday in November. The house had been "whispering" worse than ever lately, and, even in spite of his luck, Paul could not bear up against it. He was very anxious to see the effect of the birthday letter telling his mother about the thousand pounds.

170   When there were no visitors, Paul now took his meals with his parents, as he was beyond the nursery control. His mother went into town nearly every day. She had discovered that she had an odd knack of sketching furs and dress materials, so she worked secretly in the studio of a friend who was the chief "artist" for the leading drapers. She drew the figures of ladies in furs and ladies in silk and sequins for the newspaper advertisements. This young woman artist earned several thousand pounds a year, but Paul's mother only made several hundreds, and she was again dissatisfied. She so wanted to be first in something, and she did not succeed, even in making sketches for drapery advertisements.

She was down to breakfast on the morning of her birthday. Paul watched her face as she read her letters. He knew the lawyer's letter. As his mother read it, her face hardened and became more expressionless. Then a cold, determined look came on her mouth. She hid the letter under the pile of others, and said not a word about it.

"Didn't you have anything nice in the post for your birthday, mother?" said Paul.

"Quite moderately nice," she said, her voice cold and absent.

She went away to town without saying more.

175   But in the afternoon Uncle Oscar appeared. He said Paul's mother had had a long interview with the lawyer, asking if the whole five thousand could be advanced at once, as she was in debt.

"What do you think, uncle?" said the boy.

"I leave it to you, son."

"Oh, let her have it, then! We can get some more with the other," said the boy.

"A bird in the hand is worth two in the bush, laddie!" said Uncle Oscar.

180   "But I'm sure to know for the Grand National; or the Lincolnshire; or else the Derby. I'm sure to know for one of them," said Paul.

So Uncle Oscar signed the agreement, and Paul's mother touched the whole five thousand. Then something very curious happened. The voices in the house suddenly went mad, like a chorus of frogs on a spring evening. There were certain new furnishings, and Paul had a tutor. He was really going to Eton,° his father's school, in the following autumn. There were flowers in the winter, and a blossoming of the luxury Paul's mother had been used to. And yet the voices in the house, behind the sprays of mimosa and almond blossom, and from under the piles of iridescent cushions, simply trilled and screamed in a sort of ecstasy: "There must be more money! Oh-h-h, there must be more money. Oh, now, now-w! Now-w-w—there must be more money—more than ever! More than ever!"

It frightened Paul terribly. He studied away at his Latin and Greek with his tutor. But his intense hours were spent with Bassett. The Grand National had gone by: he had not "known," and had lost a hundred pounds. Summer

Eton: England's most prestigious privately supported school

was at hand. He was in agony for the Lincoln. But even for the Lincoln he didn't "know" and he lost fifty pounds. He became wild-eyed and strange, as if something were going to explode in him.

"Let it alone, son! Don't you bother about it!" urged Uncle Oscar. But it was as if the boy couldn't really hear what his uncle was saying.

"I've got to know for the Derby! I've got to know for the Derby!" the child reiterated, his big blue eyes blazing with a sort of madness.

His mother noticed how overwrought he was.   185

"You'd better go to the seaside. Wouldn't you like to go now to the seaside, instead of waiting? I think you'd better," she said, looking down at him anxiously, her heart curiously heavy because of him.

But the child lifted his uncanny blue eyes.

"I couldn't possibly go before the Derby, mother!" he said. "I couldn't possibly!"

"Why not?" she said, her voice becoming heavy when she was opposed. "Why not? You can still go from the seaside to see the Derby with your Uncle Oscar, if that's what you wish. No need for you to wait here. Besides, I think you care too much about these races. It's a bad sign. My family has been a gambling family, and you won't know till you grow up how much damage it has done. But it has done damage. I shall have to send Bassett away, and ask Uncle Oscar not to talk racing to you, unless you promise to be reasonable about it; go away to the seaside and forget it. You're all nerves!"

"I'll do what you like, mother, so long as you don't send me away till   190 after the Derby," the boy said.

"Send you away from where? Just from this house?"

"Yes," he said, gazing at her.

"Why, you curious child, what makes you care about this house so much, suddenly? I never knew you loved it."

He gazed at her without speaking. He had a secret within a secret, something he had not divulged, even to Bassett or to his Uncle Oscar.

But his mother, after standing undecided and a little bit sullen for some   195 moments, said:

"Very well, then! Don't go to the seaside till after the Derby, if you don't wish it. But promise me you won't let your nerves go to pieces. Promise you won't think so much about horse racing and events, as you call them!"

"Oh, no," said the boy casually. "I won't think much about them, mother. You needn't worry. I wouldn't worry, mother, if I were you."

"If you were me and I were you," said his mother, "I wonder what we should do!"

"But you know you needn't worry, mother, don't you?" the boy repeated.

"I should be awfully glad to know it," she said wearily.   200

"Oh, well, you can, you know. I mean, you ought to know you needn't worry," he insisted.

"Ought I? Then I'll see about it," she said.

Paul's secret of secrets was his wooden horse, that which had no name. Since he was emancipated from a nurse and a nursery-governess, he had had his rocking horse removed to his own bedroom at the top of the house.

"Surely, you're too big for a rocking horse!" his mother had remonstrated.

205   "Well, you see mother, till I can have a real horse, I like to have some sort of animal about," had been his quaint answer.

"Do you feel he keeps you company?" she laughed.

"Oh, yes! He's very good, he always keeps me company, when I'm there," said Paul.

So the horse, rather shabby, stood in an arrested prance in the boy's bedroom.

The Derby was drawing near, and the boy grew more and more tense. He hardly heard what was spoken to him, he was very frail, and his eyes were really uncanny. His mother had sudden seizures of uneasiness about him. Sometimes, for half-an-hour, she would feel a sudden anxiety about him that was almost anguish. She wanted to rush to him at once, and know he was safe.

210   Two nights before the Derby, she was at a big party in town, when one of her rushes of anxiety about her boy, her first-born, gripped her heart till she could hardly speak. She fought with the feeling, might and main, for she believed in common sense. But it was too strong. The children's nursery-governess was terribly surprised and startled at being rung up in the night.

"Are the children all right, Miss Wilmot?"

"Oh, yes, they are quite all right."

"Master Paul? Is he all right?"

"He went to bed as right as a trivet. Shall I run up and look at him?"

215   "No," said Paul's mother reluctantly. "No! Don't trouble. It's all right. Don't sit up. We shall be home fairly soon." She did not want her son's privacy intruded upon.

"Very good," said the governess.

It was about one o'clock when Paul's mother and father drove up to their house. All was still. Paul's mother went to her room and slipped off her white fur coat. She had told her maid not to wait up for her. She heard her husband downstairs, mixing a whiskey-and-soda.

And then, because of the strange anxiety at her heart, she stole upstairs to her son's room. Noiselessly she went along the upper corridor. Was there a faint noise? What was it?

She stood, with arrested muscles, outside his door listening. There was a strange, heavy, and yet not loud noise. Her heart stood still. It was a sound-less noise, yet rushing and powerful. Something huge, in violent, hushed motion. What was it? What in God's name was it? She ought to know. She felt that she knew the noise. She knew what it was.

220   Yet she could not place it. She couldn't say what it was. And on and on it went, like madness.

Softly, frozen with anxiety and fear, she turned the door handle.

The room was dark. Yet in the space near the window, she heard and saw something plunging to and fro. She gazed in fear and amazement.

Then suddenly she switched on the light, and saw her son, in his green pajamas, madly surging on the rocking horse. The blaze of light suddenly lit him up, as he urged the wooden horse, and lit her up, as she stood, blonde, in her dress of pale green and crystal, in the doorway.

"Paul!" she cried. "Whatever are you doing?"

"It's Malabar!" he screamed, in a powerful, strange voice. "It's   225
Malabar."

His eyes blazed at her for one strange and senseless second, as he ceased urging his wooden horse. Then he fell with a crash to the ground, and she, all her tormented motherhood flooding upon her, rushed to gather him up.

But he was unconscious, and unconscious he remained, with some brain-fever. He talked and tossed, and his mother sat stonily by his side.

"Malabar! It's Malabar! Bassett, Bassett, I know it! It's Malabar!"

So the child cried, trying to get up and urge the rocking horse that gave him his inspiration.

"What does he mean by Malabar?" asked the heart-frozen mother.   230

"I don't know," said his father stonily.

"What does he mean by Malabar?" she asked her brother Oscar.

"It's one of the horses running for the Derby," was the answer.

And, in spite of himself, Oscar Cresswell spoke to Bassett, and himself put a thousand on Malabar: at fourteen to one.

The third day of the illness was critical: they were waiting for a change.   235
The boy, with his rather long, curly hair, was tossing ceaselessly on the pillow. He neither slept nor regained consciousness, and his eyes were like blue stones. His mother sat, feeling her heart had gone, turned actually into a stone.

In the evening, Oscar Cresswell did not come, but Bassett sent a message, saying could he come up for one moment, just one moment? Paul's mother was very angry at the intrusion, but on second thought she agreed. The boy was the same. Perhaps Bassett might bring him to consciousness.

The gardener, a shortish fellow with a brown mustache, and sharp little brown eyes, tiptoed into the room, touched his imaginary cap to Paul's mother, and stole to the bedside, staring with glittering, smallish eyes, at the tossing, dying child.

"Master Paul!" he whispered. "Master Paul! Malabar came in first all right, a clean win. I did as you told me. You've made over seventy thousand pounds, you have; you've got over eighty thousand. Malabar came in all right, Master Paul."

"Malabar! Malabar! Did I say Malabar, mother? Did I say Malabar? Do you think I'm lucky, mother? I knew Malabar, didn't I? Over eighty thousand pounds! I call that lucky, don't you, mother? Over eighty thousand pounds! I knew, didn't I know I knew? Malabar came in all right. If I ride my

horse till I'm sure, then I tell you, Bassett, you can go as high as you like. Did
you go for all you were worth, Bassett?"

240   "I went a thousand on it, Master Paul."

"I never told you, mother, that if I can ride my horse, and get there, then
I'm absolutely sure—oh, absolutely! Mother, did I ever tell you? I'm lucky."

"No, you never did," said the mother.

But the boy died in the night.

And even as he lay dead, his mother heard her brother's voice saying to
her: "My God, Hester, you're eighty-odd thousand to the good and a poor
devil of a son to the bad. But, poor devil, poor devil, he's best gone out of a
life where he rides his rocking horse to find a winner."

QUESTIONS

1. In the phraseology of its beginning ("There was a woman . . ."), it's simple
   style, its direct characterization, and its use of the wish motif—especially
   that of the wish that is granted only on conditions that nullify its desirabil-
   ity (compare the story of King Midas)—this story has the qualities of a fairy
   tale. Its differences, however—in characterization, setting, and ending—
   are especially significant. What do they tell us about the purpose of the
   story?
2. Characterize the mother fully. How does she differ from the stepmothers
   in fairy tales like "Cinderella" and "Hansel and Gretel"? How does the
   boy's mistake about *filthy lucker* (paragraph 15) clarify her thinking and
   her motivations? Why had her love for her husband turned to dust? Why is
   she "unlucky"?
3. What kind of a child is Paul? What are his motivations?
4. The initial assumptions of the story are that (a) a boy might get divinatory
   powers by riding a rocking horse, (b) a house can whisper. Could the second of these be accepted as little more than a metaphor? Once we have
   granted these initial assumptions, does the story develop plausibly?
5. It is ironic that the boy's attempt to stop the whispers should only increase
   them. Is this a plausible irony? Why? What does it tell us about the theme
   of the story? Why is it ironic that the whispers should be especially audible
   at Christmas time? What irony is contained in the boy's last speech?
6. In what way is the boy's furious riding on the rocking horse an appropriate
   symbol for materialistic pursuits?
7. How might a sentimental writer have ended the story?
8. How many persons in the story are affected (or infected) by materialism?
9. What is the theme of the story?

Nathaniel Hawthorne

Young Goodman Brown

Young Goodman Brown came forth at sunset into the street of Salem village, but put his head back, after crossing the threshold, to exchange a parting kiss with his young wife. And Faith, as the wife was aptly named, thrust her own pretty head into the street, letting the wind play with the pink ribbons of her cap while she called to Goodman Brown.

"Dearest heart," whispered she softly and rather sadly when her lips were close to his ear, "prithee, put off your journey until sunrise, and sleep in your own bed tonight. A lone woman is troubled with such dreams and such thoughts that she's afeard of herself, sometimes. Pray, tarry with me this night, dear husband, of all nights in the year!"

"My love and my Faith," replied young Goodman Brown, "of all nights in the year this one must I tarry away from thee. My journey, as thou callest it, forth and back again must needs be done 'twixt now and sunrise. What, my sweet, pretty wife, dost thou doubt me already, and we but three months married!"

"Then God bless you!" said Faith with the pink ribbons, "and may you find all well when you come back."

"Amen!" cried Goodman Brown. "Say thy prayers, dear Faith, and go to bed at dusk, and no harm will come to thee."   5

So they parted; and the young man pursued his way until, being about to turn the corner by the meeting-house, he looked back and saw the head of Faith still peeping after him with a melancholy air in spite of her pink ribbons.

"Poor little Faith!" thought he, for his heart smote him. "What a wretch am I, to leave her on such an errand! She talks of dreams, too. Methought, as she spoke, there was trouble in her face, as if a dream had warned her what work is to be done tonight. But no, no! 'twould kill her to think it. Well; she's a blessed angel on earth and after this one night I'll cling to her skirts and follow her to Heaven."

With this excellent resolve for the future, Goodman Brown felt himself justified in making more haste on his present evil purpose. He had taken a dreary road, darkened by all the gloomiest trees of the forest, which barely stood aside to let the narrow path creep through, and closed immediately

YOUNG GOODMAN BROWN   First published in 1835. "Goodman" was a title of respect, but at a social rank lower than "gentleman." "Goody" (or "Goodwife") was the feminine equivalent. Deacon Gookin in the story is a historical personage (1612–1687), as are also Goody Cloyse, Goody Cory, and Martha Carrier, all three executed at the Salem witchcraft trials in 1692. Nathaniel Hawthorne (1804–1864) was born and grew up in Salem, Massachusetts, where Hawthornes had lived since the seventeenth century. One ancestor had been a judge at the Salem witch trials; another had been a leader in the persecution of Quakers. "Young Goodman Brown" is one of several stories in which Hawthorne explored the Puritan past of New England.

behind. It was all as lonely as could be; and there is this peculiarity in such a solitude, that the traveler knows not who may be concealed by the innumerable trunks and the thick boughs overhead, so that with lonely footsteps he may be passing through an unseen multitude.

"There may be a devilish Indian behind every tree," said Goodman Brown to himself; and he glanced fearfully behind him as he added, "What if the devil himself should be at my very elbow!"

10   His head being turned back, he passed a crook of the road, and looking forward again beheld the figure of a man in grave and decent attire, seated at the foot of an old tree. He rose at Goodman Brown's approach and walked onward side by side with him.

"You are late, Goodman Brown," said he. "The clock of the Old South was striking as I came through Boston, and that is full fifteen minutes agone."°

"Faith kept me back awhile," replied the young man with a tremor in his voice caused by the sudden appearance of his companion, though not wholly unexpected.

It was now deep dusk in the forest, and deepest in that part of it where these two were journeying. As nearly as could be discerned, the second traveler was about fifty years old, apparently in the same rank of life as Goodman Brown, and bearing a considerable resemblance to him, though perhaps more in expression than features. Still, they might have been taken for father and son. And yet, though the elder person was as simply clad as the younger, and as simple in manner too, he had an indescribable air of one who knew the world and would not have felt abashed at the governor's dinner table or in King William's court,° were it possible that his affairs should call him thither. But the only thing about him that could be fixed upon as remarkable was his staff, which bore the likeness of a great black snake, so curiously wrought that it might almost be seen to twist and wriggle itself like a living serpent. This, of course, must have been an ocular deception, assisted by the uncertain light.

"Come, Goodman Brown!" cried his fellow-traveler, "this is a dull pace for the beginning of a journey. Take my staff if you are so soon weary."

15   "Friend," said the other, exchanging his slow pace for a full stop, "having kept covenant by meeting thee here, it is my purpose now to return whence I came. I have scruples touching the matter thou wot'st of."

"Sayest thou so?" replied he of the serpent, smiling apart. "Let us walk on nevertheless, reasoning as we go, and if I convince thee not, thou shalt turn back. We are but a little way in the forest yet."

"Too far, too far!" exclaimed the goodman, unconsciously resuming his walk. "My father never went into the woods on such an errand, nor his father before him. We have been a race of honest men and good Christians since the

---

full fifteen minutes agone: The distance from the center of Boston to the forest was over twenty miles.   **King William's court:** William III, King of England, 1689–1702

days of the martyrs. And shall I be the first of the name of Brown that ever took this path and kept—"

"Such company, thou wouldst say," observed the elder person interrupting his pause. "Well said, Goodman Brown! I have been as well acquainted with your family as with ever a one among the Puritans, and that's no trifle to say. I helped your grandfather the constable when he lashed the Quaker woman so smartly through the streets of Salem. And it was I that brought your father a pitch-pine knot kindled at my own hearth, to set fire to an Indian village, in King Philip's war.° They were my good friends, both; and many a pleasant walk have we had along this path and returned merrily after midnight. I would fain be friends with you, for their sake."

"If it be as thou sayest," replied Goodman Brown, "I marvel they never spoke of these matters. Or, verily, I marvel not, seeing that the least rumor of the sort would have driven them from New England. We are a people of prayer, and good works to boot, and abide no such wickedness."

"Wickedness or not," said the traveler with twisted staff, "I have a general acquaintance here in New England. The deacons of many a church have drunk the communion wine with me, the selectmen of divers towns make me their chairman, and a majority of the Great and General Court° are firm supporters of my interest. The governor and I, too—but these are state secrets." 20

"Can this be so!" cried Goodman Brown with a stare of amazement at his undisturbed companion. "Howbeit, I have nothing to do with the governor and council; they have their own ways and are no rule for a simple husbandman like me. But were I to go on with thee, how should I meet the eye of that good old man, our minister, at Salem village? Oh, his voice would make me tremble, both Sabbath-day and lecture-day!"

Thus far, the elder traveler had listened with due gravity but now burst into a fit of irrepressible mirth, shaking himself so violently that his snake-like staff actually seemed to wriggle in sympathy.

"Ha! ha! ha!" shouted he, again and again; then composing himself, "Well, go on, Goodman Brown, go on; but prithee, don't kill me with laughing!"

"Well, then, to end the matter at once," said Goodman Brown, considerably nettled, "there is my wife, Faith. It would break her dear little heart, and I'd rather break my own!"

"Nay, if that be the case," answered the other, "e'en go thy ways, Goodman Brown. I would not for twenty old women like the one hobbling before us that Faith should come to any harm." 25

As he spoke he pointed his staff at a female figure on the path in whom Goodman Brown recognized a very pious and exemplary dame who had

King Philip's War: a war between the colonists and Indians, 1675–1676
Great and General Court: the legislature of the Massachusetts Bay Colony

taught him his catechism in youth and was still his moral and spiritual adviser, jointly with the minister and Deacon Gookin.

"A marvel, truly, that Goody Cloyse should be so far in the wilderness at nightfall!" said he. "But with your leave, friend, I shall take a cut through the woods until we have left this Christian woman behind. Being a stranger to you, she might ask whom I was consorting with and whither I was going."

"Be it so," said his fellow-traveler. "Betake you to the woods and let me keep the path."

Accordingly, the young man turned aside, but took care to watch his companion who advanced softly along the road until he had come within a staff's length of the old dame. She, meanwhile, was making the best of her way, with singular speed for so aged a woman, and mumbling some indistinct words, a prayer, doubtless, as she went. The traveler put forth his staff and touched her withered neck with what seemed the serpent's tail.

30   "The devil!" screamed the pious old lady.

"Then Goody Cloyse knows her old friend?" observed the traveler, confronting her and leaning on his writhing stick.

"Ah, forsooth, and is it your worship indeed?" cried the good dame. "Yea, truly is it, and in the very image of my old gossip, Goodman Brown, the grandfather of the silly fellow that now is. But would your worship believe it? my broomstick hath strangely disappeared, stolen as I suspect by that unhanged witch, Goody Cory, and that, too, when I was all anointed with the juice of smallage and cinque-foil and wolf's-bane—"

"Mingled with fine wheat and the fat of a new-born babe," said the shape of old Goodman Brown.

"Ah, your worship knows the recipe," cried the old lady, cackling aloud. "So, as I was saying, being all ready for the meeting, and no horse to ride on, I made up my mind to foot it; for they tell me there is a nice young man to be taken into communion tonight. But now your good worship will lend me your arm and we shall be there in a twinkling."

35   "That can hardly be," answered her friend. "I may not spare you my arm, Goody Cloyse, but here is my staff, if you will."

So saying, he threw it down at her feet where, perhaps, it assumed life, being one of the rods which its owner had formerly lent to the Egyptian Magi. Of this fact, however, Goodman Brown could not take cognizance. He had cast up his eyes in astonishment, and looking down again beheld neither Goody Cloyse nor the serpentine staff, but his fellow-traveler alone, who waited for him as calmly as if nothing had happened.

"That old woman taught me my catechism!" said the young man, and there was a world of meaning in this simple comment.

They continued to walk onward while the elder traveler exhorted his companion to make good speed and persevere in the path, discoursing so aptly that his arguments seemed rather to spring up in the bosom of his auditor than to be suggested by himself. As they went he plucked a branch of maple to serve for a walking-stick, and began to strip it of the twigs and little boughs which were wet with evening dew. The moment his fingers touched them they became strangely withered and dried up, as with a week's sunshine. Thus the pair proceeded at a good free pace, until suddenly, in a gloomy hollow of the road, Goodman Brown sat himself down on the stump of a tree and refused to go any farther.

"Friend," said he stubbornly, "my mind is made up. Not another step will I budge on this errand. What if a wretched old woman do choose to go to the devil when I thought she was going to Heaven! Is that any reason why I should quit my dear Faith and go after her?"

"You will think better of this by and by," said his acquaintance composedly. "Sit here and rest yourself awhile, and when you feel like moving again, there is my staff to help you along."   40

Without more words, he threw his companion the maple stick and was as speedily out of sight as if he had vanished into the deepening gloom. The young man sat a few moments by the roadside, applauding himself greatly and thinking with how clear a conscience he should meet the minister in his morning walk, nor shrink from the eye of good old Deacon Gookin. And what calm sleep would be his that very night, which was to have been spent so wickedly, but purely and sweetly now, in the arms of Faith! Amidst these pleasant and praiseworthy meditations, Goodman Brown heard the tramp of horses along the road and deemed it advisable to conceal himself within the verge of the forest, conscious of the guilty purpose that had brought him thither, though now so happily turned from it.

On came the hoof-tramps and the voices of the riders, two grave old voices conversing soberly as they drew near. These mingled sounds appeared to pass along the road within a few yards of the young man's hiding place; but owing, doubtless, to the depth of the gloom at that particular spot, neither the travelers nor their steeds were visible. Though their figures brushed the small boughs by the wayside, it could not be seen that they intercepted even for a moment the faint gleam from the strip of bright sky athwart which they must have passed. Goodman Brown alternately crouched and stood on tiptoe, pulling aside the branches and thrusting forth his head as far as he durst, without discerning so much as a shadow. It vexed him the more because he could have sworn, were such a thing possible, that he recognized the voices of the minister and Deacon Gookin, jogging along quietly as they were wont to do when bound to some ordination or ecclesiastical council. While yet within hearing, one of the riders stopped to pluck a switch.

"Of the two, reverend Sir," said the voice like the deacon's, "I had rather miss an ordination dinner than tonight's meeting. They tell me that some of our community are to be here from Falmouth and beyond, and others from Connecticut and Rhode Island, besides several of the Indian powwows who, after their fashion, know almost as much deviltry as the best of us. Moreover, there is a goodly young woman to be taken into communion."

"Mighty well, Deacon Gookin!" replied the solemn old tones of the minister. "Spur up, or we shall be late. Nothing can be done, you know, until I get on the ground."

45   The hoofs clattered again, and the voices talking so strangely in the empty air passed on through the forest where no church had ever been gathered nor solitary Christian prayed. Whither, then, could these holy men be journeying, so deep into the heathen wilderness? Young Goodman Brown caught hold of a tree for support, being ready to sink down on the ground, faint and over-burthened with the heavy sickness of his heart. He looked up to the sky, doubting whether there really was a Heaven above him. Yet there was the blue arch, and the stars brightening in it.

"With Heaven above, and Faith below, I will yet stand firm against the devil!" cried Goodman Brown.

While he still gazed upward into the deep arch of the firmament and had lifted his hands to pray, a cloud, though no wind was stirring, hurried across the zenith and hid the brightening stars. The blue sky was still visible except directly overhead, where this black mass of cloud was sweeping swiftly northward. Aloft in the air, as if from the depths of the cloud, came a confused and doubtful sound of voices. Once the listener fancied that he could distinguish the accents of townspeople of his own, men and women, both pious and ungodly, many of whom he had met at the communion-table, and had seen others rioting at the tavern. The next moment, so indistinct were the sounds, he doubted whether he had heard aught but the murmur of the old forest whispering without a wind. Then came a stronger swell of those familiar tones heard daily in the sunshine at Salem village, but never, until now, from a cloud at night. There was one voice, of a young woman uttering lamentations yet with an uncertain sorrow, and entreating for some favor, which, perhaps, it would grieve her to obtain. And all the unseen multitude, both saints and sinners, seemed to encourage her onward.

"Faith!" shouted Goodman Brown in a voice of agony and desperation; and the echoes of the forest mocked him, crying "Faith! Faith!" as if bewildered wretches were seeking her all through the wilderness.

The cry of grief, rage, and terror was yet piercing the night when the unhappy husband held his breath for a response. There was a scream, drowned immediately in a louder murmur of voices fading into far-off laughter as the dark cloud swept away leaving the clear and silent sky above Goodman Brown. But something fluttered lightly down through the air and caught on the branch of a tree. The young man seized it and beheld a pink ribbon.

50   "My Faith is gone!" cried he, after one stupefied moment. "There is no good on earth, and sin is but a name. Come, devil! for to thee is this world given."

And maddened with despair, so that he laughed loud and long, did Goodman Brown grasp his staff and set forth again at such a rate that he seemed to fly along the forest path rather than to walk or run. The road grew wilder and drearier and more faintly traced, and vanished at length, leaving him in the heart of the dark wilderness, still rushing onward with the instinct that guides mortal man to evil. The whole forest was peopled with frightful sounds—the creaking of the trees, the howling of wild beasts, and the yell of Indians; while sometimes the wind tolled like a distant church bell, and sometimes gave a broad roar around the traveler, as if all Nature were laughing him to scorn. But he was himself the chief horror of the scene, and shrank not from its other horrors.

"Ha! ha! ha!" roared Goodman Brown when the wind laughed at him. "Let us hear which will laugh loudest! Think not to frighten me with your deviltry! come witch, come wizard, come Indian powwow, come devil himself! and here comes Goodman Brown. You may as well fear him as he fear you!"

In truth, all through the haunted forest there could be nothing more frightful than the figure of Goodman Brown. On he flew among the black pines, brandishing his staff with frenzied gestures, now giving vent to an inspiration of horrid blasphemy, and now shouting forth such laughter as set all the echoes of the forest laughing like demons around him. The fiend in his own shape is less hideous than when he rages in the breast of man. Thus sped the demoniac on his course until, quivering among the trees, he saw a red light before him, as when the felled trunks and branches of a clearing have been set on fire and throw up their lurid blaze against the sky at the hour of midnight. He paused in a lull of the tempest that had driven him onward, and heard the swell of what seemed a hymn rolling solemnly from a distance with the weight of many voices. He knew the tune. It was a familiar one in the choir of the village meeting-house. The verse died heavily away, and was lengthened by a chorus not of human voices but of all the sounds of the benighted wilderness pealing in awful harmony together. Goodman Brown cried out, and his cry was lost to his own ear by its unison with the cry of the desert.

In the interval of silence he stole forward until the light glared full upon his eyes. At one extremity of an open space, hemmed in by the dark wall of the forest, arose a rock bearing some rude, natural resemblance either to an altar or a pulpit, and surrounded by four blazing pines, their tops aflame, their stems untouched, like candles at an evening meeting. The mass of foliage that had overgrown the summit of the rock was all on fire, blazing high into the night and fitfully illuminating the whole field. Each pendent twig and leafy festoon was in a blaze. As the red light arose and fell, a numerous congregation alternately shone forth, then disappeared in shadow, and again grew, as it were, out of the darkness, peopling the heart of the solitary woods at once.

"A grave and dark-clad company!" quoth Goodman Brown.   55

In truth they were such. Among them, quivering to and fro between gloom and splendor, appeared faces that would be seen next day at the council-board of the province, and others which Sabbath after Sabbath looked devoutly heavenward and benignantly over the crowded pews from the holiest pulpits in the land. Some affirm that the lady of the governor was there. At least, there were high dames well known to her, and wives of honored husbands, and widows a great multitude, and ancient maidens, all of excellent repute, and fair young girls who trembled lest their mothers should espy them. Either the sudden gleams of light flashing over the obscure field bedazzled Goodman Brown, or he recognized a score of the church members of Salem village famous for their especial sanctity. Good old Deacon Gookin had arrived and waited at the skirts of that venerable saint, his reverend pastor. But irreverently consorting with these grave, reputable, and pious people, these elders of the church, these chaste dames and dewy virgins, there were men of dissolute lives and women of spotted fame, wretches given over to all mean and filthy vice and suspected even of horrid crimes. It was strange to see that the good shrank not from the wicked, nor were the sinners abashed by the saints. Scattered also among their pale-faced enemies were the Indian priests or powwows who had often scared their native forest with more hideous incantations than any known to English witchcraft.

"But where is Faith?" thought Goodman Brown; and as hope came into his heart he trembled.

Another verse of the hymn arose, a slow and mournful strain such as the pious love, but joined to words which expressed all that our nature can conceive of sin, and darkly hinted at far more. Unfathomable to mere mortals is the lore of fiends. Verse after verse was sung, and still the chorus of the desert swelled between, like the deepest tone of a mighty organ. And with the final peal of that dreadful anthem, there came a sound as if the roaring wind, the rushing streams, the howling beasts, and every other voice of the unconverted wilderness were mingling and according with the voice of guilty man in homage to the prince of all. The four blazing pines threw up a loftier flame and obscurely discovered shapes and visages of horror on the smoke-wreaths above the impious assembly. At the same moment the fire on the rock shot redly forth and formed a glowing arch above its base, where now appeared a figure. With reverence be it spoken, the apparition bore no slight similitude both in garb and manner to some grave divine of the New England churches.

"Bring forth the converts!" cried a voice that echoed through the field and rolled into the forest.

60   At the word, Goodman Brown stepped forth from the shadow of the trees and approached the congregation, with whom he felt a loathful brotherhood by the sympathy of all that was wicked in his heart. He could have well-nigh sworn that the shape of his own dead father beckoned him to advance, looking downward from a smoke-wreath, while a woman with dim features of despair threw out her hand to warn him back. Was it his mother? But he had no power to retreat one step nor to resist, even in thought, when the minister and good old Deacon Gookin seized his arms and led him to the blazing rock. Thither came also the slender form of a veiled female led between Goody Cloyse, that pious teacher of the catechism, and Martha

Carrier, who had received the devil's promise to be queen of hell. A rampant hag was she! And there stood the proselytes beneath the canopy of fire.

"Welcome, my children," said the dark figure, "to the communion of your race! Ye have found, thus young, your nature and your destiny. My children, look behind you!"

They turned, and flashing forth as it were in a sheet of flame, the fiend-worshippers were seen; the smile of welcome gleamed darkly on every visage.

"There," resumed the sable form, "are all whom ye have reverenced from youth. Ye deemed them holier than yourselves and shrank from your own sin, contrasting it with their lives of righteousness and prayerful aspirations heavenward. Yet here are they all in my worshipping assembly! This night it shall be granted you to know their secret deeds: how hoary-bearded elders of the church have whispered wanton words to the young maids of their households; how many a woman eager for widow's weeds has given her husband a drink at bedtime, and let him sleep his last sleep in her bosom; how beardless youths have made haste to inherit their father's wealth; and how fair damsels—blush not, sweet ones!—have dug little graves in the garden and bidden me, the sole guest, to an infant's funeral. By the sympathy of your human hearts for sin, ye shall scent out all the places—whether in church, bedchamber, street, field, or forest—where crime has been committed, and shall exult to behold the whole earth one stain of guilt, one mighty blood-spot. Far more than this! It shall be yours to penetrate in every bosom the deep mystery of sin, the fountain of all wicked arts, and which inexhaustibly supplies more evil impulses than human power—than my power, at its utmost!—can make manifest in deeds. And now, my children, look upon each other."

They did so, and by the blaze of the hell-kindled torches the wretched man beheld his Faith, and the wife her husband trembling before that unhallowed altar.

"Lo! there ye stand, my children," said the figure in a deep solemn tone, 65 almost sad with its despairing awfulness, as if his once angelic nature could yet mourn for our miserable race. "Depending upon one another's hearts, ye had still hoped that virtue were not all a dream! Now are ye undeceived— Evil is the nature of mankind. Evil must be your only happiness. Welcome, again, my children, to the communion of your race!"

"Welcome!" repeated the fiend-worshippers in one cry of despair and triumph.

And there they stood, the only pair as it seemed who were yet hesitating on the verge of wickedness in this dark world. A basin was hollowed naturally in the rock. Did it contain water, reddened by the lurid light? or was it blood? or, perchance, a liquid flame? Herein did the Shape of Evil dip his hand and prepare to lay the mark of baptism upon their foreheads, that they might be partakers of the mystery of sin, more conscious of the secret guilt of others both in deed and thought than they could now be of their own. The husband cast one look at his pale wife, and Faith at him. What polluted wretches would the next glance show them to each other, shuddering alike at what they disclosed and what they saw!

"Faith! Faith!" cried the husband. "Look up to Heaven, and resist the Wicked One!"

Whether Faith obeyed he knew not. Hardly had he spoken when he found himself amid calm night and solitude, listening to a roar of the wind which died heavily away through the forest. He staggered against the rock and felt it chill and damp, while a hanging twig that had been all on fire besprinkled his cheek with the coldest dew.

70   The next morning, young Goodman Brown came slowly into the street of Salem village staring around him like a bewildered man. The good old minister was taking a walk along the graveyard to get an appetite for breakfast and meditate his sermon, and bestowed a blessing as he passed on Goodman Brown. He shrank from the venerable saint as if to avoid an anathema. Old Deacon Gookin was at domestic worship, and the holy words of his prayer were heard through the open window. "What God doth the wizard pray to?" quoth Goodman Brown. Goody Cloyse, that excellent old Christian, stood in the early sunshine at her own lattice catechizing a little girl who had brought her a pint of morning's milk. Goodman Brown snatched away the child as from the grasp of the fiend himself. Turning the corner by the meeting-house, he spied the head of Faith with the pink ribbons gazing anxiously forth, and bursting into such joy at sight of him that she skipped along the street and almost kissed her husband before the whole village. But Goodman Brown looked sternly and sadly into her face and passed on without a greeting.

Had Goodman Brown fallen asleep in the forest and only dreamed a wild dream of a witch-meeting?

Be it so, if you will. But, alas! it was a dream of evil omen for young Goodman Brown. A stern, a sad, a darkly meditative, a distrustful, if not a desperate man did he become from the night of that fearful dream. On the Sabbath-day when the congregation were singing a holy psalm, he could not listen because an anthem of sin rushed loudly upon his ear and drowned all the blessed strain. When the minister spoke from the pulpit with power and fervid eloquence and with his hand on the open Bible, of the sacred truths of our religion, and of saint-like lives and triumphant deaths, and of future bliss or misery unutterable, then did Goodman Brown turn pale, dreading lest the roof should thunder down upon the gray blasphemer and his hearers. Often awaking suddenly at midnight, he shrank from the bosom of Faith, and at morning or eventide when the family knelt down at prayer, he scowled and muttered to himself and gazed sternly at his wife and turned away. And when he had lived long and was borne to his grave a hoary corpse, followed by Faith, an aged woman, and children and grandchildren, a goodly procession, besides neighbors not a few, they carved no hopeful verse upon his tombstone, for his dying hour was gloom.

QUESTIONS

1. During what period in history does the story take place? What does Hawthorne gain by including the names of actual persons (Goody Cloyse, Goody Cory, Deacon Gookin, Martha Carrier) and places (Salem village, Boston, Old South Church)? What religion is practiced by the townspeople?
2. What is the point of view? Where does it change, and what is the result of the change?
3. What allegorical meanings may be given to Goodman Brown? His wife? The forest? Night (as opposed to day)? Brown's journey?
4. What is Brown's motive for going into the forest? What results does he expect from his journey? What does he expect the rest of his life to be like?
5. After he keeps his appointment with the traveler in the forest, Brown announces that he plans to return home. Why does he not do so immediately, and why at each stage when he renews his intention to do so does he proceed deeper into the forest? Is there any reason to suppose he does not actually see and hear what he thinks he perceives?
6. What details of the "witch-meeting" parallel those of a church communion service? Why does the congregation include "grave, reputable, and pious people" as well as known sinners (paragraph 56)?
7. What prevents Goodman Brown from receiving baptism? What does the devil promise as the result of baptism? Is that what you usually suppose is the reward for selling your soul to the devil? Why is it an appropriate reward for Goodman Brown? Since he does not receive baptism, how do you account for his behavior when he returns to the village?
8. "Had Goodman Brown . . . only dreamed a wild dream of a witch-meeting?" (paragraph 71). How are we to answer this question? Point out other places where Hawthorne leaves the interpretation of the story ambiguous. How is such ambiguity related to the story's theme?
9. Characterize the behavior of Faith and the other townspeople after Brown's return to the village. Are Brown's attitude and behavior thereafter the result of conviction or doubt? Is he completely misanthropic?
10. Does the story demonstrate the devil's claim that "Evil is the nature of mankind" (paragraph 65)?

CHAPTER NINE
The Scale of Value

Our purpose in the preceding chapters has been to develop not literary critics but proficient readers—readers who choose wisely and read well. Yet good reading involves criticism, for choice necessitates judgment. Though we need not, to read well, be able to settle the relative claims of Chekhov and Mansfield or of Porter and Hemingway, we do need to discriminate between the genuine and the spurious, the consequential and the trivial, the significant and the merely entertaining. Our first object, naturally, is enjoyment; but full development as human beings requires that we enjoy most what is most worth enjoying.

There are no easy rules for literary judgment. Such judgment depends ultimately on our perceptivity, intelligence, and experience; it is a product of how much and how alertly we have lived and how much and how well we have read. Yet at least two basic principles may be set up. First, *every story is to be initially judged by how fully it achieves its central purpose.* Each element in the story is to be judged by the effectiveness of its contribution to the central purpose. In a good story every element works with every other element for the accomplishment of this central purpose. It follows that no element in the story may be judged in isolation.

Perhaps the most frequent mistake made by less experienced readers when called upon for a judgment is to judge the elements of the story in isolation, independently of each other. For example, a student once wrote of "I'm a Fool" that it is not a very good story "because it is not written in good English." And certainly the style of the story, if judged by itself, is very poor indeed: the language is slangy and ungrammatical; the sentences are often disjointed and broken-backed; the narrator constantly digresses and is at times so incapable of expressing himself that he can only say "etc., etc., you know." But no high level of discrimination is needed to see that just such a style is essential to the purpose of the story. The uneducated race-track swipe, whose failure in school life has made him feel both scornful and envious of boys who "go to high schools and college," can hardly speak otherwise than as he does here; the digressions, moreover, are not truly digressions, for each of them supplies additional insight into the character of the swipe, which is the true subject of the story. Similarly, the varieties of "substandard" English displayed by the various characters in "Just Like a Tree" and by the narrator of "The Lesson" enrich rather than diminish the characterizations.

The principle of judgment just applied to style may be applied to every other element in a story. We cannot say that "Miss Brill" is a poor story because it does not have an exciting plot full of action and conflict: plot can only be judged in relation to the other elements in a story and to the story's central purpose, and in this relationship the plot of "Miss Brill" is a good one. We cannot say that "Just Like a Tree" is a poor story because it contains no such complex characterization as is to be found in "Defender of the Faith." The purpose of "Just Like a Tree" is to demonstrate the variety of human responses to a single event, each springing from an essentially flat characterization.

Every first-rate story is an organic whole. All its parts are related, and all are necessary to the central purpose. Near the beginning of "The Most Dangerous Game" there is a suggestion of theme. When Whitney declares that hunting is a great sport—for hunter, not for the jaguar—Rainsford replies, "Who cares how a jaguar feels? . . . They've no understanding." To this, Whitney counters: "I rather think they understand one thing—fear. The fear of pain and the fear of death." Evidently Rainsford has something to learn about how it feels to be hunted, and presumably during the hunt Rainsford learns it, for when General Zaroff turns back the first time—playing cat and mouse—we are told, "Then it was that Rainsford knew the full meaning of terror." Later, on the morning of the third day, Rainsford is awakened by the baying of hounds—"a sound that made him know that he had new things to learn about fear." But, really, little is made of Rainsford's terror during the hunt. The main interest focuses on Malay mancatchers, Burmese tiger pits, Uganda knife-throwers—in short, on what Zaroff refers to as "Your brain against mine. Your woodcraft against mine. Your strength and stamina against mine. Outdoor chess!" The story ends with the physical triumph of Rainsford over Zaroff. Has Rainsford been altered by the experience? Has he learned anything significant? Has he changed his attitudes toward hunting? We cannot answer, for the author's interest has been elsewhere. What connection has the final sentence—"He had never slept in a better bed, Rainsford decided"—to the question "Who cares how a jaguar feels?"

In "The Storm" we are presented with an experience of mounting terror in a woman who (a) returns to an empty, lonely house during the outbreak of a storm and (b) discovers that her husband is a murderer. There is, of course, no logical connection between the storm and the fact that her husband is a murderer or her discovery of that fact: the coincidence of the storm and the discovery is simply that—a coincidence. This coincidence and the author's manipulation of point of view (her temporary suppression of Janet Willsom's consciousness, in order to prolong suspense, when she sees the body in the trunk and when she recognizes the ring on her husband's finger) are partial clues that the author's purpose is not really to provide insight into human terror so much as to produce terror in the reader. In the light of this purpose, the storm and the discovery of the murder are both justified in the story, for both help to produce terror in the reader. At the same time, their co-presence largely prevents the story from being more meaningful, for what might have been either (a) a study of irrational terror in a woman left alone in an isolated house during a storm or (b) a study of rational terror in a woman who discovers that her husband is a murderer is prevented from being either. Thus "The Storm" is a skillfully written suspense story rather than a story of human insight.

Once a story has been judged successful in achieving its central purpose, we may apply a second principle of judgment. *A story, if successful, may be judged by the significance of its purpose.* If every story is to be judged by how successfully it integrates its materials into an organic unity, it is also to be judged by the extent, the range, and the value of the materials integrated. This principle returns us to our distinction between escape and interpretation. If a story's chief aim is to entertain, whether by mystifying, surprising, thrilling, provoking to laughter or tears, or furnishing a substitute dream life, we may judge it of less value than a story whose aim is to *reveal.* "Once Upon a Time," "The Storm," "The Drunkard," and "The Catbird Seat" are all successful stories if we judge them by the degree to which they fulfill their central purpose. But "Once Upon a Time" has a more significant purpose than "The Storm" and "The Drunkard," a more significant purpose than "The Catbird Seat." When a story does provide some revelation—does make some serious statement about life— we may measure it by the breadth and depth of that revelation. "The Drunkard" and "Once Upon a Time" are both fine stories, but "Once Upon a Time" attempts a deeper probing than does "The Drunkard."

The situation with which it is concerned is more crucial, cuts deeper. The story reveals a more significant range and depth of life.

Some stories, then, like "The Storm" and "The Catbird Seat" provide good fun and innocent merriment, and even may convey some measure of interpretation along the way. Others, like "The Drunkard" and "Once Upon a Time" afford the reader a deeper enjoyment through the profounder and more consistent insights they give into life. A third type, like many of the soap operas of television, offers a cheaper and less innocent pleasure by providing escape under the guise of interpretation. Such stories, while professing to present real-life situations and everyday people and happenings, actually, by their shallowness of characterization, their falsifications of plot, their use of stock themes and stock emotions, present us with dangerous oversimplifications and distortions. They seriously misrepresent life and are harmful to the extent that they keep us from a more sensitive, more discriminating response to experience.

The above types of stories do not fall into sharp, distinct categories. There are no fortified barriers running between them to inform us when we are passing from one realm into another. There are no appointed officials to whom we can apply for certain information. Our only passports are our own good judgments, based on our accumulated experience with both literature and life. Nevertheless, certain questions, if asked wisely and with consideration for the two principles developed in this chapter, may help us both to understand the stories we read and to place them with rough accuracy on a scale of value that rises through many gradations from "poor" to "good" to "great." These questions, most of them explored in the previous chapters of this book, are, for convenience, summarized here.

GENERAL EXERCISES FOR ANALYSIS AND EVALUATION

Plot
1. Who is the protagonist of the story? What are the conflicts? Are they physical, intellectual, moral, or emotional? Is the main conflict between sharply differentiated good and evil, or is it more subtle and complex?
2. Does the plot have unity? Are all the episodes relevant to the total meaning or effect of the story? Does each incident grow logically out of the preceding incident and lead naturally to the next? Is the ending happy, unhappy, or indeterminate? Is it fairly achieved?
3. What use does the story make of chance and coincidence? Are these occurrences used to initiate, to complicate, or to resolve the story? How improbable are they?

4. How is suspense created in the story? Is the interest confined to "What happens next?" or are larger concerns involved? Can you find examples of mystery? Of dilemma?
5. What use does the story make of surprise? Are the surprises achieved fairly? Do they serve a significant purpose? Do they divert the reader's attention from weaknesses in the story?
6. To what extent is this a "formula" story?

Characters

7. What means does the author use to reveal character? Are the characters sufficiently dramatized? What use is made of character contrasts?
8. Are the characters consistent in their actions? Adequately motivated? Plausible? Does the author successfully avoid stock characters?
9. Is each character fully enough developed to justify its role in the story? Are the main characters round or flat?
10. Is any of the characters a developing character? If so, is the change a large or a small one? Is it a plausible change for such a person? Is it sufficiently motivated? Is it given sufficient time?

Theme

11. Does the story have a theme? What is it? Is it implicit or explicit?
12. Does the theme reinforce or oppose popular notions of life? Does it furnish a new insight or refresh or deepen an old one?

Point of View

13. What point of view does the story use? Is it consistent in its use of this point of view? If shifts are made, are they justified?
14. What advantages has the chosen point of view? Does it furnish any clues as to the purpose of the story?
15. If the point of view is that of one of the characters, does this character have any limitations that affect her or his interpretation of events or persons?
16. Does the author use point of view primarily to reveal or conceal? Is important information known to the focal character ever unfairly withheld?

Symbol and Irony

17. Does the story make use of symbols? If so, do the symbols carry or merely reinforce the meaning of the story?
18. Does the story anywhere utilize irony of situation? Dramatic irony? Verbal irony? What functions do the ironies serve?

Emotion and Humor

19. Does the story aim directly at an emotional *effect,* or is emotion merely its natural by-product?
20. Is the emotion sufficiently dramatized? Is the author anywhere guilty of sentimentality?

Fantasy

21. Does the story employ fantasy? If so, what is the initial assumption? Does the story operate logically from this assumption?

22. Is the fantasy employed for its own sake or to express some human truth? If the latter, what truth?

General

23. Is the primary interest of the story in plot, character, theme, or some other element?
24. What contribution to the story is made by its setting? Is the particular setting essential, or could the story have happened anywhere?
25. What are the characteristics of the author's style? Are they appropriate to the nature of the story?
26. What light is thrown on the story by its title?
27. Do all the elements of the story work together to support a central purpose? Is any part irrelevant or inappropriate?
28. What do you conceive to be the story's central purpose? How fully has it achieved that purpose?
29. Does the story offer chiefly escape or interpretation? How significant is the story's purpose?
30. Does the story gain or lose on a second reading?

There is one more evaluative principle that this book cannot exemplify in full because of the restrictions of length: when we judge the significance of the purpose of a work of fiction, we inevitably must take into account its breadth. Most fiction takes the form of novels, not short stories, and while most of the aspects of fiction we have been discussing are represented in both longer and shorter forms, there is no doubt that a novel can explore more varieties of human experience, and explore them more deeply. This is not to say that length alone is a criterion of value, for a majority of novels are more escapist than interpretive, as browsing in the "romance" or "crime" sections of a bookstore will amply prove. But an interpretive writer practicing in the longer form of the novel has greater opportunities for developing varieties of character, exploring multiple themes, and providing richer and fuller experiences than the short story affords.

While this book cannot offer a group of novels for study and evaluative comparison, it does provide three stories of an intermediate length in Part 3. Once you have sharpened your judgment on the paired stories in this chapter, you may want to test your skills on the "Three Novellas" beginning on page 449.

EXERCISE

The two stories that follow have a number of plot features in common; in purpose, however, they are quite different. One attempts to reveal certain truths about aspects of human life and succeeds in doing so. The other attempts to do little more than entertain the reader, and, in achieving this end, it falsifies human life. Which story is which? Support your decision by making a thorough analysis of both.

O. Henry

A Municipal Report

> The cities are full of pride,
>   Challenging each to each—
> This from her mountainside,
>   That from her burthened beach.
>
> —R. KIPLING

Fancy a novel about Chicago or Buffalo, let us say, or Nashville, Tennessee! There are just three big cities in the United States that are "story cities"—New York, of course, New Orleans, and, best of the lot, San Francisco.—FRANK NORRIS.

East is east°, and west is San Francisco, according to Californians. Californians are a race of people; they are not merely inhabitants of a State. They are the Southerners of the West. Now, Chicagoans are no less loyal to their city; but when you ask them why, they stammer and speak of lake fish and the new Odd Fellows Building. But Californians go into detail.

Of course they have, in the climate, an argument that is good for half an hour while you are thinking of your coal bills and heavy underwear. But as soon as they come to mistake your silence for conviction, madness comes upon them, and they picture the city of the Golden Gate as the Bagdad of the New World. So far, as a matter of opinion, no refutation is necessary. But dear cousins all (from Adam and Eve descended), it is a rash one who will lay his finger on the map and say "In this town there can be no romance—what could happen here?" Yes, it is a bold and a rash deed to challenge in one sentence history, romance, and Rand and McNally.

A MUNICIPAL REPORT   First published in 1909. Rand McNally and Co. (see end of second paragraph), founded in 1856, is a well-known publisher of atlases and gazetteers. The statistical and historical notes about Nashville in the story are such as might be excerpted from one of their books. Fort Sumter, Appomattox, and Generals Hood, Thomas, Sherman, and Longstreet are all names connected with the Civil War, during which, in 1863, the slaves were emancipated. William Sydney Porter (1862–1919), who wrote under the pseudonym O. Henry, was born in North Carolina, but his immensely varied life took him to Texas, Central and South America, Mexico, Ohio, and Pittsburgh before he arrived in New York City in 1901 to become a writer very much in demand for his short stories.

East is east . . . : cf. Rudyard Kipling's poem "The Ballad of East and West"

Nashville.—A city, port of delivery, and the capital of the State of Tennessee, is on the Cumberland River and on the N.C. & St.L. and the L. & N. railroads. This city is regarded as the most important educational center in the South.

I stepped off the train at 8 P.M. Having searched the thesaurus in vain for adjectives, I must, as a substitution, hie me to comparison in the form of a recipe.

Take of London fog 30 parts; malaria 10 parts; gas leaks 20 parts; dew-   5
drops gathered in a brick yard at sunrise, 25 parts; odor of honeysuckle 15 parts. Mix.

The mixture will give you an approximate conception of a Nashville drizzle. It is not so fragrant as a moth-ball nor as thick as peasoup; but 'tis enough—'twill serve.°

I went to a hotel in a tumbril. It required strong self-suppression for me to keep from climbing to the top of it and giving an imitation of Sidney Carton.° The vehicle was drawn by beasts of a bygone era and driven by something dark and emancipated.

I was sleepy and tired, so when I got to the hotel I hurriedly paid it the fifty cents it demanded (with approximate lagniappe, I assure you). I knew its habits; and I did not want to hear it prate about its old "marster" or anything that happened "befo' de wah."

The hotel was one of the kind described as "renovated." That means $20,000 worth of new marble pillars, tiling, electric lights and brass cuspidors in the lobby, and a new L. & N. time table and a lithograph of Lookout Mountain in each one of the great rooms above. The management was without reproach, the attention full of exquisite Southern courtesy, the service as slow as the progress of a snail and as good-humored as Rip Van Winkle. The food was worth traveling a thousand miles for. There is no other hotel in the world where you can get such chicken livers *en brochette.*

At dinner I asked a Negro waiter if there was anything doing in town. He   10
pondered gravely for a minute, and then replied: "Well, boss, I don't really reckon there's anything at all doin' after sundown."

Sundown had been accomplished: it had been drowned in drizzle long before. So that spectacle was denied me. But I went forth upon the streets in the drizzle to see what might be there.

It is built on undulating grounds; and the streets are lighted by electricity at a cost of $32,470 per annum.

As I left the hotel there was a race riot. Down upon me charged a company of freedmen, or Arabs, or Zulus, armed with—no, I saw with relief

---

not so fragrant . . . 'twill serve: cf. Mercutio's dying speech, *Romeo and Juliet,* 3.1. 99–100   **Sidney Carton:** a dissipated character who dies nobly on the guillotine in Dickens's novel *A Tale of Two Cities*

that they were not rifles, but whips. And I saw dimly a caravan of black, clumsy vehicles; and at the reassuring shouts, "Kyar you anywhere in the town, boss, fuh fifty cents," I reasoned that I was merely a "fare" instead of a victim.

I walked through long streets, all leading uphill. I wondered how those streets ever came down again. Perhaps they didn't until they were "graded." On a few of the "main streets" I saw lights in stores here and there; saw street cars go by conveying worthy burghers hither and yon; saw people pass engaged in the art of conversation, and heard a burst of semi-lively laughter issuing from a soda-water and ice-cream parlor. The streets other than "main" seemed to have enticed upon their borders houses consecrated to peace and domesticity. In many of them lights shone behind discreetly drawn window shades, in a few pianos tinkled orderly and irreproachable music. There was indeed, little "doing." I wished I had come before sundown. So I returned to my hotel.

15   *In November, 1864, the Confederate General Hood advanced against Nashville, where he shut up a National force under General Thomas. The latter then sallied forth and defeated the Confederates in a terrible conflict.*

All my life I have heard of, admired, and witnessed the fine marksmanship of the South in its peaceful conflicts in the tobacco-chewing regions. But in my hotel a surprise awaited me. There were twelve bright, new, imposing, capacious brass cuspidors in the great lobby, tall enough to be called urns and so wide-mouthed that the crack pitcher of a lady baseball team should have been able to throw a ball into one of them at five paces distant. But, although a terrible battle had raged and was still raging, the enemy had not suffered. Bright, new, imposing, capacious, untouched, they stood. But, shades of Jefferson Brick!° the tile floor—the beautiful tile floor! I could not avoid thinking of the battle of Nashville, and trying to draw, as is my foolish habit, some deductions about hereditary marksmanship.

Here I first saw Major (by misplaced courtesy) Wentworth Caswell. I knew him for a type the moment my eyes suffered from the sight of him. A rat has no geographical habitat. My old friend, A. Tennyson,° said, as he so well said almost everything:

> Prophet, curse me the blabbing lip,
> And curse me the British vermin, the rat.

Let us regard the word "British" as interchangeable *ad lib.* A rat is a rat. This man was hunting about the hotel lobby like a starved dog that had

Jefferson Brick: an American journalist, "unwholesomely pale" from "excessive use of [chewing] tobacco" in Dickens's novel *Martin Chuzzlewit*
A. Tennyson: The quoted lines are from Tennyson's *Maud*, Part 2.5.6

forgotten where he had buried a bone. He had a face of great acreage, red, pulpy, and with a kind of sleepy massiveness like that of Buddha. He possessed one single virtue—he was very smoothly shaven. The mark of the beast is not indelible upon a man until he goes about with a stubble. I think that if he had not used his razor that day I would have repulsed his advances, and the criminal calendar of the world would have been spared the addition of one murder.

I happened to be standing within five feet of a cuspidor when Major   20 Caswell opened fire upon it. I had been observant enough to perceive that the attacking force was using Gatlings instead of squirrel rifles, so I sidestepped so promptly that the major seized the opportunity to apologize to a noncombatant. He had the blabbing lip. In four minutes he had become my friend and had dragged me to the bar.

I desire to interpolate here that I am a Southerner. But I am not one by profession or trade. I eschew the string tie, the slouch hat, the Prince Albert, the number of bales of cotton destroyed by Sherman, and plug chewing. When the orchestra plays "Dixie" I do not cheer. I slide a little lower on the leather-cornered seat and, well, order another Würzburger and wish that Longstreet had—but what's the use?

Major Caswell banged the bar with his fist, and the first gun at Fort Sumter re-echoed. When he fired the last one at Appomattox I began to hope. But then he began on family trees, and demonstrated that Adam was only a third cousin of a collateral branch of the Caswell family. Genealogy disposed of, he took up, to my distaste, his private family matters. He spoke of his wife, traced her descent back to Eve, and profanely denied any possible rumor that she may have had relations in the land of Nod.°

By this time I began to suspect that he was trying to obscure by noise the fact that he had ordered the drinks, on the chance that I would be bewildered into paying for them. But when they were down he crashed a silver dollar loudly upon the bar. Then, of course, another serving was obligatory. And when I had paid for that I took leave of him brusquely; for I wanted no more of him. But before I had obtained my release he had prated loudly of an income that his wife received, and showed a handful of silver money.

When I got my key at the desk the clerk said to me courteously: "If that man Caswell has annoyed you, and if you would like to make a complaint, we will have him ejected. He is a nuisance, a loafer, and without any known means of support, although he seems to have some money most of the time. But we don't seem to be able to hit upon any means of throwing him out legally."

"Why, no," said I, after some reflection; "I don't see my way clear to   25 making a complaint. But I would like to place myself on record as asserting

---

land of Nod: where Cain, the exiled son of Adam and Eve, found a wife (Genesis 4.16ff.)

that I do not care for his company. Your town," I continued, "seems to be a quiet one. What manner of entertainment, adventure, or excitement, have you to offer to the stranger within your gates?"°

"Well, sir," said the clerk, "there will be a show here next Thursday. It is—I'll look it up and have the announcement sent up to your room with the ice water. Good-night."

After I went up to my room I looked out the window. It was only about ten o'clock, but I looked upon a silent town. The drizzle continued, spangled with dim lights, as far apart as currants in a cake sold at the Ladies' Exchange.

"A quiet place," I said to myself, as my first shoe struck the ceiling of the occupant of the room beneath mine. "Nothing of the life here that gives color and good variety to the cities in the East and West. Just a good, ordinary, humdrum, business town."

> *Nashville occupies a foremost place among the manufacturing centers of the country. It is the fifth boot and shoe market in the United States, the largest candy and cracker manufacturing city in the South, and does an enormous wholesale drygoods, grocery, and drug business.*

30   I must tell you how I came to be in Nashville, and I assure you the digression brings as much tedium to me as it does to you. I was traveling elsewhere on my own business, but I had a commission from a Northern literary magazine to stop over there and establish a personal connection between the publication and one of its contributors, Azalea Adair.

Adair (there was no clue to the personality except the handwriting) had sent in some essays (lost art!) and poems that had made the editors swear approvingly over their one o'clock luncheon. So they had commissioned me to round up said Adair and corner by contract his or her output at two cents a word before some other publisher offered her ten or twenty.

At nine o'clock the next morning, after my chicken livers *en brochette* (try them if you can find that hotel), I strayed out into the drizzle, which was still on for an unlimited run. At the first corner I came upon Uncle Caesar. He was a stalwart Negro, older than the pyramids, with gray wool and a face that reminded me of Brutus,° and a second afterwards of the late King Cettiwayo.° He wore the most remarkable coat that I ever had seen or expect to see. It reached to his ankles and had once been a confederate gray in color. But rain and sun and age had so variegated it that Joseph's coat,° beside it, would have faded to a pale monochrome. I must linger with that coat, for it

---

stranger within your gates: cf. Exodus 20.10   **Brutus:** tragic hero of Shakespeare's *Julius Caesar*   **King Cettiwayo:** king of the Zulus (1872–1884)
Joseph's coat: cf. Genesis 37

has to do with the story—the story that is so long in coming, because you can hardly expect anything to happen in Nashville.

Once it must have been the military coat of an officer. The cape of it had vanished, but all adown its front it had been frogged and tasseled magnificently. But now the frogs and tassels were gone. In their stead had been patiently stitched (I surmised by some surviving "black mammy") new frogs made of cunningly twisted common hempen twine. This twine was frayed and disheveled. It must have been added to the coat as a substitute for vanished splendors, with tasteless but painstaking devotion, for it followed faithfully the curves of the long-missing frogs. And, to complete the comedy and pathos of the garment, all its buttons were gone save one. The second button from the top alone remained. The coat was fastened by other twine strings tied through the buttonholes and other holes rudely pierced in the opposite side. There was never such a weird garment so fantastically bedecked and of so many mottled hues. The lone button was the size of a half-dollar, made of yellow horn and sewed on with coarse twine.

This Negro stood by a carriage so old that Ham° himself might have started a hack line with it after he left the ark with the two animals hitched to it. As I approached he threw open the door, drew out a feather duster, waved it without using it, and said in deep, rumbling tones:

"Step right in, suh; ain't a speck of dust in it—jus' got back from a funeral, suh."   35

I inferred that on such gala occasions carriages were given an extra cleaning. I looked up and down the street and perceived that there was little choice among the vehicles for hire that lined the curb. I looked in my memorandum book for the address of Azalea Adair.

"I want to go to 861 Jessamine Street," I said, and was about to step into the hack. But for an instant the thick, long, gorilla-like arm of the Negro barred me. On his massive and saturnine face a look of sudden suspicion and enmity flashed for a moment. Then, with quickly returning conviction, he asked, blandishingly: "What are you gwine there for, boss?"

"What is that to you?" I asked, a little sharply.

"Nothin', suh, jus' nothin'. Only it's a lonesome kind of part of town and few folks ever has business out there. Step right in. The seats is clean—jus' got back from a funeral, suh."

A mile and a half it must have been to our journey's end. I could hear   40 nothing but the fearful rattle of the ancient hack over the uneven brick paving; I could smell nothing but the drizzle, now further flavored with coal smoke and something like a mixture of tar and oleander blossoms. All I could see through the streaming windows were two rows of dim houses.

Ham: son of Noah who, according to tradition, settled in Africa and was the ancestor of the black races

The city has an area of 10 square miles; 181 miles of streets, of which 137 miles are paved; a system of waterworks that cost $2,000,000, with 77 miles of mains.

Eight-six-one Jessamine Street was a decayed mansion. Thirty yards back from the street it stood, outmerged in a splendid grove of trees and untrimmed shrubbery. A row of box bushes overflowed and almost hid the paling fence from sight; the gate was kept closed by a rope noose that encircled the gate post and the first paling of the gate. But when you got inside you saw that 861 was a shell, a shadow, a ghost of former grandeur and excellence. But in the story, I have not yet got inside.

When the hack had ceased from rattling and the weary quadrupeds came to a rest I handed my jehu° his fifty cents with an additional quarter, feeling a glow of conscious generosity as I did so. He refused it.

"It's two dollars, suh," he said.

"How's that?" I asked, "I plainly heard you call at the hotel. 'Fifty cents to any part of town.'"

"It's two dollars, suh," he repeated obstinately. "It's a long ways from the hotel."

"It is within the city limits and well within them," I argued. "Don't think that you have picked up a greenhorn Yankee. Do you see those hills over there?" I went on, pointing toward the east (I could not see them, myself, for the drizzle); "well, I was born and raised on their other side. You old fool nigger, can't you tell people from other people when you see 'em?"

The grim face of King Cettiwayo softened. "Is you from the South, suh? I reckon it was them shoes of yourn' fooled me. They is somethin' sharp in the toes for a Southern gen'l'man to wear."

"Then the charge is fifty cents, I suppose?" said I, inexorably.

His former expression, a mingling of cupidity and hostility, returned, remained ten seconds, and vanished.

"Boss," he said, "fifty cents is right; but I *needs* two dollars, suh; I'm *obleeged* to have two dollars. I ain't *demandin'* it now, suh; after I knows whar you's from; I'm jus' sayin' that I *has* to have two dollars tonight and business is mighty po'."

Peace and confidence settled upon his heavy features. He had been luckier than he had hoped. Instead of having picked up a greenhorn, ignorant of rates, he had come upon an inheritance.

"You confounded old rascal," I said, reaching down to my pocket, "you ought to be turned over to the police."

For the first time I saw him smile. He knew; *he knew;* HE KNEW.

I gave him two one-dollar bills. As I handed them over I noticed that one of them had seen parlous times. Its upper right-hand corner was missing and

---

jehu: a fast driver (cf. 2 Kings 9.20)

45

50

55

it had been torn through in the middle, but joined again. A strip of blue tissue paper, pasted over the split, preserved its negotiability.

Enough of the African bandit for the present: I left him happy, lifted the rope, and opened the creaky gate.

The house, as I said, was a shell. A paint brush had not touched it in twenty years. I could not see why a strong wind should not have bowled it over like a house of cards until I looked again at the trees that hugged it close—the trees that saw the battle of Nashville and still drew their protecting branches around it against storm and enemy and cold.

Azalea Adair, fifty years old, white-haired, a descendant of the cavaliers, as thin and frail as the house she lived in, robed in the cheapest and cleanest dress I ever saw, with an air as simple as a queen's, received me.

The reception room seemed a mile square, because there was nothing in it except some rows of books on unpainted white-pine bookshelves, a cracked marble-topped table, a rag rug, a hairless horsehair sofa, and two or three chairs. Yes, there was a picture on the wall, a colored crayon drawing of a cluster of pansies. I looked around for the portrait of Andrew Jackson and the pine-cone hanging basket but they were not there.

Azalea Adair and I had conversation, a little of which will be repeated to you. She was a product of the old South, gently nurtured in the sheltered life. Her learning was not broad, but was deep and of splendid originality in its somewhat narrow scope. She had been educated at home, and her knowledge of the world was derived from inference and by inspiration. Of such is the precious, small group of essayists made. While she talked to me I kept brushing my fingers, trying, unconsciously, to rid them guiltily of the absent dust from the half-calf backs of Lamb, Chaucer, Hazlitt, Marcus Aurelius, Montaigne, and Hood. She was exquisite, she was a valuable discovery. Nearly everybody nowadays knows too much—oh, so much too much—of real life.

I could perceive clearly that Azalea Adair was very poor. A house and a dress she had, not much else, I fancied. So, divided between my duty to the magazine and my loyalty to the poets and essayists who fought Thomas in the valley of the Cumberland, I listened to her voice which was like a harpsichord's and found that I could not speak of contracts. In the presence of the nine Muses and the three Graces one hesitated to lower the topic to two cents. There would have to be another colloquy after I had regained my commercialism. But I spoke of my mission, and three o'clock of the next afternoon was set for the discussion of the business proposition.

"Your town," I said, as I began to make ready to depart (which is the time for smooth generalities), "seems to be a quiet, sedate place. A home town, I should say, where few things out of the ordinary ever happen."

It carries on an extensive trade in stoves and hollow ware with the West and South, and its flouring mills have a daily capacity of more than 2,000 barrels.

Azaela Adair seemed to reflect.

65   "I have never thought of it that way," she said, with a kind of sincere intensity that seemed to belong to her. "Isn't it in the still, quiet places that things do happen? I fancy that when God began to create the earth on the first Monday morning one could have leaned out one's window and heard the drops of mud splashing from His trowel as He built up the everlasting hills. What did the noisiest project in the world—I mean the building of the tower of Babel—result in finally? A page and a half of Esperanto in the *North American Review.*"

"Of course," said I, platitudinously, "human nature is the same every-where; but there is more color—er—more drama and movement and—er—romance in some cities than in others."

"On the surface," said Azalea Adair. "I have traveled many times around the world in a golden airship wafted on two wings—print and dreams. I have seen (on one of my imaginary tours) the Sultan of Turkey bowstring° with his own hands one of his wives who had uncovered her face in public. I have seen a man in Nashville tear up his theater tickets because his wife was going out with her face covered—with rice powder. In San Francisco's Chinatown I saw the slave girl Sing Yee dipped slowly, inch by inch, in boiling almond oil to make her swear she would never see her American lover again. She gave in when the boiling oil had reached three inches above her knees. At a euchre party in East Nashville the other night I saw Kitty Morgan cut dead by seven of her schoolmates and lifelong friends because she had married a house painter. The boiling oil was sizzling as high as her heart; but I wish you could have seen the fine little smile that she carried from table to table. Oh, yes, it is a humdrum town. Just a few miles of red brick houses and mud and stores and lumber yards."

Someone had knocked hollowly at the back of the house. Azalea Adair breathed a soft apology and went to investigate the sound. She came back in three minutes with brightened eyes, a faint flush on her cheeks, and ten years lifted from her shoulders.

"You must have a cup of tea before you go," she said, "and a sugar cake."

70   She reached and shook a little iron bell. In shuffled a small Negro girl about twelve, barefoot, not very tidy, glowering at me with thumb in mouth and bulging eyes.

Azalea Adair opened a tiny, worn purse and drew out a dollar bill, a dollar bill with the upper right-hand corner missing, torn in two pieces and pasted together again with a strip of blue tissue paper. It was one of those bills I had given the piratical Negro—there was no doubt of it.

"Go up to Mr. Baker's store on the corner, Impy," she said, handing the girl the dollar bill, "and get a quarter pound of tea—the kind he always sends me—and ten cents' worth of sugar cakes. Now, hurry. The supply of tea in the house happens to be exhausted," she explained to me.

bowstring: strangle with a bowstring

Impy left by the back way. Before the scrape of her hard, bare feet had died away on the back porch, a wild shriek—I was sure it was hers—filled the hollow house. Then the deep, gruff tones of an angry man's voice mingled with the girl's further squeals and unintelligible words.

Azalea Adair rose without surprise or emotion and disappeared. For two minutes I heard the hoarse rumble of the man's voice; then something like an oath and a slight scuffle, and she returned calmly to her chair.

"This is a roomy house," she said, "and I have a tenant for part of it. I   75 am sorry to have to rescind my invitation to tea. It is impossible to get the kind I always use at the store. Perhaps tomorrow Mr. Baker will be able to supply me."

I was sure that Impy had not had time to leave the house. I inquired concerning street-car lines and took my leave. After I was well on my way I remembered that I had not learned Azalea Adair's name. But tomorrow would do.

The same day I started in on the course of iniquity that this uneventful city forced upon me. I was in the town only two days, but in that time I managed to lie shamelessly by telegraph, and to be an accomplice—after the fact, if that is the correct legal term—to a murder.

As I rounded the corner nearest my hotel the Afrite coachman of the polychromatic, nonpareil coat seized me, swung open the dungeony door of his peripatetic sarcophagus, flirted his feather duster and began his ritual: "Step right in, boss. Carriage is clean—jus' got back from a funeral. Fifty cents to any—"

And then he knew me and grinned broadly. "'Scuse me, boss; you is de gen'l'man what rid out with me dis mawnin'. Thank you kindly, suh."

"I am going out to 861 again tomorrow afternoon at three," said I, "and   80 if you will be here, I'll let you drive me. So you know Miss Adair?" I concluded, thinking of my dollar bill.

"I belonged to her father, Judge Adair, suh," he replied.

"I judge that she is pretty poor," I said. "She hasn't much money to speak of, has she?"

For an instant I looked again at the fierce countenance of King Cettiwayo, and then he changed back to an extortionate old Negro hack driver.

"She ain't gwine to starve, suh," he said. "She has reso'ces, suh; she has reso'ces."

"I shall pay you fifty cents for the trip," said I.   85

"Dat is puffeckly correct, suh," he answered, humbly. "I just *had* to have dat two dollars dis mawnin', boss."

I went to the hotel and lied by electricity. I wired the magazine: "A. Adair holds out for eight cents a word."

The answer that came back was: "Give it to her quick, you duffer."

Just before dinner "Major" Wentworth Caswell bore down upon me with greetings of a long-lost friend. I have seen few men whom I have so instantaneously hated, and of whom it was so difficult to be rid. I was standing at the bar when he invaded me; therefore I could not wave the white ribbon in his face. I would have paid gladly for the drinks, hoping thereby to escape another; but he was one of those despicable, roaring, advertising bibbers who must have brass bands and fireworks attend upon every cent that they waste in their follies.

90   With an air of producing millions he drew two one-dollar bills from a pocket and dashed one of them upon the bar. I looked once more at the dollar bill with the upper right-hand corner missing, torn through the middle, and patched with a strip of blue tissue paper. It was my dollar again. It could have been no other.

I went up to my room. The drizzle and the monotony of a dreary, eventless Southern town had made me tired and listless. I remember that just before I went to bed I mentally disposed of the mysterious dollar bill (which might have formed the clue to a tremendously fine detective story of San Francisco) by saying to myself sleepily: "Seems as if a lot of people here own stock in the Hack-Drivers' Trust. Pays dividends promptly, too. Wonder if—" Then I fell asleep.

King Cettiwayo was at his post the next day, and rattled my bones over the stones out to 861. He was to wait and rattle me back again when I was ready.

Azalea Adair looked paler and cleaner and frailer than she had looked on the day before. After she had signed the contract at eight cents per word she grew still paler and began to slip out of her chair. Without much trouble I managed to get her up on the antediluvian horsehair sofa and then I ran out to the sidewalk and yelled to the coffee-colored Pirate to bring a doctor. With a wisdom that I had not suspected in him, he abandoned his team and struck off up the street afoot, realizing the value of speed. In ten minutes he returned with a grave, gray-haired, and capable man of medicine. In a few words (worth much less than eight cents each) I explained to him my presence in the hollow house of mystery. He bowed with stately understanding, and turned to the old Negro.

"Uncle Caesar," he said, calmly, "run up to my house and ask Miss Lucy to give you a cream pitcher full of fresh milk and half a tumbler of port wine. And hurry back. Don't drive—run. I want you to get back sometime this week."

95   It occurred to me that Dr. Merriman also felt a distrust as to the speeding powers of the land-pirate's steeds. After Uncle Caesar was gone, lumberingly, but swiftly, up the street, the doctor looked me over with great politeness and as much careful calculation until he had decided that I might do.

"It is only a case of insufficient nutrition," he said. "In other words, the result of poverty, pride, and starvation. Mrs. Caswell has many devoted friends who would be glad to aid her, but she will accept nothing except from that old Negro, Uncle Caesar, who was once owned by her family."

"Mrs. Caswell!" said I, in surprise. And then I looked at the contract and saw that she had signed it "Azalea Adair Caswell."

"I thought she was Miss Adair," I said.

"Married to a drunken, worthless loafer, sir," said the doctor. "It is said that he robs her even of the small sums that her old servant contributes toward her support."

When the milk and wine had been brought the doctor soon revived Azalea Adair. She sat up and talked of the beauty of the autumn leaves that were then in season and their height of color. She referred lightly to her fainting seizure as the outcome of an old palpitation of her heart. Impy fanned her as she lay on the sofa. The doctor was due elsewhere, and I followed him to the door. I told him that it was within my power and intentions to make a reasonable advance of money to Azalea Adair on future contributions to the magazine, and he seemed pleased. 100

"By the way," he said, "perhaps you would like to know that you have had royalty for a coachman. Old Caesar's grandfather was a king in Congo. Caesar himself has royal ways, as you may have observed."

As the doctor was moving off I heard Uncle Caesar's voice inside: "Did he get bofe of dem two dollars from you, Mis' Zalea?"

"Yes, Caesar," I heard Azalea Adair answer, weakly. And then I went in and concluded business negotiations with our contributor. I assumed the responsibility of advancing fifty dollars, putting it as a necessary formality in binding our bargain. And then Uncle Caesar drove me back to the hotel.

Here ends all of the story as far as I can witness. The rest must be only bare statements of facts.

At about six o'clock I went out for a stroll. Uncle Caesar was at his corner. 105 He threw open the door of his carriage, flourished his duster, and began his depressing formula: "Step right in, suh. Fifty cents to anywhere in the city—hack's puffickly clean, suh—jus' got back from a funeral—"

And then he recognized me. I think his eyesight was getting bad. His coat had taken on a few more faded shades of color, the twine strings were more frayed and ragged, the last remaining button—the button of yellow horn—was gone. A motley descendant of kings was Uncle Caesar!

About two hours later I saw an excited crowd besieging the front of the drug store. In a desert where nothing happens this was manna; so I wedged my way inside. On an extemporized couch of empty boxes and chairs was stretched the mortal corporeality of Major Wentworth Caswell. A doctor was testing him for the mortal ingredient. His decision was that it was conspicuous by its absence.

The erstwhile Major had been found dead on a dark street and brought by curious and ennuied citizens to the drug store. The late human being had been engaged in terrific battle—the details showed that. Loafer and reprobate though he had been, he had been also a warrior. But he had lost. His hands were yet clinched so tightly that his fingers could not be opened. The gentle citizens who had known him stood about and searched their vocabularies to find some good words, if it were possible, to speak of him. One kind-looking man said, after much thought: "When 'Cas' was about fo'teen he was one of the best spellers in the school."

While I stood there the fingers of the right hand of "the man that was," which hung down the side of a white pine box, relaxed, and dropped something at my feet. I covered it with one foot quietly, and a little later on I picked it up and pocketed it. I reasoned that in his last struggle his hand must have seized that object unwittingly and held it in a death grip.

110   At the hotel that night the main topic of conversation, with the possible exceptions of politics and prohibition, was the demise of Major Caswell. I heard one man say to a group of listeners:

"In my opinion, gentlemen, Caswell was murdered by some of these no-account niggers for his money. He had fifty dollars this afternoon which he showed to several gentlemen in the hotel. When he was found the money was not on his person."

I left the city the next morning at nine, and as the train was crossing the bridge over the Cumberland River I took out of my pocket a yellow horn overcoat button the size of a fifty-cent piece, with frayed ends of coarse twine hanging from it, and cast it out of the window into the slow, muddy waters below.

I wonder what's doing in Buffalo!

QUESTIONS

1. What is the narrator's attitude toward the South? What is his purpose in "quoting" the statistical data that intersperse the story? What type of humor does he employ?
2. What coincidences are required for the development of the plot?
3. Characterize Azalea Adair, Uncle Caesar, and Major Caswell. Are they round characters?
4. The central conflict of the story is resolved by a murder. What does the story offer in the way of analysis of the psychology or morality of murder? Is there a justification for Caesar's murder of Caswell?
5. One issue raised by the story is whether there can be "romance" in such a place as Nashville. Azalea Adair offers one answer in paragraph 67. Is that the same answer that the narrator comes to accept?

Susan Glaspell

A Jury of Her Peers

When Martha Hale opened the storm door and got a cut of the north wind, she ran back for her big woolen scarf. As she hurriedly wound that round her head her eye made a scandalized sweep of her kitchen. It was no ordinary thing that called her away—it was probably farther from ordinary than anything that had ever happened in Dickson County. But what her eye took in was that her kitchen was in no shape for leaving: her bread all ready for mixing, half the flour sifted and half unsifted.

She hated to see things half done; but she had been at that when the team from town stopped to get Mr. Hale, and then the sheriff came running in to say his wife wished Mrs. Hale would come too—adding, with a grin, that he guessed she was getting scarey and wanted another woman along. So she had dropped everything right where it was.

"Martha!" now came her husband's impatient voice. "Don't keep folks waiting out here in the cold."

She again opened the storm door, and this time joined the three men and the one woman waiting for her in the big two-seated buggy.

After she had the robes tucked around her she took another look at the   5
woman who sat beside her on the back seat. She had met Mrs. Peters the year before at the county fair, and the thing she remembered about her was that she didn't seem like a sheriff's wife. She was small and thin and didn't have a strong voice. Mrs. Gorman, sheriff's wife before Gorman went out and Peters came in, had a voice that somehow seemed to be backing up the law with every word. But if Mrs. Peters didn't look like a sheriff's wife, Peters made it up in looking like a sheriff. He was to a dot the kind of man who could get himself elected sheriff—a heavy man with a big voice, who was particularly genial with the law-abiding, as if to make it plain that he knew the difference between criminals and non-criminals. And right there it came into Mrs. Hale's mind, with a stab, that this man who was so pleasant and lively with all of them was going to the Wrights' now as a sheriff.

"The country's not very pleasant this time of year," Mrs. Peters at last ventured, as if she felt they ought to be talking as well as the men.

Mrs. Hale scarcely finished her reply, for they had gone up a little hill and could see the Wright place now, and seeing it did not make her feel like talking. It looked very lonesome this cold March morning. It had always been a lonesome-looking place. It was down in a hollow, and the poplar trees

A JURY OF HER PEERS   First published in 1917, the story is based on the author's one-act play *Trifles,* written in 1916 for the Provincetown Players. Susan Glaspell (1882–1948) lived for the first thirty-two years of her life in Iowa. She has said that *Trifles* (and hence this short story) was suggested to her by an experience she had while working for a Des Moines newspaper.

around it were lonesome-looking trees. The men were looking at it and talking about what had happened. The county attorney was bending to one side of the buggy, and kept looking steadily at the place as they drew up to it.

"I'm glad you came with me," Mrs. Peters said nervously, as the two women were about to follow the men in through the kitchen door.

Even after she had her foot on the doorstep, her hand on the knob, Martha Hale had a moment of feeling she could not cross the threshold. And the reason it seemed she couldn't cross it now was simply because she hadn't crossed it before. Time and time again it had been in her mind, "I ought to go over and see Minnie Foster"—she still thought of her as Minnie Foster, though for twenty years she had been Mrs. Wright. And then there was always something to do and Minnie Foster would go from her mind. But *now* she could come.

10   The men went over to the stove. The women stood close together by the door. Young Henderson, the county attorney, turned around and said, "Come up to the fire, ladies."

Mrs. Peters took a step forward, then stopped. "I'm not—cold," she said.

And so the two women stood by the door, at first not even so much as looking around the kitchen.

The men talked for a minute about what a good thing it was the sheriff had sent his deputy out that morning to make a fire for them, and then Sheriff Peters stepped back from the stove, unbuttoned his outer coat, and leaned his hands on the kitchen table in a way that seemed to mark the beginning of official business. "Now, Mr. Hale," he said in a sort of semiofficial voice, "before we move things about, you tell Mr. Henderson just what it was you saw when you came here yesterday morning."

The county attorney was looking around the kitchen.

15   "By the way," he said, "has anything been moved?" He turned to the sheriff. "Are things just as you left them yesterday?"

Peters looked from cupboard to sink; from that to a small worn rocker a little to one side of the kitchen table.

"It's just the same."

"Somebody should have been left here yesterday," said the county attorney.

"Oh—yesterday," returned the sheriff, with a little gesture as of yesterday having been more than he could bear to think of. "When I had to send Frank to Morris Center for that man who went crazy—let me tell you, I had my hands full *yesterday*. I knew you could get back from Omaha by today, George, and as long as I went over everything here myself—"

20   "Well, Mr. Hale," said the county attorney, in a way of letting what was past and gone go, "tell just what happened when you came here yesterday morning."

Mrs. Hale, still leaning against the door, had that sinking feeling of the mother whose child is about to speak a piece. Lewis often wandered along and got things mixed up in a story. She hoped he would tell this straight and plain, and not say unnecessary things that would just make things harder for Minnie Foster. He didn't begin at once, and she noticed that he looked queer—as if standing in that kitchen and having to tell what he had seen there yesterday morning made him almost sick.

"Yes, Mr. Hale?" the county attorney reminded.

"Harry and I had started to town with a load of potatoes," Mrs. Hale's husband began.

Harry was Mrs. Hale's oldest boy. He wasn't with them now, for the very good reason that those potatoes never got to town yesterday and he was taking them this morning, so he hadn't been home when the sheriff stopped to say he wanted Mr. Hale to come over to the Wright place and tell the county attorney his story there, where he could point it all out. With all Mrs. Hale's other emotions came the fear that maybe Harry wasn't dressed warm enough—they hadn't any of them realized how that north wind did bite.

"We come along this road," Hale was going on, with a motion of his hand to the road over which they had just come, "and as we got in sight of the house I says to Harry, 'I'm goin' to see if I can't get John Wright to take a telephone.' You see," he explained to Henderson, "unless I can get somebody to go in with me they won't come out this branch road except for a price *I* can't pay. I'd spoke to Wright about it once before; but he put me off, saying folks talked too much anyway, and all he asked was peace and quiet—guess you know about how much he talked himself. But I thought maybe if I went to the house and talked about it before his wife, and said all the women-folks liked the telephones, and that in this lonesome stretch of road it would be a good thing—well, I said to Harry that that was what I was going to say—though I said at the same time that I didn't know as what his wife wanted made much difference to John—"   25

Now, there he was!—saying things he didn't need to say. Mrs. Hale tried to catch her husband's eye, but fortunately the county attorney interrupted with:

"Let's talk about that a little later, Mr. Hale. I do want to talk about that, but I'm anxious now to get along to just what happened when you got here."

When he began this time, it was very deliberately and carefully:

"I didn't see or hear anything. I knocked at the door. And still it was all quiet inside. I knew they must be up—it was past eight o'clock. So I knocked again, louder, and I thought I heard somebody say 'Come in.' I wasn't sure—I'm not sure yet. But I opened the door—this door," jerking a hand toward the door by which the two women stood, "and there, in that rocker"—pointing to it—"sat Mrs. Wright."

Every one in the kitchen looked at the rocker. It came into Mrs. Hale's mind that that rocker didn't look in the least like Minnie Foster—the Minnie Foster of twenty years before. It was a dingy red, with wooden rungs up the back, and the middle rung was gone, and the chair sagged to one side.   30

"How did she—look?" the county attorney was inquiring.

"Well," said Hale, "she looked—queer."

"How do you mean—queer?"

As he asked it he took out a notebook and pencil. Mrs. Hale did not like the sight of that pencil. She kept her eye fixed on her husband, as if to keep him from saying unnecessary things that would go into that notebook and make trouble.

35   Hale did speak guardedly, as if the pencil had affected him too.

"Well, as if she didn't know what she was going to do next. And kind of—done up."

"How did she seem to feel about your coming?"

"Why, I don't think she minded—one way or other. She didn't pay much attention. I said, 'Ho' do, Mrs. Wright? It's cold, ain't it?' And she said, 'Is it?'—and went on pleatin' at her apron.

"Well, I was surprised. She didn't ask me to come up to the stove, or to sit down, but just set there, not even lookin' at me. And so I said: 'I want to see John.'

40   "And then she—laughed. I guess you would call it a laugh.

"I thought of Harry and the team outside, so I said, a little sharp, 'Can I see John?' 'No,' says she—kind of dull like. 'Ain't he home?' says I. Then she looked at me. 'Yes,' says she, 'he's home.' 'Then why can't I see him?' I asked her, out of patience with her now. ''Cause he's dead,' says she, just as quiet and dull—and fell to pleatin' her apron. 'Dead?' says I, like you do when you can't take in what you've heard.

"She just nodded her head, not getting a bit excited, but rockin' back and forth.

"'Why—where is he?' says I, not knowing *what* to say.

"She just pointed upstairs—like this"—pointing to the room above.

45   "I got up, with the idea of going up there myself. By this time I—didn't know what to do. I walked from there to here; then I says: 'Why, what did he die of?'

"'He died of a rope around his neck,' says she; and just went on pleatin' at her apron."

Hale stopped speaking, and stood staring at the rocker, as if he were still seeing the woman who had sat there the morning before. Nobody spoke; it was as if every one were seeing the woman who had sat there the morning before.

"And what did you do then?" the county attorney at last broke the silence.

"I went out and called Harry. I thought I might—need help. I got Harry in, and we went upstairs." His voice fell almost to a whisper. "There he was—lying over the—"

50   "I think I'd rather have you go into that upstairs," the county attorney interrupted, "where you can point it all out. Just go on now with the rest of the story."

"Well, my first thought was to get that rope off. It looked—"

He stopped, his face twitching.

"But Harry, he went up to him, and he said, 'No, he's dead all right, and we'd better not touch anything.' So we went downstairs.

"She was still sitting that same way. 'Has anybody been notified?' I asked. 'No,' says she, unconcerned."

"'Who did this, Mrs. Wright?' said Harry. He said it businesslike, and she   55
stopped pleatin' at her apron. 'I don't know,' she says. 'You don't *know?*' says Harry. 'Weren't you sleepin' in the bed with him?' 'Yes,' says she, 'but I was on the inside.' 'Somebody slipped a rope round his neck and strangled him, and you didn't wake up?' says Harry. 'I didn't wake up,' she said after him.

"We may have looked as if we didn't see how that could be, for after a minute she said, 'I sleep sound.'

"Harry was going to ask her more questions, but I said maybe that weren't our business; maybe we ought to let her tell her story first to the coroner or the sheriff. So Harry went fast as he could over to High Road— the Rivers's place, where there's a telephone."

"And what did she do when she knew you had gone for the coroner?" The attorney got his pencil in his hand all ready for writing.

"She moved from that chair to this one over here"—Hale pointed to a small chair in the corner—"and just sat there with her hands held together and looking down. I got a feeling that I ought to make some conversation, so I said I had come in to see if John wanted to put in a telephone; and at that she started to laugh, and then she stopped and looked at me—scared."

At the sound of a moving pencil the man who was telling the story   60
looked up.

"I dunno—maybe it wasn't scared," he hastened; "I wouldn't like to say it was. Soon Harry got back, and then Dr. Lloyd came, and you, Mr. Peters, and so I guess that's all I know that you don't."

He said that last with relief, and moved a little, as if relaxing. Every one moved a little. The county attorney walked toward the stair door.

"I guess we'll go upstairs first—then out to the barn and around there."

He paused and looked around the kitchen.

"You're convinced there was nothing important here?" he asked the   65
sheriff. "Nothing that would—point to any motive?"

The sheriff too looked all around, as if to re-convince himself.

"Nothing here but kitchen things," he said, with a little laugh for the insignificance of kitchen things.

The county attorney was looking at the cupboard—a peculiar, ungainly structure, half closet and half cupboard, the upper part of it being built in the wall, and the lower part just the old-fashioned kitchen cupboard. As if its queerness attracted him, he got a chair and opened the upper part and looked in. After a moment he drew his hand away sticky.

"Here's a nice mess," he said resentfully.

70   The two women had drawn nearer, and now the sheriff's wife spoke.

"Oh—her fruit," she said, looking to Mrs. Hale for sympathetic understanding. She turned back to the county attorney and explained: "She worried about that when it turned so cold last night. She said the fire would go out and her jars might burst."

Mrs. Peters's husband broke into a laugh.

"Well, can you beat the women! Held for murder, and worrying about her preserves!"

The young attorney set his lips.

75   "I guess before we're through with her she may have something more serious than preserves to worry about."

"Oh, well," said Mrs. Hale's husband, with good-natured superiority, "women are used to worrying over trifles."

The two women moved a little closer together. Neither of them spoke. The county attorney seemed suddenly to remember his manners—and think of his future.

"And yet," said he, with the gallantry of a young politician, "for all their worries, what would we do without the ladies?"

The women did not speak, did not unbend. He went to the sink and began washing his hands. He turned to wipe them on the roller wheel— whirled it for a cleaner place.

80   "Dirty towels! Not much of a housekeeper, would you say, ladies?"

He kicked his foot against some dirty pans under the sink.

"There's a great deal of work to be done on a farm," said Mrs. Hale stiffly.

"To be sure. And yet"—with a little bow to her—"I know there are some Dickson County farmhouses that do not have such roller towels." He gave it a pull to expose its full length again.

"Those towels get dirty awful quick. Men's hands aren't always as clean as they might be."

85   "Ah, loyal to your sex, I see," he laughed. He stopped and gave her a keen look. "But you and Mrs. Wright were neighbors. I suppose you were friends, too."

Martha Hale shook her head.

"I've seen little enough of her of late years. I've not been in this house— it's more than a year."

"And why was that? You didn't like her?"

"I liked her well enough," she replied with spirit. "Farmers' wives have their hands full, Mr. Henderson. And then"—She looked around the kitchen.

90   "Yes?" he encouraged.

"It never seemed a very cheerful place," said she, more to herself than to him.

"No," he agreed; "I don't think any one would call it cheerful. I shouldn't say she had the homemaking instinct."

"Well, I don't know as Wright had, either," she muttered.

"You mean they didn't get on very well?" he was quick to ask.

"No; I don't mean anything," she answered, with decision. As she   95
turned a little away from him, she added: "But I don't think a place would be
any the cheerfuler for John Wright's bein' in it."

"I'd like to talk to you about that a little later, Mrs. Hale," he said. "I'm
anxious to get the lay of things upstairs now."

He moved toward the stair door, followed by the two men.

"I suppose anything Mrs. Peters does'll be all right?" the sheriff inquired. "She was to take in some clothes for her, you know—and a few little
things. We left in such a hurry yesterday."

The county attorney looked at the two women whom they were leaving
alone there among the kitchen things.

"Yes—Mrs. Peters," he said, his glance resting on the woman who was   100
not Mrs. Peters, the big farmer woman who stood behind the sheriff's wife.
"Of course Mrs. Peters is one of us," he said, in a manner of entrusting
responsibility. "And keep your eye out, Mrs. Peters, for anything that might
be of use. No telling; you women might come upon a clue to the motive—
and that's the thing we need."

Mr. Hale rubbed his face after the fashion of a show man getting ready
for a pleasantry.

"But would the women know a clue if they did come upon it?" he said;
and, having delivered himself of this, he followed the others through the
stair door.

The women stood motionless and silent, listening to the footsteps, first
upon the stairs, then in the room above them.

Then, as if releasing herself from something strange, Mrs. Hale began to
arrange the dirty pans under the sink, which the county attorney's disdainful
push of the foot had deranged.

"I'd hate to have men comin' into my kitchen," she said testily—   105
"snoopin' round and criticizin'."

"Of course it's no more than their duty," said the sheriff's wife, in her
manner of timid acquiescence.

"Duty's all right," replied Mrs. Hale bluffly; "but I guess that deputy
sheriff that come out to make the fire might have got a little of this on." She
gave the roller towel a pull. "Wish I'd thought of that sooner! Seems mean to
talk about her for not having things slicked up, when she had to come away
in such a hurry."

She looked around the kitchen. Certainly it was not "slicked up." Her
eye was held by a bucket of sugar on a low shelf. The cover was off the
wooden bucket, and beside it was a paper bag—half full.

Mrs. Hale moved toward it.

"She was putting this in here," she said to herself—slowly.   110

She thought of the flour in her kitchen at home—half sifted, half not
sifted. She had been interrupted, and had left things half done. What had

interrupted Minnie Foster? Why had that work been left half done? She made a move as if to finish it,—unfinished things always bothered her,—and then she glanced around and saw that Mrs. Peters was watching her—and she didn't want Mrs. Peters to get that feeling she had got of work begun and then—for some reason—not finished.

"It's a shame about her fruit," she said, and walked toward the cupboard that the county attorney had opened, and got on the chair, murmuring: "I wonder if it's all gone."

It was a sorry enough looking sight, but "Here's one that's all right," she said at last. She held it toward the light. "This is cherries, too." She looked again. "I declare I believe that's the only one."

With a sigh, she got down from the chair, went to the sink, and wiped off the bottle.

115   "She'll feel awful bad, after all her hard work in the hot weather. I remember the afternoon I put up my cherries last summer."

She set the bottle on the table, and, with another sigh, started to sit down in the rocker. But she did not sit down. Something kept her from sitting down in that chair. She straightened—stepped back, and, half turned away, stood looking at it, seeing the woman who sat there "pleatin' at her apron."

The thin voice of the sheriff's wife broke in upon her: "I must be getting those things from the front room closet." She opened the door into the other room, started in, stepped back. "You coming with me, Mrs. Hale?" she asked nervously. "You—you could help me get them."

They were soon back—the stark coldness of that shut-up room was not a thing to linger in.

"My!" said Mrs. Peters, dropping the things on the table and hurrying to the stove.

120   Mrs. Hale stood examining the clothes the woman who was being detained in town had said she wanted.

"Wright was close!" she exclaimed, holding up a shabby black skirt that bore the marks of much making over. "I think maybe that's why she kept so much to herself. I s'pose she felt she couldn't do her part; and then, you don't enjoy things when you feel shabby. She used to wear pretty clothes and be lively—when she was Minnie Foster, one of the town girls, singing in the choir. But that—oh, that was twenty years ago."

With a carefulness in which there was something tender, she folded the shabby clothes and piled them at one corner of the table. She looked at Mrs. Peters, and there was something in the other woman's look that irritated her.

"She don't care," she said to herself. "Much difference it makes to her whether Minnie Foster had pretty clothes when she was a girl."

Then she looked again, and she wasn't so sure; in fact, she hadn't at any time been perfectly sure about Mrs. Peters. She had that shrinking manner, and yet her eyes looked as if they could see a long way into things.

125   "This all you was to take in?" asked Mrs. Hale.

"No," said the sheriff's wife; "she said she wanted an apron. Funny thing to want," she ventured in her nervous little way, "for there's not much to get you dirty in jail, goodness knows. But I suppose just to make her feel more natural. If you're used to wearing an apron—. She said they were in the bottom drawer of this cupboard. Yes—here they are. And then her little shawl that always hung on the stair door."

She took the small gray shawl from behind the door leading upstairs, and stood a minute looking at it.

Suddenly Mrs. Hale took a quick step toward the other woman.

"Mrs. Peters!"

"Yes, Mrs. Hale?"   130

"Do you think she—did it?"

A frightened look blurred the other things in Mrs. Peters's eyes.

"Oh, I don't know," she said, in a voice that seemed to shrink away from the subject.

"Well, I don't think she did," affirmed Mrs. Hale stoutly. "Asking for an apron, and her little shawl. Worryin' about her fruit."

"Mr. Peters says—." Footsteps were heard in the room above; she   135
stopped, looked up, then went on in a lowered voice: "Mr. Peters says—it looks bad for her. Mr. Henderson is awful sarcastic in a speech, and he's going to make fun of her saying she didn't—wake up."

For a moment Mrs. Hale had no answer. Then, "Well, I guess John Wright didn't wake up—when they was slippin' that rope under his neck," she muttered.

"No, it's *strange*," breathed Mrs. Peters. "They think it was such a— funny way to kill a man."

She began to laugh; at the sound of the laugh, abruptly stopped.

"That's just what Mr. Hale said," said Mrs. Hale, in a resolutely natural voice. "There was a gun in the house. He says that's what he can't understand."

"Mr. Henderson said, coming out, that what was needed for the case was   140
a motive. Something to show anger—or sudden feeling."

"Well, I don't see any signs of anger around here," said Mrs. Hale. "I don't—"

She stopped. It was as if her mind tripped on something. Her eye was caught by a dish-towel in the middle of the kitchen table. Slowly she moved toward the table. One half of it was wiped clean, the other half messy. Her eyes made a slow, almost unwilling turn to the bucket of sugar and the half empty bag beside it. Things begun—and not finished.

After a moment she stepped back, and said, in that manner of releasing herself:

"Wonder how they're finding things upstairs? I hope she had it a little more red up° up there. You know,"—she paused, and feeling gathered,—"it seems kind of *sneaking; locking her up in town and coming out here to get her own house to turn against her!"

"But, Mrs. Hale," said the sheriff's wife, "the law is the law."   145

red up: neatened, readied (dialect)

"I s'pose 'tis," answered Mrs. Hale shortly.

She turned to the stove, saying something about that fire not being much to brag of. She worked with it a minute, and when she straightened up she said aggressively:

"The law is the law—and a bad stove is a bad stove. How'd you like to cook on this?"—pointing with the poker to the broken lining. She opened the oven door and started to express her opinion of the oven; but she was swept into her own thoughts, thinking of what it would mean, year after year, to have that stove to wrestle with. The thought of Minnie Foster trying to bake in that oven—and the thought of her never going over to see Minnie Foster—.

She was startled by hearing Mrs. Peters say: "A person gets discouraged—and loses heart."

150   The sheriff's wife had looked from the stove to the sink—to the pail of water which had been carried in from outside. The two women stood there silent, above them the footsteps of the men who were looking for evidence against the woman who had worked in that kitchen. That look of seeing into things, of seeing through a thing to something else, was in the eyes of the sheriff's wife now. When Mrs. Hale next spoke to her, it was gently:

"Better loosen up your things, Mrs. Peters. We'll not feel them when we go out."

Mrs. Peters went to the back of the room to hang up the fur tippet she was wearing. A moment later she exclaimed, "Why, she was piecing a quilt," and held up a large sewing basket piled high with quilt pieces.

Mrs. Hale spread some of the blocks on the table.

"It's log-cabin pattern," she said, putting several of them together. "Pretty, isn't it?"

155   They were so engaged with the quilt that they did not hear the footsteps on the stairs. Just as the stair door opened Mrs. Hale was saying:

"Do you suppose she was going to quilt it or just knot it?"

The sheriff threw up his hands.

"They wonder whether she was going to quilt it or just knot it!"

There was a laugh for the ways of women, a warming of hands over the stove, and then the county attorney said briskly:

160   "Well, let's go right out to the barn and get that cleared up."

"I don't see as there's anything so strange," Mrs. Hale said resentfully, after the outside door had closed on the three men—"our taking up our time with little things while we're waiting for them to get the evidence. I don't see as it's anything to laugh about."

"Of course they've got awful important things on their minds," said the sheriff's wife apologetically.

They returned to an inspection of the blocks for the quilt. Mrs. Hale was looking at the fine, even sewing, and preoccupied with thoughts of the woman who had done that sewing, when she heard the sheriff's wife say, in a queer tone:

"Why, look at this one."

She turned to take the block held out to her.   165

"The sewing," said Mrs. Peters, in a troubled way. "All the rest of them have been so nice and even—but—this one. Why, it looks as if she didn't know what she was about!"

Their eyes met—something flashed to life, passed between them; then, as if with an effort, they seemed to pull away from each other. A moment Mrs. Hale sat there, her hands folded over that sewing which was so unlike all the rest of the sewing. Then she had pulled a knot and drawn the threads.

"Oh, what are you doing, Mrs. Hale?" asked the sheriff's wife, startled.

"Just pulling out a stitch or two that's not sewed very good," said Mrs. Hale mildly.

"I don't think we ought to touch things," Mrs. Peters said, a little   170
helplessly.

"I'll just finish up this end," answered Mrs. Hale, still in that mild, matter-of-fact fashion.

She threaded a needle and started to replace bad sewing with good. For a little while she sewed in silence. Then, in that thin, timid voice, she heard:

"Mrs. Hale!"

"Yes, Mrs. Peters?"

"What do you suppose she was so—nervous about?"   175

"Oh, *I* don't know," said Mrs. Hale, as if dismissing a thing not important enough to spend much time on. "I don't know as she was—nervous. I sew awful queer sometimes when I'm just tired."

She cut a thread, and out of the corner of her eye looked up at Mrs. Peters. The small, lean face of the sheriff's wife seemed to have tightened up. Her eyes had that look of peering into something. But the next moment she moved, and said in her thin, indecisive way:

"Well, I must get those clothes wrapped. They may be through sooner than we think. I wonder where I could find a piece of paper—and string."

"In that cupboard, maybe," suggested Mrs. Hale, after a glance around.

One piece of the crazy sewing remained unripped. Mrs. Peters's back   180
turned, Martha Hale now scrutinized that piece, compared it with the dainty, accurate sewing of the other blocks. The difference was startling. Holding this block made her feel queer, as if the distracted thoughts of the woman who had perhaps turned to it to try and quiet herself were communicating themselves to her.

Mrs. Peters's voice roused her.

"Here's a birdcage," she said. "Did she have a bird, Mrs. Hale?"

"Why, I don't know whether she did or not." She turned to look at the cage Mrs. Peters was holding up. "I've not been here in so long." She sighed. "There was a man round last year selling canaries cheap—but I don't know as she took one. Maybe she did. She used to sing real pretty herself."

Mrs. Peters looked around the kitchen.

185   "Seems kind of funny to think of a bird here." She half laughed—an attempt to put up a barrier. "But she must have had one—or why would she have a cage? I wonder what happened to it."

"I suppose maybe the cat got it," suggested Mrs. Hale, resuming her sewing.

"No, she didn't have a cat. She's got that feeling some people have about cats—being afraid of them. When they brought her to our house yesterday, my cat got in the room, and she was real upset and asked me to take it out."

"My sister Bessie was like that," laughed Mrs. Hale.

The sheriff's wife did not reply. The silence made Mrs. Hale turn around. Mrs. Peters was examining the birdcage.

190   "Look at this door," she said slowly. "It's broke. One hinge has been pulled apart."

Mrs. Hale came nearer.

"Looks as if some one must have been—rough with it."

Again their eyes met—startled, questioning, apprehensive. For a moment neither spoke nor stirred. Then Mrs. Hale, turning away, said brusquely:

"If they're going to find any evidence, I wish they'd be about it. I don't like this place."

195   "But I'm awful glad you came with me, Mrs. Hale." Mrs. Peters put the birdcage on the table and sat down. "It would be lonesome for me—sitting here alone."

"Yes, it would, wouldn't it?" agreed Mrs. Hale, a certain determined naturalness in her voice. She picked up the sewing, but now it dropped in her lap, and she murmured in a different voice: "But I tell you what I *do* wish, Mrs. Peters. I wish I had come over sometimes when she was here. I wish—I had."

"But of course you were awful busy, Mrs. Hale. Your house—and your children."

"I could've come," retorted Mrs. Hale shortly. "I stayed away because it weren't cheerful—and that's why I ought to have come. I"—she looked around—"I've never liked this place. Maybe because it's down in a hollow and you don't see the road. I don't know what it is, but it's a lonesome place, and always was. I wish I had come over to see Minnie Foster sometimes. I can see now—" She did not put it into words.

"Well, you mustn't reproach yourself," counseled Mrs. Peters. "Somehow, we just don't see how it is with other folks till—something comes up."

200   "Not having children makes less work," mused Mrs. Hale, after a silence, "but it makes a quiet house—and Wright out to work all day—and no company when he did come in. Did you know John Wright, Mrs. Peters?"

"Not to know him. I've seen him in town. They say he was a good man."

"Yes—good," conceded John Wright's neighbor grimly. "He didn't drink, and kept his word as well as most, I guess, and paid his debts. But he was a hard man, Mrs. Peters. Just to pass the time of day with him—." She stopped, shivered a little. "Like a raw wind that gets to the bone." Her eye fell upon the cage on the table before her, and she added, almost bitterly: "I should think she would've wanted a bird!"

Suddenly she leaned forward, looking intently at the cage. "But what do you s'pose went wrong with it?"

"I don't know," returned Mrs. Peters; "unless it got sick and died."

But after she said it she reached over and swung the broken door. Both   205
women watched it as if somehow held by it.

"You didn't know—her?" Mrs. Hale asked, a gentler note in her voice.

"Not till they brought her yesterday," said the sheriff's wife.

"She—come to think of it, she was kind of like a bird herself. Real sweet and pretty, but kind of timid and—fluttery. How—she—did—change."

That held her for a long time. Finally, as if struck with a happy thought and relieved to get back to everyday things, she exclaimed:

"Tell you what, Mrs. Peters, why don't you take the quilt in with you? It   210
might take up her mind."

"Why, I think that's a real nice idea, Mrs. Hale," agreed the sheriff's wife, as if she too were glad to come into the atmosphere of a simple kindness. "There couldn't possibly be any objection to that, could there? Now, just what will I take? I wonder if her patches are in here—and her things."

They turned to the sewing basket.

"Here's some red," said Mrs. Hale, bringing out a roll of cloth. Underneath that was a box. "Here, maybe her scissors are in here—and her things." She held it up. "What a pretty box! I'll warrant that was something she had a long time ago—when she was a girl."

She held it in her hand a moment; then, with a little sigh, opened it.

Instantly her hand went to her nose.   215

"Why—!"

Mrs. Peters drew nearer—then turned away.

"There's something wrapped up in this piece of silk," faltered Mrs. Hale.

"This isn't her scissors," said Mrs. Peters in a shrinking voice.

Her hand not steady, Mrs. Hale raised the piece of silk. "Oh, Mrs.   220
Peters!" she cried. "It's—"

Mrs. Peters bent closer.

"It's the bird," she whispered.

"But, Mrs. Peters!" cried Mrs. Hale. "*Look* at it! Its neck—look at its neck! It's all—other side *to.*"

She held the box away from her.

The sheriff's wife again bent closer.   225

"Somebody wrung its neck," said she, in a voice that was slow and deep.

And then again the eyes of the two women met—this time clung together in a look of dawning comprehension, of growing horror. Mrs. Peters looked from the dead bird to the broken door of the cage. Again their eyes met. And just then there was a sound at the outside door.

Mrs. Hale slipped the box under the quilt pieces in the basket, and sank into the chair before it. Mrs. Peters stood holding to the table. The county attorney and the sheriff came in from outside.

"Well, ladies," said the county attorney, as one turning from serious things to little pleasantries, "have you decided whether she was going to quilt it or knot it?"

230   "We think," began the sheriff's wife in a flurried voice, "that she was going to—knot it."

He was too preoccupied to notice the change that came in her voice on that last.

"Well, that's very interesting, I'm sure," he said tolerantly. He caught sight of the birdcage. "Has the bird flown?"

"We think the cat got it," said Mrs. Hale in a voice curiously even.

He was walking up and down, as if thinking something out.

235   "Is there a cat?" he asked absently.

Mrs. Hale shot a look up at the sheriff's wife.

"Well, not *now*," said Mrs. Peters. "They're superstitious, you know; they leave."

She sank into the chair.

The county attorney did not heed her. "No sign at all of any one having come in from the outside," he said to Peters, in the manner of continuing an interrupted conversation. "Their own rope. Now let's go upstairs again and go over it, piece by piece. It would have to have been some one who knew just the—"

240   The stair door closed behind them and their voices were lost.

The two women sat motionless, not looking at each other, but as if peering into something and at the same time holding back. When they spoke now it was as if they were afraid of what they were saying, but as if they could not help saying it.

"She liked the bird," said Martha Hale, low and slowly. "She was going to bury it in that pretty box."

"When I was a girl," said Mrs. Peters, under her breath, "my kitten— there was a boy took a hatchet, and before my eyes—before I could get there—" She covered her face an instant. "If they hadn't held me back I would have"—she caught herself, looked upstairs where footsteps were heard, and finished weakly—"hurt him."

Then they sat without speaking or moving.

245   "I wonder how it would seem," Mrs. Hale at last began, as if feeling her way over strange ground—"never to have had any children around?" Her eyes made a slow sweep of the kitchen, as if seeing what that kitchen had meant through all the years. "No, Wright wouldn't like the bird," she said after that—"a thing that sang. She used to sing. He killed that too." Her voice tightened.

Mrs. Peters moved uneasily.

"Of course we don't know who killed the bird."

"I knew John Wright," was Mrs. Hale's answer.

"It was an awful thing was done in this house that night, Mrs. Hale," said the sheriff's wife. "Killing a man while he slept—slipping a thing round his neck that choked the life out of him."

Mrs. Hale's hand went out to the birdcage.   250

"His neck. Choked the life out of him."

"We don't *know* who killed him," whispered Mrs. Peters wildly. "We don't *know.*"

Mrs. Hale had not moved. "If there had been years and years of—nothing, then a bird to sing to you, it would be awful—still—after the bird was still."

It was as if something within her not herself had spoken, and it found in Mrs. Peters something she did not know as herself.

"I know what stillness is," she said, in a queer, monotonous voice.   255
"When we homesteaded in Dakota, and my first baby died—after he was two years old—and me with no other then—"

Mrs. Hale stirred.

"How soon do you suppose they'll be through looking for evidence?"

"I know what stillness is," repeated Mrs. Peters, in just that same way. Then she too pulled back. "The law has got to punish crime, Mrs. Hale," she said in her tight little way.

"I wish you'd seen Minnie Foster," was the answer, "when she wore a white dress with blue ribbons, and stood up there in the choir and sang."

The picture of that girl, the fact that she had lived neighbor to that girl   260
for twenty years, and had let her die for lack of life, was suddenly more than she could bear.

"Oh, I *wish* I'd come over here once in a while!" she cried. "That was a crime! That was a crime! Who's going to punish that?"

"We mustn't take on," said Mrs. Peters, with a frightened look toward the stairs.

"I might 'a' *known* she needed help! I tell you, it's *queer,* Mrs. Peters. We live close together, and we live far apart. We all go through the same things—it's all just a different kind of the same thing! If it weren't— why do you and I *understand?* Why do we *know*—what we know this minute?"

She dashed her hand across her eyes. Then, seeing the jar of fruit on the table, she reached for it and choked out:

"If I was you I wouldn't *tell* her her fruit was gone! Tell her it *ain't.* Tell   265
her it's all right—all of it. Here—take this in to prove it to her! She—she may never know whether it was broke or not."

She turned away.

Mrs. Peters reached out for the bottle of fruit as if she were glad to take it—as if touching a familiar thing, having something to do, could keep her from something else. She got up, looked about for something to wrap the fruit in, took a petticoat from the pile of clothes she had brought from the front room, and nervously started winding that round the bottle.

"My!" she began, in a high, false voice, "it's a good thing the men couldn't hear us! Getting all stirred up over a little thing like a—dead canary." She hurried over that. "As if that could have anything to do with—with— My, wouldn't they *laugh?*"

Footsteps were heard on the stairs.

270   "Maybe they would," muttered Mrs. Hale—"maybe they wouldn't."

"No, Peters," said the county attorney incisively; "it's all perfectly clear, except the reason for doing it. But you know juries when it comes to women. If there was some definite thing—something to show. Something to make a story about. A thing that would connect up with this clumsy way of doing it."

In a covert way Mrs. Hale looked at Mrs. Peters. Mrs. Peters was looking at her. Quickly they looked away from each other. The outer door opened and Mr. Hale came in.

"I've got the team round now," he said. "Pretty cold out there."

"I'm going to stay here awhile by myself," the county attorney suddenly announced. "You can send Frank out for me, can't you?" he asked the sheriff. "I want to go over everything. I'm not satisfied we can't do better."

275   Again, for one brief moment, the two women's eyes found one another. The sheriff came up to the table.

"Did you want to see what Mrs. Peters was going to take in?"

The county attorney picked up the apron. He laughed.

"Oh, I guess they're not very dangerous things the ladies have picked out."

280   Mrs. Hale's hand was on the sewing basket in which the box was concealed. She felt that she ought to take her hand off the basket. She did not seem able to. He picked up one of the quilt blocks which she had piled on to cover the box. Her eyes felt like fire. She had a feeling that if he took up the basket she would snatch it from him.

But he did not take it up. With another little laugh, he turned away, saying:

"No; Mrs. Peters doesn't need supervising. For that matter, a sheriff's wife is married to the law. Ever think of it that way, Mrs. Peters?"

Mrs. Peters was standing beside the table. Mrs. Hale shot a look up at her; but she could not see her face. Mrs. Peters had turned away. When she spoke, her voice was muffled.

"Not—just that way," she said.

285   "Married to the law!" chuckled Mrs. Peters's husband. He moved toward the door into the front room, and said to the county attorney:

"I just want you to come in here a minute, George. We ought to take a look at these windows."

"Oh—windows," said the county attorney scoffingly.

"We'll be right out, Mr. Hale," said the sheriff to the farmer, who was still waiting by the door.

Hale went to look after the horses. The sheriff followed the county attorney into the other room. Again—for one moment—the two women were alone in that kitchen.

290   Martha Hale sprang up, her hands tight together, looking at that other woman, with whom it rested. At first she could not see her eyes, for the sheriff's wife had not turned back since she turned away at that suggestion of

being married to the law. But now Mrs. Hale made her turn back. Her eyes made her turn back. Slowly, unwillingly, Mrs. Peters turned her head until her eyes met the eyes of the other woman. There was a moment when they held each other in a steady, burning look in which there was no evasion nor flinching. Then Martha Hale's eyes pointed the way to the basket in which was hidden the thing that would make certain the conviction of the other woman—that woman who was not there and yet who had been there with them all through the hour.

For a moment Mrs. Peters did not move. And then she did it. With a rush forward, she threw back the quilt pieces, got the box, tried to put it in her handbag. It was too big. Desperately she opened it, started to take the bird out. But there she broke—she could not touch the bird. She stood helpless, foolish.

There was the sound of a knob turning in the inner door. Martha Hale snatched the box from the sheriff's wife, and got it in the pocket of her big coat just as the sheriff and the county attorney came back into the kitchen.

"Well, Henry," said the county attorney facetiously, "at least we found out that she was not going to quilt it. She was going to—what is it you call it, ladies?"

Mrs. Hale's hand was against the pocket of her coat.

"We call it—knot it, Mr. Henderson."   295

QUESTIONS

1. At the time this story was published, women were not entitled to vote or sit on juries. The title alludes to the concept in common law (encoded in Magna Carta, 1215) that an accused *man* has the right to be judged by his peers. Given these facts, what ironies are suggested by the title and the decision reached by Mrs. Hale and Mrs. Peters? Do they find that Mrs. Wright killed her husband? Do they judge her guilty of murder?
2. In what various ways are Mrs. Hale and Mrs. Peters "peers" of Mrs. Wright?
3. What common assumptions about women are shared by the men in the story? How do they try to show that they do not think women to be their inferiors? How are their assumptions ironic?
4. Since no one seems to doubt that Mrs. Wright killed her husband (there are no other suspects, and she is already being held for the crime), how does this story create suspense?
5. Compare Mrs. Wright's motives for killing to Uncle Caesar's. Compare Major Caswell to Mr. Wright. Compare the decision made at the end by the narrator of "A Municipal Report" to that of Mrs. Hale and Mrs. Peters. How do these comparisons make the purposes of these two stories clearer?

EXERCISE

The two stories by William Faulkner that follow, both revolving around an animal chase and financial transactions related thereto, are both comic interpretive stories of indisputable merit. The majority of qualified judges, however, would rank one story higher on the scale of literary value than the other. Which story, in your estimation, deserves the higher ranking? Support your decision with a reasoned and thorough analysis, using the study questions for what help they may provide.

William Faulkner

Spotted Horses

1

Yes, sir. Flem Snopes has filled that whole country full of spotted horses. You can hear folks running them all day and all night, whooping and hollering, and the horses running back and forth across them little wooden bridges ever now and then kind of like thunder. Here I was this morning pretty near half way to town, with the team ambling along and me setting in the buckboard about half asleep, when all of a sudden something come swurging up outen the bushes and jumped the road clean, without touching hoof to it. It flew right over my team, big as a billboard and flying through the air like a hawk. It taken me thirty minutes to stop my team and untangle the harness and the buckboard and hitch them up again.

That Flem Snopes. I be dog if he ain't a case, now. One morning about ten years ago, the boys was just getting settled down on Varner's porch for a little talk and tobacco, when here come Flem from behind the counter, with his coat off and his hair all parted, like he might have been clerking for Varner for ten years already. Folks all knowed him; it was a big family of them about five miles down the bottom. That year, at least. Sharecropping. They never stayed on any place over a year. Then they would move on to another place, with the chap or maybe the twins of that year's litter. It was a regular nest of them. But Flem. The rest of them stayed tenant farmers, moving every year, but here come Flem one day, walking out from behind Jody Varner's counter like he owned it. And he wasn't there but a year or two before folks knowed that, if him and Jody was both still in that store in ten years more, it would be Jody clerking for Flem Snopes. Why, that fellow could make a nickel where it wasn't but four cents to begin with. He skun me in two trades, myself, and the fellow that can do that, I just hope he'll get rich before I do; that's all.

All right. So here Flem was, clerking at Varner's, making a nickel here and there and not telling nobody about it. No, sir. Folks never knowed when

---

SPOTTED HORSES   First published in 1931. An expanded, considerably altered version of the story constitutes Book 4, Chapter 1, of *The Hamlet* (1940), part of a trilogy with *The Town* and *The Mansion*. These three books chart the spread of the Snopes tribe and the rise of Flem Snopes, son of a tenant farmer, to the foremost position of power and wealth in the county. For the setting of many of his novels and stories Faulkner created the mythical Yoknapatawpha County, Mississippi, where this story takes place. Its county seat, Jefferson, is roughly based on Oxford, Mississippi, of which Faulkner (1897–1962) was a lifelong resident.

Flem got the better of somebody lessen the fellow he beat told it. He'd just set there in the store-chair, chewing his tobacco and keeping his own business to hisself, until about a week later we'd find out it was somebody else's business he was keeping to hisself—provided the fellow he trimmed was mad enough to tell it. That's Flem.

We give him ten years to own ever thing Jody Varner had. But he never waited no ten years. I reckon you-all know that gal of Uncle Billy Varner's, the youngest one; Eula. Jody's sister. Ever Sunday ever yellow-wheeled buggy and curried riding horse in that country would be hitched to Bill Varner's fence, and the young bucks setting on the porch, swarming around Eula like bees around a honey pot. One of these here kind of big, soft-looking gals that could giggle richer than plowed new-ground. Wouldn't none of them leave before the others, and so they would set there on the porch until time to go home, with some of them with nine or ten miles to ride and then get up tomorrow and go back to the field. So they would all leave together and they would ride in a clump down to the creek ford and hitch them curried horses and yellow-wheeled buggies and get out and fight one another. Then they would get in the buggies again and go on home.

Well, one day about a year ago, one of them yellow-wheeled buggies and one of them curried saddle-horses quit this country. We heard they was heading for Texas. The next day Uncle Billy and Eula and Flem come in to town in Uncle Bill's surrey, and when they come back, Flem and Eula was married. And on the next day we heard that two more of them yellow-wheeled buggies had left the country. They mought have gone to Texas, too. It's a big place. 5

Anyway, about a month after the wedding, Flem and Eula went to Texas, too. They was gone pretty near a year. Then one day last month, Eula come back, with a baby. We figgured up, and we decided that it was as well-growed a three-months-old baby as we ever see. It can already pull up on a chair. I reckon Texas makes big men quick, being a big place. Anyway, if it keeps on like it started, it'll be chewing tobacco and voting time it's eight years old.

And so last Friday here come Flem himself. He was on a wagon with another fellow. The other fellow had one of these two-gallon hats and a ivory-handled pistol and a box of gingersnaps sticking out of his hind pocket, and tied to the tail-gate of the wagon was about two dozen of them Texas ponies, hitched to one another with barbed wire. They was colored like parrots and they was quiet as doves, and ere a one of them would kill you quick as a rattlesnake. Nere a one of them had two eyes the same color, and nere a one of them had ever see a bridle, I reckon; and when that Texas man got down offen the wagon and walked up to them to show how gentle they was, one of them cut his vest clean offen him, same as with a razor.

Flem had done already disappeared; he had went on to see his wife, I reckon, and to see if that ere baby had done gone on to the field to help Uncle Billy plow maybe. It was the Texas man that taken the horses on to Mrs. Littlejohn's lot. He had a little trouble at first, when they come to the gate, because they hadn't never see a fence before, and when he finally got them in and taken a pair of wire cutters and unhitched them and got them into the barn and poured some shell corn into the trough, they durn nigh tore down the barn. I reckon they thought that shell corn was bugs, maybe. So he left them in the lot and he announced that the auction would begin at sunup to-morrow.

That night we was setting on Mrs. Littlejohn's porch. You-all mind the moon was nigh full that night, and we could watch them spotted varmints swirling along the fence and back and forth across the lot same as minnows in a pond. And then now and then they would all kind of huddle up against the barn and rest themselves by biting and kicking one another. We would hear a squeal, and then a set of hoofs would go Bam! against the barn, like a pistol. It sounded just like a fellow with a pistol, in a nest of cattymounts, taking his time.

2

10   It wasn't ere a man knowed yet if Flem owned them things or not. They just knowed one thing: that they wasn't never going to know for sho if Flem did or not, or if maybe he didn't just get on that wagon at the edge of town, for the ride or not. Even Eck Snopes didn't know, Flem's own cousin. But wasn't nobody surprised at that. We knowed that Flem would skin Eck quick as he would ere a one of us.

They was there by sunup next morning, some of them come twelve and sixteen miles, with seed-money tied up in tobacco sacks in their overalls, standing along the fence, when the Texas man come out of Mrs. Littlejohn's after breakfast and clumb onto the gate post with that ere white pistol butt sticking outen his hind pocket. He taken a new box of gingersnaps outen his pocket and bit the end offen it like a cigar and spit out the paper, and said the auction was open. And still they was coming up in wagons and a horse- and mule-back and hitching the teams across the road and coming to the fence. Flem wasn't nowhere in sight.

But he couldn't get them started. He began to work on Eck, because Eck holp him last night to get them into the barn and feed them that shell corn. Eck got out just in time. He come outen that barn like a chip on the crest of a busted dam of water, and clumb into the wagon just in time.

He was working on Eck when Henry Armstid come up in his wagon. Eck was saying he was skeered to bid on one of them, because he might get it, and the Texas man says, "Them ponies? Them little horses?" He clumb down offen the gate post and went toward the horses. They broke and run, and him following them, kind of chirping to them, with his hand out like he was fixing to catch a fly, until he got three or four of them cornered. Then he jumped into them, and then we couldn't see nothing for a while because of the dust. It was a big cloud of it, and them blare-eyed, spotted things swoaring outen it twenty foot to a jump, in forty directions without counting up.

Then the dust settled and there they was, the Texas man and the horse. He had its head twisted clean around like a owl's head. Its legs was braced and it was trembling like a bride and groaning like a saw mill, and him holding its head wrung clean around on its neck so it was snuffing sky. "Look it over," he says, with his heels dug too and that white pistol sticking outen his pocket and his neck swole up like a spreading adder's until you could just tell what he was saying, cussing the horse and talking to us all at once: "Look him over, the fiddle-headed son of fourteen fathers. Try him, buy him; you will get the best—" Then it was all dust again, and we couldn't see nothing but spotted hide and mane, and that ere Texas man's boot-heels like a couple of walnuts on two strings, and after a while that two-gallon hat come sailing out like a fat old hen crossing a fence.

When the dust settled again, he was just getting outen the far fence corner, brushing himself off. He come and got his hat and brushed it off and come and clumb onto the gate post again. He was breathing hard. He taken the gingersnap box outen his pocket and et one, breathing hard. The hammer-head horse was still running round and round the lot like a merry-go-round at a fair. That was when Henry Armstid come shoving up to the gate in them patched overalls and one of them dangle-armed shirts of hisn. Hadn't nobody noticed him until then. We was all watching the Texas man and the horses. Even Mrs. Littlejohn; she had done come out and built a fire under the wash-pot in her back yard, and she would stand at the fence a while and then go back into the house and come out again with a arm full of wash and stand at the fence again. Well, here come Henry shoving up, and then we see Mrs. Armstid right behind him, in that ere faded wrapper and sunbonnet and them tennis shoes. "Git on back to that wagon," Henry says.

"Henry," she says.   15

"Here, boys," the Texas man says; "make room for missus to git up and see. Come on, Henry," he says; "here's your chance to buy that saddle-horse missus has been wanting. What about ten dollars, Henry?"

"Henry," Mrs. Armstid says. She put her hand on Henry's arm. Henry knocked her hand down.

"Git on back to that wagon, like I told you," he says.

Mrs. Armstid never moved. She stood behind Henry, with her hands rolled into her dress, not looking at nothing. "He hain't no more despair than to buy one of them things," she says. "And us not five dollars ahead of the pore house, he hain't no more despair." It was the truth, too. They ain't never made more than a bare living offen that place of theirs, and them with four chaps and the very clothes they wears she earns by weaving by the firelight at night while Henry's asleep.

"Shut your mouth and git on back to that wagon," Henry says. "Do you   20
want I taken a wagon stake to you here in the big road?"

Well, that Texas man taken one look at her. Then he begun on Eck again, like Henry wasn't even there. But Eck was skeered. "I can git me a snapping turtle or a water moccasin for nothing. I ain't going to buy none."

So the Texas man said he would give Eck a horse. "To start the auction, and because you holp me last night. If you'll start the bidding on the next horse," he says, "I'll give you that fiddle-head horse."

I wish you could have seen them, standing there with their seed-money in their pockets, watching that Texas man give Eck Snopes a live horse, all fixed to call him a fool if he taken it or not. Finally Eck says he'll take it. "Only I just starts the bidding," he says. "I don't have to buy the next one lessen I ain't overtopped." The Texas man said all right, and Eck bid a dollar on the next one, with Henry Armstid standing there with his mouth already open, watching Eck and the Texas man like a mad-dog or something. "A dollar," Eck says.

The Texas man looked at Eck. His mouth was already open too, like he had started to say something and what he was going to say had up and died on him. "A dollar?" he says. "One dollar? You mean, *one* dollar, Eck?"

25   "Durn it," Eck says; "two dollars, then."

Well, sir, I wish you could a seen that Texas man. He taken out that gingersnap box and held it up and looked into it, careful, like it might have been a diamond ring in it, or a spider. Then he throwed it away and wiped his face with a bandanna. "Well," he says. "Well. Two dollars. Two dollars. Is your pulse all right, Eck?" he says. "Do you have ager-sweats at night, maybe?" he says. "Well," he says, "I got to take it. But are you boys going to stand there and see Eck get two horses at a dollar a head?"

That done it. I be dog if he wasn't nigh as smart as Flem Snopes. He hadn't no more than got the words outen his mouth before here was Henry Armstid, waving his hand. "Three dollars," Henry says. Mrs. Armstid tried to hold him again. He knocked her hand off, shoving up to the gate post.

"Mister," Mrs. Armstid says, "we got chaps in the house and not corn to feed the stock. We got five dollars I earned my chaps a-weaving after dark, and him snoring in the bed. And he hain't no more despair."

"Henry bids three dollars," the Texas man says. "Raise him a dollar, Eck, and the horse is yours."

30   "Henry," Mrs. Armstid says.

"Raise him, Eck," the Texas man says.

"Four dollars," Eck says.

"Five dollars," Henry says, shaking his fist. He shoved up right under the gate post. Mrs. Armstid was looking at the Texas man too.

"Mister," she says, "if you take that five dollars I earned my chaps a-weaving for one of them things, it'll be a curse onto you and yourn during all the time of man."

35   But it wasn't no stopping Henry. He had shoved up, waving his fist at the Texas man. He opened it; the money was in nickels and quarters, and one dollar bill that looked like a cow's cud. "Five dollars," he says. "And the man that raises it'll have to beat my head off, or I'll beat hisn."

"All right," the Texas man says. "Five dollars is bid. But don't you shake your hand at me."

3

It taken till nigh sundown before the last one was sold. He got them hotted up once and the bidding got up to seven dollars and a quarter, but most of them went around three or four dollars, him setting on the gate post and picking the horses out one at a time by mouth-word, and Mrs. Littlejohn pumping up and down at the tub and stopping and coming to the fence for a while and going back to the tub again. She had done got done too, and the wash was hung on the line in the back yard, and we could smell supper cooking. Finally they was all sold; he swapped the last two and the wagon for a buckboard.

We was all kind of tired, but Henry Armstid looked more like a mad-dog then ever. When he bought, Mrs. Armstid had went back to the wagon, setting in it behind them two rabbit-sized bone-pore mules, and the wagon itself looking like it would fall all to pieces soon as the mules moved. Henry hadn't even waited to pull it outen the road; it was still in the middle of the road and her setting in it, not looking at nothing, ever since this morning.

Henry was right up against the gate. He went up to the Texas man. "I bought a horse and I paid cash," Henry says. "And yet you expect me to stand around here until they are all sold before I can get my horse. I'm going to take my horse outen that lot."

The Texas man looked at Henry. He talked like he might have been   40
asking for a cup of coffee at the table. "Take your horse," he says.

Then Henry quit looking at the Texas man. He begun to swallow, holding onto the gate. "Ain't you going to help me?" he says.

"It ain't my horse," the Texas man says.

Henry never looked at the Texas man again, he never looked at nobody. "Who'll help me catch my horse?" he says. Never nobody said nothing. "Bring the plowline," Henry says. Mrs. Armstid got outen the wagon and brought the plowline. The Texas man got down off the post. The woman made to pass him, carrying the rope.

"Don't you go in there, missus," the Texas man says.

Henry opened the gate. He didn't look back. "Come on here," he says.   45
"Don't you go in there, missus," the Texas man says.

Mrs. Armstid wasn't looking at nobody, neither, with her hands across her middle, holding the rope. "I reckon I better," she says. Her and Henry went into the lot. The horses broke and run. Henry and Mrs. Armstid followed.

"Get him into the corner," Henry says. They got Henry's horse cornered finally, and Henry taken the rope, but Mrs. Armstid let the horse get out. They hemmed it up again, but Mrs. Armstid let it get out again, and Henry turned and hit her with the rope. "Why didn't you head him back?" Henry says. He hit her again. "Why didn't you?" It was about that time I looked around and see Flem Snopes standing there.

It was the Texas man that done something. He moved fast for a big man. He caught the rope before Henry could hit the third time, and Henry whirled and made like he would jump at the Texas man. But he never jumped. The Texas man went and taken Henry's arm and led him outen the lot. Mrs. Armstid come behind them and the Texas man taken some money outen his pocket and he give it into Mrs. Armstid's hand. "Get him into the wagon and take him on home," the Texas man says, like he might have been telling them he enjoyed his supper.

50   Then here come Flem. "What's that for, Buck?" Flem says.

"Thinks he bought one of them ponies," the Texas man says. "Get him on away, missus."

But Henry wouldn't go. "Give him back that money," he says. "I bought that horse and I aim to have him if I have to shoot him."

And there was Flem, standing there with his hands in his pockets, chewing, like he had just happened to be passing.

"You take your money and I take my horse," Henry says. "Give it back to him," he says to Mrs. Armstid.

55   "You don't own no horse of mine," the Texas man says. "Get him on home, missus."

Then Henry seen Flem. "You got something to do with these horses," he says. "I bought one. Here's the money for it." He taken the bill outen Mrs. Armstid's hand. He offered it to Flem. "I bought one. Ask him. Here. Here's the money," he says, giving the bill to Flem.

When Flem taken the money, the Texas man dropped the rope he had snatched outen Henry's hand. He had done sent Eck Snopes's boy up to the store for another box of gingersnaps, and he taken the box outen his pocket and looked into it. It was empty and he dropped it on the ground. "Mr. Snopes will have your money for you to-morrow," he says to Mrs. Armstid. "You can get it from him to-morrow. He don't own no horse. You get him into the wagon and get him on home." Mrs. Armstid went back to the wagon and got in. "Where's that ere buckboard I bought?" the Texas man says. It was after sundown then. And then Mrs. Littlejohn come out on the porch and rung the supper bell.

4

I come on in and et supper. Mrs. Littlejohn would bring in a pan of bread or something, then she would go out to the porch a minute and come back and tell us. The Texas man had hitched his team to the buckboard he had swapped them last two horses for, and him and Flem had gone, and then she told that the rest of them that never had ropes had went back to the store with I. O. Snopes to get some ropes, and wasn't nobody at the gate but Henry Armstid, and Mrs. Armstid setting in the wagon in the road, and Eck Snopes and that boy of hisn. "I don't care how many of them fool men gets killed by them things," Mrs. Littlejohn says, "but I ain't going to let Eck Snopes take that boy into that lot again." So she went down to the gate, but she come back without the boy or Eck neither.

"It ain't no need to worry about that boy," I says. "He's charmed." He was right behind Eck last night when Eck went to help feed them. The whole drove of them jumped clean over that boy's head and never touched him. It was Eck that touched him. Eck snatched him into the wagon and taken a rope and frailed the tar out of him.

So I had done et and went to my room and was undressing, long as I had a long trip to make the next day; I was trying to sell a machine to Mrs. Bundren up past Whiteleaf; when Henry Armstid opened that gate and went in by hisself. They couldn't make him wait for the balance of them to get back with their ropes. Eck Snopes said he tried to make Henry wait, but Henry wouldn't do it. Eck said Henry walked right up to them and that when they broke, they run clean over Henry like a hay-mow breaking down. Eck said he snatched that boy of hisn out of the way just in time and that them things went through the gate like a creek flood and into the wagons and teams hitched side the road, busting wagon tongues and snapping harness like it was fishing-line, with Mrs. Armstid still setting in their wagon in the middle of it like something carved outen wood. Then they scattered, wild horses and tame mules with pieces of harness and single-trees dangling offen them, both ways up and down the road.

"There goes ourn, paw!" Eck says his boy said. "There it goes, into Mrs. Littlejohn's house." Eck says it run right up the steps and into the house like a boarder late for supper. I reckon so. Anyway, I was in my room, in my underclothes, with one sock on and one sock in my hand, leaning out the window when the commotion busted out, when I heard something run into the melodeon in the hall; it sounded like a railroad engine. Then the door to my room come sailing in like when you throw a tin bucket top into the wind and I looked over my shoulder and see something that looked like a fourteen-foot pinwheel a-blaring its eyes at me. It had to blare them fast, because I was already done jumped out the window.

I reckon it was anxious, too. I reckon it hadn't never seen barbed wire or shell corn before, but I know it hadn't never seen underclothes before, or maybe it was a sewing-machine agent it hadn't never seen. Anyway, it swirled and turned to run back up the hall and outen the house, when it met Eck Snopes and that boy just coming in, carrying a rope. It swirled again and run down the hall and out the back door just in time to meet Mrs. Littlejohn. She had just gathered up the clothes she had washed, and she was coming onto the back porch with a armful of washing in one hand and a scrubbing-board in the other, when the horse skidded up to her, trying to stop and swirl again. It never taken Mrs. Littlejohn no time a-tall.

"Git outen here, you son," she says. She hit it across the face with the scrubbing board; that ere scrubbing-board split as neat as ere a axe could

60

have done it, and when the horse swirled to run back up the hall, she hit it again with what was left of the scrubbing-board, not on the head this time. "And stay out," she says.

Eck and that boy was half-way down the hall by this time. I reckon that horse looked like a pinwheel to Eck too. "Git to hell outen here, Ad!" Eck says. Only there wasn't time. Eck dropped flat on his face, but the boy never moved. The boy was about a yard tall maybe, in overhalls just like Eck's; that horse swoared over his head without touching a hair. I saw that, because I was just coming back up the front steps, still carrying that ere sock and still in my underclothes, when the horse come onto the porch again. It taken one look at me and swirled again and run to the end of the porch and jumped the banisters and the lot fence like a hen-hawk and lit in the lot running and went out the gate again and jumped eight or ten upside-down wagons and went on down the road. It was a full moon then. Mrs. Armstid was still setting in the wagon like she had done been carved outen wood and left there and forgot.

65   That horse. It ain't never missed a lick. It was going about forty miles a hour when it come to the bridge over the creek. It would have had a clear road, but it so happened that Vernon Tull was already using the bridge when it got there. He was coming back from town; he hadn't heard about the auction; him and his wife and three daughters and Mrs. Tull's aunt, all setting in chairs in the wagon bed, and all asleep, including the mules. They waked up when the horse hit the bridge one time, but Tull said the first he knew was when the mules tried to turn the wagon around in the middle of the bridge and he seen that spotted varmint run right twixt the mules and run up the wagon tongue like a squirrel. He said he just had time to hit it across the face with his whip-stock, because about that time the mules turned the wagon around on that ere one-way bridge and that horse clumb across one of the mules and jumped down onto the bridge again and went on, with Vernon standing up in the wagon and kicking at it.

Tull said the mules turned in the harness and clumb back into the wagon too, with Tull trying to beat them out again, with the reins wrapped around his wrist. After that he says all he seen was overturned chairs and women-folks' legs and white drawers shining in the moonlight, and his mules and that spotted horse going on up the road like a ghost.

The mules jerked Tull outen the wagon and drug him a spell on the bridge before the reins broke. They thought at first that he was dead, and while they was kneeling around him, picking the bridge splinters outen him, here come Eck and that boy, still carrying the rope. They was running and breathing a little hard. "Where'd he go?" Eck says.

5

I went back and got my pants and shirt and shoes on just in time to go and help get Henry Armstid outen the trash in the lot. I be dog if he didn't look like he was dead, with his head hanging back and his teeth showing in the moonlight, and a little rim of white under his eyelids. We could still hear them horses, here and there; hadn't none of them got more than four-five miles away yet, not knowing the country, I reckon. So we could hear them and folks yelling now and then: "Whooey. Head him!"

We toted Henry into Mrs. Littlejohn's. She was in the hall; she hadn't put down the armful of clothes. She taken one look at us, and she laid down the busted scrubbing-board and taken up the lamp and opened a empty door. "Bring him in here," she says.

We toted him in and laid him on the bed. Mrs. Littlejohn set the lamp on the   70
dresser, still carrying the clothes. "I'll declare, you men," she says. Our shadows was way up the wall, tiptoeing too; we could hear ourselves breathing. "Better get his wife," Mrs. Littlejohn says. She went out, carrying the clothes.

"I reckon we had," Quick says. "Go get her, somebody."

"Whyn't you go?" Winterbottom says.

"Let Ernest git her," Durley says. "He lives neighbors with them."

Ernest went to fetch her. I be dog if Henry didn't look like he was dead. Mrs. Littlejohn come back, with a kettle and some towels. She went to work on Henry, and then Mrs. Armstid and Ernest come in. Mrs. Armstid come to the foot of the bed and stood there, with her hands rolled into her apron, watching what Mrs. Littlejohn was doing, I reckon.

"You men git outen the way," Mrs. Littlejohn says. "Git outside," she   75
says. "See if you can't find something else to play with that will kill some more of you."

"Is he dead?" Winterbottom says.

"It ain't your fault if he ain't," Mrs. Littlejohn says. "Go tell Will Varner to come up here. I reckon a man ain't so different from a mule, come long come short. Except maybe a mule's got more sense."

We went to get Uncle Billy. It was a full moon. We could hear them, now and then, four mile away: "Whooey. Head him." The country was full of them, one on ever wooden bridge in the land, running across it like thunder: "Whooey. There he goes. Head him."

We hadn't got far before Henry begun to scream. I reckon Mrs. Littlejohn's water had brung him to; anyway, he wasn't dead. We went on to Uncle Billy's. The house was dark. We called to him, and after a while the window opened and Uncle Billy put his head out, peart as a peckerwood, listening. "Are they still trying to catch them durn rabbits?" he says.

He come down, with his britches on over his night-shirt and his sus-   80
penders dangling, carrying his horse-doctoring grip. "Yes, sir," he says, cocking his head like a woodpecker; "they're still a-trying."

We could hear Henry before we reached Mrs. Littlejohn's. He was going Ah-Ah-Ah. We stopped in the yard. Uncle Billy went on in. We could hear Henry. We stood in the yard, hearing them on the bridges, this-a-way and that: "Whooey. Whooey."

"Eck Snopes ought to caught hisn," Ernest says.

"Looks like he ought," Winterbottom said.

Henry was going Ah-Ah-Ah steady in the house; then he begun to scream. "Uncle Billy's started," Quick says. We looked into the hall. We could see the light where the door was. Then Mrs. Littlejohn come out.

85   "Will needs some help," she says. "You, Ernest. You'll do." Ernest went into the house.

"Hear them?" Quick said. "That one was on Four Mile bridge." We could hear them; it sounded like thunder a long way off; it didn't last long. "Whooey."

We could hear Henry: "Ah-Ah-Ah-Ah-Ah."

"They are both started now," Winterbottom says. "Ernest too."

90   That was early in the night. Which was a good thing, because it taken a long night for folks to chase them things right and for Henry to lay there and holler, being as Uncle Billy never had none of this here chloryfoam to set Henry's leg with. So it was considerate in Flem to get them started early. And what do you reckon Flem's com-ment was?

That's right. Nothing. Because he wasn't there. Hadn't nobody see him since that Texas man left.

6

That was Saturday night. I reckon Mrs. Armstid got home about day-light, to see about the chaps. I don't know where they thought her and Henry was. But lucky the oldest one was a gal, about twelve, big enough to take care of the little ones. Which she did for the next two days. Mrs. Armstid would nurse Henry all night and work in the kitchen for hern and Henry's keep, and in the afternoon she would drive home (it was about four miles) to see to the chaps. She would cook up a pot of victuals and leave it on the stove, and the gal would bar the house and keep the little ones quiet. I would hear Mrs. Littlejohn and Mrs. Armstid talking in the kitchen. "How are the chaps making out?" Mrs. Littlejohn says.

"All right," Mrs. Armstid says.

"Don't they git skeered at night?" Mrs. Littlejohn says.

95   "Ina May bars the door when I leave," Mrs. Armstid says. "She's got the axe in bed with her. I reckon she can make out."

I reckon they did. And I reckon Mrs. Armstid was waiting for Flem to come back to town; hadn't nobody seen him until this morning; to get her money the Texas man said Flem was keeping for her. Sho. I reckon she was.

Anyway, I heard Mrs. Armstid and Mrs. Littlejohn talking in the kitchen this morning while I was eating breakfast. Mrs. Littlejohn had just told Mrs. Armstid that Flem was in town. "You can ask him for that five dollars," Mrs. Littlejohn says.

"You reckon he'll give it to me?" Mrs. Armstid says.

Mrs. Littlejohn was washing dishes, washing them like a man, like they was made out of iron. "No," she says. "But asking him won't do no hurt. It might shame him. I don't reckon it will, but it might."

"If he wouldn't give it back, it ain't no use to ask," Mrs. Armstid says.   100

"Suit yourself," Mrs. Littlejohn says. "It's your money."

I could hear the dishes.

"Do you reckon he might give it back to me?" Mrs. Armstid says. "That Texas man said he would. He said I could get it from Mr. Snopes later."

"Then go and ask him for it," Mrs. Littlejohn says.

I could hear the dishes.   105

"He won't give it back to me," Mrs. Armstid says.

"All right," Mrs. Littlejohn says. "Don't ask him for it, then."

I could hear the dishes; Mrs. Armstid was helping. "You don't reckon he would, do you?" she says. Mrs. Littlejohn never said nothing. It sounded like she was throwing the dishes at one another. "Maybe I better go and talk to Henry about it," Mrs. Armstid says.

"I would," Mrs. Littlejohn says. I be dog if it didn't sound like she had two plates in her hands, beating them together. "Then Henry can buy another five-dollar horse with it. Maybe he'll buy one next time that will out and out kill him. If I thought that, I'd give you back the money, myself."

"I reckon I better talk to him first," Mrs. Armstid said. Then it sounded   110 like Mrs. Littlejohn taken up all the dishes and throwed them at the cook-stove and I come away.

That was this morning. I had been up to Bundren's and back, and I thought that things would have kind of settled down. So after breakfast, I went up to the store. And there was Flem, setting in the store-chair and whittling, like he might not have ever moved since he come to clerk for Jody Varner. I. O. was leaning in the door, in his shirt sleeves and with his hair parted too, same as Flem was before he turned the clerking job over to I. O. It's a funny thing about them Snopes: they all looks alike, yet there ain't ere a two of them that claims brothers. They're always just cousins, like Flem and Eck and Flem and I. O. Eck was there too, squatting against the wall, him and that boy, eating cheese and crackers outen a sack; they told me that Eck hadn't been home a-tall. And that Lon Quick hadn't got back to town, even. He followed his horse clean down to Samson's Bridge, with a wagon and a camp outfit. Eck finally caught one of hisn. It run into a blind lane at Free-man's and Eck and the boy taken and tied their rope across the end of the lane, about three foot high. The horse come to the end of the lane and whirled and run back without ever stopping. Eck says it never seen the rope a-tall. He says it looked just like one of these here Christmas pinwheels. "Didn't it try to run again?" I says.

"No," Eck says, eating a bite of cheese offen his knife blade. "Just kicked some."

"Kicked some?" I says.

"It broke its neck," Eck says.

115   Well, they was squatting there, about six of them, talking, talking at Flem; never nobody knowed yet if Flem had ere a interest in them horses or not. So finally I come right out and asked him. "Flem's done skun all of us so much," I says, "that we're proud of him. Come on, Flem," I says, "how much did you and that Texas man make offen them horses? You can tell us. Ain't nobody here but Eck that bought one of them; the others ain't got back to town yet, and Eck's your own cousin; he'll be proud to hear, too. How much did you-all make?"

They was all whittling, not looking at Flem, making like they was studying. But you could a heard a pin drop. And I. O. He had been rubbing his back up and down on the door, but he stopped now, watching Flem like a pointing dog. Flem finished cutting the sliver offen his stick. He spit across the porch, into the road. "'Twarn't none of my horses," he says.

I. O. cackled, like a hen, slapping his legs with both hands. "You boys might just as well quit trying to get ahead of Flem," he said.

Well, about that time I see Mrs. Armstid come outen Mrs. Littlejohn's gate, coming up the road. I never said nothing. I says, "Well, if a man can't take care of himself in a trade, he can't blame the man that trims him."

Flem never said nothing, trimming at the stick. He hadn't seen Mrs. Armstid. "Yes, sir," I says. "A fellow like Henry Armstid ain't got nobody but hisself to blame."

120   "Course he ain't," I. O. says. He ain't seen her, neither. "Henry Armstid's a born fool. Always is been. If Flem hadn't a got his money, somebody else would."

We looked at Flem. He never moved. Mrs. Armstid come on up the road.

"That's right," I says. "But, come to think of it, Henry never bought no horse." We looked at Flem; you could a heard a match drop. "That Texas man told her to get that five dollars back from Flem next day. I reckon Flem's done already taken that money to Mrs. Littlejohn's and give it to Mrs. Armstid."

We watched Flem. I. O. quit rubbing his back against the door again. After a while Flem raised his head and spit across the porch, into the dust. I. O. cackled, just like a hen. "Ain't he a beating fellow, now?" I. O. says.

Mrs. Armstid was getting closer, so I kept on talking, watching to see if Flem would look up and see her. But he never looked up. I went on talking about Tull, about how he was going to sue Flem, and Flem setting there, whittling his stick, not saying nothing else after he said they wasn't none of his horses.

125   Then I. O. happened to look around. He seen Mrs. Armstid. "Psssst!" he says. Flem looked up. "Here she comes!" I. O. says. "Go out the back. I'll tell her you done went in to town to-day."

But Flem never moved. He just set there, whittling, and we watched Mrs. Armstid come up onto the porch, in that ere faded sunbonnet and wrapper and them tennis shoes that made a kind of hissing noise on the porch. She come onto the porch and stopped, her hands rolled into her dress in front, not looking at nothing.

"He said Saturday," she says, "that he wouldn't sell Henry no horse. He said I could get the money from you."

Flem looked up. The knife never stopped. It went on trimming off a sliver same as if he was watching it. "He taken that money off with him when he left," Flem says.

Mrs. Armstid never looked at nothing. We never looked at her, neither, except that boy of Eck's. He had a half-et cracker in his hand, watching her, chewing.

"He said Henry hadn't bought no horse," Mrs. Armstid says. "He said   130 for me to get the money from you to-day."

"I reckon he forgot about it," Flem said. "He taken that money off with him Saturday." He whittled again. I. O. kept on rubbing his back, slow. He licked his lips. After a while the woman looked up the road, where it went on up the hill, toward the graveyard. She looked up that way for a while, with that boy of Eck's watching her and I. O. rubbing his back slow against the door. Then she turned back toward the steps.

"I reckon it's time to get dinner started," she says.

"How's Henry this morning, Mrs. Armstid?" Winterbottom says.

She looked at Winterbottom; she almost stopped. "He's resting, I thank you kindly," she says.

Flem got up, outen the chair, putting the knife away. He spit across the   135 porch. "Wait a minute, Mrs. Armstid," he says. She stopped again. She didn't look at him. Flem went on into the store, with I. O. done quit rubbing his back now, with his head craned after Flem, and Mrs. Armstid standing there with her hands rolled into her dress, not looking at nothing. A wagon come up the road and passed; it was Freeman, on the way to town. Then Flem come out again, with I. O. still watching him. Flem had one of these little striped sacks of Jody Varner's candy; I bet he still owes Jody that nickel, too. He put the sack into Mrs. Armstid's hand, like he would have put it into a hollow stump. He spit again across the porch. "A little sweetening for the chaps," he says.

"You're right kind," Mrs. Armstid says. She held the sack of candy in her hand, not looking at nothing. Eck's boy was watching the sack, the half-et cracker in his hand; he wasn't chewing now. He watched Mrs. Armstid roll the sack into her apron. "I reckon I better get on back and help with dinner," she says. She turned and went back across the porch. Flem set down in the chair again and opened his knife. He spit across the porch again, past Mrs. Armstid where she hadn't went down the steps yet. Then she went on, in that ere sunbonnet and wrapper all the same color, back down the road toward Mrs. Littlejohn's. You couldn't see her dress move, like a natural woman walking. She looked like a old snag still standing up and moving along on a high water. We watched her turn in at Mrs. Littlejohn's and go outen sight. Flem was whittling. I. O. begun to rub his back on the door. Then he begun to cackle, just like a durn hen.

"You boys might just as well quit trying," I. O. says. "You can't git ahead of Flem. You can't touch him. Ain't he a sight, now?"

I be dog if he ain't. If I had brung a herd of wild cattymounts into town and sold them to my neighbors and kinfolks, they would have lynched me. Yes, sir.

QUESTIONS

1. Characterize Flem Snopes and trace his history in the story. What is his principal motivation? What inferences may be drawn about his marriage? About his involvement in the auction? Is there any point in the story where Flem can be proved to be lying? Are any of his actions motivated by generosity? How is he regarded by his cousins? Why?
2. Who is the narrator of the story? Characterize him as a person and comment on his abilities as a story-teller, illustrating particularly by an analysis of some single paragraph (e.g., the opening one). What kind of story, as he tells it, is this—comic? tragic? pathetic? horrifying? What kind would it be if told by Mrs. Armstid? By Mr. Armstid? How does the narrator regard his characters? What is his attitude toward Flem? What are the chief sources of his humor?
3. Characterize the Texan. How is he different from Flem? What details of his characterization make him memorable?
4. Characterize Mrs. Armstid. What characteristics individuate her and make her more than just a "victim" of social and marital injustice? Is she a sympathetic character? What are her values and loyalties? How is she regarded by (a) her husband, (b) the Texan, (c) Flem, (d) Mrs. Littlejohn, (e) the narrator?
5. For a story of its length, this story has an unusual number of characters. How many are more than mere names? Identify each of the following, characterize each briefly, and comment on characteristics that make them memorable in any way: (a) Henry Armstid, (b) Mrs. Littlejohn, (c) Eck Snopes, (d) Eck's son, Ad, (e) I. O. Snopes, (f) Eula Varner, (g) "Uncle" Billy Varner, (h) the spotted horses. What is the irony of Vernon Tull's role in the story?
6. Who is the protagonist? Who are the antagonists? Who is victorious in their conflict? Does the story have a happy ending?

William Faulkner

Mule in the Yard

It was a gray day in late January, though not cold because of the fog. Old Het, just walked in from the poorhouse, ran down the hall toward the kitchen, shouting in a strong, bright, happy voice. She was about seventy probably, though by her own counting, calculated from the ages of various housewives in the town from brides to grandmothers whom she claimed to have nursed in infancy, she would have to be around a hundred and at least triplets. Tall, lean, fog-beaded, in tennis shoes and a long rat-colored cloak trimmed with what forty or fifty years ago had been fur, a modish though not new purple toque set upon her headrag and carrying (time was when she made her weekly rounds from kitchen to kitchen carrying a brocaded carpet-bag though since the advent of the ten-cent stores the carpetbag became an endless succession of the convenient paper receptacles with which they supply their customers for a few cents) the shopping-bag, she ran into the kitchen and shouted with strong and childlike pleasure: "Miss Mannie! Mule in de yard!"

Mrs. Hait, stooping to the stove, in the act of drawing from it a scuttle of live ashes, jerked upright; clutching the scuttle, she glared at old Het, then she too spoke at once, strong too, immediate. "Them sons of bitches," she said. She left the kitchen, not running exactly, yet with a kind of outraged celerity, carrying the scuttle—a compact woman of forty-odd, with an air of indomitable yet relieved bereavement, as though that which had relicted her had been a woman and a not particularly valuable one at that. She wore a calico wrapper and a sweater coat, and a man's felt hat which they in the town knew had belonged to her ten years' dead husband. But the man's shoes had not belonged to him. They were high shoes which buttoned, with toes like small tulip bulbs, and in the town they knew that she had bought them new for herself. She and old Het ran down the kitchen steps and into the fog. That's why it was not cold: as though there lay supine and prisoned between earth and mist the long winter night's suspiration of the sleeping town in dark, close rooms—the slumber and the rousing; the stale waking thermo-static, by reheating heat-engendered: it lay like a scum of cold grease upon the steps and the wooden entrance to the basement and upon the narrow plank walk which led to a shed building in the corner of the yard: upon these planks, running and still carrying the scuttle of live ashes, Mrs. Hait skated viciously.

"Watch out!" old Het, footed securely by her rubber soles, cried happily. "Dey in de front!" Mrs. Hait did not fall. She did not even pause. She

MULE IN THE YARD   First published in 1934. A considerably altered version of the story is incorporated in Chapter 16 of *The Town* (1957). The action of the story occurs many years after that of "Spotted Horses." The town is Jefferson, the county seat of Faulkner's fictitious Yoknapatawpha County.

took in the immediate scene with one cold glare and was running again when there appeared at the corner of the house and apparently having been born before their eyes of the fog itself, a mule. It looked taller than a giraffe. Longheaded, with a flying halter about its scissorlike ears, it rushed down upon them with violent and apparitionlike suddenness.

"Dar hit!" old Het cried, waving the shopping-bag. "Hoo!" Mrs. Hait whirled. Again she skidded savagely on the greasy planks as she and the mule rushed parallel with one another toward the shed building, from whose open doorway there now projected the static and astonished face of a cow. To the cow the fog-born mule doubtless looked taller and more incredibly sudden than a giraffe even, and apparently bent upon charging right through the shed as though it were made of straw or were purely and simply mirage. The cow's head likewise had a quality transient and abrupt and unmundane. It vanished, sucked into invisibility like a match flame, though the mind knew and the reason insisted that she had withdrawn into the shed, from which, as proof's burden, there came an indescribable sound of shock and alarm by shed and beast engendered, analogous to a single note from a profoundly struck lyre or harp. Toward this sound Mrs. Hait sprang, immediately, as if by pure reflex, as though in invulnerable compact of female with female against a world of mule and man. She and the mule converged upon the shed at top speed, the heavy scuttle poised lightly in her hand to hurl. Of course it did not take this long, and likewise it was the mule which refused the gambit. Old Het was still shouting "Dar hit! Dar hit!" when it swerved and rushed at her where she stood tall as a stove pipe, holding the shopping-bag which she swung at the beast as it rushed past her and vanished beyond the other corner of the house as though sucked back into the fog which had produced it, profound and instantaneous and without any sound.

5   With that unhasteful celerity Mrs. Hait turned and set the scuttle down on the brick coping of the cellar entrance and she and old Het turned the corner of the house in time to see the now wraithlike mule at the moment when its course converged with that of a choleric-looking rooster and eight Rhode Island Red hens emerging from beneath the house. Then for an instant its progress assumed the appearance and trappings of an apotheosis: hell-born and hell-returning, in the act of dissolving completely into the fog, it seemed to rise vanishing into a sunless and dimensionless medium borne upon and enclosed by small winged goblins.

"Dey's mo in de front!" old Het cried.

"Them sons of bitches," Mrs. Hait said, again in that grim, prescient voice without rancor or heat. It was not the mules to which she referred; it was not even the owner of them. It was her whole town-dwelling history as dated from that April dawn ten years ago when what was left of Hait had been gathered from the mangled remains of five mules and several feet of new Manila rope on a blind curve of the railroad just out of town; the geographical hap of her very home; the very components of her bereavement— the mules, the defunct husband, and the owner of them. His name was

Snopes; in the town they knew about him too—how he bought his stock at the Memphis market and brought it to Jefferson and sold it to farmers and widows and orphans black and white, for whatever he could contrive—down to a certain figure; and about how (usually in the dead season of winter) teams and even small droves of his stock would escape from the fenced pasture where he kept them and, tied one to another with sometimes quite new hemp rope (and which item Snopes included in the subsequent claim), would be annihilated by freight trains on the same blind curve which was to be the scene of Hait's exit from this world; once a town wag sent him through the mail a printed train schedule for the division. A squat, pasty man perennially tieless and with a strained, harried expression, at stated intervals he passed athwart the peaceful and somnolent life of the town in dust and uproar, his advent heralded by shouts and cries, his passing marked by a yellow cloud filled with tossing jug-shaped heads and clattering hooves and the same forlorn and earnest cries of the drovers; and last of all and well back out of the dust, Snopes himself moving at a harried and panting trot, since it was said in the town that he was deathly afraid of the very beasts in which he cleverly dealt.

The path which he must follow from the railroad station to his pasture crossed the edge of town near Hait's home; Hait and Mrs. Hait had not been in the house a week before they waked one morning to find it surrounded by galloping mules and the air filled with the shouts and cries of the drovers. But it was not until that April dawn some years later, when those who reached the scene first found what might be termed foreign matter among the mangled mules and the savage fragments of new rope, that the town suspected that Hait stood in any closer relationship to Snopes and the mules than that of helping at periodical intervals to drive them out of his front yard. After that they believed that they knew; in a three days' recess of interest, surprise, and curiosity they watched to see if Snopes would try to collect on Hait also.

But they learned only that the adjuster appeared and called upon Mrs. Hait and that a few days later she cashed a check for eight thousand five hundred dollars, since this was back in the old halcyon days when even the companies considered their southern branches and divisions the legitimate prey of all who dwelt beside them. She took the cash: she stood in her sweater coat and the hat which Hait had been wearing on the fatal morning a week ago and listened in cold, grim silence while the teller counted the money and the president and the cashier tried to explain to her the virtues of a bond, then of a savings account, then of a checking account, and departed with the money in a salt sack under her apron; after a time she painted her house: that serviceable and time-defying color which the railroad station was painted, as though out of sentiment or (as some said) gratitude.

The adjuster also summoned Snopes into conference, from which he   10
emerged not only more harried-looking than ever, but with his face stamped with a bewildered dismay which it was to wear from then on, and that was

the last time his pasture fence was ever to give inexplicably away at dead of night upon mules coupled in threes and fours by adequate rope even though not always new. And then it seemed as though the mules themselves knew this, as if, even while haltered at the Memphis block at his bid, they sensed it somehow as they sensed that he was afraid of them. Now, three or four times a year and as though by fiendish concord and as soon as they were freed of the box car, the entire uproar—the dust cloud filled with shouts earnest, harried, and dismayed, with plunging demoniac shapes—would become translated in a single burst of perverse and uncontrollable violence, without any intervening contact with time, space, or earth, across the peaceful and astonished town and into Mrs. Hait's yard, where, in a certain hapless despair which abrogated for the moment even physical fear, Snopes ducked and dodged among the thundering shapes about the house (for whose very impervious paint the town believed that he felt he had paid and whose inmate lived within it a life of idle and queenlike ease on money which he considered at least partly his own) while gradually that section and neighborhood gathered to look on from behind adjacent window curtains and porches screened and not, and from the sidewalks and even from halted wagons and cars in the street—housewives in the wrappers and boudoir caps of morning, children on the way to school, casual Negroes and casual whites in static and entertained repose.

They were all there when, followed by old Het and carrying the stub of a worn-out broom, Mrs. Hait ran around the next corner and onto the handkerchief-sized plot of earth which she called her front yard. It was small; any creature with a running stride of three feet could have spanned it in two paces, yet at the moment, due perhaps to the myopic and distortive quality of the fog, it seemed to be as incredibly full of mad life as a drop of water beneath the microscope. Yet again she did not falter. With the broom clutched in her hand and apparently with a kind of sublime faith in her own invulnerability, she rushed on after the haltered mule which was still in that arrested and wraithlike process of vanishing furiously into the fog, its wake indicated by the tossing and dispersing shapes of the nine chickens like so many jagged scraps of paper in the dying air blast of an automobile, and the madly dodging figure of a man. The man was Snopes; beaded too with moisture, his wild face gaped with hoarse shouting and the two heavy lines of shaven beard descending from the corners of it as though in alluvial retrospect of years of tobacco, he screamed at her: "Fore God, Miz Hait! I done everything I could!" She didn't even look at him.

"Ketch that big un with the bridle on," she said in her cold, panting voice. "Git that big un outen here."

"Sho!" Snopes shrieked. "Jest let um take their time. Jest don't git um excited now."

"Watch out!" old Het shouted. "He headin fer de back again!"

"Git the rope," Mrs. Hait said, running again. Snopes glared back at old Het.

"Fore God, where is ere rope?" he shouted.

"In de cellar fo God!" old Het shouted, also without pausing. "Go roun de udder way en head um." Again she and Mrs. Hait turned the corner in time to see again the still-vanishing mule with the halter once more in the act of floating lightly onward on its cloud of chickens with which, they being able to pass under the house and so on the chord of a circle while it had to go around on the arc, it had once more coincided. When they turned the next corner they were in the back yard again.

"Fo God!" old Het cried. "He fixin' to misuse de cow!" For they had gained on the mule now, since it had stopped. In fact, they came around the corner on a tableau. The cow now stood in the center of the yard. She and the mule faced one another a few feet apart. Motionless, with lowered heads and braced forelegs, they looked like two book ends from two distinct pairs of a general pattern which some one of amateurly bucolic leanings might have purchased, and which some child had salvaged, brought into idle juxtaposition and then forgotten; and, his head and shoulders projecting above the back-flung slant of the cellar entrance where the scuttle still sat, Snopes standing as though buried to the armpits for a Spanish-Indian-American suttee. Only again it did not take this long. It was less than tableau; it was one of those things which later even memory cannot quite affirm. Now and in turn, man and cow and mule vanished beyond the next corner, Snopes now in the lead, carrying the rope, the cow next with her tail rigid and raked slightly like the stern staff of a boat. Mrs. Hait and old Het ran on, passing the open cellar gaping upon its accumulation of human necessities and widowed womanyears—boxes of kindling wood, old papers and magazines, the broken and outworn furniture and utensils which no woman ever throws away; a pile of coal and another of pitch pine for priming fires—and ran on and turned the next corner to see man and cow and mule all vanishing now in the wild cloud of ubiquitous chickens which had once more crossed beneath the house and emerged. They ran on, Mrs. Hait in grim and unflagging silence, old Het with the eager and happy amazement of a child. But when they gained the front again they saw only Snopes. He lay flat on his stomach, his head and shoulders upreared by his outstretched arms, his coat tail swept forward by its own arrested momentum about his head so that from beneath it his slack-jawed face mused in wild repose like that of a burlesqued nun.

"Whar'd dey go?" old Het shouted at him. He didn't answer.

"Dey tightenin' on de curves!" she cried. "Dey already in de back again!" That's where they were. The cow made a feint at running into her shed, but deciding perhaps that her speed was too great, she whirled in a final desperation of despair-like valor. But they did not see this, nor see the mule, swerving to pass her, crash and blunder for an instant at the open cellar door before going on. When they arrived, the mule was gone. The scuttle was gone too, but they did not notice it; they saw only the cow standing in the center of the yard as before, panting, rigid, with braced forelegs and lowered head facing nothing, as if the child had returned and removed one of the book ends for some newer purpose or game. They ran on. Mrs. Hait ran heavily now, her mouth too open, her face putty-colored and one hand pressed to her side. So slow was their progress that the mule in its third circuit of the house overtook them from behind and soared past with un-diminished speed, with brief demon thunder and a keen ammonia-sweet reek of sweat sudden and sharp as a jeering cry, and was gone. Yet they ran doggedly on around the next corner in time to see it succeed at last in vanish-ing into the fog; they heard its hoofs, brief, staccato, and derisive, on the paved street, dying away.

"Well," old Het said, stopping. She panted, happily. "Gentlemen, hush! Ain't we had—" Then she became stone still; slowly her head turned, high-nosed, her nostrils pulsing; perhaps for the instant she saw the open cellar door as they had last passed it, with no scuttle beside it. "Fo God I smells smoke!" she said. "Chile, run, git yo money."

That was still early, not yet ten o'clock. By noon the house had burned to the ground. There was a farmers' supply store where Snopes could be usu-ally found; more than one had made a point of finding him there by that time. They told him about how when the fire engine and the crowd reached the scene, Mrs. Hait, followed by old Het carrying her shopping-bag in one hand and a framed portrait of Mr. Hait in the other, emerged with an um-brella and wearing a new, dun-colored, mail-order coat, in one pocket of which lay a fruit jar filled with smoothly rolled banknotes and in the other a heavy, nickel-plated pistol, and crossed the street to the house opposite, where with old Het beside her in another rocker, she had been sitting ever since on the veranda, grim, inscrutable, the two of them rocking steadily, while hoarse and tireless men hurled her dishes and furniture and bedding up and down the street.

"What are you telling me for?" Snopes said. "Hit warn't me that set that ere scuttle of live fire where the first thing that passed would knock hit into the cellar."

"It was you that opened the cellar door, though."

25   "Sho. And for what? To git that rope, her own rope, where she told me to get it."

"To catch your mule with, that was trespassing on her property. You can't get out of it this time, I. O. There ain't a jury in the county that won't find for her."

"Yes. I reckon not. And just because she is a woman. That's why. Be-cause she is a durn woman. All right. Let her go to her durn jury with hit. I can talk too; I reckon hit's a few things I could tell a jury myself about—" He ceased. They were watching him.

"What? Tell a jury about what?"

"Nothing. Because hit ain't going to no jury. A jury between her and me? Me and Mannie Hait? You boys don't know her if you think she's going to make trouble over a pure acci-dent couldn't nobody help. Why, there ain't a fairer, finer woman in the county than Miz Mannie Hait. I just wisht I had a opportunity to tell her so." The opportunity came at once. Old Het was behind her, carrying the shopping-bag. Mrs. Hait looked once, quietly, about at the faces, making no response to the murmur of curious salutation, then not again. She didn't look at Snopes long either, nor talk to him long.

"I come to buy that mule," she said.   30

"What mule?" They looked at one another. "You'd like to own that mule?" She looked at him. "Hit'll cost you a hundred and fifty, Miz Mannie."

"You mean dollars?"

"I don't mean dimes nor nickels neither, Miz Mannie."

"Dollars," she said. "That's more than mules was in Hait's time."

"Lots of things is different since Hait's time. Including you and me."   35

"I reckon so," she said. Then she went away. She turned without a word, old Het following.

"Maybe one of them others you looked at this morning would suit you," Snopes said. She didn't answer. Then they were gone.

"I don't know as I would have said that last to her," one said.

"What for?" Snopes said. "If she was aiming to law something outen me about that fire, you reckon she would have come and offered to pay me money for hit?" That was about one o'clock. About four o'clock he was shouldering his way through a throng of Negroes before a cheap grocery store when one called his name. It was old Het, the now bulging shopping-bag on her arm, eating bananas from a paper sack.

"Fo God I wuz jest dis minute huntin fer you," she said. She handed the   40 banana to a woman beside her and delved and fumbled in the shopping-bag and extended a greenback. "Miz Mannie gimme dis to give you; I wuz just on de way to de sto whar you stay at. Here." He took the bill.

"What's this? From Miz Hait?"

"Fer de mule." The bill was for ten dollars. "You don't need to gimme no receipt. I kin be de witness I give hit to you."

"Ten dollars? For that mule? I told her a hundred and fifty dollars."

"You'll have to fix dat up wid her yo'self. She just gimme dis to give ter you when she sot out to fetch de mule."

"Set out to fetch— She went out there herself and taken my mule   45 outen my pasture?"

"Lawd, chile," old Het said, "Miz Mannie ain't skeered of no mule. Ain't you done foun dat out?"

And then it became late, what with the yet short winter days; when she came in sight of the two gaunt chimneys against the sunset, evening was already finding itself. But she could smell the ham cooking before she came in sight of the cow shed even, though she could not see it until she came around in front where the fire burned beneath an iron skillet set on bricks and where nearby Mrs. Hait was milking the cow. "Well," old Het said, "you is settled down, ain't you?" She looked into the shed, neated and raked and swept even, and floored now with fresh hay. A clean new lantern burned on a box, beside it a pallet bed was spread neatly on the straw and turned neatly back for the night. "Why, you is fixed up," she said with pleased astonishment. Within the door was a kitchen chair. She drew it out and sat down beside the skillet and laid the bulging shopping-bag beside her.

"I'll tend dis meat whilst you milks. I'd offer to strip dat cow fer you ef I wuzn't so wo out wid all dis excitement we been had." She looked around her. "I don't believe I sees yo new mule, dough." Mrs. Hait grunted, her head against the cow's flank. After a moment she said,

"Did you give him that money?"

50   "I give um ter him. He ack surprise at first, lak maybe he think you didn't aim to trade dat quick. I tole him to settle de details wid you later. He taken de money, dough. So I reckin dat's offen his mine en yo'n bofe." Again Mrs. Hait grunted. Old Het turned the ham in the skillet. Beside it the coffee pot bubbled and steamed. "Cawfee smell good too," she said. "I ain't had no appetite in years now. A bird couldn't live on de vittles I eats. But jest lemme git a whiff er cawfee en seem lak hit always whets me a little. Now, ef you jest had nudder little piece o dis ham, now— Fo God, you got company aready." But Mrs. Hait did not even look up until she had finished. Then she turned without rising from the box on which she sat.

"I reckon you and me better have a little talk," Snopes said. "I reckon I got something that belongs to you and I hear you got something that belongs to me." He looked about, quickly, ceaselessly, while old Het watched him. He turned to her. "You go away, aunty. I don't reckon you want to set here and listen to us."

"Lawd, honey," old Het said. "Don't you mind me. I done already had so much troubles myself dat I kin set en listen to udder folks' widout hit worryin me a-tall. You gawn talk whut you came ter talk; I jest set here en tend de ham." Snopes looked at Mrs. Hait.

"Ain't you going to make her go away?" he said.

"What for?" Mrs. Hait said. "I reckon she ain't the first critter that ever come on this yard when hit wanted and went or stayed when hit liked." Snopes made a gesture, brief, fretted, restrained.

55   "Well," he said. "All right. So you taken the mule."

"I paid you for it. She give you the money."

"Ten dollars. For a hundred-and-fifty-dollar mule. Ten dollars."

"I don't know anything about hundred-and-fifty-dollar mules. All I know is what the railroad paid." Now Snopes looked at her for a full moment.

"What do you mean?"

60   "Them sixty dollars a head the railroad used to pay for mules back when you and Hait— —"

"Hush," Snopes said; he looked about again, quick, ceaseless. "All right. Even call it sixty dollars. But you just sent me ten."

"Yes. I sent you the difference." He looked at her, perfectly still. "Between that mule and what you owed Hait."

"What I owed— —"

"For getting them five mules onto the tr— —"

"Hush!" he cried. "Hush!" Her voice went on, cold, grim, level.   65

"For helping you. You paid him fifty dollars each time, and the railroad paid you sixty dollars a head for the mules. Ain't that right?" He watched her. "That last time you never paid him. So I taken that mule instead. And I sent you the ten dollars difference."

"Yes," he said in a tone of quiet, swift, profound bemusement; then he cried: "But look! Here's where I got you. Hit was our agreement that I wouldn't never owe him nothing until after the mules was— —"

"I reckon you better hush yourself," Mrs. Hait said.

"—until hit was over. And this time, when over had come, I never owed nobody no money because the man hit would have been owed to wasn't nobody," he cried triumphantly. "You see?" Sitting on the box, motionless, downlooking, Mrs. Hait seemed to muse. "So you just take your ten dollars back and tell me where my mule is and we'll just go back good friends to where we started at. Fore God, I'm as sorry as ere a living man about that fire— —"

"Fo God!" old Het said, "hit was a blaze, wuzn't it?"   70

"—but likely with all that ere railroad money you still got, you just been wanting a chance to build new, all along. So here. Take hit." He put the money into her hand. "Where's my mule?" But Mrs. Hait didn't move at once.

"You want to give it back to me?" she said.

"Sho. We been friends all the time; now we'll just go back to where we left off being. I don't hold no hard feelings and don't you hold none. Where you got the mule hid?"

"Up at the end of that ravine ditch behind Spilmer's," she said.

"Sho. I know. A good, sheltered place, since you ain't got nere barn.   75
Only if you'd a just left hit in the pasture, hit would a saved us both trouble. But hit ain't no hard feelings though. And so I'll bid you goodnight. You're all fixed up, I see. I reckon you could save some more money by not building no house a-tall."

"I reckon I could," Mrs. Hait said. But he was gone.

"Whut did you leave de mule dar fer?" old Het said.

"I reckon that's far enough," Mrs. Hait said.

"Fer enough?" But Mrs. Hait came and looked into the skillet, and old Het said, "Wuz hit me er you dat mentioned something erbout er nudder piece o dis ham?" So they were both eating when in the not-quite-yet accomplished twilight Snopes returned. He came up quietly and stood, holding his hands to the blaze as if he were quite cold. He did not look at any one now.

"I reckon I'll take that ere ten dollars," he said.   80

"What ten dollars?" Mrs. Hait said. He seemed to muse upon the fire. Mrs. Hait and old Het chewed quietly, old Het alone watching him.

"You ain't going to give hit back to me?" he said.

"You was the one that said to let's go back to where we started," Mrs. Hait said.

"Fo God you wuz, en dat's de fack," old Het said. Snopes mused upon the fire; he spoke in a tone of musing and amazed despair:

85   "I go to the worry and the risk and the agoment for years and years and I get sixty dollars. And you, one time, without no trouble and no risk, without even knowing you are going to git it, git eighty-five hundred dollars. I never begrudged hit to you; can't nere a man say I did, even if hit did seem a little strange that you should git it all when he wasn't working for you and you never even knowed where he was at and what doing; that all you done to git it was to be married to him. And now, after all these ten years of not begrudging you hit, you taken the best mule I had and you ain't even going to pay me ten dollars for hit. Hit ain't right. Hit ain't justice."

"You got de mule back, en you ain't satisfried yit," old Het said. "Whut does you want?" Now Snopes looked at Mrs. Hait.

"For the last time I ask hit," he said. "Will you or won't you give hit back?"

"Give what back?" Mrs. Hait said. Snopes turned. He stumbled over something—it was old Het's shopping-bag—and recovered and went on. They could see him in silhouette, as though framed by the two blackened chimneys against the dying west; they saw him fling up both clenched hands in a gesture almost Gallic, of resignation and impotent despair. Then he was gone. Old Het was watching Mrs. Hait.

"Honey," she said. "Whut did you do wid de mule?" Mrs. Hait leaned forward to the fire. On her plate lay a stale biscuit. She lifted the skillet and poured over the biscuit the grease in which the ham had cooked.

90   "I shot it," she said.

"You which?" old Het said. Mrs. Hait began to eat the biscuit. "Well," old Het said, happily, "de mule burnt de house en you shot de mule. Dat's whut I calls justice." It was getting dark fast now, and before her was still the three-mile walk to the poorhouse. But the dark would last a long time in January, and the poorhouse too would not move at once. She sighed with weary and happy relaxation. "Gentlemen, hush! Ain't we had a day!"

QUESTIONS

1. This story has one character in common with "Spotted Horses." Is he a logical projection of the character as seen in that story? How is he like and unlike his cousin Flem? How does he make his living?
2. Characterize Mrs. Hait. Explain in detail her final transactions with I. O.
3. Characterize Old Het. What race is she?

4. From what point of view is this story told? Compare and contrast its narrative style with that of "Spotted Horses." Give specific examples.
5. What are the chief sources of comedy in this story? Is there any difference in the flavor of its humor?
6. Who is the protagonist? Who is the antagonist? Which is successful in their conflict?
7. Like "Spotted Horses," this is a comic story involving an animal chase. Which story is more powerful, broader in scope, deeper in insight and effect? Justify your answer.

Stories for
Further Reading

Margaret Atwood

When It Happens

Mrs. Burridge is putting up green tomato pickles. There are twelve quarts in each lot with a bit left over, and that is the end of the jars. At the store they tell her there's a strike on at the factory where they get made. She doesn't know anything about that but you can't buy them anywhere, and even before this they were double what they were last year; she considers herself lucky she had those in the cellar. She has a lot of green tomatoes because she heard on the weather last night there was going to be a killer frost, so she put on her parka and her work gloves and took the lantern out to the garden in the pitch dark and picked off all the ones she could see, over three bushels. She can lift the full baskets herself but she asked Frank to carry them in for her; he grumbles, but he likes it when she asks. In the morning the news said the growers had been hit and that would shoot the price up, not that the growers would get any of it themselves, everyone knows it's the stores that make the money.

She feels richer than she did yesterday, but on the other hand there isn't that much you can do with green tomatoes. The pickles hardly made a dint in them, and Frank has said, as he does every year, that they will never eat twenty-four quarts of green tomato pickle with just the two of them and the children gone. Except when they come to visit and eat me out of house and home, Mrs. Burridge adds silently. The truth is she has always made two batches and the children never liked it anyway, it was Frank ate them all and she knows perfectly well he'll do it again, without even noticing. He likes it on bread and cheese when he's watching the hockey games, during every commercial he goes out to the kitchen and makes himself another slice, even if he's just had a big meal, leaving a trail of crumbs and bits of pickle from the counter across the floor and over the front room rug to his big chair. It used to annoy Mrs. Burridge, especially the crumbs, but now she watches him with a kind of sadness; she once thought their life together would go on forever but she has come to realize this is not the case.

She doesn't even feel like teasing him about his spare tire any more, though she does it all the same because he would miss it if she stopped. "There you go," she says, in the angular, prodding, metallic voice she cannot change because everyone expects it from her, if she spoke any other way they would think she was ill, "you keep on munching away like that and it'll be easy for me to get you out of bed in the mornings, I'll just give

WHEN IT HAPPENS   Published in *Dancing Girls and Other Stories* in 1977. Margaret Atwood was born in 1939 in Ottawa, and grew up there, in Sault Ste. Marie, and in Toronto, all in Ontario. She was educated at the University of Toronto, Radcliffe, and Harvard. She has published several novels, collections of short stories, and volumes of poetry.

you a push and you'll roll all the way down the stairs like a barrel." And he answers in his methodical voice, pretending to be lazy even though he isn't, "You need a little fun in life," as though his pickles and cheese are slightly disreputable, almost like an orgy. Every year he tells her she's made too much but there would be a fuss all right if he went down to the cellar one day and there wasn't any left.

Mrs. Burridge has made her own pickles since 1952, which was the first year she had the garden. She remembers it especially because her daughter Sarah was on the way and she had trouble bending down to do the weeding. When she herself was growing up everyone did their own pickles, and their own canning and preserving too. But after the war most women gave it up, there was more money then and it was easier to buy things at the store. Mrs. Burridge never gave it up, though most of her friends thought she was wasting her time, and now she is glad she didn't, it kept her in practice while the others were having to learn all over again. Though with the sugar going up the way it is, she can't understand how long anyone is going to be able to afford even the homemade things.

5   On paper Frank is making more money than he ever has; yet they seem to have less to spend. They could always sell the farm, she supposes, to people from the city who would use it as a weekend place; they could get what seems like a very high price, several of the farms south of them have gone that way. But Mrs. Burridge does not have much faith in money; also it is a waste of the land, and this is her home, she has it arranged the way she wants it.

When the second batch is on and simmering she goes to the back door, opens it, and stands with her arms folded across her stomach, looking out. She catches herself doing this four or five times a day now and she doesn't quite know why. There isn't much to see, just the barn and the back field with the row of dead elms Frank keeps saying he's going to cut down, and the top of Clarke's place sticking over the hill. She isn't sure what she is looking for but she has the odd idea she may see something burning, smoke coming up from the horizon, a column of it or perhaps more than one column, off to the south. This is such a peculiar thought for her to have that she hasn't told it to anyone else. Yesterday Frank saw her standing at the back door and asked her about it at dinner; anything he wants to talk to her about he saves up till dinner, even if he thinks about it in the morning. He wondered why she was at the back door, doing nothing at all for over ten minutes, and Mrs. Burridge told him a lie, which made her very uneasy. She said she heard a strange dog barking, which wasn't a good story because their own dogs were right there and they didn't notice a thing. But Frank let it pass; perhaps he thinks she is getting funny in her old age and doesn't want to call attention to it, which would be like him. He'll track mud all over her nice shiny kitchen floor but he'd hate to hurt anyone's feelings. Mrs. Burridge decides, a little wistfully, that despite his pig-headedness he is a kind and likable man, and for her this is like renouncing a cherished and unquestionable belief, such as the flatness of the earth. He has made her angry so many times.

When the pickles are cool she labels them as she always does with the name and the date and carries them down the cellar stairs. The cellar is the old kind, with stone walls and a dirt floor. Mrs. Burridge likes to have everything neat—she still irons her sheets—so she had Frank build her some shelves right after they were married. The pickles go on one side, jams and jellies on the other, and the quarts of preserves along the bottom. It used to make her feel safe to have all that food in the cellar; she would think to herself, well, if there's a snowstorm or anything and we're cut off, it won't be so bad. It doesn't make her feel safe any more. Instead she thinks that if she has to leave suddenly she won't be able to take any of the jars with her, they'd be too heavy to carry.

She comes back up the stairs after the last trip. It's not as easy as it used to be, her knee still bothers her as it has ever since she fell six years ago, she tripped on the second-last step. She's asked Frank a million times to fix the stairs but he hasn't done it, that's what she means by pig-headed. If she asks him more than twice to do something he calls it nagging, and maybe it is, but who's going to do it if he won't? The cold vacant hole at the back of this question is too much for her.

She has to stop herself from going to the back door again. Instead she goes to the back window and looks out, she can see almost the same things anyway. Frank is going towards the barn, carrying something, it looks like a wrench. The way he walks, slower than he used to, bent forward a little— from the back he's like an old man, how many years has he been walking that way?—makes her think, *He can't protect me.* She doesn't think this on purpose, it simply occurs to her, and it isn't only him, it's all of them, they've lost the power, you can tell by the way they walk. They are all waiting, just as Mrs. Burridge is, for whatever it is to happen. Whether they realize it or not. Lately when she's gone to the Dominion Store in town she has seen a look on the faces of the women there—she knows most of them, she wouldn't be mistaken—an anxious, closed look, as if they are frightened of something but won't talk about it. They're wondering what they will do, perhaps they think there's nothing they can do. This air of helplessness exasperates Mrs. Burridge, who has always been practical.

For weeks she has wanted to go to Frank and ask him to teach her how   10
to use the gun. In fact he has two guns, a shotgun and a twenty-two rifle; he used to like going after a few ducks in the fall, and of course there are the groundhogs, they have to be shot because of the holes they make in the fields Frank drives over on the tractor five or six times a year. A lot of men get injured by overturning tractors. But she can't ask him because she can't explain to him why she needs to know, and if she doesn't explain he will only tease. "Anyone can shoot a gun," he'll say, "all you have to do is pull the trigger . . . oh, you mean you want to hit something, well now, that's different, who you planning to kill?" Perhaps he won't say that; perhaps

this is only the way he talked twenty years ago, before she stopped taking an interest in things outside the house. But Mrs. Burridge will never know because she will never ask. She doesn't have the heart to say to him, *Maybe you'll be dead. Maybe you'll go off somewhere when it happens, maybe there will be a war.* She can remember the last war.

Nothing has changed outside the window, so she turns away and sits down at the kitchen table to make out her shopping list. Tomorrow is their day for going into town. She tries to plan the day so she can sit down at intervals; otherwise her feet start swelling up. That began with Sarah and got worse with the other two children and it's never really gone away. All her life, ever since she got married, she has made lists of things that have to be bought, sewed, planted, cooked, stored; she already has her list made for next Christmas, all the names and the gift she will buy for each, and the list of what she needs for Christmas dinner. But she can't seem to get interested in it, it's too far away. She can't believe in a distant future that is orderly like the past, she no longer seems to have the energy; it's as if she is saving it up for when she will have to use it.

She is even having trouble with the shopping list. Instead of concentrating on the paper—she writes on the backs of the used-up days off the page-a-day calendar Frank gives her every New Year's—she is gazing around the kitchen, looking at all the things she will have to leave behind when she goes. That will be the hardest part. Her mother's china, her silver, even though it is an old-fashioned pattern and the silver is wearing off, the egg timer in the shape of a chicken Sarah gave her when she was twelve, the ceramic salt-and-pepper shakers, green horses with perforated heads, that one of the other children brought back from the Ex. She thinks of walking up the stairs, the sheets folded in the chest, the towels stacked neatly on the shelves, the beds made, the quilt that was her grandmother's, it makes her want to cry. On her bureau, the wedding picture, herself in a shiny satin gown (the satin was a mistake, it emphasized her hips), Frank in the suit he has not worn since except to funerals, his hair cut too short on the sides and a surprising tuft at the top, like a woodpecker's. The children when they were babies. She thinks of her girls now and hopes they will not have babies; it is no longer the right time for it.

Mrs. Burridge wishes someone would be more precise, so she could make better plans. Everyone knows something is going to happen, you can tell by reading the newspapers and watching the television, but nobody is sure what it will be, nobody can be exact. She has her own ideas about it though. At first it will simply become quieter. She will have an odd feeling that something is wrong but it will be a few days before she is able to pin it down. Then she will notice that the planes are no longer flying over on their way to the Malton Airport, and that the noise from the highway two miles away, which is quite distinct when the leaves are off the trees, has almost disappeared. The television will be non-committal about it; in fact, the television, which right now is filled with bad news, of strikes, shortages,

famines, layoffs and price increases, will become sweet-tempered and pla-
cating, and long intervals of classical music will appear on the radio. About
this time Mrs. Burridge will realize that the news is being censored as it
was during the war.

Mrs. Burridge is not positive about what will happen next; that is, she
knows what will happen but she is not positive about the order. She expects it will be the gas and oil: the oil delivery man will simply not turn up
at his usual time, and one morning the corner filling station will be closed.
Just that, no explanations, because of course they—she does not know
who "they" are, but she has always believed in their existence—they do
not want people to panic. They are trying to keep things looking normal,
possibly they have already started on this program and that is in fact why
things still do look normal. Luckily she and Frank have the diesel fuel tank
in the shed, it is three-quarters full, and they don't use the filling station
anyway, they have their own gas pump. She has Frank bring in the old
wood stove, the one they stored under the barn when they had the furnace
and the electricity put in, and for once she blesses Frank's habit of putting
things off. She was after him for years to take that stove to the dump. He
cuts down the dead elms, finally, and they burn them in the stove.

The telephone wires are blown down in a storm and no one comes to   15
fix them; or this is what Mrs. Burridge deduces. At any rate, the phone
goes dead. Mrs. Burridge doesn't particularly mind, she never liked using
the phone much anyway, but it does make her feel cut off.

About now men begin to appear on the back road, the gravel road
that goes past the gate, walking usually by themselves, sometimes in pairs.
They seem to be heading north. Most of them are young, in their twenties, Mrs. Burridge would guess. They are not dressed like the men around
here. It's been so long since she has seen anyone *walking* along this road
that she becomes alarmed. She begins leaving the dogs off their chains, she
has kept them chained at night ever since one of them bit a Jehovah's Witness early one Sunday morning. Mrs. Burridge doesn't hold with the Witnesses—she is United—but she respects their perseverance, at least they
have the courage of their convictions which is more than you can say for
some members of her own church, and she always buys a *Watchtower.*
Maybe they have been right all along.

It is about this time too that she takes one of the guns, she thinks it will
be the shotgun as she will have a better chance of hitting something, and
hides it, along with the shells, under a piece of roofing behind the barn. She
does not tell Frank; he will have the twenty-two. She has already picked
out the spot.

They do not want to waste the little gasoline they still have left in the
pump so they do not make unnecessary trips. They begin to eat the chickens, which Mrs. Burridge does not look forward to. She hates cleaning and
plucking them, and the angriest she ever got at Frank was the time he and
Henry Clarke decided to go into turkey farming. They did it too, despite

all she had to say against it, and she had to cope with the turkeys escaping and scratching in the garden and impossible to catch, in her opinion they were the stupidest birds in God's creation, and she had to clean and pluck a turkey a week until luckily the blackhead wiped out a third of the flock, which was enough to discourage them, they sold off the rest at a loss. It was the only time she was actually glad to see Frank lose money on one of his ventures.

Mrs. Burridge will feel things are getting serious on the day the electricity goes off and does not come back on. She knows, with a kind of fatalism, that this will happen in November, when the freezer is full of the vegetables but before it is cold enough to keep the packages frozen outside. She stands and looks at the pliofilm bags of beans and corn and spinach and carrots, melting and sodden, and thinks, *Why couldn't they have waited till spring.* It is the waste, of food and also of her hard work, that aggravates her the most. She salvages what she can. During the Depression, she remembers, they used to say those on farms were better off than those in the city, because at least they had food; if you could keep the farm, that is; but she is no longer sure this is true. She feels beleaguered, isolated, like someone shut up inside a fortress, though no one has bothered them, in fact no one has passed their way for days, not even any of the solitary walking men.

20   With the electricity off they can no longer get the television. The radio stations, when they broadcast at all, give out nothing but soothing music, which Mrs. Burridge does not find soothing in the least.

One morning she goes to the back door and looks out and there are the columns of smoke, right where she's been expecting to see them, off to the south. She calls Frank and they stand watching. The smoke is thick and black, oily, as though something has exploded. She does not know what Frank is thinking; she herself is wondering about the children. She has had no news of them in weeks, but how could she? They stopped delivering mail some time ago.

Fifteen minutes later, Henry Clarke drives into the yard in his half-ton truck. This is very unusual as no one has been driving anywhere lately. There is another man with him, and Mrs. Burridge identifies him as the man three farms up who moved in four or five years ago. Frank goes out and talks with them, and they drive over to the gas pump and start pumping the rest of the precious gas into the truck. Frank comes back to the house. He tells her there's a little trouble down the road, they are going along to see about it and she isn't to worry. He goes into the back room, comes out with the twenty-two, asks her where the shotgun is. She says she doesn't know. He searches for it, fruitlessly—she can hear him swearing, he does not swear in her presence—until he gives up. He comes out, kisses her goodbye, which is unusual too, and says he'll be back in a couple of hours. She watches the three of them drive off in Henry Clarke's truck, towards the smoke; she knows he will not come back. She supposes she ought to feel more emotional about it, but she is well prepared, she has been saying goodbye to him silently for years.

She re-enters the house and closes the door. She is fifty-one, her feet hurt, and she does not know where she can go, but she realizes she cannot stay here. There will now be a lot of hungry people, those that can make it this far out of the cities will be young and tough, her house is a beacon, signalling warmth and food. It will be fought over, but not by her.

She goes upstairs, searches in the cupboard, and puts on her heavy slacks and her two thickest sweaters. Downstairs she gathers up all the food that will be light enough for her to carry: raisins, cooking chocolate, dried prunes and apricots, half a loaf of bread, some milk powder which she puts into a quart freezer bag, a piece of cheese. Then she unearths the shotgun from behind the barn. She thinks briefly of killing the livestock, the chickens, the heifers and the pig, so no one will do it who does not know the right way; but she herself does not know the right way, she has never killed anything in her life, Frank always did it, so she contents herself with opening the henhouse door and the gate into the back field. She hopes the animals will run away but she knows they probably will not.

She takes one last look around the house. As an afterthought, she adds   25
her toothbrush to the bundle: she does not like the feel of unbrushed teeth. She does not go down into the cellar but she has an image of her carefully sealed bottles and jars, red and yellow and purple, shattered on the floor, in a sticky puddle that looks like blood. Those who come will be wasteful, what they cannot eat themselves they will destroy. She thinks about setting fire to the house herself, before anyone else can do it.

Mrs. Burridge sits at her kitchen table. On the back of her calendar page, it's for a Monday, she has written *Oatmeal,* in her evenly spaced public school handwriting that always got a star and has not changed very much since then. The dogs are a problem. After some thought she unchains them, but she does not let them past the gate: at a crucial moment they might give her away. She walks north in her heavy boots, carrying her parka because it is not yet cold enough to put it on, and her package of food and the shotgun which she has taken care to load. She passes the cemetery where her father and mother and her grandmother and grandfather are buried; the church used to be there but it burned down sixteen years ago and was rebuilt closer to the highway. Frank's people are in the other cemetery, his go back to the great-grandfather but they are Anglican, not that he kept it up. There is no one else on the road; she feels a little foolish. What if she is wrong and Frank comes back after all, what if nothing, really, is the matter? *Shortening,* she writes. She intends to make a lemon meringue pie for Sunday, when two of the children are coming up from the city for dinner.

It is almost evening and Mrs. Burridge is tired. She is in a part of the country she cannot remember, though she has stayed on the same road and it is a road she knows well; she has driven along it many times with

Frank. But walking is not the same as driving. On one side there is a field, no buildings, on the other a woodlot; a stream flows through a culvert under the road. Mrs. Burridge kneels down to drink: the water is ice-cold and tastes of iron. Later there will be a frost, she can feel it. She puts on her parka and her gloves, and turns into the forest where she will not be seen. There she will eat some raisins and cheese and try to rest, waiting for the moon to rise so she can continue walking. It is now quite dark. She smells earth, wood, rotting leaves.

Suddenly her eye is caught by a flicker of red, and before she can turn back—how can this happen so quickly?—it takes shape, it is a small fire, off to the right, and two men are crouching near it. They have seen her, too: one of them rises and comes towards her. His teeth bare, he is smiling; he thinks she will be easy, an old woman. He says something but she cannot imagine what it is, she does not know how people dressed like that would talk.

They have spotted her gun, their eyes have fastened on it, they want it. Mrs. Burridge knows what she must do. She must wait until they are close enough and then she must raise the gun and shoot them, using one barrel for each, aiming at the faces. Otherwise they will kill her, she has no doubt about that. She will have to be fast, which is too bad because her hands feel thick and wooden; she is afraid, she does not want the loud noise or the burst of red that will follow, she has never killed anything in her life. She has no pictures beyond this point. You never know how you will act in a thing like that until it actually happens.

30   Mrs. Burridge looks at the kitchen clock. On her list she writes *Cheese*, they are eating more cheese now than they used to because of the price of meat. She gets up and goes to the kitchen door.

Ann Beattie

Janus

The bowl was perfect. Perhaps it was not what you'd select if you faced a shelf of bowls, and not the sort of thing that would inevitably attract a lot of attention at a crafts fair, yet it had real presence. It was as predictably admired as a mutt who has no reason to suspect he might be funny. Just such a dog, in fact, was often brought out (and in) along with the bowl.

JANUS   First published in 1985. Ann Beattie was born in 1947 in Chevy Chase, Maryland, and earned degrees from American University and the University of Connecticut. She has taught creative writing at Harvard and the University of Virginia, and has published four novels in addition to her five short story collections. "Janus" was the Roman god of beginnings and of the rising and setting of the sun, as well as of doorways and other means of entrance or exit. He was often portrayed with two faces, one looking forward and the other backward. The term *Janus-faced* means deceitful ("two-faced") or having two contrasting aspects.

Andrea was a real-estate agent, and when she thought that some prospective buyers might be dog-lovers, she would drop off her dog at the same time she placed the bowl in the house that was up for sale. She would put a dish of water in the kitchen for Mondo, take his squeaking plastic frog out of her purse and drop it on the floor. He would pounce delightedly, just as he did every day at home, batting around his favorite toy. The bowl usually sat on a coffee table, though recently she had displayed it on top of a pine blanket chest and on a lacquered table. It was once placed on a cherry table beneath a Bonnard still-life, where it held its own.

Everyone who has purchased a house or who has wanted to sell a house must be familiar with some of the tricks used to convince a buyer that the house is quite special: a fire in the fireplace in early evening; jonquils in a pitcher on the kitchen counter, where no one ordinarily has space to put flowers; perhaps the slight aroma of spring, made by a single drop of scent vaporizing from a lamp bulb.

The wonderful thing about the bowl, Andrea thought, was that it was both subtle and noticeable—a paradox of a bowl. Its glaze was the color of cream and seemed to glow no matter what light it was placed in. There were a few bits of color in it—tiny geometric flashes—and some of these were tinged with flecks of silver. They were as mysterious as cells seen under a microscope; it was difficult not to study them, because they shimmered, flashing for a split second, and then resumed their shape. Something about the colors and their random placement suggested motion. People who liked country furniture always commented on the bowl, but then it turned out that people who felt comfortable with Biedermeier loved it just as much. But the bowl was not at all ostentatious, or even so noticeable that anyone would suspect that it had been put in place deliberately. They might notice the height of the ceiling on first entering a room, and only when their eye moved down from that, or away from the refraction of sunlight on a pale wall, would they see the bowl. Then they would go immediately to it and comment. Yet they always faltered when they tried to say something. Perhaps it was because they were in the house for a serious reason, not to notice some object.

Once, Andrea got a call from a woman who had not put in an offer on   5
a house she had shown her. That bowl, she said—would it be possible to find out where the owners had bought that beautiful bowl? Andrea pretended that she did not know what the woman was referring to. A bowl, somewhere in the house? Oh, on a table under the window. Yes, she would ask, of course. She let a couple of days pass, then called back to say that the bowl had been a present and the people did not know where it had been purchased.

When the bowl was not being taken from house to house, it sat on Andrea's coffee table at home. She didn't keep it carefully wrapped (although she transported it that way, in a box); she kept it on the table, because she liked to see it. It was large enough so that it didn't seem fragile, or particularly vulnerable if anyone sideswiped the table or Mondo blundered into it at play. She had asked her husband to please not drop his house key in it. It was meant to be empty.

When her husband first noticed the bowl, he had peered into it and smiled briefly. He always urged her to buy things she liked. In recent years, both of them had acquired many things to make up for all the lean years when they were graduate students, but now that they had been comfortable for quite a while, the pleasure of new possessions dwindled. Her husband had pronounced the bowl "pretty," and he had turned away without picking it up to examine it. He had no more interest in the bowl than she had in his new Leica.

She was sure that the bowl brought her luck. Bids were often put in on houses where she had displayed the bowl. Sometimes the owners, who were always asked to be away or to step outside when the house was being shown, didn't even know that the bowl had been in their house. Once—she could not imagine how—she left it behind, and then she was so afraid that something might have happened to it that she rushed back to the house and sighed with relief when the woman owner opened the door. The bowl, Andrea explained—she had purchased a bowl and set it on the chest for safekeeping while she toured the house with the prospective buyers, and she . . . She felt like rushing past the frowning woman and seizing her bowl. The owner stepped aside, and it was only when Andrea ran to the chest that the lady glanced at her a little strangely. In the few seconds before Andrea picked up the bowl, she realized that the owner must have just seen that it had been perfectly placed, that the sunlight struck the bluer part of it. Her pitcher had been moved to the far side of the chest, and the bowl predominated. All the way home, Andrea wondered how she could have left the bowl behind. It was like leaving a friend at an outing—just walking off. Sometimes there were stories in the paper about families forgetting a child somewhere and driving to the next city. Andrea had only gone a mile down the road before she remembered.

In time, she dreamed of the bowl. Twice, in a waking dream—early in the morning, between sleep and a last nap before rising—she had a clear vision of it. It came into sharp focus and startled her for a moment—the same bowl she looked at every day.

10   She had a very profitable year selling real estate. Word spread, and she had more clients than she felt comfortable with. She had the foolish thought that if only the bowl were an animate object she could thank it. There were times when she wanted to talk to her husband about the bowl. He was a stockbroker, and sometimes told people that he was fortunate to be married to a woman who had such a fine aesthetic sense and yet could also function in the real world. They were a lot alike, really—they had agreed on that. They were both quiet people—reflective, slow to make value judgments, but almost intractable once they had come to a conclusion. They both liked details, but while ironies attracted her, he was more impatient

and dismissive when matters became many-sided or unclear. But they both knew this; it was the kind of thing they could talk about when they were alone in the car together, coming home from a party or after a weekend with friends. But she never talked to him about the bowl. When they were at dinner, exchanging their news of the day, or while they lay in bed at night listening to the stereo and murmuring sleepy disconnections, she was often tempted to come right out and say that she thought that the bowl in the living room, the cream-colored bowl, was responsible for her success. But she didn't say it. She couldn't begin to explain it. Sometimes in the morning, she would look at him and feel guilty that she had such a constant secret.

Could it be that she had some deeper connection with the bowl—a relationship of some kind? She corrected her thinking: how could she imagine such a thing, when she was a human being and it was a bowl? It was ridiculous. Just think of how people lived together and loved each other . . . But was that always so clear, always a relationship? She was confused by these thoughts, but they remained in her mind. There was something within her now, something real, that she never talked about.

The bowl was a mystery, even to her. It was frustrating, because her involvement with the bowl contained a steady sense of unrequited good fortune; it would have been easier to respond if some sort of demand were made in return. But that only happened in fairy tales. The bowl was just a bowl. She did not believe that for one second. What she believed was that it was something she loved.

In the past, she had sometimes talked to her husband about a new property she was about to buy or sell—confiding some clever strategy she had devised to persuade owners who seemed ready to sell. Now she stopped doing that, for all her strategies involved the bowl. She became more deliberate with the bowl, and more possessive. She put it in houses only when no one was there, and removed it when she left the house. Instead of just moving a pitcher or a dish, she would remove all the other objects from a table. She had to force herself to handle them carefully, because she didn't really care about them. She just wanted them out of sight.

She wondered how the situation would end. As with a lover, there was no exact scenario of how matters would come to a close. Anxiety became the operative force. It would be irrelevant if the lover rushed into someone else's arms, or wrote her a note and departed to another city. The horror was the possibility of the disappearance. That was what mattered.

She would get up at night and look at the bowl. It never occurred to her that she might break it. She washed and dried it without anxiety, and she moved it often, from coffee table to mahogany corner table or wherever, without fearing an accident. It was clear that she would not be the one who would do anything to the bowl. The bowl was only handled by her, set safely on one surface or another; it was not very likely that anyone would break it. A bowl was a poor conductor of electricity: it would not be

15

hit by lightning. Yet the idea of damage persisted. She did not think be-yond that—to what her life would be without the bowl. She only contin-ued to fear that some accident would happen. Why not, in a world where people set plants where they did not belong, so that visitors touring a house would be fooled into thinking that dark corners got sunlight—a world full of tricks?

She had first seen the bowl several years earlier, at a crafts fair she had visited half in secret, with her lover. He had urged her to buy the bowl. She didn't *need* any more things, she told him. But she had been drawn to the bowl, and they had lingered near it. Then she went on to the next booth, and he came up behind her, tapping the rim against her shoulder as she ran her fingers over a wood carving. "You're still insisting that I buy that?" she said. "No," he said. "I bought it for you." He had bought her other things before this—things she liked more, at first—the child's ebony-and-turquoise ring that fitted her little finger; the wooden box, long and thin, beautifully dovetailed, that she used to hold paper clips; the soft gray sweater with a pouch pocket. It was his idea that when he could not be there to hold her hand she could hold her own—clasp her hands inside the lone pocket that stretched across the front. But in time she became more attached to the bowl than to any of his other presents. She tried to talk her-self out of it. She owned other things that were more striking or valuable. It wasn't an object whose beauty jumped out at you; a lot of people must have passed it by before the two of them saw it that day.

Her lover had said that she was always too slow to know what she re-ally loved. Why continue with her life the way it was? Why be two-faced, he asked her. He had made the first move toward her. When she would not decide in his favor, would not change her life and come to him, he asked her what made her think she could have it both ways. And then he made the last move and left. It was a decision meant to break her will, to shatter her intransigent ideas about honoring previous commitments.

Time passed. Alone in the living room at night, she often looked at the bowl sitting on the table, still and safe, unilluminated. In its way, it was perfect: the world cut in half, deep and smoothly empty. Near the rim, even in dim light, the eye moved toward one small flash of blue, a vanish-ing point on the horizon.

Raymond Carver

The Father

The baby lay in a basket beside the bed, dressed in a white bonnet and sleeper. The basket had been newly painted and tied with ice blue ribbons and padded with blue quilts. The three little sisters and the mother, who had just gotten out of bed and was still not herself, and the grandmother all stood around the baby, watching it stare and sometimes raise its fist to its mouth. He did not smile or laugh, but now and then he blinked his eyes and flicked his tongue back and forth through his lips when one of the girls rubbed his chin.

The father was in the kitchen and could hear them playing with the baby.

"Who do you love, baby?" Phyllis said and tickled his chin.

"He loves us all," Phyllis said, "but he really loves Daddy because Daddy's a boy too!"

The grandmother sat down on the edge of the bed and said, "Look at   5
its little arm! So fat. And those little fingers! Just like its mother."

"Isn't he sweet?" the mother said. "So healthy, my little baby." And bending over, she kissed the baby on its forehead and touched the cover over its arm. "We love him too."

"But who does he look like, who does he look like?" Alice cried, and they all moved up closer around the basket to see who the baby looked like.

"He has pretty eyes," Carol said.

"*All* babies have pretty eyes," Phyllis said.

"He has his grandfather's lips," the grandmother said. "Look at those   10
lips."

"I don't know . . ." the mother said. "I wouldn't say."

"The nose! The nose!" Alice cried.

"What about his nose?" the mother asked.

"It looks like somebody's nose," the girl answered.

"No, I don't know," the mother said. "I don't think so."   15

"Those lips . . ." the grandmother murmured. "Those little fingers . . ."
she said, uncovering the baby's hand and spreading out its fingers.

"Who does the baby look like?"

"He doesn't look like anybody," Phyllis said. And they moved even closer.

THE FATHER   First published in 1968. Raymond Carver (1939–1988) was born in a logging town south of Portland, Oregon. He married his first wife shortly after graduating from high school, and they had two children. He received a B.A. from Humboldt State College in California, attended the University of Iowa, and worked at a number of miscellaneous jobs. The success of his short stories and poems led to many awards and prizes, among them a five-year fellowship from the American Academy of Arts and Letters in 1983 that allowed him to give up his teaching at Syracuse University and write full time.

"*I* know! *I* know!" Carol said. "He looks like *Daddy!*" Then they looked closer at the baby.

20   "But who does Daddy *look* like?" Phyllis asked.

"Who does Daddy *look* like?" Alice repeated, and they all at once looked through to the kitchen where the father was sitting at the table with his back to them.

"Why, nobody!" Phyllis said and began to cry a little.

"Hush," the grandmother said and looked away and then back at the baby.

"Daddy doesn't look like *anybody!*" Alice said.

25   "But he has to look like *somebody,*" Phyllis said, wiping her eyes with one of the ribbons. And all of them except the grandmother looked at the father, sitting at the table.

He had turned around in his chair and his face was white and without expression.

John Cheever

The Swimmer

It was one of those midsummer Sundays when everyone sits around saying "I *drank* too much last night." You might have heard it whispered by the parishioners leaving church, heard it from the lips of the priest himself, struggling with his cassock in the *vestiarium,* heard it from the golf links and the tennis courts, heard it from the wildlife preserve where the leader of the Audubon group was suffering from a terrible hangover. "I *drank* too much," said Donald Westerhazy. "We all *drank* too much," said Lucinda Merrill. "It must have been the wine," said Helen Westerhazy. "I *drank* too much of that claret."

This was at the edge of the Westerhazy's pool. The pool, fed by an artesian well with a high iron content, was a pale shade of green. It was a fine day. In the west there was a massive stand of cumulus clouds so like a city seen from a distance—from the bow of an approaching ship—that it might have had a name. Lisbon. Hackensack. The sun was hot. Neddy Merrill sat by the green water, one hand in it, one around a glass of gin. He was a slender man—he seemed to have the especial slenderness of youth—and while he was far from young he had slid down his banister that morning and given the bronze backside of Aphrodite on the hall table a smack, as he jogged toward the smell of coffee in his dining room. He might have been compared to a summer's day, particularly the last hours of one, and while he lacked a tennis

THE SWIMMER First published in 1964. John Cheever (1912–1982) was born in Quincy, Massachusetts. After being expelled from a private school at seventeen, he went to New York City and published his first story later that year. He lived in various New England and New York towns, especially in commuter towns near New York City.

racket or a sail bag the impression was definitely one of youth, sport, and clement weather. He had been swimming and now he was breathing deeply, stertorously as if he could gulp into his lungs the components of that moment, the heat of the sun, the intenseness of his pleasure. It all seemed to flow into his chest. His own house stood in Bullet Park, eight miles to the south, where his four beautiful daughters would have had their lunch and might be playing tennis. Then it occurred to him that by taking a dogleg to the southwest he could reach his home by water.

His life was not confining and the delight he took in this observation could not be explained by its suggestion of escape. He seemed to see, with a cartographer's eye, that string of swimming pools, that quasi-subterranean stream that curved across the county. He had made a discovery, a contribution to modern geography; he would name the stream Lucinda after his wife. He was not a practical joker nor was he a fool but he was determinedly original and had a vague and modest idea of himself as a legendary figure. The day was beautiful and it seemed to him that a long swim might enlarge and celebrate its beauty.

He took off a sweater that was hung over his shoulders and dove in. He had an inexplicable contempt for men who did not hurl themselves into pools. He swam a choppy crawl, breathing either with every stroke or every fourth stroke and counting somewhere well in the back of his mind the one-two one-two of a flutter kick. It was not a serviceable stroke for long distances but the domestication of swimming had saddled the sport with some customs and in his part of the world a crawl was customary. To be embraced and sustained by the light green water was less a pleasure, it seemed, than the resumption of a natural condition, and he would have liked to swim without trunks, but this was not possible, considering his project. He hoisted himself up on the far curb—he never used the ladder—and started across the lawn. When Lucinda asked where he was going he said he was going to swim home.

The only maps and charts he had to go by were remembered or imaginary but these were clear enough. First there were the Grahams, the Hammers, the Lears, the Howlands, and the Crosscups. He would cross Ditmar Street to the Bunkers and come, after a short portage, to the Levys, the Welchers, and the public pool in Lancaster. Then there were the Hallorans, the Sachses, the Biswangers, Shirley Adams, the Gilmartins, and the Clydes. The day was lovely, and that he lived in a world so generously supplied with water seemed like a clemency, a beneficence. His heart was high and he ran across the grass. Making his way home by an uncommon route gave him the feeling that he was a pilgrim, an explorer, a man with a destiny, and he knew that he would find friends all along the way; friends would line the banks of the Lucinda River. 5

He went through a hedge that separated the Westerhazys' land from the Grahams', walked under some flowering apple trees, passed the shed that housed their pump and filter, and came out at the Grahams' pool. "Why,

Neddy," Mrs. Graham said, "what a marvelous surprise. I've been trying to get you on the phone all morning. Here, let me get you a drink." He saw then, like any explorer, that the hospitable customs and traditions of the natives would have to be handled with diplomacy if he was ever going to reach his destination. He did not want to mystify or seem rude to the Grahams nor did he have the time to linger there. He swam the length of their pool and joined them in the sun and was rescued, a few minutes later, by the arrival of two carloads of friends from Connecticut. During the uproarious reunions he was able to slip away. He went down by the front of the Grahams' house, stepped over a thorny hedge, and crossed a vacant lot to the Hammers'. Mrs. Hammer, looking up from her roses, saw him swim by although she wasn't quite sure who it was. The Lears heard him splashing past the open windows of their living room. The Howlands and the Crosscups were away. After leaving the Howlands' he crossed Ditmar Street and started for the Bunkers', where he could hear, even at that distance, the noise of a party.

The water refracted the sound of voices and laughter and seemed to suspend it in midair. The Bunkers' pool was on a rise and he climbed some stairs to a terrace where twenty-five or thirty men and women were drinking. The only person in the water was Rusty Towers, who floated there on a rubber raft. Oh, how bonny and lush were the banks of the Lucinda River! Prosperous men and women gathered by the sapphire-colored waters while caterer's men in white coats passed them cold gin. Overhead a red de Haviland trainer was circling around and around and around in the sky with something like the glee of a child in a swing. Ned felt a passing affection for the scene, a tenderness for the gathering, as if it was something he might touch. In the distance he heard thunder. As soon as Enid Bunker saw him she began to scream: "Oh, look who's here! What a marvelous surprise! When Lucinda said that you couldn't come I thought I'd *die*." She made her way to him through the crowd, and when they had finished kissing she led him to the bar, a progress that was slowed by the fact that he stopped to kiss eight or ten other women and shake the hands of as many men. A smiling bartender he had seen at a hundred parties gave him a gin and tonic and he stood by the bar for a moment, anxious not to get stuck in any conversation that would delay his voyage. When he seemed about to be surrounded he dove in and swam close to the side to avoid colliding with Rusty's raft. At the far end of the pool he bypassed the Tomlinsons with a broad smile and jogged up the garden path. The gravel cut his feet but this was the only unpleasantness. The party was confined to the pool, and as he went toward the house he heard the brilliant, watery sound of voices fade, heard the noise of a radio from the Bunkers' kitchen, where someone was listening to a ball game. Sunday afternoon. He made his way through the parked cars and down the grassy border of their driveway to Alewives Lane. He did not want to be seen on the road in his bathing trunks but there was no traffic and he made the short distance to the Levys' driveway, marked with a PRIVATE

PROPERTY sign and a green tube for *The New York Times*. All the doors and windows of the big house were open but there were no signs of life; not even a dog barked. He went around the side of the house to the pool and saw that the Levys had only recently left. Glasses and bottles and dishes of nuts were on a table at the deep end, where there was a bathhouse or gazebo, hung with Japanese lanterns. After swimming the pool he got himself a glass and poured a drink. It was his fourth or fifth drink and he had swum nearly half the length of the Lucinda River. He felt tired, clean, and pleased at that moment to be alone; pleased with everything.

It would storm. The stand of cumulus cloud—that city—had risen and darkened, and while he sat there he heard the percussiveness of thunder again. The de Haviland trainer was still circling overhead and it seemed to Ned that he could almost hear the pilot laugh with pleasure in the afternoon; but when there was another peal of thunder he took off for home. A train whistle blew and he wondered what time it had gotten to be. Four? Five? He thought of the provincial station at that hour, where a waiter, his tuxedo concealed by a raincoat, a dwarf with some flowers wrapped in newspaper, and a woman who had been crying would be waiting for the local. It was suddenly growing dark; it was that moment when the pinheaded birds seem to organize their song into some acute and knowledgeable recognition of the storm's approach. Then there was a fine noise of rushing water from the crown of an oak at his back, as if a spigot there had been turned. Then the noise of fountains came from the crowns of all the tall trees. Why did he love storms, what was the meaning of his excitement when the door sprang open and the rain wind fled rudely up the stairs, why had the simple task of shutting the windows of an old house seemed fitting and urgent, why did the first watery notes of a storm wind have for him the unmistakable sound of good news, cheer, glad tidings? Then there was an explosion, a smell of cordite, and rain lashed the Japanese lanterns that Mrs. Levy had bought in Kyoto the year before last, or was it the year before that?

He stayed in the Levys' gazebo until the storm had passed. The rain had cooled the air and he shivered. The force of the wind had stripped a maple of its red and yellow leaves and scattered them over the grass and the water. Since it was midsummer the tree must be blighted, and yet he felt a peculiar sadness at this sign of autumn. He braced his shoulders, emptied his glass, and started for the Welchers' pool. This meant crossing the Lindleys' riding ring and he was surprised to find it overgrown with grass and all the jumps dismantled. He wondered if the Lindleys had sold their horses or gone away for the summer and put them out to board. He seemed to remember having heard something about the Lindleys and their horses but the memory was unclear. On he went, barefoot through the wet grass, to the Welchers', where he found their pool was dry.

This breach in his chain of water disappointed him absurdly, and he felt like some explorer who seeks a torrential headwater and finds a dead stream. He was disappointed and mystified. It was common enough to go away for

10

the summer but no one ever drained his pool. The Welchers had definitely gone away. The pool furniture was folded, stacked, and covered with a tarpaulin. The bathhouse was locked. All the windows of the house were shut, and when he went around to the driveway in front he saw a FOR SALE sign nailed to a tree. When had he last heard from the Welchers—when, that is, had he and Lucinda last regretted an invitation to dine with them? It seemed only a week or so ago. Was his memory failing or had he so disciplined it in the repression of unpleasant facts that he had damaged his sense of the truth? Then in the distance he heard the sound of a tennis game. This cheered him, cleared away all his apprehensions and let him regard the overcast sky and the cold air with indifference. This was the day that Neddy Merrill swam across the county. That was the day! He started off then for his most difficult portage.

Had you gone for a Sunday afternoon ride that day you might have seen him, close to naked, standing on the shoulders of Route 424, waiting for a chance to cross. You might have wondered if he was the victim of foul play, had his car broken down, or was he merely a fool. Standing barefoot in the deposits of the highway—beer cans, rags, and blowout patches—exposed to all kinds of ridicule, he seemed pitiful. He had known when he started that this was a part of his journey—it had been on his maps—but confronted with the lines of traffic, worming through the summery light, he found himself unprepared. He was laughed at, jeered at, a beer can was thrown at him, and he had no dignity or humor to bring to the situation. He could have gone back, back to the Westerhazys', where Lucinda would still be sitting in the sun. He had signed nothing, vowed nothing, pledged nothing, not even to himself. Why, believing as he did, that all human obduracy was susceptible to common sense, was he unable to turn back? Why was he determined to complete his journey even if it meant putting his life in danger? At what point had this prank, this joke, this piece of horseplay become serious? He could not go back, he could not even recall with any clearness the green water at the Westerhazys', the sense of inhaling the day's components, the friendly and relaxed voices saying that they had *drunk* too much. In the space of an hour, more or less, he had covered a distance that made his return impossible.

An old man, tooling down the highway at fifteen miles an hour, let him get to the middle of the road, where there was a grass divider. Here he was exposed to the ridicule of the northbound traffic, but after ten or fifteen minutes he was able to cross. From here he had only a short walk to the Recreation Center at the edge of the village of Lancaster, where there were some handball courts and a public pool.

The effect of the water on voices, the illusion of brilliance and suspense, was the same here as it had been at the Bunkers' but the sounds here were louder, harsher, and more shrill, and as soon as he entered the crowded enclosure he was confronted with regimentation. "ALL SWIMMERS MUST

TAKE A SHOWER BEFORE USING THE POOL. ALL SWIMMERS MUST USE THE
FOOTBATH. ALL SWIMMERS MUST WEAR THEIR IDENTIFICATION DISKS."
He took a shower, washed his feet in a cloudy and bitter solution, and made
his way to the edge of the water. It stank of chlorine and looked to him like a
sink. A pair of lifeguards in a pair of towers blew police whistles at what
seemed to be regular intervals and abused the swimmers through a public
address system. Neddy remembered the sapphire water at the Bunkers' with
longing and thought that he might contaminate himself—damage his own
prosperousness and charm—by swimming in this murk, but he reminded
himself that he was an explorer, a pilgrim, and that this was merely a stag-
nant bend in the Lucinda River. He dove, scowling with distaste, into the
chlorine and had to swim with his head above water to avoid collisions, but
even so he was bumped into, splashed, and jostled. When he got to the
shallow end both lifeguards were shouting at him: "Hey, you, you without
the identification disk, get outa the water." He did, but they had no way of
pursuing him and he went through the reek of suntan oil and chlorine out
through the hurricane fence and passed the handball courts. By crossing the
road he entered the wooded part of the Halloran estate. The woods were not
cleared and the footing was treacherous and difficult until he reached the
lawn and the clipped beech hedge that encircled their pool.

The Hallorans were friends, an elderly couple of enormous wealth who
seemed to bask in the suspicion that they might be Communists. They were
zealous reformers but they were not Communists, and yet when they were accused, as they sometimes were, of subversion, it seemed to gratify and excite
them. Their beech hedge was yellow and he guessed this had been blighted
like the Levys' maple. He called hullo, hullo, to warn the Hallorans of his
approach, to palliate his invasion of their privacy. The Hallorans, for reasons
that had never been explained to him, did not wear bathing suits. No explanations were in order, really. Their nakedness was a detail in their uncompromising zeal for reform and he stepped politely out of his trunks before he
went through the opening in the hedge.

Mrs. Halloran, a stout woman with white hair and a serene face, was   15
reading the *Times.* Mr. Halloran was taking beech leaves out of the water
with a scoop. They seemed not surprised or displeased to see him. Their pool
was perhaps the oldest in the county, a fieldstone rectangle, fed by a brook. It
had no filter or pump and its waters were the opaque gold of the stream.

"I'm swimming across the county," Ned said.

"Why, I didn't know one could," exclaimed Mrs. Halloran.

"Well, I've made it from the Westerhazys'," Ned said. "That must be
about four miles."

He left his trunks at the deep end, walked to the shallow end, and swam
this stretch. As he was pulling himself out of the water he heard Mrs.
Halloran say, "We've been *terribly* sorry to hear about all your misfortunes,
Neddy."

"My misfortunes?" Ned asked. "I don't know what you mean."   20

"Why, we heard that you'd sold the house and that your poor children . . . "

"I don't recall having sold the house," Ned said, "and the girls are at home."

"Yes," Mrs. Halloran sighed. "Yes . . ." Her voice filled the air with an unseasonable melancholy and Ned spoke briskly. "Thank you for the swim."

"Well, have a nice trip," said Mrs. Halloran.

25   Beyond the hedge he pulled on his trunks and fastened them. They were loose and he wondered if, during the space of an afternoon, he could have lost some weight. He was cold and he was tired and the naked Hallorans and their dark water had depressed him. The swim was too much for his strength but how could he have guessed this, sliding down the banister that morning and sitting in the Westerhazys' sun? His arms were lame. His legs felt rubbery and ached at the joints. The worst of it was the cold in his bones and the feeling that he might never be warm again. Leaves were falling down around him and he smelled wood smoke on the wind. Who would be burning wood at this time of year?

He needed a drink. Whiskey would warm him, pick him up, carry him through the last of his journey, refresh his feeling that it was original and valorous to swim across the county. Channel swimmers took brandy. He needed a stimulant. He crossed the lawn in front of the Hallorans' house and went down a little path to where they had built a house for their only daughter, Helen, and her husband, Eric Sachs. The Sachses' pool was small and he found Helen and her husband there.

"Oh, *Neddy,*" Helen said. "Did you lunch at Mother's?"

"Not *really,*" Ned said. "I *did* stop to see your parents." This seemed to be explanation enough. "I'm terribly sorry to break in on you like this but I've taken a chill and I wonder if you'd give me a drink."

"Why, I'd *love* to," Helen said, "but there hasn't been anything in this house to drink since Eric's operation. That was three years ago."

30   Was he losing his memory, had his gift for concealing painful facts let him forget that he had sold his house, that his children were in trouble, and that his friend had been ill? His eyes slipped from Eric's face to his abdomen, where he saw three pale, sutured scars, two of them at least a foot long. Gone was his navel, and what, Neddy thought, would the roving hand, bed-checking one's gifts at 3 A.M., make of a belly with no navel, no link to birth, this breach in the succession?

"I'm sure you can get a drink at the Biswangers'," Helen said. "They're having an enormous do. You can hear it from here. Listen!"

She raised her head and from across the road, the lawns, the gardens, the woods, the fields, he heard again the brilliant noise of voices over water. "Well, I'll get wet," he said, still feeling that he had no freedom of choice about his means of travel. He dove into the Sachses' cold water and, gasping, close to drowning, made his way from one end of the pool to the other. "Lucinda and I want *terribly* to see you," he said over his shoulder, his face set toward the Biswangers'. "We're sorry it's been so long and we'll call you *very* soon."

He crossed some fields to the Biswangers' and the sounds of revelry there. They would be honored to give him a drink, they would be happy to give him a drink. The Biswangers invited him and Lucinda for dinner four times a year, six weeks in advance. They were always rebuffed and yet they continued to send out their invitations, unwilling to comprehend the rigid and undemocratic realities of their society. They were the sort of people who discussed the price of things at cocktails, exchanged market tips during dinner, and after dinner told dirty stories to mixed company. They did not belong to Neddy's set—they were not even on Lucinda's Christmas card list. He went toward their pool with feelings of indifference, charity, and some unease, since it seemed to be getting dark and these were the longest days of the year. The party when he joined it was noisy and large. Grace Biswanger was the kind of hostess who asked the optometrist, the veterinarian, the real-estate dealer, and the dentist. No one was swimming and the twilight, reflected on the water of the pool, had a wintry gleam. There was a bar and he started for this. When Grace Biswanger saw him she came toward him, not affectionately as he had every right to expect, but bellicosely.

"Why, this party has everything," she said loudly, "including a gate crasher."

She could not deal him a social blow—there was no question about this   35
and he did not flinch. "As a gate crasher," he asked politely, "do I rate a drink?"

"Suit yourself," she said. "You don't seem to pay much attention to invitations."

She turned her back on him and joined some guests, and he went to the bar and ordered a whiskey. The bartender served him but he served him rudely. His was a world in which the caterer's men kept the social score, and to be rebuffed by a part-time barkeep meant that he had suffered some loss of social esteem. Or perhaps the man was new and uninformed. Then he heard Grace at his back say: "They went for broke overnight—nothing but income—and he showed up drunk one Sunday and asked us to loan him five thousand dollars. . . ." She was always talking about money. It was worse than eating your peas off a knife. He dove into the pool, swam its length and went away.

The next pool on his list, the last but two, belonged to his old mistress, Shirley Adams. If he had suffered any injuries at the Biswangers' they would be cured here. Love—sexual roughhouse in fact—was the supreme elixir, the pain killer, the brightly colored pill that would put the spring back into his step, the joy of life in his heart. They had had an affair last week, last month, last year. He couldn't remember. It was he who had broken it off, his was the upper hand, and he stepped through the gate of the wall that surrounded her pool with nothing so considered as self-confidence. It seemed in a way to be his pool, as the lover, particularly the illicit lover, enjoys the possessions of his mistress with an authority unknown to holy matrimony. She was there, her hair the color of brass, but her figure, at the edge of the lighted, cerulean water, excited in him no profound memories. It had been, he thought, a lighthearted affair, although she had wept when he broke it off. She seemed confused to see him and he wondered if she was still wounded. Would she, God forbid, weep again?

"What do you want?" she asked.

40   "I'm swimming across the county."

"Good Christ. Will you ever grow up?"

"What's the matter?"

"If you've come here for money," she said, "I won't give you another cent."

"You could give me a drink."

45   "I could but I won't. I'm not alone."

"Well, I'm on my way."

He dove in and swam the pool, but when he tried to haul himself up onto the curb he found that the strength in his arms and shoulders had gone, and he paddled to the ladder and climbed out. Looking over his shoulder he saw, in the lighted bathhouse, a young man. Going out onto the dark lawn he smelled chrysanthemums or marigolds—some stubborn autumnal fragrance—on the night air, strong as gas. Looking overhead he saw that the stars had come out, but why should he seem to see Andromeda, Cepheus, and Cassiopeia? What had become of the constellations of midsummer? He began to cry.

It was probably the first time in his adult life that he had ever cried, certainly the first time in his life that he had ever felt so miserable, cold, tired, and bewildered. He could not understand the rudeness of the caterer's barkeep or the rudeness of a mistress who had come to him on her knees and showered his trousers with tears. He had swum too long, he had been immersed too long, and his nose and his throat were sore from the water. What he needed then was a drink, some company, and some clean, dry clothes, and while he could have cut directly across the road to his home he went on to the Gilmartins' pool. Here, for the first time in his life, he did not dive but went down the steps into the icy water and swam a hobbled sidestroke that he might have learned as a youth. He staggered with fatigue on his way to the Clydes' and paddled the length of their pool, stopping again and again with his hand on the curb to rest. He climbed up the ladder and wondered if he had the strength to get home. He had done what he wanted, he had swum the county, but he was so stupefied with exhaustion that his triumph seemed vague. Stooped, holding on to the gateposts for support, he turned up the driveway of his own house.

The place was dark. Was it so late that they had all gone to bed? Had Lucinda stayed at the Westerhazys' for supper? Had the girls joined her there or gone someplace else? Hadn't they agreed, as they usually did on

Sunday, to regret all their invitations and stay at home? He tried the garage doors to see what cars were in but the doors were locked and rust came off the handles onto his hands. Going toward the house, he saw that the force of the thunderstorm had knocked one of the rain gutters loose. It hung down over the front door like an umbrella rib, but it could be fixed in the morning. The house was locked, and he thought that the stupid cook or the stupid maid must have locked the place up until he remembered that it had been some time since they had employed a maid or a cook. He shouted, pounded on the door, tried to force it with his shoulder, and then, looking in at the windows, saw the place was empty.

Stephen Crane

The Bride Comes to Yellow Sky

1

The great Pullman was whirling onward with such dignity of motion that a glance from the window seemed simply to prove that the plains of Texas were pouring eastward. Vast flats of green grass, dull-hued spaces of mesquite and cactus, little groups of frame houses, woods of light and tender trees, all were sweeping into the east, sweeping over the horizon, a precipice.

A newly married pair had boarded this coach at San Antonio. The man's face was reddened from many days in the wind and sun, and a direct result of his new black clothes was that his brick-colored hands were constantly performing in a most conscious fashion. From time to time he looked down respectfully at his attire. He sat with a hand on each knee, like a man waiting in a barber's shop. The glances he devoted to other passengers were furtive and shy.

The bride was not pretty, nor was she very young. She wore a dress of blue cashmere, with small reservations of velvet here and there, and with steel buttons abounding. She continually twisted her head to regard her puff sleeves, very stiff, straight, and high. They embarrassed her. It was quite apparent that she had cooked, and that she expected to cook, dutifully. The blushes caused by the careless scrutiny of some passengers as she had entered the car were strange to see upon this plain, underclass countenance, which was drawn in placid, almost emotionless lines.

They were evidently very happy. "Ever been in a parlor car before?" he asked, smiling with delight.

THE BRIDE COMES TO YELLOW SKY   First published in 1898. Stephen Crane (1871–1900), son of a Methodist minister, grew up in New Jersey and New York State and did his early writing in New York City. A newspaper assignment in the West (including Texas, Arizona, Nevada, and Mexico) in the early months of 1895 provided background for this story.

5   "No," she answered, "I never was. It's fine, ain't it?"

"Great! And then after a while we'll go forward to the diner, and get a big lay-out. Finest meal in the world. Charge a dollar."

"Oh, do they?" cried the bride. "Charge a dollar? Why, that's too much—for us—ain't it, Jack?"

"Not this trip, anyhow," he answered bravely. "We're going to go the whole thing."

Later he explained to her about the trains. "You see, it's a thousand miles from one end of Texas to the other; and this train runs right across it, and never stops but four times." He had the pride of an owner. He pointed out to her the dazzling fittings of the coach; and in truth her eyes opened wider as she contemplated the sea-green figured velvet, the shining brass, silver, and glass, the wood that gleamed as darkly brilliant as the surface of a pool of oil. At one end a bronze figure sturdily held a support for a separated chamber, and at convenient places on the ceiling were frescos in olive and silver.

10   To the minds of the pair, their surroundings reflected the glory of their marriage that morning in San Antonio; this was the environment of their new estate; and the man's face in particular beamed with an elation that made him appear ridiculous to the Negro porter. This individual at times surveyed them from afar with an amused and superior grin. On other occasions he bullied them with skill in ways that did not make it exactly plain to them that they were being bullied. He subtly used all the manners of the most unconquerable kind of snobbery. He oppressed them; but of this oppression they had small knowledge, and they speedily forgot that infrequently a number of travelers covered them with stares of derisive enjoyment. Historically there was supposed to be something infinitely humorous in their situation.

"We are due in Yellow Sky at 3:42," he said, looking tenderly into her eyes.

"Oh, are we?" she said, as if she had not been aware of it. To evince surprise at her husband's statement was part of her wifely amiability. She took from a pocket a little silver watch; and as she held it before her, and stared at it with a frown of attention, the new husband's face shone.

"I bought it in San Anton' from a friend of mine," he told her gleefully.

"It's seventeen minutes past twelve," she said, looking up at him with a kind of shy and clumsy coquetry. A passenger, noting this play, grew excessively sardonic, and winked at himself in one of the numerous mirrors.

15   At last they went to the dining car. Two rows of Negro waiters, in glowing white suits, surveyed their entrance with the interest, and also the equanimity, of men who had been forewarned. The pair fell to the lot of a waiter who happened to feel pleasure in steering them through their meal. He viewed them with the manner of a fatherly pilot, his countenance radiant with benevolence. The patronage, entwined with the ordinary deference, was not plain to them. And yet, as they returned to their coach, they showed in their faces a sense of escape.

To the left, miles down a long purple slope, was a little ribbon of mist where moved the keening Rio Grande. The train was approaching it at an angle, and the apex was Yellow Sky. Presently it was apparent that, as the distance from Yellow Sky grew shorter, the husband became commensurately restless. His brick-red hands were more insistent in their prominence. Occasionally he was even rather absent-minded and faraway when the bride leaned forward and addressed him.

As a matter of truth, Jack Potter was beginning to find the shadow of a deed weigh upon him like a leaden slab. He, the town marshal of Yellow Sky, a man known, liked, and feared in his corner, a prominent person, had gone to San Antonio to meet a girl he believed he loved, and there, after the usual prayers, had actually induced her to marry him, without consulting Yellow Sky for any part of the transaction. He was now bringing his bride before an innocent and unsuspecting community.

Of course people in Yellow Sky married as it pleased them, in accordance with a general custom; but such was Potter's thought of his duty to his friends, or of their idea of his duty, or of an unspoken form which does not control men in these matters, that he felt he was heinous. He had committed an extraordinary crime. Face to face with this girl in San Antonio, and spurred by his sharp impulse, he had gone headlong over all the social hedges. At San Antonio he was like a man hidden in the dark. A knife to sever any friendly duty, any form, was easy to his hand in that remote city. But the hour of Yellow Sky—the hour of daylight—was approaching.

He knew full well that his marriage was an important thing to his town. It could only be exceeded by the burning of the new hotel. His friends could not forgive him. Frequently he had reflected on the advisability of telling them by telegraph, but a new cowardice had been upon him. He feared to do it. And now the train was hurrying him toward a scene of amazement, glee, and reproach. He glanced out of the window at the line of haze swinging slowly in toward the train.

Yellow Sky had a kind of brass band, which played painfully, to the delight of the populace. He laughed without heart as he thought of it. If the citizens could dream of his prospective arrival with his bride, they would parade the band at the station and escort them, amid cheers and laughing congratulations, to his adobe home.

He resolved that he would use all the devices of speed and plains-craft in making the journey from the station to his house. Once within that safe citadel, he could issue some sort of vocal bulletin, and then not go among the citizens until they had time to wear off a little of their enthusiasm.

The bride looked anxiously at him. "What's worrying you, Jack?"

He laughed again. "I'm not worrying, girl; I'm only thinking of Yellow Sky."

She flushed in comprehension.

A sense of mutual guilt invaded their minds and developed a finer tenderness. They looked at each other with eyes softly aglow. But Potter often laughed the same nervous laugh; the flush upon the bride's face seemed quite permanent.

The traitor to the feelings of Yellow Sky narrowly watched the speeding landscape. "We're nearly there," he said.

Presently the porter came and announced the proximity of Potter's home. He held a brush in his hand, and, with all his airy superiority gone, he brushed Potter's new clothes as the latter slowly turned this way and that way. Potter fumbled out a coin and gave it to the porter, as he had seen others do. It was a heavy and muscle-bound business, as that of a man shoeing his first horse.

The porter took their bag, and as the train began to slow they moved forward to the hooded platform of the car. Presently the two engines and their long string of coaches rushed into the station of Yellow Sky.

"They have to take water here," said Potter, from a constricted throat and in mournful cadence, as one announcing death. Before the train stopped, his eye had swept the length of the platform, and he was glad and astonished to see there was none upon it but the station agent, who, with a slightly hurried and anxious air, was walking toward the water tanks. When the train had halted, the porter alighted first, and placed in position a little temporary step.

30   "Come on, girl," said Potter, hoarsely. As he helped her down they each laughed on a false note. He took the bag from the Negro, and bade his wife cling to his arm. As they slunk rapidly away, his hangdog glance perceived that they were unloading the two trunks, and also that the station agent, far ahead near the baggage car, had turned and was running toward him, making gestures. He laughed, and groaned as he laughed, when he noted the first effect of his marital bliss upon Yellow Sky. He gripped his wife's arm firmly to his side, and they fled. Behind them the porter stood, chuckling fatuously.

2

The California Express on the Southern Railway was due at Yellow Sky in twenty-one minutes. There were six men at the bar of the Weary Gentleman saloon. One was a drummer° who talked a great deal and rapidly; three were Texans who did not care to talk at that time; and two were Mexican sheepherders, who did not talk as a general practice in the Weary Gentleman saloon. The barkeeper's dog lay on the boardwalk that crossed in front of the door. His head was on his paws, and he glanced drowsily here and there with the constant vigilance of a dog that is kicked on occasion. Across the sandy street were some vivid green grass-plots, so wonderful in appearance, amid the sands that burned near them in a blazing sun, that they caused a doubt in the mind. They exactly resembled the grass mats used to represent lawns on

drummer: traveling salesman

the stage. At the cooler end of the railway station, a man without a coat sat in a tilted chair and smoked his pipe. The fresh-cut bank of the Rio Grande circled near the town, and there could be seen beyond it a great plum-colored plain of mesquite.

Save for the busy drummer and his companions in the saloon, Yellow Sky was dozing. The newcomer leaned gracefully upon the bar, and recited many tales with the confidence of a bard who has come upon a new field.

"—and at the moment that the old man fell downstairs with the bureau in his arms, the old woman was coming up with two scuttles of coal, and of course—"

The drummer's tale was interrupted by a young man who suddenly appeared in the open door. He cried: "Scratchy Wilson's drunk, and has turned loose with both hands." The two Mexicans at once set down their glasses and faded out of the rear entrance of the saloon.

The drummer, innocent and jocular, answered: "All right, old man.   35 S'pose he has? Come in and have a drink, anyhow."

But the information had made such an obvious cleft in every skull in the room that the drummer was obliged to see its importance. All had become instantly solemn. "Say," said he, mystified, "what is this?" His three companions made the introductory gesture of eloquent speech; but the young man at the door forestalled them.

"It means, my friend," he answered, as he came into the saloon, "that for the next two hours this town won't be a health resort."

The barkeeper went to the door, and locked and barred it; reaching out of the window, he pulled in heavy wooden shutters, and barred them. Immediately a solemn, chapel-like gloom was upon the place. The drummer was looking from one to another.

"But say," he cried, "what is this anyhow? You don't mean there is going to be a gun fight?"

"Don't know whether there'll be a fight or not," answered one man,   40 grimly, "but there'll be some shootin'—some good shootin'."

The young man who had warned them waved his hand. "Oh, there'll be a fight fast enough, if anyone wants it. Anybody can get a fight out there in the street. There's a fight just waiting."

The drummer seemed to be swayed between the interest of a foreigner and a perception of personal danger.

"What did you say his name was?" he asked.

"Scratchy Wilson," they answered in chorus.

"And will he kill anybody? What are you going to do? Does this happen   45 often? Does he rampage around like this once a week or so? Can he break in that door?"

"No, he can't break down that door," replied the barkeeper. "He's tried it three times. But when he comes you'd better lay down on the floor, stranger. He's dead sure to shoot at it, and a bullet may come through."

Thereafter the drummer kept a strict eye upon the door. The time had not yet been called for him to hug the floor, but, as a minor precaution, he sidled near to the wall. "Will he kill anybody?" he said again.

The men laughed low and scornfully at the question.

"He's out to shoot, and he's out for trouble. Don't see any good in experimentin' with him."

50   "But what do you do in a case like this? What do you do?"

A man responded: "Why, he and Jack Potter—"

"But," in chorus the other men interrupted, "Jack Potter's in San Anton'."

"Well, who is he? What's he got to do with it?"

"Oh, he's the town marshal. He goes out and fights Scratchy when he gets on one of these tears."

55   "Wow!" said the drummer, mopping his brow. "Nice job he's got."

The voices had toned away to mere whisperings. The drummer wished to ask further questions, which were born of an increasing anxiety and bewilderment; but when he attempted them, the men merely looked at him in irritation and motioned him to remain silent. A tense waiting hush was upon them. In the deep shadows of the room their eyes shone as they listened for sounds from the street. One man made three gestures at the barkeeper; and the latter, moving like a ghost, handed him a glass and a bottle. The man poured a full glass of whisky, and set down the bottle noiselessly. He gulped the whisky in a swallow, and turned again toward the door in immovable silence. The drummer saw that the barkeeper, without a sound, had taken a Winchester from beneath the bar. Later he saw this individual beckoning to him, so he tip-toed across the room.

"You better come with me back of the bar."

"No, thanks," said the drummer, perspiring; "I'd rather be where I can make a break for the back door."

Whereupon the man of bottles made a kindly but peremptory gesture. The drummer obeyed it, and, finding himself seated on a box with his head below the level of the bar, balm was laid upon his soul at sight of various zinc and copper fittings that bore a resemblance to armor plate. The barkeeper took a seat comfortably upon an adjacent box.

60   "You see," he whispered, "this here Scratchy Wilson is a wonder with a gun—a perfect wonder; and when he goes on the war-trail, we hunt our holes—naturally. He's about the last one of the old gang that used to hang out along the river here. He's a terror when he's drunk. When he's sober he's all right—kind of simple—wouldn't hurt a fly—nicest fellow in town. But when he's drunk—whoo!"

There were periods of stillness. "I wish Jack Potter was back from San Anton'," said the barkeeper. "He shot Wilson up once—in the leg—and he would sail in and pull out the kinks in this thing."

Presently they heard from a distance the sound of a shot, followed by three wild yowls. It instantly removed a bond from the men in the darkened saloon. There was a shuffling to feet. They looked at each other. "Here he comes," they said.

3

A man in a maroon-colored flannel shirt, which had been purchased for purposes of decoration, and made principally by some Jewish women on the east side of New York, rounded a corner and walked into the middle of the main street of Yellow Sky. In either hand the man held a long, heavy, blue-black revolver. Often he yelled, and these cries rang through a semblance of a deserted village, shrilly flying over the roofs in a volume that seemed to have no relation to the ordinary vocal strength of a man. It was as if the surrounding stillness formed the arch of a tomb over him. These cries of ferocious challenge rang against walls of silence. And his boots had red tops with gilded imprints, of the kind beloved in winter by little sledding boys on the hillsides of New England.

The man's face flamed in a rage begot of whisky. His eyes, rolling, and yet keen for ambush, hunted the still doorways and windows. He walked with the creeping movement of the midnight cat. As it occurred to him, he roared menacing information. The long revolvers in his hands were as easy as straws; they were moved with an electric swiftness. The little fingers of each hand played sometimes in a musician's way. Plain from the low collar of the shirt, the cords of his neck straightened and sank, straightened and sank, as passion moved him. The only sounds were his terrible invitations. The calm adobes preserved their demeanor at the passing of this small thing in the middle of the street.

There was no offer of fight—no offer of fight. The man called to the sky. 65
There were no attractions. He bellowed and fumed and swayed his revolvers here and everywhere.

The dog of the barkeeper of the Weary Gentleman saloon had not appreciated the advance of events. He yet lay dozing in front of his master's door. At sight of the dog, the man paused and raised his revolver humorously. At sight of the man, the dog sprang up and walked diagonally away, with a sullen head, and growling. The man yelled, and the dog broke into a gallop. As it was about to enter an alley, there was a loud noise, a whistling, and something spat the ground directly before it. The dog screamed, and, wheeling in terror, galloped headlong in a new direction. Again there was a noise, a whistling, and sand was kicked viciously before it. Fear-stricken, the dog turned and flurried like an animal in a pen. The man stood laughing, his weapons at his hips.

Ultimately the man was attracted by the closed door of the Weary Gentleman saloon. He went to it and, hammering with a revolver, demanded drink.

The door remaining imperturbable, he picked a bit of paper from the walk, and nailed it to the framework with a knife. He then turned his back contemptuously upon this popular resort and, walking to the opposite side of the street and spinning there on his heel quickly and lithely, fired at the bit of paper. He missed it by a half-inch. He swore at himself, and went away. Later he comfortably fusilladed the windows of his most intimate friend. The man was playing with this town; it was a toy for him.

But still there was no offer of fight. The name of Jack Potter, his ancient antagonist, entered his mind, and he concluded that it would be a glad thing if he should go to Potter's house, and by bombardment induce him to come out and fight. He moved in the direction of his desire, chanting Apache scalp-music.

70   When he arrived at it, Potter's house presented the same still, calm front as had the other adobes. Taking up a strategic position, the man howled a challenge. But this house regarded him as might a great stone god. It gave no sign. After a decent wait, the man howled further challenges, mingling with them wonderful epithets.

Presently there came the spectacle of a man churning himself into deepest rage over the immobility of a house. He fumed at it as the winter wind attacks a prairie cabin in the North. To the distance there should have gone the sound of a tumult like the fighting of two hundred Mexicans. As necessity bade him, he paused for breath or to reload his revolvers.

4

Potter and his bride walked sheepishly and with speed. Sometimes they laughed together shamefacedly and low.

"Next corner, dear," he said finally.

They put forth the efforts of a pair walking bowed against a strong wind. Potter was about to raise a finger to point the first appearance of the new home when, as they circled the corner, they came face to face with a man in a maroon-colored shirt, who was feverishly pushing cartridges into a large revolver. Upon the instant the man dropped this revolver to the ground and, like lightning, whipped another from its holster. The second weapon was aimed at the bridegroom's chest.

75   There was a silence. Potter's mouth seemed to be merely a grave for his tongue. He exhibited an instinct to at once loosen his arm from the woman's grip, and he dropped the bag to the sand. As for the bride, her face had gone as yellow as old cloth. She was a slave to hideous rites, gazing at the apparitional snake.

The two men faced each other at a distance of three paces. He of the revolver smiled with a new and quiet ferocity.

"Tried to sneak up on me," he said. "Tried to sneak up on me!" His eyes grew more baleful. As Potter made a slight movement, the man thrust his revolver venomously forward. "No, don't you do it, Jack Potter. Don't you move a finger toward a gun just yet. Don't you move an eyelash. The time has come for me to settle with you, and I'm goin' to do it my own way, and loaf along with no interferin'. So if you don't want a gun bent on you, just mind what I tell you."

Potter looked at his enemy. "I ain't got a gun on me, Scratchy," he said. "Honest, I ain't." He was stiffening and steadying, but yet somewhere at the back of his mind a vision of the Pullman floated, the sea-green figured velvet, the shining brass, silver, and glass, the wood that gleamed as darkly brilliant as the surface of a pool of oil—all the glory of the marriage, the environment of the new estate. "You know I fight when it comes to fighting, Scratchy Wilson, but I ain't got a gun on me. You'll have to do all the shootin' yourself."

His enemy's face went livid. He stepped forward and lashed his weapon to and fro before Potter's chest. "Don't you tell me you ain't got no gun on you, you whelp. Don't tell me no lie like that. There ain't a man in Texas ever seen you without no gun. Don't take me for no kid." His eyes blazed with light, and his throat worked like a pump.

"I ain't takin' you for no kid," answered Potter. His heels had not moved an inch backward. "I'm takin' you for a damn fool. I tell you I ain't got a gun, and I ain't. If you're goin' to shoot me up, you better begin now; you'll never get a chance like this again." 80

So much enforced reasoning had told on Wilson's rage; he was calmer. "If you ain't got a gun, why ain't you got a gun?" he sneered. "Been to Sunday school?"

"I ain't got a gun because I've just come from San Anton' with my wife. I'm married," said Potter. "And if I'd thought there was going to be any galoots like you prowling around when I brought my wife home, I'd had a gun, and don't you forget it."

"Married!" said Scratchy, not at all comprehending.

"Yes, married. I'm married," said Potter, distinctly.

"Married?" said Scratchy. Seemingly for the first time, he saw the drooping, drowning woman at the other man's side. "No!" he said. He was like a creature allowed a glimpse of another world. He moved a pace backward, and his arm with the revolver dropped to his side. "Is this—is this the lady?" he asked. 85

"Yes, this is the lady," answered Potter.

There was another period of silence.

"Well," said Wilson at last, slowly, "I s'pose it's all off now."

"It's all off if you say so, Scratchy. You know I didn't make the trouble." Potter lifted his valise.

"Well, I 'low it's off Jack," said Wilson. He was looking at the ground. "Married!" He was not a student of chivalry; it was merely that in the presence of this foreign condition he was a simple child of the earlier plains. He picked up his starboard revolver, and, placing both weapons in their holsters, he went away. His feet made funnel-shaped tracks in the heavy sand. 90

Dagoberto Gilb

Love in L.A.

Jake slouched in a clot of near motionless traffic, in the peculiar gray of concrete, smog, and early morning beneath the overpass of the Hollywood Freeway on Alvarado Street. He didn't really mind because he knew how much worse it could be trying to make a left onto the onramp. He certainly didn't do that everyday of his life, and he'd assure anyone who'd ask that he never would either. A steady occupation had its advantages and he couldn't deny thinking about that too. He needed an FM radio in something better than this '58 Buick he drove. It would have crushed velvet interior with electric controls for the LA summer, a nice warm heater and defroster for the winter drives at the beach, a cruise control for those longer trips, mellow speakers front and rear of course, windows that hum closed, snuffing out that nasty exterior noise of freeways. The fact was that he'd probably have to change his whole style. Exotic colognes, plush, dark nightclubs, maitais and daquiris, necklaced ladies in satin gowns, misty and sexy like in a tequila ad. Jake could imagine lots of possibilities when he let himself, but none that ended up with him pressed onto a stalled freeway.

Jake was thinking about this freedom of his so much that when he glimpsed its green light he just went ahead and stared bye bye to the steadily employed. When he turned his head the same direction his windshield faced, it was maybe one second too late. He pounced the brake pedal and steered the front wheels away from the tiny brakelights but the smack was unavoidable. Just one second sooner and it would only have been close. One second more and he'd be crawling up the Toyota's trunk. As it was, it seemed like only a harmless smack, much less solid than the one against his back bumper.

Jake considered driving past the Toyota but was afraid the traffic ahead would make it too difficult. As he pulled up against the curb a few carlengths ahead, it occurred to him that the traffic might have helped him get away too. He slammed the car door twice to make sure it was closed fully and to give himself another second more, then toured front and rear of his Buick for damage on or near the bumpers. Not an impressionable scratch even in the chrome. He perked up. Though the car's beauty was secondary to its ability to start and move, the body and paint were clean except for a few minor dings. This stood out as one of his few clearcut accomplishments over the years.

LOVE IN L.A.   First published in 1986. Dagoberto Gilb, born in Los Angeles in 1950, is a Chicano of Anglo and Mexican heritage. He is a journeyman carpenter and worked for a few years as a carpenter in the construction of highrise buildings in Los Angeles County. He earned B.A. and M.A. degrees from the University of California, has taught in the writing programs of the universities of Arizona, Wyoming, and Texas (Austin), and lives in El Paso.

Before he spoke to the driver of the Toyota, whose looks he could see might present him with an added complication, he signaled to the driver of the car that hit him, still in his car and stopped behind the Toyota, and waved his hands and shook his head to let the man know there was no problem as far as he was concerned. The driver waved back and started his engine.

"It didn't even scratch my paint," Jake told her in that way of his. "So   5 how you doin? Any damage to the car? I'm kinda hoping so, just so it takes a little more time and we can talk some. Or else you can give me your phone number now and I won't have to lay my regular b.s. on you to get it later."

He took her smile as a good sign and relaxed. He inhaled her scent like it was clean air and straightened out his less than new but not unhip clothes.

"You've got Florida plates. You look like you must be Cuban."

"My parents are from Venezuela."

"My name's Jake." He held out his hand.

"Mariana."   10

They shook hands like she'd never done it before in her life.

"I really am sorry about hitting you like that." He sounded genuine. He fondled the wide dimple near the cracked taillight. "It's amazing how easy it is to put a dent in these new cars. They're so soft they might replace waterbeds soon." Jake was confused about how to proceed with this. So much seemed so unlikely, but there was always possibility. "So maybe we should go out to breakfast somewhere and talk it over."

"I don't eat breakfast."

"Some coffee then."

"Thanks, but I really can't."   15

"You're not married, are you? Not that that would matter that much to me. I'm an openminded kinda guy."

She was smiling. "I have to get to work."

"That sounds boring."

"I better get your driver's license," she said.

Jake nodded, disappointed. "One little problem," he said. "I didn't bring   20 it. I just forgot it this morning. I'm a musician," he exaggerated greatly, "and, well, I dunno, I left my wallet in the pants I was wearing last night. If you have some paper and a pen I'll give you my address and all that."

He followed her to the glove compartment side of her car.

"What if we don't report it to the insurance companies? I'll just get it fixed for you."

"I don't think my dad would let me do that."

"Your dad? It's not your car?"

"He bought it for me. And I live at home."   25

"Right." She was slipping away from him. He went back around to the back of her new Toyota and looked over the damage again. There was the trunk lid, the bumper, a rear panel, a taillight.

"You do have insurance?" she asked, suspicious, as she came around the back of the car.

"Oh yeah," he lied.

"I guess you better write the name of that down too."

30   He made up a last name and address and wrote down the name of an insurance company an old girlfriend once belonged to. He considered giving a real phone number but went against that idea and made one up.

"I act too," he lied to enhance the effect more. "Been in a couple of movies."

She smiled like a fan.

"So how about your phone number?" He was rebounding maturely. She gave it to him.

35   "Mariana, you are beautiful," he said in his most sincere voice.

"Call me," she said timidly.

Jake beamed. "We'll see you, Mariana," he said holding out his hand. Her hand felt so warm and soft he felt like he'd been kissed.

Back in his car he took a moment or two to feel both proud and sad about his performance. Then he watched the rear view mirror as Mariana pulled up behind him. She was writing down the license plate numbers on his Buick, ones that he'd taken off a junk because the ones that belonged to his had expired so long ago. He turned the ignition key and revved the big engine and clicked into drive. His sense of freedom swelled as he drove into the now moving street traffic, though he couldn't stop the thought about that FM stereo radio and crushed velvet interior and the new car smell that would even make it better.

Zora Neale Hurston

The Gilded Six-Bits

It was a Negro yard around a Negro house in a Negro settlement that looked to the payroll of the G and G Fertilizer works for its support.

But there was something happy about the place. The front yard was parted in the middle by a sidewalk from gate to door-step, a sidewalk edged on either side by quart bottles driven neck down into the ground on a slant. A mess of homey flowers planted without a plan but blooming

---

THE GILDED SIX-BITS   First published in 1933. Zora Neale Hurston (1891–1960), the daughter of a preacher and of a teacher who died when Neale was thirteen, was raised in Eatonville, Florida, the setting of this story. Her schooling was repeatedly interrupted, but included a high school diploma in 1918 and college studies at Howard University in Washington and Barnard College in New York. She did extensive field research in the folkways of African Americans in the South and in the Caribbean; by the time she wrote this story, she had married and divorced her first husband. In slang, a "bit" was twelve and a half cents, but was used only in multiples of two; "six-bits" refers to the two gilded coins used for ornaments by Mr. Slemmons, his twenty-five-cent stickpin and the fifty-cent coin on his watch chain.

cheerily from their helter-skelter places. The fence and house were white-washed. The porch and steps scrubbed white.

The front door stood open to the sunshine so that the floor of the front room could finish drying after its weekly scouring. It was Saturday. Everything clean from the front gate to the privy house. Yard raked so that the strokes of the rake would make a pattern. Fresh newspaper cut in fancy edge on the kitchen shelves.

Missie May was bathing herself in the galvanized washtub in the bedroom. Her dark-brown skin glistened under the soapsuds that skittered down from her wash rag. Her stiff young breasts thrust forward aggressively like broad-based cones with the tips lacquered in black.

She heard men's voices in the distance and glanced at the dollar clock 5 on the dresser.

"Humph! Ah'm way behind time t'day! Joe gointer be heah 'fore Ah git mah clothes on if Ah don't make haste."

She grabbed the clean meal sack at hand and dried herself hurriedly and began to dress. But before she could tie her slippers, there came the ring of singing metal on wood. Nine times.

Missie May grinned with delight. She had not seen the big tall man come stealing in the gate and creep up the walk grinning happily at the joyful mischief he was about to commit. But she knew that it was her husband throwing silver dollars in the door for her to pick up and pile beside her plate at dinner. It was this way every Saturday afternoon. The nine dollars hurled into the open door, he scurried to a hiding place behind the cape jasmine bush and waited.

Missie May promptly appeared at the door in mock alarm.

"Who dat chunkin' money in mah do'way?" she demanded. No answer 10 from the yard. She leaped off the porch and began to search the shrubbery. She peeped under the porch and hung over the gate to look up and down the road. While she did this, the man behind the jasmine darted to the china berry tree. She spied him and gave chase.

"Nobody ain't gointer be chunkin' money at me and Ah not do 'em nothin'," she shouted in mock anger. He ran around the house with Missie May at his heels. She overtook him at the kitchen door. He ran inside but could not close it after him before she crowded in and locked with him in a rough and tumble. For several minutes the two were a furious mass of male and female energy. Shouting, laughing, twisting, turning, tussling, tickling each other in the ribs; Missie May clutching onto Joe and Joe trying, but not too hard, to get away.

"Missie May, take yo' hand out mah pocket!" Joe shouted out between laughs.

"Ah ain't, Joe, not lessen you gwine gimme whateve' it is good you got in yo' pocket. Turn it go, Joe, do Ah'll tear yo' clothes."

"Go on tear 'em. You de one dat pushes de needles round heah. Move yo' hand Missie May."

"Lemme git dat paper sack out yo' pocket. Ah bet its candy kisses." 15

"Tain't. Move yo' hand. Woman ain't got no business in a man's clothes nohow. Go way."

Missie May gouged way down and gave an upward jerk and triumphed.

"Unhhunh! Ah got it. It 'tis so candy kisses. Ah knowed you had somethin' for me in yo' clothes. Now Ah got to see whut's in every pocket you got."

Joe smiled indulgently and let his wife go through all of his pockets and take out the things that he had hidden there for her to find. She bore off the chewing gum, the cake of sweet soap, the pocket handkerchief as if she had wrested them from him, as if they had not been bought for the sake of this friendly battle.

20   "Whew! dat play-fight done got me all warmed up," Joe exclaimed. "Got me some water in de kittle?"

"Yo' water is on de fire and yo' clean things is cross de bed. Hurry up and wash yo'self and git changed so we kin eat. Ah'm hongry." As Missie said this, she bore the steaming kettle into the bedroom.

"You ain't hongry, sugar," Joe contradicted her. "Youse jes' a little empty. Ah'm de one whut's hongry. Ah could eat up camp meetin', back off 'ssociation, and drink Jurdan dry. Have it on de table when Ah git out de tub."

"Don't you mess wid mah business, man. You git in yo' clothes. Ah'm a real wife, not no dress and breath. Ah might not look lak one, but if you burn me, you won't git a thing but wife ashes."

Joe splashed in the bedroom and Missie May fanned around in the kitchen. A fresh red and white checked cloth on the table. Big pitcher of buttermilk beaded with pale drops of butter from the churn. Hot fried mullet, crackling bread, ham hock atop a mound of string beans and new potatoes, and perched on the window-sill a pone of spicy potato pudding.

25   Very little talk during the meal but that little consisted of banter that pretended to deny affection but in reality flaunted it. Like when Missie May reached for a second helping of the tater pone. Joe snatched it out of her reach.

After Missie May had made two or three unsuccessful grabs at the pan, she begged, "Aw, Joe gimme some mo' dat tater pone."

"Nope, sweetenin' is for us men-folks. Y'all pritty lil frail eels don't need nothin' lak dis. You too sweet already."

"Please, Joe."

"Naw, naw. Ah don't want you to git no sweeter than whut you is already. We goin' down de road a lil piece t'night so you go put on yo' Sunday-go-to-meetin' things."

30   Missie May looked at her husband to see if he was playing some prank. "Sho nuff, Joe?"

"Yeah. We goin' to de ice cream parlor."

"Where de ice cream parlor at, Joe?"

"A new man done come heah from Chicago and he done got a place and took and opened it up for a ice cream parlor, and bein' as it's real swell,

Ah wants you to be one de first ladies to walk in dere and have some set down."

"Do Jesus, Ah ain't knowed nothin' 'bout it. Who de man done it?"

"Mister Otis D. Slemmons, of spots and places—Memphis, Chicago, 35 Jacksonville, Philadelphia and so on."

"Dat heavy-set man wid his mouth full of gold teethes?"

"Yeah. Where did you see 'im at?"

"Ah went down to de sto' tuh git a box of lye and Ah seen 'im standin' on de corner talkin' to some of de mens, and Ah come on back and went to scrubbin' de floor, and he passed and tipped his hat whilst Ah was scourin' de steps. Ah thought Ah never seen *him* befo'."

Joe smiled pleasantly. "Yeah, he's up to date. He got de finest clothes Ah ever seen on a colored man's back."

"Aw, he don't look no better in his clothes than you do in yourn. He 40 got a puzzlegut on 'im and he so chuckle-headed, he got a pone behind his neck."

Joe looked down at his own abdomen and said wistfully, "Wisht Ah had a build on me lak he got. He ain't puzzlegutted, honey. He jes' got a corperation. Dat make 'm look lak a rich white man. All rich mens is got some belly on 'em."

"Ah seen de pitchers of Henry Ford and he's a spare-built man and Rockefeller look lak he ain't got but one gut. But Ford and Rockefeller and dis Slemmons and all de rest kin be as many-gutted as dey please, Ah'm satisfied wid you jes' lak you is, baby. God took pattern after a pine tree and built you noble. Youse a pritty man, and if Ah knowed any way to make you mo' pritty still Ah'd take and do it."

Joe reached over gently and toyed with Missie May's ear. "You jes' say dat cause you love me, but Ah know Ah can't hold no light to Otis D. Slemmons. Ah ain't never been nowhere and Ah ain't got nothin' but you."

Missie May got on his lap and kissed him and he kissed back in kind. Then he went on. "All de womens is crazy 'bout 'im everywhere he go."

"How you know dat, Joe?" 45

"He tole us so hisself."

"Dat don't make it so. His mouf is cut cross-ways, ain't it? Well, he kin lie jes' lak anybody else."

"Good Lawd, Missie! You womens sho is hard to sense into things. He's got a five-dollar gold piece for a stick-pin and he got a ten-dollar gold piece on his watch chain and his mouf is jes' crammed full of gold teethes. Sho wisht it wuz mine. And whut make it so cool, he got money 'cumulated. And womens give it all to 'im."

"Ah don't see whut de womens see on 'im. Ah wouldn't give 'im a wink if de sheriff wuz after 'im."

"Well, he tole us how de white womens in Chicago give 'im all dat gold 50 money. So he don't 'low nobody to touch it at all. Not even put dey finger on it. Dey tole 'im not to. You kin make 'miration at it, but don't tetch it."

"Whyn't he stay up dere where dey so crazy 'bout 'im?"

"Ah reckon dey done made 'im vast-rich and he wants to travel some. He say dey wouldn't leave 'im hit a lick of work. He got mo' lady people crazy 'bout him than he kin shake a stick at."

"Joe, Ah hates to see you so dumb. Dat stray nigger jes' tell y'all anything and y'all b'lieve it."

"Go 'head on now, honey and put on yo' clothes. He talkin' 'bout his pritty womens—Ah want 'im to see *mine*."

55   Missie May went off to dress and Joe spent the time trying to make his stomach punch out like Slemmons' middle. He tried the rolling swagger of the stranger, but found that his tall bone-and-muscle stride fitted ill with it. He just had time to drop back into his seat before Missie May came in dressed to go.

On the way home that night Joe was exultant. "Didn't Ah say ole Otis was swell? Can't he talk Chicago talk? Wuzn't dat funny whut he said when great big fat ole Ida Armstrong come in? He asted me, 'Who is dat broad wid de forte shake?' Dat's a new word. Us always thought forty was a set of figgers but he showed us where it means a whole heap of things. Sometimes he don't say forty, he jes' say thirty-eight and two and dat mean de same thing. Know whut he tole me when Ah wuz payin' for our ice cream? He say, 'Ah have to hand it to you, Joe. Dat wife of yours is jes' thirty-eight and two. Yessuh, she's forte!' Ain't he killin'?"

"He'll do in case of a rush. But he sho is got uh heap uh gold on 'im. Dat's de first time Ah ever seed gold money. It lookted good on him sho nuff, but it'd look a whole heap better on you."

"Who, me? Missie May youse crazy! Where would a po' man lak me git gold money from?"

Missie May was silent for a minute, then she said, "Us might find some goin' long de road some time. Us could."

60   "Who would be losin' gold money round heah? We ain't even seen none dese white folks wearin' no gold money on dey watch chain. You must be figgerin' Mister Packard or Mister Cadillac goin' pass through heah."

"You don't know whut been lost 'round heah. Maybe somebody way back in memorial times lost they gold money and went on off and it ain't never been found. And then if we wuz to find it, you could wear some 'thout havin' no gang of womens lak dat Slemmons say he got."

Joe laughed and hugged her. "Don't be so wishful 'bout me. Ah'm satisfied de way Ah is. So long as Ah be yo' husband, Ah don't keer 'bout nothin' else. Ah'd ruther all de other womens in de world to be dead than for you to have de toothache. Less we go to bed and git our night rest."

It was Saturday night once more before Joe could parade his wife in Slemmons' ice cream parlor again. He worked the night shift and Saturday was his only night off. Every other evening around six o'clock he left home, and dying dawn saw him hustling home around the lake where the challenging sun flung a flaming sword from east to west across the trembling water.

That was the best part of life—going home to Missie May. Their white-washed house, the mock battle on Saturday, the dinner and ice cream parlor afterwards, church on Sunday nights when Missie out-dressed any woman in town—all, everything was right.

One night around eleven the acid ran out at the G. and G. The fore-man knocked off the crew and let the steam die down. As Joe rounded the lake on his way home, a lean moon rode the lake in a silver boat. If any-body had asked Joe about the moon on the lake, he would have said he hadn't paid it any attention. But he saw it with his feelings. It made him yearn painfully for Missie. Creation obsessed him. He thought about chil-dren. They had been married more than a year now. They had money put away. They ought to be making little feet for shoes. A little boy child would be about right.

He saw a dim light in the bedroom and decided to come in through the kitchen door. He could wash the fertilizer dust off himself before present-ing himself to Missie May. It would be nice for her not to know that he was there until he slipped into his place in bed and hugged her back. She al-ways liked that.

He eased the kitchen door open slowly and silently, but when he went to set his dinner bucket on the table he bumped it into a pile of dishes, and something crashed to the floor. He heard his wife gasp in fright and hur-ried to reassure her.

"Iss me, honey. Don't git skeered."

There was a quick, large movement in the bedroom. A rustle, a thud, and a stealthy silence. The light went out.

What? Robbers? Murderers? Some varmint attacking his helpless wife, perhaps. He struck a match, threw himself on guard and stepped over the door-sill into the bedroom.

The great belt on the wheel of Time slipped and eternity stood still. By the match light he could see the man's legs fighting with his breeches in his frantic desire to get them on. He had both chance and time to kill the in-truder in his helpless condition—half in and half out of his pants—but he was too weak to take action. The shapeless enemies of humanity that live in the hours of Time had waylaid Joe. He was assaulted in his weakness. Like Samson awakening after his haircut. So he just opened his mouth and laughed.

The match went out and he struck another and lit the lamp. A howling wind raced across his heart, but underneath its fury he heard his wife sob-bing and Slemmons pleading for his life. Offering to buy it with all that he had. "Please, suh, don't kill me. Sixty-two dollars at de sto'. Gold money."

Joe just stood. Slemmons looked at the window, but it was screened. Joe stood out like a rough-backed mountain between him and the door. Barring him from escape, from sunrise, from life.

He considered a surprise attack upon the big clown that stood there laughing like a chessy cat. But before his fist could travel an inch, Joe's own rushed out to crush him like a battering ram. Then Joe stood over him.

75   "Git into yo' damn rags, Slemmons, and dat quick."

Slemmons scrambled to his feet and into his vest and coat. As he grabbed his hat, Joe's fury overrode his intentions and he grabbed at Slemmons with his left hand and struck at him with his right. The right landed. The left grazed the front of his vest. Slemmons was knocked a somersault into the kitchen and fled through the open door. Joe found himself alone with Missie May, with the golden watch charm clutched in his left fist. A short bit of broken chain dangled between his fingers.

Missie May was sobbing. Wails of weeping without words. Joe stood, and after awhile he found out that he had something in his hand. And then he stood and felt without thinking and without seeing with his natural eyes. Missie May kept on crying and Joe kept on feeling so much and not knowing what to do with all his feelings, he put Slemmons' watch charm in his pants pocket and took a good laugh and went to bed.

"Missie May, whut you cryin' for?"

"Cause Ah love you so hard and Ah know you don't love *me* no mo'."

80   Joe sank his face into the pillow for a spell then he said huskily, "You don't know de feelings of dat yet, Missie May."

"Oh Joe, honey, he said he wuz gointer give me dat gold money and he jes' kept on after me——"

Joe was very still and silent for a long time. Then he said, "Well, don't cry no mo', Missie May. Ah got yo' gold piece for you."

The hours went past on their rusty ankles. Joe still and quiet on one bed-rail and Missie May wrung dry of sobs on the other. Finally the sun's tide crept upon the shore of night and drowned all its hours. Missie May with her face stiff and streaked towards the window saw the dawn come into her yard. It was day. Nothing more. Joe wouldn't be coming home as usual. No need to fling open the front door and sweep off the porch, making it nice for Joe. Never no more breakfast to cook; no more washing and starching of Joe's jumper-jackets and pants. No more nothing. So why get up?

With this strange man in her bed, she felt embarrassed to get up and dress. She decided to wait till he had dressed and gone. Then she would get up, dress quickly and be gone forever beyond reach of Joe's looks and laughs. But he never moved. Red light turned to yellow, then white.

85   From beyond the no-man's land between them came a voice. A strange voice that yesterday had been Joe's.

"Missie May, ain't you gonna fix me no breakfus'?"

She sprang out of bed. "Yeah, Joe. Ah didn't reckon you wuz hongry."

No need to die today. Joe needed her for a few more minutes anyhow.

Soon there was a roaring fire in the cook stove. Water bucket full and two chickens killed. Joe loved fried chicken and rice. She didn't deserve a thing and good Joe was letting her cook him some breakfast. She rushed hot biscuits to the table as Joe took his seat.

90   He ate with his eyes in his plate. No laughter, no banter.

"Missie May, you ain't eatin' yo' breakfus'."

"Ah don't choose none, Ah thank yuh."

His coffee cup was empty. She sprang to refill it. When she turned from the stove and bent to set the cup beside Joe's plate, she saw the yellow coin on the table between them.

She slumped into her seat and wept into her arms.

Presently Joe said calmly, "Missie May, you cry too much. Don't look back lak Lot's wife and turn to salt." 95

The sun, the hero of every day, the impersonal old man that beams as brightly on death as on birth, came up every morning and raced across the blue dome and dipped into the sea of fire every evening. Water ran down hill and birds nested.

Missie knew why she didn't leave Joe. She couldn't. She loved him too much, but she could not understand why Joe didn't leave her. He was polite, even kind at times, but aloof.

There were no more Saturday romps. No ringing silver dollars to stack beside her plate. No pockets to rifle. In fact the yellow coin in his trousers was like a monster hiding in the cave of his pockets to destroy her.

She often wondered if he still had it, but nothing could have induced her to ask nor yet to explore his pockets to see for herself. Its shadow was in the house whether or no.

One night Joe came home around midnight and complained of pains in the back. He asked Missie to rub him down with liniment. It had been three months since Missie had touched his body and it all seemed strange. But she rubbed him. Grateful for the chance. Before morning, youth triumphed and Missie exulted. But the next day, as she joyfully made up their bed, beneath her pillow she found the piece of money with the bit of chain attached. 100

Alone to herself, she looked at the thing with loathing, but look she must. She took it into her hands with trembling and saw first thing that it was no gold piece. It was a gilded half dollar. Then she knew why Slemmons had forbidden anyone to touch his gold. He trusted village eyes at a distance not to recognize his stick-pin as a gilded quarter, and his watch charm as a four-bit piece.

She was glad at first that Joe had left it there. Perhaps he was through with her punishment. They were man and wife again. Then another thought came clawing at her. He had come home to buy from her as if she were any woman in the long house. Fifty cents for her love. As if to say that he could pay as well as Slemmons. She slid the coin into his Sunday pants pocket and dressed herself and left his house.

Half way between her house and the quarters she met her husband's mother, and after a short talk she turned and went back home. Never would she admit defeat to that woman who prayed for it nightly. If she had not the substance of marriage she had the outside show. Joe must leave *her*. She let him see she didn't want his gold four-bits too.

She saw no more of the coin for some time though she knew that Joe could not help finding it in his pocket. But his health kept poor, and he came home at least every ten days to be rubbed.

105   The sun swept around the horizon, trailing its robes of weeks and days. One morning as Joe came in from work, he found Missie May chopping wood. Without a word he took the ax and chopped a huge pile before he stopped.

"You ain't got no business choppin' wood, and you know it."

"How come? Ah been choppin' it for de last longest."

"Ah ain't blind. You makin' feet for shoes."

"Won't you be glad to have a lil baby chile, Joe?"

110   "You know dat 'thout astin' me."

"Iss gointer be a boy chile and de very spit of you."

"You reckon, Missie May?"

"Who else could it look lak?"

Joe said nothing, but he thrust his hand deep into his pocket and fingered something there.

115   It was almost six months later Missie May took to bed and Joe went and got his mother to come wait on the house.

Missie May was delivered of a fine boy. Her travail was over when Joe came in from work one morning. His mother and the old women were drinking great bowls of coffee around the fire in the kitchen.

The minute Joe came into the room his mother called him aside.

"How did Missie May make out?" he asked quickly.

"Who, dat gal? She strong as a ox. She gointer have plenty mo'. We done fixed her wid de sugar and lard to sweeten her for de nex' one."

120   Joe stood silent awhile.

"You ain't ast 'bout de baby, Joe. You oughter be mighty proud cause he sho is de spittin' image of yuh, son. Dat's yourn all right, if you never git another one, dat un is yourn. And you know Ah'm mighty proud too, son, cause Ah never thought well of you marryin' Missie May cause her ma used tuh fan her foot round° right smart and Ah been mighty skeered dat Missie May wuz gointer git misput on her road."

Joe said nothing. He fooled around the house till late in the day then just before he went to work, he went and stood at the foot of the bed and asked his wife how she felt. He did this every day during the week.

On Saturday he went to Orlando to make his market. It had been a long time since he had done that.

Meat and lard, meal and flour, soap and starch. Cans of corn and tomatoes. All the staples. He fooled around town for awhile and bought bananas and apples. Way after while he went around to the candy store.

125   "Hello, Joe," the clerk greeted him. "Ain't seen you in a long time."

"Nope, Ah ain't been heah. Been round in spots and places."

"Want some of them molasses kisses you always buy?"

"Yessuh." He threw the gilded half dollar on the counter. "Will dat spend?"

fan . . . round: run around on her husband

"Whut is it, Joe? Well, I'll be doggone! A gold-plated four-bit piece. Where'd you git it, Joe?"

"Offen a stray nigger dat come through Eatonville. He had it on his   130
watch chain for a charm—goin' round making out iss gold money. Ha ha! He had a quarter on his tie pin and it wuz all golded up too. Tryin' to fool people. Makin' out he so rich and everything. Ha! Ha! Tryin' to tole off folkses wives from home."

"How did you git it, Joe? Did he fool you, too?"

"Who, me? Naw suh! He ain't fooled me none. Know whut Ah done? He come round me wid his smart talk. Ah hauled off and knocked 'im down and took his old four-bits way from 'im. Gointer buy my wife some good ole lasses kisses wid it. Gimme fifty cents worth of dem candy kisses."

"Fifty cents buys a mighty lot of candy kisses, Joe. Why don't you split it up and take some chocolate bars, too. They eat good, too."

"Yessuh, dey do, but Ah wants all dat in kisses. Ah got a lil boy chile home now. Tain't a week old yet, but he kin suck a sugar tit and maybe eat one them kisses hisself."

Joe got his candy and left the store. The clerk turned to the next cus-   135
tomer. "Wisht I could be like these darkies. Laughin' all the time. Nothin' worries 'em."

Back in Eatonville, Joe reached his own front door. There was the ring of singing metal on wood. Fifteen times. Missie May couldn't run to the door, but she crept there as quickly as she could.

"Joe Banks, Ah hear you chunkin' money in mah do'way. You wait till Ah got mah strength back and Ah'm gointer fix you for dat."

Shirley Jackson

The Lottery

The morning of June 27th was clear and sunny, with the fresh warmth of a full-summer day; the flowers were blossoming profusely and the grass was richly green. The people of the village began to gather in the square, between the post office and the bank, around ten o'clock; in some towns there were so many people that the lottery took two days and had to be started on June 26th, but in this village, where there were only about three hundred people, the whole lottery took less than two hours, so it could begin at ten o'clock in the morning and still be through in time to allow the villagers to get home for noon dinner.

The children assembled first, of course. School was recently over for the summer, and the feeling of liberty sat uneasily on most of them; they tended

THE LOTTERY   First published in 1948. Shirley Jackson (1919–1965) was born in San Francisco and spent most of her early life in California. After her marriage in 1940 she lived in a quiet rural community in Vermont.

to gather together quietly for a while before they broke into boisterous play, and their talk was still of the classroom and the teacher, of books and reprimands. Bobby Martin had already stuffed his pockets full of stones, and the other boys soon followed his example, selecting the smoothest and roundest stones; Bobby and Harry Jones and Dickie Delacroix—the villagers pronounced this name "Dellacroy"—eventually made a great pile of stones in one corner of the square and guarded it against the raids of the other boys. The girls stood aside, talking among themselves, looking over their shoulders at the boys, and the very small children rolled in the dust or clung to the hands of their older brothers or sisters.

Soon the men began to gather, surveying their own children, speaking of planting and rain, tractors and taxes. They stood together, away from the pile of stones in the corner, and their jokes were quiet and they smiled rather than laughed. The women, wearing faded house dresses and sweaters, came shortly after their menfolk. They greeted one another and exchanged bits of gossip as they went to join their husbands. Soon the women, standing by their husbands, began to call to their children, and the children came reluctantly, having to be called four or five times. Bobby Martin ducked under his mother's grasping hand and ran, laughing, back to the pile of stones. His father spoke up sharply, and Bobby came quickly and took his place between his father and his oldest brother.

The lottery was conducted—as were the square dances, the teen-age club, the Halloween program—by Mr. Summers, who had time and energy to devote to civic activities. He was a round-faced, jovial man and he ran the coal business, and people were sorry for him, because he had no children and his wife was a scold. When he arrived in the square, carrying the black wooden box, there was a murmur of conversation among the villagers, and he waved and called, "Little late today, folks." The postmaster, Mr. Graves, followed him, carrying a three-legged stool, and the stool was put in the center of the square and Mr. Summers set the black box down on it. The villagers kept their distance, leaving a space between themselves and the stool, and when Mr. Summers said, "Some of you fellows want to give me a hand?" there was a hesitation before two men, Mr. Martin and his oldest son, Baxter, came forward to hold the box steady on the stool while Mr. Summers stirred up the papers inside it.

5   The original paraphernalia for the lottery had been lost long ago, and the black box now resting on the stool had been put into use even before Old Man Warner, the oldest man in town, was born. Mr. Summers spoke frequently to the villagers about making a new box, but no one liked to upset even as much tradition as was represented by the black box. There was a story that the present box had been made with some pieces of the box that had preceded it, the one that had been constructed when the first people settled down to make a village here. Every year, after the lottery, Mr. Summers began talking again about a new box, but every year the subject was

allowed to fade off without anything's being done. The black box grew shabbier each year; by now it was no longer completely black but splintered badly along one side to show the original wood color, and in some places faded or stained.

Mr. Martin and his oldest son, Baxter, held the black box securely on the stool until Mr. Summers had stirred the papers thoroughly with his hand. Because so much of the ritual had been forgotten or discarded, Mr. Summers had been successful in having slips of paper substituted for the chips of wood that had been used for generations. Chips of wood, Mr. Summers had argued, had been all very well when the village was tiny, but now that the population was more than three hundred and likely to keep on growing, it was necessary to use something that would fit more easily into the black box. The night before the lottery, Mr. Summers and Mr. Graves made up the slips of paper and put them in the box, and it was then taken to the safe of Mr. Summers's coal company and locked up until Mr. Summers was ready to take it to the square next morning. The rest of the year, the box was put away, sometimes one place, sometimes another; it had spent one year in Mr. Graves's barn and another year underfoot in the post office, and sometimes it was set on a shelf in the Martin grocery and left there.

There was a great deal of fussing to be done before Mr. Summers declared the lottery open. There were the lists to make up—of heads of families, heads of households in each family, members of each household in each family. There was the proper swearing-in of Mr. Summers by the postmaster, as the official of the lottery; at one time, some people remembered, there had been a recital of some sort, performed by the official of the lottery, a perfunctory, tuneless chant that had been rattled off duly each year; some people believed that the official of the lottery used to stand just so when he said or sang it, others believed that he was supposed to walk among the people, but years and years ago this part of the ritual had been allowed to lapse. There had been, also, a ritual salute, which the official of the lottery had had to use in addressing each person who came up to draw from the box, but this also had changed with time, until now it was felt necessary only for the official to speak to each person approaching. Mr. Summers was very good at all this; in his clean white shirt and blue jeans, with one hand resting carelessly on the black box, he seemed very proper and important as he talked interminably to Mr. Graves and the Martins.

Just as Mr. Summers finally left off talking and turned to the assembled villagers, Mrs. Hutchinson came hurriedly along the path to the square, her sweater thrown over her shoulders, and slid into place in the back of the crowd. "Clean forgot what day it was," she said to Mrs. Delacroix, who stood next to her, and they both laughed softly. "Thought my old man was out back stacking wood," Mrs. Hutchinson went on, "and then I looked out the window and the kids were gone, and then I remembered it was the twenty-seventh and came a-running." She dried her hands on her apron, and Mrs. Delacroix said, "You're in time, though. They're still talking away up there."

Mrs. Hutchinson craned her neck to see through the crowd and found her husband and children standing near the front. She tapped Mrs. Delacroix on the arm as a farewell and began to make her way through the crowd. The people separated good-humoredly to let her through; two or three people said, in voices just loud enough to be heard across the crowd, "Here comes your Missus, Hutchinson," and "Bill, she made it after all." Mrs. Hutchinson reached her husband, and Mr. Summers, who had been waiting, said cheerfully, "Thought we were going to have to get on without you, Tessie." Mrs. Hutchinson said, grinning, "Wouldn't have me leave m'dishes in the sink, now, would you, Joe?" and soft laughter ran through the crowd as the people stirred back into position after Mrs. Hutchinson's arrival.

10   "Well, now," Mr. Summers said soberly, "guess we better get started, get this over with, so's we can go back to work. Anybody ain't here?"

"Dunbar," several people said. "Dunbar, Dunbar."

Mr. Summers consulted his list. "Clyde Dunbar," he said. "That's right. He's broke his leg, hasn't he? Who's drawing for him?"

"Me, I guess," a woman said, and Mr. Summers turned to look at her. "Wife draws for her husband," Mr. Summers said. "Don't you have a grown boy to do it for you, Janey?" Although Mr. Summers and everyone else in the village knew the answer perfectly well, it was the business of the official of the lottery to ask such questions formally. Mr. Summers waited with an expression of polite interest while Mrs. Dunbar answered.

"Horace's not but sixteen yet," Mrs. Dunbar said regretfully. "Guess I gotta fill in for the old man this year."

15   "Right," Mr. Summers said. He made a note on the list he was holding. Then he asked, "Watson boy drawing this year?"

A tall boy in the crowd raised his hand. "Here," he said. "I'm drawing for m'mother and me." He blinked his eyes nervously and ducked his head as several voices in the crowd said things like "Good fellow, Jack," and "Glad to see your mother's got a man to do it."

"Well," Mr. Summers said, "guess that's everyone. Old Man Warner make it?"

"Here," a voice said, and Mr. Summers nodded.

A sudden hush fell on the crowd as Mr. Summers cleared his throat and looked at the list. "All ready?" he called. "Now, I'll read the names—heads of families first—and the men come up and take a paper out of the box. Keep the paper folded in your hand without looking at it until everyone has had a turn. Everything clear?"

20   The people had done it so many times that they only half listened to the directions; most of them were quiet, wetting their lips, not looking around. Then Mr. Summers raised one hand high and said, "Adams." A man disen-

gaged himself from the crowd and came forward. "Hi, Steve," Mr. Summers said, and Mr. Adams said, "Hi, Joe." They grinned at one another humorlessly and nervously. Then Mr. Adams reached into the black box and took out a folded paper. He held it firmly by one corner as he turned and went hastily back to his place in the crowd, where he stood a little apart from his family, not looking down at his hand.

"Allen," Mr. Summers said. "Anderson . . . Bentham."

"Seems like there's no time at all between lotteries any more," Mrs. Delacroix said to Mrs. Graves in the back row. "Seems like we got through with the last one only last week."

"Time sure goes fast," Mrs. Graves said.

"Clark . . . Delacroix."

"There goes my old man," Mrs. Delacroix said. She held her breath   25
while her husband went forward.

"Dunbar," Mr. Summers said, and Mrs. Dunbar went steadily to the box while one of the women said, "Go on, Janey," and another said, "There she goes."

"We're next," Mrs. Graves said. She watched while Mr. Graves came around from the side of the box, greeted Mr. Summers gravely, and selected a slip of paper from the box. By now, all through the crowd there were men holding the small folded papers in their large hands, turning them over and over nervously. Mrs. Dunbar and her two sons stood together, Mrs. Dunbar holding the slip of paper.

"Harburt . . . Hutchinson."

"Get up there, Bill," Mrs. Hutchinson said, and the people near her laughed.

"Jones."   30

"They do say," Mr. Adams said to Old Man Warner, who stood next to him, "that over in the north village they're talking of giving up the lottery."

Old Man Warner snorted. "Pack of crazy fools," he said. "Listening to the young folks, nothing's good enough for *them*. Next thing you know, they'll be wanting to go back to living in caves, nobody work any more, live *that* way for a while. Used to be a saying about 'Lottery in June, corn be heavy soon.' First thing you know, we'd all be eating stewed chickweed and acorns. There's *always* been a lottery," he added petulantly. "Bad enough to see young Joe Summers up there joking with everybody."

"Some places have already quit lotteries," Mrs. Adams said.

"Nothing but trouble in *that*," Old Man Warner said stoutly. "Pack of young fools."

"Martin." And Bobby Martin watched his father go forward. "Overdyke   35
. . . Percy."

"I wish they'd hurry," Mrs. Dunbar said to her older son. "I wish they'd hurry."

"They're almost through," her son said.

"You get ready to run tell Dad," Mrs. Dunbar said.

Mr. Summers called his own name and then stepped forward precisely and selected a slip from the box. Then he called, "Warner."

40   "Seventy-seventh year I been in the lottery," Old Man Warner said as he went through the crowd. "Seventy-seventh time."

"Watson." The tall boy came awkwardly through the crowd. Someone said, "Don't be nervous, Jack," and Mr. Summers said, "Take your time, son."

"Zanini."

After that, there was a long pause, a breathless pause, until Mr. Summers, holding his slip of paper in the air, said, "All right, fellows." For a minute, no one moved, and then all the slips of paper were opened. Suddenly, all the women began to speak at once, saying, "Who is it?" "Who's got it?" "Is it the Dunbars?" "Is it the Watsons?" Then the voices began to say, "It's Hutchinson. It's Bill," "Bill Hutchinson's got it."

"Go tell your father," Mrs. Dunbar said to her older son.

45   People began to look around to see the Hutchinsons. Bill Hutchinson was standing quiet, staring down at the paper in his hand. Suddenly, Tessie Hutchinson shouted to Mr. Summers. "You didn't give him time enough to take any paper he wanted. I saw you. It wasn't fair."

"Be a good sport, Tessie," Mrs. Delacroix called, and Mrs. Graves said, "All of us took the same chance."

"Shut up, Tessie," Bill Hutchinson said.

"Well, everyone," Mr. Summers said, "that was done pretty fast, and now we've got to be hurrying a little more to get done in time." He consulted his next list. "Bill," he said, "you draw for the Hutchinson family. You got any other households in the Hutchinsons?"

"There's Don and Eva," Mrs. Hutchinson yelled. "Make *them* take their chance!"

50   "Daughters draw with their husband's families, Tessie," Mr. Summers said gently. "You know that as well as anyone else."

"It wasn't *fair*," Tessie said.

"I guess not, Joe," Bill Hutchinson said regretfully. "My daughter draws with her husband's family, that's only fair. And I've got no other family except the kids."

"Then, as far as drawing for families is concerned, it's you." Mr. Summers said in explanation, "and as far as drawing for households is concerned, that's you, too. Right?"

"Right," Bill Hutchinson said.

55   "How many kids, Bill?" Mr. Summers asked formally.

"Three," Bill Hutchinson said. "There's Bill, Jr., and Nancy, and little Dave. And Tessie and me."

"All right, then," Mr. Summers said. "Harry, you got their tickets back?"

Mr. Graves nodded and held up the slips of paper. "Put them in the box, then," Mr. Summers directed. "Take Bill's and put it in."

"I think we ought to start over," Mrs. Hutchinson said, as quietly as she could. "I tell you it wasn't *fair.* You didn't give him time enough to choose. *Every*body saw that."

Mr. Graves had selected the five slips and put them in the box, and he dropped all the papers but those onto the ground, where the breeze caught them and lifted them off.   60

"Listen, everybody," Mrs. Hutchinson was saying to the people around her.

"Ready, Bill?" Mr. Summers asked, and Bill Hutchinson, with one quick glance around at his wife and children, nodded.

"Remember," Mr. Summers said, "take the slips and keep them folded until each person has taken one. Harry, you help little Dave." Mr. Graves took the hand of the little boy, who came willingly with him up to the box. "Take a paper out of the box, Davy," Mr. Summers said. Davy put his hand into the box and laughed. "Take just *one* paper," Mr. Summers said. "Harry, you hold it for him." Mr. Graves took the child's hand and removed the folded paper from the tight fist and held it while little Dave stood next to him and looked up at him wonderingly.

"Nancy next," Mr. Summers said. Nancy was twelve, and her school friends breathed heavily as she went forward, switching her skirt, and took a slip daintily from the box. "Bill, Jr.," Mr. Summers said, and Billy, his face red and his feet over-large, nearly knocked the box over as he got a paper out. "Tessie," Mr. Summers said. She hesitated for a minute, looking around defiantly, and then set her lips and went up to the box. She snatched a paper out and held it behind her.

"Bill," Mr. Summers said, and Bill Hutchinson reached into the box and felt around, bringing his hand out at last with the slip of paper in it.   65

The crowd was quiet. A girl whispered, "I hope it's not Nancy," and the sound of the whisper reached the edges of the crowd.

"It's not the way it used to be," Old Man Warner said clearly. "People ain't the way they used to be."

"All right," Mr. Summers said. "Open the papers. Harry, you open little Dave's."

Mr. Graves opened the slip of paper and there was a general sigh through the crowd as he held it up and everyone could see that it was blank. Nancy and Bill, Jr., opened theirs at the same time, and both beamed and laughed, turning around to the crowd and holding their slips of paper above their heads.

"Tessie," Mr. Summers said. There was a pause, and then Mr. Summers looked at Bill Hutchinson, and Bill unfolded his paper and showed it. It was blank.   70

"It's Tessie," Mr. Summers said, and his voice was hushed. "Show us her paper, Bill."

Bill Hutchinson went over to his wife and forced the slip of paper out of her hand. It had a black spot on it, the black spot Mr. Summers had made the night before with the heavy pencil in the coal-company office. Bill Hutchinson held it up, and there was a stir in the crowd.

"All right, folks," Mr. Summers said. "Let's finish quickly."

Although the villagers had forgotten the ritual and lost the original black box, they still remembered to use stones. The pile of stones the boys had made earlier was ready; there were stones on the ground with the blowing scraps of paper that had come out of the box. Mrs. Delacroix selected a stone so large she had to pick it up with both hands and turned to Mrs. Dunbar. "Come on," she said. "Hurry up."

75   Mrs. Dunbar had small stones in both hands, and she said, gasping for breath, "I can't run at all. You'll have to go ahead and I'll catch up with you."

The children had stones already, and someone gave little Davy Hutchinson a few pebbles.

Tessie Hutchinson was in the center of a cleared space by now, and she held her hands out desperately as the villagers moved in on her. "It isn't fair," she said. A stone hit her on the side of the head.

Old Man Warner was saying, "Come on, come on, everyone." Steve Adams was in front of the crowd of villagers, with Mrs. Graves beside him.

"It isn't fair, it isn't right," Mrs. Hutchinson screamed, and then they were upon her.

James Joyce

Eveline

She sat at the window watching evening invade the avenue. Her head was leaned against the window curtains and in her nostrils was the odor of dusty cretonne. She was tired.

Few people passed. The man out of the last house passed on his way home; she heard his footsteps clacking along the concrete pavement and afterwards crunching on the cinder path before the new red houses. One time there used to be a field there in which they used to play every evening with other people's children. Then a man from Belfast bought the field and built houses in it—not like their little brown houses but bright brick houses with shining roofs. The children of the avenue used to play together in that field—the Devines, the Waters, the Dunns, little Keogh the cripple, she and

EVELINE   First published in 1904. James Joyce (1882–1941) was born and lived in Dublin, Ireland, until 1904 when he went to the continent, and for the rest of his life he lived abroad and wrote about Dublin. Eveline's weekly wages working as a sales clerk in "the Stores" are the equivalent of less than ten dollars. The "night boat" that she and Frank are planning to take departed from a dock called "the North Wall" for Liverpool, England; presumably Frank has planned to take a ship from there to Argentina with her.

her brothers and sisters. Ernest, however, never played: he was too grown up. Her father used often to hunt them in out of the field with his blackthorn stick; but usually little Keogh used to keep *nix* and call out when he saw her father coming. Still they seemed to have been rather happy then. Her father was not so bad then; and besides, her mother was alive. That was a long time ago; she and her brothers and sisters were all grown up; her mother was dead. Tizzie Dunn was dead, too, and the Waters had gone back to England. Everything changes. Now she was going to go away like the others, to leave her home.

Home! She looked round the room, reviewing all its familiar objects which she had dusted once a week for so many years, wondering where on earth all the dust came from. Perhaps she would never see again those familiar objects from which she had never dreamed of being divided. And yet during all those years she had never found out the name of the priest whose yellowing photograph hung on the wall above the broken harmonium beside the colored print of the promises made to Blessed Margaret Mary Alacoque. He had been a school friend of her father. Whenever he showed the photograph to a visitor her father used to pass it with a casual word:

"He is in Melbourne now."

She had consented to go away, to leave her home. Was that wise? She   5
tried to weigh each side of the question. In her home anyway she had shelter and food; she had those whom she had known all her life about her. Of course she had to work hard both in the house and at business. What would they say of her in the Stores when they found out that she had run away with a fellow? Say she was a fool, perhaps; and her place would be filled up by advertisement. Miss Gavan would be glad. She had always had an edge on her, especially whenever there were people listening.

"Miss Hill, don't you see these ladies are waiting?"

"Look lively, Miss Hill, please."

She would not cry many tears at leaving the Stores.

But in her new home, in a distant unknown country, it would not be like that. Then she would be married—she, Eveline. People would treat her with respect then. She would not be treated as her mother had been. Even now, though she was over nineteen, she sometimes felt herself in danger of her father's violence. She knew it was that that had given her the palpitations When they were growing up he had never gone for her, like he used to go for Harry and Ernest, because she was a girl; but latterly he had begun to threaten her and say what he would do to her only for her dead mother's sake. And now she had nobody to protect her. Ernest was dead and Harry, who was in the church decorating business, was nearly always down somewhere in the country. Besides, the invariable squabble for money on Saturday nights had begun to weary her unspeakably. She always gave her entire wages—seven shillings—and Harry always sent up what he could but the trouble was to get any money from her father. He said she used to squander the money, that she had no head, that he wasn't going to give her his hard-earned money to throw about the streets, and much more, for he was usually fairly bad of a Saturday night. In the end he would give her the money and ask her had she any intention of buying Sunday's dinner. Then she had to rush out as quickly as she could and do her marketing, holding her black leather purse tightly in her hand as she elbowed her way through the crowds and returning home late under her load of provisions. She had hard work to keep the house together and to see that the two young children who had been left to her charge went to school regularly and got their meals regularly. It was hard work—a hard life—but now that she was about to leave it she did not find it a wholly undesirable life.

10   She was about to explore another life with Frank. Frank was very kind, manly, open-hearted. She was to go away with him by the night-boat to be his wife and to live with him in Buenos Aires where he had a home waiting for her. How well she remembered the first time she had seen him; he was lodging in a house on the main road where she used to visit. It seemed a few weeks ago. He was standing at the gate, his peaked cap pushed back on his head and his hair tumbled forward over a face of bronze. Then they had come to know each other. He used to meet her outside the Stores every evening and see her home. He took her to see *The Bohemian Girl* and she felt elated as she sat in an unaccustomed part of the theater with him. He was awfully fond of music and sang a little. People knew that they were courting and, when he sang about the lass that loves a sailor, she always felt pleasantly confused. He used to call her Poppens out of fun. First of all it had been an excitement for her to have a fellow and then she had begun to like him. He had tales of distant countries. He had started as a deck boy at a pound a month on a ship of the Allan Line going out to Canada. He told her the names of the ships he had been on and the names of the different services. He had sailed through the Straits of Magellan and he told her stories of the terrible Patagonians. He had fallen on his feet in Buenos Aires, he said, and had come over to the old country just for a holiday. Of course, her father had found out the affair and had forbidden her to have anything to say to him.

"I know these sailor chaps," he said.

One day he had quarrelled with Frank and after that she had to meet her lover secretly.

The evening deepened in the avenue. The white of two letters in her lap grew indistinct. One was to Harry; the other was to her father. Ernest had been her favorite but she liked Harry too. Her father was becoming old lately, she noticed; he would miss her. Sometimes he could be very nice. Not long before, when she had been laid up for a day, he had read her out a ghost story and made toast for her at the fire. Another day, when their mother was alive, they had all gone for a picnic to the Hill of Howth. She remembered her father putting on her mother's bonnet to make the children laugh.

Her time was running out but she continued to sit by the window, leaning her head against the window curtain, inhaling the odor of dusty cretonne. Down far in the avenue she could hear a street organ playing. She knew the air. Strange that it should come that very night to remind her of the promise to her mother, her promise to keep the home together as long as she could. She remembered the last night of her mother's illness; she was again in the close dark room at the other side of the hall and outside she heard a melancholy air of Italy. The organ-player had been ordered to go away and given sixpence. She remembered her father strutting back into the sickroom saying:

"Damned Italians! coming over here!"   15

As she mused the pitiful vision of her mother's life laid its spell on the very quick of her being—that life of commonplace sacrifices closing in final craziness. She trembled as she heard again her mother's voice saying constantly with foolish insistence:

"Derevaun Seraun! Derevaun Seraun!"°

She stood up in a sudden impulse of terror. Escape! She must escape! Frank would save her. He would give her life, perhaps love, too. But she wanted to live. Why should she be unhappy? She had a right to happiness. Frank would take her in his arms, fold her in his arms. He would save her.

She stood among the swaying crowd in the station at the North Wall. He held her hand and she knew that he was speaking to her, saying something about the passage over and over again. The station was full of soldiers with brown baggages. Through the wide doors of the sheds she caught a glimpse of the black mass of the boat, lying in beside the quay wall, with illumined portholes. She answered nothing. She felt her cheek pale and cold and, out of a maze of distress, she prayed to God to direct her, to show her what was her duty. The boat blew a long mournful whistle into the mist. If she went, tomorrow she would be on the sea with Frank, steaming towards Buenos Aires. Their passage had been booked. Could she still draw back after all he had done for her? Her distress awoke a nausea in her body and she kept moving her lips in silent fervent prayer.

A bell clanged upon her heart. She felt him seize her hand: 20

"Come!"

All the seas of the world tumbled about her heart. He was drawing her into them: he would drown her. She gripped with both hands at the iron railing.

"Come!"

No! No! No! It was impossible. Her hands clutched the iron in frenzy. Amid the seas she sent a cry of anguish!

"Eveline! Evvy!"   25

He rushed beyond the barrier and called to her to follow. He was shouted at to go on but he still called to her. She set her white face to him, passive, like a helpless animal. Her eyes gave him no sign of love or farewell or recognition.

Derevaun Seraun!: This has been interpreted as a slurred Gaelic phrase meaning either "the end of pleasure is pain" or "the end of song is raving madness."

Edgar Allan Poe

The Cask of Amontillado

The thousand injuries of Fortunato I had borne as I best could; but when he ventured upon insult, I vowed revenge. You, who so well know the nature of my soul, will not suppose, however, that I gave utterance to a threat. *At length* I would be avenged; this was a point definitively settled—but the very definitiveness with which it was resolved precluded the idea of risk. I must not only punish, but punish with impunity. A wrong is unredressed when retribution overtakes its redresser. It is equally unredressed when the avenger fails to make himself felt as such to him who has done the wrong.

It must be understood, that neither by word nor deed had I given Fortunato cause to doubt my good will. I continued, as was my wont, to smile in his face, and he did not perceive that my smile *now* was at the thought of his immolation.

He had a weak point—this Fortunato—although in other regards he was a man to be respected and even feared. He prided himself on his connoisseurship in wine. Few Italians have the true virtuoso spirit. For the most part their enthusiasm is adopted to suit the time and opportunity—to practise imposture upon the British and Austrian *millionaires*. In painting and gemmary Fortunato, like his countrymen, was a quack—but in the matter of old wines he was sincere. In this respect I did not differ from him materially: I was skillful in the Italian vintages myself, and bought largely whenever I could.

It was about dusk, one evening during the supreme madness of the carnival season, that I encountered my friend. He accosted me with excessive warmth, for he had been drinking much. The man wore motley. He had on a tight-fitting parti-striped dress, and his head was surmounted by the conical cap and bells. I was so pleased to see him, that I thought I should never have done wringing his hand.

5   I said to him—"My dear Fortunato, you are luckily met. How remarkably well you are looking today! But I have received a pipe of what passes for Amontillado, and I have my doubts."

"How?" said he. "Amontillado? A pipe? Impossible! And in the middle of the carnival!"

THE CASK OF AMONTILLADO   First published in 1846. Edgar Allan Poe (1809–1849) was one of the first modern practitioners and theorists of the short story as a literary form, prescribing as its highest goal the creation of "a certain unique or single effect." His own achievement best matches his theory in his horror tales, of which this is an example. Poe was born in Boston, abandoned at the age of three by his father after the death of his mother, and raised by adoptive parents in Virginia. As a young man he failed in attempts at education at the University of Virginia and at West Point. Difficulty with alcohol combined with nervous sensitivity led to continuing health problems and perhaps to his early death. "Amontillado" is a dry Spanish sherry wine; "carnival" is the festive season preceding Lent.

"I have my doubts," I replied; "and I was silly enough to pay the full Amontillado price without consulting you in the matter. You were not to be found, and I was fearful of losing a bargain."

"Amontillado!"

"I have my doubts."

"Amontillado!"   10

"And I must satisfy them."

"Amontillado!"

"As you are engaged, I am on my way to Luchesi. If anyone has a critical turn, it is he. He will tell me—"

"Luchesi cannot tell Amontillado from Sherry."

"And yet some fools will have it that his taste is a match for your own."   15

"Come, let us go."

"Whither?"

"To your vaults."

"My friend, no; I will not impose upon your good nature. I perceive you have an engagement. Luchesi—"

"I have no engagement;—come."   20

"My friend, no. It is not the engagement, but the severe cold with which I perceive you are afflicted. The vaults are insufferably damp. They are encrusted with niter."

"Let us go, nevertheless. The cold is merely nothing. Amontillado! You have been imposed upon. And as for Luchesi, he cannot distinguish Sherry from Amontillado."

Thus speaking, Fortunato possessed himself of my arm. Putting on a mask of black silk, and drawing a *roquelaire*° closely about my person, I suffered him to hurry me to my palazzo.

There were no attendants at home; they had absconded to make merry in honor of the time. I had told them that I should not return until the morning, and had given them explicit orders not to stir from the house. These orders were sufficient, I well knew, to insure their immediate disappearance, one and all, as soon as my back was turned.

I took from their sconces two flambeaux, and giving one to Fortunato,   25 bowed him through several suites of rooms to the archway that led into the vaults. I passed down a long and winding staircase, requesting him to be cautious as he followed. We came at length to the foot of the descent, and stood together on the damp ground of the catacombs of the Montresors.

The gait of my friend was unsteady, and the bells upon his cap jingled as he strode.

"The pipe," said he.

"It is farther on," said I; "but observe the white web-work which gleams from these cavern walls."

He turned towards me, and looked into my eyes with two filmy orbs that distilled the rheum of intoxication.

---

roquelaire: a knee-length cloak worn in the eighteenth century

30   "Niter?" he asked, at length.

"Niter," I replied. "How long have you had that cough?"

"Ugh! ugh! ugh!—ugh! ugh! ugh!—ugh! ugh! ugh!—ugh! ugh! ugh!—ugh! ugh! ugh!"

My poor friend found it impossible to reply for many minutes.

"It is nothing," he said, at last.

35   "Come," I said, with decision, "we will go back; your health is precious. You are rich, respected, admired, beloved; you are happy, as once I was. You are a man to be missed. For me it is no matter. We will go back; you will be ill, and I cannot be responsible. Beside, there is Luchesi—"

"Enough," he said; "the cough is a mere nothing; it will not kill me. I shall not die of a cough."

"True—true," I replied; "and, indeed, I had no intention of alarming you unnecessarily—but you should use all proper caution. A draught of this Medoc will defend us from the damps."

Here I knocked off the neck of a bottle which I drew from a long row of its fellows that lay upon the mold.

"Drink," I said, presenting him the wine.

40   He raised it to his lips with a leer. He paused and nodded to me familiarly, while his bells jingled.

"I drink," he said, "to the buried that repose around us."

"And I to your long life."

He again took my arm, and we proceeded.

"These vaults," he said, "are extensive."

45   "The Montresors," I replied, "were a great and numerous family."

"I forget your arms."

"A huge human foot d'or, in a field azure; the foot crushes a serpent rampant whose fangs are imbedded in the heel."

"And the motto?"

"*Nemo me impune lacessit.*"°

50   "Good!" he said.

The wine sparkled in his eyes and the bells jingled. My own fancy grew warm with the Medoc. We had passed through walls of piled bones, with casks and puncheons intermingling, into the inmost recesses of the catacombs. I paused again, and this time I made bold to seize Fortunato by an arm above the elbow.

"The niter!" I said; "see, it increases. It hangs like moss upon the vaults. We are below the river's bed. The drops of moisture trickle among the bones. Come, we will go back ere it is too late. Your cough—"

"It is nothing," he said; "let us go on. But first, another draught of the Medoc."

I broke and reached him a flacon of De Grâve. He emptied it at a breath. His eyes flashed with a fierce light. He laughed and threw the bottle upwards with a gesticulation I did not understand.

Nemo ... lacessit: No one can provoke me and get away with it.

I looked at him in surprise. He repeated the movement—a grotesque one.   55
"You do not comprehend?" he said.

"Not I," I replied.

"Then you are not of the brotherhood."

"How?"

"You are not of the masons."   60

"Yes, yes," I said, "yes, yes."

"You? Impossible! A mason?"

"A mason," I replied.

"A sign," he said.

"It is this," I answered, producing a trowel from beneath the folds of my   65
roquelaire.

"You jest," he exclaimed, recoiling a few paces. "But let us proceed to
the Amontillado."

"Be it so," I said, replacing the tool beneath the cloak, and again offering
him my arm. He leaned upon it heavily. We continued our route in search of
the Amontillado. We passed through a range of low arches, descended,
passed on, and descending again, arrived at a deep crypt, in which the foul-
ness of the air caused our flambeaux rather to glow than flame.

At the most remote end of the crypt there appeared another less spacious. Its walls had been lined with human remains, piled to the vault
overhead, in the fashion of the great catacombs of Paris. Three sides of
this interior crypt were still ornamented in this manner. From the fourth
the bones had been thrown down, and lay promiscuously upon the earth,
forming at one point a mound of some size. Within the wall thus exposed
by the displacing of the bones, we perceived a still interior recess, in
depth about four feet, in width three, in height six or seven. It seemed to
have been constructed for no especial use within itself, but formed
merely the interval between two of the colossal supports of the roof of the
catacombs, and was backed by one of their circumscribing walls of solid
granite.

It was in vain that Fortunato, uplifting his dull torch, endeavored to pry
into the depth of the recess. Its termination the feeble light did not enable us
to see.

"Proceed," I said; "herein is the Amontillado. As for Luchesi—"   70

"He is an ignoramus," interrupted my friend, as he stepped unsteadily
forward, while I followed immediately at his heels. In an instant he had
reached the extremity of the niche, and finding his progress arrested by the
rock, stood stupidly bewildered. A moment more and I had fettered him to
the granite. In its surface were two iron staples, distant from each other
about two feet, horizontally. From one of these depended a short chain, from
the other a padlock. Throwing the links about his waist, it was but the work
of a few seconds to secure it. He was too much astounded to resist. Withdrawing the key I stepped back from the recess.

"Pass your hand," I said, "over the wall; you cannot help feeling the
niter. Indeed it is *very* damp. Once more let me *implore* you to return. No?

Then I must positively leave you. But I must first render you all the little attentions in my power."

"The Amontillado!" ejaculated my friend, not yet recovered from his astonishment.

"True," I replied; "the Amontillado."

75   As I said these words, I busied myself among the pile of bones of which I have before spoken. Throwing them aside, I soon uncovered a quantity of building stone and mortar. With these materials and with the aid of my trowel, I began vigorously to wall up the entrance of the niche.

I had scarcely laid the first tier of the masonry when I discovered that the intoxication of Fortunato had in a great measure worn off. The earliest indication I had of this was a low moaning cry from the depth of the recess. It was *not* the cry of a drunken man. There was then a long and obstinate silence. I laid the second tier, and the third, and the fourth; and then I heard the furious vibrations of the chain. The noise lasted for several minutes, during which, that I might harken to it with the more satisfaction, I ceased my labors and sat down upon the bones. When at last the clanking subsided, I resumed the trowel, and finished without interruption the fifth, the sixth, and the seventh tier. The wall was now nearly upon a level with my breast. I again paused, and holding the flambeaux over the masonwork, threw a few feeble rays upon the figure within.

A succession of loud and shrill screams, bursting suddenly from the throat of the chained form, seemed to thrust me violently back. For a brief moment I hesitated—I trembled. Unsheathing my rapier, I began to grope with it about the recess: but the thought of an instant reassured me. I placed my hand upon the solid fabric of the catacombs, and felt satisfied. I reapproached the wall. I replied to the yells of him who clamored. I re-echoed—I aided—I surpassed them in volume and in strength. I did this, and the clamorer grew still.

It was now midnight, and my task was drawing to a close. I had completed the eighth, the ninth, and the tenth tier. I had finished a portion of the last and the eleventh; there remained but a single stone to be fitted and plastered in. I struggled with its weight; I placed it partially in its destined position. But now there came from out the niche a low laugh that erected the hairs upon my head. It was succeeded by a sad voice, which I had difficulty in recognising as that of the noble Fortunato. The voice said—

"Ha! ha! ha!—he! he!—a very good joke indeed—an excellent jest. We will have many a rich laugh about it at the palazzo—he! he! he!—over our wine—he! he! he!"

80   "The Amontillado!" I said.

"He! he! he!—he! he! he!—yes, the Amontillado. But is it not getting late? Will not they be awaiting us at the palazzo, the Lady Fortunato and the rest? Let us be gone."

"Yes," I said, "let us be gone."

"For the love of God, Montresor!"

"Yes," I said, "for the love of God!"

But to these words I harkened in vain for a reply. I grew impatient. I   85
called aloud—

"Fortunato!"

No answer. I called again—

"Fortunato!"

No answer still. I thrust a torch through the remaining aperture and let it
fall within. There came forth in return only a jingling of the bells. My heart
grew sick—on account of the dampness of the catacombs. I hastened to
make an end of my labor. I forced the last stone into its position; I plastered it
up. Against the new masonry I re-erected the old rampart of bones. For the
half of a century no mortal has disturbed them. *In pace requiescat!*°

Eudora Welty

A Worn Path

It was December—a bright frozen day in the early morning. Far out in
the country there was an old Negro woman with her head tied in a red rag,
coming along a path through the pinewoods. Her name was Phoenix Jackson. She was very old and small and she walked slowly in the dark pine
shadows, moving a little from side to side in her steps, with the balanced
heaviness and lightness of a pendulum in a grandfather clock. She carried a
thin, small cane made from an umbrella, and with this she kept tapping the
frozen earth in front of her. This made a grave and persistent noise in the still
air, that seemed meditative like the chirping of a solitary little bird.

She wore a dark striped dress reaching down to her shoe tops, and an
equally long apron of bleached sugar sacks, with a full pocket: all neat and
tidy, but every time she took a step she might have fallen over her shoelaces,
which dragged from her unlaced shoes. She looked straight ahead. Her eyes
were blue with age. Her skin had a pattern all its own of numberless branch-
ing wrinkles and as though a whole little tree stood in the middle of her
forehead, but a golden color ran underneath, and the two knobs of her
cheeks were illumined by a yellow burning under the dark. Under the red
rag her hair came down on her neck in the frailest of ringlets, still black, and
with an odor like copper.

A WORN PATH   First published in 1941. Eudora Welty was born in 1909 in Jackson,
Mississippi, where she was raised and to which she returned after studying at the University of Wisconsin and Columbia University. In the mid-1930s she was employed by
the federal Work Projects Administration (WPA) to travel throughout Mississippi writing newspaper copy and taking photographs, a job that enabled her to observe many varieties of rural life in her native state.

In pace requiescat!: May he rest in peace!

Now and then there was a quivering in the thicket. Old Phoenix said, "Out of my way, all you foxes, owls, beetles, jack rabbits, coons, and wild animals! . . . Keep out from under these feet, little bobwhites. . . . Keep the big wild hogs out of my path. Don't let none of those come running my direction. I got a long way." Under her small black-freckled hand her cane, limber as a buggy whip, would switch at the brush as if to rouse up any hiding things.

On she went. The woods were deep and still. The sun made the pine needles almost too bright to look at, up where the wind rocked. The cones dropped as light as feathers. Down in the hollow was the mourning dove—it was not too late for him.

5   The path ran up a hill. "Seem like there is chains about my feet, time I get this far," she said, in the voice of argument old people keep to use with themselves. "Something always take a hold of me on this hill—pleads I should stay."

After she got to the top she turned and gave a full, severe look behind her where she had come. "Up through pines," she said at length. "Now down through oaks."

Her eyes opened their widest, and she started down gently. But before she got to the bottom of the hill a bush caught her dress.

Her fingers were busy and intent, but her skirts were full and long, so that before she could pull them free in one place they were caught in another. It was not possible to allow the dress to tear. "I in the thorny bush," she said. "Thorns, you doing your appointed work. Never want to let folks pass, no sir. Old eyes thought you was a pretty little *green* bush."

Finally, trembling all over, she stood free, and after a moment dared to stoop for her cane.

10   "Sun so high!" she cried, leaning back and looking, while the thick tears went over her eyes. "The time getting all gone here."

At the foot of this hill was a place where a log was laid across the creek.

"Now comes the trial," said Phoenix.

Putting her right foot out, she mounted the log and shut her eyes. Lifting her skirt, leveling her cane fiercely before her, like a festival figure in some parade, she began to march across. Then she opened her eyes and she was safe on the other side.

"I wasn't as old as I thought," she said.

15   But she sat down to rest. She spread her skirts on the bank around her and folded her hands over her knees. Up above her was a tree in a pearly cloud of mistletoe. She did not dare to close her eyes, and when a little boy brought her a plate with a slice of marble-cake on it she spoke to him. "That would be acceptable," she said. But when she went to take it there was just her own hand in the air.

So she left that tree, and had to go through a barbed-wire fence. There she had to creep and crawl, spreading her knees and stretching her fingers like a baby trying to climb the steps. But she talked loudly to herself: she could not let her dress be torn now, so late in the day, and she could not pay for having her arm or her leg sawed off if she got caught fast where she was.

At last she was safe through the fence and risen up out in the clearing. Big dead trees, like black men with one arm, were standing in the purple stalks of the withered cotton field. There sat a buzzard.

"Who you watching?"

In the furrow she made her way along.

"Glad this not the season for bulls," she said, looking sideways, "and the good Lord made his snakes to curl up and sleep in the winter. A pleasure I don't see no two-headed snake coming around that tree, where it come once. It took a while to get by him, back in the summer."

She passed through the old cotton and went into a field of dead corn. It whispered and shook and was taller than her head. "Through the maze now," she said, for there was no path.

Then there was something tall, black, and skinny there, moving before her.

At first she took it for a man. It could have been a man dancing in the field. But she stood still and listened, and it did not make a sound. It was as silent as a ghost.

"Ghost," she said sharply, "who be you the ghost of? For I have heard of nary death close by."

But there was no answer—only the ragged dancing in the wind.

She shut her eyes, reached out her hand, and touched a sleeve. She found a coat and inside that an emptiness, cold as ice.

"You scarecrow," she said. Her face lighted. "I ought to be shut up for good," she said with laughter. "My senses is gone. I too old. I the oldest people I ever know. Dance, old scarecrow," she said, "while I dancing with you."

She kicked her foot over the furrow, and with mouth drawn down, shook her head once or twice in a little strutting way. Some husks blew down and whirled in streamers about her skirts.

Then she went on, parting her way from side to side with the cane, through the whispering field. At last she came to the end, to a wagon track where the silver grass blew between the red ruts. The quail were walking around like pullets, seeming all dainty and unseen.

"Walk pretty," she said. "This the easy place. This the easy going."

She followed the track, swaying through the quiet bare fields, through the little strings of trees silver in their dead leaves, past cabins silver from weather, with the doors and windows boarded shut, all like old women under a spell sitting there. "I walking in their sleep," she said, nodding her head vigorously.

In a ravine she went where a spring was silently flowing through a hollow log. Old Phoenix bent and drank. "Sweet-gum makes the water sweet," she said, and drank more. "Nobody know who made this well, for it was here when I was born."

The track crossed a swampy part where the moss hung as white as lace from every limb. "Sleep on, alligators, and blow your bubbles." Then the track went into the road.

Deep, deep the road went down between the high green-colored banks. Overhead the live-oaks met, and it was as dark as a cave.

35   A black dog with a lolling tongue came up out of the weeds by the ditch. She was meditating, and not ready, and when he came at her she only hit him a little with her cane. Over she went in the ditch, like a little puff of milkweed.

Down there, her senses drifted away. A dream visited her, and she reached her hand up, but nothing reached down and gave her a pull. So she lay there and presently went to talking. "Old woman," she said to herself, "that black dog come up out of the weeds to stall you off, and now there he sitting on his fine tail, smiling at you."

A white man finally came along and found her—a hunter, a young man, with his dog on a chain.

"Well, Granny!" he laughed. "What are you doing there?"

"Lying on my back like a June-bug waiting to be turned over, mister," she said, reaching up her hand.

40   He lifted her up, gave her a swing in the air, and set her down. "Anything broken, Granny?"

"No sir, them old dead weeds is springy enough," said Phoenix, when she had got her breath. "I thank you for your trouble."

"Where do you live, Granny?" he asked, while the two dogs were growling at each other.

"Away back yonder, sir, behind the ridge. You can't even see it from here."

"On your way home?"

45   "No sir, going to town."

"Why, that's too far! That's as far as I walk when I come out myself, and I get something for my trouble." He patted the stuffed bag he carried, and there hung down a little closed claw. It was one of the bobwhites, with its beak hooked bitterly to show it was dead. "Now you go on home, Granny!"

"I bound to go to town, mister," said Phoenix. "The time come around."

He gave another laugh, filling the whole landscape. "I know you old colored people! Wouldn't miss going to town to see Santa Claus!"

But something held old Phoenix very still. The deep lines in her face went into a fierce and different radiation. Without warning, she had seen with her own eyes a flashing nickel fall out of the man's pocket onto the ground.

50   "How old are you, Granny?" he was saying.

"There is no telling, mister," she said, "no telling."

Then she gave a little cry and clapped her hands and said, "Git on away from here, dog! Look! Look at that dog!" She laughed as if in admiration. "He ain't scared of nobody. He a big black dog." She whispered, "Sic him!"

"Watch me get rid of that cur," said the man. "Sic him, Pete! Sic him!"

Phoenix heard the dogs fighting, and heard the man running and throwing sticks. She even heard a gunshot. But she was slowly bending forward by that time, further and further forward, the lids stretched down over her eyes, as if she were doing this in her sleep. Her chin was lowered almost to her knees. The yellow palm of her hand came out from the fold of her apron. Her fingers slid down and along the ground under the piece of money with the grace and care they would have in lifting an egg from under a setting hen. Then she slowly straightened up, she stood erect, and the nickel was in her apron pocket. A bird flew by. Her lips moved. "God watching me the whole time. I come to stealing."

The man came back, and his own dog panted about them. "Well, I 55
scared him off that time," he said, and then he laughed and lifted his gun and pointed it at Phoenix.

She stood straight and faced him.

"Doesn't the gun scare you?" he said, still pointing it.

"No, sir, I seen plenty go off closer by, in my day, and for less than what I done," she said, holding utterly still.

He smiled, and shouldered the gun. "Well, Granny," he said, "you must be a hundred years old, and scared of nothing. I'd give you a dime if I had any money with me. But you take my advice and stay home, and nothing will happen to you."

"I bound to go on my way, mister," said Phoenix. She inclined her head 60
in the red rag. Then they went in different directions, but she could hear the gun shooting again and again over the hill.

She walked on. The shadows hung from the oak trees to the road like curtains. Then she smelled wood-smoke, and smelled the river, and she saw a steeple and the cabins on their steep steps. Dozens of little black children whirled around her. There ahead was Natchez shining. Bells were ringing. She walked on.

In the paved city it was Christmas time. There were red and green electric lights strung and crisscrossed everywhere, and all turned on in the daytime. Old Phoenix would have been lost if she had not distrusted her eyesight and depended on her feet to know where to take her.

She paused quietly on the sidewalk where people were passing by. A lady came along in the crowd, carrying an armful of red-, green-, and silver-wrapped presents; she gave off perfume like the red roses in hot summer, and Phoenix stopped her.

"Please, missy, will you lace up my shoe?" She held up her foot.

"What do you want, Grandma?" 65

"See my shoe," said Phoenix. "Do all right for out in the country, but wouldn't look right to go in a big building."

"Stand still then, Grandma," said the lady. She put her packages down on the sidewalk beside her and laced and tied both shoes tightly.

"Can't lace 'em with a cane," said Phoenix. "Thank you, missy. I doesn't mind asking a nice lady to tie up my shoe, when I gets out on the street."

Moving slowly and from side to side, she went into the big building, and into a tower of steps, where she walked up and around and around until her feet knew to stop.

70   She entered a door, and there she saw nailed up on the wall the document that had been stamped with the gold seal and framed in the gold frame, which matched the dream that was hung up in her head.

"Here I be," she said. There was a fixed and ceremonial stiffness over her body.

"A charity case, I suppose," said an attendant who sat at the desk before her.

But Phoenix only looked above her head. There was sweat on her face, the wrinkles in her skin shone like a bright net.

"Speak up, Grandma," the woman said. "What's your name? We must have your history, you know. Have you been here before? What seems to be the trouble with you?"

75   Old Phoenix only gave a twitch to her face as if a fly were bothering her.

"Are you deaf?" cried the attendant.

But then the nurse came in.

"Oh, that's just old Aunt Phoenix," she said. "She doesn't come for herself—she has a little grandson. She makes these trips just as regular as clockwork. She lives away back off the Old Natchez Trace." She bent down. "Well, Aunt Phoenix, why don't you just take a seat? We won't keep you standing after your long trip." She pointed.

The old woman sat down, bolt upright in the chair.

80   "Now, how is the boy?" asked the nurse.

Old Phoenix did not speak.

"I said, how is the boy?"

But Phoenix only waited and stared straight ahead, her face very solemn and withdrawn into rigidity.

"Is his throat any better?" asked the nurse. "Aunt Phoenix, don't you hear me? Is your grandson's throat any better since the last time you came for the medicine?"

85   With her hands on her knees, the old woman waited, silent, erect and motionless, just as if she were in armor.

"You mustn't take up our time this way, Aunt Phoenix," the nurse said. "Tell us quickly about your grandson, and get it over. He isn't dead, is he?"

At last there came a flicker and then a flame of comprehension across her face, and she spoke.

"My grandson. It was my memory had left me. There I sat and forgot why I made my long trip."

"Forgot?" The nurse frowned. "After you came so far?"

Then Phoenix was like an old woman begging a dignified forgiveness for   90
waking up frightened in the night. "I never did go to school, I was too old at
the Surrender," she said in a soft voice. "I'm an old woman without an education. It was my memory fail me. My little grandson, he is just the same,
and I forgot it in the coming."

"Throat never heals, does it?" said the nurse, speaking in a loud, sure
voice to old Phoenix. By now she had a card with something written on it, a
little list. "Yes. Swallowed lye. When was it?—January—two, three years
ago—?"

Phoenix spoke unasked now. "No, missy, he not dead, he just the same.
Every little while his throat begin to close up again, and he not able to swallow. He not get his breath. He not able to help himself. So the time come
around, and I go on another trip for the soothing medicine."

"All right. The doctor said as long as you came to get it, you could have
it," said the nurse. "But it's an obstinate case."

"My little grandson, he sit up there in the house all wrapped up, waiting
by himself," Phoenix went on. "We is the only two left in the world. He
suffer and it don't seem to put him back at all. He got a sweet look. He going
to last. He wear a little patch quilt and peep out holding his mouth open like
a little bird. I remembers so plain now. I not going to forget him again, no,
the whole enduring time. I could tell him from all the others in creation."

"All right." The nurse was trying to hush her now. She brought her a   95
bottle of medicine. "Charity," she said, making a check mark in a book.

Old Phoenix held the bottle close to her eyes, and then carefully put it
into her pocket.

"I thank you," she said.

"It's Christmas time, Grandma," said the attendant. "Could I give you a
few pennies out of my purse?"

"Five pennies is a nickel," said Phoenix stiffly.

"Here's a nickel," said the attendant.   100

Phoenix rose carefully and held out her hand. She received the nickel
and then fished the other nickel out of her pocket and laid it beside the new
one. She stared at her palm closely, with her head on one side.

Then she gave a tap with her cane on the floor.

"This is what come to me to do," she said. "I going to the store and buy
my child a little windmill they sells, made out of paper. He going to find it
hard to believe there such a thing in the world. I'll march myself back where
he waiting, holding it straight up in this hand."

She lifted her free hand, gave a little nod, turned around, and walked out
of the doctor's office. Then her slow step began on the stairs, going down.

Tobias Wolff

Say Yes

They were doing the dishes, his wife washing while he dried. He'd washed the night before. Unlike most men he knew, he really pitched in on the housework. A few months earlier he'd overheard a friend of his wife's congratulate her on having such a considerate husband, and he thought, *I try.* Helping out with the dishes was a way he had of showing how considerate he was.

They talked about different things and somehow got on the subject of whether white people should marry black people. He said that all things considered, he thought it was a bad idea.

"Why?" she asked.

Sometimes his wife got this look where she pinched her brows together and bit her lower lip and stared down at something. When he saw her like this he knew he should keep his mouth shut, but he never did. Actually it made him talk more. She had that look now.

5   "Why?" she asked again, and stood there with her hand inside a bowl, not washing it but just holding it above the water.

"Listen," he said, "I went to school with blacks and I've worked with blacks and lived on the same street with blacks and we've always gotten along just fine. I don't need you coming along now and implying that I'm a racist."

"I didn't imply anything," she said, and began washing the bowl again, turning it around in her hand as though she were shaping it. "I just don't see what's wrong with a white person marrying a black person, that's all."

"They don't come from the same culture as we do. Listen to them sometime—they even have their own language. That's okay with me. I *like* hearing them talk"—he did; for some reason it always made him feel happy—"but it's different. A person from their culture and a person from our culture could never really *know* each other."

"Like you know me?" his wife asked.

10   "Yes. Like I know you."

"But if they love each other," she said. She was washing faster now, not looking at him.

Oh boy, he thought. He said, "Don't take my word for it. Look at the statistics. Most of those marriages break up."

SAY YES   First published in 1985. Tobias Wolff was born in 1945 in Birmingham, Alabama, and raised in the state of Washington. He dropped out of high school and worked as an apprentice seaman, then joined the U.S. Army Special Forces in 1964. He served as a paratrooper in Vietnam, and was a first lieutenant when he left the army in 1968. He then earned degrees at Oxford University and Stanford, and now teaches at Syracuse, where he lives with his wife and two sons. This story is from his collection titled *Back in the World,* a phrase used by the military in Vietnam to signify a return to civilian life.

"Statistics." She was piling dishes on the drainboard at a terrific rate, just swiping at them with the cloth. Many of them were greasy, and there were flecks of food between the tines of the forks. "All right," she said, "what about foreigners? I suppose you think the same thing about two foreigners getting married."

"Yes," he said, "as a matter of fact I do. How can you understand someone who comes from a completely different background?"

"Different," said his wife. "Not the same, like us."   15

"Yes, different," he snapped, angry with her for resorting to this trick of repeating his words so that they sounded crass, or hypocritical. "These are dirty," he said, and dumped all the silverware back into the sink.

The water had gone flat and grey. She stared down at it, her lips pressed tight together, then plunged her hands under the surface. "Oh!" she cried, and jumped back. She took her right hand by the wrist and held it up. Her thumb was bleeding.

"Ann, don't move," he said. "Stay right there." He ran upstairs to the bathroom and rummaged in the medicine chest for alcohol, cotton, and a Band-Aid. When he came back down she was leaning against the refrigerator with her eyes closed, still holding her hand. He took the hand and dabbed at her thumb with the cotton. The bleeding had stopped. He squeezed it to see how deep the wound was and a single drop of blood welled up, trembling and bright, and fell to the floor. Over the thumb she stared at him accusingly. "It's shallow," he said. "Tomorrow you won't even know it's there." He hoped that she appreciated how quickly he had come to her aid. He'd acted out of concern for her, with no thought of getting anything in return, but now the thought occurred to him that it would be a nice gesture on her part not to start up that conversation again, as he was tired of it. "I'll finish up here," he said. "You go and relax."

"That's okay," she said. "I'll dry."

He began to wash the silverware again, giving a lot of attention to the   20
forks.

"So," she said, "you wouldn't have married me if I'd been black."

"For Christ's sake, Ann!"

"Well, that's what you said, didn't you?"

"No, I did not. The whole question is ridiculous. If you had been black we probably wouldn't even have met. You would have had your friends and I would have had mine. The only black girl I ever really knew was my partner in the debating club, and I was already going out with you by then."

"But if we had met, and I'd been black?"   25

"Then you probably would have been going out with a black guy." He picked up the rinsing nozzle and sprayed the silverware. The water was so hot that the metal darkened to pale blue, then turned silver again.

"Let's say I wasn't," she said. "Let's say I am black and unattached and we meet and fall in love."

He glanced over at her. She was watching him and her eyes were bright. "Look," he said, taking a reasonable tone, "this is stupid. If you were black you wouldn't be you." As he said this he realized it was absolutely true. There was no possible way of arguing with the fact that she would not be herself if she were black. So he said it again: "If you were black you wouldn't be you."

"I know," she said, "but let's just say."

30   He took a deep breath. He had won the argument but he still felt cornered. "Say what?" he asked.

"That I'm black, but still me, and we fall in love. Will you marry me?"

He thought about it.

"Well?" she said, and stepped close to him. Her eyes were even brighter. "Will you marry me?"

"I'm thinking," he said.

35   "You won't, I can tell. You're going to say no."

"Let's not move too fast on this," he said. "There are lots of things to consider. We don't want to do something we would regret for the rest of our lives."

"No more considering. Yes or no."

"Since you put it that way—"

"Yes or no."

40   "Jesus, Ann. All right. No."

She said, "Thank you," and walked from the kitchen into the living room. A moment later he heard her turning the pages of a magazine. He knew that she was too angry to be actually reading it, but she didn't snap through the pages the way he would have done. She turned them slowly, as if she were studying every word. She was demonstrating her indifference to him, and it had the effect he knew she wanted it to have. It hurt him.

He had no choice but to demonstrate his indifference to her. Quietly, thoroughly, he washed the rest of the dishes. Then he dried them and put them away. He wiped the counters and the stove and scoured the linoleum where the drop of blood had fallen. While he was at it, he decided he might as well mop the whole floor. When he was done the kitchen looked new, the way it looked when they were first shown the house, before they had ever lived here.

He picked up the garbage pail and went outside. The night was clear and he could see a few stars to the west, where the lights of the town didn't blur them out. On El Camino the traffic was steady and light, peaceful as a river. He felt ashamed that he had let his wife get him into a fight. In another thirty years or so they would both be dead. What would all that stuff matter then? He thought of the years they had spent together and how close they were and how well they knew each other, and his throat tightened so that he could hardly breathe. His face and neck began to tingle. Warmth flooded his chest. He stood there for a while, enjoying these sensations, then picked up the pail and went out the back gate.

The two mutts from down the street had pulled over the garbage can again. One of them was rolling around on his back and the other had something in her mouth. Growling, she tossed it into the air, leaped up and caught it, growled again and whipped her head from side to side. When they saw him coming they trotted away with short, mincing steps. Normally he would heave rocks at them, but this time he let them go.

The house was dark when he came back inside. She was in the bathroom.   45
He stood outside the door and called her name. He heard bottles clinking, but she didn't answer him. "Ann, I'm really sorry," he said. "I'll make it up to you, I promise."

"How?" she asked.

He wasn't expecting this. But from a sound in her voice, a level and definite note that was strange to him, he knew that he had come up with a right answer. He leaned against the door. "I'll marry you," he whispered.

"We'll see," she said. "Go on to bed. I'll be out in a minute."

He undressed and got under the covers. Finally he heard the bathroom door open and close.

"Turn off the light," she said from the hallway.   50

"What?"

"Turn off the light."

He reached over and pulled the chain on the bedside lamp. The room went dark. "All right," he said. He lay there, but nothing happened. "All right," he said again. Then he heard a movement across the room. He sat up but he couldn't see a thing. The room was silent. His heart pounded the way it had on their first night together, the way it still did when he woke at a noise in the darkness and waited to hear it again—the sound of someone moving through the house, a stranger.

Three Novellas

Herman Melville

Bartleby the Scrivener

A Story of Wall Street

I am a rather elderly man. The nature of my avocations for the last thirty years has brought me into more than ordinary contact with what would seem an interesting and somewhat singular set of men of whom as yet nothing that I know of has ever been written—I mean the law-copyists or scriveners. I have known very many of them, professionally and privately, and if I pleased could relate diverse histories at which good-natured gentlemen might smile and sentimental souls might weep. But I waive the biographies of all other scriveners for a few passages in the life of Bartleby, who was a scrivener the strangest I ever saw or heard of. While of other law-copyists I might write the complete life, of Bartleby nothing of that sort can be done. I believe that no materials exist for a full and satisfactory biography of this man. It is an irreparable loss to literature. Bartleby was one of those beings of whom nothing is ascertainable except from the original sources, and in his case those are very small. What my own astonished eyes saw of Bartleby, *that* is all I know of him except, indeed, one vague report which will appear in the sequel.

Ere introducing the scrivener as he first appeared to me, it is fit I make some mention of myself, my employees, my business, my chambers, and general surroundings, because some such description is indispensable to an adequate understanding of the chief character about to be presented.

Imprimis: I am a man who from his youth upwards has been filled with a profound conviction that the easiest way of life is the best. Hence, though I belong to a profession proverbially energetic and nervous, even to turbulence at times, yet nothing of that sort have I ever suffered to invade my peace. I am one of those unambitious lawyers who never addresses a jury or in any way draws down public applause, but in the cool tranquility of a snug retreat do a snug business among rich men's bonds and mortgages and title-deeds. All who know me consider me an eminently *safe* man. The late John Jacob Astor, a personage little given to poetic enthusiasm, had no hesitation

BARTLEBY THE SCRIVENER First published in 1853. Herman Melville (1819–1891) was born in New York City. After working as a farmhand, clerk, bookkeeper, and teacher, he went to sea in 1837, where his adventures and observations supplied him with the material for several novels of the sea including *Moby Dick* (1851). The lack of financial success of that book and later works of fiction, including *Piazza Tales,* which reprinted "Bartleby the Scrivener," led Melville eventually to write poetry instead. By the time of the story, Wall Street had become the financial and business center of New York City. In the days before the invention of the typewriter, official documents and legal papers had to be copied by hand—the job of a "scrivener." "The Tombs" (paragraph 11 and thereafter) was the vivid nickname of the city prison, properly called the Halls of Justice.

in pronouncing my first grand point to be prudence; my next, method. I do not speak it in vanity but simply record the fact that I was not unemployed in my profession by the late John Jacob Astor, a name which, I admit, I love to repeat, for it hath a rounded and orbicular sound to it and rings like unto bullion. I will freely add that I was not insensible to the late John Jacob Astor's good opinion.

Sometime prior to the period at which this little history begins, my avocations had been largely increased. The good old office now extinct in the State of New York of a Master in Chancery had been conferred upon me. It was not a very arduous office but very pleasantly remunerative. I seldom lose my temper; much more seldom indulge in dangerous indignation at wrongs and outrages; but I must be permitted to be rash here and declare that I consider the sudden and violent abrogation of the office of Master in Chancery by the new Constitution as a ——— premature act, inasmuch as I had counted upon a life-lease of the profits, whereas I only received those of a few short years. But this is by the way.

5   My chambers were upstairs at No. — Wall Street. At one end they looked upon the white wall of the interior of a spacious skylight shaft penetrating the building from top to bottom. This view might have been considered rather tame than otherwise, deficient in what landscape painters call "life." But if so, the view from the other end of my chambers offered at least a contrast, if nothing more. In that direction my windows commanded an unobstructed view of a lofty brick wall, black by age and everlasting shade, which wall required no spy-glass to bring out its lurking beauties, but for the benefit of all near-sighted spectators was pushed up to within ten feet of my window panes. Owing to the great height of the surrounding buildings, and my chambers being on the second floor, the interval between this wall and mine not a little resembled a huge square cistern.

At the period just preceding the advent of Bartleby, I had two persons as copyists in my employment and a promising lad as an office boy. First, Turkey; second, Nippers; third, Ginger Nut. These may seem names the like of which are not usually found in the Directory. In truth they were nicknames mutually conferred upon each other by my three clerks, and were deemed expressive of their respective persons or characters. Turkey was a short, pursy Englishman of about my own age, that is, somewhere not far from sixty. In the morning, one might say, his face was of a fine florid hue, but after twelve o'clock, meridian—his dinner hour—it blazed like a grate full of Christmas coals, and continued blazing—but as it were with a gradual wane—till 6 o'clock P.M. or thereabouts, after which I saw no more of the proprietor of the face, which gaining its meridian with the sun, seemed to set with it, to rise, culminate, and decline the following day, with the like regularity and undiminished glory. There are many singular coincidences I have known in the course of my life, not the least among which was the fact that exactly when Turkey displayed his fullest beams from his red and radiant countenance, just then, too, at the critical moment began the daily period when I considered his business capacities as seriously disturbed for the remainder of the twenty-four hours. Not that he was absolutely idle or averse to business then; far from it. The difficulty was, he was apt to be altogether too energetic. There was a strange, inflamed, flurried, flighty recklessness of activity about him. He would be incautious in dipping his pen into his inkstand. All his blots upon my documents were dropped there after twelve o'clock, meridian. Indeed not only would he be reckless and sadly given to making blots in the afternoon, but some days he went further and was rather noisy. At such times, too, his face flamed with augmented blazonry, as if cannel coal had been heaped on anthracite. He made an unpleasant racket with his chair; spilled his sand-box°; in mending his pens, impatiently split them all to pieces, and threw them on the floor in a sudden passion; stood up and leaned over his table, boxing his papers about in a most indecorous manner, very sad to behold in an elderly man like him. Nevertheless, as he was in many ways a most valuable person to me, and all the time before twelve o'clock, meridian, was the quickest, steadiest creature too, accomplishing a great deal of work in a style not easy to be matched—for these reasons, I was willing to overlook his eccentricities, though indeed occasionally I remonstrated with him. I did this very gently, however, because though the civilest, nay, the blandest and most reverential of men in the morning, yet in the afternoon he was disposed upon provocation to be slightly rash with his tongue, in fact insolent. Now valuing his morning services as I did, and resolved not to lose them; yet at the same time made uncomfortable by his inflamed ways after twelve o'clock; and being a man of peace, unwilling by my admonitions to call forth unseemly retorts from him, I took upon me one Saturday noon (he was always worse on Saturdays) to hint to him very kindly that perhaps now that he was growing old, it might be well to abridge his labors; in short, he need not come to my chambers after twelve o'clock but, dinner over, had best go home to his lodgings and rest himself till tea-time. But no; he insisted upon his afternoon devotions. His countenance became intolerably fervid as he oratorically assured me— gesticulating with a long ruler at the other end of the room—that if his services in the morning were useful, how indispensable, then, in the afternoon?

"With submission, sir," said Turkey on this occasion. "I consider myself your right-hand man. In the morning I but marshal and deploy my columns, but in the afternoon I put myself at their head and gallantly charge the foe, thus!"—and he made a violent thrust with the ruler.

"But the blots, Turkey," intimated I.

"True,—but, with submission, sir, behold these hairs! I am getting old. Surely, sir, a blot or two of a warm afternoon is not to be severely urged against gray hairs. Old age—even if it blot the page—is honorable. With submission, sir, we *both* are getting old."

sand-box: sand kept in a shaker and used for blotting wet ink

10   This appeal to my fellow-feeling was hardly to be resisted. At all events, I
saw that go he would not. So I made up my mind to let him stay, resolving
nevertheless to see to it that during the afternoon he had to do with my less
important papers.

Nippers, the second on my list, was a whiskered, sallow, and upon the
whole rather piratical-looking young man of about five and twenty. I always
deemed him the victim of two evil powers—ambition and indigestion. The
ambition was evinced by a certain impatience of the duties of a mere copyist,
an unwarrantable usurpation of strictly professional affairs such as the original drawing up of legal documents. The indigestion seemed betokened in an
occasional nervous testiness and grinning irritability causing the teeth to
audibly grind together over mistakes committed in copying; unnecessary
maledictions hissed rather than spoken in the heat of business; and especially by a continual discontent with the height of the table where he worked.
Though of a very ingenious mechanical turn, Nippers could never get this
table to suit him. He put chips under it, blocks of various sorts, bits of
pasteboard, and at last went so far as to attempt an exquisite adjustment by
final pieces of folded blotting-paper. But no invention would answer. If for
the sake of easing his back he brought the table lid at a sharp angle well up
towards his chin, and wrote there like a man using the steep roof of a Dutch
house for his desk, then he declared that it stopped the circulation in his
arms. If now he lowered the table to his waistbands and stooped over it in
writing, then there was a sore aching in his back. In short, the truth of the
matter was Nippers knew not what he wanted. Or if he wanted anything, it
was to be rid of a scrivener's table altogether. Among the manifestations
of his diseased ambition was a fondness he had for receiving visits from certain ambiguous-looking fellows in seedy coats, whom he called his clients.
Indeed I was aware that not only was he at times considerable of a ward-
politician, but he occasionally did a little business at the Justices' courts and
was not unknown on the steps of the Tombs. I have good reason to believe
however that one individual who called upon him at my chambers and who
with a grand air he insisted was his client was no other than a dun, and the
alleged title-deed, a bill. But with all his failings, and the annoyances he
caused me, Nippers, like his compatriot Turkey, was a very useful man to
me; wrote a neat, swift hand; and, when he chose, was not deficient in a
gentlemanly sort of deportment. Added to this, he always dressed in a gentlemanly sort of way, and so incidentally reflected credit upon my chambers.
Whereas with respect to Turkey, I had much ado to keep him from being a
reproach to me. His clothes were apt to look oily and smell of eating-houses.
He wore his pantaloons very loose and baggy in the summer. His coats were
execrable, his hat not to be handled. But while the hat was a thing of indifference to me inasmuch as his natural civility and deference as a dependent
Englishman always led him to doff it the moment he entered the room, yet
his coat was another matter. Concerning his coats, I reasoned with him, but
with no effect. The truth was I suppose that a man with so small an income

could not afford to sport such a lustrous face and a lustrous coat at one and the same time. As Nippers once observed, Turkey's money went chiefly for red ink. One winter day I presented Turkey with a highly respectable looking coat of my own, a padded gray coat of a most comfortable warmth and which buttoned straight up from the knee to the neck. I thought Turkey would appreciate the favor and abate his rashness and obstreperousness of afternoons. But no. I verily believe that buttoning himself up in so downy and blanket-like a coat had a pernicious effect upon him, upon the same principle that too much oats are bad for horses. In fact, precisely as a rash, restive horse is said to feel his oats, so Turkey felt his coat. It made him insolent. He was a man whom prosperity harmed.

Though concerning the self-indulgent habits of Turkey I had my own private surmises, yet touching Nippers I was well persuaded that whatever might be his faults in other respects, he was at least a temperate young man. But indeed, nature herself seemed to have been his vintner and at his birth charged him so thoroughly with an irritable, brandy-like disposition that all subsequent potations were needless. When I consider how amid the stillness of my chambers Nippers would sometimes impatiently rise from his seat and stooping over his table spread his arms wide apart, seize the whole desk, and move it, and jerk it, with a grim, grinding motion on the floor, as if the table were a perverse voluntary agent intent on thwarting and vexing him, I plainly perceive that for Nippers, brandy and water were altogether superfluous.

It was fortunate for me that, owing to its peculiar cause—indigestion— the irritability and consequent nervousness of Nippers were mainly observable in the morning, while in the afternoon he was comparatively mild. So that Turkey's paroxysms only coming on about twelve o'clock, I never had to do with their eccentricities at one time. Their fits relieved each other like guards. When Nippers's was on, Turkey's was off, and vice versa. This was a good natural arrangement under the circumstances.

Ginger Nut, the third on my list, was a lad some twelve years old. His father was a carman,° ambitious of seeing his son on the bench instead of a cart before he died. So he sent him to my office as student at law, errand boy, and cleaner and sweeper, at the rate of one dollar a week. He had a little desk to himself but he did not use it much. Upon inspection, the drawer exhibited a great array of the shells of various sorts of nuts. Indeed, to this quick-witted youth the whole noble science of the law was contained in a nutshell. Not the least among the employments of Ginger Nut, as well as one which he discharged with the most alacrity, was his duty as cake and apple purveyor for Turkey and Nippers. Copying law papers being proverbially a dry, husky sort of business, my two scriveners were fain to moisten their mouths very often with Spitzenbergs° to be had at the numerous stalls nigh the Custom House and Post Office. Also, they sent Ginger Nut very frequently for that

carman: a cart driver   **Spitzenbergs:** a variety of apples

peculiar cake—small, flat, round, and very spicy—after which he had been named by them. Of a cold morning when business was but dull, Turkey would gobble up scores of these cakes as if they were mere wafers—indeed they sell them at the rate of six or eight for a penny—the scrape of his pen blending with the crunching of the crisp particles in his mouth. Of all the fiery afternoon blunders and flurried rashnesses of Turkey was his once moistening a ginger cake between his lips and clapping it on to a mortgage for a seal. I came within an ace of dismissing him then. But he mollified me by making an oriental bow and saying—"With submission, sir, it was generous of me to find you in stationery on my own account."

15   Now my original business—that of a conveyancer and title hunter, and drawer-up of recondite documents of all sorts—was considerably increased by receiving the master's office. There was now great work for scriveners. Not only must I push the clerks already with me, but I must have additional help. In answer to my advertisement, a motionless young man one morning stood upon my office threshold, the door being open, for it was summer. I can see that figure now—pallidly neat, pitiably respectable, incurably forlorn! It was Bartleby.

After a few words touching his qualifications I engaged him, glad to have among my corps of copyists a man of so singularly sedate an aspect, which I thought might operate beneficially upon the flighty temper of Turkey and the fiery one of Nippers.

I should have stated before that ground glass folding doors divided my premises into two parts, one of which was occupied by my scriveners, the other by myself. According to my humor I threw open these doors, or closed them. I resolved to assign Bartleby a corner by the folding doors, but on my side of them so as to have this quiet man within easy call in case any trifling thing was to be done. I placed his desk close up to a small side window in that part of the room, a window which originally had afforded a lateral view of certain grimy backyards and bricks, but which owing to subsequent erections commanded at present no view at all, though it gave some light. Within three feet of the panes was a wall, and the light came down from far above between two lofty buildings as from a very small opening in a dome. Still further to a satisfactory arrangement, I procured a high green folding screen which might entirely isolate Bartleby from my sight though not remove him from my voice. And thus, in a manner privacy and society were conjoined.

At first Bartleby did an extraordinary quantity of writing. As if long famishing for something to copy, he seemed to gorge himself on my documents. There was no pause for digestion. He ran a day and night line, copying by sunlight and by candlelight. I should have been quite delighted with his application had he been cheerfully industrious. But he wrote on silently, palely, mechanically.

It is of course an indispensable part of a scrivener's business to verify the accuracy of his copy, word by word. Where there are two or more scriveners in an office, they assist each other in this examination, one reading from the copy, the other holding the original. It is a very dull, wearisome, and le-thargic affair. I can readily imagine that to some sanguine temperaments it would be altogether intolerable. For example, I cannot credit that the met-tlesome poet Byron would have contentedly sat down with Bartleby to exam-ine a law document of, say, five hundred pages closely written in a crimpy hand.

Now and then in the haste of business, it had been my habit to assist in   20
comparing some brief document myself, calling Turkey or Nippers for this purpose. One object I had in placing Bartleby so handy to me behind the screen was to avail myself of his services on such trivial occasions. It was on the third day, I think, of his being with me, and before any necessity had arisen for having his own writing examined, that being much hurried to complete a small affair I had in hand, I abruptly called to Bartleby. In my haste and natural expectancy of instant compliance, I sat with my head bent over the original on my desk and my right hand sideways and somewhat nervously extended with the copy, so that immediately upon emerging from his retreat Bartleby might snatch it and proceed to business without the least delay.

In this very attitude did I sit when I called to him, rapidly stating what it was I wanted him to do—namely, to examine a small paper with me. Imagine my surprise, nay my consternation, when without moving from his privacy Bartleby in a singularly mild, firm voice replied, "I would prefer not to."

I sat awhile in perfect silence, rallying my stunned faculties. Imme-diately it occurred to me that my ears had deceived me, or Bartleby had entirely misunderstood my meaning. I repeated my request in the clearest tone I could assume. But in quite as clear a one came the previous reply, "I would prefer not to."

"Prefer not to," echoed I, rising in high excitement and crossing the room with a stride, "What do you mean? Are you moonstruck? I want you to help me compare this sheet here—take it," and I thrust it towards him.

"I would prefer not to," said he.

I looked at him steadfastly. His face was leanly composed, his gray eye   25
dimly calm. Not a wrinkle of agitation rippled him. Had there been the least uneasiness, anger, impatience or impertinence in his manner, in other words had there been anything ordinarily human about him, doubtless I should have violently dismissed him from the premises. But as it was, I should have as soon thought of turning my pale plaster-of-paris bust of Cicero out of doors. I stood gazing at him awhile as he went on with his own writing, and then reseated myself at my desk. This is very strange, thought I. What had one best do? But my business hurried me. I concluded to forget the matter for the present, reserving it for my future leisure. So calling Nippers from the other room, the paper was speedily examined.

A few days after this Bartleby concluded four lengthy documents, being quadruplicates of a week's testimony taken before me in my High Court of Chancery. It became necessary to examine them. It was an important suit and great accuracy was imperative. Having all things arranged I called Turkey, Nippers and Ginger Nut from the next room, meaning to place the four copies in the hands of my four clerks while I should read from the original. Accordingly Turkey, Nippers and Ginger Nut had taken their seats in a row, each with his document in hand, when I called to Bartleby to join this interesting group.

"Bartleby! quick, I am waiting."

I heard a slow scrape of his chair legs on the unscraped floor, and soon he appeared standing at the entrance of his hermitage.

"What is wanted?" said he mildly.

30   "The copies, the copies," said I hurriedly. "We are going to examine them. There"—and I held towards him the fourth quadruplicate.

"I would prefer not to," he said, and gently disappeared behind the screen.

For a few moments I was turned into a pillar of salt° standing at the head of my seated column of clerks. Recovering myself, I advanced towards the screen and demanded the reason for such extraordinary conduct.

"*Why* do you refuse?"

"I would prefer not to."

35   With any other man I should have flown outright into a dreadful passion, scorned all further words, and thrust him ignominiously from my presence. But there was something about Bartleby that not only strangely disarmed me, but in a wonderful manner touched and disconcerted me. I began to reason with him.

"These are your own copies we are about to examine. It is labor saving to you, because one examination will answer for your four papers. It is common usage. Every copyist is bound to help examine his copy. Is it not so? Will you not speak? Answer!"

"I prefer not to," he replied in a flute-like tone. It seemed to me that while I had been addressing him, he carefully revolved every statement that I made, fully comprehended the meaning, could not gainsay the irresistible conclusion, but at the same time some paramount consideration prevailed with him to reply as he did.

"You are decided, then, not to comply with my request—a request made according to common usage and common sense?"

He briefly gave me to understand that on that point my judgment was sound. Yes: his decision was irreversible.

40   It is not seldom the case that when a man is browbeaten in some unprecedented and violently unreasonable way he begins to stagger in his own plainest faith. He begins, as it were, vaguely to surmise that wonderful as it may be, all the justice and all the reason is on the other side. Accordingly, if any disinterested persons are present he turns to them for some reinforcement for his own faltering mind.

"Turkey," said I, "what do you think of this? Am I not right?"

pillar of salt: See Genesis 19.26.

"With submission, sir," said Turkey with his blandest tone, "I think that you are."

"Nippers," said I, "what do *you* think of it?"

"I think I should kick him out of the office."

(The reader of nice perceptions will here perceive that, it being morning,   45
Turkey's answer is couched in polite and tranquil terms, but Nippers replies in ill-tempered ones. Or, to repeat a previous sentence, Nippers's ugly mood was on duty, and Turkey's off.)

"Ginger Nut," said I, willing to enlist the smallest suffrage in my behalf, "what do *you* think of it?"

"I think, sir, he's a little *loony*," replied Ginger Nut, with a grin.

"You hear what they say," said I, turning towards the screen, "come forth and do your duty."

But he vouchsafed no reply. I pondered a moment in sore perplexity. But once more business hurried me. I determined again to postpone the consideration of this dilemma to my future leisure. With a little trouble we made out to examine the papers without Bartleby, though at every page or two, Turkey deferentially dropped his opinion that this proceeding was quite out of the common, while Nippers, twitching in his chair with a dyspeptic nervousness, ground out between his set teeth occasional hissing maledictions against the stubborn oaf behind the screen. And for his (Nippers's) part, this was the first and the last time he would do another man's business without pay.

Meanwhile Bartleby sat in his hermitage, oblivious to everything but his   50
own peculiar business there.

Some days passed, the scrivener being employed upon another lengthy work. His late remarkable conduct led me to regard his way narrowly. I observed that he never went to dinner, indeed that he never went anywhere. As yet I had never of my personal knowledge known him to be outside of my office. He was a perpetual sentry in the corner. At about eleven o'clock though, in the morning, I noticed that Ginger Nut would advance toward the opening in Bartleby's screen as if silently beckoned thither by a gesture invisible to me where I sat. That boy would then leave the office jingling a few pence and reappear with a handful of ginger nuts which he delivered in the hermitage, receiving two of the cakes for his trouble.

He lives then on ginger nuts, thought I; never eats a dinner, properly speaking; he must be a vegetarian then, but no, he never eats even vegetables, he eats nothing but ginger nuts. My mind then ran on in reveries concerning the probable effects upon the human constitution of living entirely on ginger nuts. Ginger nuts are so called because they contain ginger as one of their peculiar constituents, and the final flavoring one. Now what was ginger? A hot, spicy thing. Was Bartleby hot and spicy? Not at all. Ginger, then, had no effect upon Bartleby. Probably he preferred it should have none.

Nothing so aggravates an earnest person as a passive resistance. If the individual so resisted be of a not inhumane temper, and the resisting one perfectly harmless in his passivity, then in the better moods of the former, he will endeavor charitably to construe to his imagination what proves impossible to be solved by his judgment. Even so for the most part I regarded Bartleby and his ways. Poor fellow! thought I, he means no mischief; it is plain he intends no insolence; his aspect sufficiently evinces that his eccentricities are involuntary. He is useful to me. I can get along with him. If I turn him away, the chances are he will fall in with some less indulgent employer, and then he will be rudely treated and perhaps driven forth miserably to starve. Yes. Here I can cheaply purchase a delicious self-approval. To befriend Bartleby, to humor him in his strange wilfulness, will cost me little or nothing, while I lay up in my soul what will eventually prove a sweet morsel for my conscience. But this mood was not invariable with me. The passiveness of Bartleby sometimes irritated me. I felt strangely goaded on to encounter him in new opposition, to elicit some angry spark from him answerable to my own. But indeed I might as well have essayed to strike fire with my knuckles against a bit of Windsor soap. But one afternoon the evil impulse in me mastered me, and the following little scene ensued:

"Bartleby," said I, "when those papers are all copied I will compare them with you."

55　　"I would prefer not to."

"How? Surely you do not mean to persist in that mulish vagary?"

No answer.

I threw open the folding doors nearby, and turning upon Turkey and Nippers, exclaimed in an excited manner—

"He says, a second time, he won't examine his papers. What do you think of it, Turkey?"

60　　It was afternoon, be it remembered. Turkey sat glowing like a brass boiler, his bald head steaming, his hands reeling among his blotted papers.

"Think of it?" roared Turkey, "I think I'll just step behind his screen and black his eyes for him!"

So saying, Turkey rose to his feet and threw his arms into a pugilistic position. He was hurrying away to make good his promise when I detained him, alarmed at the effect of incautiously rousing Turkey's combativeness after dinner.

"Sit down, Turkey," said I, "and hear what Nippers has to say. What do you think of it, Nippers? Would I not be justified in immediately dismissing Bartleby?"

"Excuse me, that is for you to decide, sir. I think his conduct quite unusual, and indeed unjust as regards Turkey and myself. But it may only be a passing whim."

65　　"Ah," exclaimed I, "you have strangely changed your mind then—you speak very gently of him now."

"All beer," cried Turkey, "gentleness is effects of beer—Nippers and I dined together today. You see how gentle I am, sir. Shall I go and black his eyes?"

"You refer to Bartleby, I suppose. No, not today, Turkey," I replied, "pray, put up your fists."

I closed the doors, and again advanced towards Bartleby. I felt additional incentives tempting me to my fate. I burned to be rebelled against again. I remembered that Bartleby never left the office.

"Bartleby," said I, "Ginger Nut is away; just step round to the post office, won't you? (it was but a three minutes walk) and see if there is anything for me."

"I would prefer not to." 70

"You *will* not?"

"I *prefer* not."

I staggered to my desk and sat there in a deep study. My blind inveteracy returned. Was there any other thing in which I could procure myself to be ignominiously repulsed by this lean, penniless wight?—my hired clerk? What added thing is there, perfectly reasonable, that he will be sure to refuse to do?

"Bartleby!"

No answer. 75

"Bartleby," in a louder tone.

No answer.

"Bartleby," I roared.

Like a very ghost, agreeably to the laws of magical invocation, at the third summons he appeared at the entrance of his hermitage.

"Go to the next room, and tell Nippers to come to me." 80

"I prefer not to," he respectfully and slowly said, and mildly disappeared.

"Very good, Bartleby," said I, in a quiet sort of serenely severe self-possessed tone, intimating the unalterable purpose of some terrible retribution very close at hand. At the moment I half intended something of the kind. But upon the whole, as it was drawing towards my dinner hour, I thought it best to put on my hat and walk home for the day, suffering much from perplexity and distress of mind.

Shall I acknowledge it? The conclusion of this whole business was that it soon became a fixed fact of my chambers that a pale young scrivener by the name of Bartleby had a desk there; that he copied for me at the usual rate of four cents a folio (one hundred words); but he was permanently exempt from examining the work done by him, that duty being transferred to Turkey and Nippers, one of compliment doubtless to their superior acuteness; moreover, said Bartleby was never on any account to be dispatched on the most trivial errand of any sort, and that even if entreated to take upon him such a matter, it was generally understood that he would prefer not to—in other words, that he would refuse point-blank.

As days passed on, I became considerably reconciled to Bartleby. His steadiness, his freedom from all dissipation, his incessant industry (except when he chose to throw himself into a standing revery behind his screen), his great stillness, his unalterableness of demeanor under all circumstances, made him a valuable acquisition. One prime thing was this—*he was always there*—first in the morning, continually through the day, and the last at night. I had a singular confidence in his honesty. I felt my most precious papers perfectly safe in his hands. Sometimes to be sure I could not for the very soul of me avoid falling into sudden spasmodic passions with him. For it was exceeding difficult to bear in mind all the time those strange peculiarities, privileges, and unheard of exemptions forming the tacit stipulations on Bartleby's part under which he remained in my office. Now and then in the eagerness of dispatching pressing business, I would inadvertently summon Bartleby, in a short rapid tone, to put his finger, say, on the incipient tie of a bit of red tape with which I was about compressing some papers. Of course, from behind the screen the usual answer, "I prefer not to," was sure to come, and then how could a human creature with the common infirmities of our nature, refrain from bitterly exclaiming upon such perverseness—such unreasonableness? However, every added repulse of this sort which I received only tended to lessen the probability of my repeating the inadvertence.

85   Here it must be said that according to the custom of most legal gentlemen occupying chambers in densely populated law buildings, there were several keys to my door. One was kept by a woman residing in the attic, which person weekly scrubbed and daily swept and dusted my apartments. Another was kept by Turkey for convenience sake. The third I sometimes carried in my own pocket. The fourth I knew not who had.

Now one Sunday morning I happened to go to Trinity Church° to hear a celebrated preacher, and finding myself rather early on the ground I thought I would walk round to my chambers for a while. Luckily I had my key with me, but upon applying it to the lock, I found it resisted by something inserted from the inside. Quite surprised, I called out, when to my consternation a key was turned from within, and thrusting his lean visage at me and holding the door ajar, the apparition of Bartleby appeared, in his shirt sleeves, and otherwise in a strangely tattered dishabille, saying quietly that he was sorry but he was deeply engaged just then and—preferred not admitting me at present. In a brief word or two, he moreover added that perhaps I had better walk round the block two or three times, and by that time he would probably have concluded his affairs.

Now, the utterly unsurmised appearance of Bartleby tenanting my law-chambers of a Sunday morning with his cadaverously gentlemanly nonchalance, yet withal firm and self-possessed, had such a strange effect upon me that incontinently I slunk away from my own door and did as desired. But not without sundry twinges of impotent rebellion against the mild effrontery of this unaccountable scrivener. Indeed it was his wonderful mildness chiefly which not only disarmed me but unmanned me, as it were. For I consider that one, for the time, is a sort of unmanned when he tranquilly permits his

Trinity Church: located at the corner of Broadway and Wall Street

hired clerk to dictate to him and order him away from his own premises. Furthermore, I was full of uneasiness as to what Bartleby could possibly be doing in my office in his shirt sleeves and in an otherwise dismantled condition of a Sunday morning. Was anything amiss going on? Nay, that was out of the question. It was not to be thought of for a moment that Bartleby was an immoral person. But what could he be doing there?—copying? Nay again, whatever might be his eccentricities, Bartleby was an eminently decorous person. He would be the last man to sit down to his desk in any state approaching to nudity. Besides, it was Sunday, and there was something about Bartleby that forbade the supposition that he would by any secular occupation violate the proprieties of the day.

Nevertheless, my mind was not pacified; and full of a restless curiosity, at last I returned to the door. Without hindrance I inserted my key, opened it, and entered. Bartleby was not to be seen. I looked round anxiously, peeped behind his screen, but it was very plain that he was gone. Upon more closely examining the place, I surmised that for an indefinite period Bartleby must have ate, dressed, and slept in my office, and that too without plate, mirror, or bed. The cushioned seat of a rickety old sofa in one corner bore the faint impress of a lean, reclining form. Rolled away under his desk I found a blanket; under the empty grate, a blacking box and brush; on a chair, a tin basin with soap and a ragged towel; in a newspaper a few crumbs of ginger nuts and a morsel of cheese. Yes, thought I, it is evident enough that Bartleby has been making his home here, keeping bachelor's hall all by himself. Immediately then the thought came sweeping across me, what miserable friendlessness and loneliness are here revealed! His poverty is great; but his solitude, how horrible! Think of it. Of a Sunday, Wall Street is deserted as Petra, and every night of every day it is an emptiness. This building too which of weekdays hums with industry and life at nightfall echoes with sheer vacancy, and all through Sunday is forlorn. And here Bartleby makes his home, sole spectator of a solitude which he has seen all populous—a sort of innocent and transformed Marius brooding among the ruins of Carthage!

For the first time in my life a feeling of overpowering stinging melancholy seized me. Before I had never experienced aught but a not unpleasing sadness. The bond of a common humanity now drew me irresistibly to gloom. A fraternal melancholy! For both I and Bartleby were sons of Adam. I remembered the bright silks and sparkling faces I had seen that day in gala trim, swan-like sailing down the Mississippi of Broadway; and I contrasted them with the pallid copyist, and thought to myself, Ah, happiness courts the light, so we deem the world is gay; but misery hides aloof, so we deem that misery there is none. These sad fancyings—chimeras doubtless of a sick and silly brain—led on to other and more special thoughts concerning the eccentricities of Bartleby. Presentiments of strange discoveries hovered round me. The scrivener's pale form appeared to me laid out, among uncaring strangers, in its shivering winding sheet.

90   Suddenly I was attracted by Bartleby's closed desk, the key in open sight left in the lock.

I mean no mischief, seek the gratification of no heartless curiosity, thought I; besides, the desk is mine, and its contents too, so I will make bold to look within. Everything was methodically arranged, the papers smoothly placed. The pigeon holes were deep, and removing the files of documents, I groped into their recesses. Presently I felt something there and dragged it out. It was an old bandanna handkerchief, heavy and knotted. I opened it, and saw it was a savings bank.

I now recalled all the quiet mysteries which I had noted in the man. I remembered that he never spoke but to answer; that though at intervals he had considerable time to himself, yet I had never seen him reading—no, not even a newspaper; that for long periods he would stand looking out, at his pale window behind the screen, upon the dead brick wall; I was quite sure he never visited any refectory or eating house, while his pale face clearly indicated that he never drank beer like Turkey, or tea and coffee even, like other men; that he never went anywhere in particular that I could learn, never went out for a walk, unless indeed that was the case at present; that he had declined telling who he was or whence he came or whether he had any relatives in the world; that though so thin and pale, he never complained of ill health. And more than all, I remembered a certain unconscious air of pallid—how shall I call it?—of pallid haughtiness, say, or rather an austere reserve about him, which had positively awed me into my tame compliance with his eccentricities when I had feared to ask him to do the slightest incidental thing for me, even though I might know from his long-continued motionlessness that behind his screen he must be standing in one of those dead-wall reveries of his.

Revolving all these things, and coupling them with the recently discovered fact that he made my office his constant abiding place and home, and not forgetful of his morbid moodiness; revolving all these things, a prudential feeling began to steal over me. My first emotions had been those of pure melancholy and sincerest pity; but just in proportion as the forlornness of Bartleby grew and grew to my imagination, did that same melancholy merge into fear, that pity into repulsion. So true it is, and so terrible too, that up to a certain point the thought or sight of misery enlists our best affections; but in certain special cases, beyond that point it does not. They err who would assert that invariably this is owing to the inherent selfishness of the human heart. It rather proceeds from a certain hopelessness of remedying excessive and organic ill. To a sensitive being, pity is not seldom pain. And when at last it is perceived that such pity cannot lead to effectual succor, common sense bids the soul be rid of it. What I saw that morning persuaded me that the scrivener was the victim of innate and incurable disorder. I might give alms to his body, but his body did not pain him; it was his soul that suffered, and his soul I could not reach.

I did not accomplish the purpose of going to Trinity Church that morning. Somehow, the things I had seen disqualified me for the time from church-going. I walked homeward, thinking what I would do with Bartleby. Finally I resolved upon this:—I would put certain calm questions to him the next morning, touching his history, &c., and if he declined to answer them openly and unreservedly (and I supposed he would prefer not), then to give him a twenty dollar bill over and above whatever I might owe him, and tell him his services were no longer required; but that if in any other way I could assist him, I would be happy to do so, especially if he desired to return to his native place, wherever that might be, I would willingly help to defray the expenses. Moreover, if after reaching home he found himself at any time in want of aid, a letter from him would be sure of a reply.

The next morning came.   95

"Bartleby," said I, gently calling to him behind his screen.

No reply.

"Bartleby," said I, in a still gentler tone, "come here; I am not going to ask you to do anything you would prefer not to do—I simply wish to speak to you."

Upon this he noiselessly slid into view.

"Will you tell me, Bartleby, where you were born?"   100

"I would prefer not to."

"Will you tell me *anything* about yourself?"

"I would prefer not to."

"But what reasonable objection can you have to speak to me? I feel friendly towards you."

He did not look at me while I spoke, but kept his glance fixed upon my   105
bust of Cicero, which as I then sat was directly behind me, some six inches above my head.

"What is your answer, Bartleby?" said I, after waiting a considerable time for a reply, during which his countenance remained immovable, only there was the faintest conceivable tremor of the white attenuated mouth.

"At present I prefer to give no answer," he said, and retired into his hermitage.

It was rather weak in me I confess, but his manner on this occasion nettled me. Not only did there seem to lurk in it a certain disdain, but his perverseness seemed ungrateful, considering the undeniable good usage and indulgence he had received from me.

Again I sat ruminating what I should do. Mortified as I was at his behavior, and resolved as I had been to dismiss him when I entered my office, nevertheless I strangely felt something superstitious knocking at my heart, and forbidding me to carry out my purpose, and denouncing me for a villain if I dared to breathe one bitter word against this forlornest of mankind. At last, familiarly drawing my chair behind his screen, I sat down and said: "Bartleby, never mind then about revealing your history; but let me entreat you, as a friend, to comply as far as may be with the usages of this office. Say now you will help to examine papers tomorrow or next day: in short, say now that in a day or two you will begin to be a little reasonable:—say so, Bartleby."

110   "At present I would prefer not to be a little reasonable," was his mildly cadaverous reply.

Just then the folding doors opened, and Nippers approached. He seemed suffering from an unusually bad night's rest, induced by severer indigestion than common. He overheard those final words of Bartleby.

"*Prefer not,* eh?" gritted Nippers—"I'd *prefer* him, if I were you, sir," addressing me—"I'd *prefer* him; I'd give him preferences, the stubborn mule! What is it, sir, pray, that he *prefers* not to do now?"

Bartleby moved not a limb.

"Mr. Nippers," said I, "I'd prefer that you would withdraw for the present."

115   Somehow, of late I had got into the way of involuntarily using this word "prefer" upon all sorts of not exactly suitable occasions. And I trembled to think that my contact with the scrivener had already and seriously affected me in a mental way. And what further and deeper aberration might it not yet produce? This apprehension had not been without efficacy in determining me to summary means.

As Nippers, looking very sour and sulky, was departing, Turkey blandly and deferentially approached.

"With submission, sir," said he, "yesterday I was thinking about Bartleby here, and I think that if he would but prefer to take a quart of good ale every day, it would do much towards mending him and enabling him to assist in examining his papers."

"So you have got the word too," said I, slightly excited.

"With submission, what word, sir?" asked Turkey, respectfully crowding himself into the contracted space behind the screen, and by so doing making me jostle the scrivener. "What word, sir?"

120   "I would prefer to be left alone here," said Bartleby, as if offended at being mobbed in his privacy.

"*That's* the word, Turkey," said I—"*that's* it."

"Oh, *prefer?* oh yes—queer word. I never use it myself. But, sir, as I was saying, if he would but prefer—"

"Turkey," interrupted I, "you will please withdraw."

"Oh certainly, sir, if you prefer that I should."

125   As he opened the folding door to retire, Nippers at his desk caught a glimpse of me and asked whether I would prefer to have a certain paper copied on blue paper or white. He did not in the least roguishly accent the word prefer. It was plain that it involuntarily rolled from his tongue. I thought to myself, surely I must get rid of a demented man who already has in some degree turned the tongues if not the heads of myself and clerks. But I thought it prudent not to break the dismission at once.

The next day I noticed that Bartleby did nothing but stand at his window in his dead-wall revery. Upon my asking him why he did not write, he said that he had decided upon doing no more writing.

"Why, how now? what next?" exclaimed I, "do no more writing?"

"No more."

"And what is the reason?"

"Do you not see the reason for yourself?" he indifferently replied.   130

I looked steadfastly at him, and perceived that his eyes looked dull and glazed. Instantly it occurred to me that his unexampled diligence in copying by his dim window for the first few weeks of his stay with me might have temporarily impaired his vision.

I was touched. I said something in condolence with him. I hinted that of course he did wisely in abstaining from writing for a while, and urged him to embrace that opportunity of taking wholesome exercise in the open air. This, however, he did not do. A few days after this, my other clerks being absent, and being in a great hurry to dispatch certain letters by the mail, I thought that, having nothing else earthly to do, Bartleby would surely be less inflexible than usual and carry these letters to the post office. But he blankly declined. So, much to my inconvenience, I went myself.

Still added days went by. Whether Bartleby's eyes improved or not, I could not say. To all appearance, I thought they did. But when I asked him if they did, he vouchsafed no answer. At all events, he would do no copying. At last, in reply to my urgings, he informed me that he had permanently given up copying.

"What!" exclaimed I; "suppose your eyes should get entirely well—better than ever before—would you not copy then?"

"I have given up copying," he answered, and slid aside.   135

He remained as ever, a fixture in my chamber. Nay—if that were possible—he became still more of a fixture than before. What was to be done? He would do nothing in the office: why should he stay there? In plain fact, he had now become a millstone to me, not only useless as a necklace but afflictive to bear. Yet I was sorry for him. I speak less than truth when I say that on his own account, he occasioned me uneasiness. If he would but have named a single relative or friend, I would instantly have written and urged their taking the poor fellow away to some convenient retreat. But he seemed alone, absolutely alone in the universe. A bit of wreck in the mid-Atlantic. At length, necessities connected with my business tyrannized over all other considerations. Decently as I could, I told Bartleby that in six days' time he must unconditionally leave the office. I warned him to take measures, in the interval, for procuring some other abode. I offered to assist him in this endeavor, if he himself would but take the first step towards a removal. "And when you finally quit me, Bartleby," added I, "I shall see that you go not away entirely unprovided. Six days from this hour, remember."

At the expiration of that period I peeped behind the screen, and lo! Bartleby was there.

I buttoned up my coat, balanced myself, advanced slowly towards him, touched his shoulder, and said, "The time has come; you must quit this place; I am sorry for you; here is money; but you must go."

"I would prefer not," he replied, with his back still towards me.

140   "You *must.*"

He remained silent.

Now I had an unbounded confidence in this man's common honesty. He had frequently restored to me six pences and shillings carelessly dropped upon the floor, for I am apt to be very reckless in such shirt-button affairs. The proceeding then which followed will not be deemed extraordinary.

"Bartleby," said I, "I owe you twelve dollars on account; here are thirty-two; the odd twenty are yours. Will you take it?" and I handed the bills towards him.

But he made no motion.

145   "I will leave them here then," putting them under a weight on the table. Then taking my hat and cane and going to the door I tranquilly turned and added, "After you have removed your things from these offices, Bartleby, you will of course lock the door—since every one is now gone for the day but you—and if you please, slip your key underneath the mat so that I may have it in the morning. I shall not see you again, so good-bye to you. If hereafter in your new place of abode I can be of any service to you, do not fail to advise me by letter. Good-bye, Bartleby, and fare you well."

But he answered not a word; like the last column of some ruined temple, he remained standing mute and solitary in the middle of the otherwise deserted room.

As I walked home in a pensive mood, my vanity got the better of my pity. I could not but highly plume myself on my masterly management in getting rid of Bartleby. Masterly I call it, and such it must appear to any dispassionate thinker. The beauty of my procedure seemed to consist in its perfect quietness. There was no vulgar bullying, no bravado of any sort, no choleric hectoring and striding to and fro across the apartment, jerking out vehement commands for Bartleby to bundle himself off with his beggarly traps.° Nothing of the kind. Without loudly bidding Bartleby depart—as an inferior genius might have done—I *assumed* the ground that depart he must, and upon the assumption built all I had to say. The more I thought over my procedure, the more I was charmed with it. Nevertheless, next morning, upon awakening, I had my doubts—I had somehow slept off the fumes of vanity. One of the coolest and wisest hours a man has is just after he awakes in the morning. My procedure seemed as sagacious as ever—but only in theory. How it would prove in practice—there was the rub. It was truly a beautiful thought to have assumed Bartleby's departure; but after all, that assumption was simply my own, and none of Bartleby's. The great point was not whether I had assumed that he would quit me, but whether he would prefer so to do. He was more a man of preferences than assumptions.

After breakfast, I walked downtown, arguing the probabilities *pro* and *con.* One moment I thought it would prove a miserable failure, and Bartleby would be found all alive at my office as usual; the next moment it seemed certain that I should see his chair empty. And so I kept veering about. At the

traps: belongings

corner of Broadway and Canal Street, I saw quite an excited group of people standing in earnest conversation.

"I'll take odds he doesn't," said a voice as I passed.

"Doesn't go?—done!" said I, "put up your money."   150

I was instinctively putting my hand in my pocket to produce my own, when I remembered that this was an election day. The words I had overheard bore no reference to Bartleby, but to the success or non-success of some candidate for the mayoralty. In my intent frame of mind, I had, as it were, imagined that all Broadway shared in my excitement and were debating the same question with me. I passed on, very thankful that the uproar of the street screened my momentary absent-mindedness.

As I had intended, I was earlier than usual at my office door. I stood listening for a moment. All was still. He must be gone. I tried the knob. The door was locked. Yes, my procedure had worked to a charm; he indeed must be vanished. Yet a certain melancholy mixed with this: I was almost sorry for my brilliant success. I was fumbling under the door mat for the key which Bartleby was to have left there for me when accidentally my knee knocked against a panel, producing a summoning sound, and in response a voice came to me from within—"Not yet; I am occupied."

It was Bartleby.

I was thunderstruck. For an instant I stood like the man who, pipe in mouth, was killed one cloudless afternoon long ago in Virginia, by summer lightning; at his own warm open window he was killed, and remained leaning out there upon the dreamy afternoon till someone touched him, when he fell.

"Not gone!" I murmured at last. But again obeying that wondrous as-   155
cendancy which the inscrutable scrivener had over me, and from which ascendancy, for all my chafing, I could not completely escape, I slowly went downstairs and out into the street, and while walking round the block, considered what I should next do in this unheard of perplexity. Turn the man out by an actual thrusting I could not; to drive him away by calling him hard names would not do; calling in the police was an unpleasant idea; and yet, permit him to enjoy his cadaverous triumph over me?—this too I could not think of. What was to be done? or if nothing could be done, was there anything further that I could *assume* in the matter? Yes, as before I had prospectively assumed that Bartleby would depart, so now I might retrospectively assume that departed he was. In the legitimate carrying out of this assumption, I might enter my office in a great hurry, and pretending not to see Bartleby at all, walk straight against him as if he were air. Such a proceeding would in a singular degree have the appearance of a home-thrust. It was hardly possible that Bartleby could withstand such an application of the doctrine of assumptions. But upon second thoughts the success of the plan seemed rather dubious. I resolved to argue the matter over with him again.

"Bartleby," said I, entering the office with a quietly severe expression, "I am seriously displeased. I am pained, Bartleby. I had thought better of you. I had imagined you of such a gentlemanly organization that in my delicate dilemma a slight hint would suffice—in short, an assumption. But it appears I am deceived. Why," I added, unaffectedly starting, "you have not even touched that money yet," pointing to it just where I had left it the evening previous.

He answered nothing.

"Will you, or will you not, quit me?" I now demanded in a sudden passion, advancing close to him.

"I would prefer *not* to quit you," he replied, gently emphasizing the *not*.

160   "What earthly right have you to stay here? Do you pay any rent? Do you pay my taxes? Or is this property yours?"

He answered nothing.

"Are you ready to go on and write now? Are your eyes recovered? Could you copy a small paper for me this morning? or help examine a few lines? or step round to the post office? In a word, will you do anything at all to give a coloring to your refusal to depart the premises?"

He silently retired into his hermitage.

I was now in such a state of nervous resentment that I thought it but prudent to check myself at present from further demonstrations. Bartleby and I were alone. I remembered the tragedy of the unfortunate Adams and the still more unfortunate Colt° in the solitary office of the latter; and how poor Colt, being dreadfully incensed by Adams, and imprudently permitting himself to get wildly excited, was at unawares hurried into his fatal act—an act which certainly no man could possibly deplore more than the actor himself. Often it had occurred to me in my ponderings upon the subject that had that altercation taken place in the public street, or at a private residence, it would not have terminated as it did. It was the circumstance of being alone in a solitary office, upstairs, of a building entirely unhallowed by humanizing domestic associations—an uncarpeted office, doubtless, of a dusty haggard sort of appearance—this it must have been which greatly helped to enhance the irritable desperation of the hapless Colt.

165   But when this old Adam of resentment rose in me and tempted me concerning Bartleby, I grappled him and threw him. How? Why, simply by recalling the divine injunction: "A new commandment° give I unto you, that ye love one another." Yes, this it was that saved me. Aside from higher considerations, charity often operates as a vastly wise and prudent principle—a great safeguard to its possessor. Men have committed murder for jealousy's sake, and anger's sake, and hatred's sake, and selfishness' sake, and spiritual pride's sake; but no man that ever I heard of ever committed a diabolical murder for sweet charity's sake. Mere self-interest, then, if no better motive can be enlisted, should, especially with high-tempered men, prompt all beings to charity and philanthropy. At any rate, upon the occasion in question, I strove to drown my exasperated feelings towards the scrivener by benevolently construing his conduct. Poor fellow, poor fellow! thought I, he don't

---

Colt: In a famous murder case in 1841, John Colt used a hatchet to kill Samuel Adams, who owed him money.   **commandment:** See John 15.12.

mean anything; and besides, he has seen hard times, and ought to be indulged.

I endeavored also immediately to occupy myself, and at the same time to comfort my despondency. I tried to fancy that in the course of the morning, at such time as might prove agreeable to him, Bartleby of his own free accord would emerge from his hermitage and take up some decided line of march in the direction of the door. But no. Half-past twelve o'clock came; Turkey began to glow in the face, overturn his inkstand, and become generally obstreperous; Nippers abated down into quietude and courtesy; Ginger Nut munched his noon apple; and Bartleby remained standing at his window in one of his profoundest dead-wall reveries. Will it be credited? Ought I to acknowledge it? That afternoon I left the office without saying one further word to him.

Some days now passed, during which at leisure intervals I looked a little into "Edwards on the Will," and "Priestly on Necessity."° Under the circumstances, those books induced a salutary feeling. Gradually I slid into the persuasion that these troubles of mine touching the scrivener had been all predestinated from eternity, and Bartleby was billeted upon me for some mysterious purpose of an all-wise Providence which it was not for a mere mortal like me to fathom. Yes, Bartleby, stay there behind your screen, thought I; I shall persecute you no more; you are harmless and noiseless as any of these old chairs; in short, I never feel so private as when I know you are here. At least I see it, I feel it; I penetrate to the predestinated purpose of my life. I am content. Others may have loftier parts to enact; but my mission in this world, Bartleby, is to furnish you with office-room for such period as you may see fit to remain.

I believe that this wise and blessed frame of mind would have continued with me had it not been for the unsolicited and uncharitable remarks obtruded upon me by my professional friends who visited the rooms. But thus it often is, that the constant friction of illiberal minds wears out at last the best resolves of the more generous. Though to be sure, when I reflected upon it, it was not strange that people entering my office should be struck by the peculiar aspect of the unaccountable Bartleby, and so be tempted to throw out some sinister observations concerning him. Sometimes an attorney having business with me, and calling at my office, and finding no one but the scrivener there, would undertake to obtain some sort of precise information from him touching my whereabouts; but without heeding his idle talk, Bartleby would remain standing immovable in the middle of the room. So after contemplating him in that position for a time, the attorney would depart, no wiser than he came.

Also, when a reference was going on, and the room full of lawyers and witnesses and business was driving fast, some deeply occupied legal gentleman present seeing Bartleby wholly unemployed would request him to run

---

"Edwards . . . Necessity": writings by eighteenth-century philosophers who took the position that free will does not exist

round to his (the legal gentleman's) office and fetch some papers for him. Thereupon, Bartleby would tranquilly decline, and remain idle as before. Then the lawyer would give a great stare and turn to me. And what could I say? At last I was made aware that all through the circle of my professional acquaintance, a whisper of wonder was running round having reference to the strange creature I kept at my office. This worried me very much. And as the idea came upon me of his possibly turning out a long-lived man, and keep occupying my chambers, and denying my authority, and perplexing my visitors, and scandalizing my professional reputation, and casting a general gloom over the premises, keeping soul and body together to the last upon his savings (for doubtless he spent but half a dime a day), and in the end perhaps outliving me, and claiming possession of my office by right of his perpetual occupancy: as all these dark anticipations crowded upon me more and more, and my friends continually intruded their relentless remarks upon the apparition in my room, a great change was wrought in me. I resolved to gather all my faculties together, and forever rid me of this intolerable incubus.

170   Ere revolving any complicated project, however, adapted to this end, I first simply suggested to Bartleby the propriety of his permanent departure. In a calm and serious tone, I commended the idea to his careful and mature consideration. But having taken three days to meditate upon it, he apprised me that his original determination remained the same, in short, that he still preferred to abide with me.

What shall I do? I now said to myself, buttoning up my coat to the last button. What shall I do? what ought I do? what does conscience say I *should* do with this man, or rather ghost? Rid myself of him, I must; go, he shall. But how? You will not thrust him, the poor, pale, passive mortal—you will not thrust such a helpless creature out of your door? you will not dishonor yourself by such cruelty? No, I will not, I cannot do that. Rather would I let him live and die here, and then mason up his remains in the wall. What then will you do? For all your coaxing, he will not budge. Bribes he leaves under your own paperweight on your table; in short, it is quite plain that he prefers to cling to you.

Then something severe, something unusual must be done. What! surely you will not have him collared by a constable, and commit his innocent pallor to the common jail? And upon what ground could you procure such a thing to be done?—a vagrant, is he? What! he a vagrant, a wanderer, who refuses to budge? It is because he will *not* be a vagrant, then, that you seek to count him *as* a vagrant. That is too absurd. No visible means of support: there I have him. Wrong again: for indubitably he *does* support himself, and that is the only unanswerable proof that any man can show of his possessing the means so to do. No more then. Since he will not quit me, I must quit him. I will change my offices; I will move elsewhere, and give him fair notice that if I find him on my new premises I will then proceed against him as a common trespasser.

Acting accordingly, next day I thus addressed him: "I find these chambers too far from the City Hall; the air is unwholesome. In a word, I propose to remove my offices next week, and shall no longer require your services. I tell you this now, in order that you may seek another place."

He made no reply, and nothing more was said.

On the appointed day I engaged carts and men, proceeded to my chambers, and having but little furniture, everything was removed in a few hours. Throughout, the scrivener remained standing behind the screen, which I directed to be removed the last thing. It was withdrawn, and being folded up like a huge folio, left him the motionless occupant of a naked room. I stood in the entry watching him a moment, while something from within me upbraided me. 175

I re-entered, with my hand in my pocket—and—and my heart in my mouth.

"Good-bye, Bartleby; I am going—good-bye, and God some way bless you; and take that," slipping something in his hand. But it dropped upon the floor, and then—strange to say—I tore myself from him whom I had so longed to be rid of.

Established in my new quarters, for a day or two I kept the door locked, and started at every footfall in the passages. When I returned to my rooms after any little absence, I would pause at the threshold for an instant, and attentively listen ere applying my key. But these fears were needless. Bartleby never came nigh me.

I thought all was going well, when a perturbed looking stranger visited me inquiring whether I was the person who had recently occupied rooms at No.— Wall Street.

Full of forebodings, I replied that I was. 180

"Then sir," said the stranger, who proved a lawyer, "you are responsible for the man you left there. He refuses to do any copying; he refuses to do anything; he says he prefers not to; and he refuses to quit the premises."

"I am very sorry, sir," said I, with assumed tranquility, but an inward tremor, "but, really, the man you allude to is nothing to me—he is no relation or apprentice of mine, that you should hold me responsible for him."

"In mercy's name, who is he?"

"I certainly cannot inform you. I know nothing about him. Formerly I employed him as a copyist, but he has done nothing for me now for some time past."

"I shall settle him then—good morning, sir." 185

Several days passed, and I heard nothing more; and though I often felt a charitable prompting to call at the place and see poor Bartleby, yet a certain squeamishness of I know not what withheld me.

All is over with him by this time, thought I at last, when through another week no further intelligence reached me. But coming to my room the day after, I found several persons waiting at my door in a high state of nervous excitement.

"That's the man—here he comes," cried the foremost one, whom I recognized as the lawyer who had previously called upon me alone.

"You must take him away, sir, at once," cried a portly person among them, advancing upon me, and whom I knew to be the landlord of No.— Wall Street. "These gentlemen, my tenants, cannot stand it any longer; Mr. B—" pointing to the lawyer, "has turned him out of his room, and he now persists in haunting the building generally, sitting upon the banisters of the stairs by day, and sleeping in the entry by night. Everybody is concerned; clients are leaving the offices; some fears are entertained of a mob; something you must do, and that without delay."

190   Aghast at this torrent, I fell back before it, and would fain have locked myself in my new quarters. In vain I persisted that Bartleby was nothing to me—no more than to anyone else. In vain—I was the last person known to have anything to do with him, and they held me to the terrible account. Fearful then of being exposed in the papers (as one person present obscurely threatened), I considered the matter, and at length said that if the lawyer would give me a confidential interview with the scrivener, in his (the lawyer's) own room, I would that afternoon strive my best to rid them of the nuisance they complained of.

Going upstairs to my old haunt, there was Bartleby silently sitting upon the banister at the landing.

"What are you doing here, Bartleby?" said I.

"Sitting upon the banister," he mildly replied.

I motioned him into the lawyer's room, who then left us.

195   "Bartleby," said I, "are you aware that you are the cause of great tribulation to me, by persisting in occupying the entry after being dismissed from the office?"

No answer.

"Now one of two things must take place. Either you must do something or something must be done to you. Now what sort of business would you like to engage in? Would you like to re-engage in copying for someone?"

"No; I would prefer not to make any change."

"Would you like a clerkship in a dry-goods store?"

200   "There is too much confinement about that. No, I would not like a clerkship; but I am not particular."

"Too much confinement," I cried, "why you keep yourself confined all the time!"

"I would prefer not to take a clerkship," he rejoined, as if to settle that little item at once.

"How would a bar-tender's business° suit you? There is no trying of the eyesight in that."

"I would not like it at all; though, as I said before, I am not particular."

205   His unwonted wordiness inspirited me. I returned to the charge.

bar-tender's business: work as an attendant in a courtroom

"Well then, would you like to travel through the country collecting bills for the merchants? That would improve your health."

"No, I would prefer to be doing something else."

"How then would going as a companion to Europe, to entertain some young gentleman with your conversation—how would that suit you?"

"Not at all. It does not strike me that there is anything definite about that. I like to be stationary. But I am not particular."

"Stationary you shall be then," I cried, now losing all patience, and for   210
the first time in all my exasperating connection with him fairly flying into a passion. "If you do not go away from these premises before night, I shall feel bound—indeed I *am* bound—to—to—to quit the premises myself!" I rather absurdly concluded, knowing not with what possible threat to try to frighten his immobility into compliance. Despairing of all further efforts, I was precipitately leaving him, when a final thought occurred to me—one which had not been wholly unindulged before.

"Bartleby," said I, in the kindest tone I could assume under such exciting circumstances, "will you go home with me now—not to my office, but my dwelling—and remain there till we can conclude upon some convenient arrangement for you at our leisure? Come, let us start now, right away."

"No: at present I would prefer not to make any change at all."

I answered nothing, but effectually dodging everyone by the suddenness and rapidity of my flight, rushed from the building, ran up Wall Street towards Broadway, and jumping into the first omnibus was soon removed from pursuit. As soon as tranquility returned I distinctly perceived that I had now done all that I possibly could, both in respect to the demands of the landlord and his tenants, and with regard to my own desire and sense of duty, to benefit Bartleby and shield him from rude persecution. I now strove to be entirely carefree and quiescent; and my conscience justified me in the attempt though indeed it was not so successful as I could have wished. So fearful was I of being again hunted out by the incensed landlord and his exasperated tenants that, surrendering my business to Nippers, for a few days I drove about the upper part of the town and through the suburbs in my rockaway; crossed over to Jersey City and Hoboken, and paid fugitive visits to Manhattanville and Astoria. In fact I almost lived in my rockaway for the time.

When again I entered my office, lo, a note from the landlord lay upon the desk. I opened it with trembling hands. It informed me that the writer had sent to the police and had Bartleby removed to the Tombs as a vagrant. Moreover, since I knew more about him than anyone else, he wished me to appear at that place and make a suitable statement of the facts. These tidings had a conflicting effect upon me. At first I was indignant, but at last almost approved. The landlord's energetic, summary disposition had led him to adopt a procedure which I do not think I would have decided upon myself; and yet as a last resort, under such peculiar circumstances, it seemed the only plan.

215   As I afterwards learned, the poor scrivener, when told that he must be conducted to the Tombs, offered not the slightest obstacle, but in his pale unmoving way, silently acquiesced.

Some of the compassionate and curious bystanders joined the party; and headed by one of the constables arm in arm with Bartleby, the silent procession filed its way through all the noise, and heat, and joy of the roaring thoroughfares at noon.

The same day I received the note I went to the Tombs or, to speak more properly, the Halls of Justice. Seeking the right officer, I stated the purpose of my call, and was informed that the individual I described was indeed within. I then assured the functionary that Bartleby was a perfectly honest man, and greatly to be compassionated, however unaccountably eccentric. I narrated all I knew, and closed by suggesting the idea of letting him remain in as indulgent confinement as possible till something less harsh might be done—though indeed I hardly knew what. At all events, if nothing else could be decided upon, the alms-house must receive him. I then begged to have an interview.

Being under no disgraceful charge, and quite serene and harmless in all his ways, they had permitted him freely to wander about the prison, and especially in the inclosed grass-platted yards thereof. And so I found him there, standing all alone in the quietest of the yards, his face towards a high wall, while all around, from the narrow slits of the jail windows, I thought I saw peering out upon him the eyes of murderers and thieves.

"Bartleby!"

220   "I know you," he said, without looking around—"and I want nothing to say to you."

"It was not I that brought you here, Bartleby," said I, keenly pained at his implied suspicion. "And to you, this should not be so vile a place. Nothing reproachful attaches to you by being here. And see, it is not so sad a place as one might think. Look, there is the sky, and here is the grass."

"I know where I am," he replied, but would say nothing more, and so I left him.

As I entered the corridor again, a broad meat-like man in an apron accosted me, and jerking his thumb over his shoulder said—"Is that your friend?"

"Yes."

225   "Does he want to starve? If he does, let him live on the prison fare, that's all."

"Who are you?" asked I, not knowing what to make of such an unofficially speaking person in such a place.

"I am the grub-man. Such gentlemen as have friends here, hire me to provide them with something good to eat."

"Is this so?" said I, turning to the turnkey.

He said it was.

"Well, then," said I, slipping some silver into the grub-man's hands (for   230
so they called him), "I want you to give particular attention to my friend
there; let him have the best dinner you can get. And you must be as polite to
him as possible."

"Introduce me, will you?" said the grub-man, looking at me with an
expression which seemed to say he was all impatience for an opportunity to
give a specimen of his breeding.

Thinking it would prove of benefit to the scrivener, I acquiesced, and
asking the grub-man his name, went up with him to Bartleby.

"Bartleby, this is a friend; you will find him very useful to you."

"Your sarvant, sir, your sarvant," said the grub-man making a low salutation behind his apron. "Hope you find it pleasant here, sir—spacious
grounds—cool apartments, sir—hope you'll stay with us some time—try to
make it agreeable. What will you have for dinner today?"

"I prefer not to dine today," said Bartleby, turning away. "It would   235
disagree with me; I am unused to dinners." So saying he slowly moved
to the other side of the enclosure, and took up a position fronting the
dead wall.

"How's this?" said the grub-man, addressing me with a stare of astonishment. "He's odd, ain't he?"

"I think he is a little deranged," said I, sadly.

"Deranged? deranged is it? Well now, upon my word, I thought that
friend of yourn was a gentleman forger; they are always pale and genteel-
like, them forgers. I can't help pity 'em—can't help it, sir. Did you know
Monroe Edwards?" he added touchingly, and paused. Then, laying his hand
pityingly on my shoulder, sighed, "he died of consumption at Sing-Sing. So
you weren't acquainted with Monroe?"

"No, I was never socially acquainted with any forgers. But I cannot stop
longer. Look to my friend yonder. You will not lose by it. I will see you
again."

Some few days after this, I again obtained admission to the Tombs, and   240
went through the corridors in quest of Bartleby, but without finding him.

"I saw him coming from his cell not long ago," said a turnkey, "maybe
he's gone to loiter in the yards."

So I went in that direction.

"Are you looking for the silent man?" said another turnkey passing me.
"Yonder he lies—sleeping in the yard there. 'Tis not twenty minutes since I
saw him lie down."

The yard was entirely quiet. It was not accessible to the common prisoners. The surrounding walls, of amazing thickness, kept off all sound behind them. The Egyptian character of the masonry weighed upon me with
its gloom. But a soft imprisoned turf grew under foot. The heart of the
eternal pyramids, it seemed, wherein, by some strange magic, through the
clefts, grass-seed dropped by birds had sprung.

245   Strangely huddled at the base of the wall, his knees drawn up, and lying on his side, his head touching the cold stones, I saw the wasted Bartleby. But nothing stirred. I paused; then went close up to him; stooped over, and saw that his dim eyes were open; otherwise he seemed profoundly sleeping. Something prompted me to touch him. I felt his hand, when a tingling shiver ran up my arm and down my spine to my feet.

The round face of the grub-man peered upon me now. "His dinner is ready. Won't he dine today, either? Or does he live without dining?"

"Lives without dining," said I, and closed the eyes.

"Eh!—He's asleep, ain't he?"

"With kings and counselors,"° murmured I.

250   There would seem little need for proceeding further in this history. Imagination will readily supply the meager recital of poor Bartleby's interment. But ere parting with the reader, let me say that if this little narrative has sufficiently interested him to awaken curiosity as to who Bartleby was, and what manner of life he led prior to the present narrator's making his acquaintance, I can only reply that in such curiosity I fully share, but am wholly unable to gratify it. Yet here I hardly know whether I should divulge one little item of rumor which came to my ear a few months after the scrivener's decease. Upon what basis it rested, I could never ascertain; and hence how true it is I cannot now tell. But inasmuch as this vague report has not been without a certain strange suggestive interest to me, however sad, it may prove the same with some others; and so I will briefly mention it. The report was this: that Bartleby had been a subordinate clerk in the Dead Letter Office at Washington, from which he had been suddenly removed by a change in the administration. When I think over this rumor, I cannot adequately express the emotions which seize me. Dead letters! does it not sound like dead men? Conceive a man by nature and misfortune prone to a pallid hopelessness, can any business seem more fitted to heighten it than that of continually handling these dead letters and assorting them for the flames? For by the cart-load they are annually burned. Sometimes from out the folded paper the pale clerk takes a ring—the finger it was meant for, perhaps, moulders in the grave; a bank note sent in swiftest charity— he whom it would relieve, nor eats nor hungers any more; pardon for those who died despairing; hope for those who died unhoping; good tidings for those who died stifled by unrelieved calamities. On errands of life, these letters speed to death.

Ah, Bartleby! Ah, humanity!

"With . . . counselors": Job 3.14

Katherine Anne Porter

Noon Wine

TIME: *1896–1905*
PLACE: *Small South Texas Farm*

The two grubby small boys with tow-colored hair who were digging among the ragweed in the front yard sat back on their heels and said, "Hello," when the tall bony man with straw-colored hair turned in at their gate. He did not pause at the gate; it had swung back, conveniently half open, long ago, and was now sunk so firmly on its broken hinges no one thought of trying to close it. He did not even glance at the small boys, much less give them good-day. He just clumped down his big square dusty shoes one after the other steadily, like a man following a plow, as if he knew the place well and knew where he was going and what he would find there. Rounding the right-hand corner of the house under the row of china-berry trees, he walked up to the side porch where Mr. Thompson was pushing a big swing churn back and forth.

Mr. Thompson was a tough weather-beaten man with stiff black hair and a week's growth of black whiskers. He was a noisy proud man who held his neck so straight his whole face stood level with his Adam's apple, and the whiskers continued down his neck and disappeared into a black thatch under his open collar. The churn rumbled and swished like the belly of a trotting horse, and Mr. Thompson seemed somehow to be driving a horse with one hand, reining it in and urging it forward; and every now and then he turned halfway around and squirted a tremendous spit of tobacco juice out over the steps. The door stones were brown and gleaming with fresh tobacco juice. Mr. Thompson had been churning quite a while and he was tired of it. He was just fetching a mouthful of juice to squirt again when the stranger came around the corner and stopped. Mr. Thompson saw a narrow-chested man with blue eyes so pale they were almost white, looking and not looking at him from a long gaunt face, under white eyebrows. Mr. Thompson judged him to be another of these Irishmen, by his long upper lip.

"Howdy do, sir," said Mr. Thompson politely, swinging his churn.

"I need work," said the man, clearly enough but with some kind of foreign accent Mr. Thompson couldn't place. It wasn't Cajun and it wasn't Nigger and it wasn't Dutch, so it had him stumped. "You need a man here?"

NOON WINE First published in 1937 in the depths of the Great Depression. Katherine Anne Porter (1890–1980) was born in a small town in south Texas near San Antonio, and was educated at private schools in Texas and Louisiana. She worked as a journalist in Chicago, Fort Worth, Mexico, and New York City, and published her first book of fiction in 1930.

5   Mr. Thompson gave the churn a great shove and it swung back and forth several times on its own momentum. He sat on the steps, shot his quid into the grass, and said, "Set down. Maybe we can make a deal. I been kinda lookin' round for somebody. I had two niggers but they got into a cutting scrape up in the creek last week, one of 'em dead now and the other in the hoosegow at Cold Springs. Neither one of 'em worth killing, come right down to it. So it looks like I'd better get somebody. Where'd you work last?"

"North Dakota," said the man, folding himself down on the other end of the steps, but not as if he were tired. He folded up and settled down as if it would be a long time before he got up again. He never had looked at Mr. Thompson, but there wasn't anything sneaking in his eye, either. He didn't seem to be looking anywhere else. His eyes sat in his head and let things pass by them. They didn't seem to be expecting to see anything worth looking at. Mr. Thompson waited a long time for the man to say something more, but he had gone into a brown study.

"North Dakota," said Mr. Thompson, trying to remember where that was. "That's a right smart distance off, seems to me."

"I can do everything on farm," said the man; "cheap. I need work."

Mr. Thompson settled himself to get down to business. "My name's Thompson, Mr. Royal Earle Thompson," he said.

10   "I'm Mr. Helton," said the man, "Mr. Olaf Helton." He did not move.

"Well, now," said Mr. Thompson in his most carrying voice, "I guess we'd better talk turkey."

When Mr. Thompson expected to drive a bargain he always grew very hearty and jovial. There was nothing wrong with him except that he hated like the devil to pay wages. He said so himself. "You furnish grub and a shack," he said, "and then you got to pay 'em besides. It ain't right. Besides the wear and tear on your implements," he said, "they just let everything go to rack and ruin." So he began to laugh and shout his way through the deal.

"Now, what I want to know is, how much you fixing to gouge outa me?" he brayed, slapping his knee. After he had kept it up as long as he could, he quieted down, feeling a little sheepish, and cut himself a chew. Mr. Helton was staring out somewhere between the barn and the orchard, and seemed to be sleeping with his eyes open.

"I'm good worker," said Mr. Helton as from the tomb. "I get dollar a day."

15   Mr. Thompson was so shocked he forgot to start laughing again at the top of his voice until it was nearly too late to do any good. "Haw, haw," he bawled. "Why, for a dollar a day I'd hire out myself. What kinda work is it where they pay you a dollar a day?"

"Wheatfields, North Dakota," said Mr. Helton, not even smiling.

Mr. Thompson stopped laughing. "Well, this ain't any wheatfield by a long shot. This is more of a dairy farm," he said, feeling apologetic. "My wife, she was set on a dairy, she seemed to like working around with cows and calves, so I humored her. But it was a mistake," he said. "I got nearly everything to do, anyhow. My wife ain't very strong. She's sick today, that's a fact. She's been porely for the last few days. We plant a little feed, and a corn patch, and there's the orchard, and a few pigs and chickens, but our main hold is the cows. Now just speakin' as one man to another, there ain't any money in it. Now I can't give you no dollar a day because ackshally I don't make that much out of it. No, sir, we get along on a lot less than a dollar a day, I'd say, if we figger up everything in the long run. Now, I paid seven dollars a month to the two niggers, three-fifty each, and grub, but what I say is, one middlin'-good white man ekals a whole passel of niggers any day in the week, so I'll give you seven dollars and you eat at the table with us, and you'll be treated like a white man, as the feller says—"

"That's all right," said Mr. Helton. "I take it."

"Well, now I guess we'll call it a deal, hey?" Mr. Thompson jumped up as if he had remembered important business. "Now, you just take hold of that churn and give it a few swings, will you, while I ride to town on a coupla little errands. I ain't been able to leave the place all week. I guess you know what to do with butter after you get it, don't you?"

"I know," said Mr. Helton without turning his head. "I know butter   20
business." He had a strange drawling voice, and even when he spoke only two words his voice waved slowly up and down and the emphasis was in the wrong place. Mr. Thompson wondered what kind of foreigner Mr. Helton could be.

"Now just where did you say you worked last?" he asked, as if he expected Mr. Helton to contradict himself.

"North Dakota," said Mr. Helton.

"Well, one place is good as another once you get used to it," said Mr. Thompson, amply. "You're a forriner, ain't you?"

"I'm a Swede," said Mr. Helton, beginning to swing the churn.

Mr. Thompson let forth a booming laugh, as if this was the best joke on   25
somebody he'd ever heard. "Well, I'll be damned," he said at the top of his voice. "A Swede: well, now, I'm afraid you'll get pretty lonesome around here. I never seen any Swedes in this neck of the woods."

"That's all right," said Mr. Helton. He went on swinging the churn as if he had been working on the place for years.

"In fact, I might as well tell you, you're practically the first Swede I ever laid eyes on."

"That's all right," said Mr. Helton.

Mr. Thompson went into the front room where Mrs. Thompson was lying down, with the green shades drawn. She had a bowl of water by her on the table and a wet cloth over her eyes. She took the cloth off at the sound of Mr. Thompson's boots and said, "What's all the noise out there? Who is it?"

"Got a feller out there says he's a Swede, Ellie," said Mr. Thompson;   30
"says he knows how to make butter."

"I hope it turns out to be the truth," said Mrs. Thompson. "Looks like my head never will get any better."

"Don't you worry," said Mr. Thompson. "You fret too much. Now I'm gointa ride into town and get a little order of groceries."

"Don't you linger, now, Mr. Thompson," said Mrs. Thompson. "Don't go to the hotel." She meant the saloon; the proprietor also had rooms for rent upstairs.

"Just a coupla little toddies," said Mr. Thompson, laughing loudly, "never hurt anybody."

35   "I never took a dram in my life," said Mrs. Thompson, "and what's more I never will."

"I wasn't talking about the womenfolks," said Mr. Thompson.

The sound of the swinging churn rocked Mrs. Thompson first into a gentle doze, then a deep drowse from which she waked suddenly knowing that the swinging had stopped a good while ago. She sat up shading her weak eyes from the flat strips of late summer sunlight between the sill and the lowered shades. There she was, thank God, still alive, with supper to cook but no churning on hand, and her head still bewildered, but easy. Slowly she realized she had been hearing a new sound even in her sleep. Somebody was playing a tune on the harmonica, not merely shrilling up and down making a sickening noise, but really playing a pretty tune, merry and sad.

She went out through the kitchen, stepped off the porch, and stood facing the east, shading her eyes. When her vision cleared and settled, she saw a long, pale-haired man in blue jeans sitting in the doorway of the hired man's shack, tilted back in a kitchen chair, blowing away at the harmonica with his eyes shut. Mrs. Thompson's heart fluttered and sank. Heavens, he looked lazy and worthless, he did, now. First a lot of no-count fiddling darkies and then a no-count white man. It was just like Mr. Thompson to take on that kind. She did wish he would be more considerate, and take a little trouble with his business. She wanted to believe in her husband, and there were too many times when she couldn't. She wanted to believe that tomorrow, or at least the day after, life, such a battle at best, was going to be better.

She walked past the shack without glancing aside, stepping carefully, bent at the waist because of the nagging pain in her side, and went to the springhouse, trying to harden her mind to speak very plainly to that new hired man if he had not done his work.

40   The milk house was only another shack of weather-beaten boards nailed together hastily years before because they needed a milk house; it was meant to be temporary, and it was; already shapeless, leaning this way and that over a perpetual cool trickle of water that fell from a little grot, almost choked with pallid ferns. No one else in the whole countryside had such a spring on his land. Mr. and Mrs. Thompson felt they had a fortune in that spring, if ever they get around to doing anything with it.

Rickety wooden shelves clung at hazard in the square around the small pool where the larger pails of milk and butter stood, fresh and sweet in the cold water. One hand supporting her flat, pained side, the other shading her eyes, Mrs. Thompson leaned over and peered into the pails. The cream had been skimmed and set aside, there was a rich roll of butter, the wooden molds and shallow pans had been scrubbed and scalded for the first time in who knows when, the barrel was full of buttermilk ready for the pigs and the weanling calves, the hard packed-dirt floor had been swept smooth. Mrs. Thompson straightened up again, smiling tenderly. She had been ready to scold him, a poor man who needed a job, who had just come there and who might not have been expected to do things properly at first. There was nothing she could do to make up for the injustice she had done him in her thoughts but to tell him how she appreciated his good clean work, finished already, in no time at all. She ventured near the door of the shack with her careful steps; Mr. Helton opened his eyes, stopped playing, and brought his chair down straight, but did not look at her, or get up. She was a little frail woman with long thick brown hair in a braid, a suffering patient mouth and diseased eyes which cried easily. She wove her fingers into an eyeshade, thumbs on temples, and, winking her tearful lids, said with a polite little manner, "Howdy do, sir. I'm Miz Thompson, and I wanted to tell you I think you did real well in the milk house. It's always been a hard place to keep."

He said, "That's all right," in a slow voice, without moving.

Mrs. Thompson waited a moment. "That's a pretty tune you're playing. Most folks don't seem to get much music out of a harmonica."

Mr. Helton sat humped over, long legs sprawling, his spine in a bow, running his thumb over the square mouth-stops; except for his moving hand he might have been asleep. The harmonica was a big shiny new one, and Mrs. Thompson, her gaze wandering about, counted five others, all good and expensive, standing in a row on the shelf beside his cot. "He must carry them around in his jumper pocket," she thought, and noted there was not a sign of any other possession lying about. "I see you're mighty fond of music," she said. "We used to have an old accordion, and Mr. Thompson could play it right smart, but the little boys broke it up."

Mr. Helton stood up rather suddenly, the chair clattered under him, his knees straightened though his shoulders did not, and he looked at the floor as if he were listening carefully. "You know how little boys are," said Mrs. Thompson. "You'd better set them harmonicas on a high shelf or they'll be after them. They're great hands for getting into things. I try to learn 'em, but it don't do much good."

Mr. Helton, in one wide gesture of his long arms, swept his harmonicas up against his chest, and from there transferred them in a row to the ledge where the roof joined to the wall. He pushed them back almost out of sight.

"That'll do, maybe," said Mrs. Thompson. "Now I wonder," she said, turning and closing her eyes helplessly against the stronger western light,

45

"I wonder what became of them little tads. I can't keep up with them." She had a way of speaking about her children as if they were rather troublesome nephews on a prolonged visit.

"Down by the creek," said Mr. Helton, in his hollow voice. Mrs. Thompson, pausing confusedly, decided he had answered her question. He stood in silent patience, not exactly waiting for her to go, perhaps, but pretty plainly not waiting for anything else. Mrs. Thompson was perfectly accustomed to all kinds of men full of all kinds of cranky ways. The point was, to find out just how Mr. Helton's crankiness was different from any other man's, and then get used to it, and let him feel at home. Her father had been cranky, her brothers and uncles had all been set in their ways and none of them alike; and every hired man she'd ever seen had quirks and crotchets of his own. Now here was Mr. Helton, who was a Swede, who wouldn't talk, and who played the harmonica besides.

"They'll be needing something to eat," said Mrs. Thompson in a vague friendly way, "pretty soon. Now I wonder what I ought to be thinking about for supper? Now what do you like to eat, Mr. Helton? We always have plenty of good butter and milk and cream, that's a blessing. Mr. Thompson says we ought to sell all of it, but I say my family comes first." Her little face went all out of shape in a pained blind smile.

50   "I eat anything," said Mr. Helton, his words wandering up and down.

He *can't* talk, for one thing, thought Mrs. Thompson; it's a shame to keep at him when he don't know the language good. She took a slow step away from the shack, looking back over her shoulder. "We usually have cornbread except on Sundays," she told him. "I suppose in your part of the country you don't get much good cornbread."

Not a word from Mr. Helton. She saw from her eye-corner that he had sat down again, looking at his harmonica, chair tilted. She hoped he would remember it was getting near milking time. As she moved away, he started playing again, the same tune.

Milking time came and went. Mrs. Thompson saw Mr. Helton going back and forth between the cow barn and the milk house. He swung along in an easy lope, shoulders bent, head hanging, the big buckets balancing like a pair of scales at the ends of his bony arms. Mr. Thompson rode in from town sitting straighter than usual, chin in, a towsack full of supplies swung behind the saddle. After a trip to the barn, he came into the kitchen full of good will, and gave Mrs. Thompson a hearty smack on the cheek after dusting her face off with his tough whiskers. He had been to the hotel, that was plain. "Took a look around the premises, Ellie," he shouted. "That Swede sure is grinding out the labor. But he is the closest mouthed feller I ever met up with in all my days. Looks like he's scared he'll crack his jaw if he opens his front teeth."

Mrs. Thompson was stirring up a big bowl of buttermilk cornbread. "You smell like a toper, Mr. Thompson," she said with perfect dignity. "I wish you'd get one of the little boys to bring me in an extra load of fire-wood. I'm thinking about baking a batch of cookies tomorrow."

Mr. Thompson, all at once smelling the liquor on his own breath, 55
sneaked out, justly rebuked, and brought in the firewood himself. Arthur and Herbert, grubby from thatched head to toes, from skin to shirt, came stamping in yelling for supper. "Go wash your faces and comb your hair," said Mrs. Thompson, automatically. They retired to the porch. Each one put his hand under the pump and wet his forelock, combed it down with his fingers, and returned at once to the kitchen, where all the fair prospects of life were centered. Mrs. Thompson set an extra plate and commanded Arthur, the eldest, eight years old, to call Mr. Helton for supper.

Arthur, without moving from the spot, bawled like a bull calf, "Saaaaaay, Hellllllton, suuuuuupper's ready!" and added in a lower voice, "You big Swede!"

"Listen to me," said Mrs. Thompson, "that's no way to act. Now you go out there and ask him decent, or I'll get your daddy to give you a good licking."

Mr. Helton loomed, long and gloomy, in the doorway. "Sit right there," boomed Mr. Thompson, waving his arm. Mr. Helton swung his square shoes across the kitchen in two steps, slumped onto the bench and sat. Mr. Thompson occupied his chair at the head of the table, the two boys scrambled into place opposite Mr. Helton, and Mrs. Thompson sat at the end nearest the stove. Mrs. Thompson clasped her hands, bowed her head and said aloud hastily, "Lord, for all these and Thy other blessings we thank Thee in Jesus' name, amen," trying to finish before Herbert's rusty little paw reached the nearest dish. Otherwise she would be duty-bound to send him away from the table, and growing children need their meals. Mr. Thompson and Arthur always waited, but Herbert, aged six, was too young to take training yet.

Mr. and Mrs. Thompson tried to engage Mr. Helton in conversation, but it was a failure. They tried first the weather, and then the crops, and then the cows, but Mr. Helton simply did not reply. Mr. Thompson then told something funny he had seen in town. It was about some of the other old grangers at the hotel, friends of his, giving beer to a goat, and the goat's subsequent behavior. Mr. Helton did not seem to hear. Mrs. Thompson laughed dutifully, but she didn't think it was very funny. She had heard it often before, though Mr. Thompson, each time he told it, pretended it had happened that self-same day. It must have happened years ago if it ever happened at all, and it had never been a story that Mrs. Thompson thought suitable for mixed company. The whole thing came of Mr. Thompson's weakness for a dram too much now and then, though he voted for local op-tion at every election. She passed the food to Mr. Helton, who took a help-ing of everything, but not much, not enough to keep him up to his full powers if he expected to go on working the way he had started.

60   At last, he took a fair-sized piece of cornbread, wiped his plate up as
clean as if it had been licked by a hound dog, stuffed his mouth full, and,
still chewing, slid off the bench and started for the door.

"Good night, Mr. Helton," said Mrs. Thompson, and the other Thompsons took it up in a scattered chorus, "Good night, Mr. Helton!"

"Good night," said Mr. Helton's wavering voice grudgingly from the
darkness.

"Gude not," said Arthur, imitating Mr. Helton.

"Gude not," said Herbert, the copy-cat.

65   "You don't do it right," said Arthur. "Now listen to me. Guuuuuude
naht," and he ran a hollow scale in a luxury of successful impersonation.
Herbert almost went into a fit with joy.

"Now you *stop* that," said Mrs. Thompson. "He can't help the way he
talks. You ought to be ashamed of yourselves, both of you, making fun of a
poor stranger like that. How'd you like to be a stranger in a strange land?"

"I'd like it," said Arthur. "I think it would be fun."

"They're both regular heathens, Ellie," said Mr. Thompson. "Just plain
ignoramuses." He turned the face of awful fatherhood upon his young.
"You're both going to get sent to school next year, and that'll knock some
sense into you."

"I'm going to git sent to the 'formatory when I'm old enough," piped
up Herbert. "That's where I'm goin'."

70   "Oh, you are, are you?" asked Mr. Thompson. "Who says so?"

"The Sunday School Supintendant," said Herbert, a bright boy showing off.

"You see?" said Mr. Thompson, staring at his wife. "What did I tell
you?" He became a hurricane of wrath. "Get to bed, you two," he roared
until his Adam's apple shuddered. "Get now before I take the hide off you!"
They got, and shortly from their attic bedroom the sounds of scuffling and
snorting and giggling and growling filled the house and shook the kitchen
ceiling.

Mrs. Thompson held her head and said in a small uncertain voice, "It's
no use picking on them when they're so young and tender. I can't stand it."

"My goodness, Ellie," said Mr. Thompson, "we've got to raise 'em. We
can't just let 'em grow up hog wild."

75   She went on in another tone. "That Mr. Helton seems all right, even if
he can't be made to talk. Wonder how he comes to be so far from home."

"Like I said, he isn't no whamper-jaw," said Mr. Thompson, "but he
sure knows how to lay out the work. I guess that's the main thing around
here. Country's full of fellers trampin' round looking for work."

Mrs. Thompson was gathering up the dishes. She now gathered up Mr.
Thompson's plate from under his chin. "To tell you the honest truth," she
remarked, "I think it's a mighty good change to have a man round the place
who knows how to work and keep his mouth shut. Means he'll keep out of
our business. Not that we've got anything to hide, but it's convenient."

"That's a fact," said Mr. Thompson. "Haw, haw," he shouted suddenly. "Means you can do all the talking, huh?"

"The only thing," went on Mrs. Thompson, "is this: he don't eat hearty enough to suit me. I like to see a man set down and relish a good meal. My granma used to say it was no use putting dependence on a man who won't set down and make out his dinner. I hope it won't be that way this time."

"Tell *you* the truth, Ellie," said Mr. Thompson, picking his teeth with a   80 fork and leaning back in the best of good humors, "I always thought your granma was a ter'ble ole fool. She'd just say the first thing that popped into her head and call it God's wisdom."

"My granma wasn't anybody's fool. Nine times out of ten she knew what she was talking about. I always say, the first thing you think is the best thing you can say."

"Well," said Mr. Thompson, going into another shout, "You're so ree-fined about that goat story, you just try speaking out in mixed comp'ny sometime! You just try it. S'pose you happened to be thinking about a hen and a rooster, hey? I reckon you'd shock the Babtist preacher!" He gave her a good pinch on her thin little rump. "No more meat on you than a rabbit," he said, fondly. "Now I like 'em cornfed."

Mrs. Thompson looked at him open-eyed and blushed. She could see better by lamplight. "Why, Mr. Thompson, sometimes I think you're the evilest-minded man that ever lived." She took a handful of hair on the crown of his head and gave it a good, slow pull. "That's to show you how it feels, pinching so hard when you're supposed to be playing," she said, gently.

In spite of his situation in life, Mr. Thompson had never been able to outgrow his deep conviction that running a dairy and chasing after chickens was woman's work. He was fond of saying that he could plow a furrow, cut sorghum, shuck corn, handle a team, build a corn crib, as well as any man. Buying and selling, too, were man's work. Twice a week he drove the spring wagon to market with the fresh butter, a few eggs, fruits in their proper season, sold them, pocketed the change, and spent it as seemed best, being careful not to dig into Mrs. Thompson's pin money.

But from the first the cows worried him, coming up regularly twice a   85 day to be milked, standing there reproaching him with their smug female faces. Calves worried him, fighting the rope and strangling themselves until their eyes bulged, trying to get at the teat. Wrestling with a calf unmanned him, like having to change a baby's diaper. Milk worried him, coming bitter sometimes, drying up, turning sour. Hens worried him, cackling, clucking, hatching out when you least expected it and leading their broods into the barnyard where the horses could step on them; dying of roup and wryneck and getting plagues of chicken lice; laying eggs all over God's creation so that half of them were spoiled before a man could find them, in spite of a rack of nests Mrs. Thompson had set out for them in the feed room. Hens were a blasted nuisance.

Slopping hogs was hired man's work, in Mr. Thompson's opinion. Killing hogs was a job for the boss, but scraping them and cutting them up was for the hired man again; and again woman's proper work was dressing meat, smoking, pickling, and making lard and sausage. All his carefully limited fields of activity were related somehow to Mr. Thompson's feeling for the appearance of things, his own appearance in the sight of God and man. "It don't *look* right," was his final reason for not doing anything he did not wish to do.

It was his dignity and his reputation that he cared about, and there were only a few kinds of work manly enough for Mr. Thompson to undertake with his own hands. Mrs. Thompson, to whom so many forms of work would have been becoming, had simply gone down on him early. He saw, after a while, how short-sighted it had been of him to expect much from Mrs. Thompson; he had fallen in love with her delicate waist and lace-trimmed petticoats and big blue eyes, and, though all those charms had disappeared, she had in the meantime become Ellie to him, not at all the same person as Miss Ellen Bridges, popular Sunday School teacher in the Mountain City First Baptist Church, but his dear wife, Ellie, who was not strong. Deprived as he was, however, of the main support in life which a man might expect in marriage, he had almost without knowing it resigned himself to failure. Head erect, a prompt payer of taxes, yearly subscriber to the preacher's salary, land owner and father of a family, employer, a hearty good fellow among men, Mr. Thompson knew, without putting it into words, that he had been going steadily down hill. God amighty, it did look like somebody around the place might take a rake in hand now and then and clear up the clutter around the barn and the kitchen steps. The wagon shed was so full of broken-down machinery and ragged harness and old wagon wheels and battered milk pails and rotting lumber you could hardly drive in there any more. Not a soul on the place would raise a hand to it, and as for him, he had all he could do with his regular work. He would sometimes in the slack season sit for hours worrying about it, squirting tobacco on the ragweeds growing in a thicket against the wood pile, wondering what a fellow could do, handicapped as he was. He looked forward to the boys growing up soon; he was going to put them through the mill just as his own father had done with him when he was a boy; they were going to learn how to take hold and run the place right. He wasn't going to overdo it, but those two boys were going to earn their salt, or he'd know why. Great big lubbers sitting around whittling! Mr. Thompson sometimes grew quite enraged with them, when imagining their possible future, big lubbers sitting around whittling or thinking about fishing trips. Well, he'd put a stop to that, mighty damn quick.

As the seasons passed, and Mr. Helton took hold more and more, Mr. Thompson began to relax in his mind a little. There seemed to be nothing the fellow couldn't do, all in the day's work and as a matter of course. He got up at five o'clock in the morning, boiled his own coffee and fried his own bacon and was out in the cow lot before Mr. Thompson had even begun to yawn, stretch, groan, roar and thump around looking for his jeans. He milked the cows, kept the milk house, and churned the butter; rounded the hens up and somehow persuaded them to lay in the nests, not under the house and behind haystacks; he fed them regularly and they hatched out until you couldn't set a foot down for them. Little by little the piles of trash around the barns and house disappeared. He carried buttermilk and corn to the hogs, and curried cockleburs out of the horses' manes. He was gentle with the calves, if a little grim with the cows and hens; judging by his conduct, Mr. Helton had never heard of the difference between man's and woman's work on a farm.

In the second year, he showed Mr. Thompson the picture of a cheese press in a mail order catalogue, and said, "This is a good thing. You buy this, I make cheese." The press was bought and Mr. Helton did make cheese, and it was sold, along with the increased butter and the crates of eggs. Sometimes Mr. Thompson felt a little contemptuous of Mr. Helton's ways. It did seem kind of picayune for a man to go around picking up a half dozen ears of corn that had fallen off the wagon on the way from the field, gathering up fallen fruit to feed to the pigs, storing up old nails and stray parts of machinery, spending good time stamping a fancy pattern on the butter before it went to market. Mr. Thompson, sitting up high on the spring-wagon seat, with the decorated butter in a five-gallon lard can wrapped in wet towsack, driving to town, chirruping to the horses and snapping the reins over their backs, sometimes thought that Mr. Helton was a pretty meeching sort of fellow; but he never gave way to these feelings, he knew a good thing when he had it. It was a fact the hogs were in better shape and sold for more money. It was a fact that Mr. Thompson stopped buying feed, Mr. Helton managed the crops so well. When beef- and hog-slaughtering time came, Mr. Helton knew how to save the scraps that Mr. Thompson had thrown away, and wasn't above scraping guts and filling them with sausages that he made by his own methods. In all, Mr. Thompson had no grounds for complaint. In the third year, he raised Mr. Helton's wages, though Mr. Helton had not asked for a raise. The fourth year, when Mr. Thompson was not only out of debt but had a little cash in the bank, he raised Mr. Helton's wages again, two dollars and a half a month each time.

"The man's worth it, Ellie," said Mr. Thompson, in a glow of self- 90 justification for his extravagance. "He's made this place pay, and I want him to know I appreciate it."

Mr. Helton's silence, the pallor of his eyebrows and hair, his long, glum jaw and eyes that refused to see anything, even the work under his hands, had grown perfectly familiar to the Thompsons. At first, Mrs. Thompson complained a little. "It's like sitting down at the table with a disembodied spirit," she said. "You'd think he'd find something to say, sooner or later."

"Let him alone," said Mr. Thompson. "When he gets ready to talk, he'll talk."

The years passed, and Mr. Helton never got ready to talk. After his work was finished for the day, he would come up from the barn or the milk house or the chicken house, swinging his lantern, his big shoes clumping like pony hoofs on the hard path. They, sitting in the kitchen in the winter, or on the back porch in summer, would hear him drag out his wooden chair, hear the creak of it tilted back, and then for a little while he would play his single tune on one or another of his harmonicas. The harmonicas were in different keys, some lower and sweeter than the others, but the same changeless tune went on, a strange tune, with sudden turns in it, night after night, and sometimes even in the afternoons when Mr. Helton sat down to catch his breath. At first the Thompsons liked it very much, and always stopped to listen. Later there came a time when they were fairly sick of it, and began to wish to each other that he would learn a new one. At last they did not hear it any more, it was as natural as the sound of the wind rising in the evenings, or the cows lowing, or their own voices.

Mrs. Thompson pondered now and then over Mr. Helton's soul. He didn't seem to be a church-goer, and worked straight through Sunday as if it were any common day of the week. "I think we ought to invite him to go to hear Dr. Martin," she told Mr. Thompson. "It isn't very Christian of us not to ask him. He's not a forward kind of man. He'd wait to be asked."

95 "Let him alone," said Mr. Thompson. "The way I look at it, his religion is every man's own business. Besides, he ain't got any Sunday clothes. He wouldn't want to go to church in them jeans and jumpers of his. I don't know what he does with his money. He certainly don't spend it foolishly."

Still, once the notion got into her head, Mrs. Thompson could not rest until she invited Mr. Helton to go to church with the family next Sunday. He was pitching hay into neat little piles in the field back of the orchard. Mrs. Thompson put on smoked glasses and a sunbonnet and walked all the way down there to speak to him. He stopped and leaned on his pitchfork, listening, and for a moment Mrs. Thompson was almost frightened at his face. The pale eyes seemed to glare past her, the eyebrows frowned, the long jaw hardened. "I got work," he said bluntly, and lifting his pitchfork he turned from her and began to toss the hay. Mrs. Thompson, her feelings hurt, walked back thinking that by now she should be used to Mr. Helton's ways, but it did seem like a man, even a foreigner, could be just a little polite when you gave him a Christian invitation. "He's not polite, that's the only thing I've got against him," she said to Mr. Thompson. "He just can't seem to behave like other people. You'd think he had a grudge against the world," she said. "I sometimes don't know what to make of it."

In the second year something had happened that made Mrs. Thompson uneasy, the kind of thing she could not put into words, hardly into thoughts, and if she had tried to explain to Mr. Thompson it would have sounded worse than it was, or not bad enough. It was that kind of queer thing that seems to be giving a warning, and yet, nearly always nothing comes of it. It was on a hot, still spring day, and Mrs. Thompson had been down to the garden patch to pull some new carrots and green onions and string beans for dinner. As she worked, sunbonnet low over her eyes, putting each kind of vegetable in a pile by itself in her basket, she noticed how neatly Mr. Helton weeded, and how rich the soil was. He had spread it all over with manure from the barns, and worked it in, in the fall, and the vegetables were coming up fine and full. She walked back under the nubbly little fig trees where the unpruned branches leaned almost to the ground, and the thick leaves made a cool screen. Mrs. Thompson was always looking for shade to save her eyes. So she, looking idly about, saw through the screen a sight that struck her as very strange. If it had been a noisy spectacle, it would have been quite natural. It was the silence that struck her. Mr. Helton was shaking Arthur by the shoulders, ferociously, his face most terribly fixed and pale. Arthur's head snapped back and forth and he had not stiffened in resistance, as he did when Mrs. Thompson tried to shake him. His eyes were rather frightened, but surprised, too, probably more surprised than anything else. Herbert stood by meekly, watching. Mr. Helton dropped Arthur, and seized Herbert, and shook him with the same methodical ferocity, the same face of hatred. Herbert's mouth crumpled as if he would cry, but he made no sound. Mr. Helton let him go, turned and strode into the shack, and the little boys ran, as if for their lives, without a word. They disappeared around the corner to the front of the house.

Mrs. Thompson took time to set her basket on the kitchen table, to push her sunbonnet back on her head and draw it forward again, to look in the stove and make certain the fire was going, before she followed the boys. They were sitting huddled together under a clump of chinaberry trees in plain sight of her bedroom window, as if it were a safe place they had discovered.

"What are you doing?" asked Mrs. Thompson.

They looked hang-dog from under their foreheads and Arthur   100
mumbled, "Nothin'."

"Nothing *now*, you mean," said Mrs. Thompson, severely. "Well, I have plenty for you to do. Come right in here this minute and help me fix vegetables. This minute."

They scrambled up very eagerly and followed her close. Mrs. Thompson tried to imagine what they had been up to; she did not like the notion of Mr. Helton taking it on himself to correct her little boys, but she was afraid to ask them for reasons. They might tell her a lie, and she would have to overtake them in it, and whip them. Or she would have to pretend to believe them, and they would get in the habit of lying. Or they might tell her the truth, and it would be something she would have to whip them for. The very thought of it gave her a headache. She supposed she might ask Mr. Helton, but it was not her place to ask. She would wait and tell Mr. Thompson, and let him get at the bottom of it. While her mind ran on, she kept the little boys hopping. "Cut those carrot tops closer, Herbert, you're just being careless. Arthur, stop breaking up the beans so little. They're little enough already. Herbert, you go get an armload of wood. Arthur, you take these onions and wash them under the pump. Herbert, as soon as you're done here, you get a broom and sweep out this kitchen. Arthur, you get a shovel and take up the ashes. Stop picking your nose, Herbert. How often must I tell you? Arthur, you go look in the top drawer of my bureau, left-hand side, and bring me the vaseline for Herbert's nose. Herbert, come here to me. . . ."

They galloped through their chores, their animal spirits rose with activity, and shortly they were out in the front yard again, engaged in a wrestling match. They sprawled and fought, scrambled, clutched, rose and fell shouting, as aimlessly, noisily, monotonously as two puppies. They imitated various animals, not a human sound from them, and their dirty faces were streaked with sweat. Mrs. Thompson, sitting at her window, watched them with baffled pride and tenderness, they were so sturdy and healthy and growing so fast; but uneasily, too, with her pained little smile and the tears rolling from her eyelids that clinched themselves against the sunlight. They were so idle and careless, as if they had no future in this world, and no immortal souls to save, and oh, what had they been up to that Mr. Helton had shaken them, with his face positively dangerous?

In the evening before supper, without a word to Mr. Thompson of the curious fear the sight had caused her, she told him that Mr. Helton had shaken the little boys for some reason. He stepped out to the shack and spoke to Mr. Helton. In five minutes he was back, glaring at his young. "He says them brats been fooling with his harmonicas, Ellie, blowing in them and getting them all dirty and full of spit and they don't play good."

105   "Did he say all that?" asked Mrs. Thompson. "It doesn't seem possible."

"Well, that's what he meant, anyhow," said Mr. Thompson. "He didn't say it just that way. But he acted pretty worked up about it."

"That's a shame," said Mrs. Thompson, "a perfect shame. Now we've got to do something so they'll remember they mustn't go into Mr. Helton's things."

"I'll tan their hides for them," said Mr. Thompson. "I'll take a calf rope to them if they don't look out."

"Maybe you'd better leave the whipping to me," said Mrs. Thompson. "You haven't got a light enough hand for children."

110   "That's just what's the matter with them now," shouted Mr. Thompson, "rotten spoiled and they'll wind up in the penitentiary. You don't half whip 'em. Just little love taps. My pa used to knock me down with a stick of stove wood or anything else that came handy."

"Well, that's not saying it's right," said Mrs. Thompson. "I don't hold with that way of raising children. It makes them run away from home. I've seen too much of it."

"I'll break every bone in 'em," said Mr. Thompson, simmering down, "if they don't mind you better and stop being so bull-headed."

"Leave the table and wash your face and hands," Mrs. Thompson commanded the boys, suddenly. They slunk out and dabbled at the pump and slunk in again, trying to make themselves small. They had learned long ago that their mother always made them wash when there was trouble ahead. They looked at their plates. Mr. Thompson opened up on them.

"Well, now, what you got to say for yourselves about going into Mr. Helton's shack and ruining his harmonicas?"

The two little boys wilted, their faces drooped into the grieved hope- 115 less lines of children's faces when they are brought to the terrible bar of blind adult justice; their eyes telegraphed each other in panic, "Now we're really going to catch a licking"; in despair, they dropped their buttered cornbread on their plates, their hands lagged on the edge of the table.

"I ought to break your ribs," said Mr. Thompson, "and I'm a good mind to do it."

"Yes, sir," whispered Arthur, faintly.

"Yes, sir," said Herbert, his lip trembling.

"Now, papa," said Mrs. Thompson in a warning tone. The children did not glance at her. They had no faith in her good will. She had betrayed them in the first place. There was no trusting her. Now she might save them and she might not. No use depending on her.

"Well, you ought to get a good thrashing. You deserve it, don't you, 120 Arthur?"

Arthur hung his head. "Yes, sir."

"And the next time I catch either of you hanging around Mr. Helton's shack, I'm going to take the hide off *both* of you, you hear me, Herbert?"

Herbert mumbled and choked, scattering his cornbread. "Yes, sir."

"Well, now sit up and eat your supper and not another word out of you," said Mr. Thompson, beginning on his own food. The little boys perked up somewhat and started chewing, but every time they looked around they met their parents' eyes, regarding them steadily. There was no telling when they would think of something new. The boys ate warily, trying not to be seen or heard, the cornbread sticking, the buttermilk gurgling, as it went down their gullets.

"And something else, Mr. Thompson," said Mrs. Thompson after a 125 pause. "Tell Mr. Helton he's to come straight to us when they bother him, and not to trouble shaking them himself. Tell him we'll look after that."

"They're so mean," answered Mr. Thompson, staring at them. "It's a wonder he don't just kill 'em off and be done with it." But there was some-thing in the tone that told Arthur and Herbert that nothing more worth worrying about was going to happen this time. Heaving deep sighs, they sat up, reaching for the food nearest them.

"Listen," said Mrs. Thompson, suddenly. The little boys stopped eat-ing. "Mr. Helton hasn't come for his supper. Arthur, go and tell Mr. Hel-ton he's late for supper. Tell him nice, now."

Arthur, miserably depressed, slid out of his place and made for the door, without a word.

There were no miracles of fortune to be brought to pass on a small dairy farm. The Thompsons did not grow rich, but they kept out of the poor house, as Mr. Thompson was fond of saying, meaning he had got a little foothold in spite of Ellie's poor health, and unexpected weather, and strange declines in market prices, and his own mysterious handicaps which weighed him down. Mr. Helton was the hope and the prop of the family, and all the Thompsons became fond of him, or at any rate they ceased to regard him as in any way peculiar, and looked upon him, from a distance they did not know how to bridge, as a good man and a good friend. Mr. Helton went his way, worked, played his tune. Nine years passed. The boys grew up and learned to work. They could not remember the time when Ole Helton hadn't been there: a grouchy cuss, Brother Bones; Mr. Helton, the dairymaid; that Big Swede. If he had heard them, he might have been annoyed at some of the names they called him. But he did not hear them, and besides they meant no harm—or at least such harm as existed was all there, in the names; the boys referred to their father as the Old Man, or the Old Geezer, but not to his face. They lived through by main strength all the grimy, secret, oblique phases of growing up and got past the crisis safely if anyone does. Their parents could see they were good solid boys with hearts of gold in spite of their rough ways. Mr. Thompson was relieved to find that, without knowing how he had done it, he had succeeded in raising a set of boys who were not trifling whittlers. They were such good boys Mr. Thompson began to believe they were born that way, and that he had never spoken a harsh word to them in their lives, much less thrashed them. Herbert and Arthur never disputed his word.

130   Mr. Helton, his hair wet with sweat, plastered to his dripping forehead, his jumper streaked dark and light blue and clinging to his ribs, was chopping a little firewood. He chopped slowly, struck the ax into the end of the chopping log, and piled the wood up neatly. He then disappeared round the house into his shack, which shared with the wood pile a good shade from a row of mulberry trees. Mr. Thompson was lolling in a swing chair on the front porch, a place he had never liked. The chair was new, and Mrs. Thompson had wanted it on the front porch, though the side porch was the place for it, being cooler; and Mr. Thompson wanted to sit in the chair, so there he was. As soon as the new wore off of it, and Ellie's pride in it was exhausted, he would move it round to the side porch. Meantime the August heat was almost unbearable, the air so thick you could poke a hole in it. The dust was inches thick on everything, though Mr. Helton sprinkled the whole yard regularly every night. He even shot the hose upward and washed the tree tops and the roof of the house. They had laid waterpipes to the kitchen and an outside faucet. Mr. Thompson must have dozed, for he opened his eyes and shut his mouth just in time to save his face before a stranger who had driven up to the front gate. Mr. Thompson stood up, put on his hat, pulled up his jeans, and watched while the stranger tied his team, attached to a light spring wagon, to the hitching post. Mr. Thompson recognized the team and wagon. They were from a

livery stable in Buda. While the stranger was opening the gate, a strong gate that Mr. Helton had built and set firmly on its hinges several years back, Mr. Thompson strolled down the path to greet him and find out what in God's world a man's business might be that would bring him out at this time of day, in all this dust and welter.

He wasn't exactly a fat man. He was more like a man who had been fat recently. His skin was baggy and his clothes were too big for him, and he somehow looked like a man who should be fat, ordinarily, but who might have just got over a spell of sickness. Mr. Thompson didn't take to his looks at all, he couldn't say why.

The stranger took off his hat. He said in a loud hearty voice, "Is this Mr. Thompson, Mr. Royal Earle Thompson?"

"That's my name," said Mr. Thompson, almost quietly, he was so taken aback by the free manner of the stranger.

"My name is Hatch," said the stranger, "Mr. Homer T. Hatch, and I've come to see you about buying a horse."

"I expect you've been misdirected," said Mr. Thompson. "I haven't got   135
a horse for sale. Usually if I've got anything like that to sell," he said, "I tell the neighbors and tack up a little sign on the gate."

The fat man opened his mouth and roared with joy, showing rabbit teeth brown as shoeleather. Mr. Thompson saw nothing to laugh at, for once. The stranger shouted, "That's just an old joke of mine." He caught one of his hands in the other and shook hands with himself heartily. "I always say something like that when I'm calling on a stranger, because I've noticed that when a feller says he's come to buy something nobody takes him for a suspicious character. You see? Haw, haw, haw."

His joviality made Mr. Thompson nervous, because the expression in the man's eyes didn't match the sounds he was making. "Haw, haw," laughed Mr. Thompson obligingly, still not seeing the joke. "Well, that's all wasted on me because I never take any man for a suspicious character 'til he shows hisself to be one. Says or does something," he explained. "Until that happens, one man's as good as another, so far's *I'm* concerned."

"Well," said the stranger, suddenly very sober and sensible, "I ain't come neither to buy nor sell. Fact is, I want to see you about something that's of interest to us both. Yes, sir, I'd like to have a little talk with you, and it won't cost you a cent."

"I guess that's fair enough," said Mr. Thompson, reluctantly. "Come on around the house where there's a little shade."

They went round and seated themselves on two stumps under a china-   140
berry tree.

"Yes, sir, Homer T. Hatch is my name and America is my nation," said the stranger. "I reckon you must know the name? I used to have a cousin named Jameson Hatch lived up the country a ways."

"Don't think I know the name," said Mr. Thompson. "There's some Hatchers settled somewhere around Mountain City."

"Don't know the old Hatch family," cried the man in deep concern. He seemed to be pitying Mr. Thompson's ignorance. "Why, we came over from Georgia fifty years ago. Been here long yourself?"

"Just all my whole life," said Mr. Thompson, beginning to feel peevish. "And my pa and my grampap before me. Yes, sir, we've been right here all along. Anybody wants to find a Thompson knows where to look for him. My grampap immigrated in 1836."

145   "From Ireland, I reckon?" said the stranger.

"From Pennsylvania," said Mr. Thompson. "Now what makes you think we came from Ireland?"

The stranger opened his mouth and began to shout with merriment, and he shook hands with himself as if he hadn't met himself for a long time. "Well, what I always says is, a feller's got to come from *somewhere*, ain't he?"

While they were talking, Mr. Thompson kept glancing at the face near him. He certainly did remind Mr. Thompson of somebody, or maybe he really had seen the man himself somewhere. He couldn't just place the features. Mr. Thompson finally decided it was just that all rabbit-teethed men looked alike.

"That's right," acknowledged Mr. Thompson, rather sourly, "but what I always say is, Thompsons have been settled here for so long it don't make much difference any more *where* they come from. Now a course, this is the slack season, and we're all just laying around a little, but nevertheless we've all got our chores to do, and I don't want to hurry you, and so if you've come to see me on business maybe we'd better get down to it."

150   "As I said, it's not in a way, and again in a way it is," said the fat man. "Now I'm looking for a man named Helton, Mr. Olaf Eric Helton, from North Dakota, and I was told up around the country a ways that I might find him here, and I wouldn't mind having a little talk with him. No, siree, I sure wouldn't mind, if it's all the same to you."

"I never knew his middle name," said Mr. Thompson, "but Mr. Helton is right here, and been here now for going on nine years. He's a mighty steady man, and you can tell anybody I said so."

"I'm glad to hear that," said Mr. Homer T. Hatch. "I like to hear of a feller mending his ways and settling down. Now when I knew Mr. Helton he was pretty wild, yes, sir, wild is what he was, he didn't know his own mind atall. Well, now, it's going to be a great pleasure to me to meet up with an old friend and find him all settled down and doing well by hisself."

"We've all got to be young once," said Mr. Thompson. "It's like the measles, it breaks out all over you, and you're a nuisance to yourself and everybody else, but it don't last, and it usually don't leave no ill effects." He was so pleased with this notion he forgot and broke into a guffaw. The stranger folded his arms over his stomach and went into a kind of fit, roaring until he had tears in his eyes. Mr. Thompson stopped shouting and eyed the stranger uneasily. Now he liked a good laugh as well as any man, but there ought to be a little moderation. Now this feller laughed like a perfect lunatic, that was a fact. And he wasn't laughing because he really thought things were funny, either. He was laughing for reasons of his own. Mr. Thompson fell into a moody silence, and waited until Mr. Hatch settled down a little.

Mr. Hatch got out a very dirty blue cotton bandanna and wiped his eyes. "That joke just about caught me where I live," he said, almost apologetically. "Now I wish I could think up things as funny as that to say. It's a gift. It's . . ."

"If you want to speak to Mr. Helton, I'll go and round him up," said   155
Mr. Thompson, making motions as if he might get up. "He may be in the milk house and he may be setting in his shack this time of day." It was drawing towards five o'clock. "It's right around the corner," he said.

"Oh, well, there ain't no special hurry," said Mr. Hatch. "I've been wanting to speak to him for a good long spell now and I guess a few minutes more won't make no difference. I just more wanted to locate him, like. That's all."

Mr. Thompson stopped beginning to stand up, and unbuttoned one more button of his shirt, and said, "Well, he's here, and he's this kind of man, that if he had any business with you he'd like to get it over. He don't dawdle, that's one thing you can say for him."

Mr. Hatch appeared to sulk a little at these words. He wiped his face with the bandanna and opened his mouth to speak, when round the house there came the music of Mr. Helton's harmonica. Mr. Thompson raised a finger. "There he is," said Mr. Thompson. "Now's your time."

Mr. Hatch cocked an ear towards the east side of the house and listened for a few seconds, a very strange expression on his face.

"I know that tune like I know the palm of my own hand," said Mr.   160
Thompson, "but I never heard Mr. Helton say what it was."

"That's a kind of Scandahoovian song," said Mr. Hatch. "Where I come from they sing it a lot. In North Dakota, they sing it. It says something about starting out in the morning feeling so good you can't hardly stand it, so you drink up all your likker before noon. All the likker, y' understand, that you was saving for the noon lay-off. The words ain't much, but it's a pretty tune. It's a kind of drinking song." He sat there drooping a little, and Mr. Thompson didn't like his expression. It was a satisfied expression, but it was more like the cat that et the canary.

"So far as I know," said Mr. Thompson, "he ain't touched a drop since he's been on the place, and that's nine years this coming September. Yes, sir, nine years, so far as I know, he ain't wetted his whistle once. And that's more than I can say for myself," he said, meekly proud.

"Yes, that's a drinking song," said Mr. Hatch. "I used to play 'Little Brown Jug' on the fiddle when I was younger than I am now," he went on, "but this Helton, he just keeps it up. He just sits and plays it by himself."

"He's been playing it off and on for nine years right here on the place," said Mr. Thompson, feeling a little proprietary.

165   "And he was certainly singing it as well, fifteen years before that, in North Dakota," said Mr. Hatch. "He used to sit up in a straitjacket, practically, when was in the asylum—"

"What's that you say?" said Mr. Thompson. "What's that?"

"Shucks, I didn't mean to tell you," said Mr. Hatch, a faint leer of regret in his drooping eyelids. "Shucks, that just slipped out. Funny, now I'd made up my mind I wouldn' say a word, because it would just make a lot of excitement, and what I say is, if a man has lived harmless and quiet for nine years it don't matter if he *is* loony, does it? So long's he keeps quiet and don't do nobody harm."

"You mean they had him in a straitjacket?" asked Mr. Thompson, uneasily. "In a lunatic asylum?"

"They sure did," said Mr. Hatch. "That's right where they had him, from time to time."

170   "They put my Aunt Ida in one of them things in the State asylum," said Mr. Thompson. "She got vi'lent, and they put her in one of these jackets with long sleeves and tied her to an iron ring in the wall, and Aunt Ida got so wild she broke a blood vessel and when they went to look after her she was dead. I'd think one them things was dangerous."

"Mr. Helton used to sing his drinking song when he was in a straitjacket," said Mr. Hatch. "Nothing ever bothered him, except if you tried to make him talk. That bothered him, and he'd get vi'lent, like your Aunt Ida. He'd get vi'lent and then they'd put him in the jacket and go off and leave him, and he'd lay there perfickly contented, so fars you could see, singing his song. Then one night he just disappeared. Left, you might say, just went, and nobody ever saw hide or hair of him again. And then I come along and find him here," said Mr. Hatch, "all settled down and playing the same song."

"He never acted crazy to me," said Mr. Thompson. "He always acted like a sensible man, to me. He never got married, for one thing, and he works like a horse, and I bet he's got the first cent I paid him when he landed here, and he don't drink, an he never says a word, much less swear, and he don't waste time runnin' around Saturday nights, and if he's crazy," said Mr. Thompson, "why, I think I'll go crazy myself for a change."

"Haw, ha," said Mr. Hatch, "heh, he, that's good! Ha, ha, ha, I hadn't thought of it jes like that. Yeah, that's right! Let's all go crazy and get rid of our wives and save our money, hey?" He smiled unpleasantly, showing his little rabbit teeth.

Mr. Thompson felt he was being misunderstood. He turned around and motioned toward the open window back of the honeysuckle trellis. "Let's move off down here a little," he said. "I oughta thought of that before." His visitor bothered Mr. Thompson. He had a way of taking the words out of Mr. Thompson's mouth, turning them around and mixing them up until Mr. Thompson didn't know himself what he had said. "My wife's not very strong," said Mr. Thompson. "She's been kind of invalid now goin' on fourteen years. It's mighty tough on a poor man, havin' sickness in the family. She had four operations," he said proudly, "one right after the other, but they didn't do any good. For five years hand-runnin', I just turned every nickel I made over to the doctors. Upshot is, she's a mighty delicate woman."

"My old woman," said Mr. Homer T. Hatch, "had a back like a mule,   175 yes, sir. That woman could have moved the barn with her bare hands if she'd ever took the notion. I used to say, it was a good thing she didn't know her own stren'th. She's dead now, though. That kind wear out quicker than the puny ones. I never had much use for a woman always complainin'. I'd get rid of her mighty quick, yes, sir, mighty quick. It's just as you say: a dead loss, keepin' one of 'em up."

This was not at all what Mr. Thompson had heard himself say; he had been trying to explain that a wife as expensive as his was a credit to a man. "She's a mighty reasonable woman," said Mr. Thompson, feeling baffled, "but I wouldn't answer for what she'd say or do if she found out we'd had a lunatic on the place all this time." They had moved away from the window; Mr. Thompson took Mr. Hatch the front way, because if he went the back way they would have to pass Mr. Helton's shack. For some reason he didn't want the stranger to see or talk to Mr. Helton. It was strange, but that was the way Mr. Thompson felt.

Mr. Thompson sat down again, on the chopping log, offering his guest another tree stump. "Now, I mighta got upset myself at such a thing, once," said Mr. Thompson, "but now I *deefy* anything to get me lathered up." He cut himself an enormous plug of tobacco with his horn-handled pocketknife, and offered it to Mr. Hatch, who then produced his own plug and, opening a huge bowie knife with a long blade sharply whetted, cut off a large wad and put it in his mouth. They then compared plugs and both of them were astonished to see how different men's ideas of good chewing tobacco were.

"Now, for instance," said Mr. Hatch, "mine is lighter colored. That's because, for one thing, there ain't any sweetenin' in this plug. I like it dry, natural leaf, medium strong."

"A little sweetenin' don't do no harm so far as I'm concerned," said Mr. Thompson, "but it's got to be mighty little. But with me, now, I want a strong leaf, I want it heavy-cured, as the feller says. There's a man near here, named Williams, Mr. John Morgan Williams, who chews a plug— well, sir, it's black as your hat and soft as melted tar. It fairly drips with molasses, jus' plain molasses, and it chews like licorice. Now, I don't call that a good chew."

"One man's meat," said Mr. Hatch, "is another man's poison. Now,   180 such a chew would simply gag me. I couldn't begin to put it in my mouth."

"Well," said Mr. Thompson, a tinge of apology in his voice, "I jus' barely tasted it myself, you might say. Just took a little piece in my mouth and spit it out again."

"I'm dead sure I couldn't even get that far," said Mr. Hatch. "I like a dry natural chew without any artificial flavorin' of any kind."

Mr. Thompson began to feel that Mr. Hatch was trying to make out he had the best judgment in tobacco, and was going to keep up the argument until he proved it. He began to feel seriously annoyed with the fat man. After all, who was he and where did he come from? Who was he to go around telling other people what kind of tobacco to chew?

"Artificial flavorin'," Mr. Hatch went on, doggedly, "is jes put in to cover up a cheap leaf and make a man think he's gettin' somethin' more than he *is* gettin'. Even a little sweetenin' is a sign of a cheap leaf, you can mark my words."

185   "I've always paid a fair price for my plug," said Mr. Thompson, stiffly. "I'm not a rich man and I don't go round settin' myself up for one, but I'll say this, when it comes to such things as tobacco, I buy the best on the market."

"Sweetenin', even a little," began Mr. Hatch, shifting his plug and squirting tobacco juice at a dry-looking little rose bush that was having a hard enough time as it was, standing all day in the blazing sun, its roots clenched in the baked earth, "is the sign of—"

"About this Mr. Helton, now," said Mr. Thompson, determinedly, "I don't see no reason to hold it against a man because he went loony once or twice in his lifetime and so I don't expect to take no steps about it. Not a step. I've got nothin' against the man, he's always treated me fair. They's things and people," he went on, "'nough to drive any man loony. The wonder to me is, more men don't wind up in straitjackets, the way things are going these days and times."

"That's right," said Mr. Hatch, promptly, entirely too promptly, as if he were turning Mr. Thompson's meaning back on him. "You took the words right out of my mouth. There ain't every man in a straitjacket that ought to be there. Ha, ha, you're right all right. You got the idea."

Mr. Thompson sat silent and chewed steadily and stared at a spot on the ground about six feet away and felt a slow muffled resentment climbing from somewhere deep down in him, climbing and spreading all through him. What was this fellow driving at? What was he trying to say? It wasn't so much his words, but his looks and his way of talking: that droopy look in the eye, that tone of voice, as if he was trying to mortify Mr. Thompson about something. Mr. Thompson didn't like it, but he couldn't get hold of it either. He wanted to turn around and shove the fellow off the stump, but it wouldn't look reasonable. Suppose something happened to the fellow when he fell off the stump, just for instance, if he fell on the ax and cut himself, and then someone should ask Mr. Thompson why he shoved him, and what could a man say? It would look mighty funny, it would sound mighty strange to say, Well him and me fell out over a plug of tobacco. He might just shove him anyhow and then tell people he was a fat man not used to the heat and while he was talking he got dizzy and fell off by himself, or something like that, and it wouldn't be the truth either, because it wasn't the heat and it wasn't the tobacco. Mr. Thompson made up his mind to get the fellow off the place pretty quick, without seeming to be anxious, and watch him sharp till he was out of sight. It doesn't pay to be friendly with strangers from another part of the country. They're always up to something, or they'd stay at home where they belong.

"And they's some people," said Mr. Hatch, "would jus' as soon have a loonatic around their house as not, they can't see no difference between them and anybody else. I always say, if that's the way a man feels, don't care who he associates with, why, why, that's his business, not mine. I don't wanta have a thing to do with it. Now back home in North Dakota, we don't feel that way. I'd like to a seen anybody hiring a loonatic there, aspecially after what he done." 190

"I didn't understand your home was North Dakota," said Mr. Thompson. "I thought you said Georgia."

"I've got a married sister in North Dakota," said Mr. Hatch, "married a Swede, but a white man if ever I saw one. So I say *we* because we got into a little business together out that way. And it seems like home, kind of."

"What did he do?" asked Mr. Thompson, feeling very uneasy again.

"Oh, nothin' to speak of," said Mr. Hatch, jovially, "jus' went loony one day in the hayfield and shoved a pitchfork right square through his brother, when they was makin' hay. They was goin' to execute him, but they found out he had went crazy with the heat, as the feller says, and so they put him in the asylum. That's all he done. Nothin' to get lathered up about, ha, ha, ha!" he said, and taking out his sharp knife he began to slice off a chew as carefully as if he were cutting cake.

"Well," said Mr. Thompson, "I don't deny that's news. Yes, sir, news. But I still say somethin' must have drove him to it. Some men make you feel like giving 'em a good killing just by lookin' at you. His brother may a been a mean ornery cuss." 195

"Brother was going to get married," said Mr. Hatch; "used to go courtin' his girl nights. Borrowed Mr. Helton's harmonica to give her a serenade one evenin', and lost it. Brand new harmonica."

"He thinks a heap of his harmonicas," said Mr. Thompson. "Only money he ever spends, now and then he buys hisself a new one. Must have a dozen in that shack, all kinds and sizes."

"Brother wouldn't buy him a new one," said Mr. Hatch, "so Mr. Helton just ups, as I says, and runs his pitchfork through his brother. Now you know he musta been crazy to get all worked up over a little thing like that."

"Sounds like it," said Mr. Thompson, reluctant to agree in anything with this intrusive and disagreeable fellow. He kept thinking he couldn't remember when he had taken such a dislike to a man on first sight.

"Seems to me you'd get pretty sick of hearin' the same tune year in, year out," said Mr. Hatch. 200

"Well, sometimes I think it wouldn't do no harm if he learned a new one," said Mr. Thompson, "but he don't, so there's nothin' to be done about it. It's a pretty good tune, though."

"One of the Scandahoovians told me what it meant, that's how I come to know," said Mr. Hatch. "Especially that part about getting so gay you jus' go ahead and drink up all the likker you got on hand before noon. It seems like up in them Swede countries a man carries a bottle of wine around with him as a matter of course, at least that's the way I understood it. Those fellers will tell you anything, though—" He broke off and spat.

The idea of drinking any kind of liquor in this heat made Mr. Thompson dizzy. The idea of anybody feeling good on a day like this, for instance, made him tired. He felt he was really suffering from the heat. The fat man looked as if he had grown to the stump; he slumped there in his damp, dark clothes too big for him, his belly slack in his pants, his wide black felt hat pushed off his narrow forehead red with prickly heat. A bottle of good cold beer, now, would be a help, thought Mr. Thompson, remembering the four bottles sitting deep in the pool at the springhouse, and his dry tongue squirmed in his mouth. He wasn't going to offer this man anything, though, not even a drop of water. He wasn't even going to chew any more tobacco with him. He shot out his quid suddenly, and wiped his mouth on the back of his hand, and studied the head near him attentively. The man was no good, and he was there for no good, but what was he up to? Mr. Thompson made up his mind he'd give him a little more time to get his business, whatever it was, with Mr. Helton over, and then if he didn't get off the place he'd kick him off.

Mr. Hatch, as if he suspected Mr. Thompson's thoughts, turned his eyes, wicked and pig-like, on Mr. Thompson. "Fact is," he said, as if he had made up his mind about something, "I might need your help in the little matter I've got on hand, but it won't cost you any trouble. Now, this Mr. Helton here, like I tell you, he's a dangerous escaped loonatic, you might say. Now fact is, in the last twelve years or so I musta rounded up twenty-odd escaped loonatics, besides a couple of escaped convicts that I just run into by accident, like. I don't make a business of it, but if there's a reward, and there usually is a reward, of course, I get it. It amounts to a tidy little sum in the long run, but that ain't the main question. Fact is, I'm for law and order, I don't like to see lawbreakers and loonatics at large. It ain't the place for them. Now I reckon you're bound to agree with me on that, aren't you?"

205   Mr. Thompson said, "Well, circumstances alters cases, as the feller says. Now, what I know of Mr. Helton, he ain't dangerous, as I told you." Something serious was going to happen, Mr. Thompson could see that. He stopped thinking about it. He'd just let this fellow shoot off his head and then see what could be done about it. Without thinking he got out his knife and plug and started to cut a chew, then remembered himself and put them back in his pocket.

"The law," said Mr. Hatch, "is solidly behind me. Now this Mr. Helton, he's been one of my toughest cases. He's kept my record from being practically one hundred per cent. I knew him before he went loony, and I know the fam'ly, so I undertook to help out rounding him up. Well, sir, he was gone slick as a whistle, for all we knew the man was as good as dead long while ago. Now we never might have caught up with him, but do you know what he did? Well, sir, about two weeks ago his old mother gets a letter from him, and in that letter, what do you reckon she found? Well, it was a check on that little bank in town for eight hundred and fifty dollars, just like that; the letter wasn't nothing much, just said he was sending her a few little savings, she might need something, but there it was, name, postmark, date, everything. The old woman practically lost her mind with joy. She's gettin' childish, and it looked like she kinda forgot that her only living son killed his brother and went loony. Mr. Helton said he was getting along all right, and for her not to tell nobody. Well, natchally, she couldn't keep it to herself, with that check to cash and everything. So that's how I come to know." His feelings got the better of him. "You coulda knocked me down with a feather." He shook hands with himself and rocked, wagging his head, going "Heh, heh," in his throat. Mr. Thompson felt the corners of his mouth turning down. Why, the dirty low-down hound, sneaking around spying into other people's business like that. Collecting blood money, that's what it was! Let him talk!

"Yea, well, that musta been a surprise all right," he said, trying to hold his voice even. "I'd say a surprise."

"Well, siree," said Mr. Hatch, "the more I got to thinking about it, the more I just come to the conclusion that I'd better look into the matter a little, and so I talked to the old woman. She's pretty decrepid, now, half blind and all, but she was all for taking the first train out and going to see her son. I put it up to her square—how she was too feeble for the trip, and all. So, just as a favor to her, I told her for my expenses I'd come down and see Mr. Helton and bring her back all the news about him. She gave me a new shirt she made herself by hand, and a big Swedish kind of cake to bring to him, but I musta mislaid them along the road somewhere. It don't reely matter, though, he prob'ly ain't in any state of mind to appreciate 'em."

Mr. Thompson sat up and turning round on the log looked at Mr. Hatch and asked as quietly as he could, "And now what are you aiming to do? That's the question."

Mr. Hatch slouched up to his feet and shook himself. "Well, I come all prepared for a little scuffle," he said. "I got the handcuffs," he said, "but I don't want no violence if I can help it. I didn't want to say nothing around the countryside, making an uproar. I figured the two of us could overpower him." He reached into his big inside pocket and pulled them out. Handcuffs, for God's sake, thought Mr. Thompson. Coming round on a peaceable afternoon worrying a man, and making trouble, and fishing handcuffs out of his pocket on a decent family homestead, as if it was all in the day's work.

Mr. Thompson, his head buzzing, got up too. "Well," he said, roundly, "I want to tell you I think you've got a mighty sorry job on hand, you sure

210

must be hard up for something to do, and now I want to give you a good piece of advice. You just drop the idea that you're going to come here and make trouble for Mr. Helton, and the quicker you drive that hired rig away from my front gate the better I'll be satisfied."

Mr. Hatch put one handcuff in his outside pocket, the other dangling down. He pulled his hat down over his eyes, and reminded Mr. Thompson of a sheriff, somehow. He didn't seem in the least nervous, and didn't take up Mr. Thompson's words. He said, "Now listen just a minute, it ain't reasonable to suppose that a man like yourself is going to stand in the way of getting an escaped loonatic back to the asylum where he belongs. Now I know it's enough to throw you off, coming sudden like this, but fact is I counted on your being a respectable man and helping me out to see that justice is done. Now a course, if you won't help, I'll have to look around for help somewheres else. It won't look very good to your neighbors that you was harbring an escaped loonatic who killed his own brother, and then you refused to give him up. It will look mighty funny."

Mr. Thompson knew almost before he heard the words that it would look funny. It would put him in a mighty awkward position. He said, "But I've been trying to tell you all along that the man ain't loony now. He's been perfectly harmless for nine years. He's—he's—"

Mr. Thompson couldn't think how to describe how it was with Mr. Helton. "Why, he's been like one of the family," he said, "the best standby a man ever had." Mr. Thompson tried to see his way out. It was a fact Mr. Helton might go loony again any minute, and now this fellow talking around the country would put Mr. Thompson in a fix. It was a terrible position. He couldn't think of any way out. "You're crazy," Mr. Thompson roared suddenly, "you're the crazy one around here, you're crazier than he ever was! You get off this place or I'll handcuff you and turn you over to the law. You're trespassing," shouted Mr. Thompson. "Get out of here before I knock you down!"

215   He took a step towards the fat man, who backed off, shrinking, "Try it, try it, go ahead!" and then something happened that Mr. Thompson tried hard afterwards to piece together in his mind, and in fact it never did come straight. He saw the fat man with his long bowie knife in his hand, he saw Mr. Helton come round the corner on the run, his long jaw dropped, his arms swinging, his eyes wild. Mr. Helton came in between them, fists doubled up, then stopped short, glaring at the fat man, his big frame seemed to collapse, he trembled like a shied horse; and then the fat man drove at him, knife in one hand, handcuffs in the other. Mr. Thompson saw it coming, he saw the blade going into Mr. Helton's stomach, he knew he had the ax out of the log in his own hands, felt his arms go up over his head and bring the ax down on Mr. Hatch's head as if he were stunning a beef.

Mrs. Thompson had been listening uneasily for some time to the voices going on, one of them strange to her, but she was too tired at first to get up and come out to see what was going on. The confused shouting that rose so suddenly brought her up to her feet and out across the front porch without her slippers, hair half-braided. Shading her eyes, she saw first Mr. Helton, running all stooped over through the orchard, running like a man with dogs after him; and Mr. Thompson supporting himself on the ax handle was leaning over shaking by the shoulder a man Mrs. Thompson had never seen, who lay doubled up with the top of his head smashed and the blood running away in a greasy-looking puddle. Mr. Thompson without taking his hand from the man's shoulder, said in a thick voice, "He killed Mr. Helton, he killed him, I saw him do it. I had to knock him out," he called loudly, "but he won't come to."

Mrs. Thompson said in a faint scream, "Why, yonder goes Mr. Helton," and she pointed. Mr. Thompson pulled himself up and looked where she pointed. Mrs. Thompson sat down slowly against the side of the house and began to slide forward on her face; she felt as if she were drowning, she couldn't rise to the top somehow, and her only thought was she was glad the boys were not there, they were out, fishing at Halifax, oh, God, she was glad the boys were not there.

Mr. and Mrs. Thompson drove up to their barn about sunset. Mr. Thompson handed the reins to his wife, got out to open the big door, and Mrs. Thompson guided old Jim in under the roof. The buggy was gray with dust and age, Mrs. Thompson's face was gray with dust and weariness, and Mr. Thompson's face, as he stood at the horse's head and began unhitching, was gray except for the dark blue of his freshly shaven jaws and chin, gray and blue and caved in, but patient, like a dead man's face.

Mrs. Thompson stepped down to the hard packed manure of the barn floor, and shook out her light flower-sprigged dress. She wore her smoked glasses, and her wide shady leghorn hat with the wreath of exhausted pink and blue forget-me-nots hid her forehead, fixed in a knot of distress.

The horse hung his head, raised a huge sigh and flexed his stiffened legs.   220
Mr. Thompson's words came up muffled and hollow. "Poor ole Jim," he said, clearing his throat, "he looks pretty sunk in the ribs. I guess he's had a hard week." He lifted the harness up in one piece, slid it off and Jim walked out of the shafts halting a little. "Well, this is the last time," Mr. Thompson said, still talking to Jim. "Now you can get a good rest."

Mrs. Thompson closed her eyes behind her smoked glasses. The last time, and high time, and they should never have gone at all. She did not need her glasses any more, now the good darkness was coming down again, but her eyes ran full of tears steadily, though she was not crying, and she felt better with the glasses, safer, hidden away behind them. She took out her handkerchief with her hands shaking as they had been shaking ever since *that day,* and blew her nose. She said, "I see the boys have lighted the lamps. I hope they've started the stove going."

She stepped along the rough path holding her thin dress and starched petticoats around her, feeling her way between the sharp small stones, leaving the barn because she could hardly bear to be near Mr. Thompson, advancing slowly towards the house because she dreaded going there. Life was all one dread, the faces of her neighbors, of her boys, of her husband, the face of the whole world, the shape of her own house in the darkness, the very smell of the grass and the trees were horrible to her. There was no place to go, only one thing to do, bear it somehow—but how? She asked herself that question often. How was she going to keep on living now? Why had she lived at all? She wished now she had died one of those times when she had been so sick, instead of living on for this.

The boys were in the kitchen; Herbert was looking at the funny pictures from last Sunday's newspapers, the Katzenjammer Kids and Happy Hooligan. His chin was in his hands and his elbows on the table, and he was really reading and looking at the pictures, but his face was unhappy. Arthur was building the fire, adding kindling a stick at a time, watching it catch and blaze. His face was heavier and darker than Herbert's, he was a little sullen by nature; Mrs. Thompson thought, he takes things harder, too. Arthur said, "Hello, Momma," and went on with his work. Herbert swept the papers together and moved over on the bench. They were big boys—fifteen and seventeen, and Arthur as tall as his father. Mrs. Thompson sat down beside Herbert, taking off her hat. She said, "I guess you're hungry. We were late today. We went the Log Hollow road, it's rougher than ever." Her pale mouth drooped with a sad fold on either side.

"I guess you saw the Mannings, then," said Herbert.

225   "Yes, and the Fergusons, and the Allbrights, and that new family McClellan."

"Anybody say anything?" asked Herbert.

"Nothing much, you know how it's been all along, some of them keeps saying, yes, they know it was a clear case and a fair trial and they say how glad they are your papa came out so well, and all that, some of 'em do, anyhow, but it looks like they don't really take sides with him. I'm about wore out," she said, the tears rolling again from under her dark glasses. "I don't know what good it does, but your papa can't seem to rest unless he's telling how it happened. I don't know."

"I don't think it does any good, not a speck," said Arthur, moving away from the stove. "It just keeps the whole question stirred up in people's minds. Everybody will go round telling what he heard, and the whole thing is going to get worse mixed up than ever. It just makes matters worse. I wish you could get Papa to stop driving round the country talking like that."

"Your papa knows best," said Mrs. Thompson. "You oughtn't to criticize him. He's got enough to put up with without that."

230   Arthur said nothing, his jaw stubborn. Mr. Thompson came in, his eyes hollowed out and dead-looking, his thick hands gray white and seamed from washing them clean every day before he started out to see the neighbors to tell them his side of the story. He was wearing his Sunday clothes, a thick pepper-and-salt-colored suit with a black string tie.

Mrs. Thompson stood up, her head swimming. "Now you-all get out of the kitchen, it's too hot in here and I need room. I'll get us a little bite of supper, if you'll just get out and give me some room."

They went as if they were glad to go, the boys outside, Mr. Thompson into his bedroom. She heard him groaning to himself as he took off his shoes, and heard the bed creak as he lay down. Mrs. Thompson opened the icebox and felt the sweet coldness flow out of it; she had never expected to have an icebox, much less did she hope to afford to keep it filled with ice. It still seemed like a miracle, after two or three years. There was the food, cold and clean, all ready to be warmed over. She would never have had that icebox if Mr. Helton hadn't happened along one day, just by the strangest luck; so saving, and so managing, so good, thought Mrs. Thompson, her heart swelling until she feared she would faint again, standing there with the door open and leaning her head upon it. She simply could not bear to remember Mr. Helton, with his long sad face and silent ways, who had always been so quiet and harmless, who had worked so hard and helped Mr. Thompson so much, running through the hot fields and woods, being hunted like a mad dog, everybody turning out with ropes and guns and sticks to catch and tie him. Oh, God, said Mrs. Thompson in a long dry moan, kneeling before the icebox and fumbling inside for the dishes, even if they did pile mattresses all over the jail floor and against the walls, and five men there to hold him to keep him from hurting himself any more, he was already hurt too badly, he couldn't have lived anyway. Mr. Barbee, the sheriff, told her about it. He said, well, they didn't aim to harm him but they had to catch him, he was crazy as a loon; he picked up rocks and tried to brain every man that got near him. He had two harmonicas in his jumper pocket, said the sheriff, but they fell out in the scuffle, and Mr. Helton tried to pick 'em up again, and that's when they finally got him. "They *had* to be rough, Miz Thompson, he fought like a wildcat." Yes, thought Mrs. Thompson again with the same bitterness, of course, they had to be rough. They always have to be rough. Mr. Thompson can't argue with a man and get him off the place peaceably; no, she thought, standing up and shutting the ice box, he has to kill somebody, he has to be a murderer and ruin his boys' lives and cause Mr. Helton to be killed like a mad dog.

Her thoughts stopped with a little soundless explosion, cleared and began again. The rest of Mr. Helton's harmonicas were still in the shack, his tune ran in Mrs. Thompson's head at certain times of the day. She missed it in the evenings. It seemed so strange she had never known the name of that song, nor what it meant, until after Mr. Helton was gone. Mrs. Thompson, trembling in the knees, took a drink of water at the sink and poured the red beans into the baking dish, and began to roll the pieces of chicken in flour to fry them. There was a time, she said to herself, when I thought I had neighbors and friends, there was a time when we could hold up our heads, there was a time when my husband hadn't killed a man and I could tell the truth to anybody about anything.

Mr. Thompson, turning on his bed, figured that he had done all he could, he'd just try to let the matter rest from now on. His lawyer, Mr. Burleigh, had told him right at the beginning, "Now you keep calm and collected. You've got a fine case, even if you haven't got witnesses. Your wife must sit in court, she'll be a powerful argument with the jury. You just plead not guilty and I'll do the rest. The trial is going to be a mere formality, you haven't got a thing to worry about. You'll be clean out of this before you know it." And to make talk Mr. Burleigh had got to telling about all the men he knew around the country who for one reason or another had been forced to kill somebody, always in self-defense, and there just wasn't anything to it at all. He even told about how his own father in the old days had shot and killed a man just for setting foot inside his gate when he told him not to. "Sure, I shot the scoundrel," said Mr. Burleigh's father, "in self-defense; I *told* him I'd shoot him if he set his foot in my yard, and he did, and I did." There had been bad blood between them for years, Mr. Burleigh said, and his father had waited a long time to catch the other fellow in the wrong, and when he did he certainly made the most of his opportunity.

235   "But Mr. Hatch, as I told you," Mr. Thompson had said, "made a pass at Mr. Helton with his bowie knife. That's why I took a hand."

"All the better," said Mr. Burleigh. "That stranger hadn't any right coming to your house on such an errand. Why, hell," said Mr. Burleigh, "that wasn't even manslaughter you committed. So now you just hold your horses and keep your shirt on. And don't say one word without I tell you."

Wasn't even manslaughter. Mr. Thompson had to cover Mr. Hatch with a piece of wagon canvas and ride to town to tell the sheriff. It had been hard on Ellie. When they got back, the sheriff and the coroner and two deputies, they found her sitting beside the road, on a low bridge over a gulley, about half a mile from the place. He had taken her up behind his saddle and got her back to the house. He had already told the sheriff that his wife had witnessed the whole business, and now he had time, getting her to her room and in bed, to tell her what to say if they asked anything. He had left out the part about Mr. Helton being crazy all along, but it came out at the trial. By Mr. Burleigh's advice Mr. Thompson had pretended to be perfectly ignorant; Mr. Hatch hadn't said a word about that. Mr. Thompson pretended to believe that Mr. Hatch had just come looking for Mr. Helton to settle old scores, and the two members of Mr. Hatch's family who had come down to try to get Mr. Thompson convicted didn't get anywhere at all. It hadn't been much of a trial, Mr. Burleigh saw to that. He had charged a reasonable fee, and Mr. Thompson had paid him and felt grateful, but after it was over Mr. Burleigh didn't seem pleased to see him when he got to dropping into the office to talk it over, telling him things that had slipped his mind at first: trying to explain what an ornery low hound Mr. Hatch had been, anyhow. Mr. Burleigh seemed to have lost his interest; he looked sour and upset when he saw Mr. Thompson at the door. Mr. Thompson kept saying to himself that he'd got off, all right, just as Mr. Burleigh had predicted, but, but—and it was right there that Mr. Thompson's mind stuck, squirming like an angleworm on a fishhook: he had killed Mr. Hatch, and he was a murderer. That was the truth about himself that Mr. Thompson couldn't grasp, even when he said the word to himself. Why, he had not even once *thought* of killing anybody, much less Mr. Hatch, and if Mr. Helton hadn't come out so unexpectedly, hearing the row, why, then—but then, Mr. Helton had come on the run that way to help him. What he couldn't understand was what happened next. He had seen Mr. Hatch go after Mr. Helton with the knife, he had seen the point, blade up, go into Mr. Helton's stomach and slice up like you slice a hog, but when they finally caught Mr. Helton there wasn't a knife scratch on him. Mr. Thompson knew he had the ax in his own hands and felt himself lifting it, but he couldn't remember hitting Mr. Hatch. He couldn't remember it. He couldn't. He remembered only that he had been determined to stop Mr. Hatch from cutting Mr. Helton. If he was given a chance he could explain the whole matter. At the trial they hadn't let him talk. They just asked questions and he answered yes or no, and they never did get to the core of the matter. Since the trial, now, every day for a week he had washed and shaved and put on his best clothes and had taken Ellie with him to tell every neighbor he had that he never killed Mr. Hatch on purpose, and what good did it do? Nobody believed him. Even when he turned to Ellie and said, "You was there, you saw it, didn't you?" and Ellie spoke up, saying, "Yes, that's the truth. Mr. Thompson was trying to save Mr. Helton's life," and he added, "If you don't believe me, you can believe my wife. She won't lie," Mr. Thompson saw something in all their faces that disheartened him, made him feel empty and tired out. They didn't believe he was not a murderer.

Even Ellie never said anything to comfort him. He hoped she would say finally, "I remember now, Mr. Thompson, I really did come round the corner in time to see everything. It's not a lie, Mr. Thompson. Don't you worry." But as they drove together in silence, with the days still hot and dry, shortening for fall, day after day, the buggy jolting in the ruts, she said nothing; they grew to dread the sight of another house, and the people in it: all houses looked alike now, and the people—old neighbors or new—had the same expression when Mr. Thompson told them why he had come and began his story. Their eyes looked as if someone had pinched the eyeball at the back; they shriveled and the light went out of them. Some of them sat with fixed tight smiles trying to be friendly. "Yes, Mr. Thompson, we know how you must feel. It must be terrible for you, Mrs. Thompson. Yes, you know, I've about come to the point where I believe in such a thing as killing in self-defense. Why, certainly, we believe you, Mr. Thompson, why shouldn't we believe you? Didn't you have a perfectly fair and above-board trial? Well, now, natchally, Mr. Thompson, we think you done right."

Mr. Thompson was satisfied they didn't think so. Sometimes the air around him was so thick with their blame he fought and pushed with his fists, and the sweat broke out all over him, he shouted his story in a dust-choked voice, he would fairly bellow at last: "My wife, here, you know her, she was there, she saw and heard it all, if you don't believe me, ask her, she won't lie!" and Mrs. Thompson, with her hands knotted together, aching, her chin trembling, would never fail to say: "Yes, that's right, that's the truth—"

240   The last straw had been laid on today, Mr. Thompson decided. Tom Allbright, an old beau of Ellie's, why, he had squired Ellie around a whole summer, had come out to meet them when they drove up, and standing there bareheaded had stopped them from getting out. He had looked past them with an embarrassed frown on his face, telling them his wife's sister was there with a raft of young ones, and the house was pretty full and everything upset, or he'd ask them to come in. "We've been thinking of trying to get up to your place one of these days," said Mr. Allbright, moving away trying to look busy, "we've been mighty occupied up here of late." So they had to say, "Well, we just happened to be driving this way," and go on. "The Allbrights," said Mrs. Thompson, "always was fair-weather friends." "They look out for number one, that's a fact," said Mr. Thompson. But it was cold comfort to them both.

Finally Mrs. Thompson had given up. "Let's go home," she said. "Old Jim's tired and thirsty, and we've gone far enough."

Mr. Thompson said, "Well, while we're out this way, we might as well stop at the McClellans'." They drove in, and asked a little cotton-haired boy if his mamma and papa were at home. Mr. Thompson wanted to see them. The little boy stood gazing with his mouth open, then galloped into the house shouting, "Mommer, Popper, come out hyah. That man that kilt Mr. Hatch has come ter see yer!"

The man came out in his sock feet, with one gallus up, the other broken and dangling, and said, "Light down, Mr. Thompson, and come in. The ole woman's washing, but she'll git here." Mrs. Thompson, feeling her way, stepped down and sat in a broken rocking-chair on the porch that sagged under her feet. The woman of the house, barefooted, in a calico wrapper, sat on the edge of the porch, her fat sallow face full of curiosity. Mr. Thompson began, "Well, as I reckon you happen to know, I've had some strange troubles lately, and, as the feller says, it's not the kind of trouble that happens to a man every day in the year, and there's some things I don't want no misunderstanding about in the neighbors' minds, so—" He halted and stumbled forward, and the two listening faces took on a mean look, a greedy, despising look, a look that said plain as day, "My, you must be a purty sorry feller to come round worrying about what *we* think, *we* know you wouldn't be here if you had anybody else to turn to—my, I wouldn't lower myself that much, myself." Mr. Thompson was ashamed of himself, he was suddenly in a rage, he'd like to knock their dirty skunk heads together, the low-down white trash—but he held himself down and went on to the end. "My wife will tell you," he said, and this was the hardest place, because Ellie always without moving a muscle seemed to stiffen as if somebody had threatened to hit her; "ask my wife, she won't lie."

"It's true, I saw it—"

"Well, now," said the man, drily, scratching his ribs inside his shirt,   245
"that sholy is too bad. Well, now, I kaint see what we've got to do with all
this here, however. I kaint see no good reason for us to git mixed up in these
murder matters, I shore kaint. Whichever way you look at it, it ain't none of
my business. However, it's mighty nice of you-all to come around and give
us the straight of it, fur we've heerd some mighty queer yarns about it,
mighty queer, I golly you couldn't hardly make head ner tail of it."

"Evvybody goin' round shootin' they heads off," said the woman.
"Now we don't hold with killin'; the Bible says—"

"Shet yer trap," said the man, "and keep it shet 'r I'll shet it fer yer. Now
it shore looks like to me—"

"We mustn't linger," said Mrs. Thompson, unclasping her hands.
"We've lingered too long now. It's getting late, and we've far to go." Mr.
Thompson took the hint and followed her. The man and the woman lolled
against their rickety porch poles and watched them go.

Now lying on his bed, Mr. Thompson knew the end had come. Now,
this minute, lying in the bed where he had slept with Ellie for eighteen
years; under this roof where he had laid the shingles when he was waiting to
get married; there as he was with his whiskers already sprouting since his
shave that morning; with his fingers feeling his bony chin, Mr. Thompson
felt he was a dead man. He was dead to his other life, he had got to the end
of something without knowing why, and he had to make a fresh start, he
did not know how. Something different was going to begin, he didn't know
what. It was in some way not his business. He didn't feel he was going to
have much to do with it. He got up, aching, hollow, and went out to the
kitchen where Mrs. Thompson was just taking up the supper.

"Call the boys," said Mrs. Thompson. They had been down to the barn,   250
and Arthur put out the lantern before hanging it on a nail near the door.
Mr. Thompson didn't like their silence. They had hardly said a word about
anything to him since that day. They seemed to avoid him, they ran the
place together as if he wasn't there, and attended to everything without asking him for any advice. "What you boys been up to?" he asked, trying to be
hearty. "Finishing your chores?"

"No, sir," said Arthur, "there ain't much to do. Just greasing some
axles." Herbert said nothing. Mrs. Thompson bowed her head: "For these
and all Thy blessings. . . . Amen," she whispered weakly, and the Thompsons sat there with their eyes down and their faces sorrowful, as if they were
at a funeral.

Every time he shut his eyes, trying to sleep, Mr. Thompson's mind
started up and began to run like a rabbit. It jumped from one thing to another, trying to pick up a trail here or there that would straighten out
what had happened that day he killed Mr. Hatch. Try as he might, Mr.
Thompson's mind would not go anywhere that it had not already been,
he could not see anything but what he had seen once, and he knew that

was not right. If he had not seen straight that first time, then everything about his killing Mr. Hatch was wrong from start to finish, and there was nothing more to be done about it, he might just as well give up. It still seemed to him that he had done, maybe not the right thing, but the only thing he could do, that day, but had he? *Did he have to kill Mr. Hatch?* He had never seen a man he hated more, the minute he laid eyes on him. He knew in his bones the fellow was there for trouble. What seemed so funny now was this: Why hadn't he just told Mr. Hatch to get out before he ever even got in?

Mrs. Thompson, her arms crossed on her breast, was lying beside him, perfectly still, but she seemed awake, somehow. "Asleep, Ellie?"

After all, he might have got rid of him peaceably, or maybe he might have had to overpower him and put those handcuffs on him and turn him over to the sheriff for disturbing the peace. The most they could have done was to lock Mr. Hatch up while he cooled off for a few days, or fine him a little something. He would try to think of things he might have said to Mr. Hatch. Why, let's see, I could just have said, Now look here, Mr. Hatch, I want to talk to you as man to man. But his brain would go empty. What could he have said or done? But if he *could* have done anything else almost except kill Mr. Hatch, then nothing would have happened to Mr. Helton. Mr. Thompson hardly ever thought of Mr. Helton. His mind just skipped over him and went on. If he stopped to think about Mr. Helton he'd never in God's world get anywhere. He tried to imagine how it might all have been, this very night even, if Mr. Helton were still safe and sound out in his shack playing his tune about feeling so good in the morning, drinking up all the wine so you'd feel even better; and Mr. Hatch safe in jail somewhere, mad as hops, maybe, but out of harm's way and ready to listen to reason and to repent of his meanness, the dirty, yellow-livered hound coming around persecuting an innocent man and ruining a whole family that never harmed him! Mr. Thompson felt the veins of his forehead start up, his fists clutched as if they seized an ax handle, the sweat broke out on him, he bounded up from the bed with a yell smothered in his throat, and Ellie started up after him, crying out, "Oh, oh, don't! Don't! Don't!" as if she were having a nightmare. He stood shaking until his bones rattled in him, crying hoarsely, "Light the lamp, light the lamp, Ellie."

255   Instead, Mrs. Thompson gave a shrill weak scream, almost the same scream he had heard on that day she came around the house when he was standing there with the ax in his hand. He could not see her in the dark, but she was on the bed, rolling violently. He felt for her in horror, and his groping hands found her arms, up, and her own hands pulling her hair straight out from her head, her neck strained back, and the tight screams strangling her. He shouted out for Arthur, for Herbert. "Your mother!" he bawled, his voice cracking. As he held Mrs. Thompson's arms, the boys came tumbling in, Arthur with the lamp above his head. By this light Mr. Thompson

saw Mrs. Thompson's eyes, wide open, staring dreadfully at him, the tears pouring. She sat up at sight of the boys, and held out one arm towards them, the hand wagging in a crazy circle, then dropped on her back again, and suddenly went limp. Arthur set the lamp on the table and turned on Mr. Thompson. "She's scared," he said, "she's scared to death." His face was in a knot of rage, his fists were doubled up, he faced his father as if he meant to strike him. Mr. Thompson's jaw fell, he was so surprised he stepped back from the bed. Herbert went to the other side. They stood on each side of Mrs. Thompson and watched Mr. Thompson as if he were a dangerous wild beast. "What did you do to her?" shouted Arthur, in a grown man's voice. "You touch her again and I'll blow your heart out!" Herbert was pale and his cheek twitched, but he was on Arthur's side; he would do what he could to help Arthur.

Mr. Thompson had no fight left in him. His knees bent as he stood, his chest collapsed. "Why, Arthur," he said, his words crumbling and his breath coming short. "She's fainted again. Get the ammonia." Arthur did not move. Herbert brought the bottle, and handed it, shrinking, to his father.

Mr. Thompson held it under Mrs. Thompson's nose. He poured a little in the palm of his hand and rubbed it on her forehead. She gasped and opened her eyes and turned her head away from him. Herbert began a doleful hopeless sniffling. "Mamma," he kept saying, "Mamma, don't die."

"I'm all right," Mrs. Thompson said. "Now don't you worry around. Now Herbert, you mustn't do that. I'm all right." She closed her eyes. Mr. Thompson began pulling on his best pants; he put on his socks and shoes. The boys sat on each side of the bed, watching Mrs. Thompson's face. Mr. Thompson put on his shirt and coat. He said, "I reckon I'll ride over and get the doctor. Don't look like all this fainting is a good sign. Now you just keep watch until I get back." They listened, but said nothing. He said, "Don't you get any notions in your head. I never did your mother any harm in my life, on purpose." He went out, and, looking back, saw Herbert staring at him from under his brows, like a stranger. "You'll know how to look after her," said Mr. Thompson.

Mr. Thompson went through the kitchen. There he lighted the lantern, took a thin pad of scratch paper and a stub pencil from the shelf where the boys kept their schoolbooks. He swung the lantern on his arm and reached into the cupboard where he kept the guns. The shotgun was there to his hand, primed and ready, a man never knows when he may need a shotgun. He went out of the house without looking around, or looking back when he had left it, passed his barn without seeing it, and struck out to the farthest end of his fields, which ran for half a mile to the east. So many blows had been struck at Mr. Thompson and from so many directions he couldn't stop any more to find out where he was hit. He walked on, over plowed ground and over meadow, going through barbed wire fences cautiously, putting his gun through first; he could almost see in the dark, now his eyes were used to it. Finally he came to the last fence; here he sat down, back against a post, lantern at his side, and, with the pad on his knee, moistened the stub pencil and began to write:

260   "Before Almighty God, the great judge of all before who I am about to appear, I do hereby solemnly swear that I did not take the life of Mr. Homer T. Hatch on purpose. It was done in defense of Mr. Helton. I did not aim to hit him with the ax but only to keep him off Mr. Helton. He aimed a blow at Mr. Helton who was not looking for it. It was my belief at the time that Mr. Hatch would of taken the life of Mr. Helton if I did not interfere. I have told all this to the judge and the jury and they let me off but nobody believes it. This is the only way I can prove I am not a cold blooded murderer like everybody seems to think. If I had been in Mr. Helton's place he would of done the same for me. I still think I done the only thing there was to do. My wife—"

Mr. Thompson stopped here to think a while. He wet the pencil point with the tip of his tongue and marked out the last two words. He sat a while blacking out the words until he had made a neat oblong patch where they had been, and started again:

"It was Mr. Homer T. Hatch who came to do wrong to a harmless man. He caused all this trouble and he deserved to die but I am sorry it was me who had to kill him."

He licked the point of his pencil again, and signed his full name carefully, folded the paper and put it in his outside pocket. Taking off his right shoe and sock, he set the butt of the shotgun along the ground with the twin barrels pointed towards his head. It was very awkward. He thought about this a little, leaning his head against the gun mouth. He was trembling and his head was drumming until he was deaf and blind, but he lay down flat on the earth on his side, drew the barrel under his chin and fumbled for the trigger with his great toe. That way he could work it.

Leo Tolstoy

The Death of Ivan Ilych

1

During an interval in the Melvinski trial in the large building of the Law Courts, the members and public prosecutor met in Ivan Egorovich Shebek's private room, where the conversation turned on the celebrated Krasovski case. Fëdor Vasilievich warmly maintained that it was not subject to their jurisdiction, Ivan Egorovich maintained the contrary, while Peter Ivanovich, not having entered into the discussion at the start, took no part in it but looked through the *Gazette* which had just been handed in.

"Gentlemen," he said, "Ivan Ilych has died!"

"You don't say so!"

"Here, read it yourself," replied Peter Ivanovich, handing Fëdor Vasilievich the paper still damp from the press. Surrounded by a black border were the words: "Praskovya Fëdorovna Golovina, with profound sorrow, informs relatives and friends of the demise of her beloved husband Ivan Ilych Golovin, Member of the Court of Justice, which occurred on February the 4th of this year 1882. The funeral will take place on Friday at one o'clock in the afternoon."

THE DEATH OF IVAN ILYCH   First published in 1886. Translated from the Russian by Louise and Aylmer Maude. Leo Tolstoy (1828–1910), a Russian nobleman, after writing his two great novels *War and Peace* (1869) and *Anna Karenina* (1877), went through a period of spiritual turmoil in which he was obsessed with answering the question, What is the meaning of life? The crisis, which reached a head in 1879, resulted in a radical acceptance and interpretation of the teaching of Christ: one must do good for others and not live for oneself. In 1890, no longer willing to own property, he divided his large estate among his wife and nine children, gave up his royalties, and tried to live like a peasant. His new principles brought him into conflict with his family, the government, and the Church, which in 1901 excommunicated him.

A note on Russian names: In Russia, a person was identified by three names—a given name (such as Ivan), a patronymic middle name (Ilych), and a family or surname (Golovin). The patronymic indicated one's father's given name, and for men was formed by adding the suffix -ch, or -ich, or -ovich; for women, the suffixes were -evna or -ovna. "Ivan Ilych" is thus Ivan, son of Ilya Golovin. Ivan Ilych's wife has the feminine surname Golovina, and is the daughter of a man named Fëdor. It was customary, even in informal address, to call a person by both the given name and the patronymic, as a sign of politeness. Children were usually called by nicknames derived from the given name, of which (as in English) there are many. Ivan Ilych as a child was called Vanya; and his schoolboy son, Vladimir Ivanich Golovin, is called Volodya by his mother and Vasya by his father. Among intimates, also, given names or nicknames are used. Thus Ivan Ilych is called Jean by his wife. (Jean is the French equivalent of Ivan—as John is the English—and the wife's use of the French form reflects the nineteenth-century Russian upper-class belief that to be civilized was to know French and French culture.) Peasants and lower servants were generally called by their given names—Peter, the footman; Gerasim, the butler's assistant.

5   Ivan Ilych had been a colleague of the gentlemen present and was liked by them all. He had been ill for some weeks with an illness said to be incurable. His post had been kept open for him, but there had been conjectures that in the case of his death Alexeev might receive his appointment, and that either Vinnikov or Shtabel would succeed Alexeev. So on receiving the news of Ivan Ilych's death the first thought of each of the gentlemen in that private room was of the changes and promotions it might occasion among themselves or their acquaintances.

"I shall be sure to get Shtabel's place or Vinnikov's," thought Fëdor Vasilievich. "I was promised that long ago, and the promotion means an extra eight hundred rubles a year for me beside the allowance."

"Now I must apply for my brother-in-law's transfer from Kaluga," thought Peter Ivanovich. "My wife will be very glad, and then she won't be able to say that I never do anything for her relations."

"I thought he would never leave his bed again," said Peter Ivanovich aloud. "It's very sad."

"But what really was the matter with him?"

10   "The doctors couldn't say—at least they could, but each of them said something different. When last I saw him I thought he was getting better."

"And I haven't been to see him since the holidays. I always meant to go."

"Had he any property?"

"I think his wife had a little—but something quite trifling."

"We shall have to go to see her, but they live so terribly far away."

15   "Far away from you, you mean. Everything's far away from your place."

"You see, he never can forgive my living on the other side of the river," said Peter Ivanovich, smiling at Shebek. Then, still talking of the distances between different parts of the city, they returned to the Court.

Besides considerations as to the possible transfers and promotions likely to result from Ivan Ilych's death, the mere fact of the death of a near acquaintance aroused, as usual, in all who heard of it the complacent feeling that, "it is he who is dead and not I."

Each one thought or felt, "Well, he's dead but I'm alive!" But the more intimate of Ivan Ilych's acquaintances, his so-called friends, could not help thinking also that they would now have to fulfill the very tiresome demands of propriety by attending the funeral service and paying a visit of condolence to the widow.

Fëdor Vasilievich and Peter Ivanovich had been his nearest acquaintances. Peter Ivanovich had studied law with Ivan Ilych and had considered himself to be under obligations to him.

20   Having told his wife at dinner-time of Ivan Ilych's death and of his conjecture that it might be possible to get her brother transferred to their circuit, Peter Ivanovich sacrificed his usual nap, put on his evening clothes, and drove to Ivan Ilych's house.

At the entrance stood a carriage and two cabs. Leaning against the wall in the hall downstairs near the cloak-stand was a coffin-lid covered with cloth of gold, ornamented with gold cord and tassels, that had been polished up with metal powder. Two ladies in black were taking off their fur cloaks. Peter Ivanovich recognized one of them as Ivan Ilych's sister, but the other was a stranger to him. His colleague Schwartz was just coming downstairs, but on seeing Peter Ivanovich enter he stopped and winked at him, as if to say: "Ivan Ilych has made a mess of things—not like you and me."

Schwartz's face, with his Piccadilly whiskers and his slim figure in evening dress, had as usual an air of elegant solemnity which contrasted with the playfulness of his character and had a special piquancy here, or so it seemed to Peter Ivanovich.

Peter Ivanovich allowed the ladies to precede him and slowly followed them upstairs. Schwartz did not come down but remained where he was, and Peter Ivanovich understood that he wanted to arrange where they should play bridge that evening. The ladies went upstairs to the widow's room, and Schwartz with seriously compressed lips but a playful look in his eyes, indicated by a twist of his eyebrows the room to the right where the body lay.

Peter Ivanovich, like everyone else on such occasions, entered feeling uncertain what he would have to do. All he knew was that at such times it is always safe to cross oneself. But he was not quite sure whether one should make obeisances while doing so. He therefore adopted a middle course. On entering the room he began crossing himself and made a slight movement resembling a bow. At the same time, as far as the motion of his head and arm allowed, he surveyed the room. Two young men— apparently nephews, one of whom was a high-school pupil—were leaving the room, crossing themselves as they did so. An old woman was standing motionless, and a lady with strangely arched eyebrows was saying something to her in a whisper. A vigorous, resolute Church Reader, in a frockcoat, was reading something in a loud voice with an expression that precluded any contradiction. The butler's assistant, Gerasim, stepping lightly in front of Peter Ivanovich, was strewing something on the floor. Noticing this, Peter Ivanovich was immediately aware of a faint odor of a decomposing body.

The last time he had called on Ivan Ilych, Peter Ivanovich had seen   25
Gerasim in the study. Ivan Ilych had been particularly fond of him and he was performing the duty of a sick nurse.

Peter Ivanovich continued to make the sign of the cross slightly inclining his head in an intermediate direction between the coffin, the Reader, and the icons on the table in a corner of the room. Afterwards, when it seemed to him that this movement of his arm in crossing himself had gone on too long, he stopped and began to look at the corpse.

The dead man lay, as dead men always lie, in a specially heavy way, his rigid limbs sunk in the soft cushions of the coffin, with the head forever bowed on the pillow. His yellow waxen brow with bald patches over his sunken temples was thrust up in the way peculiar to the dead, the protruding nose seeming to press on the upper lip. He was much changed and had grown even thinner since Peter Ivanovich had last seen him, but, as is always the case with the dead, his face was handsomer and above all more dignified than when he was alive. The expression on the face said that what was necessary had been accomplished, and accomplished rightly. Besides this there was in that expression a reproach and a warning to the living. This warning seemed to Peter Ivanovich out of place, or at least not applicable to him. He felt a certain discomfort and so he hurriedly crossed himself once more and turned and went out of the door—too hurriedly and too regardless of propriety, as he himself was aware.

Schwartz was waiting for him in the adjoining room with legs spread wide apart and both hands toying with his top-hat behind his back. The mere sight of that playful, well-groomed, and elegant figure refreshed Peter Ivanovich. He felt that Schwartz was above all these happenings and would not surrender to any depressing influences. His very look said that this incident of a church service for Ivan Ilych could not be sufficient reason for infringing the order of the session—in other words, that it would certainly not prevent his unwrapping a new pack of cards and shuffling them that evening while a footman placed four fresh candles on the table: in fact, that there was no reason for supposing that this incident would hinder their spending the evening agreeably. Indeed he said this in a whisper as Peter Ivanovich passed him, proposing that they should meet for a game at Fëdor Vasilievich's. But apparently Peter Ivanovich was not destined to play bridge that evening. Praskovya Fëdorovna (a short, fat woman who despite all efforts to the contrary had continued to broaden steadily from her shoulders downwards and who had the same extraordinary arched eyebrows as the lady who had been standing by the coffin), dressed all in black, her head covered with lace, came out of her own room with some other ladies, conducted them to the room where the dead body lay, and said: "The service will begin immediately. Please go in."

Schwartz, making an indefinite bow, stood still, evidently neither accepting nor declining this invitation. Praskovya Fëdorovna, recognizing Peter Ivanovich, sighed, went close to him, took his hand, and said: "I know you were a true friend to Ivan Ilych . . ." and looked at him awaiting some suitable response. And Peter Ivanovich knew that, just as it had been the right thing to cross himself in that room, so what he had to do here was to press her hand, sigh, and say, "Believe me. . . ." So he did all this and as he did it felt that the desired result had been achieved: that both he and she were touched.

30   "Come with me. I want to speak to you before it begins," said the widow. "Give me your arm."

Peter Ivanovich gave her his arm and they went to the inner rooms, passing Schwartz, who winked at Peter Ivanovich compassionately.

"That does for our bridge! Don't object if we find another player. Perhaps you can cut in when you do escape," said his playful look.

Peter Ivanovich sighed still more deeply and despondently, and Praskovya Fëdorovna pressed his arm gratefully. When they reached the drawing-room, upholstered in pink cretonne and lighted by a dim lamp, they sat down at the table—she on a sofa and Peter Ivanovich on a low pouffe, the springs of which yielded spasmodically under his weight. Praskovya Fëdorovna had been on the point of warning him to take another seat, but felt that such a warning was out of keeping with her present condition and so changed her mind. As he sat down on the pouffe Peter Ivanovich recalled how Ivan Ilych had arranged this room and had consulted him regarding this pink cretonne with green leaves. The whole room was full of furniture and knick-knacks, and on her way to the sofa the lace of the widow's black shawl caught on the carved edge of the table. Peter Ivanovich rose to detach it, and the springs of the pouffe, relieved of his weight, rose also and gave him a push. The widow began detaching her shawl herself, and Peter Ivanovich again sat down, suppressing the rebellious springs of the pouffe under him. But the widow had not quite freed herself and Peter Ivanovich got up again, and again the pouffe rebelled and even creaked. When this was all over she took out a clean cambric handkerchief and began to weep. The episode with the shawl and the struggle with the pouffe had cooled Peter Ivanovich's emotions and he sat there with a sullen look on his face. This awkward situation was interrupted by Sokolov, Ivan Ilych's butler, who came to report that the plot in the cemetery that Praskovya Fëdorovna had chosen would cost two hundred rubles. She stopped weeping and, looking at Peter Ivanovich with the air of a victim, remarked in French that it was very hard for her. Peter Ivanovich made a silent gesture signifying his full conviction that it must indeed be so.

"Please smoke," she said in a magnanimous yet crushed voice, and turned to discuss with Sokolov the price of the plot for the grave.

Peter Ivanovich while lighting his cigarette heard her inquiring very   35
circumstantially into the prices of different plots in the cemetery and finally decide which she would take. When that was done she gave instructions about engaging the choir. Sokolov then left the room.

"I look after everything myself," she told Peter Ivanovich, shifting the albums that lay on the table; and noticing that the table was endangered by his cigarette-ash, she immediately passed him an ash-tray, saying as she did so: "I consider it an affectation to say that my grief prevents my attending to practical affairs. On the contrary, if anything can—I won't say console me, but—distract me, it is seeing to everything concerning him." She again took out her handkerchief as if preparing to cry, but suddenly, as if mastering her feeling, she shook herself and began to speak calmly. "But there is something I want to talk to you about."

Peter Ivanovich bowed, keeping control of the springs of the pouffe, which immediately began quivering under him.

"He suffered terribly the last few days."

"Did he?" said Peter Ivanovich.

40   "Oh, terribly! He screamed unceasingly, not for minutes but for hours. For the last three days he screamed incessantly. It was unendurable. I cannot understand how I bore it; you could hear him three rooms off. Oh, what I have suffered!"

"Is it possible that he was conscious all that time?" asked Peter Ivanovich.

"Yes," she whispered. "To the last moment. He took leave of us a quarter of an hour before he died, and asked us to take Volodya away."

The thought of the sufferings of this man he had known so intimately, first as a merry little boy, then as a school-mate, and later as a grown-up colleague, suddenly struck Peter Ivanovich with horror, despite an unpleasant consciousness of his own and this woman's dissimulation. He again saw that brow, and that nose pressing down on the lip, and felt afraid for himself.

"Three days of frightful suffering and then death! Why, that might suddenly, at any time, happen to me," he thought, and for a moment felt terrified. But—he did not himself know how—the customary reflection at once occurred to him that this had happened to Ivan Ilych and not to him, and that it should not and could not happen to him, and to think that it could would be yielding to depression which he ought not to do, as Schwartz's expression plainly showed. After which reflection Peter Ivanovich felt reassured, and began to ask with interest about the details of Ivan Ilych's death, as though death was an accident natural to Ivan Ilych but certainly not to himself.

45   After many details of the really dreadful physical suffering Ivan Ilych had endured (which details he learnt only from the effect those sufferings had produced on Praskovya Fëdorovna's nerves) the widow apparently found it necessary to get to business.

"Oh, Peter Ivanovich, how hard it is! How terribly, terribly hard!" and she again began to weep.

Peter Ivanovich sighed and waited for her to finish blowing her nose. When she had done so he said, "Believe me . . ." and she again began talking and brought out what was evidently her chief concern with him— namely, to question him as to how she could obtain a grant of money from the government on the occasion of her husband's death. She made it appear that she was asking Peter Ivanovich's advice about her pension, but he soon saw that she already knew about that to the minutest detail, more even than he did himself. She knew how much could be got out of the government in consequence of her husband's death, but wanted to find out whether she could not possibly extract something more. Peter Ivanovich tried to think of some means of doing so, but after reflecting for a while and, out of propriety, condemning the government for its niggardliness, he said he thought that nothing more could be got. Then she sighed and evidently began to devise means of getting rid of her visitor. Noticing this, he put out his cigarette, rose, pressed her hand, and went out into the anteroom.

In the dining-room where the clock stood that Ivan Ilych had liked so much and had bought at an antique shop, Peter Ivanovich met a priest and a few acquaintances who had come to attend the service, and he recognized Ivan Ilych's daughter, a handsome young woman. She was in black and her slim figure appeared slimmer than ever. She had a gloomy, determined, almost angry expression, and bowed to Peter Ivanovich as though he were in some way to blame. Behind her, with the same offended look, stood a wealthy young man, an examining magistrate, whom Peter Ivanovich also knew and who was her fiancé, as he had heard. He bowed mournfully to them and was about to pass into the death-chamber, when from under the stairs appeared the figure of Ivan Ilych's schoolboy son, who was extremely like his father. He seemed a little Ivan Ilych, such as Peter Ivanovich remembered when they studied law together. His tear-stained eyes had in them the look that is seen in the eyes of boys thirteen or fourteen who are not pure-minded. When he saw Peter Ivanovich he scowled morosely and shamefacedly. Peter Ivanovich nodded to him and entered the death-chamber. The service began: candles, groans, incense, tears, and sobs. Peter Ivanovich stood looking gloomily down at his feet. He did not look once at the dead man, did not yield to any depressing influence, and was one of the first to leave the room. There was no one in the anteroom, but Gerasim darted out of the dead man's room, rummaged with strong hands among the fur coats to find Peter Ivanovich's and helped him on with it.

"Well, friend Gerasim," said Peter Ivanovich, so as to say something. "It's a sad affair, isn't it?"

"It's God's will. We shall all come to it some day," said Gerasim, dis- 50 playing his teeth—the even, white teeth of a healthy peasant—and, like a man in the thick of urgent work, he briskly opened the front door, called the coachman, helped Peter Ivanovich into the sledge, and sprang back to the porch as if in readiness for what he had to do next.

Peter Ivanovich found the fresh air particularly pleasant after the smell of incense, the dead body, and carbolic acid.

"Where to, sir?" asked the coachman.

"It's not too late even now. . . . I'll call round on Fëdor Vasilievich."

He accordingly drove there and found them just finishing the first rubber, so that it was quite convenient for him to cut in.

2

Ivan Ilych's life had been most simple and most ordinary and therefore 55 most terrible.

He had been a member of the Court of Justice, and died at the age of forty-five. His father had been an official who after serving in various ministries and departments in Petersburg had made the sort of career which brings men to positions from which by reason of their long service they cannot be dismissed, though they are obviously unfit to hold any responsible position, and for whom therefore posts are especially created, which though fictitious carry salaries of from six to ten thousand rubles that are not fictitious, and in receipt of which they live on to a great age.

Such was the Privy Councillor and superfluous member of various superfluous institutions, Ilya Epimovich Golovin.

He had three sons, of whom Ivan Ilych was second. The eldest son was following in his father's footsteps only in another department, and was already approaching that stage in the service at which a similar sinecure would be reached. The third son was a failure. He had ruined his prospects in a number of positions and was now serving in the railway department. His father and brothers, and still more their wives, not merely disliked meeting him, but avoided remembering his existence unless compelled to do so. His sister had married Baron Greff, a Petersburg official of her father's type. Ivan Ilych was *le phénix de la famille*° as people said. He was neither cold and formal as his elder brother nor as wild as the younger, but was a happy mean between them—an intelligent, polished, lively and agreeable man. He had studied with his younger brother at the School of Law, but the latter had failed to complete the course and was expelled when he was in fifth class. Ivan Ilych finished the course well. Even when he was at the School of Law he was just what he remained for the rest of his life: a capable, cheerful, good-natured, and sociable man, though strict in the fulfillment of what he considered to be his duty: and he considered his duty to be what was so considered by those in authority. Neither as a boy nor as a man was he a toady, but from early youth was by nature attracted to people of high station as a fly is drawn to the light, assimilating their ways and views of life and establishing friendly relations with them. All the enthusiasms of childhood and youth passed without leaving much trace on him; he succumbed to sensuality, to vanity, and latterly among the highest classes to liberalism, but always within limits which his instinct unfailingly indicated to him as correct.

At school he had done things which had formerly seemed to him very horrid and made him feel disgusted with himself when he did them; but when later on he saw that such actions were done by people of good position and that they did not regard them as wrong, he was able not exactly to regard them as right, but to forget about them entirely or not be at all troubled at remembering them.

60   Having graduated from the School of Law and qualified for the tenth rank of the civil service, and having received money from his father for his equipment, Ivan Ilych ordered himself clothes at Scharmer's, the fashionable tailor, hung a medallion inscribed *respice finem*° on his watch-chain, took leave of his professor and the prince who was patron of the school, had a farewell dinner with his comrades at Donon's first-class restaurant, and with his new and fashionable portmanteau, linen, clothes, shaving and

---

le phénix de la famille: the marvel of the family   ***respice finem:*** look to the end

other toilet appliances, and a traveling rug, all purchased at the best shops, he set off for one of the provinces where, through his father's influence, he had been attached to the Governor as an official for special service.

In the province Ivan Ilych soon arranged as easy and agreeable a position for himself as he had had at the School of Law. He performed his official tasks, made his career, and at the same time amused himself pleasantly and decorously. Occasionally he paid official visits to country districts, where he behaved with dignity both to his superiors and inferiors, and performed the duties entrusted to him, which related chiefly to the sectarians,° with an exactness and incorruptible honesty of which he could not but feel proud.

In official matters, despite his youth and taste for frivolous gaiety, he was exceedingly reserved, punctilious, and even severe; but in society he was often amusing and witty, and always good-natured, correct in his manner, and *bon enfant,*° as the Governor and his wife—with whom he was like one of the family—used to say of him.

In the province he had an affair with a lady who made advances to the elegant young lawyer, and there was also a milliner; and there were carousals with aides-de-camp who visited the district, and after-supper visits to a certain outlying street of doubtful reputation; and there was too some obsequiousness to his chief and even to his chief's wife, but all this was done with such a tone of good breeding that no hard names could be applied to it. It all came under the heading of the French saying: *"Il faut que jeunesse se passe."*° It was all done with clean hands, in clean linen, with French phrases, and above all among people of the best society and consequently with the approval of people of rank.

So Ivan Ilych served for five years and then came a change in his official life. The new and reformed judicial institutions were introduced, and new men were needed. Ivan Ilych became such a new man. He was offered the post of examining magistrate, and he accepted it though the post was in another province and obliged him to give up the connections he had formed and to make new ones. His friends met to give him a send-off; they had a group-photograph taken and presented him with a silver cigarette-case, and he set off to his new post.

As examining magistrate Ivan Ilych was just as *comme il faut*° and decorous a man, inspiring general respect and capable of separating his official duties from his private life, as he had been when acting as an official on special service. His duties now as examining magistrate were far more interesting and attractive than before. In his former position it had been pleasant to wear an undress uniform made by Scharmer, and to pass through the crowd of petitioners and officials who were timorously awaiting an audience with the Governor, and who envied him as with free and

65

---

sectarians: Old Believers, dissenters from the modern church   ***bon enfant:*** a good child   ***If faut . . . passe:*** You're only young once.   ***comme il faut:*** proper

easy gait he went straight into his chief's private room to have a cup of tea and a cigarette with him. But not many people had then been directly dependent on him—only police officials and the sectarians when he went on special missions—and he liked to treat them politely, almost as comrades, as if he were letting them feel that he who had the power to crush them was treating them in this simple, friendly way. There were then but few such people. But now, as an examining magistrate, Ivan Ilych felt that everyone without exception, even the most important and self-satisfied, was in his power, and that he need only write a few words on a sheet of paper with a certain heading, and this or that important, self-satisfied person would be brought before him in the role of an accused person or a witness, and if he did not choose to allow him to sit down, would have to stand before him and answer his questions. Ivan Ilych never abused his power; he tried on the contrary to soften its expression, but the consciousness of it and of the possibility of softening its effect, supplied the chief interest and attraction of his office. In his work itself, especially in his examinations, he very soon acquired a method of eliminating all considerations irrelevant to the legal aspect of the case, and reducing even the most complicated case to a form in which it would be presented on paper only in its externals, completely excluding his personal opinion of the matter, while above all observing every prescribed formality. The work was new and Ivan Ilych was one of the first men to apply the new Code of 1864.°

On taking up the post of examining magistrate in a new town, he made new acquaintances and connections, placed himself on a new footing, and assumed a somewhat different tone. He took up an attitude of rather dignified aloofness towards the provincial authorities, but picked out the best circle of legal gentlemen and wealthy gentry living in the town and assumed a tone of slight dissatisfaction with the government, of moderate liberalism, and of enlightened citizenship. At the same time, without at all altering the elegance of his toilet, he ceased shaving his chin and allowed his beard to grow as it pleased.

Ivan Ilych settled down very pleasantly in this new town. The society there, which inclined towards opposition to the Governor, was friendly, his salary was larger, and he began to play *vint,*° which he found added not a little to the pleasure of life, for he had a capacity for cards, played good-humoredly, and calculated rapidly and astutely, so that he usually won.

After living there for two years he met his future wife, Praskovya Fëdorovna Mikhel, who was the most attractive, clever, and brilliant girl of the set in which he moved, and among other amusements and relaxations from his labors as examining magistrate, Ivan Ilych established light and playful relations with her.

While he had been an official on special service he had been accustomed to dance, but now as an examining magistrate it was exceptional for him to

---

Code of 1864: reformed judicial procedures following the 1861 emancipation of the serfs   *vint:* a card game resembling bridge do so. If he danced now, he did it as if to show that though he served under the reformed order of things, and had reached the fifth official rank, yet when it came to dancing he could do it better than most people. So at the end of an evening he sometimes danced with Praskovya Fëdorovna, and it was chiefly during these dances that he captivated her. She fell in love with him. Ivan Ilych had at first no definite intention of marrying, but when the girl fell in love with him he said to himself: "Really, why shouldn't I marry?"

Praskovya Fëdorovna came of a good family, was not bad looking, and   70 had some little property. Ivan Ilych might have aspired to a more brilliant match, but even this was good. He had his salary, and she, he hoped, would have an equal income. She was well connected, and was a sweet, pretty, and thoroughly correct young woman. To say that Ivan Ilych married because he fell in love with Praskovya Fëdorovna and found that she sympathized with his views of life would be as incorrect as to say that he married because his social circle approved of the match. He was swayed by both these considerations: the marriage gave him personal satisfaction, and at the same time it was considered the right thing by the most highly placed of his associates.

So Ivan Ilych got married.

The preparations for marriage and the beginning of married life, with its conjugal caresses, the new furniture, new crockery, and new linen, were very pleasant until his wife became pregnant—so that Ivan Ilych had begun to think that marriage would not impair the easy, agreeable, gay and always decorous character of his life, approved of by society and regarded by himself as natural, but would even improve it. But from the first months of his wife's pregnancy, something new, unpleasant, depressing, and unseemly, and from which there was no way of escape, unexpectedly showed itself.

His wife, without any reason—*de gaieté de coeur*° as Ivan Ilych expressed it to himself—began to disturb the pleasure and propriety of their life. She began to be jealous without any cause, expected him to devote his whole attention to her, found fault with everything, and made coarse and ill-mannered scenes.

At first Ivan Ilych hoped to escape from the unpleasantness of this state of affairs by the same easy and decorous relation to life that had served him heretofore: he tried to ignore his wife's disagreeable moods, continued to live in his usual easy and pleasant way, invited friends to his house for a game of cards, and also tried going out to his club or spending his evenings with friends. But one day his wife began upbraiding him so vigorously, using such coarse words, and continued to abuse him every time he did not fulfill her demands, so resolutely and with such evident determination not to give way till he submitted—that is, till he stayed at home and was bored just as she was—that he became alarmed. He now realized that matrimony—

de gaieté de coeur: out of sheer wantonness

at any rate with Praskovya Fëdorovna—was not always conducive to the pleasures and amenities of life, but on the contrary often infringed both comfort and propriety, and that he must therefore entrench himself against such infringement. And Ivan Ilych began to seek for means of doing so. His official duties were the one thing that imposed upon Praskovya Fëdorovna, and by means of his official work and the duties attached to it he began struggling with his wife to secure his own independence.

75   With the birth of their child, the attempts to feed it and the various failures in doing so, and with the real and imaginary illnesses of mother and child, in which Ivan Ilych's sympathy was demanded but about which he understood nothing, the need for securing for himself an existence outside his family life became still more imperative.

As his wife grew more irritable and exacting and Ivan Ilych transferred the center of gravity of his life more and more to his official work, so did he grow to like his work better and became more ambitious than before.

Very soon, within a year of his wedding, Ivan Ilych had realized that marriage, though it may add some comforts to life, is in fact a very intricate and difficult affair towards which in order to perform one's duty, that is, to lead a decorous life approved of by society, one must adopt a definite attitude just as towards one's official duties.

And Ivan Ilych evolved such an attitude towards married life. He only required of it those conveniences—dinner at home, housewife, and bed— which it could give him, and above all that propriety of external forms required by public opinion. For the rest he looked for light-hearted pleasure and propriety, and was very thankful when he found them, but if he met with antagonism and querulousness he at once retired into his separate fenced-off world of official duties, where he found satisfaction.

Ivan Ilych was esteemed a good official, and after three years was made Assistant Public Prosecutor. His new duties, their importance, the possibility of indicting and imprisoning anyone he chose, the publicity his speeches received, and the success he had in all these things, made his work still more attractive.

80   More children came. His wife became more and more querulous and ill-tempered, but the attitude Ivan Ilych had adopted towards his home life rendered him almost impervious to her grumbling.

After seven years' service in that town he was transferred to another province as Public Prosecutor. They moved, but were short of money and his wife did not like the place they moved to. Though the salary was higher the cost of living was greater, besides which two of their children died and family life became still more unpleasant for him.

Praskovya Fëdorovna blamed her husband for every inconvenience they encountered in their new home. Most of the conversations between husband and wife, especially as to the children's education, led to topics which recalled former disputes, and those disputes were apt to flare up again at any moment. There remained only those rare periods of amorousness which still came to them at times but did not last long. These were islets at which they anchored for a while and then again set out upon that ocean of veiled hostility which showed itself in their aloofness from one another. This aloofness might have grieved Ivan Ilych had he considered that it ought not to exist, but he now regarded the position as normal, and even made it the goal at which he aimed in family life. His aim was to free himself more and more from those unpleasantnesses and to give them a semblance of harmlessness and propriety. He attained this by spending less and less time with his family, and when obliged to be at home he tried to safeguard his position by the presence of outsiders. The chief thing however was that he had his official duties. The whole interest of his life now centered in the official world and that interest absorbed him. The consciousness of his power, being able to ruin anybody he wished to ruin, the importance, even the external dignity of his entry into court, or meetings with his subordinates, his success with superiors and inferiors, and above all his masterly handling of cases, of which he was conscious—all this gave him pleasure and filled his life, together with chats with his colleagues, dinners, and bridge. So that on the whole Ivan Ilych's life continued to flow as he considered it should do—pleasantly and properly.

So things continued for another seven years. His eldest daughter was already sixteen, another child had died, and only one son was left, a schoolboy and a subject of dissension. Ivan Ilych wanted to put him in the School of Law, but to spite him Praskovya Fëdorovna entered him at the High School. The daughter had been educated at home and had turned out well: the boy did not learn badly either.

3

So Ivan Ilych lived for seventeen years after his marriage. He was already a Public Prosecutor of long standing, and had declined several proposed transfers while awaiting a more desirable post, when an unanticipated and unpleasant occurrence quite upset the peaceful course of his life. He was expecting to be offered the post of presiding judge in a university town, but Happe somehow came to the front and obtained the appointment instead. Ivan Ilych became irritable, reproached Happe, and quarreled both with him and with his immediate superiors—who became colder to him and again passed him over when other appointments were made.

This was in 1880, the hardest year of Ivan Ilych's life. It was then that it became evident on the one hand that his salary was insufficient for them to live on, and on the other that he had been forgotten, and not only this, but that what was for him the greatest and most cruel injustice appeared to others a quite ordinary occurrence. Even his father did not consider it his duty to help him. Ivan Ilych felt himself abandoned by everyone, and that they regarded his position with a salary of 3,500 rubles as quite normal and even fortunate. He alone knew that with the consciousness of the injustices done him, with his wife's incessant nagging, and with the debts he had contracted by living beyond his means, his position was far from normal.

In order to save money that summer he obtained leave of absence and went with his wife to live in the country at her brother's place.

In the country, without his work, he experienced ennui for the first time in his life, and not only ennui but intolerable depression, and he decided that it was impossible to go on living like that, and that it was necessary to take energetic measures.

Having passed a sleepless night pacing up and down the veranda, he decided to go to Petersburg and bestir himself, in order to punish those who had failed to appreciate him and to get transferred to another ministry.

Next day, despite many protests from his wife and brother, he started for Petersburg with the sole object of obtaining a post with a salary of five thousand rubles a year. He was no longer bent on any particular department, or tendency, or kind of activity. All he now wanted was an appointment to another post with a salary of five thousand rubles, either in administration, in the banks, with the railways, in one of the Empress Marya's Institutions,° or even in customs—but it had to carry with it a salary of five thousand rubles and be in a ministry other than that in which they had failed to appreciate him.

90   And this quest of Ivan Ilych's was crowned with remarkable and unexpected success. At Kursk an acquaintance of his, F. I. Ilyin, got into the first-class carriage, sat down beside Ivan Ilych, and told him of a telegram just received by the Governor of Kursk announcing that a change was about to take place in the ministry: Peter Ivanovich was to be superseded by Ivan Semënovich.

The proposed change, apart from its significance for Russia, had a special significance for Ivan Ilych, because by bringing forward a new man, Peter Petrovich, and consequently his friend Zachar Ivanovich, it was highly favorable for Ivan Ilych, since Zachar Ivanovich was a friend and colleague of his.

In Moscow this news was confirmed, and on reaching Petersburg Ivan Ilych found Zachar Ivanovich and received a definite promise of an appointment in his former department of Justice.

A week later he telegraphed to his wife: "Zachar in Miller's place. I shall receive appointment on presentation of report."

Thanks to this change of personnel, Ivan Ilych had unexpectedly obtained an appointment in his former ministry which placed him two stages above his former colleagues besides giving him five thousand rubles salary and three thousand five hundred rubles for expenses connected with his removal. All his ill humor towards his former enemies and the whole department vanished, and Ivan Ilych was completely happy.

95   He returned to the country more cheerful and contented than he had been for a long time. Praskovya Fëdorovna also cheered up and a truce was arranged between them. Ivan Ilych told of how he had been fêted by every-

Empress Marya's Institutions: orphanage-schools for girls

body in Petersburg, how all those who had been his enemies were put to shame and now fawned on him, how envious they were of his appointment, and how much everybody in Petersburg had liked him.

Praskovya Fëdorovna listened to all this and appeared to believe it. She did not contradict anything, but only made plans for their life in the town to which they were going. Ivan Ilych saw with delight that these plans were his plans, that he and his wife agreed, and that, after a stumble, his life was regaining its due and natural character of pleasant lightheartedness and decorum.

Ivan Ilych had come back for a short time only, for he had to take up his new duties on the 10th of September. Moreover, he needed time to settle into the new place, to move all his belongings from the province, and to buy and order many additional things: in a word, to make such arrangements as he had resolved on, which were almost exactly what Praskovya Fëdorovna too had decided on.

Now that everything had happened so fortunately, and that he and his wife were at one in their aims and moreover saw so little of one another, they got on together better than they had done since the first years of marriage. Ivan Ilych had thought of taking his family away with him at once, but the insistence of his wife's brother and her sister-in-law, who had suddenly become particularly amiable and friendly to him and his family, induced him to depart alone.

So he departed, and the cheerful state of mind induced by his success and by the harmony between his wife and himself, the one intensifying the other, did not leave him. He found a delightful house, just the thing both he and his wife had dreamt of. Spacious, lofty reception rooms in the old style, a convenient and dignified study, rooms for his wife and daughter, a study for his son—it might have been specially built for them. Ivan Ilych himself superintended the arrangements, chose the wallpapers, supplemented the furniture (preferably with antiques which he considered particularly *comme il faut*), and supervised the upholstering. Everything progressed and progressed and approached the ideal he had set himself: even when things were only half completed they exceeded his expectations. He saw what a refined and elegant character, free from vulgarity, it would all have when it was ready. On falling asleep he pictured to himself how the reception-room would look. Looking at the yet unfinished drawing-room he could see the fireplace, the screen, the what-nots, the little chairs dotted here and there, the dishes and plates on the walls, and the bronzes, as they would be when everything was in place. He was pleased by the thought of how his wife and daughter, who shared his taste in this matter, would be impressed by it. They were certainly not expecting as much. He had been particularly successful in finding, and buying cheaply, antiques which gave a particularly aristocratic character to the whole place. But in his letters he intentionally understated everything in order to be able to surprise them. All this so absorbed him that his new duties—though he liked his official work—interested him less than he had expected. Sometimes he even had moments of absent-mindedness during the Court Sessions, and would consider whether he should have straight or curved cornices for his curtains. He was so interested in it all that he often did things himself, rearranging the furniture, or rehanging the curtains. Once when mounting a stepladder to show the upholsterer, who did not understand, how he wanted the hangings draped, he made a false step and slipped, but being a strong and agile man he clung on and only knocked his side against the knob of the window frame. The bruised place was painful but the pain soon passed, and he felt particularly bright and well just then. He wrote: "I feel fifteen years younger." He thought he would have everything ready by September, but it dragged on till mid-October. But the result was charming not only in his eyes but to everyone who saw it.

100   In reality it was just what is usually seen in houses of people of moderate means who want to appear rich, and therefore succeed only in resembling others like themselves: there were damasks, dark wood, plants, rugs, and dull and polished bronzes—all the things people of a certain class have in order to resemble other people of that class. His house was so like the others that it would never have been noticed, but to him it all seemed to be quite exceptional. He was very happy when he met his family at the station and brought them to the newly furnished house all lit up, where a footman in a white tie opened the door into the hall decorated with plants, and when they went on into the drawing-room and the study uttering exclamations of delight. He conducted them everywhere, drank in their praises eagerly, and beamed with pleasure. At tea that evening, when Praskovya Fëdorovna among other things asked him about his fall, he laughed and showed them how he had gone flying and frightened the upholsterer.

"It's a good thing I'm a bit of an athlete. Another man might have been killed, but I merely knocked myself, just here; it hurts when touched, but it's passing off already—it's only a bruise."

So they began living in their new home—in which, as always happens, when they got thoroughly settled in they found they were just one room short—and with the increased income, which as always was just a little (some five hundred rubles) too little, but it was all very nice.

Things went particularly well at first, before everything was finally arranged and while something had still to be done: this thing bought, that thing ordered, another thing moved, and something else adjusted. Though there were some disputes between husband and wife, they were both so well satisfied and had so much to do that it all passed off without any serious quarrels. When nothing was left to arrange it became rather dull and something seemed to be lacking, but they were then making acquaintances, forming habits, and life was growing fuller.

Ivan Ilych spent his mornings at the law court and came home to dinner, and at first he was generally in a good humor, though he occasionally became irritable just on account of his house. (Every spot on the tablecloth or the upholstery, and every broken window-blind string, irritated him. He had devoted so much trouble to arranging it all that every disturbance of it distressed him.) But on the whole his life ran its course as he believed life should do: easily, pleasantly, and decorously.

He got up at nine, drank his coffee, read the paper, and then put on his undress uniform and went to the law courts. There the harness in which he worked had already been stretched to fit him and he donned it without a hitch: petitioners, inquiries at the chancery, the chancery itself, and the sittings public and administrative. In all this the thing was to exclude everything fresh and vital, which always disturbs the regular course of official business, and to admit only official relations with people, and then only on official grounds. A man would come, for instance, wanting some information. Ivan Ilych, as one in whose sphere the matter did not lie, would have nothing to do with him: but if the man had some business with him in his official capacity, something that could be expressed on officially stamped paper, he would do everything, positively everything he could within the limits of such relations, and in doing so would maintain the semblance of friendly human relations, that is, would observe the courtesies of life. As soon as the official relations ended, so did everything else. Ivan Ilych possessed this capacity to separate his real life from the official side of affairs and not mix the two, in the highest degree, and by long practice and natural aptitude had brought it to such a pitch that sometimes, in the manner of a virtuoso, he would even allow himself to let the human and official relations mingle. He let himself do this just because he felt that he could at any time he chose resume the strictly official attitude again and drop the human relation. And he did it all easily, pleasantly, correctly, and even artistically. In the intervals between the sessions he smoked, drank tea, chatted a little about politics, a little about general topics, a little about cards, but most of all about official appointments. Tired, but with the feelings of a virtuoso—one of the first violins who has played his part in an orchestra with precision—he would return home to find that his wife and daughter had been out paying calls, or had a visitor, and that his son had been to school, had done his homework with his tutor, and was duly learning what is taught at High Schools. Everything was as it should be. After dinner, if they had no visitors, Ivan Ilych sometimes read a book that was being much discussed at the time, and in the evening settled down to work, that is, read official papers, compared the depositions of witnesses, noted paragraphs of the Code applying to them. This was neither dull nor amusing. It was dull when he might have been playing bridge, but if no bridge was available it was at any rate better than doing nothing or sitting with his wife. Ivan Ilych's chief pleasure was giving little dinners to which he invited men and women of good social position, and just as his drawing-room resembled all other drawing-rooms so did his enjoyable little parties resemble all other such parties.

Once they even gave a dance. Ivan Ilych enjoyed it and everything went off well, except that it led to a violent quarrel with his wife about the cakes and sweets. Praskovya Fëdorovna had made her own plans, but Ivan Ilych insisted on getting everything from an expensive confectioner and ordered too many cakes, and the quarrel occurred because some of those cakes were left over and the confectioner's bill came to forty-five rubles. It was a great and disagreeable quarrel. Praskovya Fëdorovna called him "a fool and an imbecile," and he clutched at his head and made angry allusions to divorce.

But the dance itself had been enjoyable. The best people were there, and Ivan Ilych had danced with Princess Trufonova, a sister of the distinguished founder of the Society "Bear my Burden."

The pleasures connected with his work were pleasures of ambition; his social pleasures were those of vanity; but Ivan Ilych's greatest pleasure was playing bridge. He acknowledged that whatever disagreeable incident happened in his life, the pleasure that beamed like a ray of light above everything else was to sit down to bridge with good players, not noisy partners, and of course to four-handed bridge (with five players it was annoying to have to stand out, though one pretended not to mind), to play a clever and serious game (when the cards allowed it) and then to have supper and a glass of wine. After a game of bridge, especially if he had won a little (to win a large sum was unpleasant), Ivan Ilych went to bed in specially good humor.

So they lived. They formed a circle of acquaintances among the best people and were visited by people of importance and by young folk. In their views as to their acquaintances, husband, wife and daughter were entirely agreed, and tacitly and unanimously kept at arm's length and shook off the shabby friends and relations who, with much show of affection, gushed into the drawing-room with its Japanese plates on the walls. Soon these shabby friends ceased to obtrude themselves and only the best people remained in the Golovins' set.

110   Young men made up to Lisa, and Petrishchev, an examining magistrate and Dmitri Ivanovich Petrishchev's son and sole heir, began to be so attentive to her that Ivan Ilych had already spoken to Praskovya Fëdorovna about it, and considered whether they should not arrange a party for them, or get up some private theatricals.

So they lived, and all went well, without change, and life flowed pleasantly.

4

They were all in good health. It could not be called ill health if Ivan Ilych sometimes said that he had a queer taste in his mouth and felt some discomfort in his left side.

But this discomfort increased and, though not exactly painful, grew into a sense of pressure in his side accompanied by ill humor. And his irritability became worse and worse and began to mar the agreeable, easy, and correct life that had established itself in the Golovin family. Quarrels between husband and wife became more and more frequent, and soon the

ease and amenity disappeared and even the decorum was barely maintained. Scenes again became frequent, and very few of those islets remained on which husband and wife could meet without an explosion. Praskovya Fëdorovna now had good reason to say that her husband's temper
was trying. With characteristic exaggeration she said he had always had a
dreadful temper, and that it had needed all her good nature to put up with
it for twenty years. It was true that now the quarrels were started by him.
His bursts of temper always came just before dinner, often just as he began
to eat his soup. Sometimes he noticed that a plate or dish was chipped, or
the food was not right, or his son put his elbow on the table, or his daughter's hair was not done as he liked it, and for all this he blamed Praskovya
Fëdorovna. At first she retorted and said disagreeable things to him, but
once or twice he fell into such a rage at the beginning of dinner that she
realized it was due to some physical derangement brought on by taking
food, and so she restrained herself and did not answer but only hurried to
get the dinner over. She regarded this self-restraint as highly praiseworthy.
Having come to the conclusion that her husband had a dreadful temper and
made her life miserable, she began to feel sorry for herself, and the more
she pitied herself the more she hated her husband. She began to wish he
would die; yet she did not want him to die because then his salary would
cease. And this irritated her against him still more. She considered herself
dreadfully unhappy just because not even his death could save her, and
though she concealed her exasperation, that hidden exasperation of hers
increased his irritation also.

After one scene in which Ivan Ilych had been particularly unfair and
after which he had said in explanation that he certainly was irritable but
that it was due to his not being well, she said that if he was ill it should be
attended to, and insisted on his going to see a celebrated doctor.

He went. Everything took place as he had expected and as it always   115
does. There was the usual waiting and the important air assumed by the
doctor, with which he was so familiar (resembling that which he himself
assumed in court), and the sounding and listening, and the questions which
called for answers that were foregone conclusions and were evidently unnecessary, and the look of importance which implied that "if only you put
yourself in our hands we will arrange everything—we know indubitably
how it has to be done, always in the same way for everybody alike." It was
all just as it was in the law courts. The doctor put on just the same air
towards him as he himself put on towards an accused person.

The doctor said that so-and-so indicated that there was so-and-so inside
the patient, but if the investigation of so-and-so did not confirm this, then
he must assume that and that. If he assumed that and that, then . . . and so
on. To Ivan Ilych only one question was important: was his case serious or
not? But the doctor ignored that inappropriate question. From his point of
view it was not the one under consideration, the real question was to decide
between a floating kidney, chronic catarrh, or appendicitis. It was not a

question of Ivan Ilych's life or death, but one between a floating kidney and appendicitis. And that question the doctor solved brilliantly, as it seemed to Ivan Ilych, in favor of appendix, with the reservation that should an examination of the urine give fresh indications the matter would be reconsidered. All this was just what Ivan Ilych had himself brilliantly accomplished a thousand times in dealing with men on trial. The doctor summed up just as brilliantly, looking over his spectacles triumphantly and even gaily at the accused. From the doctor's summing up Ivan Ilych concluded that things were bad, but that for the doctor, and perhaps for everybody else, it was a matter of indifference, though for him it was bad. And this conclusion struck him painfully, arousing in him a great feeling of pity for himself and of bitterness towards the doctor's indifference to a matter of such importance.

He said nothing of this, but rose, placed the doctor's fee on the table, and remarked with a sigh: "We sick people probably often put inappropriate questions. But tell me, in general, is this complaint dangerous, or not? . . ."

The doctor looked at him sternly over his spectacles with one eye, as if to say: "Prisoner, if you will not keep to the questions put to you, I shall be obliged to have you removed from court."

"I have already told you what I consider necessary and proper. The analysis may show something more." And the doctor bowed.

120   Ivan Ilych went out slowly, seated himself disconsolately in his sledge, and drove home. All the way home he was going over what the doctor had said, trying to translate those complicated, obscure, scientific phrases into plain language and find in them an answer to the question: "Is my condition bad? Is it very bad? Or is there as yet nothing much wrong?" And it seemed to him that the meaning of what the doctor had said was that it was very bad. Everything in the streets seemed depressing. The cabmen, the houses, the passers-by, and the shops, were dismal. His ache, this dull gnawing ache that never ceased for a moment, seemed to have acquired a new and more serious significance from the doctor's dubious remarks. Ivan Ilych now watched it with a new and oppressive feeling.

He reached home and began to tell his wife about it. She listened, but in the middle of his account his daughter came in with her hat on, ready to go out with her mother. She sat down reluctantly to listen to this tedious story, but could not stand it long, and her mother too did not hear him to the end.

"Well, I am very glad," she said. "Mind now to take your medicine regularly. Give me the prescription and I'll send Gerasim to the chemist's." And she went to get ready to go out.

While she was in the room Ivan Ilych had hardly taken time to breathe, but he sighed deeply when she left it.

"Well," he thought, "perhaps it isn't so bad after all."

125   He began taking his medicine and following the doctor's directions, which had been altered after the examination of the urine. But then it

happened that there was a contradiction between the indications drawn from the examination of the urine and the symptoms that showed themselves. It turned out that what was happening differed from what the doctor had told him, and that he had either forgotten, or blundered or hidden something from him. He could not, however, be blamed for that, and Ivan Ilych still obeyed his orders implicitly and at first derived some comfort from doing so.

From the time of his visit to the doctor, Ivan Ilych's chief occupation was the exact fulfillment of the doctor's instructions regarding hygiene and the taking of medicine, and the observation of his pain and his excretions. His chief interests came to be people's ailments and people's health. When sickness, deaths, or recoveries were mentioned in his presence, especially when the illness resembled his own, he listened with agitation which he tried to hide, asked questions, and applied what he heard to his own case.

The pain did not grow less, but Ivan Ilych made efforts to force himself to think that he was better. And he could do this so long as nothing agitated him. But as soon as he had any unpleasantness with his wife, or lack of success in his official work, or held bad cards at bridge, he was at once acutely sensible of his disease. He had formerly borne such mischances, hoping soon to adjust what was wrong, to master it and attain success, or make a grand slam. But now every mischance upset him and plunged him into despair. He would say to himself: "There now, just as I was beginning to get better and the medicine had begun to take effect, comes this accursed misfortune, or unpleasantness . . ." And he was furious with the mishap, or with the people who were causing the unpleasantness and killing him, for he felt that this fury was killing him but could not restrain it. One would have thought that it should have been clear to him that this exasperation with circumstances and people aggravated his illness, and that he ought therefore to ignore unpleasant occurrences. But he drew the very opposite conclusion: he said that he needed peace, and he watched for everything that might disturb it and became irritable at the slightest infringement of it. His condition was rendered worse by the fact that he read medical books and consulted doctors. The progress of his disease was so gradual that he could deceive himself when comparing one day with another—the difference was so slight. But when he consulted the doctors it seemed to him that he was getting worse, and even very rapidly. Yet despite this he was continually consulting them.

That month he went to see another celebrity, who told him almost the same as the first had done but put his questions rather differently, and the interview with this celebrity only increased Ivan Ilych's doubts and fears. A friend of a friend of his, a very good doctor, diagnosed his illness again quite differently from the others, and though he predicted recovery, his questions and suppositions bewildered Ivan Ilych still more and increased his doubts. A homeopathist diagnosed the disease in yet another way, and prescribed medicine which Ivan Ilych took secretly for a week. But after a week, not feeling any improvement and having lost confidence both in the former doctor's treatment and in this one's, he became more despondent. One day a lady acquaintance mentioned a cure effected by a wonder-working icon. Ivan Ilych caught himself listening attentively and beginning to believe that it had occurred. This incident alarmed him. "Has my mind really weakened to such an extent?" he asked himself. "Nonsense! It's all rubbish. I mustn't give way to nervous fears but having chosen a doctor must keep strictly to his treatment. That is what I will do. Now it's all settled. I won't think about it, but will follow the treatment seriously till summer, and then we shall see. From now there must be no more of this wavering!" This was easy to say but impossible to carry out. The pain in his side oppressed him and seemed to grow worse and more incessant, while the taste in his mouth grew stranger and stranger. It seemed to him that his breath had a disgusting smell, and he was conscious of a loss of appetite and strength. There was no deceiving himself: something terrible, new, and more important than anything before in his life, was taking place within him of which he alone was aware. Those about him did not understand or would not understand it, but thought everything in the world was going on as usual. That tormented Ivan Ilych more than anything. He saw that his household, especially his wife and daughter who were in a perfect whirl of visiting, did not understand anything of it and were annoyed that he was so depressed and so exacting, as if he were to blame for it. Though they tried to disguise it he saw that he was an obstacle in their path, and that his wife had adopted a definite line in regard to his illness and kept to it regardless of anything he said or did. Her attitude was this: "You know," she would say to her friends, "Ivan Ilych can't do as other people do, and keep to the treatment prescribed for him. One day he'll take his drops and keep strictly to his diet and go to bed in good time, but the next day unless I watch him he'll suddenly forget his medicine, eat sturgeon—which is forbidden—and sit up playing cards till one o'clock in the morning."

"Oh, come, when was that?" Ivan Ilych would ask in vexation. "Only once at Peter Ivanovich's."

130   "And yesterday with Shebek."

"Well, even if I hadn't stayed up, this pain would have kept me awake."

"Be that as it may you'll never get well like that, but will always make us wretched."

Praskovya Fëdorovna's attitude to Ivan Ilych's illness, as she expressed it both to others and to him, was that it was his own fault and was another of the annoyances he caused her. Ivan Ilych felt that this opinion escaped her involuntarily—but that did not make it easier for him.

At the law courts too, Ivan Ilych noticed, or thought he noticed, a strange attitude toward himself. It sometimes seemed to him that people were watching him inquisitively as a man whose place might soon be vacant. Then again, his friends would suddenly begin to chaff him in a friendly way about his low spirits, as if the awful, horrible, and unheard-of thing that was going on within him, incessantly gnawing at him and irresistibly drawing him away, was a very agreeable subject for jests. Schwartz in particular irritated him by his jocularity, vivacity, and *savoir-faire,* which reminded him of what he himself had been ten years ago.

Friends came to make up a set and they sat down to cards. They dealt, bending the new cards to soften them, and he sorted the diamonds in his hands and found he had seven. His partner said "No trumps" and supported him with two diamonds. What more could be wished for? It ought to be jolly and lively. They would make a grand slam. But suddenly Ivan Ilych was conscious of that gnawing pain, that taste in his mouth, and it seemed ridiculous that in such circumstances he should be pleased to make a grand slam.

He looked at his partner, Mikhail Mikhaylovich, who rapped the table with his strong hand and instead of snatching up the tricks pushed the cards courteously and indulgently towards Ivan Ilych that he might have the pleasure of gathering them up without the trouble of stretching out his hand for them. "Does he think I am too weak to stretch my arm?" thought Ivan Ilych, and forgetting what he was doing he over-trumped his partner, missing the grand slam by three tricks. And what was most awful of all was that he saw how upset Mikhail Mikhaylovich was about it but did not himself care. And it was dreadful to realize why he did not care.

They all saw that he was suffering, and said: "We can stop if you are tired. Take a rest." Lie down? No, he was not at all tired, and finished the rubber. All were gloomy and silent. Ivan Ilych felt that he had diffused the gloom over them and could not dispel it. They had supper and went away, and Ivan Ilych was left alone with the consciousness that his life was poisoned and was poisoning the lives of others, and that this poison did not weaken but penetrated more and more deeply into his whole being.

With this consciousness, and with physical pain besides that terror, he must go to bed, often to lie awake the greater part of the night. Next morning he had to get up again, dress, go to the law courts, speak, and write; or if he did not go out, spend at home those twenty-four hours a day each of which was a torture. And he had to live thus all alone on the brink of an abyss, with no one who understood or pitied him.

5

So one month passed and then another. Just before the New Year his brother-in-law came to town and stayed at their house. Ivan Ilych was at the law courts and Praskovya Fëdorovna had gone shopping. When Ivan Ilych came home and entered his study he found his brother-in-law there— a healthy, florid man—unpacking his portmanteau himself. He raised his

135

head on hearing Ivan Ilych's footsteps and looked up at him for a moment without a word. That stare told Ivan Ilych everything. His brother-in-law opened his mouth to utter an exclamation of surprise but checked himself, and that action confirmed it all.

140   "I have changed, eh?"

"Yes, there is a change."

And after that, try as he would to get his brother-in-law to return to the subject of his looks, the latter would say nothing about it. Praskovya Fëdorovna came home and her brother went out to her. Ivan Ilych locked the door and began to examine himself in the glass, first full face, then in profile. He took up a portrait of himself taken with his wife, and compared it with what he saw in the glass. The change in him was immense. Then he bared his arms to the elbow, looked at them, drew the sleeves down again, sat down on an ottoman, and grew blacker than night.

"No, no, this won't do!" he said to himself, and jumped up, went to the table, took up some law papers and began to read them, but could not continue. He unlocked the door and went into the reception-room. The door leading to the drawing-room was shut. He approached it on tiptoe and listened.

"No, you are exaggerating!" Praskovya Fëdorovna was saying.

145   "Exaggerating! Don't you see it? Why, he's a dead man! Look at his eyes—there's no light in them. But what is wrong with him?"

"No one knows. Nikolaevich [that was another doctor] said something, but I don't know what. And Leshchetitsky [this was the celebrated specialist] said quite the contrary . . ."

Ivan Ilych walked away, went to his own room, lay down, and began musing: "The kidney, a floating kidney." He recalled all the doctors had told him of how it detached itself and swayed about. And by an effort of imagination he tried to catch that kidney and arrest it and support it. So little was needed for this, it seemed to him. "No, I'll go to see Peter Ivanovich again." (That was the friend whose friend was a doctor.) He rang, ordered the carriage, and got ready to go.

"Where are you going, Jean?" asked his wife, with a specially sad and exceptionally kind look.

The exceptionally kind look irritated him. He looked morosely at her.

150   "I must go to see Peter Ivanovich."

He went to see Peter Ivanovich, and together they went to see his friend, the doctor. He was in, and Ivan Ilych had a long talk with him.

Reviewing the anatomical and physiological details of what in the doctor's opinion was going on inside him, he understood it all.

There was something, a small thing, in the vermiform appendix. It might all come right. Only stimulate the energy of one organ and check the activity of another, then absorption would take place and everything would come right. He got home rather late for dinner, ate his dinner, conversed cheerfully, but could not for a long time bring himself to go back to work in his room. At last, however, he went to his study and did what was necessary, but the consciousness that he had put something aside—an important, intimate matter which he would revert to when his work was done—never left him. When he had finished his work he remembered that this intimate matter was the thought of the vermiform appendix. But he did not give himself up to it, and went to the drawing-room for tea. There were callers there, including the examining magistrate who was a desirable match for his daughter, and they were conversing, playing the piano, and singing. Ivan Ilych, as Praskovya Fëdorovna remarked, spent the evening more cheerfully than usual, but he never for a moment forgot that he had postponed the important matter of the appendix. At eleven o'clock he said good-night and went to his bedroom. Since his illness he had slept alone in a small room next to his study. He undressed and took up a novel by Zola, but instead of reading it fell into thought, and in his imagination that desired improvement in the vermiform appendix occurred. There was the absorption and evacuation and the reestablishment of normal activity. "Yes, that's it!" he said to himself. "One need only assist nature, that's all." He remembered his medicine, rose, took it, and lay down on his back watching for the beneficent action of the medicine and for it to lessen the pain. "I need only take it regularly and avoid all injurious influences. I am already feeling better, much better." He began touching his side: it was not painful to the touch. "There, I really don't feel it. It's much better already." He put out the light and turned on his side . . . "The appendix is getting better, absorption is occurring." Suddenly he felt the old familiar, dull, gnawing pain, stubborn and serious. There was the same loathsome taste in his mouth. His heart sank and he felt dazed. "My God! My God!" he muttered. "Again, again! and it will never cease." And suddenly the matter presented itself in a quite different aspect. "Vermiform appendix! Kidney!" he said to himself. "It's not a question of appendix or kidney, but of life and . . . death. Yes, life was there and now it is going, going and I cannot stop it. Yes. Why deceive myself? Isn't it obvious to everyone but me that I'm dying, and that it's only a question of weeks, days . . . it may happen this moment. There was light and now there is darkness. I was here and now I'm going there! Where?" A chill came over him, his breathing ceased, and he felt only the throbbing of his heart.

"When I am not, what will there be? There will be nothing. Then where shall I be when I am no more? Can this be dying? No, I don't want to!" He jumped up and tried to light the candle, felt for it with trembling hands, dropped the candle and the candlestick on the floor, and fell back to his pillow.

"What's the use? It makes no difference," he said to himself, staring with wide-open eyes into the darkness. "Death. Yes, death. And none of them know or wish to know it, and they have no pity for me. Now they are

155

playing." (He heard through the door the distant sound of a song and its accompaniment.) "It's all the same to them, but they will die too! Fools! I first, and they later, but it will be the same for them. And now they are merry . . . the beasts!"

Anger choked him and he was agonizingly, unbearably, miserable. "It is impossible that all men have been doomed to suffer this awful horror!" He raised himself.

"Something must be wrong. I must calm myself—must think it over from the beginning." And he again began thinking. "Yes, the beginning of my illness: I knocked my side, but I was quite well that day and the next. It hurt a little, then rather more. I saw the doctor, then followed despondency and anguish, more doctors, and I drew nearer to the abyss. My strength grew less and I kept coming nearer and nearer, and now I have wasted away and there is no light in my eyes. I think of the appendix—but this is death! I think of mending the appendix, and all the while here is death! Can it really be death?" Again terror seized him and he gasped for breath. He leant down and began feeling for the matches, pressing with his elbow on the stand beside the bed. It was in the way and hurt him, he grew furious with it, pressed on it still harder, and upset it. Breathless and in despair he fell on his back, expecting death to come immediately.

Meanwhile the visitors were leaving. Praskovya Fëdorovna was seeing them off. She heard something fall and came in.

"What has happened?"

160   "Nothing. I knocked it over accidentally."

She went out and returned with a candle. He lay there panting heavily, like a man who has run a thousand yards, and stared upwards at her with a fixed look.

"What is it, Jean?"

"No . . . o . . . thing. I upset it." ("Why speak of it? She won't understand," he thought.)

And in truth she did not understand. She picked up the stand, lit his candle, and hurried away to see another visitor off. When she came back he still lay on his back, looking upwards.

165   "What is it? Do you feel worse?"

"Yes."

She shook her head and sat down.

"Do you know, Jean, I think we must ask Leshchetitsky to come and see you here."

This meant calling in the famous specialist, regardless of expense. He smiled malignantly and said "No." She remained a little longer and then went up to him and kissed his forehead.

170   While she was kissing him he hated her from the bottom of his soul and with difficulty refrained from pushing her away.

"Good-night. Please God you'll sleep."

"Yes."

6

Ivan Ilych saw that he was dying, and he was in continual despair.

In the depth of his heart he knew he was dying, but not only was he not accustomed to the thought, he simply did not and could not grasp it.

The syllogism he had learnt from Kiezewetter's *Logic:*° "Caius is a   175 man, men are mortal, therefore Caius is mortal," had always seemed to him correct as applied to Caius, but certainly not as applied to himself. That Caius—man in the abstract—was mortal, was perfectly correct, but he was not Caius, not an abstract man, but a creature quite, quite separate from all others. He had been little Vanya, with a mamma and a papa, with Mitya and Volodya, with the toys, a coachman and a nurse, afterwards with Katenka and with all the joys, griefs, and delights of childhood, boyhood, and youth. What did Caius know of the smell of that striped leather ball Vanya had been so fond of? Had Caius kissed his mother's hand like that, and did the silk of her dress rustle so for Caius? Had he rioted like that at school when the pastry was bad? Had Caius been in love like that? Could Caius preside at a session as he did? "Caius really was mortal, and it was right for him to die; but for me, little Vanya, Ivan Ilych, with all my thoughts and emotions, it's altogether a different matter. It cannot be that I ought to die. That would be too terrible."

Such was his feeling.

"If I had to die like Caius, I should have known it was so. An inner voice would have told me so, but there was nothing of the sort in me and I and all my friends felt that our case was quite different from that of Caius. And now here it is!" he said to himself. "It can't be. It's impossible! But here it is. How is this? How is one to understand it?"

He could not understand it, and tried to drive this false, incorrect, morbid thought away and to replace it by other proper and healthy thoughts. But that thought, and not the thought only but the reality itself, seemed to come and confront him.

And to replace that thought he called up a succession of others, hoping to find in them some support. He tried to get back into the former current of thoughts that had once screened the thought of death from him. But strange to say, all that had formerly shut off, hidden, and destroyed his consciousness of death, no longer had that effect. Ivan Ilych now spent most of his time in attempting to re-establish that old current. He would say to himself: "I will take up my duties again—after all I used to live by them." And banishing all doubts he would go to the law courts, enter into conversation with his colleagues, and sit carelessly as was his wont, scanning the crowd with a thoughtful look and leaning both his emaciated arms on the arms of his oak chair; bending over as usual to a colleague and drawing his papers nearer he would interchange whispers with him, and

Kiezewetter's *Logic:* a widely used textbook

then suddenly raising his eyes and sitting erect would pronounce certain words and open the proceedings. But suddenly in the midst of those proceedings the pain in his side, regardless of the stage the proceedings had reached, would begin its own gnawing work. Ivan Ilych would turn his attention to it and try to drive the thoughts of it away, but without success. *It* would come and stand before him and look at him, and he would be petrified and the light would die out of his eyes, and he would again begin asking himself whether *It* alone was true. And his colleagues and subordinates would see with surprise and distress that he, the brilliant and subtle judge, was becoming confused and making mistakes. He would shake himself, try to pull himself together, manage somehow to bring the sitting to a close, and return home with the sorrowful consciousness that his judicial labors could not as formerly hide from him what he wanted them to hide, and could not deliver him from *It*. And what was worst of all was that *It* drew his attention to itself not in order to take some action but only that he should look at *It*, look it straight in the face: look at it without doing anything, suffer inexpressibly.

180   And to save himself from this condition Ivan Ilych looked for consolations—new screens—and new screens were found and for a while seemed to save him, but then they immediately fell to pieces or rather became transparent, as if *It* penetrated them and nothing could veil *It*.

In these latter days he would go into the drawing-room he had arranged—that drawing-room where he had fallen and for the sake of which (how bitterly ridiculous it seemed) he had sacrificed his life—for he knew that his illness originated with that knock. He would enter and see that something had scratched the polished table. He would look for the cause of this and find that it was the bronze ornamentation of an album, that had got bent. He would take up the expensive album which he had lovingly arranged, and feel vexed with his daughter and her friends for their untidiness—for the album was torn here and there and some of the photographs turned upside down. He would put it carefully in order and bend the ornamentation back into position. Then it would occur to him to place all those things in another corner of the room, near the plants. He would call the footman, but his daughter or wife would come to help him. They would not agree, and his wife would contradict him, and he would dispute and grow angry. But that was all right, for then he did not think about *It*. *It* was invisible.

But then, when he was moving something himself, his wife would say: "Let the servants do it. You will hurt yourself again." And suddenly *It* would flash through the screen and he would see it. It was just a flash, and he hoped it would disappear, but he would involuntarily pay attention to his side. "It sits there as before, gnawing just the same!" And he could no longer forget *It*, but could distinctly see it looking at him from behind the flowers. "What is it all for?"

"It really is so! I lost my life over the curtain as I might have done when storming a fort. Is that possible? How terrible and how stupid. It can't be true! It can't, but it is."

He would go to his study, lie down, and again be alone with *It:* face to face with *It.* And nothing could be done with *It* except to look at it and shudder.

7

How it happened it is impossible to say because it came about step by step, unnoticed, but in the third month of Ivan Ilych's illness, his wife, his daughter, his son, his acquaintances, the doctors, the servants, and above all he himself, were aware that the whole interest he had for other people was whether he would soon vacate his place, and at last release the living from the discomfort caused by his presence and be himself released from his sufferings.

He slept less and less. He was given opium and hypodermic injections of morphine, but this did not relieve him. The dull depression he experienced in a somnolent condition at first gave him a little relief, but only as something new, afterwards it became as distressing as the pain itself or even more so.

Special foods were prepared for him by the doctors' orders, but all those foods became increasingly distasteful and disgusting to him.

For his excretions also special arrangements had to be made, and this was a torment to him every time—a torment from the uncleanliness, the unseemliness, and the smell, and from knowing that another person had to take part in it.

But just through this most unpleasant matter, Ivan Ilych obtained comfort. Gerasim, the butler's young assistant, always came to carry the things out. Gerasim was a clean, fresh peasant lad, grown stout on town food and always cheerful and bright. At first the sight of him, in his clean Russian peasant costume, engaged in that disgusting task embarrassed Ivan Ilych.

Once when he got up from the commode too weak to draw up his trousers, he dropped into a soft armchair and looked with horror at his bare, enfeebled thighs with the muscles so sharply marked on them.

Gerasim with a firm light tread, his heavy boots emitting a pleasant smell of tar and fresh winter air, came in wearing a clean Hessian apron, the sleeves of his print shirt tucked up over his strong bare young arms; and refraining from looking at his sick master out of consideration for his feelings, and restraining the joy of life that beamed from his face, he went up to the commode.

"Gerasim!" said Ivan Ilych in a weak voice.

Gerasim started, evidently afraid he might have committed some blunder, and with a rapid movement turned his fresh, kind, simple young face which just showed the first downy signs of a beard.

"Yes, sir?"

195   "That must be very unpleasant for you. You must forgive me. I am helpless."

"Oh, why, sir," and Gerasim's eyes beamed and he showed his glistening white teeth, "what's a little trouble? It's a case of illness with you, sir."

And his deft strong hands did their accustomed task, and he went out of the room stepping lightly. Five minutes later he as lightly returned.

Ivan Ilych was still sitting in the same position in the armchair.

"Gerasim," he said when the latter had replaced the freshly-washed utensil. "Please come here and help me." Gerasim went up to him. "Lift me up. It is hard for me to get up, and I have sent Dmitri away."

200   Gerasim went up to him, grasped his master with his strong arms deftly but gently, in the same way he stepped—lifted him, supported him with one hand, and with the other drew up his trousers and would have set him down again, but Ivan Ilych asked to be led to the sofa. Gerasim, without an effort and without apparent pressure, led him, almost lifting him, to the sofa and placed him on it.

"Thank you. How easily and well you do it all!"

Gerasim smiled again and turned to leave the room. But Ivan Ilych felt his presence such a comfort that he did not want to let him go.

"One thing more, please move up that chair. No, the other one—under my feet. It is easier for me when my feet are raised."

Gerasim brought the chair, set it down gently in place, and raised Ivan Ilych's legs on to it. It seemed to Ivan Ilych that he felt better while Gerasim was holding up his legs.

205   "It's better when my legs are higher," he said. "Place that cushion under them."

Gerasim did so. He again lifted the legs and placed them, and again Ivan Ilych felt better when Gerasim held his legs. When he set them down Ivan Ilych fancied he felt worse.

"Gerasim," he said. "Are you busy now?"

"Not at all, sir," said Gerasim, who had learnt from the townfolk how to speak to gentlefolk.

"What have you still to do?"

210   "What have I to do? I've done everything except chopping the logs for tomorrow."

"Then hold my legs up a bit higher, can you?"

"Of course I can. Why not?" And Gerasim raised his master's legs higher and Ivan Ilych thought that in that position he did not feel any pain at all.

"And how about the logs?"

"Don't trouble about that, sir. There's plenty of time."

215   Ivan Ilych told Gerasim to sit down and hold his legs, and began to talk to him. And strange to say it seemed to him that he felt better while Gerasim held his legs up.

After that Ivan Ilych would sometimes call Gerasim and get him to hold his legs on his shoulders, and he liked talking to him. Gerasim did it all easily, willingly, simply, and with a good nature that touched Ivan Ilych. Health, strength, and vitality in other people were offensive to him, but Gerasim's strength and vitality did not mortify but soothed him.

What tormented Ivan Ilych most was the deception, the lie, which for some reason they all accepted, that he was not dying but was simply ill, and that he only need keep quiet and undergo a treatment and then something very good would result. He however knew that do what they would nothing would come of it, only still more agonizing suffering and death. This deception tortured him—their not wishing to admit what they all knew and what he knew, but wanting to lie to him concerning his terrible condition, and wishing and forcing him to participate in that lie. Those lies—lies enacted over him on the eve of his death and destined to degrade this awful, solemn act to the level of their visitings, their curtains, their sturgeon for dinner—were a terrible agony for Ivan Ilych. And strangely enough, many times when they were going through their antics over him he had been within a hairbreadth of calling out to them: "Stop lying! You know and I know that I am dying. Then at least stop lying about it!" But he had never had the spirit to do it. The awful, terrible act of his dying was, he could see, reduced by those about him to the level of a casual, unpleasant, and almost indecorous incident (as if someone entered a drawing-room diffusing an unpleasant odor) and this was done by that very decorum which he had served all his life long. He saw that no one felt for him, because no one even wished to grasp his position. Only Gerasim recognized it and pitied him. And so Ivan Ilych felt at ease only with him. He felt comforted when Gerasim supported his legs (sometimes all night long) and refused to go to bed, saying: "Don't you worry, Ivan Ilych. I'll get sleep enough later on," or when he suddenly became familiar and exclaimed: "If you weren't sick it would be another matter, but as it is, why should I grudge a little trouble?" Gerasim alone did not lie; everything showed that he alone understood the facts of the case and did not consider it necessary to disguise them, but simply felt sorry for his emaciated and enfeebled master. Once when Ivan Ilych was sending him away he even said straight out: "We shall all of us die, so why should I grudge a little trouble?"   expressing the fact that he did not think his work burdensome, because he was doing it for a dying man and hoped someone would do the same for him when his time came.

Apart from this lying, or because of it, what most tormented Ivan Ilych was that no one pitied him as he wished to be pitied. At certain moments after prolonged suffering he wished most of all (though he would have been ashamed to confess it) for someone to pity him as a sick child is pitied. He longed to be petted and comforted. He knew he was an important functionary, that he had a beard turning grey, and that therefore what he longed for was impossible, but still he longed for it. And in Gerasim's attitude towards him there was something akin to what he wished for, and so that attitude comforted him. Ivan Ilych wanted to weep, wanted to be petted and cried over, and then his colleague Shebek would come, and instead of weeping and being petted, Ivan Ilych would assume a serious, severe, and profound air, and by force of habit would express his opinion on a decision of the Court of Cassation° and would stubbornly insist on that view. This falsity around him and within him did more than anything else to poison his last days.

8

It was morning. He knew it was morning because Gerasim had gone, and Peter the footman had come and put out the candles, drawn back one of the curtains, and begun quietly to tidy up. Whether it was morning or evening, Friday or Sunday, made no difference, it was all just the same: the gnawing, unmitigated, agonizing pain, never ceasing for an instant, the consciousness of life inexorably waning but not yet extinguished, the approach of that ever dreadful and hateful Death which was the only reality, and always the same falsity. What were days, weeks, hours, in such a case?

220   "Will you have some tea, sir?"

"He wants things to be regular, and wishes the gentlefolk to drink tea in the morning," thought Ivan Ilych, and only said "No."

"Wouldn't you like to move onto the sofa, sir?"

"He wants to tidy up the room, and I'm in the way. I am uncleanliness and disorder," he thought, and said only:

"No, leave me alone."

225   The man went on bustling about. Ivan Ilych stretched out his hand. Peter came up, ready to help.

"What is it, sir?"

"My watch."

Peter took the watch which was close at hand and gave it to his master.

"Half-past eight. Are they up?"

230   "No, sir, except Vladimir Ivanich [the son] who has gone to school. Praskovya Fëdorovna ordered me to wake her if you asked for her. Shall I do so?"

"No, there's no need to." "Perhaps I'd better have some tea," he thought, and added aloud: "Yes, bring me some tea."

Peter went to the door, but Ivan Ilych dreaded being left alone. "How can I keep him here? Oh yes, my medicine." "Peter, give me my medicine." "Why not? Perhaps it may do me some good." He took a spoonful and swallowed it. "No, it won't help. It's all tomfoolery, all deception," he decided as soon as he became aware of the familiar, sickly, hopeless taste. "No, I can't believe in it any longer. But the pain, why this pain? If it

Court of Cassation: the highest court of appeals

would only cease just for a moment!" And he moaned. Peter turned towards him. "It's all right. Go and fetch me some tea."

Peter went out. Left alone Ivan Ilych groaned not so much with pain, terrible though that was, as from mental anguish. Always and for ever the same, always these endless days and nights. If only it would come quicker! If only *what* would come quicker? Death, darkness? . . . No, no! Anything rather than death!

When Peter returned with the tea on a tray, Ivan Ilych stared at him for a time in perplexity, not realizing who and what he was. Peter was disconcerted by that look and his embarrassment brought Ivan Ilych to himself.

"Oh, tea! All right, put it down. Only help me to wash and put on a   235
clean shirt."

And Ivan Ilych began to wash. With pauses for rest, he washed his hands and then his face, cleaned his teeth, brushed his hair, and looked in the glass. He was terrified by what he saw, especially by the limp way in which his hair clung to his pallid forehead.

While his shirt was being changed he knew that he would be still more frightened at the sight of his body, so he avoided looking at it. Finally he was ready. He drew on a dressing-gown, wrapped himself in a plaid, and sat down in the armchair to take his tea. For a moment he felt refreshed, but as soon as he began to drink the tea he was again aware of the same taste, and the pain also returned. He finished it with an effort, and then lay down stretching out his legs, and dismissed Peter.

Always the same. Now a spark of hope flashes up, then a sea of despair rages, and always pain; always pain, always despair, and always the same. When alone he had a dreadful and distressing desire to call someone, but he knew beforehand that with others present it would be still worse. "Another dose of morphine—to lose consciousness. I will tell him, the doctor, that he must think of something else. It's impossible, impossible, to go on like this."

An hour and another pass like that. But now there is a ring at the door bell. Perhaps it's the doctor? It is. He comes in fresh, hearty, plump, and cheerful, with that look on his face that seems to say: "There now, you're in a panic about something, but we'll arrange it all for you directly!" The doctor knows this expression is out of place here, but he has put it on once for all and can't take it off—like a man who has put on a frock-coat in the morning to pay a round of calls.

The doctor rubs his hands vigorously and reassuringly.   240

"Brr! How cold it is! There's such a sharp frost; just let me warm myself!" he says, as if it were only a matter of waiting till he was warm, and then he would put everything right.

"Well now, how are you?"

Ivan Ilych feels that the doctor would like to say: "Well, how are your affairs?" but that even he feels that this would not do, and says instead: "What sort of a night have you had?"

Ivan Ilych looks at him as much as to say: "Are you really never ashamed of lying?" But the doctor does not wish to understand this question, and Ivan Ilych says: "Just as terrible as ever. The pain never leaves me and never subsides. If only something . . ."

245 "Yes, you sick people are always like that . . . There, now I think I am warm enough. Even Praskovya Fëdorovna, who is so particular, could find no fault with my temperature. Well, now I can say good-morning," and the doctor presses his patient's hand.

Then, dropping his former playfulness, he begins with a most serious face to examine the patient, feeling his pulse and taking his temperature, and then begins the sounding and auscultation.

Ivan Ilych knows quite well and definitely that all this is nonsense and pure deception, but when the doctor, getting down on his knee, leans over him, putting the ear first higher then lower, and performs various gymnastic movements over him with a significant expression on his face, Ivan Ilych submits to it all as he used to submit to the speeches of the lawyers, though he knew very well they were all lying and why they were lying.

The doctor, kneeling on the sofa, is still sounding him when Praskovya Fëdorovna's silk dress rustles at the door and she is heard scolding Peter for not having let her know of the doctor's arrival.

She comes in, kisses her husband, and at once proceeds to prove that she has been up a long time already, and only owing to a misunderstanding failed to be there when the doctor arrived.

250 Ivan Ilych looks at her, scans her all over, sets against her the whiteness and plumpness and cleanness of her hands and neck, the gloss of her hair, and the sparkle of her vivacious eyes. He hates her with his whole soul. And the thrill of hatred he feels for her makes him suffer from her touch.

Her attitude towards him and his disease is still the same. Just as the doctor had adopted a certain relation to his patient which he could not abandon, so had she formed one towards him—that he was not doing something he ought to do and was himself to blame, and that she reproached him lovingly for this—and she could not now change that attitude.

"You see he doesn't listen to me and doesn't take his medicine at the proper time. And above all he lies in a position that is no doubt bad for him—with his legs up."

She described how he made Gerasim hold his legs up.

The doctor smiled with a contemptuous affability that said: "What's to be done? These sick people do have foolish fancies of that kind, but we must forgive them."

255 When the examination was over the doctor looked at his watch, and then Praskovya Fëdorovna announced to Ivan Ilych that it was of course as he pleased, but she had sent today for a celebrated specialist who would examine him and have a consultation with Michael Danilovich (their regular doctor).

"Please don't raise any objections. I am doing this for my own sake," she said ironically, letting it be felt that she was doing this for his sake and only said this to leave him no right to refuse. He remained silent, knitting his brows. He felt that he was so surrounded and involved in a mesh of falsity that it was hard to unravel anything.

Everything she did for him was entirely for her own sake, and she told him she was doing for herself what she actually was doing for herself, as if that was so incredible that he must understand the opposite.

At half-past eleven the celebrated specialist arrived. Again the sounding began and the significant conversations in his presence and in another room about the kidneys and the appendix, and the questions and answers, with such an air of importance that again, instead of the real question of life and death which now alone confronted him, the question arose of the kidney and appendix which were not behaving as they ought to and would now be attacked by Michael Danilovich and the specialist and forced to mend their ways.

The celebrated specialist took leave of him with a serious though not hopeless look, and in reply to the timid question Ivan Ilych, with eyes glistening with fear and hope, put to him as to whether there was a chance of recovery, said that he could not vouch for it but there was a possibility. The look of hope with which Ivan Ilych watched the doctor out was so pathetic that Praskovya Fëdorovna, seeing it, even wept as she left the room to hand the doctor his fee.

The gleam of hope kindled by the doctor's encouragement did not last long. The same room, the same pictures, curtains, wall-paper, medicine bottles, were all there, and the same aching suffering body, and Ivan Ilych began to moan. They gave him a subcutaneous injection and he sank into oblivion. 260

It was twilight when he came to. They brought him his dinner and he swallowed some beef tea with difficulty, and then everything was the same again and night was coming on.

After dinner, at seven o'clock, Praskovya Fëdorovna came into the room in evening dress, her full bosom pushed up by her corset, and with traces of powder on her face. She had reminded him in the morning that they were going to the theater. Sarah Bernhardt was visiting the town and they had a box, which he had insisted on their taking. Now he had forgotten about it and her toilet offended him, but he concealed his vexation when he remembered that he had himself insisted on their securing a box and going because it would be an instructive and aesthetic pleasure for the children.

Praskovya Fëdorovna came in, self-satisfied but yet with a rather guilty air. She sat down and asked how he was, but as he saw, only for the sake of asking and not in order to learn about it, knowing that there was nothing to learn—and then went on to what she really wanted to say: that she would not on any account have gone but that the box had been taken and Helen and their daughter were going, as well as Petrishchev (the examining magistrate, their daughter's fiancé) and that it was out of the question to let them go alone; but that she would have much preferred to sit with him for a while; and he must be sure to follow the doctor's orders while she was away.

"Oh, and Fëdor Petrovich [the fiancé] would like to come in. May he? And Lisa?"

265   "All right."

Their daughter came in in full evening dress, her fresh young flesh exposed (making a show of that very flesh which in his own case caused so much suffering), strong, healthy, evidently in love, and impatient with illness, suffering, and death, because they interfered with her happiness.

Fëdor Petrovich came in too, in evening dress, his hair curled *à la Capoul,* a tight stiff collar round his long sinewy neck, an enormous white shirt-front and narrow black trousers tightly stretched over his strong thighs. He had one white glove tightly drawn on, and was holding his opera hat in his hand.

Following him the schoolboy crept in unnoticed, in a new uniform, poor little fellow, and wearing gloves. Terribly dark shadows showed under his eyes, the meaning of which Ivan Ilych knew well.

His son had always seemed pathetic to him, and now it was dreadful to see the boy's frightened look of pity. It seemed to Ivan Ilych that Vasya was the only one besides Gerasim who understood and pitied him.

270   They all sat down and again asked how he was. A silence followed. Lisa asked her mother about the opera-glasses, and there was an altercation between mother and daughter as to who had taken them and where they had been put. This occasioned some unpleasantness.

Fëdor Petrovich inquired of Ivan Ilych whether he had ever seen Sarah Bernhardt. Ivan Ilych did not at first catch the question, but then replied: "No, have you seen her before?"

"Yes, in *Adrienne Lecouvreur.*"

Praskovya Fëdorovna mentioned some rôles in which Sarah Bernhardt was particularly good. Her daughter disagreed. Conversation sprang up as to the elegance and realism of her acting—the sort of conversation that is always repeated and is always the same.

In the midst of the conversation Fëdor Petrovich glanced at Ivan Ilych and became silent. Ivan Ilych was staring with glittering eyes straight before him, evidently indignant with them. This had to be rectified, but it was impossible to do so. The silence had to be broken, but for a time no one dared to break it and they all became afraid that the conventional deception would suddenly become obvious and the truth become plain to all. Lisa was the first to pluck up courage and break the silence, but by trying to hide what everybody was feeling, she betrayed it.

275   "Well, if we are going it's time to start," she said, looking at her watch, a present from her father, and with a faint and significant smile at Fëdor

Petrovich relating to something known only to them. She got up with a rustle of her dress.

They all rose, said good-night, and went away.

When they had gone it seemed to Ivan Ilych that he felt better; the falsity had gone with them. But the pain remained—that same pain and that same fear that made everything monotonously alike, nothing harder and nothing easier. Everything was worse.

Again minute followed minute and hour followed hour. Everything remained the same and there was no cessation. And the inevitable end of it all became more and more terrible.

"Yes, send Gerasim here," he replied to a question Peter asked.

9

His wife returned late at night. She came in on tiptoe, but he heard her, opened his eyes, and made haste to close them again. She wished to send Gerasim away and to sit with him herself, but he opened his eyes and said: "No, go away."

"Are you in great pain?"

"Always the same."

"Take some opium."

He agreed and took some. She went away.

Till about three in the morning he was in a state of stupefied misery. It seemed to him that he and his pain were being thrust into a narrow, deep black sack, but though they were pushed further and further in they could not be pushed to the bottom. And this, terrible enough in itself, was accompanied by suffering. He struggled but yet cooperated. And suddenly he broke through, fell, and regained consciousness. Gerasim was sitting at the foot of the bed dozing quietly, while he himself lay with his emaciated stockinged legs resting on Gerasim's shoulders; the same shaded candle was there and the same unceasing pain.

"Go away, Gerasim," he whispered.

"It's all right, sir. I'll stay a while."

"No. Go away."

He removed his legs from Gerasim's shoulders, turned sideways onto his arm, and felt sorry for himself. He only waited till Gerasim had gone into the next room and then restrained himself no longer but wept like a child. He wept on account of his helplessness, his terrible loneliness, the cruelty of man, the cruelty of God, and the absence of God.

"Why hast Thou done all this? Why hast Thou brought me here? Why, why dost Thou torment me so terribly?"

He did not expect an answer and yet wept because there was no answer and could be none. The pain grew more acute, but he did not stir and did not call. He said to himself: "Go on! Strike me! But what is it for? What have I done to Thee? What is it for?"

Then he grew quiet and not only ceased weeping but even held his breath and became all attention. It was as though he were listening not to an audible voice but to the voice of his soul, to the current of thoughts arising within him.

"What is it you want?" was the first clear conception of expression in words, that he heard.

"What do you want? What do you want?" he repeated to himself.

295   "What do I want? To live and not to suffer," he answered.

And again he listened with such concentrated attention that even his pain did not distract him.

"To live? How?" asked his inner voice.

"Why, to live as I used to—well and pleasantly."

"As you lived before, well and pleasantly?" the voice repeated.

300   And in imagination he began to recall the best moments of his pleasant life. But strange to say none of those best moments of his pleasant life now seemed at all what they had then seemed—none of them except the first recollections of childhood. There, in childhood, there had been something really pleasant with which it would be possible to live if it could return. But the child who had experienced that happiness existed no longer, it was like a reminiscence of somebody else.

As soon as the period began which had produced the present Ivan Ilych, all that had then seemed joys now melted before his sight and turned into something trivial and often nasty.

And the further he departed from childhood and the nearer he came to the present the more worthless and doubtful were the joys. This began with the School of Law. A little that was really good was still found there—there was light-heartedness, friendship, and hope. But in the upper classes there had already been fewer of such good moments. Then during the first years of his official career, when he was in the service of the Governor, some pleasant moments again occurred: they were memories of love for a woman. Then all became confused and there was still less of what was good; later on again there was still less that was good, and the further he went the less there was. His marriage, a mere accident, then the disenchantment that followed it, his wife's bad breath and the sensuality and hypocrisy: then that deadly official life and those preoccupations about money, a year of it, and two, and ten, and twenty, and always the same thing. And the longer it lasted the more deadly it became. "It is as if I had been going downhill while I imagined I was going up. And that is really what it was. I was going up in public opinion, but to the same extent life was ebbing away from me. And now it is all done and there is only death."

"Then what does it mean? Why? It can't be that life is so senseless and horrible. But if it really has been so horrible and senseless, why must I die and die in agony? There is something wrong!"

"Maybe I did not live as I ought to have done," it suddenly occurred to him. "But how could that be, when I did everything properly?" he replied,

and immediately dismissed from his mind this, the sole solution of all the
riddles of life and death, as something quite impossible.

"Then what do you want now? To live? Live how? Live as you lived in   305
the law courts when the usher proclaimed 'The judge is coming!' The judge
is coming, the judge!" he repeated to himself. "Here he is, the judge. But I
am not guilty!" he exclaimed angrily. "What is it for?" And he ceased
crying, but turning his face to the wall continued to ponder on the same
question: Why, and for what purpose, is there all this horror? But however
much he pondered he found no answer. And whenever the thought occurred to him, as it often did, that it all resulted from his not having lived
as he ought to have done, he at once recalled the correctness of his whole
life and dismissed so strange an idea.

10

Another fortnight passed. Ivan Ilych now no longer left his sofa. He
would not lie in bed but lay on the sofa, facing the wall nearly all the time.
He suffered ever the same unceasing agonies and in his loneliness pondered
always on the same insoluble question: "What is this? Can it be that it is
Death?" And the inner voice answered: "Yes, it is Death."

"Why these sufferings?" And the voice answered, "For no reason—
they just are so." Beyond and besides this there was nothing.

From the very beginning of his illness, ever since he had first been to
see the doctor, Ivan Ilych's life had been divided between two contrary and
alternating moods: now it was despair and the expectation of this uncom-
prehended and terrible death, and now hope and an intently interested
observation of the functioning of his organs. Now before his eyes there was
only a kidney or an intestine that temporarily evaded its duty, and now
only that incomprehensible and dreadful death from which it was impossible to escape.

These two states of mind had alternated from the very beginning of his
illness, but the further it progressed the more doubtful and fantastic became the conception of the kidney, and the more real the sense of impend-
ing death.

He had but to call to mind what he had been three months before and   310
what he was now, to call to mind with what regularity he had been going
downhill, for every possibility of hope to be shattered.

Latterly during that loneliness in which he found himself as he lay
facing the back of the sofa, a loneliness in the midst of a populous town and
surrounded by numerous acquaintances and relations but that yet could
not have been more complete anywhere—either at the bottom of the sea or
under the earth—during that terrible loneliness Ivan Ilych had lived only
in memories of the past. Pictures of his past rose before him one after
another. They always began with what was nearest in time and then went
back to what was the most remote—to his childhood—and rested there. If

he thought of the stewed prunes that had been offered him that day, his mind went back to the raw shriveled French plums of his childhood, their peculiar flavor and the flow of saliva when he sucked their stones, and along with the memory of that taste came a whole series of memories of those days: his nurse, his brother, and their toys. "No, I mustn't think of that . . . It is too painful," Ivan Ilych said to himself, and brought himself back to the present—to the button on the back of the sofa and the creases in its morocco. "Morocco is expensive, but it does not wear well: there had been a quarrel about it. It was a different kind of quarrel and a different kind of morocco that time when we tore father's portfolio and were punished, and Mamma brought us some tarts . . ." And again his thoughts dwelt on his childhood, and again it was painful and he tried to banish them and fix his mind on something else.

Then again together with that chain of memories another series passed through his mind—of how his illness had progressed and grown worse. There also the further back he looked the more life there had been. There had been more of what was good in life and more of life itself. The two merged together. "Just as the pain went on getting worse and worse, so my life grew worse and worse," he thought. "There is one bright spot there at the back, at the beginning of life, and afterwards all becomes blacker and blacker and proceeds more and more rapidly—in inverse ratio to the square of the distance from death," thought Ivan Ilych. And the example of a stone falling downwards with increasing velocity entered his mind. Life, a series of increasing sufferings, flies further and further towards its end—the most terrible suffering. "I am flying . . ." He shuddered, shifted himself, and tried to resist, but was already aware that resistance was impossible, and again with eyes weary of gazing but unable to cease seeing what was before them, he stared at the back of the sofa and waited—awaiting that dreadful fall and shock and destruction.

"Resistance is impossible!" he said to himself. "If I could only understand what it is all for! But that too is impossible. An explanation would be possible if it could be said that I have not lived as I ought to. But it is impossible to say that," and he remembered all the legality, correctitude, and propriety of his life. "That at any rate can certainly not be admitted," he thought, and his lips smiled ironically as if someone could see that smile and be taken in by it. "There is no explanation! Agony, death . . . What for?"

11

Another two weeks went by in this way and during that fortnight an event occurred that Ivan Ilych and his wife had desired. Petrishchev formally proposed. It happened in the evening. The next day Praskovya Fëdorovna came into her husband's room considering how best to inform him of it, but that very night there had been a fresh change for the worse in his condition. She found him lying on the sofa but in a different position. He lay on his back, groaning and staring fixedly in front of him.

She began to remind him of his medicines, but he turned his eyes to- 315
ward her with such a look that she did not finish what she was saying; so great an animosity, to her in particular, did that look express.

"For Christ's sake let me die in peace!" he said.

She would have gone away, but just then their daughter came in and went up to say good morning. He looked at her as he had done at his wife, and in reply to her inquiry about his health said dryly that he would soon free them all of himself. They were both silent and after sitting with him for a while went away.

"Is it our fault?" Lisa said to her mother. "It's as if we were to blame! I am sorry for papa, but why should we be tortured?"

The doctor came at his usual time. Ivan Ilych answered "Yes" and "No," never taking his angry eyes from him, and at last said: "You know you can do nothing for me, so leave me alone."

"We can ease your sufferings."   320

"You can't even do that. Let me be."

The doctor went into the drawing-room and told Praskovya Fëdorovna that the case was very serious and that the only resource left was opium to allay her husband's sufferings, which must be terrible.

It was true, as the doctor said, that Ivan Ilych's physical sufferings were terrible, but worse than the physical sufferings were his mental sufferings, which were his chief torture.

His mental sufferings were due to the fact that that night, as he looked at Gerasim's sleepy, good-natured face with its prominent cheek-bones, the question suddenly occurred to him: "What if my whole life has really been wrong?"

It occurred to him that what had appeared perfectly impossible before,   325
namely that he had not spent his life as he should have done, might after all be true. It occurred to him that his scarcely perceptible attempts to struggle against what was considered good by the most highly placed people, those scarcely noticeable impulses which he had immediately suppressed, might have been the real thing, and all the rest false. And his professional duties and the whole arrangement of his life and of his family, and all his social and official interests, might all have been false. He tried to defend all those things to himself and suddenly felt the weakness of what he was defending. There was nothing to defend.

"But if that is so," he said to himself, "and I am leaving this life with the consciousness that I have lost all that was given me and it is impossible to rectify it—what then?"

He lay on his back and began to pass his life in review in quite a new way. In the morning when he saw first his footman, then his wife, then his daughter, and then the doctor, their every word and movement confirmed to him the awful truth that had been revealed to him during the night. In them he saw himself—all that for which he had lived—and saw clearly that it was not real at all, but a terrible and huge deception which had hidden both life and death. This consciousness intensified his physical suffering tenfold. He groaned and tossed about, and pulled at his clothing which choked and stifled him. And he hated them on that account.

He was given a large dose of opium and became unconscious, but at noon his sufferings began again. He drove everybody away and tossed from side to side.

His wife came to him and said:

330   "Jean, my dear, do this for me. It can't do any harm and often helps. Healthy people often do it."

He opened his eyes wide.

"What? Take communion? Why? It's unnecessary! However . . ."

She began to cry.

"Yes, do, my dear. I'll send for our priest. He is such a nice man."

335   "All right. Very well," he muttered.

When the priest came and heard his confession, Ivan Ilych was softened and seemed to feel a relief from his doubts and consequently from his sufferings, and for a moment there came a ray of hope. He again began to think of the vermiform appendix and the possibility of correcting it. He received the sacrament with tears in his eyes.

When they laid him down again afterwards he felt a moment's ease, and the hope that he might live awoke in him again. He began to think of the operation that had been suggested to him. "To live! I want to live!" he said to himself.

His wife came to congratulate him after his communion, and when uttering the usual conventional words she added:

"You feel better, don't you?"

340   Without looking at her he said "Yes."

Her dress, her figure, the expression of her face, the tone of her voice, all revealed the same thing. "This is wrong, it is not as it should be. All you have lived for and still live for is falsehood and deception, hiding life and death from you." And as soon as he admitted that thought, his hatred and his agonizing physical suffering again sprang up, and with that suffering a consciousness of the unavoidable, approaching end. And to this was added a new sensation of grinding shooting pain and a feeling of suffocation.

The expression of his face when he uttered that "yes" was dreadful. Having uttered it, he looked her straight in the eyes, turned on his face with a rapidity extraordinary in his weak state and shouted:

"Go away! Go away and leave me alone!"

12

From that moment the screaming began that continued for three days, and was so terrible that one could not hear it through two closed doors without horror. At the moment he answered his wife he realized that he was lost, that there was no return, that the end had come, the very end, and his doubts were still unsolved and remained doubts.

"Oh! Oh! Oh!" he cried in various intonations. He had begun by   345
screaming "I won't" and continued screaming on the letter *O*.

For three whole days, during which time did not exist for him, he struggled in that black sack into which he was being thrust by an invisible, resistless force. He struggled as a man condemned to death struggles in the hands of the executioner, knowing that he cannot save himself. And every moment he felt that despite all his efforts he was drawing nearer and nearer to what terrified him. He felt that his agony was due to his being thrust into that black hole and still more to his not being able to get right into it. He was hindered from getting into it by his conviction that his life had been a good one. That very justification of his life held him fast and prevented his moving forward, and it caused him most torment of all.

Suddenly some force struck him in the chest and side, making it still harder to breathe, and he fell through the hole and there at the bottom was a light. What had happened to him was like the sensation one sometimes experiences in a railway carriage when one thinks one is going backwards while one is really going forwards and suddenly becomes aware of the real direction.

"Yes, it was all not the right thing," he said to himself, "but that's no matter. It can be done. But what *is* the right thing?" he asked himself, and suddenly grew quiet.

This occurred at the end of the third day, two hours before his death. Just then his schoolboy son had crept softly in and gone up to the bedside. The dying man was still screaming and waving his arms. His hand fell on the boy's head, and the boy caught it, pressed it to his lips, and began to cry.

At that very moment Ivan Ilych fell through and caught sight of the   350
light, and it was revealed to him that though his life had not been what it should have been, this could still be rectified. He asked himself, "What *is* the right thing?" and grew still, listening. Then he felt that someone was kissing his hand. He opened his eyes, looked at his son, and felt sorry for him. His wife came up to him and he glanced at her. She was gazing at him open-mouthed with undried tears on her nose and cheek and a despairing look on her face. He felt sorry for her too.

"Yes, I am making them wretched," he thought. "They are sorry, but it will be better for them when I die." He wished to say this but had not the strength to utter it. "Besides, why speak? I must act," he thought. With a look at his wife he indicated his son and said: "Take him away . . . sorry for him . . . sorry for you too . . ." He tried to add, "forgive me," but said "forgo" and waved his hand, knowing that He whose understanding mattered would understand.

And suddenly it grew clear to him that what had been oppressing him and would not leave him was dropping away at once from two sides, from ten sides, and from all sides. He was sorry for them, he must act so as not to hurt them and free himself from these sufferings. "How good and how simple!" he thought. "And the pain?" he asked himself. "What had become of it? Where are you, pain?"

He turned his attention to it.

"Yes, here it is. Well, what of it? Let the pain be."

355   "And death . . . where is it?"

He sought his former accustomed fear of death and did not find it. "Where is it? What death?" There was no fear because there was no death.

In place of death there was light.

"So that's what it is!" he suddenly exclaimed aloud. "What joy!"

To him all this happened in a single instant, and the meaning of that instant did not change. For those present his agony continued for another two hours. Something rattled in his throat, his emaciated body twitched, then the gasping and rattle became less and less frequent.

360   "It is finished!" said someone near him.

He heard these words and repeated them in his soul.

"Death is finished," he said to himself. "It is no more!"

He drew in a breath, stopped in the midst of a sigh, stretched out, and died.

POETRY

———

The Elements
of Poetry

CHAPTER ONE

What Is Poetry?

Poetry is as universal as language and almost as ancient. The most primitive peoples have used it, and the most civilized have cultivated it. In all ages and in all countries, poetry has been written, and eagerly read or listened to, by all kinds and conditions of people—by soldiers, statesmen, lawyers, farmers, doctors, scientists, clergy, philosophers, kings, and queens. In all ages it has been especially the concern of the educated, the intelligent, and the sensitive, and it has appealed, in its simpler forms, to the uneducated and to children. Why? First, because it has given pleasure. People have read it, listened to it, or recited it because they liked it—because it gave them enjoyment. But this is not the whole answer. Poetry in all ages has been regarded as important, not simply as one of several alternative forms of amusement, as one person might choose bowling, another chess, and another poetry. Rather, it has been regarded as something central to existence, something having unique value to the fully realized life, something that we are better off for having and without which we are spiritually impoverished. To understand the reasons for this, we need to have at least a provisional understanding of what poetry is—provisional, because people have always been more successful at appreciating poetry than at defining it.

Initially, poetry might be defined as a kind of language that says *more* and says it *more intensely* than does ordinary language. To understand this fully, we need to understand what poetry "says." For language is employed on different occasions to say quite different kinds of things; in other words, language has different uses.

Perhaps the commonest use of language is to communicate *information*. We say that it is nine o'clock, that we liked a certain movie, that George Washington was the first president of the United States, that bromine and iodine are members of the halogen group of chemical elements. This we might call the *practical* use of language; it helps us with the ordinary business of living.

But it is not primarily to communicate information that novels, short stories, plays, and poems are written. These exist to bring us a sense and a perception of life, to widen and sharpen our contacts with existence. Their concern is with *experience*. We all have an inner need to live more deeply and fully and with greater awareness, to know the experience of others, and to understand our own experience better. Poets, from their own store of felt, observed, or imagined experiences, select, combine, and reorganize. They create significant new experiences for their readers—significant because focused and formed—in which readers can participate and from which they may gain a greater awareness and understanding of their world. Literature, in other words, can be used as a gear for stepping up the intensity and increasing the range of our experience and as a glass for clarifying it. This is the *literary* use of language, for literature is not only an aid to living but a means of living.*

Suppose, for instance, that we are interested in eagles. If we want simply to acquire information about eagles, we may turn to an encyclopedia or a book of natural history. There we find that the family Falconidae, to which eagles belong, is characterized by imperforate nostrils, legs of medium length, a hooked bill, the hind toe inserted on a level parallel to the three front ones, and the claws roundly curved and sharp; that land eagles are feathered fully to the toes and seafishing eagles halfway to the toes; that their length is about three feet and their wingspan seven feet; that they usually build their nests on some inaccessible cliff; that the eggs are spotted and do not exceed three; and perhaps that the eagle's "great power of vision, the vast height to which it soars in the sky, the wild grandeur of its abode, have . . . commended it to the poets of all nations."†

But unless we are interested in this information only for practical purposes, we are likely to feel a little disappointed, as though we had grasped the feathers of the eagle but not its soul. True, we have learned many facts about the eagle, but we have missed somehow its

---

*A third use of language is as an instrument of persuasion. This is the use we find in advertisements, propaganda bulletins, sermons, and political speeches. These three uses of language—the practical, the literary, and the hortatory—are not sharply divided. They may be thought of as three points of a triangle; most actual specimens of written language fall somewhere within the triangle. Most poetry conveys some information, and some poetry has a design on the reader. But language becomes literature when the desire to communicate experience predominates.

†*Encyclopedia Americana* IX (1955) 473–74.

lonely majesty, its power, and the "wild grandeur" of its surroundings that would make the eagle a living creature rather than a mere museum specimen. For the living eagle we must turn to literature.

1. The Eagle

> He clasps the crag with crooked hands;
> Close to the sun in lonely lands,
> Ringed with the azure world, he stands.
>
> The wrinkled sea beneath him crawls;
> He watches from his mountain walls,   5
> And like a thunderbolt he falls.

Alfred, Lord Tennyson (1809–1892)

QUESTIONS

1. What is peculiarly effective about the expressions "crooked hands," "Close to the sun," "Ringed with the azure world," "wrinkled," "crawls," and "like a thunderbolt"?
2. Notice the formal pattern of the poem, particularly the contrast of "he stands" in the first stanza and "he falls" in the second. Is there any other contrast between the two stanzas?

When "The Eagle" has been read well, readers will feel that they have enjoyed a significant experience and understand eagles better, though in a different way, than they did from the encyclopedia article alone. For while the article *analyzes* our experience of eagles, the poem in some sense *synthesizes* such an experience. Indeed, we may say the two approaches to experience—the scientific and the literary—complement each other. And we may contend that the kind of understanding we get from the second is at least as valuable as the kind we get from the first.

Literature, then, exists to communicate significant experience—significant because concentrated and organized. Its function is not to tell us *about* experience but to allow us imaginatively to *participate* in it. It is a means of allowing us, through the imagination, to live more fully, more deeply, more richly, and with greater awareness. It can do this in two ways: by *broadening* our experience—that is, by making us acquainted with a range of experience with which, in the ordinary course of events, we might have no contact—or by *deepening* our experience—that is, by making us feel more poignantly and more understandingly the everyday experiences all of us have. It enlarges our perspectives and breaks down some of the limits we may feel.

We can avoid two limiting approaches to poetry if we keep this conception of literature firmly in mind. The first approach always looks for a lesson or a bit of moral instruction. The second expects to find poetry always beautiful. Let us consider one of the songs from Shakespeare's *Love's Labor's Lost* (5.2).

2. Winter

When icicles hang by the wall,
And Dick the shepherd blows his nail,
And Tom bears logs into the hall,
And milk comes frozen home in pail,
When blood is nipped and ways be foul,   5
Then nightly sings the staring owl,
"Tu-whit, tu-who!"
    A merry note,
    While greasy Joan doth keel° the pot.   skim

When all aloud the wind doth blow,   10
And coughing drowns the parson's saw,
And birds sit brooding in the snow,
And Marian's nose looks red and raw,
When roasted crabs° hiss in the bowl,   crab apples
Then nightly sings the staring owl,   15
"Tu-whit, tu-who!"
    A merry note,
    While greasy Joan doth keel the pot.

William Shakespeare (1564–1616)

QUESTIONS

1. Vocabulary: *saw* (11), *brooding* (12).
2. Is the owl's cry really a "merry" note? How are this adjective and the verb "sings" employed?
3. In what way does the owl's cry contrast with the other details of the poem?

In this poem Shakespeare communicates the quality of winter life around a sixteenth-century English country house. But he does not do so by telling us flatly that winter in such surroundings is cold and in many respects unpleasant, though with some pleasant features too (the adjectives *cold, unpleasant,* and *pleasant* are not even used in the poem). Instead, he provides a series of concrete homely details that suggest these qualities and enable us, imaginatively, to experience this winter life ourselves. The shepherd blows on his fingernails to warm his hands; the milk freezes in the pail between the cowshed and the kitchen; the cook is slovenly and unclean, "greasy" either from spattered cooking fat or from her own sweat as she leans over the hot fire; the roads are muddy; the folk listening to the parson have colds; the birds "sit brooding in the snow"; and the servant girl's nose is raw from cold. But pleasant things are in prospect. Tom is bringing in logs for the fire, the hot cider or ale is ready for drinking, and the soup or stew will soon be ready. In contrast to all these familiar details of country life is the mournful and eerie note of the owl.

Obviously the poem contains no moral. If we limit ourselves to looking in poetry for some lesson, message, or noble truth about life, we are bound to be disappointed. This limited approach sees poetry as a kind of sugarcoated pill—a wholesome truth or lesson made palatable by being put into pretty words. What this narrow approach really wants is a sermon—not a poem, but something inspirational. Yet "Winter," which has appealed to readers for nearly four centuries, is not inspirational and contains no moral preachment.

Neither is the poem "Winter" beautiful. Though it is appealing in its way and contains elements of beauty, there is little that is really beautiful in red, raw noses, coughing in chapel, nipped blood, foul roads, and greasy cooks. Yet the second limiting approach may lead us to feel that poetry deals exclusively with beauty—with sunsets, flowers, butterflies, love, God—and that the one appropriate response to any poem is, after a moment of awed silence, "Isn't that beautiful!" But this narrow approach excludes a large proportion of poetry. The function of poetry is sometimes to be ugly rather than beautiful. And poetry may deal with common colds and greasy cooks as legitimately as with sunsets and flowers. Consider another example:

3. Dulce et Decorum Est

Bent double, like old beggars under sacks,
Knock-kneed, coughing like hags, we cursed through sludge,
Till on the haunting flares we turned our backs,

And towards our distant rest began to trudge.
Men marched asleep. Many had lost their boots,   5
But limped on, blood-shod. All went lame, all blind;
Drunk with fatigue; deaf even to the hoots
Of gas-shells dropping softly behind.

Gas! GAS! Quick, boys!—An ecstasy of fumbling,
Fitting the clumsy helmets just in time,   10
But someone still was yelling out and stumbling
And flound'ring like a man in fire or lime.—
Dim through the misty panes and thick green light,
As under a green sea, I saw him drowning.

In all my dreams before my helpless sight   15
He plunges at me, guttering, choking, drowning.

If in some smothering dreams, you too could pace
Behind the wagon that we flung him in,
And watch the white eyes writhing in his face,
His hanging face, like a devil's sick of sin,   20
If you could hear, at every jolt, the blood
Come gargling from the froth-corrupted lungs
Bitter as the cud
Of vile, incurable sores on innocent tongues,—
My friend, you would not tell with such high zest   25
To children ardent for some desperate glory,
The old lie: *Dulce et decorum est*
Pro patria mori.

Wilfred Owen (1893–1918)

QUESTIONS

1. The Latin quotation, from the Roman poet Horace, means "It is sweet
   and becoming to die for one's country." What is the poem's comment on
   this statement?
2. List the elements of the poem that seem not beautiful and therefore "un-
   poetic." Are there any elements of beauty in the poem?
3. How do the comparisons in lines 1, 14, 20, and 23–24 contribute to the
   effectiveness of the poem?
4. What does the poem gain by moving from plural pronouns and the past
   tense to singular pronouns and the present tense?

  Poetry takes all life as its province. Its primary concern is not with
beauty, not with philosophical truth, not with persuasion, but with experience. Beauty and philosophical truth are aspects of experience,

and the poet is often engaged with them. But poetry as a whole is concerned with all kinds of experience—beautiful or ugly, strange or common, noble or ignoble, actual or imaginary. One of the paradoxes of human existence is that all experience—even painful experience—can be enjoyable when transmitted through the medium of art. In real life, death and pain and suffering are not pleasurable, but in poetry they may be. In real life, getting soaked in a rainstorm is not pleasurable, but in poetry it can be. In actual life, if we cry, usually we are unhappy; but if we cry in a movie, we are manifestly enjoying it. We do not ordinarily like to be terrified in real life, but we sometimes seek movies or books that will terrify us. We find some value in all intense living. To be intensely alive is the opposite of being dead. To be dull, to be bored, to be imperceptive is in one sense to be dead. Poetry comes to us bringing life and therefore pleasure. Moreover, art focuses and organizes experience so as to give us a better understanding of it. And to understand life is partly to be master of it.

There is no sharp distinction between poetry and other forms of imaginative literature. Although some beginning readers may believe that poetry can be recognized by the arrangement of its lines on the page or by its use of rime and meter, such superficial signs are of little worth. The Book of Job in the Bible and Melville's *Moby Dick* are highly poetical, but the familiar verse that begins: "Thirty days hath September, / April, June, and November . . ." is not. The difference between poetry and other literature is only one of degree. Poetry is the most condensed and concentrated form of literature. It is language whose individual lines, either because of their own brilliance or because they focus so powerfully on what has gone before, have a higher voltage than most language. It is language that grows frequently incandescent, giving off both light and heat.

Ultimately, therefore, poetry can be recognized only by the response made to it by a practiced reader, someone who has acquired some sensitivity to poetry. But there is a catch here. We are not all equally experienced readers. To some readers, poetry may often seem dull and boring, a fancy way of writing something that could be said more simply. So might a color-blind person deny that there is such a thing as color.

The act of communication involved in reading poetry is like the act of communication involved in receiving a message by radio. Two devices are required: a transmitting station and a receiving set. The completeness of the communication depends on both the power and clarity of the transmitter and the sensitivity and tuning of the receiver.

When a person reads a poem and no experience is received, either the poem is not a good poem or the reader is not properly tuned. With new poetry, we cannot always be sure which is at fault. With older poetry, if it has acquired critical acceptance—has been enjoyed by generations of good readers—we may assume that the receiving set is at fault. Fortunately, the fault is not irremediable. Though we cannot all become expert readers, we can become good enough to find both pleasure and value in much good poetry, or we can increase the amount of pleasure we already find in poetry and the number of kinds of poetry in which we find it. The purpose of this book is to help you increase your sensitivity and range as a receiving set.

Poetry, finally, is a kind of multidimensional language. Ordinary language—the kind that we use to communicate information—is one-dimensional. It is directed at only part of the listener, the understanding. Its one dimension is intellectual. Poetry, which is language used to communicate experience, has at least four dimensions. If it is to communicate experience, it must be directed at the *whole* person, not just at your understanding. It must involve not only your intelligence but also your senses, emotions, and imagination. To the intellectual dimension, poetry adds a sensuous dimension, an emotional dimension, and an imaginative dimension.

Poetry achieves its extra dimensions—its greater pressure per word and its greater tension per poem—by drawing more fully and more consistently than does ordinary language on a number of language resources, none of which is peculiar to poetry. These various resources form the subjects of a number of the following chapters. Among them are connotation, imagery, metaphor, symbol, paradox, irony, allusion, sound repetition, rhythm, and pattern. Using these resources and the materials of life, the poet shapes and makes a poem. Successful poetry is never effusive language. If it is to come alive it must be as cunningly put together and as efficiently organized as a tree. It must be an organism whose every part serves a useful purpose and cooperates with every other part to preserve and express the life that is within it.

---

4. Spring

> When daisies pied and violets blue,
>   And lady-smocks all silver-white,
> And cuckoo-buds of yellow hue

Do paint the meadows with delight,
The cuckoo then, on every tree,   5
Mocks married men; for thus sings he,
        "Cuckoo!
Cuckoo, cuckoo!" O word of fear,
Unpleasing to a married ear!

When shepherds pipe on oaten straws,   10
    And merry larks are plowmen's clocks,
When turtles tread, and rooks, and daws,
    And maidens bleach their summer smocks,
The cuckoo then, on every tree,
Mocks married men; for thus sings he,   15
        "Cuckoo!
Cuckoo, cuckoo!" O word of fear,
Unpleasing to a married ear!

William Shakespeare (1564–1616)

QUESTIONS

1. Vocabulary: *pied* (1), *lady-smocks* (2), *oaten straws* (10), *turtles* (12), *tread* (12), *rooks* (12), *daws* (12).
2. This song is a companion piece to "Winter." In what respects are the two poems similar? How do they contrast? What details show that this poem, like "Winter," was written by a realist, not simply by a man carried away with the beauty of spring?
3. The word "cuckoo" is "unpleasing to a married ear" because it sounds like *cuckold*. Cuckolds were a frequent butt of humor in earlier English literature. If you do not know the meaning of the word, look it up. How does this information help to shape the tone of the poem? Is it solemn? Light and semihumorous?

5. The Whipping

The old woman across the way
    is whipping the boy again
and shouting to the neighborhood
    her goodness and his wrongs.

Wildly he crashes through elephant-ears,   5
    pleads in dusty zinnias,
while she in spite of crippling fat
    pursues and corners him.

She strikes and strikes the shrilly circling
    boy till the stick breaks   10

in her hand. His tears are rainy weather
to woundlike memories:

My head gripped in bony vise
  of knees, the writing struggle
to wrench free, the blows, the fear   15
  worse than blows that hateful

Words could bring, the face that I
  no longer knew or loved . . .
Well, it is over now, it is over,
  and the boy sobs in his room,   20

And the woman leans muttering against
  a tree, exhausted, purged—
avenged in part for lifelong hidings
  she has had to bear.

                Robert Hayden (1913–1980)

QUESTIONS

1. What similarities connect the old woman, the boy, and the speaker? Can
   you say that one of them is the main subject of the poem?
2. Does this poem express any beauty? What human truth does it embody?
   Could you argue against the claim that "it is over now, it is over" (19)?

6. The Computation

For the first twenty years since yesterday
  I scarce believed thou couldst be gone away;
For forty more I fed on favors past,
  And forty on hopes that thou wouldst they might last.
Tears drowned one hundred, and sighs blew out two;   5
  A thousand, I did neither think nor do,
Or not divide, all being one thought of you.
  Or, in a thousand more, forgot that too.
Yet call not this long life; but think that I
  Am, by being dead, immortal. Can ghosts die?   10

                John Donne (1572–1631)

QUESTIONS

1. Who is the "I" of the poem? Who is the "thou" or "you"? How long have
   they been separated—literally? Figuratively?

2. Are the numbers in this "mathematical" poem used vaguely or precisely? What reasons can you find for their choice and arrangement?
3. Explain how, in the last two lines, the speaker undermines the series of overstatements just completed with another equally hyperbolic claim. Is he really dead? Of what did he "die"?

7. Hawk Roosting

I sit in the top of the wood, my eyes closed.
Inaction, no falsifying dream
Between my hooked head and hooked feet:
Or in sleep rehearse perfect kills and eat.

The convenience of the high trees!   5
The air's buoyancy and the sun's ray
Are of advantage to me;
And the earth's face upward for my inspection.

My feet are locked upon the rough bark.
It took the whole of Creation   10
To produce my foot, my each feather:
Now I hold Creation in my foot

Or fly up, and revolve it all slowly—
I kill where I please because it is all mine.
There is no sophistry in my body: 15
My manners are tearing off heads—

The allotment of death.
For the one path of my flight is direct
Through the bones of the living.
No arguments assert my right: 20

The sun is behind me.
Nothing has changed since I began.
My eye has permitted no change.
I am going to keep things like this.

Ted Hughes (b. 1930)

QUESTIONS

1. Vocabulary: *sophistry* (15).
2. Who is the speaker of this poem? Characterize his "personality." What do his errors in summing up his situation contribute to your characterization?
3. What are the similarities and differences between this poem and "The Eagle" (No. 1)?

8. Ballad of Birmingham

(On the bombing of a church in Birmingham, Alabama, 1963)

"Mother dear, may I go downtown
Instead of out to play,
And march the streets of Birmingham
In a Freedom March today?"

"No, baby, no, you may not go,   5
For the dogs are fierce and wild,
And clubs and hoses, guns and jails
Aren't good for a little child."

"But, mother, I won't be alone.
Other children will go with me,   10
And march the streets of Birmingham
To make our country free."

"No, baby, no, you may not go,
For I fear those guns will fire.
But you may go to church instead   15
And sing in the children's choir."

She has combed and brushed her night-dark hair,
And bathed rose petal sweet,
And drawn white gloves on her small brown hands,
And white shoes on her feet.   20

The mother smiled to know her child
Was in the sacred place,
But that smile was the last smile
To come upon her face.

For when she heard the explosion,   25
Her eyes grew wet and wild.
She raced through the streets of Birmingham
Calling for her child.

She clawed through bits of glass and brick,
Then lifted out a shoe.   30
"O, here's the shoe my baby wore,
But, baby, where are you?"

Dudley Randall (b. 1914)

QUESTIONS

1. This poem is based on a historical incident. Throughout 1963, Birmingham, Alabama, was the site of demonstrations and marches protesting the

racial segregation of schools and other public facilities. Although they were intended as peaceful protests, these demonstrations often erupted in violence as police attempted to disperse them with fire hoses and police dogs. On the morning of September 15, 1963, a bomb exploded during Sunday School at the 16th Street Baptist Church. Four children were killed and 14 were injured. How does the poem differ from what you would expect to find in a newspaper account of such an incident? In an encyclopedia entry? In a speech calling for the elimination of racial injustice?

2. What do the details in the fifth stanza (17–20) contribute to the effect of the poem? Is "She" (17) the mother or the child?

3. What characteristics does this poem share with "Edward" (No. 180), which is a traditional folk ballad? Why do you think this twentieth-century poet chose to write in a form that alludes to that tradition?

4. What purpose does the poem have beyond simply telling a story? How does the irony help achieve that purpose?

9. The Red Wheelbarrow

so much depends
upon

a red wheel
barrow

glazed with rain   5
water

beside the white
chickens.

William Carlos Williams (1883–1963)

QUESTIONS

1. The speaker asserts that "so much depends upon" the objects he refers to, leading the reader to ask: *How much and why?* This glimpse of a farm scene implies one kind of answer. What is the importance of the wheelbarrow, rain, and chicken to a farmer? To all of us?

2. What further importance can you infer from the references to color, shape, texture, and the juxtaposition of objects? Does the poem itself have a shape? What two ways of observing and valuing the world does the poem imply?

10. The Pasture

I'm going out to clean the pasture spring;
I'll only stop to rake the leaves away
(And wait to watch the water clear, I may):
I shan't be gone long. —You come too.

I'm going out to fetch the little calf   5
That's standing by the mother. It's so young
It totters when she licks it with her tongue.
I shan't be gone long. —You come too.

Robert Frost (1874–1963)

QUESTIONS

1. Who and what kind of person is the speaker? Who is addressed?
2. Frost characteristically strove to capture the speech rhythms and language of the speaking voice in poems retaining a metrical form. In what lines is he particularly successful at this?
3. Originally the initial poem in Frost's second volume of verse, "The Pasture" was subsequently placed as the initial poem in his collections of his verse. What additional meaning does the poem acquire from this positioning?

11. Terence, this is stupid stuff*

"Terence, this is stupid stuff:
You eat your victuals fast enough;
There can't be much amiss, 'tis clear,
To see the rate you drink your beer.
But oh, good Lord, the verse you make,   5
It gives a chap the belly-ache.
The cow, the old cow, she is dead;
It sleeps well, the horned head:
We poor lads, 'tis our turn now
To hear such tunes as killed the cow.   10
Pretty friendship 'tis to rhyme
Your friends to death before their time
Moping melancholy mad:
Come, pipe a tune to dance to, lad."

Why, if 'tis dancing you would be,   15
There's brisker pipes than poetry.
Say, for what were hop-yards meant,
Or why was Burton built on Trent?
Oh many a peer of England brews
Livelier liquor than the Muse,   20

---

*Whenever a heading duplicates the first line of the poem or a substantial portion thereof, with only the first word capitalized, it is probable that the poet left the poem untitled and that the anthologist has substituted the first line or part of it as an editorial convenience. Such a heading is not referred to as the title of the poem.

And malt does more than Milton can
To justify God's ways to man.
Ale, man, ale's the stuff to drink
For fellows whom it hurts to think:
Look into the pewter pot   25
To see the world as the world's not.
And faith, 'tis pleasant till 'tis past:
The mischief is that 'twill not last.
Oh I have been to Ludlow fair
And left my necktie God knows where,   30
And carried half-way home, or near,
Pints and quarts of Ludlow beer:
Then the world seemed none so bad,
And I myself a sterling lad;
And down in lovely muck I've lain,   35
Happy till I woke again.
Then I saw the morning sky:
Heigho, the tale was all a lie;
The world, it was the old world yet,
I was I, my things were wet,   40
And nothing now remained to do
But begin the game anew.

   Therefore, since the world has still
Much good, but much less good than ill,
And while the sun and moon endure   45
Luck's a chance, but trouble's sure,
I'd face it as a wise man would,
And train for ill and not for good.
'Tis true, the stuff I bring for sale
Is not so brisk a brew as ale: 50
Out of a stem that scored the hand
I wrung it in a weary land.
But take it: if the smack is sour,
The better for the embittered hour;
It should do good to heart and head   55
When your soul is in my soul's stead;
And I will friend you, if I may,
In the dark and cloudy day.

   There was a king reigned in the East:
There, when kings will sit to feast,   60
They get their fill before they think
With poisoned meat and poisoned drink.
He gathered all that springs to birth
From the many-venomed earth;

First a little, thence to more,   65
He sampled all her killing store;
And easy, smiling, seasoned sound,
Sate the king when healths went round.
They put arsenic in his meat
And stared aghast to watch him eat;   70
They poured strychnine in his cup
And shook to see him drink it up:
They shook, they stared as white's their shirt:
Them it was their poison hurt.
—I tell the tale that I heard told.   75
Mithridates, he died old.

A. E. Housman (1859–1936)

QUESTIONS

1. The poem opens with the speaker quoting another person whose remarks he then refutes. What is the relationship between the two? Of what has the other person been complaining? What request has he made of the speaker?
2. Hops (17) and "malt" (21) are principal ingredients of beer and ale. Burton-upon-Trent (18) is an English city famous for its breweries. Milton (21), in the invocation of his epic poem *Paradise Lost,* declares that his purpose is to "justify the ways of God to men." What, in Terence's eyes, is the efficacy of liquor in helping one live a difficult life? What is the "stuff" *he* brings "for sale" (49)?
3. "Mithridates" (76) was a king of Pontus and a contemporary of Julius Caesar; his "tale" is told in Pliny's *Natural History.* The poem is structured by its line spacing into four verse paragraphs. What is the connection of this last verse paragraph with the rest of the poem? What is the function of each of the other three?
4. Essentially, Terence assesses the value of three possible aids for worthwhile living. What are they? Which does Terence consider the best? What six lines of the poem best sum up his philosophy?
5. This poem is the second last in Housman's book *A Shropshire Lad.* The last poem also concerns poetry and its place in the world. May we consider Terence in this poem a surrogate for Housman?
6. Many people like reading material that is cheerful and optimistic; they argue that "there's enough suffering and unhappiness in the world already." What, for Housman, is the value of pessimistic and tragic literature?

12. Ars Poetica

A poem should be palpable and mute
As a globed fruit,

Dumb
As old medallions to the thumb,

Silent as the sleeve-worn stone   5
Of casement ledges where the moss has grown—

A poem should be wordless
As the flight of birds.

                              *

A poem should be motionless in time
As the moon climbs,   10

Leaving, as the moon releases
Twig by twig the night-entangled trees,

Leaving, as the moon behind the winter leaves,
Memory by memory the mind—

A poem should be motionless in time   15
As the moon climbs.

                              *

A poem should be equal to:
Not true.

For all the history of grief
An empty doorway and a maple leaf.   20

For love
The leaning grasses and two lights above the sea—

A poem should not mean
But be.

Archibald MacLeish (1892–1982)

QUESTIONS

1. How can a poem be "wordless" (7)? How can it be "motionless in time" (15)?
2. The Latin title, literally translated "The Art of Poetry," is a traditional title for works on the philosophy of poetry. What is *this* poet's philosophy of poetry? What does he mean by saying that a poem should not "mean" (23) and should not be "true" (18)?

CHAPTER TWO

Reading the Poem

The primary purpose of this book is to develop your ability to understand and appreciate poetry. Here are some preliminary suggestions:

1. Read a poem more than once. A good poem will no more yield its full meaning on a single reading than will a Beethoven symphony on a single hearing. Two readings may be necessary simply to let you get your bearings. And if the poem is a work of art, it will repay repeated and prolonged examination. One does not listen to a good piece of music once and forget it; one does not look at a good painting once and throw it away. A poem is not like a newspaper, to be hastily read and cast into the wastebasket. It is to be hung on the wall of one's mind.

2. Keep a dictionary by you and use it. It is futile to try to understand poetry without troubling to learn the meanings of the words of which it is composed. You might as well attempt to play tennis without a ball. One of your primary purposes while in college should be to build a good vocabulary, and the study of poetry gives you an excellent opportunity. A few other reference books also will be invaluable. Particularly desirable are a good book on mythology (your instructor can recommend one) and a Bible.

3. Read so as to hear the sounds of the words in your mind. Poetry is written to be heard: its meanings are conveyed through sound as well as through print. Every word is therefore important. The best way to read a poem is just the opposite of the best way to read a newspaper. One reads a newspaper as rapidly as possible; one should read a poem as slowly as possible. When you cannot read a poem aloud, lip-read it: form the words with your tongue and mouth even though you do not utter them. With ordinary reading material, lip-reading is a bad habit; with poetry, it is a good habit.

4. Always pay careful attention to what the poem is saying. Though you should be conscious of the sounds of the poem, you should never be so exclusively conscious of them that you pay no

attention to what the poem means. For some readers, reading a poem is like getting on board a rhythmical roller coaster. The car starts, and off they go, up and down, paying no attention to the landscape flashing past them, arriving at the end of the poem breathless, with no idea of what it has been about.* This is the wrong way to read a poem. One should make the utmost effort to follow the thought continuously and to grasp the full implications and suggestions. Because a poem says so much, several readings may be necessary, but on the very first reading you should determine the subjects of the verbs, the antecedents of the pronouns, and other normal grammatical facts.

5. Practice reading poems aloud. When you find one you especially like, make friends listen to it. Try to read it to them in such a way that they will like it too. (a) Read it affectionately, but not affectedly. The two extremes oral readers often fall into are equally deadly. One is to read as if one were reading a tax report or a railroad timetable, unexpressively, in a monotone. The other is to elocute, with artificial flourishes and vocal histrionics. It is not necessary to put emotion into reading a poem. The emotion is already there. It only wants a fair chance to get out. It will express *itself* if the poem is read naturally and sensitively. (b) Of the two extremes, reading too fast offers greater danger than reading too slow. Read slowly enough that each word is clear and distinct and that the meaning has time to sink in. Remember that your friends do not have the advantage, as you do, of having the text before them. Your ordinary rate of reading will probably be too fast. (c) Read the poem so that the rhythmical pattern is felt but not exaggerated. Remember that poetry, with few exceptions, is written in sentences, just as prose is, and that punctuation is a signal as to how it should be read. Give all grammatical pauses their full due. Do not distort the natural pronunciation of words or a normal accentuation of the sentence to fit into what you have decided is its metrical pattern. One of the worst ways to read a poem is to read it ta-DUM ta-DUM ta-DUM with an exaggerated emphasis on every other syllable. On the other hand, it should not be read as if it were prose. An important test of your reading will be how you handle the end of a line that lacks line-ending punctuation. A frequent mistake of the beginning reader is to treat each line as if it were a complete thought, whether grammatically complete or not, and to drop the voice at the end of it. A frequent mistake of the sophisticated reader is to take a running start upon approaching the end of a line and fly over

---

*Some poems encourage this type of reading. When this is so, usually the poet has not made the best use of rhythm to support sense.

it as if it were not there. The line is a rhythmical unit, and its end should be observed whether there is punctuation or not. If there is no punctuation, you ordinarily should observe the end of the line by the slightest of pauses or by holding on to the last word in the line just a little longer than usual, without dropping your voice. In line 12 of the following poem, you should hold on to the word "although" longer than if it occurred elsewhere in the line. But do not lower your voice on it: it is part of the clause that follows in the next stanza.

13. The Man He Killed

Had he and I but met
By some old ancient inn,
We should have sat us down to wet
Right many a nipperkin!°   half-pint cup

But ranged as infantry,   5
And staring face to face,
I shot at him as he at me,
And killed him in his place.

I shot him dead because—
Because he was my foe,   10
Just so: my foe of course he was;
That's clear enough; although

He thought he'd 'list, perhaps,
Off-hand-like—just as I—
Was out of work—had sold his traps—°   belongings 15
No other reason why.

Yes; quaint and curious war is!
You shoot a fellow down
You'd treat, if met where any bar is,
Or help to half-a-crown.   20

Thomas Hardy (1840–1928)

QUESTIONS

1. Vocabulary: *half-a-crown* (20).
2. In informational prose the repetition of a word like "because" (9–10) would be an error. What purpose does the repetition serve here? Why does the speaker repeat to himself his "clear" reason for killing a man (10–11)? The word "although" (12) gets more emphasis than it would ordinarily because it comes not only at the end of a line but at the end of

a stanza. What purpose does this emphasis serve? Can the redundancy of "old ancient" (2) be poetically justified?
3. Poetry has been defined as "the expression of elevated thought in elevated language." Comment on the adequacy of this definition in the light of Hardy's poem.

One starting point for understanding a poem at the simplest level, and for clearing up misunderstanding, is to paraphrase its content or part of its content. To **paraphrase** a poem means to restate it in different language, so as to make its prose sense as plain as possible. The paraphrase may be longer or shorter than the poem, but it should contain all the ideas in the poem in such a way as to make them clear to a puzzled reader, and to make the central idea, or **theme,** of the poem more accessible.

14. A Study of Reading Habits

When getting my nose in a book
Cured most things short of school,
It was worth ruining my eyes
To know I could still keep cool,
And deal out the old right hook   5
To dirty dogs twice my size.

Later, with inch-thick specs,
Evil was just my lark:
Me and my cloak and fangs
Had ripping times in the dark.   10
The women I clubbed with sex!
I broke them up like meringues.

Don't read much now: the dude
Who lets the girl down before
The hero arrives, the chap   15
Who's yellow and keeps the store,
Seem far too familiar. Get stewed:
Books are a load of crap.

Philip Larkin (1922–1985)

QUESTIONS

1. The three stanzas delineate three stages in the speaker's life. Describe each.
2. What kind of person is the speaker? What kinds of books does he read? May we identify him with the poet?

3. Contrast the speaker's advice in stanza 3 with Terence's counsel in "Terence, this is stupid stuff" (No. 11). Are A. E. Housman and Philip Larkin at odds in their attitudes toward drinking and reading? Discuss.

Larkin's poem may be paraphrased as follows:

There was a time when reading was one way I could avoid almost all my troubles—except for school. It seemed worth the danger of ruining my eyes to read stories in which I could imagine myself maintaining my poise in the face of threats and having the boxing skill and experience needed to defeat bullies who were twice as big as I.

Later, already having to wear thick glasses because my eyesight had become so poor, I found my delight in stories of sex and evil: imagining myself with Dracula cloak and fangs, I relished vicious nocturnal adventures. I fancied myself a rapist who beat and tortured his delectable, vulnerable victims, leaving them broken and destroyed!

I don't read much any more because now I can identify myself only with the flawed secondary characters, such as the flashy dresser who wins the heroine's confidence and then betrays her in a moment of crisis before the cowboy hero comes to her rescue, or the cowardly storekeeper who cringes behind the counter at the first sign of danger. Getting drunk is better than reading—books are just full of useless lies.

Notice that in a paraphrase, figurative language gives way to literal language; similes replace metaphors and normal word order supplants inverted syntax. But a paraphrase retains the speaker's use of first, second, and third person, and the tenses of verbs. Though it is neither necessary nor possible to avoid using some of the words found in the original, a paraphrase should strive for plain, direct diction. And since a paraphrase is prose, it does not maintain the length and position of poetic lines.

A paraphrase is useful only if you understand that it is the barest, most inadequate approximation of what the poem really "says" and is no more equivalent to the poem than a corpse is to a person. After you have paraphrased a poem, you should endeavor to see how far short of the poem it falls, and why. In what respects does Larkin's poem say more, and say it more memorably, than the paraphrase?

Does the phrase "full of useless lies" capture the impact of "a load of crap"? Furthermore, a paraphrase may fall far short of revealing the theme of a poem. "A Study of Reading Habits" represents a man summing up his reading experience and evaluating it—but in turn the poem itself evaluates *him* and his defects. A statement of the theme of the poem might be this: A person who turns to books as a source of self-gratifying fantasies may, in the course of time, discover that escapist reading no longer protects him from his awareness of his own reality, and he may out of habit have to find other, more potent, and perhaps more self-destructive means of escaping.

To aid us in the understanding of a poem, we may ask ourselves a number of questions about it. Two of the most important are *Who is the speaker?* and *What is the occasion?* A cardinal error of some readers is to assume that a speaker who uses the first person pronouns (*I, my, mine, me*) is always the poet. A less risky course would be to assume always that the speaker is someone other than the poet. Poems, like short stories, novels, and plays, belong to the world of fiction, an imaginatively conceived world that at its best is "truer" than the factually "real" world that it reflects. When poets put themselves or their thoughts into a poem, they present a *version* of themselves; that is, they present a person who in many ways is *like* themselves but who, consciously or unconsciously, is shaped to fit the needs of the poem. We must be very careful, therefore, about identifying anything in a poem with the biography of the poet.

However, caution is not prohibition. Sometimes events or ideas in a poem will help us to understand some episodes in the poet's life. More importantly for us, knowledge of the poet's life may help us understand a poem. There can be little doubt, when all the evidence is in, that "Terence, this is stupid stuff" (No. 11) is Housman's defense of the kind of poetry he writes, and that the six lines in which Terence sums up his beliefs about life and the function of poetry closely echo Housman's own beliefs. On the other hand, it would be folly to suppose that Housman ever got drunk at "Ludlow fair" and once lay down in "lovely muck" and slept all night in a roadside ditch.

We may well think of every poem, therefore, as being to some degree *dramatic*—that is, the utterance not of the person who wrote the poem but of a fictional character in a particular situation that may be inferred. Many poems are expressly dramatic. The fact that Philip Larkin was a poet and novelist, and for many years the chief administrator of a university library, underscores the wide gap between the author and speaker of "A Study of Reading Habits."

In "The Man He Killed" the speaker is a soldier; the occasion is his having been in battle and killed a man—obviously for the first time in his life. We can tell a good deal about him. He is not a career soldier: he enlisted only because he was out of work. He is a working-man: he speaks a simple and colloquial language ("nipperkin," " 'list," "off-hand-like," "traps"). He is a friendly, kindly sort who enjoys a neighborly drink of ale in a bar and will gladly lend a friend a half crown when he has it. He has known what it is to be poor. In any other circumstances he would have been horrified at taking a human life. It gives him pause even now. He is trying to figure it out. But he is not a deep thinker and thinks he has supplied a reason when he has only supplied a name: "I killed the man . . . because he was my foe." The critical question, of course, is *why* was the man his "foe"? Even the speaker is left unsatisfied by his answer, though he is not analytical enough to know what is wrong with it. Obviously this poem is expressly dramatic. We need know nothing about Thomas Hardy's life (he was never a soldier and never killed a man) to realize that the poem is dramatic. The internal evidence of the poem tells us so.

A third important question that we should ask ourselves upon reading any poem is *What is the central purpose of the poem?** The purpose may be to tell a story, to reveal human character, to impart a vivid impression of a scene, to express a mood or an emotion, or to convey vividly some idea or attitude. Whatever the purpose is, we must determine it for ourselves and define it mentally as precisely as possible. Only by relating the various details in the poem to the central purpose or theme can we fully understand their function and meaning. Only then can we begin to assess the value of the poem and determine whether it is a good one or a poor one. In "The Man He Killed" the central purpose is quite clear: it is to make us realize more keenly the irrationality of war. The puzzlement of the speaker may be our puzzlement. But even if we are able to give a more sophisticated answer than his as to why men kill each other, we ought still to have a greater awareness, after reading the poem, of the fundamental irrationality in war that makes men kill who have no grudge against each other and who might under different circumstances show each other considerable kindness.

---

*Our only reliable evidence of the poem's purpose, of course, is the poem itself. External evidence, when it exists, though often helpful, may also be misleading. Some critics have objected to the use of such terms as "purpose" and "intention" altogether; we cannot know, they maintain, what was *attempted* in the poem; we can know only what was *done*. We are concerned, however, not with the *poet's* purpose, but with the *poem's* purpose; that is, with the theme (if it has one), and this is determinable from the poem itself.

15. Is my team plowing

"Is my team plowing,
   That I was used to drive
And hear the harness jingle
   When I was man alive?"

Aye, the horses trample,   5
   The harness jingles now;
No change though you lie under
   The land you used to plow.

"Is football playing
   Along the river shore,   10
With lads to chase the leather,
   Now I stand up no more?"

Aye, the ball is flying,
   The lads play heart and soul;
The goal stands up, the keeper   15
   Stands up to keep the goal.

"Is my girl happy,
   That I thought hard to leave,
And has she tired of weeping
   As she lies down at eve?"   20

Aye, she lies down lightly,
   She lies not down to weep:
Your girl is well contented.
   Be still, my lad, and sleep.

"Is my friend hearty,   25
   Now I am thin and pine;
And has he found to sleep in
   A better bed than mine?"

Yes, lad, I lie easy,
   I lie as lads would choose;   30
I cheer a dead man's sweetheart,
   Never ask me whose.

A. E. Housman (1859–1936)

QUESTIONS

1. What is meant by "whose" in line 32?
2. Is Housman cynical in his observation of human nature and human life?

3. The word *sleep* in the concluding stanzas suggests three different meanings. What are they? How many meanings are suggested by the word *bed*?

Once we have answered the question *What is the central purpose of
the poem?* we can consider another question, equally important to full
understanding: *By what means is that purpose achieved?* It is important
to distinguish means from ends. A student on an examination once
used the poem "Is my team plowing" as evidence that A. E. Housman
believed in immortality because in it a man speaks from the grave.
This is as much a misconstruction as to say that Thomas Hardy in
"The Man He Killed" joined the army because he was out of work.
The purpose of Housman's poem is to communicate poignantly a
certain truth about human life: Life goes on after our deaths pretty
much as it did before—our dying does not disturb the universe. Further, it dramatizes that irrational sense of betrayal and guilt that may
follow the death of a friend. The poem achieves this purpose by means
of a fanciful dramatic framework in which a dead man converses with
his still-living friend. The framework tells us nothing about whether
Housman believed in immortality (as a matter of fact, he did not). It
is simply an effective means by which we *can* learn how Housman felt
a man's death affected the life he left behind. The question *By what
means is that purpose achieved?* is partially answered by describing the
poem's dramatic framework, if it has any. The complete answer requires an accounting of various resources of communication that we
will discuss in this book.

The most important preliminary advice we can give for reading
poetry is to maintain always, while reading it, the utmost mental alertness. The most harmful idea one can get about poetry is that its purpose is to soothe and relax and that the best place to read it is lying in
a hammock with a cool drink while low music plays in the background. You *can* read poetry lying in a hammock, but only if you
refuse to put your mind in the same attitude as your body. Its purpose
is not to soothe and relax but to arouse and awake, to shock us into
life, to make us more alive. Poetry is not a substitute for a sedative.

An analogy can be drawn between reading poetry and playing
tennis. Both offer great enjoyment if the game is played hard. Good
tennis players must be constantly on the tips of their toes, concentrating on their opponent's every move. They must be ready for a drive to
the right or left, a lob overhead, or a drop shot barely over the net.
They must be ready for topspin or underspin, a ball that bounces
crazily to the left or right. They must jump for the high ones and run

for the long ones. And they will enjoy the game almost exactly in proportion to the effort they put into it. The same is true of reading poetry. Great enjoyment is there, but this enjoyment demands a mental effort equivalent to the physical effort one puts into tennis.

The reader of poetry has one advantage over the tennis player: poets are not trying to win matches. They may expect the reader to stretch for their shots, but they *want* the reader to return them.

GENERAL EXERCISES FOR ANALYSIS AND EVALUATION OF POETRY

Most of the poems in this book are accompanied by study questions that are by no means exhaustive. The following is a list of questions that you may apply to any poem. You may be unable to answer many of them until you have read further into the book.

1. Who is the speaker? What kind of person is the speaker?
2. Is there an identifiable audience for the speaker? What can we know about it (her, him, or them)?
3. What is the occasion?
4. What is the setting in time (hour, season, century, and so on)?
5. What is the setting in place (indoors or out, city or country, land or sea, region, nation, hemisphere)?
6. What is the central purpose of the poem?
7. State the central idea or theme of the poem in a sentence.
8. a. Outline the poem so as to show its structure and development, or
   b. Summarize the events of the poem.
9. Paraphrase the poem.
10. Discuss the diction of the poem. Point out words that are particularly well chosen and explain why.
11. Discuss the imagery of the poem. What kinds of imagery are used? Is there a structure of imagery?
12. Point out examples of metaphor, simile, personification, and metonymy, and explain their appropriateness.
13. Point out and explain any symbols. If the poem is allegorical, explain the allegory.
14. Point out and explain examples of paradox, overstatement, understatement, and irony. What is their function?
15. Point out and explain any allusions. What is their function?
16. What is the tone of the poem? How is it achieved?
17. Point out significant examples of sound repetition and explain their function.
18. a. What is the meter of the poem?
    b. Copy the poem and mark its scansion.
19. Discuss the adaptation of sound to sense.
20. Describe the form or pattern of the poem.
21. Criticize and evaluate the poem.

16. Break of Day

'Tis true, 'tis day; what though it be?
Oh, wilt thou therefore rise from me?
Why should we rise because 'tis light?
Did we lie down because 'twas night?
Love which in spite of darkness brought us hither   5
Should, in despite of light, keep us together.

Light hath no tongue, but is all eye;
If it could speak as well as spy,
This were the worst that it could say:
That, being well, I fain would stay,   10
And that I loved my heart and honor so,
That I would not from him that had them go.

Must business thee from hence remove?
Oh, that's the worst disease of love;
The poor, the foul, the false, love can   15
Admit, but not the busied man.
He which hath business and makes love, doth do
Such wrong as when a married man doth woo.

John Donne (1572–1631)

QUESTIONS

1. Who is the speaker? Who is addressed? What is the situation? Can the speaker be identified with the poet?
2. Explain the comparison in line 7. To whom does "I" (10–12) refer? Is "love" (15) the subject or object of "can admit"?
3. Summarize the arguments used by the speaker to keep the person addressed from leaving. What is the speaker's scale of value?
4. Are the two persons married or unmarried? Justify your answer.

17. There's been a death in the opposite house

There's been a death in the opposite house
As lately as today.
I know it by the numb look
Such houses have alway.

The neighbors rustle in and out,   5
The doctor drives away.
A window opens like a pod,
Abrupt, mechanically;

Somebody flings a mattress out—
The children hurry by;   10
They wonder if it died on that—
I used to when a boy.

The minister goes stiffly in
As if the house were his,
And he owned all the mourners now,   15
And little boys besides;

And then the milliner, and the man
Of the appalling trade,
To take the measure of the house.

There'll be that dark parade   20

Of tassels and of coaches soon.
It's easy as a sign,
The intuition of the news
In just a country town.

Emily Dickinson (1830–1886)

QUESTIONS

1. What can we know about the speaker in the poem?
2. By what signs does the speaker "intuit" that a death has occurred? Explain them stanza by stanza. What does it mean that the speaker must intuit rather than simply *know* that death has taken place?
3. Comment on the words "appalling" (18) and "dark" (20).
4. What shift in the poem is signaled by the separation of line 20 from the end of stanza 5?
5. What is the speaker's attitude toward death?

18. When in Rome

Mattie dear
the box is full
take
whatever you like
to eat   5
        (an egg
        or soup
        . . . there ain't no meat.)
there's endive there
and   10

cottage cheese
(whew! if I had some
black-eyed peas . . .)
there's sardines
on the shelves   15
and such
but
don't
get my anchovies
they cost   20
too much!
(me get the
anchovies indeed!
what she think, she got—
a bird to feed?)   25
there's plenty in there
to fill you up.
(yes'm. just the
sight's
enough!   30

Hope I lives till I get
home
I'm tired of eatin'
what they eats in Rome . . .)

Mari Evans

QUESTIONS

1. Who are the two speakers? What is the situation? Why are the second speaker's words enclosed in parentheses?
2. What are the attitudes of the two speakers toward one another? What is the attitude of each to herself?
3. What implications have the title and the last two lines?

19. The River-Merchant's Wife: A Letter

While my hair was still cut straight across my forehead
I played about the front gate, pulling flowers.
You came by on bamboo stilts, playing horse,
You walked about my seat, playing with blue plums,
And we went on living in the village of Chokan: 5
Two small people, without dislike or suspicion.

At fourteen I married My Lord you.
I never laughed, being bashful.
Lowering my head, I looked at the wall.
Called to, a thousand times, I never looked back.   10

At fifteen I stopped scowling,
I desired my dust to be mingled with yours
Forever and forever and forever.
Why should I climb the lookout?

At sixteen you departed,   15
You went into far Ku-to-yen, by the river of swirling eddies,
And you have been gone five months.
The monkeys make sorrowful noise overhead.

You dragged your feet when you went out.
By the gate now, the moss is grown, the different mosses,   20
Too deep to clear them away!
The leaves fall early this autumn, in wind.
The paired butterflies are already yellow with August
Over the grass in the West garden;
They hurt me. I grow older.   25
If you are coming down through the narrows of the river Kiang,
Please let me know beforehand,
And I will come out to meet you
              As far as Cho-fu-sa.

Ezra Pound (1885–1972)

QUESTIONS

1. Trace the stages in the speaker's life. Why do you suppose the husband departed? How do the small details provide clues about the woman's emotional states in each of the stages? For example, how does "pulling flowers" (2) give insight into the life of a child?
2. This poem is a translated adaptation of a poem by the Chinese poet Li Po (701–762). What does the indirect method of presenting the events contribute to your responses to the poem? What would you say is the central purpose?

20. The Mill

The miller's wife had waited long,
    The tea was cold, the fire was dead;
And there might yet be nothing wrong

In how he went and what he said:
"There are no millers any more,"   5
    Was all that she had heard him say;
And he had lingered at the door
    So long that it seemed yesterday.

Sick with a fear that had no form
    She knew that she was there at last;   10
And in the mill there was a warm
    And mealy fragrance of the past.
What else there was would only seem
    To say again what he had meant;
And what was hanging from a beam   15
    Would not have heeded where she went.

And if she thought it followed her,
    She may have reasoned in the dark
That one way of the few there were
    Would hide her and would leave no mark: 20
Black water, smooth above the weir
    Like starry velvet in the night,
Though ruffled once, would soon appear
    The same as ever to the sight.

                          Edwin Arlington Robinson (1869–1935)

QUESTIONS

1. What is the meaning of the husband's remark in line 5? What has the husband's occupation been, and what historical developments would lead him to make that remark?
2. What does the miller's wife find in the mill in stanza 2? What does she do in stanza 3? Why?
3. Distinguish means from ends: is it the central purpose of this poem to relate the events, or to reveal the thoughts of the wife? Poets, especially modern poets, are sometimes accused of being perversely obscure. Certainly this poem tells its story in a roundabout way—by hints and implications rather than by direct statements. What is the justification for this "obscurity"?
4. What details of the poem especially bring it to life as experience?

21. Mirror   *First-"thing" POV*

literal I am silver and exact. I have no preconceptions.
personified Whatever I see I swallow immediately
        Just as it is, unmisted by love or dislike.

I am not cruel, only truthful—
The eye of a little god, four-cornered.   5
Most of the time I meditate on the opposite wall.
It is pink, with speckles. I have looked at it so long
I think it is a part of my heart. But it flickers.
Faces and darkness separate us over and over.

Now I am a lake. A woman bends over me,   10
Searching my reaches for what she really is.
Then she turns to those liars, the candles or the moon.
I see her back, and reflect it faithfully.
She rewards me with tears and an agitation of hands.
I am important to her. She comes and goes.   15
Each morning it is her face that replaces the darkness.
In me she has drowned a young girl, and in me an old woman
Rises toward her day after day, like a terrible fish.

Sylvia Plath (1932–1963)

QUESTIONS

1. Who is the speaker? What is the central purpose of the poem, and by what means is it achieved?
2. In what ways is the mirror like and unlike a person (stanza 1)? In what ways is it like a lake (stanza 2)?
3. What is the meaning of the last two lines?

22. The Subalterns

"Poor wanderer," said the leaden sky,
    "I fain would lighten thee,
But there are laws in force on high
    Which say it must not be."

"I would not freeze thee, shorn one," cried   5
    The North, "knew I but how
To warm my breath, to slack my stride;
    But I am ruled as thou."

"Tomorrow I attack thee, wight,"
    Said Sickness. "Yet I swear   10
I bear thy little ark no spite,
    But am bid enter there."

"Come hither, Son," I heard Death say;
    "I did not will a grave

Should end thy pilgrimage today,   15
  But I, too, am a slave!"

We smiled upon each other then,
  And life to me had less
Of that fell look it wore ere when
  They owned their passiveness.   20

Thomas Hardy (1840–1928)

QUESTIONS

1. Vocabulary: *subalterns* (title), *wight* (9), *ark* (11), *fell* (19), *owned* (20).
2. Paraphrase the last stanza, and explain the psychological reaction it displays.
3. Contrast the language and sentence structures of this poem to those of "The Man He Killed" (No. 13). Is there any reason to suppose that either of these poems reflects the poet's own manner of speaking? Explain.

EXERCISE

Here are three definitions of poetry, all framed by poets themselves. Which definition best fits the poems you have so far read? Discuss.

1. Poetry is Transfiguration, the transfiguration of the Actual or the Real into the Ideal, at a lofty elevation, through the medium of melodious or nobly sounding verse.   *Alfred Austin*

2. The art of poetry is simply the art of electrifying language with extraordinary meaning.   *Lascelles Abercrombie*

3. A poem consists of all the purest and most beautiful elements in the poet's nature, crystalized into the aptest and most exquisite language, and adorned with all the outer embellishment of musical cadence or dainty rhyme.   *Grant Allen*

CHAPTER THREE

Denotation and Connotation

A primary distinction between the practical use of language and the literary use is that in literature, especially in poetry, a *fuller* use is made of individual words. To understand this, we need to examine the composition of a word.

The average word has three component parts: sound, denotation, and connotation. It begins as a combination of tones and noises, uttered by the lips, tongue, and throat, for which the written word is a notation. But it differs from a musical tone or a noise in that it has a meaning attached to it. The basic part of this meaning is its **denotation** or denotations: that is, the dictionary meaning or meanings of the word. Beyond its denotations, a word may also have connotations. The **connotations** are what it suggests beyond what it expresses: its overtones of meaning. It acquires these connotations from its past history and associations, from the way and the circumstances in which it has been used. The word *home,* for instance, by denotation means only a place where one lives, but by connotation it suggests security, love, comfort, and family. The words *childlike* and *childish* both mean "characteristic of a child," but *childlike* suggests meekness, innocence, and wide-eyed wonder, while *childish* suggests pettiness, willfulness, and temper tantrums. If we list the names of different coins—nickel, peso, lira, shilling, sen, doubloon—the word *doubloon,* to four out of five readers, immediately will suggest pirates, though a dictionary definition includes nothing about pirates. Pirates are part of its connotation.

Connotation is very important in poetry, for it is one of the means by which the poet can concentrate or enrich meaning—say more in fewer words. Consider, for instance, the following short poem:

23. There is no frigate like a book

> There is no frigate like a book
> To take us lands away,
> Nor any coursers like a page

> Of prancing poetry.
> This traverse may the poorest take　　　　　5
> Without oppress of toll.
> How frugal is the chariot
> That bears the human soul!

> *Emily Dickinson (1830–1886)*

In this poem Emily Dickinson is considering the power of a book or of poetry to carry us away, to take us from our immediate surroundings into a world of the imagination. To do this she has compared literature to various means of transportation: a boat, a team of horses, a wheeled land vehicle. But she has been careful to choose kinds of transportation and names for them that have romantic connotations. "Frigate" suggests exploration and adventure; "coursers," beauty, spirit, and speed; "chariot," speed and the ability to go through the air as well as on land. (Compare "Swing Low, Sweet Chariot" and the myth of Phaëthon, who tried to drive the chariot of Apollo, and the famous painting of Aurora with her horses, once hung in almost every school.) How much of the meaning of the poem comes from this selection of vehicles and words is apparent if we were to substitute *steamship* for "frigate," *horses* for "coursers," and *streetcar* for "chariot."

QUESTIONS

1. What is lost if *miles* is substituted for "lands" (2) or *cheap* for "frugal" (7)?
2. How is "prancing" (4) peculiarly appropriate to poetry as well as to coursers? Could the poet without loss have compared a book to coursers and poetry to a frigate?
3. Is this account appropriate to all kinds of poetry or just to certain kinds? That is, was the poet thinking of poems like Wilfred Owen's "Dulce et Decorum Est" (No. 3) or of poems like Coleridge's "Kubla Khan" (No. 211) and Keats's "La Belle Dame sans Merci" (No. 247)?

Just as a word has a variety of connotations, so may it have more than one denotation. If we look up the word *spring* in the dictionary, for instance, we will find that it has between twenty-five and thirty distinguishable meanings: It may mean (1) a pounce or leap, (2) a season of the year, (3) a natural source of water, (4) a coiled elastic wire, and so forth. This variety of denotation, complicated by additional tones of connotation, makes language confusing and difficult to use. Any person using words must be careful to define precisely by context the denotation that is intended. But the difference between the writer using language to communicate and the poet is this: the practical writer will always attempt to confine words to one denotation at a time; the poet will often take advantage of the fact that the word has more than one meaning by using it to mean more than one thing at the same time. Thus when Edith Sitwell in one of her poems writes, "This is the time of the wild spring and the mating of the tigers,"* she uses the word "spring" to denote both a season of the year and a sudden leap (and she uses "tigers" rather than *deer* or *birds* because it has a connotation of fierceness and wildness that the others lack). The two denotations of "spring" are also appropriately possessed of contrasting connotations: the season is positive in its implications, while a sudden leap may connote the pouncing of a beast of prey. Similarly, in "Mirror" (No. 21), the word "swallow" in line 2 denotes both accepting without question and consuming or devouring, and so connotes both an inability to think on the one hand, and obliteration or destruction on the other.

24. When my love swears that she is made of truth

When my love swears that she is made of truth,
I do believe her, though I know she lies,
That she might think me some untutored youth,
Unlearnèd in the world's false subtleties.
Thus vainly thinking that she thinks me young,   5
Although she knows my days are past the best,
Simply I credit her false-speaking tongue;
On both sides thus is simple truth supprest.
But wherefore says she not she is unjust?°   unfaithful
And wherefore say not I that I am old?   10
Oh, love's best habit is in seeming trust,
And age in love loves not to have years told:
Therefore I lie with her and she with me,
And in our faults by lies we flattered be.

William Shakespeare (1564–1616)

QUESTIONS

1. How old is the speaker? How old is his beloved? What is the nature of their relationship?

Collected Poems (New York: Vanguard, 1954) 392.

2. How is the contradiction in line 2 to be resolved? In lines 5–6? Who is lying to whom?
3. How do "simply" (7) and "simple" (8) differ in meaning? The words "vainly" (5), "habit" (11), "told" (12), and "lie" (13) all have double denotative meanings. What are they?
4. What is the tone of the poem—that is, the attitude of the speaker toward his situation? Should line 11 be taken as an expression of (a) wisdom, (b) conscious rationalization, or (c) self-deception? In answering these questions, consider both the situation and the connotations of all the important words beginning with "swears" (1) and ending with "flattered" (14).

A frequent misconception of poetic language is that poets seek always the most beautiful or noble-sounding words. What they really seek are the most *meaningful* words, and these vary from one context to another. Language has many levels and varieties, and poets may choose from all of them. Their words may be grandiose or humble, fanciful or matter-of-fact, romantic or realistic, archaic or modern, technical or everyday, monosyllabic or polysyllabic. Usually a poem will be pitched pretty much in one key: the words in Emily Dickinson's "There is no frigate like a book" (No. 23) and those in Thomas Hardy's "The Man He Killed" (No. 13) are chosen from quite different areas of language, but both poets have chosen the words most meaningful for their own poetic context. It is always important to determine the level of diction employed in a poem, for it may provide clear insight into the purpose of the poem by helping to characterize the speaker. Sometimes a poet may import a word from one level or area of language into a poem composed mostly of words from a different level or area. If this is done clumsily, the result will be incongruous and sloppy; if it is done skillfully, the result will be a shock of surprise and an increment of meaning for the reader. In fact, the many varieties of language open to poets provide their richest resource. Their task is one of constant exploration and discovery. They search always for the secret affinities of words that allow them to be brought together with soft explosions of meaning.

25. Pathedy of Manners

At twenty she was brilliant and adored,
Phi Beta Kappa, sought for every dance;
Captured symbolic logic and the glance
Of men whose interest was their sole reward.

She learned the cultured jargon of those bred   5
To antique crystal and authentic pearls,
Scorned Wagner, praised the Degas dancing girls,
And when she might have thought, conversed instead.

She hung up her diploma, went abroad,
Saw catalogues of domes and tapestry,   10
Rejected an impoverished marquis,
And learned to tell real Wedgwood from a fraud.

Back home her breeding led her to espouse
A bright young man whose pearl cufflinks were real.
They had an ideal marriage, and ideal   15
But lonely children in an ideal house.

I saw her yesterday at forty-three,
Her children gone, her husband one year dead,
Toying with plots to kill time and re-wed
Illusions of lost opportunity.   20

But afraid to wonder what she might have known
With all that wealth and mind had offered her,
She shuns conviction, choosing to infer
Tenets of every mind except her own.

A hundred people call, though not one friend,   25
To parry a hundred doubts with nimble talk.
Her meanings lost in manners, she will walk
Alone in brilliant circles to the end.

Ellen Kay (b. 1931)

QUESTIONS

1. The title alludes to the type of drama called "comedy of manners" and coins a word combining the suffix -*edy* with the Greek root *path*- (as in *pathetic, sympathy, pathology*). How does the poem narrate a story with both comic and pathetic implications? For what might the central character be blamed? What arouses our pity for her?
2. Explore the multiple denotations and the connotations attached to each denotation of "brilliant" (both in 1 and 28), "interest" and "reward" (4), "cultured" and "jargon" (5), "circles" (28).
3. Why are the poet's words more effective than these possible synonyms: "captured" (3) rather than *learned;* "conversed" (8) rather than *chatted, gossiped,* or *talked;* "catalogues" (10) rather than *volumes* or *multitudes;* "espouse" (13) rather than *marry?* Discuss the momentary ambiguity presented by the word "re-wed" (19).

4. At what point in the poem does the speaker shift from language that represents the way the woman might have talked about herself to language that reveals how the speaker judges her? Point out examples of both kinds of language.

People using language only to convey information are usually indifferent to the sounds of the words and are hampered by their connotations and multiple denotations. They would rather confine each word to a single, exact meaning. They use, one might say, a fraction of the word and throw away the rest. Poets, on the other hand, use as much of the word as possible. They are interested in connotation and use it to enrich and convey meaning. And they may rely on more than one denotation.

The purest form of practical language is scientific language. Scientists need a precise language to convey information precisely. The existence of multiple denotations and various overtones of meaning hinders them from accomplishing their purpose. Their ideal language would be a language with a one-to-one correspondence between word and meaning; that is, every word would have only one meaning, and for every meaning there would be only one word. Since ordinary language does not fulfill these conditions, scientists have invented languages that do. A statement in one of these languages may look like this:

$$SO_2 + H_2O = H_2SO_3$$

In such a statement the symbols are entirely unambiguous; they have been stripped of all connotation and of all denotations but one. The word *sulfurous,* if it occurred in poetry, might have all kinds of connotations: fire, smoke, brimstone, hell, damnation. But H_2SO_3 means one thing and one thing only: sulfurous acid.

The ambiguity and multiplicity of meanings possessed by words are an obstacle to the scientist but a resource to the poet. Where the scientist wants singleness of meaning, the poet wants richness of meaning. Where the scientist requires and has invented a strictly one-dimensional language in which every word is confined to one denotation, the poet needs a multidimensional language and creates it partly by using a multidimensional vocabulary, in which the dimensions of connotation and sound are added to the dimension of denotation.

The poet, we may say, plays on a many-stringed instrument and sounds more than one note at a time.

The first task in reading poetry, therefore, as in reading any kind of literature, is to develop a sense of language, a feeling for words. One needs to become acquainted with their shape, their color, and their flavor. There are two ways of doing this: extensive use of the dictionary and extensive reading.

EXERCISES

1. Which word in each group has the most "romantic" connotations: (a) horse, steed, nag; (b) king, ruler, tyrant, autocrat; (c) Chicago, Pittsburgh, Samarkand, Birmingham?
2. Which word in each group is the most emotionally connotative: (a) female parent, mother, dam; (b) offspring, children, progeny; (c) brother, sibling?
3. Arrange the words in each of the following groups from most positive to most negative in connotation: (a) skinny, thin, gaunt, slender; (b) prosperous, loaded, moneyed, opulent; (c) brainy, intelligent, eggheaded, smart.
4. Of the following, which should you be less offended at being accused of: (a) having acted foolishly, (b) having acted like a fool?
5. In any competent piece of writing, the possible multiple denotations and connotations of the words used are controlled by context. The context screens out irrelevant meanings while allowing the relevant meanings to pass through. What denotation has the word *fast* in the following contexts: fast runner, fast color, fast living, fast day? What are the varying connotations of these four denotations of *fast?*
6. Explain how, in the following examples the denotation of the word *white* remains the same, but the connotations differ: (a) The young princess had blue eyes, golden hair, and a breast as white as snow; (b) Confronted with the evidence, the false princess turned as white as a sheet.

26. Naming of Parts

Today we have naming of parts. Yesterday,
We had daily cleaning. And tomorrow morning,
We shall have what to do after firing. But today,
Today we have naming of parts. Japonica
Glistens like coral in all of the neighboring gardens,   5
    And today we have naming of parts.

This is the lower sling swivel. And this
Is the upper sling swivel, whose use you will see,
When you are given your slings. And this is the piling swivel,
Which in your case you have not got. The branches   10
Hold in the gardens their silent, eloquent gestures,
    Which in our case we have not got.

This is the safety-catch, which is always released
With an easy flick of the thumb. And please do not let me
See anyone using his finger. You can do it quite easy   15
If you have any strength in your thumb. The blossoms
Are fragile and motionless, never letting anyone see
    Any of them using their finger.

And this you can see is the bolt. The purpose of this
Is to open the breech, as you see. We can slide it   20
Rapidly backwards and forwards: we call this
Easing the spring. And rapidly backwards and forwards
The early bees are assaulting and fumbling the flowers:
    They call it easing the Spring.

They call it easing the Spring: it is perfectly easy   25
If you have any strength in your thumb: like the bolt,
And the breech, and the cocking-piece, and the point of balance,
Which in our case we have not got; and the almond-blossom
Silent in all of the gardens and the bees going backwards and forwards,
    For today we have naming of parts.   30

Henry Reed (1914–1986)

QUESTIONS

1. Who is the speaker (or speakers) in the poem, and what is the situation?
2. What basic contrasts are represented by the trainees and by the gardens?
3. What is it that trainees "have not got" (28)? How many meanings have
   the phrases "easing the spring" (22) and "point of balance" (27)?
4. What differences in language and rhythm do you find between the lines
   that involve the "naming of parts" and those that describe the gardens?
5. Does the repetition of certain phrases throughout the poem have any special function or does it merely create a kind of refrain?
6. What statement does the poem make about war as it affects men and
   their lives?

27. Cross

My old man's a white old man
And my old mother's black.
If ever I cursed my white old man
I take my curses back.

If ever I cursed my black old mother   5
And wished she were in hell,

I'm sorry for that evil wish
And now I wish her well.

My old man died in a fine big house.
My ma died in a shack.   10
I wonder where I'm gonna die,
Being neither white nor black?

Langston Hughes (1902–1967)

QUESTIONS

1. What different denotations does the title have? What connotations are linked to each of them?
2. The language in this poem, such as "old man" (1, 3, 9), "ma" (10), and "gonna" (11), is plain, and even colloquial. Is it appropriate to the subject? Why or why not?

28. The world is too much with us

The world is too much with us; late and soon,
Getting and spending, we lay waste our powers:
Little we see in nature that is ours;
We have given our hearts away, a sordid boon!
This sea that bares her bosom to the moon,   5
The winds that will be howling at all hours,
And are up-gathered now like sleeping flowers,
For this, for everything, we are out of tune;
It moves us not. —Great God! I'd rather be
A pagan suckled in a creed outworn;   10
So might I, standing on this pleasant lea,
Have glimpses that would make me less forlorn;
Have sight of Proteus rising from the sea;
Or hear old Triton blow his wreathèd horn.

William Wordsworth (1770–1850)

QUESTIONS

1. Vocabulary: *boon* (4), *Proteus* (13), *Triton* (14). What two relevant denotations has "wreathèd" (14)?
2. Explain why the poet's words are more effective than these possible alternatives: *earth* for "world" (1); *selling and buying* for "getting and spending" (2); *exposes* for "bares" (5); *dozing* for "sleeping" (7); *posies* for "flowers"

(7); *nourished* for "suckled" (10); *visions* for "glimpses" (12); *sound* for "blow" (14).
3. Should "Great God!" (9) be considered as a vocative (term of address) or an expletive (exclamation)? Or something of both?
4. State the theme (central idea) of the poem in a sentence.

29. Eldorado

Gaily bedight,
A gallant knight,
In sunshine and in shadow,
Had journeyed long,
Singing a song,   5
In search of Eldorado.

But he grew old—
This knight so bold—
And o'er his heart a shadow
Fell, as he found   10
No spot of ground
That looked like Eldorado.

And, as his strength
Failed him at length,
He met a pilgrim shadow—   15
"Shadow," said he,
"Where can it be—
This land of Eldorado?"

"Over the Mountains
Of the Moon,   20
Down the Valley of the Shadow,
Ride, boldly ride,"
The shade replied,—
"If you seek for Eldorado!"

Edgar Allan Poe (1809–1849)

QUESTIONS

1. Eldorado (or El Dorado) was a legendary land of fabulous gold sought in South America by early Spanish explorers. In the poem is this land literal or symbolic—that is, is the quest portrayed as material or spiritual, unworthy or worthy?
2. The word "shadow" has different meanings (both denotative and connotative) in each stanza. Trace and account for the changes of meaning.

3. What is the meaning of the shade's reply in the last stanza? (What does the phrase "Valley of the Shadow" call to mind?) What is the central purpose of the poem?
4. The language used in this poem differs markedly from that used in "A Study of Reading Habits" (No. 14) and "Cross" (No. 27). Describe and illustrate the differences. How do they affect your responses to the themes of these poems?

30. A Hymn to God the Father

Wilt thou forgive that sin where I begun,
   Which is my sin though it were done before?
Wilt thou forgive those sins through which I run,°   ran
   And do them still, though still I do deplore?
     When thou hast done, thou hast not done,   5
      For I have more.

Wilt thou forgive that sin by which I won
   Others to sin, and made my sin their door?
Wilt thou forgive that sin which I did shun
   A year or two, but wallowed in a score?   10
     When thou hast done, thou hast not done,
      For I have more.

I have a sin of fear, that when I have spun
   My last thread, I shall perish on the shore;
Swear by thyself that at my death thy Sun   15
   Shall shine as it shines now, and heretofore;
     And having done that, thou hast done.
      I have no more.

John Donne (1572–1631)

QUESTIONS

1. In 1601, John Donne at 29 secretly married Anne More, age 17, infuriating her upper-class father, who had him imprisoned for three days. Because of the marriage, Donne lost his job as private secretary to an important official at court, and probably ruined his chances for the career at court that he desired. It was, however, a true love match. In 1615 Donne entered the church. In 1617 his wife, then 33, died after bearing twelve children. In 1621 he was appointed Dean of St. Paul's Cathedral in London and quickly won a reputation for his eloquent sermons. His religious poems differ markedly in tone from the often cynical, sometimes erotic poems of his youth. The foregoing poem was probably written during a severe illness in 1623. Is this information of any value to a reader of the poem?

2. What sin is referred to in lines 1–2? What is meant by "when I have spun / My last thread" (13–14)? By "I shall perish on the shore" (14)?
3. How do the puns on "done" (5, 11, 17), "more" (6, 12, 18), and "Sun" (15) give structure and meaning to the poem? Explain the relevance of the meanings generated by the puns.

31. One Art

The art of losing isn't hard to master;
so many things seem filled with the intent
to be lost that their loss is no disaster.

Lose something every day. Accept the fluster
of lost door keys, the hour badly spent.   5
The art of losing isn't hard to master.

Then practice losing farther, losing faster:
places, and names, and where it was you meant
to travel. None of these will bring disaster.

I lost my mother's watch. And look! my last, or   10
next-to-last, of three loved houses went.
The art of losing isn't hard to master.

I lost two cities, lovely ones. And, vaster,
some realms I owned, two rivers, a continent.
I miss them, but it wasn't a disaster.   15

—Even losing you (the joking voice, a gesture
I love) I shan't have lied. It's evident
the art of losing's not too hard to master
though it may look like (*Write* it!) like disaster.

Elizabeth Bishop (1911–1979)

QUESTIONS

1. What various denotations of "lose" and its derivative forms are relevant to the context? What connotations are attached to the separate denotative meanings?
2. Explain how "owned" (14) and "lost" (13) shift the meanings of possessing and losing.
3. What seems to be the purpose of the speaker in the first three tercets (three-line units)? How is the advice given there supported by the personal experiences related in the next two tercets?
4. The concluding quatrain (four-line unit) contains direct address to a person, as well as a command the speaker addresses to herself. How do these details reveal the real purpose of the poem? *Can* all kinds of losses be mastered with "one art of losing"?

CHAPTER FOUR

Imagery

Experience comes to us largely through the senses. Our experiences of a spring day, for instance, may consist partly of certain emotions we feel and partly of certain thoughts we think, but most of it will be a cluster of sense impressions. It will consist of *seeing* blue sky and white clouds, budding leaves and daffodils; of *hearing* robins and bluebirds singing in the early morning; of *smelling* damp earth and blossoming hyacinths; and of *feeling* a fresh wind against one's cheek. A poet seeking to express the experience of a spring day therefore provides a selection of sense impressions. So in "Spring" (No. 4) Shakespeare gives us "daisies pied" and "lady-smocks all silver-white" and "merry larks" and the song of the cuckoo and maidens bleaching their summer smocks. Had he not done so, he might have failed to evoke the emotions that accompany these sensations. The poet's language, then, is more *sensuous* than ordinary language. It is more full of imagery.

Imagery may be defined as the representation through language of sense experience. Poetry appeals directly to our senses, of course, through its music and rhythms, which we actually hear when it is read aloud. But indirectly it appeals to our senses through imagery, the representation to the imagination of sense experience. The word *image* perhaps most often suggests a mental picture, something seen in the mind's eye—and *visual* imagery is the kind of imagery that occurs most frequently in poetry. But an image may also represent a sound (*auditory imagery*); a smell (*olfactory imagery*); a taste (*gustatory imagery*); touch, such as hardness, softness, wetness, or heat and cold (*tactile imagery*); an internal sensation, such as hunger, thirst, fatigue, or nausea (*organic imagery*); or movement or tension in the muscles or joints (*kinesthetic imagery*). If we wish to be scientific, we could extend this list further, for psychologists no longer confine themselves to five or even six senses, but for purposes of discussing poetry the preceding classification should ordinarily be sufficient.

32. Meeting at Night

The gray sea and the long black land;
And the yellow half-moon large and low;
And the startled little waves that leap
In fiery ringlets from their sleep,
As I gain the cove with pushing prow,   5
And quench its speed i' the slushy sand.

Then a mile of warm sea-scented beach;
Three fields to cross till a farm appears;
A tap at the pane, the quick sharp scratch
And blue spurt of a lighted match,   10
And a voice less loud, through its joys and fears,
Than the two hearts beating each to each!

Robert Browning (1812–1889)

"Meeting at Night" is a poem about love. It makes, one might say, a number of statements about love: being in love is a sweet and exciting experience; when one is in love everything seems beautiful, and the most trivial things become significant; when one is in love one's sweetheart seems the most important thing in the world. But the poet actually *tells* us none of these things directly. He does not even use the word *love* in his poem. His business is to communicate experience, not information. He does this largely in two ways. First, he presents us with a specific situation, in which a lover goes to meet his sweetheart. Second, he describes the lover's journey so vividly in terms of sense impressions that the reader virtually sees and hears what the lover saw and heard and seems to share his anticipation and excitement.

Every line in the poem contains some image, some appeal to the senses: the gray sea, the long black land, the yellow half-moon, the startled little waves with their fiery ringlets, the blue spurt of the lighted match—all appeal to our sense of sight and convey not only shape but also color and motion. The warm sea-scented beach appeals to the senses of both smell and touch. The pushing prow of the boat on the slushy sand, the tap at the pane, the quick scratch of the match, the low speech of the lovers, and the sound of their hearts beating—all appeal to the sense of hearing.

33. Parting at Morning

Round the cape of a sudden came the sea,
And the sun looked over the mountain's rim:
And straight was a path of gold for him,
And the need of a world of men for me.

Robert Browning (1812–1889)

QUESTIONS

1. This poem is a sequel to "Meeting at Night." "[H]im" (3) refers to the sun. Does the last line mean that the lover needs the world of men or that the world of men needs the lover? Or both?
2. Does the sea *actually* come suddenly around the cape or *appear* to? Why does Browning mention the *effect* before its *cause* (the sun looking over the mountain's rim)?
3. Do these poems (32 and 33), taken together, suggest any larger truths about love? Browning, in answer to a question, said that the second part is the man's confession of "how fleeting is the belief (implied in the first part) that such raptures are self-sufficient and enduring—as for the time they appear."

The sharpness and vividness of any image will ordinarily depend on how specific it is and on the poet's use of effective detail. The word *hummingbird,* for instance, conveys a more definite image than does *bird,* and *ruby-throated hummingbird* is sharper and more specific still. However, to represent something vividly a poet need not describe it completely. One or two especially sharp and representative details will often serve, inviting the reader's imagination to fill in the rest. Tennyson in "The Eagle" (No. 1) gives only one visual detail about the eagle itself—that he clasps the crag with "crooked hands"—but this detail is an effective and memorable one. Robinson in "The Mill" (No. 20) withholds specific information about the life that the miller and his wife had shared, but the fact that she smells "a warm / And mealy fragrance of the past" when she enters the mill speaks volumes about her sense of loss. Browning, in "Meeting at Night," calls up a whole scene with "A tap at the pane, the quick sharp scratch / And blue spurt of a lighted match."

Since imagery is a peculiarly effective way of evoking vivid experience, and since it may be used to convey emotion and suggest ideas as well as to cause a mental reproduction of sensations, it is an invaluable resource of the poet. In general, the poet will seek concrete or image-bearing words in preference to abstract or non-image-bearing words. We cannot evaluate a poem, however, by the amount or quality of its imagery alone. Sense impression is only one of the elements of experience. Poetry may attain its ends by other means. We should never judge any single element of a poem except in reference to the total intent of that poem.

34. Spring

Nothing is so beautiful as spring—
    When weeds, in wheels, shoot long and lovely and lush;
    Thrush's eggs look little low heavens, and thrush
Through the echoing timber does so rinse and wring
The ear, it strikes like lightnings to hear him sing;   5
    The glassy peartree leaves and blooms, they brush
    The descending blue; that blue is all in a rush
With richness; the racing lambs too have fair their fling.

What is all this juice and all this joy?
    A strain of the earth's sweet being in the beginning   10
In Eden garden. —Have, get, before it cloy,

    Before it cloud, Christ, lord, and sour with sinning,
Innocent mind and Mayday in girl and boy,
    Most, O maid's child, thy choice and worthy the winning.

Gerard Manley Hopkins (1844–1889)

QUESTIONS

1. The first line makes an abstract statement. How is this statement brought to carry conviction?
2. The sky is described as being "all in a rush / With richness" (7–8). In what other respects is the poem "rich"?
3. To what two things does the speaker compare the spring in lines 9–14? In what ways are the comparisons appropriate?
4. Lines 11–14 might be made clearer by paraphrasing them thus: "Christ, lord, child of the Virgin: save the innocent mind of girl and boy before sin taints it, since it is most like yours and worth saving." Why are Hopkins's lines more effective, both in imagery and in syntax?

35. The Widow's Lament in Springtime

> Sorrow is my own yard
> where the new grass
> flames as it has flamed
> often before but not
> with the cold fire   5
> that closes round me this year.
> Thirtyfive years
> I lived with my husband.
> The plumtree is white today
> with masses of flowers.   10
> Masses of flowers
> load the cherry branches
> and color some bushes
> yellow and some red
> but the grief in my heart   15
> is stronger than they
> for though they were my joy
> formerly, today I notice them
> and turned away forgetting.
> Today my son told me   20
> that in the meadows,
> at the edge of the heavy woods
> in the distance, he saw
> trees of white flowers.
> I feel that I would like   25
> to go there
> and fall into those flowers
> and sink into the marsh near them.

William Carlos Williams (1883–1963)

QUESTIONS

1. Why is springtime so poignant a time for this lament? What has been the speaker's previous experience at this time of year?
2. Why does the speaker's son tell her of the flowering trees "in the distance"? What does he want her to do? Contrast the two locations in the poem—"yard" versus "meadows," "woods," and "marsh." What does the widow desire?
3. Imagery may have degrees of vividness, depending on its particularity, concreteness, and specific detail. What is the result of the contrast between the vividness of lines 2–3 and the relative flatness of lines 13–14? How does the fact that "masses" (10, 11) appeals to two senses relate to the speaker's emotional condition?

36. I felt a funeral in my brain

I felt a funeral in my brain,
And mourners to and fro
Kept treading—treading—till it seemed
That sense was breaking through.

And when they all were seated,   5
A service, like a drum,
Kept beating—beating—till I thought
My mind was going numb.

And then I heard them lift a box
And creak across my soul   10
With those same boots of lead again.
Then space began to toll,

As all the heavens were a bell
And being, but an ear,
And I and silence, some strange race,   15
Wrecked, solitary, here.

And then a plank in reason broke
And I dropped down, and down,
And hit a world at every plunge,
And finished knowing, then.   20

Emily Dickinson (1830–1886)

QUESTIONS

1. What senses are being evoked by the imagery? Can you account for the
   fact that one important sense is absent from the poem?
2. In sequence, what aspects of a funeral and burial are represented in the
   poem? Is it possible to define the sequence of mental events that are being compared to them?
3. With respect to the funeral activities in stanzas 1–3, where is the speaker
   imaginatively located?
4. What finally happens to the speaker?

37. The Forge

All I know is a door into the dark.
Outside, old axles and iron hoops rusting;
Inside, the hammered anvil's short-pitched ring,

The unpredictable fantail of sparks
Or hiss when a new shoe toughens in water. 5
The anvil must be somewhere in the center,
Horned as a unicorn, at one end square,
Set there immovable: an altar
Where he expends himself in shape and music.
Sometimes, leather-aproned, hairs in his nose, 10
He leans out on the jamb, recalls a clatter
Of hoofs where traffic is flashing in rows;
Then grunts and goes in, with a slam and flick
To beat real iron out, to work the bellows.

Seamus Heaney (b. 1939)

QUESTIONS

1. What does the speaker mean when he says that "all" he knows is "a door into the dark" (1)? What more does he know, and how does he make his knowledge evident?
2. How do the images describing the blacksmith (10–11) relate to his attitude toward his work and toward the changing times?
3. The speaker summarizes the smith's world as "shape and music" (9), terms that suggest visual and auditory imagery. What do the contrasts between visual images contribute? The contrasts between auditory images?

38. After Apple-Picking

My long two-pointed ladder's sticking through a tree
Toward heaven still,
And there's a barrel that I didn't fill
Beside it, and there may be two or three
Apples I didn't pick upon some bough. 5
But I am done with apple-picking now.
Essence of winter sleep is on the night,
The scent of apples: I am drowsing off.
I cannot rub the strangeness from my sight
I got from looking through a pane of glass 10
I skimmed this morning from the drinking trough
And held against the world of hoary grass.
It melted, and I let it fall and break.
But I was well
Upon my way to sleep before it fell, 15
And I could tell
What form my dreaming was about to take.

Magnified apples appear and disappear,
Stem end and blossom end,
And every fleck of russet showing clear.   20
My instep arch not only keeps the ache,
It keeps the pressure of a ladder-round.
I feel the ladder sway as the boughs bend.
And I keep hearing from the cellar bin
The rumbling sound   25
Of load on load of apples coming in.
For I have had too much
Of apple-picking: I am overtired
Of the great harvest I myself desired.
There were ten thousand thousand fruit to touch,   30
Cherish in hand, lift down, and not let fall.
For all
That struck the earth,
No matter if not bruised or spiked with stubble,
Went surely to the cider-apple heap   35
As of no worth.
One can see what will trouble
This sleep of mine, whatever sleep it is.
Were he not gone,
The woodchuck could say whether it's like his   40
Long sleep, as I describe its coming on,
Or just some human sleep.

Robert Frost (1874–1963)

QUESTIONS

1. How does the poet convey so vividly the experience of "apple-picking"? Point out effective examples of each kind of imagery used. What emotional responses do the images evoke?
2. How does the speaker regard his work? Has he done it well or poorly? Does he find it enjoyable or tedious? Is he dissatisfied with its results?
3. The speaker predicts what he will dream about in his sleep. Why does he shift to the present tense (18) when he begins describing a dream he has not yet had? How sharply are real experience and dream experience differentiated in the poem?
4. The poem uses the word *sleep* six times. Does it, through repetition, come to suggest a meaning beyond the purely literal? If so, what attitude does the speaker take toward this second signification? Does he fear it? Does he look forward to it? What does he expect of it?
5. If sleep is symbolic (both literal and metaphorical), other details also may take on additional meaning. If so, how would you interpret (a) the ladder, (b) the season of the year, (c) the harvesting, (d) the "pane of glass" (10)? What denotations has the word "Essence" (7)?
6. How does the woodchuck's sleep differ from "just some human sleep" (42)?

39. Those Winter Sundays

Sundays too my father got up early
and put his clothes on in the blueblack cold,
then with cracked hands that ached
from labor in the weekday weather made
banked fires blaze. No one ever thanked him.   5

I'd wake and hear the cold splintering, breaking.
When the rooms were warm, he'd call,
and slowly I would rise and dress,
fearing the chronic angers of that house,

Speaking indifferently to him,   10
who had driven out the cold
and polished my good shoes as well.
What did I know, what did I know
of love's austere and lonely offices?

Robert Hayden (1913–1980)

QUESTIONS

1. Vocabulary: *offices* (14).
2. What kind of imagery is central to the poem? How is this imagery related
   to the emotional concerns of the poem?
3. How do the subsidiary images relate to the central images?
4. From what point in time does the speaker view the subject matter of the
   poem? What has happened to him in the interval?

40. The Letter

Bad news arrives in her distinctive hand.
The cancer has returned, this time
to his brain. Surgery impossible,
treatments under way. Hair loss, bouts
of sleeplessness and agitation at night,   5
exhaustion during the day.

I snap the blue leash onto the D-ring
of the dog's collar, and we cross
Route 4, then cut through the hayfield
to the pond road, where I let him run   10
along with my morbidity.

The trees have leafed out—only just—
and the air is misty with sap.

So green, so brightly, richly succulent,
this arbor over the road . . .   15
Sunlight penetrates in golden drops.

We come to the place where a neighbor
is taking timber from his land.
There's a smell of lacerated earth
and pine. Hardwood smells different.   20
His truck is gone.

Now you can see well up the slope,
see ledges of rock and ferns breaking forth
among the stumps and cast-aside limbs
and branches.   25

The place will heal itself in time, first
with weeds—goldenrod, cinquefoil, moth
mullein—then blackberries, sapling
pine, deciduous trees . . . But for now
the dog rolls, jovial, in the pungent   30
disturbance of wood and earth.

I summon him with a word, turn back,
and we go the long way home.

Jane Kenyon (1947–1995)

QUESTIONS

1. The first six lines refer directly to the title. What is the speaker's apparent
   emotional reaction in these lines? How do you account for the lack of imagery in them?
2. Lines 10–11 seem to offer a motive for the speaker's walk. As precisely as
   you can, explain that motive.
3. Explain the connotations of "morbidity" (11), "lacerated" (19), "heal" (26).
4. From line 12, the poem is rich with imagery. What senses are evoked, and
   what emotions are conveyed?

41. Cavalry Crossing a Ford

A line in long array where they wind betwixt green islands,
They take a serpentine course, their arms flash in the sun—hark to the
   musical clank,
Behold the silvery river, in it the splashing horses loitering stop to drink,
Behold the brown-faced men, each group, each person a picture, the
   negligent rest on the saddles,

Some emerge on the opposite bank, others are just entering the
 ford—while,   5
Scarlet and blue and snowy white,
The guidon flags flutter gaily in the wind.

Walt Whitman (1819–1892)

QUESTION

There is an old Chinese proverb: "One picture is worth more than a thousand words." Like most proverbs it expresses a partial truth. What advantages would this Civil War poem have over a photograph of the same scene?
(*Hint:* What distances would be necessary between the camera and each of
the visual details?) Would a movie camera with zoom lens suffice to capture
the experience of this poem?

42. Reapers

Black reapers with the sound of steel on stones
Are sharpening scythes. I see them place the hones
In their hip-pockets as a thing that's done,
And start their silent swinging, one by one.
Black horses drive a mower through the weeds,   5
And there, a field rat, startled, squealing bleeds,
His belly close to ground. I see the blade,
Blood-stained, continue cutting weeds and shade.

Jean Toomer (1894–1967)

QUESTIONS

1. The poem presents two examples of cutting down vegetation. What contrasts are drawn between reaping and mowing? How does imagery reinforce those contrasts?
2. What is signified by the speaker's stating that the "horses drive" (5) the
   mowing machine rather than that a man is driving the team of horses?
3. For whom (or what) would the weeds represent "shade" (8)? Are the connotations of *shade* positive or negative in this context? How are the usual
   connotations of "rat" (6) altered in the poem? Characterize the speaker.

43. To Autumn

Season of mists and mellow fruitfulness,
 Close bosom-friend of the maturing sun;
Conspiring with him how to load and bless
 With fruit the vines that round the thatch-eaves run;

To bend with apples the mossed cottage-trees,   5
    And fill all fruit with ripeness to the core;
        To swell the gourd, and plump the hazel shells
With a sweet kernel; to set budding more,
    And still more, later flowers for the bees,
    Until they think warm days will never cease,   10
        For summer has o'er-brimmed their clammy cells.

Who hath not seen thee oft amid thy store?
    Sometimes whoever seeks abroad may find
Thee sitting careless on a granary floor,
    Thy hair soft-lifted by the winnowing wind;   15
Or on a half-reaped furrow sound asleep,
    Drowsed with the fume of poppies, while thy hook
        Spares the next swath and all its twinèd flowers:
And sometimes like a gleaner thou dost keep
    Steady thy laden head across a brook;   20
    Or by a cider-press, with patient look,
        Thou watchest the last oozings hours by hours.

Where are the songs of spring? Ay, where are they?
    Think not of them, thou hast thy music too,—
While barred clouds bloom the soft-dying day,   25
    And touch the stubble-plains with rosy hue;
Then in a wailful choir the small gnats mourn
    Among the river sallows, borne aloft
        Or sinking as the light wind lives or dies;
And full-grown lambs loud bleat from hilly bourn;   30
    Hedge-crickets sing; and now with treble soft
    The red-breast whistles from a garden-croft;
        And gathering swallows twitter in the skies.

John Keats (1795–1821)

QUESTIONS

1. Vocabulary: *hook* (17), *barred* (25), *sallows* (28), *bourn* (30), *croft* (32).
2. How many kinds of imagery do you find in the poem? Give examples of each.
3. Are the images arranged haphazardly or are they carefully organized? In answering this question, consider (a) what aspect of autumn each stanza particularly concerns, (b) what kind of imagery dominates each stanza, and (c) what time of the season each stanza presents. Is there any progression in time of day?
4. What is autumn personified as in stanza 2? Is there any suggestion of personification in the other two stanzas?
5. Although the poem is primarily descriptive, what attitude toward transience and passing beauty is implicit in it?

CHAPTER FIVE

Figurative Language 1

Simile, Metaphor, Personification, Apostrophe, Metonymy

> Poetry provides the one permissible way
> of saying one thing and meaning another.
> ROBERT FROST

Let us assume that your brother has just come in out of a rainstorm and you say to him, "Well, you're a pretty sight! Got slightly wet, didn't you?" And he replies, "Wet? I'm drowned! It's raining cats and dogs, and my raincoat's like a sieve!"

You and your brother probably understand each other well enough; yet if you examine this conversation literally, that is to say unimaginatively, you will find that you have been speaking nonsense. Actually you have been speaking figuratively. You have been saying less than what you mean, or more than what you mean, or the opposite of what you mean, or something other than what you mean. You did not mean that your brother was a pretty sight but that he was a wretched sight. You did not mean that he got slightly wet but that he got very wet. Your brother did not mean that he got drowned but that he got drenched. It was not raining cats and dogs; it was raining water. And your brother's raincoat is so unlike a sieve that not even a child would confuse them.

If you are familiar with Molière's play *Le Bourgeois Gentilhomme,* you will remember how delighted M. Jourdain was to discover that he had been speaking prose all his life. Many people might be equally surprised to learn that they have been speaking a kind of subpoetry all their lives. The difference between their figures of speech and the poet's is that theirs are probably worn and trite, the poet's fresh and original.

On first examination, it might seem absurd to say one thing and mean another. But we all do it—and with good reason. We do it because we can say what we want to say more vividly and forcefully by figures than we can by saying it directly. And we can say more by figurative statement than we can by literal statement. Figures of speech offer another way of adding extra dimensions to language.

Broadly defined, a **figure of speech** is any way of saying something other than the ordinary way, and some rhetoricians have classified as many as 250 separate figures. For our purposes, however, a figure of speech is more narrowly definable as a way of saying one thing and meaning another, and we need to be concerned with no more than a dozen. **Figurative language**—language using figures of speech—is language that cannot be taken literally (or should not be taken literally only).

Metaphor and **simile** are both used as a means of comparing things that are essentially unlike. The only distinction between them is that in simile the comparison is *expressed* by the use of some word or phrase, such as *like, as, than, similar to, resembles,* or *seems;* in metaphor, the comparison is not expressed but is created when a figurative term is *substituted for* or *identified with* the literal term.

44. The Guitarist Tunes Up

With what attentive courtesy he bent
Over his instrument;
Not as a lordly conqueror who could
Command both wire and wood,
But as a man with a loved woman might,   5
Inquiring with delight
What slight essential things she had to say
Before they started, he and she, to play.

Frances Cornford (1886–1960)

QUESTIONS

Explore the comparisons. Do they principally illuminate the guitarist or the lovers or both? What one word brings the figurative and literal terms together?

45. The Hound

Life the hound
Equivocal
Comes at a bound

Either to rend me
Or to befriend me.   5
I cannot tell
The hound's intent
Till he has sprung
At my bare hand
With teeth or tongue.   10
Meanwhile I stand
And wait the event.

Robert Francis (1901–1987)

QUESTIONS

What does "Equivocal" (2) mean? Show how this is the key word in the poem.
What is the effect of placing it on a line by itself?

Metaphors may take one of four forms, depending on whether the literal and figurative terms are respectively *named* or *implied.* In the first form of metaphor, as in simile, *both* the literal *and* figurative terms are *named.* In Francis's poem, for example, the literal term is "life" and the figurative term is "hound." In the second form, the literal term is *named* and the figurative term is *implied.*

46. Bereft

Where had I heard this wind before
Change like this to a deeper roar?
What would it take my standing there for,
Holding open a restive door,
Looking down hill to a frothy shore?   5
Summer was past and day was past.
Somber clouds in the west were massed.
Out in the porch's sagging floor,
Leaves got up in a coil and hissed,
Blindly struck at my knee and missed.   10
Something sinister in the tone
Told me my secret must be known:
Word I was in the house alone
Somehow must have gotten abroad,
Word I was in my life alone,   15
Word I had no one left but God.

Robert Frost (1874–1963)

QUESTIONS

1. Describe the situation precisely. What time of day and year is it? Where is the speaker? What is happening to the weather?
2. To what are the leaves in lines 9–10 compared? How does that comparison reflect the state of mind of the speaker?
3. The word "hissed" (9) is onomatopoetic (see Glossary of Terms). How is its effect reinforced in the lines following?
4. Though lines 9–10 present the clearest example of the second form of metaphor, there are others. To what is the wind ("it") compared in line 3? Why is the door "restive" (4) and what does this do (figuratively) to the door? To what is the speaker's "life" (15) compared?
5. What is the tone of the poem? How reassuring is the last line?

In the third form of metaphor, the literal term is *implied* and the figurative term is *named*. In the fourth form, *both* the literal *and* figurative terms are *implied*. The following poem exemplifies both forms:

47. It sifts from leaden sieves

It sifts from leaden sieves,
It powders all the wood.
It fills with alabaster wool
The wrinkles of the road.

It makes an even face   5
Of mountain and of plain—
Unbroken forehead from the east
Unto the east again.

It reaches to the fence,
It wraps it rail by rail   10
Till it is lost in fleeces;
It deals celestial veil

To stump and stack and stem—
A summer's empty room—
Acres of joints where harvests were,   15
Recordless,° but for them.   unrecorded

It ruffles wrists of posts
As ankles of a queen,
Then stills its artisans like ghosts,
Denying they have been.   20

Emily Dickinson (1830–1886)

QUESTIONS

1. This poem consists essentially of a series of metaphors having the same literal term identified only as "It." What is "It"?
2. In several of these metaphors the figurative term is named—"alabaster wool" (3), "fleeces" (11), "celestial veil" (12). In two of them, however, the figurative term as well as the literal term is left unnamed. To what is "It" compared in lines 1–2? In lines 17–18?
3. Comment on the additional metaphorical expressions or complications contained in "leaden sieves" (1), "alabaster wool" (3), "even face" (5), "unbroken forehead" (7), "a summer's empty room" (14), "artisans" (19).

Metaphors of the fourth form, as one might guess, are comparatively rare. An extended example, however, is provided by Dickinson's "I like to see it lap the miles" (No. 191).

Using some examples from the previous four poems, the chart below provides a visual demonstration of the figures of comparison (simile and the four forms of metaphor).

		Poem Number	Literal Term	Figurative Term
Similes (*like, as, seems,* etc.)		44	named guitarist guitarist	named conqueror man with woman
Metaphors (*is, are,* etc.)	Form 1	45	named life	named hound
	Form 2	46	named leaves	**implied** [snake] hissed
	Form 3	47	**implied** it [snow]	named wool
	Form 4	47	**implied** it [snow]	**implied** [flour] sifts

Personification consists in giving the attributes of a human being to an animal, an object, or a concept. It is really a subtype of metaphor, an implied comparison in which the figurative term of the comparison is always a human being. When Sylvia Plath makes a mirror speak and think (No. 21), she is personifying an object. When Keats describes autumn as a harvester "sitting careless on a granary floor" or "on a half-reaped furrow sound asleep" (No. 43), he is personifying a season. Personifications differ in the degree to which they ask the reader actually to visualize the literal term in human form. In

Keats's comparison, we are asked to make a complete identification of autumn with a human being. In Sylvia Plath's, though the mirror speaks and thinks, we continue to visualize it as a mirror; similarly, in Frost's "Bereft" (No. 46), the "restive" door remains in appearance a door tugged by the wind. In Browning's reference to "the startled little waves" (No. 32), a personification is barely suggested; we would make a mistake if we tried to visualize the waves in human form or even, really, to think of them as having human emotions.*

48. Scholars

Logic does well at school;
And Reason answers every question right;
Poll-parrot Memory unwinds her spool;
And Copy-cat keeps Teacher well in sight:

The Heart's a truant; nothing does by rule;   5
Safe in its wisdom, is taken for a fool;
Nods through the morning on the dunce's stool;
    And wakes to dream all night.

Walter de la Mare (1873–1956)

QUESTIONS

1. The title identifies the metaphorical context. What is it, and what language in the poem supports it? Is it the purpose of the poem to denigrate scholarly diligence?
2. Five of the capitalized "names" are personifications, and one is not. Which one, and why not?

Closely related to personification is **apostrophe,** which consists in addressing someone absent or dead or something nonhuman as if

---

*The various figures of speech blend into each other, and it is sometimes difficult to classify a specific example as definitely metaphor or symbol, symbolism or allegory, understatement or irony, irony or paradox. Often a given example may exemplify two or more figures at once. In "The Guitarist Tunes Up" (No. 44), "wire and wood" are metonymies (see page 620) for a guitar and are personified as subjects, slaves, or soldiers who could be commanded by a lordly conqueror. In "The world is too much with us" (No. 28), when the winds are described as calm, "like sleeping flowers," the flowers function as part of a simile and are personified as something that can sleep. The important consideration in reading poetry is not that we classify figures definitively but that we construe them correctly.

that person or thing were present and alive and could reply to what is being said. The speaker in A. E. Housman's "To an Athlete Dying Young" (No. 240) apostrophizes a dead runner. William Blake apostrophizes a tiger throughout his famous poem (No. 205) but does not otherwise personify it. Keats apostrophizes *and* personifies autumn (No. 43). Personification and apostrophe are both ways of giving life and immediacy to one's language, but since neither requires great imaginative power on the part of the poet—apostrophe especially does not—they may degenerate into mere mannerisms and are to be found as often in bad and mediocre poetry as in good. We need to distinguish between their effective use and their merely conventional use.

49. Western Wind

> Western wind, when wilt thou blow,
> The small rain down can rain?
> Christ! if my love were in my arms,
> And I in my bed again!

Anonymous (c. 1500)

QUESTIONS

1. Paraphrase the first two lines. What do you conceive to be the speaker's situation?
2. What is the connection between the first two lines and the last two?

In contrast to the preceding figures that compare *unlike* things are two figures that rest on congruences or correspondences. **Synecdoche** (the use of the part for the whole) and **metonymy** (the use of something closely related for the thing actually meant) are alike in that both substitute some significant detail or aspect of an experience for the experience itself. Thus Shakespeare uses synecdoche when he says that the cuckoo's song is unpleasing to a "married ear" (No. 4), for he means a married *man*. Kay uses synecdoche when she refers to "catalogues of domes" (No. 25), because what she means is "enough domed buildings to fill a catalogue," and Housman's Terence (No. 11) uses synecdoche when he declares that "malt does more than Milton can / To justify God's ways to man," for "malt" means beer or ale, of which malt is an essential ingredient. On the other hand, when Terence advises "fellows whom it hurts to think" to "Look into the pewter pot / To see the world as the world's not," he is using metonymy, for by "pewter pot" he means the ale *in* the pot, not the pot itself, and by "world" he means human life and the conditions under which it is lived. Shakespeare uses metonymy when he says that the yellow cuckoo-buds "paint the meadows with delight" (No. 4), for he means with bright color that produces delight. Robert Frost uses metonymy in "'Out, Out—'" (No. 90) when he describes an injured boy holding up his cut hand "as if to keep / The life from spilling," for literally he means to keep the blood from spilling. In each case, however, the poem gains in vividness, meaning, or compactness. Kay, by substituting one architectural detail for whole buildings, suggests the superficiality and boredom of a person who looks at many but appreciates none. Shakespeare, by referring to bright color as "delight," evokes not only the visual effect but the emotional response it arouses. Frost tells us both that the boy's hand is bleeding and that his life is in danger.

Many synecdoches and metonymies, of course, like many metaphors, have become so much a part of the language that they no longer strike us as figurative; this is the case with *redhead* for a red-haired person, *hands* for manual workers, *highbrow* for a sophisticate, *tongues* for languages, and a boiling *kettle* for the water *in* the kettle. Such figures are often referred to as *dead metaphors* (where the word *metaphor* is itself a metonymy for all figurative speech). Synecdoche and metonymy are so much alike that it is hardly worthwhile to distinguish between them, and the latter term is increasingly used for both. In this book metonymy will be used for both figures—that is, for any figure in which a part or something closely related is substituted for the thing literally meant.

We said at the beginning of this chapter that figurative language often provides a more effective means of saying what we mean than does direct statement. What are some of the reasons for that effectiveness?

First, figurative language affords us imaginative pleasure. Imagination might be described in one sense as that faculty or ability of the mind that proceeds by sudden leaps from one point to another, that goes up a stair by leaping in one jump from the bottom to the top rather than by climbing up one step at a time.* The mind takes delight in these sudden leaps, in seeing likenesses between unlike things. We have all probably taken pleasure in staring into a fire and seeing castles and cities and armies in it, or in looking into the clouds and shaping

---

*It is also the faculty of mind that is able to "picture" or "image" absent objects as if they were present. It was with imagination in this sense that we were concerned in the chapter on imagery.

them into animals or faces, or in seeing a man in the moon. We name our plants and flowers after fancied resemblances: jack-in-the-pulpit, babies'-breath, Queen Anne's lace. Figures of speech are therefore satisfying in themselves, providing us with a source of pleasure in the exercise of the imagination.

Second, figures of speech are a way of bringing additional imagery into verse, of making the abstract concrete, of making poetry more sensuous. When Tennyson's eagle falls "like a thunderbolt" (No. 1), his swooping down for his prey is charged with energy, speed, and power; the simile also recalls that the Greek god Zeus was accompanied by an eagle and armed with lightning. When Emily Dickinson compares poetry to prancing coursers (No. 23), she objectifies imaginative and rhythmical qualities by presenting them in visual terms. When Robert Browning compares the crisping waves to "fiery ringlets" (No. 32), he starts with one image and transforms it into three. Figurative language is a way of multiplying the sense appeal of poetry.

Third, figures of speech are a way of adding emotional intensity to otherwise merely informative statements and of conveying attitudes along with information. If we say, "So-and-so is a rat" or "My feet are killing me," our meaning is as much emotional as informative. When Philip Larkin's pathetic escapist metaphorically compares books to "a load of crap" (No. 14), the vulgar language not only expresses his distaste for reading, but intensifies the characterization of him as a man whose intellectual growth was stunted. As this example shows, the use of figures may be a poet's means of revealing the characteristics of a speaker—*how* he or she expresses a thought will define the attitudes or qualities as much as *what* that thought is. When Frost's speaker in "Bereft" (No. 46) sees a striking snake in an eddy of leaves he shows that he is fearful. When Wilfred Owen compares a soldier caught in a gas attack to a man drowning under a green sea (No. 3), he conveys a feeling of despair and suffocation as well as a visual image.

Fourth, figures of speech are an effective means of concentration, a way of saying much in brief compass. Like words, they may be multidimensional. Consider, for instance, the merits of comparing life to a candle, as Shakespeare does in a passage from *Macbeth* (No. 91). Life is like a candle in that it begins and ends in darkness; in that while it burns, it gives off light and energy, is active and colorful; in that it gradually consumes itself, gets shorter and shorter; in that it can be snuffed out at any moment; in that it is brief at best, burning only for a short duration. Possibly your imagination can suggest other similarities. But at any rate, Macbeth's compact, metaphorical description of life as a "brief candle" suggests certain truths about life that would require dozens of words to state in literal language. At the same time it makes the abstract concrete, provides imaginative pleasure, and adds a degree of emotional intensity.

It is as important, when analyzing and discussing a poem, to decide what it is that the figures accomplish as it is to identify them. Seeing a personification or a simile should lead to the next questions: *What use is being made of this figure? How does it contribute to the experience of the poem?*

Obviously, if we are to read poetry well, we must be able to respond to figurative language. Every use of figurative language involves a risk of misinterpretation, though the risk is well worth taking. For the person who can interpret the figure, the dividends are immense. Fortunately all people have imagination to some degree, and imagination can be cultivated. By practice, one's ability to interpret figures of speech can be increased.

EXERCISE

Identify each of the following quotations as literal or figurative. If figurative, explain what is being compared to what and explain the appropriateness of the comparison. EXAMPLE: "Talent is a cistern; genius is a fountain." ANSWER: Metaphor. Talent = cistern; genius = fountain. Talent exists in finite supply; it can be used up. Genius is inexhaustible, ever renewing.

1. O tenderly the haughty day
   Fills his blue urn with fire.   *Ralph Waldo Emerson*
2. It is with words as with sunbeams—the more
   they are condensed, the deeper they burn.   *Robert Southey*
3. Joy and Temperance and Repose
   Slam the door on the doctor's nose.   *Anonymous*
4. The pen is mightier than the sword.   *Edward Bulwer-Lytton*
5. The strongest oaths are straw
   To the fire i' the blood.   *William Shakespeare*
6. The Cambridge ladies . . . live in furnished souls.   *e. e. cummings*
7. Dorothy's eyes, with their long brown lashes,
   looked very much like her mother's.   *Laetitia Johnson*
8. The tawny-hided desert crouches watching her.   *Francis Thompson*
9. Let us eat and drink, for tomorrow we shall die.   *Isaiah 22.13*
10. Let us eat and drink, for tomorrow we may die.
                             Common misquotation of the above

50. Mind

Mind in its purest play is like some bat
That beats about in caverns all alone,
Contriving by a kind of senseless wit
Not to conclude against a wall of stone.

It has no need to falter or explore;   5
Darkly it knows what obstacles are there,
And so may weave and flitter, dip and soar
In perfect courses through the blackest air.

And has this simile a like perfection?
The mind is like a bat. Precisely. Save   10
That in the very happiest intellection
A graceful error may correct the cave.

Richard Wilbur (b. 1921)

QUESTIONS

1. A poet may use a variety of metaphors and similes in developing a subject
   or may, as Wilbur does here, develop a single figure at length (this poem
   is an example of an **extended simile**). Identify in this chapter a poem
   containing a variety of figures and define the advantages of each type of
   development.
2. Explore the similarities between the two things compared in this poem.
   In line 12, what is meant by "A graceful error" and by "correct the cave"?

51. I taste a liquor never brewed

I taste a liquor never brewed,
From tankards scooped in pearl;
Not all the vats upon the Rhine
Yield such an alcohol!

Inebriate of air am I,   5
And debauchee of dew,
Reeling, through endless summer days,
From inns of molten blue.

When landlords turn the drunken bee
Out of the foxglove's door,   10
When butterflies renounce their drams,
I shall but drink the more!

Till seraphs swing their snowy hats,
And saints to windows run,
To see the little tippler   15
Leaning against the sun!

Emily Dickinson (1830–1886)

QUESTIONS

1. Vocabulary: *debauchee* (6), *foxglove* (10).
2. In this **extended metaphor,** what is being compared to alcoholic intoxication? The clues are given in the variety of "liquors" named or implied—"air" (5), "dew" (6), and the nectar upon which birds and butterflies feed.
3. What figurative meanings have the following details: "tankards scooped in pearl" (2), "inns of molten blue" (8), "snowy hats" (13)?
4. The last stanza creates a sterotypical street scene in which neighbors observe the behavior of a drunkard. What do comic drunks lean against in the street? What unexpected attitude do the seraphs and saints display?

52. Metaphors

I'm a riddle in nine syllables,
An elephant, a ponderous house,
A melon strolling on two tendrils,
O red fruit, ivory, fine timbers!
This loaf's big with its yeasty rising.   5
Money's new-minted in this fat purse.
I'm a means, a stage, a cow in calf.
I've eaten a bag of green apples,
Boarded the train there's no getting off.

Sylvia Plath (1932–1963)

QUESTIONS

1. Like its first metaphor, this poem is a riddle to be solved by identifying the literal terms of its metaphors. After you have identified the speaker ("riddle," "elephant," "house," "melon," "stage," "cow"), identify the literal meanings of the related metaphors ("syllables," "tendrils," "fruit," "ivory," "timbers," "loaf," "yeasty rising," "money," "purse," "train"). How do you interpret line 8?
2. How does the form of the poem relate to its content? Is this poem a complaint?

53. Song: Go, lovely rose!

Go, lovely rose!
Tell her that wastes her time and me
That now she knows,
When I resemble her to thee,
How sweet and fair she seems to be.   5

Tell her that's young
And shuns to have her graces spied
That hadst thou sprung
In deserts where no men abide,
Thou must have uncommended died.   10

Small is the worth
Of beauty from the light retired.
Bid her come forth,
Suffer herself to be desired
And not blush so to be admired.   15

Then die! that she
The common fate of all things rare
May read in thee,
How small a part of time they share
That are so wondrous sweet and fair!   20

Edmund Waller (1607–1687)

QUESTIONS

1. Vocabulary: *resemble* (4), *suffer* (14).
2. The speaker addresses a rose, but his message is to a beautiful young woman. How might this indirect means of speaking to her increase the effect of his message? What is he asking her to do? What part does "time" play in the poem?
3. Rather than using apostrophe to compare his love to a rose, the speaker might have addressed her directly, making the comparison in a simile or a metaphor ("you are like a rose" or "you are a rose"), or he might have used an abstract third-person form ("she is like a rose" or "she is a rose"). What does the poem gain from apostrophe?

54. Toads

Why should I let the toad *work*
Squat on my life?
Can't I use my wit as a pitchfork
And drive the brute off?

Six days of the week it soils   5
   With its sickening poison—
Just for paying a few bills!
   That's out of proportion.

Lots of folk live on their wits:
   Lecturers, lispers,   10
Losels,° loblolly-men,° louts—   scoundrels; bumpkins
   They don't end as paupers;

Lots of folk live up lanes
   With fires in a bucket,
Eat windfalls and tinned sardines—   15
   They seem to like it.

Their nippers° have got bare feet,   children
   Their unspeakable wives
Are skinny as whippets—and yet
   No one actually *starves.*   20

Ah, were I courageous enough
   To shout *Stuff your pension!*
But I know, all too well, that's the stuff
   That dreams are made on;

For something sufficiently toad-like   25
   Squats in me, too;
Its hunkers° are heavy as hard luck,   haunches
   And cold as snow,

And will never allow me to blarney
   My way to getting   30
The fame and the girl and the money
   All at one sitting.

I don't say, one bodies the other
   One's spiritual truth;
But I do say it's hard to lose either,   35
   When you have both.

Philip Larkin (1922–1985)

QUESTIONS

1. Two "toads" are described in the poem. Where is each located? How are they described? What are the antecedents of the pronouns "one" and "the other / One's" (33–34) respectively?
2. What characteristics in common have the people mentioned in lines 9–12? Those mentioned in lines 13–20?

3. Explain the pun in lines 22–23 and the literary allusion it leads into. (If you don't recognize the allusion, check Shakespeare's *The Tempest*, Act 4, scene 1, lines 156–58).
4. The first "toad" is explicitly identified as "*work*" (1). The literal term for the second "toad" is not named. Why not? What do you take it to be?
5. What kind of person is the speaker? What are his attitudes toward work?

55. A Valediction: Forbidding Mourning

As virtuous men pass mildly away,
   And whisper to their souls to go,
While some of their sad friends do say,
   The breath goes now, and some say, no:

So let us melt, and make no noise,   5
   No tear-floods, nor sigh-tempests move;
'Twere profanation of our joys
   To tell the laity our love.

Moving of th' earth brings harms and fears,
   Men reckon what it did and meant,   10
But trepidation of the spheres,
   Though greater far, is innocent.

Dull sublunary lovers' love
   (Whose soul is sense) cannot admit
Absence, because it doth remove   15
   Those things which elemented it.

But we by a love so much refined,
   That ourselves know not what it is,
Inter-assurèd of the mind,
   Care less, eyes, lips, and hands to miss.   20

Our two souls therefore, which are one,
   Though I must go, endure not yet
A breach, but an expansion,
   Like gold to airy thinness beat.

If they be two, they are two so   25
   As stiff twin compasses are two;
Thy soul the fixed foot, makes no show
   To move, but doth, if th' other do.

And though it in the center sit,
   Yet when the other far doth roam,   30
It leans, and hearkens after it,
   And grows erect, as that comes home.

Such wilt thou be to me, who must
Like th' other foot, obliquely run;
Thy firmness makes my circle just,   35
And makes me end, where I begun.

John Donne (1572–1631)

QUESTIONS

1. Vocabulary: *valediction* (title), *mourning* (title), *profanation* (7), *laity* (8), *trepidation* (11), *innocent* (12), *sublunary* (13), *elemented* (16). Line 11 is a reference to the spheres of the Ptolemaic cosmology, whose movements caused no such disturbance as does a movement of the earth—that is, an earthquake.
2. Is the speaker in the poem about to die? Or about to leave on a journey? (The answer may be found in a careful analysis of the simile in the last three stanzas and by noticing that the idea of dying in stanza 1 is introduced in a simile.)
3. The poem is organized around a contrast of two kinds of lovers: the "laity" (8) and, as their implied opposite, the "priesthood." Are these terms literal or metaphorical? What is the essential difference between their two kinds of love? How, according to the speaker, does their behavior differ when they must separate from each other? What is the motivation of the speaker in this "valediction"?
4. Find and explain three similes and one metaphor used to describe the parting of true lovers. The figure in the last three stanzas is one of the most famous in English literature. Demonstrate its appropriateness by obtaining a drawing compass or by using two pencils to imitate the two legs.
5. What kind of language is used in the poem? Is the language consonant with the figures of speech?

56. To His Coy Mistress

Had we but world enough, and time,
This coyness, lady, were no crime.
We would sit down, and think which way
To walk, and pass our long love's day.
Thou by the Indian Ganges' side   5
Shouldst rubies find; I by the tide
Of Humber would complain. I would
Love you ten years before the Flood,
And you should, if you please, refuse
Till the conversion of the Jews.   10
My vegetable love should grow
Vaster than empires, and more slow;
An hundred years should go to praise

Thine eyes, and on thy forehead gaze;
Two hundred to adore each breast,   15
But thirty thousand to the rest;
An age at least to every part,
And the last age should show your heart.
For, lady, you deserve this state,
Nor would I love at lower rate.   20
   But at my back I always hear
Time's wingèd chariot hurrying near;
And yonder all before us lie
Deserts of vast eternity.
Thy beauty shall no more be found,   25
Nor, in thy marble vault, shall sound
My echoing song; then worms shall try
That long-preserved virginity,
And your quaint honor turn to dust,
And into ashes all my lust: 30
The grave's a fine and private place,
But none, I think, do there embrace.
   Now therefore, while the youthful hue
Sits on thy skin like morning dew,
And while thy willing soul transpires   35
At every pore with instant fires,
Now let us sport us while we may,
And now, like amorous birds of prey,
Rather at once our time devour
Than languish in his slow-chapped power.   40
Let us roll all our strength and all
Our sweetness up into one ball,
And tear our pleasures with rough strife
Thorough° the iron gates of life.   through
Thus, though we cannot make our sun   45
Stand still, yet we will make him run.

Andrew Marvell (1621–1678)

QUESTIONS

1. Vocabulary: *coy* (title), *Humber* (7), *transpires* (35). "Mistress" (title) has the now archaic meaning of *sweetheart;* "slow-chapped" (40) derives from *chap,* meaning *jaw.*
2. What is the speaker urging his sweetheart to do? Why is she being "coy"?
3. Outline the speaker's argument in three sentences that begin with the words *If, But,* and *Therefore.* Is the argument valid?
4. Explain the appropriateness of "vegetable love" (11). What simile in the third section contrasts with it and how? What image in the third section

contrasts with the distance between the Ganges and the Humber? Of what would the speaker be "complaining" by the Humber (7)?
5. Explain the figures in lines 22, 24, and 40 and their implications.
6. Explain the last two lines. For what is "sun" a metonymy?
7. Is this poem principally about love or about time? If the latter, what might making love represent? What philosophy is the poet advancing here?

57. Suum Cuique

Wilt thou seal up the avenues of ill?
Pay every debt, as if God wrote the bill.

Ralph Waldo Emerson (1803–1882)

QUESTIONS

1. The title is Latin: "to each his own." How would you interpret its relevance to the poem?
2. Discuss the metaphor in line 1 and the simile in line 2. Is "Pay every debt" literal or metaphorical? Or both?

58. after minor surgery

this is the dress rehearsal
when the body
like a constant lover
flirts for the first time
with faithlessness   5

when the body
like a passenger on a long journey
hears the conductor call out
the name
of the first stop   10

when the body
in all its fear and cunning
makes promises to me
it knows
it cannot keep   15

Linda Pastan (b. 1932)

QUESTIONS

1. Explore the metaphor in line 1: if "this is the dress rehearsal" of a drama, what is the opening night? Explore the similes in the first two stanzas (for example, if the body is "like a constant lover," what is it flirting with, and what would "faithlessness" be?).
2. What is the effect of the shift in the third stanza from the use of similes to personification?

59. Dream Deferred

What happens to a dream deferred?

Does it dry up
like a raisin in the sun?
Or fester like a sore—
And then run?   5
Does it stink like rotten meat?
Or crust and sugar over—
like a syrupy sweet?

Maybe it just sags
like a heavy load.   10

Or does it explode?

Langston Hughes (1902–1967)

QUESTIONS

1. Of the six images, five are similes. Which is a metaphor? Comment on its position and its effectiveness.
2. Since the dream could be any dream, the poem is general in its implication. What happens to your understanding of it on learning that its author was a black American?

EXERCISES

1. Robert Frost has said that "poetry is what evaporates from all translations." Why might this be true? How much of a word can be translated?
2. Ezra Pound has defined great literature as "simply language charged with meaning to the utmost possible degree." Would this be a good definition of poetry? The word "charged" is roughly equivalent to *filled*. Why is "charged" a better word in Pound's definition?

CHAPTER SIX

Figurative Language 2

Symbol, Allegory

60. The Road Not Taken

Two roads diverged in a yellow wood,
And sorry I could not travel both
And be one traveler, long I stood
And looked down one as far as I could
To where it bent in the undergrowth;   5

Then took the other, as just as fair,
And having perhaps the better claim,
Because it was grassy and wanted wear;
Though as for that the passing there
Had worn them really about the same,   10

And both that morning equally lay
In leaves no step had trodden black.
Oh, I kept the first for another day!
Yet knowing how way leads on to way,
I doubted if I should ever come back.   15

I shall be telling this with a sigh
Somewhere ages and ages hence:
Two roads diverged in a wood, and I—
I took the one less traveled by,
And that has made all the difference.   20

Robert Frost (1874–1963)

QUESTIONS

1. Does the speaker feel that he has made the wrong choice in taking the
   road "less traveled by" (19)? If not, why will he "sigh" (16)? What does he
   regret?

2. Why will the choice between two roads that seem very much alike make such a big difference many years later?

A **symbol** may be roughly defined as something that means *more* than what it is. "The Road Not Taken," for instance, concerns a choice made between two roads by a person out walking in the woods. He would like to explore both roads. He tells himself that he will explore one and then come back and explore the other, but he knows that he will probably be unable to do so. By the last stanza, however, we realize that the poem is about something more than the choice of paths in a wood, for that choice would be relatively unimportant, whereas this choice, the speaker believes, is one that will make a great difference in his life and is one that he will remember "with a sigh . . . ages and ages hence." We must interpret his choice of a road as a symbol for any choice in life between alternatives that appear almost equally attractive but will result through the years in a large difference in the kind of experience one knows.

Image, metaphor, and symbol shade into each other and are sometimes difficult to distinguish. In general, however, an image means only what it is; the figurative term in a metaphor means something other than what it is; and a symbol means what it is and something more, too. A symbol, that is, functions literally and figuratively at the same time.* If I say that a shaggy brown dog was rubbing its back against a white picket fence, I am talking about nothing but a dog (and a picket fence) and am therefore presenting an image. If I say, "Some dirty dog stole my wallet at the party," I am not talking about a dog at all and am therefore using a metaphor. But if I say, "You can't teach an old dog new tricks," I am talking not only about dogs but about living creatures of any species and am therefore speaking symbolically. Images, of course, do not cease to be images when they become incorporated in metaphors or symbols. If we are discussing the sensuous qualities of "The Road Not Taken," we should refer to the two leaf-strewn roads in the yellow wood as an image; if we are discussing the significance of the poem, we talk about the roads as symbols.

The symbol is the richest and at the same time the most difficult of the poetic figures. Both its richness and its difficulty result from its

---

*This account does not hold for nonliterary symbols such as the letters of the alphabet and algebraic signs (the symbol ∞ for infinity or $=$ for equals). With these, the symbol is meaningless except as it stands for something else, and the connection between the sign and what it stands for is purely arbitrary.

imprecision. Although the poet may pin down the meaning of a symbol to something fairly definite and precise, more often the symbol is so general in its meaning that it can suggest a great variety of specific meanings. It is like an opal that flashes out different colors when slowly turned in the light. The choice in "The Road Not Taken," for instance, concerns some choice in life, but what choice? Was it a choice of profession? A choice of residence? A choice of mate? It might be any, all, or none of these. We cannot determine what particular choice the poet had in mind, if any, and it is not important that we do so. It is enough if we see in the poem an expression of regret that the possibilities of life experience are so sharply limited. The speaker in the poem would have liked to explore both roads, but he could explore only one. The person with a craving for life, whether satisfied or dissatisfied with the choices he has made, will always long for the realms of experience that he had to forgo. Because the symbol is a rich one, the poem suggests other meanings too. It affirms a belief in the possibility of choice and says something about the nature of choice—how each choice narrows the range of possible future choices, so that we make our lives as we go, both freely choosing and being determined by past choices. Though not a philosophical poem, it obliquely comments on the issue of free will and determinism and indicates the poet's own position. It can do all these things, concretely and compactly, by its use of an effective symbol.

Symbols vary in the degree of identification and definition given them by their authors. In this poem Frost forces us to interpret the choice of roads symbolically by the degree of importance he gives it in the last stanza. Sometimes poets are much more specific in identifying their symbols. Sometimes they do not identify them at all. Consider, for instance, the next two poems.

61. A Noiseless Patient Spider

A noiseless patient spider,
I marked where on a little promontory it stood isolated,
Marked how to explore the vacant vast surrounding,
It launched forth filament, filament, filament, out of itself,
Ever unreeling them, ever tirelessly speeding them.   5

And you, O my soul where you stand,
Surrounded, detached, in measureless oceans of space,
Ceaselessly musing, venturing, throwing, seeking the spheres to
    connect them,

Till the bridge you will need be formed, till the ductile anchor hold,
Till the gossamer thread you fling catch somewhere, O my soul.   10

Walt Whitman (1819–1892)

In the first stanza the speaker describes a spider's apparently tireless effort to attach its thread to some substantial support so that it can begin constructing a web. The speaker reveals his attentive interest by the hinted personification of the spider, and his sympathy with it is expressed in the overstatement of size and distance—he is trying to perceive the world as a spider sees it from a "promontory" surrounded by vast space. He even attributes a human motive to the spider: exploration, rather than instinctive web-building. Nevertheless, the first stanza is essentially literal—the close observation of an actual spider at its task. In the second stanza the speaker explicitly interprets the symbolic meaning of what he has observed: his soul (personified by apostrophe and by the capabilities assigned to it) is like the spider in its constant striving. But the soul's purpose is to find spiritual or intellectual certainties in the vast universe it inhabits. The symbolic meaning is richer than a mere comparison; while a spider's actual purpose is limited to its instinctive drives, the human soul strives for much more, in a much more complex "surrounding." And, of course, the result of the soul's symbolized striving is much more open-ended than is the attempt of a spider to spin a web, as the paradoxical language ("Surrounded, detached," "ductile anchor") implies. *Can* the human soul connect the celestial spheres?

QUESTIONS

1. In "The Hound" (No. 45) Robert Francis compares unpredictable human life to a hound. Whitman compares the striving human soul to a spider. Why is Francis's comparison a metaphor and Whitman's a symbol? What additional comparison does Whitman make to the soul's quest? What figure of speech is it?
2. In what ways are the spider and the soul contrasted? What do the contrasts contribute to the meaning of the symbol?
3. Can the questing soul represent human actions other than the search for spiritual certainties?

62. The Sick Rose

O Rose, thou art sick!
The invisible worm

That flies in the night,
In the howling storm,

Has found out thy bed   5
Of crimson joy,
And his dark secret love
Does thy life destroy.

William Blake (1757–1827)

QUESTIONS

1. What figures of speech do you find in the poem in addition to symbol? How do they contribute to its force or meaning?
2. Several symbolic interpretations of this poem are given below. Do you think of others?
3. Should symbolic meanings be sought for the night and the storm? If so, what meanings would you suggest?

In "A Noiseless Patient Spider" the symbolic meaning of the spider is identified and named. By contrast, in "The Sick Rose" no meanings are explicitly indicated for the rose and the worm. Indeed, we are not *compelled* to assign them specific meanings. The poem is validly read as being about a rose that has been attacked on a stormy night by a cankerworm.

The organization of "The Sick Rose" is so rich, however, and its language so powerful that the rose and the worm refuse to remain *merely* a flower and an insect. The rose, apostrophized and personified in the first line, has traditionally been a symbol of feminine beauty and love, as well as of sensual pleasures. "Bed" can refer to a woman's bed as well as to a flower bed. "Crimson joy" suggests the intense pleasure of passionate lovemaking as well as the brilliant beauty of a red flower. The "dark secret love" of the "invisible worm" is more strongly suggestive of a concealed or illicit love affair than of the feeding of a cankerworm on a plant, though it fits that too. For all these reasons the rose almost immediately suggests a woman and the worm her secret lover—and the poem suggests the corruption of innocent but physical love by concealment and deceit. But the possibilities do not stop there. The worm is a common symbol or metonymy for death; and for readers steeped in Milton (as Blake was) it recalls the "undying worm" of *Paradise Lost,* Milton's metaphor for the snake (or Satan in the form of a snake) that tempted Eve. Meanings multiply also for the reader who is familiar with Blake's other writings. Thus "The Sick Rose" has been variously interpreted as referring to the destruction of joyous physical love by jealousy, deceit, concealment, or the possessive instinct; of innocence by experience; of humanity by Satan; of imagination and joy by analytic reason; of life by death. We cannot say what specifically the poet had in mind, nor need we do so. A symbol defines an *area* of meaning, and any interpretation that falls within that area is permissible. In Blake's poem the rose stands for something beautiful, or desirable, or good. The worm stands for some corrupting agent. Within these limits, the meaning is largely "open." And because the meaning is open, the reader is justified in bringing personal experience to its interpretation. Blake's poem, for instance, might remind someone of a gifted friend whose promise has been destroyed by drug addiction.

Between the extremes exemplified by "A Noiseless Patient Spider" and "The Sick Rose" a poem may exercise all degrees of control over the range and meaning of its symbolism. Consider another example.

63. Digging

Between my finger and my thumb
The squat pen rests; snug as a gun.

Under my window, a clean rasping sound
When the spade sinks into gravelly ground:
My father, digging. I look down   5

Till his straining rump among the flowerbeds
Bends low, comes up twenty years away
Stooping in rhythm through potato drills
Where he was digging.

The coarse boot nestled on the lug, the shaft   10
Against the inside knee was levered firmly.
He rooted out tall tops, buried the bright edge deep
To scatter new potatoes that we picked
Loving their cool hardness in our hands.

By God, the old man could handle a spade.   15
Just like his old man.

My grandfather cut more turf in a day
Than any other man on Toner's bog.
Once I carried him milk in a bottle
Corked sloppily with paper. He straightened up   20
To drink it, then fell to right away

Nicking and slicing neatly, heaving sods
Over his shoulder, going down and down
For the good turf. Digging.

The cold smell of potato mould, the squelch and slap   25
Of soggy peat, the curt cuts of an edge
Through living roots awaken in my head.
But I've no spade to follow men like them.

Between my finger and my thumb
The squat pen rests.   30
I'll dig with it.

Seamus Heaney (b. 1939)

QUESTIONS

1. Vocabulary: *drills* (8), *fell to* (21). In Ireland, "turf" (17) is a block of peat dug from a bog; when dried, it is used as fuel.
2. What emotional responses are evoked by the imagery?

On the literal level, this poem presents a writer who interrupts himself to have a look at his father digging in a flower garden below his window. He is reminded of his father twenty years earlier digging potatoes for harvesting, and by that memory he is drawn farther back to his grandfather digging peat from a bog for fuel. The memories are vivid and appealing and rich in imagery, but the writer is not like his forebears, he has "no spade to follow" their examples. And so, with a trace of regret, he decides that his writing will have to be his substitute for their manual tasks.

But the title and the emphasis on varieties of the same task carried out in several different ways over a span of generations alert the reader to the need to discover the further significance of this literal statement. The last line is metaphorical, comparing digging to writing (and thus is itself not symbolic, for on a literal level one cannot dig with a pen). The metaphor, however, suggesting that the writer will commit himself to exploring the kinds of memories in this poem, invites an interpretation of the literal forms of digging. We notice then that the father has been involved in two sorts—the practical, backbreaking task of digging up potatoes to be gathered by the children, and twenty years later the relatively easy chore of digging in flowerbeds so as to encourage the growth of ornamental plants. There is a progression represented in the father's activities, from the necessary and arduous earlier life to the leisurely growing of flowers. Farther back in time, the grandfather's labors were deeper, heavier, and more essential, cutting and digging the material that would be used for heating and cooking—cooking potatoes, we should assume. The grandfather digs deeper and deeper, always in quest of the best peat, "the good turf."

Symbolically, then, digging has meanings that relate to basic needs—for warmth, for sustenance, for beauty, and for the personal satisfaction of doing a job well. In the concluding metaphor, another basic need is implied, the need to remember and confront one's origins, to find oneself in a continuum of meaningful activities, to assert the relevance and importance of one's vocation. And it is not coincidental that an Irish poet should find symbolic meanings in a confluence of Irish materials—from peat bogs to potatoes to poets and writers, that long-beleaguered island has asserted its special and distinct identity. Nor is it coincidental that Heaney selected this to be the opening poem in his first book of poetry: "Digging" is what his poetry does.

Meanings ray out from a symbol, like the corona around the sun or like connotations around a richly suggestive word. But the very fact that a symbol may be so rich in meanings requires that we use the greatest tact in its interpretation. Although Blake's "The Sick Rose" might, because of personal association, remind us of a friend destroyed by drug addiction, it would be unwise to say that Blake uses the rose to symbolize a gifted person succumbing to drug addiction, for this interpretation is private, idiosyncratic, and narrow. The poem allows it, but does not itself suggest it.

Moreover, we should never assume that because the meaning of a symbol is more or less open, we may make it mean anything we choose. We would be wrong, for instance, in interpreting the choice in "The Road Not Taken" as some choice between good and evil, for the poem tells us that the two roads are much alike and that both lie "In leaves no step had trodden black." Whatever the choice is, it is a choice between two goods. Whatever our interpretation of a symbolic poem, it must be tied firmly to the facts of the poem. We must not let loose of the string and let our imaginations go ballooning up among the clouds. Because the symbol is capable of adding so many dimensions to a poem, it is a peculiarly effective resource for the poet, but it is also peculiarly susceptible to misinterpretation by the incautious reader.

Accurate interpretation of the symbol requires delicacy, tact, and good sense. The reader must maintain balance while walking a tightrope between too little and too much—between underinterpretation and overinterpretation. If the reader falls off, however, it is much more desirable to fall off on the side of too little. Someone who reads "The Road Not Taken" as being only about a choice between two roads in a wood has at least understood part of the experience that the poem communicates, but the reader who reads into it anything imaginable might as well discard the poem and simply daydream.

Above all, we should avoid the disease of seeing symbols everywhere, like a person with hallucinations, whether or not there are symbols there. It is better to miss a symbol now and then than to walk constantly among shadows and mirages.

64. To the Virgins, to Make Much of Time

Gather ye rosebuds while ye may,
    Old Time is still a-flying;
And this same flower that smiles today
    Tomorrow will be dying.

The glorious lamp of heaven, the Sun,   5
    The higher he's a-getting,
The sooner will his race be run,
    And nearer he's to setting.

That age is best which is the first,
    When youth and blood are warmer;   10
But being spent, the worse, and worst
    Times still succeed the former.

Then be not coy, but use your time;
    And while ye may, go marry;
For having lost but once your prime,   15
    You may forever tarry.

Robert Herrick (1591–1674)

QUESTIONS

1. The first two stanzas might be interpreted literally if the third and fourth stanzas did not force us to interpret them symbolically. What do the "rosebuds" symbolize (stanza 1)? What does the course of a day symbolize (stanza 2)? Does the poet narrow the meaning of the rosebud symbol in the last stanza or merely name *one* of its specific meanings?

2. How does the title help us interpret the meaning of the symbol? Why is "virgins" a more meaningful word than, for example, *maidens*?

3. Why is such haste necessary in gathering the rosebuds? True, the blossoms die quickly, but they are replaced by others. Who *really* is dying?
4. What are "the worse, and worst" times (11)? Why?
5. Why is the wording of the poem better than these possible alternatives: *blooms* for "smiles" (3); *course* for "race" (7); *used* for "spent" (11); *spend* for "use" (13)?

Allegory is a narrative or description that has a second meaning beneath the surface. Although the surface story or description may have its own interest, the author's major interest is in the ulterior meaning. When Pharoah in the Bible, for instance, has a dream in which seven fat kine are devoured by seven lean kine, the story does not really become significant until Joseph interprets its allegorical meaning: that Egypt is to enjoy seven years of fruitfulness and prosperity followed by seven years of famine. Allegory has been defined sometimes as an extended metaphor and sometimes as a series of related symbols. But it is usually distinguishable from both of these. It is unlike extended metaphor in that it involves a *system* of related comparisons rather than one comparison drawn out. It differs from symbolism in that it puts less emphasis on the images for their own sake and more on their ulterior meanings. Also, these meanings are more fixed. In allegory there is usually a one-to-one correspondence between the details and a single set of ulterior meanings. In complex allegories the details may have more than one meaning, but these meanings tend to be definite. Meanings do not ray out from allegory as they do from a symbol.

Allegory is less popular in modern literature than it was in medieval and Renaissance writing, and it is much less often found in short poems than in long narrative works such as *The Faerie Queene, Everyman,* and *Pilgrim's Progress.* It has sometimes, especially with political allegory, been used to disguise meaning rather than reveal it (or, rather, to disguise it from some people while revealing it to others). Though less rich than the symbol, allegory is an effective way of making the abstract concrete and has occasionally been used effectively even in fairly short poems.

65. Peace

Sweet Peace, where dost thou dwell? I humbly crave,
Let me once know.
I sought thee in a secret cave,

And asked if Peace were there.
A hollow wind did seem to answer, "No,   5
Go seek elsewhere."

I did, and going did a rainbow note.
"Surely," thought I,
"This is the lace of Peace's coat;
I will search out the matter."   10
But while I looked, the clouds immediately
Did break and scatter.

Then went I to a garden, and did spy
A gallant flower,
The Crown Imperial. "Sure," said I,   15
"Peace at the root must dwell."
But when I digged, I saw a worm devour
What showed so well.

At length I met a reverend good old man,
Whom when for Peace   20
I did demand, he thus began:
"There was a prince of old
At Salem dwelt, who lived with good increase
Of flock and fold.

"He sweetly lived; yet sweetness did not save   25
His life from foes.
But after death out of his grave
There sprang twelve stalks of wheat;
Which many wondering at, got some of those
To plant and set.   30

"It prospered strangely, and did soon disperse
Through all the earth,
For they that taste it do rehearse
That virtue lies therein,
A secret virtue, bringing peace and mirth   35
By flight of sin.

"Take of this grain, which in my garden grows,
And grows for you;
Make bread of it; and that repose
And peace, which everywhere   40
With so much earnestness you do pursue,
Is only there."

George Herbert (1593–1633)

QUESTIONS

1. Vocabulary: *gallant* (14), *rehearse* (33), *virtue* (34). "Crown Imperial" (15) is a garden flower, fritillary; "Salem" (23) is Jerusalem.
2. Identify the "prince" (22), his "flock and fold" (24), the "twelve stalks of wheat" (28), the "grain" (37), and the "bread" (39).
3. Should the "secret cave" (stanza 1), the "rainbow" (stanza 2), and the flower "garden" (stanza 3) be understood merely as places where the speaker searched or do they have more precise meanings?
4. Who is the "reverend good old man" (19), and what is *his* garden (37)?

---

66. Fire and Ice

Some say the world will end in fire,
Some say in ice.
From what I've tasted of desire
I hold with those who favor fire.
But if it had to perish twice,   5
I think I know enough of hate
To say that for destruction ice
Is also great
And would suffice.

Robert Frost (1874–1963)

QUESTIONS

1. Who are "Some" (1–2)? To which two theories do lines 1–2 refer? (In answering, it might help you to know that the poem was published in 1920.)
2. What do "fire" and "ice" respectively symbolize? What two meanings has "the world"?
3. The poem ends with an *understatement* (see Chapter 7). How does it affect the tone of the poem?

67. Ulysses

It little profits that an idle king,
By this still hearth, among these barren crags,
Matched with an agèd wife, I mete and dole
Unequal laws unto a savage race,
That hoard, and sleep, and feed, and know not me.   5

I cannot rest from travel; I will drink
Life to the lees. All times I have enjoyed
Greatly, have suffered greatly, both with those
That loved me, and alone; on shore, and when
Through scudding drifts the rainy Hyades   10
Vext the dim sea. I am become a name;
For always roaming with a hungry heart
Much have I seen and known,—cities of men,
And manners, climates, councils, governments,
Myself not least, but honored of them all;   15
And drunk delight of battle with my peers,
Far on the ringing plains of windy Troy.
I am a part of all that I have met;
Yet all experience is an arch wherethrough
Gleams that untraveled world, whose margin fades   20
For ever and for ever when I move.
How dull it is to pause, to make an end,
To rust unburnished, not to shine in use!
As though to breathe were life! Life piled on life
Were all too little, and of one to me   25
Little remains; but every hour is saved
From that eternal silence, something more,
A bringer of new things; and vile it were
For some three suns to store and hoard myself,
And this gray spirit yearning in desire   30
To follow knowledge like a sinking star,
Beyond the utmost bound of human thought.

This is my son, mine own Telemachus,
To whom I leave the scepter and the isle—
Well-loved of me, discerning to fulfil   35
This labor, by slow prudence to make mild
A rugged people, and through soft degrees
Subdue them to the useful and the good.
Most blameless is he, centered in the sphere
Of common duties, decent not to fail   40
In offices of tenderness, and pay
Meet adoration to my household gods,
When I am gone. He works his work, I mine.

There lies the port; the vessel puffs her sail:
There gloom the dark, broad seas. My mariners,   45
Souls that have toiled, and wrought, and thought with me—
That ever with a frolic welcome took
The thunder and the sunshine, and opposed

Free hearts, free foreheads—you and I are old;
Old age hath yet his honor and his toil.   50
Death closes all; but something ere the end,
Some work of noble note, may yet be done,
Not unbecoming men that strove with Gods.
The lights begin to twinkle from the rocks;
The long day wanes; the slow moon climbs; the deep   55
Moans round with many voices. Come, my friends,
'Tis not too late to seek a newer world.
Push off, and sitting well in order smite
The sounding furrows; for my purpose holds
To sail beyond the sunset, and the baths   60
Of all the western stars, until I die.
It may be that the gulfs will wash us down;
It may be we shall touch the Happy Isles,
And see the great Achilles, whom we knew.
Though much is taken, much abides; and though   65
We are not now that strength which in old days
Moved earth and heaven, that which we are, we are:
One equal temper of heroic hearts,
Made weak by time and fate, but strong in will
To strive, to seek, to find, and not to yield.   70

Alfred, Lord Tennyson (1809–1892)

QUESTIONS

1. Vocabulary: *lees* (7), *Hyades* (10), *meet* (42).
2. Ulysses, king of Ithaca, is a legendary Greek hero, a major figure in Homer's *Iliad,* the hero of Homer's *Odyssey,* and a minor figure in Dante's *Divine Comedy.* After ten years at the siege of Troy, Ulysses set sail for home but, having incurred the wrath of the god of the sea, he was subjected to storms and vicissitudes and was forced to wander for another ten years, having many adventures and seeing most of the Mediterranean world before again reaching Ithaca, his wife, and his son. Once back home, according to Dante, he still wished to travel and "to follow virtue and knowledge." In Tennyson's poem, Ulysses is represented as about to set sail on a final voyage from which he will not return. Locate Ithaca on a map. Where exactly, in geographical terms, does Ulysses intend to sail (59–64)? (The Happy Isles were the Elysian fields, or Greek paradise; Achilles was another Greek prince, the hero of the *Iliad,* who was killed at the siege of Troy.)
3. Ulysses's speech is divided into three sections, beginning at lines 1, 33, and 44. What is the topic or purpose of each section? To whom, specifically, is the third section addressed? To whom, would you infer, are sections 1 and 2 addressed? Where do you visualize Ulysses as standing during his speech?
4. Characterize Ulysses. What kind of person is he as Tennyson represents him?

5. What way of life is symbolized by Ulysses? Find as many evidences as you can that Ulysses's desire for travel represents something more than mere wanderlust and wish for adventure.
6. Give two symbolic implications of the westward direction of Ulysses's journey.
7. Interpret lines 18–21 and 26–29. What metaphor is implied in line 23? What is symbolized by "The thunder and the sunshine" (48)? What do the two metonymies in line 49 stand for?

68. Curiosity

may have killed the cat; more likely
the cat was just unlucky, or else curious
to see what death was like, having no cause
to go on licking paws, or fathering
litter on litter of kittens, predictably.   5

Nevertheless, to be curious
is dangerous enough. To distrust
what is always said, what seems,
to ask odd questions, interfere in dreams,
leave home, smell rats, have hunches   10
do not endear cats to those doggy circles
where well-smelt baskets, suitable wives, good lunches
are the order of things, and where prevails
much wagging of incurious heads and tails.

Face it. Curiosity   15
will not cause us to die—
only lack of it will.
Never to want to see
the other side of the hill
or that improbable country   20
where living is an idyll
(although a probable hell)
would kill us all.
Only the curious
have, if they live, a tale   25
worth telling at all.

Dogs say cats love too much, are irresponsible,
are changeable, marry too many wives,
desert their children, chill all dinner tables
with tales of their nine lives.   30

Well, they are lucky. Let them be
nine-lived and contradictory,
curious enough to change, prepared to pay
the cat price, which is to die
and die again and again,   35
each time with no less pain.
A cat minority of one
is all that can be counted on
to tell the truth. And what cats have to tell
on each return from hell   40
is this: that dying is what the living do,
that dying is what the loving do,
and that dead dogs are those who do not know
that dying is what, to live, each has to do.

Alastair Reid (b. 1926)

QUESTIONS

1. On the surface this poem is a dissertation on cats. What deeper comments does it make? Of what are cats and dogs, in this poem, symbols?
2. In what different senses are the words *death, die,* and *dying* here used?
3. Compare and contrast this poem in meaning and manner with "Ulysses."

69. Discovery of the New World

The creatures that we met this morning
    marveled at our green skins
        and scarlet eyes.
They lack antennae
    and can't be made to grasp   5
        your proclamation that they are
our lawful food and prey and slaves,
        nor can they seem to learn
    their body-space is needed to materialize
        our oxygen absorbers—   10
which they conceive are breathing
        and thinking creatures whom they implore
at first as angels or (later) as devils
        when they are being snuffed out
            by an absorber swelling   15
                into their space.
Their history bled from one this morning

while we were tasting his brain
   in holographic rainbows
  which we assembled into quite an interesting   20
      set of legends—
         that's all it came to, though
   the colors were quite lovely before we
  poured them into our time;
      the blue shift bleached away   25
meaningless circumstance and they would not fit
  any of our truth-matrices—
     there was, however,
  a curious visual echo in their history
     of our own coming to their earth;   30
a certain General Sherman
    had said concerning a group of them
      exactly what we were saying to you
  about these creatures:
it is our destiny to asterize this planet,   35
  and they will not be asterized,
    so they must be wiped out.
We need their space and oxygen
  which they do not know how to use,
    yet they will not give up their gas unforced,   40
and we feel sure,
    whatever our "agreements" made this morning,
   we'll have to kill them all:
    the more we cook this orbit,
   the fewer next time around.   45
We've finished burning all their crops
   and killed their cattle.
  They'll have to come into our pens
  and then we'll get to study
the way our heart attacks and cancers spread among them, 50
  since they seem not immune to these.
If we didn't have this mission it might be sad
  to see such helpless creatures die,
    but never fear,
the riches of this place are ours   55
  and worth whatever pain others may have to feel.
    We'll soon have it cleared
as in fact it is already, at the poles.
   Then we will be safe, and rich, and happy here forever.

Carter Revard (b. 1931)

QUESTIONS

1. Vocabulary: *asterize* (35) is a word coined from the common prefix *aster-* or *astro-;* what would you surmise it to mean? "[M]aterialize / our oxygen absorbers" (9–10) and "truth-matrices" (27) are similarly devised terms whose meanings you should easily infer. What does the poem gain from this stretching of normal language?
2. Who (or what) is the speaker? Who (or what) is being addressed, and for what purpose?
3. "[A] certain General Sherman," some of whose attitudes are adapted beginning in line 35, was William Tecumseh Sherman (1820–1891), the Union general who after the Civil War was sent on a mission to control the native Americans in the West. Sherman was both praised and criticized for his accomplishment but took pride in having confined so many "Indians" to reservations. How does this poem allegorize that aspect of American history?
4. Does this allegory have meaning beyond its reflection of history and its fanciful imagination of a future?

70. Hymn to God My God, in My Sickness

Since I am coming to that holy room
    Where, with thy choir of saints for evermore,
I shall be made thy music, as I come
    I tune the instrument here at the door,
    And what I must do then, think now before.   5

Whilst my physicians by their love are grown
    Cosmographers, and I their map, who lie
Flat on this bed, that by them may be shown
    That this is my southwest discovery,
    Per fretum febris,° by these straits to die,   through the 10
                                      raging of fever
I joy that in these straits I see my west;
    For though those currents yield return to none,
What shall my west hurt me? As west and east
    In all flat maps (and I am one) are one,
    So death doth touch the resurrectiön.   15

Is the Pacific Sea my home? Or are
    The eastern riches? Is Jerusalem?
Anyan° and Magellan and Gibraltar,   Bering Strait
    All straits, and none but straits, are ways to them,
    Whether there Japhet dwelt, or Cham, or Shem.   20

We think that Paradise and Calvary,
  Christ's cross and Adam's tree, stood in one place;
Look, Lord, and find both Adams met in me;
  As the first Adam's sweat surrounds my face,
  May the last Adam's blood my soul embrace.   25

So, in his purple wrapped receive me, Lord;
  By these his thorns give me his other crown;
And as to others' souls I preached thy word,
  Be this my text, my sermon to mine own:
  Therefore that he may raise, the Lord throws down.   30

John Donne (1572–1631)

QUESTIONS

1. Vocabulary: *Cosmographers* (7).
2. For the last ten years of his life John Donne was Dean of St. Paul's Cathedral in London, and he is famous for his sermons (see lines 28–30) as well as his poems. According to his earliest biographer (though some scholars disagree), this poem was written eight days before Donne's death. What are "that holy room" (1) and "the instrument" (4)? What is the speaker doing in stanza 1?
3. During Donne's lifetime such explorers as Henry Hudson and Martin Frobisher sought a Northwest Passage to the East Indies to match Magellan's discovery in 1520 of a southwest passage through the straits that bear his name. Why is "southwest" more appropriate to the speaker's condition than "northwest"? In what ways is his raging fever like a strait? What different meanings of the word "straits" (10) are operative here? What do the straits symbolize?
4. In what ways does the speaker's body resemble a map?
5. Although the map is metaphorical, its parts are symbolic. What does the west symbolize? The east? The fact that west and east are one?
6. What meanings has the word "return" (12)? (Compare line 17.)
7. Japhet, Cham (or Ham), and Shem (20)—the sons of Noah—are in Christian legend the ancestors of the three races of man, roughly identifiable with the populations of Europe, Africa, and Asia. What must one go through, according to the speaker, to reach any place important? In what ways are the Pacific Ocean, the East Indies, and Jerusalem (16–17) each a fitting symbol for the speaker's own destination?
8. The locations of the garden of Eden and of Calvary (21) were identical according to early Christian scholars. How does this tie in with the poem's geographical symbolism? What connection is there between Adam's "sweat" (24) and Christ's "blood" (25)? Because Adam is said in the Bible to prefigure Christ (Romans 5:12–21), Christ is sometimes called the second Adam. How do the two Adams meet in the speaker? What do blood and sweat (together and separately) symbolize?

9. For what are "eastern riches" (17), "his purple" (26), and "his thorns" (27) respectively metonymies? What do "purple" and "thorns" symbolize? What is Christ's "other crown" (27)?
10. With what earlier paradoxes (see Chapter 7) in the poem does the paradox in the final line (very roughly paraphrased from Psalms 146.8) tie in? How does the poem explain human suffering and give it meaning?

71. Our journey had advanced

Our journey had advanced.
Our feet were almost come
To that odd fork in Being's road
"Eternity" by term.

Our pace took sudden awe.   5
Our feet reluctant led.
Before were cities, but between
The forest of the dead.

Retreat was out of hope,
Behind, a sealed route,   10
"Eternity's" white flag before,
And God at every gate.

Emily Dickinson (1830–1886)

QUESTIONS

1. Identify the "journey" (1), the "road" (3), the "forest" (8), and the speaker's destination in this allegory. What literal human experience is the subject of the poem?
2. Explain the implications of the plural forms: "Our" (1–2, 5–6), "cities" (7), "every gate" (12).
3. What is the underlying metaphor implied in the last stanza by "Retreat" (9), "flag" (11), "gate" (12)? Does the "white flag" signify surrender?

72.   Dust of Snow

The way a crow
Shook down on me
The dust of snow
From a hemlock tree

Has given my heart   5
A change of mood
And saved some part
Of a day I had rued.

Robert Frost (1874–1963)

73. Soft Snow

I walked abroad in a snowy day;
I asked the soft snow with me to play;
She played and she melted in all her prime,
And the winter called it a dreadful crime.

William Blake (1757–1827)

QUESTION

In what respects are the two preceding poems alike? In what respects are
they essentially different?

EXERCISES

1. Determine whether "sleep," in the following poems, is literal, a symbol, or
   a metaphor (or simile).
   a. "Stopping by Woods on a Snowy Evening" (No. 105)
   b. "The Chimney Sweeper" (No. 78)
   c. "Is my team plowing" (No. 15)
   d. "The Second Coming" (No. 298)
2. Shapiro's "The Fly" (No. 278) and Shaw's "Shut In" (No. 139) deal with
   a common subject. Which of them is symbolic? Explain your choice.
3. What does Blake's tiger symbolize (No. 205)?
4. Determine whether the following poems are predominantly symbolic or
   literal.
   a. "Because I could not stop for Death" (No. 151)
   b. "The Snow Man" (No. 283)
   c. "The Darkling Thrush" (No. 235)
   d. "Song: Go and catch a falling star" (No. 219)
   e. "Blackberry Eating" (No. 165)
   f. "Musée des Beaux Arts" (No. 202)
   g. "Richard Cory" (No. 271)
   h. "The Wild Swans at Coole" (No. 299)
   i. "Poem: As the cat" (No. 291)
   j. "To Waken an Old Lady" (No. 293)
   k. "Desert Places" (No. 224)
   l. "Never Again Would Birds' Song Be the Same" (No. 226)
   m. "Constantly risking absurdity" (No. 150)

CHAPTER SEVEN

Figurative Language 3

Paradox, Overstatement, Understatement, Irony

Aesop tells the tale of a traveler who sought refuge with a Satyr on a bitter winter night. On entering the Satyr's lodging, he blew on his fingers, and was asked by the Satyr why he did it. "To warm them up," he explained. Later, on being served a piping-hot bowl of porridge, he blew also on it, and again was asked why he did it. "To cool it off," he explained. The Satyr thereupon thrust him out of doors, for he would have nothing to do with a man who could blow hot and cold with the same breath.

A **paradox** is an apparent contradiction that is nevertheless somehow true. It may be either a situation or a statement. Aesop's tale of the traveler illustrates a paradoxical situation. As a figure of speech, paradox is a statement. When Alexander Pope wrote that a literary critic of his time would "damn with faint praise," he was using a verbal paradox, for how can a man damn by praising?

When we understand all the conditions and circumstances involved in a paradox, we find that what at first seemed impossible is actually entirely plausible and not strange at all. The paradox of the cold hands and hot porridge is not strange to anyone who knows that a stream of air directed upon an object of different temperature will tend to bring that object closer to its own temperature. And Pope's paradox is not strange when we realize that *damn* is being used figuratively, and that Pope means only that a too reserved praise may damage an author with the public almost as much as adverse criticism. In a paradoxical statement the contradiction usually stems from one of the words being used figuratively or with more than one denotation.

The value of paradox is its shock value. Its seeming impossibility startles the reader into attention and, by the fact of its apparent absurdity, underscores the truth of what is being said.

74. Much madness is divinest sense

Much madness is divinest sense
To a discerning eye,
Much sense, the starkest madness.
'Tis the majority
In this, as all, prevail: 5
Assent, and you are sane;
Demur, you're straightway dangerous
And handled with a chain.

Emily Dickinson (1830–1886)

QUESTIONS

1. This poem presents the two sides of a paradoxical proposition: that insanity is good sense, and that good sense is insane. How do the concepts implied by the words "discerning" (2) and "majority" (4) provide the resolution of this paradox?
2. How do we know that the speaker does not believe that the majority is correct? How do the last five lines extend the subject beyond a contrast between sanity and insanity?

Overstatement, understatement, and verbal irony form a continuous series, for they consist, respectively, of saying more, saying less, and saying the opposite of what one really means.

Overstatement, or *hyperbole,* is simply exaggeration, but exaggeration in the service of truth. It is not the same as a fish story. If you say, "I'm starved!" or "You could have knocked me over with a feather!" or "I'll die if I don't pass this course!" you do not expect to be taken literally; you are merely adding emphasis to what you really mean. (And if you say, "There were literally millions of people at the beach!" you are merely piling one overstatement on top of another, for you really mean, "There were figuratively millions of people at the beach," or, literally, "The beach was very crowded.") Like all figures of speech, overstatement may be used with a variety of effects. It may be humorous or grave, fanciful or restrained, convincing or unconvincing. When Tennyson says of his eagle (No. 1) that it is "*Close* to the sun in lonely lands," he says what appears to be literally true, though we know from our study of astronomy that it is not. When Kay reports that her character in "Pathedy of Manners" (No. 25) "Saw *catalogues* of domes" on her European trip she implies the superficiality of a person for whom visiting a few churches and palaces seemed like enough architecture to fill catalogues. When Frost says, at the conclusion of "The Road Not Taken" (No. 60),

> I shall be telling this with a sigh
> Somewhere *ages and ages hence*

we are scarcely aware of the overstatement, so quietly is the assertion made. Unskillfully used, however, overstatement may seem strained and ridiculous, leading us to react as Gertrude does to the player-queen's speeches in *Hamlet:* "The lady doth protest too much."

It is paradoxical that one can emphasize a truth either by overstating it or by understating it. **Understatement,** or saying less than one means, may exist in what one says or merely in how one says it. If, for instance, upon sitting down to a loaded dinner plate, you say, "This looks like a nice snack," you are actually stating less than the truth; but if you say, with Artemus Ward, that a man who holds his hand for half an hour in a lighted fire will experience "a sensation of excessive and disagreeable warmth," you are stating what is literally true but with a good deal less force than the situation warrants.

75. The Sun Rising

> Busy old fool, unruly sun,
>   Why dost thou thus
> Through windows and through curtains call on us?
> Must to thy motions lovers' seasons run?
>   Saucy pedantic wretch, go chide   5
>   Late schoolboys and sour 'prentices,
>   Go tell court-huntsmen that the king will ride,
>   Call country ants to harvest offices;
> Love, all alike, no season knows, nor clime,
> Nor hours, days, months, which are the rags of time.   10
>
>   Thy beams so reverend and strong
>   Why shouldst thou think?
> I could eclipse and cloud them with a wink,
> But that I would not lose her sight so long;
>   If her eyes have not blinded thine,   15
>   Look, and tomorrow late tell me
>   Whether both th' Indias of spice and mine
>   Be where thou left'st them, or lie here with me.
> Ask for those kings whom thou saw'st yesterday,
> And thou shalt hear, "All here in one bed lay."   20

> She's all states, and all princes I;
>   Nothing else is.
> Princes do but play us; compared to this,
> All honor's mimic, all wealth alchemy.
>   Thou, sun, art half as happy as we,   25
>   In that the world's contracted thus;
>   Thine age asks ease, and since thy duties be
>   To warm the world, that's done in warming us.
> Shine here to us, and thou art everywhere;
> This bed thy center is, these walls thy sphere.   30

John Donne (1572–1631)

QUESTIONS

1. Vocabulary: *offices* (8), *alchemy* (24).
2. As precisely as possible, identify the time of day and the locale. What three "persons" does the poem involve?
3. What is the speaker's attitude toward the sun in stanzas 1 and 2? How and why does it change in stanza 3?
4. Does the speaker understate or overstate the actual qualities of the sun? Point out specific examples. Identify the overstatements in lines 9–10, 13, 15, 16–20, 21–24, 29–30. What do these overstatements achieve?
5. Line 17 introduces a geographical image referring to the East and West Indies, sources respectively of spices and gold. What relationship between the lovers and the rest of the world is expressed in lines 15–22?
6. Who is actually the intended listener for this extended apostrophe? What is the speaker's purpose? What is the poem's purpose?

76. Incident

> Once riding in old Baltimore
>   Heart-filled, head-filled with glee,
> I saw a Baltimorean
>   Keep looking straight at me.
>
> Now I was eight and very small,   5
>   And he was no whit bigger,
> And so I smiled, but he poked out
>   His tongue, and called me, "Nigger."
>
> I saw the whole of Baltimore
>   From May until December;   10
> Of all the things that happened there
>   That's all that I remember.

Countee Cullen (1903–1946)

QUESTION

What accounts for the effectiveness of the last stanza? Comment on the title.
Is it in key with the meaning of the poem?

Like paradox, **irony** has meanings that extend beyond its use
merely as a figure of speech.

Verbal irony, saying the opposite of what one means, is often
confused with sarcasm and with satire, and for that reason it may be
well to look at the meanings of all three terms. Sarcasm and satire
both imply ridicule, one on the colloquial level, the other on the literary
level. **Sarcasm** is simply bitter or cutting speech, intended to wound
the feelings (it comes from a Greek word meaning to tear flesh). **Satire**
is a more formal term, usually applied to written literature rather than
to speech and ordinarily implying a higher motive: it is ridicule (either
bitter or gentle) of human folly or vice, with the purpose of bringing
about reform or at least of keeping other people from falling into similar folly or vice. Irony, on the other hand, is a literary device or figure
that may be used in the service of sarcasm or ridicule or may not. It is
popularly confused with sarcasm and satire because it is so often used
as their tool; but irony may be used without either sarcastic or satirical intent, and sarcasm and satire may exist (though they do not usually) without irony. If, for instance, one of the members of your class
raises his hand on the discussion of this point and says, "I don't understand," and your instructor replies, with a tone of heavy disgust in
his voice, "Well, I wouldn't expect *you* to," he is being sarcastic but
not ironic; he means exactly what he says. But if, after you have done
particularly well on an examination, your instructor brings your test
papers into the classroom saying, "Here's some *bad* news for you: you
all got As and Bs!" he is being ironic but not sarcastic. Sarcasm, we
may say, is cruel, as a bully is cruel: it intends to give hurt. Satire is
both cruel and kind, as a surgeon is cruel and kind: it gives hurt in the
interest of the patient or of society. Irony is neither cruel nor kind: it is
simply a device, like a surgeon's scalpel, for performing any operation
more skillfully.

Though verbal irony always implies the opposite of what is said, it
has many gradations, and only in its simplest forms does it mean *only*
the opposite of what is said. In more complex forms it means both
what is said and the opposite of what is said, at once, though in different ways and with different degrees of emphasis. When Terence's critic,
in "Terence, this is stupid stuff" (No. 11) says, "*Pretty* friendship 'tis

to rhyme / Your friends to death before their time" (11–12), we may substitute the literal *sorry* for the ironic "pretty" with little or no loss of meaning. When Terence speaks in reply, however, of the pleasure of drunkenness—"And down in *lovely* muck I've lain, / Happy till I woke again" (35–36)—we cannot substitute *loathsome* for "lovely" without considerable loss of meaning for, while muck is actually extremely unpleasant to lie in, it may *seem* lovely to an intoxicated person. Thus two meanings—one the opposite of the other—operate at once.

Like all figures of speech, verbal irony runs the danger of being misunderstood. With irony, the risks are perhaps greater than with other figures for, if metaphor is misunderstood, the result may be simply bewilderment; but if irony is misunderstood, the reader goes away with exactly the opposite idea from what the user meant to convey. The results of misunderstanding if, for instance, you ironically called someone a villain, might be calamitous. For this reason the user of irony must be very skillful in its use, conveying by an altered tone, or by a wink of the eye or pen, that irony is intended; and the reader of literature must be always alert to recognize the subtle signs of irony.

No matter how broad or obvious the irony, a number of people in any large audience always will misunderstand. The humorist Artemus Ward used to protect himself against these people by writing at the bottom of his newspaper column, "This is writ ironical." But irony is most delightful and most effective when it is subtlest. It sets up a special understanding between writer and reader that may add either grace or force. If irony is too obvious, it sometimes seems merely crude. But if effectively used, it, like all figurative language, is capable of adding extra dimensions to meaning.

77. One Perfect Rose

A single flow'r he sent me, since we met.
    All tenderly his messenger he chose;
Deep-hearted, pure, with scented dew still wet—
    One perfect rose.

I knew the language of the floweret;   5
    "My fragile leaves," it said, "his heart enclose."
Love long has taken for his amulet
    One perfect rose.

Why is it no one ever sent me yet
　　One perfect limousine, do you suppose?　　　　　10
Ah no, it's always just my luck to get
　　One perfect rose.

Dorothy Parker (1893–1967)

QUESTIONS

1. Comment on the contrast in diction between stanzas 1–2 and 3.
2. At what or whom is this satire directed? For a partial answer, review "Song: Go, lovely rose!" (No. 53).

The term *irony* always implies some sort of discrepancy or incongruity. In verbal irony the discrepancy is between what is said and what is meant. In other forms the discrepancy may be between appearance and reality or between expectation and fulfillment. These other forms of irony are, on the whole, more important resources for the poet than is verbal irony. Two types are especially important.

In **dramatic irony*** the discrepancy is not between what the speaker says and what the speaker means but between what the speaker says and what the poem means. The speaker's words may be perfectly straightforward, but the author, by putting these words in a particular speaker's mouth, may be indicating to the reader ideas or attitudes quite opposed to those the speaker is voicing. This form of irony is more complex than verbal irony and demands a more complex response from the reader. It may be used not only to convey attitudes but also to illuminate character, for the author who uses it is indirectly commenting not only upon the value of the ideas uttered but also upon the nature of the person who utters them. Such comment may be harsh, gently mocking, or sympathetic.

---

*The term *dramatic irony,* which stems from Greek tragedy, often connotes something more specific and perhaps a little different from what I am developing here. It describes a speech or an action in a story that has much greater significance to the audience than to the character who speaks or performs it, because the audience possesses knowledge the character does not have, as when the enemies of Ulysses, in the *Odyssey,* wish good luck and success to a man who the reader knows is Ulysses himself in disguise, or as when Oedipus, in the play by Sophocles, bends every effort to discover the murderer of Laius so that he may avenge the death, not knowing, as the audience does, that Laius is the man whom he himself once slew. I have appropriated the term for a perhaps slightly different situation because no other suitable term exists. Both uses have the common characteristic—that the author conveys to the reader something different, or at least something more, than the character himself intends or understands.

78. The Chimney Sweeper

When my mother died I was very young,
And my father sold me while yet my tongue
Could scarcely cry "'weep! 'weep! 'weep! 'weep!"
So your chimneys I sweep, and in soot I sleep.

There's little Tom Dacre, who cried when his head,   5
That curled like a lamb's back, was shaved; so I said,
"Hush, Tom! never mind it, for, when your head's bare,
You know that the soot cannot spoil your white hair."

And so he was quiet, and that very night,
As Tom was asleeping, he had such a sight!   10
That thousands of sweepers, Dick, Joe, Ned, and Jack,
Were all of them locked up in coffins of black.

And by came an Angel who had a bright key,
And he opened the coffins and set them all free;
Then down a green plain leaping, laughing, they run,   15
And wash in a river, and shine in the sun.

Then naked and white, all their bags left behind,
They rise upon clouds and sport in the wind;
And the Angel told Tom, if he'd be a good boy,
He'd have God for his father, and never want joy.   20

And so Tom awoke, and we rose in the dark,
And got with our bags and our brushes to work.
Though the morning was cold, Tom was happy and warm;
So if all do their duty they need not fear harm.

William Blake (1757–1827)

QUESTIONS

1. In the eighteenth century small boys, sometimes no more than four or
   five years old, were employed to climb up the narrow chimney flues and
   clean them, collecting the soot in bags. Such boys, sometimes sold to the
   master sweepers by their parents, were miserably treated by their masters
   and often suffered disease and physical deformity. Characterize the boy
   who speaks in this poem. How do his and the poet's attitudes toward his
   lot in life differ? How, especially, are the meanings of the poet and the
   speaker different in lines 3, 7–8, and 24?
2. The dream in lines 11–20, besides being a happy dream, can be interpreted allegorically. Point out possible significances of the sweepers' being
   "locked up in coffins of black" (12) and the Angel's releasing them with a
   bright key to play upon green plains.

A third type of irony, **irony of situation,** occurs when a discrepancy exists between the actual circumstances and those that would seem appropriate or between what one anticipates and what actually comes to pass. If a man and his second wife, on the first night of their honeymoon, are accidentally seated at the theater next to the man's first wife, we should call the situation ironic. When, in O. Henry's famous short story "The Gift of the Magi" a poor young husband pawns his most prized possession, a gold watch, in order to buy his wife a set of combs for her hair for Christmas, and his wife sells her most prized possession, her long brown hair, in order to buy a fob for her husband's watch, we call the situation ironic. When King Midas, in the famous fable, is granted his fondest wish, that anything he touch turn to gold, and then finds that he cannot eat because even his food turns to gold, we call the situation ironic. When Coleridge's Ancient Mariner finds himself in the middle of the ocean with "Water, water, everywhere," but not a "drop to drink," we call the situation ironic. In each case the circumstances are not what would seem appropriate or what we would expect.

Dramatic irony and irony of situation are powerful devices for poetry for, like symbol, they enable a poem to suggest meanings without stating them—to communicate a great deal more than is said. We have seen one effective use of irony of situation in "The Widow's Lament in Springtime" (No. 35). Another is in "Ozymandias," which follows.

Irony and paradox may be trivial or powerful devices, depending on their use. At their worst they may degenerate into mere mannerism and mental habit. At their best they may greatly extend the dimensions of meaning in a work of literature. Because irony and paradox demand an exercise of critical intelligence, they are particularly valuable as safeguards against sentimentality.

79. Ozymandias

I met a traveler from an antique land
Who said: Two vast and trunkless legs of stone
Stand in the desert . . . Near them, on the sand,
Half sunk, a shattered visage lies, whose frown,
And wrinkled lip, and sneer of cold command,   5
Tell that its sculptor well those passions read
Which yet survive, stamped on these lifeless things,
The hand that mocked them, and the heart that fed;
And on the pedestal these words appear:

"My name is Ozymandias, king of kings;   10
Look on my works, ye Mighty, and despair!"
Nothing beside remains. Round the decay
Of that colossal wreck, boundless and bare
The lone and level sands stretch far away.

Percy Bysshe Shelley (1792–1822)

QUESTIONS

1. "[S]urvive" (7) is a transitive verb with "hand" and "heart" as direct objects. Whose hand? Whose heart? What figure of speech is exemplified in "hand" and "heart"?
2. Characterize Ozymandias.
3. Ozymandias was an ancient Egyptian tyrant. This poem was first published in 1817. Of what is Ozymandias a *symbol?* What contemporary reference might the poem have had in Shelley's time?
4. What is the theme of the poem and how is it "stated"?

EXERCISE

Identify the figure in each of the following quotations as paradox, overstatement, understatement, or irony—and explain the use to which the figure is put (emotional emphasis, humor, satire, etc.).

1. Poetry is a language that tells us, through a more or less emotional reaction, something that cannot be said.   *Edwin Arlington Robinson*
2. Christians have burnt each other, quite persuaded
   That all the Apostles would have done as they did.   *Lord Byron*
3. A man who could make so vile a pun would not scruple to pick a pocket.
                                                         John Dennis
4. Last week I saw a woman flayed, and you will hardly believe how much it altered her person for the worse.   *Jonathan Swift*
5. . . . Where ignorance is bliss, / 'Tis folly to be wise.   *Thomas Gray*
6. All night I made my bed to swim; with my tears I dissolved my couch.
                                                         Psalms 6.6
7. Believe him, he has known the world too long,
   And seen the death of much immortal song.   *Alexander Pope*
8. Cowards die many times before their deaths;
   The valiant never taste of death but once.   *William Shakespeare*
9. . . . all men would be cowards if they durst.   *John Wilmot, Earl of Rochester*

80. Batter my heart, three-personed God

Batter my heart, three-personed God; for you
As yet but knock, breathe, shine, and seek to mend;

That I may rise and stand, o'erthrow me, and bend
Your force to break, blow, burn, and make me new.
I, like an usurped town, to another due,   5
Labor to admit you, but oh, to no end;
Reason, your viceroy in me, me should defend,
But is captived, and proves weak or untrue.
Yet dearly I love you and would be lovèd fain,°   gladly
But am betrothed unto your enemy;   10
Divorce me, untie or break that knot again,
Take me to you, imprison me, for I,
Except° you enthrall me, never shall be free,   unless
Nor ever chaste, except you ravish me.

John Donne (1572–1631)

QUESTIONS

1. In this sonnet (one in a group called "Holy Sonnets") the speaker addresses God in a series of metaphors and paradoxes. What is the paradox in the first quatrain? To what is the "three-personed God" metaphorically compared? To what is the speaker compared? Can the first three verbs of the parallel lines 2 and 4 be taken as addressed to specific "persons" of the Trinity (Father, Son, Holy Spirit)? If so, to which are "knock" and "break" addressed? "breathe" and "blow"? "shine" and "burn"? (What concealed pun helps in the attribution of the last pair? What etymological pun in the attribution of the second pair?)
2. To what does the speaker compare himself in the second quatrain? To what is God compared? Who is the usurper? What role does "Reason" (7) play in this political metaphor, and why is it a weak one?
3. To what does the speaker compare himself in the sestet (lines 9–14)? To what does he compare God? Who is the "enemy" (10)? Resolve the paradox in lines 12–13 by explaining the double meaning of "enthrall." Resolve the paradox in line 14 by explaining the double meaning of "ravish."

81. Sorting Laundry

Folding clothes,
I think of folding you
into my life.

Our king-sized sheets
like tablecloths
for the banquets of giants,   5

pillowcases, despite so many
washings, seams still
holding our dreams.

Towels patterned orange and green,   10
flowered pink and lavender,
gaudy, bought on sale,

reserved, we said, for the beach,
refusing, even after years,
to bleach into respectability.   15

So many shirts and skirts and pants
recycling week after week, head over heels
recapitulating themselves.

All those wrinkles
to be smoothed, or else   20
ignored; they're in style.

Myriad uncoupled socks
which went paired into the foam
like those creatures in the ark.

And what's shrunk   25
is tough to discard
even for Goodwill.

In pockets, surprises:
forgotten matches,
lost screws clinking on enamel;   30

paper clips, whatever they held
between shiny jaws, now
dissolved or clogging the drain;

well-washed dollars, legal tender
for all debts public and private,   35
intact despite agitation;

and, gleaming in the maelstrom,
one bright dime,
broken necklace of good gold

you brought from Kuwait,   40
the strangely tailored shirt
left by a former lover. . . .

If you were to leave me,
if I were to fold
only my own clothes,   45

the convexes and concaves
of my blouses, panties, stockings, bras
turned upon themselves,

a mountain of unsorted wash
could not fill   50
the empty side of the bed.

Elisavietta Ritchie (b. 1932)

QUESTIONS

1. Explain the metaphor in the first stanza. Where does the poem explicitly
   return to it? What psychological association connects lines 41–42 to
   line 43?
2. Explain how the length of the poem supports the overstatement in line
   49. What is the speaker's attitude toward the "you" in the poem, and toward her role as housekeeper?

82. The Unknown Citizen

(To JS/07/M/378 This Marble Monument Is Erected by the State)

He was found by the Bureau of Statistics to be
One against whom there was no official complaint,
And all the reports on his conduct agree
That, in the modern sense of an old-fashioned word, he was a saint,
For in everything he did he served the Greater Community.   5
Except for the War till the day he retired
He worked in a factory and never got fired,
But satisfied his employers, Fudge Motors Inc.
Yet he wasn't a scab or odd in his views,
For his Union reports that he paid his dues   10
(Our report on his Union shows it was sound),
And our Social Psychology workers found
That he was popular with his mates and liked a drink.
The Press are convinced that he bought a paper every day
And that his reactions to advertisements were normal in every way. 15
Policies taken out in his name prove that he was fully insured,
And his Health-card shows he was once in hospital but left it cured.
Both Producers Research and High-Grade Living declare
He was fully sensible to the advantages of the Installment Plan
And had everything necessary to the Modern Man,   20
A phonograph, a radio, a car and a frigidaire.
Our researchers into Public Opinion are content
That he held the proper opinions for the time of year;
When there was peace, he was for peace; when there was war, he went.
He was married and added five children to the population,   25
Which our Eugenist says was the right number for a parent of his
   generation,

And our teachers report that he never interfered with their education.
Was he free? Was he happy? The question is absurd:
Had anything been wrong, we should certainly have heard.

W. H. Auden (1907–1973)

QUESTIONS

1. Vocabulary: *scab* (9), *Eugenist* (26).
2. Explain the allusion and the irony in the title. Why was the citizen "unknown"?
3. This obituary of an unknown state "hero" was apparently prepared by a functionary of the state. Give an account of the citizen's life and character from Auden's own point of view.
4. What trends in modern life and social organization does the poem satirize?

83. Departmental

An ant on the tablecloth
Ran into a dormant moth
Of many times his size.
He showed not the least surprise.
His business wasn't with such.   5
He gave it scarcely a touch,
And was off on his duty run.
Yet if he encountered one
Of the hive's enquiry squad
Whose work is to find out God   10
And the nature of time and space,
He would put him onto the case.
Ants are a curious race;
One crossing with hurried tread
The body of one of their dead   15
Isn't given a moment's arrest—
Seems not even impressed.
But he no doubt reports to any
With whom he crosses antennae,
And they no doubt report   20
To the higher up at court.
Then word goes forth in Formic:
"Death's come to Jerry McCormic,
Our selfless forager Jerry.
Will the special Janizary   25
Whose office it is to bury
The dead of the commissary

Go bring him home to his people.
Lay him in state on a sepal.
Wrap him for shroud in a petal.   30
Embalm him with ichor of nettle.
This is the word of your Queen."
And presently on the scene
Appears a solemn mortician;
And taking formal position   35
With feelers calmly atwiddle,
Seizes the dead by the middle,
And heaving him high in air,
Carries him out of there.
No one stands round to stare.   40
It is nobody else's affair.

It couldn't be called ungentle.
But how thoroughly departmental.

Robert Frost (1874–1963)

QUESTIONS

1. Vocabulary: *dormant* (2), *Formic* (22), *Janizary* (25), *commissary* (27),
   sepal (29), *ichor* (31).
2. The poem is ostensibly about ants. Is it ultimately about ants? Give reasons to support your view that it is or is not.
3. What is the author's attitude toward the "departmental" (43) organization of ant society? How is it indicated? Could this poem be described as
   "gently satiric"? If so, in what sense?
4. Compare and contrast this poem with "The Unknown Citizen" in content and manner.

84. The State

When they killed my mother it made me nervous;
I thought to myself, it was *right*:
Of course she was crazy, and how she ate!
And she died, after all, in her way, for the State.
But I minded: how queer it was to stare   5
At one of them not sitting there.

When they drafted Sister I said all night,
"It's healthier there in the fields";
And I'd think, "Now I'm helping to win the War,"
When the neighbors came in, as they did, with my meals.   10

And I was, I was; but I was scared
With only one of them sitting there.

When they took my cat for the Army Corps
Of Conservation and Supply,
I thought of him there in the cold with the mice   15
And I cried, and I cried, and I wanted to die.
They were there, and I saw them, and that is my life.
Now there's nothing. I'm dead, and I want to die.

Randall Jarrell (1914–1965)

QUESTIONS

1. Point out examples of overstatement and understatement. Do they create
   verbal irony, or dramatic irony? Resolve the paradox in line 18.
2. Compare the purpose of this poem to that of "The Unknown Citizen"
   and "Departmental." In what ways are they similar? In what ways are
   they dissimilar?

85. Grace to Be Said at the Supermarket

That God of ours, the Great Geometer,
Does something for us here, where He hath put
(if you want to put it that way) things in shape,
Compressing the little lambs in orderly cubes,
Making the roast a decent cylinder,   5
Fairing the tin ellipsoid of a ham,
Getting the luncheon meat anonymous
In squares and oblongs with the edges bevelled
Or rounded (streamlined, maybe, for greater speed).

Praise Him, He hath conferred aesthetic distance   10
Upon our appetites, and on the bloody
Mess of our birthright, our unseemly need,
Imposed significant form. Through Him the brutes
Enter the pure Euclidean kingdom of number,
Free of their bulging and blood-swollen lives   15
They come to us holy, in cellophane
Transparencies, in the mystical body,

That we may look unflinchingly on death
As the greatest good, like a philosopher should.

Howard Nemerov (1920–1991)

QUESTIONS

1. In this poem "God" is a metaphor for meatpackers and the rest of those who are involved in the display of packaged meat products in the supermarkets. Does the poem satirize "us" for eating meat, or is it aimed at our denial of "our unseemly need" (12)?
2. How does meat in supermarket coolers suggest "the pure Euclidean kingdom of number" (14)?
3. Point out examples of overstatement, understatement, and paradox. Is the irony in this poem verbal or dramatic?

86. in the inner city

in the inner city
or
like we call it
home
we think a lot about uptown   5
and the silent nights
and the houses straight as
dead men
and the pastel lights
and we hang on to our no place   10
happy to be alive
and in the inner city
or
like we call it
home   15

Lucille Clifton (b. 1936)

QUESTION

Is the irony in this poem verbal or dramatic?

87. Mr. Z

Taught early that his mother's skin was the sign of error,
He dressed and spoke the perfect part of honor;
Won scholarships, attended the best schools,
Disclaimed kinship with jazz and spirituals;
Chose prudent, raceless views of each situation,   5
Or when he could not cleanly skirt dissension,

Faced up to the dilemma, firmly seized
Whatever ground was Anglo-Saxonized.

In diet, too, his practice was exemplary:
Of pork in its profane forms he was wary;   10
Expert in vintage wines, sauces and salads,
His palate shrank from cornbread, yams and collards.

He was as careful whom he chose to kiss:
His bride had somewhere lost her Jewishness,
But kept her blue eyes; an Episcopalian   15
Prelate proclaimed them matched chameleon.
Choosing the right addresses, here, abroad,
They shunned those places where they might be barred;
Even less anxious to be asked to dine
Where hosts catered to kosher accent or exotic skin.   20

And so he climbed, unclogged by ethnic weights,
An airborne plant, flourishing without roots.
Not one false note was struck—until he died:
His subtly grieving widow could have flayed
The obit writers, ringing crude changes on a clumsy phrase: 25
"One of the most distinguished members of his race."

M. Carl Holman (1919–1988)

QUESTIONS

1. Vocabulary: *profane* (10), *kosher* (20), *exotic* (20), *ethnic* (21), *obit* (25).
2. Explain Mr. Z's motivation and the strategies he used to achieve his goal.
3. What is the author's attitude toward Mr. Z? Is he satirizing him or the society that produced him? Why does he not give Mr. Z a name?
4. What judgments on Mr. Z are implied by the metaphors in lines 16 and 22? Explain them.
5. What kind of irony is operating in the last line? As you reread the poem, where else do you detect ironic overtones?
6. What is Mr. Z's color?

88. Southern Cop

Let us forgive Ty Kendricks.
The place was Darktown. He was young.
His nerves were jittery. The day was hot.
The Negro ran out of the alley.
And so Ty shot.   5

Let us understand Ty Kendricks.
The Negro must have been dangerous,
Because he ran;
And here was a rookie with a chance
To prove himself a man.   10

Let us condone Ty Kendricks
If we cannot decorate.
When he found what the Negro was running for,
It was too late;
And all we can say for the Negro is   15
It was unfortunate.

Let us pity Ty Kendricks.
He has been through enough,
Standing there, his big gun smoking,
Rabbit-scared, alone,   20
Having to hear the wenches wail
And the dying Negro moan.

Sterling A. Brown (1901–1989)

QUESTIONS

1. Explain the poem in terms of irony and understatement. Is the irony verbal
   or dramatic? Trace the slight changes in the irony from stanza to stanza.
2. To what extent does the poem create sympathy for Ty Kendricks? How
   does it do so? Does that sympathy mean that we should "forgive" (1) or
   "condone" (11) his actions?

89. My Last Duchess

Ferrara

That's my last duchess painted on the wall,
Looking as if she were alive. I call
That piece a wonder, now; Fra Pandolf's hands
Worked busily a day, and there she stands.
Will 't please you sit and look at her? I said   5
"Fra Pandolf" by design, for never read
Strangers like you that pictured countenance,
The depth and passion of its earnest glance,
But to myself they turned (since none puts by
The curtain I have drawn for you, but I)   10
And seemed as they would ask me, if they durst,
How such a glance came there; so, not the first

Are you to turn and ask thus. Sir, 'twas not
Her husband's presence only, called that spot
Of joy into the Duchess' cheek; perhaps   15
Fra Pandolf chanced to say, "Her mantle laps
Over my lady's wrist too much," or, "Paint
Must never hope to reproduce the faint
Half-flush that dies along her throat." Such stuff
Was courtesy, she thought, and cause enough   20
For calling up that spot of joy. She had
A heart—how shall I say?—too soon made glad,
Too easily impressed; she liked whate'er
She looked on, and her looks went everywhere.
Sir, 'twas all one! My favor at her breast,   25
The dropping of the daylight in the West,
The bough of cherries some officious fool
Broke in the orchard for her, the white mule
She rode with round the terrace—all and each
Would draw from her alike the approving speech,   30
Or blush, at least. She thanked men—good! but thanked
Somehow—I know not how—as if she ranked
My gift of a nine-hundred-years-old name
With anybody's gift. Who'd stoop to blame
This sort of trifling? Even had you skill   35
In speech—which I have not—to make your will
Quite clear to such an one, and say, "Just this
Or that in you disgusts me; here you miss,
Or there exceed the mark"—and if she let
Herself be lessoned so, nor plainly set   40
Her wits to yours, forsooth, and made excuse—
E'en then would be some stooping; and I choose
Never to stoop. Oh, sir, she smiled, no doubt,
Whene'er I passed her; but who passed without
Much the same smile? This grew; I gave commands;   45
Then all smiles stopped together. There she stands
As if alive. Will 't please you rise? We'll meet
The company below, then. I repeat,
The Count your master's known munificence
Is ample warrant that no just pretense   50
Of mine for dowry will be disallowed;
Though his fair daughter's self, as I avowed
At starting, is my object. Nay, we'll go
Together down, sir. Notice Neptune, though,
Taming a sea-horse, thought a rarity,   55
Which Claus of Innsbruck cast in bronze for me!

Robert Browning (1812–1889)

QUESTIONS

1. Vocabulary: *officious* (27), *munificence* (49).
2. Ferrara is in Italy. The time is during the Renaissance, probably the six-teenth century. To whom is the Duke speaking? What is the occasion? Are the Duke's remarks about his last Duchess a digression, or do they have some relation to the business at hand?
3. Characterize the Duke as fully as you can. How does your characteriza-tion differ from the Duke's opinion of himself? What kind of irony is this?
4. Why was the Duke dissatisfied with his last Duchess? Was it sexual jeal-ousy? What opinion do you get of the Duchess's personality, and how does it differ from the Duke's opinion?
5. What characteristics of the Italian Renaissance appear in the poem (marriage customs, social classes, art)? What is the Duke's attitude to-ward art? Is it insincere?
6. What happened to the Duchess? Should Browning have told us?

ADDITIONAL EXERCISE

Follow the instructions for the exercise on page 668, of which this is a con-tinuation.

10. Whoe'er their crimes for interest only quit,
    Sin on in virtue, and good deeds *commit*.   *Edward Young*
11. No doubt but ye are the people, and wisdom shall die with you.
                                                        Book of Job, 12.1
12. One soul was ours, one mind, one heart devoted,
    That, wisely doting, asked not why it doted.   *Hartley Coleridge*
13. Give me my Romeo: and, when he shall die,
    Take him and cut him out in little stars,
    And he will make the face of heaven so fine
    That all the world will be in love with night,
    And pay no worship to the garish sun.   *Juliet,* in *Shakespeare*
14. Have not the Indians been kindly and justly treated? Have not the tem-poral things, the vain baubles and filthy lucre of this world, which were too apt to engage their worldy and selfish thoughts, been benevolently taken from them? And have they not instead thereof, been taught to set their affections on things above?   *Washington Irving*
15. There lives more faith in honest doubt,
    Believe me, than in half the creeds.   *Alfred, Lord Tennyson*

CHAPTER EIGHT

Allusion

The famous English diplomat and letter writer Lord Chesterfield once was invited to a great dinner given by the Spanish ambassador. At the conclusion of the meal the host rose and proposed a toast to his master, the king of Spain, whom he compared to the sun. The French ambassador followed with a health to the king of France, whom he likened to the moon. It was then Lord Chesterfield's turn. "Your excellencies have taken from me," he said, "all the greatest luminaries of heaven, and the stars are too small for me to make a comparison of my royal master; I therefore beg leave to give your excellencies— Joshua!"*

For a reader familiar with the Bible—that is, for one who recognizes the biblical allusion—Lord Chesterfield's story will come as a stunning revelation of his wit. For an **allusion**—a reference to something in history or previous literature—is, like a richly connotative word or a symbol, a means of suggesting far more than it says. The one word "Joshua," in the context of Chesterfield's toast, calls up in the reader's mind the whole biblical story of how the Israelite captain stopped the sun and the moon in order that the Israelites might finish a battle and conquer their enemies before nightfall.† The force of the toast lies in its extreme economy; it says so much in so little, and it exercises the mind of the reader to make the connection for himself.

The effect of Chesterfield's allusion is chiefly humorous or witty, but allusions may also have a powerful emotional effect. The essayist William Hazlitt writes of addressing a fashionable audience about the lexicographer Samuel Johnson. Speaking of Johnson's great heart and of his charity to the unfortunate, Hazlitt recounted how, finding a drunken prostitute lying in Fleet Street late at night, Johnson carried her on his broad back to the address she managed to give him. The audience, unable to face the picture of the famous dictionary-maker

---

*Samuel Shellabarger, *Lord Chesterfield and His World* (Boston: Little, Brown, 1951) 132.

†Joshua 10.12–14.

doing such a thing, broke out in titters and expostulations, whereupon
Hazlitt simply said: "I remind you, ladies and gentlemen, of the parable
of the Good Samaritan." The audience was promptly silenced.*

Allusions are a means of reinforcing the emotion or the ideas of
one's own work with the emotion or ideas of another work or occasion. Because they may compact so much meaning in so small a
space, they are extremely useful to the poet.

90. "Out, Out—"

The buzz-saw snarled and rattled in the yard
And made dust and dropped stove-length sticks of wood,
Sweet-scented stuff when the breeze drew across it.
And from there those that lifted eyes could count
Five mountain ranges one behind the other   5
Under the sunset far into Vermont.
And the saw snarled and rattled, snarled and rattled,
As it ran light, or had to bear a load.
And nothing happened: day was all but done.
Call it a day, I wish they might have said   10
To please the boy by giving him the half hour
That a boy counts so much when saved from work.
His sister stood beside them in her apron
To tell them "Supper." At the word, the saw,
As if to prove saws knew what supper meant,   15
Leaped out at the boy's hand, or seemed to leap—
He must have given the hand. However it was,
Neither refused the meeting. But the hand!
The boy's first outcry was a rueful laugh,
As he swung toward them holding up the hand   20
Half in appeal, but half as if to keep
The life from spilling. Then the boy saw all—
Since he was old enough to know, big boy
Doing a man's work, though a child at heart—
He saw all spoiled. "Don't let him cut my hand off—   25
The doctor, when he comes. Don't let him, sister!"
So. But the hand was gone already.
The doctor put him in the dark of ether.
He lay and puffed his lips out with his breath.
And then—the watcher at his pulse took fright.   30
No one believed. They listened at his heart.

*Jacques Barzun, *Teacher in America* (Boston: Little, Brown, 1945) 160.

Little—less—nothing!—and that ended it.
No more to build on there. And they, since they
Were not the one dead, turned to their affairs.

Robert Frost (1874–1963)

QUESTIONS

1. How does this poem differ from a newspaper account that might have dealt with the same incident?
2. To whom does "They" (33) refer? The boy's family? The doctor and medical attendants? Casual onlookers? Need we assume that all these people—whoever they are—turned immediately "to their affairs" (34)? Does the ending of this poem seem to you callous or merely realistic? Would a more tearful and sentimental ending have made the poem better or worse?
3. What figure of speech is used in lines 21–22?

Allusions vary widely in the burden put on them by the poet to convey meaning. Lord Chesterfield risked his whole meaning on his hearers' recognizing his allusion. Robert Frost in "'Out, Out—'" makes his meaning entirely clear even for the reader who does not recognize the allusion contained in the poem's title. His theme is the uncertainty and unpredictability of life, which may be ended accidentally at any moment, and the tragic waste of human potentiality that takes place when such premature deaths occur. A boy who is already "Doing a man's work" and gives every promise of having a useful life ahead of him is suddenly wiped out. There seems no rational explanation for either the accident or the death. The only comment to be made is, "No more to build on there."

Frost's title, however, is an allusion to one of the most famous passages in all English literature, and it offers a good illustration of how a poet may use allusion not only to reinforce emotion but also to help define his theme. The passage is that in *Macbeth* in which Macbeth has just been informed of his wife's death. A good many readers will recall the key phrase, "Out, out, brief candle!" with its underscoring of the tragic brevity and uncertainty of life. For some readers, however, the allusion will summon up the whole passage in Act 5, scene 5, in which this phrase occurs. Macbeth's words are:

91.   She should have died hereafter;
There would have been a time for such a word.
Tomorrow, and tomorrow, and tomorrow

Creeps in this petty pace from day to day
To the last syllable of recorded time;   5
And all our yesterdays have lighted fools
The way to dusty death. Out, out, brief candle!
Life's but a walking shadow, a poor player,
That struts and frets his hour upon the stage
And then is heard no more. It is a tale   10
Told by an idiot, full of sound and fury,
Signifying nothing.

Macbeth's first words underscore the theme of premature death. The boy also "should have died hereafter." The rest of the passage, with its marvelous evocation of the vanity and meaninglessness of life, expresses neither Shakespeare's philosophy nor, ultimately, Frost's, but it is Macbeth's philosophy at the time of his bereavement, and it is likely to express the feelings of us all when such tragic accidents occur. Life does indeed seem cruel and meaningless, "a tale / Told by an idiot," signifying nothing, when human life and potentiality are thus without explanation so suddenly ended.

QUESTION

Examine Macbeth's speech for examples of personification, apostrophe, and metonymy. How many metaphors for an individual human life does it present?

Allusions also vary widely in the number of readers to whom they will be familiar. Poets, in using an allusion, as in using a figure of speech, are always in danger of being misunderstood. What appeals powerfully to one reader may lose another reader altogether. But poets must assume a certain fund of common experience in readers. They could not even write about the ocean unless they could assume that readers have seen the ocean or pictures of it. In the same way poets assume a certain common fund of literary experience, most frequently of classical mythology, Shakespeare, or the Bible—particularly the King James Version. Poets are often justified in expecting a rather wide range of literary experience in readers, for the people who read poetry for pleasure are generally intelligent and well-read. But, obviously, beginning readers will not have this range, just as they will not know the meanings of as many words as will more mature readers. Students should therefore be prepared to look up certain allusions, just as they should be eager to look up in their dictionaries the meanings of unfamiliar words. They will find that every increase in knowledge broadens their base for understanding both literature and life.

---

92. in Just-

in Just-
spring   when the world is mud-
luscious the little
lame balloonman

whistles   far   and wee   5

and eddieandbill come
running from marbles and
piracies and it's
spring

when the world is puddle-wonderful   10

the queer
old balloonman whistles
far   and   wee
and bettyandisbel come dancing

from hop-scotch and jump-rope and   15

it's
spring
and
    the

            goat-footed   20

balloonMan   whistles
far
and
wee

e. e. cummings (1894–1962)

QUESTION

Why is the balloonman called "goat-footed" (20)? How does the identification made by this mythological allusion enrich the meaning of the poem?

93. On His Blindness

When I consider how my light is spent
　Ere half my days in this dark world and wide,
　And that one talent which is death to hide
　Lodged with me useless, though my soul more bent
To serve therewith my Maker, and present　　　　　5
　My true account, lest he returning chide,
　"Doth God exact day-labor, light denied?"
　I fondly ask. But Patience, to prevent
That murmur, soon replies, "God doth not need
　Either man's work or his own gifts. Who best　　　10
　Bear his mild yoke, they serve him best. His state
Is kingly: thousands at his bidding speed,
　And post o'er land and ocean without rest;
　They also serve who only stand and wait."

John Milton (1608–1674)

QUESTIONS

1. Vocabulary: *spent* (1), *fondly* (8), *prevent* (8), *post* (13).
2. What two meanings has "talent" (3)? What is Milton's "one talent"?
3. The poem is unified and expanded in its dimensions by a biblical allusion that Milton's original readers would have recognized immediately. What is it? If you do not know, look up Matthew 25.14–30. In what ways is the situation in the poem similar to that in the parable? In what ways is it different?
4. What is the point of the poem?

94. Hero and Leander

Both robbed of air, we both lie in one ground,
Both whom one fire had burnt, one water drowned.

John Donne (1572–1631)

QUESTIONS

1. After looking up the story of Hero and Leander (if necessary), explain each of the four parts into which this epigram is divided by its punctuation. Which parts are literal? Which are metaphorical?
2. The subject of the poem is taken from Greek legend; its structure is based on Greek science. Explain.

95. Miniver Cheevy

Miniver Cheevy, child of scorn,
    Grew lean while he assailed the seasons;
He wept that he was ever born,
    And he had reasons.

Miniver loved the days of old   5
    When swords were bright and steeds were prancing;
The vision of a warrior bold
    Would set him dancing.

Miniver sighed for what was not,
    And dreamed, and rested from his labors;   10
He dreamed of Thebes and Camelot,
    And Priam's neighbors.

Miniver mourned the ripe renown
    That made so many a name so fragrant;
He mourned Romance, now on the town,   15
    And Art, a vagrant.

Miniver loved the Medici,
    Albeit he had never seen one;
He would have sinned incessantly
    Could he have been one.   20

Miniver cursed the commonplace
    And eyed a khaki suit with loathing;
He missed the medieval grace
    Of iron clothing.

Miniver scorned the gold he sought,   25
    But sore annoyed was he without it;
Miniver thought, and thought, and thought,
    And thought about it.

Miniver Cheevy, born too late,
    Scratched his head and kept on thinking;   30
Miniver coughed, and called it fate,
    And kept on drinking.

Edwin Arlington Robinson (1869–1935)

QUESTIONS

1. Vocabulary: *khaki* (22). The phrase "on the town" (15) means "on charity" or "down and out."

2. Identify Thebes, Camelot (11), Priam (12), and the Medici (17). What names and what sort of life does each call up? What does Miniver's love of these names tell about him?

3. Discuss the phrase "child of scorn" (1). What does it mean? In how many ways is it applicable to Miniver?

4. What is Miniver's attitude toward material wealth?

5. The phrase "rested from his labors" (10) alludes to the Bible *and* to Greek mythology. Explore the ironic effect of comparing Miniver to the Creator (Genesis 2.2) and to Hercules. Point out other examples of irony in the poem and discuss their importance.

6. Can we call this a poem about a man whose "fate" was to be "born too late"? Explain your answer.

96. Leda and the Swan

A sudden blow: the great wings beating still
Above the staggering girl, her thighs caressed
By the dark webs, her nape caught in his bill,
He holds her helpless breast upon his breast.

How can those terrified vague fingers push   5
The feathered glory from her loosening thighs?
And how can body, laid in that white rush,
But feel the strange heart beating where it lies?

A shudder in the loins engenders there
The broken wall, the burning roof and tower   10
And Agamemnon dead.
                              Being so caught up,
So mastered by the brute blood of the air,
Did she put on his knowledge with his power
Before the indifferent beak could let her drop?

William Butler Yeats (1865–1939)

QUESTIONS

1. What is the connection between Leda and "The broken wall, the burning roof and tower / And Agamemnon dead"? If you do not know, look up the myth of Leda and, if necessary, the story of Agamemnon.

2. How does this poem do more than evoke an episode out of mythology? What is the significance of the question asked in the last two lines? How would you answer it?

97. Leda's Sister and the Geese

All the boys always wanted her, so
it was no surprise about the swan-
man, god, whatever he was. That day

I was stuck at home, as usual, while
she got to moon around the lake   5
supposedly picking lilies for dye. Think *I*

would have let some pair of wings catch me,
bury me under the weight of the sky?
She came home whimpering, whined out

the whole story, said she was "sore afraid"   10
she'd got pregnant. Hunh. "Sore"
I'll bet, the size she described, and

pregnant figures: no guess who'll get
to help her with the kid or, Hera forbid,
more than one (twins run in our damned   15

family). "Never you mind, dear," Mother said.
"Your sister will take on your chores."
Sure. As though I wasn't already doing

twice as many of my own. So now
I clean, I spin, I weave, I bake,   20
fling crusts to feed these birds I wish

to Hades every day; while she sits smug
in a wicker chair, and eats sweetmeats,
and combs and combs that ratty golden hair.

Katharyn Howd Machan (b. 1952)

QUESTIONS

1. What does this humorous version of the Leda/Zeus story add to your
   perspective on that grand myth? How does the language create humor?
2. "[S]ore afraid" (10) is an allusion to Luke 2.9. How does the poem make
   use of it? What purpose is served by this vulgarized link between two inci-
   dences of divine birth?

98. An altered look about the hills

An altered look about the hills—
A Tyrian light the village fills—
A wider sunrise in the morn—

A deeper twilight on the lawn—
A print of a vermilion foot— 5
A purple finger on the slope—
A flippant fly upon the pane—
A spider at his trade again—
An added strut in chanticleer—
A flower expected everywhere— 10
An axe shrill singing in the woods—
Fern odors on untraveled roads—
All this and more I cannot tell—
A furtive look you know as well—
And Nicodemus's mystery 15
Receives its annual reply!

Emily Dickinson (1830–1886)

QUESTIONS

1. Vocabulary: *Tyrian* (2), *chanticleer* (9).
2. What does the list of natural changes indicate? How is that an answer to
   Nicodemus's questions to Jesus? (If you are not familiar with the allusion,
   see John 3.4.) Does the meaning of this poem concur or contrast with the
   meaning of the biblical passage?

99. Abraham to kill him

Abraham to kill him
Was distinctly told.
Isaac was an urchin,
Abraham was old.

Not a hesitation— 5
Abraham complied.
Flattered by obeisance,
Tyranny demurred.

Isaac, to his children
Lived to tell the tale. 10
Moral: with a mastiff
Manners may prevail.

Emily Dickinson (1830–1886)

QUESTIONS

1. Vocabulary: *obeisance* (7), *demurred* (8).
2. To whom or to what do "Tyranny" (8) and "mastiff" (11) refer? What
   figure of speech is each?

3. Who are Abraham and Isaac? What, in the context of the original story, does "demurred" mean? If you cannot answer these questions, read Genesis 22.1–18.
4. What is the reaction of the poet to this Bible story?

100. Jack, eating rotten cheese, did say

> Jack, eating rotten cheese, did say,
> Like Samson I my thousands slay;
> I vow, quoth Roger, so you do.
> And with the self-same weapon, too.

Benjamin Franklin (1706–1790)

QUESTION

If you cannot identify the allusion, see Judges 15.15–16.

101. A monkey sprang down from a tree

> A monkey sprang down from a tree
> And angrily cursed Charles D.
>   "I hold with the Bible,"
>   He cried. "It's a libel
> That man is descended from me!"

Laurence Perrine (1915–1995)

102. Two brothers devised what at sight

> Two brothers devised what at sight
> Seemed a bicycle crossed with a kite.
>   They predicted—rash pair!
>   It would fly through the air!
> And what do you know? They were Wright!

Laurence Perrine (1915–1995)

QUESTION

One of the two preceding allusive limericks is little more than a clever pun, the other poses a theme in a witty form. Which is which?

CHAPTER NINE

Meaning and Idea

103. Little Jack Horner

> Little Jack Horner
> Sat in a corner
> Eating a Christmas pie.
> He stuck in his thumb
> And pulled out a plum   5
> And said, "What a good boy am I!"

Anonymous

The meaning of a poem is the experience it expresses—nothing less. But readers who, baffled by a particular poem, ask perplexedly, "What does it *mean?*" are usually after something more specific than this. They want something they can grasp entirely with their minds. We may therefore find it useful to distinguish the **total meaning** of a poem—the experience it communicates (and which can be communicated in no other way)—from its **prose meaning**—the ingredient that can be separated out in the form of a prose paraphrase (see Chapter 2). If we make this distinction, however, we must be careful not to confuse the two kinds of meaning. The prose meaning is no more the poem than a plum is a pie or than a prune is a plum.

The prose meaning will not necessarily or perhaps even usually be an idea. It may be a story, a description, a statement of emotion, a presentation of human character, or some combination of these. "The Mill" (No. 20) tells a story; "The Eagle" (No. 1) is primarily descriptive; "Western Wind" (No. 49) is an expression of emotion; "My Last Duchess" (No. 89) is an account of human character. None of these poems is directly concerned with ideas. Message-hunters will be baffled and disappointed by poetry of this kind because they will not find what they are looking for, and they may attempt to read some idea into the poem that is really not there. Yet ideas are also part of human experience, and therefore many poems are concerned, at least partially, with presenting ideas. But with these poems message-hunting is an even more dangerous activity, for the message-hunters are likely to think that the whole object of reading the poem is to find the message—that the idea is really the only important thing in it. Like Little Jack Horner, they will reach in and pluck out the idea and say, "What a good boy am I!" as if the pie existed for the plum.

The idea in a poem is only part of the total experience that it communicates. The value and worth of the poem are determined by the value of the total experience, not by the truth or the nobility of the idea itself. This is not to say that the truth of the idea is unimportant, or that its validity should not be examined and appraised. But a good idea alone will not make a good poem, nor need an idea with which the reader does not agree ruin one. Good readers of poetry are receptive to all kinds of experience. They are able to make that "willing suspension of disbelief" that Coleridge characterized as constituting poetic faith. When one attends a performance of *Hamlet*, one is willing to forget for the time being that such a person as Hamlet never existed and that the events on the stage are fictions. Likewise, poetry readers should be willing to entertain imaginatively, for the time being, ideas they objectively regard as untrue. It is one way of better understanding these ideas and of enlarging the reader's own experience. The person who believes in God should be able to enjoy a good poem expressing atheistic ideas, just as the atheist should be able to appreciate a good poem in praise of God. The optimist should be able to find pleasure in pessimistic poetry, and the pessimist in optimistic poetry. The teetotaler should be able to enjoy *The Rubáiyát of Omar Khayyám,* and the winebibber a good poem in praise of austerity. The primary value of a poem depends not so much on the truth of the idea presented as on the power with which it is communicated and on its being made a convincing part of a meaningful total experience. We must feel that the idea has been truly and deeply *felt* by the poet, and that the poet is doing something more than merely moralizing. The plum must be made part of a pie. If the plum is properly combined with other ingredients and if the pie is well baked, it should be enjoyable even for persons who do not care for the type of plums from which it is made. Consider, for instance, the following two poems.

104. Loveliest of Trees

Loveliest of trees, the cherry now
Is hung with bloom along the bough,
And stands about the woodland ride
Wearing white for Eastertide.

Now, of my threescore years and ten,   5
Twenty will not come again,
And take from seventy springs a score,
It only leaves me fifty more.

And since to look at things in bloom
Fifty springs are little room,   10
About the woodlands I will go
To see the cherry hung with snow.

A. E. Housman (1859–1936)

QUESTIONS

1. Very briefly, this poem presents a philosophy of life. In a sentence, what is it?
2. How old is the speaker? Why does he assume that his life will be seventy years in length? What is surprising about the words "only" (8) and "little" (10)?
3. A good deal of ink has been spilt over whether "snow" (12) is literal or figurative. What do you say? Justify your answer.

105. Stopping by Woods on a Snowy Evening

Whose woods these are I think I know.
His house is in the village though;
He will not see me stopping here
To watch his woods fill up with snow.

My little horse must think it queer   5
To stop without a farmhouse near
Between the woods and frozen lake
The darkest evening of the year.

He gives his harness bells a shake
To ask if there is some mistake.   10
The only other sound's the sweep
Of easy wind and downy flake.

> The woods are lovely, dark and deep,
> But I have promises to keep,
> And miles to go before I sleep,   15
> And miles to go before I sleep.

Robert Frost (1874–1963)

QUESTIONS

1. How do these two poems differ in idea?
2. What contrasts are suggested between the speaker in the second poem
   and (a) his horse and (b) the owner of the woods?

Both of these poems present ideas, the first more or less explicitly, the second symbolically. Perhaps the best way to get at the idea of the second poem is to ask two questions. First, why does the speaker stop? Second, why does he go on? He stops, we answer, to watch the woods fill up with snow—to observe a scene of natural beauty. He goes on, we answer, because he has "promises to keep"—that is, he has obligations to fulfill. He is momentarily torn between his love of beauty and these other various and complex claims that life has upon him. The small conflict in the poem is symbolic of a larger conflict in life. One part of the sensitive, thinking person would like to give up his life to the enjoyment of beauty and art. But another part is aware of larger duties and responsibilities—responsibilities owed, at least in part, to other human beings. The speaker in the poem would like to satisfy both impulses. But when the two conflict, he seems to suggest, the "promises" must take precedence.

The first poem also presents a philosophy but it is an opposing one. For the twenty-year-old speaker, the appreciation of beauty is of such importance that he will make it his lifelong dedication, filling his time with enjoying whatever the seasons bring. The metaphor comparing white cherry blossoms to snow suggests that each season has its own special beauty, though the immediate season is spring. In a limited life, one should seek out and delight in whatever beauty is present. Thoughtful readers will have to choose between these two philosophies—to commit themselves to one or the other—but this commitment should not destroy for them their enjoyment of either poem. If it does, they are reading for plums and not for pies.

Nothing we have said so far in this chapter should be construed as meaning that the truth or falsity of the idea in a poem is a matter of no importance. *Other things being equal,* good readers naturally will, and properly should, value more highly the poem whose idea they feel to be more mature and nearer to the heart of human experience. Some ideas, moreover, may seem so vicious or so foolish or so beyond the pale of normal human decency as to discredit *by themselves* the poems in which they are found. A rotten plum may spoil a pie. But good readers strive for intellectual flexibility and tolerance, and are able to entertain sympathetically ideas other than their own. They often will like a poem whose idea they disagree with better than one with an idea they accept. And, above all, they will not confuse the prose meaning of any poem with its total meaning. They will not mistake plums for pies.

106. To a Waterfowl

Whither, midst falling dew,
While glow the heavens with the last steps of day,
Far, through their rosy depths, dost thou pursue
   Thy solitary way?

Vainly the fowler's eye   5
Might mark thy distant flight to do thee wrong,
As, darkly painted on the crimson sky,
   Thy figure floats along.

Seek'st thou the plashy brink
Of weedy lake, or marge of river wide,   10
Or where the rocking billows rise and sink
   On the chafed ocean side?

There is a Power whose care
Teaches thy way along that pathless coast—
The desert and illimitable air—   15
   Lone wandering, but not lost.

All day thy wings have fanned,
At that far height, the cold, thin atmosphere,
Yet stoop not, weary, to the welcome land,
   Though the dark night is near.   20

And soon that toil shall end;
Soon shalt thou find a summer home, and rest,
And scream among thy fellows; reeds shall bend,
   Soon, o'er thy sheltered nest.

Thou'rt gone, the abyss of heaven   25
Hath swallowed up thy form; yet, on my heart
Deeply has sunk the lesson thou hast given,
    And shall not soon depart.

He who, from zone to zone,
Guides through the boundless sky thy certain flight,   30
In the long way that I must tread alone,
    Will lead my steps aright.

William Cullen Bryant (1794–1878)

QUESTIONS

1. Vocabulary: *fowler* (5), *desert* (15), *stoop* (19).
2. What figure of speech unifies the poem?
3. Where is the waterfowl flying? Why? What is "that pathless coast" (14)?
4. What "Power" (13) "Guides" (30) the waterfowl to its destination? How does it do so?
5. What lesson does the poet derive from his observations?

107. Design

I found a dimpled spider, fat and white,
On a white heal-all, holding up a moth
Like a white piece of rigid satin cloth—
Assorted characters of death and blight
Mixed ready to begin the morning right,   5
Like the ingredients of a witches' broth—
A snow-drop spider, a flower like a froth,
And dead wings carried like a paper kite.

What had that flower to do with being white,
The wayside blue and innocent heal-all?   10
What brought the kindred spider to that height,
Then steered the white moth thither in the night?
What but design of darkness to appall?—
If design govern in a thing so small.

Robert Frost (1874–1963)

QUESTIONS

1. Vocabulary: *characters* (4), *snow-drop* (7).
2. The heal-all is a wildflower, usually blue or violet but occasionally white, found blooming along roadsides in the summer. It was once supposed to

have healing qualities, hence its name. Of what significance, scientific and poetic, is the fact that the spider, the heal-all, and the moth are all white? Of what poetic significance is the fact that the spider is "dimpled" and "fat" and like a "snow-drop," and that the flower is "innocent" and named "heal-all"?

3. The "argument from design"—that the manifest existence of design in the universe implies the existence of a Great Designer—was a favorite eighteenth-century argument for the existence of God. What twist does Frost give the argument? What answer does he suggest to the question in lines 11–12? How comforting is the apparent concession in line 14?

4. Contrast Frost's poem in content and emotional effect with "To a Water-fowl." Is it possible to like both?

108. The Indifferent

"I can love both fair and brown,
Her whom abundance melts, and her whom want betrays,
Her who loves loneness best, and her who masks and plays,
    Her whom the country formed, and whom the town,
        Her who believes, and her who tries,°   tests 5
        Her who still weeps with spongy eyes,
    And her who is dry cork and never cries;
    I can love her, and her, and you, and you;
    I can love any, so she be not true.°   faithful

"Will no other vice content you?   10
Will it not serve your turn to do as did your mothers?
Or have you all old vices spent, and now would find out others?
    Or doth a fear that men are true torment you?
        Oh, we are not; be not you so.
        Let me, and do you, twenty know.   15
    Rob me, but bind me not, and let me go.
    Must I, who came to travail thorough° you,   through
    Grow your fixed subject because you are true?"

Venus heard me sing this song,
And by love's sweetest part, variety, she swore   20
She heard not this till now, and that it should be so no more.
    She went, examined, and returned ere long,
        And said, "Alas, some two or three
        Poor heretics in love there be,
    Which think to 'stablish dangerous constancy,   25
    But I have told them, 'Since you will be true,
    You shall be true to them who are false to you.'"

John Donne (1572–1631)

QUESTIONS

1. Vocabulary: *Indifferent* (title), *know* (15), *travail* (17).
2. Who is the speaker? To whom is he speaking? About what is he "indifferent"? What one qualification does he insist on in a lover? Why?
3. Of what vice does he accuse the women of his generation in line 10? How, in his opinion, do they differ from their mothers? Why?
4. Why does Venus investigate the speaker's complaint? Does her investigation confirm or refute his accusation? Who are the "heretics in love" (24) whom she discovers? What punishment does she decree for them?

109. Love's Deity

I long to talk with some old lover's ghost
  Who died before the god of love was born.
I cannot think that he who then loved most
  Sunk so low as to love one which did scorn.
But since this god produced a destiny,   5
And that vice-nature, custom, lets it be,
      I must love her that loves not me.

Sure, they which made him god meant not so much,
  Nor he in his young godhead practiced it.
But when an even flame two hearts did touch,   10
  His office was indulgently to fit
Actives to passives. Correspondency
Only his subject was. It cannot be
      Love till I love her that loves me.

But every modern god will° now extend   wants to 15
  His vast prerogative as far as Jove.
To rage, to lust, to write to, to commend,
  All is the purlieu of the god of love.
Oh, were we wakened by this tyranny
To ungod this child again, it could not be   20
      I should love her who loves not me.

Rebel and atheist too, why murmur I
  As though I felt the worst that Love could do?
Love might make me leave loving, or might try
  A deeper plague, to make her love me too,   25
Which, since she loves before, I am loath to see.
Falsehood is worse than hate, and that must be
      If she whom I love should love me.

John Donne (1572–1631)

QUESTIONS

1. Vocabulary: *vice-* (6), *even* (10), *purlieu* (18).
2. Who is the modern "god of love" (2)? Why is he called a "child" (20)? What did "they which made him god" (8) intend to be his duties? How has he gone beyond these duties? Why does the speaker long to talk with some lover's ghost who died before this god was born (1–2)?
3. What is the speaker's situation? Whom does the speaker call "Rebel and atheist" (22)? Why?
4. Why does the speaker rebuke himself for "murmuring" in the final stanza? What two things could Love do to him that have not been done already? Why are they worse? Explain the words "before" (26) and "Falsehood" (27). To which word in the first stanza does "hate" (27) correspond?
5. How does the speaker define "love" in this poem? Is he consistent in his use of the term? How does he differ from the speaker in "The Indifferent" in his conception of love?
6. How do you explain the fact that "Love's Deity" and "The Indifferent," though both by the same poet, express opposite opinions about the value of fidelity in love?

110. To the Mercy Killers

If ever mercy move you murder me,
I pray you, kindly killers, let me live.
Never conspire with death to set me free,
but let me know such life as pain can give.
Even though I be a clot, an aching clench,   5
a stub, a stump, a butt, a scab, a knob,
a screaming pain, a putrefying stench,
still let me live, so long as life shall throb.
Even though I turn such traitor to myself
as beg to die, do not accomplice me.   10
Even though I seem not human, a mute shelf
of glucose, bottled blood, machinery
to swell the lung and pump the heart—even so,
do not put out my life. Let me still glow.

Dudley Randall (b. 1914)

QUESTIONS

1. In form this is a Shakespearean sonnet (see page 887), consisting of three quatrains and a concluding couplet (units of 4, 4, 4, and 2 lines each); but in structure (organization of thought) it follows the Italian model of an octave and sestet (8- and 6-line units) in which the first eight lines

introduce a thought and the sestet produces some kind of counterthought. What "turn" of thought occurs at the end of line 8 in this sonnet?

2. Identify the paradox in line 2 that introduces the central topic of the poem. (It is also stated in the title, but line 2 states it more effectively because of its alliteration.)

3. Is the speaker advocating a universal standard of conduct or merely expressing his personal desire?

111. How Annandale Went Out

"They called it Annandale—and I was there
To flourish, to find words, and to attend:
Liar, physician, hypocrite, and friend,
I watched him; and the sight was not so fair
As one or two that I have seen elsewhere: 5
An apparatus not for me to mend—
A wreck, with hell between him and the end,
Remained of Annandale; and I was there.

"I knew the ruin as I knew the man;
So put the two together, if you can,   10
Remembering the worst you know of me.
Now view yourself as I was, on the spot—
With a slight kind of engine. Do you see?
Like this . . . You wouldn't hang me? I thought not."

Edwin Arlington Robinson (1869–1935)

QUESTIONS

1. George Annandale is the central character in two longish poems by Robinson. In one of these, after a visit to his closest friend (who is also his doctor), Annandale is maimed and almost killed in an automobile accident. The doctor hears "a sick crash in the street" and finds his friend in a condition for which there can be no healing and which will only entail intense suffering while he lives. This information, though not essential to understanding Robinson's sonnet, may make it easier. Who is the speaker? Whom is he addressing? Why?

2. Discuss the role of overstatement and understatement in the poem. Why does the speaker call himself a "Liar" and "hypocrite" (3)? What does he mean by lines 4–5? What does he mean by line 9? What nouns and pronouns does he use in referring to Annandale?

3. Why does he repeat "and I was there" (1, 8)? What meanings has "on the spot" (12)?

4. What is the "slight kind of engine" (13)? What gesture does he make with his hand in explaining it? What has he done—something legal or illegal? Moral or immoral? What is his motivation in revealing what he has done?

5. Does his auditor approve of his action? Does Robinson?
6. Compare or contrast the attitudes expressed in this poem and in "To the Mercy Killers."

112. The Caged Skylark

As a dare-gale skylark scanted in a dull cage
   Man's mounting spirit in his bone-house, mean house, dwells—
   That bird beyond the remembering his free fells;
This in drudgery, day-laboring-out life's age.

Though aloft on turf or perch or poor low stage,   5
   Both sing sometimes the sweetest, sweetest spells,
   Yet both droop deadly sometimes in their cells
Or wring their barriers in bursts of fear or rage.

Not that the sweet-fowl, song-fowl, needs no rest—
Why, hear him, hear him babble and drop down to his nest,   10
   But his own nest, wild nest, no prison.

Man's spirit will be flesh-bound when found at best,
But uncumbered: meadow-down is not distressed
   For a rainbow footing it nor he for his bones risen.

Gerard Manley Hopkins (1844–1889)

QUESTIONS

1. Vocabulary: *scanted* (1), *fells* (3). What meanings of "mean" (2) are appropriate here? "[T]urf" (5) is a piece of sod placed in a cage.
2. The speaker expresses a belief in the Christian doctrine of the resurrection of the body. According to this belief, the immortal soul, after death, will be ultimately reunited with the body; this body, however, will be a weightless, perfected, glorified body, not the gross imperfect body of mortal life. Express the analogy in the poem as a pair of mathematical statements of proportion (in the form $a:b = c:d$ and $e:f = g:h = i:j$), using the following terms: caged skylark, mortal body, meadow-down, cage, rainbow, spirit-in-life, nest, immortal spirit, wild skylark, resurrected body.
3. Discuss the image of the last two lines as a figure for weightlessness. Why would a shadow not have been as apt as a rainbow for this comparison?

113. No worst, there is none

    No worst, there is none. Pitched past pitch of grief,
    More pangs will, schooled at forepangs, wilder wring.
    Comforter, where, where is your comforting?

Mary, mother of us, where is your relief?
My cries heave, herds-long; huddle in a main, a chief-   5
woe, world-sorrow; on an age-old anvil wince and sing—
Then lull, then leave off. Fury had shrieked "No ling-
ering! Let me be fell: force,° I must be brief."   perforce
O the mind, mind has mountains; cliffs of fall
Frightful, sheer, no-man-fathomed. Hold them cheap   10
May who ne'er hung there. Nor does long our small
Durance° deal with that steep or deep. Here! creep,   endurance
Wretch, under a comfort serves in a whirlwind: all
Life death does end and each day dies with sleep.

Gerard Manley Hopkins (1844–1889)

QUESTIONS

1. Vocabulary: *fell* (8). "Comforter" (3) refers to the Holy Spirit; "herds-
   long" and "huddle in a main" (5) evoke two images of flocks of sheep.
2. Examine the auditory and visual imagery.
3. What is gained by the failure to identify a particular cause of the speaker's
   pain and terror? Do the religious references in lines 3 and 4 and the pastoral images in line 5 suggest a context?
4. What are the emotional contrasts between this and the preceding poem,
   and how are they expressed? What lines in "The Caged Skylark" might
   allude to the ideas presented here? Determine the extent of the contrasts
   between them.

114. Alter! When the hills do

Alter! When the hills do.
Falter! When the sun
Question if his glory
Be the perfect one.

Surfeit! When the daffodil   5
Doth of the dew.
Even as herself, Sir,
I will of you.

Emily Dickinson (1830–1886)

QUESTIONS

Who is speaking to whom? What assertion does the speaker make?

115. We outgrow love

We outgrow love like other things
And put it in the drawer,
Till it an antique fashion shows
Like costumes grandsires wore.

Emily Dickinson (1830–1886)

QUESTIONS

1. To what is love metaphorically compared?
2. How does the assertion made in this poem differ from that in the preceding poem? Can you account for the difference?

EXERCISE

Explore the contrasting ideas in the following pairs of poems:
1. "Spring" (No. 4) and "Spring and All" (No. 292).
2. "Good Times" (No. 209) and "Nikki-Rosa" (No. 229).
3. "Low Barometer" (No. 206) and "Allegory of the Wolf Boy" (No. 230).
4. "The Dead" (No. 207) and "The Death of a Soldier" (No. 281).
5. "Woman Work" (No. 200) and "A Work of Artifice" (No. 263).
6. "To a Daughter Leaving Home" (No. 149) and "Offspring" (No. 253).
7. "Those Winter Sundays" (No. 39) and "Life with Father" (No. 254).

CHAPTER TEN

Tone

Tone, in literature, may be defined as the writer's or speaker's attitude toward his subject, his audience, or himself. It is the emotional coloring, or the emotional meaning, of the work and is an extremely important part of the full meaning. In spoken language it is indicated by the inflections of the speaker's voice. If, for instance, a friend tells you, "I'm going to get married today," the facts of the statement are entirely clear. But the emotional meaning of the statement may vary widely according to the tone of voice with which it is uttered. The tone may be ecstatic ("Hooray! I'm going to get married today!"); it may be incredulous ("I can't believe it! I'm going to get married today"); it may be despairing ("Horrors! I'm going to get married today"); it may be resigned ("Might as well face it. I'm going to get married today"). Obviously, a correct interpretation of the tone will be an important part of understanding the full meaning. It may even have rather important consequences. If someone calls you a fool, your interpretation of the tone may determine whether you roll up your sleeves for a fight or walk off with your arm around his shoulder. If a woman says "No" to a proposal of marriage, the man's interpretation of her tone may determine whether he asks her again or starts going with someone else.

In poetry tone is likewise important. We have not really understood a poem unless we have accurately sensed whether the attitude it manifests is playful or solemn, mocking or reverent, calm or excited. But the correct determination of tone in literature is a much more delicate matter than it is in spoken language, for we do not have the speaker's voice to guide us. We must learn to recognize tone by other means. Almost all of the elements of poetry help to indicate its tone: connotation, imagery, and metaphor; irony and understatement; rhythm, sentence construction, and formal pattern. There is therefore no simple formula for recognizing tone. It is an end product of all the elements in a poem. The best we can do is illustrate.

Robert Frost's "Stopping by Woods on a Snowy Evening" (No. 105) seems a simple poem, but it has always afforded trouble to beginning readers. A very good student, asked to interpret it, once wrote this: "The poem means that we are forever passing up pleasures to go onward to what we wrongly consider our obligations. We would like to watch the snow fall on the peaceful countryside, but we always have to rush home to supper and other engagements. Frost feels that the average person considers life too short to stop and take time to appreciate true pleasures." This student did a good job in recognizing the central conflict of the poem but went astray in recognizing its tone. Let's examine why.

In the first place, the fact that the speaker in the poem *does* stop to watch the snow fall in the woods immediately establishes him as a human being with more sensitivity and feeling for beauty than most. He is not one of the people of Wordsworth's sonnet (No. 28) who, "Getting and spending," have laid waste their powers and lost the capacity to be stirred by nature. Frost's speaker is contrasted with his horse, who, as a creature of habit and an animal without esthetic perception, cannot understand the speaker's reason for stopping. There is also a suggestion of contrast with the "owner" of the woods, who, if he saw the speaker stopping, might be as puzzled as the horse. (Who most truly "profits" from the woods—its absentee owner or the person who can enjoy its beauty?) The speaker goes on because he has "promises to keep." But the word "promises," though it may here have a wry ironic undertone of regret, has a favorable connotation: people almost universally agree that promises ought to be kept. If the poet had used a different term, say, "things to do," or "business to attend to," or "financial affairs to take care of," or "money to make," the connotations would have been quite different. As it is, the tone of the poem tells us that the poet is sympathetic to the speaker; Frost is endorsing rather than censuring the speaker's action. Perhaps we may go even further. In the concluding two lines, because of their climactic position, because they are repeated, and because "sleep" in poetry is often used figuratively to refer to death, there is a suggestion of symbolic interpretation: "and many years to live before I die." If we accept this interpretation, it poses a parallel between giving oneself up to contemplation of the woods and dying. The poet's total implication would seem to be that beauty is a distinctively human value that deserves its place in a full life but that to devote one's life to its pursuit, at the expense of other obligations and duties, is tantamount to one's death as a responsible being. The poet therefore accepts the choice the speaker makes, though not without a touch of regret.

Differences in tone, and their importance, can perhaps be studied best in poems with similar content. Consider, for instance, the following pair.

116. For a Lamb

I saw on the slant hill a putrid lamb,
Propped with daisies. The sleep looked deep,
The face nudged in the green pillow
But the guts were out for crows to eat.

Where's the lamb? whose tender plaint   5
Said all for the mute breezes.
Say he's in the wind somewhere,
Say, there's a lamb in the daisies.

Richard Eberhart (b. 1904)

QUESTION

What connotative force do these words possess: "putrid" (1), "guts" (4), "mute" (6), "lamb" (1), "daisies" (2), "pillow" (3), "tender" (5)? Give two relevant denotations of "a lamb in the daisies" (8).

117. Apparently with no surprise

Apparently with no surprise
To any happy flower,
The frost beheads it at its play
In accidental power.

The blond assassin passes on,   5
The sun proceeds unmoved
To measure off another day
For an approving God.

Emily Dickinson (1830–1886)

QUESTIONS

1. What is the "blond assassin" (5)?
2. What ironies are involved in this poem?

Both of these poems are concerned with natural process; both use contrast as their basic organizing principle—a contrast between life and death, innocence and destruction, joy and tragedy. But in tone the two poems are sharply different. The first is realistic and resigned; its tone is wistful but not pessimistic. The second, though superficially fanciful, is basically grim, almost savage; its tone is horrified. Let's examine the difference.

The title, "For a Lamb," invites associations of innocent, frolicsome youthfulness, with the additional force of traditional Christian usage. These expectations are shockingly halted by the word "putrid." Though the speaker tries to overcome the shock with the more comforting personification implied in "face" and "pillow," the truth is undeniable: the putrefying animal is food for scavengers. The second stanza comes to grips with this truth, and also with the speaker's desire that the lamb might still represent innocence and purity in nature. It mingles fact and desire by hoping that what the lamb represented is still "somewhere" in the wind, that the lamb is both lying in the daisy field and will, in nature's processes, be transformed into the daisies. The reader shares the speaker's sad acceptance of reality.

The second poem makes the same contrast between joyful innocence ("happy flower . . . at its play") and fearful destruction ("beheads it"). The chief difference would seem to be that the cause of destruction—"the blond assassin"—is specifically identified, while the lamb seems to have died in its sleep, pillowed as it is in grass and surrounded by flowers. But the metaphorical sleep is no less a death than that delivered by an assassin—lambs *do* die, and frost actually *does* destroy flowers. In the second poem, what makes the horror of the killing worse is that nothing else in nature is disturbed by it or seems even to notice it. The sun "proceeds unmoved / To measure off another day." Nothing in nature stops or pauses. The flower itself is not surprised. And even God—the God who we have been told is benevolent and concerned over the least sparrow's fall—seems to approve of what has happened, for He shows no displeasure, and He supposedly created the frost as well as the flower. Further irony lies in the fact that the "assassin" (the word's connotations are of terror and violence) is not dark but "blond," or white (the connotations here are of innocence and beauty). The destructive agent, in other words, is among the most exquisite creations of God's handiwork. The poet, then, is shocked by what has happened, and is even more shocked that nothing else in nature is shocked. What has happened seems inconsistent with a rule of benevolence in the universe. In her ironic reference to an "approving God," therefore, the poet is raising a dreadful question: are the forces that created and govern the universe actually benevolent? And if we think that the poet is unduly disturbed over the death of a flower, we may consider that what is true for the flower is true throughout nature. Death—even early or accidental death, in terrible juxtaposition with beauty—is its constant condition; the fate that befalls the flower befalls us all. In Dickinson's poem, that is the end of the process. In Eberhart's, the potentially terrible irony is directed into a bittersweet acceptance of both death and beauty as natural.

These two poems, then, though superficially similar, are basically as different as night and day. And the difference is primarily one of tone.

We have been discussing tone as if every poem could be distinguished by a single tone. But varying or shifting tones in a single poem are often a valuable means for achieving the poet's purpose, and indeed may create the dramatic structure of a poem. Consider the following.

118. Since there's no help

Since there's no help, come let us kiss and part;
Nay, I have done, you get no more of me,
And I am glad, yea, glad with all my heart
That thus so cleanly I myself can free;
Shake hands forever, cancel all our vows,   5
And when we meet at any time again,
Be it not seen in either of our brows
That we one jot of former love retain.
Now, at the last gasp of Love's latest breath,
When, his pulse failing, Passion speechless lies,   10
When Faith is kneeling by his bed of death,
And Innocence is closing up his eyes,
Now, if thou wouldst, when all have given him over,
From death to life thou mightst him yet recover.

Michael Drayton (1563–1631)

QUESTIONS

1. What difference in tone do you find between the first eight lines and the last six? In which part is the speaker more sincere? What differences in rhythm and language help to establish the difference in tone?

2. How many figures are there in the allegorical scene in lines 9–12? What do the pronouns "his" and "him" in lines 10–14 refer to? What is dying? Why? How might the person addressed still restore it from death to life?
3. Define the dramatic situation as precisely as possible, taking into consideration both the man's attitude and the woman's.

Accurately determining tone, whether it be the tone of a rejected marriage proposal or of an insulting remark, is extremely important, both when reading poetry and in real life. For the experienced reader it will be instinctive and automatic. For the beginning reader it will require study. But beyond the general suggestions for reading that we already have made, there are no specific instructions we can give. Recognition of tone requires an increasing familiarity with the meanings and connotations of words, alertness to the presence of irony and other figures, and, above all, careful reading. Poetry cannot be read as one would skim a newspaper or a mystery novel looking merely for facts.

---

119. The Coming of Wisdom with Time

Though leaves are many, the root is one;
Through all the lying days of my youth
I swayed my leaves and flowers in the sun;
Now I may wither into the truth.

William Butler Yeats (1865–1939)

QUESTIONS

Is the poet exulting over a gain or lamenting over a loss? Is there a single tone in this poem?

120. Crossing the Bar

Sunset and evening star,
    And one clear call for me!
And may there be no moaning of the bar
    When I put out to sea,

But such a tide as moving seems asleep,   5
   Too full for sound and foam,
When that which drew from out the boundless deep
   Turns again home.

Twilight and evening bell,
   And after that the dark!   10
And may there be no sadness of farewell
   When I embark;

For though from out our bourne of Time and Place
   The flood may bear me far,
I hope to see my Pilot face to face   15
   When I have crossed the bar.

Alfred, Lord Tennyson (1809–1892)

QUESTIONS

1. Vocabulary: *bourne* (13).
2. What two sets of figures does Tennyson use for approaching death? What is the precise moment of death in each set?
3. In troubled weather the wind and waves above the sandbar across a harbor's mouth make a moaning sound. What metaphorical meaning has the "moaning of the bar" (3) here? For what kind of death is the speaker wishing? Why does he want "no sadness of farewell" (11)?
4. What is "that which drew from out the boundless deep" (7)? What is "the boundless deep"? To what is it opposed in the poem? Why is "Pilot" (15) capitalized?

121. The Oxen

Christmas Eve, and twelve of the clock.
   "Now they are all on their knees,"
An elder said as we sat in a flock
   By the embers in hearthside ease.

We pictured the meek mild creatures where   5
   They dwelt in their strawy pen,
Nor did it occur to one of us there
   To doubt they were kneeling then.

So fair a fancy few would weave
   In these years! Yet, I feel,   10
If someone said on Christmas Eve,
   "Come; see the oxen kneel

"In the lonely barton° by yonder coomb°   farm; valley
    Our childhood used to know,"
I should go with him in the gloom,   15
    Hoping it might be so.

Thomas Hardy (1840–1928)

QUESTIONS

1. Is the simple superstition referred to in this poem opposed to, or identified with, religious faith? With what implications for the meaning of the poem?
2. What are "these years" (10) and how do they contrast with the years of the poet's boyhood? What event in intellectual history between 1840 and 1915 (the date Hardy composed this poem) was most responsible for the change?
3. Both "Crossing the Bar" and "The Oxen" in their last lines use a form of the verb *hope*. By fully discussing tone, establish the precise meaning of hope in each poem. What degree of expectation does it imply? How should the word be handled in reading Tennyson's poem aloud?

122. One dignity delays for all

One dignity delays for all,
One mitred afternoon.
None can avoid this purple,
None evade this crown.

Coach, it insures, and footmen,   5
Chamber, and state, and throng—
Bells, also, in the village,
As we ride grand along!

What dignified attendants!
What service when we pause!   10
How loyally at parting
Their hundred hats they raise!

How pomp surpassing ermine
When simple you and I
Present our meek escutcheon   15
And claim the rank to die!

Emily Dickinson (1830–1886)

QUESTIONS

1. Vocabulary: *mitred* (2), *state* (6), *escutcheon* (15).
2. What is the "dignity" that delays for all? What is its nature? What is being described in stanzas 2 and 3?
3. What figures of speech are combined in "our meek escutcheon" (15)? What does it represent metaphorically?

123. 'Twas warm at first like us

'Twas warm at first like us,
Until there crept upon
A chill, like frost upon a glass,
Till all the scene be gone.

The forehead copied stone,   5
The fingers grew too cold
To ache, and like a skater's brook
The busy eyes congealed.

It straightened—that was all.
It crowded cold to cold.   10
It multiplied indifference
As pride were all it could.

And even when with cords
'Twas lowered like a weight,
It made no signal, nor demurred,   15
But dropped like adamant.

Emily Dickinson (1830–1886)

QUESTIONS

1. Vocabulary: *adamant* (16).
2. What is "It" in the opening line? What is being described in the poem, and between which points in time?
3. How would you describe the tone of this poem? How does it contrast with that of the preceding poem?

124. The Apparition

When by thy scorn, O murderess, I am dead,
        And that thou thinkst thee free
From all solicitatïon from me,

Then shall my ghost come to thy bed,
And thee, feigned vestal, in worse arms shall see;   5
Then thy sick taper° will begin to wink,   candle
And he, whose thou art then, being tired before,
Will, if thou stir, or pinch to wake him, think
       Thou call'st for more,
And in false sleep will from thee shrink.   10
And then, poor aspen wretch, neglected, thou,
Bathed in a cold quicksilver sweat, wilt lie
       A verier° ghost than I.   truer
What I will say, I will not tell thee now,
Lest that preserve thee; and since my love is spent,   15
I had rather thou shouldst painfully repent,
Than by my threatenings rest still innocent.

John Donne (1572–1631)

QUESTIONS

1. Vocabulary: *feigned* (5), *aspen* (11), *quicksilver* (12). Are the latter two words used literally or figuratively? Explain.
2. What has been the past relationship between the speaker and the woman addressed? How does a "solicitatïon" differ from a proposal? Why does he call her a "murderess"? What threat does he make against her?
3. In line 15 the speaker proclaims that his love for the woman "is spent." Does the tone of the poem support this contention? Discuss.
4. In line 5 why does the speaker use the word "vestal" instead of *virgin?* Does he believe her not to be a virgin? Of what is he accusing her? (In ancient Rome the vestal virgins tended the perpetual fire in the temple of Vesta. They entered this service between the ages of six and ten, and served for a term of thirty years, during which they were bound to virginity.)
5. The implied metaphor in line 1—that a woman who will not satisfy her lover's desires is "killing" him—was a cliché of Renaissance poetry. What original twist does Donne give it to make it fresh and new?
6. In the scene imagined by the speaker of his ghost's visit to the woman's bed, he finds her "in worse arms"—worse than whose? In what respect? By what will this other man have been "tired before"? Of what will he think she is calling for "more"? What is the speaker implying about himself and the woman in these lines?
7. Why (according to the speaker) will the woman *really* be trying to wake up her bedmate? Why, when she fails, will she be a "verier" ghost than the speaker?
8. What will the ghost say to her that he will not now reveal lest his telling it "preserve" her? Can we know? Does *he* know? Why does he make this undefined threat?
9. For what does the speaker say he wants the woman to "painfully repent"? Of what crime or sin would she remain "innocent" if he revealed now what his ghost would say? What is the speaker's real objective?

125. The Flea

Mark but this flea, and mark in this
How little that which thou deny'st me is;
It sucked me first, and now sucks thee,
And in this flea our two bloods mingled be;
Thou know'st that this cannot be said   5
A sin, nor shame, nor loss of maidenhead;
   Yet this enjoys before it woo,
   And pampered swells with one blood made of two,
   And this, alas, is more than we would do.

Oh stay, three lives in one flea spare,   10
Where we almost, yea more than married are.
This flea is you and I, and this
Our marriage bed and marriage temple is;
Though parents grudge, and you, we are met
And cloistered in these living walls of jet.   15
   Though use° make you apt to kill me,   habit
   Let not to that, self-murder added be,
   And sacrilege, three sins in killing three.

Cruel and sudden, hast thou since
Purpled° thy nail in blood of innocence?   crimsoned   20
Wherein could this flea guilty be,
Except in that drop which it sucked from thee?
Yet thou triumph'st and say'st that thou
Find'st not thyself, nor me, the weaker now.
   'Tis true. Then learn how false fears be: 25
   Just so much honor, when thou yield'st to me,
   Will waste, as this flea's death took life from thee.

John Donne (1572–1631)

QUESTIONS

1. In many respects this poem is like a miniature play: it has two characters, dramatic conflict, dialogue (though we hear only one speaker), and stage action. The action is indicated by stage directions embodied in the dialogue. What has happened just *preceding* the first line of the poem? What happens *between* the first and second stanzas? What happens *between* the second and third? How does the female character behave and what does she say *during* the third stanza?
2. What has been the past relationship of the speaker and the woman? What has she denied him (2)? How has she habitually "kill[ed]" him (16)? Why has she done so? How does it happen that he is still alive? What is his objective in the poem?

3. According to a traditional Renaissance belief, the bloods of lovers "mingled" during sexual intercourse. What is the speaker's argument in stanza 1? Reduce it to paraphrase. How logical is it?

4. What do "parents grudge, and you" in stanza 2? What are the "living walls of jet" (15)? What three things will the woman kill by crushing the flea? What three sins will she commit (18)?

5. Why and how does the woman "triumph . . ." in stanza 3? What is the speaker's response? How logical is his concluding argument?

6. What action, if any, would you infer, follows the conclusion of the poem?

7. "The Apparition" and "The Flea" may both be classified as "seduction poems." How do they differ in tone?

126. Dover Beach

The sea is calm tonight,
The tide is full, the moon lies fair
Upon the straits;—on the French coast the light
Gleams and is gone; the cliffs of England stand,
Glimmering and vast, out in the tranquil bay.   5
Come to the window, sweet is the night-air!
Only, from the long line of spray
Where the sea meets the moon-blanched land,
Listen! you hear the grating roar
Of pebbles which the waves draw back, and fling,   10
At their return, up the high strand,
Begin, and cease, and then again begin,
With tremulous cadence slow, and bring
The eternal note of sadness in.

Sophocles long ago   15
Heard it on the Aegean, and it brought
Into his mind the turbid ebb and flow
Of human misery; we
Find also in the sound a thought,
Hearing it by this distant northern sea.   20

The Sea of Faith
Was once, too, at the full, and round earth's shore
Lay like the folds of a bright girdle furled.
But now I only hear
Its melancholy, long, withdrawing roar,   25
Retreating, to the breath
Of the night-wind, down the vast edges drear
And naked shingles° of the world.   pebbled beaches

Ah, love, let us be true
To one another! for the world, which seems   30
To lie before us like a land of dreams,
So various, so beautiful, so new,
Hath really neither joy, nor love, nor light,
Nor certitude, nor peace, nor help for pain;
And we are here as on a darkling plain   35
Swept with confused alarms of struggle and flight,
Where ignorant armies clash by night.

Matthew Arnold (1822–1888)

QUESTIONS

1. Vocabulary: *strand* (11), *girdle* (23), *darkling* (35). Identify the physical locale of the cliffs of Dover and their relation to the French coast; identify
   the Aegean and Sophocles.
2. As precisely as possible, define the implied scene: What is the speaker's
   physical location? Whom is he addressing? What is the time of day and
   the state of the weather?
3. Discuss the visual and auditory images of the poem and their relation to
   illusion and reality.
4. The speaker is lamenting the decline of religious faith in his time. Is he
   himself a believer? Does he see any medicine for the world's maladies?
5. Discuss in detail the imagery in the last three lines. Are the "armies" figurative or literal? What makes these lines so effective?
6. What term or terms would you choose to describe the overall tone of
   the poem?

127. Church Going

Once I am sure there's nothing going on
I step inside, letting the door thud shut.
Another church: matting, seats, and stone,
And little books; sprawlings of flowers, cut
For Sunday, brownish now; some brass and stuff   5
Up at the holy end; the small neat organ;
And a tense, musty, unignorable silence,
Brewed God knows how long. Hatless, I take off
My cycle-clips in awkward reverence,

Move forward, run my hand around the font.   10
From where I stand, the roof looks almost new—
Cleaned, or restored? Someone would know: I don't.
Mounting the lectern, I peruse a few

Hectoring large-scale verses, and pronounce
"Here endeth" much more loudly than I'd meant.   15
The echoes snigger briefly. Back at the door
I sign the book, donate an Irish sixpence,
Reflect the place was not worth stopping for.

Yet stop I did: in fact I often do,
And always end much at a loss like this,   20
Wondering what to look for, wondering, too,
When churches fall completely out of use
What we shall turn them into, if we shall keep
A few cathedrals chronically on show,
Their parchment, plate and pyx in locked cases,   25
And let the rest rent-free to rain and sheep.
Shall we avoid them as unlucky places?

Or, after dark, will dubious women come
To make their children touch a particular stone;
Pick simples for a cancer; or on some   30
Advised night see walking a dead one?
Power of some sort or other will go on
In games, in riddles, seemingly at random;
But superstition, like belief, must die,
And what remains when disbelief has gone?   35
Grass, weedy pavement, brambles, buttress, sky,

A shape less recognizable each week,
A purpose more obscure. I wonder who
Will be the last, the very last, to seek
This place for what it was; one of the crew   40
That tap and jot and know what rood-lofts were?
Some ruin-bibber, randy for antique,
Or Christmas-addict, counting on a whiff
Of gown-and-bands and organ-pipes and myrrh?
Or will he be my representative,   45

Bored, uninformed, knowing the ghostly silt
Dispersed, yet tending to this cross of ground
Through suburb scrub because it held unspilt
So long and equably what since is found
Only in separation—marriage, and birth,   50
And death, and thoughts of these—for whom was built
This special shell? For though I've no idea
What this accoutered frowsty barn is worth,
It pleases me to stand in silence here;

A serious house on serious earth it is,   55
In whose blent air all our compulsions meet,
Are recognized, and robed as destinies.
And that much never can be obsolete,
Since someone will forever be surprising
A hunger in himself to be more serious,   60
And gravitating with it to this ground,
Which, he once heard, was proper to grow wise in,
If only that so many dead lie round.

Philip Larkin (1922–1985)

QUESTIONS

1. Vocabulary: *Hectoring* (14), *pyx* (25), *dubious* (28), *simples* (30), *accoutered* (53), *frowsty* (53), *blent* (56). *Large-scale* (14) indicates a print size suited to oral reading; an *Irish sixpence* (17) was a small coin not legal tender in England, the scene of the poem; *rood-lofts* (41) are architectural features found in many early Christian churches; *bibber* and *randy* (42) are figurative, literally meaning "drunkard" and "lustful"; *gown-and-bands* (44) are ornate robes worn by church officials in religious ceremonies.

2. Like "Dover Beach" (first published in 1867), "Church Going" (1954) is concerned with belief and disbelief. In modern England the landscape is dotted with small churches, often charming in their combination of stone (outside) and intricately carved wood (inside). Some are in ruins, some are badly in need of repair, and some are well tended by parishioners who keep them dusted and provide fresh flowers for the diminishing attendance at Sunday services. These churches invariably have by the entrance a book that visitors can sign as a record of their having been there and a collection box with a sign urging them to drop in a few coins for upkeep, repair, or restoration. In small towns and villages the church is often the chief or only building of architectural or historical interest, and tourist visitors may outnumber parishioners. To which of the three categories of churches mentioned here does Larkin's poem refer?

3. What different denotations does the title contain?

4. In what activity has the speaker been engaging when he stops to see the church? How is it revealed? Why does he stop? Is he a believer? How involved is he in inspecting this church building?

5. Compare the language used by the speakers in "Dover Beach" and "Church Going." Which speaker is more eloquent? Which is more informal and conversational? Without looking back at the texts, try to assign the following words to one poem or the other: *moon-blanched, cycle-clips, darkling, hath, snigger, whiff, drear, brownish, tremulous, glimmering, frowsty, stuff.* Then go back and check your success.

6. Define the tone (the attitude of the speaker or author toward the subject) of "Church Going" as precisely as possible. Compare this tone to that of "Dover Beach."

128. Getting Out

That year we hardly slept, waking like inmates
who beat the walls. Every night
another refusal, the silent work
of tightening the heart.
Exhausted, we gave up; escaped   5
to the apartment pool, swimming those laps
until the first light relieved us.

Days were different: FM and full-blast
blues, hours of guitar "you gonna miss me
when I'm gone." Think how you tried   10
to pack up and go, for weeks stumbling
over piles of clothing, the unstrung tennis rackets.
Finally locked into blame, we paced
that short hall, heaving words like furniture.

I have the last unshredded pictures   15
of our matching eyes and hair. We've kept
to separate sides of the map,
still I'm startled by men who look like you.
And in the yearly letter, you're sure to say
you're happy now. Yet I think of the lawyer's bewilderment   20
when we cried, the last day. Taking hands
we walked apart, until our arms stretched
between us. We held on tight, and let go.

Cleopatra Mathis (b. 1947)

QUESTIONS

1. Consider the shifting pronouns as you answer the following: Does the poem assign blame to one or the other of this couple? Can you tell whether either or both were involved in "the silent work / of tightening the heart" (3–4)?
2. The poem contains only one detail about the marriage before it began to collapse—the "matching eyes and hair" (16) of the two people. Does that detail help to explain why the marriage came to seem too confining? What kind of emotional maturity does it signify? How does the last line contribute to this idea?
3. Should "inmates" (1) be interpreted as imprisonment or confinement to a mental hospital? Explain your choice.
4. Explain the shift in tone from line 14 to line 15. What emotions do these people feel for each other now? How do you know?

129. A tiny cry within the night

A tiny cry within the night,
A mother's touch, a gentle light,
A rocking chair, a cheek caressed,
A baby to a bosom pressed,
A bundle in a cot replaced,   5
A mother's footsteps, soft, retraced—
She whispers as the shadows creep . . .
"Now let me sleep! Please, let me sleep!!!"

Lynn Johnston (b. 1947)

QUESTION

The radical shift in tone changes the whole meaning of the poem. Without the last line, what would it mean?

EXERCISES

1. Marvell's "To His Coy Mistress" (No. 56), Herrick's "To the Virgins, to Make Much of Time" (No. 64), and Housman's "Loveliest of Trees" (No. 104) all treat a traditional poetic theme known as the *carpe diem* ("seize the day") theme. They differ sharply, however, in tone. Characterize the tone of each, and point out the differences in poetic technique that account for the differences in tone.
2. Describe and account for the differences in tone between the following pairs:
   a. "The Lamb" (No. 204) and "The Tiger" (No. 205).
   b. "The Unknown Citizen" (No. 82) and "Departmental" (No. 83).
   c. "It sifts from leaden sieves" (No. 47) and "The Snowstorm" (No. 136).
   d. "Leda and the Swan" (No. 96) and "Leda's Sister and the Geese" (No. 97).
   e. "Nothing Gold Can Stay" (No. 141) and "Never Again Would Birds' Song Be the Same" (No. 226).
   f. "An altered look about the hills" (No. 98) and "The Sheaves" (No. 272).
   g. "Ballad of Birmingham" (No. 8) and "Southern Cop" (No. 88).
   h. "The Whipping" (No. 5) and "The Beating" (No. 280).

CHAPTER ELEVEN

Musical Devices

Poetry obviously makes a greater use of the "music" of language than does language that is not poetry. The poet, unlike the person who uses language to convey only information, chooses words for sound as well as for meaning, and uses the sound as a means of reinforcing meaning. So prominent is this musical quality of poetry that some writers have made it the distinguishing term in their definitions of poetry. Edgar Allan Poe, for instance, describes poetry as "music . . . combined with a pleasurable idea." Whether or not it deserves this much importance, verbal music, like connotation, imagery, and figurative language, is one of the important resources that enable the poet to do more than communicate mere information. The poet may indeed sometimes pursue verbal music for its own sake; more often, at least in first-rate poetry, it is an adjunct to the total meaning or communication of the poem.

The poet achieves musical quality in two broad ways: by the choice and arrangement of sounds and by the arrangement of accents. In this chapter we will consider the first of these.

An essential element in all music is repetition. In fact, we might say that all art consists of giving structure to two elements: repetition and variation. All things we enjoy greatly and lastingly have these two elements. We enjoy the sea endlessly because it is always the same yet always different. We enjoy a baseball game because it contains the same complex combination of pattern and variation. Our love of art, then, is rooted in human psychology. We like the familiar, we like variety, but we like them combined. If we get too much sameness, the result is monotony and tedium; if we get too much variety, the result is bewilderment and confusion. The composer of music, therefore, repeats certain musical tones; repeats them in certain combinations, or chords; and repeats them in certain patterns, or melodies. The poet likewise repeats certain sounds in certain combinations and arrangements, and thus adds musical meaning to verse. Consider the following short example.

130. The Turtle

> The turtle lives 'twixt plated decks
> Which practically conceal its sex.
> I think it clever of the turtle
> In such a fix to be so fertile.

> *Ogden Nash (1902–1971)*

Here is a little joke, a paradox of animal life to which the author has cleverly drawn our attention. An experiment will show us, however, that much of its appeal lies not so much in what it says as in the manner in which it says it. If, for instance, we recast the verse as prose: "The turtle lives in a shell which almost conceals its sex. It is ingenious of the turtle, in such a situation, to be so prolific," the joke falls flat. Some of its appeal must lie in its metrical form. So now we cast it in unrimed verse:

> Because he lives between two decks,
> It's hard to tell a turtle's gender.
> The turtle is a clever beast
> In such a plight to be so fertile.

Here, perhaps, is *some* improvement over the prose version, but still the piquancy of the original is missing. Much of that appeal must have consisted in the use of rime—the repetition of sound in "decks" and "sex," "turtle" and "fertile." So we try once more.

> The turtle lives 'twixt plated decks
> Which practically conceal its sex.
> I think it clever of the turtle
> In such a plight to be so fertile.

But for perceptive readers there is still something missing—they may not at first see what—but some little touch that makes the difference between a good piece of verse and a little masterpiece of its kind. And then they see it: "plight" has been substituted for "fix."

But why should "fix" make such a difference? Its meaning is little different from that of "plight"; its only important difference is in sound. But there we are. The final x in "fix" catches up the concluding consonant sound in "sex," and its initial f is repeated in the initial consonant sound of "fertile." Not only do these sound recurrences provide a subtle gratification to the ear, but they also give the verse structure; they emphasize and draw together the key words of the piece: "sex," "fix," and "fertile."

Poets may repeat any unit of sound from the smallest to the largest. They may repeat individual vowel and consonant sounds, whole syllables, words, phrases, lines, or groups of lines. In each instance, in a good poem, the repetition will serve several purposes: it will please the ear, it will emphasize the words in which the repetition occurs, and it will give structure to the poem. The popularity and initial impressiveness of such repetitions are evidenced by their becoming in many instances embedded in the language as clichés like "wild and woolly," "first and foremost," "footloose and fancy-free," "penny-wise, pound-foolish," "dead as a doornail," "might and main," "sink or swim," "do or die," "pell-mell," "helter-skelter," "harum-scarum," "hocus-pocus." Some of these kinds of repetition have names, as we will see.

A syllable consists of a vowel sound that may be preceded or followed by consonant sounds. Any of these sounds may be repeated. The repetition of initial consonant sounds, as in "tried and true," "safe and sound," "fish or fowl," "rime or reason," is **alliteration.** The repetition of vowel sounds, as in "mad as a hatter," "time out of mind," "free and easy," "slapdash," is **assonance.** The repetition of final consonant sounds, as in "first and last," "odds and ends," "short and sweet," "a stroke of luck," or Shakespeare's "struts and frets" (No. 91) is **consonance.***

Repetitions may be used alone or in combination. Alliteration and assonance are combined in such phrases as "time and tide," "thick and thin," "kith and kin," "alas and alack," "fit as a fiddle," and Edgar Allan Poe's famous line, "The viol, the violet, and the vine." Alliteration and consonance are combined in such phrases as "crisscross," "last but not least," "lone and lorn," "good as gold," Housman's "malt does more than Milton can" (No. 11), and Kay's "meanings lost in manners" (No. 25). The combination of assonance and consonance is rime.

Rime is the repetition of the accented vowel sound and all succeeding sounds. It is called **masculine** when the rime sounds involve only one syllable, as in *decks* and *sex* or *support* and *retort*. It is

---

*There is no established terminology for these various repetitions. *Alliteration* is used by some writers to mean any repetition of consonant sounds. *Assonance* has been used to mean the similarity as well as the identity of vowel sounds, or even the similarity of any sounds whatever. *Consonance* has often been reserved for words in which both the initial *and* final consonant sounds correspond, as in *green* and *groan, moon* and *mine. Rime* (or *rhyme*) has been used to mean any sound repetition, including alliteration, assonance, and consonance. In the absence of clear agreement on the meanings of these terms, the terminology chosen here has appeared most useful, with support in usage. Labels are useful in analysis. However, the student should learn to recognize the devices and, more important, should learn to see their function, without worrying too much over nomenclature.

feminine when the rime sounds involve two or more syllables, as in *turtle* and *fertile* or *spitefully* and *delightfully*. It is referred to as **internal rime** when one or more riming words are *within* the line and as **end rime** when the riming words are at the *ends* of lines. End rime is probably the most frequently used and most consciously sought sound repetition in English poetry. Because it comes at the end of the line, it receives emphasis as a musical effect and perhaps contributes more than any other musical resource except rhythm and meter to give poetry its musical effect as well as its structure. There exists, however, a large body of poetry that does not employ rime and for which rime would not be appropriate. Also, there has always been a tendency, especially noticeable in modern poetry, to substitute approximate rimes for perfect rimes at the ends of lines. **Approximate rimes** (also called slant rimes) include words with any kind of sound similarity, from close to fairly remote. Under approximate rime we include alliteration, assonance, and consonance or their combinations when used at the end of the line; half-rime (feminine rimes in which only half of the word rimes—the accented half, as in *lightly* and *frightful,* or the unaccented half, as in *yellow* and *willow*); and other similarities too elusive to name. "'Twas warm at first like us" (No. 123), "Toads" (No. 54), and "Mr. Z" (No. 87), to different degrees, all employ various kinds of approximate end rime.

131. That night when joy began

That night when joy began
Our narrowest veins to flush,
We waited for the flash
Of morning's leveled gun.

But morning let us pass,   5
And day by day relief
Outgrows his nervous laugh,
Grown credulous of peace,

As mile by mile is seen
No trespasser's reproach,   10
And love's best glasses reach
No fields but are his own.

W. H. Auden (1907–1973)

QUESTIONS

1. What has been the past experience with love of the two people in the poem? What is their present experience? What precisely is the tone of the poem?
2. What basic metaphor underlies the poem? Work it out stanza by stanza. What is "the flash of morning's leveled gun" (3–4)? Does line 10 mean that no trespasser reproaches the lovers or that no one reproaches the lovers for being trespassers? Does "glasses" (11) refer to spectacles, tumblers, mirrors, or field glasses? Point out three personifications.
3. The rime pattern in the poem is intricate and exact. Work it out, considering alliteration, assonance, and consonance.

In addition to the repetition of individual sounds and syllables, the poet may repeat whole words, phrases, lines, or groups of lines. When such repetition is done according to some fixed pattern, it is called a **refrain.** The refrain is especially common in songlike poetry. Shakespeare's "Winter" (No. 2) and "Spring" (No. 4) furnish examples of refrains.

132. Ettrick

When we first rade° down Ettrick,   rode
Our bridles were ringing, our hearts were dancing,
The waters were singing, the sun was glancing,
An' blithely our voices rang out thegither,°   together
As we brushed the dew frae° the blooming heather,   from   5
    When we first rade down Ettrick.

When we next rade down Ettrick,
The day was dying, the wild birds calling,
The wind was sighing, the leaves were falling,
An' silent an' weary, but closer thegither,   10
We urged our steeds thro' the faded heather,
    When we next rade down Ettrick.

When I last rade down Ettrick,
The winds were shifting, the storm was waking,
The snow was drifting, my heart was breaking,   15
For we never again were to ride thegither,
In sun or storm on the mountain heather,
    When I last rade down Ettrick.

Alicia Ann Spottiswood ("Lady John Scott") (1810–1900)

QUESTIONS

1. Ettrick is the name of a small village (and mountain and valley) near Selkirk in the "Border" district of southern Scotland, an area famed for its folk ballads. Some of the characteristics of the **ballad** are the use of refrain, local dialects, and songlike rhythms and rimes, in narratives that show emotional linkages between nature and human emotions and that omit definitive explanations for events. For an example of a true folk ballad, see "Edward" (No. 180). This poem is an imitation or "literary ballad"; discuss the characteristics of the folk ballad that it exhibits.
2. What stages in the development of love are represented in the three stanzas? How does nature reflect those stages? What do the changes in the refrains contribute?

We have not nearly exhausted the possibilities of sound repetition by giving names to a few of the more prominent kinds. The complete study of possible kinds of sound repetition in poetry would be so complex, however, that it would break down under its own machinery. Some of the subtlest and loveliest effects escape our net of names. In as short a phrase as this from the prose of John Ruskin—"ivy as light and lovely as the vine"—we notice alliteration in *light* and *lovely*, assonance in *ivy*, *light*, and *vine*, and consonance in *ivy* and *lovely*, but we have no name to connect the *v* in *vine* with the *v*s in *ivy* and *lovely*, or the second *l* in *lovely* with the first *l*, or the final syllables of *ivy* and *lovely* with each other; yet these are all an effective part of the music of the line. Also contributing to the music of poetry is the linking of related rather than identical sounds, such as *m* and *n*, or *p* and *b*, or the vowel sounds in *boat*, *boot*, and *book*.

These various musical repetitions, for trained readers, will ordinarily make an almost subconscious contribution to their reading of the poem: readers will feel their effect without necessarily being aware of what has caused it. There is value, however, in occasionally analyzing a poem for these devices in order to increase awareness of them. A few words of caution are necessary. First, the repetitions are entirely a matter of sound; spelling is irrelevant. *Bear* and *pair* are rimes, but *through* and *rough* are not. *Cell* and *sin*, *folly* and *philosophy* alliterate, but *sin* and *sugar*, *gun* and *gem* do not. Second, alliteration, assonance, consonance, and masculine rime are matters that ordinarily involve only stressed or accented syllables; for only such syllables ordinarily make enough impression on the ear to be significant in the sound pattern of the poem. For instance, we should hardly consider *which* and *its* in the second line of "The Turtle" an example of assonance, for neither word is stressed enough in the reading to make it significant as a sound. Third, the words involved in these repetitions must be close enough together that the ear retains the sound, consciously or subconsciously, from its first occurrence to its second. This distance varies according to circumstances, but for alliteration, assonance, and consonance the words ordinarily have to be in the same line or adjacent lines. End rime bridges a longer gap.

133. God's Grandeur

The world is charged with the grandeur of God.
    It will flame out, like shining from shook foil;
    It gathers to a greatness, like the ooze of oil
Crushed. Why do men then now not reck his rod?
Generations have trod, have trod, have trod;   5
    And all is seared with trade; bleared, smeared with toil;
    And wears man's smudge and shares man's smell: the soil
Is bare now, nor can foot feel, being shod.

And for all this, nature is never spent;
    There lives the dearest freshness deep down things;   10
And though the last lights off the black West went
    Oh, morning, at the brown brink eastward, springs—
Because the Holy Ghost over the bent
    World broods with warm breast and with ah! bright wings.

Gerard Manley Hopkins (1844–1889)

QUESTIONS

1. What is the theme of this sonnet?
2. The image in lines 3–4 possibly refers to olive oil being collected in great vats from crushed olives, but the image is much disputed. Explain the simile in line 2 and the symbols in lines 7–8 and 11–12.
3. Explain "reck his rod" (4), "spent" (9), "bent" (13).
4. Using different-colored pencils, encircle and connect examples of alliteration, assonance, consonance, and internal rime. Do these help to carry the meaning?

    We should not leave the impression that the use of these musical devices is necessarily or always valuable. Like the other resources of poetry, they can be judged only in the light of the poem's total intention. Many of the greatest works of English poetry—for instance,

Hamlet and *King Lear* and *Paradise Lost*—do not employ end rime. Both alliteration and rime, especially feminine rime, become humorous or silly if used excessively or unskillfully. If the intention is humorous, the result is delightful; if not, fatal. Shakespeare, who knew how to use all these devices to the utmost advantage, parodied their unskillful use in lines like "The preyful princess pierced and pricked a pretty pleasing prickett" in *Love's Labor's Lost* and

> Whereat with blade, with bloody, blameful blade,
> He bravely broached his boiling bloody breast

in *A Midsummer Night's Dream*. Swinburne parodied his own highly alliterative style in "Nephelidia" with lines like "Life is the lust of a lamp for the light that is dark till the dawn of the day when we die." Used skillfully and judiciously, however, musical devices provide a palpable and delicate pleasure to the ear and, even more important, add dimension to meaning.

134. We Real Cool

The Pool Players.
Seven At The Golden Shovel.

> We real cool. We
> Left school. We
>
> Lurk late. We
> Strike straight. We
>
> Sing sin. We   5
> Thin gin. We
>
> Jazz June. We
> Die soon.

Gwendolyn Brooks (b. 1917)

QUESTIONS

1. In addition to end rime, what other musical devices does this poem employ?
2. Try reading this poem with the pronouns at the beginning of the lines instead of at the end. What is lost?

3. English teachers in a certain urban school were once criticized for having their students read this poem: it was said to be immoral. Was the criticism justified? Why or why not?

135. Blackberry Sweet

Black girl black girl
lips as curved as cherries
full as grape bunches
sweet as blackberries

Black girl black girl   5
when you walk you are
magic as a rising bird
or a falling star

Black girl black girl
what's your spell to make   10
the heart in my breast
jump   stop   shake

Dudley Randall (b. 1914)

QUESTIONS

1. Refrains traditionally are placed at the ends of stanzas. How does this poem differ? With what effect?
2. Discuss the relation of form and content in the poem. How are the separate stanzas unified in themselves and yet linked to the others? How does each stanza achieve climax? How does the poem as a whole achieve climax?

136. The Snowstorm

Announced by all the trumpets of the sky,
Arrives the snow, and, driving o'er the fields,
Seems nowhere to alight: the whited air
Hides hills and woods, the river, and the heaven,
And veils the farmhouse at the garden's end.   5
The sled and traveler stopped, the courier's feet
Delayed, all friends shut out, the housemates sit
Around the radiant fireplace, enclosed
In a tumultuous privacy of storm.

Come see the north wind's masonry.   10
Out of an unseen quarry evermore
Furnished with tile, the fierce artificer
Curves his white bastions with projected roof
Round every windward stake, or tree, or door.
Speeding, the myriad-handed, his wild work   15
So fanciful, so savage, nought cares he
For number or proportion. Mockingly,
On coop or kennel he hangs Parian wreaths;
A swan-like form invests the hidden thorn;
Fills up the farmer's lane from wall to wall,   20
Maugre the farmer's sighs; and, at the gate,
A tapering turret overtops the work.
And when his hours are numbered and the world
Is all his own, retiring as he were not,
Leaves, when the sun appears, astonished Art   25
To mimic in slow structures, stone by stone,
Built in an age, the mad wind's night-work,
The frolic architecture of the snow.

Ralph Waldo Emerson (1803–1882)

QUESTIONS

1. Vocabulary: *Parian* (18); *thorn* (19); *Maugre* (21); "as he were not" (24)
   means "as if he had not existed."
2. From line 10 the poem presents an extended metaphor in the form of a
   personification. As what is the snowstorm personified? How do subsidiary
   metaphors support that personification (e.g., explain how "quarry" and
   "tile" [11–12] are used)?
3. The last sentence (23–28) has "he" as an understood subject, and introduces a second personification, "Art." Paraphrase the sentence and discuss how it extends the meaning of this descriptive poem.
4. The poem contains no end rime, but compensates with a richness of
   alliteration, assonance, consonance, and internal rime. Find as many
   examples as you can.

137. As imperceptibly as grief

As imperceptibly as grief
The summer lapsed away,
Too imperceptible at last
To seem like perfidy.

A quietness distilled   5
As twilight long begun,
Or nature spending with herself
Sequestered afternoon.

The dusk drew earlier in,
The morning foreign shone —   10
A courteous, yet harrowing grace,
As guest who would be gone.

And thus, without a wing
Or service of a keel,
Our summer made her light escape
Into the beautiful.

Emily Dickinson (1830–1886)

QUESTIONS

1. What are the subject and tone of the poem? Explain its opening simile.
2. Discuss the ways in which approximate rimes, alliteration, and the consonant sounds in the last stanza contribute to the meaning and tone.
3. What possible meanings have the last two lines?

138. Seal Lullaby

Oh! hush thee, my baby, the night is behind us,
    And black are the waters that sparkled so green.
The moon, o'er the combers, looks downward to find us
    At rest in the hollows that rustle between.
Where billow meets billow, there soft be thy pillow;   5
    Ah, weary wee flipperling, curl at thy ease!
The storm shall not wake thee, nor shark overtake thee
    Asleep in the arms of the slow-swinging seas.

Rudyard Kipling (1865–1936)

QUESTIONS

1. Identify speaker, listener, and situation. "[F]lipperling" (6) is a coined
   word; what does it mean?
2. Identify the musical devices (noticing where internal rime is introduced).
3. A feminine rime that involves two syllables is known also as a **double
   rime**. Find examples in the poem of double rimes. Which lines employ
   masculine or **single rimes**?

139. Shut In

Like many of us, born too late,
(like all of us, fenced in by fate),
    the late October fly
    will fondly live and die

insensible of the allure   5
of carrion or cow manure.
    Withindoors day and night,
    propelled by appetite,

he circles with approving hums
a morning's manna-fall of crumbs   10
    hoping to find a smear
    of jelly somewhere near.

In such an easeful habitat
while autumn wanes he waxes fat
    and languorous, but not   15
    enough to let the swat

of hasty, rolled-up magazine
eliminate him from the scene.
    Outside, the air is chill.
    Inside, he's hard to kill.   20

Patrolling with adhesive feet
the ceiling under which we eat,
    he captures at a glance
    the slightest threat or chance,

and flaunts the facets of his eyes   25
that make him prince of household spies.
    And as he watches, we,
    if we look up, will see

a life of limits, like our own,
enclosed within a temperate zone,   30
    not harsh, not insecure,
    no challenge to endure,

but yet, with every buzz of need,
by trifles running out of speed.
    One day he will be gone.   35
    Then the real cold comes on.

Robert B. Shaw (b. 1947)

QUESTIONS

1. What is the central figure of speech? Explain the similarities drawn between the fly and us. What are the two contrasting connotations of the title?
2. Comment on the musical devices. Where is the only approximate rime in the poem?

140. Traveling through the dark

Traveling through the dark I found a deer
dead on the edge of the Wilson River road.
It is usually best to roll them into the canyon:
that road is narrow; to swerve might make more dead.

By glow of the tail-light I stumbled back of the car   5
and stood by the heap, a doe, a recent killing;
she had stiffened already, almost cold.
I dragged her off; she was large in the belly.

My fingers touching her side brought me the reason —
her side was warm; her fawn lay there waiting,   10
alive, still, never to be born.
Beside that mountain road I hesitated.

The car aimed ahead its lowered parking lights;
under the hood purred the steady engine.
I stood in the glare of the warm exhaust turning red;   15
around our group I could hear the wilderness listen.

I thought hard for us all — my only swerving —,
then pushed her over the edge into the river.

William Stafford (1914–1993)

QUESTIONS

1. State precisely the speaker's dilemma. What kind of person is he? Does he make the right decision? Why does he call his hesitation "my only swerving" (17), and how does this connect with the word "swerve" in line 4?
2. What different kinds of imagery and of image contrasts give life to the poem? Do any of the images have symbolic overtones?
3. At first glance this poem may appear to be without end rime. Looking closer, do you find any correspondences between lines 2 and 4 in each stanza? Between the final words of the concluding couplet? Can you find any line-end in the poem without some connection in sound to another line-end in its stanza?

141. Nothing Gold Can Stay

Nature's first green is gold,
Her hardest hue to hold.
Her early leaf's a flower;
But only so an hour.
Then leaf subsides to leaf.   5
So Eden sank to grief,
So dawn goes down to day.
Nothing gold can stay.

Robert Frost (1874–1963)

QUESTIONS

1. Explain the paradoxes in lines 1 and 3.
2. Discuss the poem as a series of symbols. What are the symbolic meanings of "gold" in the final line of the poem?
3. Discuss the contributions of alliteration, assonance, consonance, rime, and other repetitions to the effectiveness of the poem.

EXERCISE

Discuss the various ways in which the following poems make use of refrain:
1. "Winter" (No. 2)
2. "Spring" (No. 4)
3. "Southern Cop" (No. 88)
4. "in Just-" (No. 92)
5. "Edward" (No. 180)
6. "The Lamb" (No. 204)
7. "Riddle" (No. 238)
8. "Adieu, farewell, earth's bliss" (No. 256)
9. "Fear no more" (No. 274)
10. "Do Not Go Gentle into That Good Night" (No. 286)

CHAPTER TWELVE

Rhythm and Meter

Our love of rhythm is rooted even deeper in us than our love for musical repetition. It is related to the beat of our hearts, the pulse of our blood, the intake and outflow of air from our lungs. Everything that we do naturally and gracefully we do rhythmically. There is rhythm in the way we walk, the way we swim, the way we ride a horse, the way we swing a golf club or a baseball bat. So native is rhythm to us that we read it, when we can, into the mechanical world around us. Our clocks go tick-tick-tick, but we hear tick-tock, tick-tock. The click of railway wheels beneath us patterns itself into a tune in our heads. There is a strong appeal for us in language that is rhythmical.

The term **rhythm** refers to any wavelike recurrence of motion or sound. In speech it is the natural rise and fall of language. All language is to some degree rhythmical, for all language involves alternations between accented and unaccented syllables. Language varies considerably, however, in the degree to which it exhibits rhythm. Sometimes in speech the rhythm is so unobtrusive or so unpatterned that we are scarcely aware of it. Sometimes, as in rap or in oratory, the rhythm is so pronounced that we may be tempted to tap our feet to it.

In every word of more than one syllable, one or more syllables are **accented** or **stressed;** that is, given more prominence in pronunciation than the rest.* We say toDAY, toMORrow, YESterday, interVENE. These accents within individual words are indicated by stress marks in dictionaries, and with many words of more than two syllables primary and secondary stresses are shown (in′-ter-vene″). When words are arranged into a sentence, we give certain words or syllables more prominence in pronunciation than the rest. We say: "He WENT to the

---

*Though the words *accent* and *stress* generally are used interchangeably, as here, a distinction is sometimes made between them in technical discussions. **Accent,** the relative prominence given a syllable in relation to its neighbors, is then said to result from one or more of four causes: *stress,* or force of utterance, producing loudness; *duration; pitch;* and *juncture,* the manner of transition between successive sounds. Of these, *stress,* in English verse, is the most important.

STORE" or "ANN is DRIVing her CAR." There is nothing mysterious about this; it is the normal process of language. The only difference between prose and verse is that in prose these accents occur more or less haphazardly; in verse the poet may arrange them to occur at regular intervals.

In poetry as in prose, the rhythmic effects depend almost entirely on what a statement means, and different intended meanings will produce different rhythms even in identical statements. If I say "I don't believe YOU," I mean something different from "*I* don't believe you" or from "I don't beLIEVE you." In speech, these are **rhetorical stresses,** which we use to make our intentions clear. Stressing "I" separates me from others who do believe you; stressing "you" separates you from others whom I do believe; stressing "believe" intensifies my statement of disbelief. Such rhetorical stressing comes as naturally to us as language itself, and is at least as important in poetry as it is in expressive speaking. It is also basic to understanding the rhythm of poetry, for poetic rhythm depends on the plain, rhetorical stresses to communicate its meaning. We must be able to recognize the meaning of a line of poetry before we can determine its rhythm.

In addition to accent or stress, rhythm is based on pauses. In poetry as in prose or speech, pauses are the result of natural speech rhythms and the structure of sentences. Periods and commas create pauses, but so does the normal flow of phrases and clauses. Poetry, however, adds another kind of pause arising from the fact that poetry is written in lines. The poetic line is a unit that creates pauses in the flow of speech, sometimes slight and sometimes large. Poets have at their disposal a variety of possibilities when ending a line. An **end-stopped line** is one in which the end of the line corresponds with a natural speech pause; a **run-on line** is one in which the sense of the line hurries on into the next line. (There are of course all degrees of end-stop and run-on. A line ending with a period or semicolon is heavily end-stopped. A line without punctuation at the end is normally considered a run-on line, but it is less forcibly run-on if it ends at a natural speech pause—as between subject and predicate—than if it ends, say, between an article and its noun, between an auxiliary and its verb, or between a preposition and its object.) In addition there are pauses that occur in the middle of lines, either grammatical or rhetorical. These are called **caesuras,** and are another resource for varying the rhythm of lines.

The poetic line is the basic rhythmic unit in **free verse,** the predominating type of poetry now being written. Except for its line arrangement there are no necessary differences between the rhythms of free verse and the rhythms of prose, so our awareness of the line as a rhythmic unit is essential. Consider the rhythmic contrast between end-stopped lines and run-on lines in these two excerpts from poems presented earlier, and notice how the caesuras (marked ‖) help to vary the rhythms:

A noiseless patient spider,

I marked where on a little promontory it stood isolated,

Marked how to explore the vacant vast surrounding,

It launched forth filament, ‖ filament, ‖ filament, ‖ out of itself,

Ever unreeling them, ‖ ever tirelessly speeding them.

(from Poem No. 61)

Sorrow is my own yard

where the new grass

flames ‖ as it has flamed

often before ‖ but not

with the cold fire

that closes round me this year.

(from Poem No. 35)

There is another sort of poetry that depends entirely on ordinary prose rhythms—the **prose poem** exemplified by Carolyn Forché's "The Colonel" (No. 222). Having dispensed even with the line as a unit of rhythm, the prose poem lays its claim to being poetry by its attention to many of the poetic elements presented earlier in this book: connotation, imagery, figurative language, and the concentration of meaning in evocative language.

But most often, when people think of poetry they think of the two broad branches, free verse and metrical verse, which are distinguished mainly by the absence or presence of meter. **Meter** is the identifying characteristic of rhythmic language that we can tap our feet to. When verse is metrical, the accents of language are so arranged as to occur at apparently equal intervals of time, and it is this interval we mark off with the tap of a foot.

The study of meter is fascinating but highly complex. It is by no means an absolute prerequisite to an enjoyment, even a rich enjoyment, of poetry, any more than is the ability to identify by name the multiplicity of figures of speech. But a knowledge of the fundamentals of meter does have value. It can make the beginning reader more aware of the rhythmical effects of poetry and of how poetry should be read. It can enable the more advanced reader to analyze how certain effects are achieved, to see how rhythm interacts with meaning, and to explain what makes one poem (in this respect) better than another. The beginning student ought to have at least an elementary knowledge of the subject. And it is not so difficult as its traditional terminology might suggest.

Even for the beginner, one essential distinction must be understood: although the terms *rhythm* and *meter* are sometimes used interchangeably, they mean different things. Rhythm designates the flow of actual, pronounced sound (or sound heard in the mind's ear), whereas meter refers to the patterns that sounds follow when a poet has arranged them into metrical verse. This may be illustrated by an analogy of a well-designed building and the architect's blueprint for its construction. The building, like rhythmic sound, is actual and real; the blueprint for it is an abstract, idealized pattern, like metrical form. When we look at a building, we see the actuality, but we also recognize that it is based on a pattern. The actuality of the building goes beyond the idealized blueprint in a number of ways—it presents us with texture, with color, with varying effects depending upon light and shade, with contrasts of building materials. In poetry, the actuality is language arranged in sentences, with a progression through time, with varying emotions, dramatic contrasts of meaning and tone, the revelation of the speaker's situation, and so forth. All these are expressed through the sounds of language, which are constantly shifting to create meanings and implications.

The word *meter* comes from a word meaning "measure" (the word *rhythm* from a word meaning "flow," as in waves). To measure something we must have a unit of measurement. For measuring length we use the inch, foot, yard; for measuring time we use the second, minute, hour. For measuring verse we use the foot, the line, and (sometimes) the stanza.

One basic unit of meter, the **foot,** consists normally of one accented syllable plus one or two unaccented syllables, though occasionally there may be no unaccented syllables. Determining which syllable in a foot is accented, we compare its sound with that of the other syllables *within the foot,* not with the sounds of syllables in other feet within a line. In fact, because of the varying stresses on syllables in a spoken sentence, it is very unusual for all of the stressed syllables in a line to be equally stressed.

For diagramming the metrical form of verse, various systems of visual symbols have been devised. In this book we shall use a breve (⌣) to indicate an unstressed syllable, an ictus (′) to indicate a stressed syllable, and a vertical bar to indicate the division between feet. The basic kinds of feet are as follows:

Examples	Name of foot	Adjectival form*	
to-dáy, the sún	Iamb	Iambic	⎤
dái-ly, went to	Trochee	Trochaic	⎦ Duple meters
in-ter-véne, in the dárk	Anapest	Anapestic	⎤
múl-ti-ple, cól-or of	Dactyl	Dactylic	⎦ Triple meters
trúe-blúe	Spondee	Spondaic	

Two kinds of examples are given here, whole words and phrases, to indicate the fact that one must not assume that every individual word will be a foot, nor that divisions between feet necessarily fall between words. In actual lines, one might for example find the word *intervene* constituting parts of two different feet:

I wánt | to in- | ter-véne.

As this example demonstrates, in diagramming meters we must sometimes acknowledge the primary and secondary stresses provided by dictionaries: the word *intervene* provides the stresses for two consecutive feet.

The other basic unit of measurement in metrical verse is the line, which has the same properties as in free verse—it may be end-stopped or run-on, and its phrasing and punctuation will create caesuras. The difference between metrical and free verse lines is that

---

*In the spondee the accent is thought of as being distributed equally or almost equally over the two syllables and is sometimes referred to as a hovering accent. No whole poems are written in spondees. Hence there are only four basic meters: iambic, trochaic, anapestic, and dactylic. Iambic and trochaic are called duple because they employ two-syllable feet, anapestic and dactylic triple because they employ three-syllable feet. Of the four standard meters, iambic is by far the most common, followed by anapestic. Trochaic occurs relatively infrequently as the meter of poems, and dactylic is so rare as to be almost a museum specimen.

metrical lines are measured by naming the number of feet in them. The following names are used to indicate number:

Monometer	one foot	Tetrameter	four feet
Dimeter	two feet	Pentameter	five feet
Trimeter	three feet	Hexameter	six feet

The third unit of measurement, the **stanza,** consists of a group of lines whose metrical pattern is repeated throughout the poem. Since much verse is not written in stanzas, we shall save our discussion of this unit till a later chapter.

Although metrical form is potentially uniform in its regularity, the poet may introduce **metrical variations,** which call attention to some of the sounds because they depart from what is regular. Three means for varying meter are **substitution** (replacing the regular foot with another one), **extra-metrical syllables** added at the beginnings or endings of lines, and **anacrusis** (the omission of an unaccented syllable at the beginning of a line). Because these represent clear changes in the pattern, they are usually obvious and striking. But even metrical regularity rarely creates a monotonous rhythm because rhythm is the actuality in sound, not the pattern or blueprint of meter. The rhythm of a line of poetry, like the actuality of a building, depends on the components of sound mentioned above—stress, duration, pitch, and juncture—as these are presented in rhetorically stressed sentences. We may diagram the metrical form of a line, but because no two sentences in English are identical in sound, there can be no formulas or mechanical systems for indicating rhythm. Rhythm must be described rather than formulated.

The process of defining the metrical form of a poem is called **scansion.** To *scan* any specimen of verse, we do three things: (1) we identify the prevailing foot; (2) we name the number of feet in a line—if this length follows any regular pattern; and (3) we describe the stanzaic pattern—if there is one. We may try out our skill on the following poem:

142. Virtue

Sweet day, so cool, so calm, so bright,
The bridal of the earth and sky;

The dew shall weep thy fall to night,
　　For thou must die.

Sweet rose, whose hue, angry and brave,　　　　　5
　　Bids the rash gazer wipe his eye;
Thy root is ever in its grave,
　　And thou must die.

Sweet spring, full of sweet days and roses,
　　A box where sweets compacted lie;　　　　　10
My music shows ye have your closes,
　　And all must die.

Only a sweet and virtuous soul,
　　Like seasoned timber, never gives;
But though the whole world turn to coal,　　　15
　　Then chiefly lives.

George Herbert (1593–1633)

QUESTIONS

1. Vocabulary: *bridal* (2), *brave* (5), *closes* (11), *coal* (15).
2. How are the four stanzas interconnected? How do they build to a climax? How does the fourth contrast with the first three?

The first step in scanning a poem is to read it normally, according to its prose meaning, listening to where the accents fall naturally, and perhaps beating time with the hand. If we have any doubt about how a line should be marked, we should skip it temporarily and go on to lines where we feel greater confidence; that is, to those lines which seem most regular, with accents that fall unmistakably at regular intervals—for we are seeking the poem's pattern, which will be revealed by what is regular in it. In "Virtue" lines 3, 10, and 14 clearly fall into this category, as do the short lines 4, 8, and 12. Lines 3, 10, and 14 may be marked as follows.

The dĕw | shăll wéep | thy̆ fáll | tŏ níght, |　　　　　3

Ă bóx | whĕre swéets | cŏm-páct- | ĕd líe; |　　　　　10

Lĭke séa- | sŏned tím- | bĕr, név- | ĕr gíves |　　　　　14

Lines 4, 8, and 12 are so nearly identical that we may use line 4 to represent all three.

For thou must die.   4

Surveying what we have done so far, we may with some confidence say that the prevailing metrical foot of the poem is iambic; and we may reasonably hypothesize that the second and third lines of each stanza are tetrameter (four-foot) lines and the fourth line dimeter. What about the first lines? Line 1 contains eight syllables, and since the poem is iambic, we may mark them into four feet. The last six syllables clearly constitute three iambic feet (as a general rule, the last few feet in a line tend to reflect the prevailing meter of a poem).

Sweet day, so cool, so calm, so bright   1

This too, then, is a tetrameter line, and the only question is whether to mark the first foot as another iamb or as a spondee—that is, whether it conforms to the norm established by the iambic meter, or is a substituted foot. The adjective "Sweet" is certainly more important in the line than the repeated adverb "so," and ought to receive more stress than the adverbs on the principle of *rhetorical stress,* by which the plain prose sense governs the pronunciation. But we must remember that in marking metrical stresses, we are only comparing the syllables *within a foot,* so the comparison with the repeated "so" is irrelevant. The real question is whether "Sweet" receives as much emphasis as "day."

As another general rule (but by no means an absolute one), a noun usually receives more stress than an adjective that modifies it, a verb more than its adverbs, an adjective more than an adverb that modifies it—except when the modifying word points to an unusual or unexpected condition. If the phrase were "fat day" or "red day," we would probably feel that those adjectives were odd enough to warrant stressing them. "Sweet day" does not strike us as particularly unusual, so the noun ought to receive stress. Further, as we notice that each of the first three stanzas begins with "Sweet" modifying different nouns, we recognize that the statement of the poem is drawing attention to the similarities (and differences) of three things that can be called *sweet*— "day," "rose," and "spring." By its repetition before those three nouns, the word *sweet* may come to seem formulary, and the nouns the object of attention. On the other hand, the repetition of "Sweet" may seem emphatic, and lead us to give approximately equal stress to both the noun and its adjective. As our purpose is to detect the *pattern* of sounds in the poem, the most likely result of this study will be to mark it iambic. However, judging it to be spondaic would not be incorrect, for ultimately we are reporting what we *hear,* and there is room for subjective differences.

The first feet of lines 5 and 9 raise the same problem as line 1 and should be marked in the same way. Choices of a similar sort occur in other lines (15 and 16). Many readers will quite legitimately perceive line 16 as parallel to lines 4, 8, and 12. Others, however, may argue that the world "then"—emphasizing what happens to the virtuous soul when everything else has perished—has an importance that should be reflected in both the reading and the scansion, and will therefore mark the first foot of this line as a spondee:

Then chief-ly lives.   16

These readers also will hear the third foot in line 15 as a spondee:

But though the whole world turn to coal   15

Lines 2 and 7 introduce a different problem. Most readers, if they encountered these lines in a paragraph of prose, would read them thus:

The BRIdal of the EARTH and SKY   2

Thy ROOT is EVer in its GRAVE   7

But this reading leaves us with an anomalous situation. First, we have only three stresses where our pattern calls for four. Second, we have three unaccented syllables occurring together, a situation almost never found in verse of duple meter. From this situation we may learn an important principle. Though normal reading of the sentences in a poem establishes its metrical pattern, the metrical pattern so established in turn influences the reading. An interactive process is at work. In this poem the pressure of the pattern will cause most practiced readers to stress the second of the three unaccented syllables in both lines slightly more than those on either side of it. In scansion, comparing the syllables within the individual foot, we acknowledge that slight increase of stress by marking those syllables as stressed (remember, the marking of the accent does not indicate a *degree* of stress in comparison with other accents in the line). We mark them thus:

The bri-dal of the earth and sky   2

Thy root is ev-er in its grave   7

Line 5 presents a situation about which there can be no dispute. The word "angry," though it occurs in a position where we would expect an iamb, by virtue of its normal pronunciation *must* be accented on the first syllable, and thus must be marked a trochee:

Sweet rose, | whose hue, | an-gry | and brave   5

There is little question also that the following line begins with a trochee, but the second foot ("rash gaz-") must be examined, for we may wonder whether the adjective *rash* presents an unexpected modification for the noun *gazer*. Since the possibilities seem about equal, I prefer to let the pattern again take precedence, although a spondee would be acceptable:

Bids the | rash gaz- | er wipe | his eye   6

Similarly, the word "Only," beginning line 13, must be accented on the first syllable, thus introducing a trochaic substitution in the first foot of the line. Line 13 also presents another problem. A modern reader perceives the word "virtuous" as a three-syllable word, but the poet writing in the seventeenth century when metrical requirements were stricter than they are today would probably have meant the word to be pronounced as two syllables: *ver- tyus*. Following the tastes of this century, I mark it as three syllables, so introducing an anapest instead of the expected iamb in the last foot:

On- ly | a sweet | and vir- | tu-ous soul   13

In doing this, however, I am consciously modernizing—altering the probable practice of the poet for the sake of a contemporary audience.

One problem of scansion remains: in the third stanza, lines 9 and 11 differ from the other lines of the poem in two respects—(a) they contain an uneven number of syllables (nine rather than the expected eight); (b) they end on unaccented syllables:

Sweet spring, | full of | sweet days | and ros- | es,   9

My mu- | sic shows | ye have | your clos- | es   11

Such leftover unaccented syllables at line ends are examples of extrametrical syllables and are not counted in identifying and naming the meter. These lines are both tetrameter, and if we tap our feet when reading them, we shall tap four times. Metrical verse will often have one and sometimes two leftover unaccented syllables. In iambic and anapestic verse they will come at the end of the lines; in trochaic and dactyllic at the beginning. They never occur in the middle of a line.

Our metrical analysis of "Virtue" is completed. Though (mainly for ease of discussion) we have skipped about, we have indicated a scansion for all its lines. "Virtue" is written in iambic meter (meaning that most of its feet are iambs), and is composed of four-line stanzas, the first three lines tetrameter, the final line dimeter. We are now ready to make a few generalizations about scansion.

1. Good readers will not ordinarily stop to scan a poem they are reading, and they certainly will not read a poem aloud with the exaggerated emphasis on accented syllables that we sometimes give them in order to make the metrical pattern more apparent. However, occasional scansion of a poem has value, as will be indicated in the next chapter, which discusses the relation of sound and meter to sense. Just one example here. The structure of meaning of "Virtue" is unmistakable; three parallel stanzas concerning things that die are followed by a contrasting fourth stanza concerning the one thing that does not die. The first three stanzas all begin with the word "Sweet" preceding a noun, and the first metrical foot in these stanzas is either an iamb or a spondee. The contrasting fourth stanza, however, begins with a trochee, thus departing both from the previous pattern and from the basic meter of the poem. This departure is significant, for the word *only* is the hinge upon which the structure of the poem turns, and the metrical reversal gives it emphasis. Thus meter serves meaning.

2. Scansion only begins to reveal the rhythmical quality of a poem. It simply involves classifying all syllables as either accented or unaccented and ignores the sometimes considerable differences between degrees of accent. Whether we call a syllable accented or unaccented depends only on its degree of accent relative to the other syllable(s) in its foot. In lines 2 and 7 of "Virtue," the accents on "of" and "in" are obviously much lighter than on the other accented syllables in the line. Further, unaccented syllables also vary in weight. In line 5 "whose" is clearly heavier than (-gry) or "and," and is arguably even heavier than the accented "of" and "in" of lines 2 and 7. It is not unusual, either, to find the unaccented syllable of a foot receiving more stress than the accented syllable immediately preceding it in another foot, as in this line by Ben Jonson (No. 245):

Drink to | me on- | ly with | thine eyes |

The last four syllables of the line, two perfectly regular iambs, are actually spoken as a sequence of four increasingly stressed accents. A similar sequence of increasing accents occurs in lines 4, 8, and 12 of "Virtue"

For thŏu̍ mŭst díe̍

since the necessity expressed in the word "must" makes it more heavily stressed than the pronoun "thou." The point is that metrical scansion is incapable of describing subtle rhythmic effects in poetry. It is nevertheless a useful and serviceable tool, for by showing us the metrical *pattern,* it draws attention to the way in which the actuality of sound follows the pattern even while departing from it; that is, recognizing the meter, we can more clearly hear rhythms. The *idea* of regularity helps us be aware of the *actuality* of sounds.

3. Notice that the divisions between feet have no meaning except to help us identify the meter. They do not correspond to the speech rhythms in the line. In the third foot of line 14 of "Virtue," a syntactical pause occurs *within* the foot; and, indeed, feet divisions often fall in the middle of a word. It is sometimes a mistake of beginners to expect the word and the foot to be identical units. We mark the feet divisions only to reveal regularity or pattern, not to indicate rhythm. But in "Virtue," if we examine all of the two-syllable words, we find that all eleven of them as isolated words removed from their lines would be called *trochaic.* Yet only two of them—"angry" (5) and "only" (13)—actually occur as trochaic feet. All the rest are divided in the middle between two iambic feet. This calls for two observations: (a) the rhythm of the poem, the *heard* sound, often runs counter to the meter—iambic feet have what is called a "rising" pattern, yet these words individually and as they are spoken have a "falling" rhythm; and (b) the trochaic hinge word "only" thus has rhythmic echoes throughout the poem, those preceding it yielding a kind of predictive power, and those following it reinforcing the fact that the sense of the poem turns at that word. This rhythmic effect is especially pronounced in the simile of line 14:

Lĭke séa̍ sŏned tím̍ ber, né̍v er gíves̍

Echoing the key word "only," this line contains three disyllabic words, each of them having a falling rhythm running counter to the iambic meter.

4. Finally—and this is the most important generalization of all— perfect regularity of meter is no criterion of merit. Inexperienced readers sometimes get the notion that it is. If the meter is regular, and the rhythm mirrors that regularity in sound, they may feel that the poet has handled the meter successfully and deserves all credit for it. Actually there is nothing easier for any moderately talented versifier than to make language go ta-DUM ta-DUM ta-DUM. But there are two reasons why this is not generally desirable. The first is that, as we have said, all art consists essentially of repetition and variation. If a rhythm alternates too regularly between light and heavy beats, the result is to banish variation; the rhythm mechanically follows the meter and becomes monotonous. But used occasionally or emphatically, a monotonous rhythm can be very effective, as in the triumphant last line of Tennyson's "Ulysses" (No. 67):

To strive, to seek, to find, and not to yield.

The second reason is that, once a basic meter has been established, deviations from it become highly significant and are a means by which the poet can reinforce meaning. If a meter is too regular, and the rhythm shows little deviation from it, the probability is that the poet, instead of adopting rhythm to meaning, has simply forced the meaning into a metrical straitjacket.

Actually what gives the skillful use of meter its greatest effectiveness is to be found in the distinction between meter and rhythm. Once we have determined the basic meter of a poem, say iambic tetrameter, we have an expectation that the rhythm will coincide with it—that the pattern will be identical to the actual sound. Thus a silent drumbeat is set up in our minds, and this drumbeat constitutes an expected rhythm. But the actual rhythm of the words—the heard rhythm—will sometimes confirm this expected rhythm and sometimes not. Thus the two, meter and rhythm, are counterpointed, and the appeal of the verse is magnified just as when two melodies are counterpointed in music, or as when we see two swallows flying together and round each other, following the same general course but with individual variations and so making a more eye-catching pattern than one swallow flying alone. If the heard rhythm conforms too closely to the expected rhythm (meter), the poem becomes dull and uninteresting rhythmically. If it departs too far from the meter, there ceases to be an expected rhythm and the result is likely to be a muddle.

There are several ways by which variation can be introduced into a poem's rhythm. The most obvious way, as we have said, is by the substitution of other kinds of feet for the basic foot. Such metrical variation will always be reflected as a rhythmic variation. In our scansion of line 13 of "Virtue," for instance, we found a trochee and an anapest substituted for the expected iambs in the first and last feet. A less obvious but equally important means of variation is through varying degrees of accent arising from the prose meaning of phrases—from the rhetorical stressing. Though we began our scansion of "Virtue" by marking lines 3, 10, and 14 as perfectly regular metrically, there is actually a considerable rhythmic difference between them. Line 3 is quite regular because the rhythmic phrasing corresponds to the metrical pattern, and the line can be read ta-DUM ta-DUM ta-DUM ta-DUM (The DEW shall WEEP thy FALL to NIGHT). Line 10 is less regular, for the three-syllable word "compacted" cuts across the division between two feet. This should be read ta-DUM ta-DUM ta-DUMP-ty DUM (A BOX where SWEETS comPACTed LIE). Line 14 is the least regular of these three because here there is no correspondence between rhythmic phrasing and metrical division. This should be read ta-DUMP-ty DUMP-ty, DUMP-ty DUM (Like SEAsoned TIMber, NEVer GIVES). Finally, variation can be introduced by **grammatical** and **rhetorical pauses,** whether or not signaled by punctuation (punctuated pauses are usually of longer duration than those occasioned only by syntax and rhetoric, and pauses for periods are longer than those for commas). The comma in line 14, by introducing a grammatical pause (in the middle of a foot), provides an additional variation from its perfect regularity. Probably the most violently irregular line in the poem is line 5,

Sweet rose, | whose hue, | an- gry | and brave, |

for here the unusual trochaic substitution in the second from last foot of an iambic line (a rare occurrence) is set off and emphasized by the grammatical pause, and also as we have noted the unaccented "whose" is considerably heavier than the other unaccented syllables in the line. This trochee "angry" is the first unquestionable metrical substitution in the poem. It occurs in a line which, because it opens a stanza, is subconsciously compared to the first line of the first stanza—an example of regularity with its grammatical pauses separating all four of its feet. Once we have noticed that the first line of the second stanza contains a metrical variation, our attention is called to the fact that after the first, each stanza opens with a line containing a trochee—and that these trochees are moved forward one foot in each of the successive stanzas, from the third position in stanza two, to the second in four, and finally to the first in the concluding stanza. This pattern itself tends to add even more emphasis to the climactic change signaled by the final trochee, "only." Again, meter and rhythm serve meaning.

The effects of rhythm and meter are several. Like the musical repetitions of sound, the musical repetitions of accent can be pleasing for their own sake. In addition, rhythm works as an emotional stimulus and heightens our awareness of what is going on in a poem. Finally, a poet can adapt the sound of the verse to its content and thus make meter a powerful reinforcement of meaning. We should avoid, however, the notion that there is any mystical correspondence between certain meters or rhythms and certain emotions. There are no "happy" meters and no "melancholy" meters. The "falling" rhythm of line 14 of "Virtue," counterpointed against its "rising" meter, does not indicate a depression of mood or feeling—the line has quite the opposite emotional tone. Poets' choice of meter is probably less important than how they handle it after they have chosen it. In all great poetry, meter and rhythm work intimately with the other elements of the poem to produce the total effect.

And because of the importance of free verse today, we must not forget that poetry need not be metrical at all. Like alliteration and rime, like metaphor and irony, like even imagery, meter is simply *one* resource poets may or may not use. Their job is to employ their resources to the best advantage for the object they have in mind—the kind of experience they wish to express. And on no other basis should they be judged.

EXERCISES

1. A term that every student of poetry should know (and should be careful not to confuse with *free verse*) is blank verse. **Blank verse** has a very specific meter: it is *iambic pentameter, unrimed.* It has a special name because it is the principal English meter; that is, the meter that has been used for a large proportion of the greatest English poetry, including the plays of Shakespeare and the epics of Milton. Iambic pentameter in English seems especially suitable for the serious treatment of serious themes. The natural movement of the English language tends to be iambic. Lines shorter than pentameter tend to be songlike, or at least less suited to sustained treatment of serious material. Lines longer than pentameter tend to break up into shorter units, the hexameter line being read as two three-foot units.

Rime, while highly appropriate to most short poems, often proves a handicap for a long and lofty work. (The word *blank* indicates that the end of the line is "blank," that is, bare of rime.)

Of the following poems, four are in blank verse, two are in other meters, and four are in free verse. Determine in which category each belongs.

a. "Break of Day" (No. 16)
b. "The River-Merchant's Wife: A Letter" (No. 19)
c. "Mirror" (No. 21)
d. "Ulysses" (No. 67)
e. "The Unknown Citizen" (No. 82)
f. "Grace to Be Said at the Supermarket" (No. 85)
g. "'Out, Out—'" (No. 90)
h. "Dover Beach" (No. 126)
i. "Getting Out" (No. 128)
j. "Living in Sin" (No. 268)

2. Examine "My Last Duchess" (No. 89) and "Sound and Sense" (No. 158). Both are written in the same meter (iambic pentameter, rimed in couplets) but their general rhythmical effect is markedly different. What accounts for the difference? How does the contrast support our statement that the way poets handle meter is more important than their choice of a meter?

3. Examine "The Widow's Lament in Springtime" (No. 35), "The Hound" (No. 45), and "The Dance" (No. 167). Which is the most forcibly run-on in the majority of its lines? Describe the differences in effect.

---

143. "Introduction" to *Songs of Innocence*

Piping down the valleys wild,
Piping songs of pleasant glee,
On a cloud I saw a child,
And he laughing said to me:

"Pipe a song about a Lamb."   5
So I piped with merry cheer.
"Piper, pipe that song again."
So I piped; he wept to hear.

"Drop thy pipe, thy happy pipe;
Sing thy songs of happy cheer."   10
So I sung the same again
While he wept with joy to hear.

"Piper, sit thee down and write
In a book that all may read."
So he vanished from my sight,   15
And I plucked a hollow reed,

And I made a rural pen,
And I stained the water clear,
And I wrote my happy songs
Every child may joy to hear.   20

William Blake (1757–1827)

QUESTIONS

1. Poets have traditionally been thought of as inspired by one of the Muses (Greek female divinities whose duties were to nurture the arts). Blake's *Songs of Innocence,* a book of poems about childhood and the state of innocence, includes "The Chimney Sweeper" (No. 78) and "The Lamb" (No. 204). In this introductory poem to the book, what function is performed by the child upon a cloud?
2. What is symbolized by "a Lamb" (5)?
3. What three stages of poetic composition are suggested in stanzas 1–2, 3, and 4–5 respectively?
4. What features of the poems in his book does Blake hint at in this "Introduction"? Name at least four.
5. Mark the stressed and unstressed syllables in lines 1–2 and 9–10. Do they establish the basic meter of the poem? If so, is that meter iambic or trochaic? Or could it be either? Some metrists have discarded the distinction between iambic and trochaic, and between anapestic and dactylic, as being artificial. The important distinction, they feel, is between duple and triple meters. Does this poem support their claim?

144. It takes all sorts

It takes all sorts of in and outdoor schooling
To get adapted to my kind of fooling.

Robert Frost (1874–1963)

QUESTIONS

1. What is the poet saying about the nature of his poetry?
2. Scan the poem. Is it iambic or trochaic? Or could it be either? How does this poem differ from Blake's "Introduction" in illustrating the ambiguity of the distinction between the two meters?

145. Epitaph on an Army of Mercenaries

These, in the day when heaven was falling,
   The hour when earth's foundations fled,
Followed their mercenary calling
   And took their wages and are dead.

Their shoulders held the sky suspended;   5
   They stood, and earth's foundations stay;
What God abandoned, these defended,
   And saved the sum of things for pay.

A. E. Housman (1859–1936)

QUESTIONS

1. The Battle of Ypres (October 31, 1914), early in World War I, pitted a
   small army of British "regulars" against a much larger force of German
   volunteers. German newspapers described the conflict as one between
   young German volunteers and British "mercenaries." Housman first published this poem in the London *Times* on October 31, 1917, the third anniversary of the battle. Who are "These" (1)? Is the tone of the poem one
   of tribute or one of cynical scorn for "These"? How does the poet use the
   word "mercenary" (3)?
2. In scanning Herbert's "Virtue," we discovered two lines that had an unaccented syllable left over at the end that we did not count in determining the meter. How does this poem differ from "Virtue" in its use of such
   lines? The meter of this poem is iambic tetrameter. Does this sufficiently
   describe its metrical form?

146. Had I the Choice

Had I the choice to tally greatest bards,
To limn their portraits, stately, beautiful, and emulate at will,
Homer with all his wars and warriors—Hector, Achilles, Ajax,
Or Shakespeare's woe-entangled Hamlet, Lear, Othello—Tennyson's
   fair ladies,
Meter or wit the best, or choice conceit to wield in perfect rhyme,
   delight of singers;   5
These, these, O sea, all these I'd gladly barter,
Would you the undulation of one wave, its trick to me transfer,
Or breathe one breath of yours upon my verse,
And leave its odor there.

Walt Whitman (1819–1892)

QUESTIONS

1. Vocabulary: *tally* (1), *limn* (2), *conceit* (5).
2. What poetic qualities does Whitman propose to barter in exchange for what? What qualities do the sea and its waves symbolize?
3. Is this free verse, or metrical verse in duple meter? In what way might this be taken as an imitation of the rhythms of the sea?

147. The Aim Was Song

Before man came to blow it right
   The wind once blew itself untaught,
And did its loudest day and night
   In any rough place where it caught.

Man came to tell it what was wrong: 5
   It hadn't found the place to blow;
It blew too hard—the aim was song.
   And listen—how it ought to go!

He took a little in his mouth,
   And held it long enough for north   10
To be converted into south,
   And then by measure blew it forth.

By measure. It was word and note,
   The wind the wind had meant to be—
A little through the lips and throat.   15
   The aim was song—the wind could see.

Robert Frost (1874–1963)

QUESTIONS

1. Frost invents a myth about the origin of poetry. What implications does it suggest about the relation of man to nature and of poetry to nature?
2. Contrast the thought and form of this poem with Whitman's.
3. Scan the poem and identify its meter. How does the poet give variety to a regular metrical pattern?

148. Nevertheless

you've seen a strawberry
   that's had a struggle; yet
   was, where the fragments met,

a hedgehog or a star-
   fish for the multitude   5
   of seeds. What better food

than apple seeds—the fruit
   within the fruit—locked in
   like counter-curved twin

hazelnuts? Frost that kills   10
   the little rubber-plant-
   leaves of *kok-saghyz*-stalks, can't

harm the roots; they still grow
   in frozen ground. Once where
   there was a prickly-pear-   15

leaf clinging to barbed wire,
   a root shot down to grow
   in the earth two feet below;

as carrots form mandrakes
   or a ram's-horn root some-   20
   times. Victory won't come

to me unless I go
   to it; a grape tendril
   ties a knot in knots till

knotted thirty times—so   25
   the bound twig that's undergone and over-gone, can't stir.

The weak overcomes its
   menace, the strong overcomes itself. What is there   30

like fortitude! What sap
   went through that little thread
   to make the cherry red!

                    Marianne Moore (1887–1972)

QUESTIONS

1. Vocabulary: *kok-saghyz* (12), *prickly-pear* (15), *mandrakes* (19).
2. This apparently random collection of examples from botanical nature actually proceeds through a sequence that begins with two types of seed-bearing fruit. Where does it go from there, and what does it end up with?
3. What human meaning does the speaker draw from these botanical examples? How do the examples support that meaning?

4. This poem is an example of **syllabic verse,** which counts only the number of syllables per line regardless of accents. (Sylvia Plath's "Metaphors"
[No. 52] is another example.) Describe its formal pattern, including its
rime scheme. Although the form appears arbitrary in its line breaks and
stanza breaks, it is in fact tightly formalized. How is such a form appropriate to the meaning of the poem?

149. To a Daughter Leaving Home

When I taught you
at eight to ride
a bicycle, loping along
beside you
as you wobbled away   5
on two round wheels,
my own mouth rounding
in surprise when you pulled
ahead down the curved
path of the park,   10
I kept waiting
for the thud
of your crash as I
sprinted to catch up,
while you grew   15
smaller, more breakable
with distance,
pumping, pumping
for your life, screaming
with laughter,   20
the hair flapping
behind you like a
handkerchief waving
goodbye.

Linda Pastan (b. 1932)

QUESTIONS

1. How does the discrepancy between the title and the event create meaning? Which details of the poem take on symbolic meaning?
2. Write out this poem as prose, ignoring line ends. What poetic effect has
been lost? Which of the original line ends are particularly important to
meaning and feeling?

150. Constantly risking absurdity

Constantly risking absurdity
                          and death
        whenever he performs
                    above the heads
                              of his audience   5
    the poet like an acrobat
                  climbs on rime
                          to a high wire of his own making
and balancing on eyebeams
                          above a sea of faces   10
        paces his way
                      to the other side of day
    performing entrechats
                      and sleight-of-foot tricks
    and other high theatrics   15
                          and all without mistaking
            any thing
                    for what it may not be
        For he's the super realist
                          who must perforce perceive   20
        taut truth
                    before the taking of each stance or step
    in his supposed advance
                          toward that still higher perch
where Beauty stands and waits   25
                      with gravity
                              to start her death-defying leap
        And he
                a little charleychaplin man
                          who may or may not catch   30
            her fair eternal form
                          spreadeagled in the empty air
            of existence

Lawrence Ferlinghetti (b. 1919)

QUESTIONS

1. Vocabulary: *entrechats* (13). Explain the meanings of "above the heads" (4),
   "sleight-of-foot tricks" (14), "high theatrics" (15), and "with gravity" (26).
2. The poet "climbs on rime" (7), the poem asserts. To what extent does
   this poem utilize rime and other musical devices?
3. What statement does the poem make about poetry, truth, and beauty?

4. How do the rhythms created by the length and placement of lines reinforce the meanings of the poem? Does this poem take poets and poetry
seriously? Solemnly?

151. Because I could not stop for Death

Because I could not stop for Death,
He kindly stopped for me;
The carriage held but just ourselves
And Immortality.

We slowly drove; he knew no haste,   5
And I had put away
My labor and my leisure too,
For his civility.

We passed the school, where children strove,
At recess, in the ring,   10
We passed the fields of gazing grain,
We passed the setting sun,

Or rather, he passed us;
The dews drew quivering and chill;
For only gossamer, my gown;   15
My tippet, only tulle.

We paused before a house that seemed
A swelling of the ground;
The roof was scarcely visible.
The cornice, in the ground.   20

Since then, 'tis centuries, and yet
Feels shorter than the day
I first surmised the horses' heads
Were toward eternity.

Emily Dickinson (1830–1886)

QUESTIONS

1. Vocabulary: *gossamer* (15); *tippet, tulle* (16); *surmised* (23).
2. What allegorical meanings are attached to this ride? What does the alliteration in line 7 say about the quality of the speaker's life? Explain the irony
of "kindly" (2) and "civility" (8). As what is Death personified? What is
the "house" (17)?

3. The fourth stanza alters the metrical pattern of the poem. What aspect of this hypothetical experience is emphasized by the alteration?

152. Break, break, break

Break, break, break,
   On thy cold gray stones, O sea!
And I would that my tongue could utter
   The thoughts that arise in me.

O, well for the fisherman's boy,   5
   That he shouts with his sister at play!
O, well for the sailor lad,
   That he sings in his boat on the bay!

And the stately ships go on
   To their haven under the hill;   10
But O for the touch of a vanished hand,
   And the sound of a voice that is still!

Break, break, break,
   At the foot of thy crags, O sea!
But the tender grace of a day that is dead   15
   Will never come back to me.

Alfred, Lord Tennyson (1809–1892)

QUESTIONS

1. In lines 3–4 the speaker wishes he could put his thoughts into words. Does he make those thoughts explicit in the course of the poem?
2. What aspects of life are symbolized by the two images in stanza 2? By the image in lines 9–10? How do lines 11–12 contrast with those images?
3. The basic meter of this poem is anapestic, and all but two lines are trimeter. Which two? What other variations from a strict anapestic trimeter do you find? How many lines (and which ones) display a strict anapestic pattern? With this much variation, would you be justified in calling the poem free verse? Do the departures from a strict metrical norm contribute to the meaning?

CHAPTER THIRTEEN

Sound and Meaning

Rhythm and sound cooperate to produce what we call the music of poetry. This music, as we have pointed out, may serve two general functions: it may be enjoyable in itself, or it may be used to reinforce meaning and intensify the communication.

Pure pleasure in sound and rhythm exists from a very early age in the human being—probably from the age the baby first starts cooing in its cradle, certainly from the age that children begin chanting nursery rimes and skipping rope. The appeal of the following verse, for instance, depends almost entirely on its "music":

153.
Pease porridge hot,
Pease porridge cold,
Pease porridge in the pot
Nine days old.

There is very little sense here; the attraction comes from the emphatic rhythm, the emphatic rimes (with a strong contrast between the short vowel and short final consonant of *hot–pot* and the long vowel and long final consonant combination of *cold–old*), and the heavy alliteration (exactly half the words begin with *p*). From nonsense rimes such as this, many of us graduate to a love of more meaningful poems whose appeal resides largely in the sound they make. Much of the pleasure that we find in poems like Vachel Lindsay's "The Congo" and Edgar Allan Poe's "The Bells" lies in their musical qualities.

The peculiar function of poetry as distinguished from music, however, is to convey not sounds but meaning or experience *through* sounds. In third- and fourth-rate poetry, sound and rhythm sometimes distract attention from sense. In first-rate poetry the sound exists not for its own sake nor for mere decoration, but as a medium of meaning. Its function is to support the leading player, not to steal the scene.

The poet may reinforce meaning through sound in numerous ways. Without claiming to exhaust them, perhaps we can include most of the chief means under four general headings.

First, the poet can choose words whose sound in some degree suggests their meaning. In its narrowest sense this is called onomatopoeia. **Onomatopoeia,** strictly defined, means the use of words which, at least supposedly, sound like what they mean, such as *hiss, snap,* and *bang.*

154. Song: Come unto these yellow sands

Come unto these yellow sands,
   And then take hands.
Curtsied when you have and kissed,
   The wild waves whist,°   being hushed
Foot it featly° here and there,   nimbly 5
And, sweet sprites, the burden° bear.   refrain
   Hark, hark!
      Bow-wow.
   The watch-dogs bark!
      Bow-wow.   10
Hark, hark! I hear
The strain of strutting chanticleer
Cry, "Cock-a-doodle-doo!"

William Shakespeare (1564–1616)

In these lines, "bark," "bow-wow," and "Cock-a-doodle-doo" are onomatopoetic words. In addition, Shakespeare has reinforced the onomatopoetic effect with the repeated use of "hark," which sounds like *bark.* The usefulness of onomatopoeia, of course, is strictly limited, because it can be used only where the poet is describing sound, and most poems do not describe sound. And the use of pure onomatopoeia, as in the preceding example, is likely to be fairly trivial except as it forms an incidental part of a more complex poem. But by combining onomatopoeia with other devices that help convey meaning, the poet can achieve subtle and beautiful effects whose recognition is one of the keenest pleasures in reading poetry.

In addition to onomatopoetic words there is another group of words, sometimes called **phonetic intensives,** whose sound, by a process as yet obscure, to some degree connects with their meaning. An initial *fl-* sound, for instance, is often associated with the idea of moving light, as in *flame, flare, flash, flicker, flimmer.* An initial *gl-* also frequently accompanies the idea of light, usually unmoving, as in *glare, gleam, glint, glow, glisten.* An initial *sl-* often introduces words meaning "smoothly wet," as in *slippery, slick, slide, slime, slop, slosh, slobber, slushy.* An initial *st-* often suggests strength, as in *staunch, stalwart, stout, sturdy, stable, steady, stocky, stern, strong, stubborn, steel.* Short *-i-* often goes with the idea of smallness, as in *inch, imp, thin, slim, little, bit, chip, sliver, chink, slit, sip, whit, tittle, snip, wink, glint, glimmer, flicker, pigmy, midge, chick, kid, kitten, minikin, miniature.* Long *-o-* or *-oo-* may suggest melancholy or sorrow, as in *moan, groan, woe, mourn, forlorn, toll, doom, gloom, moody.* Final *-are* sometimes goes with the idea of a big light or noise, as *flare, glare, stare, blare.* Medial *-att-* suggests some kind of particled movement as in *spatter, scatter, shatter, chatter, rattle, prattle, clatter, batter.* Final *-er* and *-le* indicate repetition, as in *glitter, flutter, shimmer, whisper, jabber, chatter, clatter, sputter, flicker, twitter, mutter,* and *ripple, bubble, twinkle, sparkle, rattle, rumble, jingle.*

None of these various sounds is invariably associated with the idea that it seems to suggest and, in fact, a short *-i-* is found in *thick* as well as *thin,* in *big* as well as *little.* Language is a complex phenomenon. But there is enough association between these sounds and ideas to suggest some sort of intrinsic if obscure relationship. A word like *flicker,* though not onomatopoetic (because it does not refer to sound) would seem somehow to suggest its sense, with the *fl-* suggesting moving light, the *-i-* suggesting smallness, the *-ck-* suggesting sudden cessation of movement (as in *crack, peck, pick, hack,* and *flick*), and the *-er* suggesting repetition. The above list of sound-idea correspondences is only a very partial one. A complete list, though it would involve only a small proportion of words in the language, would probably be a longer list than that of the more strictly onomatopoetic words, to which they are related.

155. Splinter

The voice of the last cricket
across the first frost
is one kind of good-by.
It is so thin a splinter of singing.

Carl Sandburg (1878–1967)

QUESTIONS

1. Why is "so thin a splinter" a better choice of metaphor than *so small an atom* or *so meager a morsel?*
2. How does the poet intensify the effect of the two phonetic intensives in line 4?

A second and far more important way that the poet can reinforce meaning through sound is to choose sounds and group them so that the effect is smooth and pleasant sounding (*euphonious*) or rough and harsh sounding (*cacophonous*). Vowels are in general more pleasing than consonants, for vowels are musical tones, whereas consonants are merely noises. A line with a high percentage of vowel sounds in proportion to consonant sounds will therefore tend to be more melodious than one in which the proportion is low. The vowels and consonants themselves differ considerably in quality. The "long" vowels, such as those in *fate, reed, rime, coat, food,* and *dune* are fuller and more resonant than the "short" vowels, as in *fat, red, rim, cot, foot,* and *dun.* Of the consonants, some are fairly mellifluous, such as the "liquids," *l, m, n,* and *r;* the soft *v* and *f* sounds; the semivowels *w* and *y;* and such combinations as *th* and *wh.* Others, such as the "plosives," *b, d, g, k, p,* and *t,* are harsher and sharper in their effect. These differences in sound are the poet's materials. Good poets, however, will not necessarily seek out the sounds that are pleasing and attempt to combine them in melodious combinations. Rather, they will use **euphony** and **cacophony** as they are appropriate to content. Consider, for instance, the following poem.

156. Upon Julia's Voice

So smooth, so sweet, so silvery is thy voice,
As, could they hear, the Damned would make no noise,
But listen to thee (walking in thy chamber)
Melting melodious words to Lutes of Amber.

Robert Herrick (1591–1674)

QUESTION

Literally, an amber lute is as nonsensical as a silver voice. What connotations do "Amber" and "silvery" have that contribute to the meaning of this poem?

There are no strictly onomatopoetic words in this poem, and yet the sound seems marvelously adapted to the sense. Especially remarkable are the first and last lines, those most directly concerned with Julia's voice. In the first line the sounds that most strike the ear are the unvoiced *s*'s and the soft *v*'s, supported by voiced *th:* "So *s*mooth, *s*o *s*weet, *s*o *s*ilvery is thy voice." (A voiced consonant sound is accompanied by vibration of the vocal cords—*then* is voiced, *thin* not. Notice that the terminal *-ce* in "voice" is an example of the unvoiced *s* sound: as with alliteration, spelling is irrelevant.) In the fourth line the predominating sounds are the liquid consonants *m, l,* and *r,* supported by a *w:* "*Mel*ting *mel*odious *w*ords to *L*utes of A*m*ber." The least euphonious line in the poem, on the other hand, is the second, where the subject is the tormented in hell, not Julia's voice. Here the prominent sounds are the *d*s, supported by a voiced *s* (a voiced *s* buzzes, unlike the sibilant unvoiced *s*s in line 1), and two *k* sounds: "A*s*, *c*ould they hear, the *D*amned woul*d* ma*k*e no noi*s*e." Throughout the poem there is a remarkable correspondence between the pleasant-sounding and the pleasant in idea, the unpleasant-sounding and the unpleasant in idea.

A third way in which a poet can reinforce meaning through sound is by controlling the speed and movement of the lines by the choice and use of meter, by the choice and arrangement of vowel and consonant sounds, and by the disposition of pauses. In meter the unaccented syllables usually go faster than the accented syllables; hence the triple meters are swifter than the duple. But the poet can vary the tempo of any meter by the use of substitute feet. Generally, whenever two or more unaccented syllables come together, the effect will be to speed up the pace of the line; when two or more accented syllables come together, the effect will be to slow it down. This pace will also be affected by the vowel lengths and by whether the sounds are easily run together. The long vowels take longer to pronounce than the short ones. Some words are easily run together, while others demand that the position of the mouth be re-formed before the next word is uttered. It takes much longer, for instance, to say, "Watch dogs catch much meat" than to say, "My aunt is away," though the number of syllables is the same. And finally the poet can slow down the speed of a line through the introduction of grammatical and rhetorical pauses. Consider lines 54–56 from Tennyson's "Ulysses" (No. 67):

The lights be-gín to twin-kle from the rocks;
The long day wanes; the slow moon climbs; the deep   55
Moans round with man-y voi-ces. . . .

In these lines Tennyson wished the movement to be slow, in accordance with the slow waning of the long day and the slow climbing of the moon. His meter is iambic pentameter. This is not a swift meter, but in lines 55–56 he slows it down further, (a) by introducing three spondaic feet, thus bringing three accented syllables together in two separate places; (b) by choosing for his accented syllables words that have long vowel sounds or dipthongs that the voice hangs on to: "long," "day," "wanes," "slow," "moon," "climbs," "deep," "Moans," "round"; (c) by choosing words that are not easily run together (except for "day" and "slow," each of these words begins and ends with consonant sounds that require varying degrees of readjustment of the mouth before pronunciation can continue); and (d) by introducing two grammatical pauses, after "wanes" and "climbs," and a rhetorical pause after "deep." The result is an extremely effective use of the movement of the verse to accord with the movement suggested by the words.*

A fourth way for a poet to fit sound to sense is to control both sound and meter in such a way as to emphasize words that are important in meaning. This can be done by highlighting such words through alliteration, assonance, consonance, or rime; by placing them before a pause; or by skillfully placing or displacing them in the metrical scheme. We have already seen how Ogden Nash uses alliteration and consonance to emphasize and link the three major words ("sex," "fix," and "fertile") in his little verse "The Turtle" (No. 130), and how George Herbert pivots the structure of meaning in "Virtue" (No. 142) on a trochaic substitution in the initial foot of his final stanza. For an additional example, let us look again at "Since there's no help" (No. 118). This poem is a sonnet—fourteen lines of iambic pentameter—in which a lover threatens to leave his sweetheart forever if she will not go to bed with him. In the first eight lines he pretends to be *glad* that they are breaking off their relationship so cleanly. In the last six lines, however, he paints a vivid picture of the death of his personified Love/Passion for her but intimates that even at this last moment ("Now") she could restore it to life again—by satisfying his sexual desires.

> Now, at the last gasp of Love's la-test breath,
> When, his pulse failing, Passion speechless lies,   10
> When Faith is kneeling by his bed of death,

---

*In addition, Tennyson uses one onomatopoetic word ("Moans") and one phonetic intensive ("twinkle").

And In-͝no-cence is clos-ing up his eyes,
Now, if thou wouldst, when all have given him o-ver,*
From death to life thou mightst him yet re-cov-er.

The emphasis is on *Now*. In a matter of seconds, the speaker indicates, it will be too late: his Love/Passion will be dead, and he himself will be gone. The word "Now" begins line 9. It also begins a new sentence and a new direction in the poem. It is separated from what has gone before by a period at the end of the preceding line. Metrically it initiates a trochee, thus breaking away from the poem's basic iambic meter (line 8 is perfectly regular). In all these ways—its initial position in line, sentence, and thought, and its metrical irregularity—the word "Now" is given extraordinary emphasis appropriate to its importance in the context. Its repetition in line 13 reaffirms this importance, and there again it is given emphasis by its positional and metrical situation. It begins both a line and the final riming couplet, is separated by punctuation from the line before, and participates in a metrical inversion. (The lines before and after are metrically regular.)

While Herbert and Drayton use metrical deviation to give emphasis to important words, Tennyson, in the concluding line of "Ulysses," (No. 67) uses marked regularity, plus skillful use of grammatical pauses, to achieve the same effect.

We are not now that strength which in old days
Moved earth and heav-en, that which we are, we are:
One e-qual tem-per of he-ro-ic hearts,
Made weak by time and fate, but strong in will
To strive, to seek, to find, and not to yield.   70

The blank verse rhythm throughout "Ulysses" is remarkably subtle and varied, but the last line is not only regular in its scansion but heavily regular, for a number of reasons. First, all the words are monosyllables. Second, the unaccented syllables are all very small and unimportant words—four *to*s and one *and*—whereas the accented syllables consist of four important verbs and a very important *not*. Third, each of the verbs is followed by a grammatical pause pointed off by a mark of punctuation. The result is to cause a pronounced alternation between light and heavy syllables that brings the accent

*Drayton probably intended "given" to be pronounced as one syllable (*giv'n*), and most sixteenth-century readers would have pronounced it thus in this poem.

down on the four verbs and the *not* with sledgehammer blows. The line rings out like a challenge, which it is.

157. The Span of Life

The old dog barks backward without getting up.
I can remember when he was a pup.

Robert Frost (1874–1963)

QUESTIONS

1. Is the dog a dog only or also a symbol?
2. The first line presents a visual and auditory image; the second line makes a comment. But does the second line *call up images?* Does it suggest more than it says? Would the poem have been more or less effective if the second line had been, "He was frisky and lively when he was a pup"?

We may well conclude our discussion of the adaptation of sound to sense by analyzing this very brief poem. It consists of one riming anapestic tetrameter couplet. Its content is a contrast between the decrepitude of an old dog and his friskiness as a pup. The scansion is as follows:

The old ˈdog barks back-ˈward with-out ˈget-ting up.
I can ˈre-mem-ˈber when he ˈwas a pup.ˈ

How is sound fitted to sense? In the first place, the triple meter chosen by the poet is a swift meter, but in the first line he has jammed it up in a remarkable way by substituting a kind of foot so rare that English prosody has no name for it (the Greeks, who "measured" their verse by duration of syllables rather than accent, called it a *molussus*); at any rate, it is a foot in which the accent is distributed over three syllables. This foot, following the accented syllable in the first foot, creates a situation where four accented syllables are pushed up together. In addition, each of these accented syllables begins and ends with a strong consonant sound or cluster of consonant sounds, so that they cannot be run together in pronunciation—the mouth must be reformed between syllables: "The old *dog barks back-*." The result is to slow down the line drastically, to damage its rhythmical quality severely, and to make it difficult to utter. Indeed, the line is as decrepit as the old dog who turns his head to greet his master but does not get up. When we get to the second line, however, the contrast is startling. The rhythm is swift and regular, the syllables end in vowels or liquid consonants that are easily run together, the whole line ripples fluently off the tongue. In addition, where the first line has a high proportion of explosive and cacophonous consonants—"The ol*d d*og *b*ar*k*s *b*ack-war*d* withou*t* ge*tt*ing u*p*"—the consonants in the second line are predominantly smoother and more graceful—"I ca*n* re*m*e*m*ber *wh*e*n h*e *w*as a pup." Thus the motion and the sound of the lines are remarkably in accord with the visual images they suggest. In addition, in the first line the poet has supported the onomatopoetic word *barks* with a near echo *back*, so that the sound reinforces the auditory image. If the poem does a great deal in just two lines, this skillful adaptation of sound to sense is one very important reason.

In analyzing verse for correspondence between sound and sense, we need to be very cautious not to make exaggerated claims. A great deal of nonsense has been written about the moods of certain meters and the effects of certain sounds, and it is easy to suggest correspondences that exist only in our imaginations. Nevertheless, the first-rate poet has nearly always an instinctive tact about handling sound so that it in some degree supports meaning; the inferior poet is usually obtuse to these correspondences. One of the few absolute rules that can be applied to the judgment of poetry is that the form should be adequate to the content. This rule does not mean that there must always be a close and easily demonstrable correspondence. It does mean that there will be no glaring discrepancies. Poor poets, and even good poets in their third-rate work, sometimes go horribly wrong.

The two selections that introduce this chapter illustrate, first, the use of sound in verse almost purely for its own sake ("Pease porridge hot") and, second, the use of sound in verse almost purely to *imitate* meaning ("Hark, hark! Bow-wow"), and they are, as significant poetry, among the most trivial passages in the whole book. But in between these extremes there is an abundant range of poetic possibilities where sound is pleasurable for itself without violating meaning and where sound to varying degrees corresponds with and corroborates meaning; and in this rich middle range lie many of the greatest pleasures of reading poetry.

EXERCISE

In each of the following paired quotations, the named poet wrote the version that more successfully adapts sound to sense. As specifically as possible, account for the superiority of the better version.

1. a. Go forth—and Virtue, ever in your sight,
   Shall be your guide by day, your guard by night.
   b. Go forth—and Virtue, ever in your sight,
   Shall point your way by day, and keep you safe at night.

   Charles Churchill

2. a. How charming is divine philosophy!
   Not harsh and rough as foolish men suppose
   But musical as is the lute of Phoebus.
   b. How charming is divine philosophy!
   Not harsh and crabbed as dull fools suppose
   But musical as is Apollo's lute.　　　　*John Milton*

3. a. All day the fleeing crows croak hoarsely over the snow.
   b. All day the out-cast crows croak hoarsely across the whiteness.

   Elizabeth Coatsworth

4. a. Your talk attests how bells of singing gold
   Would sound at evening over silent water.
   b. Your low voice tells how bells of singing gold
   Would sound at twilight over silent water.　*Edwin Arlington Robinson*

5. a. A thousand streamlets flowing through the lawn,
   The moan of doves in gnarled ancient oaks,
   And quiet murmuring of countless bees.
   b. Myriads of rivulets hurrying through the lawn,
   The moan of doves in immemorial elms,
   And murmuring of innumerable bees.　　*Alfred, Lord Tennyson*

6. a. It is the lark that sings so out of tune,
   Straining harsh discords and unpleasing sharps.
   b. It is the lark that warbles out of tune
   In harsh discordant tones with doleful flats.　*William Shakespeare*

7. a. "Artillery" and "armaments" and "implements of war"
   Are phrases too severe to please the gentle Muse.
   b. Bombs, drums, guns, bastions, batteries, bayonets, bullets, —
   Hard words, which stick in the soft Muses' gullets.　*Lord Byron*

8. a. The hands of the sisters Death and Night incessantly softly wash
   again, and ever again, this soiled world.
   b. The hands of the soft twins Death and Night repeatedly wash again,
   and ever again, this dirty world.　　*Walt Whitman*

9. a. The curfew sounds the knell of parting day,
   The lowing cattle slowly cross the lea,
   The plowman goes wearily plodding his homeward way,
   Leaving the world to the darkening night and me.
   b. The curfew tolls the knell of parting day,
   The lowing herd wind slowly o'er the lea,
   The plowman homeward plods his weary way,
   And leaves the world to darkness and to me.　*Thomas Gray*

10. a. Let me chastise this odious, gilded bug,
   This painted son of dirt, that smells and bites.
   b. Yet let me flap this bug with gilded wings,
   This painted child of dirt, that stinks and stings.　*Alexander Pope*

158. Sound and Sense

True ease in writing comes from art, not chance,
As those move easiest who have learned to dance.
'Tis not enough no harshness gives offense,
The sound must seem an echo to the sense:
Soft is the strain when Zephyr gently blows,   5
And the smooth stream in smoother numbers flows;
But when loud surges lash the sounding shore,
The hoarse, rough verse should like the torrent roar;
When Ajax strives some rock's vast weight to throw,
The line too labors, and the words move slow;   10
Not so, when swift Camilla scours the plain,
Flies o'er the unbending corn, and skims along the main.
Hear how Timotheus' varied lays surprise,
And bid alternate passions fall and rise!

Alexander Pope (1688–1744)

QUESTIONS

1. Vocabulary: *numbers* (6), *lays* (13).
2. This excerpt is from a long poem (called *An Essay on Criticism*) on the arts
   of writing and judging poetry. Which line states the thesis of the passage?
3. There are four classical allusions: Zephyr (5) was god of the west wind;
   Ajax (9), a Greek warrior noted for his strength; Camilla (11), a legendary
   queen reputedly so fleet of foot that she could run over a field of grain
   without bending the blades or over the sea without wetting her feet;
   Timotheus (13), a famous Greek rhapsodic poet. How do these allusions
   enable Pope to achieve greater economy?
4. Copy the passage and scan it. Then, considering both meter and sounds,
   show how Pope practices what he preaches. (Incidentally, on which syllable should "alternate" in line 14 be accented? Does the meter help you
   to know the pronunciation of "Timotheus'" in line 13?)

159. I heard a fly buzz when I died

I heard a fly buzz when I died.
The stillness in the room
Was like the stillness in the air
Between the heaves of storm.

The eyes around had wrung them dry,   5
And breaths were gathering firm
For that last onset when the king
Be witnessed in the room.

I willed my keepsakes, signed away
What portion of me be   10
Assignable; and then it was
There interposed a fly

With blue, uncertain, stumbling buzz
Between the light and me;
And then the windows failed, and then   15
I could not see to see.

Emily Dickinson (1830–1886)

QUESTIONS

1. It is important to understand the sequence of events in this deathbed
   scene. Arrange the following events in correct chronological order: (a) the
   willing of keepsakes, (b) the weeping of mourners, (c) the appearance of
   the fly, (d) the preternatural stillness in the room.
2. What or who are the "eyes" and the "breaths" in lines 5–6? What figures
   of speech are involved in these lines? Is the speaker making out her will in
   lines 9–11? What *is* she doing?
3. What sort of expectation is set up by phrases like "last onset" (7), "the
   king" (7), and "be witnessed" (8)?
4. Explain "the windows failed" (15) and "I could not see to see" (16).
5. What is the rime scheme? What kinds of rime are employed? Explain
   the marvelous effectiveness of line 13 in terms of both imagery and
   sound.
6. Explain the point of the poem. How do you interpret the fly?

160. Heaven-Haven

A Nun Takes the Veil

I have desired to go
    Where springs not fail,
To fields where flies no sharp and sided hail
    And a few lilies blow.

And I have asked to be   5
    Where no storms come,
Where the green swell is in the havens dumb,
    And out of the swing of the sea.

Gerard Manley Hopkins (1844–1889)

QUESTIONS

1. Vocabulary: *blow* (4).
2. Who is the speaker and what is the situation? Explain the metaphors that form the substance of the poem. What things are being compared?
3. Comment on the meaning of "springs" (2) and on the effectiveness of the poet's choice of "lilies" (4).
4. How do the sound repetitions of the title reinforce the meaning? Are there other instances in the poem where sound reinforces meaning?
5. Scan the poem. (The meter is basically iambic, but there is a great deal of variation.) How does the meter reinforce meaning, especially in the last line? What purpose is served by the displacement of "not" (2) from its normal word order?

161. Anthem for Doomed Youth

What passing-bells for these who die as cattle?
Only the monstrous anger of the guns.
Only the stuttering rifles' rapid rattle
Can patter out their hasty orisons.
No mockeries now for them; no prayers nor bells,   5
Nor any voice of mourning save the choirs—
The shrill, demented choirs of wailing shells;
And bugles calling for them from sad shires.

What candles may be held to speed them all?
Not in the hands of boys, but in their eyes   10
Shall shine the holy glimmers of good-byes.
The pallor of girls' brows shall be their pall;
Their flowers the tenderness of patient minds,
And each slow dusk a drawing-down of blinds.

Wilfred Owen (1893–1918)

QUESTIONS

1. Vocabulary: *passing-bells* (1), *orisons* (4), *shires* (8), *pall* (12). It was the custom during World War I to draw down the blinds in homes where a son had been lost (14).
2. How do the octave and the sestet of this sonnet differ in (a) geographical setting, (b) subject matter, (c) kind of imagery used, and (d) tone? Who are the "boys" (10) and "girls" (12) referred to in the sestet?
3. What central metaphorical image runs throughout the poem? What secondary metaphors build up the central one?

4. Why are the "doomed youth" said to die "as cattle" (1)? Why would prayers, bells, and so on, be "mockeries" for them (5)?
5. Show how sound is adapted to sense throughout the poem.

162. Landcrab

A lie, that we come from water.
The truth is we were born
from stones, dragons, the sea's
teeth, as you testify,
with your crust and jagged scissors.   5

Hermit, hard socket
for a timid eye
you're a soft gut scuttling
sideways, a bone skull,
round bone on the prowl.   10
Wolf of treeroots and gravelly holes,
a mount on stilts,
the husk of a small demon.

Attack, voracious
eating, and flight: 15
it's a sound routine
for staying alive on edges.
Then there's the tide, and that dance
you do for the moon
on wet sand, claws raised   20
to fend off your mate,
your coupling a quick
dry clatter of rocks.
For mammals
with their lobes and bulbs,   25
scruples and warm milk,
you've nothing but contempt.

Here you are, a frozen scowl
targeted in flashlight,
then gone: a piece of what   30
we are, not all,
my stunted child, my momentary
face in the mirror,
my tiny nightmare.

Margaret Atwood (b. 1939)

QUESTIONS

1. What theory of the origin of human life is alluded to in line 1? Line 3 alludes to two Greek myths, of Deucalion sowing stones and Cadmus sowing dragon's teeth. If these are unfamiliar, look them up. What do theories about the origins of humankind have to do with the speaker's description of the landcrab? How do lines 30–34 return to that subject?
2. What do the free-verse rhythms contribute to the experience of the poem? Discuss the cacophony and euphony in lines 22–25. Where do you find other examples?

163. Eight O'Clock

He stood, and heard the steeple
   Sprinkle the quarters on the morning town.
One, two, three, four, to market-place and people
   It tossed them down.

Strapped, noosed, nighing his hour,   5
   He stood and counted them and cursed his luck;
And then the clock collected in the tower
   Its strength, and struck.

A. E. Housman (1859–1936)

QUESTIONS

1. Vocabulary: *quarters* (2).
2. Eight A.M. was the traditional hour in England for putting condemned men to death. Discuss the force of "morning" (2) and "struck" (8). Discuss the appropriateness of the image of the clock collecting its strength. Can you suggest any reason for the use of "nighing" (5) rather than *nearing*?
3. Scan the poem and note its musical devices. Comment on the adaptation of sound to sense.

164. At the round earth's imagined corners

At the round earth's imagined corners, blow
Your trumpets, angels; and arise, arise
From death, you numberless infinities
Of souls, and to your scattered bodies go:
All whom the flood did, and fire shall, o'erthrow,   5
All whom war, dearth, age, agues, tyrannies,

Despair, law, chance hath slain, and you whose eyes
Shall behold God and never taste death's woe.
But let them sleep, Lord, and me mourn a space;
For if above all these, my sins abound,   10
'Tis late to ask abundance of thy grace
When we are there. Here on this lowly ground,
Teach me how to repent; for that's as good
As if thou hadst sealed my pardon with thy blood.

John Donne (1572–1631)

QUESTIONS

1. For a note on the belief in the resurrection of the body, see question 2,
   page 701. The poem contains several allusions to the Bible: line 1, Revelation 7.1; lines 2–4, Job 19.25–26; lines 10–11, Romans 6.1. What is
   the speaker calling for in lines 1–8? Why does he change his plea in lines
   9–12? Where is "there" (12)?
2. Scan lines 1–8. How do the rhythms reinforce the meanings in these
   lines? What is the effect of the placement of "blow" (1)? Scan lines 11–12.
   What do the lack of a caesura in line 11 and the emphatic caesura in line 12
   contribute to meaning? Comment on the trochaic substitution in line 12.

165. Blackberry Eating

I love to go out in late September
among fat, overripe, icy, black blackberries
to eat blackberries for breakfast,
the stalks very prickly, a penalty
they earn for knowing the black art   5
of blackberry-making; and as I stand among them
lifting the stalks to my mouth, the ripest berries
fall almost unbidden to my tongue,
as words sometimes do, certain peculiar words
like *strengths* or *squinched*,   10
many-lettered, one-syllabled lumps,
which I squeeze, squinch open, and splurge well
in the silent, startled, icy, black language
of blackberry-eating in late September.

Galway Kinnell (b. 1927)

QUESTIONS

1. Vocabulary: *black art* (5), *squinched* (10).
2. What comparison does the poet find between "certain peculiar words"
   (9) and blackberries? How appropriate is it?

3. Is the poem free verse or metrical? How do various musical devices reinforce its meaning?

166. The Bench of Boors

In bed I muse on Teniers' boors,
Embrowned and beery losels all:
  A wakeful brain
  Elaborates pain:
Within low doors the slugs of boors   5
Laze and yawn and doze again.

In dreams they doze, the drowsy boors,
Their hazy hovel warm and small:
  Thought's ampler bound
  But chill is found: 10
Within low doors the basking boors
Snugly hug the ember-mound.

Sleepless, I see the slumberous boors
Their blurred eyes blink, their eyelids fall:
  Thought's eager sight   15
  Aches—overbright!
Within low doors the boozy boors
Cat-naps take in pipe-bowl light.

Herman Melville (1819–1891)

QUESTIONS

1. Vocabulary: *boors* (title), *losels* (2), *slugs* (5).
2. David Teniers the Younger, a seventeenth-century Flemish painter, was famous for his genre paintings of peasant life. What was the essential characteristic of this life according to the poem? What symbolism do you find in the fifth line of each stanza?
3. What is the relation of the third and fourth lines of each stanza to the speaker? To the boors? How does the form of the stanza emphasize the contrast in thought?
4. Comment on other correspondences between sound and meaning.

167. The Dance

In Breughel's great picture, The Kermess,
the dancers go round, they go round and
around, the squeal and the blare and the

tweedle of bagpipes, a bugle and fiddles
tipping their bellies (round as the thick- 5
sided glasses whose wash they impound)
their hips and their bellies off balance
to turn them. Kicking and rolling about
the Fair Grounds, swinging their butts, those
shanks must be sound to bear up under such 10
rollicking measures, prance as they dance
in Breughel's great picture, The Kermess.

William Carlos Williams (1883–1963)

QUESTIONS

1. Peter Breughel the Elder was a sixteenth-century Flemish painter of peasant life. A *kermess* is an annual outdoor festival or fair. How do the form,
the meter, and the sounds of this poem reinforce its content?
2. Explore the similarities and differences between this poem and the preceding one, both as to form and content.

ADDITIONAL EXERCISE

Follow the instructions for the exercise on page 768.
11. a. Like an iron-clanging anvil banged / With hammers.
    b. Like a massive iron anvil hit / With sledges.   *Alfred, Lord Tennyson*
12. a. I am quiet sand / In an hourglass.
    b. I am soft silt / In an hourglass.   *Gerard Manley Hopkins*
13. a. Dress! arm! mount!—away!
       Save my castle before the day
       Turns to blue from silver gray.
    b. Boot, saddle, to horse, and away!
       Rescue my castle before the hot day
       Brightens to blue from its silvery gray.   *Robert Browning*
14. a. The lilies and languors of virtue,
       . . . the roses and raptures of vice.
    b. The lilies and boredom of virtue,
       . . . the roses and pleasures of evil.   *Algernon Charles Swinburne*
15. a. And still she lulled him to asleep.
    b. And yet she conjured him to sleep.   *Anonymous*

CHAPTER FOURTEEN

Pattern

Art, ultimately, is organization. It is a searching after order, after form. Many consider the primal artistic act to have been God's creation of the universe out of chaos, shaping the formless into form; and every artist since, on a lesser scale, has sought to imitate that act—to reduce the chaotic in experience to a meaningful and pleasing order by means of selection and arrangement. For this reason we evaluate a poem partially by the same criteria that an English instructor uses to evaluate a theme—by its unity, its coherence, and its proper placing of emphasis. A well-constructed poem contains neither too little nor too much; every part of the poem belongs where it is and could be placed nowhere else; any interchanging of two stanzas, two lines, or even two words, would to some extent damage the poem and make it less effective. We come to feel, with a truly first-rate poem, that the choice and placement of every word is inevitable, that it could not be otherwise.

In addition to the internal ordering of materials—the arrangement of ideas, images, and thoughts, which we may refer to as the poem's **structure**—the poet may impose some external pattern on a poem, may give it not only an inside logical order but an outside symmetry, or **form.** Such formality appeals to the human instinct for design, the instinct that has prompted people, at various times, to tattoo and paint their bodies, to decorate their swords and armor with beautiful and complex tracery, and to choose patterned fabrics for their clothing, carpets, curtains, and wallpapers. The poet appeals to our love of the shapely.

In general, a poem may be cast in one of the three broad kinds of form: continuous form, stanzaic form, and fixed form. In **continuous form,** as illustrated by "The Widow's Lament in Springtime" (No. 35), "After Apple-Picking" (No. 38), "Ulysses" (No. 67), and "My Last Duchess" (No. 89), the element of design is slight. The lines follow each other without formal grouping, the only breaks being dictated by units of meaning, as paragraphs are in prose. But even here there are degrees of pattern. "The Widow's Lament in Springtime" has neither regular meter nor rime. "After Apple-Picking," on the other hand, is metrical; it has no regularity in length of line, but the meter is prevailingly iambic; also every line rimes with another, though not according to any fixed pattern. "Ulysses" is regular in both meter and length of line: it is unrimed iambic pentameter, or blank verse. And to these regularities "My Last Duchess" adds regularity of rime, for it is written in riming pentameter couplets. Thus, in increasing degrees, the authors of "After Apple-Picking," "Ulysses," and "My Last Duchess" have chosen a predetermined pattern in which to cast their work.

In **stanzaic form** the poet writes in a series of **stanzas;** that is, repeated units having the same number of lines, usually the same metrical pattern, and often an identical rime scheme. The poet may choose some traditional stanza pattern (poetry, like colleges, is rich in tradition) or invent an original one. The traditional stanza patterns (for example, terza rima, ballad meter, rime royal, Spenserian stanza) are many, and the student specializing in literature will wish to become familiar with some of them; the general student should know that they exist. Often the use of one of these traditional stanza forms constitutes a kind of literary allusion. The reader who is conscious of its traditional use or of its use by a previous great poet will be aware of subtleties in the communication that a less-well-read reader may miss.

Stanzaic form, like continuous form, exhibits degrees of formal pattern. The poem "in Just-" (No. 92) is divided into alternating stanzas of four lines and one line, but neither the four-line stanzas nor the one-line stanzas have any resemblance to each other. In "Poem in October" (No. 174) the stanzas are alike in length of line but are without a regular pattern of rime. In "The Aim Was Song" (No. 147) a rime pattern is added to a metrical pattern. In Shakespeare's "Winter" (No. 2) and "Spring" (No. 4), a refrain is employed in addition to the patterns of meter and rime. The following poem illustrates additional elements of design.

168. These are the days when birds come back

These are the days when birds come back—
A very few—a bird or two—
To take a backward look.

These are the days when skies resume
The old, old sophistries of June—   5
A blue and gold mistake.

Oh fraud that cannot cheat the bee,
Almost thy plausibility
Induces my belief,

Till ranks of seeds their witness bear,   10
And softly through the altered air
Hurries a timid leaf.

Oh sacrament of summer days,
Oh last communion in the haze,
Permit a child to join,   15

Thy sacred emblems to partake,
Thy consecrated bread to take,
And thine immortal wine!

Emily Dickinson (1830–1886)

QUESTIONS

1. Vocabulary: *sophistries* (5). The "fraud that cannot cheat the bee" (6) is probably an allusion to one of the apocryphal tales of Solomon who distinguished between real and artificial flowers by putting a bee into the room; the bee of course flew to the real.
2. If you have difficulty determining the time of year, examine the terms "backward" (3) and "resume" (4), and the evidence provided by "seeds" and "leaf" (10–12). Why is that time of year a "fraud" (7)? What is it pretending to be? In the final metaphor, how is that time of year like a "last communion" (14)?
3. The rime scheme of these stanzas is *aab*, in two lines of iambic tetrameter followed by one of iambic trimeter; several of its rimes are approximate, especially in the first two stanzas. An additional complication is that the first of the stanzas is a variant, riming *aba*. To find the form at its purest, examine stanzas 3 and 4. What you will also notice is that the *b* rimes of those stanzas rime with each other, creating a two-stanza unit. That pattern may then be observed in approximate *b* rimes in stanzas 1–2 and 5–6. How is the *structure* of the poem linked to the formal division into these three two-stanza units? What repetitions other than rime reinforce the meanings?

A stanza form may be described by designating four things: the rime scheme (if there is one), the position of the refrain (if there is one), the prevailing metrical foot, and the number of feet in each line. Rime scheme is traditionally designated by using letters of the alphabet to indicate the riming lines, and *x* for unrimed lines. Refrain lines may be indicated by a capital letter, and the number of feet in the line by a numerical exponent after the letter. Thus the stanza pattern of

Browning's "Meeting at Night" (No. 32) is iambic tetrameter $abccba$ (or iambic $abccba^4$); that of "These are the days when birds come back" is iambic aa^4b^3; that of Donne's "A Hymn to God the Father" (No. 30) is iambic $abab^5A^4B^2$. Stanzaic poetry not written in traditional metrical feet can be described similarly: Moore's "Nevertheless" (No. 148) is syllabic xaa^6.

A **fixed form** is a traditional pattern that applies to a whole poem. In French poetry many fixed forms have been widely used: rondeaus, rondels, villanelles, triolets, sestinas, ballades, double ballades, and others. In English poetry, though most of the fixed forms have been experimented with, perhaps only two—the limerick and the sonnet—have really taken hold.

The **limerick,** though really a subliterary form, will serve to illustrate the fixed form in general. Its pattern is anapestic $aa^3bb^2a^3$. The form freely allows the use of a substitute foot for the first foot in any line but insists as a rule on strict adherence to anapestic meter thereafter:

169. An epicure dining at Crewe

An epi-i-cure din-ing at Crewe
Found a rath-er large mouse in his stew.
Said the wait-er, "Don't shout
And wave it a-bout
Or the rest will be want-ing one too."   5

Anonymous

The limerick form is used exclusively for humorous and nonsense verse, for which, with its short lines, swift catchy meter, and emphatic rimes, it is particularly suitable. By trying to recast these little jokes and bits of nonsense in a different meter and pattern or into prose, we may discover how much of their effect they owe particularly to the limerick form. There is, of course, no magical or mysterious identity between certain forms and certain types of content, but there may be more or less correspondence. A form may be appropriate or inappropriate. The limerick form is inappropriate for the serious treatment of serious material.

The **sonnet** is less rigidly prescribed than the limerick. It must be fourteen lines in length, and it almost always is iambic pentameter, but in structure and rime scheme there may be considerable leeway. Most sonnets, however, conform more or less closely to one of two general models or types: the Italian and the English.

The **Italian** or *Petrarchan* **sonnet** (so-called because the Italian poet Petrarch practiced it so extensively) is divided usually between eight lines called the **octave,** using two rimes arranged *abbaabba,* and six lines called the **sestet,** using any arrangement of either two or three rimes: *cdcdcd* and *cdecde* are common patterns. The division between octave and sestet in the Italian sonnet (indicated by the rime scheme and sometimes marked off in printing by a space) usually corresponds to a division of thought. The octave may, for instance, present a situation and the sestet a comment, or the octave an idea and the sestet an example, or the octave a question and the sestet an answer. Thus the form reflects the structure.

170. On First Looking into Chapman's Homer

Much have I traveled in the realms of gold,
   And many goodly states and kingdoms seen;
   Round many western islands have I been
Which bards in fealty to Apollo hold.
Oft of one wide expanse had I been told   5
   That deep-browed Homer ruled as his demesne;
   Yet did I never breathe its pure serene
Till I heard Chapman speak out loud and bold:
Then felt I like some watcher of the skies
   When a new planet swims into his ken;   10
Or like stout Cortez when with eagle eyes
   He stared at the Pacific—and all his men
Looked at each other with a wild surmise—
   Silent, upon a peak in Darien.

John Keats (1795–1821)

QUESTIONS

1. Vocabulary: *fealty* (4), *Apollo* (4), *demesne* (6), *ken* (10). *Darien* (14) is an ancient name for the Isthmus of Panama.
2. John Keats, at twenty-one, could not read Greek and was probably acquainted with Homer's *Iliad* and *Odyssey* only through the translations of Alexander Pope, which to him very likely seemed prosy and stilted. Then

one day he and a friend found a vigorous poetic translation by the
Elizabethan poet George Chapman. Keats and his friend, enthralled, sat
up late at night excitedly reading aloud to each other from Chapman's
book. Toward morning Keats walked home and, before going to bed,
wrote the above sonnet and sent it to his friend. What common ideas underlie the three major figures of speech in the poem?
3. What is the rime scheme? What division of thought corresponds to the division between octave and sestet?
4. Balboa, not Cortez, discovered the Pacific. How seriously does this mistake detract from the value of the poem?

The **English** or *Shakespearean* **sonnet** (invented by the English
poet Surrey and made famous by Shakespeare) is composed of three
quatrains and a concluding couplet, riming *abab cdcd efef gg*. Again,
the units marked off by the rimes and the development of the thought
often correspond. The three quatrains, for instance, may present three
examples and the couplet a conclusion or (as in the following example) the quatrains three metaphorical statements of one idea and
the couplet an application.

171. That time of year

That time of year thou mayst in me behold
When yellow leaves, or none, or few, do hang
Upon those boughs which shake against the cold,
Bare ruined choirs where late the sweet birds sang.
In me thou see'st the twilight of such day   5
As after sunset fadeth in the west,
Which by and by black night doth take away,
Death's second self, that seals up all in rest.
In me thou see'st the glowing of such fire,
That on the ashes of his youth doth lie   10
As the deathbed whereon it must expire,
Consumed with that which it was nourished by.
This thou perceivest, which makes thy love more strong,
To love that well which thou must leave ere long.

William Shakespeare (1564–1616)

QUESTIONS

1. What are the three major images introduced by the three quatrains? What
do they have in common? Can you see any reason for presenting them in
this particular order, or might they be rearranged without loss?

2. Each of the images is to some degree complicated rather than simple. For instance, what additional image is introduced by "Bare ruined choirs" (4)? Explain its appropriateness.
3. What additional comparisons are introduced in the second and third quatrains? Explain line 12.
4. Whom does the speaker address? What assertion does he make in the concluding couplet, and with what degree of confidence? Paraphrase these lines so as to state their meaning as clearly as possible.

Initially, it may seem absurd that poets should choose to confine themselves in an arbitrary fourteen-line mold with prescribed meter and rime scheme. They do so partly from the desire to carry on a tradition, as all of us carry out certain traditions for their own sake, else why should we bring a tree indoors at Christmas time? But, in addition, the tradition of the sonnet has proved useful because, like the limerick, it seems effective for certain types of subject matter and treatment. Though these cannot be as narrowly limited or as rigidly described as for the limerick, the sonnet is usually most effective when used for the serious treatment of love but has also been used for the discussion of death, religion, political situations, and related subjects. Again, there is no magical affinity between form and subject, or treatment, and excellent sonnets have been written outside these traditional areas. The sonnet tradition has also proved useful because it has provided a challenge to the poet. Inferior poets, of course, are often defeated by that challenge: they will use unnecessary words to fill out the meter or inappropriate words for the sake of rime. Good poets are inspired by the challenge: it will call forth ideas and images that might not otherwise have come. They will subdue the form rather than be subdued by it; they will make it do what they require. There is no doubt that the presence of a net makes good tennis players more precise in their shots than they otherwise would be. And finally, there is in all form the pleasure of form itself.

EXERCISES

1. Examine the following sonnets; classify each (when possible) as primarily Italian or primarily English; then specify how closely in form and structure each adheres to or how far it departs from the polarities represented by "On First Looking into Chapman's Homer" and "That time of year":
   a. "The world is too much with us" (No. 28)
   b. "The Caged Skylark" (No. 112)
   c. "Design" (No. 107)
   d. From *Romeo and Juliet* (No. 175)
   e. "Since there's no help" (No. 118)

    f. "The Dead" (No. 207)
    g. "Batter my heart, three-personed God" (No. 80)
    h. "Ozymandias" (No. 79)
    i. "Leda and the Swan" (No. 96)
    j. "How Annandale Went Out" (No. 111)
    k. "Anthem for Doomed Youth" (No. 161)
2. "The Story We Know" (No. 179), "One Art" (No. 31), "The Freaks at
    Spurgin Road Field" (No. 243), and "Do Not Go Gentle into That Good
    Night" (No. 286) are all examples of a French fixed form known as the
    villanelle. After studying their formal features, formulate a definition for
    the villanelle. *Hint:* Start with No. 286, the "purest" example of the form;
    then examine the extent to which the others conform to or depart from
    that norm.

---

172. A Handful of Limericks

There was a young lady from Niger
Who smiled as she road on a tiger;
   They returned from the ride
   With the lady inside
And the smile on the face of the tiger.

Anonymous

A tutor who tooted the flute
Tried to teach two young tooters to toot.
   Said the two to the tutor,
   "Is it harder to toot, or
To tutor two tooters to toot?"

Carolyn Wells (1862–1942)

There was a young fellow named Hall
Who fell in the spring in the fall;
   'Twould have been a sad thing
   Had he died in the spring,
But he didn't, he died in the fall.

Anonymous

An amoeba named Sam and his brother
Were having a drink with each other.
   In the midst of their quaffing
   They split themselves laughing,
And each of them now is a mother.

Anonymous

A goat on a stroll near a brook
Found an old movie film and partook.
  "Was it good?" asked his mate.
  Said the goat, "Second-rate!
Not nearly as good as the book!"

Martin Bristow Smith (b. 1916)

A cannibal said to her mate
Who was in a deplorable state
  Of discomfort, "My dear,
  Do you think it's the beer
Or is it just someone you ate?"

A. N. Wilkins (b. 1925)

The limerick's never averse
To expressing itself in a terse
  Economical style
  And yet, all the while,
The limerick's *always* a verse.

Laurence Perrine (1915–1995)

173. Two Japanese Haiku

The lightning flashes!
And slashing through the darkness,
  A night-heron's screech.

A lightning gleam:
  into darkness travels
  a night heron's scream.

Matsuo Bashō (1644–1694)

The falling flower
I saw drift back to the branch
  Was a butterfly.

Fallen flowers rise
  back to the branch—I watch:
  oh . . . butterflies!

Moritake (1452–1540)

QUESTION

The **Haiku,** a Japanese form, consists of three lines of five, seven, and five syllables each. The translators of the versions on the left (Earl Miner and Babette Deutsch respectively) preserve this syllable count; the translator of the right-hand versions (Harold G. Henderson) seeks to preserve the sense of formal structure by making the first and last lines rime. Moritake's haiku, as Miss Deutsch points out, "refers to the Buddhist proverb that the fallen

flower never returns to the branch; the broken mirror never again reflects."
From these two examples, what would you say are the characteristics of
effective haiku?

174. Poem in October

It was my thirtieth year to heaven
Woke to my hearing from harbor and neighbor wood
   And the mussel pooled and the heron
       Priested shore
     The morning beckon   5
With water praying and call of seagull and rook
And the knock of sailing boats on the net webbed wall
    Myself to set foot
     That second
In the still sleeping town and set forth.   10

My birthday began with the water-
Birds and the birds of the winged trees flying my name
   Above the farms and the white horses
     And I rose
    In rainy autumn   15
And walked abroad in a shower of all my days.
High tide and the heron dived when I took the road
    Over the border
     And the gates
Of the town closed as the town awoke.   20

A springful of larks in a rolling
Cloud and the roadside bushes brimming with whistling
   Blackbirds and the sun of October
     Summery
     On the hill's shoulder,   25
Here were fond climates and sweet singers suddenly
Come in the morning where I wandered and listened
    To the rain wringing
     Wind blow cold
In the woods faraway under me.   30

Pale rain over the dwindling harbor
And over the sea wet church the size of a snail
   With its horns through mist and the castle
     Brown as owls
     But all the gardens   35
Of spring and summer were blooming in the tall tales

Beyond the border and under the lark full cloud.
   There could I marvel
     My birthday
Away but the weather turned around.   40

   It turned away from the blithe country
And down the other air and the blue altered sky
   Streamed again a wonder of summer
     With apples
     Pears and red currants   45
And I saw in the turning so clearly a child's
Forgotten mornings when he walked with his mother
    Through the parables
     Of sun light
And the legends of the green chapels   50

   And the twice told fields of infancy
That his tears burned my cheeks and his heart moved in mine.
   These were the woods the river and sea
     Where a boy
     In the listening   55
Summertime of the dead whispered the truth of his joy
To the trees and the stones and the fish in the tide.
    And the mystery
     Sang alive
Still in the water and singingbirds.   60

   And there could I marvel my birthday
Away but the weather turned around. And the true
   Joy of the long dead child sang burning
     In the sun.
     It was my thirtieth   65
Year to heaven stood there then in the summer noon
Though the town below lay leaved with October blood.
    O may my heart's truth
     Still be sung
On this high hill in a year's turning.   70

Dylan Thomas (1914–1953)

QUESTIONS

1. The setting is a small fishing village on the coast of Wales. The poet's first name in Welsh means "water" (12). Trace the poet's walk in relation to the village, the weather, and the time of day.

2. "The weather turned around" (40, 62) is an expression indicating a change in the weather or the direction of the wind. In what psychological

sense does the weather turn around during the poet's walk? Who is "the long dead child" (63), and what kind of child was he? With what wish does the poem close?
3. Explain "thirtieth year to heaven" (1), "horns" (33), "tall tales" (36), "green chapels" (50), "October blood" (67).
4. The elaborate stanza pattern in this poem is based not on the meter (which is very free) but on a syllable count. How many syllables are there in each line of the stanza? (In line 1 "thirtieth" may be counted as only two syllables.) Notice that stanzas 1 and 3 consist of exactly one sentence each.
5. The poem makes considerable use of approximate rime, though not according to a regular pattern. Point out examples.

175. From *Romeo and Juliet*

ROMEO   If I profane with my unworthiest hand
   This holy shrine, the gentle sin is this:
   My lips, two blushing pilgrims, ready stand
   To smooth that rough touch with a tender kiss.
JULIET   Good pilgrim, you do wrong your hand too much,   5
   Which mannerly devotion shows in this;
   For saints have hands that pilgrims' hands do touch,
   And palm to palm is holy palmers' kiss.
ROMEO   Have not saints lips, and holy palmers too?
JULIET   Ay, pilgrim, lips that they must use in prayer.   10
ROMEO   O! then, dear saint, let lips do what hands do;
   They pray, grant thou, lest faith turn to despair.
JULIET   Saints do not move,° though grant for prayer's   *propose, instigate*
   sake.
ROMEO   Then move not, while my prayer's effect I take.

William Shakespeare (1564–1616)

QUESTIONS

1. These fourteen lines have been lifted out of Act 1, scene 5, of Shakespeare's play. They are the first words exchanged between Romeo and Juliet, who are meeting, for the first time, at a masquerade ball given by her father. Struck by Juliet's beauty, Romeo has come up to greet her. What stage action accompanies this passage?
2. What is the basic metaphor created by such religious terms as "profane" (1), "shrine" (2), "pilgrims" (3), "holy palmers" (8)? How does this metaphor affect the tone of the relationship between Romeo and Juliet?
3. What play on words do you find in lines 8 and 13–14? What two meanings has line 11?
4. By meter and rime scheme, these lines form a sonnet. Do you think this was coincidental or intentional on Shakespeare's part? Discuss.

176. Death, be not proud

Death, be not proud, though some have callèd thee
Mighty and dreadful, for thou art not so;
For those whom thou think'st thou dost overthrow
Die not, poor death, nor yet canst thou kill me.
From rest and sleep, which but thy pictures be,   5
Much pleasure—then, from thee much more must flow;
And soonest° our best men with thee do go,   readiest
Rest of their bones and soul's delivery.
Thou art slave to fate, chance, kings, and desperate men,
And dost with poison, war, and sickness dwell;   10
And poppy or charms can make us sleep as well,
And better than thy stroke. Why swell'st thou then?
One short sleep passed, we wake eternally,
And death shall be no more; death, thou shalt die.

John Donne (1572–1631)

QUESTIONS

1. What two figures of speech dominate the poem?
2. Why should death not be proud? List the speaker's major reasons. Are they consistent? Logical? Persuasive?
3. Discuss the tone of the poem. Is the speaker (a) a man of assured faith with a firm conviction that death is not to be feared or (b) a man desperately trying to convince himself that there is nothing to fear in death?
4. In form this sonnet blends the English and Italian models. Explain. Is its organization of thought closer to the Italian or the English sonnet?

177. A Wreath

A wreathèd garland of deservèd praise,
Of praise deservèd, unto thee I give,
I give to thee, who knowest all my ways,
My crooked winding ways, wherein I live,
Wherein I die, not live: for "live" is straight,   5
Straight as a line, and ever tends to thee,
To thee who art more far above deceit
Than deceit seems above simplicity.
Give me simplicity that I may live,
So live and like, that I may know thy ways,   10
Know them and practise them: then shall I give
For this poor wreath, give thee a crown of praise.

George Herbert (1593–1633)

QUESTIONS

1. The extended metaphor of the poem compares praise for God to a wreath or crown the speaker is twining with his words. Noting the repetition of words or phrases from line to line, trace how the poem finally creates a circle. How are the rimes of the last four lines related to those of the first four?
2. At the center of the poem is an idea that contrasts to the movement of wreathing or twining. What additional meaning is introduced by "Straight as a line" (6)? In what way is "winding" (4) like "deceit" (7)? How are structure, form, and meaning related here?

178. Acquainted with the Night

I have been one acquainted with the night.
I have walked out in rain—and back in rain.
I have outwalked the furthest city light.

I have looked down the saddest city lane.
I have passed by the watchman on his beat   5
And dropped my eyes, unwilling to explain.

I have stood still and stopped the sound of feet
When far away an interrupted cry
Came over houses from another street,

But not to call me back or say good-by;   10
And further still at an unearthly height,
One luminary clock against the sky

Proclaimed the time was neither wrong nor right.
I have been one acquainted with the night.

Robert Frost (1874–1963)

QUESTIONS

1. How does the speaker reveal the strength of his purpose in his night-walking? Can you specify what that purpose is? What symbolic meanings does the night hold?
2. How is the poem structured into sentences? What is the effect of repeating the phrase "I have"? Of repeating line 1 at the conclusion? How do these repetitions affect the tone of the poem?
3. Some critics have interpreted the "luminary clock" (12) literally—as the illuminated dial of a tower clock; others have interpreted it figuratively as the full moon. Of what, in either case, is it a symbol? Does the clock tell accurate chronometric time? What kind of "time" is it proclaiming in line 13? Is knowing *that* kind of time the speaker's quest?

4. The poem contains 14 lines—like a sonnet. But its rime scheme is **terza rima,** an interlocking scheme with the pattern *aba bcb cdc,* etc., a formal arrangement that implies continual progression. How does Frost bring the progression to an end? Terza rima was the form memorably employed by Dante for his *Divine Comedy,* of which the *Inferno* is the best-known section. In what ways does Frost's poem allude to the subject and framework of that poem?

179. The Story We Know

The way to begin is always the same. Hello,
Hello. Your hand, your name. So glad, Just fine,
and Good-bye at the end. That's every story we know,

and why pretend? But lunch tomorrow? No?
Yes? An omelette, salad, chilled white wine?   5
The way to begin is simple, sane, Hello,

and then it's Sunday, coffee, the *Times,* a slow
day by the fire, dinner at eight or nine
and Good-bye. In the end, this is a story we know

so well we don't turn the page, or look below   10
the picture, or follow the words to the next line:
The way to begin is always the same Hello.

But one night, through the latticed window, snow
begins to whiten the air, and the tall white pine.
Good-bye is the end of every story we know   15

that night, and when we close the curtains, oh,
we hold each other against that cold white sign
of the way we all begin and end. *Hello,*
Good-bye is the only story. We know, we know.

Martha Collins (b. 1940)

QUESTIONS

1. What have lines 1, 6, 12, and 18 in common? What have lines 3, 9, 15, and 19 in common?
2. What is the rime scheme?
3. Show how the words "Hello" and "Good-bye" acquire deeper meanings as the poem progresses. What do they refer to or symbolize in the last two lines? Why is the phrase "we know" repeated in the last line?
4. This poem is a villanelle. How closely does it conform to the definition of a villanelle that you formulated on page 784?

180. Edward

"Why does your sword so drip with blood,
    Edward, Edward,
Why does your sword so drip with blood,
    And why so sad go ye, O?"
"O I have killed my hawk so good,   5
    Mother, Mother,
O I have killed my hawk so good,
    And I had no more but he, O."

"Your hawk's blood was never so red,
    Edward, Edward,   10
Your hawk's blood was never so red,
    My dear son, I tell thee, O."
"O I have killed my red-roan steed,
    Mother, Mother,
O I have killed my red-roan steed,   15
    That once was so fair and free, O."

"Your steed was old, and ye have got more,
    Edward, Edward,
Your steed was old, and ye have got more,
    Some other grief ye feel, O."   20
"O I have killed my father dear,
    Mother, Mother,
O I have killed my father dear,
    Alas, and woe is me, O!"

"And what penance will ye do for that,   25
    Edward, Edward,
And what penance will ye do for that,
    My dear son, now tell me, O."
"I'll set my feet in yonder boat,
    Mother, Mother,   30
I'll set my feet in yonder boat,
    And I'll fare over the sea, O."

"And what will ye do with your towers and your hall,
    Edward, Edward,
And what will ye do with your towers and your hall,   35
    That were so fair to see, O?"
"I'll let them stand till they down fall,
    Mother, Mother,
I'll let them stand till they down fall,
    For here nevermore must I be, O."   40

"And what will ye leave to your children and wife,
    Edward, Edward,
And what will ye leave to your children and wife,
    When ye go over the sea, O?"
"The world is large, let them beg through life,   45
    Mother, Mother,
The world is large, let them beg through life,
    For them nevermore will I see, O."

"And what will ye leave to your own mother dear,
    Edward, Edward,   50
And what will ye leave to your own mother dear?
    My dear son, now tell me, O."
"The curse of hell from me shall ye bear,
    Mother, Mother,
The curse of hell from me shall ye bear,   55
    Such counsels you gave to me, O."

Anonymous

QUESTIONS

1. What has Edward done and why? Where do the two climaxes of the poem occur?
2. Tell as much as you can about Edward and his feelings toward what he has done. From what class of society is he? Why does he at first give false answers to his mother's questions? What reversal of feelings and loyalties has he undergone? Do his answers about his hawk and steed perhaps indicate his present feelings toward his father? How do you explain his behavior to his wife and children? What are his present feelings toward his mother?
3. Tell as much as you can about Edward's mother. Why does she ask what Edward has done—doesn't she already know? Is there any clue as to the motivation of her counsel? How skillful is she in her questioning? What do we learn about her from her dismissal of Edward's steed as "old" (17) and only one of many? From her asking Edward what penance *he* will do for his act (25)? From her reference to herself as Edward's "own mother dear" (49)?
4. Structure and form are both important in this poem. Could any of the stanzas be interchanged without loss, or do they build up steadily to the two climaxes? What effect has the constant repetition of the two short refrains, "Edward, Edward" and "Mother, Mother"? What is the effect of the final "O" at the end of each speech? Does the repetition of each question and answer simply waste words or does it add to the suspense and emotional intensity? (Read the poem omitting the third and seventh lines of each stanza. Is it improved or weakened?)
5. Much of what happened is implied; much is omitted. Does the poem gain anything in power from what is *not* told?

181. A Christmas Tree

Star,
If you are
A love compassionate,
You will walk with us this year.
We face a glacial distance, who are here   5
Huddld
At your feet.

William Burford (b. 1927)

QUESTION

Why do you think the author misspelled "Huddled" (6)?

EXERCISE

The typographical shape of a poem on the page (whether, for example, it is printed with a straight left-hand margin or with a system of indentations) is determined sometimes by the poet, sometimes by the printer, sometimes by an editor. Examine each of the following poems and try to deduce what *principle* (if any) determined its typographical design:
1. "The Mill" (No. 20)
2. "To His Coy Mistress" (No. 56)
3. "Dream Deferred" (No. 59)
4. "To a Waterfowl" (No. 106)
5. "Constantly risking absurdity" (No. 150)
6. "Poem in October" (No. 174)
7. "The Lamb" (No. 204)
8. "Offspring" (No. 253)

CHAPTER FIFTEEN

Bad Poetry and Good

The attempt to evaluate a poem should never be made before the poem is understood; and, unless one has developed the capacity to feel some poetry deeply, any judgments one makes will be worthless. A person who likes no wines can hardly be a judge of them. But the ability to make judgments, to discriminate between good and bad, great and good, good and half-good, is surely a primary object of all liberal education, and one's appreciation of poetry is incomplete unless it includes discrimination. Of the mass of verse that appears in print each year, most is "stale, flat, and unprofitable"; a very, very little is of any enduring value.

In judging a poem, as in judging any work of art, we need to ask three basic questions: (1) *What is its central purpose?* (2) *How fully has this purpose been accomplished?* (3) *How important is this purpose?* We need to answer the first question in order to understand the poem. Questions 2 and 3 are those by which we evaluate it. Question 2 measures the poem on a scale of perfection. Question 3 measures it on a scale of significance. The area of a rectangle is determined by multiplying its measurements on two scales, breadth and height; in an analogous way, the greatness of a poem is determined by multiplying its measurements on two scales, perfection and significance. If the poem measures well on the first of these scales, we call it a good poem, at least of its kind. If it measures well on both scales, we call it a great poem.*

The measurement of a poem is a much more complex process, of course, than is the measurement of a rectangle. It cannot be done as

---

*As indicated in the footnote on page 584, some objection has been made to the use of the term "purpose" in literary criticism. For the two evaluative criteria suggested above may be substituted these two: (1) *How thoroughly are the materials of the poem integrated or unified?* (2) *How many and how diverse are the materials that it integrates?* Thus a poem becomes successful in proportion to the tightness of its organization—that is, according to the degree to which all its elements work together and require each other to produce the total effect—and it becomes great in proportion to its scope—that is, according to the amount and diversity of the material it amalgamates into unity.

exactly. Agreement on the measurements will never be complete. Yet over a period of time the judgments of qualified readers* tend to coalesce: there comes to be more agreement than disagreement. There is almost universal agreement, for instance, that Shakespeare is the greatest of English poets. Although qualified readers might disagree sharply as to whether Donne or Keats is the superior poet—or Wordsworth or Chaucer, or Shelley or Pope—they nearly all agree that each of these is superior to Kipling or Longfellow. And there is almost universal agreement that Kipling and Longfellow are superior to James Whitcomb Riley or Rod McKuen.

But your problem is to be able to discriminate, not between already established reputations, but between poems—poems you have not seen before and of which, perhaps, you do not even know the author. Here, of course, you will not always be right—even the most qualified readers occasionally go badly astray—but you should, we hope, be able to make broad distinctions with a higher average of success than you could when you began this book. And, unless you allow yourself to petrify, your ability to do this should improve throughout your college years and beyond.

For answering the first of our evaluative questions, *How fully has the poem's purpose been accomplished?* there are no easy yardsticks that we can apply. We cannot ask: Is the poem melodious? Does it have smooth meter? Does it use good grammar? Does it contain figures of speech? Are the rimes perfect? Excellent poems exist without any of these attributes. We can judge any element in a poem only as it contributes or fails to contribute to the achievement of the central purpose; and we can judge the total poem only as these elements work together to form an integrated whole. But we can at least attempt a few generalizations. A perfect poem contains no excess words, no words that do not bear their full weight in contributing to the total meaning, and no words that are used just to fill out the meter. Each word is the best word for expressing the total meaning: there are no inexact words forced by the rime scheme or the metrical pattern. The word order is the best order for expressing the author's total meaning; distortions or departures from normal order are for emphasis or some other meaningful purpose. The diction, the images, and the figures of speech are fresh, not trite (except, of course, when the poet uses trite language deliberately for purposes of irony). The sound of the poem

---

*Throughout this discussion the term "qualified reader" is of utmost importance. By a qualified reader we mean briefly a person with considerable experience of literature and considerable experience of life: a person of intelligence, sensitivity, and knowledge.

does not clash with its sense, or the form with its content; and in general both sound and pattern are used to support meaning. The organization of the poem is the best possible organization: images and ideas are so effectively arranged that any rearrangement would be harmful to the poem. Always remember, however, that a good poem may have flaws. We should never damn a poem for its flaws if these flaws are amply compensated for by positive excellence.

If a poem is to have true excellence, it must be in some sense a "new" poem; it must exact a fresh response from the qualified reader. It will neither be merely imitative of previous literature nor appeal to stock, preestablished ways of thinking and feeling that in some readers are automatically stimulated by words like *mother, baby, home, country, faith,* or *God,* much as a vending machine dispenses a product when the right amount is inserted in the slot.

And here, perhaps, we should discuss the kinds of poems that most frequently "fool" inexperienced readers (and occasionally a few experienced ones) and sometimes achieve tremendous popularity without winning the respect of most good readers. These poems are frequently published on greeting cards or in anthologies entitled *Poems of Inspiration, Poems of Courage,* or *Heart-Throbs.* The people who write such poems and the people who like them are often the best of people, but they are not poets or lovers of poetry in any genuine sense. They are lovers of conventional ideas or sentiments or feelings, which they like to see expressed with the adornment of rime and meter, and which, when so expressed, they respond to in predictable ways.

Of the several varieties of inferior poetry, we shall concern ourselves with three: the sentimental, the rhetorical, and the purely didactic. All three are perhaps unduly dignified by the name of poetry. They might more aptly be described as verse.

Sentimentality is indulgence in emotion for its own sake, or expression of more emotion than an occasion warrants. Sentimentalists are gushy, stirred to tears by trivial or inappropriate causes; they weep at all weddings and all funerals; they are made ecstatic by manifestations of young love; they clip locks of hair, gild baby shoes, and talk baby talk; they grow compassionate over hardened criminals when they are punished. Their opposites are callous or unfeeling people. The ideal is the person who responds sensitively on appropriate occasions and feels deeply on occasions that deserve deep feeling, but who has nevertheless a certain amount of emotional reserve, a certain command over feelings. Sentimental *literature* is "tear-jerking" literature. It aims primarily at stimulating the emotions directly rather than at communicating experience truly and freshly; it depends on trite and well-tried formulas for exciting emotion; it revels in old oaken buckets, rocking chairs, mother love, and the pitter-patter of little feet; it over-simplifies; it is unfaithful to the full complexity of human experience. In this book the best example of sentimental verse is the first seven lines of Johnston's "A tiny cry within the night" (No. 129). If this verse had ended as it began, it would have been pure sentimentalism. The eighth line redeems it by making us realize that the speaker is not an idealized mother but a real person and thus transfers the piece from the classification of sentimental verse to that of humorous verse.

Rhetorical poetry uses a language more glittering and high-flown than its substance warrants. It offers a spurious vehemence of language—language without a corresponding reality of emotion or thought underneath. It is oratorical, overelegant, artificially eloquent. It is superficial and, again, often basically trite. It loves rolling phrases like "from the rocky coast of Maine to the sun-washed shores of California" and "our heroic dead" and "Old Glory." It deals in generalities. At its worst it is bombast. In this book an example is offered by the two lines quoted from the play within a play in Shakespeare's *A Midsummer Night's Dream:*

> Whereat with blade, with bloody, blameful blade,
> He bravely broached his boiling bloody breast.

Another example may be found in the player's recitation in *Hamlet* (in Act 2, scene 2):

> Out, out, thou strumpet Fortune! All you gods,
> In general synod take away her power,
> Break all the spokes and fellies from her wheel,
> And bowl the round nave down the hill of heaven
> As low as to the fiends!

Didactic poetry has as a primary purpose to teach or preach. It is probable that all the very greatest poetry teaches in subtle ways, without being expressly didactic; and much expressly didactic poetry ranks high in poetic excellence: that is, it accomplishes its teaching without ceasing to be poetry. But when the didactic purpose supersedes the poetic purpose, when the poem communicates information or moral instruction only, then it ceases to be didactic poetry and becomes didactic verse. Such verse appeals to people who read poetry primarily for noble thoughts or inspiring lessons and like them prettily expressed. It is recognizable often by its lack of any specific situation, the flatness of its diction, the poverty of its imagery and figurative language, its emphasis on moral platitudes, its lack of poetic freshness. It is either very trite or has little to distinguish it from informational prose except rime or meter. Bryant's "To a Waterfowl" (No. 106) is an example of didactic *poetry*. The familiar couplet

> Early to bed and early to rise,
> Makes a man healthy, wealthy, and wise

is more aptly characterized as didactic *verse*.

Undoubtedly, so far in this chapter, we have spoken too categorically, have made our distinctions too sharp and definite. All poetic excellence is a matter of degree. There are no absolute lines between sentimentality and true emotion, artificial and genuine eloquence, didactic verse, and didactic poetry. Though the difference between extreme examples is easy to recognize, subtler discriminations are harder to make. But a primary distinction between the educated person and the ignorant one is the ability to make informed judgments.

A final caution to students: when making judgments on literature, always be honest. Do not pretend to like what you do not like. Do not be afraid to admit a liking for what you do like. A genuine enthusiasm for the second-rate is much better than false enthusiasm or no enthusiasm at all. Be neither hasty nor timorous in making your judgments. When you have attentively read a poem and thoroughly considered it, decide what you think. Do not hedge, equivocate, or try to find out others' opinions before forming your own. But, having formed an opinion and expressed it, do not allow it to petrify. Compare your opinion *then* with the opinions of others; allow yourself to change it when convinced of its error: in this way you learn. Honesty, courage, and humility are the necessary moral foundations for all genuine literary judgment.

In the poems for comparison that follow in this chapter, the distinction to be made is not always between bad and good; it may be between varying degrees of poetic merit.

---

182. God's Will for You and Me

> Just to be tender, just to be true,
> Just to be glad the whole day through,
> Just to be merciful, just to be mild,
> Just to be trustful as a child,
> Just to be gentle and kind and sweet,   5

Just to be helpful with willing feet,
Just to be cheery when things go wrong,
Just to drive sadness away with a song,
Whether the hour is dark or bright,
Just to be loyal to God and right,   10
Just to believe that God knows best,
Just in his promises ever to rest—
Just to let love be our daily key,
That is God's will for you and me.

183. Pied Beauty

Glory be to God for dappled things—
   For skies of couple-color as a brinded cow;
     For rose-moles all in stipple upon trout that swim;
Fresh-firecoal chestnut-falls; finches' wings;
   Landscape plotted and pieced—fold, fallow and plow;   5
   And all trades, their gear and tackle and trim.

All things counter, original, spare, strange;
   Whatever is fickle, freckled (who knows how?)
     With swift, slow; sweet, sour; adazzle, dim;
He fathers-forth whose beauty is past change: 10
       Praise him.

QUESTION

Which is the superior poem? Explain in full.

184. A Poison Tree

I was angry with my friend:
I told my wrath, my wrath did end.
I was angry with my foe:
I told it not, my wrath did grow.

And I watered it in fears,   5
Night and morning with my tears;
And I sunnèd it with smiles,
And with soft deceitful wiles.

And it grew both day and night
Till it bore an apple bright;   10
And my foe beheld it shine,
And he knew that it was mine,

And into my garden stole
When the night had veiled the pole:°   sky
In the morning glad I see   15
My foe outstretched beneath the tree.

185. The Most Vital Thing in Life

When you feel like saying something
   That you know you will regret,
Or keenly feel an insult
   Not quite easy to forget,
That's the time to curb resentment   5
   And maintain a mental peace,
For when your mind is tranquil
   All your ill-thoughts simply cease.

It is easy to be angry
   When defrauded or defied,   10
To be peeved and disappointed
   If your wishes are denied;
But to win a worthwhile battle
   Over selfishness and spite,
You must learn to keep strict silence   15
   Though you know you're in the right.

So keep your mental balance
   When confronted by a foe,
Be it enemy in ambush
   Or some danger that you know.   20
If you are poised and tranquil
   When all around is strife,
Be assured that you have mastered
   The most vital thing in life.

QUESTION

Which poem has more poetic merit? Explain.

186. Longing

Come to me in my dreams, and then
By day I shall be well again!
For then the night will more than pay
The hopeless longing of the day.

Come, as thou cam'st a thousand times,   5
A messenger from radiant climes,
And smile on thy new world, and be
As kind to others as to me!

Or, as thou never cam'st in sooth,
Come now, and let me dream it truth;   10
And part my hair, and kiss my brow,
And say: *My love! why sufferest thou?*

Come to me in my dreams, and then
By day I shall be well again!
For then the night will more than pay   15
The hopeless longing of the day.

187. To Marguerite

Yes! in the sea of life enisled,
With echoing straits between us thrown,
Dotting the shoreless watery wild,
We mortal millions live *alone*.
The islands feel the enclasping flow   5
And then their endless bounds they know.

But when the moon their hollows lights,
And they are swept by balms of spring,
And in their glens, on starry nights,
The nightingales divinely sing;   10
And lovely notes, from shore to shore,
Across the sounds and channels pour—

Oh! then a longing like despair
Is to their farthest caverns sent;
For surely once, they feel, we were   15
Parts of a single continent!
Now round us spreads the watery plain—
Oh might our marges meet again!

Who ordered that their longing's fire
Should be, as soon as kindled, cooled?   20
Who renders vain their deep desire?—
A God, a God their severance ruled!
And bade betwixt their shores to be
The unplumbed, salt, estranging sea.

QUESTION

Both poems are by Matthew Arnold (1822–1888). Which of the two could
have been written only by a great poet? Explain.

188. The Long Voyage

Not that the pines were darker there,
nor mid-May dogwood brighter there,
nor swifts more swift in summer air;
    it was my own country,

having its thunderclap of spring,   5
its long midsummer ripening,
its corn hoar-stiff at harvesting,
    almost like any country,

yet being mine; its face, its speech,
its hills bent low within my reach,   10
its river birch and upland beech
    were mine, of my own country.

Now the dark waters at the bow
fold back, like earth against the plow;
foam brightens like the dogwood now   15
    at home, in my own country.

189. Breathes there the man

Breathes there the man, with soul so dead,
Who never to himself hath said,
    This is my own, my native land!
Whose heart hath ne'er within him burned,
As home his footsteps he hath turned,   5
    From wandering on a foreign strand?
If such there breathe, go, mark him well;

For him no minstrel raptures swell;
High though his titles, proud his name,
Boundless his wealth as wish can claim—   10
Despite those titles, power, and pelf,
The wretch, concentered all in self,
Living, shall forfeit fair renown,
And, doubly dying, shall go down
To the vile dust from whence he sprung,   15
Unwept, unhonored, and unsung.

QUESTION

Which poem communicates the more genuine poetic emotion? Which is
more rhetorical? Justify your answer.

190. The Engine

Into the gloom of the deep, dark night,
    With panting breath and a startled scream,
Swift as a bird in sudden flight
    Darts this creature of steel and steam.

Awful dangers are lurking nigh,   5
    Rocks and chasms are near the track,
But straight by the light of its great white eye
    It speeds through the shadows, dense and black.

Terrible thoughts and fierce desires
    Trouble its mad heart many an hour,   10
Where burn and smoulder the hidden fires,
    Coupled ever with might and power.

It hates, as a wild horse hates the rein,
    The narrow track by vale and hill,
And shrieks with a cry of startled pain,   15
    And longs to follow its own wild will.

191. I like to see it lap the miles

I like to see it lap the miles,
And lick the valleys up,
And stop to feed itself at tanks,
And then, prodigious, step

Around a pile of mountains,   5
And, supercilious, peer
In shanties by the sides of roads,
And then a quarry pare

To fit its ribs,
And crawl between,   10
Complaining all the while
In horrid, hooting stanza,
Then chase itself down hill

And neigh like Boanerges;
Then, punctual as a star,   15
Stop—docile and omnipotent—
At its own stable door.

QUESTION

Which of these poems is more rhetorical in its language?

192. Little Boy Blue

The little toy dog is covered with dust,
  But sturdy and staunch he stands;
And the little toy soldier is red with rust,
  And his musket moulds in his hands.
Time was when the little toy dog was new,   5
  And the soldier was passing fair;
And that was the time when our Little Boy Blue
  Kissed them and put them there.

"Now, don't you go till I come," he said,
  "And don't you make any noise!"   10
So, toddling off to his trundle-bed,
  He dreamt of the pretty toys;
And, as he was dreaming, an angel song
  Awakened our Little Boy Blue—
Oh! the years are many, the years are long,   15
  But the little toy friends are True!

Ay, faithful to Little Boy Blue they stand
  Each in the same old place—
Awaiting the touch of a little hand,

> The smile of a little face;   20
>   And they wonder, as waiting the long years through
>   In the dust of that little chair,
>   What has become of our Little Boy Blue,
>   Since he kissed them and put them there.

193. The Toys

> My little Son, who looked from thoughtful eyes
> And moved and spoke in quiet grown-up wise,
> Having my law the seventh time disobeyed,
> I struck him, and dismissed
> With hard words and unkissed,   5
> His Mother, who was patient, being dead.
> Then, fearing lest his grief should hinder sleep,
> I visited his bed,
> But found him slumbering deep,
> With darkened eyelids, and their lashes yet   10
> From his late sobbing wet.
> And I, with moan,
> Kissing away his tears, left others of my own;
> For, on a table drawn beside his head,
> He had put, within his reach,   15
> A box of counters and a red-veined stone,
> A piece of glass abraded by the beach,
> And six or seven shells,
> A bottle with bluebells,
> And two French copper coins, ranged there with careful art,   20
> To comfort his sad heart.
> So when that night I prayed
> To God, I wept, and said:
> Ah, when at last we lie with trancèd breath,
> Not vexing Thee in death,   25
> And thou rememberest of what toys
> We made our joys,
> How weakly understood
> Thy great commanded good,
> Then, fatherly not less   30
> Than I whom Thou has moulded from the clay,
> Thou'lt leave Thy wrath, and say,
> "I will be sorry for their childishness."

QUESTION

One of these poems has an obvious appeal for the beginning reader. The
other is likely to have more meaning for the mature reader. Try to explain in
terms of sentimentality and honesty.

194. Song: Sweetest love, I do not go

Sweetest love, I do not go
    For weariness of thee,
Nor in hope the world can show
    A fitter love for me;
        But since that I   5
Must die at last, 'tis best
To use my self in jest
        Thus by feigned deaths to die.

Yesternight the sun went hence,
    And yet is here today,   10
He hath no desire nor sense,
    Nor half so short a way:
        Then fear not me,
But believe that I shall make
Speedier journeys, since I take   15
        More wings and spurs than he.

O how feeble is man's power,
    That if good fortune fall,
Cannot add another hour,
    Nor a lost hour recall!   20
        But come bad chance,
And we join it to our strength,
And we teach it art and length,
        Itself o'er us to advance.

When thou sigh'st, thou sigh'st not wind,   25
    But sigh'st my soul away;
When thou weep'st, unkindly kind,
    My life's blood doth decay.
        It cannot be
That thou lov'st me, as thou say'st,   30
If in thine my life thou waste;
        Thou art the best of me.

Let not thy divining° heart   prophetic
    Forethink me any ill;
Destiny may take thy part,   35
    And may thy fears fulfill;
    But think that we
Are but turned aside to sleep;
They who one another keep
Alive, ne'er parted be.   40

195. Song: Sweetest love, return again

Sweetest love, return again,
    Make not too long a stay,
Killing mirth and forcing pain,
    Sorrow leading way.
Let us not thus parted be: 5
Love and absence ne'er agree.

But since you must needs depart,
    And me hapless leave,
In your journey take my heart,
    Which will not deceive.   10
Yours it is, to you it flies,
Joying in those lovèd eyes.

So in part we shall not part,
    Though we absent be:
Time, nor place, nor greatest smart   15
    Shall my bands° make free.   bonds
Tied I am, yet think it gain:
In such knots I feel no pain.

But can I live, having lost
    Chiefest part of me?   20
Heart is fled, and sight is crossed,
    These my fortunes be.
Yet dear heart go, soon return:
As good there as here to burn.

QUESTION

Which is the superior poem, and why?

partly a native endowment, partly the product of experience, partly the achievement of conscious study, training, and intellectual effort. They cannot be achieved suddenly or quickly; they can never be achieved in perfection. The pull is a long and a hard one. But success, even relative success, brings enormous rewards in enrichment and command of life.

196. The Canonization

For God's sake, hold your tongue, and let me love!
   Or chide my palsy or my gout,
My five gray hairs or ruined fortune flout;
With wealth your state, your mind with arts improve,
    Take you a course,° get you a place,   career 5
    Observe his honor° or his grace,°   judge; bishop
Or the king's real or his stamped face°   on a coin
    Contemplate; what you will, approve,°   try out
    So you will let me love.

Alas, alas, who's injured by my love?   10
   What merchant ships have my sighs drowned?
Who says my tears have overflowed his ground?
When did my colds a forward° spring remove?   early
    When did the heats which my veins fill
    Add one more to the plaguy bill?   15
Soldiers find wars, and lawyers find out still
    Litigious men which quarrels move,
    Though she and I do love.

Call us what you will, we are made such by love.
    Call her one, me another fly;°   moth 20
We are tapers too, and at our own cost die;
And we in us find the eagle and the dove;
    The phoenix riddle hath more wit°   meaning
    By us; we two, being one, are it.
So to one neutral thing both sexes fit.   25
    We die and rise the same, and prove
    Mysterious by this love.

We can die by it, if not live by love,
    And if unfit for tombs and hearse
Our legend be, it will be fit for verse;   30

And if no piece of chronicle° we prove,	history
We'll build in sonnets pretty rooms:	
As well a well-wrought urn becomes	
The greatest ashes as half-acre tombs,	
And by these hymns all shall approve°	confirm 35
Us canonized for love,	

And thus invoke us: "You whom reverend love	
Made one another's hermitage,	
You to whom love was peace, that now is rage,	
Who did the whole world's soul contract, and drove	40
Into the glasses of your eyes	
(So made such mirrors and such spies	
That they did all to you epitomize)	
Countries, towns, courts: beg from above	
A pattern of your love!"	45

John Donne (1572–1631)

QUESTIONS

1. Vocabulary: *canonization* (title), *tapers* (21), *phoenix* (23), *invoke* (37), *epitomize* (43). "[R]eal" (7), pronounced as two syllables, puns on *royal*. The "plaguy bill" (15) is a list of plague victims. The word "die" (21, 26, 28) in seventeenth-century slang meant to experience the sexual climax. To understand lines 21 and 28, one also needs to be familiar with the Renaissance superstition that every act of sexual intercourse shortened one's life by one day. The "eagle" and the "dove" (22) are symbols for strength and mildness. "[P]attern" (45) is a model that one can copy.
2. Who is the speaker and what is his condition? How old is he? To whom is he speaking? What has his auditor been saying to him before the opening of the poem? What sort of values can we ascribe to the auditor by inference from the first stanza? What value does the speaker oppose to these? How does the stanzaic pattern of the poem emphasize this value?
3. The sighs, tears, fevers, and chills in the second stanza were commonplace in the love poetry of Donne's time. How does Donne make them fresh? What is the speaker's argument in this stanza? How does it begin to turn from pure defense to offense in the last three lines of the stanza?
4. How are the things to which the lovers are compared in the third stanza *arranged?* Does their ordering reflect in any way the arrangement of the whole poem? Elucidate line 21. Interpret or paraphrase lines 23–27.
5. Explain the first line of the fourth stanza. What status does the speaker claim for himself and his beloved in the last line of this stanza?
6. In what sense is the last stanza an invocation? Who speaks in it? To whom? What powers are ascribed to the lovers in it?
7. What do the following words from the poem have in common: "Mysterious" (27), "hymns" (35), "canonized" (36), "reverend" (37), "hermitage" (38)? What judgment about love does the speaker make by the use of these words?

197. Home Burial

He saw her from the bottom of the stairs
Before she saw him. She was starting down,
Looking back over her shoulder at some fear.
She took a doubtful step and then undid it
To raise herself and look again. He spoke   5
Advancing toward her: "What is it you see
From up there always—for I want to know."
She turned and sank upon her skirts at that,
And her face changed from terrified to dull.
He said to gain time: "What is it you see,"   10
Mounting until she cowered under him.
"I will find out now—you must tell me, dear."
She, in her place, refused him any help
With the least stiffening of her neck and silence.
She let him look, sure that he wouldn't see,   15
Blind creature; and awhile he didn't see.
But at last he murmured, "Oh," and again, "Oh."

"What is it—what?" she said.

                            "Just that I see."

"You don't," she challenged. "Tell me what it is."

"The wonder is I didn't see at once.   20
I never noticed it from here before.
I must be wonted to it—that's the reason.
The little graveyard where my people are!
So small the window frames the whole of it.
Not so much larger than a bedroom, is it?   25
There are three stones of slate and one of marble,
Broad-shouldered little slabs there in the sunlight
On the sidehill. We haven't to mind *those*.
But I understand: it is not the stones,
But the child's mound—"

                            "Don't, don't, don't,
        don't," she cried.   30

She withdrew, shrinking from beneath his arm
That rested on the banister, and slid downstairs;
And turned on him with such a daunting look,
He said twice over before he knew himself:
"Can't a man speak of his own child he's lost?"   35

"Not you! Oh, where's my hat? Oh, I don't need it!
I must get out of here. I must get air.
I don't know rightly whether any man can."

"Amy! Don't go to someone else this time.
Listen to me. I won't come down the stairs."   40
He sat and fixed his chin between his fists.
"There's something I should like to ask you, dear."

"You don't know how to ask it."

                          "Help me, then."

Her fingers moved the latch for all reply.

"My words are nearly always an offense.   45
I don't know how to speak of anything
So as to please you. But I might be taught,
I should suppose. I can't say I see how.
A man must partly give up being a man
With women-folk. We could have some arrangement   50
By which I'd bind myself to keep hands off
Anything special you're a-mind to name.
Though I don't like such things 'twixt those that love.
Two that don't love can't live together without them.
But two that do can't live together with them."   55
She moved the latch a little. "Don't—don't go.
Don't carry it to someone else this time.
Tell me about it if it's something human.
Let me into your grief. I'm not so much
Unlike other folks as your standing there   60
Apart would make me out. Give me my chance.
I do think, though, you overdo it a little.
What was it brought you up to think it the thing
To take your mother-loss of a first child
So inconsolably—in the face of love.   65
You'd think his memory might be satisfied—"

"There you go sneering now!"

                          "I'm not, I'm not!
You make me angry. I'll come down to you.
God, what a woman! And it's come to this,
A man can't speak of his own child that's dead."   70

"You can't because you don't know how to speak.
If you had any feelings, you that dug
With your own hand—how could you?—his little grave;

I saw you from that very window there,
Making the gravel leap and leap in air,   75
Leap up, like that, like that, and land so lightly
And roll back down the mound beside the hole.
I thought, Who is that man? I didn't know you.
And I crept down the stairs and up the stairs
To look again, and still your spade kept lifting.   80
Then you came in. I heard your rumbling voice
Out in the kitchen, and I don't know why,
But I went near to see with my own eyes.
You could sit there with the stains on your shoes
Of the fresh earth from your own baby's grave   85
And talk about your everyday concerns.
You had stood the spade up against the wall
Outside there in the entry, for I saw it."

"I shall laugh the worst laugh I ever laughed.
I'm cursed. God, if I don't believe I'm cursed."   90

"I can repeat the very words you were saying:
'Three foggy mornings and one rainy day
Will rot the best birch fence a man can build.'
Think of it, talk like that at such a time!
What had how long it takes a birch to rot   95
To do with what was in the darkened parlor?
You *couldn't* care! The nearest friends can go
With anyone to death, comes so far short
They might as well not try to go at all.
No, from the time when one is sick to death,   100
One is alone, and he dies more alone.
Friends make pretense of following to the grave,
But before one is in it, their minds are turned
And making the best of their way back to life
And living people, and things they understand.   105
But the world's evil. I won't have grief so
If I can change it. Oh, I won't, I won't!"

"There, you have said it all and you feel better.
You won't go now. You're crying. Close the door.
The heart's gone out of it: why keep it up?   110
Amy! There's someone coming down the road!"

"*You*—oh, you think the talk is all. I must go—
Somewhere out of this house. How can I make you—"
"If—you—do!" She was opening the door wider.

"Where do you mean to go? First tell me that.   115
I'll follow and bring you back by force. I *will!*—"

Robert Frost (1874–1963)

QUESTIONS

1. Vocabulary: *wonted* (22).
2. The poem centers on a conflict between husband and wife. What causes the conflict? Why does Amy resent her husband? What is *his* dissatisfaction with Amy?
3. Characterize the husband and wife respectively. What is the chief difference between them? Does the poem take sides? Is either presented more sympathetically than the other?
4. The poem does not say how long the couple have been married or how long the child has been buried. Does it contain suggestions from which we may make rough inferences?
5. The husband and wife both generalize on the other's faults during the course of the poem, attributing them to all men or to all women or to people in general. Point out these generalizations. Are they valid?
6. Finish the unfinished sentences in lines 30, 66, 113, 114.
7. Comment on the function of lines 25, 39, 92–93.
8. Following are three paraphrased and abbreviated versions of statements made in published discussions of the poem. Which would you support? Why?
   a. The young wife is gradually persuaded by her husband's kind yet firm reasonableness to express her feelings in words and to recognize that human nature is limited and cannot sacrifice everything to sorrow. Though she still suffers from excess grief, the crisis is past, and she will eventually be brought back to life.
   b. At the end, the whole poem is epitomized by the door that is neither open nor shut. The wife cannot really leave; the husband cannot really make her stay. Neither husband nor wife is capable of decisive action, of either self-liberation or liberation of the other.
   c. Her husband's attempt to talk, since it is the wrong kind of talk, only leads to her departure at the poem's end.

198. The Love Song of J. Alfred Prufrock

S'io credesse che mia risposta fosse
A persona che mai tornasse al mondo,
Questa fiamma staria senza piu scosse.
Ma perciocche giammai di questo fondo
Non torno vivo alcun, s'i'odo il vero,
Senza tema d'infamia ti rispondo.

Let us go then, you and I,
When the evening is spread out against the sky

Like a patient etherized upon a table;
Let us go, through certain half-deserted streets,
The muttering retreats   5
Of restless nights in one-night cheap hotels
And sawdust restaurants with oyster-shells:
Streets that follow like a tedious argument
Of insidious intent
To lead you to an overwhelming question . . .   10
Oh, do not ask, "What is it?"
Let us go and make our visit.

    In the room the women come and go
Talking of Michelangelo.

    The yellow fog that rubs its back upon the window-panes,   15
The yellow smoke that rubs its muzzle on the window-panes
Licked its tongue into the corners of the evening,
Lingered upon the pools that stand in drains,
Let fall upon its back the soot that falls from chimneys,
Slipped by the terrace, made a sudden leap,   20
And seeing that it was a soft October night,
Curled once about the house, and fell asleep.

    And indeed there will be time
For the yellow smoke that slides along the street,
Rubbing its back upon the window-panes;   25
There will be time, there will be time
To prepare a face to meet the faces that you meet;
There will be time to murder and create,
And time for all the works and days of hands
That lift and drop a question on your plate;   30
Time for you and time for me,
And time yet for a hundred indecisions,
And for a hundred visions and revisions,
Before the taking of a toast and tea.

    In the room the women come and go   35
Talking of Michelangelo.

    And indeed there will be time
To wonder, "Do I dare?" and "Do I dare?"
Time to turn back and descend the stair,
With a bald spot in the middle of my hair—   40
(They will say: "How his hair is growing thin!")
My morning coat, my collar mounting firmly to the chin,
My necktie rich and modest, but asserted by a simple pin—

(They will say: "But how his arms and legs are thin!")
Do I dare   45
Disturb the universe?
In a minute there is time
For decisions and revisions which a minute will reverse.

    For I have known them all already, known them all:—
Have known the evenings, mornings, afternoons,   50
I have measured out my life with coffee spoons;
I know the voices dying with a dying fall
Beneath the music from a farther room.
    So how should I presume?

    And I have known the eyes already, known them all—   55
The eyes that fix you in a formulated phrase,
And when I am formulated, sprawling on a pin,
When I am pinned and wriggling on the wall,
Then how should I begin
To spit out all the butt-ends of my days and ways?   60
    And how should I presume?

    And I have known the arms already, known them all—
Arms that are braceleted and white and bare
(But in the lamplight, downed with light brown hair!)
Is it perfume from a dress   65
That makes me so digress?
Arms that lie along a table, or wrap about a shawl.
    And should I then presume?
    And how should I begin?

         *   *   *

Shall I say, I have gone at dusk through narrow streets   70
And watched the smoke that rises from the pipes
Of lonely men in shirt-sleeves, leaning out of windows? . . .

    I should have been a pair of ragged claws
Scuttling across the floors of silent seas.

         *   *   *

And the afternoon, the evening, sleeps so peacefully!   75
Smoothed by long fingers,
Asleep . . . tired . . . or it malingers,
Stretched on the floor, here beside you and me.
Should I, after tea and cakes and ices,
Have the strength to force the moment to its crisis?   80
But though I have wept and fasted, wept and prayed,
Though I have seen my head (grown slightly bald) brought in upon a platter,
I am no prophet—and here's no great matter;

I have seen the moment of my greatness flicker,
And I have seen the eternal Footman hold my coat, and snicker,   85
And in short, I was afraid.

And would it have been worth it, after all,
After the cups, the marmalade, the tea,
Among the porcelain, among some talk of you and me,
Would it have been worth while,   90
To have bitten off the matter with a smile,
To have squeezed the universe into a ball
To roll it toward some overwhelming question,
To say: "I am Lazarus, come from the dead,
Come back to tell you all, I shall tell you all"—   95
If one, settling a pillow by her head,
Should say: "That is not what I meant at all.
That is not it, at all."

And would it have been worth it, after all,
Would it have been worth while,   100
After the sunsets and the dooryards and the sprinkled streets,
After the novels, after the teacups, after the skirts that trail along the floor—
And this, and so much more?—
It is impossible to say just what I mean!
But as if a magic lantern threw the nerves in patterns on a screen: 105
Would it have been worth while
If one, settling a pillow or throwing off a shawl,
And turning toward the window, should say:
"That is not it at all,
That is not what I meant, at all."   110

                *   *   *

No! I am not Prince Hamlet, nor was meant to be;
Am an attendant lord, one that will do
To swell a progress, start a scene or two,
Advise the prince; no doubt, an easy tool,
Deferential, glad to be of use,   115
Politic, cautious, and meticulous:
Full of high sentence, but a bit obtuse;
At times, indeed, almost ridiculous—
Almost, at times, the Fool.

I grow old . . . I grow old . . .   120
I shall wear the bottoms of my trousers rolled.°   cuffed

Shall I part my hair behind? Do I dare to eat a peach?
I shall wear white flannel trousers, and walk upon the beach.
I have heard the mermaids singing, each to each.

I do not think that they will sing to me.   125

I have seen them riding seaward on the waves
Combing the white hair of the waves blown back
When the wind blows the water white and black.

We have lingered in the chambers of the sea
By sea-girls wreathed with seaweed red and brown   130
Till human voices wake us, and we drown.

T. S. Eliot (1888–1965)

QUESTIONS

1. Vocabulary: *insidious* (9), *Michelangelo* (14, 35), *muzzle* (16), *malingers* (77), *progress* (113), *Deferential* (115), *Politic* (116), *meticulous* (116), *sentence* (117).
2. This poem may be for some readers the most difficult in the book because it uses a "stream of consciousness" technique (that is, it presents the apparently random thoughts going through a person's head within a certain time interval), in which the transitional links are psychological rather than logical, and also because it uses allusions you may be unfamiliar with. Even if you do not at first understand the poem in detail, you should be able to get from it a quite accurate picture of Prufrock's character and personality. What kind of person is he (answer this as fully as possible)? From what class of society does he come? What one line especially well sums up the nature of his past life? A brief initial orientation may be helpful: Prufrock is apparently on his way, at the beginning of the poem, to a late afternoon tea, at which he wishes (or does he?) to make a declaration of love to some lady who will be present. The "you and I" of the first line are divided parts of Prufrock's own nature, for he is experiencing internal conflict. Does he or does he not make the declaration? Where does the climax of the poem come? If the portion leading up to the climax is devoted to Prufrock's effort to prepare himself psychologically to make the declaration (or to postpone such effort), what is the portion after the climax devoted to?
3. The poem contains a number of striking or unusual figures of speech. Most of them in some way reflect Prufrock's own nature or his desires or fears. From this point of view discuss lines 2–3; 15–22 and 75–78; 57–58; 73–74; and 124–31. What figure of speech is lines 73–74? In what respect is the title ironic?
4. The poem makes extensive use of literary allusion. The Italian epigraph is a passage from Dante's *Inferno* in which a man in Hell tells a visitor that he would never tell his story if there were a chance that it would get back to living ears. In line 29 the phrase "works and days" is the title of a long poem—a description of agricultural life and a call to toil—by the early Greek poet Hesiod. Line 52 echoes the opening speech of Shakespeare's *Twelfth Night*. The prophet of lines 81–83 is John the Baptist, whose head was delivered to Salome by Herod as a reward for her dancing (Matthew 14.1–11, and Oscar Wilde's play *Salome*). Line 92 echoes the closing six lines of Marvell's "To His Coy Mistress" (No. 56). Lazarus (94–95) may be either the beggar Lazarus (of Luke 16) who was not permitted to return

from the dead to warn a rich man's brothers about Hell, the Lazarus (of John 11) whom Christ raised from death, or both. Lines 111–19 allude to a number of characters from Shakespeare's *Hamlet:* Hamlet himself, the chamberlain Polonius, and various minor characters including probably Rosencrantz, Guildenstern, and Osric. "Full of high sentence" (117) echoes Chaucer's description of the Clerk of Oxford in the Prologue to *The Canterbury Tales.* Relate as many of these allusions as you can to the character of Prufrock. How is Prufrock particularly like Hamlet, and how is he unlike him? Contrast Prufrock with the speaker in "To His Coy Mistress."

199. Sunday Morning

1

Complacencies of the peignoir, and late
Coffee and oranges in a sunny chair,
And the green freedom of a cockatoo
Upon a rug mingle to dissipate
The holy hush of ancient sacrifice.   5
She dreams a little, and she feels the dark
Encroachment of that old catastrophe,
As a calm darkens among water-lights.
The pungent oranges and bright, green wings
Seem things in some procession of the dead,   10
Winding across wide water, without sound.
The day is like wide water, without sound,
Stilled for the passing of her dreaming feet
Over the seas, to silent Palestine,
Dominion of the blood and sepulchre.   15

2

Why should she give her bounty to the dead?
What is divinity if it can come
Only in silent shadows and in dreams?
Shall she not find in comforts of the sun,
In pungent fruit and bright, green wings, or else   20
In any balm or beauty of the earth,
Things to be cherished like the thought of heaven?
Divinity must live within herself:
Passions of rain, or moods in falling snow;
Grievings in loneliness, or unsubdued   25
Elations when the forest blooms; gusty

Emotions on wet roads on autumn nights;
All pleasures and all pains, remembering
The bough of summer and the winter branch.
These are the measures destined for her soul.   30

3

Jove in the clouds had his inhuman birth.
No mother suckled him, no sweet land gave
Large-mannered motions to his mythy mind.
He moved among us, as a muttering king,
Magnificent, would move among his hinds,   35
Until our blood, commingling, virginal,
With heaven, brought such requital to desire
The very hinds discerned it, in a star.
Shall our blood fail? Or shall it come to be
The blood of paradise? And shall the earth   40
Seem all of paradise that we shall know?
The sky will be much friendlier then than now,
A part of labor and a part of pain,
And next in glory to enduring love,
Not this dividing and indifferent blue.   45

4

She says, "I am content when wakened birds,
Before they fly, test the reality
Of misty fields, by their sweet questionings;
But when the birds are gone, and their warm fields
Return no more, where, then, is paradise?"   50
There is not any haunt of prophecy,
Nor any old chimera of the grave,
Neither the golden underground, nor isle
Melodious, where spirits gat them home,
Nor visionary south, nor cloudy palm   55
Remote on heaven's hill, that has endured
As April's green endures; or will endure
Like her remembrance of awakened birds,
Or her desire for June and evening, tipped
By the consummation of the swallow's wings.   60

5

She says, "But in contentment I still feel
The need of some imperishable bliss."

Death is the mother of beauty; hence from her,
Alone, shall come fulfillment to our dreams
And our desires. Although she strews the leaves   65
Of sure obliteration on our paths,
The path sick sorrow took, the many paths
Where triumph rang its brassy phrase, or love
Whispered a little out of tenderness,
She makes the willow shiver in the sun   70
For maidens who were wont to sit and gaze
Upon the grass, relinquished to their feet.
She causes boys to pile new plums and pears
On disregarded plate. The maidens taste
And stray impassioned in the littering leaves.   75

6

Is there no change of death in paradise?
Does ripe fruit never fall? Or do the boughs
Hang always heavy in that perfect sky,
Unchanging, yet so like our perishing earth,
With rivers like our own that seek for seas   80
They never find, the same receding shores
That never touch with inarticulate pang?
Why set the pear upon those river-banks
Or spice the shores with odors of the plum?
Alas, that they should wear our colors there,   85
The silken weavings of our afternoons,
And pick the strings of our insipid lutes!
Death is the mother of beauty, mystical,
Within whose burning bosom we devise
Our earthly mothers waiting, sleeplessly.   90

7

Supple and turbulent, a ring of men
Shall chant in orgy on a summer morn
Their boisterous devotion to the sun,
Not as a god, but as a god might be,
Naked among them, like a savage source.   95
Their chant shall be a chant of paradise,
Out of their blood, returning to the sky;
And in their chant shall enter, voice by voice,
The windy lake wherein their lord delights,
The trees, like serafin, and echoing hills,   100
That choir among themselves long afterward.

They shall know well the heavenly fellowship
Of men that perish and of summer morn.
And whence they came and whither they shall go
The dew upon their feet shall manifest.   105

8

She hears, upon that water without sound,
A voice that cries, "The tomb in Palestine
Is not the porch of spirits lingering.
It is the grave of Jesus, where he lay."
We live in an old chaos of the sun,   110
Or old dependency of day and night,
Or island solitude, unsponsored, free,
Of that wide water, inescapable.
Deer walk upon our mountains, and the quail
Whistle about us their spontaneous cries;   115
Sweet berries ripen in the wilderness;
And, in the isolation of the sky,
At evening, casual flocks of pigeons make
Ambiguous undulations as they sink,
Downward to darkness, on extended wings.   120

Wallace Stevens (1879–1955)

QUESTIONS

1. Vocabulary: *peignoir* (1), *hinds* (35, 38), *requital* (37), *chimera* (52), *con-summation* (60), *obliteration* (66), *serafin* (seraphim) (100). "[G]at" (54) is an obsolete past tense of "get."
2. The poem presents a woman meditating on questions of death, mutability, and permanence, beginning with a stanza that sets the stage and shows her being drawn to these questions beyond her conscious will. The meditation proper is structured as a series of questions and answers stated in direct or indirect quotations, with the answer to a preceding question suggesting a further question, and so forth. In reading through the poem, paraphrase the sequence of implied or stated questions, and the answers to them.
3. The opening scene (stanza 1), in a collection of images and details, indicates the means the woman has chosen to avoid thinking of the typical "Sunday morning" topic, the Christian religion. Define the means she employs. Trace the further references to fruits and birds throughout the poem, and explain the ordering principle that ties them together (for example, what development of idea or attitude is implied in the sequence oranges/plums and pears/wild berries?).
4. What symbolic meanings are implied by the images of (a) water, (b) the sun, and (c) birds and other animals?

5. Why does the woman give up her desire for unchanging permanence? With what does she replace it? What is her final attitude toward a world that includes change and death? What is meant by "Death is the mother of beauty" (63, 88)?

6. The poet wrote, "This is not essentially a woman's meditation on religion and the meaning of life. It is anybody's meditation" (*Letters of Wallace Stevens,* ed. Holly Stevens [New York: Knopf, 1966] 250). Can you justify that claim?

7. "The Canonization," "Home Burial," "The Love Song of J. Alfred Prufrock," and "Sunday Morning" are all dramatic poems. "The Canonization" is a dramatic monologue (one person is speaking to another, whose replies we do not hear). Frost's poem (though it has a slight narrative element) is largely a dialogue between two speakers who speak in their own voices. Eliot's poem is a highly allusive soliloquy, or interior monologue. "Sunday Morning" combines descriptive scene-setting with an interior debate of question and answer. In what ways do the dramatic structures of these poems facilitate what they have to say?

Poems for
Further Reading

200. Woman Work

I've got the children to tend
The clothes to mend
The floor to mop
The food to shop
Then the chicken to fry   5
The baby to dry
I got company to feed
The garden to weed
I've got the shirts to press
The tots to dress   10
The cane to be cut
I gotta clean up this hut
Then see about the sick
And the cotton to pick.

Shine on me, sunshine   15
Rain on me, rain
Fall softly, dewdrops
And cool my brow again.

Storm, blow me from here
With your fiercest wind   20
Let me float across the sky
'Til I can rest again.

Fall gently, snowflakes
Cover me with white
Cold icy kisses and   25
Let me rest tonight.

Sun, rain, curving sky
Mountain, oceans, leaf and stone
Star shine, moon glow
You're all that I can call my own.   30

Maya Angelou (b. 1928)

201. Siren Song

This is the one song everyone
would like to learn: the song
that is irresistible:

the song that forces men
to leap overboard in squadrons   5
even though they see the beached skulls

the song nobody knows
because anyone who has heard it
is dead, and the others can't remember.

Shall I tell you the secret   10
and if I do, will you get me
out of this bird suit?

I don't enjoy it here
squatting on this island
looking picturesque and mythical   15

with these two feathery maniacs,
I don't enjoy singing
this trio, fatal and valuable.

I will tell the secret to you,
to you, only to you.   20
Come closer. This song

is a cry for help: Help me!
Only you, only you can,
you are unique

at last. Alas   25
It is a boring song
but it works every time.

Margaret Atwood (b. 1939)

Siren (title): In Greek mythology, the sirens (sometimes pictured as birds with women's heads) were creatures whose beautiful singing lured sailors to their deaths.

202. Musée des Beaux Arts

About suffering they were never wrong,
The Old Masters: how well they understood
Its human position; how it takes place
While someone else is eating or opening a window or just walking
    dully along;
How, when the aged are reverently, passionately waiting   5
For the miraculous birth, there always must be

Children who did not specially want it to happen, skating
On a pond at the edge of the wood:
They never forgot
That even the dreadful martyrdom must run its course   10
Anyhow in a corner, some untidy spot
Where the dogs go on with their doggy life and the torturer's horse
Scratches its innocent behind on a tree.

In Brueghel's *Icarus,* for instance: how everything turns away
Quite leisurely from the disaster; the plowman may   15
Have heard the splash, the forsaken cry,
But for him it was not an important failure; the sun shone
As it had to on the white legs disappearing into the green
Water; and the expensive delicate ship that must have seen
Something amazing, a boy falling out of the sky,   20
Had somewhere to get to and sailed calmly on.

W. H. Auden (1907–1973)

203. On Reading Poems to a Senior Class at South High

Before
I opened my mouth
I noticed them sitting there
as orderly as frozen fish
in a package.   5

Slowly water began to fill the room
though I did not notice it
till it reached
my ears

and then I heard the sounds   10
of fish in an aquarium
and I knew that though I had
tried to drown them
with my words
that they had only opened up   15
like gills for them
and let me in.

Together we swam around the room
like thirty tails whacking words
till the bell rang   20

puncturing
a hole in the door

where we all leaked out

They went to another class
I suppose and I home   25

where Queen Elizabeth
my cat met me
and licked my fins
till they were hands again.

D. C. Berry (b. 1942)

204. The Lamb

Little Lamb, who made thee?
Dost thou know who made thee?
Gave thee life and bid thee feed
By the stream and o'er the mead;
Gave thee clothing of delight,   5
Softest clothing wooly bright;
Gave thee such a tender voice,
Making all the vales rejoice!
  Little Lamb, who made thee?
  Dost thou know who made thee?   10

Little Lamb, I'll tell thee,
Little Lamb, I'll tell thee!
He is callèd by thy name,
For he calls himself a Lamb;
He is meek and he is mild,   15
He became a little child;
I a child and thou a lamb,
We are callèd by his name.
  Little Lamb, God bless thee.
  Little Lamb, God bless thee.   20

William Blake (1757–1827)

205. The Tiger

Tiger! Tiger! burning bright
In the forests of the night,

What immortal hand or eye
Could frame thy fearful symmetry?

In what distant deeps or skies   5
Burnt the fire of thine eyes?
On what wings dare he aspire?
What the hand dare seize the fire?

And what shoulder, and what art,
Could twist the sinews of thy heart?   10
And when thy heart began to beat,
What dread hand forged thy dread feet?

What the hammer? what the chain?
In what furnace was thy brain?
What the anvil? what dread grasp   15
Dare its deadly terrors clasp?

When the stars threw down their spears,
And watered heaven with their tears,
Did he smile his work to see?
Did he who made the Lamb make thee?   20

Tiger! Tiger! burning bright
In the forests of the night,
What immortal hand or eye
Dare frame thy fearful symmetry?

William Blake (1757–1827)

206. Low Barometer

The south wind strengthens to a gale,
Across the moon the clouds fly fast,
The house is smitten as with a flail,
The chimney shudders to the blast.

On such a night, when air has loosed   5
Its guardian grasp on blood and brain,
Old terrors then of god or ghost
Creep from their caves to life again;

And reason kens he herits° in   inherits
A haunted house. Tenants unknown   10
Assert their squalid lease of sin
With earlier title than his own.

Unbodied presences, the packed
Pollution and remorse of time,
Slipped from oblivion, reenact   15
The horrors of unhouseled° crime.   unforgiven

Some men would quell the thing with prayer
Whose sightless footsteps pad the floor,
Whose fearful trespass mounts the stair
Or bursts the locked forbidden door.   20

Some have seen corpses long interred
Escape from hallowing control,
Pale charnel forms—nay, ev'n have heard
The shrilling of a troubled soul,

That wanders till the dawn hath crossed   25
The dolorous dark, or earth hath wound
Closer her storm-spread cloak, and thrust
The baleful phantoms under ground.

Robert Bridges (1844–1930)

207. The Dead

These hearts were woven of human joys and cares,
    Washed marvelously with sorrow, swift to mirth.
The years had given them kindness. Dawn was theirs,
    And sunset, and the colors of the earth.
These had seen movement, and heard music; known   5
    Slumber and waking; loved; gone proudly friended;
Felt the quick stir of wonder; sat alone;
    Touched flowers and furs and cheeks. All this is ended.

There are waters blown by changing winds to laughter
And lit by the rich skies, all day. And after,   10
    Frost, with a gesture, stays the winds that dance
And wandering loveliness. He leaves a white
    Unbroken glory, a gathered radiance,
A width, a shining peace, under the night.

Rupert Brooke (1887–1915)

208. If thou must love me

If thou must love me, let it be for naught
Except for love's sake only. Do not say

"I love her for her smile—her look—her way
Of speaking gently—for a trick of thought
That falls in well with mine, and certes brought   5
A sense of pleasant ease on such a day"—
For these things in themselves, Beloved, may
Be changed, or change for thee—and love, so wrought,
May be unwrought so. Neither love me for
Thine own dear pity's wiping my cheeks dry—   10
A creature might forget to weep, who bore
Thy comfort long, and lose thy love thereby!
But love me for love's sake, that evermore
Thou mayst love on, through love's eternity.

Elizabeth Barrett Browning (1806–1861)

209. Good Times

My Daddy has paid the rent
and the insurance man is gone
and the lights is back on
and my uncle Brud has hit
for one dollar straight   5
and they is good times
good times
good times

My Mama has made bread
and Grampaw has come   10
and everybody is drunk
and dancing in the kitchen
and singing in the kitchen
oh these is good times
good times   15
good times

oh children think about the
good times

Lucille Clifton (b. 1936)

210. The Lost Baby Poem

the time i dropped your almost body down
down to meet the waters under the city
and run one with the sewage to the sea

what did i know about waters rushing back
what did i know about drowning   5
or being drowned

you would have been born into winter
in the year of the disconnected gas
and no car   we would have made the thin
walk over Genesee Hill into Canada wind   10
to watch you slip like ice into strangers' hands
you would have fallen naked as snow into winter
if you were here i could tell you these
and some other things

if i am ever less than a mountain   15
for your definite brothers and sisters
let the rivers pour over my head
let the sea take me for a spiller
of seas   let black men call me stranger
always   for your never named sake   20

Lucille Clifton (b. 1936)

211. Kubla Khan

In Xanadu did Kubla Khan
A stately pleasure-dome decree:
Where Alph, the sacred river, ran
Through caverns measureless to man
    Down to a sunless sea.   5
So twice five miles of fertile ground
With walls and towers were girdled round:
And here were gardens bright with sinuous rills,
Where blossomed many an incense-bearing tree;
And here were forests ancient as the hills,   10
Enfolding sunny spots of greenery.

But oh! that deep romantic chasm which slanted
Down the green hill athwart a cedarn cover!
A savage place! as holy and enchanted
As e'er beneath a waning moon was haunted   15
By woman wailing for her demon-lover!
And from this chasm, with ceaseless turmoil seething,
As if this earth in fast thick pants were breathing,
A mighty fountain momently was forced:

Amid whose swift half-intermitted burst   20
Huge fragments vaulted like rebounding hail,
Or chaffy grain beneath the thresher's flail:
And 'mid these dancing rocks at once and ever
It flung up momently the sacred river.
Five miles meandering with a mazy motion   25
Through wood and dale the sacred river ran,
Then reached the caverns measureless to man,
And sank in tumult to a lifeless ocean:
And 'mid this tumult Kubla heard from far
Ancestral voices prophesying war!   30

   The shadow of the dome of pleasure
   Floated midway on the waves;
   Where was heard the mingled measure
   From the fountain and the caves.
It was a miracle of rare device,   35
A sunny pleasure-dome with caves of ice!

   A damsel with a dulcimer
   In a vision once I saw:
   It was an Abyssinian maid,
   And on her dulcimer she played,   40
   Singing of Mount Abora.
   Could I revive within me
   Her symphony and song,
To such a deep delight, 'twould win me,
That with music loud and long,   45
I would build that dome in air,
That sunny dome! those caves of ice!
And all who heard should see them there,
And all should cry, Beware! Beware!
His flashing eyes, his floating hair!   50
Weave a circle round him thrice,
And close your eyes with holy dread,
For he on honey-dew hath fed,
And drunk the milk of Paradise.

Samuel Taylor Coleridge (1772–1834)

212. Money

   At first it will seem tame,
   willing to be domesticated.

It will nest
in your pocket
or curl up in a corner   5
reciting softly to itself
the names of the presidents.

It will delight your friends,
shake hands with men
like a dog and lick   10
the legs of women.

But like an amoeba
it makes love
in secret
only to itself.   15

Fold it frequently;
it needs exercise.

Water it every three days
and it will repay you
with displays of affection.   20

Then one day when you think
you are its master
it will turn its head
as if for a kiss
and bite you gently   25
on the hand.

There will be no pain
but in thirty seconds
the poison will reach your heart.

Victor Contoski (b. 1936)

213. The Listeners

"Is there anybody there?" said the Traveler,
    Knocking on the moonlit door;
And his horse in the silence champed the grasses
    Of the forest's ferny floor:
And a bird flew up out of the turret,   5
    Above the Traveler's head:
And he smote upon the door again a second time;

"Is there anybody there?" he said.
But no one descended to the Traveler;
   No head from the leaf-fringed sill   10
Leaned over and looked into his grey eyes,
   Where he stood perplexed and still.
But only a host of phantom listeners
   That dwelt in the lone house then
Stood listening in the quiet of the moonlight   15
   To that voice from the world of men:
Stood thronging the faint moonbeams on the dark stair,
   That goes down to the empty hall,
Hearkening in an air stirred and shaken
   By the lonely Traveler's call.   20
And he felt in his heart their strangeness,
   Their stillness answering his cry,
While his horse moved, cropping the dark turf,
   'Neath the starred and leafy sky;
For he suddenly smote on the door, even   25
   Louder, and lifted his head:—
"Tell them I came, and no one answered,
   That I kept my word," he said.
Never the least stir made the listeners,
   Though every word he spake   30
Fell echoing through the shadowiness of the still house
   From the one man left awake:
Ay, they heard his foot upon the stirrup,
   And the sound of iron on stone,
And how the silence surged softly backward,   35
   When the plunging hoofs were gone.

Walter de la Mare (1873–1956)

214. A light exists in spring

A light exists in spring
Not present on the year
At any other period.
When March is scarcely here

A color stands abroad   5
On solitary fields
That science cannot overtake
But human nature feels.

It waits upon the lawn,
It shows the furthest tree   10
Upon the furthest slope you know.
It almost speaks to you.

Then as horizons step
Or noons report away,
Without the formula of sound   15
It passes, and we stay—

A quality of loss
Affecting our content
As trade had suddenly encroached
Upon a sacrament.   20

Emily Dickinson (1830–1886)

215. A narrow fellow in the grass

A narrow fellow in the grass
Occasionally rides—
You may have met him? Did you not,
His notice instant is:

The grass divides as with a comb,   5
A spotted shaft is seen,
And then it closes at your feet
And opens further on.

He likes a boggy acre,
A floor too cool for corn,   10
But when a boy, and barefoot,
I more than once at noon

Have passed, I thought, a whip-lash
Unbraiding in the sun,
When, stooping to secure it,   15
It wrinkled, and was gone.

Several of nature's people
I know, and they know me;
I feel for them a transport
Of cordiality;   20

But never met this fellow,
Attended or alone,
Without a tighter breathing
And zero at the bone.

Emily Dickinson (1830–1886)

216. There's a certain slant of light

There's a certain slant of light,
Winter afternoons,
That oppresses like the heft
Of cathedral tunes.

Heavenly hurt it gives us.   5
We can find no scar
But internal difference
Where the meanings are.

None may teach it any—
'Tis the seal despair,   10
An imperial affliction
Sent us of the air.

When it comes the landscape listens,
Shadows hold their breath.
When it goes 'tis like the distance   15
On the look of death.

Emily Dickinson (1830–1886)

217. The Lipstick on the Mirror

For years the Mirror reported her doings
With every appearance of respect:
What is the Wicked Queen wearing tonight?
Where did she buy her adorable shoes?
How large are her sapphires? How rare   5
Her pearls? Girls throughout the realm
Would lap it up, gazing in their lesser
Mirrors to see themselves in royal attire,
Diadems of diamonds replacing buns

And braids. Her teeth and décolletage   10
Were the envy of women half her age,
Whose compact mirrors would whisper:
Crone, you'd seem chiseled of the same Parian,
With a milder soap, a better dentrifice.
Try these. Buy this. Inhale her fragrance.   15
Industries sprang up like bramble. Families
Grew rich from the sale of ribbons and laces,
Enhancers and foundation creams,
Hosiery and bras, as consumers, enchanted,
Near and far, lavished endearments   20
On softer skin, more sparkling eyes.
In Bogotá, in Marrakesh, among the Slovaks
and the Esths, the face of the distant
Sovereign began to melt and coalesce
With the faces of all women fair and rich: 25
Movie starlets, heiresses, cruel
Dictatrices,° anchorwomen, teen murderesses   female dictators
Able to sell their tales to Hollywood.
In powders and vials the Wicked Queen's
Essence was suffused like a scentless gas   30
Throughout her realm, democratizing
Vanity. Ah, but still, insatiate,
She sits before her Mirror and crimson lips
Tense in a smile to ask her confidante
Who is fairest of them all, and still the lips   35
In the silvered glass reply, "Thou, Majesty, thou."

Tom Disch (b. 1940)

218. The Good-Morrow

I wonder, by my troth, what thou and I
Did till we loved? were we not weaned till then,
But sucked on country pleasures childishly?
Or snorted we in the seven sleepers' den?
'Twas so; but this, all pleasures fancies be.   5
If ever any beauty I did see,
Which I desired, and got, 'twas but a dream of thee.

And now good-morrow to our waking souls,
Which watch not one another out of fear;
For love all love of other sights controls,   10

And makes one little room an everywhere.
Let sea-discoverers to new worlds have gone;
Let maps to other,° worlds on worlds have shown;   others
Let us possess one world; each hath one, and is one.

My face in thine eye, thine in mine appears,   15
And true plain hearts do in the faces rest;
Where can we find two better hemispheres
Without sharp north, without declining west?
Whatever dies was not mixed equally;
If our two loves be one, or thou and I   20
Love so alike that none can slacken, none can die.

                                John Donne (1572–1631)

(4) *seven sleepers' den:* a cave where, according to Christian legend, seven youths escaped persecution and slept for two centuries.

219. Song: Go and catch a falling star

Go and catch a falling star,
    Get with child a mandrake root,
Tell me where all past years are,
    Or who cleft the devil's foot,
Teach me to hear mermaids singing,   5
    Or to keep off envy's stinging,
            And find
            What wind
Serves to advance an honest mind.

If thou be'st born to strange sights,   10
    Things invisible to see,
Ride ten thousand days and nights,
    Till age snow white hairs on thee,
Thou, when thou return'st, wilt tell me
    All strange wonders that befell thee,   15
            And swear
            No where
Lives a woman true and fair.

If thou find'st one, let me know;
    Such a pilgrimage were sweet.   20
Yet do not; I would not go,
    Though at next door we might meet.

> Though she were true when you met her,
>> And last till you write your letter,
>>> Yet she   25
>>>> Will be
>> False, ere I come, to two or three.

John Donne (1572–1631)

(2) *mandrake:* supposed to resemble a human being because of its forked root.

220. The Triple Fool

> I am two fools, I know,
>> For loving, and for saying so
>>> In whining poetry.
> But where's the wiseman that would not be I
>> If she did not deny?   5
> Then, as the earth's inward, narrow, crooked lanes
> Do purge sea water's fretful salt away,
>> I thought if I could draw my pains
> Through rhyme's vexations, I should them allay.
> Grief brought to numbers° cannot be so fierce,   verse   10
> For he tames it that fetters it in verse.

> But when I have done so,
>> Some man, his art and voice to show,
>>> Doth set and sing my pain,
> And by delighting many, frees again   15
>> Grief, which verse did restrain.
> To love and grief tribute of verse belongs,
> But not of such which pleases when 'tis read;°   read aloud
>> Both are increasèd by such songs,
> For both their triumphs so are publishèd.   20
> And I, which was two fools, do so grow three.
> Who are a little wise, the best fools be.

John Donne (1572–1631)

221. Vergissmeinnicht

> Three weeks gone and the combatants gone,
> returning over the nightmare ground
> we found the place again, and found
> the soldier sprawling in the sun.

The frowning barrel of his gun   5
overshadowing. As we came on
that day, he hit my tank with one
like the entry of a demon.

Look. Here in the gunpit spoil
the dishonored picture of his girl   10
who has put: *Steffi.*° *Vergissmeinnicht*   a girl's name
in a copybook gothic script.

We see him almost with content
abased, and seeming to have paid
and mocked at by his own equipment   15
that's hard and good when he's decayed.

But she would weep to see today
how on his skin the swart flies move;
the dust upon the paper eye
and the burst stomach like a cave.   20

For here the lover and killer are mingled
who had one body and one heart.
And death who had the soldier singled
has done the lover mortal hurt.

Keith Douglas (1920–1944)

The German title means "Forget me not." The author, an English poet, fought with a
tank battalion in World War II.

222. The Colonel

What you have heard is true. I was in his house. His wife carried a tray of
coffee and sugar. His daughter filed her nails, his son went out for the
night. There were daily papers, pet dogs, a pistol on the cushion beside
him. The moon swung bare on its black cord over the house. On the television was a cop show. It was in English. Broken bottles were embedded
in the walls around the house to scoop the kneecaps from a man's legs or
cut his hands to lace. On the windows there were gratings like those in
liquor stores. We had dinner, rack of lamb, good wine, a gold bell was on
the table for calling the maid. The maid brought green mangoes, salt, a
type of bread. I was asked how I enjoyed the country. There was a brief
commercial in Spanish. His wife took everything away. There was some
talk then of how difficult it had become to govern. The parrot said hello
on the terrace. The colonel told it to shut up, and pushed himself from

the table. My friend said to me with his eyes: say nothing. The colonel returned with a sack used to bring groceries home. He spilled many human
ears on the table. They were like dried peach halves. There is no other way
to say this. He took one of them in his hands, shook it in our faces, dropped
it into a water glass. It came alive there. I am tired of fooling around he
said. As for the rights of anyone, tell your people they can go fuck themselves. He swept the ears to the floor with his arm and held the last of his
wine in the air. Something for your poetry, no? he said. Some of the ears
on the floor caught this scrap of his voice. Some of the ears on the floor
were pressed to the ground.

May 1978

Carolyn Forché (b. 1950)

223. Birches

When I see birches bend to left and right
Across the lines of straighter darker trees,
I like to think some boy's been swinging them.
But swinging doesn't bend them down to stay
As ice-storms do. Often you must have seen them   5
Loaded with ice a sunny winter morning
After a rain. They click upon themselves
As the breeze rises, and turn many-colored
As the stir cracks and crazes their enamel.
Soon the sun's warmth makes them shed crystal shells   10
Shattering and avalanching on the snow-crust—
Such heaps of broken glass to sweep away
You'd think the inner dome of heaven had fallen.
They are dragged to the withered bracken by the load,
And they seem not to break; though once they are bowed   15
So low for long, they never right themselves:
You may see their trunks arching in the woods
Years afterwards, trailing their leaves on the ground
Like girls on hands and knees that throw their hair
Before them over their heads to dry in the sun.   20
But I was going to say when Truth broke in
With all her matter-of-fact about the ice-storm
I should prefer to have some boy bend them
As he went out and in to fetch the cows—
Some boy too far from town to learn baseball,   25
Whose only play was what he found himself,
Summer or winter, and could play alone.

One by one he subdued his father's trees
By riding them down over and over again
Until he took the stiffness out of them,   30
And not one but hung limp, not one was left
For him to conquer. He learned all there was
To learn about not launching out too soon
And so not carrying the tree away
Clear to the ground. He always kept his poise   35
To the top branches, climbing carefully
With the same pains you use to fill a cup
Up to the brim, and even above the brim.
Then he flung outward, feet first, with a swish,
Kicking his way down through the air to the ground.   40
So was I once myself a swinger of birches.
And so I dream of going back to be.
It's when I'm weary of considerations,
And life is too much like a pathless wood
Where your face burns and tickles with the cobwebs   45
Broken across it, and one eye is weeping
From a twig's having lashed across it open.
I'd like to get away from earth awhile
And then come back to it and begin over.
May no fate willfully misunderstand me   50
And half grant what I wish and snatch me away
Not to return. Earth's the right place for love:
I don't know where it's likely to go better.
I'd like to go by climbing a birch tree,
And climb black branches up a snow-white trunk   55
Toward heaven, till the tree could bear no more,
But dipped its top and set me down again.
That would be good both going and coming back.
One could do worse than be a swinger of birches.

Robert Frost (1874–1963)

224. Desert Places

Snow falling and night falling fast, oh, fast
In a field I looked into going past,
And the ground almost covered smooth in snow,
But a few weeds and stubble showing last.

The woods around it have it—it is theirs.   5
All animals are smothered in their lairs.

I am too absent-spirited to count;
The loneliness includes me unawares.

And lonely as it is that loneliness
Will be more lonely ere it will be less—   10
A blanker whiteness of benighted snow
With no expression, nothing to express.

They cannot scare me with their empty spaces
Between stars—on stars where no human race is.
I have it in me so much nearer home   15
To scare myself with my own desert places.

Robert Frost (1874–1963)

225. Mending Wall

Something there is that doesn't love a wall,
That sends the frozen-ground-swell under it,
And spills the upper boulders in the sun;
And makes gaps even two can pass abreast.
The work of hunters is another thing: 5
I have come after them and made repair
Where they have left not one stone on a stone,
But they would have the rabbit out of hiding,
To please the yelping dogs. The gaps I mean,
No one has seen them made or heard them made,   10
But at spring mending-time we find them there.
I let my neighbor know beyond the hill;
And on a day we meet to walk the line
And set the wall between us once again.
We keep the wall between us as we go.   15
To each the boulders that have fallen to each.
And some are loaves and some so nearly balls
We have to use a spell to make them balance:
"Stay where you are until our backs are turned!"
We wear our fingers rough with handling them.   20
Oh, just another kind of outdoor game,
One on a side. It comes to little more:
There where it is we do not need the wall:
He is all pine and I am apple orchard.
My apple trees will never get across   25
And eat the cones under his pines, I tell him.
He only says, "Good fences make good neighbors."
Spring is the mischief in me, and I wonder

If I could put a notion in his head:
"*Why* do they make good neighbors? Isn't it   30
Where there are cows? But here there are no cows.
Before I built a wall I'd ask to know
What I was walling in or walling out,
And to whom I was like to give offense.
Something there is that doesn't love a wall,   35
That wants it down." I could say "Elves" to him,
But it's not elves exactly, and I'd rather
He said it for himself. I see him there,
Bringing a stone grasped firmly by the top
In each hand, like an old-stone savage armed.   40
He moves in darkness as it seems to me,
Not of woods only and the shade of trees.
He will not go behind his father's saying,
And he likes having thought of it so well
He says again, "Good fences make good neighbors."   45

Robert Frost (1874–1963)

226. Never Again Would Birds' Song Be the Same

He would declare and could himself believe
That the birds there in all the garden round
From having heard the daylong voice of Eve
Had added to their own an oversound,
Her tone of meaning but without the words.   5
Admittedly an eloquence so soft
Could only have had an influence on birds
When call or laughter carried it aloft.
Be that as may be, she was in their song.
Moreover her voice upon their voices crossed   10
Had now persisted in the woods so long
That probably it never would be lost.
Never again would birds' song be the same.
And to do that to birds was why she came.

Robert Frost (1874–1963)

227. The Oven Bird

There is a singer everyone has heard,
Loud, a mid-summer and a mid-wood bird,
Who makes the solid tree trunks sound again.

He says that leaves are old and that for flowers
Mid-summer is to spring as one to ten.   5
He says the early petal-fall is past,
When pear and cherry blooms went down in showers
On sunny days a moment overcast;
And comes that other fall we name the fall.
He says the highway dust is over all.   10
The bird would cease and be as other birds
But that he knows in singing not to sing.
The question that he asks in all but words
Is what to make of a diminished thing.

Robert Frost (1874–1963)

228. Pushing

Me and my brother would jump off the porch
mornings for a better view of the cars
that raced around the corner up Olds Ave.,
naming the make and year; this was '58
and his voice still young enough to wait for   5
how I'd say the names right to the air.
Cold mornings in Lansing we'd stop the mile
to school in the high-priced grocery nearly there
and the owner, maybe a decent White man
whose heavy dark hair and far Lebanese look   10
had caught too many kids at his candy,
would follow us down the aisles and say,
"I know what you boys is up to, big-eyed
and such, so you better be going your way—
buy something or else you got to leave."   15
We'd rattle the pennies we had and go
but coming home buy some nutchews to stay
and try his nerve again, because we didn't steal
but warmed ourselves till Ray would ask me why—
till, like big brothers will, one day I guessed,   20
"Some things you do because you want to.
Some things you do because you can't."
In what midwest warmth there was we'd laugh,
throw some snowballs high where the sun was
breaking up the clouds.   25

Christopher Gilbert (b. 1945)

229. Nikki-Rosa

childhood remembrances are always a drag
if you're Black
you always remember things like living in Woodlawn
with no inside toilet
and if you become famous or something   5
they never talk about how happy you were to have your mother
all to your self and
how good the water felt when you got your bath from one of those
big tubs that folk in chicago barbecue in
and somehow when you talk about home   10
it never gets across how much you
understood their feelings
as the whole family attended meetings about Hollydale
and even though you remember
your biographers never understand   15
your father's pain as he sells his stock
and another dream goes
and though you're poor it isn't poverty that
concerns you
and though they fought a lot   20
it isn't your father's drinking that makes any difference
but only that everybody is together and you
and your sister have happy birthdays and very good christmasses
and I really hope no white person ever has cause to write about me
because they never understand Black love is Black wealth
      and they'll   25
probably talk about my hard childhood and never understand that
all the while I was quite happy.

Nikki Giovanni (b. 1943)

230. The Allegory of the Wolf Boy

The causes are in Time; only their issue
Is bodied in the flesh, the finite powers.
And how to guess he hides in that firm tissue
Seeds of division? At tennis and at tea
Upon the gentle lawn, he is not ours,   5
But plays us in a sad duplicity.

Tonight the boy, still boy open and blond,
Breaks from the house, wedges his clothes between

Two moulded garden urns, and goes beyond
His understanding, through the dark and dust: 10
Fields of sharp stubble, abandoned by machine
To the whirring enmity of insect lust.

As yet ungolden in the dense, hot night
The spikes enter his feet: he seeks the moon,
Which, with the touch of its infertile light,   15
Shall loose desires hoarded against his will
By the long urging of the afternoon.
Slowly the hard rim shifts above the hill.

White in the beam he stops, faces it square,
And the same instant leaping from the ground   20
Feels the familiar itch of close dark hair;
Then, clean exception to the natural laws,
Only to instinct and the moon being bound,
Drops on four feet. Yet he has bleeding paws.

Thom Gunn (b. 1929)

231. On the Move

The blue jay scuffling in the bushes follows
Some hidden purpose, and the gust of birds
That spurts across the field, the wheeling swallows,
Has nested in the trees and undergrowth.
Seeking their instinct, or their poise, or both,   5
One moves with an uncertain violence
Under the dust thrown by a baffled sense
Or the dull thunder of approximate words.

On motorcycles, up the road, they come:
Small, black, as flies hanging in heat, the Boys,   10
Until the distance throws them forth, their hum
Bulges to thunder held by calf and thigh.
In goggles, donned impersonality,
In gleaming jackets trophied with the dust,
They strap in doubt—by hiding it, robust—   15
And almost hear a meaning in their noise.

Exact conclusion of their hardiness
Has no shape yet, but from known whereabouts
They ride, direction where the tires press.
They scare a flight of birds across the field: 20

Much that is natural, to the will must yield.
Men manufacture both machine and soul,
And use what they imperfectly control
To dare a future from the taken routes.

It is a part solution, after all.   25
One is not necessarily discord
On earth; or damned because, half animal,
One lacks direct instinct, because one wakes
Afloat on movement that divides and breaks.
One joins the movement in a valueless world,   30
Choosing it, till, both hurler and the hurled,
One moves as well, always toward, toward.

A minute holds them, who have come to go:
The self-defined, astride the created will
They burst away; the towns they travel through   35
Are home for neither bird nor holiness,
For birds and saints complete their purposes.
At worst, one is in motion; and at best,
Reaching no absolute, in which to rest,
One is always nearer by not keeping still.   40

Thom Gunn (b. 1929)

232. Snow White and the Seven Deadly Sins

Good Catholic girl, she didn't mind the cleaning.
All of her household chores, at first, were small
And hardly labors one could find demeaning.
One's duty was one's refuge, after all.

And if she had her doubts at certain moments   5
And once confessed them to the Father, she
Was instantly referred to texts in Romans
And Peter's First Epistle, chapter III.

Years passed. More sinful every day, the *Seven*
Breakfasted, grabbed their pitchforks, donned their horns,   10
And sped to contravene the hopes of heaven,
Sowing the neighbors' lawns with tares and thorns.

She set to work. *Pride*'s wall of looking glasses
Ogled her dimly, smeared with prints of lips;
Lust's magazines lay strewn, bare tits and asses   15
Weighted by his "devices"—chains, cuffs, whips.

Gluttony's empties covered half the table,
Mingling with *Avarice*'s cards and chips,
And she'd been told to sew a Bill Blass label
Inside the blazer *Envy*'d bought at Gyp's.   20

She knelt to the cold master bathroom floor as
If a petitioner before the Pope,
Retrieving several pairs of *Sloth*'s soiled drawers,
A sweat-sock and a cake of hairy soap.

Then, as she wiped the Windex from the mirror   25
She noticed, and the vision made her cry,
How much she'd grayed and paled, and how much clearer
Festered the bruise of *Wrath* beneath her eye.

"No poisoned apple needed for this Princess,"
She murmured, making X's with her thumb.   30
A car door slammed, bringing her to her senses:
Ho-hum. Ho-hum. It's home from work we come.

And she was out the window in a second,
In time to see a *Handsome Prince,* of course,
Who, spying her distressed condition, beckoned   35
For her to mount (What else?) his snow-white horse.

Impeccably he spoke. His smile was glowing.
So debonair! So charming! And so *Male.*
She took a step, reversed and without slowing
Beat it to St. Anne's where she took the veil.   40

                                        R. S. Gwynn (b. 1948)

233. The Red Hat

It started before Christmas. Now our son
officially walks to school alone.
Semi-alone, it's accurate to say:
I or his father track him on the way.
He walks up on the east side of West End,   5
we on the west side. Glances can extend
(and do) across the street; not eye contact.
Already ties are feeling and not fact.
Straus Park is where these parallel paths part;
he goes alone from there. The watcher's heart   10
stretches, elastic in its love and fear,

toward him as we see him disappear,
striding briskly. Where two weeks ago,
holding a hand, he'd dawdle, dreamy, slow,
he now is hustled forward by the pull   15
of something far more powerful than school.

The mornings we turn back to are no more
than forty minutes longer than before,
but they feel vastly different—flimsy, strange,
wavering in the eddies of this change,   20
empty, unanchored, perilously light
since the red hat vanished from our sight.

Rachel Hadas (b. 1948)

234. Channel Firing

That night your great guns, unawares,
Shook all our coffins as we lay,
And broke the chancel window-squares,
We thought it was the Judgment-day

And sat upright. While drearisome   5
Arose the howl of wakened hounds:
The mouse let fall the altar-crumb,
The worms drew back into the mounds,

The glebe cow drooled. Till God called, "No;
It's gunnery practice out at sea   10
Just as before you went below;
The world is as it used to be:

"All nations striving strong to make
Red war yet redder. Mad as hatters
They do no more for Christès sake   15
Than you who are helpless in such matters.

"That this is not the judgment-hour
For some of them's a blessed thing,
For if it were they'd have to scour
Hell's floor for so much threatening. . . .   20

"Ha, ha. It will be warmer when
I blow the trumpet (if indeed
I ever do; for you are men,
and rest eternal sorely need)."

So down we lay again. "I wonder,   25
Will the world ever saner be,"
Said one, "than when He sent us under
In our indifferent century!"

And many a skeleton shook his head.
"Instead of preaching forty year,"   30
My neighbor Parson Thirdly said,
"I wish I had stuck to pipes and beer."

Again the guns disturbed the hour,
Roaring their readiness to avenge,
As far inland as Stourton Tower,   35
And Camelot, and starlit Stonehenge.

April 1914

Thomas Hardy (1840–1928)

(35–36) *Stourton Tower:* memorial at the spot where Alfred the Great resisted the invading Danes in 879; *Camelot:* legendary capital of Arthur's kingdom; *Stonehenge:* mysterious circle of huge stones erected in Wiltshire by very early inhabitants of Britain. The three references move backward in time through the historic, the legendary, and the prehistoric.

235. The Darkling Thrush

I leant upon a coppice gate
    When Frost was specter-gray,
And Winter's dregs made desolate
    The weakening eye of day.
The tangled bine-stems scored the sky   5
    Like strings of broken lyres,
And all mankind that haunted nigh
    Had sought their household fires.

The land's sharp features seemed to be
    The Century's corpse outleant,   10
His crypt the cloudy canopy,
    The wind his death-lament.
The ancient pulse of germ and birth
    Was shrunken hard and dry,
And every spirit upon earth   15
    Seemed fervorless as I.

At once a voice arose among
    The bleak twigs overhead

In a full-hearted evensong
    Of joy illimited;   20
An aged thrush, frail, gaunt, and small,
    In blast-beruffled plume,
Had chosen thus to fling his soul
    Upon the growing gloom.

So little cause for carolings   25
    Of such ecstatic sound
Was written on terrestrial things
    Afar or nigh around,
That I could think there trembled through
    His happy good-night air   30
Some blessed Hope, whereof he knew
    And I was unaware.

31 December 1900

                      Thomas Hardy (1840–1928)

236. Dream of Fair Women

The lady gave her trust, an apple fell,
And guilt began, and pain, and death as well,
In stories that we tell.

The lady gave her trust, the heavens shone
Upon a maiden mother, one alone   5
In ballads we have known.

O first and second Eve, O dream of men
Believing life is good or might have been
And that we live again!

A sleeping beauty dreams her lover's grace,   10
Opens her eyes upon a human face,
Keeps up the human race.

                    Ann Hayes (b. 1924)

237. Redemption

Having been tenant long to a rich Lord,
    Not thriving, I resolvèd to be bold,
    And make a suit unto him, to afford

A new small-rented lease and cancel the old.
In heaven at his manor I him sought: 5
   They told me there that he was lately gone
   About some land which he had dearly bought
Long since on earth, to take possessiön.
I straight returned, and knowing his great birth,
   Sought him accordingly in great resorts;   10
   In cities, theaters, gardens, parks, and courts:
At length I heard a ragged noise and mirth
   Of thieves and murderers; there I him espied,
   Who straight, "Your suit is granted," said, and died.

George Herbert (1593–1633)

238. Riddle

From Belsen a crate of gold teeth,
from Dachau a mountain of shoes,
from Auschwitz a skin lampshade.
Who killed the Jews?

Not I, cries the typist,   5
not I, cries the engineer,
not I, cries Adolf Eichmann,
not I, cries Albert Speer.

My friend Fritz Nova lost his father—
a petty official had to choose.   10
My friend Lou Abrahms lost his brother.
Who killed the Jews?

David Nova swallowed gas,
Hyman Abrahms was beaten and starved.
Some men signed their papers,   15
and some stood guard,

and some herded them in,
and some dropped the pellets,
and some spread the ashes,
and some hosed the walls,   20

and some planted the wheat,
and some poured the steel,
and some cleared the rails,
and some raised the cattle.

Some smelled the smoke,   25
some just heard the news.
Were they Germans? Were they Nazis?
Were they human? Who killed the Jews?

The stars will remember the gold,
the sun will remember the shoes,   30
the moon will remember the skin.
But who killed the Jews?

William Heyen (b. 1940)

(1–3) *Belsen, Dachau, Auschwitz:* sites of Nazi concentration camps. (7) *Adolf Eichmann* (1906–1962), Nazi official who organized anti-Jewish activities, especially the shipping of Jews to the concentration camps. (8) *Albert Speer* (1905–1981), Hitler's chief architect and later minister of armaments whose efficient methods greatly improved the production of war materials.

239. Two Different Things

A coyote paces the enclosure,
his eyes looking toward the hills.
His paws had been stung by barbed wire and broken
    glass
until the pads were cracked and bloodied.
He was crying to the moon when you found him.   5
You brought fresh water, healed his paws,
And now you say you love him.

While he paces that enclosure
You cannot be free.

Part of his beauty   10
is the dream in his eyes of different places.
Whatever is human feels the need to possess
that, to tame that, to say: *he's mine,*
if only for a moment, and then let go.
He might come back: 15
depending less on gratitude and love
than on nostalgia for old places,
a familiar voice.

In the meantime, there's you on one side,
him on the other,   20
wanting two different things—always.

Something in you wishes he could be free
with your fence still around him.
Something in him will pull and tug
long after he leaves your hills.   25

Michael Hogan (b. 1943)

240. To an Athlete Dying Young

The time you won your town the race
We chaired you through the market-place;
Man and boy stood cheering by,
And home we brought you shoulder-high.

Today, the road all runners come,   5
Shoulder-high, we bring you home,
And set you at your threshold down,
Townsman of a stiller town.

Smart lad, to slip betimes away
From fields where glory does not stay   10
And early though the laurel grows
It withers quicker than the rose.

Eyes the shady night has shut
Cannot see the record cut,
And silence sounds no worse than cheers   15
After earth has stopped the ears:

Now you will not swell the rout
Of lads that wore their honors out,
Runners whom renown outran
And the name died before the man.   20

So set, before its echoes fade,
The fleet foot on the sill of shade,
And hold to the low lintel up
The still-defended challenge-cup.

And round that early-laureled head   25
Will flock to gaze the strengthless dead,
And find unwithered on its curls
The garland briefer than a girl's.

A. E. Housman (1859–1936)

241. Bredon Hill

In summertime on Bredon
  The bells they sound so clear;
Round both the shires they ring them
  In steeples far and near,
  A happy noise to hear.   5

Here of a Sunday morning
  My love and I would lie,
And see the colored counties,
  And hear the larks so high
  About us in the sky.   10

The bells would ring to call her
  In valleys miles away:
"Come all to church, good people;
  Good people, come and pray."
  But here my love would stay.   15

And I would turn and answer
  Among the springing thyme,
"Oh, peal upon our wedding,
  And we will hear the chime,
  And come to church in time."   20

But when the snows at Christmas
  On Bredon top were strown,
My love rose up so early
  And stole out unbeknown
  And went to church alone.   25

They tolled the one bell only,
  Groom there was none to see,
The mourners followed after,
  And so to church went she,
  And would not wait for me.   30

The bells they sound on Bredon,
  And still the steeples hum.
"Come all to church, good people,"—
  Oh, noisy bells, be dumb;
  I hear you, I will come.   35

A. E. Housman (1859–1936)

242. Thistles

Against the rubber tongues of cows and the hoeing hands of men
Thistles spike the summer air
Or crackle open under a blue-black pressure.

Every one a revengeful burst
Of resurrection, a grasped fistful   5
Of splintered weapons and Icelandic frost thrust up

From the underground stain of a decayed Viking.
They are like pale hair and the gutturals of dialects.
Every one manages a plume of blood.

Then they grow grey, like men.   10
Mown down, it is a feud. Their sons appear,
Stiff with weapons, fighting back over the same ground.

Ted Hughes (b. 1930)

243. The Freaks at Spurgin Road Field

The dim boy claps because the others clap.
The polite word, handicapped, is muttered in the stands.
Isn't it wrong, the way the mind moves back.

One whole day I sit, contrite, dirt, L.A.
Union Station, '46, sweating through last night.   5
The dim boy claps because the others clap.

Score, 5 to 3. Pitcher fading badly in the heat.
Isn't it wrong to be or not be spastic?
Isn't it wrong, the way the mind moves back.

I'm laughing at a neighbor girl beaten to scream   10
by a savage father and I'm ashamed to look.
The dim boy claps because the others clap.

The score is always close, the rally always short.
I've left more wreckage than a quake.
Isn't it wrong, the way the mind moves back.   15

The afflicted never cheer in unison.
Isn't it wrong, the way the mind moves back
to stammering pastures where the picnic should have worked.
The dim boy claps because the others clap.

Richard Hugo (1923–1982)

244. The Death of the Ball Turret Gunner

From my mother's sleep I fell into the State,
And I hunched in its belly till my wet fur froze.
Six miles from earth, loosed from its dream of life,
I woke to black flak and the nightmare fighters.
When I died they washed me out of the turret with a hose.   5

Randall Jarrell (1914–1965)

(Title) *Ball Turret:* the poet wrote, "A ball turret was a plexiglass sphere set into the belly of a B-17 or B-24 [bomber during World War II], and inhabited by two .50 caliber machine-guns and one man, a short small man. When this gunner tracked with his machine-guns a fighter [plane] attacking from below, he revolved with the turret; hunched in his little sphere, he looked like the fetus in the womb."

245. Song: To Celia

Drink to me only with thine eyes,
  And I will pledge with mine;
Or leave a kiss but in the cup,
  And I'll not look for wine.
The thirst that from the soul doth rise   5
  Doth ask a drink divine,
But might I of Jove's nectar sup,
  I would not change for thine.

I sent thee late° a rosy wreath,   recently
  Not so much honoring thee   10
As giving it a hope that there
  It could not withered be.
But thou thereon didst only breathe,
  And sent'st it back to me;
Since when, it grows, and smells, I swear,   15
  Not of itself, but thee.

Ben Jonson (1573?–1637)

246. Warning

When I am an old woman I shall wear purple
With a red hat which doesn't go, and doesn't suit me.
And I shall spend my pension on brandy and summer gloves

And satin sandals, and say we've no money for butter.
I shall sit down on the pavement when I'm tired   5
And gobble up samples in shops and press alarm bells
And run my stick along the public railings
And make up for the sobriety of my youth.
I shall go out in my slippers in the rain
And pick the flowers in other people's gardens   10
And learn to spit.

You can wear terrible shirts and grow more fat
And eat three pounds of sausages at a go
Or only bread and pickle for a week
And hoard pens and pencils and beermats and things in boxes.   15

But now we must have clothes that keep us dry
And pay our rent and not swear in the street
And set a good example for the children.
We must have friends to dinner and read the papers.

But maybe I ought to practice a little now?   20
So people who know me are not too shocked and surprised
When suddenly I am old, and start to wear purple.

Jenny Joseph (b. 1932)

247. La Belle Dame sans Merci

A Ballad

O, what can ail thee, knight-at-arms,
    Alone and palely loitering?
The sedge has withered from the lake,
    And no birds sing.

O, what can ail thee, knight-at-arms,   5
    So haggard and so woe-begone?
The squirrel's granary is full,
    And the harvest's done.

I see a lily on thy brow,
    With anguish moist and fever dew;   10
And on thy cheeks a fading rose
    Fast withereth too.

I met a lady in the meads,
    Full beautiful—a faery's child,
Her hair was long, her foot was light,   15
    And her eyes were wild.

I made a garland for her head,
  And bracelets too, and fragrant zone;
She looked at me as she did love,
  And made sweet moan.   20

I set her on my pacing steed,
  And nothing else saw all day long;
For sidelong would she bend, and sing
  A faery's song.

She found me roots of relish sweet,   25
  And honey wild, and manna dew,
And sure in language strange she said—
  "I love thee true."

She took me to her elfin grot,
  And there she wept and sighed full sore,   30
And there I shut her wild wild eyes
  With kisses four.

And there she lullèd me asleep
  And there I dreamed—Ah! woe betide!
The latest dream I ever dreamed   35
  On the cold hill side.

I saw pale kings and princes too,
  Pale warriors, death-pale were they all;
They cried—"La Belle Dame sans Merci
  Hath thee in thrall!"   40

I saw their starved lips in the gloam
  With horrid warning gapèd wide,
And I awoke and found me here
  On the cold hill's side.

And this is why I sojourn here   45
  Alone and palely loitering,
Though the sedge has withered from the lake,
  And no birds sing.

John Keats (1795–1821)

The title means "The beautiful lady without pity."

248. Ode on a Grecian Urn

Thou still unravished bride of quietness,
  Thou foster-child of silence and slow time,

Sylvan historian, who canst thus express
  A flowery tale more sweetly than our rhyme:
What leaf-fringed legend haunts about thy shape   5
  Of deities or mortals, or of both,
    In Tempe or the dales of Arcady?
  What men or gods are these? What maidens loth?
What mad pursuit? What struggle to escape?
    What pipes and timbrels? What wild ecstasy?   10

Heard melodies are sweet, but those unheard
  Are sweeter; therefore, ye soft pipes, play on;
Not to the sensual ear, but, more endeared,
  Pipe to the spirit ditties of no tone:
Fair youth, beneath the trees, thou canst not leave   15
  Thy song, nor ever can those trees be bare;
    Bold lover, never, never canst thou kiss,
Though winning near the goal—yet, do not grieve;
    She cannot fade, though thou hast not thy bliss,
For ever wilt thou love, and she be fair!   20

Ah, happy, happy boughs! that cannot shed
  Your leaves, nor ever bid the spring adieu;
And, happy melodist, unwearièd,
  For ever piping songs for ever new;
More happy love! more happy, happy love!   25
  For ever warm and still to be enjoyed,
    For ever panting and for ever young;
All breathing human passion far above,
  That leaves a heart high-sorrowful and cloyed,
    A burning forehead, and a parching tongue.   30

Who are these coming to the sacrifice?
  To what green altar, O mysterious priest,
Lead'st thou that heifer lowing at the skies,
  And all her silken flanks with garlands drest?
What little town by river or sea shore,   35
  Or mountain-built with peaceful citadel,
    Is emptied of its folk, this pious morn?
And, little town, thy streets for evermore
  Will silent be; and not a soul to tell
    Why thou are desolate, can e'er return.   40

O Attic shape! Fair attitude! with brede
  Of marble men and maidens overwrought,
With forest branches and the trodden weed;
  Thou, silent form, dost tease us out of thought

As doth eternity: Cold Pastoral!   45
    When old age shall this generation waste,
        Thou shalt remain, in midst of other woe
    Than ours, a friend to man, to whom thou say'st,
Beauty is truth, truth beauty,—that is all
        Ye know on earth, and all ye need to know.   50

John Keats (1795–1821)

(40–50) In the 1820 edition of Keats's poems the words "Beauty is truth, truth beauty" were enclosed in quotation marks, and the poem is often reprinted that way. It is now generally agreed, however, on the basis of contemporary transcripts of Keats's poem, that Keats intended the entire last two lines to be spoken by the urn.

249. Ode to a Nightingale

My heart aches, and a drowsy numbness pains
    My sense, as though of hemlock° I had drunk,   *a poison*
Or emptied some dull opiate to the drains
    One minute past, and Lethe-wards had sunk:
'Tis not through envy of thy happy lot,   5
    But being too happy in thine happiness,—
        That thou, light-wingèd Dryad° of the trees,   *wood nymph*
            In some melodious plot
    Of beechen green, and shadows numberless,
        Singest of summer in full-throated ease.   10

O for a draught of vintage! that hath been
    Cooled a long age in the deep-delvèd earth,
Tasting of Flora° and the country green,   *goddess of flowers*
    Dance, and Provençal song, and sunburnt mirth!
O for a beaker full of the warm South,   15
    Full of the true, the blushful Hippocrene,
        With beaded bubbles winking at the brim,
            And purple-stainèd mouth;
    That I might drink, and leave the world unseen,
        And with thee fade away into the forest dim: 20

Fade far away, dissolve, and quite forget
    What thou among the leaves hast never known,
The weariness, the fever, and the fret
    Here, where men sit and hear each other groan;
Where palsy shakes a few, sad, last gray hairs,   25
        Where youth grows pale, and specter-thin, and dies;
        Where but to think is to be full of sorrow

And leaden-eyed despairs,
  Where Beauty cannot keep her lustrous eyes,
    Or new Love pine at them beyond tomorrow.   30

Away! away! for I will fly to thee,
  Not charioted by Bacchus and his pards,
But on the viewless° wings of Poesy,   *invisible*
  Though the dull brain perplexes and retards:
Already with thee! tender is the night,   35
  And haply the Queen-Moon is on her throne,
    Clustered around by all her starry Fays;
      But here there is no light,
  Save what from heaven is with the breezes blown
    Through verdurous glooms and winding mossy ways.   40

I cannot see what flowers are at my feet,
  Nor what soft incense hangs upon the boughs,
But, in embalmèd° darkness, guess each sweet   *perfumed*
  Wherewith the seasonable mouth endows
The grass, the thicket, and the fruit-tree wild;   45
  White hawthorn, and the pastoral eglantine;
    Fast fading violets covered up in leaves;
      And mid-May's eldest child,
The coming musk-rose, full of dewy wine,
    The murmurous haunt of flies on summer eves.   50

Darkling° I listen; and, for many a time   *in darkness*
  I have been half in love with easeful Death,
Called him soft names in many a musèd rhyme,
  To take into the air my quiet breath;
Now more than ever seems it rich to die,   55
  To cease upon the midnight with no pain,
    While thou art pouring forth thy soul abroad
      In such an ecstasy!
  Still wouldst thou sing, and I have ears in vain—
    To thy high requiem become a sod.   60

Thou wast not born for death, immortal Bird!
  No hungry generations tread thee down;
The voice I hear this passing night was heard
  In ancient days by emperor and clown:
Perhaps the self-same song that found a path   65
  Through the sad heart of Ruth, when, sick for home,
    She stood in tears amid the alien corn;
      The same that oft-times hath
Charmed magic casements, opening on the foam
    Of perilous seas, in faery lands forlorn.   70

Forlorn! the very word is like a bell
  To toll me back from thee to my sole self!
Adieu! the fancy cannot cheat so well
  As she is famed to do, deceiving elf.
Adieu! adieu! thy plaintive anthem fades   75
  Past the near meadows, over the still stream,
    Up the hill-side; and now 'tis buried deep
      In the next valley-glades:
Was it a vision, or a waking dream?
  Fled is that music:—Do I wake or sleep?   80

John Keats (1795–1821)

(4) *Lethe:* river of forgetfulness in the Greek underworld. (14) *Provençal:* Provence, a wine-growing region in southern France famous, in the Middle Ages, for troubadours. (16) *Hippocrene:* fountain of the Muses on Mt. Helicon in Greece. (32) *Bacchus . . . pards:* Bacchus, god of wine, had a chariot drawn by leopards. (66) *Ruth:* see Bible, Ruth 2.

250. The warden said to me

The warden said to me the other day
(innocently, I think), "Say, etheridge,
why come the black boys don't run off
like the white boys do?"
I lowered my jaw and scratched my head   5
and said (innocently, I think), "Well, suh,
I ain't for sure, but I reckon it's cause
we ain't got no wheres to run to."

Etheridge Knight (1933–1991)

251. The Sound of Night

And now the dark comes on, all full of chitter noise.
Birds huggermugger crowd the trees,
the air thick with their vesper cries,
and bats, snub seven-pointed kites,
skitter across the lake, swing out,   5
squeak, chirp, dip, and skim on skates
of air, and the fat frogs wake and prink
wide-lipped, noisy as ducks, drunk
on the boozy black, gloating chink-chunk.

And now on the narrow beach we defend ourselves from dark.   10
The cooking done, we build our firework
bright and hot and less for outlook
than for magic, and lie in our blankets
while night nickers around us. Crickets
chorus hallelujahs; paws, quiet   15
and quick as raindrops, play on the stones
expertly soft, run past and are gone;
fish pulse in the lake; the frogs hoarsen.

Now every voice of the hour—the known, the supposed,
    the strange,
the mindless, the witted, the never seen—   20
sing, thrum, impinge, and rearrange
endlessly; and debarred from sleep we wait
for the birds, importantly silent,
for the crease of first eye-licking light,
for the sun, lost long ago and sweet.   25
By the lake, locked black away and tight,
we lie, day creatures, overhearing night.

                              Maxine Kumin (b. 1925)

252. Aubade

I work all day, and get half drunk at night.
Waking at four to soundless dark, I stare.
In time the curtain-edges will grow light.
Till then I see what's really always there:
Unresting death, a whole day nearer now,   5
Making all thought impossible but how
And where and when I shall myself die.
Arid interrogation: yet the dread
Of dying, and being dead,
Flashes afresh to hold and horrify.   10

The mind blanks at the glare. Not in remorse
—The good not done, the love not given, time
Torn off unused—nor wretchedly because
An only life can take so long to climb
Clear of its wrong beginnings, and may never;   15
But at the total emptiness for ever,
The sure extinction that we travel to
And shall be lost in always. Not to be here,
Not to be anywhere,
And soon; nothing more terrible, nothing more true.   20

This is a special way of being afraid
No trick dispels. Religion used to try,
That vast moth-eaten musical brocade
Created to pretend we never die,
And specious stuff that says *No rational being*   25
Can fear a thing it will not feel, not seeing
That this is what we fear—no sight, no sound,
No touch or taste or smell, nothing to think with,
Nothing to love or link with,
The anaesthetic from which none come round.   30

And so it stays just on the edge of vision,
A small unfocused blur, a standing chill
That slows each impulse down to indecision.
Most things may never happen: this one will,
And realization of it rages out   35
In furnace-fear when we are caught without
People or drink. Courage is no good:
It means not scaring others. Being brave
Lets no one off the grave.
Death is no different whined at than withstood.   40

Slowly light strengthens, and the room takes shape.
It stands plain as a wardrobe, what we know,
Have always known, know that we can't escape,
Yet can't accept. One side will have to go.
Meanwhile telephones crouch, getting ready to ring   45
In locked-up offices, and all the uncaring
Intricate rented world begins to rouse.
The sky is white as clay, with no sun.
Work has to be done.
Postmen like doctors go from house to house.   50

Philip Larkin (1922–1985)

253. Offspring

I tried to tell her:
　　This way the twig is bent.
　　Born of my trunk and strengthened by my roots,
　　you must stretch newgrown branches
　　closer to the sun   5
　　than I can reach.

I wanted to say:
    Extend my self to that far atmosphere
    only my dreams allow.

But the twig broke,   10
and yesterday I saw her
walking down an unfamiliar street,
    feet confident
    face slanted upward toward a threatening sky,
and   15
    she was smiling
    and she was
    her very free,
    her very individual,
    unpliable   20
    own.

Naomi Long Madgett (b. 1923)

254. Life with Father

Sunday meant sleeping in,
time to pull another quilt
and hide from whiskey
in our daddy's snoring.

Only the Sunday funnies saved us   5
after last night's raving,
proof there was a demon.
Under covers we traded peeks

at Maggie giving Jiggs
the devil, Dagwood   10
bumbling about insanely sober,
tiny Wash Tubbs with twins

he doted over. At dawn
we folded the quilts
and funnies, crept softly   15
through our chores

as if in church,
soothing the fi-foe-fum
of his slumber, fearing
the thrum of his boots   20

descending the heavy
stalk of his stupor,
fierce when he found
his dreamed gold gone.

Walter McDonald (b. 1934)

(9–12) *Maggie . . . Tubbs:* characters in comic strips called, respectively, "Bringing Up Father," "Blondie," and "Captain Easy."

255. What Are Years?

What is our innocence,
what is our guilt? All are
    naked, none is safe. And whence
is courage: the unanswered question,
the resolute doubt,—   5
dumbly calling, deafly listening—that
in misfortune, even death,
        encourages others
        and in its defeat, stirs

    the soul to be strong? He   10
sees deep and is glad, who
    accedes to mortality
and in his imprisonment rises
upon himself as
the sea in a chasm, struggling to be   15
free and unable to be,
        in its surrendering
        finds its continuing.

    So he who strongly feels,
behaves. The very bird,   20
    grown taller as he sings, steels
his form straight up. Though he is captive,
his mighty singing
says, satisfaction is a lowly
thing, how pure a thing is joy.   25
        This is mortality,
        this is eternity.

Marianne Moore (1887–1972)

256. Adieu, farewell, earth's bliss

Adieu, farewell, earth's bliss;
This world uncertain is;
Fond° are life's lustful joys;   foolish
Death proves them all but toys;°   trifles
None from his darts can fly;   5
I am sick, I must die.
      Lord, have mercy on us!

Rich men, trust not in wealth,
Gold cannot buy you health;
Physic° himself must fade.   medicine   10
All things to end are made.
The plague full swift goes by;
I am sick, I must die.
      Lord, have mercy on us!

Beauty is but a flower   15
Which wrinkles will devour;
Brightness falls from the hair;
Queens have died young and fair;
Dust hath closed Helen's eye.
I am sick, I must die.   20
      Lord, have mercy on us!

Strength stoops unto the grave,
Worms feed on Hector brave;
Swords may not fight with fate,
Earth still holds ope her gate.   25
"Come, come," the bells do cry.
I am sick, I must die.
      Lord, have mercy on us!

Wit° with his wantonness   intelligence
Tasteth death's bitterness;   30
Hell's executioner
Hath no ears for to hear
What vain art can reply.
I am sick, I must die.
      Lord, have mercy on us!   35

Haste, therefore, each degree,°   social rank
To welcome destiny;
Heaven is our heritage,
Earth but a player's stage;

Mount we unto the sky.   40
I am sick, I must die.
        Lord, have mercy on us.

                                    Thomas Nashe (1567–1601)

257. what gramma said about her grandpa

he was white grandpa
his name jim butler
he's good irish man
he was nice talk our
language   5
big man with moustache
boss of town
tonopah°   in southwest Nevada
he found silver mine
we still on reservation they   10
come tell us "your grandpa
found mine" so
we move to tonopah
he say "buy anything you want
don't buy just little things   15
don't buy just candy
buy something big"
that's what he used to say
4th of july he make
a great long table   20
put sheet over it
then put all kinds of food on it
he say "get your plate &
help yourselves"
he fed all the indians   25
he was good man
but then
he marry white woman
& we go back to reservation

                                    nila northSun (b. 1951)

258. The Victims

When Mother divorced you, we were glad. She took it and
took it, in silence, all those years and then

kicked you out, suddenly, and her
kids loved it. Then you were fired, and we
grinned inside, the way people grinned when   5
Nixon's helicopter lifted off the South
Lawn for the last time. We were tickled
to think of your office taken away,
your secretaries taken away,
your luncheons with three double bourbons,   10
your pencils, your reams of paper. Would they take your
suits back, too, those dark
carcasses hung in your closet, and the black
noses of your shoes with their large pores?
She had taught us to take it, to hate you and take it   15
until we pricked with her for your
annihilation, Father. Now I
pass the bums in doorways, the white
slugs of their bodies gleaming through slits in their
suits of compressed silt, the stained   20
flippers of their hands, the underwater
fire of their eyes, ships gone down with the
lanterns lit, and I wonder who took it and
took it from them in silence until they had
given it all away and had nothing   25
left but this.

Sharon Olds (b. 1942)

259. Speaking

I take him outside
under the trees,
have him stand on the ground.
We listen to the crickets,
cicadas, million years old sound.   5
Ants come by us.
I tell them,
"This is he, my son.
This boy is looking at you.
I am speaking for him."   10

The crickets, cicadas,
the ants, the millions of years
are watching us,
hearing us.
My son murmurs infant words,   15

speaking, small laughter
bubbles from him.
Tree leaves tremble.
They listen to this boy
speaking for me.   20

Simon J. Ortiz (b. 1941)

260. The Sad Children's Song

This house is a wreck said the children
when they came home with their children
Your papers are all over the place
The chairs are covered with books
and look   brown leaves are piled on the floor   5
under the wandering Jews

Your face is a wreck said the children
when they came home with their children
There are lines all over your face
your necks like curious turtles   10
Why did you let yourself go?
Where are you going without us?

This world is a wreck said the children
When they came home with their children
There are bombs all over the place   15
There's no water   the fields are all poisoned
Why did you leave things like this
Where can we go said the children
what can we say to our children?

Grace Paley (b. 1922)

261. The Hat Lady

In a childhood of hats—
my uncles in homburgs and derbies,
Fred Astaire in high black silk,
the yarmulke my grandfather wore
like the palm of a hand   5
cradling the back of his head—
only my father went hatless,
even in winter.

And in the spring,
when a turban of leaves appeared   10
on every tree, the Hat Lady came
with a fan of pins in her mouth
and pins in her sleeves,
the Hat Lady came—
that Saint Sebastian of pins,   15
to measure my mother's head.

I remember a hat of dove-grey felt
that settled like a bird
on the nest of my mother's hair.
I remember a pillbox that tilted   20
over one eye—pure Myrna Loy,
and a navy straw with cherries caught
at the brim that seemed real enough
for a child to want to pick.

Last year when the chemicals   25
took my mother's hair, she wrapped
a towel around her head. And the Hat Lady came,
a bracelet of needles on each arm,
and led her to a place
where my father and grandfather waited,   30
head to bare head, and Death
winked at her and tipped his cap.

                                                   Linda Pastan (b. 1932)

(3) *Fred Astaire* and (21) *Myrna Loy:* popular film stars of the mid-twentieth century.

262. The Imperfect Paradise

If God had stopped work after the fifth day
With Eden full of vegetables and fruits,
If oak and lilac held exclusive sway
Over a kingdom made of stems and roots,
If landscape were the genius of creation   5
And neither man nor serpent played a role
And God must look to wind for lamentation
And not to picture postcards of the soul,
Would he have rested on his bank of cloud
With nothing in the universe to lose,   10
Or would he hunger for a human crowd?

Which would a wise and just creator choose:
The green hosannas of a budding leaf
Or the strict contract between love and grief?

Linda Pastan (b. 1932)

263. A Work of Artifice

The bonsai tree
in the attractive pot
could have grown eighty feet tall
on the side of a mountain
till split by lightning.   5
But a gardener
carefully pruned it.
It is nine inches high.
Every day as he
whittles back the branches   10
the gardener croons,
It is your nature
to be small and cozy,
domestic and weak;
how lucky, little tree,   15
to have a pot to grow in.
With living creatures
one must begin very early
to dwarf their growth:
the bound feet,   20
the crippled brain,
the hair in curlers,
the hands you
love to touch.

Marge Piercy (b. 1934)

264. Spinster

Now this particular girl
During a ceremonious April walk
With her latest suitor
Found herself, of a sudden, intolerably struck
By the birds' irregular babel   5
And the leaves' litter.

By this tumult afflicted, she
Observed her lover's gestures unbalance the air,
His gait stray uneven
Through a rank wilderness of fern and flower.   10
She judged petals in disarray,
The whole season, sloven.

How she longed for winter then!—
Scrupulously austere in its order
Of white and black   15
Ice and rock, each sentiment within border,
And heart's frosty discipline
Exact as a snowflake.

But here—a burgeoning
Unruly enough to pitch her five queenly wits   20
Into vulgar motley—
A treason not to be borne. Let idiots
Reel giddy in bedlam spring:
She withdrew neatly.

And round her house she set   25
Such a barricade of barb and check
Against mutinous weather
As no mere insurgent man could hope to break
With curse, fist, threat
Or love, either.   30

Sylvia Plath (1932–1963)

265. Getting Through

Like a car stuck in gear,
a chicken too stupid to tell
its head is gone,
or sound ratcheting on
long after the film   5
has jumped the reel,
or a phone
ringing and ringing
in the house they have all
moved away from,   10
through rooms where dust

is a deepening skin,
and the locks unneeded,
so I go on loving you,
my heart blundering on,   15
a muscle spilling out
what is no longer wanted,
and my words hurtling past,
like a train off its track,
toward a boarded-up station,   20
closed for years,
like some last speaker
of a beautiful language
no one else can hear.

Deborah Pope

266. Bells for John Whiteside's Daughter

There was such speed in her little body,
And such lightness in her footfall,
It is no wonder her brown study
Astonishes us all.

Her wars were bruited in our high window.   5
We looked among orchard trees and beyond
Where she took arms against her shadow,
Or harried unto the pond

The lazy geese, like a snow cloud
Dripping their snow on the green grass,   10
Tricking and stopping, sleepy and proud,
Who cried in goose, Alas,

For the tireless heart within the little
Lady with rod that made them rise
From their noon apple-dreams and scuttle   15
Goose-fashion under the skies!

But now go the bells, and we are ready,
In one house we are sternly stopped
To say we are vexed at her brown study,
Lying so primly propped.   20

John Crowe Ransom (1888–1974)

267. Aunt Jennifer's Tigers

Aunt Jennifer's tigers prance across a screen,
Bright topaz denizens of a world of green.
They do not fear the men beneath the tree;
They pace in sleek chivalric certainty.

Aunt Jennifer's fingers fluttering through her wool   5
Find even the ivory needle hard to pull.
The massive weight of Uncle's wedding band
Sits heavily upon Aunt Jennifer's hand.

When Aunt is dead, her terrified hands will lie
Still ringed with ordeals she was mastered by.   10
The tigers in the panel that she made
Will go on prancing, proud and unafraid.

Adrienne Rich (b. 1929)

268. Living in Sin

She had thought the studio would keep itself;
no dust upon the furniture of love.
Half heresy, to wish the taps less vocal,
the panes relieved of grime. A plate of pears,
a piano with a Persian shawl, a cat   5
stalking the picturesque amusing mouse
had risen at his urging.
Not that at five each separate stair would writhe
under the milkman's tramp; that morning light
so coldly would delineate the scraps   10
of last night's cheese and three sepulchral bottles;
that on the kitchen shelf among the saucers
a pair of beetle-eyes would fix her own—
envoy from some village in the moldings . . .
Meanwhile, he, with a yawn,   15
sounded a dozen notes upon the keyboard,
declared it out of tune, shrugged at the mirror,
rubbed at his beard, went out for cigarettes;
while she, jeered by the minor demons,
pulled back the sheets and made the bed and found   20
a towel to dust the table-top,
and let the coffee-pot boil over on the stove.
By evening she was back in love again,
though not so wholly but throughout the night

she woke sometimes to feel the daylight coming   25
like a relentless milkman up the stairs.

Adrienne Rich (b. 1929)

269. Nani

Sitting at her table, she serves
the sopa de arroz° to me   rice soup
instinctively, and I watch her,
the absolute *mamá,* and eat words
I might have had to say more   5
out of embarrassment. To speak,
now-foreign words I used to speak,
too, dribble down her mouth as she serves
me albóndigas.° No more   spiced meatballs
than a third are easy to me.   10
By the stove she does something with words
and looks at me only with her
back. I am full. I tell her
I taste the mint, and watch her speak
smiles at the stove. All my words   15
make her smile. Nani° never serves   granny
herself, she only watches me
with her skin, her hair. I ask for more.

I watch the *mamá* warming more
tortillas for me. I watch her   20
fingers in the flame for me.
Near her mouth, I see a wrinkle speak
of a man whose body serves
the ants like she serves me, then more words
from more wrinkles about children, words   25
about this and that, flowing more
easily from these other mouths. Each serves
as a tremendous string around her,
holding her together. They speak
nani was this and that to me   30
and I wonder just how much of me
will die with her, what were the words
I could have been, was. Her insides speak
through a hundred wrinkles, now, more
than she can bear, steel around her,   35
shouting, then, What is this thing she serves?

She asks me if I want more.
I own no words to stop her.
Even before I speak, she serves.

Alberto Ríos (b. 1952)

270. Mr. Flood's Party

Old Eben Flood, climbing alone one night
Over the hill between the town below
And the forsaken upland hermitage
That held as much as he should ever know
On earth again of home, paused warily.   5
The road was his with not a native near;
And Eben, having leisure, said aloud,
For no man else in Tilbury Town to hear:

"Well, Mr. Flood, we have the harvest moon
Again, and we may not have many more;   10
The bird is on the wing, the poet says,
And you and I have said it here before.
Drink to the bird." He raised up to the light
The jug that he had gone so far to fill,
And answered huskily: "Well, Mr. Flood,   15
Since you propose it, I believe I will."

Alone, as if enduring to the end
A valiant armor of scarred hopes outworn,
He stood there in the middle of the road
Like Roland's ghost winding a silent horn.   20
Below him, in the town among the trees,
Where friends of other days had honored him,
A phantom salutation of the dead
Rang thinly till old Eben's eyes were dim.

Then, as a mother lays her sleeping child   25
Down tenderly, fearing it may awake,
He set the jug down slowly at his feet
With trembling care, knowing that most things break;
And only when assured that on firm earth
It stood, as the uncertain lives of men   30
Assuredly did not, he paced away,
And with his hand extended, paused again:

"Well, Mr. Flood, we have not met like this
In a long time; and many a change has come
To both of us, I fear, since last it was   35
We had a drop together. Welcome home!"
Convivially returning with himself,
Again he raised the jug up to the light;
And with an acquiescent quaver said:
"Well, Mr. Flood, if you insist, I might.   40

"Only a very little, Mr. Flood—
For auld lang syne. No more, sir; that will do."
So, for the time, apparently it did,
And Eben evidently thought so too;
For soon amid the silver loneliness   45
Of night he lifted up his voice and sang,
Secure, with only two moons listening,
Until the whole harmonious landscape rang—

"For auld lang syne." The weary throat gave out,
The last word wavered, and the song was done.   50
He raised again the jug regretfully
And shook his head, and was again alone.
There was not much that was ahead of him,
And there was nothing in the town below—
Where strangers would have shut the many doors   55
That many friends had opened long ago.

Edwin Arlington Robinson (1869–1935)

(11) *bird:* Mr. Flood is quoting from *The Rubáiyát of Omar Khayyám,* "The bird of
Time . . . is on the wing." (20) *Roland:* hero of the French epic poem *The Song of Roland.* He
died fighting a rearguard action for Charlemagne against the Moors in Spain; before his
death he sounded a call for help on his famous horn, but the king's army arrived too late.

271. Richard Cory

Whenever Richard Cory went down town,
We people on the pavement looked at him:
He was a gentleman from sole to crown,
Clean favored, and imperially slim.

And he was always quietly arrayed,   5
And he was always human when he talked;
But still he fluttered pulses when he said,
"Good-morning," and he glittered when he walked.

And he was rich—yes, richer than a king—
And admirably schooled in every grace: 10
In fine, we thought that he was everything
To make us wish that we were in his place.

So on we worked, and waited for the light,
And went without the meat, and cursed the bread;
And Richard Cory, one calm summer night,   15
Went home and put a bullet through his head.

Edwin Arlington Robinson (1869–1935)

272. The Sheaves

Where long the shadows of the wind had rolled,
Green wheat was yielding to the change assigned;
And as by some vast magic undivined
The world was turning slowly into gold.
Like nothing that was ever bought or sold   5
It waited there, the body and the mind;
And with a mighty meaning of a kind
That tells the more the more it is not told.

So in a land where all days are not fair,
Fair days went on till on another day   10
A thousand golden sheaves were lying there,
Shining and still, but not for long to stay—
As if a thousand girls with golden hair
Might rise from where they slept and go away.

Edwin Arlington Robinson (1869–1935)

273. I knew a woman

A knew a woman, lovely in her bones,
When small birds sighed, she would sigh back at them;
Ah, when she moved, she moved more ways than one:
The shapes a bright container can contain!
Of her choice virtues only gods should speak,   5
Or English poets who grew up on Greek
(I'd have them sing in chorus, cheek to cheek).

How well her wishes went! She stroked my chin,
She taught me Turn, and Counter-turn, and Stand;
She taught me Touch, that undulant white skin;   10
I nibbled meekly from her proffered hand;
She was the sickle; I, poor I, the rake,
Coming behind her for her pretty sake
(But what prodigious mowing we did make).

Love likes a gander, and adores a goose: 15
Her full lips pursed, the errant note to seize;
She played it quick, she played it light and loose;
My eyes, they dazzled at her flowing knees;
Her several parts could keep a pure repose,
Or one hip quiver with a mobile nose   20
(She moved in circles, and those circles moved).

Let seed be grass, and grass turn into hay:
I'm martyr to a motion not my own;
What's freedom for? To know eternity.
I swear she cast a shadow white as stone.   25
But who would count eternity in days?
These old bones live to learn her wanton ways:
(I measure time by how a body sways).

Theodore Roethke (1908–1963)

274. Fear no more

Fear no more the heat o' the sun,
   Nor the furious winter's rages;
Thou thy worldly task hast done,
   Home art gone, and ta'en thy wages.
Golden lads and girls all must,   5
As chimney-sweepers, come to dust.

Fear no more the frown o' the great;
   Thou art past the tyrant's stroke;
Care no more to clothe and eat;
   To thee the reed is as the oak.   10
The scepter, learning, physic,° must   art of healing
All follow this, and come to dust.

Fear no more the lightning-flash,
   Nor the all-dreaded thunder-stone;°   thunderbolt

Fear not slander, censure rash;   15
  Thou hast finished joy and moan.
All lovers young, all lovers must
  Consign to thee,° and come to dust.   yield to your condition

William Shakespeare (1564–1616)

275. Let me not to the marriage of true minds

Let me not to the marriage of true minds
Admit impediments. Love is not love
Which alters when it alteration finds,
Or bends with the remover to remove.
O no! it is an ever-fixèd mark   5
That looks on tempests and is never shaken;
It is the star to every wandering bark,
Whose worth's unknown, although his height be taken.
Love's not Time's fool, though rosy lips and cheeks
Within his bending sickle's compass come;   10
Love alters not with his brief hours and weeks,
But bears it out even to the edge of doom.
If this be error and upon me proved,
I never writ, nor no man ever loved.

William Shakespeare (1564–1616)

276. My mistress' eyes

My mistress' eyes are nothing like the sun;
Coral is far more red than her lips' red;
If snow be white, why then her breasts are dun;
If hairs be wires, black wires grow on her head.
I have seen roses damasked,° red and white,   of different colors
But no such roses see I in her cheeks;   6
And in some perfumes is there more delight
Than in the breath that from my mistress reeks.°   exhales
I love to hear her speak, yet well I know
That music hath a far more pleasing sound;   10
I grant I never saw a goddess go,—
My mistress, when she walks, treads on the ground.
And yet, by heaven, I think my love as rare
As any she belied with false compare.

William Shakespeare (1564–1616)

277. Shall I compare thee to a summer's day?

Shall I compare thee to a summer's day?
Thou art more lovely and more temperate:
Rough winds do shake the lovely buds of May,
And summer's lease hath all too short a date.
Sometimes too hot the eye of heaven shines,   5
And often is his gold complexion dimmed;
And every fair° from fair sometimes declines   beauty
By chance or nature's changing course untrimmed°;   stripped
But thy eternal summer shall not fade   bare
Nor lose possession of that fair thou ow'st°,   own   10
Nor shall death brag thou wand'rest in his shade
When in eternal lines to time thou grow'st.
So long as men can breathe or eyes can see,
So long lives this°, and this gives life to thee.   this poem

William Shakespeare (1564–1616)

278. The Fly

O hideous little bat, the size of snot,
With polyhedral eye and shabby clothes,
To populate the stinking cat you walk
The promontory of the dead man's nose,
Climb with the fine leg of a Duncan-Phyfe   5
   The smoking mountains of my food
      And in a comic mood
   In mid-air take to bed a wife.

Riding and riding with your filth of hair
On gluey foot or wing, forever coy,   10
Hot from the compost and green sweet decay,
Sounding your buzzer like an urchin toy—
You dot all whiteness with diminutive stool,
   In the tight belly of the dead
      Burrow with hungry head   15
   And inlay maggots like a jewel.

At your approach the great horse stomps and paws
Bringing the hurricane of his heavy tail;
Shod in disease you dare to kiss my hand
Which sweeps against you like an angry flail;   20
Still you return, return, trusting your wing

To draw you from the hunter's reach
   That learns to kill to teach
Disorder to the tinier thing.

My peace is your disaster. For your death   25
Children like spiders cup their pretty hands
And wives resort to chemistry of war.
In fens of sticky paper and quicksands
You glue yourself to death. Where you are stuck
   You struggle hideously and beg,
      You amputate your leg
Imbedded in the amber muck.

But I, a man, must swat you with my hate,
Slap you across the air and crush your flight,
Must mangle with my shoe and smear your blood,   35
Expose your little guts pasty and white,
Knock your head sidewise like a drunkard's hat,
   Pin your wings under like a crow's,
      Tear off your flimsy clothes,
   And beat you as one beats a rat.   40

Then like Gargantua I stride among
The corpses strewn like raisins in the dust,
The broken bodies of the narrow dead
That catch the throat with fingers of disgust.
I sweep. One gyrates like a top and falls   45
   And stunned, stone blind, and deaf
      Buzzes its frightful F
   And dies between three cannibals.

Karl Shapiro (b. 1913)

279. Small Town with One Road

We could be here. This is the valley
And its black strip of highway, big-eyed
With rabbits that won't get across.
Kids could make it, though.
They leap barefoot to the store—   5
Sweetness on their tongues, red stain of laughter.
They are the spectators of fun.
Hot dimes fall from their palms,
Chinks of light, and they eat

Candies all the way home   10
Where there's a dog for each hand,
Cats, chickens in the yard.
A pot bangs and water runs in the kitchen.
Beans, they think, and beans it will be,
Brown soup that's muscle for the field   15
And crippled steps to a ladder.
Okie or Mexican, Jew that got lost,
It's a hard life where the sun looks.
The cotton gin stands tall in the money dream
And the mill is a paycheck for   20
A wife—and perhaps my wife
Who, when she was a girl,
Boxed peaches and plums, hoed
Papa's field that wavered like a mirage
That wouldn't leave. We could go back.   25
I could lose my job, this easy one
That's only words, and pick up a shovel,
Hoe, broom that takes it away.
Worry is my daughter's story.
She touches my hand. We suck roadside   30
Snowcones in the shade
And look about. Behind sunglasses
I see where I stood: a brown kid
Getting across. "He's like me,"
I tell my daughter, and she stops her mouth.   35
He looks both ways and then leaps
Across the road where riches
Happen on a red tongue.

Gary Soto (b. 1952)

280. The Beating

The first blow caught me sideways, my jaw
Shifted. The second beat my skull against my
Brain. I raised my arm against the third.
Downward my wrist fell crooked. But the sliding

Flood of sense across the ribs caught in   5
My lungs. I fell for a long time,
One knee bending. The fourth blow balanced me.
I doubled at the kick against my belly.

The fifth was light. I hardly felt the
Sting. And down, breaking against my side, my   10
Thighs, my head. My eyes burst closed, my
Mouth the thick blood curds moved through. There

Were no more lights. I was flying. The
Wind, the place I lay, the silence.
My call came to a groan. Hands touched   15
My wrist. Disappeared. Something fell over me.

Now this white room tortures my eye.
The bed too soft to hold my breath,
Slung in plaster, caged in wood.
Shapes surround me.   20

No blow! No blow!
They only ask the thing I turn
Inside the black ball of my mind,
The one white thought.

                              Ann Stanford (1916–1987)

281. The Death of a Soldier

Life contracts and death is expected,
As in a season of autumn.
The soldier falls.

He does not become a three-days personage,
Imposing his separation,   5
Calling for pomp.

Death is absolute and without memorial,
As in a season of autumn,
When the wind stops,

When the wind stops and, over the heavens,   10
The clouds go, nevertheless,
In their direction.

                              Wallace Stevens (1879–1955)

282. Disillusionment of Ten O'Clock

The houses are haunted
By white night-gowns.
None are green,

Or purple with green rings,
Or green with yellow rings,   5
Or yellow with blue rings.
None of them are strange,
With socks of lace
And beaded ceintures.°   sashes
People are not going   10
To dream of baboons and periwinkles.
Only, here and there, an old sailor,
Drunk and asleep in his boots,
Catches tigers
In red weather.   15

Wallace Stevens (1879–1955)

283. The Snow Man

One must have a mind of winter
To regard the frost and the boughs
Of the pine-trees crusted with snow;

And have been cold a long time
To behold the junipers shagged with ice,   5
The spruces rough in the distant glitter

Of the January sun; and not to think
Of any misery in the sound of the wind,
In the sound of a few leaves,

Which is the sound of the land   10
Full of the same wind
That is blowing in the same bare place

For the listener, who listens in the snow,
And, nothing himself, beholds
Nothing that is not there and the nothing that is.   15

Wallace Stevens (1879–1955)

284. A Description of the Morning

Now hardly here and there a hackney-coach
Appearing, showed the ruddy morn's approach.
Now Betty from her master's bed had flown,
And softly stole to discompose her own.
The slip-shod 'prentice from his master's door   5

Had pared the dirt, and sprinkled round the floor.
Now Moll had whirled her mop with dextrous airs,
Prepared to scrub the entry and the stairs.
The youth with broomy stumps began to trace
The kennel's edge, where wheels had worn the place.   10
The small-coal man was heard with cadence deep,
Till drowned in shriller notes of chimney-sweep.
Duns at his lordship's gate began to meet;
And Brickdust Moll had screamed through half the street.
The turnkey now his flock returning sees,   15
Duly let out a-nights to steal for fees.
The watchful bailiffs take their silent stands;
And schoolboys lag with satchels in their hands.

Jonathan Swift (1667–1745)

(9) *youth:* he is apparently searching for salvage. (10) *kennel:* gutter. (14) *Brickdust:* red-complexioned.

285. From *In Memoriam A. H. H.*

Dark house, by which once more I stand
    Here in the long unlovely street,
    Doors, where my heart was used to beat
So quickly, waiting for a hand,

A hand that can be clasped no more—   5
    Behold me, for I cannot sleep,
    And like a guilty thing I creep
At earliest morning to the door.

He is not here; but far away
    The noise of life begins again,   10
    And ghastly through the drizzling rain
On the bald street breaks the blank day.

Alfred, Lord Tennyson (1809–1892)

This poem is part of a sequence composed after the death at age twenty-two of the poet's closest friend, the fiancé of his sister.

286. Do Not Go Gentle into That Good Night

Do not go gentle into that good night,
Old age should burn and rave at close of day;
Rage, rage against the dying of the light.

Though wise men at their end know dark is right,
Because their words had forked no lightning they   5
Do not go gentle into that good night.

Good men, the last wave by, crying how bright
Their frail deeds might have danced in a green bay,
Rage, rage against the dying of the light.

Wild men who caught and sang the sun in flight,   10
And learn, too late, they grieved it on its way
Do not go gentle into that good night.

Grave men, near death, who see with blinding sight
Blind eyes could blaze like meteors and be gay,
Rage, rage against the dying of the light.   15

And you, my father, there on the sad height,
Curse, bless, me now with your fierce tears, I pray.
Do not go gentle into that good night.
Rage, rage against the dying of the light.

Dylan Thomas (1914–1953)

287. Fern Hill

Now as I was young and easy under the apple boughs
About the lilting house and happy as the grass was green,
   The night above the dingle starry,
    Time let me hail and climb
   Golden in the heydays of his eyes,   5
And honored among wagons I was prince of the apple towns
And once below a time I lordly had the trees and leaves
    Trail with daisies and barley
   Down the rivers of the windfall light.

And as I was green and carefree, famous among the barns 10
About the happy yard and singing as the farm was home,
   In the sun that is young once only,
    Time let me play and be
   Golden in the mercy of his means,
And green and golden I was huntsman and herdsman, the calves 15
Sang to my horn, the foxes on the hills barked clear and cold,
    And the sabbath rang slowly
   In the pebbles of the holy streams.

All the sun long it was running, it was lovely, the hay
Fields high as the house, the tunes from the chimneys, it was air 20

And playing, lovely and watery
    And fire green as grass.
And nightly under the simple stars
As I rode to sleep the owls were bearing the farm away,
All the moon long I heard, blessed among stables, the nightjars   25
    Flying with the ricks, and the horses
       Flashing into the dark.

And then to awake, and the farm, like a wanderer white
With the dew, come back, the cock on his shoulder: it was all
    Shining, it was Adam and maiden,   30
      The sky gathered again
    And the sun grew round that very day.
So it must have been after the birth of the simple light
In the first, spinning place, the spellbound horses walking warm
    Out of the whinnying green stable   35
      On to the fields of praise.

And honored among foxes and pheasants by the gay house
Under the new made clouds and happy as the heart was long,
    In the sun born over and over,
      I ran my heedless ways,   40
    My wishes raced through the house high hay
And nothing I cared, at my sky blue trades, that time allows
In all his tuneful turning so few and such morning songs
    Before the children green and golden
      Follow him out of grace,   45

Nothing I cared, in the lamb white days, that time would take me
Up to the swallow thronged loft by the shadow of my hand,
    In the moon that is always rising,
      Nor that riding to sleep
I should hear him fly with the high fields   50
And wake to the farm forever fled from the childless land.
Oh as I was young and easy in the mercy of his means,
    Time held me green and dying
    Though I sang in my chains like the sea.

Dylan Thomas (1914–1953)

288. The Virgins

Down the dead streets of sun-stoned Frederiksted,
the first free port to die for tourism,
strolling at funeral pace, I am reminded
of life not lost to the American dream;

but my small-islander's simplicities   5
can't better our new empire's civilized
exchange of cameras, watches, perfumes, brandies
for the good life, so cheaply underpriced
that only the crime rate is on the rise
in streets blighted with sun, stone arches   10
and plazas blown dry by the hysteria
of rumor. A condominium drowns
in vacancy; its bargains are dusted,
but only a jeweled housefly drones
over the bargains. The roulettes spin   15
rustily to the wind—the vigorous trade
that every morning would begin afresh
by revving up green water round the pierhead
heading for where the banks of silver thresh.

Derek Walcott (b. 1930)

(1) *Frederiksted:* chief port of St. Croix, largest of the American Virgin Islands, a free port where goods can be bought without payment of customs duties and therefore at bargain prices. The economy of St. Croix, once based on sugar cane, is now chiefly dependent on tourism. Like the other American Virgin Islands, St. Croix has suffered from uncontrolled growth, building booms, unevenly distributed prosperity, destruction of natural beauty, and pollution. (5) *my . . . simplicities:* The poet is a native of St. Lucia in the West Indies. (16) *trade:* cf. trade wind.

289. When I Heard the Learn'd Astronomer

When I heard the learn'd astronomer,
When the proofs, the figures, were ranged in columns before me,
When I was shown the charts and diagrams, to add, divide,
    and measure them,
When I sitting heard the astronomer where he lectured with much
    applause in the lecture-room,
How soon unaccountable I became tired and sick,   5
Till rising and gliding out I wandered off by myself,
In the mystical moist night-air, and from time to time,
Looked up in perfect silence at the stars.

Walt Whitman (1819–1892)

290. The Writer

In her room at the prow of the house
Where light breaks, and the windows are tossed with linden,
My daughter is writing a story.

I pause in the stairwell, hearing
From her shut door a commotion of typewriter-keys   5
Like a chain hauled over a gunwale.

Young as she is, the stuff
Of her life is a great cargo, and some of it heavy:
I wish her a lucky passage.

But now it is she who pauses,   10
As if to reject my thought and its easy figure.
A stillness greatens, in which

The whole house seems to be thinking,
And then she is at it again with a bunched clamor
Of strokes, and again is silent.   15

I remember the dazed starling
Which was trapped in that very room, two years ago;
How we stole in, lifted a sash

And retreated, not to affright it;
And how for a helpless hour, through the crack of the door,   20
We watched the sleek, wild, dark

And iridescent creature
Batter against the brilliance, drop like a glove
To the hard floor, or the desk-top,

And wait then, humped and bloody,   25
For the wits to try it again; and how our spirits
Rose when, suddenly sure,

It lifted off from a chair-back,
Beating a smooth course for the right window
And clearing the sill of the world.   30

It is always a matter, my darling,
Of life or death, as I had forgotten. I wish
What I wished you before, but harder.

Richard Wilbur (b. 1921)

291. Poem

As the cat
climbed over
the top of

the jamcloset
first the right   5
forefoot

carefully
then the hind
stepped down

into the pit of   10
the empty
flowerpot

William Carlos Williams (1883–1963)

292. Spring and All

By the road to the contagious hospital
under the surge of the blue
mottled clouds driven from the
northeast—a cold wind. Beyond, the
waste of broad, muddy fields   5
brown with dried weeds, standing and fallen

patches of standing water
the scattering of tall trees

All along the road the reddish
purplish, forked, upstanding, twiggy   10
stuff of bushes and small trees
with dead, brown leaves under them
leafless vines—

Lifeless in appearance, sluggish
dazed spring approaches—   15

They enter the new world naked,
cold, uncertain of all
save that they enter. All about them
the cold, familiar wind—

Now the grass, tomorrow   20
the stiff curl of wildcarrot leaf
One by one objects are defined—
It quickens: clarity, outline of leaf

But now the stark dignity of
entrance—Still, the profound change   25
has come upon them: rooted they
grip down and begin to awaken

William Carlos Williams (1883–1963)

293. To Waken an Old Lady

Old age is
a flight of small
cheeping birds
skimming
bare trees   5
above a snow glaze.
Gaining and failing
they are buffeted
by a dark wind—
But what?   10
On harsh weedstalks
the flock has rested,
the snow
is covered with broken
seedhusks   15
and the wind tempered
by a shrill
piping of plenty.

William Carlos Williams (1883–1963)

294. Composed upon Westminster Bridge, September 3, 1802

Earth has not anything to show more fair:
Dull would he be of sight who could pass by
A sight so touching in its majesty:
This City now doth, like a garment, wear
The beauty of the morning; silent, bare,   5
Ships, towers, domes, theaters, and temples lie
Open unto the fields, and to the sky,
All bright and glittering in the smokeless air.
Never did sun more beautifully steep
In his first splendor, valley, rock, or hill;   10

Ne'er saw I, never felt, a calm so deep!
The river glideth at his own sweet will:
Dear God! the very houses seem asleep,
And all that mighty heart is lying still!

William Wordsworth (1770–1850)

295. I wandered lonely as a cloud

I wandered lonely as a cloud
That floats on high o'er vales and hills,
When all at once I saw a crowd,
A host, of golden daffodils;
Beside the lake, beneath the trees,   5
Fluttering and dancing in the breeze.

Continuous as the stars that shine
And twinkle on the milky way,
They stretched in never-ending line
Along the margin of a bay: 10
Ten thousand saw I at a glance,
Tossing their heads in sprightly dance.

The waves beside them danced; but they
Outdid the sparkling waves in glee;
A poet could not but be gay,   15
In such a jocund company;
I gazed—and gazed—but little thought
What wealth the show to me had brought:

For oft, when on my couch I lie
In vacant or in pensive mood,   20
They flash upon that inward eye
Which is the bliss of solitude;
And then my heart with pleasure fills,
And dances with the daffodils.

William Wordsworth (1770–1850)

296. The Solitary Reaper

Behold her, single in the field,
Yon solitary Highland lass!
Reaping and singing by herself;

Stop here, or gently pass!
Alone she cuts and binds the grain,   5
And sings a melancholy strain;
O listen! for the vale profound
Is overflowing with the sound.

No nightingale did ever chant
More welcome notes to weary bands   10
Of travelers in some shady haunt
Among Arabian sands.
A voice so thrilling ne'er was heard
In springtime from the cuckoo-bird,
Breaking the silence of the seas   15
Among the farthest Hebrides.

Will no one tell me what she sings?—
Perhaps the plaintive numbers° flow   measures
For old, unhappy, far-off things,
And battles long ago.   20
Or is it some more humble lay,°   song
Familiar matter of today?
Some natural sorrow, loss, or pain
That has been, and may be again?

Whate'er the theme, the maiden sang   25
As if her song could have no ending;
I saw her singing at her work,
And o'er the sickle bending—
I listened, motionless and still;
And, as I mounted up the hill,   30
The music in my heart I bore
Long after it was heard no more.

William Wordsworth (1770–1850)

297. Sailing to Byzantium

That is no country for old men. The young
In one another's arms, birds in the trees
—Those dying generations—at their song,
The salmon-falls, the mackerel-crowded seas,
Fish, flesh, or fowl, commend all summer long   5
Whatever is begotten, born, and dies.
Caught in that sensual music all neglect
Monuments of unaging intellect.

An aged man is but a paltry thing,
A tattered coat upon a stick, unless   10
Soul clap its hands and sing, and louder sing
For every tatter in its mortal dress,
Nor is there singing school but studying
Monuments of its own magnificence;
And therefore I have sailed the seas and come   15
To the holy city of Byzantium.

O sages standing in God's holy fire
As in the gold mosaic of a wall,
Come from the holy fire, perne° in a gyre,   spin
And be the singing-masters of my soul.   20
Consume my heart away; sick with desire
And fastened to a dying animal
It knows not what it is; and gather me
Into the artifice of eternity.

Once out of nature I shall never take   25
My bodily form from any natural thing,
But such a form as Grecian goldsmiths make
Of hammered gold and gold enameling
To keep a drowsy Emperor awake;
Or set upon a golden bough to sing   30
To lords and ladies of Byzantium
Of what is past, or passing, or to come.

William Butler Yeats (1865–1939)

Byzantium: Ancient eastern capital of the Roman Empire; in this poem symbolically a
holy city of the imagination. (1) *That:* Ireland, or the ordinary sensual world. (27–31)
such . . . Byzantium: The Byzantine Emperor Theophilus had made for himself mechanical golden birds which sang upon the branches of a golden tree.

298. The Second Coming

Turning and turning in the widening gyre
The falcon cannot hear the falconer;
Things fall apart; the center cannot hold;
Mere anarchy is loosed upon the world,
The blood-dimmed tide is loosed, and everywhere   5
The ceremony of innocence is drowned;
The best lack all conviction, while the worst
Are full of passionate intensity.

Surely some revelation is at hand;
Surely the Second Coming is at hand.   10
The Second Coming! Hardly are those words out
When a vast image out of *Spiritus Mundi*
Troubles my sight: somewhere in sands of the desert
A shape with lion body and the head of a man,
A gaze blank and pitiless as the sun,   15
Is moving its slow thighs, while all about it
Reel shadows of the indignant desert birds.
The darkness drops again; but now I know
That twenty centuries of stony sleep
Were vexed to nightmare by a rocking cradle,   20
And what rough beast, its hour come round at last,
Slouches towards Bethlehem to be born?

William Butler Yeats (1865–1939)

In Christian legend the prophesied "Second Coming" may refer either to Christ or to
Antichrist. Yeats believed in a cyclical theory of history in which one historical era
would be replaced by an opposite kind of era every two thousand years. Here, the anarchy in the world following World War I (the poem was written in 1919) heralds the end
of the Christian era. (12) *Spiritus Mundi:* the racial memory or collective unconscious
mind of mankind (literally, world spirit).

299. The Wild Swans at Coole

The trees are in their autumn beauty,
The woodland paths are dry,
Under the October twilight the water
Mirrors a still sky;
Upon the brimming water among the stones   5
Are nine-and-fifty swans.

The nineteenth autumn has come upon me
Since I first made my count;
I saw, before I had well finished,
All suddenly mount   10
And scatter wheeling in great broken rings
Upon their clamorous wings.

I have looked upon those brilliant creatures,
And now my heart is sore,
All's changed since I, hearing at twilight,   15
The first time on this shore,
The bell-beat of their wings above my head,
Trod with a lighter tread.

Unwearied still, lover by lover,
They paddle in the cold   20
Companionable streams or climb the air;
Their hearts have not grown old;
Passion or conquest, wander where they will,
Attend upon them still.

But now they drift on the still water,   25
Mysterious, beautiful;
Among what rushes will they build,
By what lake's edge or pool
Delight men's eyes when I awake some day
To find they have flown away?   30

William Butler Yeats (1865–1939)

Coole Park, in County Galway, Ireland, was the estate of Lady Augusta Gregory,
Yeats's patroness and friend. Beginning in 1897, Yeats regularly summered there for
many years.

DRAMA

The Elements
of Drama

CHAPTER ONE

The Nature of Drama

Drama, like prose fiction, utilizes plot and characters, develops a theme, arouses emotion or appeals to humor, and may be either escapist or interpretive in its dealings with life.* Like poetry, it may draw upon all the resources of language, including verse. Much drama *is* poetry. But drama has one characteristic peculiar to itself. It is written primarily to be *performed,* not read. It normally presents its action (a) *through* actors, (b) *on* a stage, and (c) *before* an audience. Each of these circumstances has important consequences for the nature of drama. Each presents an author with a potentially enormous source of power, and each imposes limitations on the directions a work may take.

Because a play presents its action *through* actors, its impact is direct, immediate, and heightened by the actors' skills. Instead of responding to words on a printed page, spectators see what is done and hear what is said. The experience of the play is registered directly upon their senses. It may therefore be both fuller and more compact. Where the work of prose fiction may tell us what a man looks like in one paragraph, how he moves or speaks in a second, what he says in a third, and how his auditors respond in a fourth, the acted play presents this material all at once. Simultaneous impressions are not temporally separated. Moreover, this experience is interpreted by actors who may be highly skilled in rendering nuances of meaning and strong emotion. Through facial expression, gesture, speech rhythm, and intonation, they may be able to make a speaker's words more expressive than can the reader's unaided imagination. Thus, the performance of a play by skilled actors expertly directed gives the playwright† a tremendous source of power.

---

*Plot, character, theme, symbol, irony, and other elements of literature have been discussed in the fiction section and the poetry section.

†The word *wright*—as in *playwright, shipwright, wheelwright, cartwright,* and the common surname *Wright*—comes from an Anglo-Saxon word meaning a workman or craftsman. It is related to the verb *wrought* (a past-tense form of *work*) and has nothing whatever to do with the verb *write.*

But playwrights pay a price for this increased power. Of the four major points of view open to the fiction writer, dramatists are practically limited to one—the *objective,* or *dramatic.* They cannot directly comment on the action or the characters. They cannot enter the minds of their characters and tell us what is going on there. Although there are ways around these limitations, each has its own limitations. Authorial commentary may be placed in the mouth of a character, but only at the risk of distorting characterization and of leaving the character's reliability uncertain. (Does the character speak for the author or only for herself or himself?) Entry can be made into a character's mind through the conventions of the **soliloquy** and the **aside.** In soliloquies, characters are presented as speaking to themselves— that is, they think out loud. In asides, characters turn from the persons with whom they are conversing to speak directly to (or for the benefit of) the audience, thus letting the audience know what they are really thinking or feeling as opposed to what they pretend to be thinking or feeling. Characters speaking in soliloquy or in asides are always presumed to be telling the truth, to the extent that they know the truth. Both devices can be used very effectively in the theater, but they interrupt the action and are therefore used sparingly. Also, they are inappropriate if the playwright is working in a strictly realistic mode.

Because a play presents its action *on* a stage, it can forcefully command the spectator's attention. The stage is lighted; the theater is dark; extraneous noises are shut out; spectators are almost literally pinned to their seats; there is nowhere they can go; there is nothing else to look at; there is nothing to distract. The playwright has extraordinary means by which to command the undivided attention of the audience. Unlike the fiction writer or the poet, the playwright is not dependent on the power of words alone.

But the necessity to confine the action to a stage, rather than to the imagination's vast arena, limits the kind of materials playwrights can easily and effectively present. For the most part, they must present human beings in spoken interaction with each other. They cannot easily use materials in which the main interest is in unspoken thoughts and reflections. They cannot present complex actions that involve nonhuman creatures such as wild horses or charging bulls. They find it more difficult to shift scenes rapidly than writers of prose fiction do. The latter may whisk their readers from heaven to earth and back again in the twinkling of an eye, but playwrights must usually stick to one setting for an extended period of time and may feel constrained to do so for the whole play.* Moreover, the events they depict must be of a magnitude appropriate to the stage. They cannot present the movements of armies and warfare on the vast scale that Tolstoy uses in *War and Peace*. They cannot easily present adventures at sea or action on a ski slope. Conversely, they cannot depict a fly crawling around the rim of a saucer or falling into a cup of milk. At best they can present a general on a hilltop reporting the movements of a battle or two persons bending over a cup of milk reacting to a fly that the members of the audience cannot see.

Because a play presents its action *before* an audience, the experience it creates is a communal experience, and its impact is intensified. Reading a short story or a novel is a private transaction between the reader and a book, but the performance of a play is public. The spectator's response is affected by the presence of other spectators. A comedy becomes funnier when one hears others laughing, a tragedy more moving when others are present to carry the current of feeling. A dramatic experience, in fact, becomes more intense almost exactly to the extent that it is shared and the individual spectator becomes aware that others are having the same experience. This intensification is partly dependent on the size of the audience, but more on their sense of community with each other. A play will be more successful performed before a small audience in a packed auditorium than before a large audience in a half-filled hall.

But, again, the advantage given playwrights by the fact of theatrical performance is paid for by limitations on the material they can present. A play must be able to hold the attention of a group audience.

---

*The ease, and therefore the rapidity, with which a playwright can change from one scene to another depends, first, on the elaborateness of the stage setting and, second, on the means by which one scene is separated from another. In ancient plays and in many modern ones, stage settings have been extremely simple, depending only on a few easily moved properties or even entirely on the actors' words and the spectators' imaginations. In such cases, change of scenes is made fairly easily, especially if the actors themselves are allowed to carry on and off any properties that may be needed. Various means have been used to separate scenes from each other. In Greek plays, dancing and chanting by a chorus served as a scene divider. More recently, the closing and opening or dropping and raising of a curtain has been the means used. In contemporary theater, with its command of electrical technology, increased reliance has been placed on darkening and illuminating the stage or on darkening one part of it while lighting up another. But even where there is no stage scenery and where the shift of scene is made only by a change in lighting, the playwright can seldom change the setting as rapidly as the writer of prose fiction. On the stage, too frequent shifts of scene make a play seem jerky. A reader's imagination, on the other hand, can change from one setting to another without even shifting gears.

A higher premium than in prose fiction is placed on a well-defined plot, swift exposition, strong conflict, dramatic confrontations. Unless the play is very brief, it is usually divided into parts separated by an intermission or intermissions, and each part works up to its own climax or point of suspense. It is written so that its central meanings may be grasped in a single performance. Spectators at a play cannot back up and rerun a passage whose import they have missed; they cannot, in one night, sit through the whole performance a second time. In addition, playwrights usually avoid extensive use of materials that are purely narrative or lyrical. Long narrative passages are usually interrupted, descriptive passages kept short or eliminated altogether. Primarily, human beings are presented in spoken interaction with each other. Clearly, many of the world's literary masterpieces—stories and poems that enthrall the reader of a book—would not hold the attention of a group audience in a theater.

Drama, then, imposes sharp limitations on its writer but holds out the opportunity for extraordinary force. The successful playwright combines the power of words, the power of fiction, and the power of dramatic technique to make possible the achievement of that force.

EXERCISES AND TOPICS FOR DISCUSSION

1. Works written as short stories, novels, or poems have sometimes been dramatized for stage production. In light of the advantages and limitations discussed in this chapter, however, some are clearly more easily adapted for the stage than others. Of the following works—"Miss Brill" (page 97), "Mule in the Yard" (page 365), "The Lottery" (page 421), "The Guest" (page 190), "Hills Like White Elephants" (page 171), "To Autumn" (page 617), "Home Burial" (page 813), and "The Love Song of J. Alfred Prufrock" (page 816)—which could be most easily and effectively dramatized? Which would be possible but more difficult? Which would be impossible to dramatize? Why?

2. Write a stage adaptation of "The Ant and the Grasshopper" (page 149). What are the difficulties involved? How effective would such a presentation be?

3. Movie and broadcast (TV and radio) productions are in many ways more flexible than stage productions and are more easily brought to a mass audience. What limitations of stage performance discussed in this chapter can be minimized or circumvented in a movie or broadcast production? In view of the greater flexibility of movies and broadcasting media, why is there still an eager audience for plays? What advantages do stage performances have over moving pictures, television, and radio?

4. If plays are written to be *performed*, what justification is there for reading them?

GENERAL EXERCISES FOR ANALYSIS AND
EVALUATION OF DRAMA

As drama may combine the literary resources of both prose
fiction and poetry, many of the "General Exercises" provided for
those two genres (pages 317 and 587) may be applicable to drama—
except for those directed toward the study of point of view in fiction,
since drama always employs the objective or dramatic point of view.
Even if a drama is not written in verse, the general questions about
diction and figurative language supplied for the elements of poetry
may be applicable to drama.

In addition, the variety of dramatic forms and the special nature
of drama as a theatrical as well as a literary experience require a set of
supplementary questions. Many of these questions will become more
meaningful as you read further in the drama section of this book.
(Some terms printed in bold face are not defined in this section, but
are included in the "Glossary of Terms," pages 1483–1496.)

1. Does the play employ **realistic** or **nonrealistic** conventions? On the
   spectrum from literalistic imitation of reality to stylized or surrealistic representation, where is the play situated? Are there breaks from the conventions established as a norm in the play? If so, what is the dramatic effect of
   these departures? Are they meaningful?
2. Is the play a **tragedy** or **comedy**, a **melodrama** or a **farce**? If a comedy,
   is it primarily **romantic** or **satiric**? Does it mingle aspects of these types
   of drama? How important to experiencing the drama is the audience's
   awareness of the classification of the play?
3. Identify the **protagonist(s)** and **antagonist(s).** Are there any **foil characters?** What dramatic functions are served by the various minor characters? Do they shed light on the actions or motives of the major characters?
   Do they advance the **plot** by eliciting actions by others? Do they embody
   ideas or feelings that illuminate the major characters or the movement of
   the plot?
4. How is dramatic **suspense** created? Contrast the amount of information
   possessed by the audience as the play proceeds with the knowledge that
   various individual characters have: what is the effect of such a contrast?
5. What **themes** does the play present? To what extent do the thematic materials of the play have an effect on the dramatic experience? Does the
   power of the ideas increase or decrease the pleasure of the theatrical experience? Does the play seem either too **didactic** or insufficient in its presentation of important human concerns?
6. How do the various physical effects—theatrical components such as sets,
   lights, costuming, makeup, gestures, stage movements, musical effects of
   song or dance, and so forth—reinforce the meanings and contribute to the
   emotional effects? By what means does the playwright indicate the nature

of these physical effects—explicitly, through stage directions and set descriptions, or implicitly, through dialogue between characters?

7. What amount of time is covered in the action? How much of the action is presented as a report rather than dramatized on stage? Is there a meaning behind the selection of events to be dramatized and those to be reported? Does the play feel loose or tight in its construction? Is that feeling appropriate to the themes and dramatic effects of the play?

8. To what extent does the play employ narration as a means of **dramatic exposition?** What other expository methods does it use? Does the exposition have a function beyond communicating information about prior events? What effects on the audience do the expository methods have?

Meredith Oakes

Mind the Gap

CHARACTERS

GINNY, *a mother*   *A London Underground* GUARD
LAWRENCE, *her son, fourteen*   *Passengers*
EMMA, *another mother*

SCENE. *A station platform and the interior of a train of the Underground. The noise of the train when it is moving, and the silence when it is stopped, are central to the action. The dialogue can pause at the performers' discretion.*

LAWRENCE *and* GINNY *are waiting for a train.* GINNY *sits.* LAWRENCE *stands nearby.* EMMA *approaches them.*

EMMA (*brusque*).   Orthodontist is it?
GINNY.   Emma. I was in a different movie.°
EMMA.   What's he doing off school?
GINNY (*calls*).   Lawrence. Say hullo to Emma, darling.
LAWRENCE.   Hullo Emma darling. (*Turns away.*)
GINNY (*wearily*).   They're amusing, aren't they.
EMMA.   Mine aren't amusing.
GINNY.   But isn't Nicholas so sweet with his trombone.

MIND THE GAP   First performed in 1995. Meredith Oakes was born in 1946 in Sydney, Australia, and educated at the University of Sydney. She moved to London in 1971 and worked in music journalism. Her first play production was in 1993 at the Royal National Theatre studio, and since then she has had plays mounted by two of the most prestigious companies featuring new playwrights, the Royal Court Theatre and the Hampstead Theatre (where *Mind the Gap* was performed). She is married and the mother of two children. The title "mind the gap" quotes a recorded loudspeaker announcement in stations of the London Underground (i.e., subway) warning passengers of a dangerous space between the station platform and the cars of the train.

I was in a different movie: my mind was somewhere else

EMMA.   Lawrence doesn't play?

GINNY.   No, it seems to be weight training with us. They will pick the most expensive thing, won't they, and it's such a worry, isn't it, the brain damage, the house full of dumbbells . . .

EMMA.   Where are you taking him?

GINNY.   Lawrence, tell Emma about Mönchengladbach. He went to Mönchengladbach at Easter, didn't you Spoffy. On exchange.°

LAWRENCE.   I went to Mönchengladbach on exchange.

EMMA.   I thought Mönchengladbach was nothing but factories.

LAWRENCE.   It is.

GINNY.   Lawrence stayed with a lovely family in the hills.

EMMA.   Mönchengladbach hasn't got any hills. Why aren't you at school, Lawrence?

GINNY.   I seem to be taking him to a careers adviser. He doesn't have a clue what to do with himself and yet I'm sure there must be something . . .

EMMA (to LAWRENCE).   Haven't you had your appointment then?

GINNY.   Oh we went and saw the woman at the school. It's just the basic, though, isn't it.

EMMA.   Nothing wrong with the basic, is there?

GINNY.   Well you get what you pay for, don't you. Did you enjoy the Easter Concert? It was exhausting to organize but such fun, honestly.

EMMA.   Yes, they played well, didn't they.

GINNY.   Do you know, I didn't listen to them, I used the time to write them their thank you letters, I find I have to prioritize, don't you, I envy these women that go out to work, I'm sure they don't have nearly as much to do as us. Here's the train, goodness knows where it's been.

EMMA.   It's been to Wimbledon.

GINNY.   Are you going far?

EMMA.   Not far. Just to work.

GINNY (drops her voice).   Emma, I didn't know. (They get into the train and sit down together. Other passengers are in evidence, close enough to hear what's being said when it's stationary but not when it's moving. GINNY makes the following remark in a hushed voice.) I honestly didn't know you were working. (Pause.) Patrick's all right, is he? Things are so difficult at the moment. (EMMA nods.) Half the people we used to know are out of work. (EMMA nods.) We shan't know anyone soon. (The train starts.)

EMMA.   Patrick won't push.

GINNY.   I expect working at a job that interests you is nice, isn't it?

EMMA.   I wouldn't know.

GINNY.   Weren't you something before you were married?

EMMA.   Physiotherapist.

Mönchengladbach . . . exchange: he has been in a student exchange program in a small industrial city in northwest Germany.

GINNY.   You'd have to be so strong.

EMMA.   I am strong.

GINNY.   And caring. (EMMA *shrugs.*) So you're pummelling people into shape, are you?

EMMA.   Companies get me in to massage them. My biggest client is a debt collector. Repeated strain injury.

GINNY.   Really.

EMMA.   I can't understand how so many people in our position fail to see the writing on the wall.

GINNY.   Oh the graffitti, they never catch them do they.

EMMA.   People like us can't afford silly ideas.

GINNY.   Michael and I can still afford most things.

EMMA.   I've told the boys there's always the comprehensive.°

GINNY.   I'm sure you're exaggerating, Emma. Where would we be without your boys?

EMMA.   They'd still be here you know. They'd be changing schools, not turning into werewolves.

GINNY.   I don't know, I mean surely you could sell your lovely house.

EMMA.   Patrick needs something to cling to. He's being swallowed by the overdraft. Keep this to yourself, but we're really in deep— (*The train stops.*)

GINNY.   Southfields.

EMMA (*getting up to go*).   Have fun with the careers adviser, Lawrence.

LAWRENCE.   Yeah, thanks.

GINNY.   Let me know about your lovely house! (EMMA *is gone. Silence.*) Do you want your ticket darling?

LAWRENCE.   No thanks.

GINNY.   Silly of me, I should have given it you at the barrier.° Mothers, aren't we a pain. (*The train starts. While the train is moving,* GINNY *talks to* LAWRENCE *in a different tone.*) Of all the people who could possibly have seen us.

LAWRENCE.   What's your problem?

GINNY.   That woman is so sadistically unpretentious. I suppose those who can't pretend, don't. What am I going to do?

LAWRENCE.   She thinks it's the careers adviser.

GINNY.   She won't rest until she's found the name, she'll have her eye on us from this moment on. People are always wanting to catch one out. That's all some of these people ever think of, they imagine we have such a wonderful life you know, heaven knows I play my part.

LAWRENCE.   I told you to take the car.

---

comprehensive: state-supported secondary school
platform where tickets are inspected   **barrier:** entry to the station

GINNY. I said I'm not taking the car. (*Silence.*) You never stop, do you. You never stop getting at me until I give way to you. (*Silence.*) No car, Lawrence. We're taking the train.

LAWRENCE. If she sees you, you've only got yourself to blame, right?

GINNY. Oh no, Lawrence. Wrong. It's no use trying to twist things around to suit yourself. If it weren't for you, we wouldn't be here. Would we? (*Silence.*) There's no need to answer that.

LAWRENCE. If you don't want to be here, why are we going?

GINNY. We're going because you've made it necessary. You've left me no alternative.

LAWRENCE. So why couldn't we go in the car?

GINNY. Because I'm not taking the car to Brixton.°

LAWRENCE. Why not?

GINNY. Are you mad? Because it's not a place I want to take the car to.

LAWRENCE. Why the fuck isn't it a place you want to take the car to?

GINNY. Have you ever been to Brixton?

LAWRENCE. Yes.

GINNY. You've been to Brixton. For God's sake, Lawrence. You're fourteen.

LAWRENCE. What's wrong with Brixton?

GINNY. You're doing this deliberately.

LAWRENCE. What's wrong with Brixton?

GINNY. There's nowhere to park in Brixton.

LAWRENCE. Yes there is.

GINNY. I wouldn't know.

LAWRENCE. People park all over Brixton.

GINNY. So that's what you want me to do. The hell with everything, the hell with the car, park it all over Brixton like everyone else. I wonder why you're so determined to expose me to that.

LAWRENCE. You're so stupid. You're so fucking stupid.

GINNY. You simply can't discuss a thing sensibly, can you. Not with me. Not with your mother. You work yourself into a frenzy.

LAWRENCE. Fuck you!

GINNY. That's enough Lawrence, if you continue like this I'm going to pull the lever° and stop the train. Don't think I won't do it. I'm quite impulsive, you know.

LAWRENCE. All I'm saying is we ought to have taken the car.

GINNY. Oh for God's sake, do you think I like going to this place?

LAWRENCE. So why didn't you pick a guy near us?

Brixton: known as a rough, racially mixed working-class district   **lever:** switch to stop the train in an emergency (false alarms are heavily fined)

GINNY.   It isn't up to me to choose where the wretched man lives. (*Train is stopping. Silence.*)

LAWRENCE.   Stephen's dad's a psychiatrist. He lives in Richmond.°

GINNY.   Which one is Stephen, darling? Do I know him? I get so confused with all your friends trooping in and out. Is he the one with the ring through his nose?

LAWRENCE.   I don't know the guy, he's just a guy in my class. I only mention him because his dad's a—

GINNY.   They live in Richmond, do they? Where in Richmond?

LAWRENCE.   Fucked if I know.

GINNY.   Pardon, I didn't hear what you said.

LAWRENCE.   Look, the point I was making is that you don't have to take me all the way to Brixton just to see a—

GINNY.   What's become of your class list of addresses? Did they give you one this year? They usually type them out, don't they, and distribute them, I think it's so sensible, quite interesting to see the names, isn't it, quite multicultural your school, and of course then you can see where everyone lives. Did you give it me? I can't remember. We usually have it pinned up on the notice board in the kitchen. (*The train has started again.* GINNY *resumes her private voice.*) Do you want the whole carriage to know where you're going? You seem to be regarding this as some kind of joke. It's very far from a joke. A history of instability. That's what you're about to have.

LAWRENCE.   Do you have to keep raking over the future.

GINNY.   It's all very well for us to be enlightened about that sort of thing, which I am, because your father's poor cousin Elizabeth has been in analysis for years and you'd never know really, if she didn't insist on telling one which I always think is peculiar, she lacks the normal inhibitions . . . but I think it's terribly important for you to go into this experience in a positive frame of mind, purely for your own sake, because you want to get the most out of it, Lawrence, that's what we're paying for. I'd like to think that this young man could become a friend to you, someone to discuss things with that you might not want to say to me directly. Are there things like that Lawrence? (*Silence.*) I've done everything I could to avoid it coming to this, but all my initiatives have failed, haven't they. I shall have to admit when he questions me that all my initiatives have failed. I expect he will question me, won't he, don't you think? They like to involve the family don't they. I hope he won't ask me all sorts of embarrassing questions, the truth can be nasty, but let's leave your father out of this shall we. Anyway I defy some psychiatrist to make me talk, Lawrence.

LAWRENCE.   I defy him to make you stop.

Richmond: an upper-class suburb

GINNY.   Of course if there are things he wants to check with me, I shall cooperate. Because we don't want to be at cross purposes, do we. We want to know that everyone's being fair in what they say, we don't want this poor young man being used as an excuse to slag one another off,° Lawrence. As for my credentials as a mother, well frankly I think they'll stand up to examination. I don't feel I have anything to apologize for in that department. I wonder, should I have worn the cashmere dress, what do you think, the grey one, only I didn't want to walk in there looking like some bimbo who only ever thinks of her appearance.

LAWRENCE.   What's it matter?

GINNY.   Lawrence, I'm trying hard to be agreeable! It isn't easy! I don't know what it is that makes it so impossible for you to participate in the slightest thing that might give me pleasure.

LAWRENCE.   Like being dragged off to have my head shrunk.

GINNY.   Well you certainly haven't been worried about expanding it. (*Train is stopping. They sit in silence until it starts again.*) There's not really any reason for all this self-destructive behavior. Not if it's aimed at me, Lawrence.

LAWRENCE.   If it's aimed at you, it isn't self-destructive, is it.

GINNY.   Because if you do finally succeed in killing yourself with the life you lead I might just heave an enormous sigh of relief. What a terrible thing to say. How could I say such a terrible thing? This is what you've brought me to, Lawrence, I simply don't recognize myself any more. I was never meant to be horrid and cross and ugly, I was innocent, I was meant to be cared for. I pity any woman as stupid as I've been, all those years imagining my child would care for me. What an old-fashioned idea that's turned out to be. When I first took you to nursery school you couldn't bear me to leave you, tears flying everywhere. I'd have to change my skirt when I got home, there'd be sopping wet patches where you'd put your little face. Then one day that big teacher with the mustache said, "Don't worry Mrs. Amherst, five minutes after you're gone he's playing with the others as good as gold." Well. I didn't believe her of course. So do you know what I did? I squeezed around the side of the building and climbed on to the dustbins so I could see you all through the window. I couldn't believe my eyes, there you were running around with two other little boys, as happy as if I didn't exist. Those little drawings and messages I used to get, "Mummy I love you forever," you always knew how to make the grand gesture, didn't you. Love. You don't understand the meaning of the word. I've become bitter, Lawrence. I never expected to become a bitter person. You think you're bitter, I expect. I promise you, your bitterness is childsplay next to mine. I wanted a companion in this life to confide in, to laugh with, Lawrence, for heaven's sake, how long is it since you've

slag one another off: criticize or insult

laughed with me, why can't we laugh together for heaven's sake? All I wanted was someone to feel sorry for me when I cried and tell me when my clothes didn't suit me, to understand my side of things even when I might be hiding my feelings, because I don't complain even when there's a great deal to complain of. But let's not talk about your father. I wanted my child to see me as I really am, that's all. But you have your own view. I used to think of you as my little guardian angel. I used to think there was nothing you didn't understand. We communicated perfectly until you learned to talk. (*Silence.*) Your father and I confused you with clothes and money and electronic toys, we weakened your hold on reality. All of that is going to have to change. All of that is going to have to be earned. I'm sure the shrink in Brixton will agree. Judgment Day, Lawrence. As for the time you took money from my purse. Well of course it's symbolic.

LAWRENCE.   Symbolic, yeah.

GINNY.   The child stealing money from the mother's purse is actually trying to steal from her the love and attention which it feels for some reason it isn't able to get in the usual way. Don't ask me why you feel like that.

LAWRENCE.   I was skint.°

GINNY.   You know who Freud was, do you? Freud knew all about people like you. Freud discovered the subconscious of people like you, because what we see is only the tip of the iceberg, there's a great deal more unfortunately. Have you heard of the Oedipus Complex, in which sons want to marry their mothers it seems? Nothing to be ashamed of Lawrence, Freud says it's quite normal. But their mothers are already married, aren't they. Their mothers couldn't marry someone young enough to be their son, could they. They would have to say no, Lawrence. I'm sorry.

LAWRENCE.   Don't worry about it.

GINNY.   The point is, we understand that all this difficult behavior of yours relates to the fact that you're terribly dependent on me, if you could only admit it. If a person is the center of our lives, surely we should be able to tell them, give them some flowers, I don't know, I don't see why we have to be so repressed and English about these things, do you? If you could still say to me, as you did when you were so little and sweet, "Mummy I love you forever," it would solve so many problems. I truly believe that if you could come to terms with this thing, we shouldn't even be going on this wild goose chase to Brixton. We could get off this horrible train and take a taxi home. We'd be there in a quarter of an hour and you could still have the day off school, we could get you a video on the way and some cigarettes if you must, we could have fun together Lawrence, it feels like centuries since I've had fun. For God's sake why don't you just say the word and we'll go home.

LAWRENCE.   What word.

---

skint: out of money

GINNY.   Mummy I love you forever! (*Train stops.* GINNY *reverts to her "public" voice.*) We must get you some socks.

LAWRENCE.   My feet are growing.

GINNY.   They can't be, Spoff, not again.

LAWRENCE.   I need some boots.

GINNY.   Couldn't it be shoes this time darling. You all insist on these enormous boots. Don't you get tired lifting your feet up and down? You all look so exhausted all the time, those boots are draining you.

LAWRENCE.   Only they're getting tight.

GINNY.   Then we'd better do something about it, hadn't we. That's another blow to the poor old exchequer. Where's the best place darling, is it Kensington?

LAWRENCE.   Catford.°

GINNY.   I wish I'd been free to choose my own clothes when I was young. I think it's so important to choose one's own clothes at your age, after all you've got the rest of your life to be nicely dressed, haven't you? (*The train starts. Silence.*) Well?

LAWRENCE.   What.

GINNY.   Isn't there anything you can say?

LAWRENCE.   I don't know.

GINNY.   You don't know.

LAWRENCE.   Look. You don't make it easy. All right?

GINNY.   Oh Lawrence, let's not fight any more.

LAWRENCE.   I'm not fighting.

GINNY.   Look me in the eyes and say that.

LAWRENCE (*intensely embarrassed, looking her in the eyes*).   I'm not fighting.

GINNY.   Oh Lawrence I do love you.

LAWRENCE.   When can we get the boots then?

GINNY.   We paid sixty pounds for a new pair of boots only a month ago. I don't believe your feet have grown. You simply have no sense of proportion. I'm having to pay this man seventy you realize, this psychiatrist of yours, seventy pounds the first session is what he charges, they let you pay them for the sake of your self-respect, and I suppose one's self-respect is bound to cost, anyway there it is, I'm afraid that's your boots for this month.

LAWRENCE.   Bollocks,° you can afford it.

GINNY.   It's starting again, isn't it Lawrence.

LAWRENCE.   What is?

GINNY.   You deny it, do you? You deny that it's starting again.

LAWRENCE.   Deny what?

GINNY.   As soon as I give way to you an inch it starts. You're materialistic, Lawrence. You're absolutely hung up on possessions. Why? It's not as if you were poor or anything embarrassing like that.

Kensington . . . Catford: upper- and lower-class districts   **Bollocks:** (slang) testicles

LAWRENCE.   Oh for Christ's sake.

GINNY.   You're not very sincere, are you. You don't inspire me with much confidence honestly. I think you're cold, Lawrence. Calculating and cold. I think you'd walk over my dead body to get what you want. There isn't much you hold sacred, is there. I expect you're right Lawrence. Why should we hold a little thing like our mother and father sacred? It's every man for himself, isn't it. I ought to take a leaf out of your book. I've sacrificed myself for fifteen years and nothing to show for it, perhaps it's time I forgot about you and started looking for others to appreciate me. Don't imagine it doesn't happen. I could name you two women who are certainly no younger than I am, both with sons at the school, one of them in particular I'm thinking of, Angela met her out walking the dog and said, "How have you been keeping Helen"—never mind the name, and she replied, "I'm afraid I've been in bed all week." So naturally Angela said, oh you poor thing, this flu is really terrible, and do you know what she said, "Not with the flu, with Wayne." Wayne. A toy boy,° Lawrence. What do you think? Don't you think it would do me good? I ought to try it with your young psychiatrist perhaps, I'm sure with the benefit of all that training he'd know what I need. You haven't seen him, have you, he's blond with mobile features, well I'm still bloody mobile actually, tennis four times a week—besides men aren't choosy, are they— (*While she's saying this,* LAWRENCE *is pulling the lever to call the guard.*) Lawrence! What are you doing? Leave it alone. (*She jumps up and struggles with him. He pulls the lever and the train pulls into a station with the doors shut. Silence. When* GINNY *speaks again, she's trying to regain her "public" voice.*) What a stupid accident darling, why do you have to fidget with everything. (*She sits down.*) You've given everyone a dreadful fright.

LAWRENCE (*vaguely, to passengers staring at him*).   Sorry. Sorry.

GINNY.   Sit down Lawrence, sit down or I'll scream. There's nothing to be upset about. (*He sits.*) At least we know those peculiar things work now, I've always wondered, haven't you? (GUARD *arrives.*)

GUARD.   What's the problem here?

GINNY.   I'm terribly sorry, my son made the stupidest mistake, he honestly didn't mean it, did you Spoff, he just fell on it as the train moved.

LAWRENCE.   I did it on purpose.

GINNY.   This isn't the time for jokes, darling.

LAWRENCE.   I did it because I'm mad.

GINNY.   Stop it, Lawrence.

LAWRENCE.   She's taking me to see the shrink.

GINNY.   We're going to consult a careers adviser, his father wants him to be a lawyer, he certainly knows how to dominate a room.

LAWRENCE.   We're going to see a psychiatrist.

GUARD.   I don't give a monkeys if you're going to see Santa Claus.

LAWRENCE.   I'm in a different movie.

toy boy: young male lover

GINNY.   This is absurd, Lawrence. (*To* GUARD) You need a sense of humor, don't you.

GUARD.   You must do.

LAWRENCE.   Yes, I'm funny, aren't I, ha ha ha.

GUARD.   Do you have some form of identification, madam?

GINNY.   I'll give you my driving license, his name is Lawrence, his father's an absolute workaholic and we live in Wimbledon as you see, it isn't a flat it's a house.

GUARD.   Are you able to assume responsibility for your son, madam?

GINNY.   Do you take American Express?

LAWRENCE.   She's not my mother. She's nothing like my mother. My mother's dead. This woman is mad.

GUARD.   I have to take your particulars, madam, and you will receive a summons. (*He's writing down the name and address, using* GINNY'S *driving license as a guide.*)

LAWRENCE   (*to* GUARD).   Don't leave me alone with her. Take me with you.

GUARD.   I can't do that, you ain't housetrained.

LAWRENCE.   Scream if you're mad. (*He screams.*)

GINNY   (*in an undertone*).   Stop it. I'll get you the boots. (LAWRENCE *is about to scream again.*) And a leather jacket, all right?

LAWRENCE.   Green one.

GINNY   (*in an undertone*).   Yes.

LAWRENCE   (*to* GUARD).   Thank you for your prompt action, officer. People might have been killed.

GUARD.   We can still hope. (*He leaves.*)

LAWRENCE   (*calling after him*).   Thank you. (*As the* GUARD *regains his post, the doors open.*)

GINNY.   We do make things complicated for ourselves, don't we Lawrence. There isn't any need for things to be so complicated is there? Is there?

LAWRENCE.   No.

GINNY.   So let's keep it simple, shall we. Simple things are always so expensive. Where shall we go?

LAWRENCE.   I thought we were going to Brixton.

GINNY.   They won't have those boots in Brixton, darling, and this jacket, where can we get a green one, the Kings Road I expect, we could have a pancake.

LAWRENCE.   Hackney.°

GINNY.   Is there a train to Hackney?

LAWRENCE.   Better take the car. (*The train starts.*)

GINNY.   Yes, perhaps we'd better take the car.

King's Road . . . Hackney: a shopping street for youthful modern clothes; a working-class district northeast of London

QUESTIONS

1. What does the encounter with Emma reveal about Ginny's values? Why does Ginny speak in two voices, "public" when the train is quiet and not moving, and "private" at other times?
2. What is the significance of Ginny's concern about parking in Brixton, her description to the guard of her house in Wimbledon, the shopping areas that she offers to take Lawrence to? How are Lawrence's references to other areas relevant to the situation between him and his mother?
3. Ginny speaks of Lawrence's materialistic values and of his dependence on her. How are these remarks ironic?
4. What can you infer about the relationship between Ginny and her husband? How is it implied by Ginny's hope that Lawrence would become her "guardian angel"?
5. There is no specific information about why Lawrence is being taken to a psychiatrist. What can you infer from his mother's remarks about his behavior? What can you infer from Lawrence's speeches and actions?
6. Who seems to you to be more in need of counseling, Lawrence or Ginny? Explain.
7. The title of the play refers to the dangerous space between a station platform and the train, warning the passengers to be aware ("mind") of the physical danger of falling between them. What other kinds of "gap" is the play concerned with?

Václav Havel

Unveiling

CHARACTERS

VERA
MICHAEL
FERDINAND VANĚK

On stage is the apartment of VERA *and* MICHAEL. *It consists of a large living room, extending into a step-up dining area upstage. A serving window connects the dining area with the kitchen behind the stage. Stage right, there is*

UNVEILING Written and privately performed in the mid-1970s and first printed in 1978. Translated by Jan Novak. Václav Havel (b. 1936) was a leading Czech dissident during the stringent government crackdown imposed by the Warsaw Pact invasion in 1968 to suppress freedoms that had gradually developed in Communist Czechoslovakia. Havel was banned from public life for his writings, was imprisoned for four years, lost his position in the theater, and worked in a brewery. During the 1970s Havel created the character Vaněk for a series of one-act plays, and Vaněk was taken up as a character in other plays by his friends Pavel Landovský and Pavel Kohout, two other dissident playwrights who are named in this play. The play is set at a time when expensive luxuries and foreign travel were only available to people willing to subscribe to the rigid controls imposed by the regime. After the fall of the Communists in 1989, Havel was elected president of Czechoslovakia.

a door leading into a hallway; stage left, a large fireplace; at the center of the stage stands an antique table, surrounded by soft, modern seats. A mass of sundry antiques and curious objects decorates the room—for example, there is an Art Nouveau marquee, a Chinese vase, a limestone Baroque angel, an inlaid chest, a folkloristic painting on a glass pane, a Russian icon, old handmortars and grinders, and so on; a niche in the wall houses a wooden Gothic madonna; a rococo musical clock adorns the fireplace, and a Turkish scimitar hangs above it. The dining area is furnished in a "rustic style," with a wooden farm-cart wheel on the wall; the floor is covered with a thick, shaggy carpet, on it lie several Persian mats and, near the fireplace, a bear hide with a stuffed head; downstage left stands a filigreed wooden confessional. The room also has a hi-fi stereo and a bar cart standing near the fireplace and holding various bottles, glasses, ice cubes, as well as a bowl with stuffed oysters. As the curtain rises, VANĚK *is standing at the door, evidently having just come in.* VERA *and* MICHAEL *are facing him.* VANĚK *is holding a bouquet of flowers behind his back.*

VERA.   We're so glad that you've made it—
MICHAEL.   We were afraid that you might not make it any more—
VERA.   We've been looking forward to seeing you so much—
MICHAEL.   What can I get you? A whiskey?
VANĚK.   All right— (MICHAEL *steps over to the bar cart and starts preparing three whiskeys;* VANĚK *is momentarily at a loss about what to do, then he hands the flowers to* VERA.)
VERA.   Oh, they are lovely! (*She takes the bouquet and looks at it.*) And you never forget— (*She smells it.*) What a beautiful aroma! Thank you, Ferdinand— (VERA *walks upstage and puts the flowers into a vase;* VANĚK *looks around the apartment with curiosity. A short pause.*)
VANĚK.   It looks different here somehow—
VERA.   I hope so! Michael has poured a lot of sweat into it! You know how he is when he gets involved in something: He won't let go till he has everything just the way he's planned it—
MICHAEL.   I only finished the thing the day before yesterday: we haven't had anybody over yet, so this actually is sort of an unveiling. Ice?
VANĚK.   All right— (VERA *comes back downstage; the surprised* VANĚK *is still looking around.*) Where did you get all this?
MICHAEL.   It wasn't easy, as you can imagine. I did have a few contacts among the antique dealers and collectors. I had to establish a few more. The most important thing was not to give up when I wasn't able to get my hands on what I wanted the first time around—
VERA.   He did quite a job on this, didn't he?
VANĚK.   I guess so—
VERA.   I confess that even I didn't think it would come out this well! When you want to give your place some character, it's not merely enough to like old things—you have to know how to get them and how to present them and how to integrate them with your modern furnishings—but, it so happens that Michael is really good at that—that's why you won't find

a single goof here— (MICHAEL *hands the glasses to* VERA *and* VANĚK, *then he takes his glass, raises it, and turns to* VANĚK.)

MICHAEL.   Welcome, Ferdinand—

VERA.   We've missed you—

MICHAEL.   As I was working on this, I thought about you often— what you were going to say when you saw it all.

VANĚK.   Well, cheers— (*They all drink; a short pause.*)

MICHAEL.   Of course, if I didn't have Vera's full support, it would have never come out like this. And it wasn't just a matter of support and understanding either, she gave me direct assistance in this, too! Take that Turkish scimitar there—how do you like it?

VANĚK.   It's nice—

MICHAEL.   And how does it fit in with everything here?

VANĚK.   Very well—

MICHAEL.   You see, and it's something that Vera found on her very own, and she even put it up there, too—all the while not knowing that this was exactly the thing I had in mind for that spot over the fireplace! Isn't that awesome?

VANĚK.   That's great— (*A short, awkward pause.*)

VERA.   Have a seat—

VANĚK.   Thank you— (*They all sit down in the soft seats. A short pause.* VANĚK *is looking around again;* VERA *and* MICHAEL *watch him with satisfaction;* VANĚK *eventually notices the confessional.*) What's that?

MICHAEL.   It's what you see—a confessional—

VANĚK.   Where did you get that?

MICHAEL.   You won't believe how lucky I was. I heard that they were going to liquidate a church that'd been closed down, so I dropped everything and jumped in the car. And this is the result. I managed to get it out of the sexton for three hundred—

VANĚK.   That's all?

MICHAEL.   Not bad, is it? Pure Baroque!

VANĚK.   What are you going to do with it?

MICHAEL.   What do you mean, what are we going to do with it? You don't like it?

VANĚK.   Well I do—

MICHAEL.   Isn't that a fantastic object, we're really happy about it, aren't we, Vera?

VERA.   It really is a superb piece of craftsmanship, I'd say that Michael really got another one of his steals there— (*A short pause.*) What do you think of the dining area?

VANĚK (*turns around*).   It's cozy—

VERA.   Wasn't that a nice idea—to do it so simply—as if on a farm—

VANĚK.   Mmn— (*A short pause.*)

MICHAEL.   Do you know what I like best here?

VANĚK.   What?

MICHAEL. This Gothic madonna! I needed one that would fit into that niche, and they were all either bigger or smaller—

VANĚK. And there was no way to enlarge the niche?

MICHAEL. But that's just what I didn't want to do. It strikes me that it's got the perfect dimensions the way it is—

VERA. See, that's Michael! He'd rather wear out his feet than simply enlarge the thing! (*Pause.*)

MICHAEL. And what about you? When are you going to get started?

VANĚK. On what?

MICHAEL. On your place—

VANĚK. I don't know—

MICHAEL. You should finally do something about it! You can't go on living out of boxes forever—

VANĚK. I don't even pay any attention to it anymore—

MICHAEL. If you don't feel like tackling it yourself, why doesn't Eva do something about it? She has plenty of time on her hands—

VERA. I think Eva actually needs to get involved in something like that—it would be a good way to get her back on her feet—

MICHAEL. We would gladly come to the rescue if she found she couldn't handle something—

VERA. Michael has tons of experience with this now—he'd tell her what to do—where to start—what she'd need—

MICHAEL. I'd tell her who's got what—where to go and who to see—

VERA. That's true, Ferdinand. Why don't you put Eva in charge of it anyway?

VANĚK. It's not really Eva's cup of tea—

VERA. We know that, but if you were to waken her interest somehow—

MICHAEL. Damn it, you have to do something about that home of yours—

VERA. You know, Michael and I think that a person lives the way a person lives. When you have what we call a place with character, your whole life suddenly—like it or not—acquires a certain face, too—a sort of new dimension—a different rhythm, a different content, a different order—isn't that so, Michael?

MICHAEL. She's right, Ferdinand! One really shouldn't be indifferent to what one eats, one shouldn't be indifferent to what one eats on, and what one eats with, what one dries oneself with, what one wears, what one takes a bath in, what one sleeps on. And once any of these things starts to matter, you'll find that something else suddenly matters, too, and then another thing gets you, and so a whole sort of a chain of things develops—and if you head down that road, what else can it mean but that you're upgrading your life to another, higher level of culture—and that you raise yourself to a kind of higher harmony—which then in effect translates itself into your relationships with other people! You tell him, Vera!

VERA.   That is a fact, Ferdinand! If the two of you were to put a little more effort into the way you live, I'm sure that things would get smoother in your marriage, too—

VANĚK.   But things are smooth—

VERA.   Ferdinand!

VANĚK.   But really—

VERA.   You don't like to talk about it, I know. But you know, Michael and I have been talking about the two of you a lot lately; we've been thinking about you a lot—and we really care about how you two live!

MICHAEL.   We're only trying to help, Ferdinand!

VERA.   You're our best friend—we like you a lot—you have no idea how happy we'd be for you if your situation finally got resolved somehow!

VANĚK.   What situation?

VERA.   Let's just drop it. Shouldn't I light the fireplace?

VANĚK.   Not for me—

MICHAEL.   So I'll put on some music, all right?

VERA.   Michael has just brought a ton of new records from Switzerland—

VANĚK.   Maybe later, perhaps? (*Pause; then suddenly the musical clock on the mantelpiece breaks into a period tune, startling* VANĚK. *After a while, the clock falls silent. Pause.*)

VERA.   So tell us—how is everything with you?

VANĚK.   Well, you know—nothing's changed—

VERA.   Is it true that you've got a job in a brewery now?

VANĚK.   Yes—

VERA.   That's horrible! (*Pause. Then* VERA *points at the bar cart.*) Michael, would you—

MICHAEL.   Oh yeah— (MICHAEL *takes the bowl with oysters off the bar and stands it in front of* VANĚK.)

VERA.   Help yourself—

VANĚK.   What is it?

MICHAEL.   That's Vera's specialty: sauteed groombles—°

VANĚK.   Groombles? I never heard of this—

VERA.   We've really become very fond of them lately, Michael has just brought a whole box of them from Switzerland—

MICHAEL.   Because Vera really knows how to make them—

VERA.   What you have to do is to watch for the precise moment, when they've just stopped puffing up and before they start falling—

MICHAEL.   Taste one! (VANĚK *takes one oyster and, using a spoon, begins to scoop out its contents. He concentrates on the taste;* VERA *and* MICHAEL *watch him tensely.*) So what do you think?

VANĚK.   It's good—

groombles: this and **woodpeak** (p.929), coined words represent invented terms in the Czech text

MICHAEL.   Isn't it?

VANĚK.   You went to all the trouble of making this just for me?

VERA.   We're having our unveiling today, right?

VANĚK.   It sort of reminds me of blackberries a little bit—

VERA.   That may be because I put in a few drops of woodpeak° to help the taste—

VANĚK.   Drops of what?

MICHAEL.   Woodpeak—

VERA.   That's my original contribution—

VANĚK.   Really?

MICHAEL.   An excellent idea, isn't it? I can't help it, but Vera's really got a talent for cooking. A week doesn't go by without her making some novelty—and she always uses her imagination to improve it. Take this Saturday for example—what was it that we had now? Oh yeah, the liver with walnuts! And it was such a delicacy; anyway, would you ever think of putting woodpeak on groombles?

VANĚK.   Never—

MICHAEL.   See what I mean! (VANĚK *puts away the empty oyster shell and wipes his mouth with a napkin.*)

VERA.   Well, it's a joy cooking for Michael! He knows how to appreciate and praise even the most modest idea, and when something turns out well, he really gets off on it. If he just stuffed everything in like a mechanical pie-eater, not even knowing what it is that he's swallowing, then I probably wouldn't have so much fun with it either—

VANĚK.   I can understand that—

MICHAEL.   But there's even more to it than that. When you know that an interesting dinner, some small gourmet surprise, is waiting for you at home, you look that much more forward to getting there and you have that much less reason to go bar-hopping with your buddies. Maybe it'll strike you as being petty, but I think that these things also represent a kind of cement that holds a family together and helps to create that important feeling that you've got something to back you up at home. Don't you think?

VANĚK.   Yes, of course— (*Pause.*)

VERA.   How's Eva doing? Has she learned to cook anything yet?

VANĚK.   She's always cooked—

VERA.   Granted, but how!

VANĚK.   I pretty much like her cooking—

VERA.   Because you got used to it already. Don't get offended, but those pepper steaks she made when we were over that time before Christmas—it was before Christmas, wasn't it?

VANĚK.   Yeah—

---

woodpeak: see note on previous page

VERA.   Don't get offended, but they were dreadful! Do you remember, Michael?

MICHAEL.   How could I forget!

VANĚK.   Eva was a little nervous that time—

VERA.   I'm sorry, but something like that should never ever happen to a cook! What does she cook for you usually anyway?

VANĚK.   We tend to have cold-plate dinners—

VERA.   Even on Saturdays?

VANĚK.   Sometimes we have something warm, too—breaded cutlets, for example—

MICHAEL.   Listen, Ferdinand, it's none of my business, but why don't you send Eva to some of those courses? She has plenty of time on her hands—

VERA.   Eva? Come on! You think Eva would take any courses?

MICHAEL.   Well, that's true—

VERA.   If she did learn how to cook though, it would immediately boost her self-confidence—but she won't see the connection: She's floating around somewhere, God knows where—

VANĚK.   I think her cooking's fine—

VERA.   Ferdinand!

VANĚK.   Really, I—

MICHAEL.   You don't like to talk about it, I know. But you know Vera and I have been talking about the two of you a lot lately, we've been thinking about you a lot—and we really care about how you two live!

VERA.   We're only trying to help, Ferdinand!

MICHAEL.   You're our best friend—we like you a lot—you have no idea how happy we'd be for you if your situation finally got resolved somehow!

VANĚK.   What situation?

MICHAEL.   Let's just drop it. Shouldn't I light the fireplace?

VANĚK.   Not for me—

VERA.   So I'll put on some music, all right? Michael has just brought a ton of new records from Switzerland—

VANĚK.   Maybe later, okay? (*Pause. Then suddenly the musical clock on the mantelpiece breaks into a period tune, startling* FERDINAND. *After a while, the clock falls silent. Pause.*)

MICHAEL.   So what do you actually do there, in that brewery?

VANĚK.   I draw beer—

MICHAEL.   Into barrels?

VANĚK.   Yes—

MICHAEL.   That's got to be pretty rough, doesn't it?

VANĚK.   It's not that bad— (*Pause.*)

MICHAEL.   Are we going to show Pete to Ferdinand?

VERA.   A little later, Michael, he might still wake up right now—

VANĚK.   How is Pete doing?

MICHAEL.   He's fantastic! I'd only been gone to that Switzerland for ten days, but when I got back, I tell you I barely recognized him—that's how much of a jump he's made in that time!

VERA.   He's extremely curious—

MICHAEL.   Bright—

VERA.   Perceptive—

MICHAEL.   He has a superb memory—

VERA.   And yet he's such a good-looking kid, too!

MICHAEL.   Just to give you an example. Do you know what he asked me this morning? (*To* VERA) I forgot to tell you about that! All of a sudden, he comes to me and says, "Daddy, can a frog drown?" What do you think about that? Isn't that awesome?

VERA.   Did he really ask you that? If a frog can drown?

MICHAEL.   Imagine that! He comes to me and says, "Daddy, can a frog drown?"

VERA.   Outstanding! I don't even know if I could have thought of that. Can a frog drown! Outstanding! Outstanding!

MICHAEL.   You know, Ferdinand, sometimes I say to myself that to have a child and to bring it up is the only thing that has any meaning in life! Because it is such an awesome encounter with the mystery of life—such a lesson in life appreciation! Unless you actually go through it, you can never even understand it—

VERA.   Absolutely, Ferdinand, it's an awesomely strange and beautiful experience: One day this tiny being shows up here—and you know he is yours—that without you, he wouldn't even be here—that you've made him and now he's here—and he's living his own life—and is growing before your eyes—and then he starts to walk—and say things—and reason—and ask questions—now isn't that a miracle?

VANĚK.   Certainly is—

MICHAEL.   You know a child really changes you a lot—suddenly you begin to understand everything differently, more deeply—life—nature—people—and all of a sudden your own life—like it or not—acquires sort of a new dimension—a different rhythm, a different content, a different order—isn't that so, Vera?

VERA.   Exactly! Just take the responsibility you suddenly have. It's up to you what kind of a person he will turn out to be—what he'll feel—think—how he'll live—

MICHAEL.   But not only that: Because it was you who tossed him into this world, who offered it to him for his use and who provides him with some orientation in it, you suddenly start feeling a much greater responsibility for this world that now contains your child—do you know what I mean?

VANĚK.   I guess so—

MICHAEL.   I never believed this, but now I see how a child gives you a brand new point of view, a brand new set of values—and suddenly it begins to dawn on you that the most important thing now is what you do for that child, what sort of a home you create for him, what sort of a start you give him, what openings you provide—and in the light of this awesome responsibility you start seeing the utter insignificance of most of the things you had once thought world-shattering—

VERA.   How did he put it? Can a frog drown? Do you see what that tiny head can give birth to? Isn't that fantastic?

VANĚK.   Mmn— (*Pause.*)

MICHAEL.   So what about you two?

VANĚK.   What about us two?

MICHAEL.   Why don't you have a child yet anyway?

VANĚK.   I don't know—

VERA.   Eva probably doesn't want one, does she?

VANĚK.   Oh no—she does—

VERA.   I really don't understand that girl! Is she so afraid of all the worries that go along with having a child? Because if she really wanted a baby, you would have had one ages ago!

MICHAEL.   You are the ones who will lose out by not pursuing this—because for the two of you, a child would definitely be the best possible solution! It would help you, Ferdinand, to see many things far more sensibly, realistically, wisely—

VERA.   It would straighten out your relationship, because it would give you a common purpose in life—

MICHAEL.   And what a good thing it would be for Eva!

VERA.   You'd see how it would change her!

MICHAEL.   How it would suddenly bring out the woman in her again!

VERA.   How it would teach her to pay attention to the house—

MICHAEL.   To cleanliness—

VERA.   To routine—

MICHAEL.   To you—

VERA.   To herself—

MICHAEL.   Seriously, Ferdinand, you ought to have child, believe us!

VERA.   You have no idea how happy we'd be for you!

MICHAEL.   We really would, Ferdinand—

VANĚK.   I believe you— (*Pause.*)

VERA.   Of course, there are women who don't respond even to that—and then you really feel for the children—

MICHAEL.   Of course, just to rely on the kid as some sort of panacea that will solve all your problems, that wouldn't be right either—a certain aptitude probably already has to be there before anything else—

VERA.   Absolutely! For example, Michael here makes an ideal father: He drives himself hard at the office, till I feel really sorry for him sometimes, just so that he brings home some money—and then he still devotes almost all of his free time to the family and to the home! Just take this remodelling he did. He came from the office and instead of stretching out and relaxing, he went right back to work—just so Pete can grow up in a nice environment from the very beginning, and learn to love nice things! And even while doing all that, he still found the time for Pete—

MICHAEL.   Of course, Vera is awesome, too. Do you know what it is—to shop, take care of the kid, cook, clean up, do the laundry—while the apartment is a disaster area—despite all that to look just the way she looks right now? That really is no joke! I have to say I admire her more and more as time goes on—

VERA.   A lot of that is because our marriage is working—

MICHAEL.   Definitely! We get along just awesomely. I don't even remember us having any serious quarrels lately—

VERA.   We are interested in one another, yet we don't limit or tie each other down—

MICHAEL.   We are kind and attentive to one another without tiring each other with too much thoughtfulness—

VERA.   And we always have things to say to each other, because we're fortunate enough to have exactly the same sense of humor—

MICHAEL.   The same definition of happiness—

VERA.   The same interests—

MICHAEL.   The same taste—

VERA.   The same views on family life—

MICHAEL.   And what is extremely important: We also perfectly complement each other physically—

VERA.   That's true, it is really extremely important! And Michael is awesome in that respect—he can be wild as well as tender—honestly selfish as well as awesomely attentive and giving—passionately spontaneous as well as inventively cunning—

MICHAEL.   But Vera deserves all the credit for that, because she manages to excite and stimulate me again and again—

VERA.   You'd be surprised, Ferdinand, how often we do it! And that's only possible because we always approach it as though it were our very first time, so that it becomes something new, something different for us every time. Something unique, unforgettable. In short, we really invest ourselves fully into it, and, consequently, for us it can never become just a matter of a stereotype or a boring routine—

MICHAEL.   You see, Vera knows, too, that to be a good wife doesn't mean merely being a good homemaker and a good mother—she rightly feels that what it means more than anything else is to be a good lover! That's why she takes such wonderful care of herself. So that she keeps her sex appeal even while doing the heaviest chores—in fact, even more so then than at other times!

VERA.   Do you remember the day before yesterday, Michael—when you got home early just as I was scrubbing the floor?

MICHAEL.   It was beautiful, wasn't it?

VERA.   Why do you think Michael isn't drawn to other women? Because he knows that he doesn't have some mop-swinging wifey at home, but a real woman who knows how to take as well as give—

MICHAEL.   Of course, Vera is still just as attractive as always—I'd even say that now, after Pete, she has ripened even more—she has an astonishingly fresh and youthful body now—well, judge for yourself! (MICHAEL *undoes* VERA's *clothes, uncovering her breasts.*) Not bad, right?

VANĚK.   Great—

MICHAEL.   Do you know what I will do, for example?

VANĚK.   No—

MICHAEL.   I'll kiss her, switching from her ear to her neck and back—which really turns her on and I like it, too—like this, look! (MICHAEL *starts to kiss* VERA, *alternating between her ear and her neck;* VERA *groans excitedly.*)

VERA.   Don't darling, no—please—wait—a little later, okay—come on— (MICHAEL *stops kissing* VERA.)

MICHAEL.   We'll talk a little more first, then we'll show you more—to give you an idea of the range of our technique—

VANĚK.   Won't I make you nervous by being here?

VERA.   You silly boy! You're our best friend, right?

MICHAEL.   And we'll be happy to show you how far you can take these things! (*Pause.*)

VERA.   So what about you two?

VANĚK.   How do you mean?

VERA.   Do you still sleep with each other at all?

VANĚK.   Oh yes—now and then—

VERA.   Not too often, right?

VANĚK.   That depends—

VERA.   And how is it?

VANĚK.   I don't know—it's normal—

MICHAEL.   I'm sure you don't put any effort into it—just go through the motions, so it's over and done with—

VANĚK.   We do our best—

VERA.   I don't understand that girl at all! Why wouldn't she try a little harder at least in this—

MICHAEL.   Is it really impossible for you to get her involved in this a little more?

VANĚK.   We really don't pay that much attention to it—

VERA.   See? That's where you go wrong, ignoring such an important thing! That's why you're in the shape you're in! Yet it would require so little effort—and maybe it would pull your relationship back up on its feet again!

MICHAEL.   And what a good thing it would be for Eva—you'd see how it would change her!

VERA.   How it would bring out the woman in her again!

MICHAEL.   How it would teach her to pay attention to the house—

VERA.   To you—

MICHAEL.   To herself—

VERA.   And what a change it would effect in you! Just imagine, suddenly there are no more reasons to go bar-hopping with your cronies—

MICHAEL.   Chase waitresses—

VERA.   Drink—

VANĚK.   I don't chase waitresses—

VERA.   Ferdinand!

VANĚK.   I don't—

VERA.   You don't like to talk about it, I know. But you know Michael and I have been talking about the two of you a lot lately, we've been thinking about you a lot—and we really care about how you two live!

MICHAEL.   We're only trying to help, Ferdinand!

VERA.   You're our best friend—we like you a lot—you have no idea how happy we'd be for you if your situation finally got resolved somehow!

VANĚK.   What situation?

VERA.   Let's just drop it. Shouldn't I light the fireplace?

VANĚK.   Not for me—

MICHAEL.   So I'll put on some music, all right?

VERA.   Michael has just brought a ton of new records from Switzerland—

VANĚK.   Maybe later, okay? (*Pause. Then suddenly the musical clock on the mantelpiece breaks into a period tune, startling* VANĚK. *After a while, the clock falls silent. Pause.*)

MICHAEL.   But anyway—that's what I call art!

VANĚK.   What is?

MICHAEL.   That madonna—

VANĚK.   Mmn—

MICHAEL.   Do you realize the dramatic tension that arises between her and that scimitar?

VANĚK.   Mmn— (*Pause.*)

VERA.   You probably don't use much woodpeak, do you?

VANĚK.   Not really—

VERA.   If you'd like, Michael could bring you some from Switzerland—

VANĚK.   Oh yeah?

MICHAEL.   You know that'd be no trouble at all for me. (*Pause.*)

VERA.   Have some more—

VANĚK.   No, thank you— (*Pause.*)

MICHAEL.   Why didn't you bring Eva with you?

VANĚK.   She didn't feel well—

MICHAEL.   It's not any of my business, of course, but you should take her out now and then—give her a reason to put some nice clothes on, put on some make-up, do her hair—

VANĚK.   She does her hair—

MICHAEL.   Ferdinand!

VANĚK.   She does—

MICHAEL.   You don't like to talk about it, I know. But we're only trying to help—

VERA.   We like you a lot—

MICHAEL.   You're our best friend—

VANĔK.   I know— (*Pause; the musical clock plays its tune.*)

MICHAEL.   Did you get my card from Switzerland?

VANĔK.   That was from you?

MICHAEL.   You didn't figure that out?

VANĔK.   Should have thought of it— (*Pause.*)

VERA (*to* MICHAEL).   What did Pete ask you now? Can a frog drown?

MICHAEL.   Right, imagine that—

VERA.   Outstanding! Outstanding! (*Pause.*)

MICHAEL (*to* VANĔK).   Have some more—

VANĔK.   No, thank you— (*Pause.*)

VERA.   Do you know what we started to do again?

VANĔK.   What?

VERA.   Going to the sauna!

VANĔK.   Really?

VERA.   We've been going every week now, and you wouldn't believe how good it is for us. For the nerves, you know—

MICHAEL.   Do you want to start coming with us?

VANĔK.   Not really—

VERA.   Why not?

VANĔK.   I wouldn't have the time—

MICHAEL.   Don't get offended, Ferdinand, but you're making a mistake! It would really get you into a better shape spiritually, psychically, as well as physically, and it would definitely be better for you and cost you less time, too, than the endless tongue-thrashing in bars with all those wise-guy cronies of yours—

VANĔK.   Whom do you mean by that?

MICHAEL.   Well, all those various failures. Landovský and so on—

VANĔK.   I wouldn't call them failures—

VERA.   Ferdinand!

VANĔK.   Not at all—

VERA.   You don't like to talk about it, I know. But we're only trying to help you—

MICHAEL.   We like you a lot—

VERA.   You're our best friend—

VANĔK.   I know— (*Pause; the clock plays its tune.*)

MICHAEL.   Do you know what Vera promised me?

VANĔK.   What's that?

MICHAEL.   That she'll give me another child next year!

VANĔK.   That's nice—

VERA.   I think Michael deserves no less— (*Pause.*) Do you know what Michael brought me from Switzerland?

VANĚK.   What's that?

VERA.   An electric almond peeler—

MICHAEL.   You'll have to take a look at it, it's a beautiful thing—

VERA.   As well as practical—

MICHAEL.   Because Vera does a lot with almonds, so it saves her tons of time—

VANĚK.   I believe it— (*Pause.*)

VERA.   Have some more—

VANĚK.   No, thank you— (*Pause.*)

MICHAEL.   Listen, Ferdinand—

VANĚK.   Huh?

MICHAEL.   Do you ever write anything anymore?

VANĚK.   Not a whole lot—

MICHAEL.   That's what we thought—

VANĚK.   Now that I have that job, I don't have the time for it, nor the concentration—

MICHAEL.   But from what I hear, you weren't doing much writing anyway, even before you got this job—

VANĚK.   Not all that much—

VERA.   Listen, didn't you maybe take that job because in your own mind it gave you an excuse for not writing?

VANĚK.   Not that—

MICHAEL.   So what is your real reason for not writing? Is it just that it's not pouring out? Or are you going through some kind of a crisis?

VANĚK.   It's hard to say—the times, everything that is going on—you get this feeling of futility—

MICHAEL.   Don't get offended, Ferdinand, but I think that the times are just another excuse for you, just like the job at the brewery, and that the real problem is inside of you and nowhere else! You're just all bent out of shape, you've given up on everything, you find it too tedious to strive for anything, to fight, to wrestle with problems—

VERA.   Michael is right, Ferdinand. Somehow you should finally pull yourself together—

MICHAEL.   Take care of problems at home—with Eva—

VERA.   Start a family—

MICHAEL.   Give your place some character—

VERA.   Learn how to budget your time—

MICHAEL.   Stop carousing—

VERA.   Start going to the sauna again—

MICHAEL.   Simply begin to live a decent, healthy, rational life—

VANĚK.   I don't feel that I'm doing anything irrational—

MICHAEL.   Ferdinand!

VANĚK.   I don't—

MICHAEL.   You don't like to talk about it, I know. But we're only trying to help you—

VERA.   We like you a lot—

MICHAEL.   You're our best friend—

VERA.   You have no idea how happy we'd be for you if your situation finally got resolved somehow!

MICHAEL.   Shouldn't I light the fireplace?

VANĚK.   Not for me—

VERA.   So I'll put some music on, all right? Michael has just brought a ton of new records from Switzerland—

VANĚK.   Maybe later, okay? (*Pause; the musical clock plays its tune.*)

MICHAEL.   Listen, Ferdinand—

VANĚK.   Huh?

MICHAEL.   Listen, honestly now. Are you serious with that brewery?

VANĚK.   What do you mean?

MICHAEL.   You know, don't get offended now, but we just don't understand what the purpose of the whole thing is—

VERA.   To just throw yourself away like that—to bury yourself in a brewery somewhere—only to ruin your health—

MICHAEL.   All these gestures are completely senseless! What are you trying to prove? It's been a long time since that kind of thing impressed anybody—

VANĚK.   I'm sorry, but it was the only thing I could do in my situation—

MICHAEL.   Ferdinand! Don't tell me that you couldn't do better than that—if only you really wanted to and tried a little harder—I'm convinced that with a little more effort and a little less ego on your part, you could've long been sitting in an editorial office somewhere—

VERA.   You are, after all, basically an intelligent, hard-working person—you have talent—you have clearly proven that in the past with your writing—so why would you suddenly be afraid of confronting life?

MICHAEL.   Life is rough and the world is divided. The world doesn't give a damn about us and nobody's coming to our rescue—we're in a nasty predicament, and it will get worse and worse—and you are not going to change any of it! So why beat your head against the wall and charge the bayonets?

VERA.   What I can't understand is how could you have got mixed up with those Communists—

VANĚK.   What Communists?

VERA.   Well, that Kohout and his crowd—you don't have anything in common with them! Don't be silly, forget about them and go your own way—

MICHAEL.   We're not saying that breaking out of that charmed circle is going to be easy, but it's your only chance and nobody's going to do it for you! In these things, it's every man for himself, but you're definitely strong enough to withstand that isolation!

VERA.   Just take a look at us—you could be just as happy as we are—

MICHAEL.   You could have a home with character of your own—

VERA.   Full of nice things and good family vibrations—

MICHAEL.   A well-coiffed and elegant wife—

VERA.   A bright kid—

MICHAEL.   You could have a more appropriate job—

VERA.   Make a few crowns—

MICHAEL.   Later they'd even let you go to Switzerland—

VERA.   Eat decent food—

MICHAEL.   Dress better—

VERA.   Go to the sauna—

MICHAEL.   Now and then you could have some friends over—

VERA.   Show them your place—

MICHAEL.   Your kid—

VERA.   Put on some music for them—

MICHAEL.   Make groombles—

VERA.   In short, live a little more like humans! (VANĚK *has quietly got up and begun shyly to back up to the door. When* VERA *and* MICHAEL *notice it, they stand up in surprise.*)

MICHAEL.   Ferdinand—

VANĚK.   Mmn—

MICHAEL.   What's the matter?

VANĚK.   Nothing's the matter—

VERA.   You're leaving?

VANĚK.   I have to go now—

MICHAEL.   Go where?

VANĚK.   Home—

VERA.   Home? How come? Why?

VANĚK.   It's late—I get up early—

MICHAEL.   But you can't do this—

VANĚK.   I really have to go—

VERA.   I don't understand! Here we are in the middle of our unveiling—

MICHAEL.   We wanted to give you a tour of the place—

VERA.   Show you everything we have here—

MICHAEL.   We thought you'd finish that bottle—

VERA.   Eat the rest of the groombles—

MICHAEL.   Take a look at Pete—

VERA.   Michael wanted to tell you about Switzerland—

MICHAEL.   Vera wanted to light the fireplace—

VERA.   Michael wanted to play those new records for you—

MICHAEL.   We thought you'd stay the night—

VERA.   See how we make love—

MICHAEL.   That we'd share a little of that family warmth you don't have at home—

VERA. Get into a different frame of mind—

MICHAEL. Pull you out of that mess you're living in—

VERA. Get you back up on your feet—

MICHAEL. Suggest some ways of how you can resolve your situation—

VERA. Show you what happiness is—

MICHAEL. And love—

VERA. Family harmony—

MICHAEL. A life that has some meaning—

VERA. You know that we're only trying to help you—

MICHAEL. That we like you a lot—

VERA. That you are our best friend—

MICHAEL. You cannot be this ungrateful!

VERA. We don't deserve this—not while we're trying to do so much for you!

MICHAEL. Who did you think Vera has spent the whole afternoon baking the groombles for?

VERA. Who do you think Michael has bought that whiskey for?

MICHAEL. Who do you think we wanted to play those records for? Why do you think I wasted all that hard currency on them, and dragged them half way across Europe?

VERA. Why do you think I dressed up like this, put the make-up and the perfume on, got my hair done?

MICHAEL. Why do you think we fixed this place up like this anyway? Who do you think we're doing all this for? For ourselves? (VANĚK *is by the door now.*)

VANĚK. I'm sorry, but I'll be off now—

VERA (*agitated*). Ferdinand! You can't just leave us here! You're not going to do that to us! You can't just pick up and go now; there's so much we still wanted to tell you! What are we going to do here without you? Don't you understand that? Stay, I beg you, will you stay here with us!

MICHAEL. You haven't even seen our electric almond peeler yet!

VANĚK. See you later! And thank you for the groombles— (VANĚK *is leaving, but before he closes the door behind him,* VERA *breaks into hysterical sobs.* VANĚK *stops and looks at her, not knowing what to do.*)

VERA (*crying*). You're selfish! A disgusting, unfeeling, inhuman egotist! An ungrateful, ignorant traitor! I hate you—I hate you so much—go away! Go away! (VERA *runs to the bouquet that she got from* VANĚK, *tears it out of the vase, and throws it at* VANĚK.)

MICHAEL (*to* VANĚK). See what you're doing? Aren't you ashamed? (VANĚK *is at loss about what to do for a moment, then picks up the bouquet, carries it hesitantly to the vase, puts it back in, slowly returns to his seat, and sits down with some embarrassment.* VERA *and* MICHAEL *watch tensely to see what he will do. As soon as they see that he has sat back down, they instantly return to their old selves, smiling as they sit down, too. A short pause.*)

VERA. Michael, won't we put some music on for Ferdinand?

MICHAEL. That's a good idea— (MICHAEL *walks over to the record-player and the instant he turns it on, music starts pouring forth out of all the speakers: preferably some international hit, such as Sugar Baby Love in the interpretation of Karel Gott.° The curtain falls; the music is booming on, the same tune over and over again, until the last spectator has left the theater.*)

THE END

QUESTIONS

1. Characterize Vera and Michael. How much alike are they? What are some of their characteristic words or statements? Do they display any conflicts in their marriage? Have they had conflicts in the past?
2. Vaněk says and does very little in the play. Can you define his character? What is the essential conflict between him and the married couple? How is that conflict resolved? How do you interpret Vaněk's failure to follow through on his impulse to leave?
3. On what principle have Vera and Michael collected the items for their re-decorated apartment? How do the various items as a group express the taste and intelligence of their owners? Are they religious people?
4. At what point in the play do you begin to feel something odd or absurd about Vera and Michael?
5. In what ways can this play be interpreted as a statement of political dissent? What is being unveiled?

Karel Gott: a popular Czech singer who was permitted to move freely between the East and West, who made recordings not only in Czechoslovakia but also in Germany and Austria, and who was scorned by the intelligentsia and serious artists

Tom Stoppard

"M" Is for Moon among Other Things

A radio play

CHARACTERS

A married couple, ALFRED *and* CONSTANCE—*middle class, childless, aged 45 and 42*

Silence—a man grunts and shakes his paper—a woman flips over the pages of a book and sighs.

CONSTANCE (*sighs—thinks*).   Macbeth . . . (*Flip.*) Macedonia . . . (*Flip.*) Machine-gun . . . (*Flip.*) Magna Carta . . . (*Flip.*) Measles . . . (*Flip.*) Molluscs . . . molluscs . . .

ALFRED (*grunts—thinks*).   ". . . the girl, wearing a red skirt and black sweater, asked the court that her name should not be continued in column five, continued in column five . . ." (*Shakes paper.*)

CONSTANCE (*thinks*).   . . . Invertebrate animal . . . discovered that marine varieties . . . (*Slams book shut.*) I think enough for tonight—I wish the print wasn't so small . . . Have you seen my pills anywhere?

ALFRED.   Mmmm . . . (*Thinks*) ". . . 'anything like it in my thirty years on the Bench,' he added. 'While young louts like you are roaming the streets no girl is safe from . . .'" (*Impatiently*) Oh . . . (*Turns page.*)

CONSTANCE (*thinks*).   February the fifth, March the fifth, April, May, June, July, August . . . six.

ALFRED (*thinks*).   "A Smooth-as-Silk Beauty as Fast as they Come!"

CONSTANCE (*thinks*).   The Friday before last must have been the twenty-seventh, that's right, because the Gilberts came to dinner and that was a Friday because of Mrs. Gilbert not eating the meat, and the Encyclopedia always comes on the twenty-seventh, and it was just when the M to N came when I phoned Alfred at the office about what to give the Gilberts, so it must have been Friday the twenty-seventh. So last Sunday was the twenty-ninth, so today is twenty-nine plus seven makes thirty-six,

"M" IS FOR MOON AMONG OTHER THINGS   First broadcast in 1964. Tom Stoppard was born in Czechoslovakia in 1937, and from 1939 to 1946 lived with his family in Singapore and India before settling in England. After British schooling he became at seventeen a newspaper reporter. He wrote his first play in 1960, and in 1964 began writing a series of radio plays. At twenty-nine he wrote the first of his many successful stage plays, *Rosencrantz and Guildenstern Are Dead.* The present radio play includes stage directions pertaining to sound effects and tones of voice; for example, it requires sounds of pages being flipped, a newspaper being shaken, a book being slammed shut, and it instructs the characters sometimes to adopt a "thinking" tone of voice, and to speak "up" at other times.

so it must be the sixth, unless July has thirty-one, in which case it's the seventh, no, the fifth. Thirty days hath April, June, is it? Wait a minute, the Friday before last was the twenty-seventh . . .

ALFRED (*thinks*).   "I found her to be a smooth-as-silk beauty with the classic lines of thrust of . . ."

CONSTANCE.   Alfred, is it the fifth or the sixth?

ALFRED.   Mmm? (*Thinks*) ". . . surging to sixty mph in nine seconds . . ."

CONSTANCE.   Fifth?

ALFRED.   Fifth what?

CONSTANCE.   What's today?

ALFRED.   Sunday . . . (*Thinks*) ". . . the handbrake a touch stiff and I'd like to see an extra ashtray for the passenger but otherwise . . ." (*Up*) Oh for goodness' sake—you know I hate people looking over my shoulder. (*Turns page.*)

CONSTANCE (*thinks*).   August the fifth, nineteen sixty-two. (*Up*) Alfred, in half an hour I'll be exactly forty-two-and-a-half years old. That's a thought, isn't it?

ALFRED.   Mmmm . . . (*Thinks*) "Little old grey-haired Mrs. Winifred Garters wept last night as . . ."

CONSTANCE.   What time were you born, Alfred?

ALFRED.   What?

CONSTANCE.   I was born just as the clock struck half-past ten at night—what time were you born?

ALFRED.   I can't remember.

CONSTANCE.   Didn't anyone tell you?

ALFRED.   That's what I can't remember. (*Hall clock chiming ten.*) Oh, what's that?—ten? We haven't had the news today. I think there's one now, isn't there? Turn on the box—hang on, where's the *Radio Times?*°—ah—is this this week's?

CONSTANCE.   Forty-two-and-a-half, and all I've got is a headache.

ALFRED.   Is this the new one? "August five to twelve"—what's today?

CONSTANCE.   Sunday.

ALFRED.   No—no—no—what's—oh never mind—yes, this is it—News at five-past ten. (*Turns on TV.*) *Dial M for Murder*°—oh, that might have been good.

CONSTANCE.   It's an awful thing, you know. When you start worrying about the halves. I mean there's no purpose to make sense of it, is there? Every time it's half-past ten, it's another day older, and all I've done with it is to get up and stay up. Where's it all going? (*Bring in finish of* Dial M

Radio Times: British weekly magazine listing radio and TV schedules

Dial . . . Murder: Alfred Hitchcock's 1954 film in which a husband plots the murder of his wife

for Murder—*hold it and fade it low.* CONSTANCE *thinks*) They used to call me Millie . . . my middle name was my favorite till I was—how old was I? 17? Happy Birthday Millie, it used to be . . . Then I went over to Constance, it sounded more grown-up. Seventeen from forty-two. Twenty-five. A quarter of a century, constant Constance. . . . (*Up*) If I had a choice, perhaps I'd choose what I'm doing now. I don't care about that. But I want the choice. I don't want the moon, Alfred, all I want is the possibility of an alternative, so that I know I'm doing this because I want to instead of because there's nothing else.

ALFRED.   Sshssh—hang on, Constance, let me hear the News . . . (*Bring in opening of tape* [*if there is one*] *of the 10:05 P.M. News—5 August 1962.*)

NEWS.   The News . . . Marilyn Monroe, the actress, was found dead in her Los Angeles home today . . . (*Fade out.*)

ALFRED (*fading in with "oh's" used as a sort of dirge—thinks*).   Oh . . . oh . . . oh . . . oh . . . oh . . . poor Marilyn . . . poor poor thing . . . What have they done? . . . God, poor little thing . . . She must have been so unhappy. Oh Marilyn . . .

CONSTANCE.   She seemed so full of life, didn't she?

ALFRED (*thinks*).   Abandoned . . . no love . . . like a child . . .

CONSTANCE.   Poor thing, it's awful.

ALFRED (*thinks*).   Marilyn . . . you shouldn't have trusted them, they're all rotten . . .

CONSTANCE.   Do you suppose she meant it? Oh, wasn't she lovely, I mean a lovely *person,* she made you feel it. Doesn't it go to show?

ALFRED.   Oh, do shut up.

CONSTANCE.   Alfred!

ALFRED.   Oh, I'm sorry. I'm just tired . . . and upset.

CONSTANCE.   It's all right, Alfred.

ALFRED.   Of course she meant it. By God, you've only got to use your imagination. It's such a cold shallow world she was living in. No warmth or understanding—no one understood her, she was friendless.

CONSTANCE.   Do you think so?

ALFRED.   Of course. Hangers-on. People didn't appreciate her. Just using her. A girl like that. It's a crime . . .

CONSTANCE.   Fate.

ALFRED.   Fate! Don't be absurd!

CONSTANCE.   Please don't shout, Alfred.

ALFRED (*wearily*).   Oh damn them, dammit . . . Oh, let's go to bed. I'm tired.

CONSTANCE.   Yes. I'm worn out—hope I'll be able to sleep.

ALFRED.   I can never stay awake, and you can never get to sleep—what's the matter with you?

CONSTANCE.   I don't know—can't sleep with this headache.

ALFRED.   You know, you read too much, you're always complaining of eye strain and headaches, well it's no wonder.

CONSTANCE.   The print's too small, really. (*Flip flip flip of pages.*)

ALFRED.   The Universal Treasury of People, Places and Things: Illustrated. M to N . . . A lot of useless knowledge.

CONSTANCE.   I've got as far as Molluscs, but I'm skipping madly.

ALFRED.   You forget it all anyway.

CONSTANCE.   No I don't, not all of it.

ALFRED.   Well, you forgot about Catholics, didn't you? There must have been *something* about them under C.

CONSTANCE (*unhappy, offensive-defensive, a little desperate*).   Oh Alfred, *please*—not now again . . .

ALFRED.   *Catholics!* Catholics-don't-eat-meat-on-Fridays. Or under M—*Meat!*, what-Catholics-don't-eat-on-a-Friday. Or F—*Friday!*, the-day-Catholics-don't-eat-meat-on. Oh my God, you could probably have found it under G—*Mrs. Gilbert!*, wife to Alfred's boss *Mr.* Gilbert and a staunch Catholic who does not eat meat on a Friday! (*Pause.*) D is for Debacle—that which occurs when Mrs. Gilbert is offered meat by her husband's chief accountant's wife on a Friday!

CONSTANCE (*crying*).   Well, I wouldn't have forgotten if you hadn't been so awful on the phone—I phoned you to ask you what to get for dinner and you wouldn't give me a chance—Alfred—you were—you behaved . . .

ALFRED.   Oh, don't cry—I couldn't talk to you then . . . You had to call up just as Mr. Gilbert, Anglican, was hovering round my neck with my monthly report . . . Oh, what does it matter anyway . . . (*Pages turned.*) M is for Money . . . Universal Treasury all right . . . Two guineas a volume, a guinea per letter of the alphabet. How can you get a guinea's worth out of X? Or Z?

CONSTANCE.   It was a lovely birthday present.

ALFRED.   Well, I'm sorry I haven't got as much money as your rich brother Stanley.

CONSTANCE.   Oh, you know I didn't mean that. But it's lovely to know that every month there's another volume coming. That's the seventh, counting the A and B I got on the actual day. It's O to P this month. Oranges and Orangutans. I don't know—it's just that the time isn't all a waste, somehow, do you know what I mean?

ALFRED.   What's the capital of Mongolia?

CONSTANCE.   The point isn't to know the capital of Mongolia, Alfred—the point is to . . . Alfred, at half-past ten I'll be forty-two-and-a-half years old and it's all slipping by.

ALFRED.   Well, I'm blessed—do you know they haven't even got *her* in here.

CONSTANCE.   Who?

ALFRED.   "Monroe Doctrine . . . Monroe, James, President of the United States . . ." Universal ruddy Treasury.

CONSTANCE.   Well, they can't have everything. I remember my first ABC book—everything was so simple then. I thought that each letter only stood for the one word they gave, you know? A is for Apple, B is for Baby, C is for Cat . . . M was for Moon. It was ages before I knew that M was for anything else . . . like Millie . . . She was 36, he said, didn't he?

ALFRED.   Did he? Poor dear . . . What I meant was that it needn't have happened. That's why you can't call it fate.

CONSTANCE.   It's all right, I wasn't thinking.

ALFRED.   It was just that she had no one to recognize her needs, you see. No one to turn to, I mean. No wonder the poor girl got desperate. Those *actors*—people like that—they've got no humanity, no understanding—self, self, it's such a selfish society. A girl like that, dying with a telephone in her hand—who did she have to call who would have done her any good? No one. Perhaps that's fate.

CONSTANCE.   Yes, I suppose so.

ALFRED.   Well, let's go up. I'll lock up—you have the bathroom first.

CONSTANCE.   I wonder who she was trying to phone, though . . . (*Fade out—sound of* CONSTANCE *getting into bed*). Oooooh, bed. I feel quite worn out.

ALFRED.   You got up too early again.

CONSTANCE.   I couldn't drop off once I woke up. It's getting very tiresome.

ALFRED.   Don't those pills work?

CONSTANCE.   I suppose they must help. I think I'll take an extra one tonight.

ALFRED.   Yes, I should.

CONSTANCE.   Oh—Alfred—I forgot my glass of water. Do you mind, while you're still up.

ALFRED.   Oh, gosh, where is it?

CONSTANCE.   On the wash-stand. (*Thinks*) Oh God, if I'd been in her place I would have eaten the bloody meat and gone to confession . . . Bitch . . . I shouldn't have phoned Alfred at the office, though . . .

ALFRED.   Here you are. Got the pills? (*Clock chiming half-past ten—* ALFRED *getting into bed.*)

CONSTANCE (*thinks*).   Half-past ten, August the fifth, nineteen sixty-two. Well—Cheers! (*Gulps pill and drink.*) Happy anniversary, Millie. (*Puts glass down.*)

ALFRED.   Should I turn the light off?

CONSTANCE.   Yes. (*Click.*) (*Thinks*) Maple tree, Mozambique . . . Mandragora . . . Marzipan . . . Mother . . . Moon . . . Melon . . . Menopause . . . Mongolia . . .

ALFRED (*thinks*).   Marilyn . . . don't worry, I'm glad you phoned, . . . Don't be unhappy, love, tell me all about it and I'm sure I'll think of

something . . . Do you feel better already?—Well, it's nice to have someone you know you can count on any time, isn't it? . . . Don't cry, don't cry
any more . . . I'll make it all right . . . (*Up—sigh*) Poor old thing . . .

CONSTANCE.   Oh, you mustn't worry about me, Alfred, I'll be all
right . . . (*Thinks*) Marshmallow . . . Mickey Mouse . . . Marriage . . .
Moravia . . . Mule . . . Market . . . Mumps . . .

QUESTIONS

1. What is the overt cause of conflict between Constance and Alfred? What
   other conflicts divide them, and how are these unspoken conflicts the result of contrasts of personality or temperament?
2. In what way does the difference between their reactions to the death of the
   film star Marilyn Monroe (1926–1962) define their characters? Explore
   Constance's misunderstanding of Alfred's last remark.
3. Which of the two, Alfred or Constance, is the protagonist, which the antagonist? Explain.
4. This radio play employs a technique similar to the aside in a stage drama.
   Here the characters are said to "think" some of their lines, and sometimes
   the unspoken lines represent what they are reading. Would this technique
   be as effective on the stage or on television, where you would be able to see
   the lips move as a character "thinks"?
5. A television play lacks one of the defining characteristics of drama, the audience; a radio play lacks two of them, the audience and the stage. Basing
   your discussion on the definitions of the advantages and limitations of
   those two aspects (see pp. 910–12 of this chapter), formulate a statement
   defining the characteristics of radio drama.

Edward Albee

The Sandbox

A Brief Play, in Memory of My Grandmother (1876–1959)

PLAYERS

THE YOUNG MAN, 25, *a good-looking, well-built boy in a bathing suit*
MOMMY, 55, *a well-dressed, imposing woman*
DADDY, 60, *a small man; gray, thin*
GRANDMA, 86, *a tiny, wizened woman with bright eyes*
THE MUSICIAN, *no particular age, but young would be nice*

NOTE. *When, in the course of the play,* MOMMY *and* DADDY *call each other by these names, there should be no suggestion of regionalism. These names are of empty affection and point up the pre-senility and vacuity of their characters.*

The Scene. A bare stage, with only the following: Near the footlights, far stage-right, two simple chairs set side by side, facing the audience; near the foot-lights, far stage-left, a chair facing stage-right with a music stand before it; farther back, and stage-center, slightly elevated and raked, a large child's sandbox with a toy pail and shovel; the background is the sky, which alters from brightest day to deepest night.

At the beginning, it is brightest day; the YOUNG MAN *is alone on stage to the rear of the sandbox, and to one side. He is doing calisthenics; he does calisthenics until quite at the very end of the play. These calisthenics, employing the arms only, should suggest the beating and fluttering of wings. The* YOUNG MAN *is, after all, the Angel of Death.*

MOMMY *and* DADDY *enter from stage-left,* MOMMY *first.*

THE SANDBOX   Written in 1959. Edward Albee, abandoned by his natural parents, was adopted two weeks after birth in 1928 by a wealthy couple in Westchester County, New York, and named after his adoptive grandfather, part owner of the Keith-Albee string of movie-and-vaudeville theaters. His early schooling frequently interrupted by family va-cations, Albee attended a variety of private schools. Dismissed from Trinity College (Connecticut) after three semesters, he went to Greenwich Village, against his foster parents' wishes, determined to write. For about ten years he tried poetry and fiction while working at various odd jobs to supplement a weekly allowance from a trust fund established by his grandmother. After the success of his first play, *Zoo Story* (1959), and the completion of a second, Albee interrupted work on *The American Dream* when com-missioned to do a short play for an international theatrical festival. For this play (*The Sandbox*) he used characters from the work in progress placed in a different situation and setting. Despite its overlap of characters and themes with *The American Dream* (1961), it is a separate play, and Albee in 1966 declared it his favorite among his plays (which then numbered about ten including *Who's Afraid of Virginia Woolf?*).

MOMMY (*motioning to* DADDY).   Well, here we are; this is the beach.

DADDY (*whining*).   I'm cold.

MOMMY (*dismissing him with a little laugh*).   Don't be silly; it's as warm as toast. Look at that nice young man over there: *he* doesn't think it's cold. (*Waves to the* YOUNG MAN.) Hello.

YOUNG MAN (*with an endearing smile*).   Hi!

MOMMY (*looking about*).   This will do perfectly . . . don't you think so, Daddy? There's sand there . . . and the water beyond. What do you think, Daddy?

DADDY (*vaguely*).   Whatever you say, Mommy.

MOMMY (*with the same little laugh*).   Well, of course . . . whatever I say. Then, it's settled, is it?

DADDY (*shrugs*).   She's *your* mother, not mine.

MOMMY.   *I* know she's my mother. What do you take me for? (*A pause.*) All right, now; let's get on with it. (*She shouts into the wings, stage-left*) You! Out there! You can come in now. (*The* MUSICIAN *enters, seats himself in the chair, stage-left, places music on the music stand, is ready to play.* MOMMY *nods approvingly.*) Very nice; very nice. Are you ready, Daddy? Let's go get Grandma.

DADDY.   Whatever you say, Mommy.

MOMMY (*leading the way out, stage-left*).   Of course, whatever I say. (*To the* MUSICIAN) You can begin now. (*The* MUSICIAN *begins playing;* MOMMY *and* DADDY *exit; the* MUSICIAN, *all the while playing, nods to the* YOUNG MAN.)

YOUNG MAN (*with the same endearing smile*).   Hi! (*After a moment,* MOMMY *and* DADDY *re-enter, carrying* GRANDMA. *She is borne in by their hands under her armpits; she is quite rigid; her legs are drawn up; her feet do not touch the ground; the expression on her ancient face is that of puzzlement and fear.*)

DADDY.   Where do we put her?

MOMMY (*with the same little laugh*).   Wherever I say, of course. Let me see . . . well . . . all right, over there . . . in the sandbox. (*Pause.*) Well, what are you waiting for, Daddy? . . . The sandbox! (*Together they carry* GRANDMA *over to the sandbox and more or less dump her in.*)

GRANDMA (*righting herself to a sitting position; her voice a cross between a baby's laugh and cry*).   Ahhhhh! Graaaaa!

DADDY (*dusting himself*).   What do we do now?

MOMMY (*to the* MUSICIAN).   You can stop now. (*The* MUSICIAN *stops.*) (*Back to* DADDY) What do you mean, what do we do now? We go over there and sit down, of course. (*To the* YOUNG MAN) Hello there.

YOUNG MAN (*again smiling*).   Hi! (MOMMY *and* DADDY *move to the chairs, stage-right, and sit down. A pause.*)

GRANDMA (*same as before*).   Ahhhhhh! Ah-haaaaaa! Graaaaaa!

DADDY.   Do you think . . . do you think she's . . . comfortable?

MOMMY (*impatiently*).   How would I know?

DADDY (*pause*).   What do we do now?

MOMMY (*as if remembering*).   We . . . wait. We . . . sit here . . . and we wait . . . that's what we do.

DADDY (*after a pause*).   Shall we talk to each other?

MOMMY (*with that little laugh; picking something off her dress*).   Well, *you* can talk, if you want to . . . if you can think of anything to say . . . if you can think of anything *new*.

DADDY (*thinks*).   No . . . I suppose not.

MOMMY (*with a triumphant laugh*).   Of course not!

GRANDMA (*banging the toy shovel against the pail*).   Haaaaaa! Ah-ha-aaaaa!

MOMMY (*out over the audience*).   Be quiet, Grandma . . . just be quiet, and wait. (GRANDMA *throws a shovelful of sand at* MOMMY. *Still out over the audience*) She's throwing sand at me! You stop that, Grandma; you stop throwing sand at Mommy! (*To* DADDY) She's throwing sand at me. (DADDY *looks around at* GRANDMA, *who screams at him.*)

GRANDMA.   GRAAAAAA!

MOMMY.   Don't look at her. Just . . . sit here . . . be very still . . . and wait. (*To the* MUSICIAN) You . . . uh . . . you go ahead and do whatever it is you do. (*The* MUSICIAN *plays.* MOMMY *and* DADDY *are fixed, staring out beyond the audience.* GRANDMA *looks at them, looks at the* MUSICIAN, *looks at the sandbox, throws down the shovel.*)

GRANDMA.   Ah-haaaaaa! Graaaaaa! (*Looks for reaction; gets none. Now . . . directly to the audience*) Honestly! What a way to treat an old woman! Drag her out of the house . . . stick her in a car . . . bring her out here from the city . . . dump her in a pile of sand . . . and leave her here to set. I'm eighty-six years old! I was married when I was seventeen. To a farmer. He died when I was thirty. (*To the* MUSICIAN) Will you stop that, please? (*The* MUSICIAN *stops playing.*) I'm a feeble old woman . . . how do you expect anybody to hear me over that peep! peep! peep! (*To herself*) There's no re-spect around here. (*To the* YOUNG MAN) There's no respect around here!

YOUNG MAN (*same smile*).   Hi!

GRANDMA (*after a pause, a mild double-take, continues, to the audi-ence*).   My husband died when I was thirty (*indicates* MOMMY), and I had to raise that big cow over there all by my lonesome. You can imagine what *that* was like. Lordy! (*To the* YOUNG MAN) Where'd they get *you?*

YOUNG MAN.   Oh . . . I've been around for a while.

GRANDMA.   I'll bet you have! Heh, heh, heh. Will you look at you!

YOUNG MAN (*flexing his muscles*).   Isn't that something? (*Continues his calisthenics.*)

GRANDMA.   Boy, oh boy; I'll say. Pretty good.

YOUNG MAN (*sweetly*).   I'll say.

GRANDMA.   Where ya from?

YOUNG MAN.   Southern California.

GRANDMA (*nodding*).   Figgers; figgers. What's your name, honey?

YOUNG MAN.   I don't know . . .

GRANDMA (*to the audience*).   Bright, too!

YOUNG MAN.   I mean . . . I mean, they haven't given me one yet . . . the studio . . .

GRANDMA (*giving him the once-over*).   You don't say . . . you don't say. Well . . . uh, I've got to talk some more . . . don't you go 'way.

YOUNG MAN.   Oh, no.

GRANDMA (*turning her attention back to the audience*).   Fine; fine. (*Then, once more, back to the* YOUNG MAN) You're . . . you're an actor, hunh?

YOUNG MAN (*beaming*).   Yes. I am.

GRANDMA (*to the audience again; shrugs*).   I'm smart that way. *Anyhow,* I had to raise . . . *that* over there all by my lonesome; and what's next to her there . . . that's what she married. Rich? I tell you . . . money, money, money. They took me off the *farm* . . . which was real decent of them . . . fixed a nice place for me under the stove . . . gave me an army blanket . . . and my own dish . . . my very own dish! So, what have I got to complain about? Nothing, of course. I'm not complaining. (*She looks up at the sky, shouts to someone off stage*) Shouldn't it be getting dark now, dear? (*The lights dim; night comes on. The* MUSICIAN *begins to play; it becomes deepest night. There are spots on all the players, including the* YOUNG MAN, *who is, of course, continuing his calisthenics.*)

DADDY (*stirring*).   It's nighttime.

MOMMY.   Shhhh. Be still . . . wait.

DADDY (*whining*).   It's so hot.

MOMMY.   Shhhhhh. Be still . . . wait.

GRANDMA (*to herself*).   That's better. Night. (*To the* MUSICIAN) Honey, do you play all through this part? (*The* MUSICIAN *nods.*) Well, keep it nice and soft; that's a good boy. (*The* MUSICIAN *nods again; plays softly.*) That's nice. (*There is an off-stage rumble.*)

DADDY (*starting*).   What was that?

MOMMY (*beginning to weep*).   It was nothing.

DADDY.   It was . . . it was . . . thunder . . . or a wave breaking . . . or something.

MOMMY (*whispering, through her tears*).   It was an off-stage rumble . . . and you know what *that* means . . .

DADDY.   I forget . . .

MOMMY (*barely able to talk*).   It means the time has come for poor Grandma . . . and I can't bear it!

DADDY (*vacantly*).   I . . . I suppose you've got to be brave.

GRANDMA (*mocking*).   That's right, kid; be brave. You'll bear up, you'll get over it. (*Another off-stage rumble . . . louder.*)

MOMMY.   Ohhhhhhhhhh . . . poor Grandma . . . poor Grandma . . .

GRANDMA (*to* MOMMY).   I'm fine! I'm all right! It hasn't happened yet! (*A violent off-stage rumble. All the lights go out, save the spot on the* YOUNG MAN; *the* MUSICIAN *stops playing.*)

MOMMY.   Ohhhhhhhhh . . . Ohhhhhhhhh . . . (*Silence.*)

GRANDMA.   Don't put the lights up yet . . . I'm not ready; I'm not quite ready. (*Silence.*) All right, dear . . . I'm about done. (*The lights come up again, to brightest day; the* MUSICIAN *begins to play.* GRANDMA *is discovered, still in the sandbox, lying on her side, propped up on an elbow, half covered, busily shoveling sand over herself.*)

GRANDMA (*muttering*).   I don't know how I'm supposed to do anything with this goddam toy shovel . . .

DADDY.   Mommy! It's daylight!

MOMMY (*brightly*).   So it is! Well! Our long night is over. We must put away our tears, take off our mourning . . . and face the future. It's our duty.

GRANDMA (*still shoveling; mimicking*).   . . . take off our mourning . . . face the future . . . Lordy! (MOMMY *and* DADDY *rise, stretch.* MOMMY *waves to the* YOUNG MAN.)

YOUNG MAN (*with that smile*).   Hi! (GRANDMA *plays dead.* [!] MOMMY *and* DADDY *go over to look at her; she is a little more than half buried in the sand; the toy shovel is in her hands, which are crossed on her breast.*)

MOMMY (*before the sandbox; shaking her head*).   Lovely! It's . . . it's hard to be sad . . . she looks . . . so happy. (*With pride and conviction*) It pays to do things well. (*To the* MUSICIAN) All right, you can stop now, if you want to. I mean, stay around for a swim, or something; it's all right with us. (*She sighs heavily*) Well, Daddy . . . off we go.

DADDY.   Brave Mommy!

MOMMY.   Brave Daddy! (*They exit, stage left.*)

GRANDMA (*after they leave; lying quite still*).   It pays to do things well . . . Boy, oh boy! (*She tries to sit up*) . . . well, kids . . . (*but she finds she can't*) . . . I . . . I can't get up. I . . . I can't move . . . (*The* YOUNG MAN *stops his calisthenics, nods to the* MUSICIAN, *walks over to* GRANDMA, *kneels down by the sandbox.*)

GRANDMA.   I . . . can't move . . .

YOUNG MAN.   Shhhhh . . . be very still . . .

GRANDMA.   I . . . I can't move . . .

YOUNG MAN.   Uh . . . ma'am; I . . . I have a line here.

GRANDMA.   Oh, I'm sorry, sweetie; you go right ahead.

YOUNG MAN.   I am . . . uh . . .

GRANDMA.   Take your time, dear.

YOUNG MAN (*prepares; delivers the line like a real amateur*).   I am the Angel of Death. I am . . . uh . . . I am come for you.

GRANDMA.   What . . . wha . . . (*then, with resignation*) . . . ohhhh . . . ohhhh, I see. (*The* YOUNG MAN *bends over, kisses* GRANDMA *gently on the forehead.*)

GRANDMA (*her eyes closed, her hands folded on her breast again, the shovel between her hands, a sweet smile on her face*).   Well . . . that was very nice, dear . . .

YOUNG MAN (*still kneeling*).   Shhhhh . . . be still . . .

GRANDMA.   What I meant was . . . you did that very well, dear . . .

YOUNG MAN (*blushing*).   . . . oh . . .

GRANDMA.   No; I mean it. You've got that . . . you've got a quality.

YOUNG MAN (*with his endearing smile*).   Oh . . . thank you; thank you very much . . . ma'am.

GRANDMA (*slowly; softly—as the* YOUNG MAN *puts his hands on top of* GRANDMA's).   You're . . . you're welcome . . . dear.

(*Tableau. The* MUSICIAN *continues to play as the curtain slowly comes down.*)

QUESTIONS

1. On the face of it, this little play is absurd—absurd both in the way it is presented and in what happens in it. Is it therefore simply horseplay, or does it have a serious subject? What is its subject?
2. The word **absurd,** used above, itself demands attention, since it has been much used with reference to contemporary theater. The word suggests two different meanings: (a) funny, (b) meaningless. Do both meanings function here? Does either meaning predominate?
3. Characterize Mommy and Daddy. In what ways are they alike? In what ways are they foils? Two of Daddy's speeches are repeated. What do they tell us about his relationship to Mommy?
4. Discuss the treatment by Mommy and Daddy, especially Mommy, of Grandma and her death and burial. What discrepancy exists between appearance and reality? Is their treatment of her in death similar to or different from their treatment of her in life? What metaphor is submerged in Grandma's account of their fixing her a place under the stove with an army blanket and her own dish? What is the function of the musician?
5. How does the treatment accorded the young man by most of the characters (Mommy, the musician, Grandma) contrast with their treatment of Grandma? What accounts for the difference? What kind of person is the young man?
6. What aspects of contemporary American life are presented in the play? In answering this question, consider your answers to questions 3, 4, and 5. What judgment does the play make on contemporary American life?
7. Contrast Grandma with the young man and with Mommy and Daddy. What admirable qualities does she have? What disagreeable qualities does she have? Why? On the whole, is she presented as more, or less, worthy of respect than the other characters in the play? Why?
8. Both in the notes and in the dialogue, the young man is identified as the Angel of Death. How is he a very unusual Angel of Death? Is he a simple or a multiple symbol? What other meanings does he suggest?

9. What symbolic meanings are suggested by the following: (a) the bareness of the stage, (b) the sandbox, (c) the toy pail and shovel, (d) the dimming and extinguishing of the lights, (e) Grandma's burying herself with sand, (f) the fact that Grandma is buried before she is dead, (g) the young man's kissing Grandma? Which of them, like the young man, are multiple symbols?

10. At various points in the action the characters seem aware that they are performers in a play. What effect does this have on the audience's response?

CHAPTER TWO

Realistic and Nonrealistic Drama

Literary truth in drama (as in fiction and in poetry) is not the same as fidelity to fact. Fantasy is as much the property of the theater as of poetry or the prose tale. Shakespeare in *A Midsummer Night's Dream* and *The Tempest* uses fairies and spirits and monsters as characters, and in *Hamlet* and *Macbeth* he introduces ghosts and witches. These supernatural characters, nevertheless, serve as a vehicle for truth. When Bottom, in *A Midsummer Night's Dream,* is given an ass's head, the enchantment is a visual metaphor. The witches in *Macbeth* truthfully prefigure a tragic destiny.

Because it is written to be performed, however, drama adds still another dimension of possible unreality. It may be realistic or nonrealistic in mode of production as well as in content. Staging, makeup, costuming, and acting may all be handled in such a way as to emphasize the realistic or the fanciful.

It must be recognized, however, that all stage production, no matter how realistic, involves a certain necessary artificiality. If an indoor scene is presented on a picture-frame stage, the spectator is asked to imagine that a room with only three walls is actually a room with four walls. In an arena-type theater, where the audience is seated on all sides of the acting area, the spectator must imagine all four walls. Both types of presentation, moreover, require adjustments in the acting. In a traditional theater, the actors must be facing the missing fourth wall most of the time. In an arena-type theater, they must not turn their backs too long on any "wall." Both types of staging, in the interests of effective presentation, require the actors to depart from an absolute realism.

Beyond these basic requirements of artificiality in stagecraft, the departure from the appearance of reality may be slight or considerable. In many late nineteenth- and early twentieth-century productions, an effort was made to make stage sets as realistic as possible. If the play called for a setting in a study, there had to be real bookshelves on the wall and real books on the shelves. If the room contained a wash basin, real water had to flow from the taps. More recently, however, plays have been performed on a stage furnished only with drapes and platforms. In between these two extremes, all degrees of realism are possible. The scenery may consist of painted flats, with painted bookshelves and painted books and painted pictures on the wall, and these paintings may strive for photographic faithfulness or for an impressionistic effect. Or, instead of scenery, a play may use only a few movable properties to suggest the required setting. Thornton Wilder's *Our Town* (1938) utilized a bare stage, without curtain, with exposed ropes and backstage equipment, and with a few chairs, two ladders, and a couple of trellises as the only properties. For a scene at a soda fountain, a plank was laid across the backs of two chairs. In fact, provision of elaborately realistic stage sets has been the exception rather than the rule in the long history of the theater. Neither in Greek nor in Shakespearean theater was setting much more than suggested.

The choice of realistic or nonrealistic stage sets, costuming, and makeup may, in fact, lie with the producer rather than the playwright, and a producer may choose to disregard a playwright's directions for the sake of novelty or emphasis. When we move to the realm of language and the management of dialogue, the choice is entirely the playwright's. Here again all degrees of realism and nonrealism are possible. In the realistic theater of the twentieth century, some playwrights have made an elaborate effort to reproduce the flat quality of ordinary speech, with all its stumblings and inarticulateness, its slang and its mispronunciations. Others go even further in imitating reality, even at the risk of offending some members of the audience, and reproduce the vulgarities of the language of the streets and the contemporary habit of using obscene terms simply to add force to a statement. In real life, of course, few lovers speak with the eloquence of Romeo and Juliet, and many people, in daily conversation, have difficulty getting through a grammatically correct sentence of any length or complexity. They break off, they begin again, they end lamely like the swipe in "I'm a Fool" (page 81) with "etc., etc., you know." Such unimaginative and inadequate speech, skillfully used by the playwright, may faithfully render the quality of human life at some levels, yet its limitations for expressing the heights and depths of human experience are obvious. Most dramatic dialogue, even when most realistic, is more coherent and expressive than speech in actual life. Art is always a heightening or an intensification of reality; else it would have no value. The heightening may be little or great. It is greatest in poetic drama. The love exchanges of Romeo and Juliet, spoken in rhymed iambic pentameter and at one point taking the form of a perfect sonnet (see page 788), are absurdly unrealistic if judged as an imitation of actual speech, but they vividly express the emotional truth of passionate, idealistic young love.* It is no criticism of Shakespearean tragedy, therefore, to say that in real life people do not speak in blank verse. The deepest purpose of the playwright is not to imitate actual human speech but to give accurate and powerful expression to human thought and emotion.

All drama asks us to accept certain departures from reality—certain **dramatic conventions.** That a room with three walls or fewer may represent one with four walls, that the actors speak in the language of the audience whatever the nationality of the persons they play, that the actors stand or sit so as to face the audience most of the time—these are all necessary conventions. Other conventions are optional—for example, that the characters may reveal their inner thoughts through soliloquies and asides or may speak in the heightened language of poetry. Playwrights working in a strictly realistic mode will avoid the optional conventions, for these conflict with the realistic method that they have chosen to achieve their purposes. Playwrights working in a freer mode may choose to use any or all of them, for they make possible the revelation of dimensions of reality unreachable by a strictly realistic method. Václav Havel's Vera and Michael seem realistic as a married couple in employing the same vocabulary ("awesome" is a favorite word), but when they literally repeat the same passage of dialogue several times (beginning "You don't like to talk about it," and climaxing with the striking of the musical clock), we recognize that realism is shifting into nonrealism as a means of expressing their mechanical attitudes. Hamlet's famous soliloquy that begins "To be or not to be," in which he debates in blank verse the merits of onerous life and untimely death, is nonrealistic on two counts, but it enables Shakespeare to present Hamlet's introspective mind more powerfully than he might have done otherwise. The characteristic device of Greek drama, a **chorus**—a group of actors speaking in unison, often in a

---

*The term *unrealistic* used in this sentence should not be confused with the term *nonrealistic* as it is being defined here. *Nonrealistic* and *realistic* describe qualities of dramatic presentation; *unrealistic* is a term that judges peoples' actions on a scale of good sense and practicality. It is useful in discussing drama only when you are considering a character's grasp of reality—for example, a drama (whether realistic or nonrealistic) might portray a character who is unrealistic in outlook, such as a hopeless optimist or an incorrigible sentimentalist.

chant, while going through the steps of an elaborate formalized dance—is another nonrealistic device but a useful one for conveying communal or group emotion. It has been revived, in different forms, in many modern plays. The use of a **narrator,** as in *Our Town,* is a related nonrealistic device that has served playwrights as a vehicle for dramatic truth.

The history of the drama might be told in a history of conventions that have arisen, flourished, and been replaced; and those readers and audiences who experience plays most fully are those who have learned to understand the main conventions of its various periods and major dramatists. The less experienced reader or spectator may judge a play defective because it makes use of conventions other than those in common current acceptance (whether or not consciously recognized as such). Most contemporary audiences, for example, have been trained by their experience with movies and television, two media based on the realistic conventions of photography. Few people pause to consider that looking at a photograph, whether filmed by a still camera or a movie camera, requires the acceptance of the simple convention that three-dimensional reality is being represented two-dimensionally, or that the full spectrum of color may be represented by shades of white, gray, or black. We accept these conventions without question, as we also accept in cinema and television the emotional reinforcement that comes with a musical background even though there is no justification for the presence of an orchestra in a living room or on a beach. The study of drama requires the purposeful learning of its conventions, both realistic and nonrealistic.

In most plays, the world into which we are taken—however unreal it may be—is treated as self-contained, and we are asked to regard it temporarily as a real world. Thus Shakespeare's world of fairies in *A Midsummer Night's Dream* is real to us while we watch the play. Because of Shakespeare's magic, we quite willingly make that "temporary suspension of disbelief" that, according to Coleridge, "constitutes poetic faith." And the step from accepting Bottom as real, though we know in fact he is only a dressed-up actor, to crediting Bottom with an ass's head as real is a relatively small one. But some playwrights abandon even this much attempt to give their work an illusion of reality. They deliberately violate the self-containment of the fictional world and keep reminding us that we are only seeing a play. Thus Edward Albee, in *The Sandbox,* not only presents as his main character a Grandma who buries herself alive and speaks after she is presumably dead, but he also systematically breaks down the barriers between his fictional world and the real one. The musician, instead of being concealed in an orchestra pit, is summoned onstage and told by Mommy and Grandma when to play and when not to play. Grandma addresses herself much of the time directly to the audience and at one time shouts to the electricians offstage, instructing them to dim the lights. The young man reminds us that he is an actor by telling Grandma that he has "a line here" and by delivering the line "like a real amateur." When Mommy and Daddy hear a noise offstage, Daddy thinks it may be thunder or a breaking wave, but Mommy says, with literal accuracy, "It was an off-stage rumble." In short, Albee keeps reminding us that this is a play—not reality—and not even an imitation of reality, but a symbolic representation of it. The effects he gains thereby are various: partly comic, partly antisentimental, partly intellectual; and the play that results is both theatrically effective and dramatically significant.

The adjective *realistic*, then, as applied to literature, must be regarded as a descriptive, not an evaluative, term. When we call a play realistic, we are saying something about its mode of presentation, not praising nor dispraising it. Realism indicates fidelity to the outer appearances of life. Serious dramatists are interested in life's inner meanings, which they may approach through either realistic or nonrealistic presentation. Great plays have been written in both the realistic and the nonrealistic modes. It is not without significance, however, that the greatest plays in this book are probably *Oedipus Rex, Othello,* and *The Misanthrope*—one originally written in quantitative Greek verse, one in English blank verse, and one in French rimed couplets. Human truth, rather than fidelity to fact, is the highest achievement of literary art.

EXERCISES

1. In any classification of plays, Oakes's *Mind the Gap* would undoubtedly be called realistic, Albee's *The Sandbox* nonrealistic. How would you classify the other plays in Chapter One, based on the criterion of faithfulness "to the outer appearances of life"? How would you rank the plays in that chapter for their presentation of "life's inner meanings"—their revelation of "human truth"? Although four short plays is scarcely a good sampling, could you create an hypothesis about the correlation between realistic conventions and significant insights?
2. Through the centuries, theatrical producers and writers have sometimes sought to modernize older plays, chiefly by recasting them in the

conventions of contemporary theater. Perhaps the most famous literary example (as distinct from matters of staging alone) was John Dryden's *All for Love*, a recasting of Shakespeare's *Antony and Cleopatra*. As you proceed through this book, consider what would be necessary in modernizing *Oedipus Rex*, *Othello*, and *The Misanthrope*. What might be gained, and what lost, by such an adaptation? Identify as well the nonrealistic elements in more modern plays (*The Glass Menagerie* and *Death of a Salesman*) and imagine how they would gain or suffer from the substitution of realistic equivalents.

J.e. FRANKLIN
Two Mens'es Daughter

A Ten-Minute Play

CHARACTERS

GOLDIE
ADDIE

SCENE. AUNT GOLDIE'*s place has the look of a monastic cell, but it is not drab or claustrophobic. In fact, there is a good deal of light in the room. We are simply given to know that all of* GOLDIE'*s activities take place in this room: toileting, cat-bathing, religious activity, etc. This is because* GOLDIE *can't get around like she used to.*

She is a woman of around sixty; it is important that she be light-skinned enough to pass for white.

She is sitting on the bed at the start of the action. She takes her snuff can, stretches her bottom lip to form a cup, and taps some snuff into the space.

GOLDIE *is spitting into her spittoon—a rusty lard-bucket near her bed— when she hears someone come in, and instinctively reaches for some object (ashtray, hairbrush, book, etc.). She goes through a few choices before* ADDIE *shows herself, a young woman of around twenty.*

ADDIE.   Don't shoot, Aunt Goldie, it's me—Addie!
GOLDIE.   Don't tell me they done sent you over here 'bout that mess, too!
ADDIE.   No-mam, Aunt Goldie, not me! I'm on your side.

TWO MENS'ES DAUGHTER   First performed in 1990. J. e. Franklin was born in 1937 in Houston, Texas, and graduated from the University of Texas. She has taught at the University of Iowa and the City University of New York, and has been resident director in the drama department of Skidmore College and resident playwright at Brown University. She wrote her most celebrated play, *Black Girl*, first as a television drama, then developed it for stage and screen production, and published an autobiographical account of that process.

GOLDIE.   Next one come over here devlin' me 'bout goin' to some funeral, I'm gonna throw something at 'em and try my best to kill 'em!

ADDIE.   Then there'll be two funerals, huh, Aunt Goldie?

GOLDIE.   Hit shore will.

ADDIE.   I just got through telling 'em they better leave you alone.

GOLDIE.   Don't tell 'em nothing . . . let 'em keep it up. They the ones always saying "one monkey don't stop no show," so let 'em ca'ry on without me.

ADDIE.   They over there saying they can't, Aunt Goldie. They saying according to the will, you knocking them out-a their parts, too, by not going to the funeral.

GOLDIE.   Yeah, hit's a part, all right! I bet hit ain't nothing but chicken-feed!

ADDIE.   That ol' Avrill-Morrow come calling 'em while ago, said the lawyer told him Aunt Tootie and Uncle-Cecil-David was left $10,000 a piece . . . say you was left the most but he wouldn't say how much.

GOLDIE.   Bet'cha he didn't tell how much him and them others was left. Why'n he tell that? Naw, let him bury all of it with his so-called daddy to keep him in cigars down in hell.

ADDIE.   They saying even if their part ain't but ten dollars, if their daddy left it to 'em, they want it. They real mad at you, Aunt Goldie.

GOLDIE.   You ever knowed your auntie to care 'bout somebody being mad at her?

ADDIE.   N'ome.

GOLDIE.   Well, then! Let 'em be mad and sad, and scratch up their ass till they get glad. They daddy! Which one of 'em over there calling him "daddy?" I 'members the time he was Old-Low-Down-Peckerwood-Cecil-Morrow and any other name they could think of, but they was too chicken-shit to say it to his face, too busy putting me up to doing it. (ADDIE *busies herself with tasks, performed routinely for her aunt: emptying wastebaskets, dusting.*)

ADDIE.   When I was little, I remember I used to hear y'awl! That's why they could-a knocked me over with a feather while ago when Aunt Tootie and Uncle-Cecil-David told me that, all this time, Old-Mister-Cecil-Morrow was y'awl's daddy!

GOLDIE.   What y'awl? He might'a been your Aunt Tootie and your Uncle-Cecil-David's daddy, but he wasn't no daddy 'a-mines. The onliest daddy I ever recognized was *Mister* Emmanuel Henry Randall!

ADDIE.   I hear you, Aunt Goldie!

GOLDIE.   And Daddy Randall is the onliest daddy they ever knowed, too. Would you call some "white grasshopper" daddy just cause he gave you a few nickels ever' now and then . . . just cause you *heard* he was your daddy?

ADDIE.   N'ome. I wouldn't.

GOLDIE. See, you got sense. Them fools over there ain't got none.

ADDIE. You better tell 'em not to be putting your name on that obituary, Aunt Goldie.

GOLDIE. Say they puttin' my name on the 'bituary?!

ADDIE. As one of Old-Man-Morrow's children.

GOLDIE. My name done already 'peared on the 'bituary as one a Daddy Randall's chill'un . . . how I'm gonna be two mens'es daughter?

ADDIE. I don't reckon you can be, 'less'n you got a holy-ghost daddy.

GOLDIE. Where 'bouts they at puttin' my name on a 'bituary? I'll roll out this bed and roll over 'em like the rock a-ages!

ADDIE. I ain't calling no name, Aunt Goldie. I just heard a certain person on the phone telling Sister Hayes their daddy . . . I mean, Old-Man-Morrow is survived by five children and . . .

GOLDIE. Hit was old Tootie, wasn't it? You ain't gotta tell me . . . I know that heifer the ring-tail leader . . . old ass-licker! I done told her to keep my name out-a her dev'lish mouth.

ADDIE. I ain't saying she called your name, Aunt Goldie, but there's ol' Avrill-Morrow and Miss Pam by the white mother . . . where do five come from if they ain't counting Aunt Tootie and Uncle-Cecil-David . . . and you?

GOLDIE. I swear on my dead mama's grave, I'll show up at that church-house, all right, but not for the reason they want! I'll stand up and give a testimony'll make they so-called daddy rise up out that casket and curse the day he ever laid eyes on my dark mother!

ADDIE. I know you shore will do it, too, Aunt Goldie!

GOLDIE. You think your auntie is playing?

ADDIE. N'ome. I remember that time Rev. Hill come preaching at everybody about fornicating, and you got up and told the whole church you saw him sneaking out the back door of Sister Leach's house.

GOLDIE. Well, then! I'm too old a cat to be called a kitten!

ADDIE. I was just a little bitty thing, but I remember it.

GOLDIE. That's why auntie don't hardly go to none a these churches like she used to . . . they filled with hypocrites and 'publicans!

ADDIE. You something else, Aunt Goldie!

GOLDIE. I ain't never set-foot inside no white church-house before, but this'll be one time I'll set-foot in one . . . they put my name on that 'bituary, you gonna hear auntie preach a sermon they won't never forget.

ADDIE. I shore would stand by your side while you preached it, too, Aunt Goldie. But I can't pass for white like you and Aunt Tootie and Uncle-Cecil-David, and they might not let me in.

GOLDIE. I ain't never tried to pass for white, me. Old Tootie n'em they walk in a white place just as big-and-bold and act like they white . . . I don't wanna go nowhere all my peoples can't go . . . I tell's 'em in a minute, I'm Colored and proud of it.

ADDIE.   I'm surprised Old-Man-Morrow wanted y'awl at his funeral . . . be more likely he'd-a tried to hide the fact he had outside children at all, and especially by a Colored woman.

GOLDIE.   Hide it from who? His wife? Ha ha!

ADDIE.   She knew?!

GOLDIE.   I wish I had a nickel for every white woman what knows her husband is fooling 'round with Colored womens! He want us at his funeral to get back at her for something . . . trying to get back at me, too . . . mad cause I wouldn't bow down to him in his life and figure that mess he got in his will gonna make me do it, but he got another thought coming!

ADDIE.   This put me in the mind of that big case years ago of that white man in Louisiana, died and left a whole pile of money. His will said his white children couldn't get any of it, either, unless his Colored children came to his funeral.

GOLDIE.   So he done tried to copy off-a that! That was him, all right! Old copy-cat!

ADDIE.   Seem like he should-a known better then to try to tempt you with money, Aunt Goldie! But I guess he didn't know you ain't never cared nothing for money. Ever' since I was little, I've seen how you just give it away. Anytime one of us needed it, if you had it, we had it.

GOLDIE.   I 'member one time I gave this woman the last pair good drawers I had 'cause the rubber in hers had popped. 'Cause I shore don't care. We all come in the world nekked and although we sees people with clothes on when they gets funeralized, I done heard tell they digs them graves up after everybody leave and takes even them few rags off they ass.

ADDIE.   I guess Mr. Cecil-Morrow didn't think you'd stay away and keep the others from getting their money, huh, Aunt Goldie?

GOLDIE.   What I wanna put myself out for them for? They ain't never did nothing for me. What little money they do get it all go downtown to that bail-bondsman to get Sonny Jr. out-a jail for something he done got into.

ADDIE.   Uncle-Cecil-David gonna gamble his all away . . . his'll be gone in a week.

GOLDIE.   Sooner than that, honey . . . then all of 'em be over here begging me for whatever I had.

ADDIE.   And you'd give it all to 'em little by little until it was all gone . . . cause you just good-hearted like that, Aunt Goldie . . . you good as gold. That's why I'll do anything in the world for you.

GOLDIE.   Aunt Goldie shore do love you, honey. You the onliest one understand.

ADDIE.   At first I wished you would go to Mr. Cecil-Morrow's funeral so you could get that money. But I'm glad you ain't gonna show up 'cause that'll keep ol' Avrill-Morrow from getting his share. That'll pay him back for what he did to me last week.

GOLDIE.   What he done to you?

ADDIE.   He goes out to the University now, and last week he saw me scrubbing the floors in one-a the buildings and got a cupful-a dirt and threw it on the floor, then said, "Clean it up, nigger," in front of a whole bunch of people . . . they laughed at me.

GOLDIE.   Why, that little pissy-ass bastard! Why'n you come tell auntie?!

ADDIE.   You always say every dog'll have his day and a good dog'll have two days . . . I just asked my supervisor, let me clean inside the rooms.

GOLDIE.   Next time he call you a name, ask him ain't he the one shit on hisself when his pappy brought him out here one time, wouldn't ca'ry him home to his own mammy to clean, naw, wanted my mama to do it!

ADDIE.   Did Grandma Randall clean him, Aunt Goldie?

GOLDIE.   Mama was just good-hearted like that . . . Daddy Randall always said I took after her, but I know I wasn't fit to eat her doo-doo! When people did mama wrong, she'd forgive 'em . . . me, I'd lay in wait for 'em for years, killing 'em in my heart long after they be done forgot about it. Then I'd make 'em sorry they ever crossed me!

ADDIE.   One day I'll be walking across that campus with books in my arms, just like ol' Avrill-Morrow, cause the papers say Colored can go to school out there, come next semester. I hope he still be going there by the time I save enough money to go. If I had the money, I'd enroll out there now.

GOLDIE.   I believes I did see something in The Informer 'bout they gonna let Colored go out to the University!

ADDIE.   Come next semester, Aunt Goldie. Miss Kemp's daughter gonna enroll in the nursing school, and Sister Williams' nephew, Isaac, say he gonna study engineering out there.

GOLDIE (*after a beat*).   Well, bless they hearts!

ADDIE.   I would study the law . . . but they say that cost more than any of the other courses, 'cause it's so many books to buy.

GOLDIE (*a beat*).   Bless your heart! Wanna study the law!

ADDIE.   Has anybody in our family ever gone to college, Aunt Goldie?

GOLDIE.   None that I knows of. Mama wanted me to go to mission-ary school, but, honey, I ain't wanna be no nun. And they said I'd have to give up my snuff, too! Bad enough I'd have to give up my chuchie!°

ADDIE.   I'd give up almost anything to get to go to college. But I wouldn't want you giving up your pride and going to no ol' funeral just so I could go, Aunt Goldie. I'll find a way.

GOLDIE (*a beat*).   How much do it cost?

ADDIE.   A whole lot, Aunt Goldie . . . two thousand a semester for state residents. And I would study hard, day and night . . . and make you proud of me . . . make the whole family proud.

GOLDIE.   That'll show the little puny-ass Avrill something, all right, and make you-know-who turn over in his grave. He didn't mind sleeping

chuchie: i.e., sexual pleasures

with Colored women and having us crying over his casket, but just say white and Colored settin' in a school-room together and he'd have a fit!

ADDIE.   From what I heard about him, though, Aunt Goldie—and I know I didn't hear much—seem like he respected the ones who stood up for their rights. Seem like he shore respected you.

GOLDIE (*a beat, as* GOLDIE *communes with some moment*).   How they say they planning on gettin' to that thing?

ADDIE.   Avrill-Morrow told 'em over the phone a car is being sent to pick everybody up and bring 'em back here.

GOLDIE.   No doubt it's gonna be some ol' piecy trap they got off the junkyard.

ADDIE.   N'ome. Aunt Tootie say they told her it's gonna be a Cadillac . . . brand new!

GOLDIE.   No doubt they gonna put us at the back-a the whole funeral-train.

ADDIE.   N'ome. They say Mr. Cecil-Morrow's will want the car with you and Aunt Tootie and Uncle-Cecil-David right behind the hearse. (GOLDIE*'s muscles twitch reflexively. She averts her look, communes with a private moment.*)

GOLDIE.   Think I'm gonna feel something for him in his death that I didn't feel in his life . . . humph! I say!

ADDIE.   I always wanted to ask you why you hated him so, but I was scared to. I just figured he must-a done something to you he had no business doing.

GOLDIE.   All of 'em should-a hated him, the way he treated Daddy Randall, never puttin' no handle on his name, coming out here like he owned mama . . . ! (*This beat is longer than the others, as* GOLDIE *struggles with her feelings.* ADDIE *is at a loss initially, unsure of exactly how she should respond to a* GOLDIE *she is seeing for the first time. She sits next to her on the bed and gently takes her hand.*)

GOLDIE. Mama wasn't nothing but a kid when she went to work for him. Everywhere she turned, there he was, even after Daddy Randall married her. Ain't many Colored men wants a Colored woman got white men's chill'un, but Daddy Randall loved us just like we was his'n. Old Cecil-Morrow wanted to get even, cheated him out-a some money, mad cause he married mama. What could a Colored man do back then? He didn't have no rights a white man was bound to respect. I hadn't even quit peeing-the-bed yet the first time I cussed him. I didn't know what I was saying . . . just repeating words I'd heard the grown-folks use. He told mama to beat me but she wouldn't. That let me know I could keep it up, even after he told me he was my daddy. I told him, "You might-a been the one sired me, but you ain't my daddy. If I pass on the road and see you laying in a gully dying, I'll pass on by like I don't even know you and let you die!" Me being the baby, I could get away with anything, but even after I got grown. Tootie and Cecil-David thought he'd sic the Ku-Klux-Klan on me, but he didn't. I didn't care. Something had a-holt a me.

Mama'd say, real quite, "Don't do evil for evil, baby. When somebody do you evil, do 'em good." But I knowed her heart . . . or thought I did . . . 'til one day she told me I had ways just like him. I'm shamed to even repeat what I said to my mama. I know I hurt her to her heart cause she just left me to God then. The Bible tell you not to cuss your mama . . . and your daddy . . . or your lamp be put out in everlasting darkness. That's why I stays in this room, guess I'm just waiting for the lamp to go out . . . cause God don't like ugly. He just don't!

ADDIE (*quietly, respecting* GOLDIE'S *mood*).   Back in high school, Aunt Goldie . . . we had to learn this Langston Hughes poem° that put me in the mind-a you, and went:

> *My old man was a white old man*
> *And my old mama was black.*
> *If ever I cursed my white old man*
> *I take my curses back.*
>
> *If ever I cursed my black old mother*
> *And wished her soul in hell*
> *I'm sorry for that evil wish*
> *And now I wish them well.*

(GOLDIE *weeps quietly.* ADDIE *kisses the top of her aunt's head and then enfolds her lovingly in her arms.*)

ADDIE.   Aw, Aunt Goldie, they forgive you . . . both of 'em forgive you . . . I know they do!

(*Curtain.*)

QUESTIONS

1. What strengths and weaknesses of character does Goldie have? By what means are these revealed? How just is her self-condemnation?
2. Explain the relationships between Goldie, her mother, her stepfather, and the man who "sired" her. Goldie believes she knows why her biological father wanted her to attend his funeral; can you offer other explanations that would be consistent with what you know of him?
3. Compared to the motives of her sister and brother (Aunt Tootie and Uncle-Cecil-David), is Goldie's refusal to attend the funeral admirable? Do you think that Addie's wish to go to the university will finally change Goldie's mind about the funeral? Would her motive for going be entirely altruistic, if she does go?
4. Is Addie attempting to manipulate her aunt?
5. What are the realistic elements of this play? Is it more or less realistic than Oakes's *Mind the Gap?* than Stoppard's *"M" Is for Moon among Other Things?*

Langston Hughes poem: Addie partially remembers the poem "Cross" (printed on p. 602 of this book)

Henrik Ibsen

A Doll House

CHARACTERS

TORVALD HELMER, *a lawyer*
NORA, *his wife*
DR. RANK
MRS. LINDE
KROGSTAD

THE HELMERS' THREE SMALL
    CHILDREN
ANNE-MARIE, *the children's nurse*
A HOUSEMAID
A PORTER

SCENE. *The Helmers' living room.*

ACT 1

A pleasant, tastefully but not expensively furnished, living room. A door on the rear wall, right, leads to the front hall, another door, left, to HELMER'*s study. Between the two doors a piano. A third door in the middle of the left wall; further front a window. Near the window a round table and a small couch. Towards the rear of the right wall a fourth door; further front a tile stove with a rocking chair and a couple of armchairs in front of it. Between the stove and the door a small table. Copperplate etchings on the walls. A whatnot with porcelain figurines and other small objects. A small bookcase with deluxe editions. A rug on the floor; fire in the stove. Winter day.*

The doorbell rings, then the sound of the front door opening. NORA *dressed for outdoors, enters, humming cheerfully. She carries several packages, which she puts down on the table, right. She leaves the door to the front hall open; there a* PORTER *is seen holding a Christmas tree and a basket. He gives them to the* MAID *who has let them in.*

NORA.   Be sure to hide the Christmas tree, Helene. The children mustn't see it before tonight when we've trimmed it. (*Opens her purse; to the* PORTER) How much?
PORTER.   Fifty øre.

A DOLL HOUSE   First published and then performed in 1879. English translation by Otto Reinert. Henrik Ibsen (1828–1906), widely regarded as one of the founders of modern drama, was born in Norway. Between 1851 and 1864, while employed at theaters in Bergen and Christiana (now Oslo), Ibsen gained experience but little financial success (he had known little but poverty since his early childhood, when his extravagant father went bankrupt). As a consequence of his promising achievement as a poet and playwright, a traveling grant and then a small annual stipend from the Norwegian government permitted him to move with his family to Rome, where he took up permanent residence in 1864. By the time he wrote this play, Ibsen had long been interested in women's rights.

NORA.   Here's a crown.° No, keep the change. (*The* PORTER *thanks her, leaves.* NORA *closes the door. She keeps laughing quietly to herself as she takes off her coat, etc. She takes a bag of macaroons from her pocket and eats a couple. She walks cautiously over to the door to the study and listens.*) Yes, he's home. (*Resumes her humming, walks over to the table, right.*)

HELMER (*in his study*).   Is that my little lark twittering out there?

NORA (*opening some packages*).   That's right.

HELMER.   My squirrel bustling about?

NORA.   Yes.

HELMER.   When did squirrel come home?

NORA.   Just now. (*Puts the bag of macaroons back in her pocket, wipes her mouth.*) Come out here, Torvald. I want to show you what I've bought.

HELMER.   I'm busy! (*After a little while he opens the door and looks in, pen in hand.*) Bought, eh? All that? So little wastrel has been throwing money around again?

NORA.   Oh but Torvald, this Christmas we can be a little extravagant, can't we? It's the first Christmas we don't have to scrimp.

HELMER.   I don't know about that. We certainly don't have money to waste.

NORA.   Yes, Torvald, we do. A little, anyway. Just a tiny little bit? Now that you're going to get that big salary and make lots and lots of money.

HELMER.   Starting at New Year's, yes. But payday isn't till the end of the quarter.

NORA.   That doesn't matter. We can always borrow.

HELMER.   Nora! (*Goes over to her and playfully pulls her ear.*) There you go being irresponsible again. Suppose I borrowed a thousand crowns today and you spent it all for Christmas and on New Year's Eve a tile hit me in the head and laid me out cold?

NORA (*putting her hand over his mouth*).   I won't have you say such horrid things.

HELMER.   But suppose it happened. Then what?

NORA.   If it did, I wouldn't care whether we owed money or not.

HELMER.   But what about the people I had borrowed from?

NORA.   Who cares about them! They are strangers.

HELMER.   Nora, Nora, you *are* a woman! No, really! You know how I feel about that. No debts! A home in debt isn't a free home, and if it isn't free it isn't beautiful. We've managed nicely so far, you and I, and that's the way we'll go on. It won't be for much longer.

NORA (*walks over toward the stove*).   All right, Torvald. Whatever you say.

HELMER (*follows her*).   Come, come my little songbird mustn't droop her wings. What's this? Can't have a pouty squirrel in the house, you know. (*Takes out his wallet.*) Nora, what do you think I have here?

NORA (*turns around quickly*).   Money!

Fifty øre . . . a crown: A crown was 100 øre.

HELMER.   Here. (*Gives her some bills.*) Don't you think I know Christmas is expensive?

NORA (*counting*).   Ten—twenty—thirty—forty. Thank you, thank you, Torvald. This helps a lot.

HELMER.   I certainly hope so.

NORA.   It does, it does. But I want to show you what I got. It was cheap, too. Look. New clothes for Ivar. And a sword. And a horse and trumpet for Bob. And a doll and a little bed for Emmy. It isn't any good, but it wouldn't last, anyway. And here's some dress material and scarves for the maids. I feel bad about old Anne-Marie, though. She really should be getting much more.

HELMER.   And what's in here?

NORA (*cries*).   Not till tonight!

HELMER.   I see. But now what does my little prodigal have in mind for herself?

NORA.   Oh, nothing. I really don't care.

HELMER.   Of course you do. Tell me what you'd like. Within reason.

NORA.   Oh, I don't know. Really, I don't. The only thing—

HELMER.   Well?

NORA (*fiddling with his buttons, without looking at him*).   If you really want to give me something, you might—you could—

HELMER.   All right, let's have it.

NORA (*quickly*).   Some money, Torvald. Just as much as you think you can spare. Then I'll buy myself something one of these days.

HELMER.   No, really Nora—

NORA.   Oh yes, please, Torvald. Please? I'll wrap the money in pretty gold paper and hang it on the tree. Won't that be nice?

HELMER.   What's the name for little birds that are always spending money?

NORA.   Wastrels, I know. But please let's do it my way, Torvald. Then I'll have time to decide what I need most. Now that's sensible, isn't it?

HELMER (*smiling*).   Oh, very sensible. That is, if you really bought yourself something you could use. But it all disappears in the household expenses or you buy things you don't need. And then you come back to me for more.

NORA.   Oh, but Torvald—

HELMER.   That's the truth, dear little Nora, and you know it. (*Puts his arm around her.*) My wastrel is a little sweetheart, but she *does* go through an awful lot of money awfully fast. You've no idea how expensive it is for a man to keep a wastrel.

NORA.   That's not fair, Torvald. I really save all I can.

HELMER (*laughs*).   Oh, I believe that. All you can. Meaning, exactly nothing!

NORA (*hums, smiles mysteriously*).   You don't know all the things we songbirds and squirrels need money for, Torvald.

HELMER.   You know, you're funny. Just like your father. You're always looking for ways to get money, but as soon as you do it runs through your fingers and you can never say what you spent it for. Well, I guess I'll just have to take you the way you are. It's in your blood. Yes, that sort of thing is hereditary, Nora.

NORA.   In that case, I wish I had inherited many of Daddy's qualities.

HELMER.   And I don't want you any different from just what you are— my own sweet little songbird. Hey!—I think I just noticed something. Aren't you looking—what's the word?—a little—sly—?

NORA.   I am?

HELMER.   You definitely are. Look at me.

NORA (*looks at him*).   Well?

HELMER (*wagging a finger*).   Little sweet-tooth hasn't by any chance been on a rampage today, has she?

NORA.   Of course not. Whatever makes you think that?

HELMER.   A little detour by the pastry shop maybe?

NORA.   No, I assure you, Torvald—

HELMER.   Nibbled a little jam?

NORA.   Certainly not!

HELMER.   Munched a macaroon or two?

NORA.   No, really, Torvald, I honestly—

HELMER.   All right. Of course I was only joking.

NORA (*walks toward the table, right*).   You know I wouldn't do anything to displease you.

HELMER.   I know. And I have your promise. (*Over to her.*) All right, keep your little Christmas secrets to yourself, Nora darling. They'll all come out tonight, I suppose, when we light the tree.

NORA.   Did you remember to invite Rank?

HELMER.   No, but there's no need to. He knows he'll have dinner with us. Anyway, I'll see him later this morning. I'll ask him then. I did order some good wine. Oh Nora, you've no idea how much I'm looking forward to tonight!

NORA.   Me, too. And the children Torvald! They'll have such a good time!

HELMER.   You know it *is* nice to have a good, safe job and a comfortable income. Feels good just thinking about it. Don't you agree?

NORA.   Oh, it's wonderful.

HELMER.   Remember last Christmas? For three whole weeks you shut yourself up every evening till long after midnight making ornaments for the Christmas tree and I don't know what else. Some big surprise for all of us, anyway. I'll be damned if I've ever been so bored in my whole life!

NORA.   I wasn't bored at all!

HELMER (*smiling*).   But you've got to admit you didn't have much to show for it in the end.

NORA.   Oh, don't tease me again about that! Could I help it that the cat got in and tore up everything?

HELMER. Of course you couldn't, my poor little Nora. You just wanted to please the rest of us, and that's the important thing. But I *am* glad the hard times are behind us. Aren't you?

NORA. Oh yes. I think it's just wonderful.

HELMER. This year, I won't be bored and lonely. And you won't have to strain your dear eyes and your delicate little hands—

NORA (*claps her hands*). No I won't, will I Torvald? Oh, how wonderful, how lovely, to hear you say that! (*Puts her arm under his.*) Let me tell you how I think we should arrange things, Torvald. Soon as Christmas is over— (*The doorbell rings.*) Someone's at the door. (*Straightens things up a bit.*) A caller, I suppose. Bother!

HELMER. Remember, I'm not home for visitors.

MAID (*in the door to the front hall*). Ma'am, there's a lady here—

NORA. All right. Ask her to come in.

MAID (*to* HELMER). And the Doctor just arrived.

HELMER. Is he in the study?

MAID. Yes, sir. (HELMER *exits into his study. The* MAID *shows* MRS. LINDE *in and closes the door behind her as she leaves.* MRS. LINDE *is in travel dress.*)

MRS. LINDE (*timid and a little hesitant*). Good morning, Nora.

NORA (*uncertainly*). Good morning.

MRS. LINDE. I don't believe you know who I am.

NORA. No—I'm not sure— Though I know I should— Of course! Kristine! It's you!

MRS. LINDE. Yes, it's me.

NORA. And I didn't even recognize you! I had no idea! (*In a lower voice.*) You've changed, Kristine.

MRS. LINDE. I'm sure I have. It's been nine or ten long years.

NORA. Has it really been that long? Yes, you're right. I've been so happy these last eight years. And now you're here. Such a long trip in the middle of winter. How brave!

MRS. LINDE. I got in on the steamer this morning.

NORA. To have some fun over the holidays, of course. That's lovely. For we are going to have fun. But take off your coat! You aren't cold, are you? (*Helps her.*) There, now! Let's sit down here by the fire and just relax and talk. No, you sit there. I want the rocking chair. (*Takes her hands.*) And now you've got your old face back. It was just for a minute, right at first— Though you are a little more pale, Kristine. And maybe a little thinner.

MRS. LINDE. And much, much older, Nora.

NORA. Maybe a little older. Just a teeny-weeny bit, not much. (*Interrupts herself, serious.*) Oh, but how thoughtless of me, chatting away like this! Sweet, good Kristine, can you forgive me?

MRS. LINDE. Forgive you what, Nora?

NORA (*in a low voice*). You poor dear, you lost your husband, didn't you?

MRS. LINDE. Three years ago, yes.

NORA.   I know. I saw it in the paper. Oh please believe me, Kristine. I really meant to write you, but I never got around to it. Something was always coming up.

MRS. LINDE.   Of course, Nora. I understand.

NORA.   No, that wasn't very nice of me. You poor thing, all you must have been through. And he didn't leave you much, either, did he?

MRS. LINDE.   No.

NORA.   And no children?

MRS. LINDE.   No.

NORA.   Nothing at all, in other words?

MRS. LINDE.   Not so much as a sense of loss—a grief to live on—

NORA (*incredulous*).   But Kristine, how can that be?

MRS. LINDE (*with a sad smile, strokes* NORA'S *hair*).   That's the way it sometimes is, Nora.

NORA.   All alone. How awful for you. I have three darling children. You can't see them right now, though; they're out with their nurse. But now you must tell me everything—

MRS. LINDE.   No, no; I'd rather listen to you.

NORA.   No, you begin. Today I won't be selfish. Today I'll think only of you. Except there's one thing I've just got to tell you first. Something marvelous that's happened to us just these last few days. You haven't heard, have you?

MRS. LINDE.   No; tell me.

NORA.   Just think. My husband's been made manager of the Mutual Bank.

MRS. LINDE.   Your husband—! Oh, I'm so glad!

NORA.   Yes, isn't that great? You see, private law practice is so uncertain, especially when you won't have anything to do with cases that aren't—you know—quite nice. And of course Torvald won't do that and I quite agree with him. Oh, you've no idea how delighted we are! He takes over at New Year's, and he'll be getting a big salary and all sorts of extras. From now on we'll be able to live in quite a different way—exactly as we like. Oh, Kristine! I feel so carefree and happy! It's lovely to have lots and lots of money and not have to worry about a thing! Don't your agree?

MRS. LINDE.   It would be nice to have enough at any rate.

NORA.   No, I don't mean just enough. I mean lots and lots!

MRS. LINDE (*smiles*).   Nora, Nora, when are you going to be sensible? In school you spent a great deal of money.

NORA (*quietly laughing*).   Yes, and Torvald says I still do. (*Raising her finger at* MRS. LINDE.) But "Nora, Nora" isn't so crazy as you all think. Believe me, we've had nothing to be extravagant with. We've both had to work.

MRS. LINDE.   You too?

NORA.   Yes. Oh, it's been little things, mostly—sewing, crocheting, embroidery—that sort of thing. (*Casually*) And other things too. You know of course, that Torvald left government service when we got married? There was no chance of promotion in his department, and of course he had to make more money than he had been making. So for the first few years he worked altogether too hard. He had to take jobs on the side and work night and day. It turned out to be too much for him. He became seriously ill. The doctors told him he needed to go south.

MRS. LINDE.   That's right, you spent a year in Italy, didn't you?

NORA.   Yes, we did. But you won't believe how hard it was to get away. Ivar had just been born. But of course we had to go. Oh, it was a wonderful trip. And it saved Torvald's life. But it took a lot of money, Kristine.

MRS. LINDE.   I'm sure it did.

NORA.   Twelve hundred specie dollars. Four thousand eight hundred crowns. That's a lot of money.

MRS. LINDE.   Yes. So it's lucky you have it when something like that happens.

NORA.   Well, actually we got the money from Daddy.

MRS. LINDE.   I see. That was about the time your father died, I believe.

NORA.   Yes, just about then. And I couldn't even go and take care of him. I was expecting little Ivar any day. And I had poor Torvald to look after, desperately sick and all. My dear, good Daddy! I never saw him again, Kristine. That's the saddest thing that's happened to me since I got married.

MRS. LINDE.   I know you were very fond of him. But then you went to Italy?

NORA.   Yes, for now we had the money and the doctors urged us to go. So we left about a month later.

MRS. LINDE.   And when you came back your husband was well again?

NORA.   Healthy as a horse!

MRS. LINDE.   But—the doctor?

NORA.   What do you mean?

MRS. LINDE.   I thought the maid said it was the doctor, that gentleman who came the same time I did.

NORA.   Oh, that's Dr. Rank. He doesn't come as a doctor. He's our closest friend. He looks in at least once every day. No, Torvald hasn't been sick once since then. And the children are strong and healthy, too, and so am I. (*Jumps up and claps her hands.*) Oh God, Kristine! Isn't it wonderful to be alive and happy! Isn't it just lovely!— But now I'm being mean again, talking only about myself and my things. (*Sits down on a footstool close to* MRS. LINDE *and puts her arms on her lap.*) Please don't be angry with me! Tell me, is it really true that you didn't care for your husband? Then why did you marry him?

MRS. LINDE.   Mother was still alive then, but she was bedridden and helpless. And I had my two younger brothers to look after. I didn't think I had the right to turn him down.

NORA.   No, I suppose not. So he had money then?

MRS. LINDE.   He was quite well off, I think. But it was an uncertain business, Nora. When he died, the whole thing collapsed and there was nothing left.

NORA.   And then—?

MRS. LINDE.   Well, I had to manage as best I could. With a little store and a little school and anything else I could think of. The last three years have been one long workday for me, Nora, without any rest. But now it's over. My poor mother doesn't need me any more. She's passed away. And the boys are on their own too. They've both got jobs and support themselves.

NORA.   What a relief for you—

MRS. LINDE.   No, not relief. Just a great emptiness. Nobody to live for any more. (*Gets up restlessly.*) That's why I couldn't stand it any longer in that little hole. Here in town it has to be easier to find something to keep me busy and occupy my thoughts. With a little luck I should be able to find a permanent job, something in an office—

NORA.   Oh but Kristine, that's exhausting work, and you look worn out already. It would be much better for you to go to a resort.

MRS. LINDE (*walks over to the window*).   I don't have a Daddy who can give me the money, Nora.

NORA (*getting up*).   Oh, don't be angry with me.

MRS. LINDE (*over to her*).   Dear Nora, don't *you* be angry with *me.* That's the worst thing about my kind of situation: you become so bitter. You've nobody to work for, and yet you have to look out for yourself, somehow. You've got to keep on living, and so you become selfish. Do you know—when you told me about your husband's new position I was delighted not so much for your sake as for my own.

NORA.   Why was that? Oh, I see. You think maybe Torvald can give you a job?

MRS. LINDE.   That's what I had in mind.

NORA.   And he will too, Kristine. Just leave it to me. I'll be ever so subtle about it. I'll think of something nice to tell him, something he'll like. Oh I so much want to help you.

MRS. LINDE.   That's very good of you, Nora—making an effort like that for me. Especially since you've known so little trouble and hardship in your own life.

NORA.   I—?—have known so little—?

MRS. LINDE (*smiling*).   Oh well, a little sewing or whatever it was. You're still a child, Nora.

NORA (*with a toss of her head, walks away*).   You shouldn't sound so superior.

MRS. LINDE.   I shouldn't?

NORA.   You're just like all the others. None of you think I'm good for anything really serious.

MRS. LINDE.   Well, now—

NORA.   That I've never been through anything difficult.

MRS. LINDE.   But Nora! You just told me all your troubles!

NORA.   That's nothing! (*Lowers her voice*) I haven't told you about *it*.

MRS. LINDE.   It? What's that? What do you mean?

NORA.   You patronize me, Kristine, and that's not fair. You're proud that you worked so long and so hard for your mother.

MRS. LINDE.   I don't think I patronize anyone. But it *is* true that I'm both proud and happy that I could make mother's last years comparatively easy.

NORA.   And you're proud of all you did for your brothers.

MRS. LINDE.   I think I have a right to be.

NORA.   And so do I. But now I want to tell you something, Kristine. I have something to be proud and happy about too.

MRS. LINDE.   I don't doubt that for a moment. But what exactly do you mean?

NORA.   Not so loud! Torvald mustn't hear—not for anything in the world. Nobody must know about this, Kristine. Nobody but you.

MRS. LINDE.   But what is it?

NORA.   Come here. (*Pulls her down on the couch beside her.*) You see, I *do* have something to be proud and happy about. I've saved Torvald's life.

MRS. LINDE.   Saved—? How do you mean—"saved"?

NORA.   I told you about our trip to Italy. Torvald would have died if he hadn't gone.

MRS. LINDE.   I understand that. And so your father gave you the money you needed.

NORA (*smiles*).   Yes, that's what Torvald and all the others think. But—

MRS. LINDE.   But what?

NORA.   Daddy didn't give us a penny. *I* raised that money.

MRS. LINDE.   *You* did? That whole big amount?

NORA.   Twelve hundred specie dollars. Four thousand eight hundred crowns. *Now* what do you say?

MRS. LINDE.   But Nora, how could you? Did you win in the state lottery?

NORA (*contemptuously*).   State lottery! (*Snorts.*) What is so great about that?

MRS. LINDE.   Where did it come from then?

NORA (*humming and smiling, enjoying her secret*).   Hmmm. Tra-la-la-la-la!

MRS. LINDE.   You certainly couldn't have borrowed it.

NORA.   Oh? And why not?

MRS. LINDE.   A wife can't borrow money without her husband's consent.

NORA (*with a toss of her head*).   Oh, I don't know—take a wife with a little bit of a head for business—a wife who knows how to manage things—

MRS. LINDE.   But Nora, I don't understand at all—

NORA.   You don't have to. I didn't say I borrowed the money, did I? I could have gotten it some other way. (*Leans back.*) An admirer may have given it to me. When you're as tolerably good-looking as I am—

MRS. LINDE.   Oh, you're crazy.

NORA.   I think you're dying from curiosity, Kristine.

MRS. LINDE.   I'm beginning to think you've done something very foolish, Nora.

NORA (*sits up*).   Is it foolish to save your husband's life?

MRS. LINDE.   I say it's foolish to act behind his back.

NORA.   But don't you see: he couldn't be told! You're missing the whole point, Kristine. We couldn't even let him know how seriously ill he was. The doctors came to *me* and told me his life was in danger, that nothing could save him but a stay in the south. Don't you think I tried to work on him? I told him how lovely it would be if I could go abroad like other young wives. I cried and begged. I said he'd better remember what condition I was in, that he had to be nice to me and do what I wanted. I even hinted he could borrow the money. But that almost made him angry with me. He told me I was being irresponsible and that it was his duty as my husband not to give in to my moods and whims—I think that's what he called it. All right, I said to myself, you've got to be saved somehow, and so I found a way—

MRS. LINDE.   And your husband never learned from your father that the money didn't come from him?

NORA.   Never. Daddy died that same week. I thought of telling him all about it and asking him not to say anything. But since he was so sick— It turned out I didn't have to—

MRS. LINDE.   And you've never told your husband?

NORA.   Of course not! Good heavens, how could I? He, with his strict principles! Besides, you know how men are. Torvald would find it embarrassing and humiliating to learn that he owed me anything. It would upset our whole relationship. Our happy, beautiful home would no longer be what it is.

MRS. LINDE.   Aren't you ever going to tell him?

NORA (*reflectively, half smiling*).   Yes—one day, maybe. Many, many years from now, when I'm no longer young and pretty. Don't laugh! I mean when Torvald no longer feels about me the way he does now, when he no longer thinks it's fun when I dance for him and put on costumes and recite for him. Then it will be good to have something in reverse—(*Interrupts herself.*) Oh, I'm just being silly! That day will never come.—Well, now, Kristine, what do you think of my great secret? Don't you think I'm good for something too?— By the way, you wouldn't believe all the worry I've had because of it. It's been very hard to meet my obligations on schedule. You see, in business there's something called quarterly interest and something called installments on the principal, and those are terribly hard to come up with. I've had to save a little here and a little there, whenever I could. I couldn't use much of the housekeeping money, for Torvald has to eat well. And I couldn't use what I got for clothes for the children. They have to look nice, and I didn't think it would be right to spend less than I got—the sweet little things!

MRS. LINDE.   Poor Nora! So you had to take it from your allowance!

NORA.   Yes, of course. After all, it was my affair. Every time Torvald gave me money for a new dress and things like that, I never used more than half of it. I always bought the cheapest, simplest things for myself. Thank God, everything looks good on me, so Torvald never noticed. But it was hard many times, Kristine, for it's fun to have pretty clothes. Don't you think?

MRS. LINDE.   Certainly.

NORA.   Anyway, I had other ways of making money too. Last winter I was lucky enough to get some copying work. So I locked the door and sat up writing every night till quite late. God! I often got so tired—! But it was great fun, too, working and making money. It was almost like being a man.

MRS. LINDE.   But how much have you been able to pay off this way?

NORA.   I couldn't tell you exactly. You see, it's very difficult to keep track of business like that. All I know is I have been paying off as much as I've been able to scrape together. Many times I just didn't know what to do. (*Smiles.*) Then I used to imagine a rich old gentleman had fallen in love with me—

MRS. LINDE.   What! What old gentleman?

NORA.   Phooey! And now he was dead and they were reading his will, and there it said in big letters, "All my money is to be paid in cash immediately to the charming Mrs. Nora Helmer."

MRS. LINDE.   But dearest Nora—who *was* this old gentleman?

NORA.   For heaven's sake, Kristine, don't you see? There *was* no old gentleman. He was just somebody I made up when I couldn't think of any way to raise the money. But never mind him. The old bore can be anyone he likes to for all I care. I have no use for him or his last will, for now I don't have a single worry in the world. (*Jumps up.*) Dear God, what a lovely thought this is! To be able to play and have fun with the children, to have everything nice and pretty in the house, just the way Torvald likes it! Not a care! And soon spring will be here, and the air will be blue and high. Maybe we can travel again. Maybe I'll see the ocean again! Oh, yes, yes!—it's wonderful to be alive and happy! (*The doorbell rings.*)

MRS. LINDE (*getting up*).   There's the doorbell. Maybe I better be going.

NORA.   No, please stay. I'm sure it's just someone for Torvald—

MAID (*in the hall door*).   Excuse me, ma'am. There's a gentleman here who'd like to see Mr. Helmer.

NORA.   You mean the bank manager.

MAID.   Sorry, ma'am; the bank manager. But I didn't know—since the Doctor is with him—

NORA.   Who is the gentleman?

KROGSTAD (*appearing in the door*).   It's just me, Mrs. Helmer. (MRS. LINDE *starts, looks, turns away toward the window.*)

NORA (*takes a step toward him, tense, in a low voice*).   You? What do you want? What do you want with my husband?

KROGSTAD.   Bank business—in a way. I have a small job in the Mutual, and I understand your husband is going to be our new boss—

NORA.   So it's just—

KROGSTAD.   Just routine business, ma'am. Nothing else.

NORA.   All right. In that case, why don't you go through the door to the office. (*Dismisses him casually as she closes the door. Walks over to the stove and tends the fire.*)

MRS. LINDE.   Nora—who was that man?

NORA.   His name is Krogstad. He's a lawyer.

MRS. LINDE.   So it *was* him.

NORA.   Do you know him?

MRS. LINDE.   I used to—many years ago. For a while he clerked in our part of the country.

NORA.   Right. He did.

MRS. LINDE.   He has changed a great deal.

NORA.   I believe he had a very unhappy marriage.

MRS. LINDE.   And now he's a widower, isn't he?

NORA.   With many children. There now; it's burning nicely again. (*Closes the stove and moves the rocking chair a little to the side.*)

MRS. LINDE.   They say he's into all sorts of business.

NORA.   Really? Maybe so. I wouldn't know. But let's not think about business. It's such a bore.

DR. RANK (*appears in the door to* HELMER'S *study*).   No, I don't want to be in the way. I'd rather talk to your wife a bit. (*Closes the door and notices* MRS. LINDE.) Oh, I beg your pardon. I believe I'm in the way here, too.

NORA.   No, not at all. (*Introduces them.*) Dr. Rank, Mrs. Linde.

RANK.   Aha. A name often heard in this house. I believe I passed you on the stairs coming up.

MRS. LINDE.   Yes. I'm afraid I climb stairs very slowly. They aren't good for me.

RANK.   I see. A slight case of inner decay, perhaps?

MRS. LINDE.   Overwork, rather.

RANK.   Oh, is that all? And now you've come to town to relax at all the parties?

MRS. LINDE.   I have come to look for a job.

RANK.   A proven cure for overwork, I take it?

MRS. LINDE.   One has to live, Doctor.

RANK.   Yes, that seems to be the common opinion.

NORA.   Come on, Dr. Rank—you want to live just as much as the rest of us.

RANK.   Of course I do. Miserable as I am, I prefer to go on being tortured as long as possible. All my patients feel the same way. And that's true of the moral invalids too. Helmer is talking with a specimen right this minute.

MRS. LINDE (*in a low voice*).   Ah!

NORA.   What do you mean?

RANK.   Oh, this lawyer, Krogstad. You don't know him. The roots of his character are decayed. But even he began by saying something about having *to live*—as if it were a matter of the highest importance.

NORA.   Oh? What did he want with Torvald?

RANK.   I don't really know. All I heard was something about the bank.

NORA.   I didn't know that Krog—that this Krogstad had anything to do with the Mutual Bank.

RANK.   Yes, he seems to have some kind of job there. (*To* MRS. LINDE) I don't know if you are familiar in your part of the country with the kind of person who is always running around trying to sniff out cases of moral decrepitude and as soon as he finds one puts the individual under observation in some excellent position or other. All the healthy ones are left out in the cold.

MRS. LINDE.   I should think it's the sick who need looking after the most.

RANK (*shrugs his shoulders*).   There we are. That's the attitude that turns society into a hospital. (NORA, *absorbed in her own thoughts, suddenly starts giggling and clapping her hands.*) What's so funny about that? Do you even know what society is?

NORA.   What do I care about your stupid society! I laughed at something entirely different—something terribly amusing. Tell me, Dr. Rank—all the employees in the Mutual Bank, from now on they'll all be dependent on Torvald, right?

RANK.   Is that what you find so enormously amusing?

NORA (*smiles and hums*).   That's my business, that's my business! (*Walks around.*) Yes, I do think it's fun that we—that Torvald is going to have so much influence on so many people's lives. (*Brings out the bag of macaroons.*) Have a macaroon, Dr. Rank.

RANK.   Well, well—macaroons. I thought they were banned around here.

NORA.   Yes, but these were some Kristine gave me.

MRS. LINDE.   What! I?

NORA.   That's all right. Don't look so scared. You couldn't know that Torvald won't let me have them. He's afraid they'll ruin my teeth. But who cares! Just once in a while—! Right, Dr. Rank? Have one! (*Puts a macaroon into his mouth.*) You too, Kristine. And one for me. A very small one. Or at most two. (*Walks around again.*) Yes, I really feel very, very happy. Now there's just one thing I'm dying to do.

RANK.   Oh? And what's that?

NORA.   Something I'm dying to say so Torvald could hear.

RANK.   And why can't you?

NORA.   I don't dare to, for it's not nice.

MRS. LINDE.   Not nice?

RANK.   In that case, I guess you'd better not. But surely to the two of us—? What is it you'd like to say for Helmer to hear?

NORA.   I want to say, "Goddammit!"

RANK.   Are you out of your mind!

MRS. LINDE.   For heaven's sakes, Nora!

RANK.   Say it. Here he comes.

NORA (*hiding the macaroons*).   Shhh! (HELMER *enters from his study, carrying his hat and overcoat.* NORA *goes to him.*) Well, dear, did you get rid of him?

HELMER.   Yes, he just left.

NORA.   Torvald, I want you to meet Kristine. She's just come to town.

HELMER.   Kristine—? I'm sorry; I don't think—

NORA.   Mrs. Linde, Torvald dear. Mrs. Kristine Linde.

HELMER.   Ah, yes. A childhood friend of my wife's, I suppose.

MRS. LINDE.   Yes, we've known each other for a long time.

NORA.   Just think; she has come all this way just to see you.

HELMER.   I'm not sure I understand—

MRS. LINDE.   Well, not really—

NORA.   You see, Kristine is an absolutely fantastic secretary, and she would so much like to work for a competent executive and learn more than she knows already—

HELMER.   Very sensible, I'm sure, Mrs. Linde.

NORA.   So when she heard about your appointment—there was a wire—she came here as fast as she could. How about it, Torvald? Couldn't you do something for Kristine? For my sake. Please?

HELMER.   Quite possibly. I take it you're a widow, Mrs. Linde?

MRS. LINDE.   Yes.

HELMER.   And you've had office experience?

MRS. LINDE.   Some—yes.

HELMER.   In that case I think it's quite likely that I'll be able to find you a position.

NORA (*claps her hands*).   I knew it! I knew it!

HELMER.   You've arrived at a most opportune time, Mrs. Linde.

MRS. LINDE.   Oh, how can I ever thank you—

HELMER.   Not at all, not at all. (*Puts his coat on.*) But today you'll have to excuse me—

RANK.   Wait a minute; I'll come with you. (*Gets his fur coat from the front hall, warms it by the stove.*)

NORA.   Don't be long, Torvald.

HELMER.   An hour or so; no more.

NORA.   Are you leaving, too, Kristine?

MRS. LINDE (*putting on her things*).   Yes, I'd better go and find a place to stay.

HELMER.   Good. Then we'll be going the same way.

NORA (*helping her*).   I'm sorry this place is so small, but I don't think we very well could—

MRS. LINDE.   Of course! Don't be silly, Nora. Goodbye, and thank you for everything.

NORA.   Goodbye. We'll see you soon. You'll be back this evening, of course. And you too, Dr. Rank; right? If you feel well enough? Of course you will. Just wrap yourself up. (*General small talk as all exit into the hall. CHILDREN's voices are heard on the stairs.*) There they are! There they are! (*She runs and opens the door. The nurse ANNE-MARIE enters with the CHILDREN.*)

NORA.   Come in! Come in! (*Bends over and kisses them.*) Oh, you sweet, sweet darlings! Look at them, Kristine! Aren't they beautiful?

RANK.   No standing around in the draft!

HELMER.   Come along, Mrs. Linde. This place isn't fit for anyone but mothers right now. (DR. RANK, HELMER, *and* MRS. LINDE *go down the stairs. The* NURSE *enters the living room with the children.* NORA *follows, closing the door behind her.*)

NORA.   My, how nice you all look! Such red cheeks! Like apples and roses. (*The* CHILDREN *all talk at the same time.*) You've had so much fun? I bet you have. Oh, isn't that nice! You pulled both Emmy and Bob on your sleigh? Both at the same time? That's very good, Ivar. Oh, let me hold her for a minute, Anne-Marie. My sweet little doll baby! (*Takes the smallest of the children from the* NURSE *and dances with her.*) Yes, yes, of course; Mama'll dance with you too, Bob. What? You threw snowballs? Oh, I wish I'd been there! No, no; *I* want to take their clothes off, Anne-Marie. Please let me; I think it's so much fun. You go on in. You look frozen. There's hot coffee on the stove. (*The* NURSE *exits into the room to the left.* NORA *takes the* CHILDREN's *wraps off and throws them all around. They all keep telling her things at the same time.*)

NORA.   Oh, really? A big dog ran after you? But it didn't bite you. Of course not. Dogs don't bite sweet little doll babies. Don't peek at the packages, Ivar! What's in them? Wouldn't you like to know! No, no; that's something terrible! Play? You want to play? What do you want to play? Okay, let's play hide-and-seek. Bob hides first. You want *me* to? All right. I'll go first. (*Laughing and shouting,* NORA *and the* CHILDREN *play in the living room and in the adjacent room, right. Finally,* NORA *hides herself under the table; the* CHILDREN *rush in, look for her, can't find her. They hear her low giggle, run to the table, lift the rug that covers it, see her. General hilarity. She crawls out, pretends to scare them. New delight. In the meantime there has been a knock on the door between the living room and the front hall, but nobody has noticed. Now the door is opened halfway;* KROGSTAD *appears. He waits a little. The play goes on.*)

KROGSTAD.   Pardon me, Mrs. Helmer—

NORA (*with a muted cry turns around, jumps up*).   Ah! What do you want?

KROGSTAD.   I'm sorry. The front door was open. Somebody must have forgotten to close it—

NORA (*standing up*).   My husband isn't here, Mr. Krogstad.

KROGSTAD.   I know.

NORA.   So what do you want?

KROGSTAD.   I'd like a word with you.

NORA.   With—? (*To the* CHILDREN) Go in to Anne-Marie. What? No, the strange man won't do anything bad to Mama. When he's gone we'll play some more. (*She takes the* CHILDREN *into the room to the left and closes the door. She turns—tense, troubled.*) You want to speak with me?

KROGSTAD.   Yes I do.

NORA.   Today—? It isn't the first of the month yet.

KROGSTAD.   No, it's Christmas Eve. It's up to you what kind of holiday you'll have.

NORA.   What do you want? I can't possibly—

KROGSTAD.   Let's not talk about that just yet. There's something else. You do have a few minutes, don't you?

NORA.   Yes. Yes, of course. That is,—

KROGSTAD.   Good. I was sitting in Olsen's restaurant when I saw your husband go by.

NORA.   Yes—?

KROGSTAD.   —with a lady.

NORA.   What of it?

KROGSTAD.   May I be so free as to ask: wasn't that lady Mrs. Linde?

NORA.   Yes.

KROGSTAD.   Just arrived in town?

NORA.   Yes, today.

KROGSTAD.   She's a good friend of yours, I understand?

NORA.   Yes, she is. But I fail to see—

KROGSTAD.   I used to know her myself.

NORA.   I know that.

KROGSTAD.   So you know about that. I thought as much. In that case, let me ask you a simple question. Is Mrs. Linde going to be employed in the bank?

NORA.   What makes you think you have the right to cross-examine me like this, Mr. Krogstad—you, one of my husband's employees? But since you ask, I'll tell you. Yes, Mrs. Linde is going to be working in the bank. And it was I who recommended her, Mr. Krogstad. Now you know.

KROGSTAD.   So I was right.

NORA (*walks up and down*).   After all, one does have a little influence, you know. Just because you're a woman, it doesn't mean that— Really, Mr. Krogstad, people in a subordinate position should be careful not to offend someone who—oh well—

KROGSTAD.   —has influence?

NORA.   Exactly.

KROGSTAD (*changing his tone*).   Mrs. Helmer, I must ask you to be good enough to use your influence on my behalf.

NORA.   What do you mean?

KROGSTAD.   I want you to make sure that I am going to keep my subordinate position in the bank.

NORA.   I don't understand. Who is going to take your position away from you?

KROGSTAD.   There's no point in playing ignorant with me, Mrs. Helmer. I can very well appreciate that your friend will find it unpleasant to run into me. So now I know who I can thank for my dismissal.

NORA.   But I assure you—

KROGSTAD.   Never mind. Just want to say you still have time. I advise you to use your influence to prevent it.

NORA.   But Mr. Krogstad, I don't have any influence—none at all.

KROGSTAD.   No? I thought you just said—

NORA.   Of course I didn't mean it that way. I! Whatever makes you think that I have any influence of that kind on my husband?

KROGSTAD.   I went to law school with your husband. I have no reason to think that the bank manager is less susceptible than other husbands.

NORA.   If you're going to insult my husband, I'll ask you to leave.

KROGSTAD.   You're brave, Mrs. Helmer.

NORA.   I'm not afraid of you any more. After New Year's I'll be out of this thing with you.

KROGSTAD (*more controlled*).   Listen, Mrs. Helmer. If necessary I'll fight as for my life to keep my little job in the bank.

NORA.   So it seems.

KROGSTAD.   It isn't just the money; that's really the smallest part of it. There is something else—Well, I guess I might as well tell you. It's like this. I'm sure you know, like everybody else, that some years ago I committed— an impropriety.

NORA.   I believe I've heard it mentioned.

KROGSTAD.   The case never came to court, but from that moment all doors were closed to me. So I took up the kind of business you know about. I had to do something, and I think I can say about myself that I have not been among the worst. But now I want to get out of all that. My sons are growing up. For their sake I must get back as much of my good name as I can. This job in the bank was like the first rung on the ladder. And now your husband wants to kick me down and leave me back in the mud again.

NORA.   But I swear to you, Mr. Krogstad; it's not at all in my power to help you.

KROGSTAD.   That's because you don't want to. But I have the means to force you.

NORA.   You don't mean you're going to tell my husband I owe you money?

KROGSTAD.   And if I did?

NORA.   That would be a mean thing to do. (*Almost crying.*) That secret, which is my joy and my pride—for him to learn about it in such a coarse and ugly manner—to learn it from *you*—! It would be terribly unpleasant for me.

KROGSTAD.   Just unpleasant?

NORA (*heatedly*).   But go ahead! Do it! It will be worse for you than for me. When my husband realizes what a bad person you are you'll be sure to lose your job.

KROGSTAD.   I asked you if it was just domestic unpleasantness you were afraid of?

NORA.   When my husband finds out, of course he'll pay off the loan, and then we won't have anything more to do with you.

KROGSTAD (*stepping closer*).   Listen, Mrs. Helmer—either you have a very bad memory, or you don't know much about business. I think I had better straighten you out on a few things.

NORA.   What do you mean?

KROGSTAD.   When your husband was ill, you came to me to borrow twelve hundred dollars.

NORA.   I knew nobody else.

KROGSTAD.   I promised to get you the money on certain conditions. At the time you were so anxious about your husband's health and so set on getting him away that I doubt very much that you paid much attention to the details of our transaction. That's why I remind you of them now. Anyway, I promised to get you the money if you would sign an I.O.U., which I drafted.

NORA.   And which I signed.

KROGSTAD.   Good. But below your signature I added a few lines making your father security for the loan. Your father was supposed to put his signature to those lines.

NORA.   Supposed to—? He did.

KROGSTAD.   I had left the date blank. That is, your father was to date his own signature. You recall that, don't you, Mrs. Helmer?

NORA.   I guess so—

KROGSTAD.   I gave the note to you. You were to mail it to your father. Am I correct?

NORA.   Yes.

KROGSTAD.   And of course you did so right away, for no more than five or six days later you brought the paper back to me, signed by your father. Then I paid you the money.

NORA.   Well? And haven't I been keeping up with the payments?

KROGSTAD.   Fairly well, yes. But to get back to what we were talking about—those were difficult days for you, weren't they, Mrs. Helmer?

NORA.   Yes, they were.

KROGSTAD.   Your father was quite ill, I believe.

NORA.   He was dying.

KROGSTAD.   And died shortly afterwards?

NORA.   That's right.

KROGSTAD.   Tell me, Mrs. Helmer; do you happen to remember the date of your father's death? I mean the exact day of the month?

NORA.   Daddy died on September 29.

KROGSTAD.   Quite correct. I have ascertained that fact. That's why there is something peculiar about this (*takes out a piece of paper*), which I can't account for.

NORA.   Peculiar? How? I don't understand—

KROGSTAD.   It seems very peculiar, Mrs. Helmer, that your father signed this promissory note three days after his death.

NORA.   How so? I don't see what—

KROGSTAD.   Your father died on September 29. Now look. He has dated his signature October 2. Isn't that odd? (NORA *remains silent.*) Can you explain it? (NORA *is still silent.*) I also find it striking that the date and the month and the year are not in your father's handwriting but in a hand I think I recognize. Well, that might be explained. Your father may have forgotten to date his signature and somebody else may have done it here, guessing at the date before he had learned of your father's death. That's all right. It's only the signature itself that matters. And that is genuine, isn't it, Mrs. Helmer? Your father *did* put his name to this note?

NORA (*after a brief silence tosses her head back and looks defiantly at him*).   No, he didn't. *I* wrote Daddy's name.

KROGSTAD.   Mrs. Helmer—do you realize what a dangerous admission you just made?

NORA.   Why? You'll get your money soon.

KROGSTAD.   Let me ask you something. Why didn't you mail this note to your father?

NORA.   Because it was impossible. Daddy was sick—you know that. If I had asked him to sign it, I would have had to tell him what the money was for. But I couldn't tell him, as sick as he was, that my husband's life was in danger. That was impossible. Surely you can see that.

KROGSTAD.   Then it would have been better for you if you had given up your trip abroad.

NORA.   No, that was impossible! That trip was to save my husband's life. I couldn't give it up.

KROGSTAD.   But didn't you realize that what you did amounted to fraud against me?

NORA.   I couldn't let that make any difference. I didn't care about you at all. I hated the way you made all those difficulties for me, even though you knew the danger my husband was in. I thought you were cold and unfeeling.

KROGSTAD.   Mrs. Helmer, obviously you have no clear idea of what you have done. Let me tell you that what I did that time was no more and no worse. And it ruined my name and reputation.

NORA.   You! Are you trying to tell me that you did something brave once in order to save your wife's life?

KROGSTAD.   The law doesn't ask motives.

NORA.   Then it's a bad law.

KROGSTAD.   Bad or not—if I produce this note in court you'll be judged according to the law.

NORA.   I refuse to believe you. A daughter shouldn't have the right to spare her dying old father worry and anxiety? A wife shouldn't have the right to save her husband's life? I don't know the laws very well, but I'm sure that somewhere they make allowances for cases like that. And you, a lawyer, don't know that? I think you must be a bad lawyer, Mr. Krogstad.

KROGSTAD.   That may be. But business—the kind of business you and I have with one another—don't you think I know something about that? Very well. Do what you like. But let me tell you this: if I'm going to be kicked out again, you'll keep me company. (*He bows and exits through the front hall.*)

NORA (*pauses thoughtfully; then, with a defiant toss of her head*).   Oh, nonsense! Trying to scare me like that! I'm not all that silly. (*Starts picking up the* CHILDREN'S *clothes; soon stops.*) But—? No! That's impossible! I did it for love!

THE CHILDREN (*in the door to the left*).   Mama, the strange man just left. We saw him.

NORA.   Yes, yes; I know. But don't tell anybody about the strange man. Do you hear? Not even Daddy.

CHILDREN.   We won't. But now you'll play with us again, won't you, mama?

NORA.   No, not right now.

CHILDREN.   But Mama—you promised.

NORA.   I know, but I can't just now. Go to your own room. I've so much to do. Be nice now, my little darlings. Do as I say. (*She nudges them gently into the other room and closes the door. She sits down on the couch, picks up a piece of embroidery, makes a few stitches, then stops.*) No! (*Throws the embroidery down, goes to the hall door and calls out.*) Helene! Bring the Christmas tree in here, please! (*Goes to the table, left, opens the drawer, halts.*) No—that's impossible!

MAID (*with the Christmas tree*).   Where do you want it, ma'am?

NORA.   There. The middle of the floor.

MAID.   You want anything else?

NORA.   No, thanks. I have everything I need. (*The* MAID *goes out.* NORA *starts trimming the tree.*) I want candles—and flowers— That awful man! Oh nonsense! There's nothing wrong. This will be a lovely tree. I'll do everything you want me to, Torvald. I'll sing for you—dance for you—

(HELMER, *a bundle of papers under his arm, enters from outside.*) Ah—you're back already?

HELMER.   Yes. Has anybody been here?

NORA.   Here? No.

HELMER.   That's funny. I saw Krogstad leaving just now.

NORA.   Oh? Oh yes, that's right. Krogstad was here for just a moment.

HELMER.   I can tell from your face that he came to ask you to put in a word for him.

NORA.   Yes.

HELMER.   And it was supposed to be your own idea, wasn't it? You were not to tell me he'd been here. He asked you that too, didn't he?

NORA.   Yes, Torvald, but—

HELMER.   Nora, Nora, how could you! Talk to a man like that and make him promises! And lying to me about it afterward—!

NORA.   Lying—?

HELMER.   Didn't you say nobody had been here? (*Shakes his finger at her.*) My little songbird must never do that again. Songbirds are supposed to have clean beaks to chirp with—no false notes. (*Puts his arm around her waist.*) Isn't that so? Of course it is. (*Lets her go.*) And that's enough about that. (*Sits down in front of the fireplace.*) Ah, it's nice and warm in here. (*Begins to leaf through his papers.*)

NORA (*busy with the tree; after a brief pause*).   Torvald.

HELMER.   Yes.

NORA.   I'm looking forward so much to the Stenborgs' costume party day after tomorrow.

HELMER.   And I can't wait to find out what you're going to surprise me with.

NORA.   Oh, that silly idea!

HELMER.   Oh?

NORA.   I can't think of anything. It all seems so foolish and pointless.

HELMER.   Ah, my little Nora admits that?

NORA (*behind his chair, her arms on the back of the chair*).   Are you very busy, Torvald?

HELMER.   Well—

NORA.   What are all those papers?

HELMER.   Bank business.

NORA.   Already?

HELMER.   I've asked the board to give me the authority to make certain changes in organization and personnel. That's what I'll be doing over the holidays. I want it all settled before New Year's.

NORA.   So that's why this poor Krogstad—

HELMER.   Hm.

NORA (*leisurely playing with the hair on his neck*).   If you weren't so busy, Torvald, I'd ask you for a great big favor.

HELMER.   Let's hear it, anyway.

NORA.   I don't know anyone with better taste than you, and I want so much to look nice at the party. Couldn't you sort of take charge of me, Torvald, and decide what I'll wear— Help me with my costume?

HELMER.   Aha! Little Lady Obstinate is looking for someone to rescue her?

NORA.   Yes, Torvald. I won't get anywhere without your help.

HELMER.   All right. I'll think about it. We'll come up with something.

NORA.   Oh, you *are* nice! (*Goes back to the Christmas tree. A pause.*) Those red flowers look so pretty.— Tell me, was it really all that bad what this Krogstad fellow did?

HELMER.   He forged signatures. Do you have any idea what that means?

NORA.   Couldn't it have been because he felt he had to?

HELMER.   Yes, or like so many others he may simply have been thoughtless. I'm not so heartless as to condemn a man absolutely because of a single imprudent act.

NORA.   Of course not, Torvald!

HELMER.   People like him can redeem themselves morally by openly confessing their crime and taking their punishment.

NORA.   Punishment—?

HELMER.   But that was not the way Krogstad chose. He got out of it with tricks and evasions. That's what has corrupted him.

NORA.   So you think that if—?

HELMER.   Can't you imagine how a guilty person like that has to lie and fake and dissemble wherever he goes—putting on a mask before everybody he's close to, even his own wife and children. It's the thing with the children that's the worst part of it, Nora.

NORA.   Why is that?

HELMER.   Because when a man lives inside such a circle of stinking lies he brings infection into his own home and contaminates his whole family. With every breath of air his children inhale the germs of something ugly.

NORA (*moving closer behind him*).   Are you so sure of that?

HELMER.   Of course I am. I have seen enough examples of that in my work. Nearly all young criminals have had mothers who lied.

NORA.   Why mothers—particularly?

HELMER.   Most often mothers. But of course fathers tend to have the same influence. Every lawyer knows that. And yet, for years this Krogstad has been poisoning his own children in an atmosphere of lies and deceit. That's why I call him a lost soul morally. (*Reaches out for her hands.*) And that's why my sweet little Nora must promise me never to take his side again. Let's shake on that.— What? What's this? Give me your hand. There! Now that's settled. I assure you, I would find it impossible to work in the same room with that man. I feel literally sick when I'm around people like that.

NORA (*withdraws her hand and goes to the other side of the Christmas tree*).   It's so hot in here. And I have so much to do.

HELMER (*gets up and collects his papers*).   Yes, and I really should try to get some of this reading done before dinner. I must think about your costume too. And maybe just possibly I'll have something to wrap in gilt paper and hang on the Christmas tree. (*Puts his hand on her head.*) Oh my adorable little songbird! (*Enters his study and closes the door.*)

NORA (*after a pause, in a low voice*).   It's all a lot of nonsense. It's not that way at all. It's impossible. It has to be impossible.

NURSE (*in the door, left*).   The little ones are asking ever so nicely if they can't come in and be with their mamma.

NORA.   No, no, no! Don't let them in here! You stay with them, Anne-Marie.

NURSE.   If you say so, ma'am. (*Closes the door.*)

NORA (*pale with terror*).   Corrupt my little children—! Poison my home—? (*Brief pause; she lifts her head.*) That's not true. Never. Never in a million years.

ACT 2

The same room. The Christmas tree is in the corner by the piano, stripped shabby-looking, with burnt-down candles. NORA'S outside clothes are on the couch. NORA is alone. She walks around restlessly. She stops by the couch and picks up her coat.

NORA (*drops the coat again*).   There's somebody now! (*Goes to the door, listens.*) No. Nobody. Of course not—not on Christmas. And not tomorrow either.*— But perhaps— (*Opens the door and looks.*) No, nothing in the mailbox. All empty. (*Comes forward.*) How silly I am! Of course he isn't serious. Nothing like that could happen. After all, I have three small children. (*The NURSE enters from the room, left, carrying a big carton.*)

NURSE.   Well, at last I found it—the box with your costume.

NORA.   Thanks. Just put it on the table.

NURSE (*does so*).   But it's all a big mess, I'm afraid.

NORA.   Oh, I wish I could tear the whole thing to little pieces!

NURSE.   Heavens! It's not as bad as all that. It can be fixed all right. All it takes is a little patience.

NORA.   I'll go over and get Mrs. Linde to help me.

NURSE.   Going out again? In this awful weather? You'll catch a cold.

NORA.   That might not be such a bad thing. How are the children?

NURSE.   The poor little dears are playing with their presents, but—

NORA.   Do they keep asking for me?

NURSE.   Well, you know, they're used to being with their mamma.

NORA.   I know. But Anne-Marie, from now on I can't be with them as much as before.

*In Norway both Christmas and the day after are legal holidays.

NURSE.   Oh well. Little children get used to everything.

NORA.   You think so? Do you think they'd forget their mamma if I were gone altogether?

NURSE.   Goodness me—gone altogether?

NORA.   Listen, Anne-Marie—something I've wondered about. How could you bring yourself to leave your child with strangers?

NURSE.   But I had to, if I were to nurse you.

NORA.   Yes, but how could you *want* to?

NURSE.   When I could get such a nice place? When something like that happens to a poor young girl, she'd better be grateful for whatever she gets. For *he* didn't do a thing for me—the louse!

NORA.   But your daughter has forgotten all about you, hasn't she?

NURSE.   Oh no! Not at all! She wrote to me both when she was confirmed and when she got married.

NORA (*putting her arms around her neck*).   You dear old thing—you were a good mother to me when I was little.

NURSE.   Poor little Nora had no one else, you know.

NORA.   And if my little ones didn't, I know you'd—oh, I'm being silly! (*Opens the carton.*) Go in to them, please. I really should—. Tomorrow you'll see how pretty I'll be.

NURSE.   I know. There won't be anybody at that party half as pretty as you, ma'am. (*Goes out, left.*)

NORA (*begins to take clothes out of the carton; in a moment she throws it all down*).   If only I dared to go out. If only I knew nobody would come. That nothing would happen while I was gone.— How silly! Nobody'll come. Just don't think about it. Brush the muff. Beautiful gloves. Beautiful gloves. Forget it. Forget it. One, two, three, four, five, six—(*Cries out.*) There they are! (*NORA moves toward the door, stops irresolutely.* MRS. LINDE *enters from the hall. She has already taken off her coat.*) Oh, it's you, Kristine. There's no one else out there, is there? I'm so glad you're here.

MRS. LINDE.   They told me you'd asked for me.

NORA.   I just happened to walk by. I need your help with something—badly. Let's sit here on the couch. Look. Torvald and I are going to a costume party tomorrow night—at Consul Stenborg's upstairs—and Torvald wants me to go as a Neapolitan fisher girl and dance the tarantella. I learned it when we were on Capri.

MRS. LINDE.   Well, well! So you'll be putting on a whole show?

NORA.   Yes. Torvald thinks I should. Look, here's the costume. Torvald had it made for me while we were there. But it's all torn and everything. I just don't know—

MRS. LINDE.   Oh, that can be fixed. It's not that much. The trimmings have come loose in a few places. Do you have needle and thread? Ah, here we are. All set.

NORA.   I really appreciate it, Kristine.

MRS. LINDE (*sewing*).   So you'll be in disguise tomorrow night, eh? You know—I may come by for just a moment, just to look at you.— Oh dear. I haven't even thanked you for the nice evening last night.

NORA (*gets up, moves around*).   Oh, I don't know. I don't think last night was as nice as it usually is.— You should have come to town a little earlier, Kristine.— Yes, Torvald knows how to make it nice and pretty around here.

MRS. LINDE.   You too, I should think. After all, you're your father's daughter. By the way, is Dr. Rank always as depressed as he was last night?

NORA.   No, last night was unusual. He's a very sick man, you know— very sick. Poor Rank, his spine is rotting away. Tuberculosis, I think. You see, his father was a nasty old man with mistresses and all that sort of thing. Rank has been sickly ever since he was a little boy.

MRS. LINDE (*dropping her sewing to her lap*).   But dearest Nora, where have you learned about things like that?

NORA (*still walking about*).   Oh, you know—with three children you sometimes get to talk with—other wives. Some of them know quite a bit about medicine. So you pick up a few things.

MRS. LINDE (*resumes her sewing; after a brief pause*).   Does Dr. Rank come here every day?

NORA.   Every single day. He's Torvald's oldest and best friend, after all. And my friend too, for that matter. He's part of the family, almost.

MRS. LINDE.   But tell me, is he quite sincere? I mean, isn't he the kind of man who likes to say nice things to people?

NORA.   No, not at all. Rather the opposite, in fact. What makes you say that?

MRS. LINDE.   When you introduced me yesterday, he told me he'd often heard my name mentioned in the house. But later on it was quite obvious your husband really had no idea who I was. So how could Dr. Rank—?

NORA.   You're right, Kristine, but I can explain that. You see, Torvald loves me so very much that he wants me all to himself. That's what he says. When we were first married he got almost jealous when I as much as mentioned anybody from back home that I was fond of. So of course I soon stopped doing that. But with Dr. Rank I often talk about home. You see, he likes to listen to me.

MRS. LINDE.   Look here, Nora. In many ways you're still a child. After all, I'm quite a bit older than you and have had more experience. I want to give you a piece of advice. I think you should get out of this thing with Dr. Rank.

NORA.   Get out of what thing?

MRS. LINDE.   Several things in fact, if you want my opinion. Yesterday you said something about a rich admirer who was going to give you money—

NORA.   One who doesn't exist, unfortunately. What of it?

MRS. LINDE.   Does Dr. Rank have money?

NORA.   Yes, he does.

MRS. LINDE.   And no dependents?

NORA.   No. But—?

MRS. LINDE.   And he comes here every day?

NORA.   Yes, I told you that already.

MRS. LINDE.   But how can that sensitive man be so tactless?

NORA.   I haven't the slightest idea what you're talking about.

MRS. LINDE.   Don't play games with me, Nora. Don't you think I know who you borrowed the twelve hundred dollars from?

NORA.   Are you out of your mind! The very idea—! A friend of both of us who sees us every day—! What a dreadfully uncomfortable position that would be!

MRS. LINDE.   So it really isn't Dr. Rank?

NORA.   Most certainly not! I would never have dreamed of asking him—not for a moment. Anyway, he didn't have any money then. He inherited it afterwards.

MRS. LINDE.   Well, I still think it may have been lucky for you, Nora dear.

NORA.   The idea! It would never have occurred to me to ask Dr. Rank—. Though I'm sure that if I *did* ask him—

MRS. LINDE.   But of course you wouldn't.

NORA.   Of course not. I can't imagine that that would ever be necessary. But I am quite sure that if I told Dr. Rank—

MRS. LINDE.   Behind your husband's back?

NORA.   I must get out of—this other thing. That's also behind his back. I *must* get out of it.

MRS. LINDE.   That's what I told you yesterday. But—

NORA (*walking up and down*).   A man manages these things so much better than a woman—

MRS. LINDE.   One's husband, yes.

NORA.   Silly, silly! (*Stops.*) When you've paid off all you owe, you get your I.O.U. back; right?

MRS. LINDE.   Yes, of course.

NORA.   And you can tear it into a hundred thousand little pieces and burn it—that dirty, filthy, paper!

MRS. LINDE (*looks hard at her, puts down her sewing, rising slowly*). Nora—you're hiding something from me.

NORA.   Can you tell?

MRS. LINDE.   Something's happened to you, Nora, since yesterday morning. What is it?

NORA (*going to her*).   Kristine! (*Listens.*) Shhh. Torvald just came back. Listen. Why don't you go in to the children for a while. Torvald can't stand having sewing around. Get Anne-Marie to help you.

MRS. LINDE (*gathers some of the sewing things together*).   All right, but I'm not leaving here till you and I have talked. (*She goes out left, just as* HELMER *enters from the front hall.*)

NORA (*towards him*).   I have been waiting and waiting for you, Torvald.

HELMER.   Was that the dressmaker?

NORA.   No, it was Kristine. She's helping me with my costume. Oh Torvald, just wait till you see how nice I'll look!

HELMER.   I told you. Pretty good idea I had, wasn't it?

NORA.   Lovely! And wasn't it nice of me to go along with it?

HELMER (*his hand under her chin*).   Nice? To do what your husband tells you? All right, you little rascal; I know you didn't mean it that way. But don't let me interrupt you. I suppose you want to try it on.

NORA.   And you'll be working?

HELMER.   Yes. (*Shows her a pile of papers.*) Look. I've been down to the bank. (*Is about to enter his study.*)

NORA.   Torvald.

HELMER (*halts*).   Yes?

NORA.   What if your little squirrel asked you ever so nicely—

HELMER.   For what?

NORA.   Would you do it?

HELMER.   Depends on what it is.

NORA.   Squirrel would run around and do all sorts of fun tricks if you'd be nice and agreeable.

HELMER.   All right. What is it?

NORA.   Lark would chirp and twitter in all the rooms, up and down—

HELMER.   So what? Lark does that anyway.

NORA.   I'll be your elfmaid and dance for you in the moonlight, Torvald.

HELMER.   Nora, don't tell me it's the same thing you mentioned this morning?

NORA (*closer to him*).   Yes, Torvald. I beg you!

HELMER.   You really have the nerve to bring that up again?

NORA.   Yes. You've just got to do as I say. You *must* let Krogstad keep his job.

HELMER.   My dear Nora. It's his job I intend to give to Mrs. Linde.

NORA.   I know. And that's ever so nice of you. But can't you just fire someone else?

HELMER.   This is incredible! You just don't give up do you? Because you make some foolish promise, *I* am supposed to—!

NORA.   That's not the reason, Torvald. It's for your own sake. That man writes for the worst newspapers. You've said so yourself. There's no telling what he may do to you. I'm scared to death of him.

HELMER.   Ah, I understand. You're afraid because of what happened before.

NORA.   What do you mean?

HELMER.   You're thinking of your father, of course.

NORA.   Yes. You're right. Remember the awful things they wrote about Daddy in the newspapers. I really think they might have forced him to resign if the ministry hadn't sent you to look into the charges and if you hadn't been so helpful and understanding.

HELMER.   My dear little Nora, there is a world of difference between your father and me. Your father's official conduct was not above reproach. Mine is, and I intend for it to remain that way as long as I hold my position.

NORA.   Oh, but you don't know what vicious people like that may think of. Oh, Torvald! Now all of us could be so happy together here in our own home, peaceful and carefree. Such a good life, Torvald, for you and me and the children! That's why I implore you—

HELMER.   And it's exactly because you plead for him that you make it impossible for me to keep him. It's already common knowledge in the bank that I intend to let Krogstad go. If it gets out that the new manager has changed his mind because of his wife—

NORA.   Yes? What then?

HELMER.   No, of course, that wouldn't matter at all as long as little Mrs. Pighead here got her way! Do you want me to make myself look ridiculous before my whole staff—make people think I can be swayed by just anybody—by outsiders? Believe me, I would soon enough find out what the consequences would be! Besides, there's another thing that makes it absolutely impossible for Krogstad to stay on in the bank now that I'm in charge.

NORA.   What's that?

HELMER.   I suppose in a pinch I could overlook his moral shortcomings—

NORA.   Yes, you could; couldn't you, Torvald?

HELMER.   And I understand he's quite a good worker, too. But we've known each other for a long time. It's one of those imprudent relationships you get into when you're young that embarrass you for the rest of your life. I guess I might as well be frank with you: he and I are on a first-name basis. And that tactless fellow never hides the fact even when other people are around. Rather, he seems to think it entitles him to be familiar with me. Every chance he gets he comes out with his damn "Torvald, Torvald." I'm telling you, I find it most awkward. He would make my position in the bank intolerable.

NORA.   You don't really mean any of this, Torvald.

HELMER.   Oh? I don't? And why not?

NORA.   No, for it's all so petty.

HELMER.   What! Petty? You think I'm being petty!

NORA.   No, I *don't* think you are petty, Torvald dear. That's exactly why I—

HELMER.   Never mind. You think my reasons are petty, so it follows that I must be petty too. Petty! Indeed! By God, I'll put an end to this right now! (*Opens the door to the front hall and calls out.*) Helene!

NORA.   What are you doing?

HELMER (*searching among his papers*).   Making a decision. (*The* MAID *enters.*) Here. Take this letter. Go out with it right away. Find somebody to deliver it. But quick. The address is on the envelope. Wait. Here's money.

MAID.   Very good sir. (*She takes the letter and goes out.*)

HELMER (*collecting his papers*).   There now, little Mrs. Obstinate!

NORA (*breathless*).   Torvald—what was that letter?

HELMER.   Krogstad's dismissal.

NORA.   Call it back, Torvald! There's still time! Oh Torvald, please—call it back! For my sake, for your own sake, for the sake of the children! Listen to me, Torvald! Do it! You don't know what you're doing to all of us!

HELMER.   Too late.

NORA.   Yes. Too late.

HELMER.   Dear Nora, I forgive you this fear you're in, although it really is an insult to me. Yes, it is! It's an insult to think that I am scared of a shabby scrivener's revenge. But I forgive you, for it's such a beautiful proof of how much you love me. (*Takes her in his arms.*) And that's the way it should be, my sweet darling. Whatever happens you'll see that when things get really rough I have both strength and courage. You'll find out that I am man enough to shoulder the whole burden.

NORA (*terrified*).   What do you mean by that?

HELMER.   All of it, I tell you—

NORA (*composed*).   You'll never have to do that.

HELMER.   Good. Then we'll share the burden, Nora—like husband and wife, the way it ought to be. (*Caresses her.*) Now are you satisfied? There, there, there. Not that look in your eyes—like a frightened dove. It's all your own foolish imagination.—Why don't you practice the tarantella—and your tambourine, too. I'll be in the inner office and close both doors, so I won't hear you. You can make as much noise as you like. (*Turning in the doorway.*) And when Rank comes, tell him where to find me. (*He nods to her, enters his study carrying his papers, and closes the door.*)

NORA (*transfixed by terror, whispers*).   He would do it. He'll do it. He'll do it in spite of the whole world.— No, this mustn't happen. Anything rather than that! There must be a way—! (*The doorbell rings.*) Dr. Rank! Anything rather than that! Anything—anything at all! (*She passes her hand over her face, pulls herself together, and opens the door to the hall.* DR. RANK *is out there, hanging up his coat. Darkness begins to fall during the following scene.*) Hello there, Dr. Rank. I recognized your ringing. Don't go in to Torvald yet. I think he's busy.

RANK.   And you?

NORA (*as he enters and she closes the door behind him*).   You know I always have time for you.

RANK.   Thanks. I'll make use of that as long as I can.

NORA.   What do you mean by that— As long as you can?

RANK.   Does that frighten you?

NORA.   Well, it's a funny expression. As if something was going to happen.

RANK.   Something is going to happen that I've long been expecting. But I admit I hadn't thought it would come quite so soon.

NORA (*seizes his arm*).   What is it you've found out? Dr. Rank—tell me!

RANK (*sits down by the stove*).   I'm going downhill fast. There's nothing to do about that.

NORA (*with audible relief*).   So it's *you*—

RANK.   Who else? No point in lying to myself. I'm in worse shape than any of my other patients, Mrs. Helmer. These last few days I've been making up my inner status. Bankrupt. Chances are that within a month I'll be rotting up in the cemetery.

NORA.   Shame on you! Talking that horrid way!

RANK.   The thing itself is horrid—damn horrid. The worst of it, though, is all that other horror that comes first. There is only one more test I need to make. After that I'll have a pretty good idea when I'll start coming apart. There is something I want to say to you. Helmer's refined nature can't stand anything hideous. I don't want him in my sick room.

NORA.   Oh, but Dr. Rank—

RANK.   I don't want him there. Under no circumstance. I'll close my door to him. As soon as I have full certainty that the worst is about to begin I'll give you my card with a black cross on it. Then you'll know the last horror of destruction has started.

NORA.   Today you're really quite impossible. And I had hoped you'd be in a particularly good mood.

RANK.   With death on my hands? Paying for someone else's sins? Is there justice in that? And yet there isn't a single family that isn't ruled by the same law of ruthless retribution, in one way or another.

NORA (*puts her hands over her ears*).   Poppycock! Be fun! Be fun!

RANK.   Well, yes. You may just as well laugh at the whole thing. My poor, innocent spine is suffering from my father's frolics as a young lieutenant.

NORA (*over by the table, left*).   Right. He was addicted to asparagus and goose liver paté, wasn't he?

RANK.   And truffles.

NORA.   Of course. Truffles. And oysters too, I think.

RANK.   And oysters. Obviously.

NORA.   And all the port and champagne that go with it. It's really too bad that goodies like that ruin your backbone.

RANK.   Particularly an unfortunate backbone that never enjoyed any of it.

NORA.   Ah yes, that's the saddest part of all.

RANK (*looks searchingly at her*).   Hm—

NORA (*after a brief pause*).   Why did you smile just then?

RANK.   No, it was you that laughed.

NORA.   No, it was you that smiled, Dr. Rank!

RANK (*gets up*).   You're more of a mischief-maker than I thought.

NORA.   I feel in the mood for mischief today.

RANK.   So it seems.

NORA (*with both her hands on his shoulders*).   Dear, dear Dr. Rank, don't you go and die and leave Torvald and me.

RANK.   Oh, you won't miss me for very long. Those who go away are soon forgotten.

NORA (*with an anxious look*).   Do you believe that?

RANK.   You'll make new friends, and then—

NORA.   Who'll make new friends?

RANK.   Both you and Helmer, once I'm gone. You yourself seem to have made a good start already. What was this Mrs. Linde doing here last night?

NORA.   Aha—Don't tell me you're jealous of poor Kristine?

RANK.   Yes, I am. She'll be my successor in this house. As soon as I have made my excuses, that woman is likely to—

NORA.   Shh—not so loud. She's in there.

RANK.   Today too? There you are!

NORA.   She's mending my costume. My God, you really *are* unreasonable. (*Sits down on the couch.*) Now be nice, Dr. Rank. Tomorrow you'll see how beautifully I'll dance, and then you are to pretend I'm dancing just for you—and for Torvald too, of course. (*Takes several items out of the carton.*) Sit down, Dr. Rank; I want to show you something.

RANK (*sitting down*).   What?

NORA.   Look.

RANK.   Silk stockings.

NORA.   Flesh-colored. Aren't they lovely? Now it's getting dark in here, but tomorrow— No, no. You only get to see the foot. Oh well, you might as well see all of it.

RANK.   Hmm.

NORA.   Why do you look so critical? Don't you think they'll fit?

RANK.   That's something I can't possibly have a reasoned opinion about.

NORA (*looks at him for a moment*).   Shame on you. (*Slaps his ear lightly with the stocking.*) That's what you get. (*Puts the things back in the carton.*)

RANK.   And what other treasures are you going to show me?

NORA.   Nothing at all, because you're naughty. (*She hums a little and rummages in the carton.*)

RANK (*after a brief silence*).   When I sit here like this, talking confidently with you, I can't imagine—I can't possibly imagine what would have become of me if I hadn't had you and Helmer.

NORA (*smiles*).   Well, yes—I do believe you like being with us.

RANK (*in a lower voice, lost in thought*).   And then to have to go away from it all—

NORA.   Nonsense. You are not going anywhere.

RANK (*as before*).   —and not to leave behind as much as a poor little token of gratitude, hardly a brief memory of someone missed, nothing but a vacant place that anyone can fill.

NORA.   And what if I were to ask you—? No—

RANK.   Ask me what?

NORA.   For a great proof of your friendship—

RANK.   Yes, yes—?

NORA.   No, I mean—for an enormous favor—

RANK.   Would you really for once make me as happy as all that?

NORA.   But you don't even know what it is.

RANK.   Well, then; tell me.

NORA.   Oh, but I can't, Dr. Rank. It's altogether too much to ask— It's advice and help and a favor—

RANK.   So much the better. I can't even begin to guess what it is you have in mind. So for heaven's sake tell me! Don't you trust me?

NORA.   Yes, I trust you more than anyone else I know. You are my best and most faithful friend. I know that. So I will tell you. All right, Dr. Rank. There is something you can help me prevent. You know how much Torvald loves me—beyond all words. Never for a moment would he hesitate to give his life for me.

RANK (*leaning over to her*).   Nora—do you really think he's the only one?

NORA (*with a slight start*).   Who—?

RANK.   —would gladly give his life for you.

NORA (*heavily*).   I see.

RANK.   I have sworn an oath to myself to tell you before I go. I'll never find a better occasion.— All right, Nora; now you know. And now you also know that you can confide in me more than in anyone else.

NORA (*gets up; in a calm, steady voice*).   Let me get by.

RANK (*makes room for her but remains seated*).   Nora—

NORA (*in the door to the front hall*).   Helene, bring the lamp in here, please. (*Walks over to the stove.*) Oh, dear Dr. Rank. That really wasn't very nice of you.

RANK (*gets up*).   That I have loved you as much as anybody—was that not nice?

NORA.   No; not that. But that you told me. There was no need for that.

RANK.   What do you mean? Have you known—? (*The* MAID *enters with the lamp, puts it on the table, and goes out.*) Nora—Mrs. Helmer—I'm asking you: did you know?

NORA.   Oh, how can I tell what I knew and didn't know! I really can't say— But that you could be so awkward, Dr. Rank! Just when everything was so comfortable.

RANK.   Well, anyway, now you know that I'm at your service with my life and soul. And now you must speak.

NORA (*looks at him*).   After what just happened?

RANK.   I beg of you—let me know what it is.

NORA.   There is nothing I can tell you now.

RANK.   Yes, yes. You mustn't punish me this way. Please let me do for you whatever anyone *can* do.

NORA.   Now there is nothing you can do. Besides, I don't think I really need any help, anyway. It's probably just my imagination. Of course that's all it is. I'm sure of it! (*Sits down in the rocking chair, looks at him, smiles.*) Well, well, well, Dr. Rank! What a fine gentleman you turned out to be! Aren't you ashamed of yourself, now that we have light?

RANK.   No, not really. But perhaps I ought to leave—and not come back?

NORA.   Don't be silly; of course not! You'll come here exactly as you have been doing. You know perfectly well that Torvald can't do without you.

RANK.   Yes, but what about you?

NORA.   Oh, I always think it's perfectly delightful when you come.

RANK.   That's the very thing that misled me. You are a riddle to me. It has often seemed to me that you'd just as soon be with me as with Helmer.

NORA.   Well, you see, there are people you love, and then there are other people you'd almost rather be with.

RANK.   Yes, there is something in that.

NORA.   When I lived at home with Daddy, of course I loved him most. But I always thought it was so much fun to sneak off down to the maids' room, for they never gave me advice and they always talked about such fun things.

RANK.   Aha! So it's *their* place I have taken.

NORA (*jumps up and goes over to him*).   Oh dear, kind Dr. Rank, you know very well I didn't mean it that way. Can't you see that with Torvald it is the way it used to be with Daddy? (*The* MAID *enters from the front hall.*)

MAID.   Ma'am! (*Whispers to her and gives her a caller's card.*)

NORA (*glances at the card*).   Ah! (*Puts it in her pocket.*)

RANK.   Anything wrong?

NORA.   No, no; not at all. It's nothing—just my new costume—

RANK.   But your costume is lying right there!

NORA.   Oh yes, that one. But this is another one. I ordered it. Torvald mustn't know—

RANK.   Aha. So that's the great secret.

NORA.   That's it. Why don't you go in to him, please. He's in the inner office. And keep him there for a while—

RANK.   Don't worry. He won't get away. (*Enters* HELMER'S *study.*)

NORA (*to the* MAID).   You say he's waiting in the kitchen?

MAID.   Yes. He came up the back stairs.

NORA.   But didn't you tell him there was somebody with me?

MAID.   Yes, but he wouldn't listen.

NORA.   He won't leave?

MAID.   No, not till he's had a word with you, ma'am.

NORA.   All right. But try not to make any noise. And, Helene—don't tell anyone he's here. It's supposed to be a surprise for my husband.

MAID.   I understand ma'am— (*She leaves.*)

NORA.   The terrible is happening. It's happening after all. No, no, no. It can't happen. It won't happen. (*She bolts the study door. The* MAID *opens the front hall door for* KROGSTAD *and closes the door behind him. He wears a fur coat for traveling, boots, and a fur hat.* NORA *goes toward him.*) Keep your voice down. My husband's home.

KROGSTAD.   That's all right.

NORA.   What do you want?

KROGSTAD.   To find out something.

NORA.   Be quick, then. What is it?

KROGSTAD.   I expect you know I've been fired.

NORA.   I couldn't prevent it, Mr. Krogstad. I fought for you as long and as hard as I could but it didn't do any good.

KROGSTAD.   Your husband doesn't love you any more than that? He knows what I can do to you, and yet he runs the risk—

NORA.   Surely you didn't think I'd tell him?

KROGSTAD.   No, I really didn't. It wouldn't be like Torvald Helmer to show that kind of guts—

NORA.   Mr. Krogstad, I insist that you show respect for my husband.

KROGSTAD.   By all means. All due respect. But since you're so anxious to keep this a secret, may I assume that you are a little better informed than yesterday about exactly what you have done?

NORA.   Better than *you* could ever teach me.

KROGSTAD.   Of course. Such a bad lawyer as I am—

NORA.   What do you want of me?

KROGSTAD.   I just wanted to find out how you are, Mrs. Helmer. I've been thinking about you all day. You see, even a bill collector, a pen pusher, a—anyway, someone like me—even he has a little of what they call a heart.

NORA.   Then show it. Think of my little children.

KROGSTAD.   Have you and your husband thought of mine? Never mind. All I want to tell you is that you don't need to take this business too seriously. I have no intentions of bringing charges right away.

NORA.   Oh no, you wouldn't; would you? I knew you wouldn't.

KROGSTAD.   The whole thing can be settled quite amiably. Nobody else needs to know anything. It will be between the three of us.

NORA.   My husband must never find out about this.

KROGSTAD.   How are you going to prevent that? Maybe you can pay me the balance of your loan?

NORA.   No, not right now.

KROGSTAD.   Or do you have a way of raising the money one of these next few days?

NORA.   None I intend to make use of.

KROGSTAD.   It wouldn't do you any good anyway. Even if you had the cash in your hand right this minute, I wouldn't give you your note back. It wouldn't make any difference *how* much money you offered me.

NORA.   Then you'll have to tell what you plan to use the note *for.*

KROGSTAD.   Just keep it; that's all. Have it on hand, so to speak. I won't say a word to anybody else. So if you've been thinking about doing something desperate—

NORA.   I have.

KROGSTAD.   —like leaving house and home—

NORA.   I have.

KROGSTAD.   —or even something worse—

NORA.   How did you know?

KROGSTAD.   —then: don't.

NORA.   How did you know I was thinking of *that?*

KROGSTAD.   Most of us do, right at first. I did, too, but when it came down to it I didn't have the courage—

NORA (*tonelessly*).   Nor do I.

KROGSTAD (*relieved*).   See what I mean? I thought so. You don't either.

NORA.   I don't. I don't.

KROGSTAD.   Besides, it would be very silly of you. Once that first domestic blowup is behind you—. Here in my pocket is a letter for your husband.

NORA.   Telling him everything?

KROGSTAD.   As delicately as possible.

NORA (*quickly*).   He mustn't get that letter. Tear it up. I'll get you the money somehow.

KROGSTAD.   Excuse me, Mrs. Helmer, I thought I just told you—

NORA.   I'm not talking about the money I owe you. Just let me know how much money you want from my husband, and I'll get it for you.

KROGSTAD.   I want no money from your husband.

NORA.   Then, what *do* you want?

KROGSTAD.   I'll tell you, Mrs. Helmer. I want to rehabilitate myself; I want to get up in the world; and your husband is going to help me. For a year and a half I haven't done anything disreputable. All that time I have been struggling with the most miserable circumstances. I was content to work my way up step by step. Now I've been kicked out, and I'm no longer satisfied just getting my old job back. I want more than that; I want to get to the top. I'm being quite serious. I want the bank to take me back but in a higher position. I want your husband to create a new job for me—

NORA.   He'll never do that!

KROGSTAD.   He will. I know him. He won't dare not to. And once I'm back inside and he and I are working together, you'll see! Within a year I'll be the manager's right hand. It will be Nils Krogstad and not Torvald Helmer who'll be running the Mutual Bank!

NORA.   You'll never see that happen!

KROGSTAD.   Are you thinking of—?

NORA.   Now I *do* have the courage.

KROGSTAD.   You can't scare me. A fine, spoiled lady like you—

NORA.   You'll see, you'll see!

KROGSTAD.   Under the ice, perhaps? Down into that cold, black water? Then spring comes and you float up again—hideous, can't be identified, hair all gone—

NORA.   You don't frighten me.

KROGSTAD.   Nor you me. One doesn't do that sort of thing, Mrs. Helmer. Besides, what good would it do? He'd still be in my power.

NORA.   Afterwards? When I'm no longer—?

KROGSTAD.   Aren't you forgetting that your reputation would be in my hands? (NORA *stares at him, speechless.*) All right; now I've told you what to expect. So don't do anything foolish. When Helmer gets my letter I expect to hear from him. And don't you forget that it's your husband himself who forces me to use such means again. That I'll never forgive him. Goodbye, Mrs. Helmer. (*Goes out through the hall.*)

NORA (*at the door, opens it a little, listens*).   He's going. And no letter. Of course not! That would be impossible! (*Opens the door more.*) What's he doing? He's still there. Doesn't go down. Having second thoughts—? Will he—? (*The sound of a letter dropping into the mailbox. Then* KROGSTAD'S *steps are heard going down the stairs, gradually dying away. With a muted cry* NORA *runs forward to the table by the couch; brief pause.*) In the mailbox. (*Tiptoes back to the door to the front hall.*) There it is. Torvald, Torvald—now we're lost!

MRS. LINDE (*enters from the left, carrying* NORA'S *Capri costume*). There now. I think it's all fixed. Why don't we try it on you—

NORA (*in a low, hoarse voice*).   Kristine, come here.

MRS. LINDE.   What's wrong with you? You look quite beside yourself.

NORA.   Come over here. Do you see that letter? There, look—through the glass in the mailbox.

MRS. LINDE.   Yes, yes; I see it.

NORA.   That letter is from Krogstad.

MRS. LINDE.   Nora—it was Krogstad who lent you the money!

NORA.   Yes, and now Torvald will find out about it.

MRS. LINDE.   Oh believe me, Nora. That's the best thing for both of you.

NORA.   There's more to it than you know. I forged a signature—

MRS. LINDE.   Oh my God—!

NORA.   I just want to tell you this, Kristine, that you must be my witness.

MRS. LINDE.   Witness? How? Witness to what?

NORA.   If I lose my mind—and that could very well happen—

MRS. LINDE.   Nora!

NORA.   —or if something were to happen to me—something that made it impossible for me to be here—.

MRS. LINDE.   Nora, Nora! You're not yourself!

NORA.   —and if someone were to take all the blame, assume the whole responsibility— Do you understand—?

MRS. LINDE.   Yes, yes; but how can you think—!

NORA.   Then you are to witness that that's not so, Kristine. I am not beside myself. I am perfectly rational, and what I'm telling you is that nobody else has known about this. I've done it all by myself, the whole thing. Just remember that.

MRS. LINDE.   I will. But I don't understand any of it.

NORA.   Oh, how could you! For it's the wonderful that's about to happen.

MRS. LINDE.   The wonderful?

NORA.   Yes, the wonderful. But it's so terrible, Kristine. It mustn't happen for anything in the whole world.

MRS. LINDE.   I'm going over to talk to Krogstad right now.

NORA.   No, don't. Don't go to him. He'll do something bad to you.

MRS. LINDE.   There was a time when he would have done anything for me.

NORA.   He!

MRS. LINDE.   Where does he live?

NORA.   Oh, I don't know— Yes, wait a minute— (*Reaches into her pocket.*) Here's his card.— But the letter, the letter—!

HELMER (*in his study, knocks on the door*).   Nora!

NORA (*cries out in fear*).   Oh, what is it? What do you want?

HELMER.   That's all right. Nothing to be scared about. We're not coming in. For one thing, you've bolted the door, you know. Are you modeling your costume?

NORA.   Yes, yes; I am. I'm going to be so pretty, Torvald!

MRS. LINDE (*having looked at the card*).   He lives just around the corner.

NORA.   Yes, but it's no use. Nothing can save us now. The letter is in the mailbox.

MRS. LINDE.   And your husband has the key?

NORA.   Yes. He always keeps it with him.

MRS. LINDE.   Krogstad must ask for his letter back, unread. He's got to think up some pretext or other—

NORA.   But this is just the time of day when Torvald—

MRS. LINDE.   Delay him. Go in to him. I'll be back as soon as I can. (*She hurries out through the hall door.*)

NORA (*walks over to* HELMER'S *door, opens it, and peeks in*) Torvald.

HELMER (*still offstage*).   Well, well! So now one's allowed in one's own living room again. Come on, Rank. Now we'll see— (*In the doorway.*) But what's this?

NORA.   What, Torvald dear?

HELMER.   Rank prepared me for a splendid metamorphosis.

RANK (*in the doorway*).   That's how I understood it. Evidently I was mistaken.

NORA.   Nobody gets to admire me in my costume before tomorrow.

HELMER.   But, dearest Nora—you look all done in. Have you been practicing too hard?

NORA.   No, I haven't practiced at all.

HELMER.   But you'll have to, you know.

NORA.   I know it, Torvald. I simply must. But I can't do a thing unless you help me. I have forgotten everything.

HELMER.   Oh it will all come back. We'll work on it.

NORA.   Oh yes, please, Torvald. You just have to help me. Promise? I am so nervous. That big party—. You mustn't do anything else tonight. Not a bit of business. Don't even touch a pen. Will you promise, Torvald?

HELMER.   I promise. Tonight I'll be entirely at your service—you helpless little thing.— Just a moment, though. First I want to— (*Goes to the door to the front hall.*)

NORA.   What are you doing out there?

HELMER.   Just looking to see if there's any mail.

NORA.   No, no! Don't, Torvald!

HELMER.   Why not?

NORA.   Torvald, I beg you. There is no mail.

HELMER.   Let me just look, anyway. (*Is about to go out.* NORA *by the piano, plays the first bars of the tarantella dance.* HELMER *halts at the door.*) Aha!

NORA.   I won't be able to dance tomorrow if I don't get to practice with you.

HELMER (*goes to her*).   Are you really all that scared, Nora dear?

NORA.   Yes, so terribly scared. Let's try it right now. There's still time before we eat. Oh please sit down and play for me, Torvald. Teach me, coach me, the way you always do.

HELMER.   Of course I will, my darling, if that's what you want. (*Sits down at the piano.* NORA *takes the tambourine out of the carton, as well as a long, many-colored shawl. She quickly drapes the shawl around herself, then leaps into the middle of the floor.*)

NORA.   Play for me! I want to dance! (HELMER *plays and* NORA *dances.* DR. RANK *stands by the piano behind* HELMER *and watches.*)

HELMER (*playing*).   Slow down, slow down!

NORA.   Can't!

HELMER.   Not so violent, Nora!

NORA.   It has to be this way.

HELMER (*stops playing*).   No, no. This won't do at all.

NORA (*laughing, swinging her tambourine*).   What did I tell you?

RANK.   Why don't you let me play?

HELMER (*getting up*).   Good idea. Then I can direct her better. (RANK *sits down at the piano and starts playing.* NORA *dances more and more wildly.* HELMER *stands over by the stove, repeatedly correcting her. She doesn't seem to hear. Her hair comes loose and falls down over her shoulders. She doesn't notice but keeps on dancing.* MRS. LINDE *enters.*)

MRS. LINDE (*stops by the door, dumbfounded*).   Ah—!

NORA (*dancing*).   We're having such fun, Kristine!

HELMER.   My dearest Nora, you're dancing as if it were a matter of life and death!

NORA.   It is! It is!

HELMER.   Rank, stop. This is sheer madness. Stop I say! (RANK *stops playing;* NORA *suddenly stops dancing.* HELMER *goes over to her.*) If I hadn't seen it I wouldn't have believed it. You've forgotten every single thing I ever taught you.

NORA (*tosses away the tambourine*).   See? I told you.

HELMER.   Well! You certainly need coaching.

NORA.   Didn't I tell you I did? Now you've seen for yourself. I'll need your help till the very minute we're leaving for the party. Will you promise, Torvald?

HELMER.   You can count on it.

NORA.   You're not to think of anything except me—not tonight and not tomorrow. You're not to read any letters—not to look in the mailbox—

HELMER.   Ah, I see. You're still afraid of that man.

NORA.   Yes—yes, that too.

HELMER.   Nora, I can tell from looking at you. There's a letter from him out there.

NORA.   I don't know. I think so. But you're not to read it now. I don't want anything ugly to come between us before it's all over.

RANK (*to* HELMER *in a low voice*).   Better not argue with her.

HELMER (*throws his arm around her*).   The child shall have her way. But tomorrow night, when you've done your dance—

NORA.   Then you'll be free.

MAID (*in the door, right*).   Dinner can be served any time, ma'am.

NORA.   We want champagne, Helene.

MAID.   Very good, ma'am. (*Goes out.*)

HELMER.   Aha! Having a party, eh?

NORA.   Champagne from now till sunrise! (*Calls out.*) And some macaroons, Helene. Lots!—just this once.

HELMER (*taking her hands*).   There, there—I don't like this wild—frenzy— Be my own sweet little lark again, the way you always are.

NORA.   Oh, I will. But you go on in. You too, Dr. Rank. Kristine, please help me put up my hair.

RANK (*in a low voice to* HELMER *as they go out*).   You don't think she is—you know—expecting—?

HELMER.   Oh no. Nothing like that. It's just this childish fear I was telling you about. (*They go out, right.*)

NORA.   Well?

MRS. LINDE.   Left town.

NORA.   I saw it in your face.

MRS. LINDE.   He'll be back tomorrow night. I left him a note.

NORA.   You shouldn't have. I don't want you to try to stop anything. You see, it's kind of ecstasy, too, this waiting for the wonderful.

MRS. LINDE.   But what is it you're waiting *for*?

NORA.   You wouldn't understand. Why don't you go in to the others. I'll be there in a minute. (MRS. LINDE *enters the dining room, right.* NORA *stands still for a little while, as if collecting herself; she looks at her watch.*) Five o'clock. Seven hours till midnight. Twenty-four more hours till next midnight. Then the tarantella is over. Twenty-four plus seven—thirty-one more hours to live.

HELMER (*in the door, right*).   What's happening to my little lark?

NORA (*to him, with open arms*).   Here's your lark!

ACT 3

The same room. The table by the couch and the chairs around it have been moved to the middle of the floor. A lighted lamp is on the table. The door to the front hall is open. Dance music is heard from upstairs.

MRS. LINDE *is seated by the table, idly leafing through the pages of a book. She tries to read but seems unable to concentrate. Once or twice she turns her head in the direction of the door, anxiously listening.*

MRS. LINDE (*looks at her watch*).   Not yet. It's almost too late. If only he hasn't— (*Listens again.*) Ah! There he is. (*She goes to the hall and opens the front door carefully. Quiet footsteps on the stairs. She whispers.*) Come in. There's nobody here.

KROGSTAD (*in the door*).   I found your note when I got home. What's this all about?

MRS. LINDE.   I've got to talk to you.

KROGSTAD.   Oh? And it has to be here?

MRS. LINDE.   It couldn't be at my place. My room doesn't have a separate entrance. Come in. We're quite alone. The maid is asleep and the Helmers are at a party upstairs.

KROGSTAD (*entering*).   Really? The Helmers are dancing tonight, are they?

MRS. LINDE.   And why not?

KROGSTAD.   You're right. Why not, indeed.

MRS. LINDE.   All right, Krogstad. Let's talk, you and I.

KROGSTAD.   I didn't know we had anything to talk about.

MRS. LINDE.   We have much to talk about.

KROGSTAD.   I didn't think so.

MRS. LINDE.   No, because you've never really understood me.

KROGSTAD.   What was there to understand? What happened was perfectly commonplace. A heartless woman jilts a man when she gets a more attractive offer.

MRS. LINDE.   Do you think I'm all that heartless? And do you think it was easy for me to break with you?

KROGSTAD.   No?

MRS. LINDE.   You really thought it was?

KROGSTAD.   If it wasn't, why did you write the way you did that time?

MRS. LINDE.   What else could I do? If I had to make a break, I also had the duty to destroy whatever feelings you had for me.

KROGSTAD (*clenching his hands*).   So that's the way it was. And you did—*that*—just for money!

MRS. LINDE.   Don't forget I had a helpless mother and two small brothers. We couldn't wait for you, Krogstad. You know yourself how uncertain your prospects were then.

KROGSTAD.   All right. But you still didn't have the right to throw me over for somebody else.

MRS. LINDE.   I don't know. I have asked myself that question many times. Did I have that right?

KROGSTAD (*in a lower voice*).   When I lost you I lost my footing. Look at me now. A shipwrecked man on a raft.

MRS. LINDE.   Rescue may be near.

KROGSTAD.   It *was* near. Then you came between.

MRS. LINDE.   I didn't know that, Krogstad. Only today did I find out it's your job I'm taking over in the bank.

KROGSTAD.   I believe you when you say so. But now that you *do* know, aren't you going to step aside?

MRS. LINDE.   No, for it wouldn't do you any good.

KROGSTAD.   Whether it would or not—*I* would do it.

MRS. LINDE.   I have learned common sense. Life and hard necessity have taught me that.

KROGSTAD.   And life has taught me not to believe in pretty speeches.

MRS. LINDE.   Then life has taught you a very sensible thing. But you do believe in actions, don't you?

KROGSTAD.   How do you mean?

MRS. LINDE.   You referred to yourself just now as a shipwrecked man.

KROGSTAD.   It seems to me I had every reason to do so.

MRS. LINDE.   And I am a shipwrecked woman. No one to grieve for, no one to care for.

KROGSTAD.   You made your choice.

MRS. LINDE.   I had no other choice that time.

KROGSTAD.   Let's say you didn't. What then?

MRS. LINDE.   Krogstad, how would it be if we two shipwrecked people got together?

KROGSTAD.   What's this!

MRS. LINDE.   Two on one wreck are better off than each on his own.

KROGSTAD.   Kristine!

MRS. LINDE.   Why do you think I came to town?

KROGSTAD.   Surely not because of me?

MRS. LINDE.   If I'm going to live at all I must work. All my life, for as long as I can remember, I have worked. That's been my one and only pleasure. But now that I'm all alone in the world I feel nothing but this terrible emptiness and desolation. There is no joy in working just for yourself. Krogstad—give me someone and something to work for.

KROGSTAD.   I don't believe this. Only hysterical females go in for that kind of high-minded self-sacrifice.

MRS. LINDE.   Did you ever know me to be hysterical?

KROGSTAD.   You really could do this? Listen—do you know about my past? All of it?

MRS. LINDE.   Yes, I do.

KROGSTAD.   Do you also know what people think of me around here?

MRS. LINDE.   A little while ago you sounded as if you thought that together with me you might have become a different person.

KROGSTAD.   I'm sure of it.

MRS. LINDE.   Couldn't that still be?

KROGSTAD.   Kristine—do you know what you are doing? Yes, I see you do. And you think you have the courage—?

MRS. LINDE.   I need someone to be a mother to, and your children need a mother. You and I need one another. Nils, I believe in you—in the real you. Together with you I dare to do anything.

KROGSTAD (*seizes her hands*).   Thanks, thanks, Kristine—now I know I'll raise myself in the eyes of others— Ah, but I forget—!

MRS. LINDE (*listening*).   Shhh!— There's the tarantella. You must go; hurry!

KROGSTAD.   Why? What is it?

MRS. LINDE.   Do you hear what they're playing up there? When that dance is over they'll be down.

KROGSTAD.   All right. I'm leaving. The whole thing is pointless, anyway. Of course you don't know what I'm doing to the Helmers.

MRS. LINDE.   Yes, Krogstad; I do know.

KROGSTAD.   Still, you're brave enough—?

MRS. LINDE.   I very well understand to what extremes despair can drive a man like you.

KROGSTAD.   If only it could be undone!

MRS. LINDE.   It could, for your letter is still out there in the mailbox.

KROGSTAD.   Are you sure?

MRS. LINDE.   Quite sure. But—

KROGSTAD (*looks searchingly at her*).   Maybe I'm beginning to understand. You want to save your friend at any cost. Be honest with me. That's it, isn't it.

MRS. LINDE.   Krogstad, you may sell yourself once for somebody else's sake, but you don't do it twice.

KROGSTAD.   I'll demand my letter back.

MRS. LINDE.   No, no.

KROGSTAD.   Yes, of course. I'll wait here till Helmer comes down. Then I'll ask him for my letter. I'll tell him it's just about my dismissal—that he shouldn't read it.

MRS. LINDE.   No, Krogstad. You are not to ask for that letter back.

KROGSTAD.   But tell me—wasn't that the real reason you wanted to meet me here?

MRS. LINDE.   At first it was, because I was so frightened. But that was yesterday. Since then I have seen the most incredible things going on in this house. Helmer must learn the whole truth. This miserable secret must come out in the open; those two must come to a full understanding. They simply can't continue with all this concealment and evasion.

KROGSTAD.   All right; if you want to take that chance. But there is one thing I *can* do, and I'll do that right now.

MRS. LINDE (*listening*).   But hurry! Go! The dance is over. We aren't safe another minute.

KROGSTAD.   I'll be waiting for you downstairs.

MRS. LINDE.   Yes, do. You must see me home.

KROGSTAD.   I've never been so happy in my whole life. (*He leaves through the front door. The door between the living room and the front hall remains open.*)

MRS. LINDE (*straightens up the room a little and gets her things ready*). What a change! Oh yes!—what a change! People to work for—to live for—a home to bring happiness to. I can't wait to get to work—! If only they'd come soon— (*Listens.*) Ah, there they are. Get my coat on— (*Puts on her coat and hat. HELMER'S and NORA'S voices are heard outside. A key is turned in the lock, and HELMER almost forces NORA into the hall. She is dressed in her Italian costume, with a big black shawl over her shoulders. He is in evening dress under an open black cloak.*)

NORA (*in the door, still resisting*).   No, no, no! I don't want to! I want to go back upstairs. I don't want to leave so early.

HELMER.   But dearest Nora—

NORA.   Oh please, Torvald—please! I'm asking you as nicely as I can—just another hour!

HELMER.   Not another minute, sweet. You know we agreed. There now. Get inside. You'll catch a cold out here. (*She still resists, but he guides her gently into the room.*)

MRS. LINDE.   Good evening.

NORA.   Kristine!

HELMER.   Ah, Mrs. Linde. Still here?

MRS. LINDE.   I know. I really should apologize, but I so much wanted to see Nora in her costume.

NORA.   You've been waiting up for me?

MRS. LINDE.   Yes, unfortunately I didn't get here in time. You were already upstairs, but I just didn't feel like leaving till I had seen you.

HELMER (*removing* NORA'S *shawl*). Yes, do take a good look at her, Mrs. Linde. I think I may say she's worth looking at. Isn't she lovely?

MRS. LINDE.   She certainly is—

HELMER.   Isn't she a miracle of loveliness, though? That was the general opinion at the party, too. But dreadfully obstinate—that she is, the sweet little thing. What can we do about that? Will you believe it—I practically had to use force to get her away.

NORA.   Oh Torvald, you're going to be sorry you didn't give me even half an hour more.

HELMER.   See what I mean, Mrs. Linde? She dances the tarantella— she is a tremendous success—quite deservedly so, though perhaps her performance was a little too natural—I mean, more than could be reconciled with the rules of art. But all right! The point is: she's a success, a tremendous success. So should I let her stay after that? Weaken the effect? Of course not. So I take my lovely little Capri girl—I might say, my capricious little Capri girl—under my arm—a quick turn around the room—a graceful bow in all directions, and—as they say in the novels—the beautiful apparition is gone. A finale should always be done for effect, Mrs. Linde, but there doesn't seem to be any way of getting that into Nora's head. Poooh—! It's hot in here. (*Throws his cloak down on a chair and opens the door to his room.*) Why, it's dark in here! Of course. Excuse me— (*Goes inside and lights a couple of candles.*)

NORA (*in a hurried, breathless whisper*).   Well?

MRS. LINDE (*in a low voice*).   I have talked to him.

NORA.   And—?

MRS. LINDE.   Nora—you've got to tell your husband everything.

NORA (*no expression in her voice*).   I knew it.

MRS. LINDE.   You have nothing to fear from Krogstad. But you must speak.

NORA.   I'll say nothing.

MRS. LINDE.   Then the letter will.

NORA.   Thank you, Kristine. Now I know what I have to do. Shh!

HELMER (*returning*).   Well, Mrs. Linde, have you looked your fill?

MRS. LINDE.   Yes. And now I'll say goodnight.

HELMER.   So soon? Is that your knitting?

MRS. LINDE (*takes it*).   Yes, thank you. I almost forgot.

HELMER.   So you knit, do you?

MRS. LINDE.   Oh yes.

HELMER.   You know—you ought to take up embroidery instead.

MRS. LINDE.   Oh? Why?

HELMER.   Because it's so much more beautiful. Look. You hold the embroidery so—in your left hand. Then with your right you move the needle—like this—in an easy, elongated arc—you see?

MRS. LINDE.   Maybe you're right—

HELMER.   Knitting, on the other hand, can never be anything but ugly. Look here: arms pressed close to the sides—the needles going up and down—there's something Chinese about it somehow—. That really was an excellent champagne they served us tonight.

MRS. LINDE.   Well, goodnight, Nora. And don't be obstinate any more.

HELMER.   Well said, Mrs. Linde!

MRS. LINDE.   Goodnight, sir.

HELMER (*sees her to the front door*).   Goodnight, goodnight. I hope you'll get home all right? I'd be very glad to—but of course you don't have far to walk, do you? Goodnight, goodnight. (*She leaves. He closes the door behind her and returns to the living room.*) There! At last we got rid of her. She really is an incredible bore, that woman.

NORA.   Aren't you very tired, Torvald?

HELMER.   No, not in the least.

NORA.   Not sleepy either?

HELMER.   Not at all. Quite the opposite. I feel enormously—animated. How about you? Yes, you do look tired and sleepy.

NORA.   Yes, I am very tired. Soon I'll be asleep.

HELMER.   What did I tell you? I was right, wasn't I? Good thing I didn't let you stay any longer.

NORA.   Everything you do is right.

HELMER (*kissing her forehead*).   Now my little lark is talking like a human being. But did you notice what splendid spirits Rank was in tonight?

NORA.   Was he? I didn't notice. I didn't get to talk with him.

HELMER.   Nor did I—hardly. But I haven't seen him in such a good mood for a long time. (*Looks at her, comes closer to her.*) Ah! It does feel good to be back in our own home again, to be quite alone with you—my young, lovely, ravishing woman!

NORA.   Don't look at me like that, Torvald!

HELMER.   Am I not to look at my most precious possession? All that loveliness that is mine, nobody's but mine, all of it mine.

NORA (*walks to the other side of the table*).   I won't have you talk to me like that tonight.

HELMER (*follows her*).   The tarantella is still in your blood. I can tell. That only makes you all the more alluring. Listen! The guests are beginning to leave. (*Softly.*) Nora—soon the whole house will be quiet.

NORA.   Yes, I hope so.

HELMER.   Yes, don't you, my darling? Do you know—when I'm at a party with you, like tonight—do you know why I hardly ever talk to you, why I keep away from you, only look at you once in a while—a few stolen glances—do you know why I do that? It's because I pretend that you are my secret love, my young, secret bride-to-be, and nobody has the slightest suspicion that there is anything between us.

NORA.   Yes, I know. All your thoughts are with me.

HELMER.   Then when we're leaving and I lay your shawl around your delicate young shoulders—around that wonderful curve of your neck—then I imagine you're my young bride, that we're coming away from the wedding, that I am taking you to my home for the first time—that I am alone with you for the first time—quite alone with you, you young, trembling beauty! I have desired you all evening—there hasn't been a longing in me that hasn't been for you. When you were dancing the tarantella, chasing, inviting—my blood was on fire; I couldn't stand it any longer—that's why I brought you down so early—

NORA.   Leave me now, Torvald. Please! I don't want all this.

HELMER.   What do you mean? You're only playing your little teasing bird game with me; aren't you, Nora? Don't want to? I'm your husband, aren't I? (*There is a knock on the front door.*)

NORA (*with a start*).   Did you hear that—?

HELMER (*on his way to the hall*).   Who is it?

RANK (*outside*).   It's me. May I come in for a moment?

HELMER (*in a low voice, annoyed*).   Oh, what does he want now? (*Aloud*) Just a minute. (*Opens the door.*) Well! How good of you not to pass by our door.

RANK.   I thought I heard your voice, so I felt like saying hello. (*Looks around.*) Ah yes—this dear, familiar room. What a cozy, comfortable place you have here, you two.

HELMER.   Looked to me as if you were quite comfortable upstairs too.

RANK.   I certainly was. Why not? Why not enjoy all you can in this world? As much as you can for as long as you can, anyway. Excellent wine.

HELMER.   The champagne, particularly.

RANK.   You noticed that too? Incredible how much I managed to put away.

NORA.   Torvald drank a lot of champagne tonight, too.

RANK.   Did he?

NORA.   Yes, he did, and then he's always so much fun afterwards.

RANK.   Well, why not have some fun in the evening after a well spent day?

HELMER.   Well spent? I'm afraid I can't claim that.

RANK (*slapping him lightly on the shoulder*).   But you see, I can!

NORA.   Dr. Rank, I believe you must have been conducting a scientific test today.

RANK.   Exactly.

HELMER.   What do you know—little Nora talking about scientific tests.

NORA.   May I congratulate you on the result?

RANK.   You may indeed.

NORA.   It was a good one?

RANK.   The best possible for both doctor and patient—certainty.

NORA (*a quick query*).   Certainty?

RANK.   Absolute certainty. So why shouldn't I have myself an enjoyable evening afterwards?

NORA.   I quite agree with you, Dr. Rank. You should.

HELMER.   And so do I. If only you don't pay for it tomorrow.

RANK.   Oh well—you get nothing for nothing in this world.

NORA.   Dr. Rank—you are fond of costume parties, aren't you?

RANK.   Yes, particularly when there is a reasonable number of amusing disguises.

NORA.   Listen—what are the two of us going to be the next time?

HELMER.   You frivolous little thing? Already thinking about the next party!

RANK.   You and I? That's easy. You'll be Fortune's Child.

HELMER.   Yes, but what is a fitting costume for that?

RANK.   Let your wife appear just the way she always is.

HELMER.   Beautiful. Very good indeed. But how about yourself? Don't you know what you'll go as?

RANK.   Yes, my friend. I know precisely what I'll be.

HELMER.   Yes?

RANK.   At the next masquerade I'll be invisible.

HELMER.   That's a funny idea.

RANK.   There's a certain black hat—you've heard about the hat that makes you invisible, haven't you? You put that on, and nobody can see you.

HELMER (*suppressing a smile*).   I guess that's right.

RANK.   But, I'm forgetting what I came for. Helmer, give me a cigar—one of your dark Havanas.

HELMER.   With the greatest pleasure. (*Offers him his case.*)

RANK (*takes one and cuts off the tip*).   Thanks.

NORA (*striking a match*).   Let me give you a light.

RANK.   Thanks. (*She holds the match; he lights his cigar.*) And now goodbye!

HELMER.   Goodbye, goodbye, my friend.

NORA.   Sleep well, Dr. Rank.

RANK.   I thank you.

NORA.   Wish me the same.

RANK.   You? Well, if you really want me to—. Sleep well. And thanks for the light. (*He nods to both of them and goes out.*)

HELMER (*in a low voice*).   He had had quite a bit to drink.

NORA (*absently*).   Maybe so. (HELMER *takes out his keys and goes out into the hall.*) Torvald—what are you doing out there?

HELMER.   Emptying the mailbox. It is quite full. There wouldn't be room for the newspapers in the morning—

NORA.   Are you going to work tonight?

HELMER.   You know very well I won't.— Say! What's this? Somebody's been at the lock.

NORA.   The lock—?

HELMER.   Yes. Why, I wonder. I hate to think that any of the maids—. Here's a broken hairpin. It's one of yours, Nora.

NORA (*quickly*).   Then it must be one of the children.

HELMER.   You better make damn sure they stop that. Hm, hm.—
There! I got it open, finally. (*Gathers up the mail, calls out to the kitchen.*)
Helene— Oh Helene—turn out the light here in the hall, will you? (*He
comes back into the living room and closes the door.*) Look how it's been piling
up. (*Shows her the bundle of letters. Starts leafing through it.*) What's this?

NORA (*by the window*).   The letter! Oh no, no, Torvald!

HELMER.   Two calling cards—from Rank.

NORA.   From Dr. Rank?

HELMER (*looking at them*).   "Doctor medicinae Rank." They were on
top. He must have put them there when he left just now.

NORA.   Anything written on them?

HELMER.   A black cross above the name. What a macabre idea. Like
announcing his own death.

NORA.   That's what it is.

HELMER.   Hm? You know about this? Has he said anything to you?

NORA.   That card means he has said goodbye to us. He'll lock himself
up to die.

HELMER.   My poor friend. I knew of course he wouldn't be with me
very long. But so soon—. And hiding himself away like a wounded animal—

NORA.   When it has to be, it's better it happens without words. Don't
you think so, Torvald?

HELMER (*walking up and down*).   He'd grown so close to us. I find it
hard to think of him as gone. With his suffering and loneliness he was like a
clouded background for our happy sunshine. Well, it may be better this way.
For him, at any rate. (*Stops.*) And perhaps for us, too, Nora. For now we
have nobody but each other. (*Embraces her.*) Oh you—my beloved wife! I
feel I just can't hold you close enough. Do you know, Nora—many times I
have wished some great danger threatened you, so I could risk my life and
blood and everything—everything, for your sake.

NORA (*frees herself and says in a strong and firm voice*).   I think you
should go and read your letters now, Torvald.

HELMER.   No, no—not tonight. I want to be with you, my darling.

NORA.   With the thought of your dying friend—?

HELMER.   You are right. This has shaken both of us. Something not
beautiful has come between us. Thoughts of death and dissolution. We must
try to get over it—out of it. Till then—we'll each go to our own room.

NORA (*her arms around his neck*).   Torvald—goodnight! Goodnight!

HELMER (*kisses her forehead*).   Goodnight, my little songbird. Sleep
well, Nora. Now I'll read my letters. (*He goes into his room, carrying the mail.
Closes the door.*)

NORA (*her eyes desperate, her hands groping, finds* HELMER's *black cloak
and throws it around her; she whispers, quickly, brokenly, hoarsely*).   Never see
him again. Never. Never. Never. (*Puts her shawl over her head.*) And never
see the children again, either. Never; never.— The black, icy water—fathomless—this—! If only it was all over.— Now he has it. Now he's reading it.

No, no; not yet. Torvald—goodbye—you—the children— (*She is about to hurry through the hall, when* HELMER *flings open the door to his room and stands there with an open letter in his hand.*)

HELMER. Nora!

NORA (*cries out*). Ah—!

HELMER. What is it? You know what's in this letter?

NORA. Yes, I do! Let me go! Let me out!

HELMER (*holds her back*). Where do you think you're going?

NORA (*trying to tear herself loose from him*). I won't let you save me, Torvald!

HELMER (*tumbles back*). True! Is it true what he writes? Oh my God! No, no—this can't possibly be true.

NORA. It is true. I have loved you more than anything else in the whole world.

HELMER. Oh, don't give me any silly excuses.

NORA (*taking a step towards him*). Torvald—!

HELMER. You wretch! What have you done!

NORA. Let me go. You are not to sacrifice yourself for me. You are not to take the blame.

HELMER. No more playacting. (*Locks the door to the front hall.*) You'll stay here and answer me. Do you understand what you have done? Answer me! Do you understand?

NORA (*gazes steadily at him with an increasingly frozen expression*). Yes. Now I'm beginning to understand.

HELMER (*walking up and down*). What a dreadful awakening. All these years—all these eight years—she, my pride and my joy—a hypocrite, a liar—oh worse! worse!—a criminal! Oh, the bottomless ugliness in all this! Damn! Damn! Damn! (NORA, *silent, keeps gazing at him.* HELMER *stops in front of her.*) I ought to have guessed that something like this would happen. I should have expected it. All your father's loose principles— Silence! You have inherited every one of your father's loose principles. No religion, no morals, no sense of duty—. Now I am being punished for my leniency with him. I did it for your sake, and this is how you pay me back.

NORA. Yes. This is how.

HELMER. You have ruined all my happiness. My whole future—that's what you have destroyed. Oh, it's terrible to think about. I am at the mercy of an unscrupulous man. He can do with me whatever he likes, demand anything of me, command me and dispose of me just as he pleases— I dare not say a word! To go down so miserably, to be destroyed—all because of an irresponsible woman!

NORA. When I am gone from the world, you'll be free.

HELMER. No noble gestures, please. Your father was always full of such phrases too. What good would it do me if you were gone from the world, as you put it? Not the slightest good at all. He could still make the whole thing public, and if he did, people would be likely to think I had been your accomplice. They might even think it was my idea—that it was I who urged you to do it! And for all this I have you to thank—you, whom I've borne on my hands through all the years of our marriage. *Now* do you understand what you've done to me?

NORA (*with cold calm*).   Yes.

HELMER.   I just can't get it into my head that this is happening; it's all so incredible. But we have to come to terms with it somehow. Take your shawl off. Take it off, I say! I have to satisfy him one way or another. The whole affair must be kept quiet at whatever cost.— And as far as you and I are concerned, nothing must seem to have changed. I'm talking about appearances, of course. You'll go on living here; that goes without saying. But I won't let you bring up the children; I dare not trust you with them.— Oh! Having to say this to one I have loved so much, and whom I still—! But all that is past. It's not a question of happiness any more but of hanging on to what can be salvaged—pieces, appearances— (*The doorbell rings.* HELMER *jumps.*) What's that? So late. Is the worst—? Has he—! Hide, Nora! Say you're sick. (NORA *doesn't move.* HELMER *opens the door to the hall.*)

MAID (*half dressed, out in the hall*).   A letter for your wife, sir.

HELMER.   Give it to me. (*Takes the letter and closes the door.*) Yes, it's from him. But I won't let you have it. I'll read it myself.

NORA.   Yes—you read it.

HELMER (*by the lamp*).   I hardly dare. Perhaps we're lost, both you and I. No; I've got to know. (*Tears the letter open, glances through it, looks at an enclosure; a cry of joy.*) Nora! (NORA *looks at him with a question in her eyes.*) Nora!—No, I must read it again.—Yes, yes; it is so! I'm saved! Nora, I'm saved!

NORA.   And I?

HELMER.   You too, of course; we're both saved, both you and I. Look! He's returning your note. He writes that he's sorry, he regrets, a happy turn in his life—oh, it doesn't matter what he writes. We're saved, Nora! Nobody can do anything to you now. Oh Nora, Nora—. No, I want to get rid of this disgusting thing first. Let me see— (*Looks at the signature.*) No, I don't want to see it. I don't want it to be more than a bad dream, the whole thing. (*Tears up the note and both letters, throws the pieces in the stove, and watches them burn.*) There! Now it's gone.— He wrote that ever since Christmas Eve—. Good God, Nora, these must have been three terrible days for you.

NORA.   I have fought a hard fight these last three days.

HELMER.   And been in agony and seen no other way out than—. No, we won't think of all that ugliness. We'll just rejoice and tell ourselves it's over, it's all over! Oh, listen to me, Nora. You don't seem to understand. It's over. What *is* it? Why do you look like that—that frozen expression on your face? Oh my poor little Nora, don't you think I know what it is? You can't make yourself believe that I have forgiven you. But I have, Nora; I swear to you, I have forgiven you for everything. Of course I know that what you did was for love of me.

NORA.   That is true.

HELMER.   You have loved me the way a wife ought to love her husband. You just didn't have the wisdom to judge the means. But do you think I love you any less because you don't know how to act on your own? Of course not. Just lean on me. I'll advise you; I'll guide you. I wouldn't be a man if I didn't find you twice as attractive because of your womanly helplessness. You mustn't pay any attention to the hard words I said to you right at first. It was just that first shock when I thought everything was collapsing all around me. I have forgiven you, Nora. I swear to you—I really have forgiven you.

NORA.   I thank you for your forgiveness. (*She goes out through the door, right.*)

HELMER.   No, stay— (*Looks into the room she entered.*) What are you doing in there?

NORA (*within*).   Getting out of my costume.

HELMER (*by the open door*).   Good, good. Try to calm down and compose yourself, my poor little frightened songbird. Rest safely; I have broad wings to cover you with. (*Walks around near the door.*) What a nice and cozy home we have, Nora. Here's shelter for you. Here I'll keep you safe like a hunted dove I have rescued from the hawk's talons. Believe me: I'll know how to quiet your beating heart. It will happen by and by, Nora; you'll see. Why, tomorrow you'll look at all this in quite a different light. And soon everything will be just the way it was before. I won't need to keep reassuring you that I have forgiven you; you'll feel it yourself. Did you really think I could have abandoned you, or even reproached you? Oh, you don't know a real man's heart, Nora. There is something unspeakably sweet and satisfactory for a man to know deep in himself that he has forgiven his wife—forgiven her in all the fullness of his honest heart. You see, that way she becomes his very own all over again—in a double sense, you might say. He has, so to speak, given her a second birth; it is as if she had become his wife and his child, both. From now on that's what you'll be to me, you lost and helpless creature. Don't worry about a thing, Nora. Only be frank with me, and I'll be your will and your conscience.— What's this? You're not in bed? You've changed your dress—!

NORA (*in everyday dress*).   Yes, Torvald. I have changed my dress.

HELMER.   But why—now—this late?

NORA.   I'm not going to sleep tonight.

HELMER.   But my dear Nora—

NORA (*looks at her watch*).   It isn't all that late. Sit down here with me, Torvald. You and I have much to talk about. (*Sits down at the table.*)

HELMER.   Nora—what is this all about? That rigid face—

NORA.   Sit down. This will take a while. I have much to say to you.

HELMER (*sits down, facing her across the table*).   You worry me, Nora. I don't understand you.

NORA.   No, that's just it. You don't understand me. And I have never understood you—not till tonight. No, don't interrupt me. Just listen to what I have to say.— This is a settling of accounts, Torvald.

HELMER.   What do you mean by that?

NORA (*after a brief silence*).   Doesn't one thing strike you, now that we are sitting together like this?

HELMER.   What would that be?

NORA.   We have been married for eight years. Doesn't it occur to you that this is the first time that you and I, husband and wife, are having a serious talk?

HELMER.   Well—serious—. What do you mean by that?

NORA.   For eight whole years—longer, in fact—ever since we first met we have never talked seriously to each other about a single serious thing.

HELMER.   You mean I should forever have been telling you about worries you couldn't have helped me with anyway?

NORA.   I am not talking about worries. I'm saying we have never tried seriously to get to the bottom of anything together.

HELMER.   But dearest Nora, I hardly think that would have been something *you*—

NORA.   That's the whole point. You have never understood me. Great wrong has been done to me, Torvald. First by Daddy and then by you.

HELMER.   What! By us two? We who have loved you more deeply than anyone else?

NORA (*shakes her head*).   You never loved me—neither Daddy nor you. You only thought it was fun to be in love with me.

HELMER.   But, Nora—what an expression to use!

NORA.   That's the way it has been, Torvald. When I was home with Daddy, he told me all his opinions, and so they became my opinions too. If I disagreed with him I kept it to myself, for he wouldn't have liked that. He called me his little doll baby, and he played with me the way I played with my dolls. Then I came to your house—

HELMER.   What a way to talk about our marriage!

NORA (*imperturbably*).   I mean that I passed from Daddy's hands into yours. You arranged everything according to your taste, and so I came to share it—or I pretended to; I'm not sure which. I think it was a little of both, now one and now the other. When I look back on it now, it seems to me I've been living here like a pauper—just a hand-to-mouth kind of existence. I have earned my keep by doing tricks for you, Torvald. But that's the way you wanted it. You have great sins against me to answer for, Daddy and you. It's your fault that nothing has become of me.

HELMER.   Nora, you're being both unreasonable and ungrateful. Haven't you been happy here?

NORA.   No, never. I thought I was, but I wasn't.

HELMER.   Not—not happy!

NORA.   No; just having fun. And you have always been very good to me. But our home has never been more than a playroom. I have been your doll wife here, just the way I used to be Daddy's doll child. And the children have been my dolls. I thought it was fun when you played with me, just as they thought it was fun when I played with them. That's been our marriage, Torvald.

HELMER.   There is something in what you are saying—exaggerated and hysterical though it is. But from now on things will be different. Playtime is over; it's time for growing up.

NORA.   Whose growing up—mine or the children's?

HELMER.   Both yours and the children's, Nora darling.

NORA.   Oh Torvald, you're not the man to bring me up to be the right kind of wife for you.

HELMER.   How can you say that?

NORA.   And I—? What qualifications do I have for bringing up the children?

HELMER.   Nora!

NORA.   You said so yourself a minute ago—that you didn't dare to trust me with them.

HELMER.   In the first flush of anger, yes. Surely, you're not going to count that.

NORA.   But you were quite right. I am *not* qualified. Something else has to come first. Somehow I have to grow up myself. And you are not the man to help me do that. That's a job I have to do by myself. And that's why I'm leaving you.

HELMER (*jumps up*).   What did you say!

NORA.   I have to be by myself if I am to find out about myself and about all the other things too. So I can't stay here with you any longer.

HELMER.   Nora, Nora!

NORA.   I'm leaving now. I'm sure Kristine will put me up for tonight.

HELMER.   You're out of your mind! I won't let you! I forbid you!

NORA.   You can't forbid me anything any more; it won't do any good. I'm taking my own things with me. I won't accept anything from you, either now or later.

HELMER.   But this is madness!

NORA.   Tomorrow I'm going home— I mean back to my old home town. It will be easier for me to find some kind of job there.

HELMER.   Oh, you blind, inexperienced creature—!

NORA.   I must see to it that I get experience, Torvald.

HELMER.   Leaving your home, your husband, your children! Not a thought of what people will say!

NORA.   I can't worry about that. All I know is that I have to leave.

HELMER.   Oh, this is shocking! Betraying your most sacred duties like this!

NORA.   And what do you consider my most sacred duties?

HELMER.   Do I need to tell you that? They are your duties to your husband and your children.

NORA.   I have other duties equally sacred.

HELMER.   You do not. What duties would they be?

NORA.   My duties to myself.

HELMER.   You are a wife and a mother before you are anything else.

NORA.   I don't believe that any more. I believe I am first of all a human being, just as much as you—or at any rate that I must try to become one. Oh, I know very well that most people agree with you, Torvald, and that it says something like that in all the books. But what people say and what the books say is no longer enough for me. I have to think about these things myself and see if I can't find the answers.

HELMER.   You mean to tell me you don't know what your proper place in your own home is? Don't you have a reliable guide in such matters? Don't you have religion?

NORA.   Oh but Torvald—I don't really know what religion is.

HELMER.   What are you saying!

NORA.   All I know is what the Reverend Hansen told me when he prepared me for confirmation. He said that religion was *this* and it was *that.* When I get by myself, away from here, I'll have to look into that, too. I have to decide if what the Reverend Hansen said was right, or anyway if it is right for *me.*

HELMER.   Oh, this is unheard of in a young woman! If religion can't guide you, let me appeal to your conscience. For surely you have moral feelings? Or—answer me—maybe you don't?

NORA.   Well, you see, Torvald, I don't really know what to say. I just don't know. I am confused about these things. All I know is that my ideas are quite different from yours. I have just found out that the laws are different from what I thought they were, but in no way can I get it into my head that those laws are right. A woman shouldn't have the right to spare her dying old father or save her husband's life! I just can't believe that.

HELMER.   You speak like a child. You don't understand the society you live in.

NORA.   No, I don't. But I want to find out about it. I have to make up my mind who is right, society or I.

HELMER.   You are sick, Nora; you have a fever. I really don't think you are in your right mind.

NORA.   I have never felt so clearheaded and sure of myself as I do tonight.

HELMER.   And clearheaded and sure of yourself you're leaving your husband and children?

NORA.   Yes.

HELMER.   Then there is only one possible explanation.

NORA.   What?

HELMER.   You don't love me any more.

NORA.   No, that's just it.

HELMER.   Nora! Can you say that?

NORA.   I am sorry, Torvald, for you have always been so good to me. But I can't help it. I don't love you any more.

HELMER (*with forced composure*).   And this too is a clear and sure conviction?

NORA.   Completely clear and sure. That's why I don't want to stay here any more.

HELMER.   And are you ready to explain to me how I came to forfeit your love?

NORA.   Certainly I am. It was tonight, when the wonderful didn't happen. That was when I realized you were not the man I thought you were.

HELMER.   You have to explain. I don't understand.

NORA.   I have waited patiently for eight years, for I wasn't such a fool that I thought the wonderful is something that happens any old day. Then this—thing—came crashing in on me, and then there wasn't a doubt in my mind that now—now comes the wonderful. When Krogstad's letter was in that mailbox, never for a moment did it even occur to me that you would submit to his conditions. I was so absolutely certain that you would say to him: make the whole thing public—tell everybody. And when that had happened—

HELMER.   Yes, then what? When I surrendered my wife to shame and disgrace—!

NORA.   When that had happened, I was absolutely certain that you would stand up and take the blame and say, "I'm the guilty one."

HELMER.   Nora!

NORA.   You mean I never would have accepted such a sacrifice from you? Of course not. But what would my protests have counted against yours? *That* was the wonderful I was hoping for in terror. And to prevent that I was going to kill myself.

HELMER.   I'd gladly work nights and days for you, Nora—endure sorrow and want for your sake. But nobody sacrifices his *honor* for his love.

NORA.   A hundred thousand women have done so.

HELMER.   Oh, you think and talk like a silly child.

NORA.   All right. But you don't think and talk like the man I can live with. When you had gotten over your fright—not because of what threatened *me* but because of the risk to *you*—and the whole danger was past, then you acted as if nothing at all had happened. Once again I was your little songbird, your doll, just as before, only now you had to handle her even more carefully, because she was so frail and weak. (*Rises.*) Torvald—that moment I realized that I had been living here for eight years with a stranger and had borne him three children— Oh, I can't stand thinking about it! I feel like tearing myself to pieces!

HELMER (*heavily*).   I see it, I see it. An abyss has opened up between us. —Oh but Nora—surely it can be filled?

NORA.   The way I am now I am no wife for you.

HELMER.   I have it in me to change.

NORA.   Perhaps—if your doll is taken from you.

HELMER.   To part—to part from you! No, no, Nora! I can't grasp that thought!

NORA (*goes out, right*).   All the more reason why it has to be. (*She returns with her outdoor clothes and a small bag, which she sets down on the chair by the table.*)

HELMER.   Nora, Nora! Not now! Wait till tomorrow.

NORA (*putting on her coat*).   I can't spend the night in a stranger's rooms.

HELMER.   But couldn't we live here together like brother and sister—?

NORA (*tying on her hat*).   You know very well that wouldn't last long—. (*Wraps her shawl around her.*) Goodbye, Torvald. I don't want to see the children. I know I leave them in better hands than mine. The way I am now I can't be anything to them.

HELMER.   But some day, Nora—some day—?

NORA.   How can I tell? I have no idea what's going to become of me.

HELMER.   But you're still my wife, both as you are now and as you will be.

NORA.   Listen, Torvald—when a wife leaves her husband's house, the way I am doing now, I have heard he has no more legal responsibilities for her. At any rate, I now release you from all responsibility. You are not to feel yourself obligated to me for anything, and I have no obligations to you. There has to be full freedom on both sides. Here is your ring back. Now give me mine.

HELMER.   Even this?

NORA.   Even this.

HELMER.   Here it is.

NORA.   There. So now it's over. I'm putting the keys here. The maids know everything about the house—better than I. Tomorrow, after I'm gone, Kristine will come over and pack my things from home. I want them sent after me.

HELMER.   Over! It's all over! Nora, will you never think of me?

NORA.   I'm sure I'll often think of you and the children and this house.

HELMER.   May I write to you, Nora?

NORA.   No—never. I won't have that.

HELMER.   But send you things—? You must let me—

NORA.   Nothing, nothing.

HELMER.   —help you, when you need help—

NORA.   I told you, no; I won't have it. I'll accept nothing from strangers.

HELMER.   Nora—can I never again be more to you than a stranger?

NORA (*picks up her bag*).   Oh Torvald—then the most wonderful of all would have to happen—

HELMER.   Tell me what that would be—!

NORA.   For that to happen, both you and I would have to change so that— Oh Torvald, I no longer believe in the wonderful.

HELMER.   But I *will* believe. Tell me! Change, so that—?

NORA.   So that our living together would become a true marriage. Goodbye. (*She goes out through the hall.*)

HELMER (*sinks down on a chair near the door and covers his face with his hands*).   Nora! Nora! (*Looks around him and gets up.*) All empty. She's gone. (*With sudden hope.*) The most wonderful—?!

(*From downstairs comes the sound of a heavy door slamming shut.*)

QUESTIONS

1. How do the following contribute to the characterizations of Nora at the beginning of the play: (a) her husband's nicknames for her, (b) her fondness for sweets, (c) her games with her children, (d) her prodigality with money, and (e) her deceptions? What evidence is there that these characteristics may reflect both her own nature and conformity to her husband's expectations of her? What definition of marriage does she imply in her remarks to Mrs. Linde about how she may continue to act as long as she remains "young and pretty" (page 976)? It was socially proper at the time of the play for Norwegian wives to address their husbands by their last names; what does Nora's use of Helmer's first name suggest about their relationship?

2. What are the various functions of Nora's conversation with Mrs. Linde in act 1? Consider it from these perspectives: (a) the exposition of prior events and the definition of Nora's dilemma; (b) further revelations of Nora's character, both in the past and during the conversation; (c) the insight into herself that Nora gains from Mrs. Linde's history; (d) definitions of legal and moral standards of the time indicated by the prior actions of both women.

3. What are the symbolic meanings of the title? Why is it more appropriate than *A Doll's House*? Is Nora the only "doll" in the play?

4. How much time passes during the present action of the play, from the opening of act 1 to the final curtain? What events that occurred before the first act may be considered causes for the present action? What events that take place during the present are reported rather than dramatized on the stage?

5. What is the significance of Mrs. Linde's former and present relationship to Krogstad? To what extent can Krogstad be labeled "villain"? Compare his motives and actions (in the past and in the present) to those of Helmer. To those of Dr. Rank.

6. Characterize Dr. Rank. What are his strengths? Weaknesses? Structurally and morally he may be contrasted to Krogstad—but is he a model of virtue?

7. The major characters can be described thus: Nora and Helmer are protagonist and antagonist; Mrs. Linde is a foil to Nora; and both Krogstad and Dr. Rank are foils to Helmer. By evaluating the actions and motives

of the foil characters, locate Nora and Helmer on a scale of human value. To what extent do the foil characters offer models for the central characters? To what extent do they offer them examples of actions to be avoided?

8. What positive gains does Nora make in the course of the action? What must she learn in order to perform her final act? Is that act a triumph, or a failure, or some of both? (For the play's first performance in Berlin, Ibsen was pressured into creating a conventionally "happy ending"—Nora is persuaded by Helmer not to leave him for the sake of their children, and so sacrifices herself to their need for a mother. Why is the present ending truer to the themes Ibsen presents?)

9. Compare Nora and Helmer as developing characters. What opportunities for change does Helmer have? How does he respond to them? Consider the extent to which Nora and Helmer share the responsibility for having created "a doll house" of their marriage. Evaluate Nora's leaving him as an opportunity for Helmer.

10. From the first moments of the play, money is a recurring topic. Consider the importance it has in the motivations and actions of the five major characters. Can you establish a rank-order of more or less admirable attitudes toward it? Can you separate examples of genuine need from examples of desire for gain? Is the influence of money on the lives of these characters limited to the time and society in which they lived, or are there parallels to our time?

11. Consider the ways in which the marriage of Nora and Helmer is typical rather than uniquely theirs.

12. Assess the thematic importance of deception and honesty, of self-deception and self-discovery.

13. Explore the implications of this interpretation: "*A Doll House* represents a woman imbued with the idea of becoming a person, but it proposes nothing categorical about women becoming people; in fact, its real theme has nothing to do with the sexes. It is the irrepressible conflict of two different personalities which have founded themselves on two radically different estimates of reality" (Robert M. Adams, "Ibsen on the Contrary," in *Modern Drama*, ed. Anthony Caputi [New York: Norton, 1966], 345).

Tennessee Williams

The Glass Menagerie

CHARACTERS

AMANDA WINGFIELD, *the mother, a little woman of great but confused vitality clinging frantically to another time and place. Her characterization must be carefully created, not copied from type. She is not paranoiac, but her life is paranoia. There is much to admire in* AMANDA, *and as much to love and pity as there is to laugh at. Certainly she has endurance and a kind of heroism, and though her foolishness makes her unwittingly cruel at times, there is tenderness in her slight person.*

LAURA WINGFIELD, *her daughter.* AMANDA, *having failed to establish contact with reality, continues to live vitally in her illusions, but* LAURA'S *situation is even graver. A childhood illness has left her crippled, one leg slightly shorter than the other, and held in a brace. This defect need not be more than suggested on the stage. Stemming from this,* LAURA'S *separation increases till she is like a piece of her own glass collection, too exquisitely fragile to move from the shelf.*

TOM WINGFIELD, *her son and the narrator of the play. A poet with a job in a warehouse. His nature is not remorseless, but to escape from a trap he has to act without pity.*

JIM O'CONNOR, *the gentleman caller, a nice, ordinary, young man.*

SCENE.   *An alley in St. Louis.*

Part 1. Preparation for a gentleman caller.
Part 2. The gentleman calls.

Time: Now and the Past.

THE GLASS MENAGERIE   First performed in 1944; developed from a short story, "Portrait of a Girl in Glass" (published later in *One Arm and Other Stories*). Tennessee Williams (1911–1983) was born Thomas Lanier Williams in Mississippi, the son of a traveling salesman. In 1918 the family moved to St. Louis when the father was made a sales manager of International Shoe Company. Here, while the family lived in a succession of rented apartments, Tom published his first story at sixteen, graduated from high school, attended the University of Missouri for three years, worked at a menial job in the shoe company (1932–1935), had a nervous breakdown, finished his education at Washington University and the University of Iowa. Adopting "Tennessee" as his writing name, he then embarked on a life that took him to Chicago, New Orleans, Los Angeles, Mexico City, New York, Key West, and other cities while he wrote steadily, supporting himself at odd jobs. *The Glass Menagerie*, his first commercial success, rescued him from penury. The play reflects his St. Louis years, although his real father (given to alcoholic excess) never disappeared from home; his sister (two years his elder) did have dates, was not handicapped, and did not have a glass collection; a younger brother (eight years Tom's junior) does not appear; and "Miss Edwina" (Williams's mother and his guest at the first performance) has written, "The only resemblance I have to Amanda is that we both like jonquils."

SCENE 1

The Wingfield apartment is in the rear of the building, one of those vast hive-like conglomerations of cellular living-units that flower as warty growths in over-crowded urban centers of lower middle-class population and are symptomatic of the impulse of this largest and fundamentally enslaved section of American society to avoid fluidity and differentiation and to exist and function as one interfused mass of automatism.

The apartment faces an alley and is entered by a fire-escape, a structure whose name is a touch of accidental poetic truth, for all of these huge buildings are always burning with the slow and implacable fires of human desperation. The fire-escape is part of what we see—that is, the landing of it and steps descending from it.

The scene is memory and is therefore nonrealistic. Memory takes a lot of poetic license. It omits some details; others are exaggerated, according to the emotional value of the articles it touches, for memory is seated predominantly in the heart. The interior is therefore rather dim and poetic.

At the rise of the curtain, the audience is faced with the dark, grim rear wall of the Wingfield tenement. This building is flanked on both sides by dark, narrow alleys which run into murky canyons of tangled clotheslines, garbage cans and the sinister latticework of neighboring fire-escapes. It is up and down these side alleys that exterior entrances and exits are made, during the play. At the end of TOM'S opening commentary, the dark tenement wall slowly becomes transparent and re-veals the interior of the ground floor Wingfield apartment.

Nearest the audience is the living room, which also serves as a sleeping room for LAURA, the sofa unfolding to make her bed. Just beyond, separated from the living room by a wide arch or second proscenium with transparent faded portieres (or second curtain), is the dining room. In an old-fashioned what-not in the living room are seen scores of transparent glass animals. A blown-up photograph of the father hangs on the wall of the living room to the left of the archway. It is the face of a very handsome young man in a doughboy's First World War cap. He is gallantly smiling, ineluctably smiling, as if to say, "I will be smiling forever."

Also hanging on the wall, near the photograph, are a typewriter keyboard chart and a Gregg shorthand diagram. An upright typewriter on a small table stands beneath the charts.

The audience hears and sees the opening scene in the dining room through both the transparent fourth wall of the building and the transparent gauze portieres of the dining-room arch. It is during this revealing scene that the fourth wall slowly ascends, out of sight. This transparent exterior wall is not brought down again until the very end of the play, during TOM'S final speech.

The narrator is an undisguised convention of the play. He takes whatever license with dramatic convention as is convenient to his purposes.

TOM enters, dressed as a merchant sailor, and strolls across the front of the stage to the fire-escape. There he stops and lights a cigarette. He addresses the audience.

Tom.   Yes, I have tricks in my pocket, I have things up my sleeve. But I am the opposite of a stage magician. He gives you illusion that has the appearance of truth. I give you truth in the pleasant disguise of illusion.

To begin with, I turn back time. I reverse it to that quaint period, the thirties, when the huge middle class of America was matriculating in a school for the blind. Their eyes had failed them, or they had failed their eyes, and so they were having their fingers pressed forcibly down on the fiery Braille alphabet of a dissolving economy.

In Spain there was revolution. Here there was only shouting and confusion. In Spain there was Guernica.° Here there were disturbances of labor, sometimes pretty violent, in otherwise peaceful cities such as Chicago, Cleveland, Saint Louis . . . This is the social background of the play. (*Music.*)

The play is memory. Being a memory play, it is dimly lighted, it is sentimental, it is not realistic. In memory everything seems to happen to music. That explains the fiddle in the wings.

I am the narrator of the play, and also a character in it. The other characters are my mother, Amanda, my sister, Laura, and a gentleman caller who appears in the final scenes. He is the most realistic character in the play, being an emissary from a world of reality that we were somehow set apart from. But since I have a poet's weakness for symbols, I am using this character also as a symbol; he is the long delayed but always expected something that we live for.

There is a fifth character in the play who doesn't appear except in this larger-than-life-size photograph over the mantel. This is our father who left us a long time ago. He was a telephone man who fell in love with long distances; he gave up his job with the telephone company and skipped the light fantastic out of town . . .

The last we heard of him was a picture post-card from Mazatlán, on the Pacific coast of Mexico, containing a message of two words—"Hello— Good-bye!" and no address.

I think the rest of the play will explain itself . . . (Amanda's *voice becomes audible through the portieres.* Tom *divides the portieres and enters the upstage area.* Amanda *and* Laura *are seated at a drop-leaf table. Eating is indicated by gestures without food or utensils.* Amanda *faces the audience.* Tom *and* Laura *are seated in profile. The interior has lit up softly and through the scrim we see* Amanda *and* Laura *seated at the table in the upstage area.*)

Amanda (*calling*).   Tom?

Tom.   Yes, Mother.

Amanda.   We can't say grace until you come to the table!

Tom.   Coming, Mother. (*He bows slightly and withdraws, reappearing a few moments later in his place at the table.*)

Guernica: a town in northern Spain destroyed in 1937 during the Spanish Civil War by German bombers, in the first mass air attack on an urban community

AMANDA (*to her son*).   Honey, don't *push* with your *fingers.* If you have to push with something, the thing to push with is a crust of bread. And chew—chew! Animals have sections in their stomachs which enable them to digest food without mastication, but human beings are supposed to chew their food before they swallow it down. Eat food leisurely, son, and really enjoy it. A well-cooked meal has lots of delicate flavors that have to be held in the mouth for appreciation. So chew your food and give your salivary glands a chance to function!

TOM (*deliberately lays his imaginary fork down and pushes his chair back from the table*).   I haven't enjoyed one bite of this dinner because of your constant directions on how to eat it. It's you that makes me rush through meals with your hawk-like attention to every bite I take. Sickening—spoils my appetite—all this discussion of—animals' secretion—salivary glands—mastication!

AMANDA (*lightly*).   Temperament like a Metropolitan star! (*He rises and crosses downstage.*) You're not excused from the table.

TOM.   I'm getting a cigarette.

AMANDA.   You smoke too much.

LAURA (*rises*).   I'll bring in the blancmange. (TOM *remains standing with his cigarette by the portieres during the following.*)

AMANDA (*rising*).   No, sister, no, sister—you be the lady this time and I'll be the darky.

LAURA.   I'm already up.

AMANDA.   Resume your seat, little sister—I want you fresh and pretty—for gentlemen callers!

LAURA.   I'm not expecting any gentleman callers.

AMANDA (*crossing out to kitchenette. Airily*).   Sometimes they come when they are least expected! Why, I remember one Sunday afternoon in Blue Mountain—(*enters kitchenette*).

TOM.   I know what's coming!

LAURA.   Yes. But let her tell it.

TOM.   Again?

LAURA.   She loves to tell it.

AMANDA (*returning with a bowl of dessert*).   One Sunday afternoon in Blue Mountain—your mother received—*seventeen!*—gentlemen callers! Why, sometimes there weren't chairs enough to accommodate them all. We had to send the nigger over to bring in folding chairs from the parish house.

TOM (*remaining at portieres*).   How did you entertain those gentlemen callers?

AMANDA.   I understood the art of conversation!

TOM.   I bet you could talk.

AMANDA.   Girls in those days *knew* how to talk, I can tell you.

TOM.   Yes?

AMANDA. They knew how to entertain their gentlemen callers. It wasn't enough for a girl to be possessed of a pretty face and a graceful figure—although I wasn't slighted in either respect. She also needed to have a nimble wit and a tongue to meet all occasions.

TOM. What did you talk about?

AMANDA. Things of importance going on in the world! Never anything coarse or common or vulgar. (*She addresses* TOM *as though he were seated in the vacant chair at the table though he remains by the portieres. He plays this scene as though he held the book.*) My callers were gentlemen—all! Among my callers were some of the most prominent young planters of the Mississippi Delta—planters and sons of planters! (TOM *motions for music and a spot of light on* AMANDA. *Her eyes lift, her face glows, her voice becomes rich and elegiac.*)

There was young Champ Laughlin who later became vice-president of the Delta Planters Bank. Hadley Stevenson who was drowned in Moon Lake and left his widow one hundred and fifty thousand in Government bonds. There were the Cutrere brothers, Wesley and Bates. Bates was one of my bright particular beaux! He got in a quarrel with that wild Wainwright boy. They shot it out on the floor of Moon Lake Casino. Bates was shot through the stomach. Died in the ambulance on his way to Memphis. His widow was so well-provided for, came into eight or ten thousand acres, that's all. She married him on the rebound—never loved her—carried my picture on him the night he died! And there was that boy that every girl in the Delta had set her cap for! That beautiful, brilliant young Fitzhugh boy from Greene County!

TOM. What did he leave his widow?

AMANDA. He never married! Gracious, you talk as though all of my old admirers had turned up their toes to the daisies!

TOM. Isn't this the first you've mentioned that still survives?

AMANDA. That Fitzhugh boy went North and made a fortune—came to be known as the Wolf of Wall Street! He had the Midas touch, whatever he touched turned to gold! And I could have been Mrs. Duncan J. Fitzhugh, mind you! But—I picked your *father!*

LAURA (*rising*). Mother, let me clear the table.

AMANDA. No, dear, you go in front and study your typewriter chart. Or practice your shorthand a little. Stay fresh and pretty!—It's almost time for our gentlemen callers to start arriving. (*She flounces girlishly toward the kitchenette.*) How many do you suppose we're going to entertain this afternoon? (TOM *throws down the paper and jumps up with a groan.*)

LAURA (*alone in the dining room*). I don't believe we're going to receive any, Mother.

AMANDA (*reappearing, airily*). What? No one—not one? You must be joking! (LAURA *nervously echoes her laugh. She slips in a fugitive manner through the half-open portieres and draws them gently behind her. A shaft of very clear light is thrown on her face against the faded tapestry of the curtains. Music: "The Glass Menagerie"° under faintly. Lightly)* Not one gentleman caller? It can't be true! There must be a flood, there must have been a tornado!

LAURA.   It isn't a flood, it's not a tornado, Mother. I'm just not popular like you were in Blue Mountain . . . (TOM *utters another groan.* LAURA *glances at him with a faint, apologetic smile. Her voice catching a little.)* Mother's afraid I'm going to be an old maid. (*The scene dims out with "Glass Menagerie" music.*)

SCENE 2

LAURA *is seated in the delicate ivory chair at the small claw-foot table. She wears a dress of soft violet material for a kimono—her hair tied back from her forehead with a ribbon. She is washing and polishing her collection of glass.* AMANDA *appears on the fire-escape steps. At the sound of her ascent,* LAURA *catches her breath, thrusts the bowl of ornaments away and seats herself stiffly before the diagram of the typewriter keyboard as though it held her spellbound. Something has happened to* AMANDA. *It is written in her face as she climbs to the landing: a look that is grim and hopeless and a little absurd. She has on one of those cheap or imitation velvety-looking cloth coats with imitation fur collar. Her hat is five or six years old, one of those dreadful cloche hats that were worn in the late twenties, and she is clasping an enormous black patent-leather pocketbook with nickel clasps and initials. This is her full-dress outfit, the one she usually wears to the D.A.R. Before entering she looks through the door. She purses her lips, opens her eyes very wide, rolls them upward and shakes her head. Then she slowly lets herself in the door. Seeing her mother's expression* LAURA *touches her lips with a nervous gesture.*

LAURA.   Hello, Mother, I was— (*She makes a nervous gesture toward the chart on the wall.* AMANDA *leans against the shut door and stares at* LAURA *with a martyred look.*)

AMANDA.   Deception? Deception? (*She slowly removes her hat and gloves, continuing the sweet suffering stare. She lets the hat and gloves fall on the floor—a bit of acting.*)

LAURA (*shakily*).   How was the D.A.R. meeting? (AMANDA *slowly opens her purse and removes a dainty white handkerchief which she shakes out delicately and delicately touches to her lips and nostrils.*) Didn't you go to the D.A.R. meeting, Mother?

AMANDA (*faintly, almost inaudibly*).   —No.—No. (*Then more forcibly*) I did not have the strength—to go to the D.A.R. In fact, I did not have the courage! I wanted to find a hole in the ground and hide myself in it forever! (*She crosses slowly to the wall and removes the diagram of the typewriter key-*

Music . . . : Music for the play, including "The Glass Menagerie" theme, was composed by Paul Bowles (b. 1910), American composer, novelist, and short story writer.

board. She holds it in front of her for a second, staring at it sweetly and sor-rowfully—then bites her lips and tears it in two pieces.)

LAURA (*faintly*).   Why did you do that, Mother? (AMANDA *repeats the same procedure with the chart of the Gregg Alphabet.*) Why are you—

AMANDA.   Why? Why? How old are you, Laura?

LAURA.   Mother, you know my age.

AMANDA.   I thought you were an adult; it seems that I was mistaken. (*She crosses slowly to the sofa and sinks down and stares at* LAURA.)

LAURA.   Please don't stare at me, Mother. (AMANDA *closes her eyes and lowers her head. There is a ten-second pause.*)

AMANDA.   What are we going to do, what is going to become of us, what is the future? (*There is another pause.*)

LAURA.   Has something happened, Mother? (AMANDA *draws a long breath and takes out the handkerchief again. Dabbing process.*) Mother, has—something happened?

AMANDA.   I'll be all right in a minute, I'm just bewildered—(*she hesi-tates*)—by life.

LAURA.   Mother, I wish that you would tell me what's happened!

AMANDA.   As you know, I was supposed to be inducted into my office at the D.A.R. this afternoon. But I stopped off at Rubicam's Business Col-lege to speak to your teachers about your having a cold and ask them what progress they thought were you making down there.

LAURA.   Oh . . .

AMANDA.   I went to the typing instructor and introduced myself as your mother. She didn't know who you were. "Wingfield," she said. "We don't have any such student enrolled at the school!"

I assured her she did, that you had been going to classes since early in January.

"I wonder," she said, "if you could be talking about that terribly shy little girl who dropped out of school after only a few days' attendance?"

"No," I said, "Laura, my daughter, has been going to school every day for the past six weeks!"

"Excuse me," she said. She took the attendance book out and there was your name, unmistakably printed, and all the dates you were absent until they decided that you had dropped out of school.

I still said, "No, there must have been some mistake! There must have been some mix-up in the records!"

And she said, "No—I remember her perfectly now. Her hands shook so that she couldn't hit the right keys! The first time we gave a speed-test, she broke down completely—was sick at the stomach and almost had to be car-ried into the wash-room! After that morning she never showed up any more. We phoned the house but never got any answer"—While I was working at Famous and Barr, I suppose, demonstrating those—

Oh! (*She indicates a brassiere with her hands.*) I felt so weak I could barely keep on my feet! I had to sit down while they got me a glass of water! Fifty dollars' tuition, all of our plans—my hopes and ambitions for you—just gone up the spout, just gone up the spout like that. (LAURA *draws a long breath and gets awkwardly to her feet. She crosses to the victrola and winds it up.*) What are you doing?

LAURA.   Oh! (*She releases the handle and returns to her seat.*)

AMANDA.   Laura, where have you been going when you've gone out pretending that you were going to business college?

LAURA.   I've just been going out walking.

AMANDA.   That's not true.

LAURA.   It is. I just went walking.

AMANDA.   Walking? Walking? In winter? Deliberately courting pneumonia in that light coat? Where did you walk to, Laura?

LAURA.   All sorts of places—mostly in the park.

AMANDA.   Even after you'd started catching that cold?

LAURA.   It was the lesser of two evils, Mother. I couldn't go back up. I—threw up—on the floor!

AMANDA.   From half past seven till after five every day you mean to tell me you walked around in the park, because you wanted me to think that you were still going to Rubicam's Business College?

LAURA.   It wasn't as bad as it sounds. I went inside places to get warmed up.

AMANDA.   Inside where?

LAURA.   I went in the art museum and the bird-houses at the Zoo. I visited the penguins every day! Sometimes I did without lunch and went to the movies. Lately I've been spending most of my afternoons in the Jewel-box, that big glass house where they raise the tropical flowers.

AMANDA.   You did all this to deceive me, just for deception? (LAURA *looks down.*) Why?

LAURA.   Mother, when you're disappointed, you get that awful suffering look on your face, like the picture of Jesus's mother in the museum!

AMANDA.   Hush!

LAURA.   I couldn't face it. (*Pause. A whisper of strings.*)

AMANDA (*hopelessly fingering the huge pocketbook*).   So what are we going to do the rest of our lives? Stay home and watch the parades go by? Amuse ourselves with the glass menagerie, darling? Eternally play those worn-out phonograph records your father left as a painful reminder of him? We won't have a business career—we've given that up because it gave us nervous indigestion! (*Laughs wearily.*) What is there left but dependency all our lives? I know so well what becomes of unmarried women who aren't prepared to occupy a position. I've seen such pitiful cases in the South— barely tolerated spinsters living upon the grudging patronage of sister's husband or brother's wife!—stuck away in some little mouse-trap of a room— encouraged by one in-law to visit another—little birdlike women without any nest—eating the crust of humility all their life!

Is that the future that we've mapped out for ourselves? I swear it's the only alternative I can think of! (*She pauses.*) It isn't a very pleasant alternative, is it? (*She pauses again.*) Of course—some girls *do* marry. (LAURA *twists her hands nervously.*) Haven't you ever liked some boy?

LAURA.   Yes. I liked one once. (*Rises.*) I came across his picture a while ago.

AMANDA (*with some interest*).   He gave you his picture?

LAURA.   No, it's in the year-book.

AMANDA (*disappointed*).   Oh—a high-school boy.

LAURA.   Yes. His name was Jim. (LAURA *lifts the heavy annual from the claw-foot table.*) Here he is in *The Pirates of Penzance.*

AMANDA (*absently*).   The what?

LAURA.   The operetta the senior class put on. He had a wonderful voice and we sat across the aisle from each other Mondays, Wednesdays and Fridays in the Aud. Here he is with the silver cup for debating! See his grin?

AMANDA (*absently*).   He must have had a jolly disposition.

LAURA.   He used to call me—Blue Roses.

AMANDA.   Why did he call you such a name as that?

LAURA.   When I had that attack of pleurosis—he asked me what was the matter when I came back. I said pleurosis—he thought that I said Blue Roses! So that's what he always called me after that. Whenever he saw me, he'd holler, "Hello, Blue Roses!" I didn't care for the girl he went out with. Emily Meisenbach. Emily was the best-dressed girl at Soldan. She never struck me, though, as being sincere . . . It says in the Personal Section— they're engaged. That's—six years ago! They must be married by now.

AMANDA.   Girls that aren't cut out for business careers usually wind up married to some nice man. (*Gets up with a spark of revival.*) Sister, that's what you'll do! (LAURA *utters a startled, doubtful laugh. She reaches quickly for a piece of glass.*)

LAURA.   But, Mother—

AMANDA.   Yes? (*Crossing to photograph.*)

LAURA (*in a tone of frightened apology*).   I'm—crippled!

AMANDA.   Nonsense! Laura, I've told you never, never to use that word. Why, you're not crippled, you just have a little defect—hardly noticeable, even! When people have some slight disadvantage like that, they cultivate other things to make up for it—develop charm—and vivacity—and —*charm!* That's all you have to do! (*She turns again to the photograph.*) One thing your father had *plenty of*—was *charm!* (TOM *motions to the fiddle in the wings. The scene fades out with music.*)

SCENE 3

Tom speaks from the fire-escape landing.

TOM.   After the fiasco at Rubicam's Business College, the idea of getting a gentleman caller for Laura began to play a more and more important part in Mother's calculations. It became an obsession. Like some archetype of the universal unconscious, the image of the gentleman caller haunted our small apartment . . .

An evening at home rarely passed without some allusion to this image, this specter, this hope . . . Even when he wasn't mentioned, his presence hung in Mother's preoccupied look and in my sister's frightened, apologetic manner—hung like a sentence passed upon the Wingfields!

Mother was a woman of action as well as words. She began to take logical steps in the planned direction. Late that winter and in the early spring—realizing that extra money would be needed to properly feather the nest and plume the bird—she conducted a vigorous campaign on the telephone, roping in subscribers to one of those magazines for matrons called *The Home-maker's Companion,* the type of journal that features the serialized sublimations of ladies of letters who think in terms of delicate cup-like breasts, slim, tapering waists, rich, creamy thighs, eyes like woodsmoke in autumn, fingers that soothe and caress like strains of music, bodies as powerful as Etruscan sculpture. (AMANDA *enters with phone on long extension cord. She is spotted in the dim stage.*)

AMANDA.   Ida Scott? This is Amanda Wingfield! We *missed* you at the D.A.R. last Monday! I said to myself: She's probably suffering with that sinus condition! How is the sinus condition?

Horrors! Heaven have mercy!—You're a Christian martyr, yes, that's what you are, a Christian martyr!

Well, I just now happened to notice that your subscription to the *Companion's* about to expire! Yes, it expires with the next issue, honey!—just when that wonderful new serial by Bessie Mae Hopper is getting off to such an exciting start. Oh, honey, it's something that you can't miss! You remember how *Gone with the Wind* took everybody by storm? You simply couldn't go out if you hadn't read it. All everybody *talked* was Scarlett O'Hara. Well, this is a book that critics already compare to *Gone with the Wind.* It's the *Gone with the Wind* of the post–World War generation—What?—Burning?—Oh, honey, don't let them burn, go take a look in the oven and I'll hold the wire! Heavens—I think she's hung up!

(*Before the stage is lighted, the violent voices of* TOM *and* AMANDA *are heard. They are quarreling behind the portieres. In front of them stands* LAURA *with clenched hands and panicky expression. A clear pool of light on her figure throughout this scene.*)

TOM.   What in Christ's name am I—

AMANDA (*shrilly*).   Don't you use that—

TOM.   Supposed to do!

AMANDA.   Expression! Not in my—

TOM.   Ohhh!

AMANDA.   Presence! Have you gone out of your senses?

TOM.   I have, that's true, *driven* out!

AMANDA.   What is the matter with you, you—big—big—IDIOT!

TOM.   Look!—I've got *no thing,* no single thing—

AMANDA. Lower your voice!

TOM. In my life here that I can call my OWN! Everything is—

AMANDA. Stop that shouting!

TOM. Yesterday you confiscated my books! You have the nerve to—

AMANDA. I took that horrible novel back to the library—yes! That hideous book by that insane Mr. Lawrence.° (TOM *laughs wildly.*) I cannot control the output of diseased minds or people who cater to them—(TOM *laughs still more wildly.*) BUT I WON'T ALLOW SUCH FLITH BROUGHT INTO MY HOUSE! No, no, no, no, no!

TOM. House, house! Who pays rent on it, who makes a slave of himself to—

AMANDA (*fairly screeching*). Don't you DARE to—

TOM. No, no, *I* mustn't say things. *I've* got to just—

AMANDA. Let me tell you—

TOM. I don't want to hear any more! (*He tears the portieres open. The upstage area is lit with a turgid smoky red glow.* AMANDA'S *hair is in metal curlers and she wears a very old bathrobe, much too large for her slight figure, a relic of the faithless Mr. Wingfield. An upright typewriter and a wild disarray of manuscripts is on the drop-leaf table. The quarrel was probably precipitated by* AMANDA'S *interruption of his creative labor. A chair lies overthrown on the floor. Their gesticulating shadows are cast on the ceiling by the fiery glow.*)

AMANDA. You *will* hear more, you—

TOM. No, I won't hear more, I'm going out!

AMANDA. You come right back in—

TOM. Out, out, out! Because I'm—

AMANDA. Come back here, Tom Wingfield! I'm not through talking to you!

TOM. Oh, go—

LAURA (*desperately*). —Tom!

AMANDA. You're going to listen, and no more insolence from you! I'm at the end of my patience!

TOM (*comes back toward her*). What do you think I'm at? Aren't I supposed to have any patience to reach the end of, Mother? I know, I know. It seems unimportant to you, what I'm *doing*—what I *want* to do—having a little *difference* between them! You don't think that—

AMANDA. I think you've been doing things that you're ashamed of. That's why you act like this. I don't believe that you go every night to the movies. Nobody goes to the movies night after night. Nobody in their right minds goes to the movies as often as you pretend to. People don't go to the movies at nearly midnight, and movies don't let out at two A.M. Come in stumbling. Muttering to yourself like a maniac! You get three hours' sleep and then go to work. Oh, I can picture the way you're doing down there. Moping, doping, because you're in no condition.

Mr. Lawrence: D. H. Lawrence, author of "The Rocking-Horse Winner" (page 290), emphasized in his novels the force and importance of sexuality in human life.

TOM (*wildly*).   No, I'm in no condition!

AMANDA.   What right have you got to jeopardize your job? Jeopardize the security of all of us? How do you think we'd manage if you were—

TOM.   Listen! You think I'm crazy *about* the *warehouse*? (*He bends fiercely toward her slight figure.*) You think I'm in love with the Continental Shoemakers? You think I want to spend fifty-five *years* down there in that— *celotex interior!* with—*fluorescent*—*tubes!* Look! I'd rather somebody picked up a crowbar and battered out my brains—than go back mornings! I *go!* Every time you come in yelling that God damn "*Rise and Shine!*" "*Rise and Shine!*" I say to myself, "How *lucky dead* people are!" But I get up. I *go!* For sixty-five dollars a month I give up all that I dream of doing and being *ever!* And you say self—*self's* all I ever think of. Why, listen, if self is what I thought of, Mother, I'd be where he is—GONE! (*Pointing to father's picture.*) As far as the system of transportation reaches! (*He starts past her. She grabs his arm.*) Don't grab at me, Mother!

AMANDA.   Where are you going?

TOM.   I'm going to the *movies!*

AMANDA.   I don't believe that lie!

TOM (*crouching toward her, overtowering her tiny figure. She backs away, gasping*).   I'm going to opium dens! Yes, opium dens, dens of vice and criminals' hang-outs, Mother. I've joined the Hogan gang, I'm a hired assassin, I carry a tommy-gun in a violin case! I run a string of cat-houses in the Valley! They call me Killer, Killer Wingfield, I'm leading a double-life, a simple, honest warehouse worker by day, by night a dynamic *czar* of the *underworld, Mother.* I go to gambling casinos, I spin away fortunes on the roulette table! I wear a patch over one eye and a false mustache, sometimes I put on green whiskers. On those occasions they call me—*El Diablo!* Oh, I could tell you things to make you sleepless! My enemies plan to dynamite this place. They're going to blow us all sky-high some night! I'll be glad, very happy, and so will you! You'll go up, up on a broomstick, over Blue Mountain with seventeen gentlemen callers! You ugly—babbling old—*witch* . . . (*He goes through a series of violent, clumsy movements, seizing his overcoat, lunging to the door, pulling it fiercely open. The women watch him, aghast. His arm catches in the sleeve of the coat as he struggles to pull it on. For a moment he is pinioned by the bulky garment. With an outraged groan he tears the coat off again, splitting the shoulder of it, and hurls it across the room. It strikes against the shelf of LAURA'S glass collection, there is a tinkle of shattering glass. LAURA cries out as if wounded. Music: "The Glass Menagerie."*)

LAURA (*shrilly*).   My glass!—menagerie . . . (*She covers her face and turns away. But AMANDA is still stunned and stupefied by the "ugly witch" so that she barely notices this occurrence. Now she recovers her speech.*)

AMANDA (*in an awful voice*).   I won't speak to you—until you apologize!

(*She crosses through the portieres and draws them together behind her. TOM is left with LAURA. LAURA clings weakly to the mantel with her face averted. TOM stares at her stupidly for a moment. Then he crosses to shelf. Drops awkwardly on knees to collect the fallen glass, glancing at* LAURA *as if he would speak but couldn't. "The Glass Menagerie" steals in as the scene dims out.*)

SCENE 4

The interior of the apartment is dark. There is a faint light in the alley. A deep-voiced bell in a church is tolling the hour of five as the scene commences.

TOM *appears at the top of the alley. After each solemn boom of the bell in the tower, he shakes a little noise-maker or rattle as if to express the tiny spasm of man in contrast to the sustained power and dignity of the Almighty. This and the unsteadiness of his advance make it evident that he has been drinking. As he climbs the few steps to the fire-escape landing, light steals up inside.* LAURA *appears in night-dress, observing* TOM'S *empty bed in the front room.* TOM *fishes in his pockets for his door-key, removing a motley assortment of articles in the search, including a perfect shower of movie-ticket stubs and an empty bottle. At last he finds the key, but just as he is about to insert it, it slips from his fingers. He strikes a match and crouches below the door.*

TOM (*bitterly*).   One crack—and it falls through!

LAURA (*opens the door*).   Tom! Tom, what are you doing?

TOM.   Looking for a door-key.

LAURA.   Where have you been all this time?

TOM.   I have been to the movies.

LAURA.   All this time at the movies?

TOM.   There was a very long program. There was a Garbo picture and a Mickey Mouse and a travelogue and a newsreel and a preview of coming attractions. And there was an organ solo and a collection for the milk-fund—simultaneously—which ended up in a terrible fight between a fat lady and an usher!

LAURA (*innocently*).   Did you have to stay through everything?

TOM.   Of course! And, oh, I forgot! There was a big stage show! The headliner on this stage show was Malvolio the Magician. He performed wonderful tricks, many of them, such as pouring water back and forth between pitchers. First it turned to wine and then it turned to beer and then it turned to whiskey. I know it was whiskey it finally turned into because he needed somebody to come up out of the audience to help him, and I came up—both shows! It was Kentucky Straight Bourbon. A very generous fellow, he gave souvenirs. (*He pulls from his back pocket a shimmering rainbow-colored scarf.*) He gave me this. This is his magic scarf. You can have it, Laura. You wave it over a canary cage and you get a bowl of goldfish. You wave it over the goldfish bowl and they fly away canaries . . . But the wonderfullest trick of all was the coffin trick. We nailed him into a coffin and he got out of the coffin without removing one nail. (*He has come inside.*) There is a trick that would come in handy for me—get me out of this 2 by 4 situation! (*Flops onto bed and starts removing shoes.*)

LAURA.   Tom—Shhh!

Tom.   What're you shushing me for?

Laura.   You'll wake up Mother.

Tom.   Goody, goody! Pay 'er back for all those "Rise an' Shines." (*Lies down, groaning.*) You know it don't take much intelligence to get yourself into a nailed-up coffin, Laura. But who in hell ever got himself out of one without removing one nail? (*As if in answer, the father's grinning photograph lights up. Scene dims out. Immediately following the church bell is heard striking six. At the sixth stroke the alarm clock goes off in* AMANDA'S *room, and after a few moments we hear her calling: "Rise and Shine! Rise and Shine! Laura, go tell your brother to rise and shine!"*)

Tom (*sitting up slowly*).   I'll rise—but I won't shine. (*The light increases.*)

Amanda.   Laura, tell your brother his coffee is ready.

Laura (*slips into front room*).   Tom!—It's nearly seven. Don't make Mother nervous. (*He stares at her stupidly. Beseechingly*) Tom, speak to Mother this morning. Make up with her, apologize, speak to her!

Tom.   She won't to me. It's her that started not speaking.

Laura.   If you just say you're sorry she'll start speaking.

Tom.   Her not speaking—is that such a tragedy?

Laura.   Please—please!

Amanda (*calling from kitchenette*).   Laura, are you going to do what I asked you to do, or do I have to get dressed and go out myself?

Laura.   Going, going—soon as I get on my coat! (*She pulls on a shapeless felt hat with nervous, jerky movement, pleadingly glancing at* Tom. *Rushes awkwardly for coat. The coat is one of* AMANDA'S, *inaccurately made-over, the sleeves too short for* Laura.) Butter and what else?

Amanda (*entering upstage*).   Just butter. Tell them to charge it.

Laura.   Mother, they make such faces when I do that.

Amanda.   Sticks and stones can break our bones, but the expression on Mr. Garfinkel's face won't harm us! Tell your brother his coffee is getting cold.

Laura (*at door*).   Do what I asked you, will you, will you, Tom? (*He looks sullenly away.*)

Amanda.   Laura, go now or just don't go at all!

Laura (*rushing out*).   Going—going! (*A second later she cries out.* Tom *springs up and crosses to door.* Amanda *rushes anxiously in.* Tom *opens the door.*)

Tom.   Laura?

Laura.   I'm all right. I slipped, but I'm all right.

Amanda (*peering anxiously after her*).   If anyone breaks a leg on those fire-escape steps, the landlord ought to be sued for every cent he possesses! (*She shuts door. Remembers she isn't speaking and returns to the other room.*)

(*As* Tom *enters listlessly for his coffee, she turns her back to him and stands rigidly facing the window on the gloomy gray vault of the areaway. Its light on her face with its aged but childish features is cruelly sharp, satirical as a Daumier print.*

(*Music under: "Ave Maria."*

(TOM *glances sheepishly but sullenly at her averted figure and slumps at the table. The coffee is scalding hot; he sips it and gasps and spits it back in the cup. At his gasp,* AMANDA *catches her breath and half turns. Then catches herself and turns back to window.* TOM *blows on his coffee, glancing sidewise at his mother. She clears her throat.* TOM *clears his. He starts to rise. Sinks back down again, scratches his head, clears his throat again.* AMANDA *coughs.* TOM *raises his cup in both hands to blow on it, his eyes staring over the rim of it at his mother for several moments. Then he slowly sets the cup down and awkwardly and hesitantly rises from the chair.*)

TOM (*hoarsely*). Mother. I—I apologize, Mother. (AMANDA *draws a quick, shuddering breath. Her face works grotesquely. She breaks into childlike tears.*) I'm sorry for what I said, for everything that I said, I didn't mean it.

AMANDA (*sobbingly*). My devotion has made me a witch and so I make myself hateful to my children!

TOM. *No,* you *don't.*

AMANDA. I worry so much, don't sleep, it makes me nervous!

TOM (*gently*). I understand that.

AMANDA. I've had to put up a solitary battle all these years. But you're my right-hand bower! Don't fall down, don't fail!

TOM (*gently*). I try, Mother.

AMANDA (*with great enthusiasm*). Try and you will SUCCEED! (*The notion makes her breathless.*) Why, you—you're just *full* of natural endowments! Both of my children—they're *unusual* children! Don't you think I know it? I'm so—*proud!* Happy and—feel I've—so much to be thankful for but— Promise me one thing, son!

TOM. What, Mother?

AMANDA. Promise, son, you'll—never be a drunkard!

TOM (*turns to her grinning*). I will never be a drunkard, Mother.

AMANDA. That's what frightened me so, that you'd been drinking. Eat a bowl of Purina!

TOM. Just coffee, Mother.

AMANDA. Shredded wheat biscuit?

TOM. No. No, Mother, just coffee.

AMANDA. You can't put in a day's work on an empty stomach. You've got ten minutes—don't gulp! Drinking too-hot liquids makes cancer of the stomach . . . Put cream in.

TOM. No, thank you.

AMANDA. To cool it.

TOM. No! No, thank you, I want it black.

AMANDA. I know, but it's not good for you. We have to do all that we can to build ourselves up. In these trying times we live in, all that we have to cling to is—each other . . . That's why it's so important to—Tom, I—I sent out your sister so I could discuss something with you. If you hadn't spoken I would have spoken to you. (*Sits down.*)

TOM (*gently*). What is it, Mother, that you want to discuss?

AMANDA. *Laura!*

TOM (*puts his cup down slowly. Music: "The Glass Menagerie"*).   Oh.— Laura . . .

AMANDA (*touching his sleeve*).   You know how Laura is. So quiet but— still water runs deep! She notices things and I think she—broods about them. (TOM *looks up.*) A few days ago I came in and she was crying.

TOM.   What about?

AMANDA.   You.

TOM.   Me?

AMANDA.   She has an idea that you're not happy here.

TOM.   What gave her that idea?

AMANDA.   What gives her any idea? However, you do act strangely. I— I'm not criticizing, understand *that!* I know your ambitions do not lie in the warehouse, that like everybody in the whole wide world—you've had to— make sacrifices, but—Tom—Tom—life's not easy, it calls for—Spartan en- durance! There's so many things in my heart that I cannot describe to you! I've never told you but I—*loved* your father . . .

TOM (*gently*).   I know that, Mother.

AMANDA.   And you—when I see you taking after his ways! Staying out late—and—well, you *had* been drinking the night you were in that—terrify- ing condition! Laura says that you hate the apartment and that you go out nights to get away from it! Is that true, Tom?

TOM.   No. You say thee's so much in your heart that you can't describe to me. That's true of me, too. There's so much in my heart that I can't describe to *you!* So let's respect each other's—

AMANDA.   But, why—*why,* Tom—are you always so *restless?* Where do you *go* to, nights?

TOM.   I—go to the movies.

AMANDA.   Why do you go to the movies so much, Tom?

TOM.   I go to the movies because—I like adventure. Adventure is some- thing I don't have much of at work, so I go to the movies.

AMANDA.   But, Tom, you go to the movies *entirely* too *much!*

TOM.   I like a lot of adventure. (AMANDA *looks baffled, then hurt. As the familiar inquisition resumes he becomes hard and impatient again.* AMANDA *slips back to her querulous attitude toward him.*)

AMANDA.   Most young men find adventure in their careers.

TOM.   Then most young men are not employed in a warehouse.

AMANDA.   The world is full of young men employed in warehouses and offices and factories.

TOM.   Do all of them find adventure in their careers?

AMANDA.   They do or they do without it! Not everybody has a craze for adventure.

TOM.   Man is by instinct a lover, a hunter, a fighter, and none of those instincts are given much play at the warehouse!

AMANDA.   Man is by instinct! Don't quote instincts to me! Instinct is something that people have got away from! It belongs to animals! Christian adults don't want it!

TOM.   What do Christian adults want, then, Mother?

AMANDA.   Superior things! Things of the mind and the spirit! Only animals have to satisfy instincts! Surely your aims are somewhat higher than theirs! Than monkeys—pigs—

TOM.   I reckon they're not.

AMANDA.   You're joking. However, that isn't what I wanted to discuss.

TOM (*rising*).   I haven't much time.

AMANDA (*pushing his shoulders*).   Sit down.

TOM.   You want me to punch in red at the warehouse, Mother?

AMANDA.   You have five minutes. I want to talk about Laura.

TOM.   All right! What about Laura?

AMANDA.   We have to be making some plans and provisions for her. She's older than you, two years, and nothing has happened. She just drifts along doing nothing. It frightens me terribly how she just drifts along.

TOM.   I guess she's the type that people call home girls.

AMANDA.   There's no such type, and if there is, it's a pity! That is unless the home is hers, with a husband!

TOM.   What?

AMANDA.   Oh, I can see the handwriting on the wall as plain as I see the nose in front of my face! It's terrifying! More and more you remind me of your father! He was out all hours without explanation!—Then *left!* *Goodbye!* And me with the bag to hold. I saw that letter you got from the Merchant Marine. I know what you're dreaming of. I'm not standing here blindfolded. (*She pauses.*) Very well, then. Then *do* it! But not till there's somebody to take your place.

TOM.   What do you mean?

AMANDA.   I mean that as son as Laura has got somebody to take care of her, married, a home of her own, independent—why, then you'll be free to go wherever you please, on land, on sea, whichever way the wind blows you! But until that time you've got to look out for your sister. I don't say me because I'm old and don't matter! I say your sister because she's young and dependent.

I put her in business college—a dismal failure! Frightened her so it made her sick at the stomach. I took her over to the Young People's League at the church. Another fiasco. She spoke to nobody, nobody spoke to her. Now all she does is fool with those pieces of glass and play those worn-out records. What kind of a life is that for a girl to lead?

TOM.   What can I do about it?

AMANDA.   Overcome selfishness! Self, self, self is all that you ever think of! (TOM *springs up and crosses to get his coat. It is ugly and bulky. He pulls on a cap with earmuffs.*) Where is your muffler Put your wool muffler on! (*He snatches it angrily from the closet and tosses it about his neck and pulls both ends tight.*) Tom! I haven't said what I had in mind to ask you.

TOM.   I'm too late to—

AMANDA (*catching his arm—very importunately. Then shyly*).   Down at the warehouse, aren't there some—nice young men?

TOM.   No!

AMANDA.   There *must* be—*some* . . .

TOM.   Mother—(*Gesture.*)

AMANDA.   Find out one that's clean-living—doesn't drink and—ask him out for sister!

TOM.   What?

AMANDA.   For *sister!* To *meet!* Get *acquainted!*

TOM (*stamping to door*).   Oh, my *go-osh!*

AMANDA.   Will you? (*He opens door. Imploringly*) Will you? (*He starts down.*) Will you? Will you, dear?

TOM (*calling back*).   YES! (AMANDA *closes the door hesitantly and with a troubled but faintly hopeful expression.*)

AMANDA (*moves into spotlight at the phone*).   Ella Cartwright? This is Amanda Wingfield!

How are you, honey?

How is that kidney condition? (*There is a five-second pause.*)

Horrors! (*There is another pause.*)

You're a Christian martyr, yes, honey, that's what you are, a Christian martyr! Well, I just now happened to notice in my little red book that your subscription to the *Companion* has just run out! I knew that you wouldn't want to miss out on the wonderful serial starting in this new issue. It's by Bessie Mae Hopper, the first thing she's written since *Honeymoon for Three.* Wasn't that a strange and interesting story? Well, this one is even lovelier, I believe. It has a sophisticated, society background. It's all about the horsey set on Long Island!

SCENE 5

It is early dusk of a spring evening. Supper has just been finished in the Wingfield apartment. AMANDA *and* LAURA *in light-colored dresses are removing dishes from the table, in the upstage area, which is shadowy, their movements formalized almost as a dance or ritual, their moving forms as pale and silent as moths.* TOM, *in white shirt and trousers, rises from the table and crosses toward the fire-escape.*

AMANDA (*as he passes her*).   Son, will you do me a favor?

TOM.   What?

AMANDA.   Comb your hair! You look so pretty when your hair is combed! (TOM *slouches on sofa with evening paper. Enormous caption "Franco Triumphs."*) There is only one respect in which I would like you to emulate your father.

TOM.   What respect is that?

AMANDA.   The care he always took of his appearance. He never allowed himself to look untidy. (*He throws down the paper and crosses to fire-escape.*) Where are you going?

TOM.   I'm going out to smoke.

AMANDA.   You smoke too much. A pack a day at fifteen cents a pack. How much would that amount to in a month? Thirty times fifteen is how much, Tom? Figure it out and you will be astounded at what you could save. Enough to give you a night-school course in accounting at Washington U! Just think what a wonderful thing that would be for you, Son!

TOM.   I'd rather smoke. (*He steps out on landing, letting the screen door slam.*)

AMANDA (*sharply*).   I know! That's the tragedy of it . . . (*Alone, she turns to look at her husband's picture. Dance music: "All the World Is Waiting for the Sunrise!"*)

TOM (*to the audience*).   Across the alley from us was the Paradise Dance Hall. On evenings in spring the windows and doors were open and the music came outdoors. Sometimes the lights were turned out except for a large glass sphere that hung from the ceiling. It would turn slowly about and filter the dusk with delicate rainbow colors. Then the orchestra played a waltz or a tango, something that had a slow and sensuous rhythm. Couples would come outside, to the relative privacy of the alley. You could see them kissing behind ash-pits and telephone poles. This was the compensation for lives that passed like mine, without any change or adventure. Adventure and change were imminent in this year. They were waiting around the corner for all these kids. Suspended in the mist over Berchtesgaden,° caught in the folds of Chamberlain's umbrella—.° In Spain there was Guernica! But here there was only hot swing music and liquor, dance halls, bars, and movies, and sex that hung in the gloom like a chandelier and flooded the world with brief, deceptive rainbows . . . All the world was waiting for bombardments! (AMANDA *turns from the picture and comes outside.*)

AMANDA (*sighing*).   A fire-escape landing's a poor excuse for a porch. (*She spreads a newspaper on a step and sits down, gracefully and demurely as if she were settling into a swing on a Mississippi veranda.*) What are you looking at?

TOM.   The moon.

AMANDA.   Is there a moon this evening?

TOM.   It's rising over Garfinkel's Delicatessen.

Berchtesgaden: Hitler's Bavarian summer retreat   **Chamberlain's umbrella:** Neville Chamberlain, British prime minister (1937–1940), who always carried a furled umbrella, and whose name has become a symbol for appeasement, returned from a conference with Hitler in Munich in 1938 with a signed agreement which he proclaimed meant "Peace in our time." One year later, German troops invaded Poland, beginning World War II.

AMANDA.   So it is! A little silver slipper of a moon. Have you made a wish on it yet?

TOM.   Um-hum.

AMANDA.   What did you wish for?

TOM.   That's a secret.

AMANDA.   A secret, huh? Well, I won't tell mine either. I will be just as mysterious as you.

TOM.   I bet I can guess what yours is.

AMANDA.   Is my head so transparent?

TOM.   You're not a sphinx.

AMANDA.   No, I don't have secrets. I'll tell you what I wished for on the moon. Success and happiness for my precious children! I wish for that whenever there's a moon, and when there isn't a moon, I wish for it, too.

TOM.   I thought perhaps you wished for a gentleman caller.

AMANDA.   Why do you say that?

TOM.   Don't you remember asking me to fetch one?

AMANDA.   I remember suggesting that it would be nice for your sister if you brought home some nice young man from the warehouse. I think that I've made that suggestion more than once.

TOM.   Yes, you have made it repeatedly.

AMANDA.   Well?

TOM.   We are going to have one.

AMANDA.   *What?*

TOM.   A gentleman caller! (*The annunciation is celebrated with music.* AMANDA *rises.*)

AMANDA.   You mean you have asked some nice young man to come over?

TOM.   Yep. I've asked him to dinner.

AMANDA.   You really did?

TOM.   I did!

AMANDA.   You did, and did he—*accept?*

TOM.   He did!

AMANDA.   Well, well—well, well! That's—lovely!

TOM.   I thought that you would be pleased.

AMANDA.   It's definite, then?

TOM.   Very definite.

AMANDA.   Soon?

TOM.   Very soon.

AMANDA.   For heaven's sake, stop putting on and tell me some things, will you?

TOM.   What things do you want me to tell you?

AMANDA.   *Naturally* I would like to know when he's *coming!*

TOM.   He's coming tomorrow.

AMANDA.   *Tomorrow?*

TOM.   Yep. Tomorrow.

AMANDA.   But, Tom!

TOM.   Yes, Mother?

AMANDA.   Tomorrow gives me no time!

TOM.   Time for what?

AMANDA.   Preparations! Why didn't you phone me at once, as soon as you asked him, the minute that he accepted? Then, don't you see, I could have been getting ready!

TOM.   You don't have to make any fuss.

AMANDA.   Oh, Tom, Tom, Tom, of course I have to make a fuss! I want things nice, not sloppy! Not thrown together. I'll certainly have to do some fast thinking, won't I?

TOM.   I don't see why you have to think at all.

AMANDA.   You just don't know. We can't have a gentleman caller in a pig-sty! All my wedding silver has to be polished, the monogrammed table linen ought to be laundered! The windows have to be washed and fresh curtains put up. And how about clothes? We have to *wear* something, don't we?

TOM.   Mother, this boy is no one to make a fuss over!

AMANDA.   Do you realize he's the first young man we've introduced to your sister?

It's terrible, dreadful, disgraceful that poor little sister has never received a single gentleman caller! Tom, come inside! (*She opens the screen door.*)

TOM.   What for?

AMANDA.   I want to ask you some things.

TOM.   If you're going to make such a fuss, I'll call it off, I'll tell him not to come!

AMANDA.   You certainly won't do anything of the kind. Nothing offends people worse than broken engagements. It simply means I'll have to work like a Turk! We won't be brilliant, but we'll pass inspection. Come on inside. (TOM *follows, groaning.*) Sit down.

TOM.   Any particular place you would like me to sit?

AMANDA.   Thank heavens I've got the new sofa! I'm also making payments on a floor lamp I'll have sent out! And put the chintz covers on, they'll brighten things up! Of course I'd hope to have these walls repapered . . . What is the young man's name?

TOM.   His name is O'Connor.

AMANDA.   That, of course, means fish—tomorrow is Friday! I'll have that salmon loaf—with Durkee's dressing! What does he do? He works at the warehouse?

TOM.   Of course! How else would I—

AMANDA.   Tom, he—doesn't drink?

TOM.   Why do you ask me that?

AMANDA.   Your father *did!*

TOM.   Don't get started on that!

AMANDA.   He *does* drink, then?

TOM.   Not that I know of!

AMANDA.   Make sure, be certain! The last thing I want for my daughter's a boy who drinks!

TOM.   Aren't you being a little bit premature? Mr. O'Connor has not yet appeared on the scene!

AMANDA.   But will tomorrow. To meet your sister, and what do I know about his character? Nothing! Old maids are better off than wives of drunkards!

TOM.   Oh, my God!

AMANDA.   Be still!

TOM (*leaning forward to whisper*).   Lots of fellows meet girls whom they don't marry!

AMANDA.   Oh, talk sensibly, Tom—and don't be sarcastic! (*She has gotten a hairbrush.*)

TOM.   What are you doing?

AMANDA.   I'm brushing that cow-lick down! What is this young man's position at the warehouse?

TOM (*submitting grimly to the brush and the interrogation*).   This young man's position is that of a shipping clerk, Mother.

AMANDA.   Sounds to me like a fairly responsible job, the sort of a job *you* would be in if you just had more *get-up*. What is his salary? Have you any idea?

TOM.   I would judge it to be approximately eight-five dollars a month.

AMANDA.   Well—not princely, but—

TOM.   Twenty more than I make.

AMANDA.   Yes, how well I know! But for a family man, eighty-five dollars a month is not much more than you can just get by on . . .

TOM.   Yes, but Mr. O'Connor is not a family man.

AMANDA.   He might be, mightn't he? Some time in the future?

TOM.   I see. Plans and provisions.

AMANDA.   You are the only young man that I know of who ignores the fact that the future becomes the present, the present the past, and the past turns into everlasting regret if you don't plan for it!

TOM.   I will think that over and see what I can make of it.

AMANDA.   Don't be supercilious with your mother! Tell me some more about this—what do you call him?

TOM.   James D. O'Connor. The D. is for Delaney.

AMANDA.   Irish on *both* sides! *Gracious!* And doesn't drink?

TOM.   Shall I call him up and ask him right this minute?

AMANDA.   The only way to find out about these things is to make discreet inquiries at the proper moment. When I was a girl in Blue Mountain and it was suspected that a young man drank, the girl whose attentions he had been receiving, if any girl *was,* would sometimes speak to the minister of his church, or rather her father would if her father was living, and sort of feel him out on the young man's character. That is the way such things are discreetly handled to keep a young woman from making a tragic mistake!

Tom.   Then how did you happen to make a tragic mistake?

Amanda.   That innocent look of your father's had everyone fooled! He *smiled*—the world was *enchanted!* No girl can do worse than put herself at the mercy of a handsome appearance! I hope that Mr. O'Connor is not too good-looking.

Tom.   No, he's not too good-looking. He's covered with freckles and hasn't too much of a nose.

Amanda.   He's not right-down homely, though?

Tom.   Not right-down homely. Just medium homely, I'd say.

Amanda.   Character's what to look for in a man.

Tom.   That's what I've always said, Mother.

Amanda.   You've never said anything of the kind and I suspect you would never give it a thought.

Tom.   Don't be so suspicious of me.

Amanda.   At least I hope he's the type that's up and coming.

Tom.   I think he really goes in for self-improvement.

Amanda.   What reason have you to think so?

Tom.   He goes to night school.

Amanda (*beaming*).   Splendid! What does he do, I mean study?

Tom.   Radio engineering and public speaking!

Amanda.   Then he has visions of being advanced in the world! Any young man who studies public speaking is aiming to have an executive job some day! And radio engineering? A thing for the future! Both of these facts are very illuminating. Those are the sort of things that a mother should know concerning any young man who comes to call on her daughter. Seriously or—not.

Tom.   One little warning. He doesn't know about Laura. I didn't let on that we had dark ulterior motives. I just said, why don't you come and have dinner with us? He said okay and that was the whole conversation.

Amanda.   I bet it was! You're eloquent as an oyster. However, he'll know about Laura when he gets here. When he sees how lovely and sweet and pretty she is, he'll thank his lucky stars he was asked to dinner.

Tom.   Mother, you mustn't expect too much of Laura.

Amanda.   What do you mean?

Tom.   Laura seems all those things to you and me because she's ours and we love her. We don't even notice she's crippled any more.

Amanda.   Don't say crippled! You know that I never allow that word to be used!

Tom.   But face facts, Mother. She is and—that's not all—

Amanda.   What do you mean "not all"?

Tom.   Laura is very different from other girls.

Amanda.   I think the difference is all to her advantage.

Tom.   Not quite all—in the eyes of others—strangers—she's terribly shy and lives in a world of her own and those things make her seem a little peculiar to people outside the house.

AMANDA.   Don't say peculiar.

TOM.   Face the facts. She is. (*The dance-hall music changes to a tango that has a minor and somewhat ominous tone.*)

AMANDA.   In what way is she peculiar—may I ask?

TOM (*gently*).   She lives in a world of her own—a world of—little glass ornaments, Mother . . . (*Gets up.* AMANDA *remains holding the brush, looking at him, troubled.*) She plays old phonograph records and—that's about all— (*He glances at himself in the mirror and crosses to door.*)

AMANDA (*sharply*).   Where are you going?

TOM.   I'm going to the movies. (*Out screen door.*)

AMANDA.   Not to the movies, every night to the movies! (*Follows quickly to screen door.*) I don't believe you always go to the movies! (*He is gone.* AMANDA *looks worriedly after him for a moment. Then vitality and optimism return and she turns from the door, crossing to portieres.*) Laura! Laura!

LAURA (*answers from kitchenette*).   Yes, Mother.

AMANDA.   Let those dishes go and come in front! (LAURA *appears with dish towel.* AMANDA *speaks to her gaily.*) Laura, come here and make a wish on the moon!

LAURA (*entering*).   Moon—moon?

AMANDA.   A little silver slipper of a moon. Look over your left shoulder, Laura, and make a wish! (LAURA *looks faintly puzzled as if called out of sleep.* AMANDA *seizes her shoulders and turns her at an angle by the door.*)

LAURA.   What shall I wish for, Mother?

AMANDA (*her voice trembling and her eyes suddenly filled with tears*). Happiness! Good fortune! (*The sound of the violin rises and the stage dims out.*)

SCENE 6

TOM.   And so the following evening I brought Jim home to dinner. I had known Jim slightly in high school. In high school Jim was a hero. He had tremendous Irish good nature and vitality with the scrubbed and polished look of white chinaware. He seemed to move in a continual spotlight. He was a star in basketball, captain of the debating club, president of the senior class and the glee club and he sang the male lead in the annual light operas. He was always running or bounding, never just walking. He seemed always at the point of defeating the law of gravity. He was shooting with such velocity through his adolescence that you would logically expect him to arrive at nothing short of the White House by the time he was thirty. But Jim apparently ran into more interference after his graduation from Soldan. His speed had definitely slowed. Six years after he left high school he was holding a job that wasn't much better than mine.

He was the only one at the warehouse with whom I was on friendly terms. I was valuable to him as someone who could remember his former glory, who had seen him win basketball games and the silver cup in debating.

He knew of my secret practice of retiring to a cabinet of the washroom to work on poems when business was slack in the warehouse. He called me Shakespeare. And while the other boys in the warehouse regarded me with suspicious hostility, Jim took a humorous attitude toward me. Gradually his attitude affected the others, their hostility wore off and they also began to smile at me as people smile at an oddly fashioned dog who trots across their paths at some distance.

I knew that Jim and Laura had known each other at Soldan, and I had heard Laura speak admiringly of his voice. I didn't know if Jim remembered her or not. In high school Laura had been as unobtrusive as Jim had been astonishing. If he did remember Laura, it was not as my sister, for when I asked him to dinner, he grinned and said, "You know, Shakespeare, I never thought of you as having folks!"

He was about to discover that I did . . .

(*The light dims out on* TOM *and comes up in the* Wingfield *living room—a delicate lemony light. It is about five on a Friday evening of late spring which comes "scattering poems in the sky."*)

(AMANDA *has worked like a Turk in preparation for the gentleman caller. The results are astonishing. The new floor lamp with its rose-silk shade is in place, a colored paper lantern conceals the broken light fixture in the ceiling, new billowing white curtains are at the windows, chintz covers are on chairs and sofa, a pair of new sofa pillows make their initial appearance. Open boxes and tissue paper are scattered on the floor.*)

(LAURA *stands in the middle with lifted arms while* AMANDA *crouches before her, adjusting the hem of a new dress, devout and ritualistic. The dress is colored and designed by memory. The arrangement of* LAURA'S *hair is changed; it is softer and more becoming. A fragile, unearthly prettiness has come out in* LAURA: *she is like a piece of translucent glass touched by light, given a momentary radiance, not actual, not lasting.*)

AMANDA (*impatiently*).   Why are you trembling?

LAURA.   Mother, you've made me nervous!

AMANDA.   How have I made you nervous?

LAURA.   By all this fuss! You make it seem so important!

AMANDA.   I don't understand you, Laura. You couldn't be satisfied with just sitting home, and yet whenever I try to arrange something for you, you seem to resist it. (*She gets up.*) Now take a look at yourself. No, wait! Wait just a moment—I have an idea!

LAURA.   What is it now? (AMANDA *produces two powder puffs which she wraps in handkerchiefs and stuffs in* LAURA'S *bosom.*)

LAURA.   Mother, what are you doing?

AMANDA.   They call them "Gay Deceivers"!

LAURA.   I won't wear them.

AMANDA.   You will!

LAURA.   Why should I?

AMANDA.   Because, to be painfully honest, your chest is flat.

LAURA.   You make it seem like we were setting a trap.

AMANDA.   All pretty girls are a trap, a pretty trap, and men expect them to be. Now look at yourself, young lady. This is the prettiest you will ever be! (*She stands back to admire* LAURA.) I've got to fix myself now! You're going to be surprised by your mother's appearance! (*She crosses through portieres, humming gaily.* LAURA *moves slowly to the long mirror and stares solemnly at herself. A wind blows the white curtain inward in a slow, graceful motion and with a faint, sorrowful sighing.* AMANDA *speaks from somewhere behind the portieres.*) It isn't dark enough yet. (LAURA *turns slowly before the mirror with a troubled look.*)

AMANDA (*laughing, still not visible*).   I'm going to show you something. I'm going to make a spectacular appearance!

LAURA.   What is it, Mother?

AMANDA.   Possess your soul in patience—you will see! Something I've resurrected from that old trunk! Styles haven't changed so terribly much after all . . . (*She parts the portieres.*) Now just look at your mother! (*She wears a girlish frock of yellow voile with a blue silk sash. She carries a bunch of jonquils—the legend of her youth is nearly revived. Now she speaks feverishly.*) This is the dress in which I led the cotillion. Won the cakewalk twice at Sunset Hill, wore one spring to the Governor's ball in Jackson! See how I sashayed around the ballroom, Laura? (*She raises her skirt and does a mincing step around the room.*) I wore it on Sundays for my gentlemen callers! I had it on the day I met your father—I had malaria fever all that spring. The change of climate from East Tennessee to the Delta—weakened resistance—I had a little temperature all the time—not enough to be serious—just enough to make me restless and giddy!—Invitations poured in—parties all over the Delta!—"Stay in bed," said Mother, "you have fever!"—but I just wouldn't.—I took quinine but kept on going, going!—Evenings, dances!—Afternoons, long, long rides! Picnics—lovely!—So lovely, that country in May.—All lacy with dogwood, literally flooded with jonquils!—That was the spring I had the craze for jonquils. Jonquils became an absolute obsession. Mother said, "Honey, there's no more room for jonquils." And still I kept on bringing in more jonquils. Whenever, wherever I saw them, I'd say, "Stop! Stop! I see jonquils!" I made the young men help me gather the jonquils! It was a joke, Amanda and her jonquils! Finally there were no more vases to hold them, every available space was filled with jonquils. No vases to hold them? All right, I'll hold them myself! And then I—(*She stops in front of the picture. Music.*) met your father! Malaria and jonquils and then—this—boy . . . (*She switches on the rose-colored lamp.*) I hope they get here before it starts to rain. (*She crosses upstage and places the jonquils in bowl on table.*) I gave your brother a little extra change so he and Mr. O'Connor could take the service car home.

LAURA (*with altered look*).   What did you say his name was?

AMANDA.   O'Connor.

LAURA.   What is his first name?

AMANDA.   I don't remember. Oh, yes, I do. It was—Jim! (LAURA *sways slightly and catches hold of a chair.*)

LAURA (*faintly*).   Not—Jim!

AMANDA.   Yes, that was it, it was Jim! I've never known a Jim that wasn't nice! (*The music becomes ominous.*)

LAURA.   Are you sure his name is Jim O'Connor?

AMANDA.   Yes. Why?

LAURA.   Is he the one that Tom used to know in high school?

AMANDA.   He didn't say so. I think he just got to know him at the warehouse.

LAURA.   There was a Jim O'Connor we both knew in high school— (*Then, with effort*) If that is the one that Tom is bringing to dinner—you'll have to excuse me, I won't come to the table.

AMANDA.   What sort of nonsense is this?

LAURA.   You asked me once if I'd ever liked a boy. Don't you remember I showed you this boy's picture?

AMANDA.   You mean the boy you showed me in the year book?

LAURA.   Yes, that boy.

AMANDA.   Laura, Laura, were you in love with that boy?

LAURA.   I don't know, Mother. All I know is I couldn't sit at the table if it was him!

AMANDA.   It won't be him! It isn't the least bit likely. But whether it is or not, you will come to the table. You will not be excused.

LAURA.   I'll have to be, Mother.

AMANDA.   I don't intend to humor your silliness, Laura. I've had too much from you and your brother, both! So just sit down and compose yourself till they come. Tom has forgotten his key so you'll have to let them in, when they arrive.

LAURA (*panicky*).   Oh, Mother—*you* answer the door!

AMANDA (*lightly*).   I'll be in the kitchen—busy!

LAURA.   Oh, Mother, please answer the door, don't make me do it!

AMANDA (*crossing into kitchenette*).   I've got to fix the dressing for the salmon. Fuss, fuss—silliness!—over a gentleman caller! (*Door swings shut. LAURA is left alone. She utters a low moan and turns off the lamp—sits stiffly on the edge of the sofa, knotting her fingers together. TOM and JIM appear on the fire-escape steps and climb to landing. Hearing their approach, LAURA rises with a panicky gesture. She retreats to the portieres. The doorbell rings. LAURA catches her breath and touches her throat. Low drums sound. AMANDA calls.*) Laura, sweetheart! The door! (*LAURA stares at it without moving.*)

JIM.   I think we just beat the rain.

TOM.   Uh-huh. (*He rings again, nervously. JIM whistles and fishes for a cigarette.*)

AMANDA (*very, very gaily*).   Laura, that is your brother and Mr. O'Connor! Will you let them in, darling? (*LAURA crosses toward kitchenette door.*)

LAURA (*breathlessly*).   Mother—you go to the door! (AMANDA *steps out of the kitchenette and stares furiously at* LAURA. *She points imperiously at the door.*) Please, please!

AMANDA (*in a fierce whisper*).   What is the matter with you, you silly thing?

LAURA (*desperately*).   Please, you answer it, *please!*

AMANDA.   I told you I wasn't going to humor you, Laura. Why have you chosen this moment to lose your mind?

LAURA.   Please, please, please, you go!

AMANDA.   You'll have to go to the door because I can't!

LAURA (*despairingly*).   I can't either!

AMANDA.   *Why?*

LAURA.   I'm *sick!*

AMANDA.   I'm sick too—of your nonsense! Why can't you and your brother be normal people? Fantastic whims and behavior. (TOM *gives a long ring.*) Preposterous goings on! Can you give me one reason—(*She calls out lyrically.*) COMING! JUST ONE SECOND!—why you should be afraid to open a door? Now you answer it, Laura!

LAURA.   Oh, oh, oh . . . (*She returns through the portieres, darts to the victrola, winds it frantically and turns it on.*)

AMANDA.   Laura Wingfield, you march right to that door!

LAURA.   Yes—yes, Mother! (*A faraway, scratchy rendition of "Dardanella" softens the air and gives her strength to move through it. She slips to the door and draws it cautiously open.* TOM *enters with the caller,* JIM O'CONNOR.)

TOM.   Laura, this is Jim. Jim, this is my sister, Laura.

JIM (*stepping inside*).   I didn't know that Shakespeare had a sister!

LAURA (*retreating stiff and trembling from the door*).   How—how do you do?

JIM (*heartily extending his hand*).   Okay! (LAURA *touches it hesitantly with hers.*) Your hand's *cold*, Laura!

LAURA.   Yes, well—I've been playing the victrola . . .

JIM.   Must have been playing classical music on it! You ought to play a little hot swing music to warm you up!

LAURA.   Excuse me—I haven't finished playing the victrola . . . (*She turns awkwardly and hurries into the front room. She pauses a second by the victrola. Then she catches her breath and darts through the portieres like a frightened deer.*)

JIM (*grinning*).   What was the matter?

TOM.   Oh—with Laura? Laura is—terribly shy.

JIM.   Shy, huh? It's unusual to meet a shy girl nowadays. I don't believe you ever mentioned you had a sister.

TOM.   Well, now you know. I have one. Here is the *Post Dispatch*. You want a piece of it?

JIM.   Uh-huh.

Tom.   What piece? The comics?

Jim.   Sports! (*Glances at it.*) Ole Dizzy Dean is on his bad behavior.

Tom (*uninterested*).   Yeah? (*Lights a cigarette and crosses back to fire-escape door.*)

Jim.   Where are *you* going?

Tom.   I'm going out on the terrace.

Jim (*goes after him*).   You know, Shakespeare—I'm going to sell you a bill of goods!

Tom.   What goods?

Jim.   A course I'm taking.

Tom.   Huh.

Jim.   In public speaking! You and me, we're not the warehouse type.

Tom.   Thanks—that's good news. But what has public speaking got to do with it?

Jim.   It fits you for—executive positions!

Tom.   Awww.

Jim.   I tell you it's done a helluva lot for me.

Tom.   In what respect?

Jim.   In every! Ask yourself what is the difference between you an' me and men in the office down front? Brains?—No!—Ability?—No! Then what? Just one little thing—

Tom.   What is that one little thing?

Jim.   Primarily it amounts to—social poise! Being able to square up to people and hold your own on any social level!

Amanda (*from the kitchenette*).   Tom?

Tom.   Yes, Mother?

Amanda.   Is that you and Mr. O'Connor?

Tom.   Yes, Mother.

Amanda.   Well, you just make yourselves comfortable in there.

Tom.   Yes, Mother.

Amanda.   Ask Mr. O'Connor if he would like to wash his hands.

Jim.   Aw, no—no—thank you—I took care of that at the warehouse. Tom—

Tom.   Yes?

Jim.   Mr. Mendoza was speaking to me about you.

Tom.   Favorably?

Jim.   What do you think?

Tom.   Well—

Jim.   You're going to be out of a job if you don't wake up.

Tom.   I am waking up—

Jim.   You show no signs.

Tom.   The signs are interior. I'm planning to change. (*He leans over the rail speaking with quiet exhilaration. The incandescent marquees and signs of the first-run movie houses light his face from across the alley. He looks like a voyager.*)

I'm right at the point of committing myself to a future that doesn't include the warehouse and Mr. Mendoza or even a night-school course in public speaking.

JIM.   What are you gassing about?

TOM.   I'm tired of the movies.

JIM.   Movies!

TOM.   Yes, movies! Look at them—(*a wave toward the marvels of Grand Avenue*) all of those glamorous people—having adventures—hogging it all, gobbling the whole thing up! You know what happens? People go to the *movies* instead of *moving!* Hollywood characters are supposed to have all the adventures for everybody in America, while everybody in America sits in a dark room and watches them have them! Yes, until there's a war. That's when adventure becomes available to the masses! *Everyone's* dish, not only Gable's! Then the people in the dark room come out of the dark room to have some adventures themselves—Goody, goody!—It's our turn now, to go to the South Sea Island—to make a safari—to be exotic, far-off!—But I'm not patient. I don't want to wait till then. I'm tired of the *movies* and I am *about* to *move!*

JIM (*incredulously*).   Move?

TOM.   Yes.

JIM.   When?

TOM.   Soon!

JIM.   Where? Where? (*The music seems to answer the question, while* TOM *thinks it over. He searches in his pockets.*)

TOM.   I'm starting to boil inside. I know I seem dreamy, but inside—well, I'm boiling!—Whenever I pick up a shoe, I shudder a little thinking how short life is and what I am doing!—Whatever that means, I know it doesn't mean shoes—except as something to wear on a traveler's feet! (*Finds paper.*) Look—

JIM.   What?

TOM.   I'm a member.

JIM (*reading*).   The Union of Merchant Seamen.

TOM.   I paid my dues this month, instead of the light bill.

JIM.   You will regret it when they turn the lights off.

TOM.   I won't be here.

JIM.   How about your mother?

TOM.   I'm like my father. The bastard son of a bastard! See how he grins? And he's been absent going on sixteen years!

JIM.   You're just talking, you drip. How does your mother feel about it?

TOM.   Shh!—Here comes Mother! Mother is not acquainted with my plans!

AMANDA (*coming through the portieres*).   Where are you all?

TOM.   On the terrace, Mother. (*They start inside. She advances to them.* TOM *is distinctly shocked at her appearance. Even* JIM *blinks a little. He is making his first contact with girlish Southern vivacity and in spite of the night-school course in public speaking is somewhat thrown off the beam by the unexpected outlay of social charm. Certain responses are attempted by* JIM *but are swept aside by* AMANDA'S *gay laughter and chatter.* TOM *is embarrassed but after the first shock* JIM *reacts very warmly. He grins and chuckles, is altogether won over.*)

AMANDA (*coyly smiling, shaking her girlish ringlets*).   Well, well, well, so this is Mr. O'Connor. Introductions entirely unnecessary. I've heard so much about you from my boy. I finally said to him, Tom—good gracious!—why don't you bring this paragon to supper? I'd like to meet this nice young man at the warehouse!—Instead of just hearing him sing your praises so much! I don't know why my son is so stand-offish—that's not Southern behavior! Let's sit down and—I think we could stand a little more air in here! Tom, leave the door open. I felt a nice fresh breeze a moment ago. Where has it gone? Mmm, so warm already! And not quite summer, even. We're going to burn up when summer really gets started. However, we're having—we're having a very light supper. I think light things are better fo' this time of year. The same as light clothes are. Light clothes an' light food are what warm weather calls fo'. You know our blood gets so thick during th' winter—it takes a while fo' us to *adjust* ou'selves!—when the season changes . . . It's come so quick this year. I wasn't prepared. All of a sudden—heavens! Already summer!—I ran to the trunk an' pulled out this light dress—Terribly old! Historical almost! But feels so good—so good an'co-ol, y' know . . .

TOM.   Mother—

AMANDA.   Yes, honey?

TOM.   How about—supper?

AMANDA.   Honey, you go ask Sister if supper is ready! You know that Sister is in full charge of supper! Tell her you hungry boys are waiting for it. (*To* JIM) Have you met Laura?

JIM.   She—

AMANDA.   Let you in? Oh, good, you've met already! It's rare for a girl as sweet an' pretty as Laura to be domestic! But Laura, is, thank heavens, not only pretty but very domestic. I'm not at all. I never was a bit. I never could make a thing but angel-food cake. Well, in the south we had so many servants. Gone, gone, gone. All vestige of gracious living! Gone completely! I wasn't prepared for what the future brought me. All of my gentlemen callers were sons of planters and so of course I assumed that I would be married to one and raise my family on a large piece of land with plenty of servants. But man proposes—and woman accepts the proposal!—to vary that old, old saying° a little bit—I married no planter! I married a man who worked for the telephone company!—That gallantly smiling gentleman over

---

old . . . saying: "Man proposes, but God disposes" (Thomas à Kempis [1380–1471], *Imitation of Christ*)

there! (*Points to the picture.*) A telephone man who—fell in love with long-distance!—Now he travels and I don't even know where!—But what am I going on for about my—tribulations? Tell me yours—I hope you don't have any! Tom?

TOM (*returning*).   Yes, Mother.

AMANDA.   Is supper nearly ready?

TOM.   It looks to me like supper is on the table.

AMANDA.   Let me look—(*She rises prettily and looks through portieres.*) Oh, lovely!—But where is Sister?

TOM.   Laura is not feeling well and she says that she thinks she'd better not come to the table.

AMANDA.   What?—Nonsense!—Laura? Oh, Laura!

LAURA (*off stage, faintly*).   Yes, Mother.

AMANDA.   You really must come to the table. We won't be seated until you come to the table! Come in, Mr. O'Connor. You sit over there, and I'll—Laura? Laura Wingfield! You're keeping us waiting, honey! We can't say grace until you come to the table! (*The kitchenette door is pushed weakly open and* LAURA *comes in. She is obviously quite faint, her lips trembling, her eyes wide and staring. She moves unsteadily toward the table. Outside a summer storm is coming abruptly. The white curtains billow inward at the windows and there is a sorrowful murmur and deep blue dusk.* LAURA *suddenly stumbles—she catches at a chair with a faint moan.*)

TOM.   Laura!

AMANDA.   Laura! (*There is a clap of thunder. Despairingly*) Why, Laura, you *are* sick, darling! Tom, help your sister into the living room, dear! Sit in the living room, Laura—rest on the sofa. Well! (*To* JIM *as* TOM *helps his sister to the sofa in the living room*) Standing over the hot stove made her ill!—I told her that it was just too warm this evening, but—(*TOM comes back to the table.*) Is Laura all right now?

TOM.   Yes.

AMANDA.   What *is* that? Rain? A nice cool rain has come up! (*She gives the gentleman caller a frightened look.*) I think we may—have grace—now . . . (*TOM looks at her stupidly.*) Tom, honey—you say grace!

TOM.   Oh . . . "For these and all thy mercies—" (*They bow their heads,* AMANDA *stealing a nervous glance at* JIM. *In the living room,* LAURA, *stretched on the sofa, clenches her hand to her lips, to hold back a shuddering sob.*) God's Holy Name be praised—(*The scene dims out.*)

SCENE 7

Half an hour later. Dinner is just being finished in the dining room. LAURA *is still huddled upon the sofa, her feet drawn under her, her head resting on a pale blue pillow, her eyes wide and mysteriously watchful. The new floor lamp with its shade of rose-colored silk gives a soft, becoming light to her face, bringing out the fragile, unearthly prettiness which usually escapes attention. There is a steady murmur of rain, but it is slackening and soon stops; the air outside becomes pale and luminous as the moon breaks out. A moment after the curtain rises, the lights in both rooms flicker and go out.*

JIM.   Hey, there, Mr. Light Bulb!

AMANDA (*laughs nervously*).   Where was Moses when the lights went out? Ha-ha. Do you know the answer to that one, Mr. O'Connor?

JIM.   No, Ma'am, what's the answer?

AMANDA.   In the dark! (JIM *laughs appreciatively.*) Everybody sit still. I'll light the candles. Isn't it lucky we have them on the table? Where's a match? Which of you gentlemen can provide a match?

JIM.   Here.

AMANDA.   Thank you, sir.

JIM.   Not at all, Ma'am!

AMANDA.   I guess the fuse has burnt out. Mr. O'Connor, can you tell a burnt-out fuse? I know I can't and Tom is a total loss when it comes to mechanics. (*They rise from the table and go into the kitchenette, from where their voices are heard.*) Oh, be careful you don't bump into something. We don't want our gentleman caller to break his neck. Now wouldn't that be a fine howdy-do?

JIM.   Ha-ha! Where is the fuse box?

AMANDA.   Right here next to the stove. Can you see anything?

JIM.   Just a minute.

AMANDA.   Isn't electricity a mysterious thing? Wasn't it Benjamin Franklin who tied a key to a kite? We live in such a mysterious universe, don't we? Some people say that science clears up all the mysteries for us. In my opinion it only creates more! Have you found it yet?

JIM.   No, Ma'am. All these fuses look okay to me.

AMANDA.   Tom!

TOM.   Yes, Mother?

AMANDA.   That light bill I gave you several days ago. The one I told you we got the notices about?

TOM.   Oh—Yeah.

AMANDA.   You didn't neglect to pay it by chance?

TOM.   Why, I—

AMANDA.   Didn't! I might have known it!

JIM.   Shakespeare probably wrote a poem on that light bill, Mrs. Wingfield.

AMANDA.   I might have known better than to trust him with it! There's such a high price for negligence in this world!

JIM.   Maybe the poem will win a ten-dollar prize.

AMANDA.   We'll just have to spend the remainder of the evening in the nineteenth century, before Mr. Edison made the Mazda lamp!

JIM.   Candlelight is my favorite kind of light.

AMANDA.   That shows you're romantic! But that's no excuse for Tom. Well, we got through dinner. Very considerate of them to let us get through dinner before they plunged us into everlasting darkness, wasn't it, Mr. O'Connor?

JIM.   Ha-ha!

AMANDA.   Tom, as a penalty for your carelessness you can help me with the dishes.

JIM.   Let me give you a hand.

AMANDA.   Indeed you will not!

JIM.   I ought to be good for something.

AMANDA.   Good for something? (*Her tone is rhapsodic.*) You? Why, Mr. O'Connor nobody, *nobody's* given me this much entertainment in years—as you have!

JIM.   Aw, now, Mrs. Wingfield!

AMANDA.   I'm not exaggerating, not one bit! But Sister is all by her lonesome. You go keep her company in the parlor! I'll give you this lovely old candelabrum that used to be on the altar at the church of the Heavenly Rest. It was melted a little out of shape when the church burnt down. Lightning struck it one spring. Gypsy Jones was holding a revival at the time and he intimated that the church was destroyed because the Episcopalians gave card parties.

JIM.   Ha-ha.

AMANDA.   And how about you coaxing Sister to drink a little wine? I think it would be good for her! Can you carry both at once?

JIM.   Sure. I'm Superman!

AMANDA.   Now, Thomas, get into this apron! (*JIM comes into the dining room, carrying the candelabrum, its candles lighted, in one hand and a glass of wine in the other. The door of the kitchenette swings closed on* AMANDA'S *gay laughter; the flickering light approaches the portieres.* LAURA *sits up nervously as he enters. Her speech at first is low and breathless from the almost intolerable strain of being alone with a stranger. At first, before* JIM'S *warmth overcomes her paralyzing shyness,* LAURA'S *voice is thin and breathless, as though she had just run up a steep flight of stairs.* JIM'S *attitude is gently humorous. While the incident is apparently unimportant, it is to* LAURA *the climax of her secret life.*)

JIM.   Hello, there, Laura.

LAURA (*faintly*).   Hello. (*She clears her throat.*)

JIM.   How are you feeling now? Better?

LAURA.   Yes. Yes, thank you.

JIM.   This is for you. A little dandelion wine. (*He extends it toward her with extravagant gallantry.*)

LAURA.   Thank you.

JIM.   Drink it—but don't get drunk! (*He laughs heartily.* LAURA *takes the glass uncertainly, laughs shyly.*) Where shall I set the candles?

LAURA.   Oh—oh, anywhere . . .

JIM.   How about here on the floor? Any objections?

LAURA.   No.

JIM.   I'll spread a newspaper to catch the drippings. I like to sit on the floor. Mind if I do?

LAURA.   Oh, no.

JIM.   Give me a pillow?

LAURA.   What?

JIM.   A pillow!

LAURA.   Oh . . . (*Hands him one quickly.*)

JIM.   How about you? Don't you like to sit on the floor?

LAURA.   Oh—yes.

JIM.   Why don't you, then?

LAURA.   I—will.

JIM.   Take a pillow! (LAURA *does. Sits on the other side of the candelabrum.* JIM *crosses his legs and smiles engagingly at her.*) I can't hardly see you sitting way over there.

LAURA.   I can—see you.

JIM.   I know, but that's not fair. I'm in the limelight. (LAURA *moves her pillow closer.*) Good! Now I can see you! Comfortable?

LAURA.   Yes.

JIM.   So am I. Comfortable as a cow! Will you have some gum?

LAURA.   No, thank you.

JIM.   I think I will indulge, with your permission. (*He musingly unwraps it and holds it up.*) Think of the fortune made by the guy that invented the first piece of chewing gum. Amazing, huh? The Wrigley Building is one of the sights of Chicago.—I saw it summer before last when I went up to the Century of Progress.° Did you take in the Century of Progress?

LAURA.   No, I didn't.

JIM.   Well, it was quite a wonderful exposition. What impressed me most was the Hall of Science. Gives you an idea of what the future will be in America, even more wonderful than the present time is! (*There is a pause.* JIM *smiles at her.*) Your brother tells me you're shy. Is that right, Laura?

LAURA.   I—don't know.

JIM.   I judge you to be an old-fashioned type of girl. Well, I think that's a pretty good type to be. Hope you don't think I'm being too personal—do you?

LAURA (*hastily, out of embarrassment*).   I believe I *will* take a piece of gum, if you—don't mind. (*Clearing her throat.*) Mr. O'Connor, have you—kept up with your singing?

JIM.   Singing? Me?

Century of Progress: World's Fair in Chicago, 1933–1934

LAURA.   Yes. I remember what a beautiful voice you had.

JIM.   When did you hear me sing?

(*Voice off stage in the pause:*

> O blow, ye winds, heigh-ho,
> A-roving I will go!
> I'm off to my love
> With a boxing glove—
> Ten thousand miles away!)

JIM.   You say you've heard me sing?

LAURA.   Oh, yes! Yes, very often . . . I—don't suppose—you remember me—at all?

JIM (*smiling doubtfully*).   You know I have an idea I've seen you before. I had that idea soon as you opened the door. It seems almost like I was about to remember your name. But the name that I started to call you—wasn't a name! And so I stopped myself before I said it.

LAURA.   Wasn't it—Blue Roses?

JIM (*springs up. Grinning*).   Blue Roses!—My gosh, yes—Blue Roses! That's what I had on my tongue when you opened the door! Isn't it funny what tricks your memory plays? I didn't connect you with high school somehow or other. But that's where it was; it was high school. I didn't even know you were Shakespeare's sister! Gosh, I'm sorry.

LAURA.   I didn't expect you to. You—barely knew me!

JIM.   But we did have a speaking acquaintance, huh?

LAURA.   Yes, we—spoke to each other.

JIM.   When did you recognize me?

LAURA.   Oh, right away!

JIM.   Soon as I came in the door?

LAURA.   When I heard your name I thought it was probably you. I knew that Tom used to know you a little in high school. So when you came in the door—well, then I was—sure.

JIM.   Why didn't you *say* something, then?

LAURA (*breathlessly*).   I didn't know what to say, I was—too surprised!

JIM.   For goodness sakes! You know, this sure is funny!

LAURA.   Yes! Yes, isn't it, though . . .

JIM.   Didn't we have a class in something together?

LAURA.   Yes, we did.

JIM.   What class was that?

LAURA.   It was—singing—chorus!

JIM.   Aw!

LAURA.   I sat across the aisle from you in the Aud.

JIM.   Aw.

LAURA.   Mondays, Wednesdays and Fridays.

JIM.   Now I remember—you always came in late.

LAURA.   Yes, it was so hard for me getting upstairs. I had that brace on my leg—it clumped so loud!

JIM.   I never heard any clumping.

LAURA (*wincing at the recollection*).   To me it sounded like—thunder!

JIM.   Well, well, well, I never even noticed.

LAURA.   And everybody was seated before I came in. I had to walk in front of all those people. My seat was in the back row. I had to go clumping all the way up the aisle with everyone watching!

JIM.   You shouldn't have been self-conscious.

LAURA.   I know, but I was. It was always such a relief when the singing started.

JIM.   Aw, yes, I've placed you now! I used to call you Blue Roses. How was it that I got started calling you that?

LAURA.   I was out of school a little while with pleurosis. When I came back you asked me what was the matter. I said I had pleurosis—you thought I said Blue Roses. That's what you always called me after that!

JIM.   I hope you didn't mind.

LAURA.   Oh, no—I liked it. You see, I wasn't acquainted with many—people . . .

JIM.   As I remember you sort of stuck by yourself.

LAURA.   I—I—never have had much luck at—making friends.

JIM.   I don't see why you wouldn't.

LAURA.   Well, I—started out badly.

JIM.   You mean being—

LAURA.   Yes, it sort of—stood between me—

JIM.   You shouldn't have let it!

LAURA.   I know, but it did, and—

JIM.   You were shy with people!

LAURA.   I tried not to be but never could—

JIM.   Overcome it?

LAURA.   No, I—I never could!

JIM.   I guess being shy is something you have to work out of kind of gradually.

LAURA (*sorrowfully*).   Yes—I guess it—

JIM.   Takes time!

LAURA.   Yes—

JIM.   People are not so dreadful when you know them. That's what you have to remember! And everybody has problems, not just you, but practically everybody has got some problems. You think of yourself as having the only problems, as being the only one who is disappointed. But just look around you and you will see lots of people as disappointed as you are. For instance, I hoped when I was going to high school that I would be further along at this time, six years later, than I am now—You remember that wonderful write-up I had in *The Torch*?

LAURA.   Yes! (*She rises and crosses to table.*)

JIM.   It said I was bound to succeed in anything I went into! (LAURA *returns with the annual.*) Holy Jeez! *The Torch!* (*He accepts it reverently. They smile across it with mutual wonder.* LAURA *crouches beside him and they begin to turn through it.* LAURA'S *shyness is dissolving in his warmth.*)

LAURA.   Here you are in *The Pirates of Penzance!*°

JIM (*wistfully*).   I sang the baritone lead in that operetta.

LAURA (*raptly*).   So—*beautifully!*

JIM (*protesting*).   Aw—

LAURA.   Yes, yes—beautifully—beautifully!

JIM.   You heard me?

LAURA.   All three times!

JIM.   No!

LAURA.   Yes!

JIM.   All three performances?

LAURA (*looking down*).   Yes.

JIM.   Why?

LAURA.   I—wanted to ask you to—autograph my program.

JIM.   Why didn't you ask me to?

LAURA.   You were always surrounded by your own friends so much that I never had a chance to.

JIM.   You should have just—

LAURA.   Well, I—thought you might think I was—

JIM.   Thought I might think you was—what?

LAURA.   Oh—

JIM (*with reflective relish*).   I was beleaguered by females in those days.

LAURA.   You were terribly popular!

JIM.   Yeah—

LAURA.   You had such a—friendly way—

JIM.   I was spoiled in high school.

LAURA.   Everybody—liked you!

JIM.   Including you?

LAURA.   I—yes, I—I did, too—(*She gentley closes the book in her lap.*)

JIM.   Well, well, well!—Give me that program, Laura. (*She hands it to him. He signs it with a flourish.*) There you are—better late than never!

LAURA.   Oh, I—what a—surprise!

JIM.   My signature isn't worth very much right now. But some day—maybe—it will increase in value! Being disappointed is one thing and being discouraged is something else. I am disappointed but I am not discouraged. I'm twenty-three years old. How old are you?

LAURA.   I'll be twenty-four in June.

JIM.   That's not old age!

LAURA.   No, but—

JIM.   You finished high school?

LAURA (*with difficulty*).   I didn't go back.

JIM.   You mean you dropped out?

The . . . Penzance: comic operetta (1880) by Gilbert and Sullivan

LAURA.   I made bad grades in my final examinations. (*She rises and replaces the book and the program. Her voice is strained.*) How is—Emily Meisenbach getting along?

JIM.   Oh, that kraut-head!

LAURA.   Why do you call her that?

JIM.   That's what she was.

LAURA.   You're not still—going with her?

JIM.   I never see her.

LAURA.   It said in the Personal Section that you were—engaged!

JIM.   I know, but I wasn't impressed by that—propaganda!

LAURA.   It wasn't—the truth?

JIM.   Only in Emily's optimistic opinion!

LAURA.   Oh—(JIM *lights a cigarette and leans indolently back on his elbows smiling at* LAURA *with a warmth and charm which lights her inwardly with altar candles. She remains by the table and turns in her hands a piece of glass to cover her tumult.*)

JIM (*after several reflective puffs on a cigarette*).   What have you done since high school? (*She seems not to hear him.*) Huh? (LAURA *looks up.*) I said what have you done since high school, Laura?

LAURA.   Nothing much.

JIM.   You must have been doing something these six long years.

LAURA.   Yes.

JIM.   Well, then, such as what?

LAURA.   I took a business course at business college—

JIM.   How did that work out?

LAURA.   Well, not very—well—I had to drop out, it gave me—indigestion—

JIM (*laughs gently*).   What are you doing now?

LAURA.   I don't do anything—much. Oh, please don't think I sit around doing nothing! My glass collection takes up a good deal of time. Glass is something you have to take good care of.

JIM.   What did you say—about glass?

LAURA.   Collection I said—I have one—(*She clears her throat and turns away again, acutely shy.*)

JIM (*abruptly*).   You know what I judge to be the trouble with you? Inferiority complex! Know what that is? That's what they call it when someone low-rates himself! I understand it because I had it, too. Although my case was not so aggravated as yours seems to be. I had it until I took up public speaking, developed my voice, and learned that I had an aptitude for science. Before that time I never thought of myself as being outstanding in any way whatsoever! Now I've never made a regular study of it, but I have a friend who says I can analyze people better than doctors that make a profession of it. I don't claim that to be necessarily true, but I can sure guess a person's psychology, Laura! (*Takes out his gum.*) Excuse me, Laura. I always take it out when the flavor is gone. I'll use this scrap of paper to wrap it in. I know how it is to get it stuck on a shoe. Yep—that's what I judge to be your principal trouble. A lack of confidence in yourself as a person. You don't have the proper amount of faith in yourself. I'm basing that fact on a number of your remarks and also on certain observations I've made. For instance that clumping you thought was so awful in high school. You say that you even dreaded to walk into class. You see what you did? You dropped out of school, you gave up an education because of a clump, which as far as I know was practically non-existent! A little physical defect is what you have. Hardly noticeable even! Magnified thousands of times by imagination! You know what my strong advice to you is? Think of yourself as *superior* in some way!

LAURA.   In what way would I think?

JIM.   Why, man alive, Laura! Just look about you a little. What do you see? A world full of common people! All of 'em born and all of 'em going to die! Which of them has one-tenth of your good points! Or mine! Or anyone else's, as far as that goes—Gosh! Everybody excels in some one thing. Some in many! (*Unconsciously glances at himself in the mirror.*) All you've got to do is discover in *what!* Take me, for instance. (*He adjusts his tie at the mirror.*) My interest happens to lie in electro-dynamics. I'm taking a course in radio engineering at night school, Laura, on top of a fairly responsible job at the warehouse. I'm taking that course and studying public speaking.

LAURA.   Ohhhh.

JIM.   Because I believe in the future of television! (*Turning back to her.*) I wish to be ready to go up right along with it. Therefore I'm planning to get in on the ground floor. In fact I've already made the right connections and all that remains is for the industry itself to get under way! Full steam—(*His eyes are starry.*) Knowledge—Zzzzzp! *Money*—Zzzzzp!—*Power!* That's the cycle democracy is built on! (*His attitude is convincingly dynamic.* LAURA *stares at him, even her shyness eclipsed in her absolute wonder. He suddenly grins.*) I guess you think I think a lot of myself?

LAURA.   No—o-o-o, I—

JIM.   Now how about you? Isn't there something you take more interest in than anything else?

LAURA.   Well, I do—as I said—have my—glass collection—(*A peal of girlish laughter from the kitchenette.*)

JIM.   I'm not right sure I know what you're talking about. What kind of glass is it?

LAURA.   Little articles of it, they're ornaments mostly! Most of them are little animals made out of glass, the tiniest little animals in the world. Mother calls them a glass menagerie! Here's an example of one, if you'd like to see it! This one is one of the oldest. It's nearly thirteen. (*Music: "The Glass Menagerie."* JIM *stretches out his hand.*) Oh, be careful—if you breathe, it breaks!

JIM.   I'd better not take it. I'm pretty clumsy with things.

LAURA.   Go on, I trust you with him! (*Places it in his palm.*) There now—you're holding him gently! Hold him over the light, he loves the light! You see how the light shines through him?

JIM.   It sure does shine!

LAURA.   I shouldn't be partial, but he is my favorite one.

JIM.   What kind of thing is this one supposed to be?

LAURA.   Haven't you noticed the single horn on his forehead?

JIM.   A unicorn, huh?

LAURA.   Mmm-hmmm!

JIM.   Unicorns, aren't they extinct in the modern world?

LAURA.   I know!

JIM.   Poor little fellow, he must feel sort of lonesome.

LAURA (*smiling*).   Well, if he does he doesn't complain about it. He stays on a shelf with some horses that don't have horns and all of them seem to get along nicely together.

JIM.   How do you know?

LAURA (*lightly*).   I haven't heard any arguments among them!

JIM (*grinning*).   No arguments, huh? Well, that's a pretty good sign! Where shall I set him?

LAURA.   Put him on the table. They all like a change of scenery once in a while!

JIM (*stretching*).   Well, well, well, well—Look how big my shadow is when I stretch!

LAURA.   Oh, oh, yes—it stretches across the ceiling!

JIM (*crossing to door*).   I think it's stopped raining. (*Opens fire-escape door.*) Where does the music come from?

LAURA.   From the Paradise Dance Hall across the alley.

JIM.   How about cutting the rug a little, Miss Wingfield?

LAURA.   Oh, I—

JIM.   Or is your program filled up? Let me have a look at it. (*Grasps imaginary card.*) Why, every dance is taken! I'll just have to scratch some out. (*Waltz music: "La Golondrina."*) Ahhh, a waltz! (*He executes some sweeping turns by himself then holds his arms toward* LAURA.)

LAURA (*breathlessly*).   I—can't dance!

JIM.   There you go, that inferiority stuff!

LAURA.   I've never danced in my life!

JIM.   Come on, try!

LAURA.   Oh, but I'd step on you!

JIM.   I'm not made out of glass.

LAURA.   How—how—how do we start?

JIM.   Just leave it to me. You hold your arms out a little.

LAURA.   Like this?

JIM.   A bit higher. Right. Now don't tighten up, that's the main thing about it—relax.

LAURA (*laughing breathlessly*).   It's hard not to.

JIM.   Okay.

LAURA.   I'm afraid you can't budge me.

JIM.   What do you bet I can't? (*He swings her into motion.*)

LAURA.   Goodness, yes, you can!

JIM.   Let yourself go, now, Laura, just let yourself go.

LAURA.   I'm—

JIM.   Come on!

LAURA.   Trying!

JIM.   Not so stiff—Easy does it!

LAURA.   I know but I'm—

JIM.   Loosen th' backbone! There now, that's a lot better.

LAURA.   Am I?

JIM.   Lots, lots better! (*He moves her about the room in a clumsy waltz.*)

LAURA.   Oh, my!

JIM.   Ha-ha!

LAURA.   Oh, my goodness!

JIM.   Ha-ha-ha! (*They suddenly bump into the table.* JIM *stops.*) What did we hit on?

LAURA.   Table.

JIM.   Did something fall off it? I think—

LAURA.   Yes.

JIM.   I hope it wasn't the little glass horse with the horn!

LAURA.   Yes.

JIM.   Aw, aw, aw. Is it broken?

LAURA.   Now it is just like all the other horses.

JIM.   It's lost its—

LAURA.   Horn! It doesn't matter. Maybe it's a blessing in disguise.

JIM.   You'll never forgive me. I bet that was your favorite piece of glass.

LAURA.   I don't have favorites much. It's no tragedy, Freckles. Glass breaks so easily. No matter how careful you are. The traffic jars the shelves and things fall off them.

JIM.   Still I'm awfully sorry that I was the cause.

LAURA (*smiling*).   I'll just imagine he had an operation. The horn was removed to make him feel less—freakish! (*They both laugh.*) Now he will feel more at home with the other horses, the ones that don't have horns . . .

JIM.   Ha-ha, that's very funny! (*Suddenly serious.*) I'm glad to see that you have a sense of humor. You know—you're—well—very different! Surprisingly different from anyone else I know! (*His voice becomes soft and hesitant with a genuine feeling.*) Do you mind me telling you that? (LAURA *is abashed beyond speech.*) I mean it in a nice way . . . (LAURA *nods shyly, looking away.*) You make me feel sort of—I don't know how to put it! I'm usually pretty good at expressing things, but—this is something that I don't know how to say! (LAURA *touches her throat and clears it—turns the broken unicorn in her hands. His voice becomes softer.*) Has anyone ever told you that you were pretty? (*Pause: music.* LAURA *looks up slowly, with wonder, and shakes her head.*)

Well, you are! In a very different way from anyone else. And all the nicer because of the difference, too. (*His voice becomes low and husky.* LAURA *turns away, nearly faint with the novelty of her emotions.*) I wish that you were my sister. I'd teach you to have some confidence in yourself. The different people are not like other people, but being different is nothing to be ashamed of. Because other people are not such wonderful people. They're one hundred times one thousand. You're one times one! They walk all over the earth. You just stay here. They're common as—weeds, but—you—well, you're—*Blue Roses!* (*Music changes.*)

LAURA.   But blue is wrong for—roses . . .

JIM.   It's right for you!—You're—pretty!

LAURA.   In what respect am I pretty?

JIM.   In all respects—believe me! Your eyes—your hair—are pretty! Your hands are pretty! (*He catches hold of her hand.*) You think I'm making this up because I'm invited to dinner and have to be nice. Oh, I could do that! I could put on an act for you, Laura, and say lots of things without being very sincere. But this time I am. I'm talking to you sincerely. I happened to notice you had this inferiority complex that keeps you from feeling comfortable with people. Somebody needs to build your confidence up and make you proud instead of shy and turning away and—blushing—Somebody—ought to—Ought to—*kiss* you, Laura! (*His hand slips slowly up her arm to her shoulder. Music swells tumultuously. He suddenly turns her about and kisses her on the lips. When he releases her,* LAURA *sinks on the sofa with a bright, dazed look.* JIM *backs away and fishes in his pocket for a cigarette.*) Stumble-john! (*He lights a cigarette, avoiding her look. There is a peal of girlish laughter from* AMANDA *in the kitchenette.* LAURA *slowly raises and opens her hand. It still contains the little broken glass animal. She looks at it with a tender, bewildered expression.*)

Stumble-john! I shouldn't have done that—That was way off beam. You don't smoke, do you? (*She looks up, smiling, not hearing the question. He sits beside her a little gingerly. She looks at him speechlessly—waiting. He coughs decorously and moves a little farther aside as he considers the situation and senses her feelings, dimly, with perturbation. He speaks gently.*) Would you—care for a—mint? (*She doesn't seem to hear him but her look grows brighter even.*) Peppermint—Life-Saver? My pocket's a regular drug store—wherever I go . . . (*He pops a mint in his mouth. Then gulps and decides to make a clean breast of it. He speaks slowly and gingerly.*) Laura, you know, if I had a sister like you, I'd do the same thing as Tom. I'd bring out fellows and—introduce her to them. The right type of boys of a type to—appreciate her. Only—well—he made a mistake with me. Maybe I've got no call to be saying this. That may not have been the idea in having me over. But what if it was? There's nothing wrong about that. The only trouble is that in my case—I'm not in a situation to—do the right thing. I can't take down your number and say I'll phone. I can't call up next week and—ask for a date. I thought I had better explain the situation in case you—misunderstood it and—hurt your feelings . . . (*Pause. Slowly, very slowly,* LAURA'S *look changes, her eyes returning slowly from his to the ornament in her palm.* AMANDA *utters another gay laugh in the kitchenette.*)

LAURA (*faintly*).   You—won't—call again?

JIM.   No, Laura, I can't. (*He rises from the sofa.*) As I was just explaining. I've—got strings on me. Laura, I've—been going steady! I go out all of the time with a girl named Betty. She's a home-girl like you, and Catholic, and Irish, and in a great many ways we—get along fine. I met her last summer on a moonlight boat trip up the river to Alton, on the *Majestic.* Well—right away from the start it was—love! (LAURA *sways slightly forward and grips the arm of the sofa. He fails to notice, now enrapt in his own comfortable being.*) Being in love has made a new man of me! (*Leaning stiffly forward, clutching the arm of the sofa,* LAURA *struggles visibly with her storm. But* JIM *is oblivious; she is a long way off.*) The power of love is really pretty tremendous! Love is something that—changes the whole world, Laura! (*The storm abates a little and* LAURA *leans back. He notices her again.*) It happened that Betty's aunt took sick, she got a wire and had to go to Centralia. So Tom—when he asked me to dinner—I naturally just accepted the invitation, not knowing that you—that he—that I—(*He stops awkwardly.*) Huh—I'm a stumblejohn! (*He flops back on the sofa. The holy candles in the altar of* LAURA'S *face have been snuffed out. There is a look of almost infinite desolation.* JIM *glances at her uneasily.*) I wish that you would—say something. (*She bites her lip which was trembling and then bravely smiles. She opens her hand again on the broken glass ornament. Then she gently takes his hand and raises it level with her own. She carefully places the unicorn in the palm of his hand, then pushes his fingers closed upon it.*) What are you—doing that for? You want me to have him— Laura? (*She nods.*) What for?

LAURA.   A—souvenir . . . (*She rises unsteadily and crouches beside the victrola to wind it up. At this moment* AMANDA *rushes brightly back into the living room. She bears a pitcher of fruit punch in an old-fashioned cut-glass pitcher and a plate of macaroons. The plate has a gold border and poppies painted on it.*)

AMANDA.   Well, well, well! Isn't the air delightful after the shower? I've made you children a little liquid refreshment. (*She turns gaily to* JIM.) Jim, do you know that song about lemonade?

> "Lemonade, lemonade,
> Made in the shade and stirred with a spade—
> Good enough for any old maid!"

JIM (*uneasily*).   Ha-ha! No—I never heard it.

AMANDA.   Why, Laura! You look so serious!

JIM.   We were having a serious conversation.

AMANDA.   Good! Now you're better acquainted!

JIM (*uncertainly*).   Ha-ha! Yes.

AMANDA.   You modern young people are much more serious-minded than my generation. I was so gay as a girl!

JIM.   You haven't changed, Mrs. Wingfield.

AMANDA.   Tonight I'm rejuvenated! The gaiety of the occasion, Mr. O'Connor! (*She tosses her head with a peal of laughter. Spills lemonade.*) Oooo! I'm baptizing myself!

JIM.   Here—let me—

AMANDA (*setting the pitcher down*).   There now. I discovered we had some maraschino cherries. I dumped them in, juice and all!

JIM.   You shouldn't have gone to that trouble, Mrs. Wingfield.

AMANDA.   Trouble, trouble? Why, it was loads of fun! Didn't you hear me cutting up in the kitchen? I bet your ears were burning! I told Tom how outdone with him I was for keeping you to himself so long a time! He should have brought you over much, much sooner! Well, now that you've found your way, I want you to be a frequent caller! Not just occasional but all the time. Oh, we're going to have a lot of gay times together! I see them coming! Mmm, just breathe that air! So fresh, and the moon's so pretty! I'll skip back out—I know where my place is when young folks are having a—serious conversation!

JIM.   Oh, don't go out, Mrs. Wingfield. The fact of the matter is I've got to be going.

AMANDA.   Going, now? You're joking! Why, it's only the shank of the evening, Mr. O'Connor!

JIM.   Well, you know how it is.

AMANDA.   You mean you're a young workingman and have to keep workingmen's hours. We'll let you off early tonight. But only on the condition that next time you stay later.

What's the best night for you? Isn't Saturday night the best night for you workingmen?

JIM.   I have a couple of time-clocks to punch, Mrs. Wingfield. One at morning, another at night!

AMANDA.   My, but you *are* ambitious! You work at night, too?

JIM.   No, Ma'am, not work but—Betty! (*He crosses deliberately to pick up his hat. The band at the Paradise Dance Hall goes into a tender waltz.*)

AMANDA.   Betty? Betty? Who's—Betty! (*There is an ominous cracking sound in the sky.*)

JIM.   Oh, just a girl. The girl I go steady with! (*He smiles charmingly. The sky falls.*)

AMANDA (*a long-drawn exhalation*).   Ohhhh. . . . Is it a serious romance, Mr. O'Connor?

JIM.   We're going to be married the second Sunday in June.

AMANDA.   Ohhhh—how nice! Tom didn't mention that you were engaged to be married.

JIM.   The cat's not out of the bag at the warehouse yet. You know how they are. They call you Romeo and stuff like that. (*He stops at the oval mirror to put on his hat. He carefully shapes the brim and the crown to give a discreetly dashing effect.*) It's been a wonderful evening, Mrs. Wingfield. I guess this is what they mean by Southern hospitality.

AMANDA.   It really wasn't anything at all.

JIM.   I hope it don't seem like I'm rushing off. But I promised Betty I'd pick her up at the Wabash depot, an' by the time I get my jalopy down there her train'll be in. Some women are pretty upset if you keep 'em waiting.

AMANDA. Yes, I know—The tyranny of women! (*Extends her hand.*) Good-bye, Mr. O'Connor. I wish you luck—and happiness—and success! All three of them, and so does Laura—Don't you Laura?

LAURA. Yes!

JIM (*taking her hand*). Good-bye Laura. I'm certainly going to treasure that souvenir. And don't you forget the good advice I gave you. (*Raises his voice to a cheery shout.*) So long, Shakespeare! Thanks again, ladies—Good night! (*He grins and ducks jauntily out. Still bravely grimacing,* AMANDA *closes the door on the gentleman caller. Then she turns back to the room with a puzzled expression. She and* LAURA *don't dare to face each other.* LAURA *crouches beside the victrola to wind it.*)

AMANDA (*faintly*). Things have a way of turning out so badly. I don't believe that I would play the victrola. Well, well—well—Our gentleman caller was engaged to be married! (*She raises her voice.*) Tom!

TOM (*from the kitchenette*). Yes, Mother?

AMANDA. Come in here a minute. I want to tell you something awfully funny.

TOM (*enters with a macaroon and a glass of lemonade*). Has the gentleman caller gotten away already?

AMANDA. The gentleman caller has made an early departure. What a wonderful joke you played on us!

TOM. How do you mean?

AMANDA. You didn't mention that he was engaged to be married.

TOM. Jim? Engaged?

AMANDA. That's what he just informed us.

TOM. I'll be jiggered! I didn't know about that.

AMANDA. That seems very peculiar.

TOM. What's peculiar about it?

AMANDA. Didn't you call him your best friend down at the warehouse?

TOM. He is, but how did I know?

AMANDA. It seems extremely peculiar that you wouldn't know your best friend was going to be married!

TOM. The warehouse is where I work, not where I know things about people!

AMANDA. You don't know things anywhere! You live in a dream; you manufacture illusions! (*He crosses to the door.*) Where are you going?

TOM. I'm going to the movies.

AMANDA. That's right, now that you've had us make such fools of ourselves. The effort, the preparations, all the expense! The new floor lamp, the rug, the clothes for Laura! All for what? To entertain some other girls' fiancé! Go to the movies, go! Don't think about us, a mother deserted, an unmarried sister who's crippled and has no job! Don't let anything interfere with your selfish pleasure! Just go, go, go—to the movies!

TOM. All right, I will! The more you shout about my selfishness to me the quicker I'll go, and I won't go to the movies!

AMANDA.   Go, then! Then go to the moon—you selfish dreamer!

(TOM *smashes his glass on the floor. He plunges out of the fire-escape, slamming the door.* LAURA *screams in fright. The dance-hall music becomes louder.* TOM *goes to the rail and grips it desperately, lifting his face in the chill white moonlight penetrating the narrow abyss of the alley.*

(TOM'S *closing speech is timed with what is happening inside the house. The interior scene is played as though viewed through soundproof glass.* AMANDA *appears to be making a comforting speech to* LAURA *who is huddled upon the sofa. Now that we cannot hear the mother's speech, her silliness is gone and she has dignity and tragic beauty.* LAURA'S *dark hair hides her face until at the end of the speech she lifts it to smile at her mother.* AMANDA'S *gestures are slow and graceful, almost dance-like, as she comforts her daughter. At the end of her speech she glances a moment at the father's picture—then withdraws through the portieres. At the close of* TOM'S *speech,* LAURA *blows out the candles, ending the play.*)

TOM.   I didn't go to the moon, I went much further—for time is the longest distance between two places—Not long after that I was fired for writing a poem on the lid of a shoe-box. I left Saint Louis. I descended the steps of this fire-escape for a last time and followed, from then on, in my father's footsteps, attempting to find in motion what was lost in space—I traveled around a great deal. The cities swept about me like dead leaves, leaves that were brightly colored but torn away from the branches. I would have stopped, but I was pursued by something. It always came upon me unawares, taking me altogether by surprise. Perhaps it was a familiar bit of music. Perhaps it was only a piece of transparent glass—Perhaps I am walking along a street at night, in some strange city, before I have found companions. I pass the lighted window of a shop where perfume is sold. The window is filled with pieces of colored glass, tiny transparent bottles in delicate colors, like bits of a shattered rainbow. Then all at once my sister touches my shoulder. I turn around and look into her eyes . . . Oh, Laura, Laura, I tried to leave you behind me, but I am more faithful than I intended to be! I reach for a cigarette, I cross the street, I run into the movies or a bar, I buy a drink, I speak to the nearest stranger—anything that can blow your candles out! (LAURA *bends over the candles.*) For nowadays the world is lit by lightning! Blow out your candles, Laura—and so goodbye . . .

(*She blows the candles out.*)

QUESTIONS

1. In presenting Scene 1, the author says: "The scene is memory and is therefore nonrealistic." To whose memory does he refer? Why should memory be nonrealistic? List the different ways in which the play is nonrealistic. What, according to Tom in his opening speech, is the ultimate aim of this nonrealistic method of presentation?

2. How does the kind of language Tom uses as a narrator differ from that he uses as a character? What would happen to the play if Tom used the first kind of language throughout?

3. What is Tom's dilemma? Why is he always quarreling with his mother? What is his attitude toward Laura? Why does he finally leave? Does he ever resolve his dilemma?

4. What qualities possessed by Tom, and by him alone, make him the proper narrator of the play?

5. Laura is the pivotal character in the play, as evidenced by its title and by the fact that the main actions of the play revolve around her. What are the symptoms and causes of her mental condition? Can they all be traced to her physical defect? What qualities make her a sympathetic character? How does her relationship with her mother differ from Tom's?

6. What symbolic meanings has Laura's glass menagerie? What, especially, is symbolized by the unicorn? How and why does her reaction to Jim's breaking the unicorn differ from her reaction to Tom's breaking several pieces at the end of Scene 3? Why does she give the broken unicorn to Jim as a souvenir? What future do you predict for her? What symbolism has her blowing out the candles at the end of the play?

7. The author tells us (page 1025) that "Amanda, having failed to establish contact with reality, continues to live vitally in her illusions." What part of this statement could be applied to Laura as well? What part could not? What are the chief instances in the play of Amanda's having lost "contact with reality"? What are her chief illusions? What are her strengths? How is she both cruel and tender with her children? What qualities has she in common with Jim, the gentleman caller? Why do you suppose her husband left her?

8. The author describes Jim O'Connor as "a nice, ordinary, young man" (page 1025). Tom (in Scene 1) describes him as "the most realistic character, being an emissary from that world of reality that we were set apart from." In what ways is Jim "nice"? In what ways is he "ordinary"? In what ways and in what sense is he more "realistic" than the Wingfields? Does this mean that he is without delusions? What would you predict for his future? Of what is he symbolic?

9. Account for Jim's treatment of Laura in Scene 7.

10. What trait do Laura, Amanda, and Tom all share, which makes Jim more realistic than they? Explain the dramatic irony in Amanda's remark to Tom, in their final dialogue, "You don't know things anywhere! You live in a dream; you manufacture illusions!"

11. What respective claims have Tom, Laura, and Amanda for being considered the protagonist of the play? For which character would it be most crucial to the success or failure of a production to obtain a highly accomplished actor or actress? Why?

12. The play is set in the 1930s. Of what significance are the many references throughout the play to its social and historical background? How are these larger events and the Wingfields' domestic lives related?

13. The play is divided into seven scenes. If you were to produce it with one intermission, where would you put the intermission? For what reasons?

Christopher Durang

Naomi in the Living Room

CHARACTERS

NAOMI
JOHN
JOHNNA

A living room. Enter NAOMI, *followed by* JOHN *and* JOHNNA, *an attractive young couple.* JOHN *has a mustache and is dressed in a suit and tie.* JOHNNA *is wearing a dress with a string of pearls.* NAOMI, *though, looks odd.* NAOMI *plants herself somewhere definitive—by the mantelpiece, for instance—and gestures out toward the room.*

NAOMI.   And this is the living room. And you've seen the dining room and the bedroom and the bathroom.

JOHN.   Yes, I know. I used to live here.

NAOMI.   The dining room is where we dine. The bedroom is where we go to bed. The bathroom is where we take a bath. The kitchen is where we . . . cook. That doesn't sound right. The kitchen is where we . . . collect kitsch. Hummel figurines, Statue of Liberty salt and pepper shakers, underpants that say Home of the Whopper, and so on. Kitsch. The kitchen is where we look at kitsch. The laundry room is where we do laundry. And the living room is where Hubert and I do all of our living. Our major living. So that's the living room.

JOHNNA.   What do you use the cellar for?

NAOMI (*suspicious*).   What?

JOHNNA.   What do you use the cellar for?

NAOMI.   We use the cellar to . . . we go to the cellar to . . . replenish our cells. We go to the attic to . . . practice our tics, our facial tics. (*Her face contorts variously.*) And we go to the carport to port the car. Whew! Please don't ask me any more questions, I'm afraid I may not have the strength to find the answers. (*Laughs uproariously.*) Please, sit down; don't let my manner make you uncomfortable. Sit on one of the sitting devices; we use them for sitting in the living room. (*There is a couch and one chair to choose from.* JOHN *and* JOHNNA *go to sit on the couch.*)

NAOMI (*screams at them*).   Don't sit there, I want to sit there! (JOHN *and* JOHNNA *stand and look frightened.* NAOMI *charges over to the couch, and* JOHN *and* JOHNNA *almost have to run to avoid being sat on by her.*) Shits! Ingrates!

NAOMI IN THE LIVING ROOM   First performed in 1991. Christopher Durang was born in 1949 in Montclair, New Jersey, and raised in upper-middle-class surroundings. He graduated from Harvard and the Yale School of Drama. His first big success was the Off-Broadway production in 1981 of *Sister Mary Ignatius Explains It All for You.* His plays often take the form of iconoclastic satires of suburban domestic life.

It's my house, it's my living room. I didn't ask you, I can ask you to leave. (JOHN *and* JOHNNA *are still standing and start to maybe edge out of the room.*) No, no, sit down. Please, make yourselves at home, this is the living room, it's where Rupert and I do all our living. (*There's only one chair, so with some hesitation* JOHNNA *sits in the chair, and* JOHN *stands behind her.* NAOMI *stretches her arms out on the couch.*) Wow. Boy oh boy. I need a big couch to sit on because *I'm a big personality!* (*Laughs uproariously.*) Tell me, are you two ever going to speak, or do I just have to go on and on by myself, or what! (NAOMI *stares at* JOHN *and* JOHNNA *intensely. They hesitate but then speak.*)

JOHNNA.   This is a very comfortable chair. I love it.

JOHN.   Yes, thank you.

NAOMI.   Go on.

JOHNNA.   Ummmm, this morning I washed my hair, and then I dried it. And we had coffee in the kitchen, didn't we, John?

JOHN.   Yes, Johnna, we did.

JOHNNA (*pause, doesn't know what else to say*).   And I love sitting in this chair.

NAOMI.   I think I want to sit in it, get up, get up. (NAOMI *charges over, and* JOHN *and* JOHNNA *move away from it, standing uncomfortably.* NAOMI *sits and moves around in the chair, luxuriating in it.*) Hmmmm, yes. Chair, chair. Chair in the living room. Hmmm, yes. (*Looks at* JOHN *and* JOHNNA, *shouts at them*) Well, go sit down on the fucking couch, you morons! (JOHN *and* JOHNNA *look startled, and sit on the couch. Screams offstage.*) Leonard! Oh, Leonard! Come on in here in the *living room* and have some conversation with us. You don't want me to soak up everything our son says all by myself, do you? (NAOMI *stands and walks over to* JOHN *and* JOHNNA *on the couch. She smiles at* JOHNNA.) You probably didn't know John was Herbert's and my son, did you?

JOHNNA.   Yes, he told me. I've met you before, you know.

NAOMI.   Shut up! (*Calls out*) Hubert! Rupert! Leonard! (*To them*) I hope he's not dead. I wouldn't know what room to put him in. We don't have a dead room. (*Smiles; screams*) *Aaaaaaaaaaaaaaaaaaahhhhhhhhh!* (*Looks at them.*) Goodness, my moods switch quickly. (NAOMI *sees a tiny stuffed pig in a Santa Claus suit perched on the mantelpiece. With momentary interest, she picks it up and looks at it, then puts it down again. Focusing on* JOHN *and* JOHNNA *again; a good hostess.*) Tell me all about yourselves, do you have children? (*Sits, listens attentively.*)

JOHNNA.   We had five children, but they all died in a car accident. The babysitter was taking them for a ride, and she was drunk. We were very upset.

NAOMI.   Uh-huh. Do you like sitting on the couch?

JOHN.   Mother, Johnna was telling you something sad.

NAOMI.   Was she? I'm sorry, Johnna, tell it to me again.

JOHNNA.   We had five children. . . .

NAOMI (*tries to concentrate, but something impinges on her consciousness*). Wait a minute, something's bothering me! (*She rushes over to the little stuffed Santa pig, snatches it up and throws it against the wall in a fury.*) This belongs in the kitchen, *not* in the living room. The living room is for living; it is not meant for sincerely designed but ludicrously corny artifacts! Kitsch! (*She sits down again.*) Do you like Hummel figurines?

JOHN.   Very much. Now that the children are dead, Johnna and I have begun to collect Hummel figurines, especially little boy shepherds and little girl shepherdesses.

NAOMI.   Uh-huh, isn't that interesting? Excuse me if I fall asleep. I'm not tired yet, but I just want to apologize in advance in case your boring talk puts me to sleep. I don't want to offend you. (*Screams*) *Aaaaaaaaaaaaaaaaahhhhhhhhh!* I'm just so bored I could scream. Did you ever hear that expression? *Aaaaaaaaaaaaaaaaahhhhhhhhhh!*

JOHN.   Excuse me, I want to change my clothes. I'm tired of my color scheme. Do you have a clothes changing room?

NAOMI.   No, I don't have a clothes changing room; you certainly are an idiot. Use the bedroom or the bathroom. Really, children these days have no sense. In my day we killed them.

JOHN (*to* JOHNNA).   Excuse me, I'll be right back.

JOHNNA.   Must you go?

JOHN.   Darling, I don't feel comfortable in these colors. They're hurting my eyes.

JOHNNA.   Well, bring it back.

JOHN.   What?

JOHNNA (*sincere, confused*).   I'm sorry, I don't know what I mean. (JOHN *exits.*) He's constantly talking about his color scheme. It's my cross to bear, I guess. That and the death of the children.

NAOMI.   So who the fuck are you, anyway?

JOHNNA.   I'm Johnna. I'm married to your son. All our children recently were killed.

NAOMI.   Stop talking about your children, I heard you the first time. God, some people can't get over their own little personal tragedies; what a great big crashing bore. Lots of people have it worse, girlie, so eat shit! (*Calls offstage*) Hey, John, where did you get this turd of a wife, at the Salvation Army? I'd bring her back! (*Laughs uproariously*) Ahahaha-hahahahaha!

JOHNNA.   I think I want to go.

NAOMI.   Boy, you can't take criticism, can you? Sit down, let's have a conversation. This is the conversation pit. You can't leave the pit until you converse on at least five subjects with me. Starting now, go: (*Waits expectantly.*)

JOHNNA.   I was reading about Dan Quayle's grandmother the other day.

NAOMI.   That's one. Go on.

JOHNNA. She said there should be prayer in the schools. . . .

NAOMI. That's two. (NAOMI *starts to remove her boots, or high-heeled shoes, in order to massage her feet.*)

JOHNNA. And that we should have a strong defense . . .

NAOMI. That's three.

JOHNNA. And that the Supreme Court should repeal the Wade versus Roe ruling that legalized abortions.

NAOMI. That's four.

JOHNNA. And that even in the case of pregnancy resulting from incest, she felt that the woman should be forced to carry the child through to term.

NAOMI. That's four-A.

JOHNNA. And then she said she hoped the mother would be forced to suffer and slave over a horrible job and take home a tiny, teeny paycheck to pay for some hovel somewhere and live in squalor with the teeny tiny baby, and that then she hoped she'd be sorry she ever had sexual intercourse.

NAOMI. That's still four-A.

JOHNNA. Don't you think she's lacking in Christian charity?

NAOMI. That's five, kind of. Yes, I do. But then so few people are true Christians anymore. I know I'm not. I'm a psychotic. (*She throws her boot in* JOHNNA'S *direction.*) Get up off the couch. I want to sit there. (NAOMI *rushes over;* JOHNNA *has to vacate fast. Then* NAOMI *starts to luxuriate in sitting in the couch, moving sensuously.*) Oh, couch, couch, big couch in the living room. I have room to spread. Couch, couch, you are my manifest destiny. Mmmmm, yes, yes. (*Calls out*) Edward, hurry out here, I'm about to have an orgasm, you don't want to miss it. (*Back to herself*) Mmmmmmm, yes, couch, couch pillows, me sitting on the couch in the living room, mmmmm, yes, mmmm . . . no. (*Calls*) Forget it! It's not happening. (*To* JOHNNA) Tell me, can you switch moods like I can? Let me see you. (JOHNNA *stares for a moment.*) No, go ahead, try.

JOHNNA. Very well. (*Happy*) I'm so happy, I'm so happy. (*Screams*) Aaaaaaah! Do you have chocolates for me? (*Desperate*) I'm so sad, I'm so sad. Drop dead! (*Laughs hysterically*) Ahahahahahahahaha! That's a good one! (*Looks at* NAOMI *for feedback.*)

NAOMI. Very phony, I didn't believe you for a moment. (*Calls offstage*) Herbert! Are you there? (*To* JOHNNA) Tell me, do you think Shubert is dead?

JOHNNA. You mean the composer?

NAOMI. Is he a composer? (*Calls out*) Lanford, are you a composer? (*Listens.*) He never answers. That's why I sometimes worry he might be dead, and as I said, I don't have a room for a dead person. We might build one on, and that would encourage the economy and prove the Republicans right, but I don't understand politics, do you?

JOHNNA. Politics?

NAOMI.   Politics, politics! What, are you deaf? Are you stupid? Are you dead? Are you sitting in a chair? (*Enter* JOHN. *He is dressed just like* JOHNNA—*the same dress, pearls, stockings, shoes. He has shaved off his mustache, and he wears a wig that resembles her hair and has a bow in it like the one she has in her hair. They look very similar.*)

JOHN.   Hello again.

NAOMI.   You took off your mustache.

JOHN.   I just feel so much better this way.

NAOMI.   Uh-huh.

JOHNNA (*deeply embarrassed*).   John and I are in couples therapy because of this. Dr. Cucharacha says his cross-dressing is an intense kind of codependence.

NAOMI.   If this Dr. Cucharacha cross-dresses, I wouldn't see him. That's what John here is doing. Too many men in women's clothing; nothing gets done!

JOHNNA (*to* JOHN).   Why do you humiliate me so this way?

JOHN.   I want to be just like you. Say something so I can copy you.

JOHNNA.   Oh, John. (*Does a feminine gesture and looks away.*)

JOHN.   Oh, John. (*Imitates her gesture.*) That doesn't give me much. Say something else.

JOHNNA.   Maybe it's in your genes.

JOHN.   Maybe it's in your genes. (JOHNNA, *in her discomfort, keeps touching her hair, her pearls, shaking her head, etc.* JOHN *imitates everything she does, glowing with glee. His imitations drive her crazy and are undoubtedly part of what has them in couples therapy.*)

NAOMI.   This is a disgusting sight. (*Calls*) Sherbert, our son is prancing out here with his wife; you should really see this. (*To them*) I find this uncomfortable. This makes me want to vomit.

JOHNNA.   Maybe we should go.

JOHN.   Maybe we should go.

NAOMI (*upset*).   How come you don't dress like me? How come you dress like her?

JOHN.   I want to be noticed, but I don't want to be considered insane.

JOHNNA.   John, please, just stay quiet and pose if you must, but no more talking.

NAOMI.   Insane? Is he referring to someone in this room as insane? (*Calls.*) Sally! Gretchen! Marsha! Felicity! (*To them*) I'm calling my army in here, and then we'll have some dead bodies.

JOHNNA.   Maybe we should go.

JOHN.   Maybe we should go. (*Keeps imitating* JOHNNA'S *movements.*)

JOHNNA.   Will you stop that? (NAOMI, *very upset and discombobulated, stands on the couch and begins to pace up and down on it.*)

NAOMI.   Insane, I'll give you insane! What's the capital of Madagascar? You don't know, do you? Now who's insane? What's the square root of 347? You don't know, do you? Well, get out of here if you think I'm so crazy. If you want to dress like her and not like me, I don't want you here. (NAOMI *lies down on the couch in a snit to continue her upset.* JOHN *begins to stride back and forth around the room, pretending he's on a fashion runway.* JOHNNA *slumps back in her chair and covers her eyes.*) I can have Christmas by myself, I can burn the Yule log by myself, I can wait for Santa by myself. I can pot geraniums. I can bob for apples. I can buy a gun in a store and shoot you. By myself! Do you get it? (*Stands and focuses back on them.*) You're dead meat with me, both of you. You're ready for the crock pot. You're a crock of shit. Leave here. I don't need you, and you're dead! (*Pause.*)

JOHNNA.   Well, I guess we should be going.

JOHN.   Well, I guess we should be going. (JOHNNA *and* JOHN, *looking the same and walking the same, leave the house.* NAOMI *chases after them to the door.*)

NAOMI.   Fuck you and the horse you came in on! (JOHN *and* JOHNNA *exit.* NAOMI *comes back into the room and is overcome with grief. She sits back on the couch and lets out enormous, heartfelt sobs. They go on for quite a bit, but when they subside, she's like an infant with a new thought, and she seems to be fairly contented.*) Well, that was a nice visit.

QUESTIONS

1. This short play of a mother, son, and daughter-in-law relies for its absurdity on exaggerations of "normal" speech and action. For example, when Naomi explains the functions of the various rooms, she is overplaying the polite hostess, and her explanations are even more ridiculous because (as John points out) he already knows his mother's house. In her pretense that she is entertaining strangers, Naomi reveals her sense of estrangement from her married son. As thoroughly as you can, ferret out the "normal" meanings of other absurd exaggerations, such as: (a) Naomi's referring to her husband by different but similar names; (b) Naomi's outbursts of obscene language; (c) Johnna's claim that her five children were killed in an auto accident; (d) John's mimicking his wife's clothes, speeches, and gestures; and others you discover.
2. What would you say is the actual situation involving these characters? What effect do the absurd exaggerations have on your response to them?
3. While the language, actions, and gestures of the play are nonrealistic, the description of the setting is not. If you were staging this play, how realistic would you make the sets, furniture, costumes, and so forth? The only description of Naomi's appearance is that she "looks odd." How would you have the actress create that impression?
4. Naomi's final outburst comes when John states that if he were to imitate her, he would "be considered insane." Is she insane?
5. State the theme of the play.

CHAPTER THREE

Tragedy and Comedy

The two masks of drama—one with the corners of its mouth turned down, the other with the corners of its mouth turned up—are familiar everywhere. Derived from masks actually worn by the actors in ancient Greek plays, they symbolize two principal modes of drama. Indeed, just as life gravitates between tears and laughter, they seem to imply that all drama is divided between tragedy and comedy.

But drama is an ancient literary form; in its development from the beginnings to the present it has produced a rich variety of plays. Can all these plays be classified under two terms? If our answer to this question is Yes, we must define the terms very broadly. If our answer is No, then how many terms do we need, and where do we stop? Polonius, in *Hamlet,* says of a visiting troupe of players that they can act "tragedy, comedy, history, pastoral, pastoral-comical, historical-pastoral, tragical-historical, tragical-comical-historical-pastoral, scene individable, or poem unlimited." Like Polonius himself, his list seems ridiculous. Moreover, even if we adopted these terms, and more, could we be sure that they would accurately classify all plays or that a new play, written tomorrow, would not demand a totally new category?

The discussion that follows proceeds on four assumptions. First, perfect definitions and an airtight system of classification are impossible. There exist no views of tragedy and comedy that have not been challenged and no classification system that unequivocally provides for all examples. Second, it is quite unnecessary that we classify each play we read or see. The most important questions to ask about a play are not "Is this a tragedy?" or "Is this a comedy?" but "Does this play furnish an enjoyable, valid, and significant experience?" Third, the quality of experience furnished by a play may be partially dependent on our perception of its relationship to earlier literary forms, and therefore familiarity with traditional notions of tragedy and comedy is important for our understanding and appreciation of plays. Many of the conventions used in specific plays have been determined by the kind of play the author intended to write. Other plays have been written in deliberate defiance of these conventions. Fourth, whether or not tragedy and comedy be taken as the two all-inclusive dramatic modes, they are certainly, as symbolized by the masks, the two principal ones, and useful points, therefore, from which to begin discussion.

The popular distinctions between comedy and tragedy are fairly simple: comedy is funny; tragedy is sad. Comedy has a happy ending, tragedy an unhappy one. The typical ending for comedy is a marriage; the typical ending for tragedy is a death. There is some truth in these notions, but only some. Some plays called comedies make no attempt to be funny. Successful tragedies, though they involve suffering and sadness, do not leave the spectator depressed. Some funny plays have sad endings: they send the viewer away with a lump in the throat. A few plays usually classified as tragedies do not have unhappy endings but conclude with the protagonist's triumph. In short, the popular distinctions are unreliable. Though we need not abandon them entirely, we must take a more complex view. Let us begin with tragedy.

The first great theorist of dramatic art was Aristotle (384–322 B.C.), whose discussion of tragedy in *Poetics* has dominated critical thought ever since. A very brief summary of Aristotle's view will be helpful.*

A tragedy, so Aristotle wrote, is the imitation in dramatic form of an action that is serious and complete, with incidents arousing pity and fear wherewith it effects a catharsis of such emotions. The language used is pleasurable and appropriate throughout to the situation in which it is used. The chief characters are noble personages ("better than ourselves," says Aristotle), and the actions they perform are noble actions. The plot involves a change in the protagonist's fortune, in which he usually, but not always, falls from happiness to misery. The protagonist, though not perfect, is hardly a bad person; his misfortunes result not from character deficiencies but rather from what Aristotle calls *hamartia*, a criminal act committed in ignorance of some material fact or even for the sake of a greater good. A tragic plot has organic unity: the events follow not just *after* one another but *because* of one another. The best tragic plots involve a reversal (a change from one state of things within the play to its opposite) or a discovery (a change from ignorance to knowledge) or both.

In the more extensive account that follows, we will not attempt to delineate the boundaries of tragedy nor necessarily to describe it at its greatest. Instead, we will describe a common understanding of tragedy

---

*The summary retains Aristotle's reference to the tragic protagonist in masculine terms. However, the definitions apply equally to female protagonists such as Sophocles's Antigone and Shakespeare's Cleopatra.

as a point of departure for further discussion. Nor shall we enter into the endless controversies over what Aristotle meant by "catharsis" or over which of his statements are meant to apply to all tragedies and which only to the best ones. The important thing is that Aristotle had important insights into the nature of some of the greatest tragedies and that, rightly or wrongly interpreted, his conceptions are the basis for a kind of archetypal notion of tragedy that has dominated critical thought. What are the central features of that archetype?

1. The tragic hero is a man of noble stature. He has a greatness about him. He is not an ordinary man but one of outstanding quality. In Greek and in Shakespearean tragedy, he is usually a prince or a king. We may, if we wish, set down this predilection of former times for kings as tragic heroes as an undemocratic prejudice that regarded some men to be of nobler "blood" than others—preeminent by virtue of their aristocratic birth. But it is only partially that. We may with equal validity regard the hero's kingship as the symbol rather than as the cause of his greatness. He is great not primarily by virtue of his kingship but by his possession of extraordinary powers, by qualities of passion or aspiration or nobility of mind. The tragic hero's kingship is also a symbol of his initial good fortune, the mark of his high position. If the hero's fall is to arouse in us the emotions of pity and fear, it must be a fall from a height.

2. The tragic hero is good, though not perfect, and his fall results from his committing what Aristotle calls "an act of injustice" (*hamartia*) either through ignorance or from a conviction that some greater good will be served. This act is, nevertheless, a criminal one, and the good hero is still responsible for it, even if he is totally unaware of its criminality and is acting out of the best intentions. Some later critics ignore Aristotle's insistence on the hero's commission of a guilty act and choose instead to blame the hero's fall on a flaw in his character or personality. Such a notion misrepresents Aristotle's view both of tragedy and of a basically just natural order. It implies a world in which personality alone, not one's actions, can bring on catastrophe.

(Aristotle notwithstanding, there is a critical tradition that attributes the fall of the hero to a so-called tragic flaw—some fault of character such as inordinate ambition, quickness to anger, a tendency to jealousy, or overweening pride. Conversely, the protagonist's vulnerability has been attributed to some excess of virtue—a nobility of character that unfits him for life among ordinary mortals. But whatever it be—a criminal act, a fault of character, or excessive virtue—the protagonist is personally responsible for his downfall.)

3. The hero's downfall, therefore, is his own fault, the result of his own free choice—not the result of pure accident or villainy or some overriding malignant fate. Accident, villainy, or fate may contribute to the downfall but only as cooperating agents: they are not alone responsible. The combination of the hero's greatness and his responsibility for his own downfall is what entitles us to describe his downfall as tragic rather than as merely pathetic. In common speech these two adjectives are often confused. If a father of ten children is accidentally killed at a street corner, the event, strictly speaking, is pathetic, not tragic. When a weak man succumbs to his weakness and comes to a bad end, the event should be called pathetic, not tragic. The tragic event involves a fall from greatness, brought about, at least partially, by the agent's free action.

4. Nevertheless, the hero's misfortune is not wholly deserved. The punishment exceeds the crime. We do not come away from tragedy with the feeling that "He got what he had coming to him" but rather with the sad sense of a waste of human potential. For what most impresses us about the tragic hero is not his weakness but his greatness. He is, in a sense, "larger than life," or, as Aristotle said, "better than ourselves." He reveals to us the dimensions of human possibility. He is a person mainly admirable, and his fall therefore fills us with pity and fear.

5. Yet the tragic fall is not pure loss. Though it may result in the protagonist's death, it involves, before his death, some increase in awareness, some gain in self-knowledge—as Aristotle puts it, some "discovery"—a change from ignorance to knowledge. On the level of plot, the discovery may be merely learning the truth about some fact or situation of which the protagonist was ignorant, but on the level of character it is accompanied or followed by a significant insight, a fuller self-knowledge, an increase not only in knowledge but in wisdom. Often this increase in wisdom involves some sort of reconciliation with the universe or with the protagonist's situation. He exits not cursing his fate but accepting it and acknowledging that it is to some degree just.

6. Though it arouses solemn emotions—pity and fear, says Aristotle, but compassion and awe might be better terms—tragedy, when well performed, does not leave its audience in a state of depression. Though we cannot be sure what Aristotle meant by his term *catharsis*, some sort of emotional release at the end is a common experience of those who witness great tragedies on the stage. They have been greatly moved by pity, fear, and associated emotions, but they are not left

emotionally beaten down or dejected. Instead, there may be a feeling almost of exhilaration. This feeling is a response to the tragic action. With the fall of the hero and his gain in wisdom or self-knowledge, there is, besides the appalling sense of human waste, a fresh recognition of human greatness, a sense that human life has unrealized potentialities. Though the hero may be defeated, he at least has dared greatly, and he gains understanding from his defeat.

Is the comic mask laughing or smiling? The question is more important than it may at first appear, for usually we laugh *at* something but smile *with* someone. The laugh expresses recognition of some absurdity in human behavior; the smile expresses pleasure in someone's company or good fortune.

The comic mask may be interpreted both ways. Comedy, Northrop Frye has said, lies between satire and romance. Historically, there have been two chief kinds of comedy—scornful comedy and romantic comedy, laughing comedy and smiling comedy. Of the two, scornful or satiric comedy is the older and probably still the more dominant.

The most essential difference between tragedy and comedy, particularly scornful comedy, is in their depiction of human nature. Where tragedy emphasizes human greatness, comedy delineates human weakness. Where tragedy celebrates human freedom, comedy points up human limitations. Wherever human beings fail to measure up to their own resolutions or to their own self-conceptions, wherever they are guilty of hypocrisy, vanity, or folly, wherever they fly in the face of good sense and rational behavior, comedy exhibits their absurdity and invites us to laugh at them. Where tragedy tends to say, with Shakespeare's Hamlet, "What a piece of work is a man! how noble in reason! how infinite in faculty! in form and moving how express and admirable! in action how like an angel! in apprehension how like a god!" comedy says, with Shakespeare's Puck, "Lord, what fools these mortals be!"

Because comedy exposes human folly, its function is partly critical and corrective. Where tragedy challenges us with a vision of human possibility, comedy reveals to us a spectacle of human ridiculousness that it makes us want to avoid. No doubt, we should not exaggerate this function of comedy. We go to the theater primarily for enjoyment, not to receive lessons in personality or character development. Nevertheless, laughter may be educative at the same time that it is enjoyable.

The comedies of Aristophanes and Molière, of Ben Jonson and Congreve, are, first of all, good fun, but, secondly, they are antidotes for human folly.

Romantic or smiling comedy, as opposed to scornful comedy, and as exemplified by many plays of Shakespeare—*As You Like It, Twelfth Night, Much Ado About Nothing, The Tempest,* for instance—puts its emphasis upon sympathetic rather than ridiculous characters. These characters—likeable, not given up to folly or vanity—are placed in various kinds of difficulties from which, at the end of the play, they are rescued, attaining their ends or having their good fortunes restored. Though different from the protagonists of scornful comedy, however, these characters are not the commanding or lofty figures that tragic protagonists are. They are sensible and good rather than noble, aspiring, and grand. They do not strike us with awe as the tragic protagonist does. They do not so challengingly test the limits of human possibility. In short, they move in a smaller world. Romantic comedies, therefore, do not occupy a different universe from satiric comedies; they simply lie at opposite sides of the same territory. The romantic comedy, moreover, though its protagonists are sympathetic, has usually a number of lesser characters whose folly is held up to ridicule. The satiric comedy, on the other hand, frequently has minor characters—often a pair of young lovers—who are sympathetic and likeable. The difference between the two kinds of comedy may be only a matter of whether we laugh at the primary or at the secondary characters.

There are other differences between comedy and tragedy. The norms of comedy are primarily social. Where tragedies tend to isolate their protagonists to emphasize their uniqueness, comedies put their protagonists in the midst of a group to emphasize their commonness. Where tragic protagonists possess overpowering individuality, so that plays are often named after them (for example, *Oedipus Rex, Othello*), comic protagonists tend to be types of individuals, and the plays in which they appear are often named for the type (for example, Molière's *The Miser,* Congreve's *The Double Dealer*). We judge tragic protagonists by absolute moral standards, by how far they soar above society. We judge comic protagonists by social standards, by how well they adjust to society and conform to the expectations of the group.

Finally, comic plots are less likely than tragic plots to exhibit the high degree of organic unity—of logical cause-and-effect progression—that Aristotle required of tragedy. Plausibility, in fact, is not usually the central characteristic of a comic plot. Unlikely coincidences, improbable disguises, mistaken identities—these are the stuff of which comedy is made; and, as long as they make us laugh and, at the same time, help to illuminate human nature and human folly, we need not greatly care. Not that plausibility is no longer important—only that other things are more important, and these other things are often achieved by the most outrageous violations of probability.

This is particularly true regarding the comic ending. Conventionally, comedies have a happy ending, but the emphasis here is on *conventionally*. The happy ending is, indeed, a *convention* of comedy, which is to say that a comedy ends happily because comedies end happily— that is the nature of the form—not necessarily because a happy ending is a plausible outcome of the events that have preceded. The greatest masters of comedy—Aristophanes, Shakespeare, Molière—have often been extremely arbitrary in the manner in which they achieved their endings. The accidental discovery of a lost will, rescue by an act of divine intervention (*deus ex machina*), the sudden reform of a mean-spirited person into a friendly person—such devices have been used by the greatest comic writers. And, even where the ending is achieved more plausibly, comedy asks us to forget for the time being that in actuality life has no endings except for death. Marriage, which provides the ending for so many comedies, is really a beginning.

And now, though we do not wish to imitate the folly of Polonius, it is well that we define two additional terms: melodrama and farce. In the two-part classification suggested by the two symbolic masks, melodrama belongs with tragedy and farce with comedy, but the differences are sufficient to make the two new terms useful.

Melodrama, like tragedy, attempts to arouse feelings of fear and pity, but it does so ordinarily through cruder means. The conflict is an oversimplified one between good and evil depicted in absolute terms. Plot is emphasized at the expense of characterization. Sensational incidents provide the staple of the plot. The young mother and her baby are evicted into a howling storm by the villain holding the mortgage; the heroine is tied to the railroad tracks as the express train approaches. Most important, good finally triumphs over evil, and the ending is happy. Typically, at the end, the hero marries the heroine; villainy is foiled or crushed. Melodrama may, of course, have different degrees of power and subtlety; it is not always as crude as its crudest examples. But, in it, moral issues are typically oversimplified, and good is finally triumphant. Melodrama does not provide the complex insights of tragedy. It is usually escapist rather than interpretive. Much of what television and films present as science fiction, police or medical dramas, and thrillers are examples of melodrama.

Farce, more consistently than comedy, is aimed at rousing explosive laughter. But again the means are cruder. The conflicts are violent and usually at the physical level. Plot is emphasized at the expense of characterization, improbable situations and coincidence at the expense of articulated plot. Comic implausibility is raised to heights of absurd impossibility. Coarse wit, practical jokes, and physical action are staples. Characters trip over benches, insult each other, run into walls, knock each other down, get into brawls. Performed with gusto, farce may be hilariously funny. Psychologically, it may boost our spirits and purge us of hostility and aggression. In content, however, like melodrama, it is usually escapist rather than interpretive. Contemporary farces are a staple of the movies.

Now we have four classifications—tragedy, comedy, melodrama, farce—the latter two as appendages of the former. But none of these classifications is rigid. They blend into each other and defy exact definition. If we take them too seriously, the tragic mask may laugh, and the comic mask weep.

Sophocles

Oedipus Rex

The plots of Greek tragedies were based on legends with which Greek audiences were more or less familiar (as American audiences, for example, would be familiar with the major events in a historical play based on the life of Lincoln). These plays often owed much of their impact to the audience's previous knowledge of the characters and their fate, for it enabled the playwright to make powerful use of dramatic irony and allusion. Much of the audience's delight, in addition, came from seeing how the playwright worked out the details of the story. The purpose of this introductory note is therefore to supply such information as the play's first audiences might be presumed to have had.

Because of a prophecy that their new son would kill his father, Laius and Jocasta, King and Queen of Thebes, gave their infant to a shepherd with orders that he be left on a mountainside to die. The shepherd, however, after having pinned the babe's ankles together, took pity on him and gave him instead to a Corinthian shepherd. This shepherd in turn presented him to Polybus and Merope, King and

Queen of Corinth, who, childless, adopted him as their own. The child was given the name Oedipus ("Swollen-foot") because of the injury to his ankles.

When grown to manhood at Polybus's court, Oedipus was accused by a drunken guest of not being his father's son. Though reassured by Polybus and Merope, he was still disturbed and traveled to consult the Delphic oracle. The oracle, without answering the question about his parentage, prophesied that Oedipus would kill his father and beget children by his mother. Horrified, resolved to avert this fate, Oedipus determined never to return to Corinth. Traveling from Delphi, he came to a place where three roads met and was ordered off the road by a man in a chariot. Blows were exchanged, and Oedipus killed the man and four of his attendants. Later, on the outskirts of Thebes, he encountered the Sphinx, a monster with the head of a woman, wings of an eagle, and body of a lion, which was terrorizing Thebes by slaying all who failed to answer her riddle ("What goes on four legs in the morning, two legs at noon, and three legs in the evening?"). When Oedipus correctly answered the riddle ("man, for he crawls as an infant, walks erect as a man, and uses a staff in old age"), the Sphinx destroyed herself. As a reward, Oedipus was named King of Thebes to replace the recently slain Laius and was given the hand of Jocasta in marriage. With her, he ruled Thebes successfully for some years and had four children—two sons and two daughters. Then the city was afflicted by a plague. It is at this point that the action of Sophocles's play begins.

The play was first performed in Athens about 430 B.C. In the present version, prepared by Dudley Fitts and Robert Fitzgerald, the translators use spellings for the proper names that are closer to the original Greek than the more familiar Anglicized spellings used in this note. Sophocles (496?–406 B.C.), an active and devoted citizen of Athens during its democratic period, served as an elected general in an Athenian military expedition and held other posts of civic responsibility, but was most importantly its leading and most prolific tragic playwright.

CHARACTERS

OEDIPUS, *King of Thebes, supposed son of Polybus and Meropê, King and Queen of Corinth*

IOKASTÊ, *wife of Oedipus and widow of the late King Laïos*

KREON, *brother of Iokastê, a prince of Thebes*

TEIRESIAS, *a blind seer who serves Apollo*

PRIEST
MESSENGER, *from Corinth*
SHEPHERD, *former servant of Laïos*
SECOND MESSENGER, *from the palace*
CHORUS OF THEBAN ELDERS
CHORAGOS, *leader of the Chorus*
ANTIGONE *and* ISMENE, *young daughters of Oedipus and Iokastê. They appear
    in the Exodus but do not speak.*
SUPPLIANTS, GUARDS, SERVANTS

THE SCENE. *Before the palace of* OEDIPUS, *King of Thebes. A central door
and two lateral doors open onto a platform which runs the length of the façade. On
the platform, right and left, are altars; and three steps lead down into the orchêstra,
or chorus-ground. At the beginning of the action these steps are crowded by suppliants who have brought branches and chaplets of olive leaves and who sit in
various attitudes of despair.* OEDIPUS *enters.*

PROLOGUE

OEDIPUS.   My children, generations of the living
    In the line of Kadmos,° nursed at his ancient hearth:
    Why have you strewn yourselves before these altars
    In supplication, with your boughs and garlands?
    The breath of incense rises from the city   5
    With a sound of prayer and lamentation.
                                        Children,
    I would not have you speak through messengers,
    And therefore I have come myself to hear you—
    I, Oedipus, who bear the famous name.
    (*To a* PRIEST) You, there, since you are eldest in the company,   10
    Speak for them all, tell me what preys upon you,
    Whether you come in dread, or crave some blessing:
    Tell me, and never doubt that I will help you
    In every way I can; I should be heartless
    Were I not moved to find you suppliant here.   15
PRIEST.   Great Oedipus, O powerful king of Thebes!
    You see how all the ages of our people
    Cling to your altar steps: here are boys
    Who can barely stand alone, and here are priests
    By weight of age, as I am a priest of God,   20
    And young men chosen from those yet unmarried;
    As for the others, all that multitude,

2. **Kadmos:** founder of Thebes

They wait with olive chaplets in the squares,
At the two shrines of Pallas, and where Apollo
Speaks in the glowing embers.
                              Your own eyes   25
Must tell you: Thebes is tossed on a murdering sea
And can not lift her head from the death surge.
A rust consumes the buds and fruits of the earth;
The herds are sick; children die unborn,
And labor is vain. The god of plague and pyre   30
Raids like detestable lightning through the city,
And all the house of Kadmos is laid waste,
All emptied, and all darkened: Death alone
Battens upon the misery of Thebes.
You are not one of the immortal gods, we know;   35
Yet we have come to you to make our prayer
As to the man surest in mortal ways
And wisest in the ways of God. You saved us
From the Sphinx, that flinty singer, and the tribute
We paid to her so long; yet you were never   40
Better informed than we, nor could we teach you:
A god's touch, it seems, enabled you to help us.

Therefore, O mighty power, we turn to you:
Find us our safety, find us a remedy,
Whether by counsel of the gods or of men.   45
A king of wisdom tested in the past
Can act in a time of troubles, and act well.
Noblest of men, restore
Life to your city! Think how all men call you
Liberator for your boldness long ago;   50
Ah, when your years of kingship are remembered,
Let them not say *We rose, but later fell*—
Keep the State from going down in the storm!
Once, years ago, with happy augury,
You brought us fortune; be the same again!   55
No man questions your power to rule the land:
But rule over men, not over a dead city!
Ships are only hulls, high walls are nothing,
When no life moves in the empty passageways.

OEDIPUS.   Poor children! You may be sure I know   60
All that you longed for in your coming here.
I know that you are deathly sick; and yet,
Sick as you are, not one is as sick as I.
Each of you suffers in himself alone

His anguish, not another's; but my spirit   65
Groans for the city, for myself, for you.

I was not sleeping, you are not waking me.
No, I have been in tears for a long while
And in my restless thought walked many ways.
In all my search I found one remedy,   70
And I have adopted it: I have sent Kreon,
Son of Menoikeus, brother of the queen,
To Delphi, Apollo's place of revelation,
To learn there, if he can,
What act or pledge of mine may save the city.   75
I have counted the days, and now, this very day,
I am troubled, for he has overstayed his time.
What is he doing? He has been gone too long.
Yet whenever he comes back, I should do ill
Not to take any action the god orders.   80
PRIEST.   It is a timely promise. At this instant
    They tell me Kreon is here.
OEDIPUS.   O Lord Apollo!
    May his news be fair as his face is radiant!
PRIEST.   Good news, I gather! he is crowned with bay,
    The chaplet is thick with berries.
OEDIPUS.   We shall soon know;   85
    He is near enough to hear us now. (*Enter* KREON.) O prince:
    Brother: son of Menoikeus:
    What answer do you bring us from the god?
KREON.   A strong one. I can tell you, great afflictions
    Will turn out well, if they are taken well.   90
OEDIPUS.   What was the oracle? These vague words
    Leave me still hanging between hope and fear.
KREON.   Is it your pleasure to hear me with all these
    Gathered around us? I am prepared to speak,
    But should we not go in?
OEDIPUS.   Speak to them all,   95
    It is for them I suffer, more than for myself.
KREON.   Then I will tell you what I heard at Delphi.
    In plain words
    The god commands us to expel from the land of Thebes
    An old defilement we are sheltering.   100
    It is a deathly thing, beyond cure;
    We must not let it feed upon us longer.
OEDIPUS.   What defilement? How shall we rid ourselves of it?
KREON.   By exile or death, blood for blood. It was
    Murder that brought the plague-wind on the city.   105

OEDIPUS.   Murder of whom? Surely the god has named him?
KREON.   My lord: Laïos once ruled this land,
    Before you came to govern us.
OEDIPUS.   I know;
    I learned of him from others; I never saw him.
KREON.   He was murdered; and Apollo commands us now   110
    To take revenge upon whoever killed him.
OEDIPUS.   Upon whom? Where are they? Where shall we find a clue
    To solve that crime after so many years?
KREON.   Here in this land, he said. Search reveals
    Things that escape an inattentive man.   115
OEDIPUS.   Tell me: Was Laïos murdered in his house,
    Or in the fields, or in some foreign country?
KREON.   He said he planned to make a pilgrimage.
    He did not come home again.
OEDIPUS.   And was there no one,
    No witness, no companion, to tell what happened?   120
KREON.   They were all killed but one, and he got away,
    So frightened that he could remember one thing only.
OEDIPUS.   What was that one thing? One may be the key
    To everything, if we resolve to use it.
KREON.   He said that a band of highwaymen attacked them,   125
    Outnumbered them, and overwhelmed the king.
OEDIPUS.   Strange, that a highwayman should be so daring—
    Unless some faction here bribed him to do it.
KREON.   We thought of that. But after Laïos' death
    New troubles arose and we had no avenger.   130
OEDIPUS.   What troubles could prevent your hunting down the killers?
KREON.   The riddling Sphinx's song
    Made us deaf to all mysteries but her own.
OEDIPUS.   Then once more I must bring what is dark to light.
    It is most fitting that Apollo shows,   135
    As you do, this compunction for the dead.
    You shall see how I stand by you, as I should,
    Avenging this country and the god as well,
    And not as though it were for some distant friend,
    But for my own sake, to be rid of evil.   140
    Whoever killed King Laïos might—who knows?—
    Lay violent hands even on me—and soon.
    I act for the murdered king in my own interest.

    Come, then, my children: leave the altar steps,
    Lift up your olive boughs!
                   One of you go   145
    And summon the people of Kadmos to gather here.

I will do all that I can; you may tell them that. (*Exit a* PAGE.)
So, with the help of God,
We shall be saved—or else indeed we are lost.
PRIEST.   Let us rise, children. It was for this we came,   150
And now the king has promised it.
Phoibos° has sent us an oracle; may he descend
Himself to save us and drive out the plague. (*Exeunt* OEDIPUS *and*
KREON *into the palace by the central door. The* PRIEST *and the* SUPPLIANTS
disperse right and left. After a short pause the CHORUS *enters the orchêstra.*)

PÁRODOS°

STROPHE 1

CHORUS.   What is God singing in his profound
Delphi of gold and shadow?   155
What oracle for Thebes, the sunwhipped city?
Fear unjoints me, the roots of my heart tremble.
Now I remember, O Healer, your power, and wonder:
Will you send doom like a sudden cloud, or weave it
Like nightfall of the past?   160
Speak to me, tell me, O
Child of golden Hope, immortal Voice.

ANTISTROPHE 1

Let me pray to Athenê, the immortal daughter of Zeus,
And to Artemis her sister
Who keeps her famous throne in the market ring,   165
And to Apollo, archer from distant heaven—
O gods, descend! Like three streams leap against
The fires of our grief, the fires of darkness;
Be swift to bring us rest!
As in the old time from the brilliant house   170

---

152. Phoibus: Apollo, god of light and truth   **Párodos:** The song or ode chanted
by the chorus on their entry. It is accompanied by dancing and music played on a
flute. The chorus, in this play, represents elders of the city of Thebes. They remain on
stage (on a level lower than the principal actors) for the remainder of the play. The
choral odes and dances serve to separate one scene from another (there was no curtain in Greek theater) as well as to comment on the action, reinforce the emotion, and
interpret the situation. The chorus also performs dance movements during certain
portions of the scenes themselves. *Strophe* and *antistrophe* are terms denoting the
movement and countermovement of the chorus from one side of their playing area to
the other. When the chorus participates in dialogue with the other characters, their
lines are spoken by the Choragos, their leader.

Of air you stepped to save us, come again!

STROPHE 2

> Now our afflictions have no end,
> Now all our stricken host lies down
> And no man fights off death with his mind;
> The noble plowland bears no grain,   175
> And groaning mothers can not bear—
> See, how our lives like birds take wing,
> Like sparks that fly when a fire soars,
> To the shore of the god of evening.

ANTISTROPHE 2

> The plague burns on, it is pitiless,   180
> Though pallid children laden with death
> Lie unwept in the stony ways,
> And old gray women by every path
> Flock to the strand about the altars
> There to strike their breasts and cry   185
> Worship of Phoibus in wailing prayers:
> Be kind, God's golden child!

STROPHE 3

> There are no swords in this attack by fire,
> No shields, but we are ringed with cries.
> Send the besieger plunging from our homes   190
> Into the vast sea-room of the Atlantic
> Or into the waves that foam eastward of Thrace—
> For the day ravages what the night spares—
> Destroy our enemy, lord of the thunder!
> Let him be riven by lightning from heaven!   195

ANTISTROPHE 3

> Phoibus Apollo, stretch the sun's bowstring,
> That golden cord, until it sing for us,
> Flashing arrows in heaven!
>   Artemis, Huntress,
> Race with flaring lights upon our mountains!
> O scarlet god,° O golden-banded brow,   200

---

200. scarlet god: Bacchos, god of wine and revelry. The Maenads were his female attendants.

O Theban Bacchos in a storm of Maenads, (*Enter* OEDIPUS, *center.*)
Whirl upon Death, that all the Undying hate!
Come with blinding torches, come in joy!

SCENE 1

OEDIPUS.   Is this your prayer? It may be answered. Come,
    Listen to me, act as the crisis demands,   205
    And you shall have relief from all these evils.

    Until now I was a stranger to this tale,
    As I had been a stranger to the crime.
    Could I track down the murderer without a clue?
    But now, friends,   210
    As one who became a citizen after the murder,
    I make this proclamation to all Thebans:
    If any man knows by whose hand Laïos, son of Labdakos,
    Met his death, I direct that man to tell me everything,
    No matter what he fears for having so long withheld it.   215
    Let it stand as promised that no further trouble
    Will come to him, but he may leave the land in safety.
    Moreover: If anyone knows the murderer to be foreign,
    Let him not keep silent: he shall have his reward from me.
    However, if he does conceal it; if any man   220
    Fearing for his friend or for himself disobeys this edict,
    Hear what I propose to do:

    I solemnly forbid the people of this country,
    Where power and throne are mine, ever to receive that man
    Or speak to him, no matter who he is, or let him   225
    Join in sacrifice, lustration, or in prayer.
    I decree that he be driven from every house,
    Being, as he is, corruption itself to us: the Delphic
    Voice of Apollo has pronounced this revelation.
    Thus I associate myself with the oracle   230
    And take the side of the murdered king.

    As for the criminal, I pray to God—
    Whether it be a lurking thief, or one of a number—
    I pray that that man's life be consumed in evil and wretchedness.
    And as for me, this curse applies no less   235
    If it should turn out that the culprit is my guest here,
    Sharing my hearth.
            You have heard the penalty.
    I lay it on you now to attend to this

For my sake, for Apollo's, for the sick
Sterile city that heaven has abandoned.   240
Suppose the oracle had given you no command:
Should this defilement go uncleansed for ever?
You should have found the murderer: your king,
A noble king, had been destroyed!
                    Now I,
Having the power that he held before me,   245
Having his bed, begetting children there
Upon his wife, as he would have, had he lived—
Their son would have been my children's brother,
If Laïos had had luck in fatherhood!
(And now his bad fortune has struck him down)—   250
I say I take the son's part, just as though
I were his son, to press the fight for him
And see it won! I'll find the hand that brought
Death to Labdakos's and Polydoros's child,
Heir of Kadmos's and Agenor's line.°   255
And as for those who fail me,
May the gods deny them the fruit of the earth,
Fruit of the womb, and may they rot utterly!
Let them be wretched as we are wretched, and worse!

For you, for loyal Thebans, and for all   260
Who find my actions right, I pray the favor
Of justice, and of all the immortal gods.
CHORAGOS.   Since I am under oath, my lord, I swear
    I did not do the murder, I can not name
    The murderer. Phoibus ordained the search;   265
    Why did he not say who the culprit was?
OEDIPUS.   An honest question. But no man in the world
    Can make the gods do more than the gods will.
CHORAGOS.   There is an alternative, I think—
OEDIPUS.   Tell me.
    Any or all, you must not fail to tell me.   270
CHORAGOS.   A lord clairvoyant to the lord Apollo,
    As we all know, is the skilled Teiresias.
    One might learn much about this from him, Oedipus.
OEDIPUS.   I am not wasting time:
    Kreon spoke of this, and I have sent for him—   275
    Twice, in fact; it is strange that he is not here.
CHORAGOS.   The other matter—that old report—seems useless.

---

255. Labdakos, Polydoros, Kadmos, and Agenor: father, grandfather, great-grandfather, and great-great-grandfather of Laïos

OEDIPUS.   What was that? I am interested in all reports.

CHORAGOS.   The king was said to have been killed by highwaymen.

OEDIPUS.   I know. But we have no witness to that.   280

CHORAGOS.   If the killer can feel a particle of dread,
>   Your curse will bring him out of hiding!

OEDIPUS.   No.
>   The man who dared that act will fear no curse.

(Enter the blind seer TEIRESIAS, *led by a* PAGE.)

CHORAGOS.   But there is one man who may detect the criminal.
>   This is Teiresias, this is the holy prophet   285
>   In whom, alone of all men, truth was born.

OEDIPUS.   Teiresias: seer: student of mysteries,
>   Of all that's taught and all that no man tells,
>   Secrets of Heaven and secrets of the earth:
>   Blind though you are, you know the city lies   290
>   Sick with plague; and from this plague, my lord,
>   We find that you alone can guard or save us.

>   Possibly you did not hear the messengers?
>   Apollo, when we sent to him,
>   Sent us back word that this great pestilence   295
>   Would lift, but only if we established clearly
>   The identity of those who murdered Laïos.
>   They must be killed or exiled.

>   Can you use
>   Birdflight° or any art of divination
>   To purify yourself, and Thebes, and me   300
>   From this contagion? We are in your hands.
>   There is no fairer duty
>   Than that of helping others in distress.

TEIRESIAS.   How dreadful knowledge of the truth can be
>   When there's no help in truth! I knew this well,   305
>   But did not act on it: else I should not have come.

OEDIPUS.   What is troubling you? Why are your eyes so cold?

TEIRESIAS.   Let me go home. Bear your own fate, and I'll
>   Bear mine. It is better so: trust what I say.

OEDIPUS.   What you say is ungracious and unhelpful   310
>   To your native country. Do not refuse to speak.

TEIRESIAS.   When it comes to speech, your own is neither temperate
>   Nor opportune. I wish to be more prudent.

OEDIPUS.   In God's name, we all beg you—

---

299. Birdflight: Prophets predicted the future or divined the unknown by observing the flight of birds.

TEIRESIAS.   You are all ignorant.
    No; I will never tell you what I know.   315
    Now it is my misery; then, it would be yours.
OEDIPUS.   What! You do know something, and will not tell us?
    You would betray us all and wreck the State?
TEIRESIAS.   I do not intend to torture myself, or you.
    Why persist in asking? You will not persuade me.   320
OEDIPUS.   What a wicked old man you are! You'd try a stone's
    Patience! Out with it! Have you no feeling at all?
TEIRESIAS.   You call me unfeeling. If you could only see
    The nature of your own feelings . . .
OEDIPUS.   Why,
    Who would not feel as I do? Who could endure   325
    Your arrogance toward the city?
TEIRESIAS.   What does it matter?
    Whether I speak or not, it is bound to come.
OEDIPUS.   Then, if "it" is bound to come, you are bound to tell me.
TEIRESIAS.   No, I will not go on. Rage as you please.
OEDIPUS.   Rage? Why not!
                  And I'll tell you what I think: 330
    You planned it, you had it done, you all but
    Killed him with your own hands: if you had eyes,
    I'd say the crime was yours, and yours alone.
TEIRESIAS.   So? I charge you, then,
    Abide by the proclamation you have made: 335
    From this day forth
    Never speak again to these men or me;
    You yourself are the pollution of this country.
OEDIPUS.   You dare say that! Can you possibly think you have
    Some way of going free, after such insolence?   340
TEIRESIAS.   I have gone free. It is the truth sustains me.
OEDIPUS.   Who taught you shamelessness? It was not your craft.
TEIRESIAS.   You did. You made me speak. I did not want to.
OEDIPUS.   Speak what? Let me hear it again more clearly.
TEIRESIAS.   Was it not clear before? Are you tempting me?   345
OEDIPUS.   I did not understand it. Say it again.
TEIRESIAS.   I say that you are the murderer whom you seek.
OEDIPUS.   Now twice you have spat out infamy. You'll pay for it!
TEIRESIAS.   Would you care for more? Do you wish to be really angry?
OEDIPUS.   Say what you will. Whatever you say is worthless.   350
TEIRESIAS.   I say you live in hideous shame with those
    Most dear to you. You can not see the evil.
OEDIPUS.   Can you go on babbling like this for ever?
TEIRESIAS.   I can, if there is power in truth.
OEDIPUS.   There is:

But not for you, not for you,   355
You sightless, witless, senseless, mad old man!
TEIRESIAS.   You are the madman. There is no one here
Who will not curse you soon, as you curse me.
OEDIPUS.   You child of total night! I would not touch you;
Neither would any man who sees the sun.   360
TEIRESIAS.   True: it is not from you my fate will come.
That lies within Apollo's competence,
As it is his concern.
OEDIPUS.   Tell me, who made
These fine discoveries? Kreon? or someone else?
TEIRESIAS.   Kreon is no threat. You weave your own doom.   365
OEDIPUS.   Wealth, power, craft of statesmanship!
Kingly position, everywhere admired!
What savage envy is stored up against these,
If Kreon, whom I trusted, Kreon my friend,
For this great office which the city once   370
Put in my hands unsought—if for this power
Kreon desires in secret to destroy me!

He has bought this decrepit fortune-teller, this
Collector of dirty pennies, this prophet fraud—
Why, he is no more clairvoyant than I am!
                                            Tell us: 375
Has your mystic mummery ever approached the truth?
When that hellcat the Sphinx was performing here,
What help were you to these people?
Her magic was not for the first man who came along:
It demanded a real exorcist. Your birds—   380
What good were they? or the gods, for the matter of that?
But I came by,
Oedipus, the simple man, who knows nothing—
I thought it out for myself, no birds helped me!
And this is the man you think you can destroy,   385
That you may be close to Kreon when he's king!
Well, you and your friend Kreon, it seems to me,
Will suffer most. If you were not an old man,
You would have paid already for your plot.
CHORAGOS.   We can not see that his words or yours   390
Have been spoken except in anger, Oedipus,
And of anger we have no need. How to accomplish
The god's will best: that is what most concerns us.
TEIRESIAS.   You are a king. But where argument's concerned
I am your man, as much a king as you.   395
I am not your servant, but Apollo's.

I have no need of Kreon or Kreon's name.

Listen to me. You mock my blindness, do you?
But I say that you, with both your eyes, are blind:
You can not see the wretchedness of your life,   400
Nor in whose house you live, no, nor with whom.
Who are your father and mother? Can you tell me?
You do not even know the blind wrongs
That you have done them, on earth and in the world below.
But the double lash of your parents' curse will whip you   405
Out of this land some day, with only night
Upon your precious eyes.
Your cries then—where will they not be heard?
What fastness of Kithairon° will not echo them?
And that bridal-descant of yours—you'll know it then,   410
The song they sang when you came here to Thebes
And found your misguided berthing.
All this, and more, that you can not guess at now,
Will bring you to yourself among your children.

Be angry, then. Curse Kreon. Curse my words.   415
I tell you, no man that walks upon the earth
Shall be rooted out more horribly than you.
OEDIPUS.   Am I to bear this from him?—Damnation
     Take you! Out of this place! Out of my sight!
TEIRESIAS.   I would not have come at all if you had not asked me.   420
OEDIPUS.   Could I have told that you'd talk nonsense, that
     You'd come here to make a fool of yourself, and of me?
TEIRESIAS.   A fool? Your parents thought me sane enough.
OEDIPUS.   My parents again!— Wait: who were my parents?
TEIRESIAS.   This day will give you a father, and break your heart.   425
OEDIPUS.   Your infantile riddles! Your damned abracadabra!
TEIRESIAS.   You were a great man once at solving riddles.
OEDIPUS.   Mock me with that if you like; you will find it true.
TEIRESIAS.   It was true enough. It brought about your ruin.
OEDIPUS.   But if it saved the town?
TEIRESIAS (*to the* PAGE).   Boy, give me your hand.   430
OEDIPUS.   Yes, boy; lead him away.
                              —While you are here
     We can do nothing. Go; leave us in peace.
TEIRESIAS.   I will go when I have said what I have to say.
     How can you hurt me? And I tell you again:
     The man you have been looking for all this time,   435

409. Kithairon: the mountain where Oedipus was taken to be exposed as an infant

The damned man, the murderer of Laïos,
That man is in Thebes. To your mind he is foreign-born,
But it will soon be shown that he is a Theban,
A revelation that will fail to please.
                    A blind man,
Who has his eyes now; a penniless man, who is rich now;   440
And he will go tapping the strange earth with his staff.
To the children with whom he lives now he will be
Brother and father—the very same; to her
Who bore him, son and husband—the very same
Who came to his father's bed, wet with his father's blood.   445
Enough. Go think that over.
If later you find error in what I have said,
You may say that I have no skill in prophecy.
(*Exit* TEIRESIAS, *led by his* PAGE. OEDIPUS *goes into the palace.*)

ODE 1

STROPHE 1

CHORUS.   The Delphic stone of prophecies
          Remembers ancient regicide   450
          And a still bloody hand.
          That killer's hour of flight has come.
          He must be stronger than riderless
          Coursers of untiring wind,
          For the son° of Zeus armed with his father's thunder   455
          Leaps in lightning after him;
          And the Furies hold his track, the sad Furies.

ANTISTROPHE 1

          Holy Parnassos'° peak of snow
          Flashes and blinds that secret man,
          That all shall hunt him down: 460
          Though he may roam the forest shade
          Like a bull gone wild from pasture
          To rage through glooms of stone,
          Doom comes down on him; flight will not avail him;
          For the world's heart calls him desolate,   465
          And the immortal voices follow, for ever follow.

STROPHE 2

          But now a wilder thing is heard
          From the old man skilled at hearing Fate in the wing-beat of a bird.

455. son: Apollo   **458. Parnassos:** mountain sacred to Apollo

Bewildered as a blown bird, my soul hovers and can not find
Foothold in this debate, or any reason or rest of mind.   470
But no man ever brought—none can bring
Proof of strife between Thebes' royal house,
Labdakos' line, and the son of Polybos;
And never until now has any man brought word
Of Laïos' dark death staining Oedipus the King.   475

ANTISTROPHE 2

Divine Zeus and Apollo hold
Perfect intelligence alone of all tales ever told;
And well though this diviner works, he works in his own night;
No man can judge that rough unknown or trust in second sight,
For wisdom changes hands among the wise.   480
Shall I believe my great lord criminal
At a raging word that a blind old man let fall?
I saw him, when the carrion woman° faced him of old,
Prove his heroic mind. These evil words are lies.

SCENE 2

KREON. Men of Thebes: 485
   I am told that heavy accusations
   Have been brought against me by King Oedipus.

   I am not the kind of man to bear this tamely.

   If in these present difficulties
   He holds me accountable for any harm to him   490
   Through anything I have said or done—why, then,
   I do not value life in this dishonor.
   It is not as though this rumor touched upon
   Some private indiscretion. The matter is grave.
   The fact is that I am being called disloyal   495
   To the State, to my fellow citizens, to my friends.
CHORAGOS.   He may have spoken in anger, not from his mind.
KREON.   But did you not hear him say I was the one
   Who seduced the old prophet into lying?
CHORAGOS.   The thing was said; I do not know how seriously.   500
KREON.   But you were watching him! Were his eyes steady?
   Did he look like a man in his right mind?
CHORAGOS.   I do not know.
   I can not judge the behavior of great men.

483. woman: the Sphinx

But here is the king himself. (*Enter* OEDIPUS.)
OEDIPUS.   So you dared come back.
   Why? How brazen of you to come to my house,   505
   You murderer!
                     Do you think I do not know
   That you plotted to kill me, plotted to steal my throne?
   Tell me, in God's name: am I coward, a fool,
   That you should dream you could accomplish this?
   A fool who could not see your slippery game?   510
   A coward, not to fight back when I saw it?
   You are the fool, Kreon, are you not? hoping
   Without support or friends to get a throne?
   Thrones may be won or bought: you could do neither.
KREON.   Now listen to me. You have talked; let me talk, too.   515
   You can not judge unless you know the facts.
OEDIPUS.   You speak well: there is one fact; but I find it hard
   To learn from the deadliest enemy I have.
KREON.   That above all I must dispute with you.
OEDIPUS.   That above all I will not hear you deny.   520
KREON.   If you think there is anything good in being stubborn
   Against all reason, then I say you are wrong.
OEDIPUS.   If you think a man can sin against his own kind
   And not be punished for it, I say you are mad.
KREON.   I agree. But tell me: what have I done to you?   525
OEDIPUS.   You advised me to send for that wizard, did you not?
KREON.   I did. I should do it again.
OEDIPUS.   Very well, Now tell me:
   How long has it been since Laïos—
KREON.   What of Laïos?
OEDIPUS.   Since he vanished in that onset by the road?
KREON.   It was long ago, a long time.
OEDIPUS.   And this prophet,   530
   Was he practicing here then?
KREON.   He was; and with honor, as now.
OEDIPUS.   Did he speak of me at that time?
KREON.   He never did,
   At least, not when I was present.
OEDIPUS.   But . . . the enquiry?
   I suppose you held one?
KREON.   We did, but we learned nothing.
OEDIPUS.   Why did the prophet not speak against me then?   535
KREON.   I do not know; and I am the kind of man
   Who holds his tongue when he has no facts to go on.
OEDIPUS.   There's one fact that you know, and you could tell it.
KREON.   What fact is that? If I know it, you shall have it.

OEDIPUS.   If he were not involved with you, he could not say   540
    That it was I who murdered Laïos.

KREON.   If he says that, you are the one that knows it!—
    But now it is my turn to question you.

OEDIPUS.   Put your questions. I am no murderer.

KREON.   First, then: You married my sister?

OEDIPUS.   I married your sister.   545

KREON.   And you rule the kingdom equally with her?

OEDIPUS.   Everything that she wants she has from me.

KREON.   And I am the third, equal to both of you?

OEDIPUS.   That is why I call you a bad friend.

KREON.   No. Reason it out, as I have done.   550
    Think of this first: Would any sane man prefer
    Power, with all a king's anxieties,
    To that same power and the grace of sleep?
    Certainly not I.
    I have never longed for the king's power—only his rights.   555
    Would any wise man differ from me in this?
    As the matters stand, I have my way in everything
    With your consent, and no responsibilities.
    If I were king, I should be a slave to policy.
    How could I desire a scepter more   560
    Than what is now mine—untroubled influence?
    No, I have not gone mad; I need no honors,
    Except those with the perquisites I have now.
    I am welcome everywhere; every man salutes me,
    And those who want your favor seek my ear,   565
    Since I know how to manage what they ask.
    Should I exchange this ease for that anxiety?
    Besides, no sober mind is treasonable.
    I hate anarchy
    And never would deal with any man who likes it.   570

    Test what I have said. Go to the priestess
    At Delphi, ask if I quoted her correctly.
    And as for this other thing: if I am found
    Guilty of treason with Teiresias,
    Then sentence me to death. You have my word   575
    It is a sentence I should cast my vote for—
    But not without evidence!
                   You do wrong
    When you take good men for bad, bad men for good.
    A true friend thrown aside—why, life itself
    Is not more precious!
                 In time you will know this well: 580

For time, and time alone, will show the just man,
Though scoundrels are discovered in a day.

CHORAGOS.   This is well said, and a prudent man would ponder it.
Judgments too quickly formed are dangerous.

OEDIPUS.   But is he not quick in his duplicity?   585
And shall I not be quick to parry him?
Would you have me stand still, hold my peace, and let
This man win everything, through my inaction?

KREON.   And you want—what is it, then? To banish me?

OEDIPUS.   No, not exile. It is your death I want,   590
So that all the world may see what treason means.

KREON.   You will persist, then? You will not believe me?

OEDIPUS.   How can I believe you?

KREON.   Then you are a fool.

OEDIPUS.   To save myself?

KREON.   In justice, think of me.

OEDIPUS.   You are evil incarnate.

KREON.   But suppose that you are wrong?   595

OEDIPUS.   Still I must rule.

KREON.   But not if you rule badly.

OEDIPUS.   O city, city!

KREON.   It is my city, too!

CHORAGOS.   Now, my lords, be still. I see the queen,
Iokastê, coming from her palace chambers;
And it is time she came, for the sake of you both.   600
This dreadful quarrel can be resolved through her. (*Enter* IOKASTÊ.)

IOKASTÊ.   Poor foolish men, what wicked din is this?
With Thebes sick to death, is it not shameful
That you should rake some private quarrel up?
(*To* OEDIPUS) Come into the house.
                                —And you, Kreon, go now: 605
Let us have no more of this tumult over nothing.

KREON.   Nothing? No, sister: what your husband plans for me
Is one of two great evils: exile or death.

OEDIPUS.   He is right.
                        Why, woman I have caught him squarely
Plotting against my life.

KREON.   No! Let me die   610
Accurst if ever I have wished you harm!

IOKASTÊ.   Ah, believe it, Oedipus!
In the name of the gods, respect this oath of his
For my sake, for the sake of these people here!

STROPHE 1

CHORAGOS.   Open your mind to her, my lord. Be ruled by her, I beg you! 615

OEDIPUS.   What would you have me do?

CHORAGOS.   Respect Kreon's word. He has never spoken like a fool,
And now he has sworn an oath.

OEDIPUS.   You know what you ask?

CHORAGOS.   I do.

OEDIPUS.   Speak on, then.

CHORAGOS.   A friend so sworn should not be baited so,
In blind malice, and without final proof.   620

OEDIPUS.   You are aware, I hope, that what you say
Means death for me, or exile at the least.

STROPHE 2

CHORAGOS.   No, I swear by Helios, first in heaven!
            May I die friendless and accurst,
            The worst of deaths, if ever I meant that!   625
            It is the withering fields
                That hurt my sick heart:
            Must we bear all these ills,
                And now your blood as well?

OEDIPUS.   Then let him go. And let me die, if I must,   630
Or be driven by him in shame from the land of Thebes.
It is your unhappiness, and not his talk,
That touches me.
                As for him—
Wherever he goes, hatred will follow him.

KREON.   Ugly in yielding, as you were ugly in rage!   635
Natures like yours chiefly torment themselves.

OEDIPUS.   Can you not go? Can you not leave me?

KREON.   I can.
You do not know me; but the city knows me,
And in its eyes I am just, if not in yours. (*Exit* KREON.)

ANTISTROPHE 1

CHORAGOS.   Lady Iokastê, did you not ask the King to go to his
        chambers?   640

IOKASTÊ.   First tell me what has happened.

CHORAGOS.   There was suspicion without evidence; yet it rankled
As even false charges will.

IOKASTÊ.   On both sides?

CHORAGOS.   On both.

IOKASTÊ.   But what was said?

CHORAGOS.   Oh let it rest, let it be done with!
Have we not suffered enough?   645

OEDIPUS.   You see to what your decency has brought you:
You have made difficulties where my heart saw none.

ANTISTROPHE 2

CHORAGOS.   Oedipus, it is not once only I have told you—
            You must know I should count myself unwise
              To the point of madness, should I now forsake you—   650
                  You, under whose hand,
                     In the storm of another time,
                 Our dear land sailed out free.
                 But now stand fast at the helm!
IOKASTÊ.   In God's name, Oedipus, inform your wife as well: 655
    Why are you so set in this hard anger?
OEDIPUS.   I will tell you, for none of these men deserves
    My confidence as you do. It is Kreon's work,
    His treachery, his plotting against me.
IOKASTÊ.   Go on, if you can make this clear to me.   660
OEDIPUS.   He charges me with the murder of Laïos.
IOKASTÊ.   Has he some knowledge? Or does he speak from hearsay?
OEDIPUS.   He would not commit himself to such a charge,
    But he has brought in that damnable soothsayer
    To tell his story.
IOKASTÊ.   Set your mind at rest.   665
    If it is a question of soothsayers, I tell you
    That you will find no man whose craft gives knowledge
    Of the unknowable.
                Here is my proof:
    An oracle was reported to Laïos once
    (I will not say from Phoibos himself, but from   670
    His appointed ministers, at any rate)
    That his doom would be death at the hands of his own son—
    His son, born of his flesh and of mine!

    Now, you remember the story: Laïos was killed
    By marauding strangers where three highways meet;   675
    But his child had not been three days in this world
    Before the king had pierced the baby's ankles
    And left him to die on a lonely mountainside.

    Thus, Apollo never caused that child
    To kill his father, and it was not Laïos' fate   680
    To die at the hands of his son, as he had feared.
    This is what prophets and prophecies are worth!
    Have no dread of them.
                It is God himself
    Who can show us what he wills, in his own way.
OEDIPUS.   How strange a shadowy memory crossed my mind,   685

Just now while you were speaking; it chilled my heart.

IOKASTÊ.   What do you mean? What memory do you speak of?

OEDIPUS.   If I understand you, Laïos was killed
    At a place where three roads meet.

IOKASTÊ.   So it was said;
    We have no later story.

OEDIPUS.   Where did it happen?   690

IOKASTÊ.   Phokis, it is called: at a place where the Theban Way
    Divides into the roads toward Delphi and Daulia.

OEDIPUS.   When?

IOKASTÊ.   We had the news not long before you came
    And proved the right to your succession here.

OEDIPUS.   Ah, what net has God been weaving for me?   695

IOKASTÊ.   Oedipus! Why does this trouble you?

OEDIPUS.   Do not ask me yet.
    First, tell me how Laïos looked, and tell me
    How old he was.

IOKASTÊ.   He was tall, his hair just touched
    With white; his form was not unlike your own.

OEDIPUS.   I think that I myself may be accurst   700
    By my own ignorant edict.

IOKASTÊ.   You speak strangely.
    It makes me tremble to look at you, my king.

OEDIPUS.   I am not sure that the blind man can not see.
    But I should know better if you were to tell me—

IOKASTÊ.   Anything—though I dread to hear you ask it.   705

OEDIPUS.   Was the king lightly escorted, or did he ride
    With a large company, as a ruler should?

IOKASTÊ.   There were five men with him in all: one was a herald;
    And a single chariot, which he was driving.

OEDIPUS.   Alas, that makes it plain enough!

                               But who—   710
    Who told you how it happened?

IOKASTÊ.   A household servant,
    The only one to escape.

OEDIPUS.   And is he still
    A servant of ours?

IOKASTÊ.   No; for when he came back at last
    And found you enthroned in the place of the dead king,
    He came to me, touched my hand with his, and begged   715
    That I would send him away to the frontier district
    Where only the shepherds go—
    As far away from the city as I could send him.
    I granted his prayer; for although the man was a slave,
    He had earned more than this favor at my hands.   720

OEDIPUS.   Can he be called back quickly?
IOKASTÊ.   Easily.
    But why?
OEDIPUS.   I have taken too much upon myself
    Without enquiry; therefore I wish to consult him.
IOKASTÊ.   Then he shall come.
                              But am I not one also
    To whom you might confide these fears of yours?   725
OEDIPUS.   That is your right; it will not be denied you,
    Now least of all; for I have reached a pitch
    Of wild foreboding. Is there anyone
    To whom I should sooner speak?

    Polybos of Corinth is my father.   730
    My mother is a Dorian: Meropê.
    I grew up chief among the men of Corinth
    Until a strange thing happened—
    Not worth my passion, it may be, but strange.
    At a feast, a drunken man maundering in his cups   735
    Cries out that I am not my father's son!

    I contained myself that night, though I felt anger
    And a sinking heart. The next day I visited
    My father and mother, and questioned them. They stormed,
    Calling it all the slanderous rant of a fool;   740
    And this relieved me. Yet the suspicion
    Remained always aching in my mind;
    I knew there was talk; I could not rest;
    And finally, saying nothing to my parents,
    I went to the shrine at Delphi.   745

    The god dismissed my question without reply;
    He spoke of other things.
                              Some were clear,
    Full of wretchedness, dreadful, unbearable:
    As, that I should lie with my own mother, breed
    Children from whom all men would turn their eyes;   750
    And that I should be my father's murderer.

    I heard all this, and fled. And from that day
    Corinth to me was only in the stars
    Descending in that quarter of the sky,
    As I wandered farther and farther on my way   755
    To a land where I should never see the evil

Sung by the oracle. And I came to this country
Where, so you say, King Laïos was killed.

I will tell you all that happened there, my lady.

There were three highways   760
Coming together at a place I passed;
And there a herald came towards me, and a chariot
Drawn by horses, with a man such as you describe
Seated in it. The groom leading the horses
Forced me off the road at his lord's command;   765
But as this charioteer lurched over towards me
I struck him in my rage. The old man saw me
And brought his double goad down upon my head
As I came abreast.
                        He was paid back, and more!
Swinging my club in this right hand I knocked him   770
Out of his car, and he rolled on the ground.
                                        I killed him.

I killed them all.
Now if that stranger and Laïos were—kin,
Where is a man more miserable than I?
More hated by the gods? Citizen and alien alike   775
Must never shelter me or speak to me—
I must be shunned by all.
                        And I myself
Pronounced this malediction upon myself!

Think of it: I have touched you with these hands,
These hands that killed your husband. What defilement!   780

Am I all evil, then? It must be so,
Since I must flee from Thebes, yet never again
See my own countrymen, my own country,
For fear of joining my mother in marriage
And killing Polybos, my father.
                        Ah,   785
If I was created so, born to this fate,
Who could deny the savagery of God?

O holy majesty of heavenly powers!
May I never see that day! Never!
Rather let me vanish from the race of men   790

Than know the abomination destined me!
CHORAGOS.   We too, my lord, have felt dismay at this.
    But there is hope: you have yet to hear the shepherd.
OEDIPUS.   Indeed, I fear no other hope is left me.
IOKASTÊ.   What do you hope from him when he comes?
OEDIPUS.   This much: 795
    If his account of the murder tallies with yours,
    Then I am cleared.
IOKASTÊ.   What was it that I said
    Of such importance?
OEDIPUS.   Why, "marauders," you said,
    Killed the king, according to this man's story.
    If he maintains that still, if there were several,   800
    Clearly the guilt is not mine: I was alone.
    But if he says one man, singlehanded, did it,
    Then the evidence all points to me.
IOKASTÊ.   You may be sure that he said there were several;
    And can he call back that story now? He can not.   805
    The whole city heard it as plainly as I.
    But suppose he alters some detail of it:
    He can not ever show that Laïos' death
    Fulfilled the oracle: for Apollo said
    My child was doomed to kill him; and my child—   810
    Poor baby!—it was my child that died first.

    No. From now on, where oracles are concerned,
    I would not waste a second thought on any.
OEDIPUS.   You may be right.
                    But come: let someone go
    For the shepherd at once. This matter must be settled.   815
IOKASTÊ.   I will send for him.
    I would not wish to cross you in anything.
    And surely not in this.—Let us go in. (*Exeunt into the palace.*)

ODE 2

STROPHE 1

CHORUS.   Let me be reverent in the ways of right,
    Lowly the paths I journey on;   820
    Let all my words and actions keep
    The laws of the pure universe
    From highest Heaven handed down
    For Heaven is their bright nurse,
    Those generations of the realms of light;   825

Ah, never of mortal kind were they begot,
Nor are they slaves of memory, lost in sleep:
Their Father is greater than Time, and ages not.

ANTISTROPHE 1

The tyrant is a child of Pride
Who drinks from his great sickening cup   830
Recklessness and vanity,
Until from his high crest headlong
He plummets to the dust of hope.
That strong man is not strong.
But let no fair ambition be denied;   835
May God protect the wrestler for the State
In government, in comely policy,
Who will fear God, and on His ordinance wait.

STROPHE 2

Haughtiness and the high hand of disdain
Tempt and outrage God's holy law;   840
And any mortal who dares hold
No immortal Power in awe
Will be caught up in a net of pain:
The price for which his levity is sold.
Let each man take due earnings, then,   845
And keep his hands from holy things,
And from blasphemy stand apart—
Else the crackling blast of heaven
Blows on his head, and on his desperate heart.
Though fools will honor impious men,   850
In their cities no tragic poet sings.

ANTISTROPHE 2

Shall we lose faith in Delphi's obscurities,
We who have heard the world's core
Discredited, and the sacred wood
Of Zeus at Elis praised no more?   855
The deeds and the strange prophecies
Must make a pattern yet to be understood.
Zeus, if indeed you are lord of all,
Throned in light over night and day,
Mirror this in your endless mind: 860
Our masters call the oracle
Words on the wind, and the Delphic vision blind!

Their hearts no longer know Apollo,
And reverence for the gods has died away.

SCENE 3

Enter IOKASTÊ.

IOKASTÊ.   Princes of Thebes, it has occurred to me   865
   To visit the altars of the gods, bearing
   These branches as a suppliant, and this incense.
   Our king is not himself: his noble soul
   Is overwrought with fantasies of dread,
   Else he would consider   870
   The new prophecies in the light of the old.
   He will listen to any voice that speaks disaster,
   And my advice goes for nothing. (*She approaches the altar, right.*)
                              To you, then, Apollo,
   Lycéan lord, since you are nearest, I turn in prayer.
   Receive these offerings, and grant us deliverance   875
   From defilement. Our hearts are heavy with fear
   When we see our leader distracted, as helpless sailors
   Are terrified by the confusion of their helmsman. (*Enter* MESSENGER.)
MESSENGER.   Friends, no doubt you can direct me:
   Where shall I find the house of Oedipus,   880
   Or, better still, where is the king himself?
CHORAGOS.   It is this very place, stranger; he is inside.
   This is his wife and mother of his children.
MESSENGER.   I wish her happiness in a happy house,
   Blest in all the fulfillment of her marriage.   885
IOKASTÊ.   I wish as much for you: your courtesy
   Deserves a like good fortune. But now, tell me:
   Why have you come? What have you to say to us?
MESSENGER.   Good news, my lady, for your house and your husband.
IOKASTÊ.   What news? Who sent you here?
MESSENGER.   I am from Corinth.   890
   The news I bring ought to mean joy for you,
   Though it may be you will find some grief in it.
IOKASTÊ.   What is it? How can it touch us in both ways?
MESSENGER.   The word is that the people of the Isthmus
   Intend to call Oedipus to be their king.   895
IOKASTÊ.   But old King Polybos—is he not reigning still?
MESSENGER.   No. Death holds him in his sepulcher.
IOKASTÊ.   What are you saying? Polybos is dead?
MESSENGER.   If I am not telling the truth, may I die myself.

IOKASTÊ (*to a* MAIDSERVANT).   Go in, go quickly; tell this to your master.   900
   O riddlers of God's will, where are you now!
   This was the man whom Oedipus, long ago,
   Feared so, fled so, in dread of destroying him—
   But it was another fate by which he died. (*Enter* OEDIPUS, *center.*)
OEDIPUS.   Dearest Iokastê, why have you sent for me?   905
IOKASTÊ.   Listen to what this man says, and then tell me
   What has become of the solemn prophecies.
OEDIPUS.   Who is this man? What is his news for me?
IOKASTÊ.   He has come from Corinth to announce your father's death!
OEDIPUS.   Is it true, stranger? Tell me in your own words.   910
MESSENGER.   I can not say it more clearly: the king is dead.
OEDIPUS.   Was it by treason? Or by an attack of illness?
MESSENGER.   A little thing brings old men to their rest.
OEDIPUS.   It was sickness, then?
MESSENGER.   Yes, and his many years.
OEDIPUS.   Ah!   915
   Why should a man respect the Pythian hearth,° or
   Give heed to the birds that jangle above his head?
   They prophesied that I should kill Polybos,
   Kill my own father; but he is dead and buried,
   And I am here—I never touched him, never,   920
   Unless he died of grief for my departure,
   And thus, in a sense, through me. No. Polybos
   Has packed the oracles off with him underground.
   They are empty words.
IOKASTÊ.   Had I not told you so?
OEDIPUS.   You had; it was my faint heart that betrayed me.   925
IOKASTÊ.   From now on never think of those things again.
OEDIPUS.   And yet—must I not fear my mother's bed?
IOKASTÊ.   Why should anyone in this world be afraid,
   Since Fate rules us and nothing can be foreseen?
   A man should live only for the present day.   930

   Have no more fear of sleeping with your mother:
   How many men, in dreams, have lain with their mothers!
   No reasonable man is troubled by such things.
OEDIPUS.   That is true; only—
   If only my mother were not still alive!   935
   But she is alive. I can not help my dread.
IOKASTÊ.   Yet this news of your father's death is wonderful.
OEDIPUS.   Wonderful. But I fear the living woman.

916. Pythian hearth: Delphi

MESSENGER.   Tell me who is this woman that you fear?
OEDIPUS.   It is Meropê, man; the wife of King Polybos.   940
MESSENGER.   Meropê? Why should you be afraid of her?
OEDIPUS.   An oracle of the gods, a dreadful saying.
MESSENGER.   Can you tell me about it or are you sworn to silence?
OEDIPUS.   I can tell you, and I will.

    Apollo said through his prophet that I was the man   945
    Who should marry his own mother, shed his father's blood
    With his own hands. And so, for all these years
    I have kept clear of Corinth, and no harm has come—
    Though it would have been sweet to see my parents again.

MESSENGER.   And is this the fear that drove you out of Corinth?   950
OEDIPUS.   Would you have me kill my father?
MESSENGER.   As for that
    You must be reassured by the news I gave you.
OEDIPUS.   If you could reassure me, I would reward you.
MESSENGER.   I had that in mind, I will confess; I thought
    I could count on you when you returned to Corinth.   955
OEDIPUS.   No: I will never go near my parents again.
MESSENGER.   Ah, son, you still do not know what you are doing—
OEDIPUS.   What do you mean? In the name of God tell me!
MESSENGER.   —If these are your reasons for not going home.
OEDIPUS.   I tell you, I fear the oracle may come true.   960
MESSENGER.   And guilt may come upon you through your parents?
OEDIPUS.   That is the dread that is always in my heart.
MESSENGER.   Can you not see that all your fears are groundless?
OEDIPUS.   Groundless? Am I not my parents' son?
MESSENGER.   Polybos was not your father.
OEDIPUS.   Not my father?   965
MESSENGER.   No more your father than the man speaking to you.
OEDIPUS.   But you are nothing to me!
MESSENGER.   Neither was he.
OEDIPUS.   Then why did he call me son?
MESSENGER.   I will tell you:
    Long ago he had you from my hands, as a gift.
OEDIPUS.   Then how could he love me so, if I was not his?   970
MESSENGER.   He had no children, and his heart turned to you.
OEDIPUS.   What of you? Did you buy me? Did you find me by chance?
MESSENGER.   I came upon you in the woody vales of Kithairon.
OEDIPUS.   And what were you doing there?
MESSENGER.   Tending my flocks.
OEDIPUS.   A wandering shepherd?
MESSENGER.   But your savior, son, that day.   975
OEDIPUS.   From what did you save me?
MESSENGER.   Your ankles should tell you that.

OEDIPUS.   Ah, stranger, why do you speak of that childhood pain?
MESSENGER.   I pulled the skewer that pinned your feet together.
OEDIPUS.   I have had the mark as long as I can remember.
MESSENGER.   That was why you were given the name you bear.   980
OEDIPUS.   God! Was it my father or my mother who did it?
    Tell me!
MESSENGER.   I do not know. The man who gave you to me
    Can tell you better than I.
OEDIPUS.   It was not you that found me, but another?
MESSENGER.   It was another shepherd gave you to me.   985
OEDIPUS.   Who was he? Can you tell me who he was?
MESSENGER.   I think he was said to be one of Laïos' people.
OEDIPUS.   You mean the Laïos who was king here years ago?
MESSENGER.   Yes; King Laïos; and the man was one of his herdsmen.
OEDIPUS.   Is he still alive? Can I see him?
MESSENGER.   These men here   990
    Know best about such things.
OEDIPUS.   Does anyone here
    Know this shepherd that he is talking about?
    Have you seen him in the fields, or in the town?
    If you have, tell me. It is time things were made plain.
CHORAGOS.   I think the man he means is that same shepherd   995
    You have already asked to see. Iokastê perhaps
    Could tell you something.
OEDIPUS.   Do you know anything
    About him, Lady? Is he the man we have summoned?
    Is that the man this shepherd means?
IOKASTÊ.   Why think of him?
    Forget this herdsman. Forget it all.   1000
    This talk is a waste of time.
OEDIPUS.   How can you say that,
    When the clues to my true birth are in my hands?
IOKASTÊ.   For God's love, let us have no more questioning!
    Is your life nothing to you?
    My own is pain enough for me to bear.   1005
OEDIPUS.   You need not worry. Suppose my mother a slave,
    And born of slaves: no baseness can touch you.
IOKASTÊ.   Listen to me, I beg you: do not do this thing!
OEDIPUS.   I will not listen; the truth must be made known.
IOKASTÊ.   Everything that I say is for your own good!
OEDIPUS.   My own good   1010
    Snaps my patience, then; I want none of it.
IOKASTÊ.   You are fatally wrong! May you never learn who you are!
OEDIPUS.   Go, one of you, and bring the shepherd here.
    Let us leave this woman to brag of her royal name.

IOKASTÊ.   Ah, miserable!   1015
    That is the only word I have for you now.
    That is the only word I can ever have. (*Exit into the palace.*)
CHORAGOS.   Why has she left us, Oedipus? Why has she gone
    In such a passion of sorrow? I fear this silence:
    Something dreadful may come of it.
OEDIPUS.   Let it come!   1020
    However base my birth, I must know about it.
    The Queen, like a woman, is perhaps ashamed
    To think of my low origin. But I
    Am a child of Luck; I can not be dishonored.
    Luck is my mother; the passing months, my brothers,   1025
    Have seen me rich and poor.
                                    If this is so,
    How could I wish that I were someone else?
    How could I not be glad to know my birth?

ODE 3

STROPHE

CHORUS.   If ever the coming time were known
    To my heart's pondering,   1030
    Kithairon, now by Heaven I see the torches
    At the festival of the next full moon,
    And see the dance, and hear the choir sing
    A grace to your gentle shade:
    Mountain where Oedipus was found,   1035
    O mountain guard of a noble race!
    May the god° who heals us lend his aid,
    And let that glory come to pass
    For our king's cradling-ground.

ANTISTROPHE

    Of the nymphs that flower beyond the years,   1040
    Who bore you,° royal child,
    To Pan of the hills or the timberline Apollo,
    Cold in delight where the upland clears,
    Or Hermês for whom Kyllenê's heights are piled?
    Or flushed as evening cloud,   1045

1037. god: Apollo   **1041. Who bore you:** The chorus is suggesting that perhaps
Oedipus is the son of one of the immortal nymphs and of a god—Pan, Apollo, Hermes,
or Dionysis. The "sweet god-ravisher" (line 1049) is the presumed mother.

Great Dionysis, roamer of mountains,
He—was it he who found you there,
And caught you up in his own proud
Arms from the sweet god-ravisher
Who laughed by the Muses' fountains?   1050

SCENE 4

OEDIPUS.   Sirs: though I do not know the man,
  I think I see him coming, this shepherd we want:
  He is old, like our friend here, and the men
  Bringing him seem to be servants of my house.
  But you can tell, if you have ever seen him.   1055
  (*Enter* SHEPHERD *escorted by* SERVANTS.)
CHORAGOS.   I know him, he was Laïos' man. You can trust him.
OEDIPUS.   Tell me first, you from Corinth: is this the shepherd
  We were discussing?
MESSENGER.   This is the very man.
OEDIPUS (*to* SHEPHERD).   Come here. No, look at me. You must answer
  Everything I ask.— You belonged to Laïos?   1060
SHEPHERD.   Yes: born his slave, brought up in his house.
OEDIPUS.   Tell me: what kind of work did you do for him?
SHEPHERD.   I was a shepherd of his, most of my life.
OEDIPUS.   Where mainly did you go for pasturage?
SHEPHERD.   Sometimes Kithairon, sometimes the hills near-by.   1065
OEDIPUS.   Do you remember ever seeing this man out there?
SHEPHERD.   What would he be doing there? This man?
OEDIPUS.   This man standing here. Have you ever seen him before?
SHEPHERD.   No. At least, not to my recollection.
MESSENGER.   And that is not strange, my lord. But I'll refresh   1070
  His memory: he must remember when we two
  Spent three whole seasons together, March to September,
  On Kithairon or thereabouts. He had two flocks;
  I had one. Each autumn I'd drive mine home
  And he would go back with his to Laïos' sheepfold.—   1075
  Is this not true, just as I have described it?
SHEPHERD.   True, yes; but it was all so long ago.
MESSENGER.   Well, then: do you remember, back in those days,
  That you gave me a baby boy to bring up as my own?
SHEPHERD.   What if I did? What are you trying to say?   1080
MESSENGER.   King Oedipus was once that little child.
SHEPHERD.   Damn you, hold your tongue!
OEDIPUS.   No more of that!
  It is your tongue needs watching, not this man's.

SHEPHERD.   My king, my master, what is it I have done wrong?
OEDIPUS.   You have not answered his question about the boy.   1085
SHEPHERD.   He does not know . . . He is only making trouble . . .
OEDIPUS.   Come, speak plainly, or it will go hard with you.
SHEPHERD.   In God's name, do not torture an old man!
OEDIPUS.   Come here, one of you; bind his arms behind him.
SHEPHERD.   Unhappy king! What more do you wish to learn?   1090
OEDIPUS.   Did you give this man the child he speaks of?
SHEPHERD.   I did.
　　　And I would to God I had died that very day.
OEDIPUS.   You will die now unless you speak the truth.
SHEPHERD.   Yet if I speak the truth, I am worse than dead.
OEDIPUS (*to* ATTENDANT).   He intends to draw it out, apparently—   1095
SHEPHERD.   No! I have told you already that I gave him the boy.
OEDIPUS.   Where did you get him? From your house? From somewhere else?
SHEPHERD.   Not from mine, no. A man gave him to me.
OEDIPUS.   Is that man here? Whose house did he belong to?
SHEPHERD.   For God's love, my king, do not ask me any more!   1100
OEDIPUS.   You are a dead man if I have to ask you again.
SHEPHERD.   Then . . . Then the child was from the palace of Laïos.
OEDIPUS.   A slave child? or a child of his own line?
SHEPHERD.   Ah, I am on the brink of dreadful speech!
OEDIPUS.   And I of dreadful hearing. Yet I must hear.   1105
SHEPHERD.   If you must be told, then . . .
　　　　　　　　　　　　　　　They said it was Laïos' child;
　　　But it is your wife who can tell you about that.
OEDIPUS.   My wife—Did she give it to you?
SHEPHERD.   My lord, she did.
OEDIPUS.   Do you know why?
SHEPHERD.   I was told to get rid of it.
OEDIPUS.   Oh heartless mother!
SHEPHERD.   But in dread of prophecies . . .   1110
OEDIPUS.   Tell me.
SHEPHERD.   It was said that the boy would kill his own father.
OEDIPUS.   Then why did you give him over to this old man?
SHEPHERD.   I pitied the baby, my king,
　　　And I thought that this man would take him far away
　　　To his own country.
　　　　　　　　　He saved him—but for what a fate!   1115
　　　For if you are what this man says you are,
　　　No man living is more wretched than Oedipus.
OEDIPUS.   Ah God!
　　　It was true!
　　　　　　All the prophecies!
　　　　　　　　　—Now,

O Light, may I look on you for the last time!   1120
I, Oedipus,
Oedipus, damned in his birth, in his marriage damned,
Damned in the blood he shed with his own hand!
(*He rushes into the palace.*)

ODE 4

STROPHE 1

CHORUS.   Alas for the seed of men.
What measure shall I give these generations   1125
That breathe on the void and are void
And exist and do not exist?
Who bears more weight of joy
Than mass of sunlight shifting in images,
Or who shall make his thought stay on   1130
That down time drifts away?
Your splendor is all fallen.
O naked brow of wrath and tears,
O change of Oedipus!
I who saw your days call no man blest—   1135
Your great days like ghósts góne.

ANTISTROPHE 1

That mind was a strong bow.
Deep, how deep you drew it then, hard archer,
At a dim fearful range,
And brought dear glory down!   1140
You overcame the stranger°—
The virgin with her hooking lion claws—
And though death sang, stood like a tower
To make pale Thebes take heart.
Fortress against our sorrow!   1145
True king, giver of laws,
Majestic Oedipus!
No prince in Thebes had ever such renown,
No prince won such grace of power.

STROPHE 2

And now of all men ever known   1150
Most pitiful is this man's story:

1141. stranger: the Sphinx

His fortunes are most changed; his state
Fallen to a low slave's
Ground under bitter fate.
O Oedipus, most royal one!   1155
The great door° that expelled you to the light
Gave at night—ah, gave night to your glory:
As to the father, to the fathering son.
All understood too late.
How could that queen whom Laïos won,   1160
The garden that he harrowed at his height,
Be silent when that act was done?

ANTISTROPHE 2

But all eyes fail before time's eye,
All actions come to justice there.
Though never willed, though far down the deep past,   1165
Your bed, your dread sirings,
Are brought to book at last.
Child by Laïos doomed to die,
Then doomed to lose that fortunate little death,
Would God you never took breath in this air   1170
That with my wailing lips I take to cry:
For I weep the world's outcast.
I was blind, and now I can tell why:
Asleep, for you had given ease of breath
To Thebes, while the false years went by.   1175

EXODOS°

Enter, from the palace, SECOND MESSENGER.

SECOND MESSENGER.   Elders of Thebes, most honored in this land,
     What horrors are yours to see and hear, what weight
     Of sorrow to be endured, if, true to your birth,
     You venerate the line of Labdakos!
     I think neither Istros nor Phasis, those great rivers,   1180
     Could purify this place of all the evil
     It shelters now, or soon must bring to light—
     Evil not done unconsciously, but willed.

     The greatest griefs are those we cause ourselves.
CHORAGOS.   Surely, friend, we have grief enough already;   1185
     What new sorrow do you mean?
SECOND MESSENGER.   The queen is dead.

1156. door: Iokastê's womb   **Exodos:** final scene

CHORAGOS.   O miserable queen! But at whose hand?
SECOND MESSENGER.   Her own.
    The full horror of what happened you can not know,
    For you did not see it; but I, who did, will tell you
    As clearly as I can how she met her death.   1190

    When she had left us,
    In passionate silence, passing through the court,
    She ran to her apartment in the house,
    Her hair clutched by the fingers of both hands.
    She closed the doors behind her; then, by that bed   1195
    Where long ago the fatal son was conceived—
    That son who should bring about his father's death—
    We heard her call upon Laïos, dead so many years,
    And heard her wail for the double fruit of her marriage,
    A husband by her husband, children by her child.   1200

    Exactly how she died I do not know:
    For Oedipus burst in moaning and would not let us
    Keep vigil to the end: it was by him
    As he stormed about the room that our eyes were caught.
    From one to another of us he went, begging a sword,   1205
    Hunting the wife who was not his wife, the mother
    Whose womb had carried his own children and himself.
    I do not know: it was none of us aided him,
    But surely one of the gods was in control!
    For with a dreadful cry   1210
    He hurled his weight, as though wrenched out of himself,
    At the twin doors: the bolts gave, and he rushed in.
    And there we saw her hanging, her body swaying
    From the cruel cord she had noosed about her neck.
    A great sob broke from him, heartbreaking to hear,   1215
    As he loosened the rope and lowered her to the ground.

    I would blot out from my mind what happened next!
    For the king ripped from her gown the golden brooches
    That were her ornament, and raised them, and plunged them down
    Straight into his own eyeballs, crying, "No more,   1220
    No more shall you look on the misery about me,
    The horrors of my own doing! Too long you have known
    The faces of those whom I should never have seen,
    Too long been blind to those for whom I was searching!
    From this hour, go in darkness!" And as he spoke,   1225
    He struck his eyes—not once, but many times;
    And the blood spattered his beard,
    Bursting from his ruined sockets like red hail.

So from the unhappiness of two this evil has sprung,
A curse on the man and woman alike. The old   1230
Happiness of the house of Labdakos
Was happiness enough: where is it today?
It is all wailing and ruin, disgrace, death—all
The misery of mankind that has a name—
And it is wholly and for ever theirs.   1235
CHORAGOS.   Is he in agony still? Is there no rest for him?
SECOND MESSENGER.   He is calling for someone to open the doors wide
So that all the children of Kadmos may look upon
His father's murderer, his mother's—no,
I can not say it!
And then he will leave Thebes,   1240
Self-exiled, in order that the curse
Which he himself pronounced may depart from the house.
He is weak, and there is none to lead him,
So terrible is his suffering.
But you will see:
Look, the doors are opening; in a moment   1245
You will see a thing that would crush a heart of stone.
(*The central door is opened;* OEDIPUS, *blinded, is led in.*)
CHORAGOS.   Dreadful indeed for me to see.
Never have my own eyes
Looked on a sight so full of fear.

Oedipus!   1250
What madness came upon you, what daemon
Leaped on your life with heavier
Punishment than a mortal man can bear?
No: I can not even
Look at you, poor ruined one.   1255
And I would speak, question, ponder,
If I were able. No.
You make me shudder.
OEDIPUS.   God. God.
Is there a sorrow greater?   1260
Where shall I find harbor in this world?
My voice is hurled far on a dark wind.
What has God done to me?
CHORAGOS.   Too terrible to think of, or to see.

STROPHE 1

OEDIPUS.   O cloud of night,   1265
Never to be turned away: night coming on,
I can not tell how: night like a shroud!

My fair winds brought me here.
                                    O God. Again
The pain of the spikes where I had sight,
The flooding pain   1270
Of memory, never to be gouged out.
CHORAGOS.   This is not strange.
    You suffer it all twice over, remorse in pain,
    Pain in remorse.

ANTISTROPHE 1

OEDIPUS.   Ah dear friend   1275
    Are you faithful even yet, you alone?
    Are you still standing near me, will you stay here,
    Patient, to care for the blind?
                                    The blind man!
    Yet even blind I know who it is attends me,
    By the voice's tone—   1280
    Though my new darkness hide the comforter.
CHORAGOS.   Oh fearful act!
    What god was it drove you to rake black
    Night across your eyes?

STROPHE 2

OEDIPUS.   Apollo. Apollo. Dear   1285
    Children, the god was Apollo.
    He brought my sick, sick fate upon me.
    But the blinding hand was my own!
    How could I bear to see
    When all my sight was horror everywhere?   1290
CHORAGOS.   Everywhere; that is true.
OEDIPUS.   And now what is left?
    Images? Love? A greeting even,
    Sweet to the senses? Is there anything?
    Ah, no, friends: lead me away.   1295
    Lead me away from Thebes.
                                    Lead the great wreck
    And hell of Oedipus, whom the gods hate.
CHORAGOS.   Your misery, you are not blind to that.
    Would God you had never found it out!

ANTISTROPHE 2

OEDIPUS.   Death take the man who unbound   1300
    My feet on that hillside
    And delivered me from death to life! What life?

If only I had died,
This weight of monstrous doom
Could not have dragged me and my darlings down.   1305
CHORAGOS.   I would have wished the same.
OEDIPUS.   Oh never to have come here
    With my father's blood upon me! Never
    To have been the man they call his mother's husband!
    Oh accurst! Oh child of evil,   1310
    To have entered that wretched bed—
                                    the selfsame one!
    More primal than sin itself, this fell to me.
CHORAGOS.   I do not know what words to offer you.
    You were better dead than alive and blind.
OEDIPUS.   Do not counsel me any more. This punishment   1315
    That I have laid upon myself is just.
    If I had eyes,
    I do not know how I could bear the sight
    Of my father, when I came to the house of Death,
    Or my mother: for I have sinned against them both   1320
    So vilely that I could not make my peace
    By strangling my own life.
                            Or do you think my children,
    Born as they were born, would be sweet to my eyes?
    Ah never, never! Nor this town with its high walls,
    Nor the holy images of the gods.
                            For I,   1325
    Thrice miserable!—Oedipus, noblest of all the line
    Of Kadmos, have condemned myself to enjoy
    These things no more, by my own malediction
    Expelling that man whom the gods declared
    To be a defilement in the house of Laïos.   1330
    After exposing the rankness of my own guilt,
    How could I look men frankly in the eyes?
    No, I swear it.
    If I could have stifled my hearing at its source,
    I would have done it and made all this body   1335
    A tight cell of misery, blank to light and sound:
    So I should have been safe in my dark mind
    Beyond external evil.
                    Ah Kithairon!
    Why did you shelter me? When I was cast upon you,
    Why did I not die? Then I should never   1340
    Have shown the world my execrable birth.

    Ah Polybos! Corinth, city that I believed
    The ancient sea of my ancestors: how fair

I seemed, your child! And all the while this evil
Was cancerous within me!
      For I am sick,   1345
In my own being, sick in my origin.

O three roads, dark ravine, woodland and way
Where three roads met: you, drinking my father's blood,
My own blood, spilled by my own hand: can you remember
The unspeakable things I did there, and the things   1350
I went on from there to do?
       O marriage, marriage!
The act that engendered me, and again the act
Performed by the son in the same bed—
         Ah, the net
Of incest, mingling fathers, brothers, sons,
With brides, wives, mothers: the last evil   1355
That can be known by men: no tongue can say
How evil!
    No. For the love of God, conceal me
Somewhere far from Thebes; or kill me; or hurl me
Into the sea, away from men's eyes for ever.

Come, lead me. You need not fear to touch me.   1360
Of all men, I alone can bear this guilt. (*Enter* KREON.)
CHORAGOS. Kreon is here now. As to what you ask,
 He may decide the course to take. He only
 Is left to protect the city in your place.
OEDIPUS. Alas, how can I speak to him? What right have I 1365
 To beg his courtesy whom I have deeply wronged?
KREON. I have not come to mock you, Oedipus,
 Or to reproach you, either.
  (*To* ATTENDANTS)   —You, standing there:
 If you have lost all respect for man's dignity,
 At least respect the flame of Lord Helios: 1370
 Do not allow this pollution to show itself
 Openly here, an affront to the earth
 And Heaven's rain and the light of day. No, take him
 Into the house as quickly as you can.
 For it is proper   1375
 That only the close kindred see his grief.
OEDIPUS. I pray you in God's name, since your courtesy
 Ignores my dark expectation, visiting
 With mercy this man of all men most execrable:
 Give me what I ask for—for your good, not for mine. 1380
KREON. And what is it that you turn to me begging for?

OEDIPUS.   Drive me out of this country as quickly as may be
 To a place where no human voice can ever greet me.
KREON.   I should have done that before now—only,
 God's will had not been wholly revealed to me.   1385
OEDIPUS.   But his command is plain: the parricide
 Must be destroyed. I am that evil man.
KREON.   That is the sense of it, yes; but as things are,
 We had best discover clearly what is to be done.
OEDIPUS.   You would learn more about a man like me?   1390
KREON.   You are ready now to listen to the god.
OEDIPUS.   I will listen. But it is to you
 That I must turn for help. I beg you, hear me.

The woman in there—
Give her whatever funeral you think proper: 1395
She is your sister.
     —But let me go, Kreon!
Let me purge my father's Thebes of the pollution
Of my living here, and go out to the wild hills,
To Kithairon, that has won such fame with me,
The tomb my mother and father appointed for me,   1400
And let me die there, as they willed I should.
And yet I know
Death will not ever come to me through sickness
Or in any natural way: I have been preserved
For some unthinkable fate. But let that be.   1405

As for my sons, you need not care for them.
They are men, they will find some way to live.
But my poor daughters, who have shared my table,
Who never before have been parted from their father—
Take care of them, Kreon; do this for me.   1410

And will you let me touch them with my hands
A last time, and let us weep together?
Be kind, my lord,
Great prince, be kind!
      Could I but touch them,
They would be mine again, as when I had my eyes.   1415
(*Enter* ANTIGONE *and* ISMENE, *attended.*)
Ah, God!
Is it my dearest children I hear weeping?
Has Kreon pitied me and sent my daughters?
KREON.   Yes, Oedipus: I knew that they were dear to you
 In the old days, and know you must love them still. 1420

OEDIPUS.   May God bless you for this—and be a friendlier
Guardian to you than he has been to me!

Children, where are you?
Come quickly to my hands: they are your brother's—
Hands that have brought your father's once clear eyes   1425
To this way of seeing—
                      Ah dearest ones,
I had neither sight nor knowledge then, your father
By the woman who was the source of his own life!
And I weep for you—having no strength to see you—
I weep for you when I think of the bitterness   1430
That men will visit upon you all your lives.
What homes, what festivals can you attend
Without being forced to depart again in tears?
And when you come to marriageable age,
Where is the man, my daughters, who would dare   1435
Risk the bane that lies on all my children?
Is there any evil wanting? Your father killed
His father; sowed the womb of her who bore him;
Engendered you at the fount of his own existence!
That is what they will say of you.

                      Then, whom   1440
Can you ever marry? There are no bridegrooms for you,
And your lives must wither away in sterile dreaming.

O Kreon, son of Menoikeus!
You are the only father my daughters have,
Since we, their parents, are both of us gone for ever.   1445
They are your own blood: you will not let them
Fall into beggary and loneliness;
You will keep them from the miseries that are mine!
Take pity on them; see, they are only children,
Friendless except for you. Promise me this,   1450
Great prince, and give me your hand in token of it.
(KREON clasps his right hand.)
Children:
I could say much, if you could understand me,
But as it is, I have only this prayer for you:
Live where you can, be as happy as you can—   1455
Happier, please God, than God has made your father.
KREON.   Enough. You have wept enough. Now go within.
OEDIPUS.   I must; but it is hard.
KREON.   Time eases all things.

OEDIPUS.   You know my mind, then?
KREON.   Say what you desire.
OEDIPUS.   Send me from Thebes!
KREON.   God grant that I may!   1460
OEDIPUS.   But since God hates me . . .
KREON.   No, he will grant your wish.
OEDIPUS.   You promise?
KREON.   I can not speak beyond my knowledge.
OEDIPUS.   Then lead me in.
KREON.   Come now, and leave your children.
OEDIPUS.   No! Do not take them from me!
KREON.   Think no longer
That you are in command here, but rather think   1465
How, when you were, you served your own destruction. (*Exeunt into
the house all but the* CHORUS; *the* CHORAGOS *chants directly to the audience.*)
CHORAGOS.   Men of Thebes: look upon Oedipus.

This is the king who solved the famous riddle
And towered up, most powerful of men.
No mortal eyes but looked on him with envy,   1470
Yet in the end ruin swept over him.

Let every man in mankind's frailty
Consider his last day; and let none
Presume on his good fortune until he find
Life, at his death, a memory without pain.   1475

QUESTIONS

1. The oracles had prophesied that Oedipus would kill his father and beget children by his mother. Is Oedipus therefore *made* to do these things? Is the play premised on the notion that Oedipus is bound or free—the puppet of fate or the creator of his own fate? Or some of each?
2. Outline the actions presented on the stage: begin where the play begins, with the people turning to their king for relief from the plague, and disregard for the moment the revelation of incidents that preceded the play. Then summarize the antecedent actions as they are gradually revealed. In what ways are Oedipus's stage actions consistent with his prior actions? In what ways are they different? How do these two sets of actions reveal him to be a person of extraordinary stature?
3. What is Oedipus's primary motivation throughout the action of the play? What were his motives in actions prior to the play? What characters try to dissuade him from pursuing his purpose, and why do they do so? How do his subjects regard him?
4. Is any common pattern of behavior exhibited in Oedipus's encounters with Laïos, with Teiresias, and with Kreon? Is there any justification for his anger with Teiresias? For his suspicion of Kreon? Why?

5. Oedipus's original question, "Who killed Laïos?" soon turns into the question "Who am I?" On the level of plot, the answer is "Son of Laïos and Iokastê, father's murderer, mother's husband." What is the answer at the level of character—that is, in a psychological or philosophical sense?

6. What philosophical issues are raised by Iokastê's judgment on the oracles (scene 2)? How does the chorus respond to her judgment? How does the play resolve these issues?

7. Why does Oedipus blind himself? Is this an act of weakness or of strength? Why does he ask Kreon to drive him from Thebes? Does he feel that his fate has been just or unjust? Is his suffering, in fact, deserved? Partially deserved? Undeserved?

8. There is a good deal in the play about seeing and blindness. What purpose does this serve? How is Oedipus contrasted with Teiresias? How does Oedipus at the beginning of the play contrast with Oedipus at the end? Why is his blinding himself dramatically appropriate?

9. In what sense may Oedipus be regarded as a better man, though a less fortunate one, at the end of the play than at the beginning? What has he gained from his experience?

10. Some critics have suggested that Oedipus's answer to the Sphinx's riddle was incomplete—that the answer should have been not just man but Oedipus himself—and that Oedipus was as ignorant of the whole truth here as he is when he lays his curse in scene 1 on the murderer of Laïos. Does this suggestion make sense? On how many legs does Oedipus walk at the end of the play?

11. If the answer to the Sphinx's riddle is not just man but Oedipus himself, may the answer to Oedipus's question "Who am I?" pertain not only to Oedipus but also to man, or at least to civilized Western man? What characteristics of Oedipus as an individual are also characteristics of man in the Western world? Is Sophocles writing only about Oedipus the king, or is he saying something about man's presumed place and his real place in the universe?

12. What purposes are served by the appearance of Antigone and Ismene in the Exodos?

13. What purposes does the chorus serve in the play? Whom does it speak for? Comment on the function of each of the four Odes.

14. What does the final speech of the Choragos tell us about human life?

15. A central formal feature of the play is its use of dramatic irony. Point out speeches by Oedipus, especially in the Prologue and scene 1, that have a different or a larger meaning for the audience than for Oedipus himself. Sophocles's title literally translates "Oedipus the Tyrant," but the word *tyrant* denoted a ruler who had earned his position through his own intelligence and strength rather than by inheritance—it was not a negative term. Given that, what ironies are suggested by Sophocles's title?

16. The plot of *Oedipus Rex* has been called one of the most perfect dramatic plots ever devised. Why is it admired? What are its outstanding characteristics?

William Shakespeare

Othello, the Moor of Venice

CHARACTERS

DUKE OF VENICE
BRABANTIO, *a Senator*
OTHER SENATORS
GRATIANO, *brother to Brabantio*
LODOVICO, *kinsman to Brabantio*
OTHELLO, *a noble Moor in the service of the Venetian state*
CASSIO, *his lieutenant*
IAGO, *his ensign*
MONTANO, *Othello's predecessor in the government of Cyprus*
RODERIGO, *a Venetian gentleman*
CLOWN, *servant to Othello*
DESDEMONA, *daughter to Brabantio and wife to Othello*
EMILIA, *wife to Iago*
BIANCA, *mistress to Cassio*
SAILOR, MESSENGER, HERALD, OFFICERS, GENTLEMEN, MUSICIANS,
    and ATTENDANTS

SCENE. *Venice, a seaport in Cyprus.*

ACT 1

SCENE 1. Venice. A street.

Enter RODERIGO *and* IAGO.

OTHELLO, THE MOOR OF VENICE First performed in 1604. The general historical background of the action is probably sometime between 1470 and 1522, a period when Venice, an independent city-state headed by a duke (or doge) elected by the heads of the noble families, was the strongest sea power of the Christian world and included Cyprus and Rhodes among its dominions. Its chief rival for power in the Mediterranean was the Turkish or Ottomite empire. Venetian law required that the commander-in-chief of its forces be an alien, not a Venetian citizen, to prevent political ambition from interfering with his duties. Othello, a black African of royal blood and a soldier of great experience, fulfills the qualifications. The events and characters of the play are fictional, and in any case Shakespeare was not overly concerned with historical accuracy.

William Shakespeare (1564–1616) was born in Stratford-on-Avon but went to London as a young man and made his fortune as an actor, playwright, and part-owner of the Globe Theatre. He did not supervise the publication of his plays, and the two earliest printings of *Othello*—the quarto of 1622 and the folio of 1623—differ in various ways. Modern editors must rely on judgment and scholarship in reconciling the two to arrive at their texts. The version presented here is that of G. B. Harrison, from *Shakespeare: The Complete Works* (New York: Harcourt, 1952). Selections from Harrison's notes are supplemented by those of the editors of this volume.

RODERIGO.   Tush, never tell me! I take it much unkindly
   That thou, Iago, who hast had my purse
   As if the strings were thine, shouldst know of this.
IAGO.   'Sblood, but you will not hear me.
   If ever I did dream of such a matter,   5
   Abhor me.
RODERIGO.   Thou told'st me thou didst hold him in thy hate.
IAGO.   Despise me if I do not. Three great ones of the city,
   In personal suit to make me his Lieutenant,
   Off-capped to him. And, by the faith of man,   10
   I know my price, I am worth no worse a place.
   But he, as loving his own pride and purposes,
   Evades them, with a bombast circumstance
   Horribly stuffed with epithets of war.
   And, in conclusion,   15
   Nonsuits° my mediators, for, "Certes," says he,
   "I have already chose my officer."
   And what was he?
   Forsooth, a great arithmetician,°
   One Michael Cassio, a Florentine,   20
   A fellow almost damned in a fair wife,°
   That never set a squadron in the field,
   Nor the division of a battle knows
   More than a spinster, unless the bookish theoric,
   Wherein the toged Consuls° can propose   25
   As masterly as he—mere prattle without practice
   Is all his soldiership. But he, sir, had the election.
   And I, of whom his° eyes had seen the proof
   At Rhodes, at Cyprus, and on other grounds
   Christian and heathen, must be beleed° and calmed   30
   By debitor and creditor. This countercaster,°
   He, in good time,° must his Lieutenant be,
   And I—God bless the mark!—his Moorship's Ancient.°
RODERIGO.   By Heaven, I rather would have been his hangman.

---

16. Nonsuits: rejects the petition of   **19. arithmetician:** Contemporary books on military tactics are full of elaborate diagrams and numerals to explain military formations. Cassio is a student of such books.   **21. almost . . . wife:** A much-disputed phrase. There is an Italian proverb, "You have married a fair wife? You are damned." If Iago has this in mind, he means by *almost* that Cassio is about to marry.   **25. toged Consuls:** senators in togas [Eds.]   **28. his:** Othello's [Eds.]   **30. beleed:** placed on the lee (or unfavorable) side   **31. countercaster:** calculator (repeating the idea of arithmetician). Counters were used in making calculations.   **32. in good time:** a phrase expressing indignation   **33. Ancient:** ensign, the third officer in the company of which Othello is Captain and Cassio Lieutenant

IAGO.   Why, there's no remedy. 'Tis the curse of service,   35
 Preferment goes by letter and affection,
 And not by old gradation,° where each second
 Stood heir to the first. Now, sir, be judge yourself
 Whether I in any just term am affined°
 To love the Moor.
RODERIGO.   I would not follow him, then.   40
IAGO.   Oh, sir, content you,
 I follow him to serve my turn upon him.
 We cannot all be masters, nor all masters
 Cannot be truly followed. You shall mark
 Many a duteous and knee-crooking knave   45
 That doting on his own obsequious bondage
 Wears out his time, much like his master's ass,
 For naught but provender, and when he's old, cashiered.
 Whip me such honest knaves. Others there are
 Who, trimmed in forms and visages of duty,   50
 Keep yet their hearts attending on themselves,
 And throwing but shows of service on their lords
 Do well thrive by them, and when they have lined their coats
 Do themselves homage. These fellows have some soul,
 And such a one do I profess myself. For, sir,   55
 It is as sure as you are Roderigo,
 Were I the Moor, I would not be Iago.
 In following him, I follow but myself.
 Heaven is my judge, not I for love and duty,
 But seeming so, for my peculiar° end.   60
 For when my outward action doth demonstrate
 The native act and figure of my heart
 In compliment extern, 'tis not long after
 But I will wear my heart upon my sleeve
 For daws to peck at. I am not what I am.   65
RODERIGO.   What a full fortune does the thick-lips owe°
 If he can carry 't thus!°
IAGO.   Call up her father,
 Rouse him. Make after him, poison his delight,
 Proclaim him in the streets. Incense her kinsmen,
 And though he in a fertile climate dwell,   70
 Plague him with flies. Though that his joy be joy,
 Yet throw such changes of vexation on 't

36–37. Preferment . . . gradation: Promotion comes through private recommenda-
tion and favoritism and not by order of seniority.   **39. affined:** tied by affection
60. peculiar: personal [Eds.]   **66. owe:** own   **67. carry 't thus:** i.e., bring off
this marriage

As it may lose some color.

RODERIGO. Here is her father's house, I'll call aloud.

IAGO. Do, with like timorous° accent and dire yell   75
    As when, by night and negligence, the fire
    Is spied in populous cities.

RODERIGO. What ho, Brabantio! Signior Brabantio, ho!

IAGO. Awake! What ho, Brabantio! Thieves! Thieves! Thieves!
    Look to your house, your daughter and your bags!°   80
    Thieves! Thieves! (BRABANTIO *appears above, at a window.*)

BRABANTIO. What is the reason of this terrible summons?
    What is the matter there?

RODERIGO. Signior, is all your family within?

IAGO. Are your doors locked?

BRABANTIO.   Why, wherefore ask you this?   85

IAGO. 'Zounds, sir, you're robbed. For shame, put on your gown,
    Your heart is burst, you have lost half your soul.
    Even now, now, very now, an old black ram
    Is tupping your white ewe. Arise, arise,
    Awake the snorting° citizens with the bell,   90
    Or else the Devil° will make a grandsire of you.
    Arise, I say.

BRABANTIO. What, have you lost your wits?

RODERIGO. Most reverend signior, do you know my voice?

BRABANTIO. Not I. What are you?

RODERIGO. My name is Roderigo.

BRABANTIO.   The worser welcome.   95
    I have charged thee not to haunt about my doors.
    In honest plainness thou hast heard me say
    My daughter is not for thee, and now, in madness,
    Being full of supper and distempering draughts,
    Upon malicious bravery° dost thou come   100
    To start° my quiet.

RODERIGO. Sir, sir, sir—

BRABANTIO.   But thou must needs be sure
    My spirit and my place have in them power
    To make this bitter to thee.

RODERIGO.   Patience, good sir.

BRABANTIO. What tell'st thou me of robbing? This is Venice,   105
    My house is not a grange.°

RODERIGO.   Most grave Brabantio,
    In simple and pure soul I come to you.

---

75. timorous: terrifying   **80. bags:** moneybags   **90. snorting:** snoring
91. Devil: The Devil in old pictures and woodcuts was represented as black.
100. bravery: defiance   **101. start:** startle   **106. grange:** lonely farm

IAGO.   'Zounds, sir, you are one of those that will not serve God if the
Devil bid you. Because we come to do you service and you think we are
ruffians, you'll have your daughter covered with a Barbary° horse, you'll
have your nephews° neigh to you, you'll have coursers for cousins,°
and jennets° for germans.°   112

BRABANTIO.   What profane wretch art thou?

IAGO.   I am one, sir, that comes to tell you your daughter and the Moor
are now making the beast with two backs.

BRABANTIO.   Thou art a villain.

IAGO.   You are—a Senator.

BRABANTIO.   This thou shalt answer. I know thee, Roderigo.

RODERIGO.   Sir, I will answer anything. But I beseech you
If 't be your pleasure and most wise consent,
As partly I find it is, that your fair daughter,   120
At this odd-even° and dull watch o' the night,
Transported with no worse nor better guard
But with a knave of common hire, a gondolier,
To the gross clasps of a lascivious Moor—
If this be known to you, and your allowance,°   125
We then have done you bold and saucy wrongs.
But if you know not this, my manners tell me
We have your wrong rebuke. Do not believe
That, from the sense of all civility,°
I thus would play and trifle with your reverence.   130
Your daughter, if you have not given her leave,
I say again, hath made a gross revolt,
Tying her duty, beauty, wit, and fortunes
In an extravagant° and wheeling° stranger
Of here and everywhere. Straight satisfy yourself.   135
If she be in her chamber or your house,
Let loose on me the justice of the state
For thus deluding you.

BRABANTIO.   Strike on the tinder,° ho!
Give me a taper!° Call up all my people!
This accident is not unlike my dream.   140
Belief of it oppresses me already.
Light, I say! Light! (*Exit above.*)

IAGO.   Farewell, for I must leave you.
It seems not meet, nor wholesome to my place,°
To be produced—as if I stay I shall—

---

110. Barbary: Moorish   **111. nephews:** grandsons   **cousins:** near relations
112. jennets: Moorish ponies   **germans:** kinsmen   **121. odd-even:** about midnight   **125. your allowance:** by your permission   **129. from . . . civility:** contrary to all decency [Eds.]   **134. extravagant:** vagabond   **wheeling:** wandering
138. tinder: the primitive method of making fire, used before the invention of
matches   **139. taper:** candle   **143. place:** i.e., as Othello's officer

Against the Moor. For I do know the state,   145
However this may gall him with some check,
Cannot with safety cast° him. For he's embarked
With such loud reason to the Cyprus wars,
Which even now stand in act,° that, for their souls,
Another of his fathom they have none   150
To lead their business. In which regard,
Though I do hate him as I do Hell pains,
Yet for necessity of present life
I must show out a flag and sign of love,
Which is indeed but sign. That you shall surely find him,   155
Lead to the Sagittary° the raisèd search,
And there will I be with him. So farewell.
    (*Exit* IAGO. *Enter, below,* BRABANTIO, *in his nightgown,*° *and* SERVANTS
with torches.)
BRABANTIO.   It is too true an evil. Gone she is,
And what's to come of my despisèd time
Is naught but bitterness. Now, Roderigo,   160
Where didst thou see her? Oh, unhappy girl!
With the Moor, say'st thou? Who would be a father!
How didst thou know 'twas she? Oh, she deceives me
Past thought! What said she to you? Get more tapers.
Raise all my kindred. Are they married, think you?   165
RODERIGO.   Truly, I think they are.
BRABANTIO.   Oh Heaven! How got she out? Oh, treason of the blood!
Fathers, from hence trust not your daughters' minds
By what you see them act. Are there not charms°
By which the property° of youth and maidhood   170
May be abused?° Have you not read, Roderigo,
Of some such thing?
RODERIGO.   Yes, sir, I have indeed.
BRABANTIO.   Call up my brother.—Oh, would you had had her!—
Some one way, some another.—Do you know
Where we may apprehend her and the Moor?   175
RODERIGO.   I think I can discover him, if you please
To get good guard and go along with me.
BRABANTIO.   Pray you, lead on. At every house I'll call,
I may command° at most. Get weapons, ho!
And raise some special officers of night.   180
On, good Roderigo, I'll deserve your pains.° (*Exeunt.*)

---

147. cast: dismiss from service   **149. stand in act:** are under way [Eds.]
156. Sagittary: presumably some inn in Venice [Eds.]   **157. s.d. nightgown:**
dressing-gown [Eds.]   **169. charms:** magic spells   **170. property:** nature
171. abused: deceived   **179. command:** find supporters   **181. deserve your
pains:** reward your labor

SCENE 2. Another street.

Enter OTHELLO, IAGO, *and* ATTENDANTS *with torches.*

IAGO.   Though in the trade of war I have slain men,
　　Yet do I hold it very stuff o' the conscience
　　To do no contrivèd murder. I lack iniquity
　　Sometimes to do me service. Nine or ten times
　　I had thought to have yerked him° here under the ribs.　　　　5
OTHELLO.   'Tis better as it is.
IAGO.　　　　　　　　　　　Nay, but he prated
　　And spoke such scurvy and provoking terms
　　Against your honor
　　That, with the little godliness I have,
　　I did full hard forbear him. But I pray you, sir,　　　　　　10
　　Are you fast married? Be assured of this,
　　That the Magnifico is much beloved,
　　And hath in his effect a voice potential
　　As double as° the Duke's. He will divorce you,
　　Or put upon you what restraint and grievance　　　　　　15
　　The law, with all his might to enforce it on,
　　Will give him cable.
OTHELLO.　　　　　　　Let him do his spite.
　　My services which I have done the signiory°
　　Shall out-tongue his complaints. 'Tis yet to know°—
　　Which, when I know that boasting is an honor,　　　　　　20
　　I shall promulgate—I fetch my life and being
　　From men of royal siege,° and my demerits°
　　May speak unbonneted to as proud a fortune
　　As this that I have reached. For know, Iago,
　　But that I love the gentle Desdemona,　　　　　　　　　25
　　I would not my unhousèd° free condition
　　Put into circumscription and confine
　　For the sea's worth. But look! What lights come yond?
IAGO.   Those are the raisèd father and his friends.
　　You were best go in.
OTHELLO.　　　　　　Not I, I must be found.　　　　　　30
　　My parts, my title, and my perfect soul°
　　Shall manifest me rightly. Is it they?
IAGO.   By Janus, I think no.
　　(*Enter* CASSIO, *and certain* OFFICERS *with torches.*)

---

5. yerked him: stabbed Brabantio [Eds.]　　**13–14. potential . . . as:** twice as
powerful as　　**18. signiory:** state of Venice　　**19. yet to know:** not widely known
[Eds.]　　**22. siege:** rank [Eds.]　　**demerits:** deserts　　**26. unhousèd:** unmarried　　**31. perfect soul:** clear conscience [Eds.]

OTHELLO.   The servants of the Duke, and my Lieutenant.
    The goodness of the night upon you, friends!   35
    What is the news?
CASSIO.   The Duke does greet you, General,
    And he requires your haste-posthaste appearance,
    Even on the instant.
OTHELLO.   What is the matter, think you?
CASSIO.   Something from Cyprus, as I may divine.
    It is a business of some heat. The galleys   40
    Have sent a dozen sequent messengers
    This very night at one another's heels,
    And many of the consuls, raised and met,
    Are at the Duke's already. You have been hotly called for
    When, being not at your lodging to be found,   45
    The Senate hath sent about three several° quests
    To search you out.
OTHELLO.   'Tis well I am found by you.
    I will but spend a word here in the house
    And go with you. (*Exit.*)
CASSIO.   Ancient, what makes he here?
IAGO.   Faith, he tonight hath boarded a land carrack.°   50
    If it prove lawful prize, he's made forever.
CASSIO.   I do not understand.
IAGO.   He's married.
CASSIO.   To who? (*Re-enter* OTHELLO.)
IAGO.   Marry°, to—Come, Captain, will you go?
OTHELLO.   Have with you.
CASSIO.   Here comes another troop to seek for you.
IAGO.   It is Brabantio. General, be advised,   55
    He comes to bad intent.
    (*Enter* BRABANTIO, RODERIGO, *and* OFFICERS *with torches and weapons.*)
OTHELLO.   Holloa! Stand there!
RODERIGO.   Signior, it is the Moor.
BRABANTIO.   Down with him, thief!
    (*They draw on both sides.*)
IAGO.   You, Roderigo! Come, sir, I am for you.
OTHELLO.   Keep up° your bright swords, for the dew will rust them.
    Good signior, you shall more command with years   60
    Than with your weapons.
BRABANTIO.   O thou foul thief, where hast thou stowed my daughter?
    Damned as thou art, thou hast enchanted her.
    For I'll refer me to all things of sense

---

46. several: separate   **50. carrack:** large merchant ship   **53. Marry:** a mild
oath [Eds.]   **59. Keep up:** sheathe

> If she in chains of magic were not bound,   65
> Whether a maid so tender, fair, and happy,
> So opposite to marriage that she shunned
> The wealthy curlèd darlings of our nation,
> Would ever have, to incur a general mock,
> Run from her guardage° to the sooty bosom   70
> Of such a thing as thou, to fear, not to delight.
> Judge me the world if 'tis not gross in sense°
> That thou hast practiced on her with foul charms,
> Abused her delicate youth with drugs or minerals
> That weaken motion.° I'll have 't disputed on,°   75
> 'Tis probable, and palpable to thinking.
> I therefore apprehend and do attach° thee
> For an abuser of the world, a practicer
> Of arts inhibited and out of warrant.°
> Lay hold upon him. If he do resist,   80
> Subdue him at his peril.

OTHELLO.   Hold your hands,
> Both you of my inclining and the rest.
> Were it my cue to fight, I should have known it
> Without a prompter. Where will you that I go
> To answer this your charge?

BRABANTIO.   To prison, till fit time   85
> Of law and course of direct session
> Call thee to answer.

OTHELLO.   What if I do obey?
> How may the Duke be therewith satisfied,
> Whose messengers are here about my side
> Upon some present business of the state   90
> To bring me to him?

FIRST OFFICER.   'Tis true, most worthy signior.
> The Duke's in council, and your noble self
> I am sure is sent for.

BRABANTIO.   How? The Duke in council?
> In this time of the night? Bring him away.
> Mine's not an idle cause. The Duke himself,   95
> Or any of my brothers of the state,
> Cannot but feel this wrong as 'twere their own.
> For if such actions may have passage free,
> Bondslaves and pagans shall our statesmen be. (*Exeunt.*)

---

70. guardage: guardianship   **72. gross in sense:** obvious [Eds.]   **75. motion:**
sense   **disputed on:** argued in the law courts [Eds.]   **77. attach:** arrest
79. inhibited . . . warrant: forbidden and illegal [Eds.]

SCENE 3. A council chamber.

The Duke *and* Senators *sitting at a table,* Officers *attending.*

Duke.   There is no composition° in these news°
    That gives them credit.
First Senator.   Indeed they are disproportioned.
    My letters say a hundred and seven galleys.
Duke.   And mine, a hundred and forty.
Second Senator.   And mine, two hundred.
    But though they jump not on a just account°—   5
    As in these cases, where the aim reports,°
    'Tis oft with difference—yet do they all confirm
    A Turkish fleet, and bearing up to Cyprus.
Duke.   Nay, it is possible enough to judgment.
    I do not so secure me in the error,°   10
    But the main article° I do approve
    In fearful° sense.
Sailor (*within*).   What ho! What ho! What ho!
First Officer.   A messenger from the galleys. (*Enter* Sailor.)
Duke.   Now, what's the business?
Sailor.   The Turkish preparation makes for Rhodes.
    So was I bid report here to the state   15
    By Signior Angelo.
Duke.   How say you by this charge?
First Senator.   This cannot be,
    By no assay of reason. 'Tis a pageant
    To keep us in false gaze. When we consider
    The importancy of Cyprus to the Turk,   20
    And let ourselves again but understand
    That as it more concerns the Turk than Rhodes,
    So may he with more facile question bear it,°
    For that it stands not in such warlike brace
    But altogether lacks the abilities   25
    That Rhodes is dressed in—if we make thought of this,
    We must not think the Turk is so unskillful
    To leave that latest which concerns him first,
    Neglecting an attempt of ease and gain
    To wake and wage a danger profitless.   30

---

1. composition: agreement   **news:** reports   **5. jump . . . account:** do not agree with an exact estimate   **6. aim reports:** i.e., intelligence reports of an enemy's intention often differ in the details   **10. I . . . error:** I do not consider myself free from danger, because the reports may not all be accurate.   **11. main article:** general report   **12. fearful:** to be feared   **23. with . . . it:** take it more easily

DUKE.   Nay, in all confidence, he's not for Rhodes.

FIRST OFFICER.   Here is more news. (*Enter a* MESSENGER.)

MESSENGER.   The Ottomites,° Reverend and Gracious,
  Steering with due course toward the isle of Rhodes,
  Have there injointed° them with an after-fleet.°   35

FIRST SENATOR.   Aye, so I thought. How many, as you guess?

MESSENGER.   Of thirty sail. And now they do restem°
  Their backward course, bearing with frank appearance
  Their purposes toward Cyprus. Signior Montano,
  Your trusty and most valiant servitor,   40
  With his free duty recommends° you thus,
  And prays you to believe him.

DUKE.   'Tis certain then for Cyprus.
  Marcus Luccicos, is not he in town?

FIRST SENATOR.   He's now in Florence.   45

DUKE.   Write from us to him, post-posthaste dispatch.

FIRST SENATOR.   Here comes Brabantio and the valiant Moor.
  (*Enter* BRABANTIO, OTHELLO, IAGO, RODERIGO, *and* OFFICERS.)

DUKE.   Valiant Othello, we must straight employ you
  Against the general enemy Ottoman.
  (*To* BRABANTIO) I did not see you. Welcome, gentle signior, 50
  We lacked your counsel and your help tonight.

BRABANTIO.   So did I yours. Good your Grace, pardon me,
  Neither my place nor aught I heard of business
  Hath raised me from my bed, nor doth the general care
  Take hold on me. For my particular° grief   55
  Is of so floodgate and o'erbearing nature
  That it engluts and swallows other sorrows,
  And it is still itself.

DUKE.   —— Why, what's the matter?

BRABANTIO.   My daughter! Oh, my daughter!

ALL.   Dead?

BRABANTIO.   Aye, to me.
  She is abused, stol'n from me and corrupted   60
  By spells and medicines bought of mountebanks.
  For nature so preposterously to err,
  Being not deficient, blind, or lame of sense,
  Sans° witchcraft could not.

DUKE.   Whoe'er he be that in this foul proceeding   65
  Hath thus beguiled your daughter of herself
  And you of her, the bloody book of law

---

33. Ottomites: Turks **35. injointed:** joined **after-fleet:** second fleet
37. restem: steer again **41. recommends:** advises [Eds.] **55. particular:**
personal **64. Sans:** without

You shall yourself read in the bitter letter
After your own sense—yea, though our proper° son
Stood in your action.
BRABANTIO.   Humbly I thank your Grace.   70
  Here is the man, this Moor, whom now, it seems,
  Your special mandate for the state affairs
  Hath hither brought.
ALL.   We are very sorry for 't.
DUKE (to OTHELLO). What in your own part can you say to this?
BRABANTIO. Nothing but this is so.   75
OTHELLO. Most potent, grave, and reverend signiors,
  My very noble and approved good masters,
  That I have ta'en away this old man's daughter,
  It is most true—true, I have married her.
  The very head and front of my offending   80
  Hath this extent, no more. Rude am I in my speech,
  And little blest with the soft phrase of peace,
  For since these arms of mine had seven years' pith
  Till now some nine moons wasted, they have used
  Their dearest action in the tented field;   85
  And little of this great world can I speak,
  More than pertains to feats of broil and battle,
  And therefore little shall I grace my cause
  In speaking for myself. Yet, by your gracious patience,
  I will a round unvarnished tale° deliver   90
  Of my whole course of love—what drugs, what charms,
  What conjuration and what mighty magic—
  For such proceeding I am charged withal—
  I won his daughter.
BRABANTIO.   A maiden never bold,
  Of spirit so still and quiet that her motion   95
  Blushed at herself, and she—in spite of nature,
  Of years, of country, credit,° everything—
  To fall in love with what she feared to look on!
  It is a judgment maimed and most imperfect
  That will confess perfection so could err   100
  Against all rules of nature, and must be driven
  To find out practices of cunning Hell
  Why this should be. I therefore vouch again
  That with some mixtures powerful o'er the blood,
  Or with some dram conjured to this effect,   105
  He wrought upon her.

---

69. proper: own   **90. round . . . tale:** direct, unadorned account
97. credit: reputation

DUKE.   To vouch this is no proof
Without more certain and more overt test
Than these thin habits and poor likelihoods
Of modern seeming° do prefer against him.
FIRST SENATOR.   But, Othello, speak.   110
Did you by indirect and forcèd courses
Subdue and poison this young maid's affections?
Or came it by request, and such fair question
As soul to soul affordeth?
OTHELLO.   I do beseech you
Send for the lady to the Sagittary,   115
And let her speak of me before her father.
If you do find me foul in her report,
The trust, the office I do hold of you,
Not only take away, but let your sentence
Even fall upon my life.
DUKE.   Fetch Desdemona hither.   120
OTHELLO.   Ancient, conduct them, you best know the place.
   (*Exeunt* IAGO *and* ATTENDANTS.)
And till she come, as truly as to Heaven
I do confess the vices of my blood,
So justly to your grave ears I'll present
How I did thrive in this fair lady's love   125
And she in mine.
DUKE.   Say it, Othello.
OTHELLO.   Her father loved me, oft invited me,
Still° questioned me the story of my life
From year to year, the battles, sieges, fortunes,
That I have passed.   130
I ran it through, even from my boyish days
To the very moment that he bade me tell it.
Wherein I spake of most disastrous chances,
Of moving accidents by flood and field,
Of hairbreadth 'scapes i' the imminent deadly breach,   135
Of being taken by the insolent foe
And sold to slavery, of my redemption thence,
And portance in my travels' history.
Wherein of antres° vast and deserts idle,
Rough quarries, rocks, and hills whose heads touch heaven,   140
It was my hint to speak—such was the process.
And of the cannibals that each other eat,
The anthropophagi,° and men whose heads

108–109. thin . . . seeming: superficial, unlikely, and trivial suppositions [Eds.]
128. Still: always   **139. antres:** caves   **143. anthropophagi:** cannibals

Do grow beneath their shoulders. This to hear
Would Desdemona seriously incline.   145
But still the house affairs would draw her thence,
Which ever as she could with haste dispatch,
She'd come again, and with a greedy ear
Devour up my discourse. Which I observing,
Took once a pliant hour and found good means   150
To draw from her a prayer of earnest heart
That I would all my pilgrimage dilate,
Whereof by parcels she had something heard,
But not intentively. I did consent,
And often did beguile her of her tears   155
When I did speak of some distressful stroke
That my youth suffered. My story being done,
She gave me for my pains a world of sighs.
She swore, in faith, 'twas strange, 'twas passing strange,
'Twas pitiful, 'twas wondrous pitiful.   160
She wished she had not heard it, yet she wished
That Heaven had made her such a man. She thanked me,
And bade me, if I had a friend that loved her,
I should but teach him how to tell my story
And that would woo her. Upon this hint° I spake.   165
She loved me for the dangers I had passed,
And I loved her that she did pity them.
This only is the witchcraft I have used.
Here comes the lady, let her witness it.
(*Enter* DESDEMONA, IAGO, *and* ATTENDANTS.)
DUKE.   I think this tale would win my daughter too.   170
Good Brabantio,
Take up this mangled matter at the best.°
Men do their broken weapons rather use
Than their bare hands.
BRABANTIO.   I pray you hear her speak.
If she confess that she was half the wooer,   175
Destruction on my head if my bad blame
Light on the man! Come hither, gentle mistress.
Do you perceive in all this noble company
Where most you owe obedience?
DESDEMONA.   My noble father,
I do perceive here a divided duty.   180
To you I am bound for life and education,
My life and education both do learn me

---

165. hint: opportunity [Eds.]   **172. Take . . . best:** make the best settlement you
can of this confused business

How to respect you; you are the lord of duty,
I am hitherto your daughter. But here's my husband,
And so much duty as my mother showed   185
To you, preferring you before her father,
So much I challenge that I may profess
Due to the Moor my lord.
BRABANTIO.   God be with you! I have done.
Please it your Grace, on to the state affairs.
I had rather to adopt a child than get° it.   190
Come hither, Moor.
I here do give thee that with all my heart
Which, but thou hast already, with all my heart
I would keep from thee. For your sake, jewel,
I am glad at soul I have no other child,   195
For thy escape would teach me tyranny,
To hang clogs on them. I have done, my lord.
DUKE.   Let me speak like yourself, and lay a sentence°
Which, as a grise° or step, may help these lovers
Into your favor.   200
When remedies are past, the griefs are ended
By seeing the worst, which late on hopes depended.
To mourn a mischief that is past and gone
Is the next way to draw new mischief on.
What cannot be preserved when fortune takes,   205
Patience her injury a mockery makes.
The robbed that smiles steals something from the thief.
He robs himself that spends a bootless grief.
BRABANTIO.   So let the Turk of Cyprus us beguile,
We lose it not so long as we can smile.   210
He bears the sentence well that nothing bears
But the free comfort which from thence he hears.
But he bears both the sentence and the sorrow
That, to pay grief, must of poor patience borrow.
These sentences, to sugar or to gall,   215
Being strong on both sides, are equivocal.
But words are words. I never yet did hear
That the bruised heart was piercèd through the ear.
I humbly beseech you, proceed to the affairs of state.
DUKE.   The Turk with a most mightly preparation makes for Cyprus.
Othello, the fortitude of the place is best known to you, and though we
have there a substitute° of most allowed sufficiency, yet opinion, a sover-
eign mistress of effects, throws a more safer voice on you. You must

---

190 get: beget   **198. sentence:** proverbial saying   **199. grise:** degree
222. substitute: deputy commander

therefore be content to slubber° the gloss of your new fortunes with this
more stubborn and boisterous expedition.   225
OTHELLO.   The tyrant custom, most grave Senators,
   Hath made the flinty and steel couch of war
   My thrice-driven bed of down. I do agnize°
   A natural and prompt alacrity
   I find in hardness,° and do undertake   230
   These present wars against the Ottomites.
   Most humbly therefore bending to your state,
   I crave fit disposition for my wife,
   Due reference of place and exhibition,°
   With such accommodation and besort°   235
   As levels with her breeding.
DUKE.   If you please,
   Be 't at her father's.
BRABANTIO.   I'll not have it so.
OTHELLO.   Nor I.
DESDEMONA.   Nor I. I would not there reside,
   To put my father in impatient thoughts
   By being in his eye. Most gracious Duke,   240
   To my unfolding lend your prosperous° ear,
   And let me find a charter in your voice
   To assist my simpleness.
DUKE.   What would you, Desdemona?
DESDEMONA.   That I did love the Moor to live with him,   245
   My downright violence and storm of fortunes
   May trumpet to the world. My heart's subdued
   Even to the very quality° of my lord.
   I saw Othello's visage in his mind,
   And to his honors and his valiant parts°   250
   Did I my soul and fortunes consecrate.
   So that, dear lords, if I be left behind,
   A moth of peace, and he go to the war,
   The rites for which I love him are bereft me,
   And I a heavy interim shall support   255
   By his dear absence. Let me go with him.
OTHELLO.   Let her have your voices.
   Vouch with me, Heaven, I therefore beg it not
   To please the palate of my appetite,
   Nor to comply with heat—the young affects   260

---

224. slubber: tarnish   **228. agnize:** confess   **230. hardness:** hardship
234. exhibition: allowance   **235. besort:** attendants   **241. prosperous:** favorable
248. quality: profession   **250. parts:** qualities

In me defunct°—and proper satisfaction,
But to be free and bounteous to her mind.°
And Heaven defend your good souls, that you think
I will your serious and great business scant
For she is with me. No, when light-winged toys   265
Of feathered Cupid seel° with wanton dullness
My speculative and officed instruments,°
That my disports° corrupt and taint my business,
Let housewives make a skillet of my helm,
And all indign° and base adversities   270
Make head against my estimation!°

DUKE.   Be it as you shall privately determine,
Either for her stay or going. The affair cries haste,
And speed must answer 't. You must hence tonight.

DESDEMONA.   Tonight, my lord?

DUKE.   This night.

OTHELLO.   With all my heart.   275

DUKE.   At nine i' the morning here we'll meet again.
Othello, leave some officer behind,
And he shall our commission bring to you,
With such things else of quality and respect
As doth import you.

OTHELLO.   So please your Grace, my Ancient,   280
A man he is of honesty and trust.
To his conveyance I assign my wife,
With what else needful your good Grace shall think
To be sent after me.

DUKE.   Let it be so.
Good night to everyone. (*To* BRABANTIO) And, noble signior,   285
If virtue no delighted beauty lack,
Your son-in-law is far more fair than black.°

FIRST SENATOR.   Adieu, brave Moor. Use Desdemona well.

BRABANTIO.   Look to her, Moor, if thou hast eyes to see.
She has deceived her father, and may thee.   290
(*Exeunt* DUKE, SENATORS, OFFICERS, *etc.*)

OTHELLO.   My life upon her faith! Honest Iago,
My Desdemona must I leave to thee.
I prithee, let thy wife attend on her,
And bring them after in the best advantage.

260–61. young . . . defunct: in me the passion of youth is dead.   262. to . . . mind:
Othello repeats Desdemona's claim that this is a marriage of minds.   266. seel:
close up   267. speculative . . . instruments: powers of sight and action; i.e., my
efficiency as your general   268. disports: amusements   270. indign: unworthy
271. estimation: reputation   286–87. If . . . black: If worthiness is a beautiful
thing in itself, your son-in-law, though black, has beauty.

Come, Desdemona, I have but an hour   295
Of love, of worldly matters and direction,
To spend with thee. We must obey the time.
(*Exeunt* OTHELLO *and* DESDEMONA.)
RODERIGO.   Iago!
IAGO.   What sayest thou, noble heart?
RODERIGO.   What will I do, thinkest thou?   300
IAGO.   Why, go to bed and sleep.
RODERIGO.   I will incontinently° drown myself.
IAGO.   If thou dost, I shall never love thee after. Why, thou silly gentleman!
RODERIGO.   It is silliness to live when to live is torment, and then have we a
prescription to die when death is our physician.   305
IAGO.   Oh, villainous! I have looked upon the world for four times seven
years, and since I could distinguish betwixt a benefit and an injury I
never found man that knew how to love himself. Ere I would say I would
drown myself for the love of a guinea hen, I would change my humanity
with a baboon.   310
RODERIGO.   What should I do? I confess it is my shame to be so fond, but it
is not in my virtue° to amend it.
IAGO.   Virtue! A fig! 'Tis in ourselves that we are thus or thus. Our bodies
are gardens, to the which our wills are gardeners. So that if we will plant
nettles or sow lettuce, set hyssop and weed up thyme, supply it with one
gender of herbs or distract it with many, either to have it sterile with
idleness or manured with industry—why, the power and corrigible° authority of this lies in our wills. If the balance of our lives had not one scale
of reason to poise another of sensuality, the blood and baseness of our
natures would conduct us to most preposterous conclusions. But we have
reason to cool our raging motions, our carnal stings, our unbitted lusts,
whereof I take this that you call love to be a sect or scion.°   322
RODERIGO.   It cannot be.
IAGO.   It is merely a lust of the blood and a permission of the will. Come,
be a man! Drown thyself? Drown cats and blind puppies! I have pro-
fessed me thy friend, and I confess me knit to thy deserving with
cables of perdurable toughness. I could never better stead thee than
now. Put money in thy purse, follow thou the wars, defeat thy favor
with an usurped beard°—I say put money in thy purse. It cannot be
that Desdemona should long continue her love to the Moor—put money
in thy purse—nor he his to her. It was a violent commencement, and
thou shalt see an answerable sequestration°—put but money in thy
purse. These Moors are changeable in their wills.°—Fill thy purse

---

302. incontinently: immediately   **312. virtue:** strength [Eds.]   **317. corrigible:**
correcting, directing   **322. sect or scion:** Both words mean a slip taken from a tree
and planted to produce a new growth.   **328–29. defeat . . . beard:** disguise your
face by growing a beard   **332. answerable sequestration:** corresponding separation; i.e., reaction   **333. wills:** desires [Eds.]

with money. The food that to him now is as luscious as locusts shall be to him shortly as bitter as coloquintida. She must change for youth. When she is sated with his body, she will find the error of her choice. She must have change, she must—therefore put money in thy purse. If thou wilt needs damn thyself, do it a more delicate way than drowning. Make all the money thou canst.° If sanctimony and a frail vow betwixt an erring° barbarian and a supersubtle Venetian be not too hard for my wits and all the tribe of Hell, thou shalt enjoy her—therefore make money. A pox of drowning thyself! It is clean out of the way. Seek thou rather to be hanged in compassing thy joy than to be drowned and go without her.   344

RODERIGO.   Wilt thou be fast to my hopes if I depend on the issue?

IAGO.   Thou art sure of me. Go, make money. I have told thee often, and I retell thee again and again, I hate the Moor. My cause is hearted,° thine hath no less reason. Let us be conjunctive in our revenge against him. If thou canst cuckold him thou dost thyself a pleasure, me a sport. There are many events in the womb of time which will be delivered. Traverse, go, provide thy money. We will have more of this tomorrow. Adieu.

RODERIGO.   Where shall we meet i' the morning?   352

IAGO.   At my lodging.

RODERIGO.   I'll be with thee betimes.

IAGO.   Go to, farewell. Do you hear, Roderigo?   355

RODERIGO.   What say you?

IAGO.   No more of drowning, do you hear?

RODERIGO.   I am changed. I'll go sell all my land. (*Exit.*)

IAGO.   Thus do I ever make my fool my purse,
For I mine own gained knowledge should profane   360
If I would time expend with such a snipe
But for my sport and profit. I hate the Moor,
And it is thought abroad that 'twixt my sheets
He's done my office. I know not if 't be true,
But I for mere suspicion in that kind   365
Will do as if for surety. He holds me well,
The better shall my purpose work on him.
Cassio's a proper° man. Let me see now,
To get his place, and to plume up° my will
In double knavery—How, how?—Let's see.—   370
After some time, to abuse Othello's ear
That he is too familiar with his wife.
He hath a person and a smooth dispose
To be suspected,° framed to make women false.
The Moor is of a free and open nature   375

---

339. Make . . . canst: turn all you can into ready cash   **340. erring:** vagabond
347. hearted: heartfelt   **368. proper:** handsome   **369. plume up:** glorify
373–74. He . . . suspected: an easy way about him that is naturally suspected

That thinks men honest that but seem to be so,
And will as tenderly be led by the nose
As asses are.
I have 't. It is engendered. Hell and night
Must bring this monstrous birth to the world's light. (*Exit.*)   380

ACT 2

SCENE 1.   A seaport in Cyprus. An open place near the wharf.

Enter MONTANO *and two* GENTLEMEN.

MONTANO.   What from the cape can you discern at sea?
FIRST GENTLEMAN.   Nothing at all. It is a high-wrought flood.
    I cannot 'twixt the heaven and the main
    Descry a sail.
MONTANO.   Methinks the wind hath spoke aloud at land,   5
    A fuller blast ne'er shook our battlements.
    If it hath ruffianed so upon the sea,
    What ribs of oak, when mountains melt on them,
    Can hold the mortise? What shall we hear of this?
SECOND GENTLEMAN.   A segregation° of the Turkish fleet.   10
    For do but stand upon the foaming shore,
    The chidden billow seems to pelt the clouds,
    The wind-shaked surge, with high and monstrous mane,
    Seems to cast water on the burning Bear,
    And quench the guards of the ever-fixèd Pole.°   15
    I never did like molestation view
    On the enchafèd flood.
MONTANO.   If that the Turkish fleet
    Be not ensheltered and embayed, they are drowned.
    It is impossible to bear it out. (*Enter a* THIRD GENTLEMAN.)
THIRD GENTLEMAN.   News, lads! Our wars are done.   20
    The desperate tempest hath so banged the Turks
    That their designment halts. A noble ship of Venice
    Hath seen a grievous wreck and sufferance°
    On most part of their fleet.
MONTANO.   How! Is this true?
THIRD GENTLEMAN.   The ship is here put in,   25
    A Veronesa. Michael Cassio,
    Lieutenant to the warlike Moor Othello,
    Is come on shore, the Moor himself at sea,
    And is in full commission here for Cyprus.
MONTANO.   I am glad on 't. 'Tis a worthy governor.   30

---

10. segregation: separation   **14–15. cast . . . Pole:** drown the constellations
[Eds.]   **23. sufferance:** damage

THIRD GENTLEMAN.   But this same Cassio, though he speak of comfort
   Touching the Turkish loss, yet he looks sadly
   And prays the Moor be safe, for they were parted
   With foul and violent tempest.
MONTANO.   Pray Heavens he be,
   For I have served him, and the man commands   35
   Like a full soldier. Let's to the seaside, ho!
   As well to see the vessel that's come in
   As to throw out our eyes for brave Othello,
   Even till we make the main and the aerial blue
   An indistinct regard.
THIRD GENTLEMAN.   Come, let's do so.   40
   For every minute is expectancy
   Of more arrivance. (*Enter* CASSIO.)
CASSIO.   Thanks, you the valiant of this warlike isle
   That so approve the Moor! Oh, let the heavens
   Give him defense against the elements,   45
   For I have lost him on a dangerous sea.
MONTANO.   Is he well shipped?
CASSIO.   His bark is stoutly timbered, and his pilot
   Of very expert and approved allowance.
   Therefore my hopes, not surfeited to death,   50
   Stand in bold cure.
   (*A cry within:* "A sail, a sail, a sail!" *Enter a* FOURTH GENTLEMAN.)
   What noise?
FOURTH GENTLEMAN.   The town is empty. On the brow o' the sea
   Stand ranks of people and they cry "A sail!"
CASSIO.   My hopes do shape him for the governor. (*Guns heard.*)   55
SECOND GENTLEMAN.   They do discharge their shot of courtesy.
   Our friends, at least.
CASSIO.   I pray you, sir, go forth,
   And give us truth who 'tis that is arrived.
SECOND GENTLEMAN.   I shall. (*Exit.*)
MONTANO.   But, good Lieutenant, is your General wived?   60
CASSIO.   Most fortunately. He hath achieved a maid
   That paragons description and wild fame,
   One that excels the quirks of blazoning pens
   And in the essential vesture of creation
   Does tire the ingener.° (*Re-enter* SECOND GENTLEMAN.)
                       How now! Who has put in?   65
SECOND GENTLEMAN.   'Tis one Iago, Ancient to the General.
CASSIO.   He has had most favorable and happy speed.

63–65. One . . . ingener: one that is too good for the fancy phrases (*quirks*) of painting pens (i.e., poets) and in her absolute perfection wearies the artist (i.e., the painter) **ingener:** inventor

Tempests themselves, high seas, and howling winds,
The guttered rocks, and congregated sands,
Traitors ensteeped to clog the guiltless keel,   70
As having sense of beauty, do omit
Their mortal° natures, letting go safely by
The divine Desdemona.
MONTANO.   What is she?
CASSIO.   She that I spake of, our great Captain's captain,
Left in the conduct of the bold Iago,   75
Whose footing here anticipates our thoughts
A sennight's° speed. Great Jove, Othello guard,
And swell his sail with thine own powerful breath,
That he may bless this bay with his tall ship,
Make love's quick pants in Desdemona's arms,   80
Give renewed fire to our extincted spirits,
And bring all Cyprus comfort.
(*Enter* DESDEMONA, EMILIA, IAGO, RODERIGO, *and* ATTENDANTS.)
                    Oh, behold,
The riches of the ship is come on shore!
Ye men of Cyprus, let her have your knees.
Hail to thee, lady! And the grace of Heaven,   85
Before, behind thee, and on every hand,
Enwheel thee round!
DESDEMONA.   I thank you, valiant Cassio.
What tidings can you tell me of my lord?
CASSIO.   He is not yet arrived, nor know I aught
But that he's well and will be shortly here.   90
DESDEMONA.   Oh, but I fear—How lost you company?
CASSIO.   The great contention of the sea and skies
Parted our fellowship.—But hark! A sail.
(*A cry within:* "A sail, a sail!" *Guns heard.*)
SECOND GENTLEMAN.   They give their greeting to the citadel.
This likewise is a friend.
CASSIO.   See for the news. (*Exit* GENTLEMAN.)   95
Good Ancient, you are welcome. (*To* EMILIA) Welcome, mistress.
Let it not gall your patience, good Iago,
That I extend my manners. 'Tis my breeding
That gives me this bold show of courtesy. (*Kissing her.*)
IAGO.   Sir, would she give you so much of her lips   100
As of her tongue she oft bestows on me,
You'd have enough.
DESDEMONA.   Alas, she has no speech.
IAGO.   In faith, too much,
I find it still when I have list° to sleep.

72. **mortal:** deadly   77. **sennight's:** week's   104. **list:** desire

Marry, before your ladyship, I grant,   105
She puts her tongue a little in her heart
And chides with thinking.
EMILIA.   You have little cause to say so.
IAGO.   Come on, come on. You are pictures° out of doors,
Bells° in your parlors, wildcats in your kitchens,   110
Saints in your injuries,° devils being offended,
Players in your housewifery, and housewives in your beds.
DESDEMONA.   Oh, fie upon thee, slanderer!
IAGO.   Nay, it is true, or else I am a Turk.
You rise to play, and go to bed to work.   115
EMILIA.   You shall not write my praise.
IAGO.   No, let me not.
DESDEMONA.   What wouldst thou write of me if thou shouldst praise
me?
IAGO.   O gentle lady, do not put me to 't,
For I am nothing if not critical.
DESDEMONA.   Come on, assay.°—There's one gone to the harbor?   120
IAGO.   Aye, madam.
DESDEMONA *(aside)*.   I am not merry, but I do beguile
The thing I am by seeming otherwise.—
Come, how wouldst thou praise me?
IAGO.   I am about it, but indeed my invention   125
Comes from my pate as birdlime does from frieze°—
It plucks out brains and all. But my Muse labors,
And thus she is delivered:
If she be fair and wise, fairness and wit,
The one's for use, the other useth it.   130
DESDEMONA.   Well praised! How if she be black° and witty?
IAGO.   If she be black, and thereto have a wit,
She'll find a white° that shall her blackness fit.
DESDEMONA.   Worse and worse.
EMILIA.   How if fair and foolish?   135
IAGO.   She never yet was foolish that was fair,
For even her folly helped her to an heir.
DESDEMONA.   These are old fond paradoxes to make fools laugh i' the ale-
house. What miserable praise hast thou for her that's foul and foolish?
IAGO.   There's none so foul, and foolish thereunto,   140
But does foul pranks which fair and wise ones do.

---

109. pictures: i.e., painted and dumb   **110. Bells:** i.e., ever clacking
111. Saints . . . injuries: saints when you hurt anyone else   **120. assay:** try
125–26. my . . . frieze: my literary effort (*invention*) is as hard to pull out of my head
as frieze (cloth with a nap) stuck to birdlime   **131. black:** brunette, dark-complex-
ioned [Eds.]   **133. white:** with a pun on *wight* (line 156), man, person

DESDEMONA. Oh, heavy ignorance! Thou praisest the worst best. But
what praise couldst thou bestow on a deserving woman indeed, one that
in the authority of her merit did justly put on the vouch of very malice
itself?°   145
IAGO. She that was ever fair and never proud,
Had tongue at will° and yet was never loud,
Never lacked gold and yet went never gay,
Fled from her wish and yet said "Now I may";
She that, being angered, her revenge being nigh,   150
Bade her wrong stay and her displeasure fly;
She that in wisdom never was so frail
To change the cod's head for the salmon's tail;°
She that could think and ne'er disclose her mind,
See suitors following and not look behind;   155
She was a wight, if ever such wight were—
DESDEMONA. To do what?
IAGO. To suckle fools and chronicle small beer.°
DESDEMONA. Oh, most lame and impotent conclusion! Do not learn of
him, Emilia, though he be thy husband. How say you, Cassio? Is he not a
most profane and liberal° counselor?   161
CASSIO. He speaks home,° madam. You may relish him more in the soldier
than in the scholar.
IAGO (*aside*). He takes her by the palm. Aye, well said, whisper. With as
little a web as this will I ensnare as great a fly as Cassio. Aye, smile upon
her, do, I will gyve thee in thine own courtship.° You say true, 'tis so
indeed. If such tricks as these strip you out of your Lieutenantry, it had
been better you had not kissed your three fingers° so oft, which now
again you are most apt to play the sir° in. Very good, well kissed! An
excellent courtesy! 'Tis so indeed. Yet again your fingers to your lips?
Would they were clyster pipes° for your sake! (*Trumpet within.*) The
Moor! I know his trumpet.   172
CASSIO. 'Tis truly so.
DESDEMONA. Let's meet him and receive him.
CASSIO. Lo where he comes! (*Enter* OTHELLO *and* ATTENDANTS.)   175
OTHELLO. O my fair warrior!°
DESDEMONA.   My dear Othello!

143–145. one . . . itself: one so deserving that even malice would declare her good
147. tongue . . . will: a ready flow of words   **153. To . . . tail:** to prefer the tail
end of a good thing to the head of a poor thing   **158. suckle . . . beer:** nurse
babies and keep petty household accounts (i.e., even the best woman belongs in the
nursery and kitchen) [Eds.]   **161. liberal:** gross   **162. home:** bluntly [Eds.]
166. gyve . . . courtship: trap you with your own show of courtesy [Eds.]   **168.
kissed . . . fingers:** a gesture of gallantry   **169. play the sir:** act the fine gentleman   **171. clyster pipes:** an enema syringe   **176. warrior:** because she is a
soldier's wife

OTHELLO.   It gives me wonder great as my content
  To see you here before me. O my soul's joy!
  If after every tempest come such calms,
  May the winds blow till they have wakened death!   180
  And let the laboring bark climb hills of seas
  Olympus-high, and duck again as low
  As Hell's from Heaven! If it were now to die,
  'Twere now to be most happy, for I fear
  My soul hath her content so absolute   185
  That not another comfort like to this
  Succeeds in unknown fate.
DESDEMONA.   The Heavens forbid
  But that our loves and comforts should increase,
  Even as our days do grow!
OTHELLO.   Amen to that, sweet powers!
  I cannot speak enough of this content.   190
  It stops me here,° it is too much of joy.
  And this, and this, the greatest discords be (*Kissing her.*)
  That e'er our hearts shall make!
IAGO (*aside*).   Oh, you are well tuned now,
  But I'll set down the pegs° that make this music,
  As honest as I am.
OTHELLO.   Come, let us to the castle.   195
  News, friends! Our wars are done, the Turks are drowned.
  How does my old acquaintance of this isle?
  Honey, you shall be well desired in Cyprus,
  I have found great love amongst them. O my sweet,
  I prattle out of fashion, and I dote   200
  In mine own comforts. I prithee, good Iago,
  Go to the bay and disembark my coffers.°
  Bring thou the master° to the citadel.
  He is a good one, and his worthiness
  Does challenge much respect. Come, Desdemona,   205
  Once more well met at Cyprus. (*Exeunt all but* IAGO *and* RODERIGO.)
IAGO.   Do thou meet me presently at the harbor. Come hither. If thou beest
  valiant—as they say base men being in love have then a nobility in their
  natures more than is native to them—list me. The Lieutenant tonight
  watches on the court of guard. First, I must tell thee this. Desdemona is
  directly in love with him.   211
RODERIGO.   With him! Why, 'tis not possible.
IAGO.   Lay thy finger thus,° and let thy soul be instructed. Mark me with
  what violence she first loved the Moor, but for bragging and telling her

191. here: i.e., in the heart   **194. set . . . pegs:** i.e., make you sing out of tune. A
stringed instrument was tuned by the pegs.   **202. coffers:** trunks   **203. master:**
captain of the ship   **213. thus:** i.e., on the lips

fantastical lies. And will she love him still for prating? Let not thy discreet heart think it. Her eye must be fed, and what delight shall she have to look on the Devil? When the blood is made dull with the act of sport, there should be, again to inflame it and to give satiety a fresh appetite, loveliness in favor,° sympathy in years, manners, and beauties, all which the Moor is defective in. Now, for want of these required conveniences, her delicate tenderness will find itself abused, begin to heave the gorge, disrelish and abhor the Moor. Very nature will instruct her in it and compel her to some second choice. Now, sir, this granted—as it is a most pregnant and unforced position°—who stands so eminently in the degree of this fortune as Cassio does? A knave very voluble, no further conscionable° than in putting on the mere form of civil and humane seeming° for the better compassing of his salt° and most hidden loose affection? Why, none, why, none. A slipper° and subtle knave, a finder-out of occasions, that has an eye can stamp and counterfeit advantages,° though true advantage never present itself. A devilish knave! Besides, the knave is handsome, young, and hath all those requisites in him that folly and green minds look after. A pestilent complete knave, and the woman hath found him already.   233

RODERIGO.   I cannot believe that in her. She's full of most blest condition.°

IAGO.   Blest fig's-end!° The wine she drinks is made of grapes. If she had been blest, she would never have loved the Moor. Blest pudding! Didst thou not see her paddle with the palm of his hand? Didst not mark that?   238

RODERIGO.   Yes, that I did, but that was but courtesy.

IAGO.   Lechery, by his hand, an index and obscure prologue to the history of lust and foul thoughts. They met so near with their lips that their breaths embraced together. Villainous thoughts, Roderigo! When these mutualities so marshal the way, hard at hand comes the master and main exercise, the incorporate° conclusion. Pish! But, sir, be you ruled by me. I have brought you from Venice. Watch you tonight. For the command, I'll lay 't upon you. Cassio knows you not. I'll not be far from you. Do you find some occasion to anger Cassio, either by speaking too loud, or tainting° his discipline, or from what other course you please which the time shall more favorably minister.

RODERIGO.   Well.   250

IAGO.   Sir, he is rash and very sudden in choler,° and haply may strike at you. Provoke him, that he may, for even out of that will I cause these of Cyprus to mutiny, whose qualification shall come into no true taste again

---

219. **favor:** face   224. **pregnant . . . position:** very significant and probable argument   225–26. **no . . . conscionable:** who has no more conscience   227. **humane seeming:** courteous appearance   227. **salt:** lecherous   228. **slipper:** slippery   229. **stamp . . . advantages:** forge false opportunities   234. **condition:** disposition   235. **fig's-end:** nonsense [Eds.]   244. **incorporate:** bodily   248. **tainting:** disparaging   251. **choler:** anger

but by the displanting of Cassio. So shall you have a shorter journey to
your desires by the means I shall then have to prefer° them, and the
impediment most profitably removed without the which there were no
expectation of our prosperity.   257

RODERIGO.   I will do this, if I can bring it to any opportunity.

IAGO.   I warrant thee. Meet me by and by at the citadel. I must fetch his
necessaries ashore. Farewell.   260

RODERIGO.   Adieu. (*Exit.*)

IAGO.   That Cassio loves her, I do well believe it.
That she loves him, 'tis apt and of great credit.°
The Moor, howbeit that I endure him not,
Is of a constant, loving, noble nature,   265
And I dare think he'll prove to Desdemona
A most dear husband. Now, I do love her too,
Not out of absolute lust, though peradventure
I stand accountant for as great a sin,
But partly led to diet° my revenge   270
For that I do suspect the lusty Moor
Hath leaped into my seat. The thought whereof
Doth like a poisonous mineral gnaw my inwards,
And nothing can or shall content my soul
Till I am evened with him, wife for wife.   275
Or failing so, yet that I put the Moor
At least into a jealousy so strong
That judgment cannot cure. Which thing to do,
If this poor trash of Venice, whom I trash
For his quick hunting,° stand the putting-on,   280
I'll have our Michael Cassio on the hip,
Abuse him to the Moor in the rank garb°—
For I fear Cassio with my nightcap too—
Make the Moor thank me, love me, and reward me
For making him egregiously an ass   285
And practicing upon his peace and quiet
Even to madness. 'Tis here, but yet confused.
Knavery's plain face is never seen till used. (*Exit.*)

SCENE 2. A street.

Enter a HERALD *with a proclamation,* PEOPLE *following.*

HERALD.   It is Othello's pleasure, our noble and valiant General, that upon
certain tidings now arrived, importing the mere perdition° of the Turkish

---

255. prefer: promote   **263. apt . . . credit:** likely and very creditable   **270.
diet:** feed   **279–80. trash . . . hunting:** hold back from outrunning the pack
[Eds.]   **282. rank garb:** gross manner; i.e., by accusing him of being Desdemona's
lover   **2. mere perdition:** absolute destruction

fleet, every man put himself into triumph°—some to dance, some to make bonfires, each man to what sport and revels his addiction leads him. For, besides these beneficial news, it is the celebration of his nuptial. So much was his pleasure should be proclaimed. All offices° are open, and there is full liberty of feasting from this present hour of five till the bell have told eleven. Heaven bless the isle of Cyprus and our noble General Othello! (*Exeunt.*)

SCENE 3. A hall in the castle.

Enter OTHELLO, DESDEMONA, CASSIO, *and* ATTENDANTS.

OTHELLO.   Good Michael, look you to the guard tonight.
Let's teach ourselves that honorable stop,
Not to outsport discretion.°
CASSIO.   Iago hath directions what to do,
But notwithstanding with my personal eye   5
Will I look to 't.
OTHELLO.   Iago is most honest.
Michael, good night. Tomorrow with your earliest
Let me have speech with you. (*To* DESDEMONA) Come, my dear love,
The purchase made, the fruits are to ensue—
That profit's yet to come 'tween me and you.   10
Good night. (*Exeunt all but* CASSIO. *Enter* IAGO.)
CASSIO.   Welcome, Iago. We must to the watch.
IAGO.   Not this hour, Lieutenant, 'tis not yet ten o'clock. Our General cast° us thus early for the love of his Desdemona, who let us not therefore blame. He hath not yet made wanton the night with her, and she is sport for Jove.   16
CASSIO.   She's a most exquisite lady.
IAGO.   And, I'll warrant her, full of game.
CASSIO.   Indeed she's a most fresh and delicate creature.
IAGO.   What an eye she has! Methinks it sounds a parley to provocation. 20
CASSIO.   An inviting eye, and yet methinks right modest.
IAGO.   And when she speaks, is it not an alarum to love?
CASSIO.   She is indeed perfection.
IAGO.   Well, happiness to their sheets! Come, Lieutenant, I have a stoup of wine, and there without are a brace of Cyprus gallants that would fain have a measure to the health of black Othello.   26
CASSIO.   Not tonight, good Iago. I have very poor and unhappy brains for drinking. I could well wish courtesy would invent some other custom of entertainment.
IAGO.   Oh, they are our friends. But one cup—I'll drink for you.   30

___

3. put . . . triumph: celebrate   **6. offices:** the kitchen and buttery—i.e., free food and drink for all   **3. outsport discretion:** let the fun go too far.   **14. cast:** dismissed

CASSIO.   I have drunk but one cup tonight, and that was craftily qualified°
too, and behold what innovation it makes here. I am unfortunate in the
infirmity, and dare not task my weakness with any more.

IAGO.   What, man! 'Tis a night of revels. The gallants desire it.

CASSIO.   Where are they?   35

IAGO.   Here at the door. I pray you call them in.

CASSIO.   I'll do 't, but it dislikes me. (*Exit.*)

IAGO.   If I can fasten but one cup upon him,
With that which he hath drunk tonight already,
He'll be as full of quarrel and offense   40
As my young mistress' dog. Now my sick fool Roderigo,
Whom love hath turned almost the wrong side out,
To Desdemona hath tonight caroused
Potations pottle-deep, and he's to watch.
Three lads of Cyprus, noble swelling spirits   45
That hold their honors in a wary distance,°
The very elements° of this warlike isle,
Have I tonight flustered with flowing cups,
And they watch too. Now, 'mongst this flock of drunkards,
Am I to put our Cassio in some action   50
That may offend the isle. But here they come.
If consequence do but approve my dream,
My boat sails freely, both with wind and stream.
(*Re-enter* CASSIO, *with him* MONTANO *and* GENTLEMEN, SERVANTS *follow-
ing with wine.*)

CASSIO.   'Fore God, they have given me a rouse already.

MONTANO.   Good faith, a little one—not past a pint, as I am a soldier.

IAGO.   Some wine, ho! (*Sings*)   56
                    "And let me the cannikin clink, clink
                    And let me the cannikin clink.
                    A soldier's a man,
                    A life's but a span.°   60
                    Why, then let a soldier drink."
Some wine, boys!

CASSIO.   'Fore God, an excellent song.

IAGO.   I learned it in England, where indeed they are most potent in potting.° Your Dane, your German, and your swag-bellied Hollander—
Drink, ho!—are nothing to your English.   66

CASSIO.   Is your Englishman so expert in his drinking?

IAGO.   Why, he drinks you with facility your Dane dead drunk, he sweats

---

31. qualified: diluted [Eds.]   **46. hold . . . distance:** are very sensitive about their
honor [Eds.]   **47. very elements:** typical specimens   **60. span:** lit., the measure between the thumb and little finger of the outstretched hand; about 9 inches
64–65. potting: drinking

not to overthrow your Almain,° he gives your Hollander a vomit° ere
the next pottle can be filled.   70
CASSIO.   To the health of our General!
MONTANO.   I am for it, Lieutenant, and I'll do you justice.
IAGO.   O sweet England! (*Sings*)
     "King Stephen was a worthy peer,
      His breeches cost him but a crown.   75
     He held them sixpence all too dear,
      With that he called the tailor lown.°

     "He was a wight of high renown,
      And thou art but of low degree.
     'Tis pride that pulls the country down.   80
      Then take thine auld cloak about thee."
  Some wine, ho!
CASSIO.   Why, this is a more exquisite song than the other.
IAGO.   Will you hear 't again?
CASSIO.   No, for I hold him to be unworthy of his place that does those
  things. Well, God's above all, and there be souls must be saved and there
  be souls must not be saved.   87
IAGO.   It's true, good Lieutenant.
CASSIO.   For mine own part—no offense to the General, nor any man of
  quality—I hope to be saved.
IAGO.   And so do I too, Lieutenant.   91
CASSIO.   Aye, but, by your leave, not before me. The Lieutenant is to be
  saved before the Ancient. Let's have no more of this, let's to our affairs.
  God forgive us our sins! Gentlemen, let's look to our business. Do not
  think, gentlemen, I am drunk. This is my Ancient, this is my right hand
  and this is my left. I am not drunk now, I can stand well enough and
  speak well enough.   97
ALL.   Excellent well.
CASSIO.   Why, very well, then, you must not think then that I am drunk.
  (*Exit.*)
MONTANO.   To the platform, masters. Come, let's set the watch.   100
IAGO.   You see this fellow that is gone before.
  He is a soldier fit to stand by Caesar
  And give direction. And do but see his vice.
  'Tis to his virtue a just equinox,
  The one as long as the other. 'Tis pity of him.   105
  I fear the trust Othello puts him in
  On some odd time of his infirmity
  Will shake this island.

69. Almain: German **gives . . . vomit:** drinks as much as will make a Dutchman
throw up **77. lown:** lout

MONTANO.   But is he often thus?
IAGO.   'Tis evermore the prologue to his sleep.
   He'll watch the horologe a double set,°   110
   If drink rock not his cradle.
MONTANO.   It were well
   The General were put in mind of it.
   Perhaps he sees it not, or his good nature
   Prizes the virtue that appears in Cassio
   And looks not on his evils. Is not this true? (*Enter* RODERIGO.)   115
IAGO (*aside to him*).   How now, Roderigo! I pray you, after the Lieutenant.
   Go. (*Exit* RODERIGO.)
MONTANO.   And 'tis great pity that the noble Moor
   Should hazard such a place as his own second
   With one of an ingraft infirmity.   120
   It were an honest action to say
   So to the Moor.
IAGO.   Not I, for this fair island.
   I do love Cassio well, and would do much
   To cure him of this evil—But hark! What noise?
   (*A cry within:* "Help! Help!" *Re-enter* CASSIO, *driving in* RODERIGO.)
CASSIO.   'Zounds! You rogue! You rascal!   125
MONTANO.   What's the matter, Lieutenant?
CASSIO.   A knave teach me my duty! But I'll beat the knave into a wicker
   bottle.
RODERIGO.   Beat me!
CASSIO.   Does thou prate, rogue? (*Striking* RODERIGO.)   130
MONTANO.   Nay, good Lieutenant (*staying him*),
                    I pray you sir, hold your hand.
CASSIO.   Let me go, sir, or I'll knock you o'er the mazzard.°
MONTANO.   Come, come, you're drunk.
CASSIO.   Drunk! (*They fight.*)
IAGO (*aside to* RODERIGO).   Away, I say. Go out and cry a mutiny.   135
   (*Exit* RODERIGO.)
   Nay, good Lieutenant! God's will, gentlemen!
   Help, ho!—Lieutenant—sir—Montano—sir—
   Help, masters!—Here's a goodly watch indeed! (*A bell rings.*)
   Who's that that rings the bell?—Diablo, ho!
   The town will rise. God's will, Lieutenant, hold—   140
   You will be ashamed forever. (*Re-enter* OTHELLO *and* ATTENDANTS.)
OTHELLO.   What is the matter here?
MONTANO.   'Zounds, I bleed still, I am hurt to death. (*Faints.*)
OTHELLO.   Hold, for your lives!

---

110. watch . . . set: stay awake the clock twice round   **132. mazzard:** head

IAGO.   Hold, ho! Lieutenant—sir—Montano—gentlemen—
    Have you forgot all sense of place and duty?   145
    Hold! The General speaks to you. Hold, hold, for shame!
OTHELLO.   Why, how now, ho! From whence ariseth this?
    Are we turned Turks, and to ourselves do that
    Which Heaven hath forbid the Ottomites?
    For Christian shame, put by this barbarous brawl.   150
    He that stirs next to carve for his own rage
    Holds his soul light, he dies upon his motion.
    Silence that dreadful bell. It frights the isle
    From her propriety. What is the matter, masters?
    Honest Iago, that look'st dead with grieving,   155
    Speak, who began this? On thy love, I charge thee.
IAGO.   I do not know. Friends all but now, even now,
    In quarter and in terms like bride and groom
    Devesting them for bed. And then, but now,
    As if some planet had unwitted men,   160
    Swords out, and tilting one at other's breast
    In opposition bloody. I cannot speak
    Any beginning to this peevish odds,
    And would in action glorious I had lost
    Those legs that brought me to a part of it!   165
OTHELLO.   How comes it, Michael, you are thus forgot?°
CASSIO.   I pray you, pardon me, I cannot speak.
OTHELLO.   Worthy Montano, you were wont be civil.
    The gravity and stillness of your youth
    The world hath noted, and your name is great   170
    In mouths of wisest censure.° What's the matter
    That you unlace your reputation thus
    And spend your rich opinion° for the name
    Of a night brawler? Give me answer to it.
MONTANO.   Worthy Othello, I am hurt to danger.   175
    Your officer, Iago, can inform you—
    While I spare speech, which something now offends me—
    Of all that I do know. Nor know I aught
    By me that's said or done amiss this night,
    Unless self-charity° be sometimes a vice,   180
    And to defend ourselves it be a sin
    When violence assails us.
OTHELLO.   Now, by Heaven,
    My blood begins my safer guides to rule,

---

166. are thus forgot: have so forgotten yourself   **171. censure:** judgment
173. opinion: reputation [Eds.]   **180. self-charity:** love for oneself

And passion, having my best judgment collied,°
Assays to lead the way. If I once stir,   185
Or do but lift this arm, the best of you
Shall sink in my rebuke. Give me to know
How this foul rout began, who set it on,
And he that is approved° in this offense,
Though he had twinned with me, both at a birth,   190
Shall lose me. What! In a town of war,
Yet wild, the people's hearts brimful of fear,
To manage private and domestic quarrel,
In night, and on the court and guard of safety!
'Tis monstrous. Iago, who began 't?   195
MONTANO.   If partially affined or leagued in office,
Thou dost deliver more or less than truth,
Thou art no soldier.
IAGO.   Touch me not so near.
I had rather have this tongue cut from my mouth
Than it should do offense to Michael Cassio.   200
Yet I persuade myself to speak the truth
Shall nothing wrong him. Thus it is, General.
Montano and myself being in speech,
There comes a fellow crying out for help,
And Cassio following him with determined sword   205
To execute upon him. Sir, this gentleman
Steps in to Cassio and entreats his pause.
Myself the crying fellow did pursue
Lest by his clamor—as it so fell out—
The town might fall in fright. He, swift of foot,   210
Outran my purpose, and I returned the rather
For that I heard the clink and fall of swords,
And Cassio high in oath, which till tonight
I ne'er might say before. When I came back—
For this was brief—I found them close together,   215
At blow and thrust, even as again they were
When you yourself did part them.
More of this matter cannot I report.
But men are men, the best sometimes forget.
Though Cassio did some little wrong to him,   220
As men in rage strike those that wish them best,
Yet surely Cassio, I believe, received
From him that fled some strange indignity,
Which patience could not pass.
OTHELLO.   I know, Iago,

184. **collied:** darkened   189. **approved:** proved guilty

Thy honesty and love doth mince this matter,   225
Making it light to Cassio. Cassio, I love thee,
But never more be officer of mine. (*Re-enter* DESDEMONA, *attended.*)
Look, if my gentle love be not raised up!
I'll make thee an example.
DESDEMONA.   What's the matter?
OTHELLO.   All's well now, sweeting. Come away to bed.   230
(*To* MONTANO, *who is led off*)
Sir, for your hurts, myself will be your surgeon.
Lead him off.
Iago, look with care about the town,
And silence those whom this vile brawl distracted.
Come, Desdemona. 'Tis the soldier's life   235
To have their balmy slumbers waked with strife.
(*Exeunt all but* IAGO *and* CASSIO.)
IAGO.   What, are you hurt, Lieutenant?
CASSIO.   Aye, past all surgery.
IAGO.   Marry, Heaven forbid!
CASSIO.   Reputation, reputation, reputation! Oh, I have lost my reputa-
tion! I have lost the immortal part of myself, and what remains is bestial.
My reputation, Iago, my reputation!   242
IAGO.   As I am an honest man, I thought you had received some bodily
wound. There is more sense in that than in reputation. Reputation is an
idle and most false imposition, oft got without merit and lost without
deserving. You have lost no reputation at all unless you repute yourself
such a loser. What, man! There are ways to recover the General again.
You are but now cast in his mood,° a punishment more in policy° than in
malice—even so as one would beat his offenseless dog to affright an im-
perious lion.° Sue to him again and he's yours.   250
CASSIO.   I will rather sue to be despised than to deceive so good a commander with so slight, so drunken, and so indiscreet an officer. Drunk?
And speak parrot°? And squabble? Swagger? Swear? And discourse fus-
tian° with one's own shadow? O thou invisible spirit of wine, if thou hast
no name to be known by, let us call thee devil!   255
IAGO.   What was he that you followed with your sword? What had he done
to you?
CASSIO.   I know not.
IAGO.   Is 't possible?
CASSIO.   I remember a mass of things, but nothing distinctly—a quarrel,
but nothing wherefore. Oh God, that men should put an enemy in their

---

248. cast . . . mood: dismissed because he is in a bad mood   **in policy:** i.e., because
he must appear to be angry before the Cypriots   **249–50. even . . . lion:** A proverb
meaning that when the lion sees the dog beaten, he will know what is coming to him
253–54. speak parrot: babble   **253–54. fustian:** nonsense

mouths to steal away their brains! That we should, with joy, pleasance, revel, and applause, transform ourselves into beasts! 263

IAGO.   Why, but you are now well enough. How came you thus recovered?

CASSIO.   It hath pleased the devil drunkenness to give place to the devil wrath. One unperfectness shows me another, to make me frankly despise myself. 267

IAGO.   Come, you are too severe a moraler. As the time, the place, and the condition of this country stands, I could heartily wish this had not befallen. But since it is as it is, mend it for your own good. 270

CASSIO.   I will ask him for my place again, he shall tell me I am a drunkard! Had I as many mouths as Hydra, such an answer would stop them all. To be now a sensible man, by and by a fool, and presently a beast! Oh, strange! Every inordinate cup is unblest, and the ingredient is a devil.

IAGO.   Come, come, good wine is a good familiar creature, if it be well used. Exclaim no more against it. And, good Lieutenant, I think you think I love you. 277

CASSIO.   I have well approved it, sir. I drunk!

IAGO.   You or any man living may be drunk at some time, man. I'll tell you what you shall do. Our General's wife is now the General. I may say so in this respect, for that he hath devoted and given up himself to the contemplation, mark, and denotement of her parts and graces. Confess yourself freely to her, importune her help to put you in your place again. She is of so free, so kind, so apt, so blessed a disposition, she holds it a vice in her goodness not to do more than she is requested. This broken joint between you and her husband entreat her to splinter° and, my fortunes against any lay° worth naming, this crack of your love shall grow stronger than it was before. 288

CASSIO.   You advise me well.

IAGO.   I protest, in the sincerity of love and honest kindness.

CASSIO.   I think it freely, and betimes in the morning I will beseech the virtuous Desdemona to undertake for me. I am desperate of my fortunes if they check me here.

IAGO.   You are in the right. Good night, Lieutenant, I must to the watch.

CASSIO.   Good night, honest Iago. (*Exit.*) 295

IAGO.   And what's he then that says I play the villain?
    When this advice is free I give and honest,
    Probal° to thinking, and indeed the course
    To win the Moor again? For 'tis most easy
    The inclining Desdemona to subdue   300
    In any honest suit. She's framed as fruitful
    As the free elements. And then for her
    To win the Moor, were 't to renounce his baptism,
    All seals and symbols of redeemèd sin,
    His soul is so enfettered to her love   305

---

286. splinter: put in splints   **287. lay:** bet   **298. Probal:** probable

That she may make, unmake, do what she list,
Even as her appetite shall play the god
With his weak function.° How am I then a villain
To counsel Cassio to this parallel course,
Directly to his good? Divinity of Hell!   310
When devils will the blackest sins put on,
They do suggest at first with heavenly shows,
As I do now. For whiles this honest fool
Plies Desdemona to repair his fortunes,
And she for him pleads strongly to the Moor,   315
I'll pour this pestilence into his ear,
That she repeals° him for her body's lust,
And by how much she strives to do him good,
She shall undo her credit with the Moor.
So will I turn her virtue into pitch,   320
And out of her own goodness make the net
That shall enmesh them all. (*Enter* RODERIGO.)
                   How now, Roderigo!
RODERIGO.   I do follow here in the chase, not like a hound that hunts but
one that fills up the cry. My money is almost spent, I have been tonight
exceedingly well cudgeled, and I think the issue will be I shall have so
much experience from my pains and so, with no money at all and a little
more wit, return again to Venice.   327
IAGO.   How poor are they that have not patience!
What wound did ever heal but by degrees?
Thou know'st we work by wit and not by witchcraft,   330
And wit depends on dilatory Time.
Does 't not go well? Cassio hath beaten thee,
And thou by that small hurt hast cashiered Cassio.
Though other things grow fair against the sun,
Yet fruits that blossom first will first be ripe.   335
Content thyself awhile, By the mass, 'tis morning.
Pleasure and action make the hours seem short.
Retire thee, go where thou art billeted.
Away, I say. Thou shalt know more hereafter.
Nay, get thee gone. (*Exit* RODERIGO.)
                  Two things are to be done: 340
My wife must move for Cassio to her mistress,
I'll set her on,
Myself the while to draw the Moor apart
And bring him jump° when he may Cassio find
Soliciting his wife. Aye, that's the way.   345
Dull not device by coldness and delay. (*Exit.*)

---

308. function: mental faculties [Eds.]   **317. repeals:** calls back   **344. jump:** at
the moment

ACT 3

SCENE 1.   Before the castle.

Enter CASSIO *and some* MUSICIANS.

CASSIO.   Masters, play here, I will content your pains°—
Something that's brief, and bid "Good morrow, General."°
(*Music. Enter* CLOWN.)
CLOWN.   Why, masters, have your instruments been in Naples, that they
speak i' the nose thus?
FIRST MUSICIAN.   How, sir, how?   5
CLOWN.   Are these, I pray you, wind instruments?
FIRST MUSICIAN.   Aye, marry are they, sir.
CLOWN.   Oh, thereby hangs a tail.
FIRST MUSICIAN.   Whereby hangs a tale, sir?
CLOWN.   Marry, sir, by many a wind instrument that I know. But, masters,
here's money for you. And the General so likes your music that he desires
you, for love's sake, to make no more noise with it.   12
FIRST MUSICIAN.   Well, sir, we will not.
CLOWN.   If you have any music that may not be heard, to 't again. But, as
they say, to hear music the General does not greatly care.   15
FIRST MUSICIAN.   We have none such, sir.
CLOWN.   Then put up your pipes in your bag, for I'll away. Go, vanish into
air, away! (*Exeunt* MUSICIANS.)
CASSIO.   Dost thou hear, my honest friend?
CLOWN.   No, I hear not your honest friend, I hear you.   20
CASSIO.   Prithee keep up thy quillets.° There's a poor piece of gold for thee.
If the gentlewoman that attends the General's wife be stirring, tell her
there's one Cassio entreats her a little favor of speech. Wilt thou do this?
CLOWN.   She is stirring, sir. If she will stir hither, I shall seem to notify
unto her.   25
CASSIO.   Do, good my friend. (*Exit* CLOWN. *Enter* IAGO.)
                              In happy time, Iago.
IAGO.   You have not been abed, then?
CASSIO.   Why, no, the day had broke
Before we parted. I have made bold, Iago,
To send in to your wife. My suit to her   30
Is that she will to virtuous Desdemona
Procure me some access.
IAGO.   I'll send her to you presently,

---

1. content your pains: reward your labor   **2. bid . . . General:** It was a common custom to play or sing a song beneath the bedroom window of a distinguished guest or of a newly wedded couple on the morning after their wedding night. **21. keep . . . quillets:** put away your wisecracks

And I'll devise a mean to draw the Moor
Out of the way, that your convérse and business
May be more free.   35
CASSIO.   I humbly thank you for 't. (*Exit* IAGO.)
                         I never knew
A Florentine more kind and honest. (*Enter* EMILIA.)
EMILIA. Good morrow, good Lieutenant. I am sorry
For your displeasure, but all will sure be well.
The General and his wife are talking of it,   40
And she speaks for you stoutly. The Moor replies
That he you hurt is of great fame in Cyprus
And great affinity,° and that in wholesome wisdom
He might not but refuse you. But he protests he loves you,
And needs no other suitor but his likings   45
To take the safest occasion by the front
To bring you in again.
CASSIO.   Yet I beseech you
If you think fit, or that it may be done,
Give me advantage of some brief discourse
With Desdemona alone.
EMILIA.   Pray you, come in.   50
I will bestow you where you shall have time
To speak your bosom freely.
CASSIO.   I am much bound to you. (*Exeunt.*)

SCENE 2. A room in the castle.

Enter OTHELLO, IAGO, *and* GENTLEMEN.

OTHELLO.   These letters give, Iago, to the pilot,
And by him do my duties to the Senate.
That done, I will be walking on the works.°
Repair there to me.
IAGO.   Well, my good lord, I'll do 't.
OTHELLO.   This fortification, gentlemen, shall we see 't?   5
GENTLEMEN.   We'll wait upon your lordship. (*Exeunt.*)

SCENE 3. The garden of the castle.

Enter DESDEMONA, CASSIO, *and* EMILIA.

DESDEMONA.   Be thou assured, good Cassio, I will do
All my abilities in thy behalf.
EMILIA.   Good madam, do. I warrant it grieves my husband
As if the case were his.

43. affinity: kindred   **3. works:** fortifications

DESDEMONA.   Oh, that's an honest fellow. Do not doubt, Cassio,   5
But I will have my lord and you again
As friendly as you were.
CASSIO.   Bounteous madam,
Whatever shall become of Michael Cassio,
He's never anything but your true servant.
DESDEMONA.   I know 't. I thank you. You do love my lord.   10
You have known him long, and be you well assured
He shall in strangeness stand no farther off
Than in a politic distance.°
CASSIO.   Aye, but lady,
That policy may either last so long,
Or feed upon such nice and waterish diet,   15
Or breed itself so out of circumstance,
That, I being absent and my place supplied,
My General will forget my love and service.
DESDEMONA.   Do not doubt° that. Before Emilia here
I give thee warrant of thy place. Assure thee,   20
If I do vow a friendship, I'll perform it
To the last article. My lord shall never rest.
I'll watch him tame and talk him out of patience,
His bed shall seem a school, his board a shrift.°
I'll intermingle every thing he does   25
With Cassio's suit. Therefore be merry, Cassio,
For thy solicitor shall rather die
Than give thy cause away. (*Enter* OTHELLO *and* IAGO, *at a distance.*)
EMILIA.   Madam, here comes my lord.
CASSIO.   Madam, I'll take my leave.   30
DESDEMONA.   Nay, stay and hear me speak.
CASSIO.   Madam, not now. I am very ill at ease,
Unfit for mine own purposes.
DESDEMONA.   Well, do your discretion. (*Exit* CASSIO.)
IAGO.   Ha! I like not that.   35
OTHELLO.   What dost thou say?
IAGO.   Nothing, my lord. Or if—I know not what.
OTHELLO.   Was not that Cassio parted from my wife?
IAGO.   Cassio, my lord! No, sure, I cannot think it,
That he would steal away so guilty-like,   40
Seeing you coming.
OTHELLO.   I do believe 'twas he.
DESDEMONA.   How now, my lord!

12–13: He . . . distance: i.e., his apparent coldness to you shall only be so much as his official position demands for reasons of policy   **19. doubt:** fear   **24. shrift:** place of confession [Eds.]

I have been talking with a suitor here,
A man that languishes in your displeasure.
OTHELLO. Who is 't you mean?   45
DESDEMONA. Why, your Lieutenant, Cassio. Good my lord,
　　If I have any grace or power to move you,
　　His present reconciliation take.°
　　For if he be not one that truly loves you,
　　That errs in ignorance and not in cunning,   50
　　I have no judgment in an honest face.
　　I prithee call him back.
OTHELLO.   Went he hence now?
DESDEMONA. Aye, sooth, so humbled
　　That he hath left part of his grief with me,
　　To suffer with him. Good love, call him back.   55
OTHELLO. Not now, sweet Desdemona, some other time.
DESDEMONA. But shall 't be shortly?
OTHELLO.   The sooner, sweet, for you.
DESDEMONA. Shall 't be tonight at supper?
OTHELLO.   No, not tonight.
DESDEMONA. Tomorrow dinner then?
OTHELLO.   I shall not dine at home.
　　I meet the captains at the citadel.   60
DESDEMONA. Why, then tomorrow night or Tuesday morn,
　　On Tuesday noon, or night, on Wednesday morn.
　　I prithee name the time, but let it not
　　Exceed three days. In faith, he's penitent,
　　And yet his trespass, in our common reason—   65
　　Save that, they say, the wars must make examples
　　Out of their best—is not almost° a fault
　　To incur a private check.° When shall he come?
　　Tell me, Othello. I wonder in my soul
　　What you would ask me that I should deny,   70
　　Or stand so mammering° on. What! Michael Cassio,
　　That came a-wooing with you, and so many a time
　　When I have spoke of you dispraisingly
　　Hath ta'en your part—to have so much to do
　　To bring him in! Trust me, I could do much—   75
OTHELLO. Prithee, no more. Let him come when he will.
　　I will deny thee nothing.
DESDEMONA.   Why, this is not a boon.
　　'Tis as I should entreat you wear your gloves,
　　Or feed on nourishing dishes, or keep you warm,

---

48. His . . . take: accept his immediate apology and forgive him　　**67. not almost:** hardly　　**68. check:** rebuke　　**71. mammering:** hesitating

Or sue to you to do a peculiar profit   80
To your own person. Nay, when I have a suit
Wherein I mean to touch your love indeed,
It shall be full of poise and difficult weight,
And fearful to be granted.
OTHELLO.   I will deny thee nothing.
Whereon I do beseech thee grant me this,   85
To leave me but a little to myself.
DESDEMONA.   Shall I deny you? No. Farewell, my lord.
OTHELLO.   Farewell, my Desdemona. I'll come to thee straight.
DESDEMONA.   Emilia, come. Be as your fancies teach you.
Whate'er you be, I am obedient.   90
(*Exeunt* DESDEMONA *and* EMILIA.)
OTHELLO.   Excellent wretch! Perdition catch my soul
But I do love thee! And when I love thee not,
Chaos is come again.
IAGO.   My noble lord—
OTHELLO.   What dost thou say, Iago?
IAGO.   Did Michael Cassio, when you wooed my lady,   95
Know of your love?
OTHELLO.   He did, from first to last. Why dost thou ask?
IAGO.   But for a satisfaction of my thought,
No further harm.
OTHELLO.   Why of thy thought, Iago?
IAGO.   I did not think he had been acquainted with her.   100
OTHELLO.   Oh yes, and went between us very oft.
IAGO.   Indeed!
OTHELLO.   Indeed! Aye, indeed. Discern'st thou aught in that?
Is he not honest?
IAGO.   Honest, my lord!
OTHELLO.   Honest! Aye, honest.
IAGO.   My lord, for aught I know.
OTHELLO.   What dost thou think?   105
IAGO.   Think, my lord!
OTHELLO.   Think, my lord! By Heaven, he echoes me
As if there were some monster in his thought
Too hideous to be shown. Thou dost mean something.
I heard thee say even now that thou likedst not that   110
When Cassio left my wife. What didst not like?
And when I told thee he was of my counsel
In my whole course of wooing, thou criedst "Indeed!"
And didst contract and purse thy brow together
As if thou then hadst shut up in thy brain   115
Some horrible conceit. If thou dost love me,
Show me thy thought.

IAGO.   My lord, you know I love you.
OTHELLO.   I think thou dost,
    And for I know thou'rt full of love and honesty
    And weigh'st thy words before thou givest them breath,   120
    Therefore these stops of thine fright me the more.
    For such things in a false disloyal knave
    Are tricks of custom, but in a man that's just
    They're close delations,° working from the heart,
    That passion cannot rule.
IAGO.   For Michael Cassio,   125
    I dare be sworn I think that he is honest.
OTHELLO.   I think so too.
IAGO.   Men should be what they seem,
    Or those that be not, would they might seem none!°
OTHELLO.   Certain, men should be what they seem.
IAGO.   Why, then I think Cassio's an honest man.   130
OTHELLO.   Nay, yet there's more in this.
    I prithee speak to me as to thy thinkings,
    As thou dost ruminate, and give thy worst of thoughts
    The worst of words.
IAGO.   Good my lord, pardon me.
    Though I am bound to every act of duty,   135
    I am not bound to that all slaves are free to.
    Utter my thoughts? Why, say they are vile and false,
    As where's that palace whereinto foul things
    Sometimes intrude not? Who has a breast so pure
    But some uncleanly apprehensions   140
    Keep leets° and law days, and in session sit
    With meditations lawful?
OTHELLO.   Thou dost conspire against thy friend, Iago,
    If thou but think'st him wronged and makest his ear
    A stranger to thy thoughts.
IAGO.   I do beseech you—   145
    Though I perchance am vicious in my guess,
    As, I confess, it is my nature's plague
    To spy into abuses, and oft my jealousy°
    Shapes faults that are not—that your wisdom yet,
    From one that so imperfectly conceits,°   150
    Would take no notice, nor build yourself a trouble
    Out of his scattering and unsure observance.°
    It were not for your quiet nor your good,

---

124. close delations: concealed accusations   **128. seem none:** i.e., not seem to be
honest men   **141. leets:** courts   **148. jealousy:** suspicion   **150. conceits:**
conceives   **152. observance:** observation

Nor for my manhood, honesty, or wisdom,
To let you know my thoughts.
OTHELLO.   What dost thou mean?   155
IAGO.   Good name in man and woman, dear my lord,
Is the immediate jewel of their souls.
Who steals my purse steals trash—'tis something, nothing,
'Twas mine, 'tis his, and has been slave to thousands—
But he that filches from me my good name   160
Robs me of that which not enriches him
And makes me poor indeed.
OTHELLO.   By Heaven, I'll know thy thoughts.
IAGO.   You cannot, if my heart were in your hand,
Nor shall not, whilst 'tis in my custody.   165
OTHELLO.   Ha!
IAGO.   Oh, beware, my lord, of jealousy.
It is the green-eyed monster which doth mock
The meat it feeds on. That cuckold lives in bliss
Who, certain of his fate, loves not his wronger.°
But, oh, what damnèd minutes tells he o'er   170
Who dotes, yet doubts, suspects, yet strongly loves!
OTHELLO.   Oh misery!
IAGO.   Poor and content is rich, and rich enough,
But riches fineless° is as poor as winter
To him that ever fears he shall be poor.   175
Good God, the souls of all my tribe defend
From jealousy!
OTHELLO.   Why, why is this?
Think'st thou I'd make a life of jealousy,
To follow still the changes of the moon
With fresh suspicions? No, to be once in doubt   180
Is once to be resolved.° Exchange me for a goat
When I shall turn the business of my soul
To such exsufflicate° and blown surmises,
Matching thy inference.° 'Tis not to make me jealous
To say my wife is fair, feeds well, loves company,   185
Is free of speech, sings, plays, and dances well.
Where virtue is, these are more virtuous.
Nor from mine own weak merits will I draw
The smallest fear or doubt of her revolt,

168–69. That . . . wronger: i.e., the cuckold who hates his wife and knows her falseness is not tormented by suspicious jealousy.   **174. fineless:** limitless
180–81. to . . . resolved: whenever I find myself in doubt I at once seek out the truth.   **182–84. When . . . inference:** when I shall allow that which concerns me most dearly to be influenced by such trifling suggestions as yours.   **exsufflicate:** blown up like a bubble

For she had eyes, and chose me. No, Iago,   190
I'll see before I doubt, when I doubt, prove,
And on the proof, there is no more but this—
Away at once with love or jealousy!
IAGO.   I am glad of it, for now I shall have reason
To show the love and duty that I bear you   195
With franker spirit. Therefore, as I am bound,
Receive it from me. I speak not yet of proof.
Look to your wife. Observe her well with Cassio.
Wear your eye thus, not jealous nor secure.°
I would not have your free and noble nature   200
Out of self-bounty° be abused. Look to 't.
I know our country disposition well.
In Venice° they do let Heaven see the pranks
They dare not show their husbands. Their best conscience
Is not to leave 't undone, but keep 't unknown.   205
OTHELLO.   Dost thou say so?
IAGO.   She did deceive her father, marrying you,
And when she seemed to shake and fear your looks,
She loved them most.
OTHELLO.   And so she did.
IAGO.   Why, go to, then.
She that so young could give out such a seeming   210
To seel° her father's eyes up close as oak—
He thought 'twas witchcraft—but I am much to blame.
I humbly do beseech you of your pardon
For too much loving you.
OTHELLO.   I am bound to thee forever.
IAGO.   I see this hath a little dashed your spirits.   215
OTHELLO.   Not a jot, not a jot.
IAGO.   I' faith, I fear it has.
I hope you will consider what is spoke
Comes from my love. But I do see you're moved.
I am to pray you not to strain my speech
To grosser issues nor to larger reach   220
Than to suspicion.
OTHELLO.   I will not.
IAGO.   Should you do so, my lord,
My speech should fall into such vile success
As my thoughts aim not at. Cassio's my worthy friend.—
My lord, I see you're moved.

---

199. secure: overconfident   **201. self-bounty:** natural goodness   **203. In Venice:** Venice was notorious for its loose women; the Venetian courtesans were among the sights of Europe and were much commented upon by travelers.   **211. seel:** blind

OTHELLO.   No, not so much moved.   225
   I do not think but Desdemona's honest.°
IAGO.   Long live she so! And long live you to think so!
OTHELLO.   And yet, how nature erring from itself—
IAGO.   Aye, there's the point. As—to be bold with you—
   Not to affect° many proposèd matches   230
   Of her own clime, complexion, and degree,
   Whereto we see in all things nature tends°—
   Foh! One may smell in such a will most rank,°
   Foul disproportion, thoughts unnatural.
   But pardon me. I do not in position   235
   Distinctly speak of her, though I may fear
   Her will, recoiling to her better judgment,
   May fall to match° you with her country forms,°
   And happily° repent.
OTHELLO.   Farewell, farewell.
   If more thou dost perceive, let me know more.   240
   Set on thy wife to observe. Leave me, Iago.
IAGO (*going*).   My lord, I take my leave.
OTHELLO.   Why did I marry? This honest creature doubtless
   Sees and knows more, much more, than he unfolds.
IAGO (*returning*).   My lord, I would I might entreat your honor   245
   To scan this thing no further. Leave it to time.
   Though it be fit that Cassio have his place,
   For sure he fills it up with great ability,
   Yet if you please to hold him off awhile,
   You shall by that perceive him and his means.   250
   Note if your lady strain his entertainment°
   With any strong or vehement importunity—
   Much will be seen in that. In the meantime,
   Let me be thought too busy in my fears—
   As worthy cause I have to fear I am—   255
   And hold her free, I do beseech your Honor.
OTHELLO.   Fear not my government.°
IAGO.   I once more take my leave. (*Exit.*)
OTHELLO.   This fellow's of exceeding honesty,
   And knows all qualities, with a learned spirit,   260
   Of human dealings. If I do prove her haggard,°

---

226. honest: When applied to Desdemona, "honest" means "chaste," but applied to
Iago it has the modern meaning of "open and sincere."   **230. affect:** be inclined
to   **232. in . . . tends:** i.e., a woman naturally marries a man of her own country,
color, and rank.   **233. will . . . rank:** desire most lustful   **238. match:** compare
country forms: the appearance of her countrymen, i.e., white men   **239. happily:**
haply, by chance   **251. strain his entertainment:** urge you to receive him
257. government: self-control   **261. haggard:** a wild hawk

Though that her jesses° were my dear heartstrings,
I'd whistle her off and let her down the wind
To prey at fortune.° Haply, for° I am black
And have not those soft parts of conversation   265
That chamberers° have, or for I am declined
Into the vale of years—yet that's not much—
She's gone, I am abused, and my relief
Must be to loathe her. Oh, curse of marriage,
That we can call these delicate creatures ours,   270
And not their appetites! I had rather be a toad
And live upon the vapor of a dungeon
Than keep a corner in the thing I love
For others' uses. Yet, 'tis the plague of great ones,
Prerogatived are they less than the base.   275
'Tis destiny unshunnable, like death.
Even then this forkèd plague° is fated to us
When we do quicken.° Desdemona comes.
(*Re-enter* DESDEMONA *and* EMILIA.)
If she be false, oh, then Heaven mocks itself!
I'll not believe 't.
DESDEMONA.   How now, my dear Othello!   280
    Your dinner, and the generous° islanders
    By you invited, do attend your presence.
OTHELLO.   I am to blame.
DESDEMONA.   Why do you speak so faintly?
    Are you not well?
OTHELLO.   I have a pain upon my forehead here.   285
DESDEMONA.   Faith, that's with watching,° 'twill away again.
    Let me but bind it hard, within this hour
    It will be well.
OTHELLO.   Your napkin° is too little,
    (*He puts the handkerchief from him, and it drops.*)
    Let it alone. Come, I'll go in with you.
DESDEMONA.   I am very sorry that you are not well.   290
    (*Exeunt* OTHELLO *and* DESDEMONA.)
EMILIA.   I am glad I have found this napkin.
    This was her first remembrance from the Moor.
    My wayward° husband hath a hundred times
    Wooed me to steal it, but she so loves the token,

261–64. If . . . fortune: Othello keeps up the imagery of falconry throughout. He means: If I find that she is wild, I'll whistle her off the game and let her go where she will, for she's not worth keeping.   **jesses:** the straps attached to a hawk's legs
264. Haply, for: perhaps, because [Eds.]   **266. chamberers:** playboys   **277.
forkèd plague:** i.e., to be a cuckold   **278. quicken:** stir in our mother's womb
281. generous: noble   **286. watching:** lack of sleep   **288. napkin:** handkerchief   **293. wayward:** unaccountable

For he conjured° her she should ever keep it,   295
That she reserves it evermore about her
To kiss and talk to. I'll have the work ta'en out,°
And give 't to Iago. What he will do with it
Heaven knows, not I.
I nothing know, but for his fantasy.° (*Re-enter* IAGO.)   300
IAGO.   How now! What do you here alone?
EMILIA.   Do not you chide, I have a thing for you.
IAGO.   A thing for me? It is a common thing—
EMILIA.   Ha!
IAGO.   To have a foolish wife.   305
EMILIA.   Oh, is that all? What will you give me now
For that same handkerchief?
IAGO.   What handkerchief?
EMILIA.   What handkerchief!
Why, that the Moor first gave to Desdemona,
That which so often you did bid me steal.   310
IAGO.   Hast stol'n it from her?
EMILIA.   No, faith, she let it drop by negligence,
And, to the advantage, I being here took 't up.
Look, here it is.
IAGO.   A good wench. Give it me.
EMILIA.   What will you do with 't, that you have been so earnest 315
To have me filch it?
IAGO (*snatching it*).   Why, what's that to you?
EMILIA.   If 't be not for some purpose of import,
Give 't me again. Poor lady, she'll run mad
When she shall lack it.
IAGO.   Be not acknown on 't,° I have use for it.   320
Go, leave me. (*Exit* EMILIA.)
I will in Cassio's lodging lose this napkin,
And let him find it. Trifles light as air
Are to the jealous confirmations strong
As proofs of Holy Writ. This may do something.   325
The Moor already changes with my poison.
Dangerous conceits° are in their natures poisons,
Which at the first are scarce found to distaste,
But, with a little, act upon the blood,
Burn like the mines of sulphur. I did say so.°   330
Look where he comes! (*Re-enter* OTHELLO.)

---

295. **conjured:** begged with an oath   297. **work . . . out:** pattern copied   **300. fantasy:** whim   320. **Be . . . 't:** Know nothing about it   327. **conceits:** ideas [Eds.]   330. **I . . . so:** As Iago says this, Othello is seen approaching, with all the signs of his agitation outwardly visible.

Not poppy,° nor mandragora,°
Nor all the drowsy syrups of the world,
Shall ever medicine thee to that sweet sleep
Which thou owedst° yesterday,
OTHELLO.   Ha! Ha! False to me?
IAGO.   Why, how now, General! No more of that.   335
OTHELLO.   Avaunt! Be gone! Thou hast set me on the rack.
I swear 'tis better to be much abused
Than but to know 't a little.
IAGO.   How now, my lord!
OTHELLO.   What sense had I of her stol'n hours of lust?
I saw 't not, thought it not, it harmed not me.   340
I slept the next night well, was free and merry.
I found not Cassio's kisses on her lips.
He that is robbed, not wanting° what is stol'n,
Let him not know 't and he's not robbed at all.
IAGO.   I am sorry to hear this.   345
OTHELLO.   I had been happy if the general camp,
Pioners° and all, had tasted her sweet body,
So I had nothing known. Oh, now forever
Farewell the tranquil mind! Farewell content!
Farewell the plumèd troop and the big wars   350
That make ambition virtue! Oh farewell,
Farewell the neighing steed and the shrill trump,
The spirit-stirring drum, the ear-piercing fife,
The royal banner, and all quality,
Pride, pomp, and circumstance of glorious war!   355
And, O you mortal engines,° whose rude throats
The immortal Jove's dread clamors counterfeit,
Farewell! Othello's occupation's gone!
IAGO.   Is 't possible, my lord?
OTHELLO.   Villain, be sure thou prove my love a whore,   360
Be sure of it, give me the ocular proof.
Or by the worth of man's eternal soul,
Thou hadst been better have been born a dog
Than answer my waked wrath!
IAGO.   Is 't come to this?
OTHELLO.   Make me to see 't, or at the least so prove it   365
That the probation° bear no hinge nor loop
To hang a doubt on, or woe upon thy life!

---

331. poppy: opium   **mandragora:** called also mandrake—a root used as a drug
to bring sleep   **334. owedst:** owned   **343. wanting:** missing   **347. Pioners:**
pioneers, the lowest type of soldier   **356. mortal engines:** deadly cannon
366. probation: proof

IAGO.   My noble lord—
OTHELLO.   If thou dost slander her and torture me,
Never pray more, abandon all remorse.°   370
On horror's head horrors accumulate,
Do deeds to make Heaven weep, all earth amazed,
For nothing canst thou to damnation add
Greater than that.
IAGO.   Oh, grace! Oh, Heaven defend me!
Are you a man? Have you a soul or sense?   375
God be wi' you, take mine office. O wretched fool,
That livest to make thine honesty a vice!
O monstrous world! Take note, take note, O world,
To be direct and honest is not safe.
I thank you for this profit, and from hence   380
I'll love no friend, sith° love breeds such offense.
OTHELLO.   Nay, stay. Thou shouldst be honest.
IAGO.   I should be wise, for honesty's a fool,
And loses that it works for.
OTHELLO.   By the world,
I think my wife be honest, and think she is not.   385
I think that thou are just, and think thou art not.
I'll have some proof. Her name, that was as fresh
As Dian's° visage, is now begrimed and black
As mine own face. If there be cords, or knives,
Poison, or fire, or suffocating streams,   390
I'll not endure it. Would I were satisfied!
IAGO.   I see, sir, you are eaten up with passion.
I do repent me that I put it to you.
You would be satisfied?
OTHELLO.   Would! Nay, I will.
IAGO.   And may, but how? How satisfied, my lord?   395
Would you, the supervisor,° grossly gape on?
Behold her topped?
OTHELLO.   Death and damnation! Oh!
IAGO.   It were a tedious difficulty, I think,
To bring them to that prospect. Damn them then,
If ever mortal eyes do see them bolster°   400
More than their own! What then? How then?
What shall I say? Where's satisfaction?
It is impossible you should see this,
Were they as prime° as goats, as hot as monkeys,
As salt° as wolves in pride,° and fools as gross   405

---

370. **remorse:** pity   381. **sith:** since   388. **Dian:** Diana, goddess of chastity
396. **supervisor:** looker-on   400. **bolster:** sleep together   404. **prime:** lustful
405. **salt:** eager   **pride:** in heat

As ignorance made drunk. But yet I say
If imputation° and strong circumstances,
Which lead directly to the door of truth,
Will give you satisfaction, you may have 't.
OTHELLO.   Give me a living reason she's disloyal.   410
IAGO.   I do not like the office.
But sith I am entered in this cause so far,
Pricked to 't by foolish honesty and love,
I will go on. I lay with Cassio lately,
And being troubled with a raging tooth,   415
I could not sleep.
There are a kind of men so loose of soul
That in their sleeps will mutter their affairs.
One of this kind is Cassio.
In sleep I heard him say "Sweet Desdemona,   420
Let us be wary, let us hide our loves."
And then, sir, would he gripe° and wring my hand,
Cry "O sweet creature!" and then kiss me hard,
As if he plucked up kisses by the roots
That grew upon my lips. Then laid his leg   425
Over my thigh, and sighed and kissed, and then
Cried "Cursed fate that gave thee to the Moor!"
OTHELLO.   Oh, monstrous! Monstrous!
IAGO.   Nay, this was but his dream.
OTHELLO.   But this denoted a foregone conclusion.
'Tis a shrewd doubt,° though it be but a dream.   430
IAGO.   And this may help to thicken other proofs
That do demonstrate thinly.
OTHELLO.   I'll tear her all to pieces.
IAGO.   Nay, but be wise. Yet we see nothing done.
She may be honest yet. Tell me this:
Have you not sometimes seen a handkerchief   435
Spotted with strawberries in your wife's hand?
OTHELLO.   I gave her such a one, 'twas my first gift.
IAGO.   I know not that. But such a handkerchief—
I am sure it was your wife's—did I today
See Cassio wipe his beard with.
OTHELLO.   If it be that—   440
IAGO.   If it be that, or any that was hers,
It speaks against her with the other proofs.
OTHELLO.   Oh, that the slave had forty thousand lives!
One is too poor, too weak, for my revenge.
Now do I see 'tis true. Look here, Iago,   445

407. **imputation:** probability   422. **gripe:** grip   430. **shrewd doubt:** bitter
suspicion

All my fond love thus do I blow to Heaven—
'Tis gone.
Arise, black Vengeance, from thy hollow cell!
Yield up, O Love, thy crown and hearted throne
To tyrannous hate! Swell, bosom, with thy fraught,° 450
For 'tis of aspics'° tongues!

IAGO.   Yet be content.

OTHELLO.   Oh, blood, blood, blood!

IAGO.   Patience, I say. Your mind perhaps may change.

OTHELLO.   Never, Iago. Like to the Pontic Sea,
Whose icy current and compulsive course 455
Ne'er feels retiring ebb but keeps due on
To the Propontic and the Hellespont;
Even so my bloody thoughts, with violent pace,
Shall ne'er look back, ne'er ebb to humble love,
Till that a capable° and wide revenge 460
Swallow them up. Now, by yond marble Heaven,
In the due reverence of a sacred vow (*kneels*)
I here engage my words.

IAGO.   Do not rise yet. (*Kneels.*)
Witness, you ever burning lights above,
You elements that clip° us round about, 465
Witness that here Iago doth give up
The execution of his wit,° hands, heart,
To wronged Othello's service! Let him command,
And to obey shall be in me remorse,°
What bloody business ever. (*They rise.*)

OTHELLO.   I greet thy love, 470
Not with vain thanks, but with acceptance bounteous,
And will upon the instant put thee to 't.
Within these three days let me hear thee say
That Cassio's not alive.

IAGO.   My friend is dead. 'Tis done at your request. 475
But let her live.

OTHELLO.   Damn her, lewd minx! Oh, damn her!
Come, go with me apart. I will withdraw,
To furnish me with some swift means of death
For the fair devil. Now art thou my Lieutenant. 480

IAGO.   I am your own forever. (*Exeunt.*)

SCENE 4. Before the castle.

Enter DESDEMONA, EMILIA, *and* CLOWN.

---

450. fraught: freight   **451. aspics':** asps'   **460. capable:** comprehensive
465. clip: embrace   **467. wit:** mind [Eds.]   **469. remorse:** solemn obligation

DESDEMONA.   Do you know, sirrah, where Lieutenant Cassio lies?
CLOWN.   I dare not say he lies anywhere.
DESDEMONA.   Why, man?
CLOWN.   He's a soldier, and for one to say a soldier lies is stabbing.
DESDEMONA.   Go to. Where lodges he?   5
CLOWN.   To tell you where he lodges is to tell you where I lie.
DESDEMONA.   Can anything be made of this?
CLOWN.   I know not where he lodges, and for me to devise a lodging, and
    say he lies here or he lies there, were to lie in mine own throat.
DESDEMONA.   Can you inquire him out and be edified by report?°   10
CLOWN.   I will catechize the world for him; that is, make questions and by
    them answer.
DESDEMONA.   Seek him, bid him come hither. Tell him I have moved my
    lord on his behalf and hope all will be well.
CLOWN.   To do this is within the compass of man's wit, and therefore I will
    attempt the doing it. (*Exit.*)   16
DESDEMONA.   Where should I lose that handkerchief, Emilia?
EMILIA.   I know not, madam.
DESDEMONA.   Believe me, I had rather have lost my purse
    Full of crusados. And, but my noble Moor   20
    Is true of mind and made of no such baseness
    As jealous creatures are, it were enough
    To put him to ill thinking.
EMILIA.   Is he not jealous?
DESDEMONA.   Who, he? I think the sun where he was born
    Drew all such humors from him.
EMILIA.   Look where he comes.   25
DESDEMONA.   I will not leave him now till Cassio
    Be called to him. (*Enter* OTHELLO.)
                                    How is 't with you, my lord?
OTHELLO.   Well, my good lady. (*Aside*) Oh, hardness to dissemble!
    How do you, Desdemona?
DESDEMONA.   Well, my good lord.
OTHELLO.   Give me your hand. This hand is moist,° my lady.   30
DESDEMONA.   It yet has felt no age nor known no sorrow.
OTHELLO.   This argues fruitfulness and liberal heart.
    Hot, hot, and moist—this hand of yours requires
    A sequester from liberty, fasting and prayer,
    Much castigation, exercise devout.   35
    For here's a young and sweating devil here,
    That commonly rebels. 'Tis a good hand,
    A frank one.

---

10. **edified by report:** enlightened by the information. Desdemona speaks with mock
pomposity.   30. **moist:** A hot moist palm was believed to show desire.

DESDEMONA.   You may indeed say so,
  For 'twas that hand that gave away my heart.
OTHELLO.   A liberal° hand. The hearts of old gave hands,   40
  But our new heraldry is hands, not hearts.°
DESDEMONA.   I cannot speak of this. Come now, your promise.
OTHELLO.   What promise, chuck?°
DESDEMONA.   I have sent to bid Cassio come speak with you.
OTHELLO.   I have a salt and sorry rheum offends me.   45
  Lend me thy handkerchief.
DESDEMONA.   Here, my lord.
OTHELLO.   That which I gave you.
DESDEMONA.   I have it not about me.
OTHELLO.   Not?
DESDEMONA.   No indeed, my lord.
OTHELLO.   That's a fault. That handkerchief
  Did an Egyptian to my mother give.   50
  She was a charmer, and could almost read
  The thoughts of people. She told her while she kept it
  'Twould make her amiable and subdue my father
  Entirely to her love, but if she lost it
  Or made a gift of it, my father's eye   55
  Should hold her loathèd and his spirits should hunt
  After new fancies. She dying gave it me,
  And bid me, when my fate would have me wive,
  To give it her. I did so. And take heed on 't,
  Make it a darling like your precious eye.   60
  To lose 't or give 't away were such perdition
  As nothing else could match.
DESDEMONA.   Is 't possible?
OTHELLO.   'Tis true. There's magic in the web of it.
  A sibyl that had numbered in the world
  The sun to course two hundred compasses   65
  In her prophetic fury sewed the work.
  The worms were hallowed that did breed the silk,
  And it was dyed in mummy which the skillful
  Conserved° of maiden's hearts.
DESDEMONA.   Indeed! Is 't true?
OTHELLO.   Most veritable, therefore look to 't well.   70
DESDEMONA.   Then would God that I had never seen 't.
OTHELLO.   Ha! Wherefore?

---

40. liberal: overgenerous   **40–41. The . . . hearts:** Once love and deeds went together, but now it is all deeds (i.e., faithlessness) and no love.   **43. chuck:** A term
of affection, but not the kind of word with which a person of Othello's dignity would
normally address his wife. He is beginning to treat her with contemptuous familiarity.
69. Conserved: prepared

DESDEMONA.   Why do you speak so startingly and rash?
OTHELLO.   Is 't lost? Is 't gone? Speak, is it out o' the way?
DESDEMONA.   Heaven bless us!   75
OTHELLO.   Say you?
DESDEMONA.   It is not lost, but what an if it were?
OTHELLO.   How!
DESDEMONA.   I say it is not lost.
OTHELLO.   Fetch 't, let me see it.
DESDEMONA.   Why, so I can, sir, but I will not now.   80
    This is a trick to put me from my suit.
    Pray you let Cassio be received again.
OTHELLO.   Fetch me the handkerchief. My mind misgives.
DESDEMONA.   Come, come,
    You'll never meet a more sufficient man.   85
OTHELLO.   The handkerchief!
DESDEMONA.   I pray talk me of Cassio.
OTHELLO.   The handkerchief!
DESDEMONA.   A man that all this time
    Hath founded his good fortunes on your love,
    Shared dangers with you—
OTHELLO.   The handkerchief!   90
DESDEMONA.   In sooth, you are to blame.
OTHELLO.   Away! (*Exit.*)
EMILIA.   Is not this man jealous?
DESDEMONA.   I ne'er saw this before.
    Sure there's some wonder in this handkerchief.   95
    I am most unhappy in the loss of it.
EMILIA.   'Tis not a year or two shows us a man.°
    They are all but stomachs and we all but food.
    They eat us hungerly, and when they are full
    They belch us. Look you, Cassio and my husband.   100
    (*Enter* CASSIO *and* IAGO.)
IAGO.   There is no other way, 'tis she must do 't.
    And, lo, the happiness!° Go and impórtune her.
DESDEMONA.   How now, good Cassio! What's the news with you?
CASSIO.   Madam, my former suit. I do beseech you
    That by your virtuous means I may again   105
    Exist, and be a member of his love
    Whom I with all the office of my heart
    Entirely honor. I would not be delayed.
    If my offense be of such mortal kind
    That nor my service past nor present sorrows   110

97. 'Tis . . . man: It does not take a couple of years to discover the nature of a man;
i.e., he soon shows his real nature.   **102. And . . . happiness:** what good luck, here
she is

Nor purposed merit in futurity
Can ransom me into his love again,
But to know so must be my benefit.
So shall I clothe me in a forced content
And shut myself up in some other course   115
To Fortune's alms.
DESDEMONA.   Alas, thrice-gentle Cassio!
My advocation° is not now in tune.
My lord is not my lord, nor should I know him
Were he in favor° as in humor altered.
So help me every spirit sanctified,   120
As I have spoken for you all my best
And stood within the blank° of his displeasure
For my free speech! You must awhile be patient.
What I can do I will, and more I will
Than for myself I dare. Let that suffice you.   125
IAGO.   Is my lord angry?
EMILIA.   He went hence but now,
And certainly in strange unquietness.
IAGO.   Can he be angry? I have seen the cannon
When it hath blown his ranks into the air,
And, like the Devil, from his very arm   130
Puffed his own brother, and can he be angry?
Something of moment then. I will go meet him.
There's matter in 't indeed if he be angry.
DESDEMONA.   I prithee do so. (*Exit* IAGO.)
                        Something sure of state,
Either from Venice, or some unhatched practice   135
Made demonstrable° here in Cyprus to him,
Hath puddled his clear spirit. And in such cases
Men's natures wrangle with inferior things,
Though great ones are their object. 'Tis even so,
For let our finger ache and it indues   140
Our other healthful members even to that sense
Of pain. Nay, we must think men are not gods,
Nor of them look for such observancy
As fits the bridal.° Beshrew me much, Emilia,
I was, unhandsome warrior° as I am,   145
Arraigning his unkindness with my soul,

---

117. **advocation:** advocacy   119. **favor:** face [Eds.]   122. **blank:** aim
135–36. unhatched . . . demonstrable: some plot, not yet matured, which has been
revealed   144. **bridal:** honeymoon   145. **unhandsome warrior:** clumsy
soldier. Desdemona continually thinks of herself as Othello's companion in arms.
Cf. 1.3.248 ff.

But now I find I had suborned the witness,°
And he's indicted falsely.
EMILIA.   Pray Heaven it be state matters, as you think,
And no conception nor no jealous toy°   150
Concerning you.
DESDEMONA.   Alas the day, I never gave him cause!
EMILIA.   But jealous souls will not be answered so.
They are not ever jealous for the cause,
But jealous for they are jealous. 'Tis a monster   155
Begot upon itself, born on itself.
DESDEMONA.   Heaven keep that monster from Othello's mind!
EMILIA.   Lady, amen.
DESDEMONA.   I will go seek him. Cassio, walk hereabout.
If I do find him fit, I'll move your suit,   160
And seek to effect it to my uttermost.
CASSIO.   I humbly thank your ladyship.
(*Exeunt* DESDEMONA *and* EMILIA. *Enter* BIANCA.)
BIANCA.   Save you, friend Cassio!
CASSIO.   What make you from home?
How is it with you, my most fair Bianca?   165
I' faith, sweet love, I was coming to your house.
BIANCA.   And I was going to your lodging, Cassio.
What, keep a week away? Seven days and nights?
Eightscore eight hours? And lovers' absent hours,
More tedious than the dial eightscore times?
Oh, weary reckoning!
CASSIO.   Pardon me, Bianca.   170
I have this while with leaden thoughts been pressed,
But I shall in a more continuate time
Strike off this score of absence. Sweet Bianca,
(*Giving her* DESDEMONA's *handkerchief*)
Take me this work out.
BIANCA.   O Cassio, whence came this?
This is some token from a newer friend.   175
To the felt absence now I feel a cause.
Is 't come to this? Well, well.
CASSIO.   Go to, woman!
Throw your vile guesses in the Devil's teeth,
From whence you have them. You are jealous now
That this is from some mistress, some remembrance.   180
No, by my faith, Bianca.
BIANCA.   Why, whose is it?

---

147. suborned the witness: corrupted the evidence; i.e., misunderstood his behavior
[Eds.]   **150. jealous toy:** silly suspicion

CASSIO. I know not, sweet. I found it in my chamber.
I like the work well. Ere it be demanded—
As like enough it will—I'd have it copied.
Take it, and do 't, and leave me for this time.   185
BIANCA. Leave you! Wherefore?
CASSIO. I do attend here on the General,
And think it no addition,° nor my wish
To have him see me womaned.°
BIANCA.   Why, I pray you?
CASSIO. Not that I love you not.
BIANCA.   But that you do not love me.   190
I pray you bring me on the way a little,
And say if I shall see you soon at night.
CASSIO. 'Tis but a little way that I can bring you,
For I attend here. But I'll see you soon.
BIANCA. 'Tis very good, I must be circumstanced.° (*Exeunt.*)   195

ACT 4

SCENE 1. Cyprus. Before the castle.

Enter OTHELLO *and* IAGO.

IAGO. Will you think so?
OTHELLO.   Think so, Iago!
IAGO.   What,
To kiss in private?
OTHELLO.   An unauthorized kiss.
IAGO. Or to be naked with her friend in bed
An hour or more, not meaning any harm?
OTHELLO. Naked in bed, Iago, and not mean harm!   5
It is hypocrisy against the Devil.
They that mean virtuously and yet do so,
The Devil their virtue tempts and they tempt Heaven.
IAGO. So they do nothing, 'tis a venial° slip.
But if I give my wife a handkerchief—   10
OTHELLO. What then?
IAGO. Why, then, 'tis hers, my lord, and being hers,
She may, I think, bestow 't on any man.
OTHELLO. She is protectress of her honor too.
May she give that?   15
IAGO. Her honor is an essence that's not seen.
They have it very oft that have it not.
But for the handkerchief—

---

188. addition: honor   **189. womaned:** with a woman   **195. circumstanced:**
put off   **9. venial:** pardonable

OTHELLO.   By Heaven, I would most gladly have forgot it.
Thou said'st—oh, it comes o'er my memory,   20
As doth the raven o'er the infected house
Boding to all°—he had my handkerchief.
IAGO.   Aye, what of that?
OTHELLO.   That's not so good now.
IAGO.   What
If I had said I had seen him do you wrong?
Or heard him say—as knaves be such abroad,   25
Who having, by their own importunate suit,
Or voluntary dotage of some mistress,
Convincèd or supplied° them, cannot choose
But they must blab—
OTHELLO.   Hath he said anything?
IAGO.   He hath, my lord, but be you well assured,   30
No more than he'll unswear.
OTHELLO.   What hath he said?
IAGO.   Faith, that he did—I know not what he did.
OTHELLO.   What? What?
IAGO.   Lie—
OTHELLO.   With her?
IAGO.   With her, on her, what you will.   34
OTHELLO.   Lie° with her! Lie on her!—We say lie on her when they belie
her.—Lie with her. 'Zounds, that's fulsome!° Handkerchief—confes-
sions—handkerchief!—To confess, and be hanged for his labor. First to
be hanged, and then to confess. I tremble at it. Nature would not invest
herself in such shadowing passion without some instruction.° It is not
words that shake me thus. Pish! Noses, ears, and lips. Is 't possible?—
Confess?—Handkerchief?—Oh, devil! (*Falls in a trance.*)   41
IAGO.   Work on,
My medicine, work! Thus credulous fools are caught,
And many worthy and chaste dames even thus,
All guiltless, meet reproach. What ho! My lord!   45
My lord, I say! Othello! (*Enter* CASSIO.)
                     How now, Cassio!
CASSIO.   What's the matter?
IAGO.   My lord is fall'n into an epilepsy.
This is his second fit, he had one yesterday.
CASSIO.   Rub him about the temples.

21–22. As doth the raven . . . all: as an evil omen (such as a raven overhead) brings
evil tidings to all who live in a plague-infested house [Eds.]   **28. Convincèd or
supplied:** overcome or satisfied their desires   **35–41. Lie . . . devil:** Othello breaks
into incoherent muttering before he falls down in a fit.   **36. fulsome:** disgusting
38–39. Nature . . . instruction: Nature would not fill me with such overwhelming
emotion unless there was some cause.

IAGO.   No, forbear,   50
The lethargy° must have his quiet course.
If not, he foams at mouth and by and by
Breaks out to savage madness. Look, he stirs.
Do you withdraw yourself a little while,
He will recover straight. When he is gone,   55
I would on great occasion speak with you. (*Exit* CASSIO.)
How is it, General? Have you not hurt your head?°
OTHELLO.   Dost thou mock me?
IAGO.   I mock you! No, by Heaven.
Would you would bear your fortune like a man!
OTHELLO.   A hornèd man's a monster and a beast.   60
IAGO.   There's many a beast, then, in a populous city,
And many a civil monster.
OTHELLO.   Did he confess it?
IAGO.   Good sir, be a man.
Think every bearded fellow that's but yoked°
May draw with you.° There's millions now alive   65
That nightly lie in those unproper beds
Which they dare swear peculiar.° Your case is better.
Oh, 'tis the spite of Hell, the Fiend's arch-mock,
To lip° a wanton in a secure couch°
And to suppose her chaste! No, let me know,   70
And knowing what I am, I know what she shall be.
OTHELLO.   Oh, thou art wise, 'tis certain.
IAGO.   Stand you awhile apart,
Confine yourself but in a patient list.°
Whilst you were here o'erwhelmèd with your grief—
A passion most unsuiting such a man—   75
Cassio came hither. I shifted him away,
And laid good 'scuse upon your ecstasy,°
Bade him anon return and here speak with me,
The which he promised. Do but encave yourself,
And mark the fleers, the gibes, and notable scorns,   80
That dwell in every region of his face.
For I will make him tell the tale anew,
Where, how, how oft, how long ago, and when
He hath and is again to cope° your wife.

---

51. lethargy: epileptic fit   **57. Have . . . head:** With brutal cynicism Iago asks
whether Othello is suffering from cuckold's headache.   **64. yoked:** married
65. draw with you: be your yoke fellow   **66–67. That . . . peculiar:** that lie
nightly in beds which they believe are their own but which others have shared
69. lip: kiss   **secure couch:** lit., a carefree bed; i.e., a bed which has been used
by the wife's lover, but secretly   **73. patient list:** confines of patience
77. ecstasy: fit   **84. cope:** encounter

I say but mark his gesture. Marry, patience,   85
Or I shall say you are all in all in spleen,
And nothing of a man.
OTHELLO.   Dost thou hear, Iago?
I will be found most cunning in my patience,
But—dost thou hear?—most bloody.
IAGO.   That's not amiss.
But yet keep time in all. Will you withdraw? (OTHELLO *retires.*)   90
Now will I question Cassio of Bianca,
A housewife° that by selling her desires
Buys herself bread and clothes. It is a creature
That dotes on Cassio, as 'tis the strumpet's plague
To beguile many and be beguiled by one.   95
He, when he hears of her, cannot refrain
From the excess of laughter. Here he comes. (*Re-enter* CASSIO.)
As he shall smile, Othello shall go mad,
And his unbookish° jealousy must construe
Poor Cassio's smiles, gestures, and light behavior   100
Quite in the wrong. How do you now, Lieutenant?
CASSIO.   The worser that you give me the addition°
Whose want even kills me.
IAGO.   Ply Desdemona well, and you are sure on 't.
Now, if this suit lay in Bianca's power,   105
How quickly should you speed!
CASSIO.   Alas, poor caitiff!°
OTHELLO.   Look how he laughs already!
IAGO.   I never knew a woman love man so.
CASSIO.   Alas, poor rogue! I think i' faith, she loves me.
OTHELLO.   Now he denies it faintly and laughs it out.   110
IAGO.   Do you hear, Cassio?
OTHELLO.   Now he impórtunes him
To tell it o'er. Go to. Well said, well said.
IAGO.   She gives it out that you shall marry her.
Do you intend to?
CASSIO.   Ha, ha, ha!   115
OTHELLO.   Do you triumph, Roman?° Do you triumph?
CASSIO.   I marry her! What, a customer!° I prithee bear some charity to my
wit. Do not think it so unwholesome. Ha, ha, ha!
OTHELLO.   So, so, so, so. They laugh that win.
IAGO.   Faith, the cry goes that you shall marry her.   120

---

92. housewife: hussy   **99. unbookish:** unlearned   **102. addition:** title (Lieutenant) which he has lost   **106. caitiff:** wretch   **116. triumph, Roman:** The
word "triumph" suggests "Roman" because the Romans celebrated their victories with
triumphs, elaborate shows, and processions.   **117. customer:** harlot

CASSIO. Prithee say true.

IAGO. I am a very villain else.

OTHELLO. Have you scored° me? Well.

CASSIO. This is the monkey's own giving out. She is persuaded I will marry
her out of her own love and flattery, not out of my promise.   125

OTHELLO. Iago beckons me, now he begins the story.

CASSIO. She was here even now. She haunts me in every place. I was the
other day talking on the sea bank with certain Venetians, and thither
comes the bauble, and, by this hand, she falls me thus about my
neck—   130

OTHELLO. Crying "O dear Cassio!" as it were. His gesture imports it.

CASSIO. So hangs and lolls and weeps upon me, so hales and pulls me. Ha,
ha, ha!

OTHELLO. Now he tells how she plucked him to my chamber. Oh, I see
that nose of yours, but not that dog I shall throw it to.   135

CASSIO. Well, I must leave her company.

IAGO. Before me!° Look where she comes.

CASSIO. 'Tis such another fitchew!° Marry, a perfumed one.

(*Enter* BIANCA.)

What do you mean by this haunting of me?

BIANCA. Let the Devil and his dam haunt you! What did you mean by that
same handkerchief you gave me even now? I was a fine fool to take it. I
must take out the work? A likely piece of work, that you should find it in
your chamber and not know who left it there! This is some minx's token,
and I must take out the work? There, give it your hobbyhorse. Where-
soever you had it, I'll take out no work on 't.   145

CASSIO. How now, my sweet Bianca! How now! How now!

OTHELLO. By Heaven, that should be my handkerchief!

BIANCA. An° you'll come to supper tonight, you may. An you will not,
come when you are next prepared for. (*Exit.*)

IAGO. After her, after her.   150

CASSIO. Faith, I must, she'll rail i' the street else.

IAGO. Will you sup there?

CASSIO. Faith, I intend so.

IAGO. Well, I may chance to see you, for I would very fain speak with
you.   155

CASSIO. Prithee, come, will you?

IAGO. Go to. Say no more. (*Exit* CASSIO.)

OTHELLO (*advancing*). How shall I murder him, Iago?

IAGO. Did you perceive how he laughed at his vice?

OTHELLO. Oh, Iago!   160

IAGO. And did you see the handkerchief?

---

123. scored: marked, as with a blow from a whip   **137. Before me:** by my soul
138. fitchew: polecat   **148. An:** if

OTHELLO. Was that mine?

IAGO. Yours, by this hand. And to see how he prizes the foolish woman
your wife? She gave it him, and he hath given it his whore.

OTHELLO. I would have him nine years a-killing. A fine woman! A fair
woman! A sweet woman!   166

IAGO. Nay, you must forget that.

OTHELLO. Aye, let her rot, and perish, and be damned tonight, for she
shall not live. No, my heart is turned to stone, I strike it and it hurts
my hand. Oh, the world hath not a sweeter creature. She might lie by an
emperor's side, and command him tasks.   171

IAGO. Nay, that's not your way.°

OTHELLO. Hang her! I do but say what she is, so delicate with her needle,
an admirable musician—oh, she will sing the savageness out of a bear—
of so high and plenteous wit and invention—   175

IAGO. She's the worse for all this.

OTHELLO. Oh, a thousand times. And then, of so gentle a condition!

IAGO. Aye, too gentle.

OTHELLO. Nay, that's certain. But yet the pity of it, Iago! O Iago, the pity
of it, Iago!   180

IAGO. If you are so fond over her iniquity, give her patent to offend, for if it
touch not you, it comes near nobody.

OTHELLO. I will chop her into messes.° Cuckold me!

IAGO. Oh, 'tis foul in her.

OTHELLO. With mine officer!   185

IAGO. That's fouler.

OTHELLO. Get me some poison, Iago, this night. I'll not expostulate with
her, lest her body and beauty unprovide my mind again. This night,
Iago.

IAGO. Do it not with poison, strangle her in her bed, even the bed she hath
contaminated.   191

OTHELLO. Good, good. The justice of it pleases. Very good.

IAGO. And for Cassio, let me be his undertaker.°
You shall hear more by midnight.

OTHELLO. Excellent good. (*A trumpet within.*) What trumpet is that same?

IAGO. Something from Venice, sure. 'Tis Lodovico   196
Come from the Duke. And see, your wife is with him.
(*Enter* LODOVICO, DESDEMONA, *and* ATTENDANTS.)

LODOVICO. God save the worthy General!

OTHELLO. With all my heart, sir.

LODOVICO. The Duke and Senators of Venice greet you. (*Gives him a letter.*)

OTHELLO. I kiss the instrument of their pleasures.   201

---

172. Nay . . . way: i.e., don't get soft thoughts about her   183. messes: mince-
meat [Eds.]   193. be his undertaker: undertake to manage his business. In
Shakespeare's plays the word does *not* mean "mortician."

(Opens the letter, and reads.)

DESDEMONA.   And what's the news, good Cousin Lodovico?

IAGO.   I am very glad to see you, signior.
   Welcome to Cyprus.

LODOVICO.   I thank you. How does Lieutenant Cassio?   205

IAGO.   Lives, sir.

DESDEMONA.   Cousin, there's fall'n between him and my lord
   An unkind breach, but you shall make all well.

OTHELLO.   Are you sure of that?

DESDEMONA.   My lord?   210

OTHELLO *(reads)*.   "This fail you not to do, as you will—"

LODOVICO.   He did not call, he's busy in the paper.
   Is there division 'twixt my lord and Cassio?

DESDEMONA.   A most unhappy one. I would do much
   To atone° them, for the love I bear to Cassio.   215

OTHELLO.   Fire and brimstone!

DESDEMONA.   My lord?

OTHELLO.   Are you wise?°

DESDEMONA.   What, is he angry?

LODOVICO.   Maybe the letter moved him,
   For, as I think, they do command him home,
   Deputing Cassio in his government.

DESDEMONA.   By my troth, I am glad on 't.

OTHELLO.   Indeed!

DESDEMONA.   My lord?   220

OTHELLO.   I am glad to see you mad.

DESDEMONA.   Why, sweet Othello?

OTHELLO.   Devil! *(Striking her.)*

DESDEMONA.   I have not deserved this.

LODOVICO.   My lord, this would not be believed in Venice
   Though I should swear I saw 't. 'Tis very much.   225
   Make her amends, she weeps.

OTHELLO.   O devil, devil!
   If that the earth could teem with a woman's tears,
   Each drop she falls would prove a crocodile.°
   Out of my sight!

DESDEMONA.   I will not stay to offend you. *(Going.)*

LODOVICO.   Truly, an obedient lady.   230
   I do beseech your lordship, call her back.

OTHELLO.   Mistress!

DESDEMONA.   My lord?

---

215. atone: reconcile   **216. Are you wise:** i.e., in saying you bear love to Cassio
227–28. If . . . crocodile: If the earth could breed from woman's tears, each tear that
she lets fall would become a crocodile. It was believed that the crocodile would cry
and sob to attract the sympathetic passer-by, who was then snapped up.

OTHELLO.   What would you with her, sir?
LODOVICO.   Who, I, my lord?
OTHELLO.   Aye, you did wish that I would make her turn.   235
   Sir, she can turn and turn, and yet go on
   And turn again. And she can weep, sir, weep.
   And she's obedient, as you say, obedient,
   Very obedient.—Proceed you in your tears—
   Concerning this, sir—oh, well-painted passion!°—   240
   I am commanded home.—Get you away.
   I'll send for you anon.—Sir, I obey the mandate,
   And will return to Venice.—Hence, avaunt! (*Exit* DESDEMONA.)
   Cassio shall have my place. And, sir, tonight,
   I do entreat that we may sup together.   245
   You are welcome, sir, to Cyprus.—Goats and monkeys! (*Exit.*)
LODOVICO.   Is this the noble Moor whom our full Senate
   Call all-in-all sufficient? This the nature
   Whom passion could not shake? Whose solid virtue
   The shot of accident nor dart of chance   250
   Could neither graze nor pierce?
IAGO.   He is much changed.
LODOVICO.   Are his wits safe? Is he not light of brain?
IAGO.   He's that he is. I may not breathe my censure°
   What he might be. If what he might he is not,
   I would to Heaven he were!
LODOVICO.   What, strike his wife!   255
IAGO.   Faith, that was not so well, yet would I knew
   That stroke would prove the worst!
LODOVICO.   Is it his use?
   Or did the letters work upon his blood,
   And new-create this fault?
IAGO.   Alas, alas!
   It is not honesty in me to speak   260
   What I have seen and known. You shall observe him,
   And his own courses will denote him so
   That I may save my speech. Do but go after,
   And mark how he continues.
LODOVICO.   I am sorry that I am deceived in him. (*Exeunt.*)   265

SCENE 2. A room in the castle.

   Enter OTHELLO *and* EMILIA.

OTHELLO.   You have seen nothing, then?
EMILIA.   Nor ever heard, nor ever did suspect.
OTHELLO.   Yes, you have seen Cassio and she together.

---

240. passion: emotion [Eds.]   **253. censure:** opinion [Eds.]

EMILIA.   But then I saw no harm, and then I heard
    Each syllable that breath made up between them.   5
OTHELLO.   What, did they never whisper?
EMILIA.   Never, my lord.
OTHELLO.   Nor send you out o' the way?
EMILIA.   Never.
OTHELLO.   To fetch her fan, her gloves, her mask, nor nothing?
EMILIA.   Never, my lord.   10
OTHELLO.   That's strange.
EMILIA.   I durst, my lord, to wager she is honest,
    Lay down my soul at stake. If you think other,
    Remove your thought, it doth abuse your bosom.
    If any wretch have put this in your head,   15
    Let Heaven requite it with the serpent's curse!
    For if she be not honest, chaste, and true,
    There's no man happy, the purest of their wives
    Is foul as slander.
OTHELLO.   Bid her come hither. Go. (*Exit* EMILIA.)
    She says enough. Yet she's a simple bawd   20
    That cannot say as much. This is a subtle whore,
    A closet lock and key of villainous secrets.
    And yet she'll kneel and pray, I have seen her do 't.
    (*Enter* DESDEMONA *with* EMILIA.)
DESDEMONA.   My lord, what is your will?
OTHELLO.   Pray, chuck, come hither.
DESDEMONA.   What is your pleasure?
OTHELLO.   Let me see your eyes.   25
    Look in my face.
DESDEMONA.   What horrible fancy's this?
OTHELLO (*to* EMILIA).   Some of your function,° mistress.
    Leave procreants alone and shut the door,
    Cough, or cry hem, if anybody come.
    Your mystery,° your mystery. Nay, dispatch. (*Exit* EMILIA.)   30
DESDEMONA.   Upon my knees, what doth your speech import?
    I understand a fury in your words,
    But not the words.
OTHELLO.   Why, what art thou?
DESDEMONA.   Your wife, my lord, your true and loyal wife.
OTHELLO.   Come, swear it, damn thyself,   35
    Lest, being like one of Heaven,° the devils themselves
    Should fear to seize thee. Therefore be double-damned.
    Swear thou art honest.

---

27. Some . . . function: Get about your business, i.e., prostitution. Othello pretends
that Emilia is keeper of a brothel and Desdemona one of the women.   **30. mystery:**
profession   **36. being . . . Heaven:** because you look like an angel

DESDEMONA.   Heaven doth truly know it.
OTHELLO.   Heaven truly knows that thou art false as Hell.
DESDEMONA.   To whom, my lord? With whom? How am I false?   40
OTHELLO.   O Desdemona! Away! Away! Away!
DESDEMONA.   Alas the heavy day! Why do you weep!
   Am I the motive of these tears, my lord?
   If haply you my father do suspect
   An instrument of this your calling-back,   45
   Lay not your blame on me. If you have lost him,
   Why, I have lost him too.
OTHELLO.   Had it pleased Heaven
   To try me with affliction, had they rained
   All kinds of sores and shames on my bare head,
   Steeped me in poverty to the very lips,   50
   Given to captivity me and my utmost hopes,
   I should have found in some place of my soul
   A drop of patience. But, alas, to make me
   A fixèd figure for the time of scorn
   To point his slow unmoving finger at!   55
   Yet could I bear that too, well, very well.
   But there where I have garnered up my heart,
   Where either I must live or bear no life,
   The fountain from the which my current runs
   Or else dries up—to be discarded thence!   60
   Or keep it as a cistern for foul toads
   To knot and gender in! Turn thy complexion there,
   Patience, thou young and rose-lipped cherubin—
   Aye, there, look grim as Hell!
DESDEMONA.   I hope my noble lord esteems me honest.   65
OTHELLO.   Oh, aye, as summer flies are in the shambles,°
   That quicken even with blowing.° O thou weed,
   Who art so lovely fair and smell'st so sweet
   That the sense aches at thee, would thou hadst ne'er been born!
DESDEMONA.   Alas, what ignorant sin have I committed?   70
OTHELLO.   Was this fair paper,° this most goodly book,
   Made to write "whore" upon? What committed!
   Committed! O thou public commoner!°
   I should make very forges of my cheeks
   That would to cinders burn up modesty   75
   Did I but speak thy deeds. What committed!
   Heaven stops the nose at it, and the moon winks.
   The bawdy wind, that kisses all it meets,

---

66. shambles: slaughterhouse   **67. quicken . . . blowing:** come to life as soon as
the eggs are laid   **71. fair paper:** i.e., her white body   **73. public commoner:**
one who offers herself to all comers

Is hushed within the hollow mine of earth
And will not hear it. What committed!   80
Impudent strumpet!
DESDEMONA.   By Heaven, you do me wrong.
OTHELLO.   Are not you a strumpet?
DESDEMONA.   No, as I am a Christian.
If to preserve this vessel for my lord
From any other foul unlawful touch
Be not to be a strumpet, I am none.   85
OTHELLO.   What, not a whore?
DESDEMONA.   No, as I shall be saved.
OTHELLO.   Is 't possible?
DESDEMONA.   Oh, Heaven forgive us!
OTHELLO.   I cry you mercy, then.
I took you for that cunning whore of Venice
That married with Othello. (*Raising his voice*) You mistress,   90
That have the office opposite to Saint Peter,
And keep the gate of Hell! (*Re-enter* EMILIA.)
                        You, you, aye, you!
We have done our course, there's money for your pains.
I pray you turn the key, and keep our counsel. (*Exit.*)
EMILIA.   Alas, what does this gentleman conceive?   95
How do you, madam? How do you, my good lady?
DESDEMONA.   Faith, half-asleep.
EMILIA.   Good madam, what's the matter with my lord?
DESDEMONA.   With who?
EMILIA.   Why, with my lord, madam.   100
DESDEMONA.   Who is thy lord?
EMILIA.   He that is yours, sweet lady.
DESDEMONA.   I have none. Do not talk to me, Emilia.
I cannot weep, nor answer have I none
But what should go by water.° Prithee tonight
Lay on my bed my wedding sheets. Remember,   105
And call thy husband hither.
EMILIA.   Here's a change indeed! (*Exit.*)
DESDEMONA.   'Tis meet I should be used so, very meet.
How have I been behaved that he might stick
The small'st opinion on my least misuse?°
(*Re-enter* EMILIA *with* IAGO.)
IAGO.   What is your pleasure, madam? How is 't with you?   110
DESDEMONA.   I cannot tell. Those that do teach young babes
Do it with gentle means and easy tasks.
He might have chid me so, for, in good faith,
I am a child to chiding.

---

104. go by water: be expressed in tears   **109. misuse:** mistake

IAGO.   What's the matter, lady?
EMILIA.   Alas, Iago, my lord hath so bewhored her,   115
  Thrown such despite and heavy terms upon her,
  As true hearts cannot bear.
DESDEMONA.   Am I that name, Iago?
IAGO.   What name, fair lady?
DESDEMONA.   Such as she says my lord did say I was.
EMILIA.   He called her whore. A beggar in his drink   120
  Could not have laid such terms upon his callet.°
IAGO.   Why did he so?
DESDEMONA.   I do not know. I am sure I am none such.
IAGO.   Do not weep, do not weep. Alas the day!
EMILIA.   Hath she forsook so many noble matches,   125
  Her father and her country and her friends,
  To be called whore? Would it not make one weep?
DESDEMONA.   It is my wretched fortune.
IAGO.   Beshrew him for 't!
  How comes this trick upon him?
DESDEMONA.   Nay, Heaven doth know.
EMILIA.   I will be hanged if some eternal villain,   130
  Some busy and insinuating rogue,
  Some cogging, cozening slave, to get some office,
  Have not devised this slander. I'll be hanged else.
IAGO.   Fie, there is no such man, it is impossible.
DESDEMONA.   If any such there be, heaven pardon him!   135
EMILIA.   A halter pardon him! And Hell gnaw his bones!
  Why should he call her whore? Who keeps her company?
  What place? What time? What form? What likelihood?
  The Moor's abused by some most villainous knave,
  Some base notorious knave, some scurvy fellow.   140
  O Heaven, that such companions° Thou'dst unfold,°
  And put in every honest hand a whip
  To lash the rascals naked through the world
  Even from the east to the west!
IAGO.   Speak withindoor.°
EMILIA.   Oh, fie upon them! Some such squire he was   145
  That turned your wit the seamy side without,
  And made you to suspect me with the Moor.
IAGO.   You are a fool. Go to.°
DESDEMONA.   O good Iago,
  What shall I do to win my lord again?
  Good friend, go to him, for, by this light of Heaven,   150

---

121. **callet:** slut [Eds.]   141. **companions:** low creatures   **unfold:** bring to light
144. **Speak withindoor:** Don't shout so loud that all the street will hear you.   148.
Go to: an expression of derision

I know not how I lost him. Here I kneel.
If e'er my will did trespass 'gainst his love
Either in discourse of thought or actual deed,
Or that mine eyes, mine ears, or any sense
Delighted them in any other form,   155
Or that I do not yet,° and ever did,
And ever will, though he do shake me off
To beggarly divorcement, love him dearly,
Comfort forswear me! Unkindness may do much,
And his unkindness may defeat my life,   160
But never taint my love. I cannot say "whore,"
It doth abhor me now I speak the word.
To do the act that might the addition° earn
Not the world's mass of vanity° could make me.
IAGO.   I pray you be content, 'tis but his humor.   165
The business of the state does him offense,
And he does chide with you.
DESDEMONA.   If 'twere no other—
IAGO.   'Tis but so, I warrant. (*Trumpets within.*)
Hark how these instruments summon to supper!
The messengers of Venice stay the meat.°   170
Go in, and weep not, all things shall be well.
(*Exeunt* DESDEMONA *and* EMILIA. *Enter* RODERIGO.)
How now, Roderigo!
RODERIGO.   I do not find that thou dealest justly with me.
IAGO.   What in the contrary?
RODERIGO.   Every day thou daffest me with some device, Iago, and rather,
as it seems to me now, keepest from me all conveniency than suppliest
me with the least advantage of hope. I will indeed no longer endure it,
nor am I yet persuaded to put up in peace what already I have foolishly
suffered.   179
IAGO.   Will you hear me, Roderigo?
RODERIGO.   Faith, I have heard too much, for your words and performances are no kin together.
IAGO.   You charge me most unjustly.
RODERIGO.   With naught but truth. I have wasted myself out of my means.
The jewels you have had from me to deliver to Desdemona would half
have corrupted a votarist.° You have told me she hath received them, and
returned me expectations and comforts of sudden respect and acquain-
tance, but I find none.   188
IAGO.   Well, go to, very well.

---

156. yet: still [Eds.]   **163. addition:** title   **164. vanity:** i.e., riches
170. meat: serving of supper   **186. votarist:** nun

RODERIGO.   Very well! Go to! I cannot go to, man, nor 'tis not very well. By this hand, I say 'tis very scurvy, and begin to find myself fopped in it.

IAGO.   Very well.   192

RODERIGO.   I tell you 'tis not very well. I will make myself known to Desdemona. If she will return me my jewels, I will give over my suit and repent my unlawful solicitation. If not, assure yourself I will seek satisfaction of you.   196

IAGO.   You have said now.°

RODERIGO.   Aye, and said nothing but what I protest intendment of doing.

IAGO.   Why, now I see there's mettle in thee, and even from this instant do build on thee a better opinion than ever before. Give me thy hand, Roderigo. Thou hast taken against me a most just exception, but yet I protest I have dealt most directly in thy affair.   202

RODERIGO.   It hath not appeared.

IAGO.   I grant indeed it hath not appeared, and your suspicion is not without wit and judgment. But, Roderigo, if thou hast that in thee indeed which I have greater reason to believe now than ever—I mean purpose, courage, and valor—this night show it. If thou the next might following enjoy not Desdemona, take me from this world with treachery and devise engines° for my life.   209

RODERIGO.   Well, what is it? Is it within reason and compass?

IAGO.   Sir, there is especial commission come from Venice to depute Cassio in Othello's place.

RODERIGO.   Is that true? Why, then Othello and Desdemona return again to Venice.   214

IAGO.   Oh, no. He goes into Mauritania, and takes away with him the fair Desdemona, unless his abode be lingered here by some accident, wherein none can be so determinate as the removing of Cassio.

RODERIGO.   How do you mean, "removing of" him?   218

IAGO.   Why, by making him uncapable of Othello's place, knocking out his brains.

RODERIGO.   And that you would have me to do?

IAGO.   Aye, if you dare do yourself a profit and a right. He sups tonight with a harlotry,° and thither will I go to him. He knows not yet of his honorable fortune. If you will watch his going thence, which I will fashion to fall out between twelve and one, you may take him at your pleasure. I will be near to second your attempt, and he shall fall between us. Come, stand not amazed at it, but go along with me. I will show you such a necessity in his death that you shall think yourself bound to put it on him. It is now high suppertime and the night grows to waste. About it.

RODERIGO.   I will hear further reason for this.   230

IAGO.   And you shall be satisfied. (*Exeunt.*)

---

197. You . . . now: or in modern slang, "Oh yeah."   **209. engines:** instruments of
torture   **223. harlotry:** harlot

SCENE 3. Another room in the castle.

Enter OTHELLO, LODOVICO, DESDEMONA, EMILIA, *and* ATTENDANTS.

LODOVICO.   I do beseech you, sir, trouble yourself no further.
OTHELLO.   Oh, pardon me, 'twill do me good to walk.
LODOVICO.   Madam, good night. I humbly thank your ladyship.
DESDEMONA.   Your Honor is most welcome.
OTHELLO.   Will you walk, sir?
   Oh—Desdemona—   5
DESDEMONA.   My lord?
OTHELLO.   Get you to bed on the instant, I will be returned forthwith.
   Dismiss your attendant there. Look it be done.
DESDEMONA.   I will, my lord.
   (*Exeunt* OTHELLO, LODOVICO, *and* ATTENDANTS.)
EMILIA.   How goes it now? He looks gentler than he did.   10
DESDEMONA.   He says he will return incontinent.°
   He hath commanded me to go to bed,
   And bade me to dismiss you.
EMILIA.   Dismiss me!
DESDEMONA.   It was his bidding, therefore, good Emilia,
   Give me my nightly wearing, and adieu.   15
   We must not now displease him.
EMILIA.   I would you had never seen him!
DESDEMONA.   So would not I. My love doth so approve him
   That even his stubbornness, his checks, his frowns—
   Prithee, unpin me—have grace and favor in them.   20
EMILIA.   I have laid those sheets you bade me on the bed.
DESDEMONA.   All's one. Good faith, how foolish are our minds!
   If I do die before thee, prithee shroud me
   In one of those same sheets.
EMILIA.   Come, come, you talk.
DESDEMONA.   My mother had a maid called Barbary.   25
   She was in love, and he she loved proved mad
   And did forsake her. She had a song of "willow"°—
   An old thing 'twas, but it expressed her fortune,
   And she died singing it. That song tonight
   Will not go from my mind. I have much to do   30
   But to go hang my head all at one side
   And sing it like poor Barbary. Prithee, dispatch.
EMILIA.   Shall I go fetch your nightgown?
DESDEMONA.   No, unpin me here.
   This Lodovico is a proper man.
EMILIA.   A very handsome man.   35
DESDEMONA.   He speaks well.

---

11. incontinent: immediately   **27. willow:** the emblem of the forlorn lover

EMILIA. I know a lady in Venice would have walked barefoot to Palestine
for a touch of his nether lip.
DESDEMONA (*singing*).
"The poor soul sat sighing by a sycamore tree,
Sing all a green willow.   40
Her hand on her bosom, her head on her knee,
Sing willow, willow, willow.
The fresh streams ran by her, and murmured her moans,
Sing willow, willow, willow.
Her salt tears fell from her, and softened the stones—"   45
Lay by these—(*singing*)
"Sing willow, willow, willow,"
Prithee, hie thee, he'll come anon.—(*singing*)
"Sing all a green willow must be my garland.
Let nobody blame him, his scorn I approve—"   50
Nay, that's not next. Hark! Who is 't that knocks?
EMILIA. It's the wind.
DESDEMONA (*singing*).
"I called my love false love, but what said he then?
Sing willow, willow, willow.
If I court moe° women, you'll couch with moe men."   55
So get thee gone, good night. Mine eyes do itch.
Doth that bode weeping?
EMILIA.   'Tis neither here nor there.
DESDEMONA. I have heard it said so. Oh, these men, these men!
Dost thou in conscience think—tell me, Emilia—
That there be women do abuse their husbands   60
In such gross kind?
EMILIA.   There be some such, no question.
DESDEMONA. Wouldst thou do such a deed for all the world?
EMILIA. Why, would not you?
DESDEMONA.   No, by this heavenly light!
EMILIA. Nor I neither by this heavenly light.
I might do 't as well i' the dark.   65
DESDEMONA. Would thou do such a deed for all the world?
EMILIA. The world's a huge thing. It is a great price
For a small vice.
DESDEMONA.   In troth, I think thou wouldst not.
EMILIA. In troth, I think I should, and undo 't when I had done. Marry, I
would not do such a thing for a joint ring,° nor for measures of lawn,° nor
for gowns, petticoats, nor caps, nor any petty exhibition;° but for the
whole world—why, who would not make her husband a cuckold to make

---

55. moe: more   **70. joint ring:** ring made in two pieces, a lover's gift
measures of lawn: lengths of finest linen [Eds.]   **71. petty exhibition:** small
allowance of money

him a monarch? I should venture Purgatory for 't.   73
DESDEMONA.   Beshrew me if I would do such a wrong for the whole
world.
EMILIA.   Why, the wrong is but a wrong i' the world, and having the world
for your labor, 'tis a wrong in your own world and you might quickly
make it right.   78
DESDEMONA.   I do not think there is any such woman.
EMILIA.   Yes, a dozen, and as many to the vantage as would store the world
they played for.
But I do think it is their husbands' faults
If wives do fall. Say that they slack their duties
And pour our treasures into foreign laps,
Or else break out in peevish jealousies,   85
Throwing restraint upon us, or say they strike us,
Or scant our former having in despite,°
Why, we have galls,° and though we have some grace,
Yet have we some revenge. Let husbands know
Their wives have sense like them. They see and smell   90
And have their palates both for sweet and sour,
As husbands have. What is it that they do
When they change us for others? Is it sport?
I think it is. And doth affection breed it?
I think it doth. Is 't frailty that thus errs?   95
It is so too. And have not we affections,
Desires for sport, and frailty, as men have?
Then let them use us well. Else let them know
The ills we do, their ills instruct us so.
DESDEMONA.   Good night, good night. Heaven me such uses send,   100
Not to pick bad from bad, but by bad mend! (*Exeunt.*)

ACT 5

SCENE 1. Cyprus. A street.

Enter IAGO *and* RODERIGO.

IAGO.   Here, stand behind this bulk, straight will he come.
Wear thy good rapier bare, and put it home.
Quick, quick, fear nothing. I'll be at thy elbow.
It makes us, or it mars us. Think on that,
And fix most firm thy resolution.   5
RODERIGO.   Be near at hand. I may miscarry in 't.
IAGO.   Here, at thy hand. Be bold, and take thy stand. (*Retires.*)

---

87. scant . . . despite: for spite cut down our allowance   **88. galls:** bile, the cause
of bitterness

RODERIGO.   I have no great devotion to the deed,
And yet he hath given me satisfying reasons.
'Tis but a man gone. Forth, my sword. He dies.   10
IAGO.   I have rubbed this young quat° almost to the sense,°
And he grows angry. Now, whether he kill Cassio,
Or Cassio him, or each do kill the other,
Every way makes my gain. Live Roderigo,°
He calls me to a restitution large   15
Of gold and jewels that I bobbed from him
As gifts to Desdemona.
It must not be. If Cassio do remain,
He hath a daily beauty in his life
That makes me ugly,° and besides, the Moor   20
May unfold me to him. There stand I in much peril.
No, he must die. Be 't so. I hear him coming. (*Enter* CASSIO.)
RODERIGO.   I know his gait, 'tis he. Villain, thou diest!
(*Makes a pass at* CASSIO.)
CASSIO.   That thrust had been mine enemy indeed
But that my coat is better than thou know'st.   25
I will make proof of thine. (*Draws, and wounds* RODERIGO.)
RODERIGO.   Oh, I am slain!
(IAGO *from behind wounds* CASSIO *in the leg, and exit.*)
CASSIO.   I am maimed for ever. Help, ho! Murder! Murder!
(*Falls. Enter* OTHELLO.)
OTHELLO.   The voice of Cassio. Iago keeps his word.
RODERIGO.   Oh, villain that I am!
OTHELLO.   It is even so.
CASSIO.   Oh, help, ho! Light! A surgeon!   30
OTHELLO.   'Tis he. O brave Iago, honest and just,
That hast such noble sense of thy friend's wrong!
Thou teachest me. Minion,° your dear friend lies dead,
And your unblest fate hies. Strumpet, I come!
Forth of my heart those charms, thine eyes, are blotted.   35
Thy bed lust-stained shall with lust's blood be spotted.
(*Exit. Enter* LODOVICO *and* GRATIANO.)
CASSIO.   What ho! No watch?° No passage?° Murder! Murder!
GRATIANO.   'Tis some mischance, the cry is very direful.
CASSIO.   Oh, help!
LODOVICO.   Hark!   40
RODERIGO.   Oh, wretched villain!

---

11. quat: pimple   **sense:** quick   **14. Live Roderigo:** if Roderigo lives [Eds.]
19–20. He . . . ugly: by comparison with him I am a poor thing. Iago is conscious of
his lack of social graces.   **33. Minion:** darling, in a bad sense   **37. watch:** police
No passage: Nobody passing

LODOVICO.   Two or three groan. It is a heavy° night.
    These may be counterfeits. Let's think 't unsafe
    To come in to the cry without more help.
RODERIGO.   Nobody come? Then I shall bleed to death.   45
LODOVICO.   Hark! (*Re-enter* IAGO, *with a light.*)
GRATIANO.   Here's one comes in his shirt, with light and weapons.
IAGO.   Who's there? Whose noise is this that cries on murder?
LODOVICO.   We do not know.
IAGO.   Did not you hear a cry?
CASSIO.   Here, here! For Heaven's sake, help me!
IAGO.   What's the matter?   50
GRATIANO.   This is Othello's Ancient, as I take it.
LODOVICO.   The same indeed, a very valiant fellow.
IAGO.   What are you here that cry so grievously?
CASSIO.   Iago? Oh, I am spoiled, undone by villains! Give me some help.
IAGO.   Oh me, Lieutenant! What villains have done this?   55
CASSIO.   I think that one of them is hereabout,
    And cannot make away.
IAGO.   Oh, treacherous villains!
    (*To* LODOVICO *and* GRATIANO) What are you there?
    Come in and give some help.
RODERIGO.   Oh, help me here!
CASSIO.   That's one of them.
IAGO.   Oh, murderous slave! Oh, villain!   60
    (*Stabs* RODERIGO.)
RODERIGO.   Oh, damned Iago! Oh, inhuman dog!
IAGO.   Kill men i' the dark! Where be these bloody thieves?
    How silent is this town! Ho! Murder! Murder!
    What may you be? Are you of good or evil?
LODOVICO.   As you shall prove us, praise us.   65
IAGO.   Signior Lodovico?
LODOVICO.   He, sir.
IAGO.   I cry your mercy. Here's Cassio hurt by villains.
GRATIANO.   Cassio!
IAGO.   How is 't, brother?   70
CASSIO.   My leg is cut in two.
IAGO.   Marry, Heaven forbid!
    Light, gentlemen. I'll bind it with my shirt. (*Enter* BIANCA.)
BIANCA.   What is the matter, ho? Who is 't that cried?
IAGO.   Who is 't that cried!
BIANCA.   Oh, my dear Cassio! My sweet Cassio!   75
    Oh, Cassio, Cassio, Cassio!
IAGO.   Oh, notable strumpet! Cassio, may you suspect

---

42. heavy: thick

Who they should be that have thus mangled you?

CASSIO.   No.

GRATIANO.   I am sorry to find you thus. I have been to seek you.   80

IAGO.   Lend me a garter. Oh, for a chair,
    To bear him easily hence!

BIANCA.   Alas, he faints! Oh, Cassio, Cassio, Cassio!

IAGO.   Gentlemen all, I do suspect this trash
    To be a party in this injury.   85
    Patience awhile, good Cassio. Come, come
    Lend me a light. Know we this face or no?
    Alas, my friend and my dear countryman
    Roderigo? No—yes, sure. Oh Heaven! Roderigo.

GRATIANO.   What, of Venice?   90

IAGO.   Even he, sir. Did you know him?

GRATIANO.   Know him! Aye.

IAGO.   Signior Gratiano? I cry you gentle pardon.
    These bloody accidents must excuse my manners,
    That so neglected you.

GRATIANO.   I am glad to see you.

IAGO.   How do you, Cassio? Oh, a chair, a chair!   95

GRATIANO.   Roderigo!

IAGO.   He, he, 'tis he. (*A chair brought in.*) Oh, that's well said, the chair.
    Some good man bear him carefully from hence.
    I'll fetch the General's surgeon. (*To* BIANCA) For you, mistress,
    Save you your labor. He that lies slain here, Cassio,   100
    Was my dear friend. What malice between you?

CASSIO.   None in the world, nor do I know the man.

IAGO (*to* BIANCA).   What, look you pale? Oh, bear him out o' the air.
    (CASSIO *and* RODERIGO *are borne off.*)
    Stay you, good gentlemen. Look you pale, mistress?
    Do you perceive the gastness of her eye?   105
    Nay, if you stare, we shall hear more anon.
    Behold her well, I pray you look upon her.
    Do you see, gentlemen? Nay, guiltiness will speak,
    Though tongues were out of use. (*Enter* EMILIA.)

EMILIA.   'Las, what's the matter? What's the matter, husband?   110

IAGO.   Cassio hath here been set on in the dark
    By Roderigo and fellows that are 'scaped.
    He's almost slain, and Roderigo dead.

EMILIA.   Alas, good gentleman! Alas, good Cassio!

IAGO.   This is the fruit of whoring. Prithee, Emilia,   115
    Go know of Cassio where he supped tonight.
    What, do you shake at that?

BIANCA.   He supped at my house, but I therefore shake not.

IAGO.   Oh, did he so? I charge you, go with me.

EMILIA.   Fie, fie upon thee, strumpet!   120
BIANCA.   I am no strumpet, but of life as honest
  As you that thus abuse me.
EMILIA.   As I! Foh! Fie upon thee!
IAGO.   Kind gentlemen, let's go see poor Cassio dressed.°
  Come, mistress, you must tell's another tale.
  Emilia, run you to the citadel,   125
  And tell my lord and lady what hath happened!
  Will you go on afore? I pray. (*Aside*) This is the night
  That either makes me or fordoes me quite. (*Exeunt.*)

SCENE 2.   *A bedchamber in the castle.* DESDEMONA *in bed asleep, a light burning.*

  Enter OTHELLO.

OTHELLO.   It is the cause,° it is the cause, my soul.
  Let me not name it to you, you chaste stars!
  It is the cause. Yet I'll not shed her blood,
  Nor scar that whiter skin of hers than snow
  And smooth as monumental alabaster.   5
  Yet she must die, else she'll betray more men.
  Put out the light, and then put out the light.
  If I quench thee, thou flaming minister,°
  I can again thy former light restore,
  Should I repent me. But once put out thy light,   10
  Thou cunning'st° pattern of excelling nature,
  I know not where is that Promethean heat
  That can thy light relume. When I have plucked the rose,
  I cannot give it vital growth again,
  It needs must wither. I'll smell it on the tree. (*Kissing her*) 15
  Ah, balmy breath, that dost almost persuade
  Justice to break her sword! One more, one more.
  Be thus when thou art dead, and I will kill thee,
  And love thee after. One more, and this the last.
  So sweet was ne'er so fatal. I must weep,   20
  But they are cruel tears. This sorrow's heavenly,
  It strikes where it doth love. She wakes.
DESDEMONA.   Who's there? Othello?
OTHELLO.   Aye, Desdemona.

---

123. dressed: i.e., his wound dressed   **1. It . . . cause:** The meaning of the opening lines of this speech has been much discussed. The *cause* is Desdemona's supposed faithlessness; Othello, at this moment, sees himself as embodied justice, the avenger of man betrayed by woman.   **8. minister:** servant   **11. cunning'st:** most skillfully made

DESDEMONA.   Will you come to bed, my lord?
OTHELLO.   Have you prayed tonight, Desdemona?
DESDEMONA.   Aye, my lord.   25
OTHELLO.   If you bethink yourself of any crime
    Unreconciled as yet to Heaven and grace,
    Solicit for it straight.
DESDEMONA.   Alas, my lord, what may you mean by that?
OTHELLO.   Well, do it, and be brief. I will walk by.   30
    I would not kill thy unpreparèd spirit.
    No, Heaven forfend! I would not kill thy soul.
DESDEMONA.   Talk you of killing?
OTHELLO.   Aye, I do.
DESDEMONA.   Then Heaven
    Have mercy on me!
OTHELLO.   Amen, with all my heart!
DESDEMONA.   If you say so, I hope you will not kill me.   35
OTHELLO.   Hum!
DESDEMONA.   And yet I fear you, for you are fatal then
    When your eyes roll so. Why I should fear I know not,
    Since guiltiness I know not, but yet I feel I fear.
OTHELLO.   Think on thy sins.
DESDEMONA.   They are loves I bear to you.   40
OTHELLO.   Aye, and for that thou diest.
DESDEMONA.   That death's unnatural that kills for loving.
    Alas, why gnaw you so your nether lip?
    Some bloody passion shakes your very frame.
    These are portents, but yet I hope, I hope,   45
    They do not point on me.
OTHELLO.   Peace, and be still!
DESDEMONA.   I will so. What's the matter?
OTHELLO.   That handkerchief which I so loved and gave thee
    Thou gavest to Cassio.
DESDEMONA.   No, by my life and soul!
    Send for the man, and ask him.
OTHELLO.   Sweet soul, take heed,   50
    Take heed of perjury, thou art on thy deathbed.
DESDEMONA.   Aye, but not yet to die.
OTHELLO.   Yes, presently.°
    Therefore confess thee freely of thy sin,
    For to deny each article with oath
    Cannot remove nor choke the strong conception   55
    That I do groan withal. Thou art to die.
DESDEMONA.   Then Lord have mercy on me!

52. presently: at once

OTHELLO.   I say amen.
DESDEMONA.   And have you mercy too! I never did
    Offend you in my life, never loved Cassio
    But with such general warranty of Heaven   60
    As I might love. I never gave him token.
OTHELLO.   By Heaven, I saw my handkerchief in 's hand.
    O perjured woman! Thou dost stone° my heart,
    And makest me call what I intend to do
    A murder, which I thought a sacrifice.   65
    I saw the handkerchief.
DESDEMONA.   He found it, then,
    I never gave it him. Send for him hither.
    Let him confess a truth.
OTHELLO.   He hath confessed.
DESDEMONA.   What, my lord?
OTHELLO.   That he hath used thee.
DESDEMONA.   How? Unlawfully?
OTHELLO.   Aye.   70
DESDEMONA.   He will not say so.
OTHELLO.   No, his mouth is stopped.
    Honest Iago hath ta'en order for 't.
DESDEMONA.   Oh, my fear interprets! What, is he dead?
OTHELLO.   Had all his hairs been lives, my great revenge
    Had stomach for them all.   75
DESDEMONA.   Alas, he is betrayed, and I undone!
OTHELLO.   Out, strumpet! Weep'st thou for him to my face?
DESDEMONA.   Oh, banish me, my lord, but kill me not!
OTHELLO.   Down, strumpet!
DESDEMONA.   Kill me tomorrow, let me live tonight!   80
OTHELLO.   Nay, if you strive—
DESDEMONA.   But half an hour!
OTHELLO.   Being done, there is no pause.
DESDEMONA.   But while I say one prayer!
OTHELLO.   It is too late. (*He stifles her.*)
EMILIA (*within*).   My lord, my lord! What ho! My lord, my lord!
OTHELLO.   What noise is this? Not dead? Not yet quite dead?   85
    I that am cruel am yet merciful,
    I would not have thee linger in thy pain.
    So, so.
EMILIA (*within*).   What ho! My lord, my lord!
OTHELLO.   Who's there?
EMILIA (*within*).   Oh, good my lord, I would speak a word with you!
OTHELLO.   Yes, 'tis Emilia. By and by. She's dead.   90
    'Tis like she comes to speak of Cassio's death.

---

63. stone: turn to stone

The noise was here. Ha! No more moving?
Still as the grave. Shall she come in? Were 't good?
I think she stirs again. No. What's best to do?
If she come in, she'll sure speak to my wife.   95
My wife! My wife! What wife? I have no wife.
Oh, insupportable! Oh, heavy hour!
Methinks it should be now a huge eclipse
Of sun and moon, and that the affrighted globe
Should yawn° at alteration.
EMILIA (*within*).   I do beseech you   100
That I may speak with you, O good my lord!
OTHELLO.   I had forgot thee. Oh, come in, Emilia.
Soft, by and by. Let me the curtains° draw.
What art thou? (*Unlocks the door. Enter* EMILIA.)
                    What's the matter with thee now?
EMILIA.   Oh, my good lord, yonder's foul murders done!   105
OTHELLO.   What, now?
EMILIA.   But now, my lord.
OTHELLO.   It is the very error of the moon.
She comes more nearer earth than she was wont
And makes men mad.   110
EMILIA.   Cassio, my lord, hath killed a young Venetian
Called Roderigo.
OTHELLO.   Roderigo killed!
And Cassio killed!
EMILIA.   No, Cassio is not killed.
OTHELLO.   Not Cassio killed! Then murder's out of tune,
And sweet revenge grows harsh.   115
DESDEMONA.   Oh, falsely, falsely murdered!
EMILIA.   Alas, what cry is that?
OTHELLO.   That! What?
EMILIA.   Out and alas! That was my lady's voice.
Help! Help, ho! Help! O lady, speak again!
Sweet Desdemona! O sweet mistress, speak!   120
DESDEMONA.   A guiltless death I die.
EMILIA.   Oh, who hath done this deed?
DESDEMONA.   Nobody, I myself. Farewell.
Commend me to my kind lord. Oh, farewell! (*Dies.*)
OTHELLO.   Why, how should she be murdered?
EMILIA.   Alas, who knows?   125
OTHELLO.   You heard her say herself it was not I.
EMILIA.   She said so. I must needs report the truth.
OTHELLO.   She's like a liar gone to burning Hell.
'Twas I that killed her.

---

100. yawn: split open in an earthquake [Eds.]   **103. curtains:** i.e., of the bed

EMILIA.   Oh, the more angel she,
   And you the blacker devil!   130
OTHELLO.   She turned to folly, and she was a whore.
EMILIA.   Thou dost belie her, and thou art a devil.
OTHELLO.   She was false as water.
EMILIA.   Thou art rash as fire to say
   That she was false. Oh, she was heavenly true!
OTHELLO.   Cassio did top her, ask thy husband else.   135
   Oh, I were damned beneath all depth in Hell
   But that I did proceed upon just grounds
   To this extremity. Thy husband knew it all.
EMILIA.   My husband!
OTHELLO.   Thy husband.   140
EMILIA.   That she was false to wedlock?
OTHELLO.   Aye, with Cassio. Nay, had she been true,
   If Heaven would make me such another world
   Of one entire and perfect chrysolite,
   I'd not have sold her for it.
EMILIA.   My husband!   145
OTHELLO.   Aye, 'twas he that told me first.
   An honest man he is, and hates the slime
   That sticks on filthy deeds.
EMILIA.   My husband!
OTHELLO.   What needs this iteration, woman? I say thy husband.
EMILIA.   Oh, mistress, villainy hath made mocks with love!   150
   My husband say that she was false!
OTHELLO.   He, woman.
   I say thy husband. Dost understand the word?
   My friend, thy husband, honest, honest Iago.
EMILIA.   If he say so, may his pernicious soul
   Rot half a grain a day! He lies to the heart.   155
   She was too fond of her most filthy bargain.
OTHELLO.   Ha!
EMILIA.   Do thy worst.
   This deed of thine is no more worthy Heaven
   Than thou wast worthy her.
OTHELLO.   Peace, you were best.   160
EMILIA.   Thou hast not half that power to do me harm
   As I have to be hurt. O gull! O dolt!
   As ignorant as dirt! Thou hast done a deed—
   I care not for thy sword, I'll make thee known,
   Though I lost twenty lives. Help! Help! ho! Help!   165
   The Moor hath killed my mistress! Murder! Murder!
   (*Enter* MONTANO, GRATIANO, IAGO, *and others.*)
MONTANO.   What is the matter? How now, General!

EMILIA.   Oh, are you come, Iago? You have done well,
   That men must lay their murders on your neck.
GRATIANO.   What is the matter?   170
EMILIA.   Disprove this villain, if thou be'st a man.
   He says thou told'st him that his wife was false.
   I know thou didst not, thou'rt not such a villain.
   Speak, for my heart is full.
IAGO.   I told him what I thought, and told no more   175
   Than what he found himself was apt and true.
EMILIA.   But did you ever tell him she was false?
IAGO.   I did.
EMILIA.   You told a lie, an odious, damnèd lie,
   Upon my soul, a lie, a wicked lie!   180
   She false with Cassio! Did you say with Cassio?
IAGO.   With Cassio, mistress. Go to, charm your tongue.°
EMILIA.   I will not charm my tongue, I am bound to speak.
   My mistress here lies murdered in her bed.
ALL.   Oh, Heavens forfend!   185
EMILIA.   And your reports have set the murder on.
OTHELLO.   Nay, stare not, masters. It is true indeed.
GRATIANO.   'Tis a strange truth.
MONTANO.   Oh, monstrous act!
EMILIA.   Villainy, villainy, villainy!
   I think upon 't. I think I smell 't. Oh, villainy!   190
   I thought so then. I'll kill myself for grief.
   Oh, villainy, villainy!
IAGO.   What, are you mad? I charge you, get you home.
EMILIA.   Good gentlemen, let me have leave to speak.
   'Tis proper I obey him, but not now.   195
   Perchance, Iago, I will ne'er go home.
OTHELLO.   Oh! Oh! Oh! (*Falling on the bed.*)
EMILIA.   Nay, lay thee down and roar,
   For thou has killed the sweetest innocent
   That e'er did lift up eye.
OTHELLO (*rising*).   Oh, she was foul!
   I scarce did know you, Uncle. There lies your niece,   200
   Whose breath indeed these hands have newly stopped.
   I know this act shows horrible and grim.
GRATIANO.   Poor Desdemona! I am glad thy father's dead.
   Thy match was mortal to him, and pure grief
   Shore his old thread in twain. Did he live now,   205
   This sight would make him do a desperate turn—

---

182. **charm your tongue:** be silent

Yea, curse his better angel from his side,
And fall to reprobation.°
OTHELLO.   'Tis pitiful, but yet Iago knows
    That she with Cassio hath the act of shame   210
    A thousand times committed. Cassio confessed it.
    And she did gratify his amorous works
    With that recognizance and pledge of love
    Which I first gave her, I saw it in his hand.
    It was a handkerchief, an antique token   215
    My father gave my mother.
EMILIA.   Oh, Heaven! Oh, heavenly powers!
IAGO.   'Zounds! Hold your peace.
EMILIA.   'Twill out, 'twill out. I peace!
    No, I will speak as liberal as the north.°
    Let Heaven and men and devils, let them all,   220
    All, all, cry shame against me, yet I'll speak.
IAGO.   Be wise, and get you home.
EMILIA.   I will not.
    (IAGO *offers to stab* EMILIA.)
GRATIANO.   Fie!
    Your sword upon a woman!
EMILIA.   O thou dull Moor! That handkerchief thou speak'st of
    I found by fortune and did give my husband,   225
    For often with a solemn earnestness,
    More than indeed belonged to such a trifle,
    He begged of me to steal it.
IAGO.   Villainous whore!
EMILIA.   She give it Cassio! No, alas, I found it,
    And I did give 't my husband.
IAGO.   Filth, thou liest!   230
EMILIA.   By Heaven, I do not, I do not, gentlemen.
    Oh, murderous coxcomb! What should such a fool
    Do with so good a wife!
OTHELLO.   Are there no stones° in Heaven
    But what serve for the thunder? Precious villain!
    (*He runs at* IAGO. IAGO, *from behind, stabs* EMILIA, *and exits.*)
GRATIANO.   The woman falls. Sure, he hath killed his wife.   235
EMILIA.   Aye. Aye. Oh, lay me by my mistress' side.
GRATIANO.   He's gone, but his wife's killed.
MONTANO.   'Tis a notorious villain. Take you this weapon,
    Which I have here recovered from the Moor.
    Come, guard the door without, let him not pass,   240

---

208. reprobation: damnation; i.e., by self-murder   **219. liberal . . . north:** as
freely as the north wind, which is loud and bitter   **233. stones:** thunderbolts

But kill him rather. I'll after that same villain,
For 'tis a damnèd slave. (*Exeunt all but* OTHELLO *and* EMILIA.)
OTHELLO.   I am not valiant neither,
But every puny whipster gets my sword.
But why should honor outlive honesty?
Let it go all.
EMILIA.   What did thy song bode, lady?   245
Hark, canst thou hear me? I will play the swan,
And die in music. (*Singing*)
                              "Willow, willow, willow."
Moor, she was chaste. She loved thee, cruel Moor,
So come my soul to bliss as I speak true.
So speaking as I think, I die, I die. (*Dies.*)   250
OTHELLO.   I have another weapon in this chamber.
It is a sword of Spain, the ice brook's temper.—
Oh, here it is. Uncle, I must come forth.
GRATIANO (*within*).   If thou attempt it, it will cost thee dear.
Thou hast no weapon, and perforce must suffer.   255
OTHELLO.   Look in upon me then, and speak with me,
Or, naked° as I am, I will assault thee. (*Re-enter* GRATIANO.)
GRATIANO.   What is the matter?
OTHELLO.   Behold, I have a weapon,
A better never did itself sustain
Upon a soldier's thigh. I have seen the day   260
That with this little arm and this good sword
I have made my way through more impediments
Than twenty times your stop. But, oh, vain boast!
Who can control his fate? 'Tis not so now.
Be not afraid, though you do see me weaponed.   265
Here is my journey's end, here is my butt°
And very sea mark of my utmost sail.
Do you go back dismayed? 'Tis a lost fear.
Man but a rush° against Othello's breast,
And he retires. Where should Othello go?   270
Now, how dost thou look now? O ill-starred wench!
Pale as thy smock! When we shall meet at compt,°
This look of thine will hurl my soul from Heaven
And fiends will snatch at it. Cold, cold, my girl!
Even like thy chastity. Oh, cursèd slave!   275
Whip me, ye devils,
From the possession of this heavenly sight!
Blow me about in winds! Roast me in sulphur!

257. naked: unarmed   **266. butt:** aim   **269. Man . . . rush:** Attack with only
a reed   **272. compt:** account; i.e., the Day of Judgment

Wash me in steep-down gulfs of liquid fire!
O Desdemona! Desdemona! Dead!   280
Oh! Oh! Oh!

(*Enter* LODOVICO, MONTANO, CASSIO *carried in a chair, and* OFFICERS
with IAGO, *prisoner.*)

LODOVICO.   Where is this rash and most unfortunate man?
OTHELLO.   That's he that was Othello. Here I am.
LODOVICO.   Where is the viper? Bring the villain forth.
OTHELLO.   I look down toward his feet,° but that's a fable.   285
    If that thou be'st a devil, I cannot kill thee. (*Wounds* IAGO.)
LODOVICO.   Wrench his sword from him.
IAGO.   I bleed, sir, but not killed.
OTHELLO.   I am not sorry neither. I'd have thee live,
    For, in my sense, 'tis happiness to die.
LODOVICO.   O thou Othello, that wert once so good,   290
    Fall'n in the practice° of a damnèd slave,
    What shall be said to thee?
OTHELLO.   Why, anything.
    An honorable murderer, if you will,
    For naught did I in hate, but all in honor.
LODOVICO.   This wretch hath part confessed his villainy.   295
    Did you and he consent in Cassio's death?
OTHELLO.   Aye.
CASSIO.   Dear General, I never gave you cause.
OTHELLO.   I do believe it, and I ask your pardon.
    Will you, I pray, demand that demi-devil   300
    Why he hath thus ensnared my soul and body?
IAGO.   Demand me nothing. What you know, you know.
    From this time forth I never will speak word.
LODOVICO.   What, not to pray?
GRATIANO.   Torments will ope your lips.
OTHELLO.   Well, thou dost best.   305
LODOVICO.   Sir, you shall understand what hath befall'n,
    Which, as I think, you know not. Here is a letter
    Found in the pocket of the slain Roderigo,
    And here another. The one of them imports
    The death of Cassio to be undertook   310
    By Roderigo.
OTHELLO.   Oh, villain!
CASSIO.   Most heathenish and most gross!
LODOVICO.   Now here's another discontented paper,
    Found in his pocket too. And this, it seems,
    Roderigo meant to have sent this damnèd villain   315

---

285. **toward his feet:** i.e., to see if he has the cloven hoof of a devil   **291. Fall'n . . .
practice:** destroyed by the plotting

But that, belike, Iago in the interim
Came in and satisfied him.
OTHELLO.   Oh, the pernicious caitiff!
How come you, Cassio, by that handkerchief
That was my wife's?
CASSIO.   I found it in my chamber.
And he himself confessed but even now   320
That there he dropped it for a special purpose
Which wrought to his desire.
OTHELLO.   O fool! Fool! Fool!
CASSIO.   There is besides in Roderigo's letter
How he upbraids Iago, that he made him
Brave° me upon the watch, whereon it came   325
That I was cast.° And even but now he spake
After long seeming dead, Iago hurt him,
Iago set him on.
LODOVICO.   You must forsake this room, and go with us.
Your power and your command is taken off,   330
And Cassio rules in Cyprus. For this slave,
If there be any cunning cruelty
That can torment him much and hold him long,°
It shall be his. You shall close prisoner rest
Till that the nature of your fault be known   335
To the Venetian state. Come, bring away.
OTHELLO.   Soft you, a word or two before you go.
I have done the state some service, and they know 't.
No more of that. I pray you, in your letters,
When you shall these unlucky deeds relate,   340
Speak of me as I am, nothing extenuate,
Nor set down aught in malice. Then must you speak
Of one that loved not wisely but too well;
Of one not easily jealous, but, being wrought,
Perplexed in the extreme; of one whose hand,   345
Like the base Indian, threw a pearl away
Richer than all his tribe; of one whose subdued eyes,
Albeit unusèd to the melting mood,
Drop tears as fast as the Arabian trees
Their medicinable gum. Set you down this,   350
And say besides that in Aleppo once,
Where a malignant and a turbaned Turk
Beat a Venetian and traduced the state,
I took by the throat the circumcisèd dog
And smote him, thus. (*Stabs himself.*)   355
LODOVICO.   Oh, bloody period!

---

325. Brave: insult   **326. cast:** dismissed   **333. long:** i.e., in dying

GRATIANO.   All that's spoke is marred.
OTHELLO.   I kissed thee ere I killed thee. No way but this,
    Killing myself, to die upon a kiss. (*Falls on the bed, and dies.*)
CASSIO.   This did I fear, but thought he had no weapon,
    For he was great of heart.
LODOVICO (*to* IAGO).   O Spartan° dog,   360
    More fell° than anguish, hunger, or the sea!
    Look on the tragic loading of this bed:
    This is thy work. The object poisons sight,
    Let it be hid.° Gratiano, keep the house,
    And seize upon the fortunes of the Moor,   365
    For they succeed on you. To you, Lord Governor,
    Remains the censure of this hellish villain,
    The time, the place, the torture.
    Oh, enforce it!
    Myself will straight aboard, and to the state   370
    This heavy act with heavy heart relate. (*Exeunt.*)

QUESTIONS

1. In what ways is Othello, in the first two acts, shown to be a person of extra-ordinary quality?

2. Is Othello a person jealous "by nature"? Does he show any disposition to jealousy in the first two acts? What does he say about himself in his final soliloquy? (There has been much critical controversy over the psychological probability of Othello's being roused so quickly to such a high pitch of jealousy in act 3. Some have explained it by attributing a predisposition to jealousy in Othello; others have attributed it to the almost superhuman Machiavellian cleverness of Iago, which would have taken in any husband. In general, however, Shakespeare was less interested in psychological consistency and the subtle tracing of motivation—which are modern interests—than he was in theatrical effectiveness and the orchestration of emotions. Perhaps the question we should properly ask is not "How probable is Othello's jealousy?" but "How vital and effective has Shakespeare rendered it?")

3. Who is more naturally suspicious of human nature—Othello or Iago?

4. Is something of Othello's nobility manifested even in the scale of his jealousy? How does he respond to his conviction that Desdemona has been unfaithful to him? Would a lesser man have responded in the same way? Why or why not?

5. How does Othello's final speech reestablish his greatness?

6. What are Iago's motivations in his actions toward Othello, Cassio, and Roderigo? What is his philosophy? How does his technique in handling Roderigo differ from his technique in handling Othello and Cassio? Why?

360. Spartan: i.e., hardhearted   **361. fell:** cruel   **364. Let . . . hid:** At these words the curtains are closed across the inner stage (or chamber, if this scene was acted aloft), concealing all three bodies.

7. In rousing Othello's suspicions against Desdemona (3.3) Iago uses the same technique, in part, that he had used with Othello in inculpating Cassio (2.3) and that he later uses with Lodovico in inculpating Othello (4.2). What is this technique? Why is it effective? How does he change his tactics in the opening of 4.1?

8. What opinions of Iago, before his exposure, are expressed by Othello, Desdemona, Cassio, and Lodovico? Is Othello the only one taken in by him? Does his own wife think him capable of villainy?

9. Though Othello is the protagonist, the majority of soliloquies and asides are given to Iago. Why?

10. The difference between Othello and Desdemona that Iago plays on most is that of color, and, reading the play today, we may be tempted to see the play as being centrally about race relations. However, only one other character, besides Othello, makes much of this difference in color. Which one? Is this character sympathetically portrayed? What attitude toward Othello himself, and his marriage, is taken by the Duke, Cassio, Lodovico, Emilia, Desdemona herself? What differences between Othello and Desdemona, besides color, are used by Iago to undermine Othello's confidence in Desdemona's fidelity? What differences does Othello himself take into account?

11. What are Desdemona's principal character traits? In what ways are she and Emilia character foils? Is she entirely discreet in pleading Cassio's case to Othello? Why or why not? Why does she lie about the handkerchief (3.4)?

12. Like Sophocles in *Oedipus Rex*, Shakespeare makes extensive use of dramatic irony in this play. Point out effective examples.

13. Unlike *Oedipus Rex*, *Othello* contains comedy. For what purposes is it used? What larger difference in effect between *Othello* and *Oedipus Rex* does this use of comedy contribute to?

14. Find several occasions when chance and coincidence are involved in the plot (for example, Bianca's entry in 4.1). How important are these to the development of the plot? To what extent do they *cause* subsequent events to happen?

15. As much responsible as any other quality for the original popularity and continued vitality of *Othello* is its poetry. What are some of the prominent characteristics of that poetry (language, imagery, rhythm)? What speeches are particularly memorable or effective? Though most of the play is written in blank verse, some passages are written in rhymed iambic pentameter couplets and others in prose. Can you suggest any reasons for Shakespeare's use of these other mediums?

16. How would the effect of the play have been different if Othello had died *before* discovering Desdemona's innocence?

Molière

The Misanthrope

CHARACTERS

ALCESTE, *in love with Célimène*	ACASTE ⎱ *marquesses*
PHILINTE, *Alceste's friend*	CLITANDRE ⎰
ORONTE, *in love with Célimène*	BASQUE, *Célimène's servant*
CÉLIMÈNE, *Alceste's beloved*	A GUARD *of the Marshalsea*
ELIANTE, *Célimène's cousin*	DUBOIS, *Alceste's valet*
ARSINOÉ, *a friend of Célimène's*	

The scene throughout is in Célimène's house at Paris.

ACT 1

SCENE 1

Enter ALCESTE *and* PHILINTE.

PHILINTE.   Now, what's got into you?
ALCESTE (*seated*).   Kindly leave me alone.
PHILINTE.   Come, come, what is it? This lugubrious tone . . .
ALCESTE.   Leave me, I said; you spoil my solitude.
PHILINTE.   Oh, listen to me, now, and don't be rude.
ALCESTE.   I choose to be rude, Sir, and to be hard of hearing.   5
PHILINTE.   These ugly moods of yours are not endearing;
   Friends though we are, I really must insist . . .
ALCESTE (*abruptly rising*).   Friends? Friends, you say? Well, cross me off
   your list.
   I've been your friend till now, as you well know;
   But after what I saw a moment ago   10
   I tell you flatly that our ways must part.
   I wish no place in a dishonest heart.
PHILINTE.   Why, what have I done, Alceste? Is this quite just?
ALCESTE.   My God, you ought to die of self-disgust.
   I call your conduct inexcusable, Sir,   15

THE MISANTHROPE   First performed in 1666 in Paris during the reign of the Sun King (Louis XIV), a time in social and aristocratic circles when great emphasis was placed on elegance in dress, manners, and taste. Translated by Richard Wilbur. Molière (1622–1673) was born Jean-Baptiste Poquelin in Paris and was given excellent schooling by his father, a successful upholsterer employed by the court. He took "Molière" as his stage name when, at the age of twenty-one, he joined a traveling group of players. The rest of his life was spent in the theater as actor, manager, and author. Though twice sent to prison for debts, and often in trouble with the civil authorities for his writing, he enjoyed a certain amount of royal favor after his establishment in Paris in 1658.

And every man of honor will concur.
I see you almost hug a man to death,
Exclaim for joy until you're out of breath,
And supplement these loving demonstrations
With endless offers, vows, and protestations;   20
Then when I ask you "Who was that?" I find
That you can barely bring his name to mind!
Once the man's back is turned, you cease to love him,
And speak with absolute indifference of him!
By God, I say it's base and scandalous   25
To falsify the heart's affections thus;
If I caught myself behaving in such a way,
I'd hang myself for shame, without delay.
PHILINTE.   It hardly seems a hanging matter to me;
I hope that you will take it graciously   30
If I extend myself a slight reprieve,
And live a little longer, by your leave.
ALCESTE.   How dare you joke about a crime so grave?
PHILINTE.   What crime? How else are people to behave?
ALCESTE.   I'd have them be sincere, and never part   35
With any word that isn't from the heart.
PHILINTE.   When someone greets us with a show of pleasure,
It's but polite to give him equal measure,
Return his love the best that we know how,
And trade him offer for offer, vow for vow.   40
ALCESTE.   No, no, this formula you'd have me follow,
However fashionable, is false and hollow,
And I despise the frenzied operations
Of all these barterers of protestations,
These lavishers of meaningless embraces,   45
These utterers of obliging commonplaces,
Who court and flatter everyone on earth
And praise the fool no less than the man of worth.
Should you rejoice that someone fondles you,
Offers his love and service, swears to be true,   50
And fills your ears with praises of your name,
When to the first damned fop he'll say the same?
No, no: no self-respecting heart would dream
Of prizing so promiscuous an esteem;
However high the praise, there's nothing worse   55
Than sharing honors with the universe.
Esteem is founded on comparison:
To honor all men is to honor none.
Since you embrace this indiscriminate vice,
Your friendship comes at far too cheap a price;   60

I spurn the easy tribute of a heart
Which will not set the worthy man apart:
I choose, Sir, to be chosen; and in fine,
The friend of mankind is no friend of mine.

PHILINTE.   But in polite society, custom decrees   65
That we show certain outward courtesies . . .

ALCESTE.   Ah, no! we should condemn with all our force
Such false and artificial intercourse.
Let men behave like men; let them display
Their inmost hearts in everything they say;   70
Let the heart speak, and let our sentiments
Not mask themselves in silly compliments.

PHILINTE.   In certain cases it would be uncouth
And most absurd to speak the naked truth;
With all respect for your exalted notions,   75
It's often best to veil one's true emotions.
Wouldn't the social fabric come undone
If we were wholly frank with everyone?
Suppose you met with someone you couldn't bear;
Would you inform him of it then and there?   80

ALCESTE.   Yes.

PHILINTE.   Then you'd tell old Emilie it's pathetic
The way she daubs her features with cosmetic
And plays the gay coquette at sixty-four?

ALCESTE.   I would.

PHILINTE.   And you'd call Dorilas a bore,
And tell him every ear at court is lame   85
From hearing him brag about his noble name?

ALCESTE.   Precisely.

PHILINTE.   Ah, you're joking.

ALCESTE.   *Au contraire:*°
In this regard there's none I'd choose to spare.
All are corrupt; there's nothing to be seen
In court or town but aggravates my spleen.   90
I fall into deep gloom and melancholy
When I survey the scene of human folly,
Finding on every hand base flattery,
Injustice, fraud, self-interest, treachery . . .
Ah, it's too much; mankind has grown so base,   95
I mean to break with the whole human race.

PHILINTE.   This philosophic rage is a bit extreme;
You've no idea how comical you seem;

87. *Au contraire:* On the contrary

Indeed, we're like those brothers in the play
Called *School for Husbands,* one of whom was prey . . .°   100
ALCESTE.   Enough, now! None of your stupid similes.
PHILINTE.   Then let's have no more tirades, if you please.
The world won't change, whatever you say or do;
And since plain speaking means so much to you,
I'll tell you plainly that by being frank   105
You've earned the reputation of a crank,
And that you're thought ridiculous when you rage
And rant against the manners of the age.
ALCESTE.   So much the better; just what I wish to hear.
No news could be more grateful to my ear.   110
All men are so detestable in my eyes,
I should be sorry if they thought me wise.
PHILINTE.   Your hatred's very sweeping, is it not?
ALCESTE.   Quite right: I hate the whole degraded lot.
PHILINTE.   Must all poor human creatures be embraced,   115
Without distinction, by your vast distaste?
Even in these bad times, there are surely a few . . .
ALCESTE.   No, I include all men in one dim view:
Some men I hate for being rogues; the others
I hate because they treat the rogues like brothers,   120
And, lacking a virtuous scorn for what is vile,
Receive the villain with a complaisant smile.
Notice how tolerant people choose to be
Toward that bold rascal who's at law with me.
His social polish can't conceal his nature;   125
One sees at once that he's a treacherous creature;
No one could possibly be taken in
By those soft speeches and that sugary grin.
The whole world knows the shady means by which
The low-brow's grown so powerful and rich,   130
And risen to a rank so bright and high
That virtue can but blush, and merit sigh.
Whenever his name comes up in conversation,
None will defend his wretched reputation;
Call him knave, liar, scoundrel, and all the rest,   135
Each head will nod, and no one will protest.

---

100. School . . . prey: *School for Husbands* is an earlier play by Molière. The chief characters are two brothers, one of whom, puritanical and suspicious, mistrusts the fashions
and customs of the world, shuts up his ward and fiancée to keep her from infection by
them, and is outwitted and betrayed by her. The other, more amiable and easygoing,
allows his ward a free rein and is rewarded with her love.

And yet his smirk is seen in every house,
He's greeted everywhere with smiles and bows,
And when there's any honor that can be got
By pulling strings, he'll get it, like as not.   140
My God! It chills my heart to see the ways
Men come to terms with evil nowadays;
Sometimes, I swear, I'm moved to flee and find
Some desert land unfouled by humankind.

PHILINTE.   Come, let's forget the follies of the times   145
And pardon mankind for its petty crimes;
Let's have an end of rantings and of railings,
And show some leniency toward human failings.
This world requires a pliant rectitude;
Too stern a virtue makes one stiff and rude;   150
Good sense views all extremes with detestation,
And bids us to be noble in moderation.
The rigid virtues of the ancient days
Are not for us; they jar with all our ways
And ask of us too lofty a perfection.   155
Wise men accept their times without objection,
And there's no greater folly, if you ask me,
Than trying to reform society.
Like you, I see each day a hundred and one
Unhandsome deeds that might be better done,   160
But still, for all the faults that meet my view,
I'm never known to storm and rave like you.
I take men as they are, or let them be,
And teach my soul to bear their frailty;
And whether in court or town, whatever the scene,   165
My phlegm's as philosophic as your spleen.

ALCESTE.   This phlegm which you so eloquently commend,
Does nothing ever rile it up, my friend?
Suppose some man you trust should treacherously
Conspire to rob you of your property,   170
And do his best to wreck your reputation?
Wouldn't you feel a certain indignation?

PHILINTE.   Why, no. These faults of which you complain
Are part of human nature, I maintain,
And it's no more a matter of disgust   175
That men are knavish, selfish and unjust,
Than that the vulture dines upon the dead,
And wolves are furious, and apes ill-bred.

ALCESTE.   Shall I see myself betrayed, robbed, torn to bits,
And not . . . Oh, let's be still and rest our wits.   180
Enough of reasoning, now. I've had my fill.

PHILINTE.   Indeed, you would do well, Sir, to be still.
  Rage less at your opponent, and give some thought
  To how you'll win this lawsuit that he's brought.
ALCESTE.   I assure you I'll do nothing of the sort.   185
PHILINTE.   Then who will plead your case before the court?
ALCESTE.   Reason and right and justice will plead for me.
PHILINTE.   Oh, Lord. What judges do you plan to see?
ALCESTE.   Why, none. The justice of my cause is clear.
PHILINTE.   Of course, man; but there's politics to fear . . .   190
ALCESTE.   No, I refuse to lift a hand. That's flat.
  I'm either right, or wrong.
PHILINTE.   Don't count on that.
ALCESTE.   No, I'll do nothing.
PHILINTE.   Your enemy's influence
  Is great, you know . . .
ALCESTE.   That makes no difference.
PHILINTE.   It will; you'll see.
ALCESTE.   Must honor bow to guile?   195
  If so, I shall be proud to lose the trial.
PHILINTE.   Oh, really . . .
ALCESTE.   I'll discover by this case
  Whether or not men are sufficiently base
  And impudent and villainous and perverse
  To do me wrong before the universe.   200
PHILINTE.   What a man!
ALCESTE.   Oh, I could wish, whatever the cost,
  Just for the beauty of it, that my trial were lost.
PHILINTE.   If people heard you talking so, Alceste,
  They'd split their sides. Your name would be a jest.
ALCESTE.   So much the worse for jesters.
PHILINTE.   May I enquire   205
  Whether this rectitude you so admire,
  And these hard virtues you're enamored of
  Are qualities of the lady whom you love?
  It much surprises me that you, who seem
  To view mankind with furious disesteem,   210
  Have yet found something to enchant your eyes
  Amidst a species which you do despise.
  And what is more amazing, I'm afraid,
  Is the most curious choice your heart has made.
  The honest Eliante is fond of you,   215
  Arsinoé, the prude, admires you too;
  And yet your spirit's been perversely led
  To choose the flighty Célimène instead,
  Whose brittle malice and coquettish ways

So typify the manners of our days.   220
How is it that the traits you most abhor
Are bearable in this lady you adore?
Are you so blind with love that you can't find them?
Or do you contrive, in her case, not to mind them?
ALCESTE.   My love for that young widow's not the kind   225
That can't perceive defects; no, I'm not blind.
I see her faults, despite my ardent love,
And all I see I fervently reprove.
And yet I'm weak; for all her falsity,
That woman knows the art of pleasing me,   230
And though I never cease complaining of her,
I swear I cannot manage not to love her.
Her charm outweighs her faults; I can but aim
To cleanse her spirit in my love's pure flame.
PHILINTE.   That's no small task; I wish you all success.   235
You think then that she loves you?
ALCESTE.   Heavens, yes!
I wouldn't love her did she not love me.
PHILINTE.   Well, if her taste for you is plain to see,
Why do these rivals cause you such despair?
ALCESTE.   True love, Sir, is possessive, and cannot bear   240
To share with all the world. I'm here today
To tell her she must send that mob away.
PHILINTE.   If I were you, and had your choice to make,
Eliante, her cousin, would be the one I'd take;
That honest heart, which cares for you alone,   245
Would harmonize far better with your own.
ALCESTE.   True, true: each day my reason tells me so;
But reason doesn't rule in love, you know.
PHILINTE.   I fear some bitter sorrow is in store;
This love . . .

*SCENE 2**

   Enter ORONTE.

ORONTE (*to* ALCESTE).   The servants told me at the door   250
That Eliante and Célimène were out,
But when I heard, dear Sir, that you were about,

---

*In English and in most modern plays, a scene is a continuous section of the action in one setting, and acts are not usually divided into scenes unless there is a shift in setting or a shift in time. In older French drama, however, a scene is any portion of the play involving one group of characters, and a new scene begins, without interruption of the action, whenever any important character enters or exits.

I came to say, without exaggeration,
That I hold you in the vastest admiration,
And that it's always been my dearest desire   255
To be the friend of one I so admire.
I hope to see my love of merit requited,
And you and I in friendship's bond united.
I'm sure you won't refuse—if I may be frank—
A friend of my devotedness—and rank. (*During this speech of* ORONTE'S,
ALCESTE *is abstracted, and seems unaware that he is being spoken to. He
only breaks off his reverie when* ORONTE *says*)
    It was for you, if you please, that my words were intended.   261
ALCESTE.   For me, Sir?
ORONTE.   Yes, for you. You're not offended?
ALCESTE.   By no means. But this much surprises me . . .
    The honor comes most unexpectedly . . .
ORONTE.   My high regard should not astonish you;   265
    The whole world feels the same. It is your due.
ALCESTE.   Sir . . .
ORONTE.   Why, in all the State there isn't one
    Can match your merits; they shine, Sir, like the sun.
ALCESTE.   Sir . . .
ORONTE.   You are higher in my estimation
    Than all that's most illustrious in the nation.   270
ALCESTE.   Sir . . .
ORONTE.   If I lie, may heaven strike me dead!
    To show you that I mean what I have said,
    Permit me, Sir, to embrace you most sincerely,
    And swear that I will prize our friendship dearly.
    Give me your hand. And now, Sir, if you choose,   275
    We'll make our vows.
ALCESTE.   Sir . . .
ORONTE.   What! You refuse?
ALCESTE.   Sir, it's a very great honor you extend:
    But friendship is a sacred thing, my friend;
    It would be profanation to bestow
    The name of friend on one you hardly know.   280
    All parts are better played when well-rehearsed;
    Let's put off friendship, and get acquainted first.
    We may discover it would be unwise
    To try to make our natures harmonize.
ORONTE.   By heaven! You're sagacious to the core;   285
    This speech has made me admire you even more.
    Let time, then, bring us closer day by day;
    Meanwhile, I shall be yours in every way.
    If, for example, there should be anything

You wish at court, I'll mention it to the King.   290
I have his ear, of course; it's quite well known
That I am much in favor with the throne.
In short, I am your servant. And now, dear friend,
Since you have such fine judgment, I intend
To please you, if I can, with a small sonnet   295
I wrote not long ago. Please comment on it,
And tell me whether I ought to publish it.
ALCESTE.   You must excuse me, Sir; I'm hardly fit
To judge such matters.
ORONTE.   Why not?
ALCESTE.   I am, I fear,
Inclined to be unfashionably sincere.   300
ORONTE.   Just what I ask; I'd take no satisfaction
In anything but your sincere reaction.
I beg you not to dream of being kind.
ALCESTE.   Since you desire it, Sir, I'll speak my mind.
ORONTE.   *Sonnet.* It's a sonnet . . . *Hope* . . . The poem's addressed 305
To a lady who wakened hopes within my breast.
Hope . . . this is not the pompous sort of thing,
Just modest little verses, with a tender ring.
ALCESTE.   Well, we shall see.
ORONTE.   *Hope* . . . I'm anxious to hear
Whether the style seems properly smooth and clear,   310
And whether the choice of words is good or bad.
ALCESTE.   We'll see, we'll see.
ORONTE.   Perhaps I ought to add
That it took me only a quarter-hour to write it.
ALCESTE.   The time's irrelevant, Sir: kindly recite it.
ORONTE (*reading*).   Hope comforts us awhile, 'tis true,   315
                Lulling our cares with careless laughter,
                And yet such joy is full of rue,
                My Phyllis, if nothing follows after.
PHILINTE.   I'm charmed by this already; the style's delightful.
ALCESTE (*sotto voce, to* PHILINTE).   How can you say that? Why, the thing is
frightful.   320
ORONTE.   Your fair face smiled on me awhile,
                But was it kindness so to enchant me?
                'Twould have been fairer not to smile,
                If hope was all you meant to grant me.
PHILINTE.   What a clever thought! How handsomely you phrase it!   325
ALCESTE (*sotto voce, to* PHILINTE).   You know the thing is trash. How dare
you praise it?
ORONTE.   If it's to be my passion's fate
                Thus everlastingly to wait,

Then death will come to set me free:
For death is fairer than the fair;   330
Phyllis, to hope is to despair
When one must hope eternally.
PHILINTE.   The close is exquisite—full of feeling and grace.
ALCESTE (*sotto voce, aside*).   Oh, blast the close; you'd better close your face
Before you send your lying soul to hell.   335
PHILINTE.   I can't remember a poem I've liked so well.
ALCESTE (*sotto voce, aside*).   Good Lord!
ORONTE (*to* PHILINTE).   I fear you're flattering me a bit.
PHILINTE.   Oh, no!
ALCESTE (*sotto voce, aside*).   What else d'you call it, you hypocrite?
ORONTE (*to* ALCESTE).   But you, Sir, keep your promise now: don't shrink
From telling me sincerely what you think.   340
ALCESTE.   Sir, these are delicate matters; we all desire
To be told that we've the true poetic fire.
But once, to one whose name I shall not mention,
I said, regarding some verse of his invention,
That gentlemen should rigorously control   345
That itch to write which often afflicts the soul;
That one should curb the heady inclination
To publicize one's little avocation;
And that in showing off one's works of art
One often plays a very clownish part.   350
ORONTE.   Are you suggesting in a devious way
That I ought not . . .
ALCESTE.   Oh, that I do not say.
Further, I told him that no fault is worse
Than that of writing frigid, lifeless verse,
And that the merest whisper of such a shame   355
Suffices to destroy a man's good name.
ORONTE.   D'you mean to say my sonnet's dull and trite?
ALCESTE.   I don't say that. But I went on to cite
Numerous cases of once-respected men
Who came to grief by taking up the pen.   360
ORONTE.   And am I like them? Do I write so poorly?
ALCESTE.   I don't say that. But I told this person, "Surely
You're under no necessity to compose;
Why you should wish to publish, heaven knows.
There's no excuse for printing tedious rot   365
Unless one writes for bread, as you do not.
Resist temptation, then, I beg of you;
Conceal your pastimes from the public view;
And don't give up, on any provocation,
Your present high and courtly reputation,   370

To purchase at a greedy printer's shop
The name of silly author and scribbling fop."
These were the points I tried to make him see.
ORONTE.   I sense that they are also aimed at me;
But now—about my sonnet—I'd like to be told . . .   375
ALCESTE.   Frankly, that sonnet should be pigeonholed.
You've chosen the worst models to imitate.
The style's unnatural. Let me illustrate:

> For example, Your fair face smiled on me awhile,
> Followed by, 'Twould have been fairer not to smile!   380
> Or this: such joy is full of rue;
> Or this: For death is fairer than the fair;
> Or, Phyllis, to hope is to despair
>   When one must hope eternally!

This artificial style, that's all the fashion,   385
Has neither taste, nor honesty, nor passion;
It's nothing but a sort of wordy play,
And nature never spoke in such a way.
What, in this shallow age, is not debased?
Our fathers, though less refined, had better taste;   390
I'd barter all that men admire today
For one old love-song I shall try to say:

> If the King had given me for my own
> Paris, his citadel,
> And I for that must leave alone   395
> Her whom I love so well,
> I'd say then to the Crown,
> Take back your glittering town;
> My darling is more fair, I swear,
> My darling is more fair.   400

The rhyme's not rich, the style is rough and old,
But don't you see that it's the purest gold
Beside the tinsel nonsense now preferred,
And that there's passion in its every word?

> If the King had given me for my own   405
> Paris, his citadel,
> And I for that must leave alone
> Her whom I love so well,
> I'd say then to the Crown,
> Take back your glittering town;   410
> My darling is more fair, I swear,
> My darling is more fair.

There speaks a loving heart. (*To* PHILINTE) You're laughing, eh?
Laugh on, my precious wit. Whatever you say,
I hold that song's worth all the bibelots   415
That people hail today with ah's and oh's.
ORONTE.   And I maintain my sonnet's very good.
ALCESTE.   It's not at all surprising that you should.
You have your reasons; permit me to have mine
For thinking that you cannot write a line.   420
ORONTE.   Others have praised my sonnet to the skies.
ALCESTE.   I lack their art of telling pleasant lies.
ORONTE.   You seem to think you've got no end of wit.
ALCESTE.   To praise your verse, I'd need still more of it.
ORONTE.   I'm not in need of your approval, Sir.   425
ALCESTE.   That's good; you couldn't have it if you were.
ORONTE.   Come now, I'll lend you the subject of my sonnet;
I'd like to see you try to improve upon it.
ALCESTE.   I might, by chance, write something just as shoddy;
But then I wouldn't show it to everybody.   430
ORONTE.   You're most opinionated and conceited.
ALCESTE.   Go find your flatterers, and be better treated.
ORONTE.   Look here, my little fellow, pray watch your tone.
ALCESTE.   My great big fellow, you'd better watch your own.
PHILINTE (*stepping between them*).   Oh, please, please, gentlemen!
This will never do.   435
ORONTE.   The fault is mine, and I leave the field to you.
I am your servant, Sir, in every way.
ALCESTE.   And I, Sir, am your most abject valet. (*Exit* ORONTE.)

SCENE 3

PHILINTE.   Well, as you see, sincerity in excess
Can get you into a very pretty mess;   440
Oronte was hungry for appreciation . . .
ALCESTE.   Don't speak to me.
PHILINTE.   What?
ALCESTE.   No more conversation.
PHILINTE.   Really, now . . .
ALCESTE.   Leave me alone.
PHILINTE.   If I . . .
ALCESTE.   Out of my sight!
PHILINTE.   But what . . .
ALCESTE.   I won't listen.
PHILINTE.   But . . .
ALCESTE.   Silence!
PHILINTE.   Now, is it polite . . .

ALCESTE.   By heaven, I've had enough. Don't follow me.   445
PHILINTE.   Ah, you're just joking. I'll keep you company. (*Exeunt.*)

ACT 2

SCENE 1

Enter ALCESTE *and* CÉLIMÈNE.

ALCESTE.   Shall I speak plainly, Madam? I confess
    Your conduct gives me infinite distress,
    And my resentment's grown too hot to smother.
    Soon, I foresee, we'll break with one another.
    If I said otherwise, I should deceive you;   5
    Sooner or later, I shall be forced to leave you,
    And if I swore that we shall never part,
    I should misread the omens of my heart.
CÉLIMÈNE.   You kindly saw me home, it would appear,
    So as to pour invectives in my ear.   10
ALCESTE.   I've no desire to quarrel. But I deplore
    Your inability to shut the door
    On all these suitors who beset you so.
    There's what annoys me, if you care to know.
CÉLIMÈNE.   Is it my fault that all these men pursue me?   15
    Am I to blame if they're attracted to me?
    And when they gently beg an audience,
    Ought I to take a stick and drive them hence?
ALCESTE.   Madam, there's no necessity for a stick;
    A less responsive heart would do the trick.   20
    Of your attractiveness I don't complain;
    But those your charms attract, you then detain
    By a most melting and receptive manner,
    And so enlist their hearts beneath your banner.
    It's the agreeable hopes which you excite   25
    That keep these lovers round you day and night;
    Were they less liberally smiled upon,
    That sighing troop would very soon be gone.
    But tell me, Madam, why it is that lately
    This man Clitandre interests you so greatly?   30
    Because of what high merits do you deem
    Him worthy of the honor of your esteem?
    Is it that your admiring glances linger
    On the splendidly long nail of his little finger?
    Or do you share the general deep respect   35
    For the blond wig he chooses to affect?

Are you in love with his embroidered hose?
Do you adore his ribbons and his bows?
Or is it that this paragon bewitches
Your tasteful eye with his vast German breeches?   40
Perhaps his giggle, or his falsetto voice,
Makes him the latest gallant of your choice?
CÉLIMÈNE.   You're much mistaken to resent him so.
Why I put up with him you surely know:
My lawsuit's very shortly to be tried,   45
And I must have his influence on my side.
ALCESTE.   Then lose your lawsuit, Madam, or let it drop;
Don't torture me by humoring such a fop.
CÉLIMÈNE.   You're jealous of the whole world, Sir.
ALCESTE.   That's true,
Since the whole world is well-received by you.   50
CÉLIMÈNE.   That my good nature is so unconfined
Should serve to pacify your jealous mind;
Were I to smile on one, and scorn the rest,
Then you might have some cause to be distressed.
ALCESTE.   Well, if I mustn't be jealous, tell me, then,   55
Just how I'm better treated than other men.
CÉLIMÈNE.   You know you have my love. Will that not do?
ALCESTE.   What proof have I that what you say is true?
CÉLIMÈNE.   I would expect, Sir, that my having said it
Might give the statement a sufficient credit.   60
ALCESTE.   But how can I be sure that you don't tell
The selfsame thing to other men as well?
CÉLIMÈNE.   What a gallant speech! How flattering to me!
What a sweet creature you make me out to be!
Well then, to save you from the pangs of doubt,   65
All that I've said I hereby cancel out;
Now, none but yourself shall make a monkey of you:
Are you content?
ALCESTE.   Why, why am I doomed to love you?
I swear that I shall bless the blissful hour
When this poor heart's no longer in your power!   70
I make no secret of it: I've done my best
To exorcise this passion from my breast;
But thus far all in vain; it will not go;
It's for my sins that I must love you so.
CÉLIMÈNE.   Your love for me is matchless, Sir; that's clear. 75
ALCESTE.   Indeed, in all the world it has no peer;
Words can't describe the nature of my passion,
And no man ever loved in such a fashion.

CÉLIMÈNE.   Yes, it's a brand-new fashion, I agree:
  You show your love by castigating me,   80
  And all your speeches are enraged and rude.
  I've never been so furiously wooed.
ALCESTE.   Yet you could calm that fury, if you chose.
  Come, shall we bring our quarrels to a close?
  Let's speak with open hearts, then, and begin . . .   85

SCENE 2

Enter BASQUE.

CÉLIMÈNE.   What is it?
BASQUE.   Acaste is here.
CÉLIMÈNE.   Well, send him in. (*Exit* BASQUE.)

SCENE 3

ALCESTE.   What! Shall we never be alone at all?
  You're always ready to receive a call,
  And you can't bear, for ten ticks of the clock,
  Not to keep open house for all who knock.   90
CÉLIMÈNE.   I couldn't refuse him: he'd be most put out.
ALCESTE.   Surely that's not worth worrying about.
CÉLIMÈNE.   Acaste would never forgive me if he guessed
  That I consider him a dreadful pest.
ALCESTE.   If he's a pest, why bother with him then?   95
CÉLIMÈNE.   Heavens! One can't antagonize such men;
  Why, they're the chartered gossips of the court,
  And have a say in things of every sort.
  One must receive them, and be full of charm;
  They're no great help, but they can do you harm,   100
  And though your influence be ever so great,
  They're hardly the best people to alienate.
ALCESTE.   I see, dear lady, that you could make a case
  For putting up with the whole human race;
  These friendships that you calculate so nicely . . .   105

SCENE 4

Enter BASQUE.

BASQUE.   Madam, Clitandre is here as well.
ALCESTE.   Precisely.
CÉLIMÈNE.   Where are you going?
ALCESTE.   Elsewhere.

CÉLIMÈNE.   Stay.
ALCESTE.   No, no.
CÉLIMÈNE.   Stay, Sir.
ALCESTE.   I can't.
CÉLIMÈNE.   I wish it.
ALCESTE.   No, I must go.
   I beg you, Madam, not to press the matter;
   You know I have no taste for idle chatter.   110
CÉLIMÈNE.   Stay: I command you.
ALCESTE.   No, I cannot stay.
CÉLIMÈNE.   Very well; you have my leave to go away.

SCENE 5

Enter ELIANTE *and* PHILINTE.

ELIANTE (*to* CÉLIMÈNE).   The Marquesses have kindly come to call.
   Were they announced?
CÉLIMÈNE.   Yes. Basque, bring chairs for all.
   (BASQUE *provides the chairs, and exits. To* ALCESTE)
   You haven't gone?
ALCESTE.   No; and I shan't depart   115
   Till you decide who's foremost in your heart.
CÉLIMÈNE.   Oh, hush.
ALCESTE.   It's time to choose; take them or me.
CÉLIMÈNE.   You're mad.
ALCESTE.   I'm not, as you shall shortly see.
CÉLIMÈNE.   Oh?
ALCESTE.   You'll decide.
CÉLIMÈNE.   You're joking now, dear friend.
ALCESTE.   No, no; you'll choose; my patience is at an end.   120
   (*Enter* CLITANDRE *and* ACASTE.)
CLITANDRE.   Madam, I come from court, where poor Cléonte
   Behaved like a perfect fool, as is his wont.
   Has he no friend to counsel him, I wonder,
   And teach him less unerringly to blunder?
CÉLIMÈNE.   It's true, the man's a most accomplished dunce;   125
   His gauche behavior charms the eye at once;
   And every time one sees him, on my word,
   His manner's grown a trifle more absurd.
ACASTE.   Speaking of dunces, I've just now conversed
   With old Damon, who's one of the very worst;   130
   I stood a lifetime in the broiling sun
   Before his dreary monologue was done.
CÉLIMÈNE.   Oh, he's a wondrous talker, and has the power
   To tell you nothing hour after hour:

If, by mistake, he ever came to the point,   135
The shock would put his jawbone out of joint.
ELIANTE (*to* PHILINTE).   The conversation takes its usual turn,
And all our dear friends' ears will shortly burn.
CLITANDRE.   Timante's a character, Madam.
CÉLIMÈNE.   Isn't he, though?
A man of mystery from top to toe,   140
Who moves about in a romantic mist
On secret missions which do not exist.
His talk is full of eyebrows and grimaces;
How tired one gets of his momentous faces;
He's always whispering something confidential   145
Which turns out to be quite inconsequential;
Nothing's too slight for him to mystify;
He even whispers when he says "good-by."
ACASTE.   Tell us about Géralde.
CÉLIMÈNE.   That tiresome ass.
He mixes only with the titled class,   150
And fawns on dukes and princes, and is bored
With anyone who's not at least a lord.
The man's obsessed with rank, and his discourses
Are all of hounds and carriages and horses;
He uses Christian names with all the great,   155
And the word Milord, with him, is out of date.
CLITANDRE.   He's very taken with Bélise, I hear.
CÉLIMÈNE.   She is the dreariest company, poor dear.
Whenever she comes to call, I grope about
To find some topic which will draw her out,   160
But, owing to her dry and faint replies,
The conversation wilts, and droops, and dies.
In vain one hopes to animate her face
By mentioning the ultimate commonplace;
But sun or shower, even hail or frost   165
Are matters she can instantly exhaust.
Meanwhile her visit, painful though it is,
Drags on and on through mute eternities,
And though you ask the time, and yawn, and yawn,
She sits there like a stone and won't be gone.   170
ACASTE.   Now for Adraste.
CÉLIMÈNE.   Oh, that conceited elf
Has a gigantic passion for himself;
He rails against the court, and cannot bear it
That none will recognize his hidden merit;
All honors given to others give offense   175
To his imaginary excellence.

CLITANDRE.   What about young Cléon? His house, they say,
   Is full of the best society, night and day.
CÉLIMÈNE.   His cook has made him popular, not he:
   It's Cléon's table that people come to see.   180
ELIANTE.   He gives a splendid dinner, you must admit.
CÉLIMÈNE.   But must he serve himself along with it?
   For my taste, he's a most insipid dish
   Whose presence sours the wine and spoils the fish.
PHILINTE.   Damis, his uncle, is admired no end.   185
   What's your opinion, Madam?
CÉLIMÈNE.   Why, he's my friend.
PHILINTE.   He seems a decent fellow, and rather clever.
CÉLIMÈNE.   He works too hard at cleverness, however.
   I hate to see him sweat and struggle so
   To fill his conversation with bons mots.   190
   Since he's decided to become a wit
   His taste's so pure that nothing pleases it;
   He scolds at all the latest books and plays,
   Thinking that wit must never stoop to praise,
   That finding fault's a sign of intellect,   195
   That all appreciation is abject,
   And that by damning everything in sight
   One shows oneself in a distinguished light.
   He's scornful even of our conversations:
   Their trivial nature sorely tries his patience;   200
   He folds his arms, and stands above the battle,
   And listens sadly to our childish prattle.
ACASTE.   Wonderful, Madam! You've hit him off precisely.
CLITANDRE.   No one can sketch a character so nicely.
ALCESTE.   How bravely, Sirs, you cut and thrust at all   205
   These absent fools, till one by one they fall:
   But let one come in sight, and you'll at once
   Embrace the man you lately called a dunce,
   Telling him in a tone sincere and fervent
   How proud you are to be his humble servant.   210
CLITANDRE.   Why pick on us? Madame's been speaking, Sir,
   And you should quarrel, if you must, with her.
ALCESTE.   No, no, by God, the fault is yours, because
   You lead her on with laughter and applause,
   And make her think that she's the more delightful   215
   The more her talk is scandalous and spiteful.
   Oh, she would stoop to malice far, far less
   If no such claque approved her cleverness.
   It's flatterers like you whose foolish praise
   Nourishes all the vices of these days.   220

PHILINTE.   But why protest when someone ridicules
    Those you'd condemn, yourself, as knaves or fools?
CÉLIMÈNE.   Why, Sir? Because he loves to make a fuss.
    You don't expect him to agree with us,
    When there's an opportunity to express   225
    His heaven-sent spirit of contrariness?
    What other people think, he can't abide;
    Whatever they say, he's on the other side;
    He lives in deadly terror of agreeing;
    'Twould make him seem an ordinary being.   230
    Indeed, he's so in love with contradiction,
    He'll turn against his most profound conviction
    And with a furious eloquence deplore it,
    If only someone else is speaking for it.
ALCESTE.   Go on, dear lady, mock me as you please;   235
    You have your audience in ecstasies.
PHILINTE.   But what she says is true: you have a way
    Of bridling at whatever people say;
    Whether they praise or blame, your angry spirit
    Is equally unsatisfied to hear it.   240
ALCESTE.   Men, Sir, are always wrong, and that's the reason
    That righteous anger's never out of season;
    All that I hear in all their conversation
    Is flattering praise or reckless condemnation.
CÉLIMÈNE.   But . . .
ALCESTE.   No, no, Madam, I am forced to state   245
    That you have pleasures which I deprecate,
    And that these others, here, are much to blame
    For nourishing the faults which are your shame.
CLITANDRE.   I shan't defend myself, Sir; but I vow
    I'd thought this lady faultless until now.   250
ACASTE.   I see her charms and graces, which are many;
    But as for faults, I've never noticed any.
ALCESTE.   I see them, Sir; and rather than ignore them,
    I strenuously criticize her for them.
    The more one loves, the more one should object   255
    To every blemish, every least defect.
    Were I this lady, I would soon get rid
    Of lovers who approved of all I did,
    And by their slack indulgence and applause
    Endorsed my follies and excused my flaws.   260
CÉLIMÈNE.   If all hearts beat according to your measure,
    The dawn of love would be the end of pleasure;
    And love would find its perfect consummation
    In ecstasies of rage and reprobation.

ELIANTE.   Love, as a rule, affects men otherwise,   265
 And lovers rarely love to criticize.
 They see their lady as a charming blur,
 And find all things commendable in her.
 If she has any blemish, fault, or shame,
 They will redeem it by a pleasing name.   270
 The pale-faced lady's lily-white, perforce;
 The swarthy one's a sweet brunette, of course;
 The spindly lady has a slender grace;
 The fat one has a most majestic pace;
 The plain one, with her dress in disarray,   275
 They classify as *beauté négligée;*°
 The hulking one's a goddess in their eyes,
 The dwarf, a concentrate of Paradise;
 The haughty lady has a noble mind;
 The mean one's witty, and the dull one's kind;   280
 The chatterbox has liveliness and verve,
 The mute one has a virtuous reserve.
 So lovers manage, in their passion's cause,
 To love their ladies even for their flaws.
ALCESTE.   But I still say . . .
CÉLIMÈNE.   I think it would be nice   285
 To stroll around the gallery once or twice.
 What! You're not going, Sirs?
CLITANDRE *and* ACASTE.   No, Madam, no.
ALCESTE.   You seem to be in terror lest they go.
 Do what you will, Sirs; leave, or linger on,
 But I shan't go till after you are gone.   290
ACASTE.   I'm free to linger, unless I should perceive
 Madame is tired, and wishes me to leave.
CLITANDRE.   And as for me, I needn't go today
 Until the hour of the King's *coucher.*°
CÉLIMÈNE (*to* ALCESTE).   You're joking, surely?
ALCESTE.   Not in the least; we'll see
 Whether you'd rather part with them, or me.   296

SCENE 6

Enter BASQUE.

BASQUE (*to* ALCESTE).   Sir, there's a fellow here who bids me state
 That he must see you, and that it can't wait.
ALCESTE.   Tell him that I have no such pressing affairs.

---

276. *beauté négligée:* careless beauty   **294. *coucher:*** bedtime (the King's going-
to-bed was a ceremonial occasion)

BASQUE.   It's a long tailcoat that this fellow wears,   300
 With gold all over.
CÉLIMÈNE (*to* ALCESTE).   You'd best go down and see.
 Or—have him enter. (*Exit* BASQUE.)

SCENE 7

 Enter GUARD.

ALCESTE (*confronting the guard*).   Well, what do you want with me?
 Come in, Sir.
GUARD.   I've a word, Sir, for your ear.
ALCESTE.   Speak it aloud, Sir; I shall strive to hear.
GUARD.   The Marshals have instructed me to say   305
 You must report to them without delay.
ALCESTE.   Who? Me, Sir?
GUARD.   Yes, Sir; you.
ALCESTE.   But what do they want?
PHILINTE (*to* ALCESTE).   To scotch your silly quarrel with Oronte.
CÉLIMÈNE (*to* PHILINTE).   What quarrel?
PHILINTE.   Oronte and he have fallen out
 Over some verse he spoke his mind about;   310
 The Marshals wish to arbitrate the matter.
ALCESTE.   Never shall I equivocate or flatter!
PHILINTE.   You'd best obey their summons; come, let's go.
ALCESTE.   How can they mend our quarrel, I'd like to know?
 Am I to make a cowardly retraction,   315
 And praise those jingles to his satisfaction?
 I'll not recant; I've judged that sonnet rightly.
 It's bad.
PHILINTE.   But you might say so more politely. . . .
ALCESTE.   I'll not back down; his verses make me sick.
PHILINTE.   If only you could be more politic!   320
 But come, let's go.
ALCESTE.   I'll go, but I won't unsay
 A single word.
PHILINTE.   Well, let's be on our way.
ALCESTE.   Till I am ordered by my lord the King
 To praise that poem, I shall say the thing
 Is scandalous, by God, and that the poet   325
 Ought to be hanged for having the nerve to show it.
 (*To* CLITANDRE *and* ACASTE, *who are laughing*)
 By heaven, Sirs, I really didn't know
 That I was being humorous.
CÉLIMÈNE.   Go, Sir, go;
 Settle your business.

ALCESTE.   I shall, and when I'm through,
  I shall return to settle things with you. (*Exeunt.*)   330

ACT 3

SCENE 1

  Enter CLITANDRE *and* ACASTE.

CLITANDRE.   Dear Marquess, how contented you appear;
  All things delight you, nothing mars your cheer.
  Can you, in perfect honesty, declare
  That you've a right to be so debonair?
ACASTE.   By Jove, when I survey myself, I find   5
  No cause whatever for distress of mind.
  I'm young and rich; I can in modesty
  Lay claim to an exalted pedigree;
  And owing to my name and my condition
  I shall not want for honors and position.   10
  Then as to courage, that most precious trait,
  I seem to have it, as was proved of late
  Upon the field of honor, where my bearing,
  They say, was very cool and rather daring.
  I've wit, of course; and taste in such perfection   15
  That I can judge without the least reflection,
  And at the theater, which is my delight,
  Can make or break a play on opening night,
  And lead the crowd in hisses or bravos,
  And generally be known as one who knows.   20
  I'm clever, handsome, gracefully polite;
  My waist is small, my teeth are strong and white;
  As for my dress, the world's astonished eyes
  Assure me that I bear away the prize.
  I find myself in favor everywhere,   25
  Honored by men, and worshiped by the fair;
  And since these things are so, it seems to me
  I'm justified in my complacency.
CLITANDRE.   Well, if so many ladies hold you dear,
  Why do you press a hopeless courtship here?   30
ACASTE.   Hopeless, you say? I'm not the sort of fool
  That likes his ladies difficult and cool.
  Men who are awkward, shy, and peasantish
  May pine for heartless beauties, if they wish,
  Grovel before them, bear their cruelties,   35
  Woo them with tears and sighs and bended knees,
  And hope by dogged faithfulness to gain

What their poor merits never could obtain.
For men like me, however, it makes no sense
To love on trust, and foot the whole expense.   40
Whatever any lady's merits be,
I think, thank God, that I'm as choice as she;
That if my heart is kind enough to burn
For her, she owes me something in return;
And that in any proper love affair   45
The partners must invest an equal share.

CLITANDRE.   You think, then, that our hostess favors you?
ACASTE.   I've reason to believe that that is true.
CLITANDRE.   How did you come to such a mad conclusion?
You're blind, dear fellow. This is sheer delusion.   50
ACASTE.   All right, then: I'm deluded and I'm blind.
CLITANDRE.   Whatever put the notion in your mind?
ACASTE.   Delusion.
CLITANDRE.   What persuades you that you're right?
ACASTE.   I'm blind.
CLITANDRE.   But have you any proofs to cite?
ACASTE.   I tell you I'm deluded.
CLITANDRE.   Have you, then,   55
Received some secret pledge from Célimène?
ACASTE.   Oh, no: she scorns me.
CLITANDRE.   Tell me the truth, I beg.
ACASTE.   She just can't bear me.
CLITANDRE.   Ah, don't pull my leg.
Tell me what hope she's given you, I pray.
ACASTE.   I'm hopeless, and it's you who win the day.   60
She hates me thoroughly, and I'm so vexed
I mean to hang myself on Tuesday next.
CLITANDRE.   Dear Marquess, let us have an armistice
And make a treaty. What do you say to this?
If ever one of us can plainly prove   65
That Célimène encourages his love,
The other must abandon hope, and yield,
And leave him in possession of the field.
ACASTE.   Now, there's a bargain that appeals to me;
With all my heart, dear Marquess, I agree.   70
But hush.

SCENE 2

Enter CÉLIMÈNE.

CÉLIMÈNE.   Still here?

CLITANDRE.   'Twas love that stayed our feet.
CÉLIMÈNE.   I think I heard a carriage in the street.
   Whose is it? D'you know?

SCENE 3

   Enter BASQUE.

BASQUE.   Arsinoé is here,
   Madame.
CÉLIMÈNE.   Arsinoé, you say? Oh, dear.
BASQUE.   Eliante is entertaining her below.   75
CÉLIMÈNE.   What brings the creature here, I'd like to know?
ACASTE.   They say she's dreadfully prudish, but in fact
   I think her piety . . .
CÉLIMÈNE.   It's all an act.
   At heart she's worldly, and her poor success
   In snaring men explains her prudishness.   80
   It breaks her heart to see the beaux and gallants
   Engrossed by other women's charms and talents,
   And so she's always in a jealous rage
   Against the faulty standards of the age.
   She lets the world believe that she's a prude   85
   To justify her loveless solitude,
   And strives to put a brand of moral shame
   On all the graces that she cannot claim.
   But still she'd love a lover; and Alceste
   Appears to be the one she'd love the best.   90
   His visits here are poison to her pride;
   She seems to think I've lured him from her side;
   And everywhere, at court or in the town,
   The spiteful, envious woman runs me down.
   In short, she's just as stupid as can be,   95
   Vicious and arrogant in the last degree,
   And . . .

SCENE 4

   Enter ARSINOÉ.

CÉLIMÈNE.   Ah! What happy chance has brought you here?
   I've thought about you ever so much, my dear.
ARSINOÉ.   I've come to tell you something you should know.
CÉLIMÈNE.   How good of you to think of doing so!   100
   (CLITANDRE *and* ACASTE *go out, laughing.*)

SCENE 5

ARSINOÉ.   It's just as well those gentlemen didn't tarry.
CÉLIMÈNE.   Shall we sit down?
ARSINOÉ.   That won't be necessary.
 Madam, the flame of friendship ought to burn
 Brightest in matters of the most concern,
 And as there's nothing which concerns us more   105
 Than honor, I have hastened to your door
 To bring you, as your friend, some information
 About the status of your reputation.
 I visited, last night, some virtuous folk,
 And, quite by chance, it was of you they spoke;   110
 There was, I fear, no tendency to praise
 Your light behavior and your dashing ways.
 The quantity of gentlemen you see
 And your by now notorious coquetry
 Were both so vehemently criticized   115
 By everyone, that I was much surprised.
 Of course, I needn't tell you where I stood;
 I came to your defense as best I could,
 Assured them you were harmless, and declared
 Your soul was absolutely unimpaired.   120
 But there are some things, you must realize,
 One can't excuse, however hard one tries,
 And I was forced at last into conceding
 That your behavior, Madam, is misleading,
 That it makes a bad impression, giving rise   125
 To ugly gossip and obscene surmise,
 And that if you were more *overtly* good,
 You wouldn't be so much misunderstood.
 Not that I think you've been unchaste—no! no!
 The saints preserve me from a thought so low!   130
 But mere good conscience never did suffice:
 One must avoid the outward show of vice.
 Madam, you're too intelligent, I'm sure,
 To think my motives anything but pure
 In offering you this counsel—which I do   135
 Out of a zealous interest in you.
CÉLIMÈNE.   Madam, I haven't taken you amiss;
 I'm very much obliged to you for this;
 And I'll at once discharge the obligation
 By telling you about *your* reputation.   140
 You've been so friendly as to let me know
 What certain people say of me, and so

I mean to follow your benign example
By offering you a somewhat similar sample.
The other day, I went to an affair   145
And I found some most distinguished people there
Discussing piety, both false and true.
The conversation soon came round to you.
Alas! Your prudery and bustling zeal
Appeared to have a very slight appeal.   150
Your affectation of a grave demeanor,
Your endless talk of virtue and of honor,
The aptitude of your suspicious mind
For finding sin where there is none to find,
Your towering self-esteem, that pitying face   155
With which you contemplate the human race,
Your sermonizings and your sharp aspersions
On people's pure and innocent diversions—
All these were mentioned, Madam, and, in fact,
Were roundly and concertedly attacked.   160
"What good," they said, "are all these outward shows,
When everything belies her pious pose?
She prays incessantly; but then, they say,
She beats her maids and cheats them of their pay;
She shows her zeal in every holy place,   165
But still she's vain enough to paint her face;
She holds that naked statues are immoral,
But with a naked *man* she'd have no quarrel."
Of course, I said to everybody there
That they were being viciously unfair;   170
But still they were disposed to criticize you,
And all agreed that someone should advise you
To leave the morals of the world alone,
And worry rather more about your own.
They felt that one's self-knowledge should be great   175
Before one thinks of setting others straight;
That one should learn the art of living well
Before one threatens other men with hell,
And that the Church is best equipped, no doubt,
To guide our souls and root our vices out.   180
Madam, you're too intelligent, I'm sure,
To think my motives anything but pure
In offering you this counsel—which I do
Out of a zealous interest in you.
ARSINOÉ.   I dared not hope for gratitude, but I   185
Did not expect so acid a reply;
I judge, since you've been so extremely tart,

That my good counsel pierced you to the heart.
CÉLIMÈNE.   Far from it, Madam. Indeed, it seems to me
    We ought to trade advice more frequently.   190
    One's vision of oneself is so defective
    That it would be an excellent corrective.
    If you are willing, Madam, let's arrange
    Shortly to have another frank exchange
    In which we'll tell each other, *entre nous,*°   195
    What you've heard tell of me, and I of you.
ARSINOÉ.   Oh, people never censure you, my dear;
    It's me they criticize. Or so I hear.
CÉLIMÈNE.   Madam, I think we either blame or praise
    According to our taste and length of days.   200
    There is a time of life for coquetry,
    And there's a season, too, for prudery.
    When all one's charms are gone, it is, I'm sure,
    Good strategy to be devout and pure:
    It makes one seem a little less forsaken.   205
    Some day, perhaps, I'll take the road you've taken:
    Time brings all things. But I have time aplenty,
    And see no cause to be a prude at twenty.
ARSINOÉ.   You give your age in such a gloating tone
    That one would think I was an ancient crone;   210
    We're not so far apart, in sober truth,
    That you can mock me with a boast of youth!
    Madam, you baffle me. I wish I knew
    What moves you to provoke me as you do.
CÉLIMÈNE.   For my part, Madam, I should like to know   215
    Why you abuse me everywhere you go.
    Is it my fault, dear lady, that your hand
    Is not, alas, in very great demand?
    If men admire me, if they pay me court
    And daily make me offers of the sort   220
    You'd dearly love to have them make to you,
    How can I help it? What would you have me do?
    If what you want is lovers, please feel free
    To take as many as you can from me.
ARSINOÉ.   Oh, come. D'you think the world is losing sleep   225
    Over that flock of lovers which you keep,
    Or that we find it difficult to guess
    What price you pay for their devotedness?
    Surely you don't expect us to suppose
    Mere merit could attract so many beaux?   230

---

195. *entre nous:* between ourselves

It's not your virtue that they're dazzled by;
Nor is it virtuous love for which they sigh.
You're fooling no one, Madam; the world's not blind;
There's many a lady heaven has designed
To call men's noblest, tenderest feelings out,   235
Who has no lovers dogging her about;
From which it's plain that lovers nowadays
Must be acquired in bold and shameless ways,
And only pay one court for such reward
As modesty and virtue can't afford.   240
Then don't be quite so puffed up, if you please,
About your tawdry little victories;
Try, if you can, to be a shade less vain,
And treat the world with somewhat less disdain.
If one were envious of your amours,   245
One soon could have a following like yours;
Lovers are no great trouble to collect
If one prefers them to one's self-respect.
CÉLIMÈNE.   Collect them then, my dear; I'd love to see
You demonstrate that charming theory;   250
Who knows, you might . . .
ARSINOÉ.   Now, Madam, that will do;
It's time to end this trying interview.
My coach is late in coming to your door,
Or I'd have taken leave of you before.
CÉLIMÈNE.   Oh, please don't feel that you must rush away;   255
I'd be delighted, Madam, if you'd stay.
However, lest my conversation bore you,
Let me provide some better company for you;
This gentleman, who comes most apropos,
Will please you more than I could do, I know.   260

SCENE 6

Enter ALCESTE.

CÉLIMÈNE.   Alceste, I have a little note to write
Which simply must go out before tonight;
Please entertain *Madame;* I'm sure that she
Will overlook my incivility. (*Exit.*)

SCENE 7

ARSINOÉ.   Well, Sir, our hostess graciously contrives   265
For us to chat until my coach arrives;
And I shall be forever in her debt

For granting me this little tête-á-tête.
We women very rightly give our hearts
To men of noble character and parts,   270
And your especial merits, dear Alceste,
Have roused the deepest sympathy in my breast.
Oh, how I wish they had sufficient sense
At court, to recognize your excellence!
They wrong you greatly, Sir. How it must hurt you   275
Never to be rewarded for your virtue!
ALCESTE.   Why, Madam, what cause have I to feel aggrieved?
What great and brilliant thing have I achieved?
What service have I rendered to the King
That I should look to him for anything?   280
ARSINOÉ.   Not everyone who's honored by the State
Has done great services. A man must wait
Till time and fortune offer him the chance.
Your merit, Sir, is obvious at a glance,
And . . .
ALCESTE.   Ah, forget my merit; I'm not neglected.   285
The court, I think, can hardly be expected
To mine men's souls for merit, and unearth
Our hidden virtues and our secret worth.
ARSINOÉ.   *Some* virtues, though, are far too bright to hide;
Yours are acknowledged, Sir, on every side.   290
Indeed, I've heard you warmly praised of late
By persons of considerable weight.
ALCESTE.   This fawning age has praise for everyone,
And all distinctions, Madam, are undone.
All things have equal honor nowadays,   295
And no one should be gratified by praise.
To be admired, one only need exist,
And every lackey's on the honors list.
ARSINOÉ.   I only wish, Sir, that you had your eye
On some position at court, however high;   300
You'd only have to hint at such a notion
For me to set the proper wheels in motion;
I've certain friendships I'd be glad to use
To get you any office you might choose.
ALCESTE.   Madam, I fear that any such ambition   305
Is wholly foreign to my disposition.
The soul God gave me isn't of the sort
That prospers in the weather of a court.
It's all too obvious that I don't possess
The virtues necessary for success.   310
My one great talent is for speaking plain;

I've never learned to flatter or to feign;
And anyone so stupidly sincere
Had best not seek a courtier's career.
Outside the court, I know, one must dispense   315
With honors, privilege, and influence;
But still one gains the right, foregoing these,
Not to be tortured by the wish to please.
One needn't live in dread of snubs and slights,
Nor praise the verse that every idiot writes,   320
Nor humor silly Marquesses, nor bestow
Politic sighs on Madam So-and-so.
ARSINOÉ.   Forget the court, then; let the matter rest.
But I've another cause to be distressed
About your present situation, Sir.   325
It's to your love affair that I refer.
She whom you love, and who pretends to love you,
Is, I regret to say, unworthy of you.
ALCESTE.   Why, Madam! Can you seriously intend
To make so grave a charge against your friend?   330
ARSINOÉ.   Alas, I must. I've stood aside too long
And let that lady do you grievous wrong;
But now my debt to conscience shall be paid:
I tell you that your love has been betrayed.
ALCESTE.   I thank you, Madam; you're extremely kind. 335
Such words are soothing to a lover's mind.
ARSINOÉ.   Yes, though she *is* my friend, I say again
You're very much too good for Célimène.
She's wantonly misled you from the start.
ALCESTE.   You may be right; who knows another's heart? 340
But ask yourself if it's the part of charity
To shake my soul with doubts of her sincerity.
ARSINOÉ.   Well, if you'd rather be a dupe than doubt her,
That's your affair. I'll say no more about her.
ALCESTE.   Madam, you know that doubt and vague suspicion 345
Are painful to a man in my position;
It's most unkind to worry me this way
Unless you've some real proof of what you say.
ARSINOÉ.   Sir, say no more: all doubt shall be removed,
And all that I've been saying shall be proved.   350
You've only to escort me home, and there
We'll look into the heart of this affair.
I've ocular evidence which will persuade you
Beyond a doubt, that Célimène's betrayed you.
Then, if you're saddened by that revelation,   355
Perhaps I can provide some consolation. (*Exeunt.*)

ACT 4

SCENE 1

Enter PHILINTE *and* ELIANTE.

PHILINTE. Madam, he acted like a stubborn child;
　　I thought they never would be reconciled;
　　In vain we reasoned, threatened, and appealed;
　　He stood his ground and simply would not yield.
　　The Marshals, I feel sure, have never heard　　　　　5
　　An argument so splendidly absurd.
　　"No, gentlemen," said he, "I'll not retract.
　　His verse is bad: extremely bad, in fact.
　　Surely it does the man no harm to know it.
　　Does it disgrace him, not to be a poet?　　　　　10
　　A gentleman may be respected still,
　　Whether he writes a sonnet well or ill.
　　That I dislike his verse should not offend him;
　　In all that touches honor, I commend him;
　　He's noble, brave, and virtuous—but I fear　　　　　15
　　He can't in truth be called a sonneteer.
　　I'll gladly praise his wardrobe; I'll endorse
　　His dancing, or the way he sits a horse;
　　But, gentlemen, I cannot praise his rhyme.
　　In fact, it ought to be a capital crime　　　　　20
　　For anyone so sadly unendowed
　　To write a sonnet, and read the thing aloud."
　　At length he fell into a gentler mood
　　And, striking a concessive attitude,
　　He paid Oronte the following courtesies:　　　　　25
　　"Sir, I regret that I'm so hard to please,
　　And I'm profoundly sorry that your lyric
　　Failed to provoke me to a panegyric."
　　After these curious words, the two embraced,
　　And then the hearing was adjourned—in haste.　　　　　30
ELIANTE. His conduct has been very singular lately;
　　Still, I confess that I respect him greatly.
　　The honesty in which he takes such pride
　　Has—to my mind—its noble, heroic side.
　　In this false age, such candor seems outrageous;　　　　　35
　　But I could wish that it were more contagious.
PHILINTE. What most intrigues me in our friend Alceste
　　Is the grand passion that rages in his breast.
　　The sullen humors he's compounded of
　　Should not, I think, dispose his heart to love;　　　　　40

But since they do, it puzzles me still more
That he should choose your cousin to adore.
ELIANTE.   It does, indeed, belie the theory
    That love is born of gentle sympathy,
    And that the tender passion must be based   45
    On sweet accords of temper and of taste.
PHILINTE.   Does she return his love, do you suppose?
ELIANTE.   Ah, that's a difficult question, Sir. Who knows?
    How can we judge the truth of her devotion?
    Her heart's a stranger to its own emotion.   50
    Sometimes it thinks it loves, when no love's there;
    At other times it loves quite unaware.
PHILINTE.   I rather thank Alceste is in for more
    Distress and sorrow than he's bargained for;
    Were he of my mind, Madam, his affection   55
    Would turn in quite a different direction,
    And we would see him more responsive to
    The kind regard which he receives from you.
ELIANTE.   Sir, I believe in frankness, and I'm inclined,
    In matters of the heart, to speak my mind.   60
    I don't oppose his love for her; indeed,
    I hope with all my heart that he'll succeed,
    And were it in my power, I'd rejoice
    In giving him the lady of his choice.
    But if, as happens frequently enough   65
    In love affairs, he meets with a rebuff—
    If Célimène should grant some rival's suit—
    I'd gladly play the role of substitute;
    Nor would his tender speeches please me less
    Because they'd once been made without success.   70
PHILINTE.   Well, Madam, as for me, I don't oppose
    Your hopes in this affair; and heaven knows
    That in my conversations with the man
    I plead your cause as often as I can.
    But if those two should marry, and so remove   75
    All chance that he will offer you his love,
    Then I'll declare my own, and hope to see
    Your gracious favor pass from him to me.
    In short, should you be cheated of Alceste,
    I'd be most happy to be second best.   80
ELIANTE.   Philinte, you're teasing.
PHILINTE.   Ah, Madam, never fear;
    No words of mine were ever so sincere,
    And I shall live in fretful expectation
    Till I can make a fuller declaration.

SCENE 2

Enter ALCESTE.

ALCESTE.   Avenge me, Madam! I must have satisfaction,   85
    Or this great wrong will drive me to distraction!
ELIANTE.   Why, what's the matter? What's upset you so?
ALCESTE.   Madam, I've had a mortal, mortal blow.
    If Chaos repossessed the universe,
    I swear I'd not be shaken any worse.   90
    I'm ruined . . . I can say no more . . . My soul . . .
ELIANTE.   Do try, Sir, to regain your self-control.
ALCESTE.   Just heaven! Why were so much beauty and grace
    Bestowed on one so vicious and so base?
ELIANTE.   Once more, Sir, tell us . . .
ALCESTE.   My world has gone to wrack;   95
    I'm— I'm betrayed; she's stabbed me in the back:
    Yes, Célimène (who would have thought it of her?)
    Is false to me, and has another lover.
ELIANTE.   Are you quite certain? Can you prove these things?
PHILINTE.   Lovers are prey to wild imaginings   100
    And jealous fancies. No doubt there's some mistake . . .
ALCESTE.   Mind your own business, Sir, for heaven's sake.
    (*To* ELIANTE) Madam, I have the proof that you demand
    Here in my pocket, penned by her own hand.
    Yes, all the shameful evidence one could want   105
    Lies in this letter written to Oronte—
    Oronte! whom I felt sure she couldn't love,
    And hardly bothered to be jealous of.
PHILINTE.   Still, in a letter, appearances may deceive;
    This may not be so bad as you believe.   110
ALCESTE.   Once more I beg you, Sir, to let me be;
    Tend to your own affairs; leave mine to me.
ELIANTE.   Compose yourself; this anguish that you feel . . .
ALCESTE.   Is something, Madam, you alone can heal.
    My outraged heart, beside itself with grief,   115
    Appeals to you for comfort and relief.
    Avenge me on your cousin, whose unjust
    And faithless nature has deceived my trust;
    Avenge a crime your pure soul must detest.
ELIANTE.   But how, Sir?
ALCESTE.   Madam, this heart within my breast   120
    Is yours; pray take it; redeem my heart from her,
    And so avenge me on my torturer.
    Let her be punished by the fond emotion,
    The ardent love, the bottomless devotion,

The faithful worship which this heart of mine   125
Will offer up to yours as to a shrine.
ELIANTE.   You have my sympathy, Sir, in all you suffer;
Nor do I scorn the noble heart you offer;
But I suspect you'll soon be mollified,
And this desire for vengeance will subside.   130
When some beloved hand has done us wrong
We thirst for retribution—but not for long;
However dark the deed that she's committed,
A lovely culprit's very soon acquitted.
Nothing's so stormy as an injured lover,   135
And yet no storm so quickly passes over.
ALCESTE.   No, Madam, no—this is no lovers' spat;
I'll not forgive her; it's gone too far for that;
My mind's made up; I'll kill myself before
I waste my hopes upon her any more.   140
Ah, here she is. My wrath intensifies.
I shall confront her with her tricks and lies,
And crush her utterly, and bring you then
A heart no longer slave to Célimène.

SCENE 3

Enter CÉLIMÈNE.

ALCESTE (*aside*).   Sweet heaven, help me to control my passion.   145
CÉLIMÈNE (*aside, to* ALCESTE).   Oh, Lord. Why stand there staring in that
    fashion?
And what d'you mean by those dramatic sighs,
And that malignant glitter in your eyes?
ALCESTE.   I mean that sins which cause the blood to freeze
Look innocent beside your treacheries;   150
That nothing Hell's or Heaven's wrath could do
Ever produced so bad a thing as you.
CÉLIMÈNE.   Your compliments were always sweet and pretty.
ALCESTE.   Madam, it's not the moment to be witty.
No, blush and hang your head; you've ample reason,   155
Since I've the fullest evidence of your treason.
Ah, this is what my sad heart prophesied;
Now all my anxious fears are verified;
My dark suspicion and my gloomy doubt
Divined the truth, and now the truth is out.   160
For all your trickery, I was not deceived;
It was my bitter stars that I believed.
But don't imagine that you'll go scot-free;
You shan't misuse me with impunity.

I know that love's irrational and blind;   165
I know the heart's not subject to the mind,
And can't be reasoned into beating faster;
I know each soul is free to choose its master;
Therefore had you but spoken from the heart,
Rejecting my attentions from the start,   170
I'd have no grievance, or at any rate
I could complain of nothing but my fate.
Ah, but so falsely to encourage me—
That was a treason and a treachery
For which you cannot suffer too severely,   175
And you shall pay for that behavior dearly.
Yes, now I have no pity, not a shred;
My temper's out of hand; I've lost my head;
Shocked by the knowledge of your double-dealings,
My reason can't restrain my savage feelings;   180
A righteous wrath deprives me of my senses,
And I won't answer for the consequences.
CÉLIMÈNE.   What does this outburst mean? Will you please explain?
      Have you, by any chance, gone quite insane?
ALCESTE.   Yes, yes, I went insane the day I fell   185
      A victim to your black and fatal spell,
      Thinking to meet with some sincerity
      Among the treacherous charms that beckoned me.
CÉLIMÈNE.   Pooh. Of what treachery can you complain?
ALCESTE.   How sly you are, how cleverly you feign!   190
      But you'll not victimize me any more.
      Look: here's a document you've seen before.
      This evidence, which I acquired today,
      Leaves you, I think, without a thing to say.
CÉLIMÈNE.   Is this what sent you into such a fit?   195
ALCESTE.   You should be blushing at the sight of it.
CÉLIMÈNE.   Ought I to blush? I truly don't see why.
ALCESTE.   Ah, now you're being bold as well as sly;
      Since there's no signature, perhaps you'll claim . . .
CÉLIMÈNE.   I wrote it, whether or not it bears my name.   200
ALCESTE.   And you can view with equanimity
      This proof of your disloyalty to me!
CÉLIMÈNE.   Oh, don't be so outrageous and extreme.
ALCESTE.   You take this matter lightly, it would seem.
      Was it no wrong to me, no shame to you,   205
      That you should send Oronte this billet-doux?
CÉLIMÈNE.   Oronte! Who said it was for him?
ALCESTE.   Why, those
      Who brought me this example of your prose.

But what's the difference? If you wrote the letter
To someone else, it pleases me no better.   210
My grievance and your guilt remain the same.
CÉLIMÈNE.   But need you rage, and need I blush for shame,
   If this was written to a *woman* friend?
ALCESTE.   Ah! Most ingenious. I'm impressed no end;
   And after that incredible evasion   215
   Your guilt is clear. I need no more persuasion.
   How dare you try so clumsy a deception?
   D'you think I'm wholly wanting in perception?
   Come, come, let's see how brazenly you'll try
   To bolster up so palpable a lie: 220
   Kindly construe this ardent closing section
   As nothing more than sisterly affection!
   Here, let me read it. Tell me, if you dare to,
   That this is for a woman . . .
CÉLIMÈNE.   I don't care to.
   What right have you to badger and berate me,   225
   And so highhandedly interrogate me?
ALCESTE.   Now, don't be angry; all I ask of you
   Is that you justify a phrase or two . . .
CÉLIMÈNE.   No, I shall not. I utterly refuse,
   And you may take those phrases as you choose.   230
ALCESTE.   Just show me how this letter could be meant
   For a woman's eyes, and I shall be content.
CÉLIMÈNE.   No, no, it's for Oronte; you're perfectly right.
   I welcome his attentions with delight,
   I prize his character and his intellect,   235
   And everything is just as you suspect.
   Come, do your worst now; give your rage free rein;
   But kindly cease to bicker and complain.
ALCESTE (*aside*).   Good God! Could anything be more inhuman?
   Was ever a heart so mangled by a woman?   240
   When I complain of how she has betrayed me,
   She bridles, and commences to upbraid me!
   She tries my tortured patience to the limit;
   She won't deny her guilt; she glories in it!
   And yet my heart's too faint and cowardly   245
   To break these chains of passion, and be free,
   To scorn her as it should, and rise above
   This unrewarded, mad, and bitter love.
   (*To* CÉLIMÈNE) Ah, traitress, in how confident a fashion
   You take advantage of my helpless passion,   250
   And use my weakness for your faithless charms
   To make me once again throw down my arms!

But do at least deny this black transgression;
Take back that mocking and perverse confession;
Defend this letter and your·innocence,   255
And I, poor fool, will aid in your defense.
Pretend, pretend, that you are just and true,
And I shall make myself believe in you.

CÉLIMÈNE.   Oh, stop it. Don't be such a jealous dunce,
Or I shall leave off loving you at once.   260
Just why should I *pretend?* What could impel me
To stoop so low as that? And kindly tell me
Why, if I loved another, I shouldn't merely
Inform you of it, simply and sincerely!
I've told you where you stand, and that admission   265
Should altogether clear me of suspicion;
After so generous a guarantee,
What right have you to harbor doubts of me?
Since women are (from natural reticence)
Reluctant to declare their sentiments,   270
And since the honor of our sex requires
That we conceal our amorous desires,
Ought any man for whom such laws are broken
To question what the oracle has spoken?
Should he not rather feel an obligation   275
To trust that most obliging declaration?
Enough, now. Your suspicions quite disgust me;
Why should I love a man who doesn't trust me?
I cannot understand why I continue,
Fool that I am, to take an interest in you.   280
I ought to choose a man less prone to doubt,
And give you something to be vexed about.

ALCESTE.   Ah, what a poor enchanted fool I am;
These gentle words, no doubt, were all a sham;
But destiny requires me to entrust   285
My happiness to you, and so I must.
I'll love you to the bitter end, and see
How false and treacherous you dare to be.

CÉLIMÈNE.   No, you don't really love me as you ought.

ALCESTE.   I love you more than can be said or thought;   290
Indeed, I wish you were in such distress
That I might show my deep devotedness.
Yes, I could wish that you were wretchedly poor,
Unloved, uncherished, utterly obscure;
That fate had set you down upon the earth   295
Without possessions, rank, or gentle birth;
Then, by the offer of my heart, I might
Repair the great injustice of your plight;

I'd raise you from the dust, and proudly prove
The purity and vastness of my love.   300
CÉLIMÈNE.   This is a strange benevolence indeed!
God grant that I may never be in need . . .
Ah, here's Monsieur Dubois, in quaint disguise.

SCENE 4

Enter DUBOIS.

ALCESTE.   Well, why this costume? Why those frightened eyes?
What ails you?
DUBOIS.   Well, Sir, things are most mysterious.   305
ALCESTE.   What do you mean?
DUBOIS.   I fear they're very serious.
ALCESTE.   What?
DUBOIS.   Shall I speak more loudly?
ALCESTE.   Yes; speak out.
DUBOIS.   Isn't there someone here, Sir?
ALCESTE.   Speak, you lout!
Stop wasting time.
DUBOIS.   Sir, we must slip away.
ALCESTE.   How's that?
DUBOIS.   We must decamp without delay.   310
ALCESTE.   Explain yourself.
DUBOIS.   I tell you we must fly.
ALCESTE.   What for?
DUBOIS.   We mustn't pause to say good-by.
ALCESTE.   Now what d'you mean by all of this, you clown?
DUBOIS.   I mean, Sir, that we've got to leave this town.
ALCESTE.   I'll tear you limb from limb and joint from joint   315
If you don't come more quickly to the point.
DUBOIS.   Well, Sir, today a man in a black suit,
Who wore a black and ugly scowl to boot,
Left us a document scrawled in such a hand
As even Satan couldn't understand.   320
It bears upon your lawsuit, I don't doubt;
But all hell's devils couldn't make it out.
ALCESTE.   Well, well, go on. What then? I fail to see
How this event obliges us to flee.
DUBOIS.   Well, Sir: an hour later, hardly more,   325
A gentleman who's often called before
Came looking for you in an anxious way.
Not finding you, he asked me to convey
(Knowing I could be trusted with the same)
The following message . . . Now, what *was* his name?   330
ALCESTE.   Forget his name, you idiot. What did he say?

DUBOIS.   Well, it was one of your friends, Sir, anyway.
    He warned you to begone, and he suggested
    That if you stay, you may well be arrested.
ALCESTE.   What? Nothing more specific? Think, man, think!   335
DUBOIS.   No, Sir. He had me bring him pen and ink,
    And dashed you off a letter which, I'm sure,
    Will render things distinctly less obscure.
ALCESTE.   Well—let me have it!
CÉLIMÈNE.   What *is* this all about?
ALCESTE.   God knows; but I have hopes of finding out.   340
    How long am I to wait, you blitherer?
DUBOIS (*after a protracted search for the letter*).   I must have left it on
    your table, Sir.
ALCESTE.   I ought to . . .
CÉLIMÈNE.   No, no, keep your self-control;
    Go find out what's behind his rigmarole.
ALCESTE.   It seems that fate, no matter what I do,   345
    Has sworn that I may not converse with you;
    But, Madam, pray permit your faithful lover
    To try once more before the day is over. (*Exeunt.*)

ACT 5

SCENE 1

Enter ALCESTE *and* PHILINTE.

ALCESTE.   No, it's too much. My mind's made up, I tell you.
PHILINTE.   Why should this blow, however hard, compel you . . .
ALCESTE.   No, no, don't waste your breath in argument;
    Nothing you say will alter my intent;
    This age is vile, and I've made up my mind   5
    To have no further commerce with mankind.
    Did not truth, honor, decency, and the laws
    Oppose my enemy and approve my cause?
    My claims were justified in all men's sight;
    I put my trust in equity and right;   10
    Yet, to my horror and the world's disgrace,
    Justice is mocked, and I have lost my case!
    A scoundrel whose dishonesty is notorious
    Emerges from another lie victorious!
    Honor and right condone his brazen fraud,   15
    While rectitude and decency applaud!
    Before his smirking face, the truth stands charmed,
    And virtue conquered, and the law disarmed!
    His crime is sanctioned by a court decree!

And not content with what he's done to me,   20
The dog now seeks to ruin me by stating
That I composed a book now circulating,
A book so wholly criminal and vicious
That even to speak its title is seditious!
Meanwhile Oronte, my rival, lends his credit   25
To the same libelous tale, and helps to spread it!
Oronte! a man of honor and of rank,
With whom I've been entirely fair and frank;
Who sought me out and forced me, willy-nilly,
To judge some verse I found extremely silly;   30
And who, because I properly refused
To flatter him, or see the truth abused,
Abets my enemy in a rotten slander!
There's the reward of honesty and candor!
The man will hate me to the end of time   35
For failing to commend his wretched rhyme!
And not this man alone, but all humanity
Do what they do from interest and vanity;
They prate of honor, truth, and righteousness,
But lie, betray, and swindle nonetheless.   40
Come then: man's villainy is too much to bear;
Let's leave this jungle and this jackal's lair.
Yes! treacherous and savage race of men,
You shall not look upon my face again.
PHILINTE.   Oh, don't rush into exile prematurely;   45
Things aren't as dreadful as you make them, surely.
It's rather obvious, since you're still at large,
That people don't believe your enemy's charge.
Indeed, his tale's so patently untrue
That it may do more harm to him than you.   50
ALCESTE.   Nothing could do that scoundrel any harm:
His frank corruption is his greatest charm,
And, far from hurting him, a further shame
Would only serve to magnify his name.
PHILINTE.   In any case, his bald prevarication   55
Has done no injury to your reputation,
And you may feel secure in that regard.
As for your lawsuit, it should not be hard
To have the case reopened, and contest
This judgment . . .
ALCESTE.   No, no, let the verdict rest.   60
Whatever cruel penalty it may bring,
I wouldn't have it changed for anything.
It shows the times' injustice with such clarity

That I shall pass it down to our posterity
As a great proof and signal demonstration   65
Of the black wickedness of this generation.
It may cost twenty thousand francs; but I
Shall pay their twenty thousand, and gain thereby
The right to storm and rage at human evil,
And send the race of mankind to the devil.   70
PHILINTE.   Listen to me . . .
ALCESTE.   Why? What can you possibly say?
  Don't argue, Sir; your labor's thrown away.
  Do you propose to offer lame excuses
  For men's behavior and the times' abuses?
PHILINTE.   No, all you say I'll readily concede: 75
  This is a low, dishonest age indeed;
  Nothing but trickery prospers nowadays,
  And people ought to mend their shabby ways.
  Yes, man's a beastly creature; but must we then
  Abandon the society of men?   80
  Here in the world, each human frailty
  Provides occasion for philosophy,
  And that is virtue's noblest exercise;
  If honesty shone forth from all men's eyes,
  If every heart were frank and kind and just,   85
  What could our virtues do but gather dust
  (Since their employment is to help us bear
  The villainies of men without despair)?
  A heart well-armed with virtue can endure . . .
ALCESTE.   Sir, you're a matchless reasoner, to be sure;   90
  Your words are fine and full of cogency;
  But don't waste time and eloquence on me.
  My reason bids me go, for my own good.
  My tongue won't lie and flatter as it should;
  God knows what frankness it might next commit,   95
  And what I'd suffer on account of it.
  Pray let me wait for Célimène's return
  In peace and quiet. I shall shortly learn,
  By her response to what I have in view,
  Whether her love for me is feigned or true.   100
PHILINTE.   Till then, let's visit Eliante upstairs.
ALCESTE.   No, I am too weighed down with somber cares.
  Go to her, do; and leave me with my gloom
  Here in the darkened corner of this room.
PHILINTE.   Why, that's no sort of company, my friend;   105
  I'll see if Eliante will not descend. (*Exit.* ALCESTE *withdraws.*)

SCENE 2

Enter ORONTE *and* CÉLIMÈNE.

ORONTE.   Yes, Madam, if you wish me to remain
Your true and ardent lover, you must deign
To give me some more positive assurance.
All this suspense is quite beyond endurance.   110
If your heart shares the sweet desires of mine,
Show me as much by some convincing sign;
And here's the sign I urgently suggest:
That you no longer tolerate Alceste,
But sacrifice him to my love, and sever   115
All your relations with the man forever.
CÉLIMÈNE.   Why do you suddenly dislike him so?
You praised him to the skies not long ago.
ORONTE.   Madam, that's not the point. I'm here to find
Which way your tender feelings are inclined.   120
Choose, if you please, between Alceste and me,
And I shall stay or go accordingly.
ALCESTE (*emerging from the corner*).   Yes, Madam, choose; this
     gentleman's demand
Is wholly just, and I support his stand.
I too am true and ardent; I too am here   125
To ask you that you make your feelings clear.
No more delays, now; no equivocation;
The time has come to make your declaration.
ORONTE.   Sir, I've no wish in any way to be
An obstacle to your felicity.   130
ALCESTE.   Sir, I've no wish to share her heart with you;
That may sound jealous, but at least it's true.
ORONTE.   If, weighing us, she leans in your direction . . .
ALCESTE.   If she regards you with the least affection . . .
ORONTE.   I swear I'll yield her to you there and then.   135
ALCESTE.   I swear I'll never see her face again.
ORONTE.   Now, Madam, tell us what we've come to hear.
ALCESTE.   Madam, speak openly and have no fear.
ORONTE.   Just say which one is to remain your lover.
ALCESTE.   Just name one name, and it will all be over.   140
ORONTE.   What! Is it possible that you're undecided?
ALCESTE.   What! Can your feelings possibly be divided?
CÉLIMÈNE.   Enough: this inquisition's gone too far:
How utterly unreasonable you are!
Not that I couldn't make the choice with ease;   145
My heart has no conflicting sympathies;

I know full well which one of you I favor,
And you'd not see me hesitate or waver.
But how can you expect me to reveal
So cruelly and bluntly what I feel?   150
I think it altogether too unpleasant
To choose between two men when both are present;
One's heart has means more subtle and more kind
Of letting its affections be divined,
Nor need one be uncharitably plain   155
To let a lover know he loves in vain.

ORONTE.   No, no, speak plainly; I for one can stand it.
I beg you to be frank.

ALCESTE.   And I demand it.
The simple truth is what I wish to know,
And there's no need for softening the blow.   160
You've made an art of pleasing everyone,
But now your days of coquetry are done:
You have no choice now, Madam, but to choose,
For I'll know what to think if you refuse;
I'll take your silence for a clear admission   165
That I'm entitled to my worst suspicion.

ORONTE.   I thank you for this ultimatum, Sir,
And I may say I heartily concur.

CÉLIMÈNE.   Really, this foolishness is very wearing:
Must you be so unjust and overbearing?   170
Haven't I told you why I must demur?
Ah, here's Eliante; I'll put the case to her.

SCENE 3

Enter ELIANTE.

CÉLIMÈNE.   Cousin, I'm being persecuted here
By these two persons, who, it would appear,
Will not be satisfied till I confess   175
Which one I love the more, and which the less,
And tell the latter to his face that he
Is henceforth banished from my company.
Tell me, has ever such a thing been done?

ELIANTE.   You'd best not turn to me; I'm not the one   180
To back you in a matter of this kind:
I'm all for those who frankly speak their mind.

ORONTE.   Madam, you'll search in vain for a defender.

ALCESTE.   You're beaten, Madam, and may as well surrender.

ORONTE.   Speak, speak, you must; and end this awful strain.   185

ALCESTE.   Or don't, and your position will be plain.
ORONTE.   A single word will close this painful scene.
ALCESTE.   But if you're silent, I'll know what you mean.

SCENE 4

Enter ACASTE, CLITANDRE, *and* ARSINOÉ.

ACASTE (*to* CÉLIMÈNE).   Madam, with all due deference, we two
    Have come to pick a little bone with you.   190
CLITANDRE (*to* ORONTE *and* ALCESTE).   I'm glad you're present, Sirs; as
    you'll soon learn,
    Our business here is also your concern.
ARSINOÉ (*to* CÉLIMÈNE).   Madam, I visit you so soon again
    Only because of these two gentlemen,
    Who came to me indignant and aggrieved   195
    About a crime too base to be believed.
    Knowing your virtue, having such confidence in it,
    I couldn't think you guilty for a minute,
    In spite of all their telling evidence;
    And, rising above our little difference,   200
    I've hastened here in friendship's name to see
    You clear yourself of this great calumny.
ACASTE.   Yes, Madam, let us see with what composure
    You'll manage to respond to this disclosure.
    You lately sent Clitandre this tender note.   205
CLITANDRE.   And this one, for Acaste, you also wrote.
ACASTE (*to* ORONTE *and* ALCESTE).   You'll recognize this writing, Sirs,
    I think;
    The lady is so free with pen and ink
    That you must know it all too well, I fear.
    But listen: this is something you should hear.   210

    "How absurd you are to condemn my lightheartedness in society, and
to accuse me of being happiest in the company of others. Nothing could
be more unjust; and if you do not come to me instantly and beg pardon for
saying such a thing, I shall never forgive you as long as I live. Our big
bumbling friend the Viscount . . ."   215

What a shame that he's not here.

    "Our big bumbling friend the Viscount, whose name stands first in
your complaint, is hardly a man to my taste; and ever since the day I
watched him spend three-quarters of an hour spitting into a well, so as to
make circles in the water, I have been unable to think highly of him. As
for the little Marquess . . ."   221

In all modesty, gentlemen, that is I.

"As for the little Marquess, who sat squeezing my hand for such a long while yesterday, I find him in all respects the most trifling creature alive; and the only things of value about him are his cape and his sword. As for the man with the green ribbons . . ."   226

(*To* ALCESTE) It's your turn now, Sir.

"As for the man with the green ribbons, he amuses me now and then with his bluntness and his bearish ill-humor; but there are many times indeed when I think him the greatest bore in the world. And as for the sonneteer . . ."   231

(*To* ORONTE) Here's your helping.

"And as for the sonneteer, who has taken it into his head to be witty, and insists on being an author in the teeth of opinion, I simply cannot be bothered to listen to him, and his prose wearies me quite as much as his poetry. Be assured that I am not always so well-entertained as you suppose; that I long for your company, more than I dare to say, at all these entertainments to which people drag me; and that the presence of those one loves is true and perfect seasoning to all one's pleasures."   239

CLITANDRE.   And now for me.

"Clitandre, whom you mention, and who so pesters me with his saccharine speeches, is the last man on earth for whom I could feel any affection. He is quite mad to suppose that I love him, and so are you, to doubt that you are loved. Do come to your senses; exchange your suppositions for his; and visit me as often as possible, to help me bear the annoyance of his unwelcome attentions."   246

It's a sweet character that these letters show,
And what to call it, Madam, you well know.
Enough. We're off to make the world acquainted
With this sublime self-portrait that you've painted.   250
ACASTE.   Madam, I'll make you no farewell oration;
No, you're not worthy of my indignation.
Far choicer hearts than yours, as you'll discover,
Would like this little Marquess for a lover. (*Exeunt* ACASTE *and*
CLITANDRE.)

SCENE 5

ORONTE.   So! After all those loving letters you wrote,   255
You turn on me like this, and cut my throat!
And your dissembling, faithless heart, I find,
Has pledged itself by turns to all mankind!

How blind I've been! But now I clearly see;
I thank you, Madam, for enlightening me.   260
My heart is mine once more, and I'm content;
The loss of it shall be your punishment.
(*To* ALCESTE) Sir, she is yours; I'll seek no more to stand
Between your wishes and this lady's hand. (*Exit.*)

SCENE 6

ARSINOÉ (*to* CÉLIMÈNE).   Madam, I'm forced to speak. I'm far too stirred   265
  To keep my counsel, after what I've heard.
  I'm shocked and staggered by your want of morals.
  It's not my way to mix in others' quarrels;
  But really, when this fine and noble spirit,
  This man of honor and surpassing merit,   270
  Laid down the offering of his heart before you,
  How *could* you . . .
ALCESTE.   Madam, permit me, I implore you,
  To represent myself in this debate.
  Don't bother, please, to be my advocate.
  My heart, in any case, could not afford   275
  To give your services their due reward;
  And if I chose, for consolation's sake,
  Some other lady, t'would not be you I'd take.
ARSINOÉ.   What makes you think you could, Sir? And how dare you
  Imply that I've been trying to ensnare you?   280
  If you can for a moment entertain
  Such flattering fancies, you're extremely vain.
  I'm not so interested as you suppose
  In Célimène's discarded gigolos.
  Get rid of that absurd illusion, do.   285
  Women like me are not for such as you.
  Stay with this creature, to whom you're so attached;
  I've never seen two people better matched. (*Exit.*)

SCENE 7

ALCESTE (*to* CÉLIMÈNE).   Well, I've been still throughout this exposé,
  Till everyone but me has said his say.   290
  Come, have I shown sufficient self-restraint?
  And may I now . . .
CÉLIMÈNE.   Yes, make your just complaint.
  Reproach me freely, call me what you will;
  You've every right to say I've used you ill.
  I've wronged you, I confess it; and in my shame   295

I'll make no effort to escape the blame.
The anger of those others I could despise;
My guilt toward you I sadly recognize.
Your wrath is wholly justified, I fear;
I know how culpable I must appear,   300
I know all things bespeak my treachery,
And that, in short, you've grounds for hating me.
Do so; I give you leave.
ALCESTE.   Ah, traitress—how,
How should I cease to love you, even now?
Though mind and will were passionately bent   305
On hating you, my heart would not consent.
(*To* ELIANTE *and* PHILINTE) Be witness to my madness, both of you;
See what infatuation drives one to;
But wait; my folly's only just begun,
And I shall prove to you before I'm done   310
How strange the human heart is, and how far
From rational we sorry creatures are.
(*To* CÉLIMÈNE) Woman, I'm willing to forget your shame,
And clothe your treacheries in a sweeter name;
I'll call them youthful errors, instead of crimes,   315
And lay the blame on these corrupting times.
My one condition is that you agree
To share my chosen fate, and fly with me
To that wild, trackless solitary place
In which I shall forget the human race.   320
Only by such a course can you atone
For those atrocious letters; by that alone
Can you remove my present horror of you,
And make it possible for me to love you.
CÉLIMÈNE.   What! *I* renounce the world at my young age,   325
And die of boredom in some hermitage?
ALCESTE.   Ah, if you really loved me as you ought,
You wouldn't give the world a moment's thought;
Must you have me, and all the world beside?
CÉLIMÈNE.   Alas, at twenty one is terrified   330
Of solitude. I fear I lack the force
And depth of soul to take so stern a course.
But if my hand in marriage will content you,
Why, there's a plan which I might well consent to,
And . . .
ALCESTE.   No, I detest you now. I could excuse   335
Everything else, but since you thus refuse
To love me wholly, as a wife should do,

And see the world in me, as I in you,
Go! I reject your hand, and disenthrall
My heart from your enchantments, once for all. (*Exit* CÉLIMÈNE.) 340

SCENE 8

ALCESTE (*to* ELIANTE).   Madam, your virtuous beauty has no peer,
Of all this world, you only are sincere;
I've long esteemed you highly, as you know;
Permit me ever to esteem you so,
And if I do not now request your hand,   345
Forgive me, Madam, and try to understand.
I feel unworthy of it; I sense that fate
Does not intend me for the married state,
That I should do you wrong by offering you
My shattered heart's unhappy residue,   350
And that in short . . .
ELIANTE.   Your argument's well taken:
Nor need you fear that I shall feel forsaken.
Were I to offer him this hand of mine,
Your friend Philinte, I think, would not decline.
PHILINTE.   Ah, Madam, that's my heart's most cherished goal,   355
For which I'd gladly give my life and soul.
ALCESTE (*to* ELIANTE *and* PHILINTE).   May you be true to all you
    now profess,
And so deserve unending happiness.
Meanwhile, betrayed and wronged in everything,
I'll flee this bitter world where vice is king,   360
And seek some spot unpeopled and apart
Where I'll be free to have an honest heart. (*Exit.*)
PHILINTE.   Come, Madam, let's do everything we can
To change the mind of this unhappy man. (*Exeunt.*)

QUESTIONS

1. How does the argument between Alceste and Philinte in the opening scene state the play's major thematic conflict? Which of the two philosophies expressed is the more idealistic? Which more realistic? Is either or are both of them extreme?
2. What are the attitudes of Célimène, Eliante, and Arsinoé toward Alceste? Do they respect him? Why or why not?
3. *The Misanthrope* is generally acknowledged to be one of the world's greatest comedies, but, at the same time, it is an atypical one, both in its hero and in its ending. In what ways does Alceste approach the stature of a tragic hero? In what way is the ending unlike a comic ending?

4. Alceste is in conflict with social convention, with social injustice, and with Célimène. Does he discriminate between them as to their relative importance? Discuss.
5. Are there any indications in the opening scene that the motivations behind Alceste's hatred of social convention are not as unmixed as he thinks them?
6. Alceste declares himself not blind to Célimène's faults. Is he blind in any way about his relationship with Célimène? If so, what does his blindness spring from?
7. What do Alceste's reasons for refusing to appeal his lawsuit (5.1) and his wish that Célimène were "Unloved, uncherished, utterly obscure" so that he might raise her "from the dust" (4.3) tell us about his character?
8. What are Célimène's good qualities? What are her bad ones? In what ways are she and Alceste foils? Might Célimène have been redeemed had Alceste been able to accept her without taking her from society?
9. How is the gossip session between Acaste, Clitandre, and Célimène (2.5) a double-edged satire? Which of Célimène's satirical portraits is the finest? How accurate is Célimène's portrait of Alceste himself?
10. Which is the more scathingly satirized—Alceste, or the society in which he lives? Why?
11. What character in the play most nearly represents a desirable norm of social behavior? Why?
12. What characteristics keep Alceste from being a tragic hero? What keeps the ending from being a tragic ending?
13. The verse form used by Richard Wilbur in translating Molière's play is quite different from that used by Shakespeare in *Othello*. Describe the differences. What relation is there between the poetic style of each play and its subject matter?
14. Compare *The Misanthrope* and *A Doll House* as plays dealing with a character in conflict with the norms of a society. How are the characters of Alceste and Nora similar? How are they different? Which is portrayed by the playwright with greater sympathy? Why?
15. Are politeness and hypocrisy the same thing? If not, distinguish between them.

Luis Valdez
Los Vendidos

CHARACTERS

HONEST SANCHO   JOHNNY PACHUCO
SECRETARY   REVOLUCIONARIO
FARMWORKER   MEXICAN-AMERICAN

SCENE: HONEST SANCHO's *Used Mexican Lot and Mexican Curio Shop. Three models are on display in* HONEST SANCHO's *shop. To the right, there is a* REVOLUCIONARIO, *complete with sombrero, carrilleras and carabina 30-30.° At center, on the floor, there is the* FARMWORKER, *under a broad straw sombrero. At stage left is the* PACHUCO, *filero° in hand.* HONEST SANCHO *is moving among his models, dusting them off and preparing for another day of business.*

SANCHO.   Bueno, bueno, mis monos, vamos a ver a quién vendemos ahora, ¿no? (*To audience*) ¡Quihubo!° I'm Honest Sancho and this is my shop. Antes fui contratista, pero ahora logré mi negocito.° All I need now is a customer. (*A bell rings offstage.*) Ay, a customer!
SECRETARY (*entering*).   Good morning, I'm Miss Jimenez from . . .
SANCHO.   Ah, una chicana! Welcome, welcome Señorita Jiménez.
SECRETARY (*Anglo pronunciation*).   JIM-enez.
SANCHO.   ¿Qué?
SECRETARY.   My name is Miss JIM-enez. Don't you speak English? What's wrong with you?
SANCHO.   Oh, nothing, Señorita JIM-enez. I'm here to help you.
SECRETARY.   That's better. As I was starting to say, I'm a secretary from Governor Reagan's office, and we're looking for a Mexican type for the administration.

LOS VENDIDOS   First performed 1967. The title may be translated both "men who are sold" and "the sellouts," i.e., traitors to the cause. Luis Valdez was born in 1940 in Delano, California, the son of migrant farmworkers (*campesinos*). Although his early education was interrupted by the need to work in the fields, he earned a B.A. in English from San Jose State College in 1964 and then joined the San Francisco Mime Troupe performing political and satirical plays in public parks. In 1965 he founded El Teatro Campesino in Delano to present satirical skits (called "Actos") in support of the farmworkers' cause and as a means of political protest. Like others of the Actos, *Los Vendidos* was presented free to an audience in a park. Subsequently, in 1972, it won an Emmy in a television production for the Corporation for Public Broadcasting. At the time of its writing, Ronald Reagan was governor of California and another film actor, George Murphy, was a U.S. Senator.

carrilleras . . . 30-30: cartridge belts and 30-30 rifle   **filero:** switchblade
Bueno . . . Quihubo!: Good, good, my cuties, let's see who we can sell now. What's going on?   **Antes fui . . . negocito:** I used to be a contractor, but now I run my little business.

SANCHO.   Well, you come to the right place, lady. This is Honest Sancho's
Used Mexican Lot, and we got all types here. Any particular type
you want?

SECRETARY.   Yes, we were looking for somebody suave . . .

SANCHO.   Suave.

SECRETARY.   Debonaire.

SANCHO.   De buen aire.

SECRETARY.   Dark.

SANCHO.   Prieto.

SECRETARY.   But of course, not too dark.

SANCHO.   No muy prieto.

SECRETARY.   Perhaps, beige.

SANCHO.   Beige, just the tone. Asi como cafecito con leche,° ¿no?

SECRETARY.   One more thing. He must be hard-working.

SANCHO.   That could only be one model. Step right over here to the center of the shop, lady. (*They cross to the* FARMWORKER.) This is our standard farmworker model. As you can see, in the words of our beloved
Senator George Murphy, he is "built close to the ground." Also, take
special notice of his 4-ply Goodyear huaraches,° made from the rain
tire. This wide-brimmed sombrero is an extra added feature; keeps off
the sun, rain and dust.

SECRETARY.   Yes, it does look durable.

SANCHO.   And our farmworker model is friendly. Muy amable.° Watch.
(*Snaps his fingers.*)

FARMWORKER (*lifts up head*).   Buenos días, señorita. (*His head drops.*)

SECRETARY.   My, he is friendly.

SANCHO.   Didn't I tell you? Loves his patrones!° But his most attractive
feature is that he's hard-working. Let me show you. (*Snaps fingers.*
FARMWORKER *stands.*)

FARMWORKER.   ¡El jale!° (*He begins to work.*)

SANCHO.   As you can see he is cutting grapes.

SECRETARY.   Oh, I wouldn't know.

SANCHO.   He also picks cotton. (*Snaps.* FARMWORKER *begins to pick cotton.*)

SECRETARY.   Versatile, isn't he?

SANCHO.   He also picks melons. (*Snaps.* FARMWORKER *picks melons.*) That's
his slow speed for late in the season. Here's his fast speed. (*Snap.* FARM-
WORKER *picks faster.*)

SECRETARY.   Chihuahua°. . . . I mean, goodness, he sure is a hardworker.

SANCHO (*pulls the* FARMWORKER *to his feet*).   And that isn't the half of it.
Do you see these little holes on his arms that appear to be pores? During those hot sluggish days in the field when the vines or the branches

---

Asi . . . leche: like coffee with milk   **huaraches:** sandals   **Muy amable:** Very
friendly   **patrones:** bosses   **El jale:** The job   **Chihuahua:** Hot damn!

get so entangled, it's almost impossible to move, these holes emit a certain grease that allows our model to slip and slide right through the crop with no trouble at all.

SECRETARY. Wonderful. But is he economical?

SANCHO. Economical? Señorita, you are looking at the Volkswagen of Mexicans. Pennies a day is all it takes. One plate of beans and tortillas will keep him going all day. That, and chile. Plenty of chile. Chile jalapeños, chile verde, chile colorado. But, of course, if you do give him chile (*Snap.* FARMWORKER *turns left face.* *Snap.* FARMWORKER *bends over.*), then you have to change his oil filter once a week.

SECRETARY. What about storage?

SANCHO. No problem. You know these new farm labor camps our Honorable Governor Reagan has built out by Parlier or Raisin City? They were designed with our model in mind. Five, six, seven, even ten in one of those shacks will give you no trouble at all. You can also put him in old barns, old cars, riverbanks. You can even leave him out in the field overnight with no worry!

SECRETARY. Remarkable.

SANCHO. And here's an added feature: every year at the end of the season, this model goes back to Mexico and doesn't return, automatically, until next spring.

SECRETARY. How about that. But tell me, does he speak English?

SANCHO. Another outstanding feature is that last year this model was programmed to go out on STRIKE! (*Snap.*)

FARMWORKER. ¡Huelga! ¡Huelga! Hermanos, sálganse de esos files.° (*Snap. He stops.*)

SECRETARY. No! Oh no, we can't strike in the State Capitol.

SANCHO. Well, he also scabs. (*Snap.*)

FARMWORKER. Me vendo barato, ¿y qué°? (*Snap.*)

SECRETARY. That's much better, but you didn't answer my question. Does he speak English?

SANCHO. Bueno . . . no, pero° he has other . . .

SECRETARY. No.

SANCHO. Other features.

SECRETARY. No! He just won't do!

SANCHO. Okay, okay, pues.° We have other models.

SECRETARY. I hope so. What we need is something a little more sophisticated.

SANCHO. Sophisti-qué?

SECRETARY. An urban model.

Huelga . . . files: Strike, strike, brothers, leave those rows **Me vendo . . . qué:** My price is cheap, so what? **Bueno . . . pero:** Well, no, but **pues:** then

SANCHO. Ah, from the city! Step right back. Over here in this corner of the shop is exactly what you're looking for. Introducing our new 1969 JOHNNY PACHUCO° model! This is our fast-back model. Streamlined. Built for speed, low-riding, city life. Take a look at some of these features. Mag shoes, dual exhausts, green chartreuse paint-job, dark-tint windshield, a little poof on top. Let me just turn him on. (*Snap.* JOHNNY *walks to stage center with a* PACHUCO *bounce.*)

SECRETARY. What was that?

SANCHO. That, señorita, was the Chicano shuffle.

SECRETARY. Okay, what does he do?

SANCHO. Anything and everything necessary for city life. For instance, survival: he knife fights. (*Snaps.* JOHNNY *pulls out a switchblade and swings at* SECRETARY. SECRETARY *screams.*) He dances. (*Snap.*)

JOHNNY (*singing*). "Angel Baby, my Angel Baby . . ." (*Snap.*)

SANCHO. And here's a feature no city model can be without. He gets arrested, but not without resisting, of course. (*Snap.*)

JOHNNY. En la madre, la placa.° I didn't do it! I didn't do it!

(JOHNNY *turns and stands up against an imaginary wall, legs spread out, arms behind his back.*)

SECRETARY. Oh no, we can't have arrests! We must maintain law and order.

SANCHO. But he's bilingual.

SECRETARY. Bilingual?

SANCHO. Simón que yes. He speaks English! Johnny, give us some English. (*Snap.*)

JOHNNY (*comes downstage*). Fuck-you!

SECRETARY (*gasps*). Oh! I've never been so insulted in my whole life!

SANCHO. Well, he learned it in your school.

SECRETARY. I don't care where he learned it.

SANCHO. But he's economical.

SECRETARY. Economical?

SANCHO. Nickels and dimes. You can keep Johnny running on hamburgers, Taco Bell tacos, Lucky Lager beer, Thunderbird wine, yesca . . .

SECRETARY. Yesca?

SANCHO. Mota.

SECRETARY. Mota?

SANCHO. Leños° . . . marijuana. (*Snap.* JOHNNY *inhales on an imaginary joint.*)

SECRETARY. That's against the law!

JOHNNY (*big smile, holding his breath*). Yeah.

SANCHO. He also sniffs glue. (*Snap.* JOHNNY *inhales glue, big smile.*)

JOHNNY. Tha's too much, man, ése.°

SECRETARY. No, Mr. Sancho, I don't think this . . .

Pachuco: a slang term for an urban tough   **En la . . . placa:** Oh, oh, the cops
Leños: joints   **ése:** man

SANCHO.   Wait a minute, he has other qualities I know you'll love. For example, an inferiority complex. (*Snap.*)

JOHNNY (*to* SANCHO).   You think you're better than me, huh, ése? (*Swings switchblade.*)

SANCHO.   He can also be beaten and he bruises. Cut him and he bleeds, kick him and he . . . (*He beats, bruises and kicks* PACHUCO.) Would you like to try it?

SECRETARY.   Oh, I couldn't.

SANCHO.   Be my guest. He's a great scapegoat.

SECRETARY.   No really.

SANCHO.   Please.

SECRETARY.   Well, all right. Just once. (*She kicks* PACHUCO.) Oh, he's so soft.

SANCHO.   Wasn't that good? Try again.

SECRETARY (*kicks* PACHUCO).   Oh, he's wonderful! (*She kicks him again.*)

SANCHO.   Okay, that's enough, lady. You'll ruin the merchandise. Yes, our Johnny Pachuco model can give you many hours of pleasure. Why, the LAPD just bought twenty of these to train their rookie cops on. And talk about maintenance. Señorita, you are looking at an entirely self-supporting machine. You're never going to find our Johnny Pachuco model on the relief rolls. No, sir, this model knows how to liberate.

SECRETARY.   Liberate?

SANCHO.   He steals. (*Snap.* JOHNNY *rushes to* SECRETARY *and steals her purse.*)

JOHNNY.   ¡Dame esa bolsa, vieja!° (*He grabs the purse and runs. Snap by* SANCHO, *he stops.* SECRETARY *runs after* JOHNNY *and grabs purse away from him, kicking him as she goes.*)

SECRETARY.   No, no, no! We can't have any more thieves in the State Administration. Put him back.

SANCHO.   Okay, we still got other models. Come on, Johnny, we'll sell you to some old lady. (SANCHO *takes* JOHNNY *back to his place.*)

SECRETARY.   Mr. Sancho, I don't think you quite understand what we need. What we need is something that will attract the women voters. Something more traditional, more romantic.

SANCHO.   Ah, a lover. (*He smiles meaningfully.*) Step right over here, señorita. Introducing our standard Revolucionario and/or Early California Bandit type. As you can see, he is well-built, sturdy, durable. This is the International Harvester of Mexicans.

SECRETARY.   What does he do?

SANCHO.   You name it, he does it. He rides horses, stays in the mountains, crosses deserts, plains, rivers, leads revolutions, follows revolutions, kills, can be killed, serves as a martyr, hero, movie star. Did I say movie star? Did you ever see *Viva Zapata? Viva Villa, Villa Rides, Pancho Villa Returns, Pancho Villa Goes Back, Pancho Villa Meets Abbott and Costello?*

SECRETARY.   I've never seen any of those.

¡Dame . . . vieja!: Give me that purse, old lady!

SANCHO.   Well, he was in all of them. Listen to this. (*Snap.*)

REVOLUCIONARIO (*scream*).   ¡Viva Villaaaaa!

SECRETARY.   That's awfully loud.

SANCHO.   He has a volume control. (*He adjusts volume. Snap.*)

REVOLUCIONARIO (*mousey voice*).   Viva Villa.

SECRETARY.   That's better.

SANCHO.   And even if you didn't see him in the movies, perhaps you saw him on TV. He makes commercials. (*Snap.*)

REVOLUCIONARIO.   Is there a Frito Bandito in your house?

SECRETARY.   Oh, yes, I've seen that one!

SANCHO.   Another feature about this one is that he is economical. He runs on raw horsemeat and tequila!

SECRETARY.   Isn't that rather savage?

SANCHO.   Al contrario,° it makes him a lover. (*Snap.*)

REVOLUCIONARIO (*to* SECRETARY).   Ay, mamasota, cochota, ven pa 'ca!° (*He grabs* SECRETARY *and folds her back, Latin-lover style.*)

SANCHO (*Snap.* REVOLUCIONARIO *goes back upright*).   Now wasn't that nice?

SECRETARY.   Well, it was rather nice.

SANCHO.   And finally, there is one outstanding feature about this model I know the ladies are going to love: he's a genuine antique! He was made in Mexico in 1910!

SECRETARY.   Made in Mexico?

SANCHO.   That's right. Once in Tijuana, twice in Guadalajara, three times in Cuernavaca.

SECRETARY.   Mr. Sancho, I thought he was an American product.

SANCHO.   No, but . . .

SECRETARY.   No, I'm sorry. We can't buy anything but American made products. He just won't do.

SANCHO.   But he's an antique!

SECRETARY.   I don't care. You still don't understand what we need. It's true we need Mexican models, such as these, but it's more important that he be American.

SANCHO.   American?

SECRETARY.   That's right, and judging from what you've shown me, I don't think you have what we want. Well, my lunch hour's almost over, I better . . .

SANCHO.   Wait a minute! Mexican but American?

SECRETARY.   That's correct.

SANCHO.   Mexican but . . . (*A sudden flash.*) American! Yeah, I think we've got exactly what you want. He just came in today! Give me a minute. (*He exits. Talks from backstage.*) Here he is in the shop. Let me just get some papers off. There. Introducing our new 1970 Mexican-

Al contrario: on the contrary   **Ay . . . pa 'ca:** Hey, c'mere, big mama!

American! Ta-ra-ra-raaaa! (SANCHO *brings out the* MEXICAN-AMERICAN *model, a clean-shaven middle class type in a business suit, with glasses.*)

SECRETARY (*impressed*).   Where have you been hiding this one?

SANCHO.   He just came in this morning. Ain't he a beauty? Feast your eyes on him! Sturdy U.S. Steel frame, streamlined, modern. As a matter of fact, he is built exactly like our Anglo models, except that he comes in a variety of darker shades: naugahyde, leather or leatherette.

SECRETARY.   Naugahyde.

SANCHO.   Well, we'll just write that down. Yes, señorita, this model represents the apex of American engineering! He is bilingual, college educated, ambitious! Say the word "acculturate" and he accelerates. He is intelligent, well-mannered, clean. Did I say clean? (*Snap.* MEXICAN-AMERICAN *raises his arm.*) Smell.

SECRETARY (*smells*).   Old Sobaco, my favorite.

SANCHO (*Snap.* MEXICAN-AMERICAN *turns toward* SANCHO).   Eric? (*To* SECRETARY) We call him Eric García. (*To* ERIC) I want you to meet Miss JIM-enez, Eric.

MEXICAN-AMERICAN.   Miss JIM-enez, I am delighted to make your acquaintance. (*He kisses her hand.*)

SECRETARY.   Oh, my, how charming!

SANCHO.   Did you feel the suction? He has seven especially engineered suction cups right behind his lips. He's a charmer all right!

SECRETARY.   How about boards, does he function on boards?

SANCHO.   You name them, he is on them. Parole boards, draft boards, school boards, taco quality control boards, surf boards, two by fours.

SECRETARY.   Does he function in politics?

SANCHO.   Señorita, you are looking at a political machine. Have you ever heard of the OEO, EOC, COD, WAR ON POVERTY? That's our model! Not only that, he makes political speeches.

SECRETARY.   May I hear one?

SANCHO.   With pleasure. (*Snap.*) Eric, give us a speech.

MEXICAN-AMERICAN.   Mr. Congressman, Mr. Chairman, members of the board, honored guests, ladies and gentlemen. (SANCHO *and* SECRETARY *applaud.*) Please, please. I come before you as a Mexican-American to tell you about the problems of the Mexican. The problems of the Mexican stem from one thing and one thing only: he's stupid. He's uneducated. He needs to stay in school. He needs to be ambitious, forward-looking, harder-working. He needs to think American, American, American, American, American! God bless America! God bless America! God bless America! (*He goes out of control.* SANCHO *snaps frantically and the* MEXICAN-AMERICAN *finally slumps forward, bending at the waist.*)

SECRETARY.   Oh my, he's patriotic too!

SANCHO.   Sí, señorita, he loves his country. Let me just make a little adjustment here. (*Stands* MEXICAN-AMERICAN *up.*)

SECRETARY.   What about upkeep? Is he economical?

SANCHO.   Well, no, I won't lie to you. The Mexican-American costs a little bit more, but you get what you pay for. He's worth every extra cent. You can keep him running on dry Martinis, Langendorf bread . . .

SECRETARY.   Apple pie?

SANCHO.   Only Mom's. Of course, he's also programmed to eat Mexican food at ceremonial functions, but I must warn you, an overdose of beans will plug up his exhaust.

SECRETARY.   Fine! There's just one more question. How much do you want for him?

SANCHO.   Well, I tell you what I'm gonna do. Today and today only, because you've been so sweet, I'm gonna let you steal this model from me! I'm gonna let you drive him off the lot for the simple price of, let's see, taxes and license included, $15,000.

SECRETARY.   Fifteen thousand dollars? For a Mexican!!!!

SANCHO.   Mexican? What are you talking about? This is a Mexican-American! We had to melt down two pachucos, a farmworker and three gabachos° to make this model! You want quality, but you gotta pay for it! This is no cheap run-about. He's got class!

SECRETARY.   Okay, I'll take him.

SANCHO.   You will?

SECRETARY.   Here's your money.

SANCHO.   You mind if I count it?

SECRETARY.   Go right ahead.

SANCHO.   Well, you'll get your pink slip in the mail. Oh, do you want me to wrap him up for you? We have a box in the back.

SECRETARY.   No, thank you. The Governor is having a luncheon this afternoon, and we need a brown face in the crowd. How do I drive him?

SANCHO.   Just snap your fingers. He'll do anything you want. (SECRETARY *snaps.* MEXICAN-AMERICAN *steps forward.*)

MEXICAN-AMERICAN.   ¡Raza querida, vamos levantando armas para liberarnos de estos desgraciados gabachos que nos explotan! Vamos . . .°

SECRETARY.   What did he say?

SANCHO.   Something about taking up arms, killing white people, etc.

SECRETARY.   But he's not supposed to say that!

SANCHO.   Look, lady, don't blame me for bugs from the factory. He's your Mexican-American, you bought him, now drive him off the lot!

SECRETARY.   But he's broken!

SANCHO.   Try snapping another finger. (SECRETARY *snaps.* MEXICAN-AMERICAN *comes to life again.*)

---

gabachos: whites   **¡Raza querida . . . Vamos:** Beloved members of our Mexican race, let's take up arms to free ourselves from those damned whites who exploit us! Let's go

MEXICAN-AMERICAN.   Esta gran humanidad ha dicho basta! ¡Y se ha puesto en marcha! ¡Basta! ¡Basta! ¡Viva la raza! ¡Viva la causa! ¡Viva la huelga! ¡Vivan los brown berets! ¡Vivan los estudiantes!° ¡Chicano power! (*The* MEXICAN-AMERICAN *turns toward the* SECRETARY, *who gasps and backs up. He keeps turning toward the* PACHUCO, FARMWORKER *and* REVOLUCIONARIO, *snapping his fingers and turning each of them on, one by one.*)

PACHUCO (*Snap. To* SECRETARY).   I'm going to get you, baby! ¡Viva la raza!

FARMWORKER (*Snap. To* SECRETARY).   ¡Viva la huelga! ¡Viva la huelga! ¡Viva la huelga!

REVOLUCIONARIO (*Snap. To* SECRETARY).   ¡Viva la revolución! (*The three models join together and advance toward the* SECRETARY, *who backs up and runs out of the shop screaming.* SANCHO *is at the other end of the shop holding his money in his hand. All freeze. After a few seconds of silence, the* PACHUCO *moves and stretches, shaking his arms and loosening up. The* FARMWORKER *and* REVOLUCIONARIO *do the same.* SANCHO *stays where he is, frozen to his spot.*)

JOHNNY.   Man, that was a long one, ése. (*Others agree with him.*)

FARMWORKER.   How did we do?

JOHNNY.   Pretty good, look at all that lana,° man! (*He goes over to* SANCHO *and removes the money from his hand.* SANCHO *stays where he is.*)

REVOLUCIONARIO.   En la madre, look at all the money.

JOHNNY.   We keep this up, we're going to be rich.

FARMWORKER.   They think we're machines.

REVOLUCIONARIO.   Burros.

JOHNNY.   Puppets.

MEXICAN-AMERICAN.   The only thing I don't like is how come I always get to play the goddamn Mexican-American?

JOHNNY.   That's what you get for finishing high school.

FARMWORKER.   How about our wages, ése?

JOHNNY.   Here it comes right now, $3,000 for you, $3,000 for you, $3,000 for you and $3,000 for me. The rest we put back into the business.

MEXICAN-AMERICAN.   Too much, man. Hey, where you vatos° going tonight?

FARMWORKER.   I'm going over to Concha's. There's a party.

JOHNNY.   Wait a minute, vatos. What about our salesman? I think he needs an oil job.

REVOLUCIONARIO.   Leave him to me. (*The* PACHUCO, FARMWORKER *and* MEXICAN-AMERICAN *exit, talking loudly about their plans for the night.*)

Esta . . . estudiantes: This great mass of humanity has done enough talking! It has begun to march! Enough! Enough! Long live our race! Long live our cause! Long live the strike! Long live the brown berets! Long live the students!   **lana:** money **vatos:** guys

The REVOLUCIONARIO *goes over to* SANCHO, *removes his derby hat and cigar, lifts him up and throws him over his shoulder.* SANCHO *hangs loose, lifeless. To audience)* He's the best model we got! ¡Ajúa!° (*Exit.*)

QUESTIONS

1. "Honest Sancho" runs his "Used Mexican Lot" like a used car lot. How is this metaphorical context developed in the play? How is the satire directed at both used car salesmen and a Mexican who has sold out his race?
2. Explore the stereotyping that characterizes the "models" that Honest Sancho offers for sale. At whom is the satire directed—the four "models," or people who stereotype others? What is the implication of these men being presented as if they were machines?
3. Of the characters in the play, only Miss Jimenez escapes being portrayed as a machine. Is she therefore treated sympathetically by the play?
4. How effective is the surprise ending?
5. How do you think an audience composed entirely of Mexican-Americans would respond to this play? an audience of Anglos? a mixed audience? Would there be differences among these audiences as to how comic the play is?

¡**Ajúa**! Wow!

Plays for
Further Reading

Anton Chekhov

The Cherry Orchard

A Comedy in Four Acts

CHARACTERS

RANYEVSKAYA, LYUBOV [LYUBA], *a widowed landowner returning home from Paris to her Russian estate*
ANYA [ANYECHKA], *her daughter, aged 17*
VARYA, *her adopted daughter, aged 24*
GAYEV, LEONID [LENYA] ANDREYICH, *Madame Ranyevskaya's brother, aged 51*
LOPAKHIN, YERMOLAY, *a businessman*
TROFIMOV, [PETYA], *a student in his late twenties, tutor of Madame Ranyevskaya's late son Grisha*
SIMEONOV-PISHCHIK, *called Pishchik, a landowner*
CHARLOTTA IVANOVNA, *Anya's governess*
YEPIKHODOV, *a clerk on the estate*
DUNYASHA, *the chambermaid*
FIRS, *the old manservant, aged 87*
YASHA, *the young footman*
A PASSER-BY; THE STATIONMASTER; THE POSTMASTER.

(Characters are listed here with the nicknames that occur in the text. For an explanation of Russian names, see page 515.)

The action takes place on Madame Ranyevskaya's estate.

ACT I

A room which is still known as the nursery. One of the doors leads to ANYA'S *room. Half-light, shortly before sunrise. It is May already, and the cherry trees*

THE CHERRY ORCHARD   First performed in Moscow in 1904. Translated by Michael Frayn. At the turn of the century Russia was in transition from a semifeudal monarchy to a modern state, and the aristocratic landowners were losing out economically to a rising business class. Various attempts at political and social reform during the preceding half-century included the freeing of the serfs in 1861, the establishment of local self-government councils in the sixties and seventies, the abolition of the poll tax in 1887, and throughout the period increasing educational opportunities at all levels—yet, in the census of 1897 for example, 74 percent of the citizens were still illiterate. Like the character Lopakhin, Anton Chekhov (1860–1904)—also author of the story "In Exile" (page 140)—was the grandson of a serf and the son of a small shopkeeper, but was educated as a physician and made enough money from his writing to buy a small country estate near Moscow in 1892.

are in blossom, but outside in the orchard it is cold, with a morning frost. The windows are closed. Enter DUNYASHA *with a candle, and* LOPAKHIN *with a book in his hand.*

LOPAKHIN.   God be praised, the train's arrived. What time is it?

DUNYASHA.   Nearly two o'clock. (*Extinguishes the candle.*) It's light already.

LOPAKHIN.   So the train's how late? Two hours, at least. (*Yawns and stretches.*) Fine one I am. Complete fool. Came all the way here to go and meet them at the station, and then just dropped off while I was sitting there. It's a shame. You might have woken me.

DUNYASHA.   I thought you'd gone. (*Listens.*) That sounds like them now.

LOPAKHIN (*listens*).   No . . . Luggage to pick up, one thing and another . . . (*Pause.*) She's lived abroad for five years—I don't know what she'll be like now . . . She's a fine woman. Easy, straightforward. I remember, when I was a boy of fifteen or so, my father—he kept a shop then in the village here—dead now, of course—he punched me in the face, and the blood started to pour out of my nose . . . For some reason we'd come into the yard here together, and he was drunk. It seems like yesterday. She was only young—such a slim young thing. She brought me in and she took me to the wash-stand in this room, in the nursery. "Don't cry, my little peasant," she says. "It'll heal in time for your wedding . . ." (*Pause.*) My little peasant . . . it's true, my father was a peasant—and here am I in a white waistcoat and yellow shoes. Like a pig in a pastry cook's . . . The only difference is I'm a rich man, plenty of money, but look twice and I'm a peasant, a real peasant . . . (*Leafs through the book.*) I was reading this book. Couldn't understand a word. Fell asleep over it. (*Pause.*)

DUNYASHA.   And the dogs, they haven't slept all night. They can sense that the mistress is coming.

LOPAKHIN.   What's the matter with you, Dunyasha?

DUNYASHA.   My hands are all of a tremble. I'm going to faint.

LOPAKHIN.   Very tender plant, aren't you, Dunyasha? Dress like a lady, do your hair like one, too. Not the way, is it? You want to remember who you are. (*Enter* YEPIKHODOV *with a bouquet. He is wearing a jacket and highly polished boots that squeak loudly. As he comes in he drops the bouquet.*)

YEPIKHODOV (*picks up the bouquet*).   The gardener sent them. He says to put them in the dining-room. (*Gives the bouquet to* DUNYASHA.)

LOPAKHIN.   And bring me some kvass.°

DUNYASHA.   Very good. (*Goes out.*)

YEPIKHODOV.   Three degrees of frost this morning, and the cherry all in blossom. I can't give our climate my seal of approval. (*Sighs.*) Indeed I can't. It never knows how to lend a helping hand at the right moment. And I

kvass: homemade beer

mean look at me—I bought myself these boots the day before yesterday, and they squeak so much, I mean it's quite impossible. I mean, put it like this— what should I grease them with?

LOPAKHIN.   Leave off, will you? Pester, pester.

YEPIKHODOV.   I don't know. Every day some disaster happens to me. Not that I complain. I'm used to it. I even smile. (*Enter* DUNYASHA. *She gives* LOPAKHIN *his kvass.*) I'll go, then. (*Stumbles against the table, which falls over.*) There you are . . . (*As if exulting in it*) You see what I'm up against! I mean, it's simply amazing! (*Goes out.*)

DUNYASHA.   To tell you the truth, he's proposed to me.

LOPAKHIN.   Ah!

DUNYASHA.   I don't know *what* to say . . . He's all right, he doesn't give any trouble, it's just sometimes when he starts to talk—you can't understand a word of it. It's very nice, and he puts a lot of feeling into it, only you can't understand it. I quite like him in a way, even. He's madly in love with me. He's the kind of person who never has any luck. Every day something happens. They tease him in our part of the house—they call him Disasters by the Dozen . . .

LOPAKHIN (*listens*).   I think they're coming.

DUNYASHA.   They're coming! What's the matter with me? I've gone all cold.

LOPAKHIN.   They are indeed coming. Let's go and meet them. Will she recognize me? Five years we haven't seen each other.

DUNYASHA (*in agitation*).   I'll faint this very minute . . . I will, I'll faint clean away! (*Two carriages can be heard coming up to the house.* LOPAKHIN *and* DUNYASHA *hurry out. The stage is empty. Then there is noise in the adjoining rooms. Across the stage, leaning on his stick, hurries* FIRS, *who has gone to the station to meet the mistress. He is wearing ancient livery and a top hat. He is saying something to himself, but not a word of it can be made out. The noise offstage grows louder and louder.*)

A VOICE (*off*).   This way, look. (*Enter* RANYEVSKAYA, ANYA, *and* CHARLOTTA IVANOVNA, *who has a little dog on a leash. All three ladies are dressed for traveling;* VARYA *wears an overcoat and shawl;* GAYEV, SIMEONOV-PISHCHIK, LOPAKHIN, DUNYASHA *with a bundle and an umbrella,* SERVANTS *carrying things—they all go across the room.*)

ANYA.   This way. Mama, do you remember which room this is?

RANYEVSKAYA (*joyfully, on the verge of tears*).   The nursery!

VARYA.   So cold. My hands are quite numb. (*To* RANYEVSKAYA) Your rooms . . . the white one and the mauve one—they've stayed just as they were, Mama.

RANYEVSKAYA.   The nursery. My own dear room, my lovely room . . . I slept in here when I was a little girl. (*Weeps.*) And now I'm like a little girl again . . . (*Kisses her brother, then* VARYA, *then her brother once more.*) And Varya's just the same as before—she looks like a nun. And Dunyasha I recognize . . . (*Kisses her.*)

GAYEV.   The train was two hours late. What do you think of that? What kind of standards do these people have?

CHARLOTTA (*to* PISHCHIK).   My dog can eat nuts even.

PISHCHIK (*surprised*).   Would you believe it! (*They all go out except* ANYA *and* DUNYASHA.)

DUNYASHA.   We waited and waited . . . (*She takes off* ANYA'S *coat and hat.*)

ANYA.   I didn't sleep on the way—I haven't slept for four nights . . . Oh, I'm completely frozen!

DUNYASHA.   You went away in Lent, with snow on the ground still, and now look at it. Oh, my dear! (*Laughs and kisses her.*) I've waited and waited for you. My own precious! My heart's delight . . . I'm going to tell you at once—I can't contain myself another minute . . .

ANYA (*inertly*).   Nothing else.

DUNYASHA.   Yepikhodov—you know who I mean, the estate clerk— just after Easter he proposed to me.

ANYA.   Still on about the same old thing . . . (*Tidying her hair.*) I've gradually lost all the pins . . . (*She is completely exhausted—unable to keep her balance, even.*)

DUNYASHA.   I don't know *what* to think. He's in love with me, so in love with me!

ANYA (*looks into her room, tenderly.*).   My room, my windows, just as if I'd never been away. I'll get up in the morning, I'll run out into the orchard . . . Oh, if only I could get to sleep! I didn't sleep all the way—I was worn out with worry.

DUNYASHA.   The day before yesterday Mr. Trofimov arrived.

ANYA (*joyfully*).   Petya!

DUNYASHA.   He's sleeping in the bath-house—he's living out there. He said he was afraid of being in the way. (*Looks at her pocket watch.*) We ought to wake him up, but Miss Varya said not to. Don't you go waking him, she says. (*Enter* VARYA, *with a bunch of keys on her belt. As household manager, she carries keys to all the cupboards.*)

VARYA.   Dunyasha, quick now—Mama's asking for coffee.

DUNYASHA.   Very good. (*Goes out.*)

VARYA.   Well, God be praised, you've got here, both of you. You're home again, Anya. (*Cuddling her*) My darling's come home! My lovely's come home again!

ANYA.   I've had a most terrible time.

VARYA.   I can imagine.

ANYA.   I set out from here in Holy Week. It was cold. Charlotta talked the whole way—she kept showing me conjuring tricks. Why on earth you saddled me with Charlotta . . .

VARYA.   You couldn't have traveled alone, my darling. Not at seventeen!

ANYA.   Anyway, we get to Paris, and it's cold, it's snowing. My French is terrible. Mama's living up on the fifth floor, and when I arrive she's got people with her—Frenchmen, I don't know who they were, and ladies, and some ancient Catholic priest holding a prayer-book—and the air's full of tobacco smoke, and it's bleak and uncomfortable. And suddenly I felt sorry for Mama. I felt so sorry for her I put my arms around her and pressed her head against me and couldn't let go. After that Mama kept hugging me, and crying . . .

VARYA (*on the verge of tears*).   Don't, don't . . .

ANYA.   She'd already sold that villa she had outside Menton.° She's nothing left, nothing. Nor have I—not a kopeck. We scarcely managed it here. And Mama doesn't understand! We'll sit down to dinner in a station restaurant, and she orders the most expensive item on the menu. Then she tips all the waiters a ruble each. Charlotta's the same. And Yasha has to be fed, too—it's simply frightful. You know Mama has this footman, Yasha. We brought him with us.

VARYA.   I've seen the rogue.

ANYA.   So what—have we paid the interest?

VARYA.   How could we?

ANYA.   Oh God, oh God . . .

VARYA.   In August they're going to sell the estate off.

ANYA.   Oh God . . .

LOPAKHIN (*looks in at the door, and moos*).   M-e-e-e . . . (*Goes out.*)

VARYA (*through her tears*).   Oh, I'd like to give him such a . . . (*Raises her fist threateningly.*)

ANYA (*embraces* VARYA—*quietly*).   Varya, has he proposed? (VARYA *shakes her head.*) Look, he loves you . . . Why don't you get things straight between you? What are you both waiting for?

VARYA.   I'll tell you what I think—I think nothing's going to come of it. He's very busy, he hasn't got time for me—he doesn't even notice. Well, good luck to him, but I can't bear the sight of him. Everyone talks about our wedding, everyone keeps congratulating me, but in fact there's nothing there—it's all a kind of dream. (*In a different tone*) You've got a bumble-bee brooch.

ANYA (*sadly*).   Mama bought it. (*Goes into her room, and speaks cheerfully, childishly.*) And in Paris I went up in an air-balloon!

VARYA   Oh, my darling's come home! My lovely's come home again! (DUNYASHA *is back with the coffee-pot. She makes the coffee.* VARYA *stands by the door to* ANYA's *room.*) Oh, my darling, I go about the house all day in a dream. If we could just get you married to some rich man, then I could be easy in my mind. I could take myself off into a retreat, then to Kiev, to Moscow, and oh, I'd walk all round the holy places . . . I'd just keep walking and walking. The glory of it!

ANYA.   The birds are singing in the orchard. What time is it now?

VARYA.   It must be after two. Time for you to sleep, my darling. (*Going in to* ANYA.) The glory of it! (*Enter* YASHA *with a rug and traveling bag.*)

Menton: town on the Mediterranean coast of France

YASHA (*crosses with delicacy*).   All right to come through?

DUNYASHA.   I shouldn't even recognize you, Yasha. You've changed so abroad!

YASHA.   Mm . . . And who are you?

DUNYASHA.   When you left I was so high . . . (*Indicates from the floor.*) Dunyasha. Fyodor Kozoyedov's daughter. You don't remember!

YASHA.   Mm . . . Quite a pippin, aren't you? (*Looks round and embraces her. She screams and drops a saucer. Exit* YASHA, *swiftly.*)

VARYA (*in the doorway, displeased*).   Now what's going on?

DUNYASHA (*through her tears*).   I've smashed the saucer . . .

VARYA.   That's good luck.

ANYA (*coming out of her room*).   We should warn Mama—Petya's here.

VARYA.   I gave orders not to wake him.

ANYA (*reflectively*).   Six years since Father died, and only a month later that Grisha was drowned in the river. My brother . . . Seven years old, and such a pretty boy. Mama couldn't bear it. She escaped—fled without so much as a backward glance . . . (*Shivers.*) I understand her so well, if only she knew! (*Pause.*) And Petya Trofimov was Grisha's tutor. He may remind her . . . (*Enter* FIRS, *in jacket and white waistcoat.*)

FIRS (*goes to the coffee-pot, preoccupied*).   The mistress will be taking it in here . . . (*Puts on white gloves.*) The coffee ready? (*To* DUNYASHA, *sternly*) What's this, girl? Where's the cream?

DUNYASHA.   Oh, my Lord . . . (*Rushes out.*)

FIRS (*busies himself with the coffee-pot*).   Oh, you sillybilly! (*Mutters to himself*) Come from Paris . . . The master went to Paris once . . . by post-chaise . . . (*Laughs.*)

VARYA.   What are you going on about, Firs?

FIRS.   What do you want? (*Joyfully*) My lady has come home! I waited for her! I can die happy . . . (*Weeps with joy. Enter* RANYEVSKAYA, GAYEV, LOPAKHIN *and* SIMEONOV-PISHCHIK *who is wearing a tight-fitting, long-waisted coat in a fine material, and wide, Oriental-looking trousers.* GAYEV, *as he comes in, makes movements with his arms and trunk as if he were playing billiards.*)

RANYEVSKAYA.   How did it go? Let's see . . . Yellow into the corner. Then off the cushion into the middle pocket.

GAYEV.   And screw back into the corner! There was a time, my sister, when you and I slept in this very room. And now I'm fifty-one already, strange as it seems.

LOPAKHIN.   Yes, the time goes by.

GAYEV.   Who?

LOPAKHIN.   I say the time goes by.

GAYEV.   It reeks of cheap scent in here, though.

ANYA.   I'm going to bed. Good night, Mama. (*Kisses her mother.*)

RANYEVSKAYA.   My beloved child. (*Kisses her hands.*) Are you pleased to be home? I don't think I shall ever manage to come down to earth.

ANYA.   Good night, Uncle.

GAYEV (*kisses her face and hands*).   The Lord guard and keep you. How like your mother you are! (*To his sister*) Lyuba, at her age you were just like that. (ANYA *gives her hand to* LOPAKHIN *and* PISHCHIK, *then goes out and closes the door behind her.*)

RANYEVSKAYA.   She's tired out.

PISHCHIK.   It's a long way to go, no doubt about it.

VARYA (*to* LOPAKHIN *and* PISHCHIK).   Well, then, gentlemen. Past two o'clock. Time to be saying goodbye.

RANYEVSKAYA (*laughs*).   Varya, you're just the same as ever. (*Draws her close and kisses her.*) I'll drink my coffee, then we'll all go. (FIRS *puts a cushion under her feet.*) Thank you, my dear. I've got into the coffee habit. I drink it day and night. Thank you, my dear old friend. (*Kisses* FIRS.)

VARYA.   I must see if they've brought all the things. (*Exits.*)

RANYEVSKAYA.   Is this really me sitting here? (*Laughs.*) I feel like leaping into the air and waving my arms about. (*Covers her face with her hands.*) Perhaps it's all a dream. Oh, but I love my country, God knows I do, I love it tenderly. I couldn't look out of the carriage window—I did nothing but weep. (*On the verge of tears*) However, the coffee has to be drunk. Thank you, Firs, thank you, my dear. I'm so glad to find you still alive.

FIRS.   The day before yesterday.

GAYEV.   His hearing's going.

LOPAKHIN.   I have to leave straight away, before five o'clock. I'm off to Kharkov. Such a shame. I just wanted to get a look at you, have a few words . . . You're still as magnificent as ever.

PISHCHIK (*breathes hard*).   You've grown even more lovely . . . Dressed in Paris fashions . . . I could throw caution to the winds.

LOPAKHIN.   In the eyes of your sort—your brother here, for instance—I'm a boor, I'm a money-grubbing peasant, but I don't give a damn about that. The only thing I want is for you to trust me as you did before, to see your amazing, heart-breaking eyes looking at me the way they used to. Merciful God! My father was a serf, and your father and grandfather owned him. But you—yes, you were the one—you did so much for me once that I've forgotten all that, and I love you like my own flesh and blood . . . more than my own flesh and blood.

RANYEVSKAYA.   I can't sit still. I'm physically incapable . . . (*Jumps up and walks about in a state of great emotion.*) I shall never survive this joy . . . Laugh at me, I'm such a fool . . . My bookcase, my own dear bookcase . . . (*Kisses the bookcase.*) My dear old table.

GAYEV.   Nanna died while you were away.

RANYEVSKAYA (*sits and drinks coffee*).   Yes, God rest her soul. They wrote and told me.

GAYEV.   And Anastasy died. Petrushka—you remember him? With the squint? He left me. Living in town now, working for the local police inspector. (*He takes a box of hard candies out of his pocket and sucks one.*)

PISHCHIK.   My daughter Dashenka—she sends her best regards . . .

LOPAKHIN.   I want to tell you some very pleasant and cheering news. (*Glances at his watch.*) I shall be leaving very shortly, we haven't time for a proper talk . . . I'll put it in two words, then. You know, of course, that your cherry orchard is to be sold to pay your debts—the sale is fixed for the twenty-second of August. But don't you worry yourself about it, my dear— sleep easy in your bed at night—there is a way out . . . This is my plan. Now listen carefully. Your estate is only thirteen miles out of town; the railway has now come through right next to it; and if the cherry orchard and the land along the river are broken up into building lots and leased out as sites for summer cottages, then you will possess an income of—at the very least— twenty-five thousand rubles a year.

GAYEV.   I'm sorry, but it's such nonsense!

RANYEVSKAYA (*to* LOPAKHIN).   I don't entirely understand you.

LOPAKHIN.   You will get from your leaseholders at the very minimum ten rubles a year per acre. And if you advertise it now, then I swear upon anything you like to name that by the autumn you won't have a single acre left—it will all have been taken up. In short—congratulations, you're saved. It's a marvelous position with this deep river. The only thing, of course, is that you need to tidy it up a bit. Remove all the old buildings, for example— like this house, which won't have any use now—and cut down the old cherry orchard.

RANYEVSKAYA.   Cut it down? My dear, forgive me, but you don't understand. If there is one thing of any interest at all in this whole province— if there is even something rather remarkable—then it's our cherry orchard.

LOPAKHIN.   There's only one thing remarkable about this orchard. It's very big. You only get a full crop every other year, and then there's nothing to do with it—no one buys it.

GAYEV.   There's even a reference to this orchard in the encyclopedia.

LOPAKHIN (*glances at his watch*).   If we don't think of something, if we don't come to some decision, then on the twenty-second of August not only the cherry orchard but the whole estate will be sold at auction. So nerve yourselves! There is no other way out, I swear to you. None whatsoever.

FIRS.   In the old days, forty, fifty years ago, they used to dry the cherries, they used to soak them, they used to pickle them, they used to make jam out of them, and year after year . . .

GAYEV.   Do be quiet, Firs.

FIRS.   And year after year they'd send off dried cherries by the cartload to Moscow and Kharkov. There was money then! And the dried cherries were soft and juicy and sweet and scented . . . They knew the recipe in those days.

RANYEVSKAYA.   And what's happened to this recipe now?

FIRS.   They've forgotten it. No one remembers it.

PISHCHIK (*to* RANYEVSKAYA).   How was it in Paris, then? Did you eat frogs?

RANYEVSKAYA.   I ate crocodiles.

PISHCHIK.   Would you believe it!

LOPAKHIN.   Up to now in the countryside we've had only the gentry and the peasants. But now a new class has appeared—the summer country-men. Every town now, even the smallest, is surrounded with summer cottages. And we may assume that over the next twenty years or so our summer countryman will be fruitful and multiply exceedingly. Now he merely sits on his verandah and drinks tea, but you know it may come to pass that he'll put his couple of acres to some use, and start to cultivate them. And then this old cherry orchard of yours will become happy and rich and luxuriant . . .

GAYEV (*exasperated*).   Such nonsense! (*Enter* VARYA *and* YASHA.)

VARYA.   Mama, there are two telegrams that came for you. (*Selects a key which clinks in the lock as she opens the antique bookcase.*) Here.

RANYEVSKAYA.   From Paris. (*Tears up the telegrams without reading them.*) Paris is over and done with.

GAYEV.   But, Lyuba, do you know how old this bookcase is? I pulled out the bottom drawer last week, and I looked, and there were some numbers burnt into the wood with a poker. This bookcase was built exactly one hundred years ago. What do you think of that? We could celebrate its centenary. It's an inanimate object, but all the same, whichever way you look at it, it's still a bookcase.

PISHCHIK (*in surprise*).   A hundred years . . . Would you believe it!

GAYEV.   Yes . . . Quite an achievement . . . (*Feels the bookcase.*) Dear bookcase! Most esteemed bookcase! I salute your existence, which for more than a hundred years now has been directed towards the shining ideals of goodness and of truth. For a hundred years your unspoken summons to fruitful labor has never faltered, upholding (*on the verge of tears*), through all the generations of our family, wisdom and faith in a better future, and foster-ing within us ideals of goodness and of social consciousness. (*Pause.*)

LOPAKHIN.   Yes . . .

RANYEVSKAYA.   You're the same as ever, Lenya.

GAYEV (*in some slight confusion*).   In off into the righthand corner! Then screw back into the middle pocket!

LOPAKHIN (*glances at his watch*).   Well, I must be on my way.

YASHA (*hands pills to* RANYEVSKAYA).   Take your pills now, perhaps . . .

PISHCHIK.   Dearest heart, you mustn't go taking medicines . . . there's neither harm nor charm in them . . . Give them here . . . Dear lady. (*Picks up the pills, tips them out on to his palm, blows on them, puts them into his mouth, and washes them down with kvass.*) There!

RANYEVSKAYA (*alarmed*).   But you've gone utterly mad!

PISHCHIK.   I've taken all the pills.

LOPAKHIN.   There's a greedyguts! (*Everyone laughs.*)

FIRS.   When he was here at Easter he put away half a bucket of pickled cucumbers . . . (*Mutters.*)

RANYEVSKAYA.   What's he going on about now?

VARYA.   He's been muttering away like this for the last three years. We've got used to it.

YASHA.   Old age, isn't it? (CHARLOTTA IVANOVNA *crosses the stage, in a white dress. She is very thin and very tightly laced, with a lorgnette hanging from her belt.*)

LOPAKHIN.   Forgive me, I haven't had a chance to say hello to you. (*Tries to kiss her hand.*)

CHARLOTTA (*taking her hand away*).   Let you kiss my hand, and next thing I know you'll be after my elbow, then my shoulder . . .

LOPAKHIN.   Not having any luck today, am I? (*Everyone laughs.*) Come on, then, show us a conjuring trick!

CHARLOTTA.   No, I just want to go to bed. (*Goes out.*)

LOPAKHIN.   Well, we'll meet again in three weeks time. (*Kisses* RANYEVSKAYA'S *hand.*) So until then. (*To* GAYEV) Goodbye. (*Exchanges kisses with* PISHCHIK.) Goodbye. (*Gives his hand to* VARYA, *then to* FIRS *and* YASHA.) I only wish I didn't have to go. (*To* RANYEVSKAYA) If you come to a decision about the houses, let me know, and I'll get you fifty thousand on account. Think about it seriously.

VARYA (*angrily*).   Oh, go on!

LOPAKHIN.   I'm going. I'm going. (*Exits.*)

GAYEV.   A boor—the man's a boor. Oh, *pardon* . . . Varya's going to marry him. He's Varya's intended.

VARYA.   Uncle, please, don't start.

RANYEVSKAYA.   Why, Varya, I shall be very happy. He's a good man.

PISHCHIK.   A most—it has to be said—worthy man. And my Dashenka . . . she also says that, well, she says various things. (*Snores, but immediately wakes up again.*) But all the same, dear lady, if you could oblige me . . . with a loan of two hundred and forty rubles . . . The interest on my mortgage is due tomorrow . . .

VARYA (*alarmed*).   No, no!

RANYEVSKAYA.   I really do have nothing.

PISHCHIK.   Well, it'll get itself found somehow. (*Laughs.*) I never lose hope. Here we are, I think to myself, everything's lost, I'm done for—but not at all, because lo and behold—the railway's come through my land, and . . . they've paid me. And by and by, you'll see, one day soon, something else will happen . . . There's two hundred thousand Dashenka's going to win— she's got a lucky ticket.

RANYEVSKAYA.   The coffee's finished. We can go to bed.

FIRS (*brushes* GAYEV; *lecturing*).   You've put the wrong trousers on again. What am I to do with you?

VARYA (*quietly*).   Anya's asleep. (*Quietly opens a window.*) The sun's up already—it's not cold. Look, Mama—what marvelous trees they are! And oh, sweet heavens, the air! And the starlings are chattering!

GAYEV (*opens another window*).   The orchard's all in white. You haven't forgotten, Lyuba? The way the long avenue there runs straight, straight, like a ribbon stretched taut, the way it shines on moonlit nights. You remember? You haven't forgotten?

RANYEVSKAYA (*looks out of the window at the orchard*).   Oh, my childhood, my innocence! In this nursery I slept, from this room I looked out at the orchard, and happiness woke with me every morning. The orchard was just the same then, nothing has changed. (*Laughs with joy.*) All, all in white! Oh, my orchard! After dark foul autumn and cold cold winter, again you're young and filled with happiness, and not abandoned by the angels. If only the millstone could be lifted from my neck. If only I could forget my past!

GAYEV.   Yes, even the orchard will be sold to meet our debts. Strange as it seems . . .

RANYEVSKAYA.   Look—there's Mama, our own dead Mama, walking through the orchard . . . in a white dress! (*Laughs with joy.*) It's her.

GAYEV.   Where?

VARYA.   God save you, Mama.

RANYEVSKAYA.   There's no one there. It just looked like it for a moment. To the right, on the turning to the summer-house—a tree bending under its blossom like the figure of a woman. (*Enter* TROFIMOV, *in a shabby student's uniform and spectacles.*) What an amazing orchard it is! The white masses of the blossom, the pale blue of the sky . . .

TROFIMOV.   Lyubov Andreyevna! (*She looks round at him.*) I'm just going to pay my respects to you, and then I'll go away and leave you in peace. (*Ardently kisses her hand.*) I was told to wait until morning, but I didn't have patience enough. (RANYEVSKAYA *gazes at him in perplexity.*)

VARYA (*on the verge of tears*).   It's Petya.

TROFIMOV.   Trofimov. Petya Trofimov. I used to be Grisha's tutor . . . Have I really changed so much? (RANYEVSKAYA *embraces him and weeps quietly.*)

GAYEV (*embarrassed*).   Come on, Lyuba. Come on, now.

VARYA (*weeps*).   Petya, I did tell you to wait until tomorrow.

RANYEVSKAYA.   My Grisha . . . my boy . . Grisha . . . my son . . .

VARYA.   What can we do, Mama? It was God's will.

TROFIMOV (*softly, on the verge of tears*).   There now . . . There, now . . .

RANYEVSKAYA (*weeps quietly*).   My boy died, my little boy was drowned . . . Why? Why, my friend? (*More quietly*) Anya's asleep in there, and here am I talking at the top of my voice . . . making a noise . . . What's this, Petya? Why have you lost your looks? Why have you aged so?

TROFIMOV.   You know what some old woman on a train the other day called me?—"That mangy-looking gentleman."

RANYEVSKAYA.   You were still only a boy before, just a nice young student. Now you've got glasses, your hair's gone thin. You're surely not still a student? (*Goes to the door.*)

TROFIMOV.   I should think I'm going to be a perpetual student. The Wandering Student, like the Wandering Jew.

RANYEVSKAYA (*kisses her brother, then* VARYA).   Well, off to bed, then . . . You've aged, too, Leonid.

PISHCHIK (*follows her*).   So, bedtime . . . Oh, my gout. I'll stay the night here, I think. (*To* RANYEVSKAYA) And in the morning, dearest heart, if you would . . . two hundred and forty rubles . . .

GAYEV.   Never gives up, does he?

PISHCHIK.   Two hundred and forty rubles . . . I have to pay the interest on my mortgage.

RANYEVSKAYA.   I have no money, my sweet.

PISHCHIK.   I'll give it back, my dear. It's the most piffling sum.

RANYEVSKAYA.   Well, all right. Leonid will give it to you. You give it to him, Leonid.

GAYEV.   If it's up to me, he can whistle for it.

RANYEVSKAYA.   What can we do? Just give it to him . . . He needs it . . . He'll give it back. (*Exeunt* RANYEVSKAYA, TROFIMOV, PISHCHIK *and* FIRS. GAYEV, VARYA *and* YASHA *remain.*)

GAYEV.   My sister still hasn't got out of the habit of flinging her money around. (*To* YASHA) Do go away, my dear good chap—you smell of chickens.

YASHA (*grinning*).   And you're just the same as you always were.

GAYEV.   Who? (*To* VARYA) What does he say?

VARYA (*to* YASHA).   Your mother's come from the village. She's been sitting in the servants' hall since yesterday waiting to see you.

YASHA.   Well, good luck to her, then.

VARYA.   Shameless, aren't you?

YASHA.   What's the point. She could just as well have come tomorrow. (*Goes out.*)

VARYA.   Mama's exactly the same as she was. She hasn't changed at all. If it was up to her she'd have given everything away.

GAYEV.   Yes . . . (*Pause.*) If for some disease a great many different remedies are proposed, then it means that the disease is incurable. I think, I cudgel my brains—I have many remedies, a great many—and what that means when you get down to it is that I haven't a solitary one. It would be a good thing if we got an inheritance from someone. It would be a good thing if we married Anya to some very rich man. It would be a good thing if we went to Yaroslavl° and tried our luck with that aunt of ours, the countess. She's very rich indeed, you know.

VARYA (*weeps*).   If only God would help.

Yaroslavl: old Russian town on the Volga River

GAYEV.   Don't howl. Aunt is very rich, but she doesn't like us. In the first place, my sister married an ordinary lawyer instead of a gentleman with property . . . (ANYA *appears in the doorway.*) She married a commoner, and the way she's behaved—well, you couldn't say it was very virtuously. She's good, she's kind, she's a splendid woman, I love her dearly, but however many extenuating circumstances you think up, the fact has to be faced: she is depraved. You can sense it in her slightest movement.

VARYA (*in a whisper*).   Anya is standing in the doorway.

GAYEV.   Who? (*Pause.*) Funny—I've got something in my right eye. I can't see properly. And on Thursday, when I was at the district court . . . (*Enter* ANYA.)

VARYA.   Why aren't you asleep, Anya?

ANYA.   I can't get to sleep.

GAYEV.   My pet. (*Kisses* ANYA'S *face and hands.*) My child . . . (*On the verge of tears*) You're not my niece at all—you're my angel. You're everything to me. Believe me. Trust me.

ANYA.   I trust you, uncle. Everyone loves you, everyone looks up to you . . . but, dear Uncle, you must be quiet, only be quiet. What were you saying just then about my mother—about your own sister? Why did you say that?

GAYEV.   Yes, yes . . . (*Covers his face with her hand.*) Really, that was terrible! God forgive me! And today I made a speech to the bookcase . . . so stupid! And only when I'd finished did I realize how stupid it was.

VARYA.   It's true, Uncle dear, you must keep quiet. Just be quiet, that's all.

ANYA.   If you're quiet, you'll be calmer in yourself, too.

GAYEV.   I am silent. (*Kisses their hands.*) Not a word. Just one thing on a matter of business. On Thursday I was at the district court, and, well, a few of us there got to talking about this and that, one thing and another, and it seems it would be possible to arrange a loan against my note of hand to pay the bank interest.

VARYA.   If only the Lord would help!

GAYEV.   On Tuesday I'll go and have another talk about it. (*To* VARYA) Don't howl. (*To* ANYA) Your mother will have a word with Lopakhin. He obviously won't refuse her. And you—as soon as you've got your breath back you'll go to Yaroslavl to see the countess, your great aunt. So we'll be operating from three sides at once—and the job's as good as done. We shall pay the interest, of that I'm convinced. (*Puts a candy in his mouth.*) I swear, upon my honor, upon whatever you like, that the estate will not be sold! (*Excitedly*) By my hope of happiness I swear it! Here's my hand on it—call me a low, dishonorable fellow if I let it go to auction! By my whole being I swear to you!

ANYA (*her calm mood has returned to her: she is happy*).   What a good man you are, Uncle, what a good and clever man! (*Embraces him.*) Now I'm calm! Quite calm! I'm happy! (*Enter* FIRS.)

FIRS (*to* GAYEV, *reproachfully*).   What? Have you no fear before God? When are you going to bed?

GAYEV.   Right now, right now. You go off. Don't worry about me, I'll undress myself. Well, night night, then, children. Details tomorrow, but now to bed. (*Kisses* ANYA *and* VARYA.) I am a man of the eighties.° Not a period they speak well of these days, but I can tell you that I have suffered not a little in this life for my convictions. It's no accident that your ordinary peasant loves me. You have to know your peasant! You have to know how to . . .

ANYA.   Uncle, you're off again!

VARYA.   Dear uncle, just be quiet.

FIRS (*angrily*).   Leonid Andreyich!

GAYEV.   I'm coming, I'm coming . . . Off to bed, then. Cushion, cushion, and into the middle pocket! Clean as a whistle . . . (*Goes out, with* FIRS *trotting behind him.*)

ANYA.   Now I'm calm. I don't want to go to Yaroslavl—I don't like our great aunt. But all the same I'm calm. Thanks to Uncle. (*Sits down.*)

VARYA.   We must get some sleep. I'm off. One rather annoying thing happened while you were away, though. You know what used to be the servants' quarters? Well, of course, it's only the elderly servants who live there now: Yefimushka, Polya, Yevstigney, oh, yes, and Karp. Well, they began to let various riff-raff in to spend the night. I said nothing about it. Only then I hear they've been spreading a rumor to the effect that I've had them fed on nothing but dried peas. Out of meanness, do you see . . . And all this is Yevstigney's doing . . . Right, I think to myself. If that's the way you want it, then just you wait. So I send for Yevstigney . . . (*Yawns.*) He comes in . . . What's all this, then, Yevstigney? I say to him . . . You're such a fool . . . (*Looks at* ANYA.) Anyechka . . . ! (*Pause.*) Asleep . . . ! (*Takes* ANYA *by the arm.*) Off to bed, then . . . off we go . . . ! (*Leads her.*) My poor precious has fallen fast asleep! Off we go . . . (*A long way away, beyond the orchard, a* SHEPHERD *plays on a reed pipe.* TROFIMOV *crosses the stage, and stops at the sight of* VARYA *and* ANYA.)

VARYA.   Sh . . . She's asleep . . . asleep . . . Off we go, my own sweet precious.

ANYA (*quietly, half asleep*).   So tired . . . I can still hear the harness bells . . . Uncle . . . dear Uncle . . . Mama and Uncle, too . . .

VARYA.   Off we go, my own sweet love. Off we go . . . (*They go into* ANYA'S *room.*)

TROFIMOV (*moved*).   My sunshine! My springtime!

---

man of the eighties: Gayev is probably taking credit for involvement in the altruistic "era of small deeds" when the gentry encouraged peasants' efforts to participate in local self-government and to improve public health, education, and local economies. Looking backward from the end of the century, the eighties seemed a time of gradual, peaceful change, in contrast to the more fervent revolutionary movement that preceded the decade, or those following it that were to culminate in the 1905 revolution the year after Chekhov's death.

ACT 2

The open fields. A wayside shrine—old, crooked, and long neglected. Beside it—a well, large slabs which were evidently once tombstones, and an old bench. A path can be seen leading to the Gayev estate. At one side rise the dark shapes of poplars; this is where the cherry orchard begins. In the distance is a row of telegraph poles, and a long way away on the horizon a large town can just be made out, visible only in very fine, clear weather. The sun is just about to set. CHARLOTTA, YASHA *and* DUNYASHA *are sitting on the bench;* YEPIKHODOV *is standing beside it, playing the guitar. They are all in a reflective mood.* CHARLOTTA *is wearing an old peaked cap. She has taken a gun off her shoulder and is adjusting the buckle on the sling.*

CHARLOTTA (*meditatively*).   I haven't got proper papers—I don't know how old I am. So I always think of myself as being young. When I was a little girl Mama and my father used to go round all the fairs giving shows. Very good shows they were, too. And I'd turn somersaults and do all kinds of little tricks. And when Papa and Mama died, some German lady took me in and began to give me an education. So, all right, I grew up, and then I went to be a governess. But where I come from and who I am, I don't know. Who my parents were—whether they were even married or not—I don't know. (*Gets a cucumber out of her pocket and eats it.*) I don't know anything. (*Pause.*) I so long to talk to someone, but there's no one to talk to. I haven't got anyone.

YEPIKHODOV (*plays the guitar and sings*).
　　　What should I care for life's clamor,
　　　What for my friend or my foe . . .
How very agreeable it is to pluck at the strings of a mandolin!

DUNYASHA.   That's not a mandolin—that's a guitar. (*Powders herself in a pocket mirror.*)

YEPIKHODOV.   For the madman who's in love it's a mandolin. (*Sings*)
　　　. . . Had I a passion requited
　　　Warming my heart with its glow? (YASHA *joins in.*)

CHARLOTTA.   Horrible way these people sing! Faugh! Like jackals howling!

DUNYASHA (*to* YASHA).   All the same, how lovely to spend some time abroad.

YASHA.   Yes, of course. I couldn't agree more. (*Yawns, and then lights a cigar.*)

YEPIKHODOV.   Oh, absolutely. Everything abroad's been in full constitution for years.

YASHA.   Obviously.

YEPIKHODOV.   Here am I—I mean, I'm a grown man—I read—I read all sorts of important books—but what I can't make out is any, I mean, kind of movement of opinion when it comes to what I personally want in life. Put it this way—do I want to go on living, or do I want to shoot myself? I mean, I always carry a revolver on me, look. (*Shows the revolver.*)

CHARLOTTA.   Done it. I'm off. (*Slings the gun on her shoulder.*) Yepikhodov, you're a genius. A terrifying genius. All the women ought to be mad about you. Brrr! (*Starts to go.*) These great brains—they're all such fools. I've no one to talk to. Alone, always alone, I haven't got anyone. And who I am and why I am remains a mystery . . . (*Goes unhurriedly off.*)

YEPIKHODOV.   I mean, leaving everything else aside, I mean just taking my own case, and I'm not going to mince my words, but, really, fate has treated me quite relentlessly. I've been tossed around like a rowing-boat in a high sea. All right, let's say I'm talking nonsense. In that case, why, just to take one example, why, when I woke up this morning, why did I find, sitting there on my chest, this enormous spider? Like this. (*Demonstrates with both hands.*) All right, take another example. I pour myself some kvass, to have a drink, and there in the glass is something really profoundly horrible. I mean, a cockroach, for example. (*Pause.*) Have you read Buckle?° The *History of Civilization?* (*Pause. To* DUNYASHA) If I might trouble you, I should appreciate the chance of a word or two.

DUNYASHA.   Go on, then.

YEPIKHODOV.   I should have been hopeful of having it in private. (*Sighs.*)

DUNYASHA (*embarrassed*).   All right—only first fetch me my cloak. You'll find it by the cupboard. It's rather damp here.

YEPIKHODOV.   Now I know what to do with my revolver . . . (*Takes his guitar and goes off playing it.*)

YASHA.   Poor old Disasters! Between you and me, that man is a fool. (*Yawns.*)

DUNYASHA.   Just so long as he doesn't go and shoot himself. (*Pause.*) I've got so nervous these days—I worry all the time. They took me into service when I was a little girl still. I've got out of the way of ordinary people's life now. Look at my hands—white as white, like a lady's. I've turned into someone all refined, someone terribly delicate and ladylike—I'm frightened of everything. It's dreadful being like this. And Yasha, if you deceive me, well, I don't know what would become of my nerves.

YASHA (*kisses her*).   Real country pippin, aren't you? Of course, every girl's got to remember who she is. If there's one thing I hate more than anything else, it's a girl who doesn't know how to behave herself.

DUNYASHA.   I'm absolutely passionately in love with you. Because you're an educated man—you can talk about anything. (*Pause.*)

YASHA (*yawns*).   Right . . . What I think is, if a girl's in love with someone then she's got no morals. (*Pause.*) Nice having a cigar in the open air . . . (*Listens.*) Someone coming . . . It's *them.* (DUNYASHA *impetuously embraces him.*) Go home as if you'd been down to the river for a swim—here, along this path. Otherwise you'll run into them and they'll think I've been seeing you. I'm not having that.

Buckle: Henry Thomas Buckle, English historian (1821–1862)

DUNYASHA (*coughs quietly*).   Your cigar's given me a headache . . . (*Goes off.* YASHA *remains, sitting beside the shrine. Enter* RANYEVSKAYA, GAYEV, *and* LOPAKHIN.)

LOPAKHIN.   It has to be settled once and for all—time won't wait. Look, it's a simple enough question. Do you agree to lease out the land for summer cottages or not? Answer me one word: yes or no? Just one word!

RANYEVSKAYA.   Who's smoking some foul cigar? (*Sits.*)

GAYEV.   It's very convenient now they've built the railway. (*Sits.*) We popped into town and had some lunch . . . Yellow into the middle pocket! I should have gone indoors first and had a quick game.

RANYEVSKAYA.   You've still got time.

LOPAKHIN.   Just one word! (*Pleading*) Give me an answer!

GAYEV (*yawns*).   Who?

RANYEVSKAYA (*looks into her purse*).   There was a lot of money in here yesterday, and today there's hardly any. My poor Varya feeds everyone on milk soup to economize—she gives the old men in the kitchen nothing but dried peas, while I somehow just go on mindlessly spending . . . (*Drops the purse and scatters gold coins.*) And now it's gone everywhere . . . (*She is annoyed.*)

YASHA.   Leave it to me—I'll do it. (*Picks up the coins.*)

RANYEVSKAYA.   Would you, Yasha? And why did I go into town for lunch? That horrible restaurant of yours with the music playing, and the tablecloths smelling of soap . . . Why do you drink so much, Lenya? Why do you eat so much? Why do you talk so much? In the restaurant today you kept talking again—and it was all so rambling. The seventies, the Decadent movement.° And who were you saying it all to? Fancy telling the waiters about the Decadents!

LOPAKHIN.   Yes.

GAYEV (*waves his hand*).   I'm incorrigible, that's obvious. (*To* YASHA, *irritated*) What is it? You're perpetually dangling in front of my eyes.

YASHA (*laughs*).   I can't hear your voice without wanting to laugh.

GAYEV (*to his sister*).   Either he goes, or I do.

RANYEVSKAYA.   Off you go, Yasha.

YASHA (*gives* RANYEVSKAYA *her purse*).   Certainly. (*Scarcely restrains himself from laughing.*) This instant. (*Goes.*)

LOPAKHIN.   Your estate is going to be bought by Deriganov. He's a very wealthy man. I gather he's coming to the sale in person.

RANYEVSKAYA.   Where did you hear that?

LOPAKHIN.   It's what they're saying in town.

GAYEV.   Our aunt in Yaroslavl has promised to send something, but when and how much—that we don't know.

Decadent movement: the Symbolist movement of French and English writers and painters in the late nineteenth century

LOPAKHIN.   What would it be? A hundred thousand? Two hundred thousand?

RANYEVSKAYA.   Ten or fifteen thousand, and lucky if we get even that.

LOPAKHIN.   Forgive me for saying this, but such frivolous people as you, such strange unbusinesslike people, I have never come across. You are told in plain language that your estate is being sold, and you simply do not understand.

RANYEVSKAYA.   What can we possibly do? Tell us.

LOPAKHIN.   I tell you every day. Every day I tell you exactly the same thing. The cherry orchard and the land along the river must be leased out for summer cottages—and it must be done now, as soon as possible—the sale is upon us! Get it into your heads! Just once make up your minds to have the houses and you will get money—as much money as you like—and you will be saved.

RANYEVSKAYA.   Summer cottages—summer people—forgive me, but it's so sordid.

GAYEV.   I agree entirely.

LOPAKHIN.   I don't know whether to scream, or to burst into tears, or to fall down in a faint. I can't go on! You reduce me to despair! (*To* GAYEV) You're an old woman!

GAYEV.   Who?

LOPAKHIN.   An old woman. You! (*Starts to go.*)

RANYEVSKAYA (*frightened*).   No, don't go. Stay with us, my dear. I beg you. Perhaps we'll think of something.

LOPAKHIN.   What is there to think of?

RANYEVSKAYA.   Don't go, I implore you. It's more fun with you here, at any rate . . . (*Pause.*) I keep waiting for something to happen—as if the house were going to come down about our ears.

GAYEV (*deep in thought*).   Red, cushion, and into the corner . . . Cushion, red, and into the corner . . .

RANYEVSKAYA.   We have sinned, and sinned greatly . . .

LOPAKHIN.   What are your sins, then?

GAYEV (*puts a candy in his mouth*).   They say I've wasted all my substance in fruit drops . . . (*Laughs.*)

RANYEVSKAYA.   Oh, my sins . . . Always I've thrown money about like a lunatic, and I married a man who made nothing of his life but debts. My husband died of champagne—he was a terrible drinker—and my misfortune then was to fall in love with someone else. I gave myself to him, and it was just at that time—and this was my first punishment, it was like a club coming down on my head—my little boy . . . in the river here . . . my little boy was drowned, and I went away, went abroad, went utterly away, went meaning never to return, never to see this river again . . . I shut my eyes, ran blindly—and *he* after me . . . pitilessly, brutally. I bought a villa outside Menton, because *he* fell sick there, and for three years I knew no rest, neither by day nor by night. For three years he was an invalid—he drained my strength—my soul shriveled within me. And last year, when the villa was sold to pay my debts, I went to Paris, and there he robbed me openly, he threw me aside, he took up with another woman. I tried to poison myself . . . So stupid, so shameful . . . And suddenly I yearned for Russia, for my homeland, for my daughter . . . (*Wipes her tears.*) Lord, Lord have mercy! Forgive me my sins! Don't punish me any more! (*Takes a telegram out of her pocket.*) I got this today from Paris . . . He begs my forgiveness, implores me to return . . . (*Tears the telegram up.*) There's a sound of music somewhere. (*Listens.*)

GAYEV.   That's our famous Jews' band. Do you remember? Four fiddles, flute, and double bass.

RANYEVSKAYA.   It still exists? We ought to get them here somehow—we ought to arrange an evening.

LOPAKHIN (*listens*).   I can't hear anything . . . (*Sings quietly*)
> Money talks, so here's poor Russkies
> Getting Frenchified by Germans.

(*Laughs.*) Very good play I saw last night. Very funny.

RANYEVSKAYA.   There's nothing funny in the world. People shouldn't watch plays. They should look at their own selves a little more often. What grey lives they all lead. How much they say that should never be said at all.

LOPAKHIN.   True. We live like complete fools, it has to be admitted. (*Pause.*) My father was a peasant. He was an idiot, he knew nothing, he taught me nothing, all he did was to take his stick to me when he was drunk. And when you get down to it, I'm just the same sort of stupid oaf myself. I've never learned anything. I write such a foul hand I'm ashamed for people to see it. I'm a pig.

RANYEVSKAYA.   What you need, my friend, is to get married.

LOPAKHIN.   Yes . . . That's true.

RANYEVSKAYA.   To Varya, why not? Our own Varya. She's a good girl.

LOPAKHIN.   Yes.

RANYEVSKAYA.   She came to me from simple people—she works the whole day long. But the main thing is, she loves you. Yes, and you've liked her for a long time now.

LOPAKHIN.   Fair enough. I've nothing against it. She's a good girl. (*Pause.*)

GAYEV.   I've been offered a job in a bank. Six thousand a year. Have you heard about that?

RANYEVSKAYA.   The idea! You just stay as you are. (*Enter* FIRS. *He has brought an overcoat.*)

FIRS (*to Gayev*).   Now will you put it on, sir, if you please, or you'll be getting damp.

GAYEV (*puts on the coat*).   Firs, my friend, you're a bore.

FIRS.   No call for that, now. You went off this morning without a word. (*Examines him.*)

RANYEVSKAYA.   You've aged, Firs, haven't you?

FIRS.   What do you want?

LOPAKHIN.   She says you've aged a lot!

FIRS.   I've lived a long life. They were marrying me off before your Papa even arrived in the world. (*Laughs.*) And when the Freedom° came, in sixty-one, I was already head valet. I didn't agree to have the Freedom—I stayed with the masters . . . (*Pause.*) And I remember, everyone was glad. But what they were glad about they didn't know themselves.

LOPAKHIN.   Lovely it was before. At least they flogged you.

FIRS (*not having heard right*).   Oh, my word, they were. The peasants belonged to the masters, and the masters to the peasants. Now it's all chippety-chippety—you can't make any sense of it.

GAYEV.   Do be quiet for a moment, Firs. Tomorrow I have to go into town. I've been promised an introduction to a general who might put up something against my note of hand.

LOPAKHIN.   Nothing's going to come of it, whatever you do. And you're not going to pay that interest, don't worry.

RANYEVSKAYA.   He's living in a dream. There's no general. (*Enter* TROFIMOV, ANYA *and* VARYA.)

GAYEV.   Some more of us coming.

ANYA.   It's Mama.

RANYEVSKAYA (*tenderly*).   Here . . . here . . . my own darlings . . . (*Embracing* ANYA *and* VARYA.) If only you knew how much I love you both! Sit next to me—here . . . (*They all settle themselves down.*)

LOPAKHIN.   Our Wandering Student always seems to be wandering with the young ladies.

TROFIMOV.   Mind your own business.

LOPAKHIN.   He'll be fifty before he knows where he is, and still a student.

TROFIMOV.   Why don't you leave off your stupid jokes?

LOPAKHIN.   Not losing your temper, are you, O weird one?

TROFIMOV.   Don't keep badgering me.

LOPAKHIN (*laughs*).   All right, then, my dear sir. What do you make of me?

TROFIMOV.   I'll tell you what I make of you, sir. You're a wealthy man—you'll soon be a millionaire. And just as there must be predatory animals to maintain nature's metabolism by devouring whatever crosses their path, so there must also be you. (*They all laugh.*)

VARYA.   Petya, I think it would be better if you told us about the planets.

RANYEVSKAYA.   No, let's go on with the conversation we were having yesterday.

TROFIMOV.   What was that about?

the Freedom: emancipation of the serfs, 1861

GAYEV.   Pride.

TROFIMOV.   We talked for a long time yesterday, but we never arrived at any conclusions. Human pride, in the sense you're using it, has some kind of mystical significance. And you may even be right, in your own fashion. But if we're going to talk about it in a down-to-earth way, without any fancy trimmings, then what sort of pride can there be—does the expression have any sense at all—if man is physiologically ill-constructed, if in the vast majority of cases he is crude and stupid and profoundly unhappy? We have to stop admiring ourselves. We have simply to work.

GAYEV.   It makes no difference—you still die.

TROFIMOV.   Who knows? And what does it mean—you die? Perhaps man has a hundred senses, and at death it's only the five we know of that perish, while the other ninety-five go on living.

RANYEVSKAYA.   What a clever man you are, Petya!

LOPAKHIN (*ironically*).   Oh, staggeringly.

TROFIMOV.   Mankind is advancing, perfecting its powers. All the things that are beyond its reach now will one day be brought close and made plain. All we have to do is to work, to bend all our strength to help those who are seeking the truth. Here in Russia very few as yet are working. Most members of the intelligentsia, so far as I know it, are seeking nothing, neither the truth nor anything else. They're doing nothing—they're still incapable of hard work. They call themselves the intelligentsia, but they treat servants like children, and peasants like animals. They don't know how to study. They never do any serious reading. They understand next to nothing about art; science they merely talk about. They're all terribly serious people with terribly stern expressions on their faces. They all talk about nothing but terribly important questions. They all philosophize away. And right in front of their eyes the whole time there are workers living on filthy food and sleeping without pillows to their heads, thirty and forty to a room—and everywhere bugs, damp, stench, and moral squalor. And all the fine conversations we have are plainly just to distract attention from it all. Our own attention, and other people's, too. Show me—where are the crèches° that everyone's always going on about—where are the reading-rooms? They're only in novels—they don't exist in reality. There's just filth and banality and barbarism. I have little love for all those serious faces; I fear those serious conversations. Better to be silent.

LOPAKHIN.   Listen, I get up before five every morning, I work all the hours God gave, I'm constantly handling money—my own and other people's—and I can't help seeing what my fellow men are like. You've only got to start trying to do something to discover how few honest, decent people there are in the world. Sometimes, when I can't sleep, I think to myself: "Lord, you gave us immense forests, boundless plains, broad horizons—living in it all we ought properly to be giants."

crèches: day nurseries

RANYEVSKAYA.   A lot of use giants would be. It's only in fairy-tales that they're all right. Anywhere else they're frightening. (YEPIKHODOV *crosses upstage, playing the guitar. Pensively*) There goes Yepikhodov . . .

ANYA (*likewise*).   There goes Yepikhodov . . .

GAYEV.   The sun has set, ladies and gentlemen.

TROFIMOV.   Yes.

GAYEV (*softly, as if declaiming*).   O nature, wondrous nature! You shine with an everlasting radiance, beautiful and indifferent; you that we call Mother unite within yourself existence and death; you give life and you destroy it . . .

VARYA (*imploringly*).   Uncle!

ANYA.   You're doing it again!

TROFIMOV.   You'd be better off potting yellow.

GAYEV.   I am silent, I am silent. (*They all sit lost in thought. Silence. All that can be heard is* FIRS *muttering quietly. Suddenly there is a distant sound, as if from the sky: the sound of a breaking string°—dying away, sad.*)

RANYEVSKAYA.   What was that?

LOPAKHIN.   I don't know. Somewhere a long way off, in the mines, a winding cable has parted. But a long, long way off.

GAYEV.   Perhaps a bird of some sort . . . something like a heron.

TROFIMOV.   Or some kind of owl.

RANYEVSKAYA (*shivers*).   Horrible, I don't know why. (*Pause.*)

FIRS.   It was the same before the troubles. The owl screeched, and the samovar moaned without stop.

GAYEV.   Before what troubles?

FIRS.   Before the Freedom. (*Pause.*)

RANYEVSKAYA.   Listen, my friends, we must be going. The night is drawing on. (*To* ANYA) There are tears in your eyes. What is it, child? (*Embraces her.*)

ANYA.   Nothing. Just tears. It doesn't matter.

TROFIMOV.   There's someone coming. (*A* PASSER-BY *appears. He is wearing an overcoat and a stolen white peaked cap; he is slightly drunk.*)

PASSER-BY.   May I ask—is this the way to the station?

GAYEV.   Along this path.

PASSER-BY.   Most profoundly grateful. (*Coughs.*) Wonderful weather . . . (*Declaims*)

> My friend, my brother, weary, suffering, sad,
> Though falsehood rule and evil triumph,
> Take courage yet and let your soul be glad . . . (*Pause.*)

> Go to the Volga. Hear again
> The song it sings, the song of groans.—

---

string: The sound indicated is that of a breaking string from a musical instrument such as a harp.

The litany of hauling men,
Groaned from weary hearts and bones.
Volga! All spring's melted snows,
And still you cannot flood your plain
As wide as this land overflows
With all its people's sea of pain . . .°

(*To* VARYA) Mademoiselle, spare a few kopeks for a starving Russian. (VARYA *is frightened, and cries out.*)

LOPAKHIN (*angrily*).   Now that's enough! There are limits!

RANYEVSKAYA (*hurriedly*).   Wait . . . here you are . . . (*Looks in her purse.*) I've no silver . . . Never mind, here—ten rubles . . . (*Gives him a gold coin.*)

PASSER-BY.   Most profoundly grateful. (*Goes off. Laughter.*)

VARYA (*frightened*).   I'm going in . . . Oh, Mama—at home there's nothing for the servants to eat, and you gave him ten rubles.

RANYEVSKAYA.   What's to be done with me?—I'm so silly! When we get home I'll give you everything I've got. (*To* LOPAKHIN) You'll lend me some more, won't you?

LOPAKHIN.   Your humble servant.

RANYEVSKAYA.   Ladies and gentlemen, it's time we were going. Oh, and Varya, while we were sitting here we quite made a match for you. So congratulations.

VARYA (*on the verge of tears*).   Don't joke about it, Mama.

LOPAKHIN.   Get thee to a nunnery, Ophelia-Ophoolia.°

GAYEV.   My hands are shaking—I've been missing my billiards.

LOPAKHIN.   Nymph, in thy orisons be all my sins dismembered!

RANYEVSKAYA.   Off we go, then. It's nearly time for supper.

VARYA.   He gave me such a fright. My heart's simply pounding.

LOPAKHIN.   Let me remind you, ladies and gentlemen: the cherry orchard will be coming up for sale on the twenty-second of August. Think about it! Think! (*They all go out except* TROFIMOV *and* ANYA.)

ANYA (*laughing*).   We ought to thank that tramp for frightening Varya. Now we're alone.

TROFIMOV.   She's afraid you and I are suddenly going to fall in love with each other. She doesn't let us out of her sight for days at a time. What she can't get into her narrow mind is that we're above such things as love. Our whole aim—the whole sense of our life—is to avoid the petty illusions that stop us being free and happy. On, on, on! We are going to that bright star that blazes from afar there, and no one can hold us back! On, on, on! In step together, friends!

My friend . . . pain: The quoted lines are from two Russian poems with contrasting content; the first poem expresses love overcoming evil, the second compares the moans of suffering people to the sounds of the Volga River.   **Ophelia-Ophoolia:** In this and his next speech Lopakhin alludes to the "nunnery scene" in *Hamlet* (3.1).

ANYA (*clasping her hands*).   How beautifully you talk! (*Pause.*) It's wonderful here today.

TROFIMOV.   Yes, amazing weather.

ANYA.   What have you done to me, Petya? Why don't I love the cherry orchard like I used to? I loved it so tenderly. I thought there was nowhere finer on earth.

TROFIMOV.   All Russia is our orchard. The earth is broad and beautiful. There are many marvelous places. (*Pause.*) Think for a moment, Anya: your grandfather, your great-grandfather—all your forebears—they were the masters of serfs. They owned living souls. Can't you see human faces, looking out at you from behind every tree-trunk in the orchard—from every leaf and every cherry. Can't you hear their voices? The possession of living souls—it's changed something deep in all of you, hasn't it. So that your mother and you and your uncle don't even notice you're living on credit, at the expense of others—at the expense of people you don't allow past the front hall . . . We're two hundred years behind the times at least. We still have nothing—no properly defined attitude to the past. We just philosophize away, and complain about our boredom or drink vodka. But it's only too clear that to start living in the present we have to redeem our past—we have to break with it. And it can be redeemed only by suffering, only by the most unheard-of, unceasing labor. You must understand that, Anya.

ANYA.   The house we live in hasn't been ours for a long time now. I'm going to leave, I give you my word.

TROFIMOV.   Throw the keys down the well, and go. Be free as the wind.

ANYA (*in delight*).   You put it so beautifully!

TROFIMOV.   Have faith in me, Anya! Have faith in me! I'm not thirty yet—I'm young—I'm still a student—but I've borne so much already! Every winter I'm hungry, sick and fearful, as poor as a beggar. And the places I've been to! The places where fate has driven me! And all the time, at every minute of the day and night, my soul has been filled with premonitions I can't explain or describe. I have a premonition of happiness, Anya. I can just see it now . . .

ANYA (*pensively*).   The moon is rising. (*There is the sound of* YEPIKHODOV *still playing the same mournful song on his guitar. The moon rises. Somewhere over by the poplar trees* VARYA *is looking for* ANYA.)

VARYA (*calling off*).   Anya! Where are you?

TROFIMOV.   Yes, the moon is rising. (*Pause.*) Here it is—happiness. Here it comes. Closer and closer. I can hear its footsteps already. And if we don't see it, if we never know its face, then what does it matter? Others will!

VARYA (*off*).   Anya! Where are you?

TROFIMOV.   There's that Varya again! (*Angrily*) It's outrageous!

ANYA.   Come on—let's go down to the river. It's nice there.

TROFIMOV.   Come on, then. (*They start to go.*)

VARYA (*off*).   Anya! Anya!

ACT 3

The drawing-room, with an archway leading through into the ballroom. The chandelier is lit. From an ante-room comes the sound of the Jews' band mentioned in act 2. Company has been invited for the evening. In the ballroom they are dancing the "grand-rond."

SIMEONOV-PISHCHIK (*off*). "Promenade à une paire!" (*The* COUPLES *emerge into the drawing-room—first* PISHCHIK *and* CHARLOTTA IVANOVNA, *second* TROFIMOV *and* RANYEVSKAYA, *third* ANYA *and the* POSTMASTER, *fourth* VARYA *and the* STATIONMASTER, *and so on.* VARYA *is quietly weeping, and wiping her eyes as she dances. In the last couple is* DUNYASHA. *They go round the room.*)

PISHCHIK. "Grand-rond balancez . . . ! Les cavaliers à genoux et remerciez vos dames!" (FIRS, *wearing a tailcoat, brings the seltzer water on a tray.* PISHCHIK *and* TROFIMOV *come into the drawing-room.*)

PISHCHIK. Blood-pressure—that's my trouble. I've had two strokes already, and I don't find dancing easy. But you know what they say—if you run with the pack you must wag your tail. I'm as strong as a horse. My late father, who was something of a humorist, God rest his soul, used to say the venerable tribe of Simeonov-Pishchik was descended from the horse that Caligula made consul° . . . (*Sits down.*) But the snag is—no money! What do people say?—A hungry dog believes only in meat . . . (*Snores and immediately wakes up again.*) Same with me—can't think about anything but money.

TROFIMOV. It's true—there is something rather horse-like about you.

PISHCHIK. Well, that's all right . . . a horse is a good beast . . . a horse can be sold. (*There is the sound of billiards being played in the next room.* VARYA *appears in the archway to the ballroom.*)

TROFIMOV (*teasing*). Madame Lopakhina! Madame Lopakhina!

VARYA (*angrily*). And who's this? The mangy-looking gentleman.

TROFIMOV. Yes, that's what I am—a mangy-looking gentleman. And proud of it!

VARYA (*reflecting bitterly*). Here we are, we've hired musicians—but what are we going to pay them with? (*Goes out.*)

TROFIMOV (*to* PISHCHIK). If all the energy you've expended during your life in the quest for money had gone on something else, you could have turned the world upside down by now.

PISHCHIK. Nietzsche—the philosopher—very great philosopher, very famous one—man of enormous intelligence—he claims in his books that it's all right to forge banknotes.

TROFIMOV. You've read Nietzsche, have you?

PISHCHIK. Well . . . my daughter Dashenka was telling me about him. Though with the position I'm in now, even if I started forging banknotes . . .

Caligula . . . consul: The first-century A.D. Roman emperor is said to have appointed his favorite horse to sit in the Senate.

I've got to pay three hundred and ten rubles the day after tomorrow . . . I've got hold of a hundred and thirty . . . (*Feels his pockets in alarm.*) The money's gone! I've lost the money! (*On the verge of tears*) Where's the money? (*Joyfully*) Here it is, in the lining . . . I'd quite come out in a sweat. (*Enter* RANYEVSKAYA *and* CHARLOTTA IVANOVNA.)

RANYEVSKAYA (*hums a Caucasian dance, the lezghinka*).   Why is Leonid taking so long? What can he be doing in town? (*To* DUNYASHA) Dunyasha, ask the musicians if they'd like some tea.

TROFIMOV.   The sale probably never took place.

RANYEVSKAYA.   It wasn't the moment to have the band, it wasn't the moment to get up a ball. Well, who cares? (*Sits down and hums quietly.*)

CHARLOTTA (*offers* PISHCHIK *a pack of cards*).   Think of a card. Any card you like.

PISHCHIK.   I've thought of one.

CHARLOTTA.   Now shuffle the pack. Good. Give it to me, then, my dear monsieur Pishchik. *Ein, zwei, drei!*° Now have a look and you'll find it in your side pocket.

PISHCHIK (*gets a card out of his side pocket*).   The eight of spades—that's absolutely right! (*Amazed*) Well, would you believe it!

CHARLOTTA (*to* TROFIMOV, *holding the pack in the palm of her hand*). The top card—quick—what is it?

TROFIMOV.   I don't know . . . oh . . . the queen of spades.

CHARLOTTA.   Right! (*To* PISHCHIK) Well? The top card?

PISHCHIK.   The ace of hearts.

CHARLOTTA.   Right! (*Claps her hands, and the pack disappears.*) Marvelous weather we're having! (*A mysterious female voice answers, apparently from under the floor.*)

VOICE.   Oh, yes, wonderful weather!

CHARLOTTA.   You are my heart's ideal!

VOICE.   Yes, I've taken rather a fancy to you.

STATIONMASTER (*applauds*).   Madame the ventriloquist! Bravo!

PISHCHIK (*amazed*).   Would you believe it! Enchanting woman! I've absolutely fallen in love with you.

CHARLOTTA.   In love? (*Shrugs her shoulders.*) Are you really capable of love?

TROFIMOV (*claps* PISHCHIK *on the shoulder*).   You're so much like a horse, you see . . .

CHARLOTTA.   Your attention please. One more trick. (*Takes a traveling rug off one of the chairs.*) I have here a very fine rug, a very fine rug for sale. (*Shakes it.*) Who'll buy this very fine rug?

PISHCHIK (*amazed*).   Would you believe it!

CHARLOTTA.   *Ein, zwei, drei!* (*She has lowered the rug; now she quickly raises it.* ANYA *is standing behind the rug. She curtseys, runs to her mother and embraces her, then runs back into the ballroom amid general delight.*)

Ein, zwei, drei: German, "one, two, three"

RANYEVSKAYA (*applauds*).   Bravo, bravo . . . !

CHARLOTTA.   Once more, now! *Ein, zwei, drei!* (*Raises the rug.* VARYA *is standing behind the rug. She bows.*)

PISHCHIK (*amazed*).   Would you believe it!

CHARLOTTA.   And that is the end of my show. (*Throws the rug at* PISHCHIK, *curtseys, and runs out into the ballroom.*)

PISHCHIK (*hurries after her*).   What a witch, though! What a witch! (*Goes.*)

RANYEVSKAYA.   And still no sign of Leonid. I don't understand what he could be doing in town for all this time. It must be over by now. Either the estate is sold, or else the sale never took place. What's the point of keeping us all in suspense?

VARYA (*trying to calm her*).   Uncle has bought it—I'm sure of that.

TROFIMOV (*sarcastically*).   Oh, of course he has.

VARYA.   Great-aunt gave him authority to purchase it in her name, and to transfer the mortgage to her. It was all for Anya's sake. And, God willing, I'm sure Uncle will have done it.

RANYEVSKAYA.   To buy this estate—and to buy it in her own name, because she doesn't trust us—your great-aunt sent fifteen thousand rubles—not enough to pay the interest. (*Covers her face with her hands.*) Today my fate is being decided. My fate . . .

TROFIMOV (*teases* VARYA).   Madame Lopakhina!

VARYA (*angrily*).   The Wandering Student! They've thrown you out of university twice already.

RANYEVSKAYA.   Why are you getting so cross, Varya? All right, he's teasing you about Lopakhin—but what of it? If you want to marry Lopakhin, then marry him. He's a good man, he's an interesting person. If you don't want to, then don't. Darling, no one's forcing you.

VARYA.   I must tell you, Mama, that this is something I take very seriously. He's a good man, and I like him.

RANYEVSKAYA.   Then marry him. Why wait? I don't understand.

VARYA.   Mama dear, *I* can't propose to *him*. For two years now everyone's been talking to me about him. Everyone's been talking except him. He either says nothing or else makes a joke of it. I see why. He's busy making his fortune—he's no time for me. If only we had some money—just a little, a hundred rubles even—I'd throw up everything, I'd go away. I'd go into a nunnery.

TROFIMOV.   The glory of it.

VARYA (*to* TROFIMOV).   I thought students were supposed to have a little sense in their heads! (*In a gentle voice, with tears in her eyes*) Oh, but Petya, you've grown so ugly, you've aged so! (*To* RANYEVSKAYA, *no longer crying*) It's just that I can't manage without things to do, Mama. Every minute of the day I must have something to do. (*Enter* YASHA.)

YASHA (*scarcely restraining himself from laughing*).   Yepikhodov's broken the billiard cue . . . ! (*Goes out.*)

VARYA.   What's Yepikhodov doing here? Who said he could play billiards? I simply don't understand these people. (*Goes out.*)

RANYEVSKAYA.   Don't tease her, Petya. You can see, she's unhappy enough as it is.

TROFIMOV.   She's very diligent, I must say that for her. Particularly at minding other people's business. All summer she's given me and Anya no peace. She's been frightened we were going to have some kind of romance. What's it to do with her? Particularly since I've shown not the slightest sign of it—I'm not given to that sort of vulgarity. We're above such things as love!

RANYEVSKAYA.   I suppose I must be beneath them. (*In great anxiety*) Why isn't Leonid back? If only I knew whether the estate was sold or not. It seems such an incredible disaster that I just can't think—I can't keep control of myself . . . I could scream as I stand here . . . I could do something quite foolish. Save me, Petya. Talk to me about something, talk to me . . .

TROFIMOV.   Does it make any difference whether the estate's been sold today or not? All that was finished with long ago—there's no way back—the path's grown over. Be calm now, my dear. Don't deceive yourself. Face up to the truth for once in your life.

RANYEVSKAYA.   Yes, but what truth? You can see which is truth and which is falsehood, but I feel as if I'd gone blind—I can't see anything at all. You boldly settle all the great questions, but my love, isn't that because you're young, isn't that because you've never had to live a single one of those questions out? You look boldly forwards, but isn't that because you have the eyes of youth, because life is still hidden from them, so that you see nothing frightening in store? You're more daring than the rest of us, you're deeper, you're more honest—but think about it for a moment, be just a touch magnanimous in your judgment, take pity on me. After all, I was born here, my father and mother lived here, my grandfather . . . I love this house. Without the cherry orchard I can't make sense of my life, and if it really has to be sold, then sell me along with it . . . (*Embraces* TROFIMOV, *and kisses him on the forehead.*) And then this is where my son was drowned . . . (*Weeps.*) You're a good man, a kind man—have pity on me.

TROFIMOV.   You know I sympathize with all my heart.

RANYEVSKAYA.   Yes, but not said like that, not like that . . . (*Takes out her handkerchief, and a telegram falls on the floor.*) There is such a weight upon my heart today, you can never know. All this noise here—my heart jumps at every sound—everything in me jumps. But to go away and be on my own—I can't, because as soon as I'm alone and surrounded by silence I'm terrified. Don't judge me, Petya. I love you as if you were my own child. I should gladly have given my consent to your marrying Anya—I truly should. Only, my precious boy, you must study, you must finish at university. It's so strange—you do nothing but get yourself tossed by fate from one place to the next. Isn't that true? Yes? And you must do something with your beard somehow to make it grow. (*Laughs.*) You are an absurd man!

TROFIMOV (*picks up the telegram*).   I've no desire to be known for my looks.

RANYEVSKAYA.   It's a telegram from Paris. Every day they come. One yesterday, another one today. That wild man—he's ill again, he's in trouble again. He begs my forgiveness, he implores me to come, and really I ought to go to Paris, I ought to be with him. You're pulling your stern face, Petya, but my dear, what can I do, what can I possibly do? He's ill, he's lonely and unhappy, and who'll look after him there, who'll keep him from making mistakes, who'll give him his medicine at the right time? And what's the point of hiding it or not talking about it?—I plainly love him. I love him, love him. He's a millstone round my neck—he'll take me to the bottom with him. But I love this millstone of mine—I can't live without it. (*Presses* TROFIMOV'S *hand*.) Don't think harsh thoughts, Petya. Don't say anything to me. Don't speak.

TROFIMOV (*on the verge of tears*).   Forgive me if I'm frank, please God forgive me, but listen—he's openly robbed you!

RANYEVSKAYA.   No, no, no, you mustn't say things like that . . . (*Covers her ears*.)

TROFIMOV.   Look, he's no good, and you're the only one who doesn't know it! He's a petty scoundrel, a nobody . . .

RANYEVSKAYA (*angry now, but restraining it*).   You're twenty-six, twenty-seven years old, and you're still a schoolboy, you're still a fifth-former.

TROFIMOV.   If you say so.

RANYEVSKAYA.   It's time you were a man. At your age you must understand people who know what it is to love. You must know what it is yourself! You must fall in love! (*Angrily*) Yes, yes! You're no more pure than I am! You're just a prig, a ridiculous freak, a monster . . . !

TROFIMOV (*in horror*).   What is she saying?

RANYEVSKAYA.   "I'm above such things as love!" You're not above anything—you're merely what our Firs calls a sillybilly. Fancy not having a mistress at your age!

TROFIMOV (*in horror*).   This is appalling! What is she saying? (*Rushes toward the ballroom, holding his head*.) Appalling . . . I can't cope with this, I shall have to go . . . (*Goes out, but immediately comes back*.) Everything is finished between us! (*Goes out into the anteroom*.)

RANYEVSKAYA (*calls after him*).   Petya, wait! You absurd man! I was joking! Petya! (*In the anteroom someone can be heard rushing downstairs, and then suddenly falling with a crash*. ANYA *and* VARYA *cry out, but then at once there is a sound of laughter*.) What's happening out there? (ANYA *runs in*.)

ANYA (*laughing*).   Petya's fallen downstairs! (*Runs out*.)

RANYEVSKAYA.   What a freak that Petya is . . . (*The* STATIONMASTER *takes up a position in the middle of the ballroom*.)

STATIONMASTER.   The Scarlet Woman. A poem in six parts by Aleksey Konstantinovich Tolstoy. Part One.

> The merry rev'llers throng the hall;
> The lute plays sweet; the cymbals brawl;
> The crystal blazes; gold shines bright;

> While 'twixt the columns, rich brocades
> Hang swagged with finely broidered braids,
> And flowering shrubs anoint the light . . .

(*People are listening to him, but from the anteroom come the sounds of a waltz, and the reading stops short. Everyone dances.* TROFIMOV, ANYA, VARYA *and* RANYEVSKAYA *emerge from the anteroom.*)

RANYEVSKAYA.   Now, Petya . . . Petya with the pure soul . . . Please forgive me. Shall we dance . . . ? (*Dances with him.* ANYA *and* VARYA *dance. Enter* FIRS. *He puts his stick next to the side door.* YASHA *has also entered, and is watching the dancing.*)

YASHA.   What's up with you, then, Grandad?

FIRS.   I'm not right in myself. When we gave a ball in the old days we used to have generals dancing here, we had barons, we had admirals. Now we send for the postmaster and the stationmaster, and even them they're none too eager. I'm not as strong as I was. The old master, her grandfather, used to treat all our ailments with a dose of sealing-wax. I've been taking sealing-wax every day for twenty years or more. Maybe that's why I'm still alive.

YASHA.   Real old bore, aren't you, Grandad? (*Yawns.*) Why don't you just drop dead?

FIRS.   Oh, you . . . sillybilly. (*Mumbles.* TROFIMOV *and* RANYEVSKAYA *dance first in the ballroom, and then in the drawing-room.*)

RANYEVSKAYA.   *Merci.* I'm going to sit down for a moment. (*Sits.*) I'm quite tired out. (*Enter* ANYA.)

ANYA (*excitedly*).   Some man just came to the kitchen saying the cherry orchard's been sold.

RANYEVSKAYA.   Sold? To whom?

ANYA.   He didn't say. He's gone now. (*Dances with* TROFIMOV. *They both go out into the ballroom.*)

YASHA.   That was just some old man gossiping. Some stranger.

FIRS.   And Leonid Andreyich still isn't here. He still hasn't come. He's wearing his light autumn coat, he'll go and catch cold. When will these young people learn?

RANYEVSKAYA.   I shall die on the spot. Yasha, go and find out who it was sold to.

YASHA.   What, from the old man? He left ages ago. (*Laughs.*)

RANYEVSKAYA (*with slight irritation*).   What are you laughing at? What are you so pleased about?

YASHA.   Very funny man, that Yepikhodov. Fatuous devil. Old Disasters by the Dozen.

RANYEVSKAYA.   Firs, if the estate is sold, where will you go?

FIRS.   Wherever you tell me to go.

RANYEVSKAYA.   Why are you pulling that face? Are you ill? You could go to bed, you know.

FIRS.   Oh, yes . . . (*Smiles.*) I go to bed, and who's going to wait on everyone, who's going to see to everything? There's only me to do the whole house.

YASHA (*to* RANYEVSKAYA).   Madam, could I ask you a special favor? If you go to Paris again, please take me with you. I can't possibly stay here. (*Looking round and lowering his voice*) I don't have to tell you—you can see it for yourself. It's an uneducated country, they're people without any morals. And then on top of that there's the boredom—and the food they give us in the kitchen, it's disgusting—and then there's Firs here wandering round all the time muttering away to himself. Take me with you! Please! (*Enter* PISHCHIK.)

PISHCHIK.   You wonderful woman, may I beg just one thing? One tiny waltz? (RANYEVSKAYA *accompanies him.*) Enchanting creature! All the same, I shall take a hundred and eighty rubles off you . . . I will, you know . . . (*He dances.*) A hundred and eighty tiny rubles . . . (*They have passed through into the ballroom.*)

YASHA (*sings quietly*).   "And will you know just how my heart beats faster . . . ?" (*In the ballroom a figure in a grey top hat and check trousers waves its arms and leaps about.*)

VOICES (*off*).   It's Charlotta Ivanovna! Bravo!

DUNYASHA (*who has stopped to powder her nose*).   Miss told me to dance because there are too many gentlemen and not enough ladies, and now my head's spinning, my heart's pounding. And the postmaster just told me something that quite took my breath away. (*The music becomes quieter.*)

FIRS.   What did he tell you?

DUNYASHA.   He said, "You're like a flower."

YASHA (*yawns*).   The ignorance of these people . . . (*Goes out.*)

DUNYASHA.   Like a flower . . . I'm such a sensitive girl—I do terribly love it when people say nice things to me.

FIRS.   You'll have your head turned, you will. (*Enter* YEPIKHODOV.)

YEPIKHODOV (*to* DUNYASHA).   You've no wish to see me, have you . . . As if I was some kind of insect. (*Sighs.*) Ah, life!

DUNYASHA.   What do you want?

YEPIKHODOV.   And you're right, no doubt, possibly. (*Sighs.*) Though, of course, if you look at it from one point of view, then I mean you have reduced me—and forgive me for saying this, but I mean I'm not going to mince my words—you have reduced me to, well, let's put it like this, to a complete and utter state of mind. I know what's in my stars—every day some disaster happens—I've long been used to it—I look upon my fate now with a smile. I mean, you gave me your word, and although I . . .

DUNYASHA.   Please, we'll talk about it later. Leave me in peace now. I'm busy dreaming. (*Plays with a fan.*)

YEPIKHODOV.   Every day another disaster, and I mean, all I do is smile. Laugh, even. (*Enter* VARYA *from the ballroom.*)

VARYA (*to* YEPIKHODOV).   Are you still here? Have you no respect? (*To* DUNYASHA) Out of here, Dunyasha. (*To* YEPIKHODOV) First you play billiards and break the cue, and now you parade about the drawing-room as if you were a guest.

YEPIKHODOV.   I'm not going to account for my behavior to you, if I may say so.

VARYA.   I'm not asking you to account for your behavior. I'm telling you. All you do is wander about from place to place. You never get down to any work. We keep a clerk, but what for, heaven only knows.

YEPIKHODOV (*offended*).   Whether I do any work or not—whether I wander about or play billiards—these are questions that can only be judged by people older and wiser than you.

VARYA.   You dare to talk to me like that! (*Flaring up*) You dare! Are you trying to tell me I don't know what's right and wrong? Clear off out of here! This minute!

YEPIKHODOV (*cowering*).   Kindly express yourself with more refinement.

VARYA (*beside herself*).   Out of here! This instant! Out! (*He goes to the door, and she after him.*) Disasters by the Dozen—that's right! I want neither sight nor sound of you in here! (YEPIKHODOV *is by now out of the room.*)

YEPIKHODOV (*off, behind the door*).   I'll tell about you!

VARYA.   Oh, coming back, are you? (*Seizes the stick that* FIRS *left beside the door.*) Come on, then . . . Come on . . . Come on . . . I'll show you . . . Are you coming? My word, you're going to be in for it . . . ! (*Raises the stick threateningly. Enter* LOPAKHIN.)

LOPAKHIN.   Thank you kindly.

VARYA (*angrily and sarcastically*).   Sorry! My mistake.

LOPAKHIN.   That's all right. I'm touched to get such a warm welcome.

VARYA.   Oh, please—think nothing of it. (*Goes away from him, then looks round and asks softly*) I didn't hurt you, did I?

LOPAKHIN.   No, no. Don't worry about it. I shall just have the most enormous bump, that's all.

VOICES (*off, in the ballroom*).   Lopakhin's arrived! Lopakhin's here! (*Enter* PISHCHIK.)

PISHCHIK.   As large as life . . . (*He and* LOPAKHIN *kiss.*) You smell of brandy, my dear fellow. And we're making merry here as well. (*Enter* RANYEVSKAYA.)

RANYEVSKAYA.   Is it him . . . ? (*To* LOPAKHIN) Why so long? Where's Leonid?

LOPAKHIN.   He arrived with me—he's just coming . . .

RANYEVSKAYA (*alarmed*).   So what happened? Did they hold the sale? Speak!

LOPAKHIN (*confused, afraid to reveal his joy*).   The sale ended just on four o'clock. We missed the train—we had to wait till half-past nine. (*Sighs heavily.*) Ouf! My head's rather going round . . . (*Enter* GAYEV. *In his left hand he is carrying his purchases; with his right he is wiping away his tears.*)

RANYEVSKAYA.   Lenya! Lenya, what happened? (*Impatiently in tears*) Quickly, for the love of God . . .

GAYEV (*gives her no reply except a flap of the hand; to* FIRS, *weeping*).   Here, take these . . . anchovies, Crimean herrings . . . I haven't eaten anything all day . . . Oh, what I've been through! (*The door into the billiard room is open; the click of balls can be heard.*)

YASHA (*off*).   Seven and eighteen! (GAYEV'S *expression changes; he is no longer weeping.*)

GAYEV.   I'm horribly tired. Help me change, will you, Firs? (*Goes off to his room by way of the ballroom, with* FIRS *after him.*)

PISHCHIK.   What happened at the sale? Tell us!

RANYEVSKAYA.   Is the cherry orchard sold?

LOPAKHIN.   It is.

RANYEVSKAYA.   Who bought it?

LOPAKHIN.   I did. (RANYEVSKAYA *is utterly cast down; if she were not standing beside the armchair and the table she would fall.* VARYA *takes the keys off her belt, throws them on the floor in the middle of the room, and goes out.*) I bought it! One moment . . . wait . . . if you would, ladies and gentlemen . . . My head's going round and round, I can't speak . . . (*Laughs.*) We got to the sale, and there was Deriganov—I told you he was going to be there. All your brother had was fifteen thousand, and Deriganov straightway bid the mortgage plus thirty. I thought, all right, if that's the way things are, and I got to grips with him—I bid forty. Him—forty-five. Me—fifty-five. So he's going up in fives, I'm going up in tens . . . Well, that was that. I bid the mortgage plus ninety, and there it stayed. So now the cherry orchard is mine! Mine! (*He gives a shout of laughter.*) Great God in heaven—the cherry orchard is mine! Tell me I'm drunk—I'm out of my mind—tell me it's all an illusion . . . (*Stamps his feet up and down.*) Don't laugh at me! If my father and grandfather could rise from their graves and see it all happening—if they could see me, their Yermolay, their beaten, half-literate Yermolay, who ran barefoot in winter—if they could see this same Yermolay buying the estate . . . The most beautiful thing in the entire world! I have bought the estate where my father and grandfather were slaves, where they weren't allowed even into the kitchens. I'm asleep—I'm imagining it—it's all inside my head . . . (*Picks up the keys, smiling tenderly.*) She threw down the keys—she wants to demonstrate she's no longer mistress here. (*Jingles the keys.*) Well, it makes no odds. (*The sound of the band tuning up.*) Hey, you in the band! Play away! I want to hear you! Everyone come and watch Yermolay Lopakhin set about the cherry orchard with his axe! Watch the trees come down! Summer cottages, we'll build summer cottages, and our grandchildren and our great-grandchildren will see a new life here . . . Music! Let's have some music! (*The music plays.* RANYEVSKAYA *has sunk down on to a chair and is weeping bitterly.* LOPAKHIN *continues reproachfully)* Why, why, why didn't you listen to me? My poor dear love, you won't bring it back now. (*In tears*) Oh, if only it were all over. If only we could somehow change this miserable, muddled life of ours.

PISHCHIK (*takes him by the arm, speaks with lowered voice*).   She's crying. We'll go next door and let her be on her own. Come on . . . (*Takes him by the arm and leads him out towards the ballroom.*)

LOPAKHIN.   What's all this? Let's hear the band play! Let's have everything the way I want it! (*Ironically*) Here comes the new landlord, the owner of the cherry orchard! (*Accidentally bangs into an occasional table, and almost overturns the candelabra.*) I can pay for it all! (*Goes out with* PISHCHIK. *There is no one in either ballroom or drawing-room except* RANYEVSKAYA, *who sits crumpled and weeping bitterly. The music plays quietly.* ANYA *and* TROFIMOV *hurry in.* ANYA *goes up to her mother and kneels before her.* TROFIMOV *remains by the archway into the ballroom.*)

ANYA.   Mama . . . ! You're crying, Mama? Dear Mama, sweet, kind, beautiful Mama—I love you and bless you. The cherry orchard's sold, it's lost and gone—that's true. But don't cry, Mama. You have life left in front of you. You still possess your own soul, your generous pure soul . . . We'll go away, love, you and me, we'll go away from here, we'll go away. We'll plant a new orchard, lovelier still, and when you see it you'll understand. And your heart will be visited by joy, a quiet, deep, joy like evening sunlight, and you'll smile again, Mama! Come, love! Come . . . !

ACT 4

The same room as act 1. There are no curtains at the window, and no pictures. A little furniture remains, stacked up in one corner, as if for a sale. You can feel the emptiness. Upstage, and by the door leading to the outside, are stacked suitcases, bundles made up for a journey, etc. The door on the left is open, and the voices of VARYA *and* ANYA *can be heard from beyond.* LOPAKHIN *stands waiting.* YASHA *is holding a tray of glasses filled with champagne. In the anteroom* YEPIKHODOV *is packing a box. From upstage off can be heard a hum of voices—the peasants who have come to say farewell.*

GAYEV (*off*).   Thank you, men. Thank you.

YASHA (*to* LOPAKHIN).   The peasants have come to make their farewells. They're a decent enough lot, if you want my opinion. They're just not very bright. (*The hum of voices dies away. Enter through the anteroom* RANYEVSKAYA *and* GAYEV. *She is not weeping, but she is pale and her face is trembling. She cannot speak.*)

GAYEV.   Lyuba, you gave them your purse! You mustn't do things like that! You really must not!

RANYEVSKAYA.   I couldn't help it! I simply couldn't help it! (*They both go out.*)

LOPAKHIN (*following them to the doorway*).   May I humbly propose a farewell drink? I didn't think to bring any from town, and I could only find one bottle at the station. Come on—have a drink! (*Pause.*) What—don't you want to? (*Moves away from the door.*) If I'd known I wouldn't have bought it. Well, I shan't have any, either. (YASHA *carefully places the tray on a chair.*) You might as well have a drink yourself, then, Yasha.

YASHA.   To all those departing! And to all those staying behind. (*Drinks.*) This isn't real champagne, I can tell you that.

LOPAKHIN.   Eight rubles a bottle. (*Pause.*) Cold as hell in here.

YASHA.   They haven't lit the stoves today. Who cares? We're leaving. (*Laughs.*)

LOPAKHIN.   What?

YASHA.   Sheer pleasure.

LOPAKHIN.   October out there, but the sun's shining, the air's still. It's like summer. Good building weather. (*Glances at his watch, and goes to the door.*) Please bear in mind, ladies and gentleman, you've only forty-six minutes before the train goes! That means we have to leave for the station in twenty minutes. Do make a little haste, now. (*Enter* TROFIMOV *from outside, wearing an overcoat.*)

TROFIMOV.   Just about time to go, isn't it? The carriages are here. Heaven knows where my galoshes are. They've vanished. (*Through the doorway*) Anya, I haven't got my galoshes! I can't find them.

LOPAKHIN.   I have to go to Kharkov—I'll be traveling on the same train as the rest of you. That's where I'm staying all winter. I've just been loafing around all this time with you people, going out of my mind with nothing to do. I can't get by without work. I don't know what to do with my hands. They look strange just hanging around like this. They look as if they belonged to somebody else.

TROFIMOV.   Well, in a minute we'll be leaving, and you'll be resuming your valuable labors.

LOPAKHIN.   Have a glass.

TROFIMOV.   I won't, thank you.

LOPAKHIN.   So, you're off to Moscow now?

TROFIMOV.   Yes, I'm going into town with them. Then tomorrow morning, on to Moscow.

LOPAKHIN.   So what, none of the professors been giving their lectures? All waiting for you to arrive, are they?

TROFIMOV.   No business of yours.

LOPAKHIN.   How many years now have you been at university?

TROFIMOV.   Oh, think up something a bit newer than that. That's an old one—old and feeble. (*Looks for his galoshes.*) Listen, we shall probably never see each other again, so allow me to give you one piece of advice as a farewell present. Don't keep waving your arms about! Break yourself of this habit of gesticulating. And all this business of building summer cottages, then calculating that eventually the people who rent them will turn into landlords themselves—that's also a form of arm-waving. All the same, I can't help liking you. You've got fine, sensitive fingers, like an artist's. You've got a fine, sensitive soul, too.

LOPAKHIN (*embraces him*).   Goodbye, then, old son. Thanks for everything. Here—just in case you need it—have some money for the journey.

TROFIMOV.   What for? I don't need it.

LOPAKHIN.   Look, you haven't got any!

TROFIMOV.   Yes, I have. Thank you. I got some for a translation I did. Here, in my pocket. (*Anxiously*) But what I haven't got is my galoshes!

VARYA (*from the next room*).   Take your junk away, will you? (*Throws out on to the stage a pair of galoshes.*)

TROFIMOV.   Why are you so cross, Varya? Oh, but these aren't my galoshes!

LOPAKHIN.   I planted nearly three thousand acres of poppy° this spring, and I've made a clear forty thousand rubles on it. But when my poppy was in bloom—what a picture! So here I am, I'm telling you, I've made forty thousand, and I'm offering you a loan because I've got it there to offer. Why turn up your nose? I'm a peasant . . . I'm not going to tie it up in pink ribbon for you.

TROFIMOV.   Your father was a peasant, and mine was a pharmacist, and from that follows absolutely nothing at all. (LOPAKHIN *takes out his wallet.*) Leave it, leave it . . . Offer me two hundred thousand if you like, and I still wouldn't take it. I'm a free man. And everything that you all value so highly and dearly—all of you, rich men and beggars alike—it hasn't the slightest power over me. It's just so much thistledown, drifting in the wind. I can manage without you—I can go round the side of you. I'm strong and proud. Mankind is marching towards a higher truth, towards a higher happiness, as high as ever may be on this earth, and I am in its foremost ranks!

LOPAKHIN.   And you'll get there, will you?

TROFIMOV.   I shall get there. (*Pause.*) Either get there, or else show others the way. (*From the distance comes the sound of an axe thudding against a tree.*)

LOPAKHIN.   Well, then, goodbye, old lad. Time to go. We turn up our noses at each other, you and me, but life goes on regardless. When I'm at work—and I can work long hours and never tire—then my thoughts run easier, and I feel I know why I exist. And how many people are there in Russia, my friend, who exist and never know the reason why? Well, it makes no odds—it doesn't stop the world going round. I'm told her brother's found a job—in a bank, apparently—six thousand a year. Only he'll never stick at it, of course—he's too lazy.

ANYA (*in the doorway*).   Mama says will they please not start cutting down the orchard until she's gone.

TROFIMOV.   For heaven's sake—how could anyone have so little tact? (*Goes out through the anteroom.*)

---

poppy: Poppies are grown for their seeds, which are used in cooking.

LOPAKHIN.   I'll see to it, I'll see to it . . . It's quite true—these people
. . . (*Goes out after him.*)

ANYA.   Has Firs been sent off to the hospital?

YASHA.   I told them this morning. I assume they sent him off.

ANYA (*to* YEPIKHODOV, *who is crossing the room*).   Ask them, will you,
please, if they've taken Firs to the hospital.

YASHA (*offended*).   I told Yegor this morning. What's the point of asking ten times over?

YEPIKHODOV.   The aged Firs, in my considered opinion, is past repair.
It's not a hospital he needs—it's gathering to his fathers. And I can only envy
him. (*Puts down the suitcase he is carrying on top of a hat-box, and crushes it.*) Of
course! Of course! I knew I was going to do that! (*Goes out.*)

YASHA (*mockingly*).   Poor old Disasters!

VARYA (*outside the door*).   Have they taken Firs to hospital?

ANYA.   Yes, they have.

VARYA.   Why didn't they take the letter to the doctor?

ANYA.   It'll have to be sent on after him, then. (*Goes out.*)

VARYA (*from the next room*).   Where's Yasha? Tell him, will you, his
mother's come. She wants to say goodbye to him.

YASHA (*flaps his hand*).   Oh, they'll drive me to drink. (DUNYASHA *all
this while been busying herself about things; now that* YASHA *is alone she goes
up to him.*)

DUNYASHA.   If only you'd just give me a glance, Yasha. You're going
away . . . abandoning me . . . (*Weeps and throws herself on his neck.*)

YASHA.   What's all the crying for? (*Drinks champagne.*) Six days from
now I'll be in Paris again. Tomorrow we'll be getting on board that express
and we'll be away like smoke. I can't believe it. *Vive la France . . .*! Not my
style, this place. I can't live here, there's no help for it. I've seen all I want to
see of ignorance—I've had my fill of it. (*Drinks champagne.*) So what's there
to cry about? Behave yourself properly, then you won't cry.

DUNYASHA (*powders herself, looking in a little mirror*).   You will write to
me from Paris, won't you? I loved you, you know, Yasha—I loved you so
much! I'm terribly tender-hearted, Yasha!

YASHA.   They're coming. (*Busies himself about the suitcase, humming
quietly. Enter* RANYEVSKAYA, GAYEV, ANYA *and* CHARLOTTA IVANOVNA.)

GAYEV.   We ought to be going. We haven't much time in hand. (*Looking
at* YASHA.) Who is it smelling of herrings?

RANYEVSKAYA.   Another ten minutes, and we'll get into the carriages
. . . (*Glances round the room.*) Farewell, dear house. Farewell, old grandfather
house. The winter will go by, spring will come, and then soon you won't be
here—they'll be pulling you down. So many things these walls have seen!
(*Fervently kisses her daughter.*) My treasure, you're radiant—your eyes are
sparkling like two diamonds. You're pleased, then? Very pleased?

ANYA.   Very pleased. There's a new life beginning, Mama!

GAYEV (*cheerfully*).   Absolutely—everything's all right now. Before the
cherry orchard was sold we were all frightfully upset, we were all suffering.

And then, as soon as the question had been finally settled, and no going back on it, we all calmed down, we got quite cheerful even . . . Here am I, I'm an old hand when it comes to banks—and now I'm a financier . . . yellow into the middle pocket . . . And Lyuba, you look better somehow, you really do.

RANYEVSKAYA.   Yes. My nerves are better, it's true. (*She is helped into her overcoat and hat.*) I'm sleeping well. Take my things out, will you, Yasha. It's time to go. (*To* ANYA) My own little girl, we'll see each other again soon. When I get to Paris I'll be living on the money your great-aunt in Yaroslavl sent to buy the estate—hurrah for her! But it won't last long.

ANYA.   Mama, you'll come back soon, soon . . . won't you? I'm going to study and take my examinations—and then I'm going to work, I'm going to help you. Mama, you and I are going to read all sorts of books together. We will, won't we? (*Kisses her mother's hands.*) We'll read in the autumn evenings, read lots and lots of books, and a marvelous new world will open up before us . . . (*Lost in her dreams.*) Come back, Mama . . .

RANYEVSKAYA.   I will, my precious. (*Embraces her. Enter* LOPAKHIN. CHARLOTTA *quietly hums a tune.*)

GAYEV.   Charlotta's happy—she's singing!

CHARLOTTA (*picks up a bundle that looks like a swaddled infant*).   My little baby! Off to bye-byes now . . .

INFANT (*cries*).   Wah! Wah!

CHARLOTTA.   Hush, my pretty one. Hush, my darling boy!

INFANT.   Wah! Wah!

CHARLOTTA.   Poor little thing! (*Tosses the bundle back where it came from.*) So you'll try to find me a place, will you, please? I can't manage otherwise.

LOPAKHIN.   We'll find something for you, never you fear.

GAYEV.   They're all leaving us. Varya's going away . . . Suddenly no one needs us any more.

CHARLOTTA.   I've nowhere to live in town. I shall have to go farther afield. (*Hums.*) But what do I care? (*Enter* PISHCHIK.)

LOPAKHIN.   Well, of all the world's wonders . . . !

PISHCHIK (*out of breath*).   Oh, let me get my breath back . . . such a state . . . my dear good people . . . water, some water . . .

GAYEV.   After money, is he? No good looking at me . . . I shall be departing from temptation. (*Goes out.*)

PISHCHIK.   Long time since I was in this house . . . wonderful woman . . . (*To* LOPAKHIN) And you're here . . . Very pleased to catch you . . . Man of enormous intelligence . . . Here . . . Take this . . . Four hundred rubles . . . Eight hundred still to come . . .

LOPAKHIN (*shrugs in bewilderment*).   It's like a dream . . . Where on earth did you get it?

PISHCHIK.   Wait . . . Hot . . . Most extraordinary thing. Some Englishmen arrived—found some kind of white clay in my land . . . (*To* RANYEVSKAYA) And four hundred for you . . . You amazing, wonderful woman . . . (*Gives her the money.*) The rest later. (*Drinks the water.*) Someone was just telling me—young man on the train—apparently there's some great philosopher who recommends jumping off the roof. "Jump!" he says—and apparently that's the whole problem in life. (*In amazement*) Would you believe it! Some more water . . .

LOPAKHIN.   Who were these Englishmen?

PISHCHIK.   I gave them a twenty-four year lease on the section with the clay in it . . . But forgive me, I can't stay now . . . I've got to gallop . . . Go and see old Znoykov . . . And Kardamonov . . . I owe money to all of them . . . (*Drinks.*) Your very good health . . . I'll look in on Thursday . . .

RANYEVSKAYA.   We're just moving into town—and tomorrow I'm going abroad.

PISHCHIK.   What? (*Alarmed*) What's this about moving into town? So that's why I can see all this furniture . . . all these suitcases . . . Well, there we are . . . (*On the verge of tears*) There we are . . . People of tremendous intelligence, these Englishmen . . . There we are . . . Be happy . . . God give you strength . . . There we are, then . . . To everything in this world there is an end . . . (*Kisses* RANYEVSKAYA'S *hand.*) And if one day the rumor reaches you that the end has come for me, then remember this old . . . this old horse, and say: "Once on this earth there was a certain Simeon-Pishchik . . . God rest his soul . . ." Most remarkable weather . . . Yes . . . (*Exits in great confusion, but at once returns and speaks from the doorway.*) Dashenka sends her regards! (*Goes out.*)

RANYEVSKAYA.   We could even be going now. I'm leaving with two things still on my mind. One is poor Firs. (*Glances at her watch.*) We could wait another five minutes . . .

ANYA.   Mama, Firs has been taken to hospital. Yasha did it this morning.

RANYEVSKAYA.   My other worry is Varya. She's used to rising early and doing a day's work. Now she has nothing to do all day she's like a fish out of water. Poor soul, she's grown thin and pale, she's forever weeping . . . (*Pause. To* LOPAKHIN) As you well know, I dreamt of . . . seeing her married to you, and everything appeared to be pointing in that direction. (*Whispers to* ANYA, *who motions to* CHARLOTTA, *whereupon both of them go out.*) She loves you—you like her—and why you seem to avoid each other like this I simply do not know. I don't understand it.

LOPAKHIN.   I don't understand it myself, I have to admit. It's all very strange. If there's still time, then I'm ready—here and now, if you like. Let's get it over with, and *basta.*° I have a feeling I'll never propose once you've gone.

RANYEVSKAYA.   Splendid. It'll only take a minute, after all. I'll call her in at once.

LOPAKHIN.   We've even got champagne, appropriately enough. (*Looks at the glasses.*) Empty. Someone's drunk the lot. (YASHA *coughs.*) Well, that really is lapping it up.

basta: Italian, "enough"

RANYEVSKAYA (*animatedly*).   Wonderful. We'll go out of the room. Yasha, *allez!*° I'll call her . . . (*Through the doorway*) Varya, leave all that and come here. Come on! (*Goes out with* YASHA.)

LOPAKHIN (*looks at his watch*).   Yes . . . (*Pause. There is stifled laughter and whispering outside the door. Finally* VARYA *comes in.*)

VARYA (*looks round the room at some length*).   That's strange. I can't find it anywhere . . .

LOPAKHIN.   What are you looking for?

VARYA.   I packed it myself and I can't remember where. (*Pause.*)

LOPAKHIN.   Where are you off to now, then?

VARYA.   Me? To the Ragulins. I've agreed to keep an eye on the running of the house for them. Well, to be housekeeper.

LOPAKHIN.   That's in Yashnevo, isn't it? What, about forty-five miles from here? (*Pause.*) Well, here we are, no more life in this house . . .

VARYA (*examining things*).   Where is it . . . ? Or perhaps I packed it in the trunk . . . No, no more life in this house. Never again.

LOPAKHIN.   And I'm off to Kharkov now . . . on this train, in fact. Lot of business to do. I'm leaving Yepikhodov in charge here. I've taken him on.

VARYA.   Really?

LOPAKHIN.   This time last year we had snow already, if you remember. Now it's calm and sunny. The only thing is the cold. Three degrees of frost.

VARYA.   I didn't look. (*Pause.*) Anyway, our thermometer's broken . . . (*Pause.*)

A VOICE (*through the door from outside*).   Where's Lopakhin?

LOPAKHIN (*as if he has been expecting this call for some time*).   Coming! (*Goes rapidly out.* VARYA, *now sitting on the floor, lays her head on a bundle of clothing, and sobs quietly. The door opens and* RANYEVSKAYA *cautiously enters.*)

RANYEVSKAYA.   What? (*Pause.*) We must go.

VARYA (*she has already stopped crying; wipes her eyes*).   Yes, Mama, dear, it's time. I'll get to the Ragulins today provided we don't miss that train . . .

RANYEVSKAYA (*through the doorway*).   Anya, get your things on! (*Enter* ANYA, *followed by* GAYEV *and* CHARLOTTA IVANOVNA. GAYEV *is wearing an overcoat with a hood. The* SERVANTS *and* CARRIERS *foregather.* YEPIKHODOV *busies himself about the things.*) Well, then, I think we can finally be on our way.

ANYA (*joyfully*).   On our way!

GAYEV.   My friends! My dear good friends! Leaving this house forever, can I stand silent, can I refrain from saying a word of farewell, from giving expression to those feelings that now invade my whole being . . . ?

ANYA (*imploringly*).   Uncle!

VARYA.   Dear uncle, don't!

GAYEV (*gloomily*).   Off the cushion and into the middle . . . I am silent. (*Enter* TROFIMOV, *followed by* LOPAKHIN.)

TROFIMOV.   What are we waiting for, then? It's time to go!

LOPAKHIN.   Yepikhodov, my coat!

allez: French, "let's go"

RANYEVSKAYA.   I'm going to stop here for one more minute. It's as if I'd never really seen before what the walls in this house were like, what the ceilings were like. And now I look at them avidly, with such a tender love.

GAYEV.   I remember, when I was six years old, sitting up on this windowsill on Trinity Sunday and watching my father go to church.

RANYEVSKAYA.   Have all the things been taken out?

LOPAKHIN.   I think the lot. (*To* YEPIKHODOV, *as he puts on his overcoat*) Have a look, though, see if everything's all right.

YEPIKHODOV (*in a hoarse voice*).   Don't worry—leave it to me!

LOPAKHIN.   Why are you talking in that sort of voice?

YEPIKHODOV.   Just drinking some water, and I swallowed something.

YASHA (*contemptuously*).   The ignorance of these people . . .

RANYEVSKAYA.   We shall depart, and not a living soul will remain behind.

LOPAKHIN.   All the way through until the spring.

VARYA (*pulls an umbrella out of one of the bundles in a way that looks as if she were raising it threateningly:* LOPAKHIN *pretends to be frightened*).   What? What are you doing . . . ? It never even entered my head.

TROFIMOV.   Ladies and gentlemen, we must get into the carriages. It really is time! The train will be arriving any minute!

VARYA.   Here they are, Petya—your galoshes, next to this suitcase. (*In tears*) And what dirty galoshes they are . . .

TROFIMOV (*putting on the galoshes*).   Off we go, then!

GAYEV (*in great confusion, afraid of bursting into tears*).   The train . . . the station . . . In off into the middle, off the cushion into the corner . . .

RANYEVSKAYA.   Off we go!

LOPAKHIN.   Are we all here? No one left behind? (*Locks the side door on the left.*) The things are all stacked in here, we must lock up. Right, off we go!

ANYA.   Farewell, old house! Farewell, old life!

TROFIMOV.   Hail, new life! (*Goes with* ANYA. VARYA *looks round the room and goes out without hurrying.* YASHA *and* CHARLOTTA *go out with her little dog.*)

LOPAKHIN.   So, until the spring. Out you go, all of you . . . Goodbye! (*Goes out.* RANYEVSKAYA *and* GAYEV *are left alone together. As if they have been waiting for this, they throw themselves on each other's necks and sob quietly, restraining themselves, afraid of being overheard.*)

GAYEV (*in despair*).   My sister, my sister . . .

RANYEVSKAYA.   Oh my dear orchard, my sweet and lovely orchard! My life, my youth, my happiness—farewell! Farewell!

ANYA (*off, calling cheerfully*).   Mama!

TROFIMOV (*off, cheerfully and excitedly*).   Hulloooo . . . !

RANYEVSKAYA.   One last look at the walls . . . the windows . . . This is the room where our mother loved to walk, our poor dead mother . . .

GAYEV.   My sister, my sister . . . !

ANYA (*off*).   Mama!

TROFIMOV (*off*). Hulloooo . . . !
RANYEVSKAYA. We're coming! (*They go out. The stage is empty. There is the sound of all the doors being locked, and then of the carriages departing. It grows quiet. Through the silence comes the dull thudding of the axe. It sounds lonely and sad. Steps are heard. From the door on the right comes* FIRS. *He is dressed as always, in jacket and white waistcoat, with his feet in slippers. He is ill.*)
    FIRS (*goes to the door and tries the handle*). Locked. They've gone. (*Sits down on the sofa.*) They've forgotten about me. Well, never mind. I'll just sit here for a bit . . . And I dare say he hasn't put his winter coat on, he's gone off in his autumn coat. (*Sighs anxiously.*) I never looked to see. When will these young people learn? (*Mutters something impossible to catch.*) My life's gone by, and it's just as if I'd never lived at all. (*Lies down.*) I'll lie down for a bit, then . . . No strength, have you? Nothing left. Nothing . . . Oh you . . . sillybilly . . . (*Lies motionless.*)

    (*A sound is heard in the distance, as if from the sky—the sound of a breaking string, dying away, sad.*
    (*Silence descends, and the only thing that can be heard, far away in the orchard, is the thudding of the axe.*)

Arthur Miller

Death of a Salesman

Certain Private Conversations in Two Acts and a Requiem

CHARACTERS

WILLY LOMAN	CHARLEY, *a neighbor*
LINDA, *his wife*	BERNARD, *Charley's son*
BIFF ⎱ *his sons*	JENNY, *Charley's secretary*
HAPPY ⎰	STANLEY, *a waiter*
UNCLE BEN, *his older brother*	MISS FORSYTHE ⎱ *young women*
HOWARD WAGNER, *his employer*	LETTA ⎰
THE WOMAN	

    The action takes place in Willy Loman's house and yard and in various places he visits in the New York and Boston of today.

DEATH OF A SALESMAN   First performed in 1949. Arthur Miller was born in 1915 in New York City, the son of a well-to-do manufacturer whose financial losses in the Depression forced a move to Brooklyn in 1929. Here Miller graduated from high school and worked in an automobile parts warehouse for two years before entering the University of Michigan, where he won three drama prizes. After graduation in 1938, he returned to Brooklyn, married, and fathered a son and daughter. *Death of a Salesman* was his third Broadway play.

ACT 1

A melody is heard, played upon a flute. It is small and fine, telling of grass and trees and the horizon. The curtain rises.

Before us is the Salesman's house. We are aware of towering, angular shapes behind it, surrounding it on all sides. Only the blue light of the sky falls upon the house and forestage; the surrounding area shows an angry glow of orange. As more light appears, we see a solid vault of apartment houses around the small, fragile-seeming home. An air of the dream clings to the place, a dream rising out of reality. The kitchen at center seems actual enough, for there is a kitchen table with three chairs, and a refrigerator. But no other fixtures are seen. At the back of the kitchen there is a draped entrance, which leads to the living-room. To the right of the kitchen, on a level raised two feet, is a bedroom furnished only with a brass bedstead and a straight chair. On a shelf over the bed a silver athletic trophy stands. A window opens onto the apartment house at the side.

Behind the kitchen, on a level raised six and a half feet, is the boys' bedroom, at present barely visible. Two beds are dimly seen, and at the back of the room a dormer window. (This bedroom is above the unseen living-room.) At the left a stairway curves up to it from the kitchen.

The entire setting is wholly, or, in some places, partially transparent. The roof-line of the house is one-dimensional; under and over it we see the apartment buildings. Before the house lies an apron, curving beyond the forestage into the orchestra. This forward area serves as the back yard as well as the locale of all WILLY'S *imaginings and of his city scenes. Whenever the action is in the present the actors observe the imaginary wall-lines, entering the house only through its door at the left. But in the scenes of the past these boundaries are broken, and characters enter or leave a room by stepping "through" a wall onto the forestage.*

From the right, WILLY LOMAN, *the Salesman, enters, carrying two large sample cases. The flute plays on. He hears but is not aware of it. He is past sixty years of age, dressed quietly. Even as he crosses the stage to the doorway of the house, his exhaustion is apparent. He unlocks the door, comes into the kitchen, and thankfully lets his burden down, feeling the soreness of his palms. A word-sigh escapes his lips—it might be "Oh, boy, oh, boy." He closes the door, then carries his cases out into the living-room, through the draped kitchen doorway.*

LINDA, *his wife, has stirred in her bed at the right. She gets out and puts on a robe, listening. Most often jovial, she has developed an iron repression of her exceptions to* WILLY'S *behavior—she more than loves him, she admires him, as though his mercurial nature, his temper, his massive dreams and little cruelties, served her only as sharp reminders of the turbulent longings within him, longings which she shares but lacks the temperament to utter and follow to their end.*

LINDA (*hearing* WILLY *outside the bedroom, calls with some trepidation*).   Willy!

WILLY.   It's all right. I came back.

LINDA.   Why? What happened? (*Slight pause.*) Did something happen, Willy?

WILLY.   No, nothing happened.

LINDA.   You didn't smash the car, did you?

WILLY (*with casual irritation*).   I said nothing happened. Didn't you hear me?

LINDA.   Don't you feel well?

WILLY.   I'm tired to the death. (*The flute has faded away. He sits on the bed beside her, a little numb.*) I couldn't make it. I just couldn't make it, Linda.

LINDA (*very carefully, delicately*).   Where were you all day? You look terrible.

WILLY.   I got as far as a little above Yonkers. I stopped for a cup of coffee. Maybe it was the coffee.

LINDA.   What?

WILLY (*after a pause*).   I suddenly couldn't drive any more. The car kept going off onto the shoulder, y'know?

LINDA (*helpfully*).   Oh. Maybe it was the steering again. I don't think Angelo knows the Studebaker.

WILLY.   No, it's me, it's me. Suddenly I realize I'm goin' sixty miles an hour and I don't remember the last five minutes. I'm—I can't seem to—keep my mind to it.

LINDA.   Maybe it's your glasses. You never went for your new glasses.

WILLY.   No, I see everything. I came back ten miles an hour. It took me nearly four hours from Yonkers.

LINDA (*resigned*).   Well, you'll just have to take a rest, Willy, you can't continue this way.

WILLY.   I just got back from Florida.

LINDA.   But you didn't rest your mind. Your mind is overactive, and the mind is what counts, dear.

WILLY.   I'll start out in the morning. Maybe I'll feel better in the morning. (*She is taking off his shoes.*) These goddam arch supports are killing me.

LINDA.   Take an aspirin. Should I get you an aspirin? It'll soothe you.

WILLY (*with wonder*).   I was driving along, you understand? And I was fine. I was even observing the scenery. You can imagine, me looking at scenery, on the road every week of my life. But it's so beautiful up there, Linda, the trees are so thick, and the sun is warm. I opened the windshield and just let the warm air bathe over me. And then all of a sudden I'm goin' off the road! I'm tellin' ya, I absolutely forgot I was driving. If I'd've gone the other way over the white line I might've killed somebody. So I went on again—and five minutes later I'm dreamin' again, and I nearly—(*He presses two fingers against his eyes.*) I have such thoughts, I have such strange thoughts.

LINDA.   Willy, dear. Talk to them again. There's no reason why you can't work in New York.

WILLY.   They don't need me in New York. I'm the New England man. I'm vital in New England.

LINDA.   But you're sixty years old. They can't expect you to keep traveling every week.

WILLY.   I'll have to send a wire to Portland. I'm supposed to see Brown and Morrison tomorrow morning at ten o'clock to show the line. Goddammit, I could sell them! (*He starts putting on his jacket.*)

LINDA (*taking the jacket from him*).   Why don't you go down to the place tomorrow and tell Howard you've simply got to work in New York? You're too accommodating, dear.

WILLY.   If old man Wagner was alive I'd a been in charge of New York now! That man was a prince, he was a masterful man. But that boy of his, that Howard, he don't appreciate. When I went north the first time, the Wagner Company didn't know where New England was!

LINDA.   Why don't you tell those things to Howard, dear?

WILLY (*encouraged*).   I will, I definitely will. Is there any cheese?

LINDA.   I'll make you a sandwich.

WILLY.   No, go to sleep. I'll take some milk. I'll be up right away. The boys in?

LINDA.   They're sleeping. Happy took Biff on a date tonight.

WILLY (*interested*).   That so?

LINDA.   It was so nice to see them shaving together, one behind the other, in the bathroom. And going out together. You notice? The whole house smells of shaving lotion.

WILLY.   Figure it out. Work a lifetime to pay off a house. You finally own it, and there's nobody to live in it.

LINDA.   Well, dear, life is a casting off. It's always that way.

WILLY.   No, no, some people—some people accomplish something. Did Biff say anything after I went this morning?

LINDA.   You shouldn't have criticized him, Willy, especially after he just got off the train. You mustn't lose your temper with him.

WILLY.   When the hell did I lose my temper? I simply asked him if he was making any money. Is that a criticism?

LINDA.   But, dear, how could he make any money?

WILLY (*worried and angered*).   There's such an undercurrent in him. He became a moody man. Did he apologize when I left this morning?

LINDA.   He was crestfallen, Willy. You know how he admires you. I think if he finds himself, then you'll both be happier and not fight any more.

WILLY.   How can he find himself on a farm? Is that a life? A farmhand? In the beginning, when he was young, I thought, well, a young man, it's good for him to tramp around, take a lot of different jobs. But it's more than ten years now and he has yet to make thirty-five dollars a week!

LINDA.   He's finding himself, Willy.

WILLY.   Not finding yourself at the age of thirty-four is a disgrace!

LINDA.   Shh!

WILLY.   The trouble is he's lazy, goddammit!

LINDA.   Willy, please!

WILLY.   Biff is a lazy bum!

LINDA.   They're sleeping. Get something to eat. Go on down.

WILLY.   Why did he come home? I would like to know what brought him home.

LINDA.   I don't know. I think he's still lost, Willy. I think he's very lost.

WILLY.   Biff Loman is lost. In the greatest country in the world a young man with such—personal attractiveness, gets lost. And such a hard worker. There's one thing about Biff—he's not lazy.

LINDA.   Never.

WILLY (*with pity and resolve*).   I'll see him in the morning; I'll have a nice talk with him. I'll get him a job selling. He could be big in no time. My God! Remember how they used to follow him around in high school? When he smiled at one of them their faces lit up. When he walked down the street . . . (*He loses himself in reminiscences.*)

LINDA (*trying to bring him out of it*).   Willy, dear, I got a new kind of American-type cheese today. It's whipped.

WILLY.   Why do you get American when I like Swiss?

LINDA.   I just thought you'd like a change—

WILLY.   I don't want change! I want Swiss cheese. Why am I always being contradicted?

LINDA (*with a covering laugh*).   I thought it would be a surprise.

WILLY.   Why don't you open a window in here, for God's sake?

LINDA (*with infinite patience*).   They're all open, dear.

WILLY.   The way they boxed us in here. Bricks and windows, windows and bricks.

LINDA.   We should've bought the land next door.

WILLY.   The street is lined with cars. There's not a breath of fresh air in the neighborhood. The grass don't grow any more, you can't raise a carrot in the back yard. They should've had a law against apartment houses. Remember those two beautiful elm trees out there? When I and Biff hung the swing between them?

LINDA.   Yeah, like being a million miles from the city.

WILLY.   They should've arrested the builder for cutting those down. They massacred the neighborhood. (*Lost*) More and more I think of those days, Linda. This time of year it was lilac and wisteria. And then the peonies would come out, and the daffodils. What fragrance in this room!

LINDA.   Well, after all, people had to move somewhere.

WILLY.   No, there's more people now.

LINDA.   I don't think there's more people. I think—

WILLY.   There's more people! That's what's ruining this country! Population is getting out of control. The competition is maddening! Smell the stink from that apartment house! And another one on the other side . . . How can they whip cheese?

(*On* WILLY'S *last line,* BIFF *and* HAPPY *raise themselves up in their beds, listening.*)

LINDA.   Go down, try it. And be quiet.

WILLY (*turning to* LINDA, *guiltily*).   You're not worried about me, are you, sweetheart?

BIFF.   What's the matter?

HAPPY.   Listen!

LINDA.   You've got too much on the ball to worry about.

WILLY.   You're my foundation and my support, Linda.

LINDA.   Just try to relax, dear. You make mountains out of molehills.

WILLY.   I won't fight with him any more. If he wants to go back to Texas, let him go.

LINDA.   He'll find his way.

WILLY.   Sure. Certain men just don't get started till later in life. Like Thomas Edison, I think. Or B. F. Goodrich. One of them was deaf. (*He starts for the bedroom doorway.*) I'll put my money on Biff.

LINDA.   And Willy—if it's warm Sunday we'll drive in the country. And we'll open the windshield, and take lunch.

WILLY.   No, the windshields don't open on the new cars.

LINDA.   But you opened it today.

WILLY.   Me? I didn't. (*He stops.*) Now isn't that peculiar! Isn't that a remarkable—(*He breaks off in amazement and fright as the flute is heard distantly.*)

LINDA.   What, darling?

WILLY.   That is the most remarkable thing.

LINDA.   What, dear?

WILLY.   I was thinking of the Chevvy. (*Slight pause.*) Nineteen twenty-eight . . . when I had that red Chevvy—(*Breaks off.*) That's funny! I coulda sworn I was driving that Chevvy today.

LINDA.   Well, that's nothing. Something must've reminded you.

WILLY.   Remarkable. Ts. Remember those days? The way Biff used to simonize that car? The dealer refused to believe there was eighty thousand miles on it. (*He shakes his head.*) Heh! (*To* LINDA) Close your eyes, I'll be right up. (*He walks out of the bedroom.*)

HAPPY (*to* BIFF).   Jesus, maybe he smashed up the car again!

LINDA (*calling after* WILLY).   Be careful on the stairs, dear! The cheese is on the middle shelf! (*She turns, goes over to the bed, takes his jacket, and goes out of the bedroom.*)

(*Light has risen on the boys' room. Unseen,* WILLY *is heard talking to himself,* "Eighty thousand miles," *and a little laugh.* BIFF *gets out of bed, comes downstage a bit, and stands attentively.* BIFF *is two years older than his brother* HAPPY, *well built, but in these days bears a worn air and seems less self-assured. He has succeeded less, and his dreams are stronger and less acceptable than* HAPPY'S. HAPPY *is tall, powerfully made. Sexuality is like a visible color on him, or a scent that many women have discovered. He, like his brother, is lost, but in a different way, for he has never allowed himself to turn his face toward defeat and is thus more confused and hard-skinned, although seemingly more content.*)

HAPPY (*getting out of bed*).   He's going to get his license taken away if he keeps that up. I'm getting nervous about him, y'know, Biff?

BIFF.   His eyes are going.

HAPPY.   No, I've driven with him. He sees all right. He just doesn't keep his mind on it. I drove into the city with him last week. He stops at a green light and then it turns red and he goes. (*He laughs.*)

BIFF.   Maybe he's color-blind.

HAPPY.   Pop? Why he's got the finest eye for color in the business. You know that.

BIFF (*sitting down on his bed*).   I'm going to sleep.

HAPPY.   You're not still sour on Dad, are you, Biff?

BIFF.   He's all right, I guess.

WILLY (*underneath them, in the living-room*).   Yes, sir, eighty thousand miles—eighty-two thousand!

BIFF.   You smoking?

HAPPY (*holding out a pack of cigarettes*).   Want one?

BIFF (*taking a cigarette*).   I can never sleep when I smell it.

WILLY.   What a simonizing job, heh!

HAPPY (*with deep sentiment*).   Funny, Biff, y'know? Us sleeping in here again? The old beds. (*He pats his bed affectionately.*) All the talk that went across those two beds, huh? Our whole lives.

BIFF.   Yeah. Lotta dreams and plans.

HAPPY (*with a deep and masculine laugh*).   About five hundred women would like to know what was said in this room. (*They share a soft laugh.*)

BIFF.   Remember that big Betsy something—what the hell was her name—over on Bushwick Avenue?

HAPPY (*combing his hair*).   With the collie dog!

BIFF.   That's the one. I got you in there, remember?

HAPPY.   Yeah, that was my first time—I think. Boy, there was a pig! (*They laugh, almost crudely.*) You taught me everything I know about women. Don't forget that.

BIFF.   I bet you forgot how bashful you used to be. Especially with girls.

HAPPY.   Oh, I still am, Biff.

BIFF.   Oh, go on.

HAPPY.   I just control it, that's all. I think I got less bashful and you got more so. What happened, Biff? Where's the old humor, the old confidence? (*He shakes* BIFF'S *knee.* BIFF *gets up and moves restlessly about the room.*) What's the matter?

BIFF.   Why does Dad mock me all the time?

HAPPY.   He's not mocking you, he—

BIFF.   Everything I say there's a twist of mockery on his face. I can't get near him.

HAPPY.   He just wants you to make good, that's all. I wanted to talk to you about Dad for a long time, Biff. Something's—happening to him. He— talks to himself.

BIFF.   I noticed that this morning. But he always mumbled.

HAPPY.   But not so noticeable. It got so embarrassing I sent him to Florida. And you know something? Most of the time he's talking to you.

BIFF.   What's he say about me?

HAPPY.   I can't make it out.

BIFF.   What's he say about me?

HAPPY.   I think the fact that you're not settled, that you're still kind of up in the air . . .

BIFF.   There's one or two other things depressing him, Happy.

HAPPY.   What do you mean?

BIFF.   Never mind. Just don't lay it all to me.

HAPPY.   But I think if you just got started—I mean—is there any future for you out there?

BIFF.   I'll tell ya, Hap, I don't know what the future is. I don't know—what I'm supposed to want.

HAPPY.   What do you mean?

BIFF.   Well, I spent six or seven years after high school trying to work myself up. Shipping clerk, salesman, business of one kind or another. And it's a measly manner of existence. To get on that subway on the hot mornings in summer. To devote your whole life to keeping stock, or making phone calls, or selling or buying. To suffer fifty weeks of the year for the sake of a two-week vacation, when all you really desire is to be outdoors, with your shirt off. And always to have to get ahead of the next fella. And still—that's how you build a future.

HAPPY.   Well, you really enjoy it on a farm? Are you content out there?

BIFF *(with rising agitation)*.   Hap, I've had twenty or thirty different kinds of jobs since I left home before the war, and it always turns out the same. I just realized it lately. In Nebraska when I herded cattle, and the Dakotas, and Arizona, and now in Texas. It's why I came home now, I guess, because I realized it. This farm I work on, it's spring there now, see? And they've got about fifteen new colts. There's nothing more inspiring or— beautiful than the sight of a mare and a new colt. And it's cool there now, see? Texas is cool now, and it's spring. And whenever spring comes to where I am, I suddenly get the feeling, my God, I'm not gettin' anywhere! What the hell am I doing, playing around with horses, twenty-eight dollars a week! I'm thirty-four years old, I oughta be makin' my future. That's when I come running home. And now, I get here, and I don't know what to do with myself. *(After a pause.)* I've always made a point of not wasting my life, and everytime I come back here I know that all I've done is to waste my life.

HAPPY.   You're a poet, you know that, Biff? You're a—you're an idealist!

BIFF.   No, I'm mixed up very bad. Maybe I oughta get married. Maybe I oughta get stuck into something. Maybe that's my trouble. I'm like a boy. I'm not married, I'm not in business, I just—I'm like a boy. Are you content, Hap? You're a success, aren't you? Are you content?

HAPPY. Hell, no!

BIFF. Why? You're making money, aren't you?

HAPPY (*moving about with energy, expressiveness*).   All I can do now is wait for the merchandise manager to die. And suppose I get to be merchandise manager? He's a good friend of mine, and he just built a terrific estate on Long Island. And he lived there about two months and sold it, and now he's building another one. He can't enjoy it once it's finished. And I know that's just what I would do. I don't know what the hell I'm workin' for. Sometimes I sit in my apartment—all alone. And I think of the rent I'm paying. And it's crazy. But then, it's what I always wanted. My own apartment, a car, and plenty of women. And still, goddammit, I'm lonely.

BIFF (*with enthusiasm*).   Listen, why don't you come out West with me?

HAPPY.   You and I, heh?

BIFF.   Sure, maybe we could buy a ranch. Raise cattle, use our muscles. Men built like we are should be working out in the open.

HAPPY (*avidly*).   The Loman Brothers, heh?

BIFF (*with vast affection*).   Sure, we'd be known all over the counties!

HAPPY (*enthralled*).   That's what I dream about, Biff. Sometimes I want to just rip my clothes off in the middle of the store and outbox that goddam merchandise manager. I mean I can outbox him, outrun, and outlift anybody in that store, and I have to take orders from those common, petty sons-of-bitches till I can't stand it any more.

BIFF.   I'm tellin' you, kid, if you were with me I'd be happy out there.

HAPPY (*enthused*).   See, Biff, everybody around me is so false that I'm constantly lowering my ideals . . .

BIFF.   Baby, together we'd stand up for one another, we'd have someone to trust.

HAPPY.   If I were around you—

BIFF.   Hap, the trouble is we weren't brought up to grub for money. I don't know how to do it.

HAPPY.   Neither can I!

BIFF.   Then let's go!

HAPPY.   The only thing is—what can you make out there?

BIFF.   But look at your friend. Builds an estate and then hasn't the peace of mind to live in it.

HAPPY.   Yeah, but when he walks into the store the waves part in front of him. That's fifty-two thousand dollars a year coming through the revolving door, and I got more in my pinky finger than he's got in his head.

BIFF.   Yeah, but you just said—

HAPPY.   I gotta show some of those pompous, self-important executives over there that Hap Loman can make the grade. I want to walk into the store the way he walks in. Then I'll go with you, Biff. We'll be together yet, I swear. But take those two we had tonight. Now weren't they gorgeous creatures?

BIFF.   Yeah, yeah, most gorgeous I've had in years.

HAPPY.   I get that any time I want, Biff. Whenever I feel disgusted. The only trouble is, it gets like bowling or something. I just keep knockin' them over and it doesn't mean anything. You still run around a lot?

BIFF.   Naa. I'd like to find a girl—steady, somebody with substance.

HAPPY.   That's what I long for.

BIFF.   Go on! You'd never come home.

HAPPY.   I would! Somebody with character, with resistance! Like Mom, y'know? You're gonna call me a bastard when I tell you this. That girl Charlotte I was with tonight is engaged to be married in five weeks. (*He tries on his new hat.*)

BIFF.   No kiddin'!

HAPPY.   Sure, the guy's in line for the vice-presidency of the store. I don't know what gets into me, maybe I just have an overdeveloped sense of competition or something, but I went and ruined her, and furthermore I can't get rid of her. And he's the third executive I've done that to. Isn't that a crummy characteristic? And to top it all, I go to their weddings! (*Indignantly, but laughing*) Like I'm not supposed to take bribes. Manufacturers offer me a hundred-dollar bill now and then to throw an order their way. You know how honest I am, but it's like this girl, see. I hate myself for it. Because I don't want the girl, and, still, I take it and—I love it!

BIFF.   Let's go to sleep.

HAPPY.   I guess we didn't settle anything, heh?

BIFF.   I just got one idea that I think I'm going to try.

HAPPY.   What's that?

BIFF.   Remember Bill Oliver?

HAPPY.   Sure, Oliver is very big now. You want to work for him again?

BIFF.   No, but when I quit he said something to me. He put his arm on my shoulder, and he said, "Biff, if you ever need anything, come to me."

HAPPY.   I remember that. That sounds good.

BIFF.   I think I'll go to see him. If I could get ten thousand or even seven or eight thousand dollars I could buy a beautiful ranch.

HAPPY.   I bet he'd back you. 'Cause he thought highly of you, Biff. I mean, they all do. You're well liked, Biff. That's why I say to come back here, and we both have the apartment. And I'm tellin' you, Biff, any babe you want . . .

BIFF.   No, with a ranch I could do the work I like and still be something. I just wonder though. I wonder if Oliver still thinks I stole that carton of basketballs.

HAPPY.   Oh, he probably forgot that long ago. It's almost ten years. You're too sensitive. Anyway, he didn't really fire you.

BIFF.   Well, I think he was going to. I think that's why I quit. I was never sure whether he knew or not. I know he thought the world of me, though. I was the only one he'd let lock up the place.

WILLY (*below*).   You gonna wash the engine, Biff?

HAPPY.   Shh! (BIFF *looks at* HAPPY, *who is gazing down, listening.* WILLY *is mumbling in the parlor.*) You hear that? (*They listen.* WILLY *laughs warmly.*)

BIFF (*growing angry*).   Doesn't he know Mom can hear that?

WILLY.   Don't get your sweater dirty, Biff! (*A look of pain crosses* BIFF'S *face.*)

HAPPY.   Isn't that terrible? Don't leave again, will you? You'll find a job here. You gotta stick around. I don't know what to do about him, it's getting embarrassing.

WILLY.   What a simonizing job!

BIFF.   Mom's hearing that!

WILLY.   No kiddin', Biff, you got a date? Wonderful!

HAPPY.   Go on to sleep. But talk to him in the morning, will you?

BIFF (*reluctantly getting into bed*).   With her in the house. Brother!

HAPPY (*getting into bed*).   I wish you'd have a good talk with him. (*The light on their room begins to fade.*)

BIFF (*to himself in bed*).   That selfish, stupid . . .

HAPPY.   Sh . . . Sleep, Biff.

(*Their light is out. Well before they have finished speaking,* WILLY'S *form is dimly seen below in the darkened kitchen. He opens the refrigerator, searches in there, and takes out a bottle of milk. The apartment houses are fading out, and the entire house and surroundings become covered with leaves. Music insinuates itself as the leaves appear.*)

WILLY.   Just wanna be careful with those girls, Biff, that's all. Don't make any promises. No promises of any kind. Because a girl, y'know, they always believe what you tell 'em, and you're very young, Biff, you're too young to be talking seriously to girls. (*Light rises on the kitchen.* WILLY, *talking, shuts the refrigerator door and comes downstage to the kitchen table. He pours milk into a glass. He is totally immersed in himself, smiling faintly.*) Too young entirely, Biff. You want to watch your schooling first. Then when you're all set, there'll be plenty of girls for a boy like you. (*He smiles broadly at a kitchen chair.*) That so? The girls pay for you? (*He laughs.*) Boy, you must really be makin' a hit. (WILLY *is gradually addressing—physically—a point offstage, speaking through the wall of the kitchen, and his voice has been rising in volume to that of a normal conversation.*) I been wondering why you polish the car so careful. Ha! Don't leave the hubcaps, boys. Get the chamois to the hubcaps. Happy, use newspaper on the windows, it's the easiest thing. Show him how to do it, Biff! You see, Happy? Pad it up, use it like a pad. That's it, that's it, good work. You're doin' all right, Hap. (*He pauses, then nods in approbation for a few seconds, then looks upward.*) Biff, first thing we gotta do when we get time is clip that big branch over the house. Afraid it's gonna fall in a storm and hit the roof. Tell you what. We get a rope and sling her around, and then we climb up there with a couple of saws and take her down. Soon as you finish the car, boys, I wanna see ya. I got a surprise for you, boys.

BIFF (*offstage*).   Whatta ya got, Dad?

WILLY.   No, you finish first. Never leave a job till you're finished—remember that. (*Looking toward the "big trees"*) Biff, up in Albany I saw a beautiful hammock. I think I'll buy it next trip, and we'll hang it right between those two elms. Wouldn't that be something? Just swingin' there under those branches. Boy, that would be . . . (YOUNG BIFF *and* YOUNG HAPPY *appear from the direction* WILLY *was addressing.* HAPPY *carries rags and a pail of water.* BIFF, *wearing a sweater with a block "S," carries a football.*)

BIFF (*pointing in the direction of the car offstage*).   How's that, Pop, professional?

WILLY.   Terrific. Terrific job, boys. Good work, Biff.

HAPPY.   Where's the surprise, Pop?

WILLY.   In the back seat of the car.

HAPPY.   Boy! (*He runs off.*)

BIFF.   What is it, Dad? Tell me, what'd you buy?

WILLY (*laughing, cuffs him*).   Never mind, something I want you to have.

BIFF (*turns and starts off*).   What is it, Hap?

HAPPY (*offstage*).   It's a punching bag!

BIFF.   Oh, Pop!

WILLY.   It's got Gene Tunney's signature on it! (HAPPY *runs onstage with a punching bag.*)

BIFF.   Gee, how'd you know we wanted a punching bag?

WILLY.   Well, it's the finest thing for the timing.

HAPPY (*lies down on his back and pedals with his feet*).   I'm losing weight, you notice, Pop?

WILLY (*to* HAPPY).   Jumping rope is good too.

BIFF.   Did you see the new football I got?

WILLY (*examining the ball*).   Where'd you get a new ball?

BIFF.   The coach told me to practice my passing.

WILLY.   That so? And he gave you the ball, heh?

BIFF.   Well, I borrowed it from the locker room. (*He laughs confidentially.*)

WILLY (*laughing with him at the theft*).   I want you to return that.

HAPPY.   I told you he wouldn't like it!

BIFF (*angrily*).   Well, I'm bringing it back!

WILLY (*stopping the incipient argument, to* HAPPY).   Sure, he's gotta practice with a regulation ball, doesn't he? (*To* BIFF) Coach'll probably congratulate you on your initiative!

BIFF.   Oh, he keeps congratulating my initiative all the time, Pop.

WILLY.   That's because he likes you. If somebody else took that ball there'd be an uproar. So what's the report, boys, what's the report?

BIFF.   Where'd you go this time, Dad? Gee, we were lonesome for you.

WILLY (*pleased, puts an arm around each boy and they come down to the apron*).   Lonesome, heh?

BIFF.   Missed you every minute.

WILLY.   Don't say? Tell you a secret, boys. Don't breathe it to a soul. Someday I'll have my own business, and I'll never have to leave home any more.

HAPPY.   Like Uncle Charley, heh?

WILLY.   Bigger than Uncle Charley! Because Charley is not—liked. He's liked, but he's not—well liked.

BIFF.   Where'd you go this time, Dad?

WILLY.   Well, I got on the road, and I went north to Providence. Met the Mayor.

BIFF.   The Mayor of Providence!

WILLY.   He was sitting in the hotel lobby.

BIFF.   What'd he say?

WILLY.   He said, "Morning!" And I said, "You got a fine city here, Mayor." And then he had coffee with me. And then I went to Waterbury. Waterbury is a fine city. Big clock city, the famous Waterbury clock. Sold a nice bill there. And then Boston—Boston is the cradle of the Revolution. A fine city. And a couple of other towns in Mass., and on to Portland and Bangor and straight home!

BIFF.   Gee, I'd love to go with you sometime, Dad.

WILLY.   Soon as summer comes.

HAPPY.   Promise?

WILLY.   You and Hap and I, and I'll show you all the towns. America is full of beautiful towns and fine, upstanding people. And they know me, boys, they know me up and down New England. The finest people. And when I bring you fellas up, there'll be open sesame for all of us, 'cause one thing, boys: I have friends. I can park my car in any street in New England, and the cops protect it like their own. This summer, heh?

BIFF *and* HAPPY (*together*).   Yeah! You bet!

WILLY.   We'll take our bathing suits.

HAPPY.   We'll carry your bags, Pop!

WILLY.   Oh, won't that be something! Me comin' into the Boston stores with you boys carryin' my bags. What a sensation! (BIFF *is prancing around, practicing passing the ball.*) You nervous, Biff, about the game?

BIFF.   Not if you're gonna be there.

WILLY.   What do they say about you in school, now that they made you captain?

HAPPY.   There's a crowd of girls behind him everytime the classes change.

BIFF (*taking* WILLY'S *hand*).   This Saturday, Pop, this Saturday—just for you, I'm going to break through for a touchdown.

HAPPY.   You're supposed to pass.

BIFF.   I'm takin' one play for Pop. You watch me, Pop, and when I take off my helmet, that means I'm breakin' out. Then you watch me crash through that line!

WILLY (*kisses* BIFF).   Oh, wait'll I tell this in Boston! (BERNARD *enters in knickers. He is younger than* BIFF, *earnest and loyal, a worried boy.*)

BERNARD.   Biff, where are you? You're supposed to study with me today.

WILLY.   Hey, looka Bernard. What're you lookin' so anemic about, Bernard?

BERNARD.   He's gotta study, Uncle Willy. He's got Regents° next week.

HAPPY (*tauntingly, spinning* BERNARD *around*).   Let's box, Bernard!

BERNARD.   Biff! (*He gets away from* HAPPY.) Listen, Biff, I heard Mr. Birnbaum say that if you don't start studyin' math he's gonna flunk you, and you won't graduate. I heard him!

WILLY.   You better study with him, Biff. Go ahead now.

BERNARD.   I heard him!

BIFF.   Oh, Pop, you didn't see my sneakers! (*He holds up a foot for* WILLY *to look at.*)

WILLY.   Hey, that's a beautiful job of printing!

BERNARD (*wiping his glasses*).   Just because he printed University of Virginia on his sneakers doesn't mean they've got to graduate him, Uncle Willy!

WILLY (*angrily*).   What're you talking about? With scholarships to three universities they're gonna flunk him?

BERNARD.   But I heard Mr. Birnbaum say—

WILLY.   Don't be a pest, Bernard! (*To his* BOYS) What an anemic!

BERNARD.   Okay, I'm waiting for you in my house, Biff. (BERNARD *goes off. The* LOMANS *laugh.*)

WILLY.   Bernard is not well liked, is he?

BIFF.   He's liked, but he's not well liked.

HAPPY.   That's right, Pop.

WILLY.   That's just what I mean. Bernard can get the best marks in school, y'understand, but when he gets out in the business world, y'understand, you are going to be five times ahead of him. That's why I thank Almighty God you're both built like Adonises. Because the man who makes an appearance in the business world, the man who creates personal interest, is the man who gets ahead. Be liked and you will never want. You take me, for instance. I never have to wait in line to see a buyer. "Willy Loman is here!" That's all they have to know, and I go right through.

BIFF.   Did you knock them dead, Pop?

WILLY.   Knocked 'em cold in Providence, slaughtered 'em in Boston.

HAPPY (*on his back, pedaling again*).   I'm losing weight, you notice, Pop? (LINDA *enters, as of old, a ribbon in her hair, carrying a basket of washing.*)

LINDA (*with youthful energy*).   Hello, dear!

WILLY.   Sweetheart!

LINDA.   How'd the Chevvy run?

Regents: a statewide proficiency examination administered in New York high schools

WILLY.   Chevrolet, Linda, is the greatest car ever built. (*To the* BOYS) Since when do you let your mother carry wash up the stairs?

BIFF.   Grab hold there, boy!

HAPPY.   Where to, Mom?

LINDA.   Hang them up on the line. And you better go down to your friends, Biff. The cellar is full of boys. They don't know what to do with themselves.

BIFF.   Ah, when Pop comes home they can wait!

WILLY (*laughs appreciatively*).   You better go down and tell them what to do, Biff.

BIFF.   I think I'll have them sweep out the furnace room.

WILLY.   Good work, Biff.

BIFF (*goes through wall-line of kitchen to doorway at back and calls down*).   Fellas! Everybody sweep out the furnace room! I'll be right down!

VOICES.   All right! Okay, Biff.

BIFF.   George and Sam and Frank, come out back! We're hangin' up the wash! Come on, Hap, on the double! (*He and* HAPPY *carry out the basket.*)

LINDA.   The way they obey him!

WILLY.   Well, that's training, the training. I'm tellin' you, I was sellin' thousands and thousands, but I had to come home.

LINDA.   Oh, the whole block'll be at that game. Did you sell anything?

WILLY.   I did five hundred gross in Providence and seven hundred gross in Boston.

LINDA.   No! Wait a minute, I've got a pencil. (*She pulls pencil and paper out of her apron pocket.*) That makes your commission . . . Two hundred—my God! Two hundred and twelve dollars!

WILLY.   Well, I didn't figure it yet, but . . .

LINDA.   How much did you do?

WILLY.   Well, I—I did—about a hundred and eighty gross in Providence. Well no—it came to—roughly two hundred gross on the whole trip.

LINDA (*without hesitation*).   Two hundred gross. That's . . . (*She figures.*)

WILLY.   The trouble was that three of the stores were half closed for inventory in Boston. Otherwise I woulda broke records.

LINDA.   Well, it makes seventy dollars and some pennies. That's very good.

WILLY.   What do we owe?

LINDA.   Well, on the first there's sixteen dollars on the refrigerator—

WILLY.   Why sixteen?

LINDA.   Well, the fan belt broke, so it was a dollar eighty.

WILLY.   But it's brand new.

LINDA.   Well, the man said that's the way it is. Till they work themselves in, y'know. (*They move through the wall-line into the kitchen.*)

WILLY.   I hope we didn't get stuck on that machine.

LINDA.   They got the biggest ads of any of them!

WILLY.   I know, it's a fine machine. What else?

LINDA.   Well, there's nine-sixty for the washing machine. And for the vacuum cleaner there's three and a half due on the fifteenth. Then the roof, you got twenty-one dollars remaining.

WILLY.   It doesn't leak, does it?

LINDA.   No, they did a wonderful job. Then you owe Frank for the carburetor.

WILLY.   I'm not going to pay that man! That goddam Chevrolet, they ought to prohibit the manufacture of that car!

LINDA.   Well, you owe him three and a half. And odds and ends, comes to around a hundred and twenty dollars by the fifteenth.

WILLY.   A hundred and twenty dollars! My God, if business don't pick up I don't know what I'm gonna do!

LINDA.   Well, next week you'll do better.

WILLY.   Oh, I'll knock 'em dead next week. I'll go to Hartford. I'm very well liked in Hartford. You know, the trouble is, Linda, people don't seem to take to me. (*They move onto the forestage.*)

LINDA.   Oh, don't be foolish.

WILLY.   I know it when I walk in. They seem to laugh at me.

LINDA.   Why? Why would they laugh at you? Don't talk that way, Willy. (WILLY *moves to the edge of the stage.* LINDA *goes into the kitchen and starts to darn stockings.*)

WILLY.   I don't know the reason for it, but they just pass me by. I'm not noticed.

LINDA.   But you're doing wonderful, dear. You're making seventy to a hundred dollars a week.

WILLY.   But I gotta be at it ten, twelve hours a day. Other men—I don't know—they do it easier. I don't know why—I can't stop myself—I talk too much. A man oughta come in with a few words. One thing about Charley. He's a man of few words, and they respect him.

LINDA.   You don't talk too much, you're just lively.

WILLY (*smiling*).   Well, I figure, what the hell, life is short, a couple of jokes. (*To himself*) I joke too much! (*The smile goes.*)

LINDA.   Why? You're—

WILLY.   I'm fat. I'm very—foolish to look at, Linda. I didn't tell you, but Christmas time I happened to be calling on F. H. Stewarts, and a salesman I know, as I was going in to see the buyer I heard him say something about—walrus. And I—I cracked him right across the face. I won't take that. I simply will not take that. But they do laugh at me. I know that.

LINDA.   Darling . . .

WILLY.   I gotta overcome it. I know I gotta overcome it. I'm not dressing to advantage, maybe.

LINDA.   Willy, darling, you're the handsomest man in the world—

WILLY.   Oh, no, Linda.

LINDA.   To me you are. (*Slight pause.*) The handsomest. (*From the darkness is heard the laughter of a woman.* WILLY *doesn't turn to it, but it continues through* LINDA'S *lines.*) And the boys, Willy. Few men are idolized by their children the way you are. (*Music is heard as, behind a scrim to the left of the house,* THE WOMAN, *dimly seen, is dressing.*)

WILLY (*with great feeling*).   You're the best there is, Linda, you're a pal, you know that? On the road—on the road I want to grab you sometimes and just kiss the life outa you.

(*The laughter is loud now, and he moves into a brightening area at the left, where* THE WOMAN *has come from behind the scrim and is standing, putting on her hat, looking into a "mirror" and laughing.*)

WILLY.   'Cause I get so lonely—especially when business is bad and there's nobody to talk to. I get the feeling that I'll never sell anything again, that I won't make a living for you, or a business, a business for the boys. (*He talks through* THE WOMAN'S *subsiding laughter;* THE WOMAN *primps at the "mirror."*) There's so much I want to make for—

THE WOMAN.   Me? You didn't make me, Willy. I picked you.

WILLY (*pleased*).   You picked me?

THE WOMAN (*who is quite proper-looking,* WILLY'S *age*).   I did. I've been sitting at that desk watching all the salesmen go by, day in, day out. But you've got such a sense of humor, and we do have such a good time together, don't we?

WILLY.   Sure, sure. (*He takes her in his arms.*) Why do you have to go now?

THE WOMAN.   It's two o'clock . . .

WILLY.   No, come on in! (*He pulls her.*)

THE WOMAN.   . . . my sisters'll be scandalized. When'll you be back?

WILLY.   Oh, two weeks about. Will you come up again?

THE WOMAN.   Sure thing. You do make me laugh. It's good for me. (*She squeezes his arm, kisses him.*) And I think you're a wonderful man.

WILLY.   You picked me, heh?

THE WOMAN.   Sure. Because you're so sweet. And such a kidder.

WILLY.   Well, I'll see you next time I'm in Boston.

THE WOMAN.   I'll put you right through to the buyers.

WILLY (*slapping her bottom*).   Right. Well, bottoms up!

THE WOMAN (*slaps him gently and laughs*).   You just kill me, Willy. (*He suddenly grabs her and kisses her roughly.*) You kill me. And thanks for the stockings. I love a lot of stockings. Well, good night.

WILLY.   Good night. And keep your pores open!

THE WOMAN.   Oh, Willy!

(THE WOMAN *bursts out laughing, and* LINDA'S *laughter blends in.* THE WOMAN *disappears into the dark. Now the area at the kitchen table brightens.* LINDA *is sitting where she was at the kitchen table, but now is mending a pair of her silk stockings.*)

LINDA.   You are, Willy. The handsomest man. You've got no reason to feel that—

WILLY (*coming out of* THE WOMAN'S *dimming area and going over to* LINDA).   I'll make it all up to you, Linda. I'll—

LINDA.   There's nothing to make up, dear. You're doing fine, better than—

WILLY (*noticing her mending*).   What's that?

LINDA.   Just mending my stockings. They're so expensive—

WILLY (*angrily, taking them from her*).   I won't have you mending stockings in this house! Now throw them out! (LINDA *puts the stockings in her pocket.*)

BERNARD (*entering on the run*).   Where is he? If he doesn't study!

WILLY (*moving to the forestage, with great agitation*).   You'll give him the answers!

BERNARD.   I do, but I can't on a Regents! That's a state exam! They're liable to arrest me!

WILLY.   Where is he? I'll whip him, I'll whip him!

LINDA.   And he'd better give back that football, Willy, it's not nice.

WILLY.   Biff! Where is he? Why is he taking everything?

LINDA.   He's too rough with the girls, Willy. All the mothers are afraid of him!

WILLY.   I'll whip him!

BERNARD.   He's driving the car without a license! (THE WOMAN'S *laugh is heard.*)

WILLY.   Shut up!

LINDA.   All the mothers—

WILLY.   Shut up!

BERNARD (*backing quietly away and out*).   Mr. Birnbaum says he's stuck up.

WILLY.   Get outa here!

BERNARD.   If he doesn't buckle down he'll flunk math! (*He goes off.*)

LINDA.   He's right, Willy, you've gotta—

WILLY (*exploding at her*).   There's nothing the matter with him! You want him to be a worm like Bernard? He's got spirit, personality . . . (*As he speaks,* LINDA, *almost in tears, exits into the living-room.* WILLY *is alone in the kitchen, wilting and staring. The leaves are gone, it is night again, and the apartment houses look down from behind.*) Loaded with it. Loaded! What is he stealing? He's giving it back, isn't he? Why is he stealing? What did I tell him? I never in my life told him anything but decent things. (HAPPY *in pajamas has come down the stairs;* WILLY *suddenly becomes aware of* HAPPY'S *presence.*)

HAPPY.   Let's go now, come on.

WILLY (*sitting down at the kitchen table*).   Huh! Why did she have to wax the floors herself? Everytime she waxes the floors she keels over. She knows that!

HAPPY.   Shh! Take it easy. What brought you back tonight?

WILLY.   I got an awful scare. Nearly hit a kid in Yonkers. God! Why didn't I go to Alaska with my brother Ben that time! Ben! That man was a genius, that man was success incarnate! What a mistake! He begged me to go.

HAPPY.   Well, there's no use in—

WILLY.   You guys! There was a man started with the clothes on his back and ended up with diamond mines!

HAPPY.   Boy, someday I'd like to know how he did it.

WILLY.   What's the mystery? The man knew what he wanted and went out and got it! Walked into a jungle, and comes out, the age of twenty-one, and he's rich! The world is an oyster, but you don't crack it open on a mattress.

HAPPY.   Pop, I told you I'm gonna retire you for life.

WILLY.   You'll retire me for life on seventy goddam dollars a week? And your women and your car and your apartment, and you'll retire me for life! Christ's sake, I couldn't get past Yonkers today! Where are you guys, where are you? The woods are burning! I can't drive a car! (CHARLEY *has appeared in the doorway. He is a large man, slow of speech, laconic, immovable. In all he says, despite what he says, there is pity, and, now, trepidation. He has a robe over pajamas, slippers on his feet. He enters the kitchen.*)

CHARLEY.   Everything all right?

HAPPY.   Yeah, Charley, everything's . . .

WILLY.   What's the matter?

CHARLEY.   I heard some noise. I thought something happened. Can't we do something about the walls? You sneeze in here, and in my house hats blow off.

HAPPY.   Let's go to bed, Dad. Come on. (CHARLEY *signals to* HAPPY *to go.*)

WILLY.   You go ahead, I'm not tired at the moment.

HAPPY (*to* WILLY).   Take it easy, huh? (*He exits.*)

WILLY.   What're you doin' up?

CHARLEY (*sitting down at the kitchen table opposite* WILLY).   Couldn't sleep good. I had a heartburn.

WILLY.   Well, you don't know how to eat.

CHARLEY.   I eat with my mouth.

WILLY.   No, you're ignorant. You gotta know about vitamins and things like that.

CHARLEY.   Come on, let's shoot. Tire you out a little.

WILLY (*hesitantly*).   All right. You got cards?

CHARLEY (*taking a deck from his pocket*).   Yeah, I got them. Someplace. What is it with those vitamins?

WILLY (*dealing*).   They build up your bones. Chemistry.

CHARLEY.   Yeah, but there's no bones in a heartburn.

WILLY.   What are you talkin' about? Do you know the first thing about it?

CHARLEY.   Don't get insulted.

WILLY.   Don't talk about something you don't know anything about.
(*They are playing. Pause.*)

CHARLEY.   What're you doin' home?

WILLY.   A little trouble with the car.

CHARLEY.   Oh. (*Pause.*) I'd like to take a trip to California.

WILLY.   Don't say.

CHARLEY.   You want a job?

WILLY.   I got a job, I told you that. (*After a slight pause*) What the hell
are you offering me a job for?

CHARLEY.   Don't get insulted.

WILLY.   Don't insult me.

CHARLEY.   I don't see no sense in it. You don't have to go on this way.

WILLY.   I got a good job. (*Slight pause.*) What do you keep coming in
here for?

CHARLEY.   You want me to go?

WILLY (*after a pause, withering*).   I can't understand it. He's going back
to Texas again. What the hell is that?

CHARLEY.   Let him go.

WILLY.   I got nothin' to give him, Charley, I'm clean, I'm clean.

CHARLEY.   He won't starve. None a them starve. Forget about him.

WILLY.   Then what have I got to remember?

CHARLEY.   You take it too hard. To hell with it. When a deposit bottle
is broken you don't get your nickel back.

WILLY.   That's easy enough for you to say.

CHARLEY.   That ain't easy for me to say.

WILLY.   Did you see the ceiling I put up in the living-room?

CHARLEY.   Yeah, that's a piece of work. To put up a ceiling is a mystery
to me. How do you do it?

WILLY.   What's the difference?

CHARLEY.   Well, talk about it.

WILLY.   You gonna put up a ceiling?

CHARLEY.   How could I put up a ceiling?

WILLY.   Then what the hell are you bothering me for?

CHARLEY.   You're insulted again.

WILLY.   A man who can't handle tools is not a man. You're disgusting.

CHARLEY.   Don't call me disgusting, Willy. (UNCLE BEN, *carrying a
valise and an umbrella, enters the forestage from around the right corner of the
house. He is a stolid man, in his sixties, with a mustache and an authoritative air.
He is utterly certain of his destiny, and there is an aura of far places about him. He
enters exactly as* WILLY *speaks.*)

WILLY.   I'm getting awfully tired, Ben. (BEN'S *music is heard.* BEN
looks around at everything.)

CHARLEY.   Good, keep playing; you'll sleep better. Did you call me
Ben? (BEN *looks at his watch.*)

WILLY.   That's funny. For a second there you reminded me of my brother Ben.

BEN.   I only have a few minutes. (*He strolls, inspecting the place.* WILLY *and* CHARLEY *continue playing.*)

CHARLEY.   You never heard from him again, heh? Since that time?

WILLY.   Didn't Linda tell you? Couple of weeks ago we got a letter from his wife in Africa. He died.

CHARLEY.   That so.

BEN (*chuckling*).   So this is Brooklyn, eh?

CHARLEY.   Maybe you're in for some of his money.

WILLY.   Naa, he had seven sons. There's just one opportunity I had with that man . . .

BEN.   I must make a train, William. There are several properties I'm looking at in Alaska.

WILLY.   Sure, sure! If I'd gone with him to Alaska that time, everything would've been totally different.

CHARLEY.   Go on, you'd froze to death up there.

WILLY.   What're you talking about?

BEN.   Opportunity is tremendous in Alaska, William. Surprised you're not up there.

WILLY.   Sure, tremendous.

CHARLEY.   Heh?

WILLY.   There was the only man I ever met who knew the answers.

CHARLEY.   Who?

BEN.   How are you all?

WILLY (*taking a pot, smiling*).   Fine, fine.

CHARLEY.   Pretty sharp tonight.

BEN.   Is Mother living with you?

WILLY.   No, she died a long time ago.

CHARLEY.   Who?

BEN.   That's too bad. Fine specimen of a lady, Mother.

WILLY (*to* CHARLEY).   Heh?

BEN.   I'd hoped to see the old girl.

CHARLEY.   Who died?

BEN.   Heard anything from Father, have you?

WILLY (*unnerved*).   What do you mean, who died?

CHARLEY (*taking a pot*).   What're you talkin' about?

BEN (*looking at his watch*).   William, it's half-past eight!

WILLY (*as though to dispel his confusion he angrily stops* CHARLEY'S *hand*). That's my build!

CHARLEY.   I put the ace—

WILLY.   If you don't know how to play the game I'm not gonna throw my money away on you!

CHARLEY (*rising*).   It was my ace, for God's sake!

WILLY.   I'm through, I'm through!

BEN.   When did Mother die?

WILLY.   Long ago. Since the beginning you never knew how to play cards.

CHARLEY (*picks up the cards and goes to the door*).   All right! Next time I'll bring a deck with five aces.

WILLY.   I don't play that kind of game!

CHARLEY (*turning to him*).   You ought to be ashamed of yourself!

WILLY.   Yeah?

CHARLEY.   Yeah! (*He goes out.*)

WILLY (*slamming the door after him*).   Ignoramus!

BEN (*as* WILLY *comes toward him through the wall-line of the kitchen*).   So you're William.

WILLY (*shaking* BEN'S *hand*).   Ben! I've been waiting for you so long! What's the answer? How did you do it?

BEN.   Oh, there's a story in that. (LINDA *enters the forestage, as of old, carrying the wash basket.*)

LINDA.   Is this Ben?

BEN (*gallantly*).   How do you do, my dear.

LINDA.   Where've you been all these years? Willy's always wondered why you—

WILLY (*pulling* BEN *away from her impatiently*).   Where is Dad? Didn't you follow him? How did you get started?

BEN.   Well, I don't know how much you remember.

WILLY.   Well, I was just a baby, of course, only three or four years old—

BEN.   Three years and eleven months.

WILLY.   What a memory, Ben!

BEN.   I have many enterprises, William, and I have never kept books.

WILLY.   I remember I was sitting under the wagon in—was it Nebraska?

BEN.   It was South Dakota, and I gave you a bunch of wild flowers.

WILLY.   I remember you walking away down some open road.

BEN (*laughing*).   I was going to find Father in Alaska.

WILLY.   Where is he?

BEN.   At that age I had a very faulty view of geography, William. I discovered after a few days that I was heading due south, so instead of Alaska, I ended up in Africa.

LINDA.   Africa!

WILLY.   The Gold Coast!

BEN.   Principally diamond mines.

LINDA.   Diamond mines!

BEN.   Yes, my dear. But I've only a few minutes—

WILLY.   No! Boys! Boys! (YOUNG BIFF *and* HAPPY *appear.*) Listen to this. This is your Uncle Ben, a great man! Tell my boys, Ben!

BEN.   Why, boys, when I was seventeen I walked into the jungle, and when I was twenty-one I walked out. (*He laughs.*) And by God I was rich.

WILLY (*to the* BOYS).   You see what I been talking about? The greatest things can happen!

BEN (*glancing at his watch*).   I have an appointment in Ketchikan Tuesday week.

WILLY.   No, Ben! Please tell about Dad. I want my boys to hear. I want them to know the kind of stock they spring from. All I remember is a man with a big beard, and I was in Mamma's lap, sitting around a fire, and some kind of high music.

BEN.   His flute. He played the flute.

WILLY.   Sure, the flute, that's right! (*New music is heard, a high, rollicking tune.*)

BEN.   Father was a very great and a very wild-hearted man. We would start in Boston, and he'd toss the whole family into the wagon, and then he'd drive the team right across the country; through Ohio and Indiana, Michigan, Illinois, and all the Western states. And we'd stop in the towns and sell the flutes that he'd made on the way. Great inventor, Father. With one gadget he made more in a week than a man like you could make in a lifetime.

WILLY.   That's just the way I'm bringing them up, Ben—rugged, well liked, all-around.

BEN.   Yeah? (*To* BIFF) Hit that, boy—hard as you can. (*He pounds his stomach.*)

BIFF.   Oh, no, sir!

BEN (*taking boxing stance*).   Come on, get to me! (*He laughs.*)

WILLY.   Go to it, Biff! Go ahead, show him!

BIFF.   Okay! (*He cocks his fists and starts in.*)

LINDA (*to* WILLY).   Why must he fight, dear?

BEN (*sparring with* BIFF).   Good boy! Good boy!

WILLY.   How's that, Ben, heh?

HAPPY.   Give him the left, Biff!

LINDA.   Why are you fighting?

BEN.   Good boy! (*Suddenly comes in, trips* BIFF, *and stands over him, the point of his umbrella poised over* BIFF'S *eye.*)

LINDA.   Look out, Biff!

BIFF.   Gee!

BEN (*patting* BIFF'S *knee*).   Never fight fair with a stranger, boy. You'll never get out of the jungle that way. (*Taking* LINDA'S *hand and bowing*) It was an honor and a pleasure to meet you, Linda.

LINDA (*withdrawing her hand coldly, frightened*).   Have a nice—trip.

BEN (*to* WILLY).   And good luck with your—what do you do?

WILLY.   Selling.

BEN.   Yes. Well . . . (*He raises his hand in farewell to all.*)

WILLY.   No, Ben, I don't want you to think . . . (*He takes* BEN'S *arm to show him.*) It's Brooklyn, I know, but we hunt too.

BEN.   Really, now.

WILLY.   Oh, sure, there's snakes and rabbits and—that's why I moved out here. Why, Biff can fell any one of these trees in no time! Boys! Go right over to where they're building the apartment house and get some sand. We're gonna rebuild the entire front stoop right now! Watch this, Ben!

BIFF.   Yes, sir! On the double, Hap!

HAPPY (*as he and* BIFF *run off*).   I lost weight, Pop, you notice? (CHARLEY *enters in knickers, even before the* BOYS *are gone.*)

CHARLEY.   Listen, if they steal any more from that building the watchman'll put the cops on them!

LINDA (*to* WILLY).   Don't let Biff . . . (BEN *laughs lustily.*)

WILLY.   You shoulda seen the lumber they brought home last week. At least a dozen six-by-tens worth all kinds a money.

CHARLEY.   Listen, if that watchman—

WILLY.   I gave them hell, understand. But I got a couple of fearless characters there.

CHARLEY.   Willy, the jails are full of fearless characters.

BEN (*clapping* WILLY *on the back, with a laugh at* CHARLEY).   And the stock exchange, friend!

WILLY (*joining in* BEN'S *laughter*).   Where are the rest of your pants?

CHARLEY.   My wife bought them.

WILLY.   Now all you need is a golf club and you can go upstairs and go to sleep. (*To* BEN) Great athlete! Between him and his son Bernard they can't hammer a nail!

BERNARD (*rushing in*).   The watchman's chasing Biff!

WILLY (*angrily*).   Shut up! He's not stealing anything!

LINDA (*alarmed, hurrying off left*).   Where is he? Biff, dear! (*She exits.*)

WILLY (*moving toward the left, away from* BEN).   There's nothing wrong. What's the matter with you?

BEN.   Nervy boy. Good!

WILLY (*laughing*).   Oh, nerves of iron, that Biff!

CHARLEY.   Don't know what it is. My New England man comes back and he's bleedin', they murdered him up there.

WILLY.   It's contacts, Charley, I got important contacts!

CHARLEY (*sarcastically*).   Glad to hear it, Willy. Come in later, we'll shoot a little casino. I'll take some of your Portland money. (*He laughs at* WILLY *and exits.*)

WILLY (*turning to* BEN).   Business is bad, it's murderous. But not for me, of course.

BEN.   I'll stop by on my way back to Africa.

WILLY (*longingly*).   Can't you stay a few days? You're just what I need, Ben, because I—I have a fine position here, but I—well, Dad left when I was such a baby and I never had a chance to talk to him and I still feel—kind of temporary about myself.

BEN.   I'll be late for my train. (*They are at opposite ends of the stage.*)

WILLY.   Ben, my boys—can't we talk? They'd go into the jaws of hell for me, but I—

BEN.   William, you're being first-rate with your boys. Outstanding, manly chaps!

WILLY (*hanging on to his words*).   Oh, Ben, that's good to hear! Because sometimes I'm afraid that I'm not teaching them the right kind of—Ben, how should I teach them?

BEN (*giving great weight to each word, and with a certain vicious audacity*).   William, when I walked into the jungle, I was seventeen. When I walked out I was twenty-one. And, by God, I was rich! (*He goes off into the darkness around the right corner of the house.*)

WILLY.   . . . was rich! That's just the spirit I want to imbue them with! To walk into a jungle! I was right! (BEN *is gone, but* WILLY *is still speaking to him as* LINDA, *in nightgown and robe, enters the kitchen, glances around for* WILLY, *then goes to the door of the house, looks out and sees him. Comes down to his left. He looks at her.*)

LINDA.   Willy, dear? Willy?

WILLY.   I was right!

LINDA.   Did you have some cheese? (*He can't answer.*) It's very late, darling. Come to bed, heh?

WILLY (*looking straight up*).   Gotta break your neck to see a star in this yard.

LINDA.   You coming in?

WILLY.   Whatever happened to that diamond watch fob? Remember? When Ben came from Africa that time? Didn't he give me a watch fob with a diamond in it?

LINDA.   You pawned it, dear. Twelve, thirteen years ago. For Biff's radio correspondence course.

WILLY.   Gee, that was a beautiful thing. I'll take a walk.

LINDA.   But you're in your slippers.

WILLY (*starting to go around the house at the left*).   I was right! I was! (*Half to* LINDA, *as he goes, shaking his head*) What a man! There was a man worth talking to. I was right!

LINDA (*calling after* WILLY).   But in your slippers, Willy! (WILLY *is almost gone when* BIFF, *in his pajamas, comes down the stairs and enters the kitchen.*)

BIFF.   What is he doing out there?

LINDA.   Sh!

BIFF.   God Almighty, Mom, how long has he been doing this?

LINDA.   Don't, he'll hear you.

BIFF.   What the hell is the matter with him?

LINDA.   It'll pass by morning.

BIFF.   Shouldn't we do anything?

LINDA.   Oh, my dear, you should do a lot of things, but there's nothing to do, so go to sleep. (HAPPY *comes down the stairs and sits on the steps.*)

HAPPY.   I never heard him so loud, Mom.

LINDA.   Well, come around more often; you'll hear him. (*She sits down at the table and mends the lining of* WILLY'S *jacket.*)

BIFF.   Why didn't you ever write me about this, Mom?

LINDA.   How would I write to you? For over three months you had no address.

BIFF.   I was on the move. But you know I thought of you all the time. You know that, don't you, pal?

LINDA.   I know, dear, I know. But he likes to have a letter. Just to know that there's still a possibility for better things.

BIFF.   He's not like this all the time, is he?

LINDA.   It's when you come home he's always the worst.

BIFF.   When I come home?

LINDA.   When you write you're coming, he's all smiles, and talks about the future, and—he's just wonderful. And then the closer you seem to come, the more shaky he gets, and then, by the time you get here, he's arguing, and he seems angry at you. I think it's just that maybe he can't bring himself to—to open up to you. Why are you so hateful to each other? Why is that?

BIFF (*evasively*).   I'm not hateful, Mom.

LINDA.   But you no sooner come in the door than you're fighting!

BIFF.   I don't know why. I mean to change. I'm tryin', Mom, you understand?

LINDA.   Are you home to stay now?

BIFF.   I don't know. I want to look around, see what's doin'.

LINDA.   Biff, you can't look around all your life, can you?

BIFF.   I just can't take hold, Mom. I can't take hold of some kind of a life.

LINDA.   Biff, a man is not a bird to come and go with the springtime.

BIFF.   Your hair . . . (*He touches her hair.*) Your hair got so gray.

LINDA.   Oh, it's been gray since you were in high school. I just stopped dyeing it, that's all.

BIFF.   Dye it again, will ya? I don't want my pal looking old. (*He smiles.*)

LINDA.   You're such a boy! You think you can go away for a year and . . . You've got to get it into your head now that one day you'll knock on this door and there'll be strange people here—

BIFF.   What are you talking about? You're not even sixty, Mom.

LINDA.   But what about your father?

BIFF (*lamely*).   Well, I meant him, too.

HAPPY.   He admires Pop.

LINDA.   Biff, dear, if you don't have any feeling for him, then you can't have any feeling for me.

BIFF.   Sure I can, Mom.

LINDA.   No. You can't just come to see me, because I love him. (*With a threat, but only a threat, of tears*) He's the dearest man in the world to me, and I won't have anyone making him feel unwanted and low and blue. You've got to make up your mind now, darling, there's no leeway any more. Either he's your father and you pay him that respect, or else you're not to come here. I know he's not easy to get along with—nobody knows that better than me— but . . .

WILLY (*from the left, with a laugh*).   Hey, hey, Biffo!

BIFF (*starting to go out after* WILLY).   What the hell is the matter with him? (HAPPY *stops him.*)

LINDA.   Don't—don't go near him!

BIFF.   Stop making excuses for him! He always, always wiped the floor with you. Never had an ounce of respect for you.

HAPPY.   He's always had respect for—

BIFF.   What the hell do you know about it?

HAPPY (*surlily*).   Just don't call him crazy!

BIFF.   He's got no character—Charley wouldn't do this. Not in his own house—spewing out that vomit from his mind.

HAPPY.   Charley never had to cope with what he's got to.

BIFF.   People are worse off than Willy Loman. Believe me, I've seen them.

LINDA.   Then make Charley your father, Biff. You can't do that, can you? I don't say he's a great man. Willy Loman never made a lot of money. His name was never in the paper. He's not the finest character that ever lived. But he's a human being, and a terrible thing is happening to him. So attention must be paid. He's not to be allowed to fall into his grave like an old dog. Attention, attention must be finally paid to such a person. You called him crazy—

BIFF.   I didn't mean—

LINDA.   No, a lot of people think he's lost his—balance. But you don't have to be very smart to know what his trouble is. The man is exhausted.

HAPPY.   Sure!

LINDA.   A small man can be just as exhausted as a great man. He works for a company thirty-six years this March, opens up unheard-of territories to their trademark, and now in his old age they take his salary away.

HAPPY (*indignantly*).   I didn't know that, Mom.

LINDA.   You never asked, my dear! Now that you get your spending money someplace else you don't trouble your mind with him.

HAPPY.   But I gave you money last—

LINDA.   Christmas time, fifty dollars! To fix the hot water it cost ninety-seven fifty! For five weeks he's been on straight commission, like a beginner, an unknown!

BIFF.   Those ungrateful bastards!

LINDA.   Are they any worse than his sons? When he brought them business, when he was young, they were glad to see him. But now his old friends, the old buyers that loved him so and always found some order to hand him in a pinch—they're all dead, retired. He used to be able to make six, seven calls a day in Boston. Now he takes his valises out of the car and puts them back and takes them out again and he's exhausted. Instead of walking he talks now. He drives seven hundred miles, and when he gets there no one knows him any more, no one welcomes him. And what goes through a man's mind, driving seven hundred miles home without having earned a cent? Why shouldn't he talk to himself? Why? When he has to go to Charley and borrow fifty dollars a week and pretend to me that it's his pay? How long can that go on? How long? You see what I'm sitting here and waiting for? And you tell me he has no character? The man who never worked a day but for your benefit? When does he get the medal for that? Is this his reward—to turn around at the age of sixty-three and find his sons, who he loved better than his life, one a philandering bum—

HAPPY.   Mom!

LINDA.   That's all you are, my baby! (*To* BIFF) And you! What happened to the love you had for him? You were such pals! How you used to talk to him on the phone every night! How lonely he was till he could come home to you!

BIFF.   All right, Mom, I'll live here in my room, and I'll get a job. I'll keep away from him, that's all.

LINDA.   No, Biff. You can't stay here and fight all the time.

BIFF.   He threw me out of this house, remember that.

LINDA.   Why did he do that? I never knew why.

BIFF.   Because I know he's a fake and he doesn't like anybody around who knows!

LINDA.   Why a fake? In what way? What do you mean?

BIFF.   Just don't lay it all at my feet. It's between me and him—that's all I have to say. I'll chip in from now on. He'll settle for half my pay check. He'll be all right. I'm going to bed. (*He starts for the stairs.*)

LINDA.   He won't be all right.

BIFF (*turning on the stairs, furiously*).   I hate this city and I'll stay here. Now what do you want?

LINDA.   He's dying, Biff. (HAPPY *turns quickly to her, shocked.*)

BIFF (*after a pause*).   Why is he dying?

LINDA.   He's been trying to kill himself.

BIFF (*with great horror*).   How?

LINDA.   I live from day to day.

BIFF.   What're you talking about?

LINDA.   Remember I wrote you that he smashed up the car again? In February?

BIFF.   Well?

LINDA.   The insurance inspector came. He said that they have evidence. That all these accidents in the last year—weren't—weren't—accidents.

HAPPY.   How can they tell that? That's a lie.

LINDA.   It seems there's a woman . . . (*She takes a breath as*)

{ BIFF (*sharply but contained*).   What woman?

{ LINDA (*simultaneously*).   . . . and this woman . . .

LINDA.   What?

BIFF.   Nothing. Go ahead.

LINDA.   What did you say?

BIFF.   Nothing. I just said what woman?

HAPPY.   What about her?

LINDA.   Well, it seems she was walking down the road and saw his car. She says that he wasn't driving fast at all, and that he didn't skid. She says he came to that little bridge, and then deliberately smashed into the railing, and it was only the shallowness of the water that saved him.

BIFF.   Oh, no, he probably just fell asleep again.

LINDA.   I don't think he fell asleep.

BIFF.   Why not?

LINDA.   Last month . . . (*With great difficulty*) Oh, boys, it's so hard to say a thing like this! He's just a big stupid man to you, but I tell you there's more good in him than in many other people. (*She chokes, wipes her eyes.*) I was looking for a fuse. The lights blew out, and I went down to the cellar. And behind the fuse box—it happened to fall out—was a length of rubber pipe—just short.

HAPPY.   No kidding?

LINDA.   There's a little attachment on the end of it. I knew it right away. And sure enough, on the bottom of the water heater there's a new little nipple on the gas pipe.

HAPPY (*angrily*).   That—jerk.

BIFF.   Did you have it taken off?

LINDA.   I'm—I'm ashamed to. How can I mention it to him? Every day I go down and take away that little rubber pipe. But, when he comes home, I put it back where it was. How can I insult him that way? I don't know what to do. I live from day to day, boys. I tell you, I know every thought in his mind. It sounds so old-fashioned and silly, but I tell you he put his whole life into you and you've turned your backs on him. (*She is bent over in the chair, weeping, her face in her hands.*) Biff, I swear to God! Biff, his life is in your hands!

HAPPY (*to* BIFF).   How do you like that damned fool!

BIFF (*kissing her*).   All right, pal, all right. It's all settled now. I've been remiss. I know that, Mom. But now I'll stay, and I swear to you, I'll apply myself. (*Kneeling in front of her, in a fever of self-reproach*) It's just—you see, Mom, I don't fit in business. Not that I won't try. I'll try, and I'll make good.

HAPPY.   Sure you will. The trouble with you in business was you never tried to please people.

BIFF.   I know, I—

HAPPY.   Like when you worked for Harrison's. Bob Harrison said you were tops, and then you go and do some damn fool thing like whistling whole songs in the elevator like a comedian.

BIFF (*against* HAPPY).   So what? I like to whistle sometimes.

HAPPY.   You don't raise a guy to a responsible job who whistles in the elevator!

LINDA.   Well, don't argue about it now.

HAPPY.   Like when you'd go off and swim in the middle of the day instead of taking the line around.

BIFF (*his resentment rising*).   Well, don't you run off? You take off some-times, don't you? On a nice summer day?

HAPPY.   Yeah, but I cover myself!

LINDA.   Boys!

HAPPY.   If I'm going to take a fade the boss can call any number where I'm supposed to be and they'll swear to him that I just left. I'll tell you something that I hate to say, Biff, but in the business world some of them think you're crazy.

BIFF (*angered*).   Screw the business world!

HAPPY.   All right, screw it! Great, but cover yourself!

LINDA.   Hap, Hap!

BIFF.   I don't care what they think! They've laughed at Dad for years, and you know why? Because we don't belong in this nuthouse of a city! We should be mixing cement on some open plain, or—or carpenters. A carpenter is allowed to whistle! (WILLY *walks in from the entrance of the house, at left.*)

WILLY.   Even your grandfather was better than a carpenter. (*Pause. They watch him.*) You never grew up. Bernard does not whistle in the elevator, I assure you.

BIFF (*as though to laugh* WILLY *out of it*).   Yeah, but you do, Pop.

WILLY.   I never in my life whistled in an elevator! And who in the business world thinks I'm crazy?

BIFF.   I didn't mean it like that, Pop. Now don't make a whole thing out of it, will ya?

WILLY.   Go back to the West! Be a carpenter, a cowboy, enjoy yourself!

LINDA.   Willy, he was just saying—

WILLY.   I heard what he said!

HAPPY (*trying to quiet* WILLY).   Hey, Pop, come on now . . .

WILLY (*continuing over* HAPPY'S *line*).   They laugh at me, heh? Go to Filene's, go to the Hub, go to Slattery's, Boston. Call out the name Willy Loman and see what happens! Big shot!

BIFF.   All right, Pop.

WILLY.   Big!

BIFF.   All right!

WILLY.   Why do you always insult me?

BIFF.   I didn't say a word. (*To* LINDA) Did I say a word?

LINDA.   He didn't say anything, Willy.

WILLY (*going to the doorway of the living-room*).   All right, good night, good night.

LINDA.   Willy, dear, he just decided . . .

WILLY (*to* BIFF).   If you get tired hanging around tomorrow, paint the ceiling I put up in the living-room.

BIFF.   I'm leaving early tomorrow.

HAPPY.   He's going to see Bill Oliver, Pop.

WILLY (*interestedly*).   Oliver? For what?

BIFF (*with reserve, but trying, trying*).   He always said he'd stake me. I'd like to go into business, so maybe I can take him up on it.

LINDA.   Isn't that wonderful?

WILLY.   Don't interrupt. What's wonderful about it? There's fifty men in the City of New York who'd stake him. (*To* BIFF) Sporting goods?

BIFF.   I guess so. I know something about it and—

WILLY.   He knows something about it! You know sporting goods better than Spalding, for God's sake! How much is he giving you?

BIFF.   I don't know, I didn't even see him yet, but—

WILLY.   Then what're you talkin' about?

BIFF (*getting angry*).   Well, all I said was I'm gonna see him, that's all!

WILLY (*turning away*).   Ah, you're counting your chickens again.

BIFF (*starting left for the stairs*).   Oh, Jesus, I'm going to sleep!

WILLY (*calling after him*).   Don't curse in this house!

BIFF (*turning*).   Since when did you get so clean?

HAPPY (*trying to stop them*).   Wait a . . .

WILLY.   Don't use that language to me! I won't have it!

HAPPY (*grabbing* BIFF, *shouts*).   Wait a minute! I got an idea. I got a feasible idea. Come here, Biff, let's talk this over now, let's talk some sense here. When I was down in Florida last time, I thought of a great idea to sell sporting goods. It just came back to me. You and I, Biff—we have a line, the Loman Line. We train a couple of weeks, and put on a couple of exhibitions, see?

WILLY.   That's an idea!

HAPPY.   Wait! We form two basketball teams, see? Two water-polo teams. We play each other. It's a million dollars' worth of publicity. Two brothers, see? The Loman Brothers. Displays in the Royal Palms—all the hotels. And banners over the ring and the basketball court: "Loman Brothers." Baby, we could sell sporting goods!

WILLY.   That is a one-million-dollar idea!

LINDA.   Marvelous!

BIFF.   I'm in great shape as far as that's concerned.

HAPPY.   And the beauty of it is, Biff, it wouldn't be like a business. We'd be out playin' ball again . . .

BIFF (*enthused*).   Yeah, that's . . .

WILLY.   Million-dollar . . .

HAPPY.   And you wouldn't get fed up with it, Biff. It'd be the family again. There'd be the old honor, and comradeship, and if you wanted to go off for a swim or somethin'—well, you'd do it! Without some smart cooky gettin' up ahead of you!

WILLY.   Lick the world! You guys together could absolutely lick the civilized world.

BIFF.   I'll see Oliver tomorrow. Hap, if we could work that out . . .

LINDA.   Maybe things are beginning to—

WILLY (*wildly enthused, to* LINDA).   Stop interrupting! (*To* BIFF) But don't wear sport jacket and slacks when you see Oliver.

BIFF.   No, I'll—

WILLY.   A business suit, and talk as little as possible, and don't crack any jokes.

BIFF.   He did like me. Always liked me.

LINDA.   He loved you!

WILLY (*to* LINDA).   Will you stop! (*To* BIFF) Walk in very serious. You are not applying for a boy's job. Money is to pass. Be quiet, fine, and serious. Everybody likes a kidder, but nobody lends him money.

HAPPY.   I'll try to get some myself, Biff. I'm sure I can.

WILLY.   I see great things for you kids, I think your troubles are over. But remember, start big and you'll end big. Ask for fifteen. How much you gonna ask for?

BIFF.   Gee, I don't know—

WILLY.   And don't say, "Gee," "Gee" is a boy's word. A man walking in for fifteen thousand dollars does not say "Gee!"

BIFF.   Ten, I think, would be top though.

WILLY.   Don't be so modest. You always started too low. Walk in with a big laugh. Don't look worried. Start off with a couple of your good stories to lighten things up. It's not what you say, it's how you say it—because personality always wins the day.

LINDA.   Oliver always thought the highest of him—

WILLY.   Will you let me talk?

BIFF.   Don't yell at her, Pop, will ya?

WILLY (*angrily*).   I was talking, wasn't I?

BIFF.   I don't like you yelling at her all the time, and I'm tellin' you, that's all.

WILLY.   What're you, takin' over this house?

LINDA.   Willy—

WILLY (*turning on her*).   Don't take his side all the time, goddammit!

BIFF (*furiously*).   Stop yelling at her!

WILLY (*suddenly pulling on his cheek, beaten down, guilt ridden*).   Give my best to Bill Oliver—he may remember me. (*He exits through the living-room doorway.*)

LINDA (*her voice subdued*).   What'd you have to start that for? (BIFF *turns away.*) You see how sweet he was as soon as you talked hopefully? (*She goes over to* BIFF.) Come up and say good night to him. Don't let him go to bed that way.

HAPPY.   Come on, Biff, let's buck him up.

LINDA.   Please, dear. Just say good night. It takes so little to make him happy. Come. (*She goes through the living-room doorway, calling upstairs from within the living-room.*) Your pajamas are hanging in the bathroom, Willy!

HAPPY (*looking toward where* LINDA *went out*).   What a woman! They broke the mold when they made her. You know that, Biff?

BIFF.   He's off salary. My God, working on commission!

HAPPY.   Well, let's face it: he's no hot-shot selling man. Except that sometimes, you have to admit, he's a sweet personality.

BIFF (*decidedly*).   Lend me ten bucks, will ya? I want to buy some new ties.

HAPPY.   I'll take you to a place I know. Beautiful stuff. Wear one of my striped shirts tomorrow.

BIFF.   She got gray. Mom got awful old. Gee, I'm gonna go in to Oliver tomorrow and knock him for a—

HAPPY.   Come on up. Tell that to Dad. Let's give him a whirl. Come on.

BIFF (*steamed up*).   You know, with ten thousand bucks, boy!

HAPPY (*as they go into the living-room*).   That's the talk, Biff, that's the first time I've heard the old confidence out of you! (*From within the living-room, fading off*) You're gonna live with me, kid, and any babe you want just say the word . . . (*The last lines are hardly heard. They are mounting the stairs to their parents' bedroom.*)

LINDA (*entering her bedroom and addressing* WILLY, *who is in the bathroom. She is straightening the bed for him*).   Can you do anything about the shower? It drips.

WILLY (*from the bathroom*).   All of a sudden everything falls to pieces! Goddam plumbing, oughta be sued, those people. I hardly finished putting it in and the thing . . . (*His words rumble off.*)

LINDA.   I'm just wondering if Oliver will remember him. You think he might?

WILLY (*coming out of the bathroom in his pajamas*).   Remember him? What's the matter with you, you crazy? If he'd've stayed with Oliver he'd be on top by now! Wait'll Oliver gets a look at him. You don't know the average caliber any more. The average young man today—(*he is getting into bed*)—is got a caliber of zero. Greatest thing in the world for him was to bum around. (BIFF *and* HAPPY *enter the bedroom. Slight pause.* WILLY *stops short, looking at* BIFF.) Glad to hear it, boy.

HAPPY.   He wanted to say good night to you, sport.

WILLY (*to* BIFF).   Yeah. Knock him dead, boy. What'd you want to tell me?

BIFF.   Just take it easy, Pop. Good night. (*He turns to go.*)

WILLY (*unable to resist*).   And if anything falls off the desk while you're talking to him—like a package or something—don't you pick it up. They have office boys for that.

LINDA.   I'll make a big breakfast—

WILLY.   Will you let me finish? (*To* BIFF) Tell him you were in the business in the West. Not farm work.

BIFF.   All right, Dad.

LINDA.   I think everything—

WILLY (*going right through her speech*).   And don't undersell yourself. No less than fifteen thousand dollars.

BIFF (*unable to bear him*).   Okay. Good night, Mom. (*He starts moving.*)

WILLY.   Because you got a greatness in you, Biff, remember that. You got all kinds of greatness . . . (*He lies back, exhausted.* BIFF *walks out.*)

LINDA (*calling after* BIFF).   Sleep well, darling!

HAPPY.   I'm going to get married, Mom. I wanted to tell you.

LINDA.   Go to sleep, dear.

HAPPY (*going*).   I just wanted to tell you.

WILLY.   Keep up the good work. (HAPPY *exits.*) God . . . remember that Ebbets Field game? The championship of the city?

LINDA.   Just rest. Should I sing to you?

WILLY.   Yeah. Sing to me. (LINDA *hums a soft lullaby.*) When that team came out—he was the tallest, remember?

LINDA.   Oh, yes. And in gold. (BIFF *enters the darkened kitchen, takes a cigarette, and leaves the house. He comes downstage into a golden pool of light. He smokes, staring at the night.*)

WILLY.   Like a young god. Hercules—something like that. And the sun, the sun all around him. Remember how he waved to me? Right up from the field, with the representatives of three colleges standing by? And the buyers I brought, and the cheers when he came out—Loman, Loman, Loman! God Almighty, he'll be great yet. A star like that, magnificent, can never really fade away! (*The light on* WILLY *is fading. The gas heater begins to glow through the kitchen wall, near the stairs, a blue flame beneath the red coils.*)

LINDA (*timidly*).   Willy dear, what has he got against you?

WILLY.   I'm so tired. Don't talk any more. (BIFF *slowly returns to the kitchen. He stops, stares toward the heater.*)

LINDA.   Will you ask Howard to let you work in New York?

WILLY.   First thing in the morning. Everything'll be all right. (BIFF *reaches behind the heater and draws out a length of rubber tubing. He is horrified and turns his head toward* WILLY'S *room, still dimly lit, from which the strains of* LINDA'S *desperate but monotonous humming rise.* WILLY *stares through the window into the moonlight.*) Gee, look at the moon moving between the buildings! (BIFF *wraps the tubing around his hand and quickly goes up the stairs.*)

ACT 2

Music is heard, gay and bright. The curtain rises as the music fades away. WILLY, *in shirt sleeves, is sitting at the kitchen table, sipping coffee, his hat in his lap.* LINDA *is filling his cup when she can.*

WILLY.   Wonderful coffee. Meal in itself.

LINDA.   Can I make you some eggs?

WILLY.   No. Take a breath.

LINDA.   You look so rested, dear.

WILLY.   I slept like a dead one. First time in months. Imagine, sleeping till ten on a Tuesday morning. Boys left nice and early, heh?

LINDA.   They were out of here by eight o'clock.

WILLY.   Good work!

LINDA.   It was so thrilling to see them leaving together. I can't get over the shaving lotion in this house!

WILLY (*smiling*).   Mmm—

LINDA.   Biff was very changed this morning. His whole attitude seemed to be hopeful. He couldn't wait to get downtown to see Oliver.

WILLY.   He's heading for a change. There's no question, there simply are certain men that take longer to get—solidified. How did he dress?

LINDA.   His blue suit. He's so handsome in that suit. He could be a— anything in that suit! (WILLY *gets up from the table.* LINDA *holds his jacket for him.*)

WILLY.   There's no question, no question at all. Gee, on the way home tonight I'd like to buy some seeds.

LINDA (*laughing*).   That'd be wonderful. But not enough sun gets back there. Nothing'll grow any more.

WILLY.   You wait, kid, before it's all over we're gonna get a little place out in the country, and I'll raise some vegetables, a couple of chickens . . .

LINDA.   You'll do it yet, dear. (WILLY *walks out of his jacket.* LINDA *follows him.*)

WILLY.   And they'll get married, and come for a weekend. I'd build a little guest house. 'Cause I got so many fine tools, all I'd need would be a little lumber and some peace of mind.

LINDA (*joyfully*).   I sewed the lining . . .

WILLY.   I would build two guest houses, so they'd both come. Did he decide how much he's going to ask Oliver for?

LINDA (*getting him into his jacket*).   He didn't mention it, but I imagine ten or fifteen thousand. You going to talk to Howard today?

WILLY.   Yeah. I'll put it to him straight and simple. He'll just have to take me off the road.

LINDA.   And, Willy, don't forget to ask for a little advance, because we've got the insurance premium. It's the grace period now.

WILLY.   That's a hundred . . . ?

LINDA.   A hundred and eight, sixty-eight. Because we're a little short again.

WILLY.   Why are we short?

LINDA.   Well, you had the motor job on the car . . .

WILLY.   That goddam Studebaker!

LINDA.   And you got one more payment on the refrigerator . . .

WILLY.   But it just broke again!

LINDA.   Well, it's old, dear.

WILLY.   I told you we should've bought a well-advertised machine. Charley bought a General Electric and it's twenty years old and it's still good, that son-of-a-bitch.

LINDA.   But, Willy—

WILLY.   Whoever heard of a Hastings refrigerator? Once in my life I would like to own something outright before it's broken! I'm always in a race with the junkyard! I just finished paying for the car and it's on its last legs. The refrigerator consumes belts like a goddam maniac. They time those things. They time them so when you finally paid for them, they're used up.

LINDA (*buttoning up his jacket as he unbuttons it*).   All told, about two hundred dollars would carry us, dear. But that includes the last payment on the mortgage. After this payment, Willy, the house belongs to us.

WILLY.   It's twenty-five years!

LINDA.   Biff was nine years old when we bought it.

WILLY.   Well, that's a great thing. To weather a twenty-five year mortgage is—

LINDA.   It's an accomplishment.

WILLY.   All the cement, lumber, the reconstruction I put in this house! There ain't a crack to be found in it any more.

LINDA.   Well, it served its purpose.

WILLY.   What purpose? Some stranger'll come along, move in, and that's that. If only Biff would take this house, and raise a family . . . (*He starts to go.*) Good-by, I'm late.

LINDA (*suddenly remembering*).   Oh, I forgot! You're supposed to meet them for dinner.

WILLY.   Me?

LINDA.   At Frank's Chop House on Forty-eighth near Sixth Avenue.

WILLY.   Is that so! How about you?

LINDA.   No, just the three of you. They're gonna blow you to a big meal!

WILLY.   Don't say! Who thought of that?

LINDA.   Biff came to me this morning, Willy, and he said, "Tell Dad, we want to blow him to a big meal." Be there six o'clock. You and your two boys are going to have dinner.

WILLY.   Gee whiz! That's really somethin'. I'm gonna knock Howard for a loop, kid. I'll get an advance, and I'll come home with a New York job. Goddammit, now I'm gonna do it!

LINDA.   Oh, that's the spirit, Willy!

WILLY.   I will never get behind a wheel the rest of my life!

LINDA.   It's changing, Willy, I can feel it changing!

WILLY.   Beyond a question. G'by, I'm late. (*He starts to go again.*)

LINDA (*calling after him as she runs to the kitchen table for a handkerchief*).   You got your glasses?

WILLY (*feels for them, then comes back in*).   Yeah, yeah, got my glasses.

LINDA (*giving him the handkerchief*).   And a handkerchief.

WILLY.   Yeah, handkerchief.

LINDA.   And your saccharine?

WILLY.   Yeah, my saccharine.

LINDA.   Be careful on the subway stairs. (*She kisses him, and a silk stocking is seen hanging from her hand.* WILLY *notices it.*)

WILLY.   Will you stop mending stockings? At least while I'm in the house. It gets me nervous. I can't tell you. Please. (LINDA *hides the stocking in her hand as she follows* WILLY *across the forestage in front of the house.*)

LINDA.   Remember, Frank's Chop House.

WILLY (*passing the apron*).   Maybe beets would grow out there.

LINDA (*laughing*).   But you tried so many times.

WILLY.   Yeah. Well, don't work hard today. (*He disappears around the right corner of the house.*)

LINDA.   Be careful! (*As* WILLY *vanishes,* LINDA *waves to him. Suddenly the phone rings. She runs across the stage and into the kitchen and lifts it.*) Hello? Oh, Biff! I'm so glad you called, I just . . . Yes, sure, I just told him. Yes, he'll be there for dinner at six o'clock, I didn't forget. Listen, I was just dying to tell you. You know that little rubber pipe I told you about? That he connected to the gas heater? I finally decided to go down the cellar this morning and take it away and destroy it. But it's gone! Imagine? He took it away himself, it isn't there! (*She listens.*) When? Oh, then you took it. Oh—nothing, it's just that I'd hoped he'd taken it away himself. Oh, I'm not worried, darling, because this morning he left in such high spirits, it was like the old days! I'm not afraid any more. Did Mr. Oliver see you? . . . Well, you wait there then. And make a nice impression on him, darling. Just don't perspire too much before you see him. And have a nice time with Dad. He may have big news too! . . . That's right, a New York job. And be sweet to him tonight, dear. Be loving to him. Because he's only a little boat looking for a harbor. (*She is trembling with sorrow and joy.*) Oh, that's wonderful, Biff, you'll save his life. Thanks, darling. Just put your arm around him when he comes into the restaurant. Give him a smile. That's the boy . . . Good-by, dear . . . You got your comb? . . . That's fine. Good-by, Biff dear.

(*In the middle of her speech,* HOWARD WAGNER, *thirty-six, wheels on a small typewriter table on which is a wire-recording machine and proceeds to plug it in. This is on the left forestage. Light slowly fades on* LINDA *as it rises on* HOWARD. HOWARD *is intent on threading the machine and only glances over his shoulder as* WILLY *appears.*)

WILLY.   Pst! Pst!

HOWARD.   Hello, Willy, come in.

WILLY.   Like to have a little talk with you, Howard.

HOWARD.   Sorry to keep you waiting. I'll be with you in a minute.

WILLY.   What's that, Howard?

HOWARD.   Didn't you ever see one of these? Wire recorder.

WILLY.   Oh. Can we talk a minute?

HOWARD.   Records things. Just got delivery yesterday. Been driving me crazy, the most terrific machine I ever saw in my life. I was up all night with it.

WILLY.   What do you do with it?

HOWARD.   I bought it for dictation, but you can do anything with it. Listen to this. I had it home last night. Listen to what I picked up. The first one is my daughter. Get this. (*He flicks the switch and "Roll Out the Barrel" is heard being whistled.*) Listen to that kid whistle.

WILLY.   That is lifelike, isn't it?

HOWARD.   Seven years old. Get that tone.

WILLY.   Ts, ts. Like to ask a little favor of you . . . (*The whistling breaks off, and the voice of* HOWARD'S *daughter is heard.*)

HIS DAUGHTER.   "Now you, Daddy."

HOWARD.   She's crazy for me! (*Again the same song is whistled.*) That's me! Ha! (*He winks.*)

WILLY.   You're very good! (*The whistling breaks off again. The machine runs silent for a moment.*)

HOWARD.   Sh! Get this now, this is my son.

HIS SON.   "The capital of Alabama is Montgomery; the capital of Arizona is Phoenix; the capital of Arkansas is Little Rock; the capital of California is Sacramento . . ." (*and on, and on*).

HOWARD (*holding up five fingers*).   Five years old, Willy!

WILLY.   He'll make an announcer some day!

HIS SON (*continuing*).   "The capital . . ."

HOWARD.   Get that—alphabetical order! (*The machine breaks off suddenly.*) Wait a minute. The maid kicked the plug out.

WILLY.   It certainly is a—

HOWARD.   Sh, for God's sake!

HIS SON.   "It's nine o'clock, Bulova watch time. So I have to go to sleep."

WILLY.   That really is—

HOWARD.   Wait a minute! The next is my wife. (*They wait.*)

HOWARD'S VOICE.   "Go on, say something." (*Pause.*) "Well, you gonna talk?"

HIS WIFE.   "I can't think of anything."

HOWARD'S VOICE.   "Well, talk—it's turning."

HIS WIFE (*shyly, beaten*).   "Hello." (*Silence.*) "Oh, Howard, I can't talk into this . . ."

HOWARD (*snapping the machine off*).   That was my wife.

WILLY.   That is a wonderful machine. Can we—

HOWARD.   I tell you, Willy, I'm gonna take my camera, and my bandsaw, and all my hobbies, and out they go. This is the most fascinating relaxation I ever found.

WILLY.   I think I'll get one myself.

HOWARD.   Sure, they're only a hundred and a half. You can't do without it. Supposing you wanna hear Jack Benny, see? But you can't be at home at that hour. So you tell the maid to turn the radio on when Jack Benny comes on, and this automatically goes on with the radio . . .

WILLY.   And when you come home you . . .

HOWARD.   You can come home twelve o'clock, one o'clock, any time you like, and you get yourself a Coke and sit yourself down, throw the switch, and there's Jack Benny's program in the middle of the night!

WILLY.   I'm definitely going to get one. Because lots of time I'm on the road, and I think to myself, what I must be missing on the radio!

HOWARD.   Don't you have a radio in the car?

WILLY.   Well, yeah, but who ever thinks of turning it on?

HOWARD.   Say, aren't you supposed to be in Boston?

WILLY.　That's what I want to talk to you about, Howard. You got a minute? (*He draws a chair in from the wing.*)

HOWARD.　What happened? What're you doing here?

WILLY.　Well . . .

HOWARD.　You didn't crack up again, did you?

WILLY.　Oh, no. No . . .

HOWARD.　Geez, you had me worried there for a minute. What's the trouble?

WILLY.　Well, tell you the truth, Howard, I've come to the decision that I'd rather not travel any more.

HOWARD.　Not travel! Well, what'll you do?

WILLY.　Remember, Christmas time, when you had the party here? You said you'd try to think of some spot for me here in town.

HOWARD.　With us?

WILLY.　Well, sure.

HOWARD.　Oh, yeah, yeah. I remember. Well, I couldn't think of anything for you, Willy.

WILLY.　I tell ya, Howard. The kids are all grown up, y'know. I don't need much any more. If I could take home—well, sixty-five dollars a week, I could swing it.

HOWARD.　Yeah, but Willy, see I—

WILLY.　I tell ya why, Howard. Speaking frankly and between the two of us, y'know—I'm just a little tired.

HOWARD.　Oh, I could understand that, Willy. But you're a road man, Willy, and we do a road business. We've only got a half-dozen salesmen on the floor here.

WILLY.　God knows, Howard, I never asked a favor of any man. But I was with the firm when your father used to carry you in here in his arms.

HOWARD.　I know that, Willy, but—

WILLY.　Your father came to me the day you were born and asked me what I thought of the name of Howard, may he rest in peace.

HOWARD.　I appreciate that, Willy, but there just is no spot here for you. If I had a spot I'd slam you right in, but I just don't have a single solitary spot. (*He looks for his lighter.* WILLY *has picked it up and gives it to him. Pause.*)

WILLY (*with increasing anger*).　Howard, all I need to set my table is fifty dollars a week.

HOWARD.　But where am I going to put you, kid?

WILLY.　Look, it isn't a question of whether I can sell merchandise, is it?

HOWARD.　No, but it's a business, kid, and everybody's gotta pull his own weight.

WILLY (*desperately*).　Just let me tell you a story, Howard—

HOWARD.　'Cause you gotta admit, business is business.

WILLY (*angrily*).　Business is definitely business, but just listen for a minute. You don't understand this. When I was a boy—eighteen, nineteen—I was already on the road. And there was a question in my mind as to whether selling had a future for me. Because in those days I had a yearning to go to Alaska. See, there were three gold strikes in one month in Alaska, and I felt like going out. Just for the ride, you might say.

HOWARD (*barely interested*).   Don't say.

WILLY.   Oh, yeah, my father lived many years in Alaska. He was an adventurous man. We've got quite a little streak of self-reliance in our family. I thought I'd go out with my older brother and try to locate him, and maybe settle in the North with the old man. And I was almost decided to go, when I met a salesman in the Parker House. His name was Dave Singleman. And he was eighty-four years old, and he'd drummed merchandise in thirty-one states. And old Dave, he'd go up to his room, y'understand, put on his green velvet slippers—I'll never forget—and pick up his phone and call the buyers, and without ever leaving his room, at the age of eighty-four, he made his living. And when I saw that, I realized that selling was the greatest career a man could want. 'Cause what could be more satisfying than to be able to go, at the age of eighty-four, into twenty or thirty different cities, and pick up a phone, and be remembered and loved and helped by so many different people? Do you know? when he died—and by the way he died the death of a salesman, in his green velvet slippers in the smoker of the New York, New Haven and Hartford, going into Boston—when he died, hundreds of salesmen and buyers were at his funeral. Things were sad on a lotta trains for months after that. (*He stands up.* HOWARD *has not looked at him.*) In those days there was personality in it, Howard. There was respect, and comradeship, and gratitude in it. Today, it's all cut and dried, and there's no chance for bringing friendship to bear—or personality. You see what I mean? They don't know me any more.

HOWARD (*moving away, to the right*).   That's just the thing, Willy.

WILLY.   If I had forty dollars a week—that's all I'd need. Forty dollars, Howard.

HOWARD.   Kid, I can't take blood from a stone, I—

WILLY (*desperation is on him now*).   Howard, the year Al Smith° was nominated, your father came to me and—

HOWARD (*starting to go off*).   I've got to see some people, kid.

WILLY (*stopping him*).   I'm talking about your father! There were promises made across this desk! You mustn't tell me you've got people to see—I put thirty-four years into this firm, Howard, and now I can't pay my insurance! You can't eat the orange and throw the peel away—a man is not a piece of fruit! (*After a pause.*) Now pay attention. Your father—in 1928 I had a big year. I averaged a hundred and seventy dollars a week in commissions.

HOWARD (*impatiently*).   Now, Willy, you never averaged—

WILLY (*banging his hand on the desk*).   I averaged a hundred and seventy dollars a week in the year of 1928! And your father came to me—or rather, I

Al Smith: Four-term governor of New York and the Democratic nominee for president in 1928 who lost to Herbert Hoover.

was in the office here—it was right over this desk—and he put his hand on my shoulder—

HOWARD (*getting up*).   You'll have to excuse me, Willy, I gotta see some people. Pull yourself together. (*Going out*) I'll be back in a little while. (*On* HOWARD'S *exit, the light on his chair grows very bright and strange.*)

WILLY.   Pull myself together! What the hell did I say to him? My God, I was yelling at him! How could I! (WILLY *breaks off, staring at the light, which occupies the chair, animating it. He approaches this chair, standing across the desk from it.*) Frank, Frank, don't you remember what you told me that time? How you put your hand on my shoulder, and Frank . . . (*He leans on the desk and as he speaks the dead man's name he accidently switches on the recorder, and instantly*)

HOWARD'S SON.   ". . . of New York is Albany. The capital of Ohio is Cincinnati, the capital of Rhode Island is . . ." (*The recitation continues.*)

WILLY (*leaping away with fright, shouting*).   Ha! Howard! Howard! Howard!

HOWARD (*rushing in*).   What happened?

WILLY (*pointing at the machine, which continues nasally, childishly, with the capital cities*).   Shut it off! Shut it off!

HOWARD (*pulling the plug out*).   Look, Willy . . .

WILLY (*pressing his hands to his eyes*).   I gotta get myself some coffee. I'll get some coffee . . . (WILLY *starts to walk out.* HOWARD *stops him.*)

HOWARD (*rolling up the cord*).   Willy, look . . .

WILLY.   I'll go to Boston.

HOWARD.   Willy, you can't go to Boston for us.

WILLY.   Why can't I go?

HOWARD.   I don't want you to represent us. I've been meaning to tell you for a long time now.

WILLY.   Howard, are you firing me?

HOWARD.   I think you need a good long rest, Willy.

WILLY.   Howard—

HOWARD.   And when you feel better, come back, and we'll see if we can work something out.

WILLY.   But I gotta earn money, Howard. I'm in no position to—

HOWARD.   Where are your sons? Why don't your sons give you a hand?

WILLY.   They're working on a very big deal.

HOWARD.   This is no time for false pride, Willy. You go to your sons and tell them that you're tired. You've got two great boys, haven't you?

WILLY.   Oh, no question, no question, but in the meantime . . .

HOWARD.   Then that's that, heh?

WILLY.   All right, I'll go to Boston tomorrow.

HOWARD.   No, no.

WILLY.   I can't throw myself on my sons. I'm not a cripple!

HOWARD.   Look, kid, I'm busy this morning.

WILLY (*grasping* HOWARD'S *arm*).   Howard, you've got to let me go to Boston!

HOWARD (*hard, keeping himself under control*).   I've got a line of people to see this morning. Sit down, take five minutes, and pull yourself together, and then go home, will ya? I need the office, Willy. (*He starts to go, turns, remembering the recorder, starts to push off the table holding the recorder.*) Oh, yeah. Whenever you can this week, stop by and drop off the samples. You'll feel better, Willy, and then come back and we'll talk. Pull yourself together, kid, there's people outside. (HOWARD *exits, pushing the table off left.* WILLY *stares into space, exhausted. Now the music is heard*—BEN'S *music—first distantly, then closer, closer. As* WILLY *speaks,* BEN *enters from the right. He carries valise and umbrella.*)

WILLY.   Oh, Ben, how did you do it? What is the answer? Did you wind up the Alaska deal already?

BEN.   Doesn't take much time if you know what you're doing. Just a short business trip. Boarding ship in an hour. Wanted to say goody-by.

WILLY.   Ben, I've got to talk to you.

BEN (*glancing at his watch*).   Haven't the time, William.

WILLY (*crossing the apron to* BEN).   Ben, nothing's working out. I don't know what to do.

BEN.   Now look here, William. I've bought timberland in Alaska and I need a man to look after things for me.

WILLY.   God, timberland! Me and my boys in those grand outdoors!

BEN.   You've a new continent at your doorstep, William. Get out of these cities, they're full of talk and time payments and courts of law. Screw on your fists and you can fight for a fortune up there.

WILLY.   Yes, yes! Linda, Linda! (LINDA *enters as of old, with the wash.*)

LINDA.   Oh, you're back?

BEN.   I haven't much time.

WILLY.   No, wait! Linda, he's got a proposition for me in Alaska.

LINDA.   But you've got—(*To* BEN) He's got a beautiful job here.

WILLY.   But in Alaska, kid, I could—

LINDA.   You're doing well enough, Willy!

BEN (*to* LINDA).   Enough for what, my dear?

LINDA (*frightened of* BEN *and angry at him*).   Don't say those things to him! Enough to be happy right here, right now. (*To* WILLY, *while* BEN *laughs*) Why must everybody conquer the world? You're well liked, and the boys love you, and someday—(*to* BEN)—why, old man Wagner told him just the other day that if he keeps it up he'll be a member of the firm, didn't he, Willy?

WILLY.   Sure, sure. I am building something with this firm, Ben, and if a man is building something he must be on the right track, mustn't he?

BEN.   What are you building? Lay your hand on it. Where is it?

WILLY (*hesitantly*).   That's true, Linda, there's nothing.

LINDA.   Why? (*To* BEN) There's a man eighty-four years old—

WILLY.   That's right, Ben, that's right. When I look at that man I say, what is there to worry about?

BEN.   Bah!

WILLY.   It's true, Ben. All he has to do is go into any city, pick up the phone, and he's making his living and you know why?

BEN (*picking up his valise*).   I've got to go.

WILLY (*holding* BEN *back*).   Look at this boy! (BIFF, *in his high-school sweater, enters carrying suitcase.* HAPPY *carries* BIFF'S *shoulder guards, gold helmet, and football pants.*) Without a penny to his name, three great universities are begging for him, and from there the sky's the limit, because it's not what you do, Ben. It's who you know and the smile on your face! It's contacts, Ben, contacts! The whole wealth of Alaska passes over the lunch table at the Commodore Hotel, and that's the wonder, the wonder of this country, that a man can end with diamonds here on the basis of being liked! (*He turns to* BIFF.) And that's why when you get out on that field today, it's important. Because thousands of people will be rooting for you and loving you. (*To* BEN, *who has again begun to leave*) And Ben! when he walks into a business office his name will sound out like a bell and all the doors will open to him! I've seen it, Ben, I've seen it a thousand times! You can't feel it with your hand like timber, but it's there!

BEN.   Good-by, William.

WILLY.   Ben, am I right? Don't you think I'm right? I value your advice.

BEN.   There's a new continent at your doorstep, William. You could walk out rich. Rich! (*He is gone.*)

WILLY.   We'll do it here, Ben! You hear me? We're gonna do it here! (YOUNG BERNARD *rushes in. The gay music of the* BOYS *is heard.*)

BERNARD.   Oh, gee, I was afraid you left already!

WILLY.   Why? What time is it?

BERNARD.   It's half-past one!

WILLY.   Well, come on, everybody! Ebbets Field° next stop! Where's the pennants? (*He rushes through the wall-line of the kitchen and out into the living-room.*)

LINDA (*to* BIFF).   Did you pack fresh underwear?

BIFF (*who has been limbering up*).   I want to go!

BERNARD.   Biff, I'm carrying your helmet, ain't I?

HAPPY.   No, I'm carrying the helmet.

BERNARD.   Oh, Biff, you promised me.

HAPPY.   I'm carrying the helmet.

BERNARD.   How am I going to get in the locker room?

LINDA.   Let him carry the shoulder guards. (*She puts her coat and hat on in the kitchen.*)

BERNARD.   Can I, Biff? 'Cause I told everybody I'm going to be in the locker room.

HAPPY.   In Ebbets Field it's the clubhouse.

Ebbets Field: A baseball stadium, the home of the Brooklyn Dodgers, torn down in 1960. Because it was used primarily for baseball, its locker rooms were called clubhouses.

BERNARD.   I meant the clubhouse, Biff!

HAPPY.   Biff!

BIFF (*grandly, after a slight pause*).   Let him carry the shoulder guards.

HAPPY (*as he gives* BERNARD *the shoulder guards*).   Stay close to us now. (WILLY *rushes in with the pennants.*)

WILLY (*handing them out*).   Everybody wave when Biff comes out on the field. (HAPPY *and* BERNARD *run off.*) You set now, boy? (*The music has died away.*)

BIFF.   Ready to go, Pop. Every muscle is ready.

WILLY (*at the edge of the apron*).   You realize what this means?

BIFF.   That's right, Pop.

WILLY (*feeling* BIFF'S *muscles*).   You're comin' home this afternoon captain of the All-Scholastic Championship Team of the City of New York.

BIFF.   I got it, Pop. And remember, pal, when I take off my helmet, that touchdown is for you.

WILLY.   Let's go! (*He is starting out, with his arms around* BIFF, *when* CHARLEY *enters, as of old, in knickers.*) I got no room for you, Charley.

CHARLEY.   Room? For what?

WILLY.   In the car.

CHARLEY.   You goin' for a ride? I wanted to shoot some casino.

WILLY (*furiously*).   Casino! (*Incredulously*) Don't you realize what to-day is?

LINDA.   Oh, he knows, Willy. He's just kidding you.

WILLY.   That's nothing to kid about!

CHARLEY.   No, Linda, what's goin' on?

LINDA.   He's playing in Ebbets Field.

CHARLEY.   Baseball in this weather?

WILLY.   Don't talk to him. Come on, come on! (*He is pushing them out.*)

CHARLEY.   Wait a minute, didn't you hear the news?

WILLY.   What?

CHARLEY.   Don't you listen to the radio? Ebbets Field just blew up.

WILLY.   You go to hell! (CHARLEY *laughs. Pushing them out*) Come on, come on! We're late.

CHARLEY (*as they go*).   Knock a homer, Biff, knock a homer!

WILLY (*the last to leave, turning to* CHARLEY).   This is the greatest day of his life.

CHARLEY.   Willy, when are you going to grow up?

WILLY.   Yeah, heh? When this game is over, Charley, you'll be laughing out the other side of your face. They'll be calling him another Red Grange.° Twenty-five thousand a year.

CHARLEY (*kidding*).   Is that so?

WILLY.   Yeah, that's so.

Red Grange: famous All-American running back at the University of Illinois (1923–1925)

CHARLEY.   Well, then, I'm sorry, Willy. But tell me something.

WILLY.   What?

CHARLEY.   Who is Red Grange?

WILLY.   Put up your hands. Goddam you, put up your hands! (CHARLEY, *chuckling, shakes his head and walks away, around the left corner of the stage.* WILLY *follows him. The music rises to a mocking frenzy.*) Who the hell do you think you are, better than anybody else? You don't know everything, you big, ignorant, stupid . . . Put up your hands!

(*Light rises, on the right side of the forestage, on a small table in the reception room of* CHARLEY'S *office. Traffic sounds are heard.* BERNARD, *now mature, sits whistling to himself. A pair of tennis rackets and an overnight bag are on the floor beside him.*)

WILLY (*offstage*).   What are you walking away for? Don't walk away! If you're going to say something say it to my face! I know you laugh at me behind my back. You'll laugh out of the other side of your goddam face after this game. Touchdown! Touchdown! Eighty thousand people! Touchdown! Right between the goal posts.

(BERNARD *is a quiet, earnest, but self-assured young man.* WILLY'S *voice is coming from right upstage now.* BERNARD *lowers his feet off the table and listens.* JENNY, *his father's secretary, enters.*)

JENNY (*distressed*).   Say, Bernard, will you go out in the hall?

BERNARD.   What is that noise? Who is it?

JENNY.   Mr. Loman. He just got off the elevator.

BERNARD (*getting up*).   Who's he arguing with?

JENNY.   Nobody. There's nobody with him. I can't deal with him any more, and your father gets all upset everytime he comes. I've got a lot of typing to do, and your father's waiting to sign it. Will you see him?

WILLY (*entering*).   Touchdown! Touch—(*He sees* JENNY.) Jenny, Jenny, good to see you. How're ya? Workin'? Or still honest?

JENNY.   Fine. How've you been feeling?

WILLY.   Not much any more, Jenny. Ha, Ha! (*He is surprised to see the rackets.*)

BERNARD.   Hello, Uncle Willy.

WILLY (*almost shocked*).   Bernard! Well, look who's here! (*He comes quickly, guiltily, to* BERNARD *and warmly shakes his hand.*)

BERNARD.   How are you? Good to see you.

WILLY.   What are you doing here?

BERNARD.   Oh, just stopped by to see Pop. Get off my feet till my train leaves. I'm going to Washington in a few minutes.

WILLY.   Is he in?

BERNARD.   Yes, he's in his office with the accountant. Sit down.

WILLY (*sitting down*).   What're you going to do in Washington?

BERNARD.   Oh, just a case I've got there, Willy.

WILLY.   That so? (*Indicating the rackets*) You going to play tennis there?

BERNARD.   I'm staying with a friend who's got a court.

WILLY.   Don't say. His own tennis court. Must be fine people, I bet.

BERNARD.   They are, very nice. Dad tells me Biff's in town.

WILLY (*with a big smile*).   Yeah, Biff's in. Working on a very big deal, Bernard.

BERNARD.   What's Biff doing?

WILLY.   Well, he's been doing very big things in the West. But he decided to establish himself here. Very big. We're having dinner. Did I hear your wife had a boy?

BERNARD.   That's right. Our second.

WILLY.   Two boys! What do you know!

BERNARD.   What kind of deal has Biff got?

WILLY.   Well, Bill Oliver—very big sporting goods man—he wants Biff very badly. Called him in from the West. Long distance, carte blanche, special deliveries. Your friends have their own private tennis court?

BERNARD.   You still with the old firm, Willy?

WILLY (*after a pause*).   I'm—I'm overjoyed to see how you made the grade, Bernard, overjoyed. It's an encouraging thing to see a young man really—really—Looks very good for Biff—very—(*He breaks off, then*) Bernard—(*He is so full of emotion, he breaks off again.*)

BERNARD.   What is it, Willy?

WILLY (*small and alone*).   What—what's the secret?

BERNARD.   What secret?

WILLY.   How—how did you? Why didn't he ever catch on?

BERNARD.   I wouldn't know that, Willy.

WILLY (*confidentially, desperately*).   You were his friend, his boyhood friend. There's something I don't understand about it. His life ended after that Ebbets Field game. From the age of seventeen nothing good ever happened to him.

BERNARD.   He never trained himself for anything.

WILLY.   But he did, he did. After high school he took so many correspondence courses. Radio mechanics; television; God knows what, and never made the slightest mark.

BERNARD (*taking off his glasses*).   Willy, do you want to talk candidly?

WILLY (*rising, faces* BERNARD).   I regard you as a very brilliant man, Bernard. I value your advice.

BERNARD.   Oh, the hell with the advice, Willy. I couldn't advise you. There's just one thing I've always wanted to ask you. When he was supposed to graduate, and the math teacher flunked him—

WILLY.   Oh, that son-of-a-bitch ruined his life.

BERNARD.   Yeah, but, Willy, all he had to do was go to summer school and make up that subject.

WILLY.   That's right, that's right.

BERNARD.   Did you tell him not to go to summer school?

WILLY.   Me? I begged him to go. I ordered him to go!

BERNARD.   Then why wouldn't he go?

WILLY.   Why? Why! Bernard, that question has been trailing me like a ghost for the last fifteen years. He flunked the subject, and laid down and died like a hammer hit him!

BERNARD.   Take it easy, kid.

WILLY.   Let me talk to you—I got nobody to talk to. Bernard, Bernard, was it my fault? Y'see? It keeps going around in my mind, maybe I did something to him. I got nothing to give him.

BERNARD.   Don't take it so hard.

WILLY.   Why did he lay down? What is the story there? You were his friend!

BERNARD.   Willy, I remember, it was June, and our grades came out. And he'd flunked math.

WILLY.   That son-of-a-bitch!

BERNARD.   No, it wasn't right then. Biff just got very angry, I remember, and he was ready to enroll in summer school.

WILLY (*surprised*).   He was?

BERNARD.   He wasn't beaten by it at all. But then, Willy, he disappeared from the block for almost a month. And I got the idea that he'd gone up to New England to see you. Did he have a talk with you then? (WILLY *stares in silence.*) Willy?

WILLY (*with a strong edge of resentment in his voice*).   Yeah, he came to Boston. What about it?

BERNARD.   Well, just that when he came back—I'll never forget this, it always mystifies me. Because I thought so well of Biff, even though he'd always taken advantage of me. I loved him. Willy, y'know? And he came back after that month and took his sneakers—remember those sneakers with "University of Virginia" printed on them? He was so proud of those, wore them every day. And he took them down in the cellar, and burned them up in the furnace. We had a fist fight. It lasted at least half an hour. Just the two of us, punching each other down the cellar, and crying right through it. I've often thought of how strange it was that I knew he'd given up his life. What happened in Boston, Willy? (WILLY *looks at him as at an intruder.*) I just bring it up because you asked me.

WILLY (*angrily*).   Nothing. What do you mean, "What happened?" What's that got to do with anything?

BERNARD.   Well, don't get sore.

WILLY.   What are you trying to do, blame it on me? If a boy lays down is that my fault?

BERNARD.   Now, Willy, don't get—

WILLY.   Well, don't—don't talk to me that way! What does that mean, "What happened?" (CHARLEY *enters. He is in his vest, and he carries a bottle of bourbon.*)

CHARLEY.   Hey, you're going to miss that train. (*He waves the bottle.*)

BERNARD.   Yeah, I'm going. (*He takes the bottle.*) Thanks, Pop. (*He picks up his rackets and bag.*) Good-by, Willy, and don't worry about it. You know, "If at first you don't succeed . . ."

WILLY. Yes, I believe in that.

BERNARD. But sometimes, Willy, it's better for a man just to walk away.

WILLY. Walk away?

BERNARD. That's right.

WILLY. But if you can't walk away?

BERNARD (*after a slight pause*). I guess that's when it's tough. (*Extending his hand*) Good-by, Willy.

WILLY (*shaking* BERNARD'S *hand*). Good-by, boy.

CHARLEY (*an arm on* BERNARD'S *shoulder*). How do you like this kid? Gonna argue a case in front of the Supreme Court.

BERNARD (*protesting*). Pop!

WILLY (*genuinely shocked, pained, and happy*). No! The Supreme Court!

BERNARD. I gotta run. 'By Dad!

CHARLEY. Knock 'em dead, Bernard! (BERNARD *goes off.*)

WILLY (*as* CHARLEY *takes out his wallet*). The Supreme Court! And he didn't even mention it!

CHARLEY (*counting out money on the desk*). He don't have to—he's gonna do it.

WILLY. And you never told him what to do, did you? You never took any interest in him.

CHARLEY. My salvation is that I never took any interest in anything. There's some money—fifty dollars. I got an accountant inside.

WILLY. Charley, look . . . (*With difficulty*) I got my insurance to pay. If you can manage it—I need a hundred and ten dollars. (CHARLEY *doesn't reply for a moment; merely stops moving.*) I'd draw it from my bank but Linda would know, and I . . .

CHARLEY. Sit down, Willy.

WILLY (*moving toward the chair*). I'm keeping an account of everything, remember. I'll pay every penny back. (*He sits.*)

CHARLEY. Now listen to me, Willy.

WILLY. I want you to know I appreciate . . .

CHARLEY (*sitting down on the table*). Willy, what're you doin'? What the hell is goin' on in your head?

WILLY. Why? I'm simply . . .

CHARLEY. I offered you a job. You can make fifty dollars a week. And I won't send you on the road.

WILLY. I've got a job.

CHARLEY. Without pay? What kind of a job is a job without pay? (*He rises.*) Now, look, kid, enough is enough. I'm no genius but I know when I'm being insulted.

WILLY. Insulted!

CHARLEY. Why don't you want to work for me?

WILLY. What's the matter with you? I've got a job.

CHARLEY. Then what're you walkin' in here every week for?

WILLY (*getting up*). Well, if you don't want me to walk in here—

CHARLEY.   I am offering you a job.

WILLY.   I don't want your goddam job!

CHARLEY.   When the hell are you going to grow up?

WILLY (*furiously*).   You big ignoramus, if you say that to me again I'll rap you one! I don't care how big you are! (*He's ready to fight. Pause.*)

CHARLEY (*kindly, going to him*).   How much do you need, Willy?

WILLY.   Charley, I'm strapped. I'm strapped. I don't know what to do. I was just fired.

CHARLEY.   Howard fired you?

WILLY.   That snotnose. Imagine that? I named him. I named him Howard.

CHARLEY.   Willy, when're you gonna realize that them things don't mean anything? You named him Howard, but you can't sell that. The only thing you got in this world is what you can sell. And the funny thing is that you're a salesman, and you don't know that.

WILLY.   I've always tried to think otherwise, I guess. I always felt that if a man was impressive, and well liked, that nothing—

CHARLEY.   Why must everybody like you? Who liked J. P. Morgan? Was he impressive? In a Turkish bath he'd look like a butcher. But with his pockets on he was very well liked. Now listen, Willy, I know you don't like me, and nobody can say I'm in love with you, but I'll give you a job be-cause—just for the hell of it, put it that way. Now what do you say?

WILLY.   I—I just can't work for you, Charley.

CHARLEY.   What're you, jealous of me?

WILLY.   I can't work for you, that's all, don't ask me why.

CHARLEY (*angered, takes out more bills*).   You been jealous of me all your life, you damned fool! Here, pay your insurance. (*He puts the money in* WILLY's *hand.*)

WILLY.   I'm keeping strict accounts.

CHARLEY.   I've got some work to do. Take care of yourself. And pay your insurance.

WILLY (*moving to the right*).   Funny, y'know? After all the highways, and the trains, and the appointments, and the years, you end up worth more dead than alive.

CHARLEY.   Willy, nobody's worth nothin' dead. (*After a slight pause.*) Did you hear what I said? (WILLY *stands still, dreaming.*) Willy!

WILLY.   Apologize to Bernard for me when you see him. I didn't mean to argue with him. He's a fine boy. They're all fine boys, and they'll end up big—all of them. Someday they'll all play tennis together. Wish me luck, Charley. He saw Bill Oliver today.

CHARLEY.   Good luck.

WILLY (*on the verge of tears*).   Charley, you're the only friend I got. Isn't that a remarkable thing? (*He goes out.*)

CHARLEY.   Jesus!

(CHARLEY *stares after him a moment and follows. All light blacks out. Sud-denly raucous music is heard, and a red glow rises behind the screen at right.*

STANLEY, *a young waiter, appears, carrying a table, followed by* HAPPY, *who is carrying two chairs.*)

STANLEY (*putting the table down*).   That's all right, Mr. Loman, I can handle it myself. (*He turns and takes the chairs from* HAPPY *and places them at the table.*)

HAPPY (*glancing around*).   Oh, this is better.

STANLEY.   Sure, in the front there you're in the middle of all kinds a noise. Whenever you got a party, Mr. Loman, you just tell me and I'll put you back here. Y'know, there's a lotta people they don't like it private, because when they go out they like to see a lotta action around them because they're sick and tired to stay in the house by theirself. But I know you, you ain't from Hackensack. You know what I mean?

HAPPY (*sitting down*).   So how's it coming, Stanley?

STANLEY.   Ah, it's a dog's life. I only wish during the war they'd a took me in the Army. I coulda been dead by now.

HAPPY.   My brother's back, Stanley.

STANLEY.   Oh, he come back, heh? From the Far West.

HAPPY.   Yeah, big cattle man, my brother, so treat him right. And my father's coming too.

STANLEY.   Oh, your father too!

HAPPY.   You got a couple of nice lobsters?

STANLEY.   Hundred per cent, big.

HAPPY.   I want them with the claws.

STANLEY.   Don't worry, I don't give you no mice. (HAPPY *laughs.*) How about some wine? It'll put a head on the meal.

HAPPY.   No. You remember, Stanley, that recipe I brought you from overseas? With the champagne in it?

STANLEY.   Oh, yeah, sure. I still got it tacked up yet in the kitchen. But that'll have to cost a buck apiece anyways.

HAPPY.   That's all right.

STANLEY.   What'd you, hit a number or somethin'?

HAPPY.   No, it's a little celebration. My brother is—I think he pulled off a big deal today. I think we're going into business together.

STANLEY.   Great! That's the best for you. Because a family business, you know what I mean?—that's the best.

HAPPY.   That's what I think.

STANLEY.   'Cause what's the difference? Somebody steals? It's in the family. Know what I mean? (*Sotto voce*) Like this bartender here. The boss is goin' crazy what kinda leak he's got in the cash register. You put it in but it don't come out.

HAPPY (*raising his head*).   Sh!

STANLEY.   What?

HAPPY.   You notice I wasn't lookin' right or left, was I?

STANLEY.   No.

HAPPY.   And my eyes are closed.

STANLEY.   So what's the—?

HAPPY.   Strudel's comin'.

STANLEY (*catching on, looks around*).   Ah, no, there's no—(*He breaks off as a furred, lavishly dressed girl enters and sits at the next table. Both follow her with their eyes.*) Geez, how'd ya know?

HAPPY.   I got radar or something. (*Staring directly at her profile*) Oooooooo . . . Stanley.

STANLEY.   I think that's for you, Mr. Loman.

HAPPY.   Look at that mouth. Oh, God. And the binoculars.

STANLEY.   Geez, you got a life, Mr. Loman.

HAPPY.   Wait on her.

STANLEY (*going to the* GIRL'S *table*).   Would you like a menu, ma'am?

GIRL.   I'm expecting someone, but I'd like a—

HAPPY.   Why don't you bring her—excuse me, miss, do you mind? I sell champagne, and I'd like you to try my brand. Bring her a champagne, Stanley.

GIRL.   That's awfully nice of you.

HAPPY.   Don't mention it. It's all company money. (*He laughs.*)

GIRL.   That's a charming product to be selling, isn't it?

HAPPY.   Oh, gets to be like everything else. Selling is selling, y'know.

GIRL.   I suppose.

HAPPY.   You don't happen to sell, do you?

GIRL.   No, I don't sell.

HAPPY.   Would you object to a compliment from a stranger? You ought to be on a magazine cover.

GIRL (*looking at him a little archly*).   I have been. (STANLEY *comes in with a glass of champagne.*)

HAPPY.   What'd I say before, Stanley? You see? She's a cover girl.

STANLEY.   Oh, I could see, I could see.

HAPPY (*to the* GIRL).   What magazine?

GIRL.   Oh, a lot of them. (*She takes the drink.*) Thank you.

HAPPY.   You know what they say in France, don't you? "Champagne is the drink of the complexion"—Hya, Biff! (BIFF *has entered and sits with* HAPPY.)

BIFF.   Hello, kid. Sorry I'm late.

HAPPY.   I just got here. Uh, Miss—?

GIRL.   Forsythe.

HAPPY.   Miss Forsythe, this is my brother.

BIFF.   Is Dad here?

HAPPY.   His name is Biff. You might've heard of him. Great football player!

GIRL.   Really? What team?

HAPPY.   Are you familiar with football?

GIRL.   No, I'm afraid I'm not.

HAPPY.   Biff is quarterback with the New York Giants.

GIRL.   Well, that is nice, isn't it? (*She drinks.*)

HAPPY.   Good health.

GIRL.   I'm happy to meet you.

HAPPY.   That's my name. Hap. It's really Harold, but at West Point they called me Happy.

GIRL (*now really impressed*).   Oh, I see. How do you do? (*She turns her profile.*)

BIFF.   Isn't Dad coming?

HAPPY.   You want her?

BIFF.   Oh, I could never make that.

HAPPY.   I remember the time that idea would never come into your head. Where's the old confidence, Biff?

BIFF.   I just saw Oliver—

HAPPY.   Wait a minute. I've got to see that old confidence again. Do you want her? She's on call.

BIFF.   Oh, no. (*He turns to look at the* GIRL.)

HAPPY.   I'm telling you. Watch this. (*Turning to the* GIRL) Honey? (*She turns to him.*) Are you busy?

GIRL.   Well, I am . . . but I could make a phone call.

HAPPY.   Do that, will you, honey? And see if you can get a friend. We'll be here for a while. Biff is one of the greatest football players in the country.

GIRL (*standing up*).   Well, I'm certainly happy to meet you.

HAPPY.   Come back soon.

GIRL.   I'll try.

HAPPY.   Don't try, honey, try hard. (*The* GIRL *exits.* STANLEY *follows, shaking his head in bewildered admiration.*) Isn't that a shame now? A beautiful girl like that? That's why I can't get married. There's not a good woman in a thousand. New York is loaded with them, kid!

BIFF.   Hap, look—

HAPPY.   I told you she was on call!

BIFF (*strangely unnerved*).   Cut it out, will ya? I want to say something to you.

HAPPY.   Did you see Oliver?

BIFF.   I saw him all right. Now look, I want to tell Dad a couple of things and I want you to help me.

HAPPY.   What? Is he going to back you?

BIFF.   Are you crazy? You're out of your goddam head, you know that?

HAPPY.   Why? What happened?

BIFF (*breathlessly*).   I did a terrible thing today, Hap. It's been the strangest day I ever went through. I'm all numb, I swear.

HAPPY.   You mean he wouldn't see you?

BIFF.   Well, I waited for six hours for him, see? All day. Kept sending my name in. Even tried to date his secretary so she'd get me to him, but no soap.

HAPPY.   Because you're not showin' the old confidence, Biff. He remembered you, didn't he?

BIFF (*stopping* HAPPY *with a gesture*).   Finally, about five o'clock, he comes out. Didn't remember who I was or anything. I felt like such an idiot, Hap.

HAPPY.   Did you tell him my Florida idea?

BIFF.   He walked away. I saw him for one minute. I got so mad I could've torn the walls down! How the hell did I ever get the idea I was a salesman there? I even believed myself that I'd been a salesman for him! And then he gave me one look and—I realized what a ridiculous lie my whole life has been! We've been talking in a dream for fifteen years. I was a shipping clerk.

HAPPY.   What'd you do?

BIFF (*with great tension and wonder*).   Well, he left, see. And the secretary went out. I was all alone in the waiting-room. I don't know what came over me, Hap. The next thing I know I'm in his office—paneled walls, everything. I can't explain it. I—Hap, I took his fountain pen.

HAPPY.   Geez, did he catch you?

BIFF.   I ran out. I ran down all eleven flights. I ran and ran and ran.

HAPPY.   That was an awful dumb—what'd you do that for?

BIFF (*agonized*).   I don't know, I just—wanted to take something, I don't know. You gotta help me, Hap, I'm gonna tell Pop.

HAPPY.   You crazy? What for?

BIFF.   Hap, he's got to understand that I'm not the man somebody lends that kind of money to. He thinks I've been spiting him all these years and it's eating him up.

HAPPY.   That's just it. You tell him something nice.

BIFF.   I can't.

HAPPY.   Say you got a lunch date with Oliver tomorrow.

BIFF.   So what do I do tomorrow?

HAPPY.   You leave the house tomorrow and come back at night and say Oliver is thinking it over. And he thinks it over for a couple of weeks, and gradually it fades away and nobody's the worse.

BIFF.   But it'll go on forever!

HAPPY.   Dad is never so happy as when he's looking forward to something! (WILLY *enters*.) Hello, scout!

WILLY.   Gee, I haven't been here in years! (STANLEY *has followed* WILLY *in and sets a chair for him*. STANLEY *starts off but* HAPPY *stops him*.)

HAPPY.   Stanley! (STANLEY *stands by, waiting for an order*.)

BIFF (*going to* WILLY *with guilt, as to an invalid*).   Sit down, Pop. You want a drink?

WILLY.   Sure, I don't mind.

BIFF.   Let's get a load on.

WILLY.   You look worried.

BIFF.   N-no. (*To* STANLEY) Scotch all around. Make it doubles.

STANLEY.   Doubles, right. (*He goes*.)

WILLY.   You had a couple already, didn't you?

BIFF.   Just a couple, yeah.

WILLY.   Well, what happened, boy? (*Nodding affirmatively, with a smile*) Everything go all right?

BIFF (*takes a breath, then reaches out and grasps* WILLY'S *hand*).   Pal . . . (*He is smiling bravely, and* WILLY *is smiling too.*) I had an experience today.

HAPPY.   Terrific, Pop.

WILLY.   That so? What happened?

BIFF (*high, slightly alcoholic, above the earth*).   I'm going to tell you everything from first to last. It's been a strange day. (*Silence. He looks around, composes himself as best he can, but his breath keeps breaking the rhythm of his voice.*) I had to wait quite a while for him, and—

WILLY.   Oliver?

BIFF.   Yeah, Oliver. All day, as a matter of cold fact. And a lot of— instances—facts, Pop, facts about my life came back to me. Who was it, Pop? Who ever said I was a salesman with Oliver?

WILLY.   Well, you were.

BIFF.   No, Dad, I was a shipping clerk.

WILLY.   But you were practically—

BIFF (*with determination*).   Dad, I don't know who said it first, but I was never a salesman for Bill Oliver.

WILLY.   What're you talking about?

BIFF.   Let's hold on to the facts tonight, Pop. We're not going to get anywhere bullin' around. I was a shipping clerk.

WILLY (*angrily*).   All right, now listen to me—

BIFF.   Why don't you let me finish?

WILLY.   I'm not interested in stories about the past or any crap of that kind because the woods are burning, boys, you understand? There's a big blaze going on all around. I was fired today.

BIFF (*shocked*).   How could you be?

WILLY.   I was fired, and I'm looking for a little good news to tell your mother, because the woman has waited and the woman has suffered. The gist of it is that I haven't got a story left in my head, Biff. So don't give me a lecture about facts and aspects. I am not interested. Now what've you got to say to me? (STANLEY *enters with three drinks. They wait until he leaves.*) Did you see Oliver?

BIFF.   Jesus, Dad!

WILLY.   You mean you didn't go up there?

HAPPY.   Sure he went up there.

BIFF.   I did. I—saw him. How could they fire you?

WILLY (*on the edge of his chair*).   What kind of a welcome did he give you?

BIFF.   He won't even let you work on commission?

WILLY.   I'm out! (*Driving*) So tell me, he gave you a warm welcome?

HAPPY.   Sure, Pop, sure!

BIFF (*driven*).   Well, it was kind of—

WILLY.   I was wondering if he'd remember you. (*To* HAPPY) Imagine, man doesn't see him for ten, twelve years and gives him that kind of a welcome!

HAPPY.   Damn right!

BIFF (*trying to return to the offensive*).   Pop look—

WILLY.   You know why he remembered you, don't you? Because you impressed him in those days.

BIFF.   Let's talk quietly and get this down to the facts, huh?

WILLY (*as though* BIFF *had been interrupting*).   Well, what happened? It's great news, Biff. Did he take you into his office or'd you talk in the waiting-room?

BIFF.   Well, he came in, see, and—

WILLY (*with a big smile*).   What'd he say? Betcha he threw his arm around you.

BIFF.   Well, he kinda—

WILLY.   He's a fine man. (*To* HAPPY) Very hard man to see, y'know.

HAPPY (*agreeing*).   Oh, I know.

WILLY (*to* BIFF).   Is that where you had the drinks?

BIFF.   Yeah, he gave me a couple of—no, no!

HAPPY (*cutting in*).   He told him my Florida idea.

WILLY.   Don't interrupt. (*To* BIFF) How'd he react to the Florida idea?

BIFF.   Dad, will you give me a minute to explain?

WILLY.   I've been waiting for you to explain since I sat down here! What happened? He took you into his office and what?

BIFF.   Well—I talked. And—and he listened, see.

WILLY.   Famous for the way he listens, y'know. What was his answer?

BIFF.   His answer was—(*He breaks off, suddenly angry.*) Dad, you're not letting me tell you what I want to tell you!

WILLY (*accusing, angered*).   You didn't see him, did you?

BIFF.   I did see him!

WILLY.   What'd you insult him or something? You insulted him, didn't you?

BIFF.   Listen, will you let me out of it, will you just let me out of it!

HAPPY.   What the hell!

WILLY.   Tell me what happened!

BIFF (*to* HAPPY).   I can't talk to him!

(*A single trumpet note jars the ear. The light of green leaves stains the house, which holds the air of night and a dream.* YOUNG BERNARD *enters and knocks on the door of the house.*)

YOUNG BERNARD (*frantically*).   Mrs. Loman, Mrs. Loman!

HAPPY.   Tell him what happened!

BIFF (*to* HAPPY).   Shut up and leave me alone!

WILLY.   No, no! You had to go and flunk math!

BIFF.   What math? What're you talking about?

YOUNG BERNARD.   Mrs. Loman, Mrs. Loman! (LINDA *appears in the house, as of old.*)

WILLY (*wildly*).   Math, math, math!

BIFF.   Take it easy, Pop!

YOUNG BERNARD.   Mrs. Loman!

WILLY (*furiously*).   If you hadn't flunked you'd've been set by now!

BIFF.   Now, look, I'm gonna tell you what happened, and you're going to listen to me.

YOUNG BERNARD.   Mrs. Loman!

BIFF.   I waited six hours—

HAPPY.   What the hell are you saying?

BIFF.   I kept sending in my name but he wouldn't see me. So finally he . . . (*He continues unheard as light fades low on the restaurant.*)

YOUNG BERNARD.   Biff flunked math!

LINDA.   No!

YOUNG BERNARD.   Birnbaum flunked him! They won't graduate him!

LINDA.   But they have to. He's gotta go to the university. Where is he? Biff! Biff!

YOUNG BERNARD.   No, he left. He went to Grand Central.

LINDA.   Grand—You mean he went to Boston!

YOUNG BERNARD.   Is Uncle Willy in Boston?

LINDA.   Oh, maybe Willy can talk to the teacher. Oh, the poor, poor boy! (*Light on house area snaps out.*)

BIFF (*at the table, now audible, holding up a gold fountain pen*).   . . . so I'm washed up with Oliver, you understand? Are you listening to me?

WILLY (*at a loss*).   Yeah, sure. If you hadn't flunked—

BIFF.   Flunked what? What're you talking about?

WILLY.   Don't blame everything on me! I didn't flunk math—you did! What pen?

HAPPY.   That was awful dumb, Biff, a pen like that is worth—

WILLY (*seeing the pen for the first time*).   You took Oliver's pen?

BIFF (*weakening*).   Dad, I just explained it to you.

WILLY.   You stole Bill Oliver's fountain pen!

BIFF.   I didn't exactly steal it! That's just what I've been explaining to you!

HAPPY.   He had it in his hand and just then Oliver walked in, so he got nervous and stuck it in his pocket!

WILLY.   My God, Biff!

BIFF.   I never intended to do it, Dad!

OPERATOR'S VOICE.   Standish Arms, good evening!

WILLY (*shouting*).   I'm not in my room!

BIFF (*frightened*).   Dad, what's the matter? (*He and HAPPY stand up.*)

OPERATOR.   Ringing Mr. Loman for you!

WILLY.   I'm not there, stop it!

BIFF (*horrified, gets down on one knee before* WILLY).   Dad, I'll make good, I'll make good. (WILLY *tries to get to his feet.* BIFF *holds him down.*) Sit down now.

WILLY.   No, you're no good, you're no good for anything.

BIFF.   I am, Dad, I'll find something else, you understand? Now don't worry about anything. (*He holds up* WILLY'S *face.*) Talk to me, Dad.

OPERATOR.   Mr. Loman does not answer. Shall I page him?

WILLY (*attempting to stand, as though to rush and silence the* OPERA-TOR).   No, no, no!

HAPPY.   He'll strike something, Pop.

WILLY.   No, no . . .

BIFF (*desperately, standing over* WILLY).   Pop, listen! Listen to me! I'm telling you something good. Oliver talked to his partner about the Florida idea. You listening? He—he talked to his partner, and he came to me . . . I'm going to be all right, you hear? Dad, listen to me, he said it was just a question of the amount!

WILLY.   Then you . . . got it?

HAPPY.   He's gonna be terrific, Pop!

WILLY (*trying to stand*).   Then you got it, haven't you? You got it! You got it!

BIFF (*agonized, holds* WILLY *down*).   No, no. Look, Pop. I'm supposed to have lunch with them tomorrow. I'm just telling you this so you'll know that I can still make an impression, Pop. And I'll make good somewhere, but I can't go tomorrow, see?

WILLY.   Why not? You simply—

BIFF.   But the pen, Pop!

WILLY.   You give it to him and tell him it was an oversight!

HAPPY.   Sure, have lunch tomorrow!

BIFF.   I can't say that—

WILLY.   You were doing a crossword puzzle and accidentally used his pen!

BIFF.   Listen, kid, I took those balls years ago, now I walk in with his fountain pen? That clinches it, don't you see? I can't face him like that! I'll try elsewhere.

PAGE'S VOICE.   Paging Mr. Loman!

WILLY.   Don't you want to be anything?

BIFF.   Pop, how can I go back?

WILLY.   You don't want to be anything, is that what's behind it?

BIFF (*now angry at* WILLY *for not crediting his sympathy*).   Don't take it that way! You think it was easy walking into that office after what I'd done to him? A team of horses couldn't have dragged me back to Bill Oliver!

WILLY.   Then why'd you go?

BIFF.   Why did I go? Why did I go! Look at you! Look at what's be-come of you! (*Off left,* THE WOMAN *laughs.*)

WILLY.   Biff, you're going to go to that lunch tomorrow, or—

BIFF.   I can't go. I've got no appointment!

HAPPY.   Biff, for . . . !

WILLY.   Are you spiting me?

BIFF.   Don't take it that way! Goddammit!

WILLY (*strikes* BIFF *and falters away from the table*).   You rotten little louse! Are you spiting me?

THE WOMAN.   Someone's at the door, Willy!

BIFF.   I'm no good, can't you see what I am?

HAPPY (*separating them*).   Hey, you're in a restaurant! Now cut it out, both of you! (*The* GIRLS *enter.*) Hello, girls, sit down. (THE WOMAN *laughs, off left.*)

MISS FORSYTHE.   I guess we might as well. This is Letta.

THE WOMAN.   Willy, are you going to wake up?

BIFF (*ignoring* WILLY).   How're ya, miss, sit down. What do you drink?

MISS FORSYTHE.   Letta might not be able to stay long.

LETTA.   I gotta get up very early tomorrow. I got jury duty. I'm so excited! Were you fellows ever on a jury?

BIFF.   No, but I been in front of them! (*The* GIRLS *laugh.*) This is my father.

LETTA.   Isn't he cute? Sit down with us, Pop.

HAPPY.   Sit him down, Biff!

BIFF (*going to him*).   Come on, slugger, drink us under the table. To hell with it! Come on, sit down, pal. (*On* BIFF'S *last insistence,* WILLY *is about to sit.*)

THE WOMAN (*now urgently*).   Willy, are you going to answer the door! (THE WOMAN'S *call puts* WILLY *back. He starts right, befuddled.*)

BIFF.   Hey, where are you going?

WILLY.   Open the door.

BIFF.   The door?

WILLY.   The washroom . . . the door . . . where's the door?

BIFF (*leading* WILLY *to the left*).   Just go straight down. (WILLY *moves left.*)

THE WOMAN.   Willy, Willy, are you going to get up, get up, get up, get up? (WILLY *exits left.*)

LETTA.   I think it's sweet you bring your daddy along.

MISS FORSYTHE.   Oh, he isn't really your father!

BIFF (*at left, turning to her resentfully*).   Miss Forsythe, you've just seen a prince walk by. A fine, troubled prince. A hard-working, unappreciated prince. A pal, you understand? A good companion. Always for his boys.

LETTA.   That's so sweet.

HAPPY.   Well, girls, what's the program? We're wasting time. Come on, Biff. Gather round. Where would you like to go?

BIFF.   Why don't you do something for him?

HAPPY.   Me!

BIFF.   Don't you give a damn for him, Hap?

HAPPY.   What're you talking about? I'm the one who—

BIFF.   I sense it, you don't give a good goddam about him. (*He takes the rolled-up hose from his pocket and puts it on the table in front of* HAPPY.) Look what I found in the cellar, for Christ's sake. How can you let it go on?

HAPPY.   Me? Who goes away? Who runs off and—

BIFF.   Yeah, but he doesn't mean anything to you. You could help him—I can't! Don't you understand what I'm talking about? He's going to kill himself, don't you know that?

HAPPY.   Don't I know it! Me!

BIFF.   Hap, help him! Jesus . . . help him . . . Help me, help me, I can't bear to look at his face! (*Ready to weep, he hurries out, up right.*)

HAPPY (*starting after him*).   Where are you going?

MISS FORSYTHE.   What's he so mad about?

HAPPY.   Come on, girls, we'll catch up with him.

MISS FORSYTHE (*as* HAPPY *pushes her out*).   Say, I don't like that temper of his!

HAPPY.   He's just a little overstrung, he'll be all right!

WILLY (*off left, as* THE WOMAN *laughs*).   Don't answer! Don't answer!

LETTA.   Don't you want to tell your father—

HAPPY.   No, that's not my father. He's just a guy. Come on, we'll catch Biff, and, honey, we're going to paint this town! Stanley, where's the check! Hey, Stanley! (*They exit,* STANLEY *looks toward left.*)

STANLEY (*calling to* HAPPY *indignantly*).   Mr. Loman! Mr. Loman! (STANLEY *picks up a chair and follows them off. Knocking is heard off left.* THE WOMAN *enters, laughing.* WILLY *follows her. She is in a black slip; he is buttoning his shirt. Raw, sensuous music accompanies their speech.*)

WILLY.   Will you stop laughing? Will you stop?

THE WOMAN.   Aren't you going to answer the door? He'll wake the whole hotel.

WILLY.   I'm not expecting anybody.

THE WOMAN.   Whyn't you have another drink, honey, and stop being so damn self-centered.

WILLY.   I'm so lonely.

THE WOMAN.   You know you ruined me, Willy? From now on, whenever you come to the office, I'll see that you go right through to the buyers. No waiting at my desk any more, Willy. You ruined me.

WILLY.   That's nice of you to say that.

THE WOMAN.   Gee, you are self-centered! Why so sad? You are the saddest, self-centeredest soul I ever did see-saw. (*She laughs. He kisses her.*) Come on inside, drummer boy. It's silly to be dressing in the middle of the night. (*As knocking is heard*) Aren't you going to answer the door?

WILLY.   They're knocking on the wrong door.

THE WOMAN.   But I felt the knocking. And he heard us talking in here. Maybe the hotel's on fire!

WILLY (*his terror rising*).   It's a mistake.

THE WOMAN.   Then tell him to go away!

WILLY.   There's nobody there.

THE WOMAN.   It's getting on my nerves, Willy. There's somebody standing out there and it's getting on my nerves!

WILLY (*pushing her away from him*).   All right, stay in the bathroom here, and don't come out. I think there's a law in Massachusetts about it, so don't come out. It may be the new room clerk. He looked very mean. So don't come out. It's a mistake, there's no fire. (*The knocking is heard again. He takes a few steps away from her, and she vanishes into the wing. The light follows him, and now he is facing* YOUNG BIFF, *who carries a suitcase.* BIFF *steps toward him. The music is gone.*)

BIFF.   Why didn't you answer?

WILLY.   Biff! What are you doing in Boston?

BIFF.   Why didn't you answer? I've been knocking for five minutes, I called you on the phone—

WILLY.   I just heard you. I was in the bathroom and had the door shut. Did anything happen home?

BIFF.   Dad—I let you down.

WILLY.   What do you mean?

BIFF.   Dad . . .

WILLY.   Biffo, what's this about? (*Putting his arm around* BIFF) Come on, let's go downstairs and get you a malted.

BIFF.   Dad, I flunked math.

WILLY.   Not for the term?

BIFF.   The term. I haven't got enough credits to graduate.

WILLY.   You mean to say Bernard wouldn't give you the answers?

BIFF.   He did, he tried, but I only got sixty-one.

WILLY.   And they wouldn't give you four points?

BIFF.   Birnbaum refused absolutely. I begged him, Pop, but he won't give me those points. You gotta talk to him before they close the school. Because if he saw the kind of man you are, and you just talked to him in your way, I'm sure he'd come through for me. The class came right before practice, see, and I didn't go enough. Would you talk to him? He'd like you, Pop. You know the way you could talk.

WILLY.   You're on. We'll drive right back.

BIFF.   Oh, Dad, good work! I'm sure he'll change it for you!

WILLY.   Go downstairs and tell the clerk I'm checkin' out. Go right down.

BIFF.   Yes, sir! See, the reason he hates me, Pop—one day he was late for class so I got up at the blackboard and imitated him. I crossed my eyes and talked with a lithp.

WILLY (*laughing*).   You did? The kids like it?

BIFF.   They nearly died laughing!

WILLY.   Yeah? What'd you do?

BIFF.   The thquare root of thixty twee is . . . (WILLY *bursts out laughing;* BIFF *joins him*). And in the middle of it he walked in! (WILLY *laughs and* THE WOMAN *joins in off-stage.*)

WILLY (*without hesitation*).   Hurry downstairs and—

BIFF.   Somebody in there?

WILLY.   No, that was next door. (THE WOMAN *laughs offstage.*)

BIFF.   Somebody got in your bathroom!

WILLY.   No, it's the next room, there's a party.

THE WOMAN (*enters, laughing. She lisps this*).   Can I come in? There's something in the bathtub, Willy, and it's moving! (WILLY *looks at* BIFF, *who is staring open-mouthed and horrified at* THE WOMAN.)

WILLY.   Ah—you better go back to your room. They must be finished painting by now. They're painting her room so I let her take a shower here. Go back, go back . . . (*He pushes her.*)

THE WOMAN (*resisting*).   But I've got to get dressed, Willy, I can't—

WILLY.   Get out of here! Go back, go back . . . (*Suddenly striving for the ordinary*) This is Miss Francis, Biff, she's a buyer. They're painting her room. Go back, Miss Francis, go back . . .

THE WOMAN.   But my clothes, I can't go out naked in the hall!

WILLY (*pushing her offstage*).   Get outa here! Go back, go back! (BIFF *slowly sits down on his suitcase as the argument continues offstage.*)

THE WOMAN.   Where's my stockings? You promised me stockings, Willy!

WILLY.   I have no stockings here!

THE WOMAN.   You had two boxes of size nine sheers for me, and I want them!

WILLY.   Here, for God's sake, will you get outa here!

THE WOMAN (*enters holding a box of stockings*).   I just hope there's nobody in the hall. That's all I hope. (*To* BIFF) Are you football or baseball?

BIFF.   Football.

THE WOMAN (*angry, humiliated*).   That's me too. G'night. (*She snatches her clothes from* WILLY *and walks out.*)

WILLY (*after a pause*).   Well, better get going. I want to get to the school first thing in the morning. Get my suits out of the closet. I'll get my valise. (BIFF *doesn't move.*) What's the matter? (BIFF *remains motionless, tears falling.*) She's a buyer. Buys for J. H. Simmons. She lives down the hall—they're painting. You don't imagine—(*He breaks off. After a pause*) Now listen, pal, she's just a buyer. She sees merchandise in her room and they have to keep it looking just so . . . (*Pause. Assuming command*) All right, get my suits. (BIFF *doesn't move.*) Now stop crying and do as I say. I gave you an order. Biff, I gave you an order! Is that what you do when I give you an order? How dare you cry! (*Putting his arm around* BIFF) Now look, Biff, when you grow up you'll understand about these things. You mustn't—you mustn't overemphasize a thing like this. I'll see Birnbaum first thing in the morning.

BIFF.   Never mind.

WILLY (*getting down beside* BIFF).   Never mind! He's going to give you those points. I'll see to it.

BIFF.   He wouldn't listen to you.

WILLY.   He certainly will listen to me. You need those points for the U. of Virginia.

BIFF.   I'm not going there.

WILLY.   Heh? If I can't get him to change that mark you'll make it up in summer school. You've got all summer to—

BIFF (*his weeping breaking from him*).   Dad . . .

WILLY (*infected by it*).   Oh, my boy . . .

BIFF.   Dad . . .

WILLY.   She's nothing to me, Biff. I was lonely, I was terribly lonely.

BIFF.   You—you gave her Mama's stockings! (*His tears break through and he rises to go.*)

WILLY (*grabbing for* BIFF).   I gave you an order!

BIFF.   Don't touch me, you—liar!

WILLY.   Apologize for that!

BIFF.   You fake! You phony little fake! You fake! (*Overcome, he turns quickly and weeping fully goes out with his suitcase.* WILLY *is left on the floor on his knees.*)

WILLY.   I gave you an order! Biff, come back here or I'll beat you! Come back here! I'll whip you! (STANLEY *comes quickly in from the right and stands in front of* WILLY, *who shouts at him.*) I gave you an order . . .

STANLEY.   Hey, let's pick it up, pick it up, Mr. Loman. (*He helps* WILLY *to his feet.*) Your boys left with the chippies. They said they'll see you home. (*A second waiter watches some distance away.*)

WILLY.   But we were supposed to have dinner together. (*Music is heard,* WILLY'S *theme.*)

STANLEY.   Can you make it?

WILLY.   I'll—sure. I can make it. (*Suddenly concerned about his clothes*) Do I—I look all right?

STANLEY.   Sure, you look all right. (*He flicks a speck off* WILLY'S *lapel.*)

WILLY.   Here—here's a dollar.

STANLEY.   Oh, your son paid me. It's all right.

WILLY (*putting it in* STANLEY'S *hand*).   No, take it. You're a good boy.

STANLEY.   Oh, no, you don't have to . . .

WILLY.   Here's some more, I don't need it any more. (*After a slight pause.*) Tell me—is there a seed store in the neighborhood?

STANLEY.   Seeds? You mean like to plant? (*As* WILLY *turns,* STANLEY *slips the money back into his jacket pocket.*)

WILLY.   Yes. Carrots, peas . . .

STANLEY.   Well, there's hardware stores on Sixth Avenue, but it may be too late now.

WILLY (*anxiously*).   Oh, I'd better hurry. I've got to get some seeds. (*He starts off to the right.*) I've got to get some seeds, right away. Nothing's planted. I don't have a thing in the ground. (WILLY *hurries out as the light goes down.* STANLEY *moves over to the right after him, watches him off. The other waiter has been staring at* WILLY.)

STANLEY (*to the waiter*).   Well, whatta you looking at?

(*The waiter picks up the chairs and moves off right.* STANLEY *takes the table and follows him. The light fades on this area. There is a long pause, the sound of the flute coming over. The light gradually rises on the kitchen, which is empty.* HAPPY *appears at the door of the house, followed by* BIFF. HAPPY *is carrying a large bunch of long-stemmed roses. He enters the kitchen, looks around for* LINDA. *Not seeing her, he turns to* BIFF, *who is just outside the house door, and makes a gesture with his hands, indicating "Not here, I guess." He looks into the living-room and freezes. Inside,* LINDA, *unseen, is seated,* WILLY'S *coat on her lap. She rises ominously and quietly and moves toward* HAPPY, *who backs up into the kitchen, afraid.*)

HAPPY.   Hey, what're you doing? (LINDA *says nothing but moves toward him implacably.*) Where's Pop? (*He keeps backing to the right, and now* LINDA *is in full view of the doorway to the living-room.*) Is he sleeping?

LINDA.   Where were you?

HAPPY (*trying to laugh it off*).   We met two girls, Mom, very fine types. Here, we brought you some flowers. (*Offering them to her*) Put them in your room, Ma. (*She knocks them to the floor at* BIFF'S *feet. He has now come inside and closed the door behind him. She stares at* BIFF, *silent.*) Now what'd you do that for? Mom, I want you to have some flowers—

LINDA (*cutting* HAPPY *off, violently to* BIFF).   Don't you care whether he lives or dies?

HAPPY (*going to the stairs*).   Come upstairs, Biff.

BIFF (*with a flare of disgust, to* HAPPY).   Go away from me! (*To* LINDA) What do you mean, lives or dies? Nobody's dying around here, pal.

LINDA.   Get out of my sight! Get out of here!

BIFF.   I wanna see the boss.

LINDA.   You're not to go near him!

BIFF.   Where is he? (*He moves into the living-room and* LINDA *follows.*)

LINDA (*shouting after* BIFF).   You invite him to dinner. He looks forward to it all day—(BIFF *appears in his parents' bedroom, looks around, and exits*)—and then you desert him there. There's no stranger you'd do that to!

HAPPY.   Why? He had a swell time with us. Listen, when I—(LINDA *comes back into the kitchen*)—desert him I hope I don't outlive the day!

LINDA.   Get out of here!

HAPPY.   Now look, Mom . . .

LINDA.   Did you have to go to women tonight? You and your lousy rotten whores! (BIFF *re-enters the kitchen.*)

HAPPY.   Mom, all we did was follow Biff around trying to cheer him up! (*To* BIFF) Boy, what a night you gave me!

LINDA.   Get out of here, both of you, and don't come back! I don't want you tormenting him any more. Go on now, get your things together! (*To* BIFF) You can sleep in his apartment. (*She starts to pick up the flowers and stops herself.*) Pick up this stuff, I'm not your maid any more. Pick it up, you bum, you! (HAPPY *turns his back to her in refusal.* BIFF *slowly moves over and gets down on his knees, picking up the flowers.*)

LINDA.   You're a pair of animals! Not one, not another living soul would have had the cruelty to walk out on that man in a restaurant!

BIFF (*not looking at her*).   Is that what he said?

LINDA.   He didn't have to say anything. He was so humiliated he nearly limped when he came in.

HAPPY.   But, Mom, he had a great time with us—

BIFF (*cutting him off violently*).   Shut up! (*Without another word,* HAPPY *goes upstairs.*)

LINDA.   You! You didn't even go in to see if he was all right!

BIFF (*still on the floor in front of* LINDA, *the flowers in his hand; with self-loathing*).   No. Didn't. Didn't do a damned thing. How do you like that, heh? Left him babbling in a toilet.

LINDA.   You louse. You . . .

BIFF.   Now you hit it on the nose! (*He gets up, throws the flowers in the wastebasket.*) The scum of the earth, and you're looking at him!

LINDA.   Get out of here!

BIFF.   I gotta talk to the boss, Mom. Where is he?

LINDA.   You're not going near him. Get out of this house!

BIFF (*with absolute assurance, determination*).   No. We're gonna have an abrupt conversation, him and me.

LINDA.   You're not talking to him! (*Hammering is heard from outside the house, off right.* BIFF *turns toward the noise.* LINDA *is suddenly pleading.*) Will you please leave him alone?

BIFF.   What's he doing out there?

LINDA.   He's planting a garden!

BIFF (*quietly*).   Now? Oh, my God! (BIFF *moves outside,* LINDA *following. The light dies down on them and comes up on the center of the apron as* WILLY *walks into it. He is carrying a flashlight, a hoe, and a handful of seed packets. He raps the top of the hoe sharply to fix it firmly, and then moves to the left, measuring off the distance with his foot. He holds the flashlight to look at the seed packets, reading off the instructions. He is in the blue of night.*)

WILLY.   Carrots . . . quarter-inch apart. Rows . . . one-foot rows. (*He measures it off.*) One foot. (*He puts down a package and measures off.*) Beets. (*He puts down another package and measures again.*) Lettuce. (*He reads the package, puts it down.*) One foot—(*He breaks off as* BEN *appears at the right and moves slowly down to him.*) What a proposition, ts, ts. Terrific, terrific. 'Cause she suffered, Ben, the woman has suffered. You understand me? A man can't go out the way he came in. Ben, a man has got to add up to something. You can't, you can't—(BEN *moves toward him as though to interrupt.*) You gotta consider, now. Don't answer so quick. Remember, it's a guaranteed twenty-thousand-dollar proposition. Now look, Ben, I want you to go through the ins and outs of this thing with me. I've got nobody to talk to, Ben, and the woman has suffered, you hear me?

BEN (*standing still, considering*).   What's the proposition?

WILLY.   It's twenty-thousand dollars on the barrelhead. Guaranteed, gilt-edged, you understand?

BEN.   You don't want to make a fool of yourself. They might not honor the policy.

WILLY.   How can they dare refuse? Didn't I work like a coolie to meet every premium on the nose? And now they don't pay off? Impossible!

BEN.   It's called a cowardly thing, William.

WILLY.   Why? Does it take more guts to stand here the rest of my life ringing up a zero?

BEN (*yielding*).   That's a point, William. (*He moves, thinking, turns.*) And twenty-thousand—that *is* something one can feel with the hand, it is there.

WILLY (*now assured, with rising power*).   Oh, Ben, that's the whole beauty of it! I can see it like a diamond shining in the dark, hard and rough, that I can pick up and touch in my hand. Not like—like an appointment! This would not be another damned-fool appointment, Ben, and it changes all the aspects. Because he thinks I'm nothing, see, and so he spites me. But the funeral—(*Straightening up*) Ben, that funeral will be massive! They'll come from Maine, Massachusetts, Vermont, New Hampshire! All the old-timers with the strange license plates—that boy will be thunderstruck, Ben, because he never realized—I am known! Rhode Island, New York, New Jersey—I am known, Ben, and he'll see it with his eyes once and for all. He'll see what I am. He's in for a shock, that boy!

BEN (*coming down to the edge of the garden*).   He'll call you a coward.

WILLY (*suddenly fearful*).   No, that would be terrible.

BEN.   Yes. And a damned fool.

WILLY.   No, no, he mustn't, I won't have it! (*He is broken and desperate.*)

BEN.   He'll hate you, William. (*The gay music of the* BOYS *is heard.*)

WILLY.   Oh, Ben, how do we get back to all the great times? Used to be so full of light, and comradeship, the sleigh-riding in winter and the ruddiness of his cheeks. And always some kind of good news coming up, always something nice coming up ahead. And never let me carry the valises in the house, and simonizing, simonizing that little red car! Why, why can't I give him something and not have him hate me?

BEN.   Let me think about it. (*He glances at his watch.*) I still have a little time. Remarkable proposition, but you've got to be sure you're not making a fool of yourself. (BEN *drifts off upstage and goes out of sight.* BIFF *comes down from the left.*)

WILLY (*suddenly conscious of* BIFF, *turns and looks up at him, then begins picking up the packages of seeds in confusion*).   Where the hell is that seed? (*Indignantly*) You can't see nothing out here! They boxed in the whole god-dam neighborhood!

BIFF.   There are people all around here. Don't you realize that?

WILLY.   I'm busy. Don't bother me.

BIFF (*taking the hoe from* WILLY).   I'm saying good-by to you, Pop. (WILLY *looks at him, silent, unable to move.*) I'm not coming back any more.

WILLY.   You're not going to see Oliver tomorrow?

BIFF.   I've got no appointment, Dad.

WILLY.   He put his arms around you, and you've got no appointment?

BIFF.   Pop, get this now, will you? Every time I've left it's been a fight that sent me out of here. Today I realized something about myself and I tried to explain it to you and I—I think I'm just not smart enough to make any sense out of it for you. To hell with whose fault it is or anything like that. (*He takes* WILLY'S *arm.*) Let's just wrap it up, heh? Come on in, we'll tell Mom. (*He gently tries to pull* WILLY *to left.*)

WILLY (*frozen, immobile, with guilt in his voice*).   No, I don't want to see her.

BIFF.   Come on! (*He pulls again, and* WILLY *tries to pull away.*)

WILLY (*highly nervous*).   No, no, I don't want to see her.

BIFF (*tries to look into* WILLY'S *face, as if to find the answer there*).   Why don't you want to see her?

WILLY (*more harshly now*).   Don't bother me, will you?

BIFF.   What do you mean, you don't want to see her? You don't want them calling you yellow do you? This isn't your fault; it's me, I'm a bum. Now come inside! (WILLY *strains to get away.*) Did you hear what I said to you? (WILLY *pulls away and quickly goes by himself into the house.* BIFF *follows.*)

LINDA (*to* WILLY).   Did you plant, dear?

BIFF (*at the door, to* LINDA).   All right, we had it out. I'm going and I'm not writing any more.

LINDA (*going to* WILLY *in the kitchen*).   I think that's the best way, dear. 'Cause there's no use drawing it out, you'll just never get along. (WILLY *does not respond.*)

BIFF.   People ask where I am and what I'm doing, you don't know, and you don't care. That way it'll be off your mind and you can start brightening up again. All right? That clears it, doesn't it? (WILLY *is silent, and* BIFF *goes to him.*) You gonna wish me luck, scout? (*He extends his hand.*) What do you say?

LINDA.   Shake his hand, Willy.

WILLY (*turning to her, seething with hurt*).   There's no necessity to mention the pen at all, y'know.

BIFF (*gently*).   I've got no appointment, Dad.

WILLY (*erupting fiercely*).   He put his arm around . . . ?

BIFF.   Dad, you're never going to see what I am, so what's the use of arguing? If I strike oil I'll send you a check. Meantime forget I'm alive.

WILLY (*to* LINDA).   Spite, see?

BIFF.   Shake hands, Dad.

WILLY.   Not my hand.

BIFF.   I was hoping not to go this way.

WILLY.   Well, this is the way you're going. Good-by. (BIFF *looks at him a moment, then turns sharply and goes to the stairs.* WILLY *stops him with*) May you rot in hell if you leave this house!

BIFF (*turning*).   Exactly what is it that you want from me?

WILLY.   I want you to know, on the train, in the mountains, in the valleys, wherever you go, that you cut down your life for spite!

BIFF.   No, no.

WILLY.   Spite, spite, is the word of your undoing! And when you're down and out, remember what did it. When you're rotting somewhere beside the railroad tracks, remember, and don't you dare blame it on me!

BIFF.   I'm not blaming it on you!

WILLY.   I won't take the rap for this, you hear? (HAPPY *comes down the stairs and stands on the bottom step, watching.*)

BIFF.   That's just what I'm telling you!

WILLY (*sinking into a chair at the table, with full accusation*).   You're trying to put a knife in me—don't think I don't know what you're doing!

BIFF.   All right, phony! Then let's lay it on the line. (*He whips the rubber tube out of his pocket and puts it on the table.*)

HAPPY.   You crazy—

LINDA.   Biff! (*She moves to grab the hose, but* BIFF *holds it down with his hand.*)

BIFF.   Leave it there! Don't move it!

WILLY (*not looking at it*).   What is that?

BIFF.   You know goddam well what that is.

WILLY (*caged, wanting to escape*).   I never saw that.

BIFF.   You saw it. The mice didn't bring it into the cellar! What is this supposed to do, make a hero out of you? This supposed to make me sorry for you?

WILLY.   Never heard of it.

BIFF.   There'll be no pity for you, you hear it? No pity!

WILLY (*to* LINDA).   You hear the spite!

BIFF.   No, you're going to hear the truth—what you are and what I am!

LINDA.   Stop it!

WILLY.   Spite!

HAPPY (*coming down toward* BIFF).   You cut it out now!

BIFF (*to* HAPPY).   The man don't know who we are! The man is gonna know! (*To* WILLY) We never told the truth for ten minutes in this house!

HAPPY.   We always told the truth!

BIFF (*turning on him*).   You big blow, are you the assistant buyer? You're one of two assistants to the assistant, aren't you?

HAPPY.   Well, I'm practically—

BIFF.   You're practically full of it! We all are! And I'm through with it. (*To* WILLY) Now hear this, Willy, this is me.

WILLY.   I know you!

BIFF.   You know why I had no address for three months? I stole a suit in Kansas City and I was in jail. (*To* LINDA, *who is sobbing*) Stop crying. I'm through with it. (LINDA *turns away from them, her hands covering her face.*)

WILLY.   I suppose that's my fault!

BIFF. I stole myself out of every job since high school!

WILLY. And whose fault is that?

BIFF. And I never got anywhere because you blew me so full of hot air I could never stand taking orders from anybody! That's whose fault it is!

WILLY. I hear that!

LINDA. Don't, Biff!

BIFF. It's goddam time you heard that! I had to be boss big shot in two weeks, and I'm through with it!

WILLY. Then hang yourself! For spite, hang yourself!

BIFF. No! Nobody's hanging himself, Willy! I ran down eleven flights with a pen in my hand today. And suddenly I stopped, you hear me? And in the middle of that office building, do you hear this? I stopped in the middle of that building and I saw—the sky. I saw the things that I love in this world. The work and the food and time to sit and smoke. And I looked at the pen and said to myself, what the hell am I grabbing this for? Why am I trying to become what I don't want to be? What am I doing in an office, making a contemptuous, begging fool of myself, when all I want is out there, waiting for me the minute I say I know who I am! Why can't I say that, Willy? (*He tries to make* WILLY *face him, but* WILLY *pulls away and moves to the left.*)

WILLY (*with hatred, threateningly*). The door of your life is wide open!

BIFF. Pop! I'm a dime a dozen, and so are you!

WILLY (*turning on him now in an uncontrolled outburst*). I am not a dime a dozen! I am Willy Loman, and you are Biff Loman! (BIFF *starts for* WILLY, *but is blocked by* HAPPY. *In his fury,* BIFF *seems on the verge of attacking his father.*)

BIFF. I am not a leader of men, Willy, and neither are you. You were never anything but a hard-working drummer who landed in the ash can like all the rest of them! I'm one dollar an hour, Willy! I tried seven states and couldn't raise it. A buck an hour! Do you gather my meaning? I'm not bringing home any prizes any more, and you're going to stop waiting for me to bring them home!

WILLY (*directly to* BIFF). You vengeful, spiteful mutt! (BIFF *breaks from* HAPPY. WILLY, *in fright, starts up the stairs.* BIFF *grabs him.*)

BIFF (*at the peak of his fury*). Pop, I'm nothing! I'm nothing, Pop. Can't you understand that? There's no spite in it any more. I'm just what I am, that's all. (BIFF'S *fury has spent itself, and he breaks down, sobbing, holding on to* WILLY, *who dumbly fumbles for* BIFF'S *face.*)

WILLY (*astonished*). What're you doing? What're you doing? (*To* LINDA) Why is he crying?

BIFF (*crying, broken*). Will you let me go, for Christ's sake? Will you take that phony dream and burn it before something happens? (*Struggling to contain himself, he pulls away and moves to the stairs.*) I'll go in the morning. Put him—put him to bed. (*Exhausted,* BIFF *moves up the stairs to his room.*)

WILLY (*after a long pause, astonished, elevated*). Isn't that—isn't that remarkable? Biff—he likes me!

LINDA.   He loves you, Willy!

HAPPY (*deeply moved*).   Always did, Pop.

WILLY.   Oh, Biff! (*Staring wildly*) He cried! Cried to me. (*He is choking with his love, and now cries out his promise.*) That boy—that boy is going to be magnificent! (BEN *appears in the light just outside the kitchen.*)

BEN.   Yes, outstanding, with twenty thousand behind him.

LINDA (*sensing the racing of his mind, fearfully, carefully*).   Now come to bed, Willy. It's all settled now.

WILLY (*finding it difficult not to rush out of the house*).   Yes, we'll sleep. Come on. Go to sleep, Hap.

BEN.   And it does take a great kind of man to crack the jungle. (*In accents of dread,* BEN'S *idyllic music starts up.*)

HAPPY (*his arm around* LINDA).   I'm getting married, Pop, don't forget it. I'm changing everything. I'm gonna run that department before the year is up. You'll see, Mom. (*He kisses her.*)

BEN.   The jungle is dark but full of diamonds, Willy. (WILLY *turns, moves, listening to* BEN.)

LINDA.   Be good. You're both good boys, just act that way, that's all.

HAPPY.   'Night, Pop. (*He goes upstairs.*)

LINDA (*to* WILLY).   Come, dear.

BEN (*with greater force*).   One must go in to fetch a diamond out.

WILLY (*to* LINDA, *as he moves slowly along the edge of the kitchen, toward the door*).   I just want to get settled down, Linda. Let me sit alone for a little.

LINDA (*almost uttering her fear*).   I want you upstairs.

WILLY (*taking her in his arms*).   In a few minutes, Linda. I couldn't sleep right now. Go on, you look awful tired. (*He kisses her.*)

BEN.   Not like an appointment at all. A diamond is rough and hard to the touch.

WILLY.   Go on now. I'll be right up.

LINDA.   I think this is the only way, Willy.

WILLY.   Sure, it's the best thing.

BEN.   Best thing!

WILLY.   The only way. Everything is gonna be—go on, kid, get to bed. You look so tired.

LINDA.   Come right up.

WILLY.   Two minutes. (LINDA *goes into the living-room, then reappears in her bedroom.* WILLY *moves just outside the kitchen door.*) Loves me. (*Wonderingly*) Always loved me. Isn't that a remarkable thing? Ben, he'll worship me for it!

BEN (*with promise*).   It's dark there, but full of diamonds.

WILLY.   Can you imagine that magnificence with twenty thousand dollars in his pocket?

LINDA (*calling from her room*).   Willy! Come up!

WILLY (*calling into the kitchen*).   Yes, yes. Coming! It's very smart, you realize that, don't you, sweetheart? Even Ben sees it. I gotta go, baby. 'By!

'By! (*Going over to* BEN, *almost dancing*) Imagine? When the mail comes he'll be ahead of Bernard again!

BEN.   A perfect proposition all around.

WILLY.   Did you see how he cried to me? Oh, if I could kiss him, Ben!

BEN.   Time, William, time!

WILLY.   Oh, Ben, I always knew one way or another we were gonna make it, Biff and I!

BEN (*looking at his watch*).   The boat. We'll be late. (*He moves slowly off into the darkness.*)

WILLY (*elegiacally, turning to the house*).   Now when you kick off, boy, I want a seventy-yard boot, and get right down the field under the ball, and when you hit, hit low and hit hard, because it's important, boy. (*He swings around and faces the audience.*) There's all kinds of important people in the stands, and the first thing you know . . . (*Suddenly realizing he is alone*) Ben! Ben, where do I . . . ? (*He makes a sudden movement of search.*) Ben, how do I . . . ?

LINDA (*calling*).   Willy, you coming up?

WILLY (*uttering a gasp of fear, whirling about as if to quiet her*).   Sh! (*He turns as if to find his way; sounds, faces, voices, seem to be swarming in upon him and he flicks at them, crying*) Sh! Sh! (*Suddenly music, faint and high, stops him. It rises in intensity, almost to an unbearable scream. He goes up and down on his toes, and rushes off around the house.*) Shhh!

LINDA.   Willy? (*There is no answer.* LINDA *waits.* BIFF *gets up off his bed. He is still in his clothes.* HAPPY *sits up.* BIFF *stands there listening.* LINDA, *with real fear*) Willy, answer me! Willy! (*There is the sound of a car starting and moving away at full speed.*) No!

BIFF (*rushing down the stairs*).   Pop!

(*As the car speeds off, the music crashes down in a frenzy of sound, which becomes the soft pulsation of a single cello string.* BIFF *slowly returns to his bedroom. He and* HAPPY *gravely don their jackets.* LINDA *slowly walks out of her room. The music has developed into a dead march. The leaves of day are appearing over everything.* CHARLEY *and* BERNARD, *somberly dressed, appear and knock on the kitchen door.* BIFF *and* HAPPY *slowly descend the stairs to the kitchen as* CHARLEY *and* BERNARD *enter. All stop a moment when* LINDA, *in clothes of mourning, bearing a little bunch of roses, comes through the draped doorway into the kitchen. She goes to* CHARLEY *and takes his arm. Now all move toward the audience, through the wall-line of the kitchen. At the limit of the apron,* LINDA *lays down the flowers, kneels, and sits back on her heels. All stare down at the grave.*)

REQUIEM

CHARLEY.   It's getting dark, Linda. (LINDA *doesn't react. She stares at the grave.*)

BIFF.   How about it, Mom? Better get some rest, heh? They'll be closing the gate soon. (LINDA *makes no move. Pause.*)

HAPPY (*deeply angered*).   He had no right to do that. There was no necessity for it. We would've helped him.

CHARLEY (*grunting*).   Hmmm.

BIFF.   Come along, Mom.

LINDA.   Why didn't anybody come?

CHARLEY.   It was a nice funeral.

LINDA.   But where are all the people he knew? Maybe they blame him.

CHARLEY.   Naa. It's a rough world, Linda. They wouldn't blame him.

LINDA.   I can't understand it. At this time especially. First time in thirty-five years we were just about free and clear. He only needed a little salary. He was even finished with the dentist.

CHARLEY.   No man only needs a little salary.

LINDA.   I can't understand it.

BIFF.   There were a lot of nice days. When he'd come home from a trip; or on Sundays, making the stoop; finishing the cellar; putting on the new porch; when he built the extra bathroom; and put up the garage. You know something, Charley, there's more of him in that front stoop than in all the sales he ever made.

CHARLEY.   Yeah. He was a happy man with a batch of cement.

LINDA.   He was so wonderful with his hands.

BIFF.   He had the wrong dreams. All, all, wrong.

HAPPY (*almost ready to fight* BIFF).   Don't say that!

BIFF.   He never knew who he was.

CHARLEY (*stopping* HAPPY's *movement and reply. To* BIFF).   Nobody dast blame this man. You don't understand: Willy was a salesman. And for a salesman, there is no rock bottom to the life. He don't put a bolt to a nut, he don't tell you the law or give you medicine. He's a man way out there in the blue, riding on a smile and a shoeshine. And when they start not smiling back—that's an earthquake. And then you get yourself a couple of spots on your hat, and you're finished. Nobody dast blame this man. A salesman is got to dream, boy. It comes with the territory.

BIFF.   Charley, the man didn't know who he was.

HAPPY (*infuriated*).   Don't say that!

BIFF.   Why don't you come with me, Happy?

HAPPY.   I'm not licked that easily. I'm staying right in this city, and I'm gonna beat this racket! (*He looks at* BIFF, *his chin is set.*) The Loman Brothers!

BIFF.   I know who I am, kid.

HAPPY.   All right, boy. I'm gonna show you and everybody else that Willy Loman did not die in vain. He had a good dream. It's the only dream you can have—to come out number-one man. He fought it out here and this is where I'm gonna win it for him.

BIFF (*with a hopeless glance at* HAPPY, *bends toward his mother*).   Let's go, Mom.

LINDA.   I'll be with you in a minute. Go on, Charley. (*He hesitates.*) I want to, just for a minute. I never had a chance to say good-by. (CHARLEY *moves away, followed by* HAPPY. BIFF *remains a slight distance up and left of*

LINDA. *She sits there, summoning herself. The flute begins, not far away, playing behind her speech.*) Forgive me, dear. I can't cry. I don't know what it is, but I can't cry. I don't understand it. Why did you ever do that? Help me, Willy, I can't cry. It seems to me that you're just on another trip. I keep expecting you. Willy, dear, I can't cry. Why did you do it? I search and search and I search, and I can't understand it, Willy. I made the last payment on the house today. Today, dear. And there'll be nobody home. (*A sob rises in her throat.*) We're free and clear. (*Sobbing more fully, released*) We're free. (BIFF *comes slowly toward her.*) We're free . . . We're free . . .

(BIFF *lifts her to her feet and moves out up right with her in his arms.* LINDA *sobs quietly.* BERNARD *and* CHARLEY *come together and follow them, followed by* HAPPY. *Only the music of the flute is left on the darkening stage as over the house the hard towers of the apartment buildings rise into sharp focus, and the curtain falls.*)

August Wilson
Fences

CHARACTERS

TROY MAXSON
JIM BONO, *Troy's friend*
ROSE, *Troy's wife*
LYONS, *Troy's oldest son by previous marriage*
GABRIEL, *Troy's brother*
CORY, *Troy and Rose's son*
RAYNELL, *Troy's daughter*

The setting is the yard which fronts the only entrance to the Maxson household, an ancient two-story brick house set back off a small alley in a big-city neighborhood. The entrance to the house is gained by two or three steps leading to a wooden porch badly in need of paint.

FENCES   First produced in 1985. The setting is a black neighborhood in Pittsburgh, reminiscent of the author's childhood home where he was one of six children raised by their mother in the absence of their white father. August Wilson (born in 1945) quit the football team and dropped out of high school when he was sixteen but continued his education by reading in the public library, where he developed the goal of being a writer. After a series of jobs, he moved to St. Paul, Minnesota, and became involved with the Playwrights Center in Minneapolis. *Fences* is one of ten projected plays dealing with African-American experience in the twentieth century (one play for each decade). The action of the play begins ten years after Jackie Robinson (1919–1972) became the first black to play major league baseball. Prior to that time blacks were limited to playing in the Negro Leagues; two of the legendary players in the Leagues were Josh Gibson (1911–1947), called "the Babe Ruth" of the Negro Leagues, and the venerable Satchel Paige (1906–1982). Probably the most celebrated black athlete of the first half of the century was the heavyweight boxing champion Joe Louis (1914–1981).

A relatively recent addition to the house and running its full width, the porch lacks congruence. It is a sturdy porch with a flat roof. One or two chairs of dubious value sit at one end where the kitchen window opens onto the porch. An old-fashioned icebox stands silent guard at the opposite end.

The yard is a small dirt yard, partially fenced, except for the last scene, with a wooden sawhorse, a pile of lumber, and other fence-building equipment set off to the side. Opposite is a tree from which hangs a ball made of rags. A baseball bat leans against the tree. Two oil drums serve as garbage receptacles and sit near the house at right to complete the setting.

Near the turn of the century, the destitute of Europe sprang on the city with tenacious claws and an honest and solid dream. The city devoured them. They swelled its belly until it burst into a thousand furnaces and sewing machines, a thousand butcher shops and bakers' ovens, a thousand churches and hospitals and funeral parlors and money-lenders. The city grew. It nourished itself and offered each man a partnership limited only by his talent, his guile, and his willingness and capacity for hard work. For the immigrants of Europe, a dream dared and won true.

The descendants of African slaves were offered no such welcome or participation. They came from places called the Carolinas and the Virginias, Georgia, Alabama, Mississippi, and Tennessee. They came strong, eager, searching. The city rejected them and they fled and settled along the riverbanks and under bridges in shallow, ramshackle houses made of sticks and tarpaper. They collected rags and wood. They sold the use of their muscles and their bodies. They cleaned houses and washed clothes, they shined shoes, and in quiet desperation and vengeful pride, they stole, and lived in pursuit of their own dream: that they could breathe free, finally, and stand to meet life with the force of dignity and whatever eloquence the heart could call upon.

By 1957, the hard-won victories of the European immigrants had solidified the industrial might of America. War had been confronted and won with new energies that used loyalty and patriotism as its fuel. Life was rich, full, and flourishing. The Milwaukee Braves won the World Series, and the hot winds of change that would make the sixties a turbulent, racing, dangerous, and provocative decade had not yet begun to blow full.

ACT 1

SCENE 1

It is 1957. TROY and BONO enter the yard, engaged in conversation. TROY is fifty-three years old, a large man with thick, heavy hands; it is this largeness that he strives to fill out and make an accommodation with. Together with his blackness, his largeness informs his sensibilities and the choices he has made in his life.

Of the two men, BONO is obviously the follower. His commitment to their friendship of thirty-odd years is rooted in his admiration of TROY'S honesty, capacity for hard work, and his strength, which BONO seeks to emulate.

It is Friday night, payday, and the one night of the week the two men engage in a ritual of talk and drink. TROY *is usually the most talkative and at times he can be crude and almost vulgar, though he is capable of rising to profound heights of expression. The men carry lunch buckets and wear or carry burlap aprons and are dressed in clothes suitable to their jobs as garbage collectors.*

BONO.   Troy, you ought to stop that lying!

TROY.   I ain't lying! The nigger had a watermelon this big. (*He indicates with his hands.*) Talking about . . . "What watermelon, Mr. Rand?" I liked to fell out! "What watermelon, Mr. Rand?" . . . And it sitting there big as life.

BONO.   What did Mr. Rand say?

TROY.   Ain't said nothing. Figure if the nigger too dumb to know he carrying a watermelon, he wasn't gonna get much sense out of him. Trying to hide that great big watermelon under his coat. Afraid to let the white man see him carry it home.

BONO.   I'm like you . . . I ain't got no time for them kind of people.

TROY.   Now what he look like getting mad cause he see the man from the union talking to Mr. Rand?

BONO.   He come to me talking about . . . "Maxson gonna get us fired." I told him to get away from me with that. He walked away from me calling you a troublemaker. What Mr. Rand say?

TROY.   Ain't said nothing. He told me to go down the Commissioner's office next Friday. They called me down there to see them.

BONO.   Well, as long as you got your complaint filed, they can't fire you. That's what one of them white fellows tell me.

TROY.   I ain't worried about them firing me. They gonna fire me 'cause I asked a question? That's all I did. I went to Mr. Rand and asked him, "Why? Why you got the white mens driving and the colored lifting?" Told him, "what's the matter, don't I count? You think only white fellows got sense enough to drive a truck. That ain't no paper job! Hell, anybody can drive a truck. How come you got all whites driving and the colored lifting?" He told me "take it to the union." Well, hell, that's what I done! Now they wanna come up with this pack of lies.

BONO.   I told Brownie if the man come and ask him any questions . . . just tell the truth! It ain't nothing but something they done trumped up on you cause you filed a complaint on them.

TROY.   Brownie don't understand nothing. All I want them to do is change the job description. Give everybody a chance to drive the truck. Brownie can't see that. He ain't got that much sense.

BONO.   How you figure he be making out with that gal be up at Taylors' all the time . . . that Alberta gal?

TROY.   Same as you and me. Getting just as much as we is. Which is to say nothing.

BONO.   It is, huh? I figure you doing a little better than me . . . and I ain't saying what I'm doing.

TROY.   Aw, nigger, look here . . . I know you. If you had got anywhere near that gal, twenty minutes later you be looking to tell somebody. And the first one you gonna tell . . . that you gonna want to brag to . . . is me.

BONO.   I ain't saying that. I see where you be eyeing her.

TROY.   I eye all the women. I don't miss nothing. Don't never let nobody tell you Troy Maxson don't eye the women.

BONO.   You been doing more than eyeing her. You done bought her a drink or two.

TROY.   Hell yeah, I bought her a drink! What that mean? I bought you one, too. What that mean cause I buy her a drink? I'm just being polite.

BONO.   It's all right to buy her one drink. That's what you call being polite. But when you wanna be buying two or three . . . that's what you call eyeing her.

TROY.   Look here, as long as you known me . . . you ever known me to chase after women?

BONO.   Hell yeah! Long as I done known you. You forgetting I knew you when.

TROY.   Naw, I'm talking about since I been married to Rose?

BONO.   Oh, not since you been married to Rose. Now, that's the truth, there. I can say that.

TROY.   All right then! Case closed.

BONO.   I see you be walking up around Alberta's house. You supposed to be at Taylors' and you be walking up around there.

TROY.   What you watching where I'm walking for? I ain't watching after you.

BONO.   I seen you walking around there more than once.

TROY.   Hell, you liable to see me walking anywhere! That don't mean nothing cause you see me walking around there.

BONO.   Where she come from anyway? She just kinda showed up one day.

TROY.   Tallahassee. You can look at her and tell she one of them Florida gals. They got some big healthy women down there. Grow them right up out the ground. Got a little bit of Indian in her. Most of them niggers down in Florida got some Indian in them.

BONO.   I don't know about that Indian part. But she damn sure big and healthy. Woman wear some big stockings. Got them great big old legs and hips as wide as the Mississippi River.

TROY.   Legs don't mean nothing. You don't do nothing but push them out of the way. But them hips cushion the ride!

BONO.   Troy, you ain't got no sense.

TROY.   It's the truth! Like you riding on Goodyears!

(ROSE *enters from the house. She is ten years younger than* TROY; *her devotion to him stems from her recognition of the possibilities of her life without him: a succession of abusive men and their babies, a life of partying and running the streets, the Church, or aloneness with its attendant pain and frustration. She recognizes* TROY'S *spirit as a fine and illuminating one and she either ignores or forgives his faults, only some of which she recognizes. Though she doesn't drink, her presence is an integral part of the Friday night rituals. She alternates between the porch and the kitchen, where supper preparations are under way.)*

ROSE. What you all out here getting into?

TROY. What you worried about what we getting into for? This is men talk, woman.

ROSE. What I care what you all talking about? Bono, you gonna stay for supper?

BONO. No, I thank you, Rose. But Lucille says she cooking up a pot of pigfeet.

TROY. Pigfeet! Hell, I'm going home with you! Might even stay the night if you got some pigfeet. You got something in there to top them pigfeet, Rose?

ROSE. I'm cooking up some chicken. I got some chicken and collard greens.

TROY. Well, go on back in the house and let me and Bono finish what we was talking about. This is men talk. I got some talk for you later. You know what kind of talk I mean. You go on and powder it up.

ROSE. Troy Maxson, don't you start that now!

TROY (*puts his arms around her*). Aw, woman . . . come here. Look here, Bono . . . when I met this woman . . . I got out that place, say, "Hitch up my pony, saddle up my mare . . . there's a woman out there for me somewhere. I looked here. Looked there. Saw Rose and latched on to her." I latched on to her and told her—I'm gonna tell you the truth—I told her, "Baby, I don't wanna marry, I just wanna be your man." Rose told me . . . tell him what you told me, Rose.

ROSE. I told him if he wasn't the marrying kind, then move out the way so the marrying kind could find me.

TROY. That's what she told me. "Nigger, you in my way. You blocking the view! Move out the way so I can find me a husband." I thought it over two or three days. Come back—

ROSE. Ain't no two or three days nothing. You was back the same night.

TROY. Come back, told her . . . "Okay, baby . . . but I'm gonna buy me a banty rooster and put him out there in the backyard . . . and when he see a stranger come, he'll flap his wings and crow . . ." Look here, Bono, I could watch the front door by myself . . . it was that back door I was worried about.

ROSE. Troy, you ought not talk like that. Troy ain't doing nothing but telling a lie.

TROY. Only thing is . . . when we first got married . . . forget the rooster . . . we ain't had no yard!

BONO. I hear you tell it. Me and Lucille was staying down there on Logan Street. Had two rooms with the outhouse in the back. I ain't mind the outhouse none. But when that goddamn wind blow through there in the winter . . . that's what I'm talking about! To this day I wonder why in the hell

I ever stayed down there for six long years. But see, I didn't know I could do no better. I thought only white folks had inside toilets and things.

ROSE.   There's a lot of people don't know they can do no better than they doing now. That's just something you got to learn. A lot of folks still shop at Bella's.

TROY.   Ain't nothing wrong with shopping at Bella's. She got fresh food.

ROSE.   I ain't said nothing about if she got fresh food. I'm talking about what she charge. She charge ten cents more than the A&P.

TROY.   The A&P ain't never done nothing for me. I spends my money where I'm treated right. I go down to Bella, say, "I need a loaf of bread, I'll pay you Friday." She give it to me. What sense that make when I got money to go and spend it somewhere else and ignore the person who done right by me? That ain't in the Bible.

ROSE.   We ain't talking about what's in the Bible. What sense it make to shop there when she overcharge?

TROY.   You shop where you want to. I'll do my shopping where the people been good to me.

ROSE.   Well, I don't think it's right for her to overcharge. That's all I was saying.

BONO.   Look here . . . I got to get on. Lucille going be raising all kind of hell.

TROY.   Where you going, nigger? We ain't finished this pint. Come here, finish this pint.

BONO.   Well, hell, I am . . . if you ever turn the bottle loose.

TROY (*hands him the bottle*).   The only thing I say about the A&P is I'm glad Cory got that job down there. Help him take care of his school clothes and things. Gabe done moved out and things getting tight around here. He got that job. . . . He can start to look out for himself.

ROSE.   Cory done went and got recruited by a college football team.

TROY.   I told that boy about that football stuff. The white man ain't gonna let him get nowhere with that football. I told him when he first come to me with it. Now you come telling me he done went and got more tied up in it. He ought to go and get recruited in how to fix cars or something where he can make a living.

ROSE.   He ain't talking about making no living playing football. It's just something the boys in school do. They gonna send a recruiter by to talk to you. He'll tell you he ain't talking about making no living playing football. It's a honor to be recruited.

TROY.   It ain't gonna get him nowhere. Bono'll tell you that.

BONO.   If he be like you in the sports . . . he's gonna be all right. Ain't but two men ever played baseball as good as you. That's Babe Ruth and Josh Gibson. Them's the only two men ever hit more home runs than you.

TROY.   What it ever get me? Ain't got a pot to piss in or a window to throw it out of.

ROSE.   Times have changed since you was playing baseball, Troy. That was before the war. Times have changed a lot since then.

TROY.   How in hell they done changed?

ROSE.   They got lots of colored boys playing ball now. Baseball and football.

BONO.   You right about that, Rose. Times have changed, Troy. You just come along too early.

TROY.   There ought not never have been no time called too early! Now you take that fellow . . . what's that fellow they had playing right field for the Yankees back then? You know who I'm talking about, Bono. Used to play right field for the Yankees.

ROSE.   Selkirk?

TROY.   Selkirk! That's it! Man batting .269, understand? .269. What kind of sense that make? I was hitting .432 with thirty-seven home runs! Man batting .269 and playing right field for the Yankees! I saw Josh Gibson's daughter yesterday. She walking around with raggedy shoes on her feet. Now I bet you Selkirk's daughter ain't walking around with raggedy shoes on her feet! I bet you that!

ROSE.   They got a lot of colored baseball players now. Jackie Robinson was the first. Folks had to wait for Jackie Robinson.

TROY.   I done seen a hundred niggers play baseball better than Jackie Robinson. Hell, I know some teams Jackie Robinson couldn't even make! What you talking about Jackie Robinson. Jackie Robinson wasn't nobody. I'm talking about if you could play ball then they ought to have let you play. Don't care what color you were. Come telling me I come along too early. If you could play . . . then they ought to have let you play. (TROY *takes a long drink from the bottle.*)

ROSE.   You gonna drink yourself to death. You don't need to be drinking like that.

TROY.   Death ain't nothing. I done seen him. Done wrassled with him. You can't tell me nothing about death. Death ain't nothing but a fastball on the outside corner. And you know what I'll do to that! Lookee here, Bono . . . am I lying? You get one of them fastballs, about waist high, over the outside corner of the plate where you can get the meat of the bat on it . . . and good god! You can kiss it goodbye. Now, am I lying?

BONO.   Naw, you telling the truth there. I seen you do it.

TROY.   If I'm lying . . . that 450 feet worth of lying! (*Pause.*) That's all death is to me. A fastball on the outside corner.

ROSE.   I don't know why you want to get on talking about death.

TROY.   Ain't nothing wrong with talking about death. That's part of life. Everybody gonna die. You gonna die, I'm gonna die. Bono's gonna die. Hell, we all gonna die.

ROSE.   But you ain't got to talk about it. I don't like to talk about it.

TROY.   You the one brought it up. Me and Bono was talking about baseball . . . you tell me I'm gonna drink myself to death. Ain't that right,

Bono? You know I don't drink this but one night out of the week. That's Friday night. I'm gonna drink just enough to where I can handle it. Then I cuts it loose. I leave it alone. So don't you worry about me drinking myself to death. 'Cause I ain't worried about Death. I done seen him. I done wrestled with him.

Look here, Bono . . . I looked up one day and Death was marching straight at me. Like Soldiers on Parade! The Army of Death was marching straight at me. The middle of July, 1941. It got real cold just like it be winter. It seem like Death himself reached out and touched me on the shoulder. He touch me just like I touch you. I got cold as ice and Death standing there grinning at me.

ROSE.   Troy, why don't you hush that talk.

TROY.   I say . . . what you want, Mr. Death? You be wanting me? You done brought your army to be getting me? I looked him dead in the eye. I wasn't fearing nothing. I was ready to tangle. Just like I'm ready to tangle now. The Bible say be ever vigilant. That's why I don't get but so drunk. I got to keep watch.

ROSE.   Troy was right down there in Mercy Hospital. You remember he had pneumonia? Laying there with a fever talking plumb out of his head.

TROY.   Death standing there staring at me . . . carrying that sickle in his hand. Finally he say, "You want bound over for another year?" See, just like that . . . "You want bound over for another year?" I told him, "Bound over hell! Let's settle this now!"

It seem like he kinda fell back when I said that, and all the cold went out of me. I reached down and grabbed that sickle and threw it just as far as I could throw it . . . and me and him commenced to wrestling.

We wrestled for three days and three nights. I can't say where I found the strength from. Every time it seemed like he was gonna get the best of me, I'd reach way down deep inside myself and find the strength to do him one better.

ROSE.   Every time Troy tell that story he find different ways to tell it. Different things to make up about it.

TROY.   I ain't making up nothing. I'm telling you the facts of what happened. I wrestled with Death for three days and three nights and I'm standing here to tell you about it. (*Pause.*) All right. At the end of the third night we done weakened each other to where we can't hardly move. Death stood up, throwed on his robe . . . had him a white robe with a hood on it. He throwed on that robe and went off to look for his sickle. Say, "I'll be back." Just like that. "I'll be back." I told him, say, "Yeah, but . . . you gonna have to find me!" I wasn't no fool. I wasn't going looking for him. Death ain't nothing to play with. And I know he's gonna get me. I know I got to join his army . . . his camp followers. But as long as I keep my strength and see him coming . . . as long as I keep up my vigilance . . . he's gonna have to fight to get me. I ain't going easy.

BONO.   Well, look here, since you got to keep up your vigilance . . . let me have the bottle.

TROY.   Aw hell, I shouldn't have told you that part. I should have left out that part.

ROSE.   Troy be talking that stuff and half the time don't even know what he be talking about.

TROY.   Bono know me better than that.

BONO.   That's right. I know you. I know you got some Uncle Remus° in your blood. You got more stories than the devil got sinners.

TROY.   Aw hell, I done seen him too! Done talked with the devil.

ROSE.   Troy, don't nobody wanna be hearing all that stuff. (LYONS *enters the yard from the street. Thirty-four years old,* TROY'S *son by a previous marriage, he sports a neatly trimmed goatee, sport coat, white shirt, tieless and buttoned at the collar. Though he fancies himself a musician, he is more caught up in the rituals and "idea" of being a musician than in the actual practice of the music. He has come to borrow money from* TROY, *and while he knows he will be successful, he is uncertain as to what extent his lifestyle will be held up to scrutiny and ridicule.*)

LYONS.   Hey, Pop.

TROY.   What you come "Hey, Popping" me for?

LYONS.   How you doing, Rose? (*He kisses her.*) Mr. Bono. How you doing?

BONO.   Hey, Lyons . . . how you been?

TROY.   He must have been doing all right. I ain't seen him around here last week.

ROSE.   Troy, leave your boy alone. He come by to see you and you wanna start all that nonsense.

TROY.   I ain't bothering Lyons. (*Offers him the bottle.*) Here . . . get you a drink. We got an understanding. I know why he come by to see me and he know I know.

LYONS.   Come on, Pop . . . I just stopped by to say hi . . . see how you was doing.

TROY.   You ain't stopped by yesterday.

ROSE.   You gonna stay for supper, Lyons? I got some chicken cooking in the oven.

LYONS.   No, Rose . . . thanks. I was just in the neighborhood and thought I'd stop by for a minute.

TROY.   You was in the neighborhood all right, nigger. You telling the truth there. You was in the neighborhood cause it's my payday.

LYONS.   Well, hell, since you mentioned it . . . let me have ten dollars.

TROY.   I'll be damned! I'll die and go to hell and play blackjack with the devil before I give you ten dollars.

Uncle Remus: black narrator of folk tales in a series of books by Joel Chandler Harris (1848–1908)

BONO.   That's what I wanna know about . . . that devil you done seen.

LYONS.   What . . . Pop done seen the devil? You too much, Pops.

TROY.   Yeah, I done seen him. Talked to him too!

ROSE.   You ain't seen no devil. I done told you that man ain't had nothing to do with the devil. Anything you can't understand, you want to call it the devil.

TROY.   Look here, Bono . . . I went down to see Hertzberger about some furniture. Got three rooms for two-ninety-eight. That what it say on the radio. "Three rooms . . . two-ninety-eight." Even made up a little song about it. Go down there . . . man tell me I can't get no credit. I'm working every day and can't get no credit. What to do? I got an empty house with some raggedy furniture in it. Cory ain't got no bed. He's sleeping on a pile of rags on the floor. Working every day and can't get no credit. Come back here—Rose'll tell you—madder than hell. Sit down . . . try to figure what I'm gonna do. Come a knock on the door. Ain't been living here but three days. Who know I'm here? Open the door . . . devil standing there bigger than life. White fellow . . . white fellow . . . got on good clothes and everything. Standing there with a clipboard in his hand. I ain't had to say nothing. First words come out of his mouth was . . . "I understand you need some furniture and can't get no credit." I liked to fell over. He say, "I'll give you all the credit you want, but you got to pay the interest on it." I told him, "Give me three rooms worth and charge whatever you want." Next day a truck pulled up here and two men unloaded them three rooms. Man what drove the truck give me a book. Say send ten dollars, first of every month to the address in the book and everything will be all right. Say if I miss a payment the devil was coming back and it'll be hell to pay. That was fifteen years ago. To this day . . . the first of the month I send my ten dollars, Rose'll tell you.

ROSE.   Troy lying.

TROY.   I ain't never seen that man since. Now you tell me who else that could have been but the devil? I ain't sold my soul or nothing like that, you understand. Naw, I wouldn't have truck with the devil about nothing like that. I got my furniture and pays my ten dollars the first of the month just like clockwork.

BONO.   How long you say you been paying this ten dollars a month?

TROY.   Fifteen years!

BONO.   Hell, ain't you finished paying for it yet? How much the man done charged you?

TROY.   Ah hell, I done paid for it. I done paid for it ten times over! The fact is I'm scared to stop paying it.

ROSE.   Troy lying. We got that furniture from Mr. Glickman. He ain't paying no ten dollars a month to nobody.

TROY.   Aw hell, woman. Bono know I ain't that big a fool.

LYONS.   I was just getting ready to say . . . I know where there's a bridge for sale.

TROY.   Look here, I'll tell you this . . . it don't matter to me if he was the devil. It don't matter if the devil give credit. Somebody has got to give it.

ROSE.   It ought to matter. You going around talking about having truck with the devil . . . God's the one you gonna have to answer to. He's the one gonna be at the Judgment.

LYONS.   Yeah, well, look here, Pop . . . let me have that ten dollars. I'll give it back to you. Bonnie got a job working at the hospital.

TROY.   What I tell you, Bono? The only time I see this nigger is when he wants something. That's the only time I see him.

LYONS.   Come on, Pop, Mr. Bono don't want to hear all that. Let me have the ten dollars. I told you Bonnie working.

TROY.   What that mean to me? "Bonnie working." I don't care if she working. Go ask her for the ten dollars if she working. Talking about "Bonnie working." Why ain't you working?

LYONS.   Aw, Pop, you know I can't find no decent job. Where am I gonna get a job at? You know I can't get no job.

TROY.   I told you I know some people down there. I can get you on the rubbish if you want to work. I told you that the last time you came by here asking me for something.

LYONS.   Naw, Pop . . . thanks. That ain't for me. I don't wanna be carrying nobody's rubbish. I don't wanna be punching nobody's time clock.

TROY.   What's the matter, you too good to carry people's rubbish? Where you think that ten dollars you talking about come from? I'm just supposed to haul people's rubbish and give my money to you cause you too lazy to work. You too lazy to work and wanna know why you ain't got what I got.

ROSE.   What hospital Bonnie working at? Mercy?

LYONS.   She's down at Passavant working in the laundry.

TROY.   I ain't got nothing as it is. I give you that ten dollars and I got to eat beans the rest of the week. Naw . . . you ain't getting no ten dollars here.

LYONS.   You ain't got to be eating no beans. I don't know why you wanna say that.

TROY.   I ain't got no extra money. Gabe done moved over to Miss Pearl's paying her the rent and things done got tight around here. I can't afford to be giving you every payday.

LYONS.   I ain't asked you to give me nothing. I asked you to loan me ten dollars. I know you got ten dollars.

TROY.   Yeah, I got it. You know why I got it? Cause I don't throw my money away out there in the streets. You living the fast life . . . wanna be a musician . . . running around in them clubs and things . . . then, you learn to take care of yourself. You ain't gonna find me going and asking nobody for nothing. I done spent too many years without.

LYONS.   You and me is two different people, Pop.

TROY.   I done learned my mistake and learned to do what's right by it. You still trying to get something for nothing. Life don't owe you nothing. You owe it to yourself. Ask Bono. He'll tell you I'm right.

LYONS.   You got your way of dealing with the world . . . I got mine. The only thing that matters to me is the music.

TROY.   Yeah, I can see that! It don't matter how you gonna eat . . . where your next dollar is coming from. You telling the truth there.

LYONS.   I know I got to eat. But I got to live too. I need something that gonna help me to get out of the bed in the morning. Make me feel like I belong in the world. I don't bother nobody. I just stay with the music 'cause that's the only way I can find to live in the world. Otherwise there ain't no telling what I might do. Now I don't come criticizing you and how you live. I just come by to ask you for ten dollars. I don't wanna hear all that about how I live.

TROY.   Boy, your mamma did a hell of a job raising you.

LYONS.   You can't change me, Pop. I'm thirty-four years old. If you wanted to change me, you should have been there when I was growing up. I come by to see you . . . ask for ten dollars and you want to talk about how I was raised. You don't know nothing about how I was raised.

ROSE.   Let the boy have ten dollars, Troy.

TROY (*to* LYONS).   What the hell you looking at me for? I ain't got no ten dollars. You know what I do with my money. (*To* ROSE) Give him ten dollars if you want him to have it.

ROSE.   I will. Just as soon as you turn it loose.

TROY (*handing* ROSE *the money*).   There it is. Seventy-six dollars and forty-two cents. You see this, Bono? Now, I ain't gonna get but six of that back.

ROSE.   You ought to stop telling that lie. Here, Lyons. (*She hands him the money.*)

LYONS.   Thanks, Rose. Look . . . I got to run . . . I'll see you later.

TROY.   Wait a minute. You gonna say, "thanks, Rose" and ain't gonna look to see where she got that ten dollars from? See how they do me, Bono?

LYONS.   I know she got it from you, Pop. Thanks. I'll give it back to you.

TROY.   There he go telling another lie. Time I see that ten dollars . . . he'll be owing me thirty more.

LYONS.   See you, Mr. Bono.

BONO.   Take care, Lyons!

LYONS.   Thanks, Pop. I'll see you again. (LYONS *exits the yard.*)

TROY.   I don't know why he don't go and get him a decent job and take care of that woman he got.

BONO.   He'll be all right, Troy. The boy is still young.

TROY.   The *boy* is thirty-four years old.

ROSE.   Let's not get off into all that.

BONO.   Look here . . . I got to be going. I got to be getting on. Lucille gonna be waiting.

TROY (*puts his arm around* ROSE).   See this woman, Bono? I love this woman. I love this woman so much it hurts. I love her so much . . . I done run out of ways of loving. So I got to go back to basics. Don't you come by my house Monday morning talking about time to go to work . . . 'cause I'm still gonna be stroking!

ROSE.   Troy! Stop it now!

BONO.   I ain't paying him no mind, Rose. That ain't nothing but gin-talk. Go on, Troy. I'll see you Monday.

TROY.   Don't you come by my house, nigger! I done told you what I'm gonna be doing. (*The lights go down to black.*)

SCENE 2

The lights come up on ROSE *hanging up clothes. She hums and sings softly to herself. It is the following morning.*

ROSE (*sings*).   Jesus, be a fence all around me every day
                Jesus, I want you to protect me as I travel on my way.
                Jesus, be a fence all around me every day.
(TROY *enters from the house.*)
                Jesus, I want you to protect me
                As I travel on my way.
(*To* TROY) 'Morning. You ready for breakfast? I can fix it soon as I finish hanging up these clothes.

TROY.   I got the coffee on. That'll be all right. I'll just drink some of that this morning.

ROSE.   That 651 hit yesterday. That's the second time this month. Miss Pearl hit for a dollar . . . seem like those that need the least always get lucky. Poor folks can't get nothing.

TROY.   Them numbers don't know nobody. I don't know why you fool with them. You and Lyons both.

ROSE.   It's something to do.

TROY.   You ain't doing nothing but throwing your money away.

ROSE.   Troy, you know I don't play foolishly. I just play a nickel here and nickel there.

TROY.   That's two nickels you done thrown away.

ROSE.   Now I hit sometimes . . . that makes up for it. It always comes in handy when I do hit. I don't hear you complaining then.

TROY.   I ain't complaining now. I just say it's foolish. Trying to guess out of six hundred ways which way the number gonna come. If I had all the money niggers, these Negroes, throw away on numbers for one week—just one week—I'd be a rich man.

ROSE.   Well, you wishing and calling it foolish ain't gonna stop folks from playing numbers. That's one thing for sure. Besides . . . some good things come from playing numbers. Look where Pope done bought him that restaurant off of numbers.

TROY.   I can't stand niggers like that. Man ain't had two dimes to rub together. He walking around with his shoes all run over bumming money for cigarettes. All right. Got lucky there and hit the numbers . . .

ROSE.   Troy, I know all about it.

TROY.   Had good sense, I'll say that for him. He ain't throwed his money away. I seen niggers hit the numbers and go through two thousand dollars in four days. Man bought him that restaurant down there . . . fixed it up real nice . . . and then didn't want nobody to come in it! A Negro go in there and can't get no kind of service. I seen a white fellow come in there and order a bowl of stew. Pope picked all the meat out the pot for him. Man ain't had nothing but a bowl of meat! Negro come behind him and ain't got nothing but the potatoes and carrots. Talking about what numbers do for people, you picked a wrong example. Ain't done nothing but make a worser fool out of him than he was before.

ROSE.   Troy, you ought to stop worrying about what happened at work yesterday.

TROY.   I ain't worried. Just told me to be down there at the Commissioner's office on Friday. Everybody think they gonna fire me. I ain't worried about them firing me. You ain't got to worry about that. (*Pause.*) Where's Cory? Cory in the house? (*Calls*) Cory?

ROSE.   He gone out.

TROY.   Out, huh? He gone out 'cause he know I want him to help me with this fence. I know how he is. That boy scared of work. (GABRIEL *enters. He comes halfway down the alley and, hearing* TROY'S *voice, stops.*) He ain't done a lick of work in his life.

ROSE.   He had to go to football practice. Coach wanted them to get in a little extra practice before the season start.

TROY.   I got his practice . . . running out of here before he get his chores done.

ROSE.   Troy, what is wrong with you this morning? Don't nothing set right with you. Go on back in there and go to bed . . . get up on the other side.

TROY.   Why something got to be wrong with me? I ain't said nothing wrong with me.

ROSE.   You got something to say about everything. First it's the numbers . . . then it's the way the man runs his restaurant . . . then you done got on Cory. What's it gonna be next? Take a look up there and see if the weather suits you . . . or is it gonna be how you gonna put up the fence with the clothes hanging in the yard.

TROY.   You hit the nail on the head then.

ROSE.   I know you like I know the back of my hand. Go on in there and get you some coffee . . . see if that straighten you up. 'Cause you ain't right this morning. (TROY *starts into the house and sees* GABRIEL. GABRIEL *starts singing.* TROY'S *brother, he is seven years younger than* TROY. *Injured in World War II, he has a metal plate in his head. He carries an old trumpet tied around his waist and believes with every fiber of his being that he is the Archangel Gabriel. He carries a chipped basket with an assortment of discarded fruits and vegetables he has picked up in the strip district and which he attempts to sell.*)

GABRIEL (*singing*).   Yes, ma'am, I got plums
               You ask me how I sell them
               Oh ten cents apiece
               Three for a quarter
               Come and buy now
               'Cause I'm here today
               And tomorrow I'll be gone
(GABRIEL *enters the yard.*) Hey, Rose!

ROSE.   How you doing, Gabe?

GABRIEL.   There's Troy . . . Hey, Troy!

TROY.   Hey, Gabe. (*Exit into kitchen.*)

ROSE (*to* GABRIEL).   What you got there?

GABRIEL.   You know what I got, Rose. I got fruits and vegetables.

ROSE (*looking in basket*).   Where's all these plums you talking about?

GABRIEL.   I ain't got no plums today, Rose. I was just singing that. Have some tomorrow. Put me in a big order for plums. Have enough plums tomorrow for St. Peter and everybody. (TROY *reenters from kitchen, crosses to steps.*) Troy's mad at me.

TROY.   I ain't mad at you. What I got to be mad at you about? You ain't done nothing to me.

GABRIEL.   I just moved over to Miss Pearl's to keep out from in your way. I ain't mean no harm by it.

TROY.   Who said anything about that? I ain't said anything about that.

GABRIEL.   You ain't mad at me, is you?

TROY.   Naw . . . I ain't mad at you, Gabe. If I was mad at you I'd tell you about it.

GABRIEL.   Got me two rooms. In the basement. Got my own door too. Wanna see my key? (*He holds up a key.*) That's my own key! Ain't nobody else got a key like that. That's my key! My two rooms!

TROY.   Well, that's good, Gabe. You got your own key . . . that's good.

ROSE.   You hungry, Gabe? I was just fixing to cook Troy his breakfast.

GABRIEL.   I'll take some biscuits. You got some biscuits? Did you know when I was in heaven . . . every morning me and St. Peter would sit down by the gate and eat some big fat biscuits? Oh, yeah! We had us a good time. We'd sit there and eat us them biscuits and then St. Peter would go off to sleep and tell me to wake him up when it's time to open the gates for the judgment.

ROSE.   Well, come on . . . I'll make up a batch of biscuits. (*Exits into the house.*)

GABRIEL.   Troy . . . St. Peter got your name in the book. I seen it. It say . . . Troy Maxson. I say . . . I know him! He got the same name like what I got. That's my brother!

TROY.   How many times you gonna tell me that, Gabe?

GABRIEL.   Ain't got my name in the book. Don't have to have my name. I done died and went to heaven. He got your name though. One morning St. Peter was looking at his book . . . marking it up for the judgment . . . and he let me see your name. Got it in there under M. Got Rose's name . . . I ain't seen it like I seen yours . . . but I know it's in there. He got a great big book. Got everybody's name what was ever been born. That's what he told me. But I seen your name. Seen it with my own eyes.

TROY.   Go on in the house there. Rose going to fix you something to eat.

GABRIEL.   Oh, I ain't hungry. I done had breakfast with Aunt Jemimah. She come by and cooked me up a whole mess of flapjacks. Remember how we used to eat them flapjacks?

TROY.   Go on in the house and get you something to eat now.

GABRIEL.   I got to sell my plums. I done sold some tomatoes. Got me two quarters. Wanna see? (*He shows* TROY *his quarters.*) I'm gonna save them and buy me a new horn so St. Peter can hear me when it's time to open the gates. (GABRIEL *stops suddenly. Listens.*) Hear that? That's the hellhounds. I got to chase them out of here. Go on get out of here! Get out! (GABRIEL *exits singing.*)

> Better get ready for the judgment
> Better get ready for the judgment
> My Lord is coming down

(ROSE *enters from the house.*)

TROY.   He's gone off somewhere.

GABRIEL (*offstage*).   Better get ready for the judgment
> Better get ready for the judgment morning
> Better get ready for the judgment
> My God is coming down.

ROSE.   He ain't eating right. Miss Pearl say she can't get him to eat nothing.

TROY.   What you want me to do about it, Rose? I done did everything I can for the man. I can't make him get well. Man got half his head blown away . . . what you expect?

ROSE.   Seem like something ought to be done to help him.

TROY.   Man don't bother nobody. He just mixed up from that metal plate he got in his head. Ain't no sense for him to go back into the hospital.

ROSE.   Least he be eating right. They can help him take care of himself.

TROY.   Don't nobody wanna be locked up, Rose. What you wanna lock him up for? Man go over there and fight the war . . . messin' around with them Japs, get half his head blown off . . . and they give him a lousy three thousand dollars. And I had to swoop down on that.

ROSE.   Is you fixing to go into that again?

TROY.   That's the only way I got a roof over my head . . . 'cause of that metal plate.

ROSE.   Ain't no sense you blaming yourself for nothing. Gabe wasn't in no condition to manage that money. You done what was right by him. Can't nobody say you ain't done what was right by him. Look how long you took care of him . . . till he wanted to have his own place and moved over there with Miss Pearl.

TROY.   That ain't what I'm saying, woman! I'm just stating the facts. If my brother didn't have that metal plate in his head . . . I wouldn't have a pot to piss in or a window to throw it out of. And I'm fifty-three years old. Now see if you can understand that! (TROY *gets up from the porch and starts to exit the yard.*)

ROSE.   Where you going off to? You been running out of here every Saturday for weeks. I thought you was gonna work on this fence?

TROY.   I'm gonna walk down to Taylors'. Listen to the ball game. I'll be back in a bit. I'll work on it when I get back. (*He exits the yard. The lights go to black.*)

SCENE 3

The lights come up on the yard. It is four hours later. ROSE *is taking down the clothes from the line.* CORY *enters carrying his football equipment.*

ROSE.   Your daddy like to had a fit with you running out of here this morning without doing your chores.

CORY.   I told you I had to go to practice.

ROSE.   He say you were supposed to help him with this fence.

CORY.   He been saying that the last four or five Saturdays, and then he don't never do nothing, but go down to Taylors'. Did you tell him about the recruiter?

ROSE.   Yeah, I told him.

CORY.   What he say?

ROSE.   He ain't said nothing too much. You get in there and get started on your chores before he gets back. Go on and scrub down them steps before he gets back here hollering and carrying on.

CORY.   I'm hungry. What you got to eat, Mama?

ROSE.   Go on and get started on your chores. I got some meat loaf in there. Go on and make you a sandwich . . . and don't leave no mess in there. (CORY *exits into the house.* ROSE *continues to take down the clothes.* TROY *enters the yard and sneaks up and grabs her from behind.*) Troy! Go on, now. You liked to scared me to death. What was the score of the game? Lucille had me on the phone and I couldn't keep up with it.

TROY.   What I care about the game? Come here, woman. (*He tries to kiss her.*)

ROSE.   I thought you went down Taylors' to listen to the game. Go on, Troy! You supposed to be putting up this fence.

TROY (*attempting to kiss her again*).   I'll put it up when I finish with what is at hand.

ROSE.   Go on, Troy. I ain't studying you.

TROY (*chasing after her*).   I'm studying you . . . fixing to do my homework!

ROSE.   Troy, you better leave me alone.

TROY.   Where's Cory? That boy brought his butt home yet?

ROSE.   He's in the house doing his chores.

TROY (*calling*).   Cory! Get your butt out here, boy! (ROSE *exits into the house with the laundry.* TROY *goes over to the pile of wood, picks up a board, and starts sawing.* CORY *enters from the house.*) You just now coming in here from leaving this morning?

CORY.   Yeah, I had to go to football practice.

TROY.   Yeah, what?

CORY.   Yessir.

TROY.   I ain't but two seconds off you noway. The garbage sitting in there overflowing . . . you ain't done none of your chores . . . and you come in here talking about "Yeah."

CORY.   I was just getting ready to do my chores now, Pop . . .

TROY.   Your first chore is to help me with this fence on Saturday. Everything else come after that. Now get that saw and cut them boards. (CORY *takes the saw and begins cutting the boards.* TROY *continues working. There is a long pause.*)

CORY.   Hey, Pop . . . why don't you buy a TV?

TROY.   What I want with a TV? What I want one of them for?

CORY.   Everybody got one. Earl, Ba Bra . . . Jesse!

TROY.   I ain't asked you who had one. I say what I want with one?

CORY.   So you can watch it. They got lots of things on TV. Baseball games and everything. We could watch the World Series.

TROY.   Yeah . . . and how much this TV cost?

CORY.   I don't know. They got them on sale for around two hundred dollars.

TROY.   Two hundred dollars, huh?

CORY.   That ain't that much, Pop.

TROY.   Naw, it's just two hundred dollars. See that roof you got over your head at night? Let me tell you something about that roof. It's been over ten years since that roof was last tarred. See now . . . the snow come this winter and sit up there on that roof like it is . . . and it's gonna seep inside. It's just gonna be a little bit . . . ain't gonna hardly notice it. Then the next thing you know, it's gonna be leaking all over the house. Then the wood rot from all that water and you gonna need a whole new roof. Now, how much you think it cost to get that roof tarred?

CORY.   I don't know.

TROY.   Two hundred and sixty-four dollars . . . cash money. While you thinking about a TV, I got to be thinking about the roof . . . and whatever else go wrong here. Now if you had two hundred dollars, what would you do . . . fix the roof or buy a TV?

CORY.   I'd buy a TV. Then when the roof started to leak . . . when it needed fixing . . . I'd fix it.

TROY.   Where you gonna get the money from? You done spent it for a TV. You gonna sit up and watch the water run all over your brand new TV.

CORY.   Aw, Pop. You got money. I know you do.

TROY.   Where I got it at, huh?

CORY.   You got it in the bank.

TROY.   You wanna see my bankbook? You wanna see that seventy-three dollars and twenty-two cents I got sitting up in there.

CORY.   You ain't got to pay for it all at one time. You can put a down payment on it and carry it on home with you.

TROY.   Not me. I ain't gonna owe nobody nothing if I can help it. Miss a payment and they come and snatch it right out your house. Then what you got? Now, soon as I get two hundred dollars clear, then I'll buy a TV. Right now, as soon as I get two hundred and sixty-four dollars, I'm gonna have this roof tarred.

CORY.   Aw . . . Pop!

TROY.   You go on and get you two hundred dollars and buy one if ya want it. I got better things to do with my money.

CORY.   I can't get no two hundred dollars. I ain't never seen two hundred dollars.

TROY.   I'll tell you what . . . you get you a hundred dollars and I'll put the other hundred with it.

CORY.   All right, I'm gonna show you.

TROY.   You gonna show me how you can cut them boards right now.

(CORY *begins to cut the boards. There is a long pause.*)

CORY.   The Pirates won today. That makes five in a row.

TROY.   I ain't thinking about the Pirates. Got an all-white team. Got that boy . . . that Puerto Rican boy . . . Clemente. Don't even half-play him. That boy could be something if they give him a chance. Play him one day and sit him on the bench the next.

CORY.   He gets a lot of chances to play.

TROY.   I'm talking about playing regular. Playing every day so you can get your timing. That's what I'm talking about.

CORY.   They got some white guys on the team that don't play every day. You can't play everybody at the same time.

TROY.   If they got a white fellow sitting on the bench . . . you can bet your last dollar he can't play! The colored guy got to be twice as good before he get on the team. That's why I don't want you to get all tied up in them sports. Man on the team and what it get him? They got colored on the team and don't use them. Same as not having them. All them teams the same.

CORY.   The Braves got Hank Aaron and Wes Covington. Hank Aaron hit two home runs today. That makes forty-three.

TROY.   Hank Aaron ain't nobody. That what you supposed to do. That's how you supposed to play the game. Ain't nothing to it. It's just a matter of timing . . . getting the right follow-through. Hell, I can hit forty-three home runs right now!

CORY.   Not off no major-league pitching, you couldn't.

TROY.   We had better pitching in the Negro leagues. I hit seven home runs off of Satchel Paige. You can't get no better than that!

CORY.   Sandy Koufax. He's leading the league in strikeouts.

TROY.   I ain't thinking of no Sandy Koufax.

CORY.   You got Warren Spahn and Lew Burdette. I bet you couldn't hit no home runs off of Warren Spahn.

TROY.   I'm through with it now. You go on and cut them boards. (*Pause.*) Your mama tell me you done got recruited by a college football team? Is that right?

CORY.   Yeah. Coach Zellman say the recruiter gonna be coming by to talk to you. Get you to sign the permission papers.

TROY.   I thought you supposed to be working down there at the A&P. Ain't you suppose to be working down there after school?

CORY.   Mr. Stawicki say he gonna hold my job for me until after the football season. Say starting next week I can work weekends.

TROY.   I thought we had an understanding about this football stuff? You suppose to keep up with your chores and hold that job down at the A&P. Ain't been around here all day on a Saturday. Ain't none of your chores done . . . and now you telling me you done quit your job.

CORY.   I'm going to be working weekends.

TROY.   You damn right you are! And ain't no need for nobody coming around here to talk to me about signing nothing.

CORY.   Hey, Pop . . . you can't do that. He's coming all the way from North Carolina.

TROY.   I don't care where he coming from. The white man ain't gonna let you get nowhere with that football noway. You go on and get your book-learning so you can work yourself up in that A&P or learn how to fix cars or build houses or something, get you a trade. That way you have something can't nobody take away from you. You go on and learn how to put your hands to some good use. Besides hauling people's garbage.

CORY.   I get good grades, Pop. That's why the recruiter wants to talk with you. You got to keep up your grades to get recruited. This way I'll be going to college. I'll get a chance . . .

TROY.   First you gonna get your butt down there to the A&P and get your job back.

CORY.   Mr. Stawicki done already hired somebody else 'cause I told him I was playing football.

TROY.   You a bigger fool than I thought . . . to let somebody take away your job so you can play some football. Where you gonna get your money to take out your girlfriend and whatnot? What kind of foolishness is that to let somebody take away your job?

CORY.   I'm still gonna be working weekends.

TROY.   Naw . . . naw. You getting your butt out of here and finding you another job.

CORY.   Come on, Pop! I got to practice. I can't work after school and play football too. The team needs me. That's what Coach Zellman say . . .

TROY.   I don't care what nobody else say. I'm the boss . . . you understand? I'm the boss around here. I do the only saying what counts.

CORY.   Come on, Pop!

TROY.   I asked you . . . did you understand?

CORY.   Yeah . . .

TROY.   What?!

CORY.   Yessir.

TROY.   You go on down there to that A&P and see if you can get your job back. If you can't do both . . . then you quit the football team. You've got to take the crookeds with the straights.

CORY.   Yessir. (*Pause.*) Can I ask you a question?

TROY.   What the hell you wanna ask me? Mr. Stawicki the one you got the questions for.

CORY.   How come you ain't never liked me?

TROY.   Liked you? Who the hell say I got to like you? What law is there say I got to like you? Wanna stand up in my face and ask a damn fool-ass question like that. Talking about liking somebody. Come here, boy, when I talk to you. (CORY *comes over to where* TROY *is working. He stands slouched over and* TROY *shoves him on his shoulder.*) Straighten up, goddammit! I asked you a question . . . what law is there say I got to like you?

CORY.   None.

TROY.   Well, all right then! Don't you eat every day? (*Pause.*) Answer me when I talk to you! Don't you eat every day?

CORY.   Yeah.

TROY.   Nigger, as long as you in my house, you put that sir on the end of it when you talk to me!

CORY.   Yes . . . sir.

TROY.   You eat every day.

CORY.   Yessir!

TROY.   Got a roof over your head.

CORY.   Yessir!

TROY.   Got clothes on your back.

CORY.   Yessir.

TROY.   Why you think that is?

CORY.   'Cause of you.

TROY.   Ah, hell I know it's 'cause of me . . . but why do you think that is?

CORY (*hesitant*).   'Cause you like me.

TROY.   Like you? I go out of here every morning . . . bust my butt . . . putting up with them crackers every day . . . 'cause I like you? You are the biggest fool I ever saw. (*Pause.*) It's my job. It's my responsibility! You understand that? A man got to take care of his family. You live in my house . . . sleep you behind on my bedclothes . . . fill you belly up with my food . . . 'cause you my son. You my flesh and blood. Not 'cause I like you! 'Cause it's my duty to take care of you. I owe a responsibility to you! Let's get this straight right here . . . before it go along any further . . . I ain't got to like you. Mr. Rand don't give me my money come payday 'cause he likes me. He give me 'cause he owe me. I done give you everything I had to give you. I gave you your life! Me and your mama worked that out between us. And liking your black ass wasn't part of the bargain. Don't you try and go through life worrying about if somebody like you or not. You best be making sure they doing right by you. You understand what I'm saying, boy?

CORY.   Yessir.

TROY.   Then get the hell out of my face, and get on down to that A&P. (ROSE *has been standing behind the screen door for much of the scene. She enters as* CORY *exits.*)

ROSE.   Why don't you let the boy go ahead and play football, Troy? Ain't no harm in that. He's just trying to be like you with the sports.

TROY.   I don't want him to be like me! I want him to move as far away from my life as he can get. You the only decent thing that ever happened to me. I wish him that. But I don't wish him a thing else from my life. I decided seventeen years ago that boy wasn't getting involved in no sports. Not after what they did to me in the sports.

ROSE.   Troy, why don't you admit you was too old to play in the major leagues? For once . . . why don't you admit that?

TROY.   What do you mean too old? Don't come telling me I was too old. I just wasn't the right color. Hell, I'm fifty-three years old and can do better than Selkirk's .269 right now!

ROSE.   How's was you gonna play ball when you were over forty? Sometimes I can't get no sense out of you.

TROY.   I got good sense, woman. I got sense enough not to let my boy get hurt over playing no sports. You been mothering that boy too much. Worried about if people like him.

ROSE.   Everything that boy do . . . he do for you. He wants you to say "Good job, son." That's all.

TROY.   Rose, I ain't got time for that. He's alive. He's healthy. He's got to make his own way. I made mine. Ain't nobody gonna hold his hand when he get out there in that world.

ROSE.   Times have changed from when you was young, Troy. People change. The world's changing around you and you can't even see it.

TROY (*slow, methodical*).   Woman . . . I do the best I can do. I come in here every Friday. I carry a sack of potatoes and a bucket of lard. You all line up at the door with your hands out. I give you the lint from my pockets. I give you my sweat and my blood. I ain't got no tears. I done spent them. We go upstairs in that room at night . . . and I fall down on you and try to blast a hole into forever. I get up Monday morning . . . find my lunch on the table. I go out. Make my way. Find my strength to carry me through to the next Friday. (*Pause.*) That's all I got, Rose. That's all I got to give. I can't give nothing else. (TROY *exits into the house. The lights go down to black.*)

SCENE 4

It is Friday. Two weeks later. CORY *starts out of the house with his football equipment. The phone rings.*

CORY (*calling*).   I got it! (*He answers the phone and stands in the screen door talking.*) Hello? Hey, Jesse. Naw . . . I was just getting ready to leave now.
ROSE (*calling*).   Cory!
CORY.   I told you, man, them spikes is all tore up. You can use them if you want, but they ain't no good. Earl got some spikes.
ROSE (*calling*).   Cory!
CORY (*calling to* ROSE).   Mam? I'm talking to Jesse. (*Into phone*) When she say that? (*Pause.*) Aw, you lying, man. I'm gonna tell her you said that.
ROSE (*calling*).   Cory, don't you go nowhere!
CORY.   I got to go to the game, Ma! (*Into the phone*) Yeah, hey, look, I'll talk to you later. Yeah, I'll meet you over Earl's house. Later. Bye, Ma. (CORY *exits the house and starts out the yard.*)
ROSE.   Cory, where you going off to? You got that stuff all pulled out and thrown all over your room.
CORY (*in the yard*).   I was looking for my spikes. Jesse wanted to borrow my spikes.
ROSE.   Get up there and get that cleaned up before your daddy get back in here.
CORY.   I got to go to the game! I'll clean it up when I get back. (CORY *exits.*)
ROSE.   That's all he need to do is see that room all messed up. (ROSE *exits into the house.* TROY *and* BONO *enter the yard.* TROY *is dressed in clothes other than his work clothes.*)
BONO.   He told him the same thing he told you. Take it to the union.
TROY.   Brownie ain't got that much sense. Man wasn't thinking about nothing. He wait until I confront them on it . . . then he wanna come crying seniority. (*Calls*) Hey, Rose!
BONO.   I wish I could have seen Mr. Rand's face when he told you.
TROY.   He couldn't get it out of his mouth! Liked to bit his tongue! When they called me down there to the Commissioner's office . . . he thought they was gonna fire me. Like everybody else.

BONO.   I didn't think they was gonna fire you. I thought they was gonna put you on the warning paper.

TROY.   Hey, Rose! (*To* BONO) Yeah, Mr. Rand like to bit his tongue. (TROY *breaks the seal on the bottle, takes a drink, and hands it to* BONO.)

BONO.   I see you run right down to Taylors' and told that Alberta gal.

TROY (*calling*).   Hey Rose! (*To* BONO) I told everybody. Hey, Rose! I went down there to cash my check.

ROSE (*entering from the house*).   Hush all that hollering, man! I know you out here. What they say down there at the Commissioner's office?

TROY.   You supposed to come when I call you, woman. Bono'll tell you that. (*To* BONO) Don't Lucille come when you call her?

ROSE.   Man, hush your mouth. I ain't no dog . . . talk about "come when you call me."

TROY (*puts his arm around* ROSE).   You hear this, Bono? I had me an old dog used to get uppity like that. You say, "C'mere, Blue!" . . . and he just lay there and look at you. End up getting a stick and chasing him away trying to make him come.

ROSE.   I ain't studying you and your dog. I remember you used to sing that old song.

TROY (*he sings*).   Hear it ring! Hear it ring! I had a dog his name was Blue.

ROSE.   Don't nobody wanna hear you sing that old song.

TROY (*sings*).   You know Blue was mighty true.

ROSE.   Used to have Cory running around here singing that song.

BONO.   Hell, I remember that song myself.

TROY (*sings*).   You know Blue was a good old dog.

      Blue treed a possum in a hollow log.

That was my daddy's song. My daddy made up that song.

ROSE.   I don't care who made it up. Don't nobody wanna hear you sing it.

TROY (*makes a song like calling a dog*).   Come here, woman.

ROSE.   You come in here carrying on, I reckon they ain't fired you. What they say down there at the Commissioner's office?

TROY.   Look here, Rose . . . Mr. Rand called me into his office today when I got back from talking to them people down there . . . it come from up top . . . he called me in and told me they was making me a driver.

ROSE.   Troy, you kidding!

TROY.   No I ain't. Ask Bono.

ROSE.   Well, that's great, Troy. Now you don't have to hassle them people no more. (LYONS *enters from the street.*)

TROY.   Aw hell, I wasn't looking to see you today. I thought you was in jail. Got it all over the front page of the *Courier* about them raiding Sefus's place . . . where you be hanging out with all them thugs.

LYONS.   Hey, Pop . . . that ain't got nothing to do with me. I don't go down there gambling. I go down there to sit in with the band. I ain't got nothing to do with the gambling part. They got some good music down there.

TROY.   They got some rogues . . . is what they got.

LYONS. How you been, Mr. Bono? Hi, Rose.

BONO. I see where you playing down at the Crawford Grill tonight.

ROSE. How come you ain't brought Bonnie like I told you? You should have brought Bonnie with you, she ain't been over in a month of Sundays.

LYONS. I was just in the neighborhood . . . thought I'd stop by.

TROY. Here he come . . .

BONO. Your daddy got a promotion on the rubbish. He's gonna be the first colored driver. Ain't got to do nothing but sit up there and read the paper like them white fellows.

LYONS. Hey, Pop . . . if you knew how to read you'd be all right.

BONO. Naw . . . naw . . . you mean if the nigger knew how to *drive* he'd be all right. Been fighting with them people about driving and ain't even got a license. Mr. Rand know you ain't got no driver's license?

TROY. Driving ain't nothing. All you do is point the truck where you want it to go. Driving ain't nothing.

BONO. Do Mr. Rand know you ain't got no driver's license? That's what I'm talking about. I ain't asked if driving was easy. I asked if Mr. Rand know you ain't got no driver's license.

TROY. He ain't got to know. The man ain't got to know my business. Time he find out, I have two or three driver's licenses.

LYONS (*going into his pocket*). Say, look here, Pop . . .

TROY. I knew it was coming. Didn't I tell you, Bono? I know what kind of "Look here, Pop" that was. The nigger fixing to ask me for some money. It's Friday night. It's my payday. All them rogues down there on the avenue . . . the ones that ain't in jail . . . and Lyons is hopping in his shoes to get down there with them.

LYONS. See, Pop . . . if you give somebody else a chance to talk sometimes, you'd see that I was fixing to pay you back your ten dollars like I told you. Here . . . I told you I'd pay you when Bonnie got paid.

TROY. Naw . . . you go ahead and keep that ten dollars. Put it in the bank. The next time you feel like you wanna come by here and ask me for something . . . you go on down there and get that.

LYONS. Here's your ten dollars, Pop. I told you I don't want you to give me nothing. I just wanted to borrow ten dollars.

TROY. Naw . . . you go on and keep that for the next time you want to ask me.

LYONS. Come on, Pop . . . here go your ten dollars.

ROSE. Why don't you go on and let the boy pay you back, Troy?

LYONS. Here you go, Rose. If you don't take it I'm gonna have to hear about it for the next six months. (*He hands her the money.*)

ROSE. You can hand yours over here too, Troy.

TROY. You see this, Bono. You see how they do me.

BONO. Yeah, Lucille do me the same way. (GABRIEL *is heard singing offstage. He enters.*)

GABRIEL. Better get ready for the Judgment! Better get ready for . . . Hey! . . . Hey! There's Troy's boy!

LYONS.   How are you doing, Uncle Gabe!

GABRIEL.   Lyons . . . The King of the Jungle! Rose . . . hey, Rose. Got a flower for you. (*He takes a rose from his pocket.*) Picked it myself. That's the same rose like you is!

ROSE.   That's right nice of you, Gabe.

LYONS.   What you been doing, Uncle Gabe?

GABRIEL.   Oh, I been chasing hellhounds and waiting on the time to tell St. Peter to open the gates.

LYONS.   You been chasing hellhounds, huh? Well . . . you doing the right thing, Uncle Gabe. Somebody got to chase them.

GABRIEL.   Oh, yeah . . . I know it. The devil's strong. The devil ain't no pushover. Hellhounds snipping at everybody's heels. But I got my trumpet waiting on the judgment time.

LYONS.   Waiting on the Battle of Armageddon, huh?

GABRIEL.   Ain't gonna be too much of a battle when God get to waving that Judgment sword. But the people's gonna have a hell of a time trying to get into heaven if them gates ain't open.

LYONS (*putting his arm around* GABRIEL).   You hear this, Pop. Uncle Gabe, you all right!

GABRIEL (*laughing with* LYONS).   Lyons! King of the Jungle.

ROSE.   You gonna stay for supper, Gabe? Want me to fix you a plate?

GABRIEL.   I'll take a sandwich, Rose. Don't want no plate. Just wanna eat with my hands. I'll take a sandwich.

ROSE.   How about you, Lyons? You staying? Got some short ribs cooking.

LYONS.   Naw, I won't eat nothing till after we finished playing. (*Pause.*) You ought to come down and listen to me play, Pop.

TROY.   I don't like that Chinese music. All that noise.

ROSE.   Go on in the house and wash up, Gabe . . . I'll fix you a sandwich.

GABRIEL (*to* LYONS, *as he exits*).   Troy's mad at me.

LYONS.   What you mad at Uncle Gabe for, Pop?

ROSE.   He thinks Troy's mad at him 'cause he moved over to Miss Pearl's.

TROY.   I ain't mad at the man. He can live where he want to live at.

LYONS.   What he move over there for? Miss Pearl don't like nobody.

ROSE.   She don't mind him none. She treats him real nice. She just don't allow all that singing.

TROY.   She don't mind that rent he be paying . . . that's what she don't mind.

ROSE.   Troy, I ain't going through that with you no more. He's over there 'cause he want to have his own place. He can come and go as he please.

TROY.   Hell, he could come and go as he please here. I wasn't stopping him. I ain't put no rules on him.

ROSE.   It ain't the same thing, Troy. And you know it. (GABRIEL *comes to the door.*) Now, that's the last I wanna hear about that. I don't wanna hear nothing else about Gabe and Miss Pearl. And next week . . .

GABRIEL.   I'm ready for my sandwich, Rose.

ROSE.   And next week . . . when that recruiter come from that school . . . I want you to sign that paper and go on and let Cory play football. Then that'll be the last I have to hear about that.

TROY (*to* ROSE *as she exits into the house*).   I ain't thinking about Cory nothing.

LYONS.   What . . . Cory got recruited? What school he going to?

TROY.   That boy walking around here smelling his piss . . . thinking he's grown. Thinking he's gonna do what he want, irrespective of what I say. Look here, Bono . . . I left the Commissioner's office and went down to the A&P . . . that boy ain't working down there. He lying to me. Telling me he got his job back . . . telling me he working weekends . . . telling me he working after school . . . Mr. Stawicki tell me he ain't working down there at all!

LYONS.   Cory just growing up. He's just busting at the seams trying to fill out your shoes.

TROY.   I don't care what he's doing. When he get to the point where he wanna disobey me . . . then it's time for him to move on. Bono'll tell you that. I bet he ain't never disobeyed his daddy without paying the consequences.

BONO.   I ain't never had a chance. My daddy came on through . . . but I ain't never knew him to see him . . . or what he had on his mind or where he went. Just moving on through. Searching out the New Land. That's what the old folks used to call it. See a fellow moving around from place to place . . . woman to woman . . . called it searching out the New Land. I can't say if he ever found it. I come along, didn't want no kids. Didn't know if I was gonna be in one place long enough to fix on them right as their daddy. I figured I was going searching too. As it turned out I been hooked up with Lucille near about as long as your daddy been with Rose. Going on sixteen years.

TROY.   Sometimes I wish I hadn't known my daddy. He ain't cared nothing about no kids. A kid to him wasn't nothing. All he wanted was for you to learn how to walk so he could start you to working. When it come time for eating . . . he ate first. If there was anything left over, that's what you got. Man would sit down and eat two chickens and give you the wing.

LYONS.   You ought to stop that, Pop. Everybody feed their kids. No matter how hard times is . . . everybody care about their kids. Make sure they have something to eat.

TROY.   The only thing my daddy cared about was getting them bales of cotton in to Mr. Lubin. That's the only thing that mattered to him. Sometimes I used to wonder why he was living. Wonder why the devil hadn't come and got him. "Get them bales of cotton in to Mr. Lubin" and find out he owe him money . . .

LYONS.   He should have just went on and left when he saw he couldn't get nowhere. That's what I would have done.

TROY.   How he gonna leave with eleven kids? And where he gonna go? He ain't knew how to do nothing but farm. No, he was trapped and I think he knew it. But I'll say this for him . . . he felt a responsibility toward us. Maybe he ain't treated us the way I felt he should have . . . but without that responsibility he could have walked off and left us . . . made his own way.

BONO.   A lot of them did. Back in those days what you talking about . . . they walk out their front door and just take on down one road or another and keep on walking.

LYONS.   There you go! That's what I'm talking about.

BONO.   Just keep on walking till you come to something else. Ain't you never heard of nobody having the walking blues? Well, that's what you call it when you just take off like that.

TROY.   My daddy ain't had them walking blues! What you talking about? He stayed right there with his family. But he was just as evil as he could be. My mama couldn't stand him. Couldn't stand that evilness. She run off when I was about eight. She sneaked off one night after he had gone to sleep. Told me she was coming back for me. I ain't never seen her no more. All his women run off and left him. He wasn't good for nobody.

When my turn come to head out, I was fourteen and got to sniffing around Joe Canewell's daughter. Had us an old mule we called Greyboy. My daddy sent me out to do some plowing and I tied up Greyboy and went to fooling around with Joe Canewell's daughter. We done found us a nice little spot, got real cozy with each other. She about thirteen and we done figured we was grown anyway . . . so we down there enjoying ourselves . . . ain't thinking about nothing. We didn't know Greyboy had got loose and wandered back to the house and my daddy was looking for me. We down there by the creek enjoying ourselves when my daddy come up on us. Surprised us. He had them leather straps off the mule and commenced to whupping me like there was no tomorrow. I jumped up, mad and embarrassed. I was scared of my daddy. When he commenced to whupping on me . . . quite naturally I run to get out of the way. (*Pause.*) Now I thought he was mad 'cause I ain't done my work. But I see where he was chasing me off so he could have the gal for himself. When I see what the matter of it was, I lost all fear of my daddy. Right there is where I become a man . . . at fourteen years of age. (*Pause.*) Now it was my turn to run him off. I picked up them same reins that he had used on me. I picked up them reins and commenced to whupping on him. The gal jumped up and run off . . . and when my daddy turned to face me, I could see why the devil had never come to get him . . . 'cause he was the devil himself. I don't know what happened. When I woke up, I was laying right there by the creek, and Blue . . . this old dog we had . . . was licking my face. I thought I was blind. I couldn't see nothing. Both my eyes were swollen shut. I laid there and cried. I didn't know what I was gonna do. The only thing I knew was the time had come for me to leave my daddy's house. And right there the world suddenly got big. And it was a long time before I could cut it down to where I could handle it.

Part of that cutting down was when I got to the place where I could feel him kicking in my blood and knew that the only thing that separated us was the matter of a few years. (GABRIEL *enters from the house with a sandwich.*)

LYONS. What you got there, Uncle Gabe?

GABRIEL. Got me a ham sandwich. Rose gave me a ham sandwich.

TROY. I don't know what happened to him. I done lost touch with everybody except Gabriel. But I hope he's dead. I hope he found some peace.

LYONS. That's a heavy story, Pop. I didn't know you left home when you was fourteen.

TROY. I didn't know nothing. The only part of the world I knew was the forty-two acres of Mr. Lubin's land. That's all I knew about life.

LYONS. Fourteen's kinda young to be out on your own. (*Phone rings.*) I don't even think I was ready to be out on my own at fourteen. I don't know what I would have done.

TROY. I got up from the creek and walked on down to Mobile. I was through with farming. Figured I could do better in the city. So I walked the two hundred miles to Mobile.

LYONS. Wait a minute . . . you ain't walked no two hundred miles, Pop. Ain't nobody gonna walk no two hundred miles. You talking about some walking there.

BONO. That's the only way you got anywhere back in them days.

LYONS. Shhh. Damn if I wouldn't have hitched a ride with somebody!

TROY. Who you gonna hitch it with? They ain't had no cars and things like they got now. We talking about 1918.

ROSE (*entering*). What you all out here getting into?

TROY (*to* ROSE). I'm telling Lyons how good he got it. He don't know nothing about this I'm talking.

ROSE. Lyons, that was Bonnie on the phone. She say you supposed to pick her up.

LYONS. Yeah, okay, Rose.

TROY. I walked on down to Mobile and hitched up with some of them fellows that was heading this way. Got up here and found out . . . not only couldn't you get a job . . . you couldn't find no place to live. I thought I was in freedom. Shhh. Colored folks living down there on the riverbanks in whatever kind of shelter they could find for themselves. Right down there under the Brady Street Bridge. Living in shacks made of sticks and tarpaper. Messed around there and went from bad to worse. Start stealing. First it was food. Then I figured, hell, if I steal money I can buy me some food. Buy me some shoes too! One thing led to another. Met your mama. I was young and anxious to be a man. Met your mama and had you. What I do that for? Now I got to worry about feeding you and her. Got to steal three times as much. Went out one day looking for somebody to rob . . . that's what I was, a robber. I'll tell you the truth. I'm ashamed of it today. But it's the truth. Went to rob this fellow . . . pulled out my knife . . . and he pulled out a gun. Shot me in the chest. I felt just like somebody had taken a hot branding iron and laid it on me. When he shot me I jumped at him with my knife. They told me I killed him and they put me in the penitentiary and locked me up for fifteen years. That's where I met Bono. That's where I learned how to play baseball. Got out that place and your mama had taken you and went on to make life without me. Fifteen years was a long time for her to wait. But that fifteen years cured me of that robbing stuff. Rose'll tell you. She asked me when I met her if I had gotten all that foolishness out of my system. And I told her, "Baby, it's you and baseball all what count with me." You hear me, Bono? I mean it too. She say, "Which one comes first?" I told her, "Baby, ain't no doubt it's baseball . . . but you stick and get old with me and we'll both outlive this baseball." Am I right, Rose? And it's true.

ROSE.   Man, hush your mouth. You ain't said no such thing. Talking about, "Baby, you know you'll always be number one with me." That's what you was talking.

TROY.   You hear that, Bono. That's why I love her.

BONO.   Rose'll keep you straight. You get off the track, she'll straighten you up.

ROSE.   Lyons, you better get on up and get Bonnie. She waiting on you.

LYONS (*gets up to go*).   Hey, Pop, why don't you come on down to the Grill and hear me play?

TROY.   I ain't going down there. I'm too old to be sitting around in them clubs.

BONO.   You got to be good to play down at the Grill.

LYONS.   Come on, Pop . . .

TROY.   I got to get up in the morning.

LYONS.   You ain't got to stay long.

TROY.   Naw, I'm gonna get my supper and go on to bed.

LYONS.   Well, I got to go. I'll see you again.

TROY.   Don't you come around my house on my payday.

ROSE.   Pick up the phone and let somebody know you coming. And bring Bonnie with you. You know I'm always glad to see her.

LYONS.   Yeah, I'll do that, Rose. You take care now. See you, Pop. See you, Mr. Bono. See you, Uncle Gabe.

GABRIEL.   Lyons! King of the Jungle! (LYONS *exits.*)

TROY.   Is supper ready, woman? Me and you got some business to take care of. I'm gonna tear it up too.

ROSE.   Troy, I done told you now!

TROY (*puts his arm around* BONO).   Aw hell, woman . . . this is Bono. Bono like family. I done known this nigger since . . . how long I done know you?

BONO.   It's been a long time.

TROY.   I done know this nigger since Skippy was a pup. Me and him done been through some times.

BONO.   You sure right about that.

TROY.   Hell, I done know him longer than I known you. And we still standing shoulder to shoulder. Hey, look here, Bono . . . a man can't ask for no more than that. (*Drinks to him.*) I love you, nigger.

BONO.   Hell, I love you too . . . I got to get home see my woman. You got yours in hand. I got to go get mine. (BONO *starts to exit as* CORY *enters the yard, dressed in his football uniform. He gives* TROY *a hard, uncompromising look.*)

CORY.   What you do that for, Pop? (*He throws his helmet down in the direction of* TROY.)

ROSE.   What's the matter? Cory . . . what's the matter?

CORY.   Papa done went up to the school and told Coach Zellman I can't play football no more. Wouldn't even let me play the game. Told him to tell the recruiter not to come.

ROSE.   Troy . . .

TROY.   What you Troying me for. Yeah, I did it. And the boy know why I did it.

CORY.   Why you wanna do that to me? That was the one chance I had.

ROSE.   Ain't nothing wrong with Cory playing football, Troy.

TROY.   The boy lied to me. I told the nigger if he wanna play football . . . to keep up his chores and hold down that job at the A&P. That was the conditions. Stopped down there to see Mr. Stawicki . . .

CORY.   I can't work after school during the football season, Pop! I tried to tell you that Mr. Stawicki's holding my job for me. You don't never want to listen to nobody. And then you wanna go and do this to me!

TROY.   I ain't done nothing to you. You done it to yourself.

CORY.   Just 'cause you didn't have a chance! You just scared I'm gonna be better than you, that's all.

TROY.   Come here.

ROSE.   Troy . . . (CORY *reluctantly crosses over to* TROY.)

TROY.   All right! See. You done made a mistake.

CORY.   I didn't even do nothing!

TROY.   I'm gonna tell you what your mistake was. See . . . you swung at the ball and didn't hit it. That's strike one. See, you in the batter's box now. You swung and you missed. That's strike one. Don't you strike out! (*Lights fade to black.*)

ACT 2

SCENE 1

The following morning. CORY *is at the tree hitting the ball with the bat. He tries to mimic* TROY, *but his swing is awkward, less sure.* ROSE *enters from the house.*

ROSE.   Cory, I want you to help me with this cupboard.

CORY.   I ain't quitting the team. I don't care what Poppa say.

ROSE.   I'll talk to him when he gets back. He had to go see about your Uncle Gabe. The police done arrested him. Say he was disturbing the peace. He'll be back directly. Come on in here and help me clean out the top of this cupboard. (CORY *exits into the house.* ROSE *sees* TROY *and* BONO *coming down the alley.*) Troy . . . what they say down there?

TROY.   Ain't said nothing. I give them fifty dollars and they let him go. I'll talk to you about it. Where's Cory?

ROSE.   He's in there helping me clean out these cupboards.

TROY.   Tell him to get his butt out here. (TROY *and* BONO *go over to the pile of wood.* BONO *picks up the saw and begins sawing. To* BONO) All they want is the money. That makes six or seven times I done went down there and got him. See me coming they stick out their *hands.*

BONO.   Yeah. I know what you mean. That's all they care about . . . that money. They don't care about what's right. (*Pause.*) Nigger, why you got to go and get some hard wood? You ain't doing nothing but building a little old fence. Get you some soft pine wood. That's all you need.

TROY.   I know what I'm doing. This is outside wood. You put pine wood inside the house. Pine wood is inside wood. This here is outside wood. Now you tell me where the fence is gonna be?

BONO.   You don't need this wood. You can put it up with pine wood and it'll stand as long as you gonna be here looking at it.

TROY.   How you know how long I'm gonna be here, nigger? Hell, I might just live forever. Live longer than old man Horsely.

BONO.   That's what Magee used to say.

TROY.   Magee's a damn fool. Now you tell me who you ever heard of gonna pull their own teeth with a pair of rusty pliers.

BONO.   The old folks . . . my granddaddy used to pull his teeth with pliers. They ain't had no dentists for the colored folks back then.

TROY.   Get clean pliers! You understand? Clean pliers! Sterilize them! Besides we ain't living back then. All Magee had to do was walk over to Doc Goldblum's.

BONO.   I see where you and that Tallahassee gal . . . that Alberta . . . I see where you all done got tight.

TROY.   What you mean "got tight"?

BONO.   I see where you be laughing and joking with her all the time.

TROY.   I laughs and jokes with all of them, Bono. You know me.

BONO.   That ain't the kind of laughing and joking I'm talking about. (CORY *enters from the house.*)

CORY.   How you doing, Mr. Bono?

TROY.   Cory? Get that saw from Bono and cut some wood. He talking about the wood's too hard to cut. Stand back there, Jim, and let that young boy show you how it's done.

BONO.   He's sure welcome to it. (CORY *takes the saw and begins to cut the wood.*) Whew-e-e! Look at that. Big old strong boy. Look like Joe Louis. Hell, must be getting old the way I'm watching that boy whip through that wood.

CORY.   I don't see why Mama want a fence around the yard noways.

TROY.   Damn if I know either. What the hell she keeping out with it? She ain't got nothing nobody want.

BONO.   Some people build fences to keep people out . . . and other people build fences to keep people in. Rose wants to hold on to you all. She loves you.

TROY.   Hell, nigger, I don't need nobody to tell me my wife loves me. Cory . . . go on in the house and see if you can find that other saw.

CORY.   Where's it at?

TROY.   I said find it! Look for it till you find it! (CORY *exits into the house.*) What's that supposed to mean? Wanna keep us in?

BONO.   Troy . . . I done known you seem like damn near my whole life. You and Rose both. I done know both of you all for a long time. I remember when you met Rose. When you was hitting them baseball out the park. A lot of them old gals was after you then. You had the pick of the litter. When you picked Rose, I was happy for you. That was the first time I knew you had any sense. I said . . . My man Troy knows what he's doing . . . I'm gonna follow this nigger . . . he might take me somewhere. I been following you too. I done learned a whole heap of things about life watching you. I done learned how to tell where the shit lies. How to tell it from the alfalfa. You done learned me a lot of things. You showed me how to not make the same mistakes . . . to take life as it comes along and keep putting one foot in front of the other. (*Pause.*) Rose a good woman, Troy.

TROY.   Hell, nigger, I know she a good woman. I been married to her for eighteen years. What you got on your mind, Bono?

BONO.   I just say she a good woman. Just like I say anything. I ain't got to have nothing on my mind.

TROY.   You just gonna say she a good woman and leave it hanging out there like that? Why you telling me she a good woman?

BONO.   She loves you, Troy. Rose loves you.

TROY.   You saying I don't measure up. That's what you trying to say. I don't measure up 'cause I'm seeing this other gal. I know what you trying to say.

BONO.   I know what Rose means to you, Troy. I'm just trying to say I don't want to see you mess up.

TROY.   Yeah, I appreciate that, Bono. If you was messing around on Lucille I'd be telling you the same thing.

BONO.   Well, that's all I got to say. I just say that because I love you both.

TROY.   Hell, you know me . . . I wasn't out there looking for nothing. You can't find a better woman than Rose. I know that. But seems like this woman just stuck onto me where I can't shake her loose. I done wrestled with it, tried to throw her off me . . . but she just stuck on tighter. Now she's stuck on for good.

BONO.   You's in control . . . that's what you tell me all the time. You responsible for what you do.

TROY.   I ain't ducking the responsibility of it. As long as it sets right in my heart . . . then I'm okay. 'Cause that's all I listen to. It'll tell me right from wrong every time. And I ain't talking about doing Rose no bad turn. I love Rose. She done carried me a long ways and I love and respect her for that.

BONO.   I know you do. That's why I don't want to see you hurt her. But what you gonna do when she find out? What you got then? If you try and juggle both of them . . . sooner or later you gonna drop one of them. That's common sense.

TROY.   Yeah, I hear what you saying, Bono. I been trying to figure a way to work it out.

BONO.   Work it out right, Troy. I don't want to be getting all up between you and Rose's business . . . but work it so it come out right.

TROY.   Ah hell, I get all up between you and Lucille's business. When you gonna get that woman that refrigerator she been wanting? Don't tell me you ain't got no money now. I know who your banker is. Mellon don't need that money bad as Lucille want that refrigerator. I'll tell you that.

BONO.   Tell you what I'll do . . . when you finish building this fence for Rose . . . I'll buy Lucille that refrigerator.

TROY.   You done stuck your foot in your mouth now! (*Grabs up a board and begins to saw.* BONO *starts to walk out of the yard.*) Hey, nigger . . . where you going?

BONO.   I'm going home. I know you don't expect me to help you now. I'm protecting my money. I wanna see you put that fence up by yourself. That's what I want to see. You'll be here another six months without me.

TROY.   Nigger, you ain't right.

BONO.   When it comes to my money . . . I'm right as fireworks on the Fourth of July.

TROY.   All right, we gonna see now. You better get out your bankbook. (BONO *exits, and* TROY *continues to work.* ROSE *enters from the house.*)

ROSE.   What they say down there? What's happening with Gabe?

TROY.   I went down there and got him out. Cost me fifty dollars. Say he was disturbing the peace. Judge set up a hearing for him in three weeks. Say to show cause why he shouldn't be recommitted.

ROSE.   What was he doing that cause them to arrest him?

TROY.   Some kids was teasing him and he run them off home. Say he was howling and carrying on. Some folks seen him and called the police. That's all it was.

ROSE.   Well, what's you say? What'd you tell the judge?

TROY.   Told him I'd look after him. It didn't make no sense to recommit the man. He stuck out his big greasy palm and told me to give him fifty dollars and take him on home.

ROSE.   Where's he at now? Where'd he go off to?

TROY.   He's gone about his business. He don't need nobody to hold his hand.

ROSE.   Well, I don't know. Seem like that would be the best place for him if they did put him into the hospital. I know what you're gonna say. But that's what I think would be best.

TROY.   The man done had his life ruined fighting for what? And they wanna take and lock him up. Let him be free. He don't bother nobody.

ROSE.   Well, everybody got their own way of looking at it I guess. Come on and get your lunch. I got a bowl of lima beans and some cornbread in the oven. Come and get something to eat. Ain't no sense you fretting over Gabe. (*Turns to go into the house.*)

TROY.   Rose . . . got something to tell you.

ROSE.   Well, come on . . . wait till I get this food on the table.

TROY.   Rose! (*She stops and turns around.*) I don't know how to say this. (*Pause.*) I can't explain it none. It just sort of grows on you till it gets out of hand. It starts out like a little bush . . . and the next thing you know it's a whole forest.

ROSE.   Troy . . . what is you talking about?

TROY.   I'm talking, woman, let me talk. I'm trying to find a way to tell you . . . I'm gonna be a daddy. I'm gonna be somebody's daddy.

ROSE.   Troy . . . you're not telling me this? You're gonna be . . . what?

TROY.   Rose . . . now . . . see . . .

ROSE.   You telling me you gonna be somebody's daddy? You telling your *wife* this? (GABRIEL *enters from the street. He carries a rose in his hand.*)

GABRIEL.   Hey, Troy! Hey, Rose!

ROSE.   I have to wait eighteen years to hear something like this.

GABRIEL.   Hey, Rose . . . I got a flower for you. (*He hands it to her.*) That's a rose. Same rose like you is.

ROSE.   Thanks, Gabe.

GABRIEL.   Troy, you ain't mad at me is you? Them bad mens come and put me away. You ain't mad at me is you?

TROY.   Naw, Gabe, I ain't mad at you.

ROSE.   Eighteen years and you wanna come with this.

GABRIEL (*takes a quarter out of his pocket*).   See what I got? Got a brand new quarter.

TROY.   Rose . . . it's just . . .

ROSE.   Ain't nothing you can say, Troy. Ain't no way of explaining that.

GABRIEL.   Fellow that give me this quarter had a whole mess of them. I'm gonna keep this quarter till it stop shining.

ROSE.   Gabe, go on in the house there. I got some watermelon in the Frigidaire. Go on and get you a piece.

GABRIEL.   Say, Rose . . . you know I was chasing hellhounds and them bad mens come and get me and take me away. Troy helped me. He come down there and told them they better let me go before he beat them up. Yeah, he did!

ROSE.   You go on and get you a piece of watermelon, Gabe. Them bad mens is gone now.

GABRIEL.   Okay, Rose . . . gonna get me some watermelon. The kind with the stripes on it. (GABRIEL *exits into the house.*)

ROSE.   Why, Troy? Why? After all these years to come dragging this in to me now. It don't make no sense at your age. I could have expected this ten or fifteen years ago, but not now.

TROY.   Age ain't got nothing to do with it, Rose.

ROSE.   I done tried to be everything a wife should be. Everything a wife could be. Been married eighteen years and I got to live to see the day you tell me you been seeing another woman and done fathered a child by her. And you know I ain't never wanted no half nothing in my family. My whole family is half. Everybody got different fathers and mothers . . . my two sisters and my brother. Can't hardly tell who's who. Can't never sit down and talk about Papa and Mama. It's your papa and your mama and my papa and my mama . . .

TROY.   Rose . . . stop it now.

ROSE.   I ain't never wanted that for none of my children. And now you wanna drag your behind in here and tell me something like this.

TROY.   You ought to know. It's time for you to know.

ROSE.   Well, I don't want to know, goddamn it!

TROY.   I can't just make it go away. It's done now. I can't wish the circumstance of the thing away.

ROSE.   And you don't want to either. Maybe you want to wish me and my boy away. Maybe that's what you want? Well, you can't wish us away. I've got eighteen years of my life invested in you. You ought to have stayed upstairs in my bed where you belong.

TROY.   Rose . . . now listen to me . . . we can get a handle on this thing. We can talk this out . . . come to an understanding.

ROSE.   All of a sudden it's "we." Where was "we" at when you was down there rolling around with some godforsaken woman? "We" should have come to an understanding before you started making a damn fool of yourself. You're a day late and a dollar short when it comes to an understanding with me.

TROY.   It's just . . . She gives me a different idea . . . a different understanding about myself. I can step out of this house and get away from the pressures and problems . . . be a different man. I ain't got to wonder how I'm gonna pay the bills or get the roof fixed. I can just be a part of myself that I ain't never been.

ROSE.   What I want to know . . . is do you plan to continue seeing her. That's all you can say to me.

TROY.   I can sit up in her house and laugh. Do you understand what I'm saying? I can laugh out loud . . . and it feels good. It reaches all the way down to the bottom of my shoes. (*Pause.*) Rose, I can't give that up.

ROSE.   Maybe you ought to go on and stay down there with her . . . if she's a better woman than me.

TROY.   It ain't about nobody being a better woman or nothing. Rose, you ain't the blame. A man couldn't ask for no woman to be a better wife than you've been. I'm responsible for it. I done locked myself into a pattern trying to take care of you all that I forgot about myself.

ROSE.   What the hell was I there for? That was my job, not somebody else's.

TROY.   Rose, I done tried all my life to live decent . . . to live a clean . . . hard . . . useful life. I tried to be a good husband to you. In every way I knew how. Maybe I come into the world backwards, I don't know. But . . . you born with two strikes on you before you come to the plate. You got to guard it closely . . . always looking for the curve ball on the inside corner. You can't afford to let none get past you. You can't afford a call strike. If you going down . . . you going down swinging. Everything lined up against you. What you gonna do? I fooled them, Rose. I bunted. When I found you and Cory and a halfway decent job . . . I was safe. Couldn't nothing touch me. I wasn't gonna strike out no more. I wasn't going back to the penitentiary. I wasn't gonna lay in the streets with a bottle of wine. I was safe. I had me a family. A job. I wasn't gonna get that last strike. I was on first looking for one of them boys to knock me in. To get me home.

ROSE.   You should have stayed in my bed, Troy.

TROY.   Then when I saw that gal . . . she firmed up my backbone. And I got to thinking that if I tried . . . I just might be able to steal second. Do you understand after eighteen years I wanted to steal second.

ROSE.   You should have held me tight. You should have grabbed me and held on.

TROY.   I stood on first base for eighteen years and I thought . . . well, goddamn it . . . go on for it!

ROSE.   We're not talking about baseball! We're talking about you going off to lay in bed with another woman . . . and then bring it home to me. That's what we're talking about. We ain't talking about no baseball.

TROY.   Rose, you're not listening to me. I'm trying the best I can to explain it to you. It's not easy for me to admit that I been standing in the same place for eighteen years.

ROSE.   I been standing with you! I been right here with you, Troy. I got a life too. I gave eighteen years of my life to stand in the same spot with you. Don't you think I ever wanted other things? Don't you think I had dreams and hopes? What about my life? What about me. Don't you think it ever crossed my mind to want to know other men? That I wanted to lay up somewhere and forget about my responsibilities? That I wanted someone to make me laugh so I could feel good? You not the only one who's got wants and needs. But I held on to you, Troy. I took all my feelings, my wants and needs, my dreams . . . and buried them inside you. I planted a seed and watched and prayed over it. I planted myself inside you and waited to bloom. And it didn't take me no eighteen years to find out the soil was hard and rocky and it wasn't never gonna bloom.

But I held on to you, Troy. I held you tighter. You was my husband. I owed you everything I had. Every part of me I could find to give you. And upstairs in that room . . . with the darkness falling in on me . . . I gave everything I had to try and erase the doubt that you wasn't the finest man in the world. And wherever you was going . . . I wanted to be there with you. 'Cause you was my husband. 'Cause that's the only way I was gonna survive as your wife. You always talking about what you give . . . and what you don't have to give. But you take too. You take . . . and don't even know nobody's giving! (*Turns to exit into the house;* TROY *grabs her arm.*)

TROY.   You say I take and don't give!

ROSE.   Troy! You're hurting me!

TROY.   You say I take and don't give!

ROSE.   Troy . . . you're hurting my arm! Let go!

TROY.   I done give you everything I got. Don't you tell that lie on me.

ROSE.   Troy!

TROY.   Don't you tell that lie on me! (CORY *enters from the house.*)

CORY.   Mama!

ROSE.   Troy. You're hurting me.

TROY.   Don't you tell me about my taking and giving. (CORY *comes up behind* TROY *and grabs him.* TROY, *surprised, is thrown off balance just as* CORY *throws a glancing blow that catches him on the chest and knocks him down.* TROY *is stunned, as is* CORY.)

ROSE.   Troy. Troy. No! (TROY *gets to his feet and starts at* CORY.) Troy . . . no. Please! Troy! (ROSE *pulls on* TROY *to hold him back.* TROY *stops himself.*)

TROY (*to* CORY).   All right. That's strike two. You stay away from around me, boy. Don't you strike out. You living with a full count. Don't you strike out. (TROY *exits out the yard as the lights go down.*)

SCENE 2

It is six months later, early afternoon. TROY *enters from the house and starts to exit the yard.* ROSE *enters from the house.*

ROSE.   Troy, I want to talk to you.

TROY.   All of a sudden, after all this time, you want to talk to me, huh? You ain't wanted to talk to me for months. You ain't wanted to talk to me last night. You ain't wanted no part of me then. What you wanna talk to me about now?

ROSE.   Tomorrow's Friday.

TROY.   I know what day tomorrow is. You think I don't know tomorrow's Friday? My whole life I ain't done nothing but look to see Friday coming and you got to tell me it's Friday.

ROSE.   I want to know if you're coming home.

TROY.   I always come home, Rose. You know that. There ain't never been a night I ain't come home.

ROSE.   That ain't what I mean . . . and you know it. I want to know if you're coming straight home after work.

TROY.   I figure I'd cash my check . . . hang out at Taylors' with the boys . . . maybe play a game of checkers . . .

ROSE.   Troy, I can't live like this. I won't live like this. You livin' on borrowed time with me. It's been going on six months now you ain't been coming home.

TROY.   I be here every night. Every night of the year. That's 365 days.

ROSE.   I want you to come home tomorrow after work.

TROY.   Rose . . . I don't mess up my pay. You know that now. I take my pay and I give it to you. I don't have no money but what you give me back. I just want to have a little time to myself . . . a little time to enjoy life.

ROSE.   What about me? When's my time to enjoy life?

TROY.   I don't know what to tell you, Rose. I'm doing the best I can.

ROSE.   You ain't been home from work but time enough to change your clothes and run out . . . and you wanna call that the best you can do?

TROY.   I'm going over to the hospital to see Alberta. She went into the hospital this afternoon. Look like she might have the baby early. I won't be gone long.

ROSE.   Well, you ought to know. They went over to Miss Pearl's and got Gabe today. She said you told them to go ahead and lock him up.

TROY.   I ain't said no such thing. Whoever told you that is telling a lie. Pearl ain't doing nothing but telling a big fat lie.

ROSE.   She ain't had to tell me. I read it on the papers.

TROY.   I ain't told them nothing of the kind.

ROSE.   I saw it right there on the papers.

TROY.   What it say, huh?

ROSE.   It said you told them to take him.

TROY.   Then they screwed that up, just the way they screw up everything. I ain't worried about what they got on the paper.

ROSE.   Say the government send part of his check to the hospital and the other part to you.

TROY.   I ain't got nothing to do with that if that's the way it works. I ain't made up the rules about how it work.

ROSE.   You did Gabe just like you did Cory. You wouldn't sign the paper for Cory . . . but you signed for Gabe. You signed that paper. (*The telephone is heard ringing inside the house.*)

TROY.   I told you I ain't signed nothing, woman! The only thing I signed was the release form. Hell, I can't read, I don't know what they had on that paper! I ain't signed nothing about sending Gabe away.

ROSE.   I said send him to the hospital . . . you said let him be free . . . now you done went down there and signed him to the hospital for half his money. You went back on yourself, Troy. You gonna have to answer for that.

TROY.   See now . . . you been over there talking to Miss Pearl. She done got mad 'cause she ain't getting Gabe's rent money. That's all it is. She's liable to say anything.

ROSE.   Troy, I seen where you signed the paper.

TROY.   You ain't seen nothing I signed. What she doing got papers on my brother anyway? Miss Pearl telling a big fat lie. And I'm gonna tell her about it too! You ain't seen nothing I signed. Say . . . you ain't seen nothing I signed. (ROSE *exits into the house to answer the telephone. Presently she returns.*)

ROSE.   Troy . . . that was the hospital. Alberta had the baby.

TROY.   What she have? What is it?

ROSE.   It's a girl.

TROY.   I better get on down to the hospital to see her.

ROSE.   Troy . . .

TROY.   Rose . . . I got to go see her now. That's only right . . . what's the matter . . . the baby's all right, ain't it?

ROSE.   Alberta died having the baby.

TROY.   Died . . . you say she's dead? Alberta's dead?

ROSE.   They said they done all they could. They couldn't do nothing for her.

TROY.   The baby? How's the baby?

ROSE.   They say it's healthy. I wonder who's gonna bury her.

TROY.   She had family, Rose. She wasn't living in the world by herself.

ROSE.   I know she wasn't living in the world by herself.

TROY.   Next thing you gonna want to know if she had any insurance.

ROSE.   Troy, you ain't got to talk like that.

TROY.   That's the first thing that jumped out your mouth. "Who's gonna bury her?" Like I'm fixing to take on that task for myself.

ROSE.   I am your wife. Don't push me away.

TROY.   I ain't pushing nobody away. Just give me some space. That's all. Just give me some room to breathe. (ROSE *exits into the house.* TROY *walks about the yard. With a quiet rage that threatens to consume him.*) All right . . . Mr. Death. See now . . . I'm gonna tell you what I'm gonna do. I'm gonna take and build me a fence around this yard. See? I'm gonna build me a fence around what belongs to me. And then I want you to stay on the other side. See? You stay over there until you're ready for me. Then you come on. Bring your army. Bring your sickle. Bring your wrestling clothes. I ain't gonna fall down on my vigilance this time. You ain't gonna sneak up on me no more. When you ready for me . . . when the top of your list say Troy Maxson . . . that's when you come around here. You come up and knock on the front door. Ain't nobody else got nothing to do with this. This is between you and me. Man to man. You stay on the other side of that fence until you ready for me. Then you come up and knock on the front door. Anytime you want. I'll be ready for you. (*The lights go down to black.*)

SCENE 3

The lights come up on the porch. It is late evening three days later. ROSE *sits listening to the ball game waiting for* TROY. *The final out of the game is made and* ROSE *switches off the radio.* TROY *enters the yard carrying an infant wrapped in blankets. He stands back from the house and calls.*

ROSE *enters and stands on the porch. There is a long, awkward silence, the weight of which grows heavier with each passing second.*

TROY.   Rose . . . I'm standing here with my daughter in my arms. She ain't but a wee bittie little old thing. She don't know nothing about grownups' business. She innocent . . . and she ain't got no mama.

ROSE.   What you telling me for, Troy? (*She turns and exits into the house.*)

TROY.   Well . . . I guess we'll just sit out here on the porch. (*He sits down on the porch. There is an awkward indelicateness about the way he handles the baby. His largeness engulfs and seems to swallow it. He speaks loud enough for* ROSE *to hear*) A man's got to do what's right for him. I ain't sorry for nothing I done. It felt right in my heart. (*To the baby*) What you smiling at? Your daddy's a big man. Got these great big old hands. But sometimes he's scared. And right now your daddy's scared 'cause we sitting out here and ain't got no home. Oh, I been homeless before. I ain't had no little baby with me. But I been homeless. You just be out on the road by your lonesome and you see one of them trains coming and you just kinda go like this . . . (*He sings as a lullaby.*)

Please, Mr. Engineer let a man ride the line

Please, Mr. Engineer let a man ride the line

I ain't got no ticket please let me ride the blinds

(ROSE *enters from the house.* TROY, *hearing her steps behind him, stands and faces her.*) She's my daughter, Rose. My own flesh and blood. I can't deny her no more than I can deny them boys. (*Pause.*) You and them boys is my family. You and them and this child is all I got in the world. So I guess what I'm saying is . . . I'd appreciate it if you'd help me take care of her.

ROSE.   Okay, Troy . . . you're right. I'll take care of your baby for you . . . 'cause . . . like you say . . . she's innocent . . . and you can't visit the sins of the father upon the child. A motherless child has got a hard time. (*She takes the baby from him.*) From right now . . . this child got a mother. But you a womanless man. (ROSE *turns and exits into the house with the baby. Lights go down to black.*)

SCENE 4

It is two months later. LYONS *enters from the street. He knocks on the door and calls.*

LYONS.   Hey, Rose! (*Pause*) Rose!

ROSE (*from inside the house*).   Stop that yelling. You gonna wake up Raynell. I just got her to sleep.

LYONS.   I just stopped by to pay Papa this twenty dollars I owe him. Where's Papa at?

ROSE.   He should be here in a minute. I'm getting ready to go down to the church. Sit down and wait on him.

LYONS.   I got to go pick up Bonnie over her mother's house.

ROSE.   Well, sit it down there on the table. He'll get it.

LYONS (*enters the house and sets the money on the table*).   Tell Papa I said thanks. I'll see you again.

ROSE.   All right, Lyons. We'll see you. (LYONS *starts to exit as* CORY *enters.*)

CORY.   Hey, Lyons.

LYONS.   What's happening, Cory? Say man, I'm sorry I missed your graduation. You know I had a gig and couldn't get away. Otherwise, I would have been there, man. So what you doing?

CORY.   I'm trying to find a job.

LYONS.   Yeah I know how that go, man. It's rough out here. Jobs are scarce.

CORY.   Yeah, I know.

LYONS.   Look here, I got to run. Talk to Papa . . . he know some people. He'll be able to help you get a job. Talk to him . . . see what he say.

CORY.   Yeah . . . all right, Lyons.

LYONS.   You take care. I'll talk to you soon. We'll find some time to talk. (LYONS *exits the yard.* CORY *wanders over to the tree, picks up the bat, and assumes a batting stance. He studies an imaginary pitcher and swings. Dissatisfied with the result, he tries again.* TROY *enters. They eye each other for a beat.* CORY *puts the bat down and exits the yard.* TROY *starts into the house as* ROSE *exits with* RAYNELL. *She is carrying a cake.*)

TROY.   I'm coming in and everybody's going out.

ROSE.   I'm taking this cake down to the church for the bake sale. Lyons was by to see you. He stopped by to pay you your twenty dollars. It's laying in there on the table.

TROY (*going into his pocket*).   Well . . . here go this money.

ROSE.   Put it in there on the table, Troy. I'll get it.

TROY.   What time you coming back?

ROSE.   Ain't no use in you studying me. It don't matter what time I come back.

TROY.   I just asked you a question, woman. What's the matter . . . can't I ask you a question?

ROSE.   Troy, I don't want to go into it. Your dinner's in there on the stove. All you got to do is heat it up. And don't you be eating the rest of them cakes in there. I'm coming back for them. We having a bake sale at the church tomorrow. (ROSE *exits the yard.* TROY *sits down on the step, takes a pint bottle from his pocket, opens it, and drinks. He begins to sing.*)

TROY.   Hear it ring! Hear it ring!

>   Had an old dog his name was Blue
>   You know Blue was mighty true
>   You know Blue was a good old dog
>   Blue trees a possum in a hollow log
>   You know from that he was a good old dog (BONO *enters the yard.*)

BONO.   Hey, Troy.

TROY.   Hey, what's happening, Bono?

BONO.   I just thought I'd stop by to see you.

TROY.   What you stop by and see me for? You ain't stopped by in a month of Sundays. Hell, I must owe you money or something.

BONO.   Since you got your promotion I can't keep up with you. Used to see you every day. Now I don't even know what route you working.

TROY.   They keep switching me around. Got me out in Greentree now . . . hauling white folks' garbage.

BONO.   Greentree, huh? You lucky, at least you ain't got to be lifting them barrels. Damn if they ain't getting heavier. I'm gonna put in my two years and call it quits.

TROY.   I'm thinking about retiring myself.

BONO.   You got it easy. You can *drive* for another five years.

TROY.   It ain't the same, Bono. It ain't like working the back of the truck. Ain't got nobody to talk to . . . feel like you working by yourself. Naw, I'm thinking about retiring. How's Lucille?

BONO.   She all right. Her arthritis get to acting up on her sometime. Saw Rose on my way in. She going down to the church, huh?

TROY.   Yeah, she took up going down there. All them preachers looking for somebody to fatten their pockets. (*Pause.*) Got some gin here.

BONO.   Naw, thanks. I just stopped by to say hello.

TROY.   Hell, nigger . . . you can take a drink. I ain't never known you to say no to a drink. You ain't got to work tomorrow.

BONO.   I just stopped by. I'm fixing to go over to Skinner's. We got us a domino game going over his house every Friday.

TROY.   Nigger, you can't play no dominoes. I used to whup you four games out of five.

BONO.   Well, that learned me. I'm getting better.

TROY.   Yeah? Well, that's all right.

BONO.   Look here . . . I got to be getting on. Stop by sometime, huh?

TROY.   Yeah, I'll do that, Bono. Lucille told Rose you bought her a new refrigerator.

BONO.   Yeah, Rose told Lucille you had finally built your fence . . . so I figured we'd call it even.

TROY.   I knew you would.

BONO.   Yeah . . . okay. I'll be talking to you.

TROY.   Yeah, take care, Bono. Good to see you. I'm gonna stop over.

BONO.   Yeah. Okay, Troy. (BONO *exits.* TROY *drinks from the bottle.*)

TROY.   Old Blue died and I dig his grave
      Let him down with a golden chain
      Every night when I hear old Blue bark
      I know Blue treed a possum in Noah's Ark.
      Hear it ring! Hear it ring!

(CORY *enters the yard. They eye each other for a beat.* TROY *is sitting in the middle of the steps.* CORY *walks over.*)

CORY.   I got to get by.

TROY.   Say what? What's you say?

CORY.   You in my way. I got to get by.

TROY.   You got to get by where? This is my house. Bought and paid for. In full. Took me fifteen years. And if you wanna go in my house and I'm sitting on the steps . . . you say excuse me. Like your mama taught you.

CORY.   Come on, Pop . . . I got to get by. (CORY *starts to maneuver his way past* TROY. TROY *grabs his leg and shoves him back.*)

TROY.   You just gonna walk over top of me?

CORY.   I live here too!

TROY (*advancing toward him*).   You just gonna walk over top of me in my own house?

CORY.   I ain't scared of you.

TROY.   I ain't asked if you was scared of me. I asked you if you was fixing to walk over top of me in my own house? That's the question. You ain't gonna say excuse me? You just gonna walk over top of me?

CORY.   If you wanna put it like that.

TROY.   How else am I gonna put it?

CORY.   I was walking by you to go into the house 'cause you sitting on the steps drunk, singing to yourself. You can put it like that.

TROY.   Without saying excuse me??? (CORY *doesn't respond.*) I asked you a question. Without saying excuse me???

CORY.   I ain't got to say excuse me to you. You don't count around here no more.

TROY.   Oh, I see . . . I don't count around here no more. You ain't got to say excuse me to your daddy. All of a sudden you done got so grown that your daddy don't count around here no more . . . Around here in his own house and yard that he done paid for with the sweat of his brow. You done got so grown to where you gonna take over. You gonna take over my house. Is that right? You gonna wear my pants. You gonna go in there and stretch out on my bed. You ain't got to say excuse me 'cause I don't count around here no more. Is that right?

CORY.   That's right. You always talking this dumb stuff. Now, why don't you just get out my way?

TROY.   I guess you got someplace to sleep and something to put in your belly. You got that, huh? You got that? That's what you need. You got that, huh?

CORY.   You don't know what I got. You ain't got to worry about what I got.

TROY.   You right! You one hundred percent right! I done spent the last seventeen years worrying about what you got. Now it's your turn, see? I'll tell you what to do. You grown . . . we done established that. You a man. Now, let's see you act like one. Turn your behind around and walk out this yard. And when you get out there in the alley . . . you can forget about this house. See? 'Cause this is my house. You go on and be a man and get your own house. You can forget about this. 'Cause this is mine. You go on and get yours 'cause I'm through with doing for you.

CORY.   You talking about what you did for me . . . what'd you ever give me?

TROY.   Them feet and bones! That pumping heart, nigger! I give you more than anybody else is ever gonna give you.

CORY.   You ain't never gave me nothing! You ain't never done nothing but hold me back. Afraid I was gonna be better than you. All you ever did was try and make me scared of you. I used to tremble every time you called my name. Every time I heard your footsteps in the house. Wondering all the time . . . what's Papa gonna say if I do this? . . . What's he gonna say if I do that? . . . What's Papa gonna say if I turn on the radio? And Mama, too . . . she tries . . . but she's scared of you.

TROY.   You leave your mama out of this. She ain't got nothing to do with this.

CORY.   I don't know how she stand you . . . after what you did to her.

TROY.   I told you to leave your mama out of this! (*He advances toward* CORY.)

CORY.   What you gonna do . . . give me a whupping? You can't whup me no more. You're too old. You just an old man.

TROY (*shoves him on his shoulder*).   Nigger! That's what you are. You just another nigger on the street to me!

CORY.   You crazy! You know that?

TROY.   Go on now! You got the devil in you. Get on away from me!

CORY.   You just a crazy old man . . . talking about I got the devil in me.

TROY.   Yeah, I'm crazy! If you don't get on the other side of that yard . . . I'm gonna show you how crazy I am! Go on . . . get the hell out of my yard.

CORY.   It ain't your yard. You took Uncle Gabe's money he got from the army to buy this house and then you put him out.

TROY (*advances on* CORY).   Get your black ass out of my yard! (TROY's *advance backs* CORY *up against the tree.* CORY *grabs up the bat.*)

CORY.   I ain't going nowhere! Come on . . . put me out! I ain't scared of you.

TROY.   That's my bat!

CORY.   Come on!

TROY.   Put my bat down!

CORY.   Come on, put me out. (*Swings at* TROY, *who backs across the yard.*) What's the matter? you so bad . . . put me out! (TROY *advances toward* CORY. *Backing up*) Come on! Come on!

TROY.   You're gonna have to use it! You wanna draw that bat back on me . . . you're gonna have to use it.

CORY.   Come on! . . . Come on! (CORY *swings the bat at* TROY *a second time. He misses.* TROY *continues to advance toward him.*)

TROY.   You're gonna have to kill me! You wanna draw that bat back on me. You're gonna have to kill me. (CORY, *backed up against the tree, can go no farther.* TROY *taunts him. He sticks out his head and offers him a target.*) Come on! Come on! (CORY *is unable to swing the bat.* TROY *grabs it.*) Then I'll show you. (CORY *and* TROY *struggle over the bat. The struggle is fierce and fully engaged.* TROY *ultimately is the stronger and takes the bat from* CORY *and stands over him ready to swing. He stops himself.*) Go on and get away from around my house. (CORY, *stung by his defeat, picks himself up, walks slowly out of the yard and up the alley.*)

CORY.   Tell Mama I'll be back for my things.

TROY.   They'll be on the other side of that fence. (CORY *exits.*) I can't taste nothing. Hallelujah! I can't taste nothing no more. (TROY *assumes a batting posture and begins to taunt Death, the fastball on the outside corner.*) Come on! It's between you and me now! Come on! Anytime you want! Come on! I be ready for you . . . but I ain't gonna be easy. (*The lights go down on the scene.*)

SCENE 5

The time is 1965. The lights come up in the yard. It is the morning of TROY'S *funeral. A funeral plaque with a light hangs beside the door. There is a small garden plot off to the side. There is noise and activity in the house as* ROSE *and* BONO *have gathered. The door opens and* RAYNELL, *seven years old, enters dressed in a flannel nightgown. She crosses to the garden and pokes around with a stick.* ROSE *calls from the house.*

ROSE.   Raynell!

RAYNELL.   Mam?

ROSE.   What you doing out there?

RAYNELL.   Nothing. (ROSE *comes to the door.*)

ROSE.   Girl, get in here and get dressed. What you doing?

RAYNELL.   Seeing if my garden growed.

ROSE.   I told you it ain't gonna grow overnight. You got to wait.

RAYNELL.   It don't look like it never gonna grow. Dag!

ROSE.   I told you a watched pot never boils. Get in here and get dressed.

RAYNELL.   This ain't even no pot, Mama.

ROSE.   You just have to give it a chance. It'll grow. Now you come on and do what I told you. We got to be getting ready. This ain't no morning to be playing around. You hear me?

RAYNELL.   Yes, mam. (ROSE *exits into the house.* RAYNELL *continues to poke at her garden with a stick.* CORY *enters. He is dressed in a Marine corporal's uniform, and carries a duffel bag. His posture is that of a military man, and his speech has a clipped sternness.*)

CORY (*to* RAYNELL).   Hi. (*Pause.*) I bet your name is Raynell.

RAYNELL.   Uh huh.

CORY.   Is your mama home? (RAYNELL *runs up on the porch and calls through the screen door.*)

RAYNELL.   Mama . . . there's some man out here. Mama? (ROSE *comes to the door.*)

ROSE.   Cory? Lord have mercy! Look here, you all! (ROSE *and* CORY *embrace in a tearful reunion as* BONO *and* LYONS *enter from the house dressed in funeral clothes.*)

BONO.   Aw, looka here . . .

ROSE.   Done got all grown up!

CORY.   Don't cry, Mama. What you crying about?

ROSE.   I'm just so glad you made it.

CORY.   Hey Lyons. How you doing, Mr. Bono. (LYONS *goes to embrace* CORY.)

LYONS.   Look at you, man. Look at you. Don't he look good, Rose. Got them Corporal stripes.

ROSE.   What took you so long?

CORY.   You know how the Marines are, Mama. They got to get all their paperwork straight before they let you do anything.

ROSE.   Well, I'm sure glad you made it. They let Lyons come. Your Uncle Gabe's still in the hospital. They don't know if they gonna let him out or not. I just talked to them a little while ago.

LYONS.   A Corporal in the United States Marines.

BONO.   Your daddy knew you had it in you. He used to tell me all the time.

LYONS.   Don't he look good, Mr. Bono?

BONO.   Yeah, he remind me of Troy when I first met him. (*Pause.*) Say, Rose, Lucille's down at the church with the choir. I'm gonna go down and get the pallbearers lined up. I'll be back to get you all.

ROSE.   Thanks, Jim.

CORY.   See you, Mr. Bono.

LYONS (*with his arm around* RAYNELL).   Cory . . . look at Raynell. Ain't she precious? She gonna break a whole lot of hearts.

ROSE.   Raynell, come and say hello to your brother. This is your brother, Cory. You remember Cory?

RAYNELL.   No, Mam.

CORY.   She don't remember me, Mama.

ROSE.   Well, we talk about you. She heard us talk about you. (*To* RAYNELL) This is your brother, Cory. Come on and say hello.

RAYNELL.   Hi.

CORY.   Hi. So you're Raynell. Mama told me a lot about you.

ROSE.   You all come on into the house and let me fix you some breakfast. Keep up your strength.

CORY.   I ain't hungry, Mama.

LYONS.   You can fix me something, Rose. I'll be in there in a minute.

ROSE.   Cory, you sure you don't want nothing? I know they ain't feeding you right.

CORY.   No, Mama . . . thanks. I don't feel like eating. I'll get something later.

ROSE.   Raynell . . . get on upstairs and get that dress on like I told you. (ROSE *and* RAYNELL *exit into the house.*)

LYONS.   So . . . I hear you thinking about getting married.

CORY.   Yeah, I done found the right one, Lyons. It's about time.

LYONS.   Me and Bonnie been split up about four years now. About the time Papa retired. I guess she just got tired of all them changes I was putting her through. (*Pause.*) I always knew you was gonna make something out yourself. Your head was always in the right direction. So . . . you gonna stay in . . . make it a career . . . put in your twenty years?

CORY.   I don't know. I got six already, I think that's enough.

LYONS.   Stick with Uncle Sam and retire early. Ain't nothing out here. I guess Rose told you what happened with me. They got me down the work-house. I thought I was being slick cashing other people's checks.

CORY.   How much time you doing?

LYONS.   They give me three years. I got that beat now. I ain't got but nine more months. It ain't so bad. You learn to deal with it like anything else. You got to take the crookeds with the straights. That's what Papa used to say. He used to say that when he struck out. I seen him strike out three times in a row . . . and the next time up he hit the ball over the grandstand. Right out there in Homestead Field. He wasn't satisfied hitting in the seats . . . he want to hit it over everything! After the game he had two hundred people standing around waiting to shake his hand. You got to take the crookeds with the straights. Yeah, Papa was something else.

CORY.   You still playing?

LYONS.   Cory . . . you know I'm gonna do that. There's some fellows down there we got us a band . . . we gonna try and stay together when we get out . . . but yeah, I'm still playing. It still helps me to get out of bed in the morning. As long as it do that I'm gonna be right there playing and trying to make some sense out of it.

ROSE (*calling*).   Lyons, I got these eggs in the pan.

LYONS.   Let me go on and get these eggs, man. Get ready to go bury Papa. (*Pause.*) How you doing? You doing all right? (CORY *nods.* LYONS *touches him on the shoulder and they share a moment of silent grief.* LYONS *exits into the house.* CORY *wanders about the yard.* RAYNELL *enters.*)

RAYNELL.   Hi.

CORY.   Hi.

RAYNELL.   Did you used to sleep in my room?

CORY.   Yeah . . . that used to be my room.

RAYNELL.   That's what Papa call it. "Cory's room." It got your football in the closet. (ROSE *comes to the door.*)

ROSE.   Raynell, get in there and get them good shoes on.

RAYNELL.   Mama, can't I wear these? Them other one hurt my feet.

Rose. Well, they just gonna have to hurt your feet for a while. You ain't said they hurt your feet when you went down to the store and got them.

Raynell. They didn't hurt then. My feet done got bigger.

Rose. Don't you give me no backtalk now. You get in there and get them shoes on. (Raynell *exits into the house.*) Ain't too much changed. He still got that piece of rag tied to that tree. He was out here swinging that bat. I was just ready to go back in the house. He swung that bat and then he just fell over. Seem like he swung it and stood there with this grin on his face . . . and then he just fell over. They carried him on down to the hospital, but I knew there wasn't no need . . . why don't you come on in the house?

Cory. Mama . . . I got something to tell you. I don't know how to tell you this . . . but I've got to tell you . . . I'm not going to Papa's funeral.

Rose. Boy, hush your mouth. That's your daddy you talking about. I don't want to hear that kind of talk this morning. I done raised you to come to this? You standing there all healthy and grown talking about you ain't going to your daddy's funeral?

Cory. Mama . . . listen . . .

Rose. I don't want to hear it, Cory. You just get that thought out of your head.

Cory. I can't drag Papa with me everywhere I go. I've got to say no to him. One time in my life I've got to say no.

Rose. Don't nobody have to listen to nothing like that. I know you and your daddy ain't seen eye to eye, but I ain't got to listen to that kind of talk this morning. Whatever was between you and your daddy . . . the time has come to put it aside. Just take it and set it over there on the shelf and forget about it. Disrespecting your daddy ain't gonna make you a man, Cory. You got to find a way to come to that on your own. Not going to your daddy's funeral ain't gonna make you a man.

Cory. The whole time I was growing up . . . living in his house . . . Papa was like a shadow that followed you everywhere. It weighed on you and sunk into your flesh. It would wrap around you and lay there until you couldn't tell which one was you anymore. That shadow digging in your flesh. Trying to crawl in. Trying to live through you. Everywhere I looked, Troy Maxson was staring back at me . . . hiding under the bed . . . in the closet. I'm just saying I've got to find a way to get rid of that shadow, Mama.

Rose. You just like him. You got him in you good.

Cory. Don't tell me that, Mama.

Rose. You Troy Maxson all over again.

Cory. I don't want to be Troy Maxson. I want to be me.

Rose. You can't be nobody but who you are, Cory. That shadow wasn't nothing but you growing into yourself. You either got to grow into it or cut it down to fit you. But that's all you got to make life with. That's all you got to measure yourself against that world out there. Your daddy wanted you to be everything he wasn't . . . and at the same time he tried to make you into everything he was. I don't know if he was right or wrong . . . but I do know he meant to do more good than he meant to do harm. He wasn't always right. Sometimes when he touched he bruised. And sometimes when he took me in his arms he cut.

When I first met your daddy I thought . . . Here is a man I can lay down with and make a baby. That's the first thing I thought when I seen him. I was thirty years old and had done seen my share of men. But when he walked up to me and said, "I can dance a waltz that'll make you dizzy," I thought, Rose Lee, here is a man that you can open yourself up to and be filled to bursting. Here is a man that can fill all them empty spaces you been tipping around the edges of. One of them empty spaces was being somebody's mother.

I married your daddy and settled down to cooking his supper and keeping clean sheets on the bed. When your daddy walked through the house he was so big he filled it up. That was my first mistake. Not to make him leave some room for me. For my part in the matter. But at that time I wanted that. I wanted a house that I could sing in. And that's what your daddy gave me. I didn't know to keep up his strength I had to give up little pieces of mine. I did that. I took on his life as mine and mixed up the pieces so that you couldn't hardly tell which was which anymore. It was my choice. It was my life and I didn't have to live it like that. But that's what life offered me in the way of being a woman and I took it. I grabbed hold of it with both hands.

By the time Raynell came into the house, me and your daddy had done lost touch with one another. I didn't want to make my blessing off of nobody's misfortune . . . but I took on to Raynell like she was all them babies I had wanted and never had. (*The phone rings.*) Like I'd been blessed to relive a part of my life. And if the Lord see fit to keep up my strength . . . I'm gonna do her just like your daddy did you . . . I'm gonna give her the best of what's in me.

RAYNELL (*entering, still with her old shoes*).   Mama . . . Reverend Tollivier on the phone. (ROSE *exits into the house.*)

RAYNELL.   Hi.

CORY.   Hi.

RAYNELL.   You in the Army or the Marines?

CORY.   Marines.

RAYNELL.   Papa said it was the Army. Did you know Blue?

CORY.   Blue? Who's Blue?

RAYNELL.   Papa's dog what he sing about all the time.

CORY (*singing*).   Hear it ring! Hear it ring!

> I had a dog his name was Blue
> You know Blue was mighty true
> You know Blue was a good old dog
> Blue treed a possum in a hollow log
> You know from that he was a good old dog.
> Hear it ring! Hear it ring! (RAYNELL *joins in singing.*)

> CORY *and* RAYNELL.   Blue treed a possum out on a limb
> Blue looked at me and I looked at him
> Grabbed that possum and put him in a sack
> Blue stayed there till I came back
> Old Blue's feets was big and round
> Never allowed a possum to touch the ground.
>
> Old Blue died and I dug his grave
> I dug his grave with a silver spade
> Let him down with a golden chain
> And every night I call his name
> Go on Blue, you good dog you
> Go on Blue, you good dog you
> RAYNELL.   Blue laid down and died like a man
> Blue laid down and died . . .
> BOTH.   Blue laid down and died like a man
> Now he's treeing possums in the Promised Land
> I'm gonna tell you this to let you know
> Blue's gone where the good dogs go
> When I hear old Blue bark
> When I hear old Blue bark
> Blue treed a possum in Noah's Ark
> Blue treed a possum in Noah's Ark.

(ROSE *comes to the screen door.*)

ROSE.   Cory, we gonna be ready to go in a minute.

CORY (*to* RAYNELL).   You go on in the house and change them shoes like Mama told you so we can go to Papa's funeral.

RAYNELL.   Okay, I'll be back. (RAYNELL *exits into the house.* CORY *gets up and crosses over to the tree.* ROSE *stands in the screen door watching him.* GABRIEL *enters from the alley.*)

GABRIEL (*calling*).   Hey, Rose!

ROSE.   Gabe?

GABRIEL.   I'm here, Rose. Hey Rose, I'm here! (ROSE *enters from the house.*)

ROSE.   Lord . . . Look here, Lyons!

LYONS.   See, I told you, Rose . . . I told you they'd let him come.

CORY.   How you doing, Uncle Gabe?

LYONS.   How you doing, Uncle Gabe?

GABRIEL.   Hey, Rose. It's time. It's time to tell St. Peter to open the gates. Troy, you ready? You ready, Troy. I'm gonna tell St. Peter to open the gates. You get ready now. (GABRIEL, *with great fanfare, braces himself to blow. The trumpet is without a mouthpiece. He puts the end of it into his mouth and blows with great force, like a man who has been waiting some twenty-odd years for this single moment. No sound comes out of the trumpet. He braces himself and blows again with the same result. A third time he blows. There is a weight of impossible description that falls away and leaves him bare and exposed to a fright- ful realization. It is a trauma that a sane and normal mind would be unable to withstand. He begins to dance. A slow, strange dance, eerie and life-giving. A dance of atavistic signature and ritual.* LYONS *attempts to embrace him.* GA- BRIEL *pushes* LYONS *away. He begins to howl in what is an attempt at song, or perhaps a song turning back into itself in an attempt at speech. He finishes his dance and the gates of heaven stand open as wide as God's closet.*) That's the way that go!

Writing about Literature

I. WHY WRITE ABOUT LITERATURE?

Written assignments in a literature class have two purposes: (a) to give you additional practice in writing clearly and persuasively, and (b) to deepen your understanding of literary works by leading you to read and think about a few works more searchingly than you might otherwise do. But these two purposes are private. To be successful, your paper must have a public purpose as well: it should be written to enlighten others besides yourself. Even if no one else ever reads your paper, you should never treat it as a private note to your instructor. You should write every paper as if it were intended for publication.

II. FOR WHOM DO YOU WRITE?

The audience for whom you write will govern both the content and expression of your paper. You need to know something about your readers' backgrounds—national, racial, social, religious—and be able to make intelligent guesses about their knowledge, interests, and previous reading. In writing about George Herbert's "Peace" (page 647) for a Hindu audience, you would need to include explanations of Christian belief and biblical stories that would be unnecessary for a Western European or American audience. In presenting Graham Greene's "The Destructors" (page 49), your editors have felt it necessary to provide information (in footnotes) that would not be needed by a British audience; for "Defender of the Faith" (page 116), footnotes provide definitions and explanations that would not be necessary for an audience familiar with Jewish religious practices. But the most crucial question about an audience is: *Has it read the work you are writing about?* The book reviewer in your Sunday paper generally writes about a newly published book that the audience has not read. A reviewer's purpose is to let readers know something of what the book is about and to give them some notion of whether they will enjoy or profit from reading it. At an opposite extreme, the scholar writing in a specialized scholarly journal can generally assume an audience that *has* read the work, that has a knowledge of previous interpretations of the work, and that is familiar with other works in its period or genre. The scholar's purpose, not infrequently, is to persuade this audience that some new information or some new way of looking at the work appreciably deepens or alters its meaning or significance.

Clearly, essays written for such different audiences and with such different purposes differ considerably in content, organization, and style. Book reviewers reviewing a new novel will include a general idea of its plot while being careful not to reveal the outcome. Scholars will assume that readers already know the plot and will have no compunction about discussing its outcome. Reviewers will try to write interestingly and engagingly about the novel and to persuade readers that they have valid grounds for their opinions of its worth, but their manner will generally be informal. Scholars are more interested in presenting a cogent argument, logically arranged, and solidly based on evidence. They will be more formal, and may use critical terms and refer to related works that would be unfamiliar to nonspecialized readers. In documentation the two types of essays will be quite different. Reviewers' only documentation is normally the identification of the novel's title, author, publisher, and price, at the top of the review. For other information and opinions they hope that a reader will rely on their intelligence, knowledge, and judgment. Scholars, on the other hand, may furnish an elaborate array of citations of other sources of information, allowing the reader to verify the accuracy or basis of any important part of their argument. Scholars expect to be challenged, and they see to it that all parts of their arguments are buttressed.

For whom, then, should *you* write? Unless your instructor stipulates (or you request) a different audience, the best plan is to assume that you are writing for the other members of your class. Pretend that your class publishes a journal of which it also constitutes the readership. Your instructor is the editor and determines editorial policy. If you write on a work that has been assigned for class reading, you assume that your audience is familiar with it. (This kind of paper is generally of the greatest educational value, for it is most open to challenge and class discussion, and places on you a heavier burden of proof.) If you compare an assigned work with one that has not been assigned, you must gauge what portion of your audience is familiar with the unassigned work, and proceed accordingly. If the unassigned story were A. Conan Doyle's "The Adventure of the Speckled Band," you would probably not need to explain that "Sherlock Holmes is a detective" and that "Dr. Watson is his friend," for you can assume that *this* audience, through movies, TV, or reading, is familiar with these characters; but you could not assume familiarity with this particular story. You know that, as members of the same class, your readers have certain backgrounds and interests in common and are at comparable levels of education. Anything you know about your audience may be important for how you write your paper and what you put in it.

Assuming members of your class as your audience carries another advantage: you can also assume that they are familiar with the definitions and examples given in this book, and therefore you can avoid wasting space by quoting or paraphrasing the book. There will be no need to tell them that an indeterminate ending is one in which the central conflict is left unresolved, or that Emily Dickinson's poems are untitled, or that Miss Brill is an unmarried Englishwoman living in France.

III. CHOOSING A TOPIC

As editor of this imaginary publication, your instructor is responsible for the nature of its contents. Instructors may be very specific in their assignments, or they may be very general, inviting you to submit a paper on any subject within a broadly defined area of interest. They will also have editorial policies concerning length of papers, preparation of manuscripts, and deadlines for submission (all of which should be meticulously heeded). Instructors may further specify whether the paper should be entirely the work of your own critical thinking, or whether it is to be an investigative assignment—that is, one involving research into what other writers have written concerning your subject and the use of their findings, where relevant, to help you support your own conclusions.

Let us consider four kinds of papers you might write: (a) papers that focus on a single literary work, (b) papers of comparison and contrast, (c) papers on a number of works by a single author, and (d) papers on a number of works having some feature other than authorship in common.

1. Papers that Focus on a Single Literary Work

If your assignment is a specific one (How is the landscape symbolic in "Hills Like White Elephants"? Who are the speakers and what is the relationship between them in Mari Evans's poem "When in Rome"? Is Addie trying to manipulate Goldie in J. e. Franklin's *Two Mens'es Daughter?*), your task is clear-cut. You have only to read the selection carefully (obviously more than once), formulate your answer, and support it with corroborating evidence from within the text as cogently and convincingly as possible. In order to convince your readers that your answer is the best one, you will need to examine and account for apparently contrary evidence as well as clearly supportive evidence; otherwise skeptical readers, reluctant to change their minds, might simply refer to "important points" that you have "overlooked."

Specific questions like these, when they are central to the work and may be a matter of dispute, make excellent topics for papers. You may discover them for yourself when you disagree with a classmate about the interpretation of a story or poem or play. The study questions following many of the selections in this anthology frequently suggest topics of this kind.

If your assignment is more general, and if you are given some choice as to what selection you wish to write on, it is usually best to choose one you enjoyed, whether or not you entirely understood it. (You are more likely to write a good paper on a selection you liked than on one you disliked, and you should arrive at a fuller understanding of it while thinking through your paper.) You must then decide what kind of paper you will write, taking into account the length and kind of selection you have chosen and the amount of space at your disposal. Probably your paper will be either an *explication* or an *analysis*.

An *explication* (literally, an "unfolding") has been defined as "an examination of a work of literature for a knowledge of each part, for the relations of these parts to each other, and for their relations to the whole."* It is a detailed elucidation of a work, sometimes line by line or word by word, which is interested not only in *what* that work means but in *how* it means what it means. It thus considers all relevant aspects of a work—speaker or point of view, connotative words and double meanings, images, figurative language, allusions, form, structure, sound, rhythm—and discusses, if not all of these, at least the most important. (There is no such thing as exhausting the meanings and the ways to those meanings in a really rich piece of literature, and the explicator must settle for something less than completeness.) Explication follows from what we sometimes call "close reading"—looking at a piece of writing, as it were, through a magnifying glass.

Clearly, the kinds of literature for which an explication is appropriate are limited. First, the work must be rich enough to repay the kind of close attention demanded. One would not think of explicating "Thirty days hath September" (unless for purposes of parody), for it

---

*George Arms, "A Note on Explication," *Western Review* 15 (1950): 57.

has no meanings that need elucidation and no "art" worthy of comment. Second, the work must be short enough to be encompassed in a relatively brief discussion. A thorough explication of *Othello* would be much longer than the play itself and would tire the patience of even the most dogged reader. Explications work best with short poems. (Sonnets like Shakespeare's "That time of year" [page 782] and Frost's "Design" [page 696] almost beg for explication.) Explication sometimes may also be appropriate for passages in long poems, as, for example, the lines spoken by Macbeth after the death of his wife (page 627) or the "sonnet" from *Romeo and Juliet* (page 788), and occasionally for exceptionally rich or crucial passages of prose, perhaps the final paragraphs of stories like "Defender of the Faith," "Paul's Case," or "Miss Brill." But explication as a critical form should perhaps be separated from explication as a method. Whenever you elucidate even a small part of a literary work by a close examination that relates it to the whole, you are essentially explicating (unfolding). For example, if you point out the double meaning in the title of *Mind the Gap* as it relates to that play's action, you are explicating the title.

For a sample of an explication, see "A Study of Reading Habits," page 1477. This book displays the explicative method frequently, but has no pure examples of explication. The discussions of "A Noiseless Patient Spider" (pages 641–43), "Digging" (pages 644–45), and "Hills Like White Elephants" (pages 183–87) come close to being explications, and might have been so had they included answers to the study questions and one or two other matters. The General Exercises for Analysis and Evaluation of Poetry on page 597 should be helpful to you in writing an explication of a poem. Not all the questions will be applicable to every poem, and you need not answer all those that are applicable, but you should start by considering all that apply and then work with those that are central and important for your explication.

An *analysis* (literally a "breaking up" or separation of something into its constituent parts), instead of trying to examine all parts of a work in relation to the whole, selects for examination *one* aspect or element or part that relates to the whole. Clearly, an analysis is a better approach to longer works and to prose works than is an explication. A literary work may be usefully approached through almost any of its elements—point of view, characterization, plot, setting, symbolism, structure, and the like—so long as you relate this element to the central meaning or the whole. (An analysis of meter is meaningless unless it shows how meter serves the meaning; an analysis of the vocabulary and grammar of "The Lesson" or *Two Mens'es Daughter* would be pointless unless related to the characterization of the speakers.) The list of General Exercises on pages 317–19 may suggest approaches to stories, plays, and narrative poems; the list on page 587 to anything written in verse; and that on pages 913–14 to dramas. As always, it is important to choose a topic appropriate to the space available. "Characterization in Flannery O'Connor's 'Greenleaf'" is too large a topic to be usefully treated in a few pages, but a character analysis of Mrs. May or of her two sons might fit the space neatly. For an example of an analysis, see "The Function of the Frame Story in 'Once Upon a Time'" (page 592).

2. Papers of Comparison and Contrast

The comparison and contrast of two stories, poems, or plays having one or more features in common may be an illuminating exercise, because the similarities highlight the differences, or vice versa, and thus lead to a better understanding not only of both pieces but of literary processes in general. The works selected may be similar in plot but different in theme, similar in subject but different in tone, similar in theme but different in literary value, or, conversely, different in plot but similar in theme, different in subject but similar in tone, and so on. In writing such a paper, it is usually best to decide first whether the similarities or the differences are more significant, begin with a brief summary of the less significant, and then concentrate on the more significant.*

3. Papers on a Number of Works by a Single Author

Most readers, when they discover a work they particularly like, look for other works by the same author. The paper that focuses on a

---

*A number of selections in this collection have been paired to encourage just this kind of study: "The Most Dangerous Game" and "The Child by Tiger" in Chapter 1 of the fiction section; "The Storm" and "Once Upon a Time," "The Catbird Seat" and "The Drunkard," "A Christmas Memory" and "The Night Old Santa Claus Came" in Chapter 7; "A Municipal Report" and "A Jury of Her Peers," "Spotted Horses" and "Mule in the Yard" in Chapter 9; in the poetry section "Ulysses" and "Curiosity," "Dust of Snow" and "Soft Snow" in Chapter 6; "The Unknown Citizen" and "Departmental" in Chapter 7; "Abraham to kill him" and "An altered look about the hills" in Chapter 8; except for "Little Jack Horner," all six pairs of poems in Chapter 9; "For a Lamb" and "Apparently with no surprise," "One dignity delays for all" and "'Twas warm at first like us," "Crossing the Bar" and "The Oxen," "The Apparition" and "The Flea," "Dover Beach" and "Church Going," in Chapter 10; "Had I the Choice" and "The Aim Was Song" in Chapter 12; and all seven pairs of poems in Chapter 15.

single author rather than a single work is the natural corollary of such an interest. The most common concern in a paper of this type is to identify the characteristics that make this author different from other authors and therefore of particular interest to the writer. What are the author's characteristic subjects, settings, or themes? With what kinds of life does the author characteristically deal? What are the author's preferred literary forms? Is the author's approach ironic, witty, serious, comic, tragic? Is the author's vision directed principally inward or outward? In short, what configuration of patterns makes the author's fingerprints unique? Your paper may consider one or more of these questions.*

A more ambitious type of paper on a single author examines the works for signs of development. The attitudes that any person, especially an author, takes toward the world may change with the passing from adolescence to adulthood to old age. So also may the author's means of expressing attitudes and judgments. Though some writers are remarkably consistent in outlook and expression throughout their careers, others manifest surprising changes. To write a paper on the development of an author's work, you must have accurate information about the dates when works were written, and the works must be read in chronological order. When you have mastered the differences, you may be able to illustrate them through close examination of two or three works, one for each stage.

When readers become especially interested in the works of a particular author, they may develop a curiosity about that author's life as well. This is a legitimate interest, and, if there is sufficient space and your editor/instructor permits it, you may want to incorporate biographical information into your paper. If so, however, you should heed three caveats. First, your main interest should be in the literature itself: the biographical material should subordinated to and used in service of your examination of the work. In general, discuss only those aspects of the author's life that bear directly on the work: biography should not be used as "filler." Second, you should be extremely cautious about identifying an event in a work with an event in the life of the author. Almost never is a story, poem, or play an exact transcription of its author's personal experience. Authors fictionalize themselves when they put themselves into imaginative works. If you consider that even in autobiographies (where they intend to give accurate accounts

*John Donne, Emily Dickinson, and Robert Frost are represented in this anthology by a sufficient number of poems to support such a paper without turning to outside sources.

of their lives) writers must select incidents from the vast complexity of their experiences, that the memory of past events may be defective, and that at best writers work from their own points of view—in short, when you realize that even autobiography cannot be an absolutely reliable transcription of historical fact—you should be more fully prepared not to expect such an equation in works whose object is imaginative truth. Third, you must document the sources of your information about the author's life (see pages 1462–68).

4. Papers on a Number of Works with Some Feature Other than Authorship in Common

Papers on works by various authors that have some feature in common—subject, form, setting, point of view, and the like—where the purpose is to discover different ways that different works may use or regard that common feature, are often illuminating. Probably the most familiar paper of this type is the one that treats works having a similar thematic concern (love, war, religious belief or doubt, art, adolescence, initiation, maturity, old age, death, parents and children, racial conflict, social injustice). But a paper may also examine particular forms of literature, for example, the Italian sonnet, the dramatic monologue, the short story with an unreliable narrator. Topics of this kind may be further limited by time or place or number—four attitudes toward death, Elizabethan love lyrics, poetry of the Vietnam war, the use of the chorus in three Greek tragedies.

IV. PROVING YOUR POINT

In writing about literature, your object generally is to convince your readers that your understanding of a work is valid and important and to lead them to share that understanding. When writing about other subjects, it may be appropriate to persuade your readers through various rhetorical means—through eloquent diction, devices of suspense, analogies, personal anecdotes, and the like. But readers of essays about literature usually look for "proof." They want you to show them *how* the work, or the element you are discussing, does what you claim it does. Like scientists who require proof of the sort that they can duplicate in their own laboratories, readers of criticism want access to the process of inference, analysis, and deduction that has led to your conclusions, so that they may respond as you have done.

To provide this proof is no easy task, for it depends on your own mastery of reading and writing. You must understand what a work means and what its effects are; you must be able to point out precisely how it communicates that meaning and how it achieves those effects; and you must be able to present your experience of it clearly and directly. When you have spent considerable time in coming to understand and respond to a work of literature, it may become so familiar that it seems self-evident to you, and you will need to "back off" sufficiently to be able to put yourself in your readers' position—they may have vague feelings about the work ("I like it" or "It moves me deeply"), without knowing what it is that produced those feelings. It is your job to refine the feelings and define away the vagueness.

Some forms of "proof" rarely do the job. Precision does not result from explaining a metaphor metaphorically ("When Shakespeare's Juliet calls parting from Romeo a 'sweet sorrow' the reader is reminded of taking bitter-tasting medicine"). Nor can you prove anything about a work by hypothesizing about what it might have been if it did not contain what it does ("If Desdemona had not lost her handkerchief, Othello would never have murdered her"—this is equivalent to saying "If the play were not what it is, it would not be what it is"). Your own personal experiences will rarely help your readers ("Drifting helplessly at sea for a week when our engine and radio were out of commission was like Madame Ranyevskaya's hopelessness as she loses her cherry orchard"). Even your personal history of coming to understand a literary work will seldom help, though you present it in more general terms ("At a first reading, the opening paragraphs of 'Hills Like White Elephants' are confusing because they do not reveal what the man wants the woman to do"—most literature does not yield up its richness on a first reading, so this approach has nothing to add to your reader's understanding). Just as in formal logic, argument by analogy is not regarded as valid, so in critical discourse analogies are usually unconvincing ("Desdemona's ignorance about adultery is like a child's inability to balance a checkbook"). These strategies all have in common the looseness and vagueness of trying to define something by saying what it is not, or what it is like, rather than dealing with what it *is*.

"Proof" in writing about literature is primarily an exercise in strict definition. Juliet's phrase "sweet sorrow" (quoted in the preceding paragraph) derives its feeling from the paradoxical linking of sweetness and grief as a representation of the conflicting emotions of love.

To provide an appropriate definition of the effect of the phrase, you would need to identify the figure of speech as paradox and to investigate the way in which love can simultaneously inflict pain and give pleasure, and you might find it useful to point to the alliteration that ties these opposites together. Obviously, comparing this kind of proof to that required by science is inexact, since what you are doing is reminding your readers, or perhaps informing them, of feelings that are associated with language, not of the properties of chemical compounds. Furthermore, a scientific proof is incomplete if it does not present every step in a process. If that requirement were placed on literary analysis, a critical essay would be interminable, since more can always be said about any interpretive point. So, rather than attempting to prove every point that you make, you should aim to demonstrate that your *method* of analysis is valid by providing persuasive proof of your major point or points. If you have shown that your handling of a major point is sound, your readers will tend to trust your judgment on lesser matters.

V. WRITING THE PAPER

The general procedures for writing a good paper on literature are much the same as the procedures for writing a good paper on any subject.

1. As soon as possible after receiving the assignment, read carefully and thoughtfully the literary materials on which it is based, mulling over the problem to be solved or—if the assignment is general—a good choice of subject, jotting down notes, and sidelining or underlining important passages with a pencil if the book is your own.* If possible, read the material more than once.

2. Then, rather than proceeding directly to the writing of the paper, put the materials aside for several days and let them steep in your mind. The advantage of this is that your subconscious mind, if you have truly placed the problem in it, will continue to work on the problem while you are engaged in other activities, indeed even while you are asleep. Repeated investigations into the psychology of creativity have shown that great solutions to scientific and artistic problems frequently occur while the scientist or artist is thinking of something

---

*If you use a library book, make notes of the page or line numbers of such passages so that you can readily find them again.

else; the answer pops into consciousness as if out of nowhere but really out of the hidden recesses of the mind where it has been quietly incubating. Whether this apparent "miracle" happens to you or not, it is probable that you will have more ideas when you sit down to write after a period of incubation than you will if you try to write your paper immediately after reading the materials.

3.   When you are ready to write (allow yourself as long an incubation period as possible, but also allow ample time for writing, looking things up, revising, copying your revision, and correcting your final copy), jot down a list of the ideas you have, select connecting ideas relevant to your problem or to a single acceptable subject, and formulate a thesis statement that will clearly express in one sentence what you wish to say about that subject. Make a rough outline, rearranging your ideas in the order that will best support your thesis. Do they make a coherent case? Have you left out anything necessary to demonstrate your thesis? If so, add it in the proper place. Then begin to write, using your rough outline as a guide. Write this first draft as swiftly as possible, not bothering about sentence structure, grammar, diction, spelling, or verification of sources. Concentrate on putting on paper what is in your head and on your outline without interrupting the flow of thought for any other purpose. If alternative ways of expressing a thought occur to you, put them all down for a later decision. Nothing is more unprofitable than staring at a blank sheet of paper, chewing on a pencil—or staring at a blank monitor, hearing the word processor's hum—wondering, *How shall I begin?* Just begin. Get something down on paper. It may look awful, but you can shape and polish it later.

4.   Once you have something on paper, it is much easier to see what should be done with it. The next step is to revise. Does your paper proceed from an introductory paragraph that either defines the problem to be solved or states your thesis, through a series of logically arranged paragraphs that advance toward a solution of the problem or demonstrate your thesis, to a final paragraph that either solves the problem or sums up and restates your thesis but in somewhat different words? If not, analyze the difficulty. Do the paragraphs need reorganization or amplification? Are more examples needed? Does the thesis itself need modification? Make whatever adjustments are necessary for a logical and convincing demonstration. This may require a rewriting of the paper, or it may call only for a few strike-outs, insertions, and circlings with arrows showing that a sentence or paragraph should be shifted from one place to another.

Notice that you are expected to organize your paper according to *your* purpose or thesis. This frequently will mean that you will not be moving paragraph-by-paragraph through a story, line-by-line through a poem, or speech-by-speech through a play, following the structure that the author created, but rather ordering your paper in the most effective way to make your point. If you do discuss a work following the order in which its materials are presented, your reader will naturally expect your thesis to include some comment on the structure of the work. The exception to this is a paper devoted entirely to explication, since in that case you will be expected to follow the structure of the poem or the passage you are explicating.

5.   In your revision (if not earlier), make sure that the stance expressed in your statements and judgments is firm and forthright, not weak and wishy-washy. Don't allow your paper to become a sump of phrases like "it seems to me that," "I think [or feel] that," "this word might connote," "this line could mean," and "in my opinion." Your readers know that the content of your paper expresses your thoughts; you need to warn them only when it expresses someone else's. And don't be weak-kneed in expressing your opinion. Even though you are not 100 percent sure of your rightness, write as if you are presenting a truth. Realizing beforehand that you will need to state your interpretations and conclusions confidently also should help you to strive for a greater degree of certainty as you read and interpret.

6.   Having revised your paper for the logic, coherence, confidence, and completeness of its argument, your next step is to revise it for effectiveness of expression. Do this slowly and carefully. How many words can you cut out without loss of meaning? Are your sentences constructed for maximum force and economy? Are they correctly punctuated? Do the pronouns have clear antecedents? Do the verbs agree with their subjects? Are the tenses consistent? Have you chosen the most exact words and spelled them correctly? Now is the time to use the dictionary, to verify quotations and other references, and to supply whatever documentation is needed. A conscientious writer may put a paper through several revisions.

7.   After all is in order, write or type your final copy, being sure to follow the editorial policies of your instructor for the submission of manuscripts.

8.   Read over your final copy slowly and carefully, and correct any mistakes (omissions, repetitions, typographical errors) you may have made in copying from your draft. This final step—too often omitted

due to haste or fatigue—is extremely important and may make the difference between an A or a C paper, or between a C paper and an F. It is easy to make careless mistakes in copying but your editor should not be counted on to recognize the difference between a copying error and one of ignorance. Moreover, the smallest error may utterly destroy the sense of what you have written: omission of a "not" may make your paper say exactly the opposite of what you meant it to say. Few editors require or want you to recopy or retype a whole page of your paper at this stage. It is enough to make neat corrections in ink on the paper itself.

VI. INTRODUCING QUOTATIONS

In writing about literature it is often desirable, sometimes imperative, to quote from the work under discussion. Quoted material is needed (a) to provide essential evidence in support of your argument, and (b) to set before your reader any passage that you are going to examine in detail. It will also keep your reader in contact with the text and allow you to use felicitous phrasing from the text to enhance your own presentation. You must, however, be careful not to overquote. If a paper consists of more than 20 percent quotation, it loses the appearance of closely knit argument and seems instead merely a collection of quotations strung together like clothes hung out on a line to dry. Avoid, especially, unnecessary use of long quotations. Readers tend to skip them. Consider carefully whether the quoted material may not be more economically presented by paraphrase, or whether the quotation, if judged necessary, may not be effectively shortened by ellipsis (see Q9 below). Readers faced with a long quotation may reasonably expect you to examine it in some detail; that is, the longer your quotation, the more you should do with it.

As a general rule in analytical writing, quotation should be included for the purpose of supporting or proving a point, not for the purpose of re-creating the experience of a work for your reader. You may assume that your reader has already read the work and does not need to have it summarized—but on the other hand, you should not send your reader back to the book to reread in order to understand what you are referring to. Analysis is the process of demonstrating how the parts work together to create the whole; it requires both the details and the way they work together. Quoting presents details, and analysis shows how the details do what you say they do. If a quotation seems entirely self-evident to you, so that you have nothing to explain about it, then it is not really worth quoting. If it is self-evident, your reader has already understood all there is to know about it.

As with every other aspect of good writing, the amount of quotation one uses and the explanation of how the quoted material works are matters of intelligence and tact and cannot be decreed. Effective use of quotation is an art.

Principles and "Rules"

There is no legislative body that establishes laws governing the formal aspects of quoting, documenting, or any other aspect of writing. The only "rules" are the editorial policies of the publisher to whom you submit your work. There is, however, a national organization—the Modern Language Association of America—that is so influential that its policies for its own publications and its recommendations for others are adopted by most journals of literary criticism and scholarship. The instructions below are in general accord with those stated in the *MLA Handbook for Writers of Research Papers*, 4th edition, by Joseph Gibaldi (New York: MLA, 1995). In your course, your instructor will inform you of any editorial policies in effect that differ from those given here or in the *MLA Handbook*. The examples we use here are all drawn from act 5, scene 2 of *Othello*.

Q1. If the quotation is short (normally not more than four typed lines of prose, not more than two or three lines of verse), put it in quotation marks and introduce it directly into the text of your essay.

a	Othello, before stabbing himself, reminds his listeners, "I have done the state some ser- vice and they know 't." He speaks of himself
b	as "one that loved not wisely but too well" and compares himself to "the base Indian"
c	who "threw a pearl away / Richer than all his tribe" (5.2.338–47).

Q2. If the quotation is long (normally more than four typed lines of prose, more than three lines of verse), begin it on a new line (and end it on its own line); double-space it (like the rest of your paper); and indent it twice as far from the left margin (ten spaces) as you do for a new paragraph (five spaces); if it is verse and has lines either too long or too short to look good with a ten-space indentation, center it between the margins. Whether verse or prose, *do not enclose it in quotation marks.* Since the indentation and the line arrangement both signal a quotation, the use of quotation marks would be redundant.

In the final scene, convinced that Desdemona is entirely innocent and having decided to kill himself, Othello says to his auditors:

> I pray you, in your letters,
> When you shall these unlucky deeds relate,
> Speak of me as I am, nothing extenuate,
> Nor set down aught in malice. (5.2.339–42)

The two boxed examples illustrate (Q1) the "run-in" quotation, where the quotation is "run in" with the writer's own text, and (Q2) the "set-off" or "block" quotation, which is separated from the writer's text.

Q3.   In quoting verse, it is extremely important to preserve the line arrangement of the original, for the verse line is a rhythmical unit and thus affects meaning. When more than one line of verse is "run in," the lines are separated by a virgule (or diagonal slash with one letter-space on each side), and capitalization after the first line follows that of the original. (See Q1.c. above.)

Q4.   In general, sentences containing a quotation are punctuated as they would be if there were no quotation. In Q1.a. above, a comma precedes the quoted statement as it would if there were no quotation marks. In Q2, a colon precedes the quoted sentence because it is long and complex. In Q1.b. and Q1.c., there is no punctuation at all before the quotation. Do not put punctuation before a quotation unless it is otherwise called for.

Q5.   Your quotation must combine with its introduction to make a grammatically correct sentence. The normal processes of grammar and syntax, like the normal processes of punctuation, are unaffected by quoting. Subjects must agree with their verbs, verbs must be consistent in tense, pronouns must have their normal relation with antecedents.

WRONG	Othello says, "One that loved not wisely but too well" (5.2.343).
	(Incomplete sentence)
RIGHT	Othello speaks of himself as "one that loved not wisely but too well" (5.2.343).

WRONG	Othello asks his auditors to "speak of me as I am" (5.2.341).
	(The pronouns "me" and "I" do not agree in person with their antecedent.)
RIGHT	Othello bids his auditors,
	Speak of me as I am, nothing extenuate,
	Nor set down aught in malice. Then must you speak
	Of one that loved not wisely but too well.
	(5.2.341–43)

WRONG	Othello says that "I have done the state some service" (5.2.338).
	(Incorrect mixture of direct and indirect quotation)
RIGHT	Othello says, "I have done the state some service" (5.2.338).

WRONG	Othello says that he "have done the state some service" (5.2.338).
	(Subject and verb of subordinate clause lack agreement.)
RIGHT	Othello says that he has "done the state some service" (5.2.338).

Q6. Your introduction must supply enough context to make the quotation meaningful. Be careful that all pronouns in the quotation have clearly identifiable antecedents.

WRONG	In the final speech of the play, Lodovico says, "Look on the tragic loading of this bed: / This is thy work" (5.2.362–63). (Whose work?)
RIGHT	In the final speech of the play, Lodovico says to Iago, "Look on the tragic loading of this bed: / This is thy work" (5.2.362–63).

Q7. The words within your quotation marks must be quoted *exactly* from the original.

WRONG	Though Iago bids his wife to "hold her peace," Emilia declares, "I will speak as liberally as the north wind" (5.2.218–19).

Q8. It is permissible to insert or supply words in a quotation *if* you enclose them within brackets. Brackets (parentheses with square corners) are used to indicate *editorial* changes or additions. If parentheses were used, the reader might interpret the enclosed material as *authorial* (as part of the quotation). Since brackets do not appear on all typewriters, you may have to put them in with a pen or pencil. Avoid excessive use of brackets: they have a pedantic air. Find other solutions. Often paraphrase will serve as well as quotation.

CORRECT	Though Iago bids his wife to "hold [her] peace," Emilia declares, "I will speak as liberal[ly] as the north [wind]" (5.2.218–19).
BETTER	Though Iago bids his wife to hold her peace, Emilia declares that she will speak as liberally as the north wind.

Notice that a word within brackets can either replace a word in the original (as in the substitution of *her* for "you" above) or be added to explain or complete the original (as with *-ly* and *wind* above). Since a reader understands that brackets signal either substitutions or additions, it is superfluous to include the words for which substitutions have been made.

WRONG | Iago bids his wife to "hold your [her] peace" (5.2.218).

Your sentences, including bracketed words, must read as if there were no brackets.

RIGHT | After Iago's treachery has been completely exposed, Lodovico tells Othello:
> You must forsake this room, and go with us.
> Your power and your command is taken off.
> And Cassio rules in Cyprus. For this slave [Iago],
> If there can be any cunning cruelty
> That can torment him much and hold him long,
> It shall be his. (5.2.329–34)

Q9. It is permissible to omit words from quoted material, but *only* if the omission is indicated. Three *spaced* periods are used to indicate the omission (technically they are called "ellipsis points"). If there are four periods, one is the normal period at the end of a sentence; the other three indicate the ellipsis.

The statement just concluded, if quoted, might be shortened in the following way: "It is permissible to omit words . . . *if* the omission is indicated. Three *spaced* periods are used to indicate the omission. . . . If there are four periods, one is the normal period at the end of a sentence."

It is usually not necessary to indicate ellipsis at the beginning or ending of a quotation (the very act of quoting implies that something

Perhaps the majority of articles published in newspapers and periodicals with wide circulation are of this kind. Informal documentation works best for essays written on a single short work, without use of secondary sources, for readers without great scholarly expectations. A first-rate paper might be written on Herman Melville's "Bartleby the Scrivener" using only textual documentation. The author's name and the title of the story mentioned somewhere near the beginning of the essay, plus a few phrases like "In the opening paragraph" or "When Bartleby answers the lawyer's advertisement for additional scriveners" or "At the story's conclusion" might provide all the documentation needed for this audience. The action of the story is straightforward enough that the reader can easily locate any detail within it. If the essay is intended for our hypothetical journal published by your literature class (all of whose members are using the same anthology and have presumably read the story), its readers can readily locate the story and its events. But textual documentation, although less appropriate, can also be used for more complex subjects, and can even accommodate secondary sources with phrases like "As Yvor Winters points out in his essay on Melville in *In Defense of Reason*, . . ."

Principles and "Rules"

TD1. Enclose titles of short stories, articles, and poems (unless they are book-length) in quotation marks; underline titles of plays, magazines, newspapers, and books. Do not underline or put the title of your own paper in quotation marks. The general principle is that titles of separate publications are underlined; titles of selections or parts of books are put within quotation marks. Full-length plays, like *Othello* and *Oedipus Rex,* though often reprinted as part of an anthology, are elsewhere published as separate books and should be underlined. Underlining, in manuscripts, is equivalent to italics in printed matter. Many word-processing programs allow the use of italics, so you should check with your instructor for the preferred style.

TD2. Capitalize the first word and all important words in titles. Do not capitalize articles, prepositions, and conjunctions except when they begin the title ("A Christmas Memory," "I'm a Fool," "To the Virgins, to Make Much of Time").

TD3. When the title above a poem is identical with its first line or a major part of its first line, there is a strong presumption that the poet left the poem untitled and the editor or anthologist has used the first line or part of it to serve as a title. In such a case you may *use* the first line as a title, but should not *refer* to it as a title (Don't write: "The poet's repetition of his title in his first line emphasizes . . ."). In using it as a title, capitalize only those words that are capitalized in the first line.

TD4.   Never use page numbers in the body of your discussion because a page is not a structural part of a story, poem, or play. You may refer in your discussions to paragraphs, sections, stanzas, lines, acts, or scenes, as appropriate, but use page numbers *only* in parenthetical documentation where a specific edition of the work has been named.

TD5.   Spell out numerical references when they precede the unit they refer to; use numbers when they follow the unit (the fifth act, or act 5; the second paragraph, or paragraph 2; the fourth line, or line 4; the tenth stanza, or stanza 10). Use the first of these alternative forms sparingly, and only with small numbers. Never write "In the thirty-fourth and thirty-fifth lines . . .," for to do so is to waste good space and irritate your reader; write "In lines 34–35. . . ."

2. Parenthetical Documentation

Parenthetical documentation makes possible fuller and more precise accrediting without a forbidding apparatus of footnotes or an extensive list of Works Cited. With a full-length play like Tennessee Williams's *The Glass Menagerie,* a phrase like "midway through scene 4" is insufficient to allow the reader to locate the passage readily. This can be done by giving a page number, within parentheses, after the passage cited. But the reader needs to know also what book or edition the page number refers to, so this information must be supplied the first time such a citation is made.

Parenthetical documentation is the method most often required for a paper using only the primary source, or, at most, two or three sources—as, for example, most of the writing assigned in an introductory literature course. The information given in parenthetical documentation should enable your reader to turn easily to the exact source of a quotation or a reference. At the first mention of a work (which may well precede the first quotation from it), full publishing details should be given, but parenthetical documentation should supplement textual documentation; that is, information provided in the text of your essay should not be repeated within the parentheses. For the readers of our hypothetical class journal, the first reference in a paper on Williams's play might look like this:

> In Tennessee Williams's *The Glass Menagerie* (reprinted in Thomas R. Arp, *Perrine's Literature: Structure, Sound, and Sense,* 7th ed. [Fort Worth: Harcourt, 1998] 1025), the playwright examines . . .

Notice in this entry that brackets are used for parentheses within parentheses. In subsequent references, provided no other source intervenes, only the page number need be given.

> Amanda defines her fear that she and Laura will be deserted when she compares Tom to his father: "He was out all hours without explanation!—Then *left! Good-bye!* And me with the bag to hold" (1041).

If more than one source is used, each must be identified (if referred to a second time) by an abbreviated version of the main entry, normally the author's last name, for example (Williams 1031), but in any case the shortest identification that will differentiate it from the other sources.

Principles and "Rules"

PD1.   For the first citation from a book, give the author's name; the title of the selection; the name of the book from which it is taken; the editor (preceded by the abbreviation ed. for "edited by") or the translator (preceded by the abbreviation trans. for "translated by"); the edition (designated by an Arabic number) if there has been more than one; the city of publication (the first one will suffice if there is more than one); the publisher (this may be given in shortened form, dropping all but the first name named); the year of publication or of most recent copyright; and the page number. The following example correctly combines textual with parenthetical documentation.

> In "Home Burial," Frost has a husband complain, "'A man must partly give up being a man / With womenfolk'" (*The Poetry of Robert Frost,* ed. Edward Connery Latham [New York: Holt, 1969] 52).

PD2.   For your principal primary source, after the first reference, only a page number is required. Since the paragraphs of the stories in this book are numbered, your instructor may prefer you to supply the paragraph number rather than the page number. For long poems, it may be useful to give line numbers or stanza numbers rather than page numbers. If a poem is short, line numbers are unnecessary and should be omitted. For plays in verse, citation by line number (preceded by act and scene number) will usually be more useful than citation by page number: *Othello* (5.2.133).

PD3.   Documentation for run-in quotations always follows the quotation marks. If the quotation ends with a period, remove it to the end of the documentation. If it ends with an exclamation point or question mark, leave it, but put a period after the documentation as well. The following examples are from *Othello:*

"She was false as water" (5.2.133).
"Alas, what cry is that?" (5.2.116).

PD4.   With block quotations, parenthetical documentation follows the last mark of punctuation without further punctuation after the parentheses:

Out and alas! That was my lady's voice.
Help! Help, ho! Help! O lady, speak again!
Sweet Desdemona! O sweet mistress, speak!
(5.2.118–20)

PD5.   Avoid cluttering your paper with excessive documentation. When possible, use one note to cover a series of short quotations. (See example, Q1.) Remember that short poems need no parenthetical documentation at all after the first reference. Do not document well-known sayings or proverbs that you use for stylistic purposes and that form no part of the substance of your investigation (and of course be wary of including hackneyed commonplaces in your formal writing).

PD6.   It is customary in a formal paper to document all quoted materials. Do not, however, fall victim to the too frequent delusion that *only* quotations need documentation. The first purpose of documentation (see page 1463) implies that any major or possibly controversial assertion concerning interpretation may need documentation. If you declare that the turning point in a long story occurs with an apparently minor event, it may be more important for the reader to have a page number for that event than for any quotation from the story. Judgment must be exercised. You cannot and should not provide page numbers for every detail of a story; but neither should you think that you have necessarily done your duty if you merely document all quotations.

VIII. STANCE AND STYLE

In section II, "For Whom Do You Write?" we discussed the assumed audience for your critical writing. Now we must consider the other half of the reader/writer equation. We might ask the parallel question "Who Are You?" except that that would imply that we are asking about your own personal identity. Rather, since we defined your audience hypothetically as members of your class, we need to define "you" in terms of the voice that your audience will expect and respond to. Certain conventional expectations are aroused when we read critical analyses of literature, and what follows are a few suggestions that may lead you to adopt the stance that your readers will expect. If these sound prescriptive (or if your instructor suggests others), remember that writing about literature is essentially persuasive writing, its purpose being to persuade your readers to agree with your interpretation; the means of persuasion are many, and the writer's stance is only one of them. What we advise here are a few "hints" that have been valuable to students in the past, and may be helpful to you.

S1. *Keep out!* This injunction warns you away from unnecessarily intruding yourself into your critical statements, with a consequent loss of power and precision. Consider the relative force of these approaches:

POOR	It seems to me that Hemingway uses the hot, arid side of the valley to symbolize sterility.
GOOD	Hemingway uses the hot, arid side of the valley to symbolize sterility.
BETTER	The hot, arid side of the valley symbolizes sterility.

The first example dilutes the statement by making it sound tentative and opinionated. It allows your reader to respond, "Why should I consider that seriously, since the writer confesses that it's only a private opinion rather than a fact?" As a critic, you should adopt the stance of the sensitive person who is confident of the accuracy of her or his insights—even when in your heart you may *feel* tentative or unsure. Say it with an air of confidence.

The third example is "better" because it observes the following suggestion:

S2.   *Write about the work.* When analyzing a work of literature or some aspect of it, you should be sure that the thesis or topic of a paragraph or essay (and its thesis sentences) focuses on your topic. You will usually not be writing about an author but about a *work,* so try to avoid using the author's name as the subject.

POOR	Hemingway uses the river valley to symbolize fertility. (This focuses on *Hemingway* [subject] and *uses* [verb].)
GOOD	The river valley symbolizes fertility. (Subject, *valley;* verb, *symbolizes.*)

Try also to avoid the verb *uses,* since your focus is not on a writer using a technical device but on the result of that use, not on an author selecting a device to achieve a purpose but on the result of that selection. The easiest way to get rid of the word *use* or the idea of *using* is simply to delete them:

POOR	Hemingway uses the river valley to symbolize . . .
GOOD	The valley symbolizes . . .

The revised version cuts the wordiness and is more direct.

S3.   *Avoid passive constructions.* In analyzing literature, the passive voice presents three potential problems: (a) it may fail to identify its subject and thus (b) may introduce vagueness, and (c) it is often a weak and wordy way to say something that can be said directly and forcefully. It may also be a roundabout way to write about an author rather than a work.

POOR	The valley of the Ebro is used as the setting of the story.
POOR	Hemingway uses the valley of the Ebro as the setting of the story.
	(Passive voice is eliminated, but a problem with S2.)
GOOD	The valley of the Ebro is the setting of the story.

S4.   *Omit praise.* Praising a writer or a work with such adverbs as "cleverly," "carefully," "remarkably," "beautifully," and so forth, usually sounds a little condescending and fatuous when you are analyzing established literature (as distinct from writing a review of a new book). It suggests that *your* estimation of the quality of Faulkner's or Dickinson's or Shakespeare's work will tip the balance in favor of immortality for them.

S5.   *Avoid preparatory circumlocution.* Don't write a "table of contents" as an introductory paragraph, and eliminate such phrases as "in order to understand X we must examine Y." Just go ahead and examine Y, and trust your reader to recognize its relevance. Another example: "Z is a significant aspect of the poem" (or, a little worse, "It is interesting to note that Z is a significant aspect"). If Z is significant, just go ahead and say what it signifies; if it is interesting, let what is interesting about it be your topic.

Such circumlocution is sometimes called "treading water," since it is generally only a way of keeping afloat on the page until you get a good idea of the direction you really want to swim. You wouldn't walk into a room and announce, "I am now going to tell you that I'm here," or "I will tell you how interested you'll be to notice that I'm here." You'd say, "Here I am!"

It is perfectly all right to use such space-wasters in preliminary drafts—as ways of keeping your pen or keyboard in action while you are figuring out which way you are going to swim. Just be sure to edit them out of your finished text.

S6. *Avoid negative hypotheses.* An example of negative hypothesis is introduced with an example on p. 1452, "Proving Your Point." Here's another: "If the girl in 'Hills Like White Elephants' were not pregnant, she and the man would not face the deterioration of their relationship." But she *is,* so a critical analysis can neither speculate about what they might have done under other circumstances, nor prove by comparison that what they are doing is better or worse—there is nothing to compare.

IX. GRAMMAR, PUNCTUATION, AND USAGE: SPECIAL PROBLEMS

1. Grammar

G1. In discussing the action of a literary work, rely primarily on the present tense (even when the work itself uses the past), keeping the past, future, and perfect tenses available for prior or subsequent actions; for example,

> When Mrs. May imagines that the bull may have gored Greenleaf and killed him, and thinks of this as the "perfect ending" for a story she has been telling her friends, the situation is highly ironic, for she does not guess that the bull will cause her own death.

G2. Do not let pronouns refer to nouns in the possessive case. Antecedents of pronouns should always hold a strong grammatical position: a possessive is a mere modifier, like an adjective.

WRONG	In Shakespeare's play *Othello,* he writes . . .
	(Antecedent of "he" is in possessive case.)
RIGHT	In his play *Othello,* Shakespeare writes . . .
	(Antecedent of "his" is the subject of the sentence.)

2. Punctuation

P1.   The insertion of a parenthetical phrase in your sentence structure (as, for example, in parenthetical documentation) does not alter the normal punctuation of the rest of the sentence. Do not, as the preceding sentence doesn't, place a comma after a parenthetical phrase unless it belonged there before the parenthesis was inserted. You wouldn't write, "Hemingway's story, is about a crisis," so don't include that comma when you insert a parenthesis.

WRONG	Hemingway's "Hills Like White Elephants" (repr. in Thomas R. Arp, *Perrine's Literature,* 7th ed. [Fort Worth: Harcourt, 1998], 170–73), is about a crisis in a relationship.
	(Delete the comma after the parenthesis.)

And it is an inflexible rule of punctuation: never place a comma immediately before a parenthesis.

P2.   Do not set off restrictive appositives with commas. A restrictive appositive is one necessary to the meaning of the sentence; a nonrestrictive appositive could be left out without changing the meaning.

WRONG	In his story, "Hills Like White Elephants," Hemingway . . .
	(The title of the story is necessary to the meaning of the statement. As punctuated, the sentence falsely implies that Hemingway wrote only one story.)
RIGHT	In his story "Hills Like White Elephants," Hemingway . . .
RIGHT	In his only story in *Perrine's Literature,* "Hills Like White Elephants," Hemingway . . .
	(The adjective "only" identifies the story. The title simply supplies additional information and could be omitted without changing the meaning.)

P3.   Words used simply as words should be either underlined, italicized, or put in quotation marks.

WRONG	The word describing the countryside is brown.
	(This statement is false; all the words in the story are black.)
RIGHT	The word describing the countryside is "brown."

Since the word "brown" is quoted from the story, it has here been put in quotation marks. However, if you list a series of words from various parts of the story, you may prefer underlining for the sake of appearance. Whichever system you choose, be consistent throughout your paper.

P4.   Observe the conventions of typed manuscripts: (a) put a space after an abbreviating period (p. 7, not p.7; pp. 10–13, not pp.10–13); (b) use two hyphens to represent a dash -- and do not put spaces before and after them.

P5.   Observe the standard for forming possessives. For a singular noun, add an apostrophe and an *s* (a student's duty, yesterday's mail, the dress's hemline). For a plural noun, add only an apostrophe (the students' duties, seven days' mail). For proper nouns, the same rules apply (Camus's "The Guest," Chekhov's "In Exile," Capps's story).

Do not confuse the contraction *it's* (it is) with the possessive *its* (belonging to it). *Its* is an exception to the general rule requiring apostrophes for possessives.

3. Usage

U1.   Though accepted usage changes with time, and the distinctions between the following pairs of words are fading, many instructors will bless you if you try to preserve them.

> *convince, persuade Convince* pertains to belief (conviction); *persuade* pertains to either action or belief. The following sentences observe the distinction. "In 'Hills Like White

Elephants,' the man tries to persuade the woman to have an abortion." "In 'Hills Like White Elephants,' the man tries to convince the woman that she will be happy after the abortion." "She is persuaded to go through with the abortion though she is not convinced that it will make her happy."

describe, define   *Describe* means to delineate the visual appearance of something; *define* means to state the meaning of a word or phrase, or to explain the essential quality of something. Reserve *describe* and *description* for talking about how things look.

disinterested, uninterested   A disinterested judge is one who has no "stake" or personal interest in the outcome of a case and who can therefore judge fairly; an uninterested judge goes to sleep on the bench. A good judge is interested in the case but disinterested in its outcome. An uninterested reader finds reading boring. A disinterested reader? Perhaps one who can enjoy a good book whatever its subject matter.

imply, infer   A writer or speaker implies; a reader or listener infers. An implication is a meaning hinted at but not stated outright. An inference is a conclusion drawn from evidence not complete enough for proof. If you imply that I am a snob, I may infer that you do not like me.

lover, beloved   In older literature, the word *lover* usually meant one of two things—a man who is sexually involved, or any person who feels affection or esteem for another person or persons. In the case of the former, *lover* generally designated the male partner and *beloved* his female partner. In the case of the latter usage, no sexual implications are involved.

quote, quotation   Quote was originally used only as a verb. Today the use of "single quotes" and "double quotes" in reference to quotation marks is almost universally accepted; but, although the use of "quote" for "quotation" is common in informal speech, it is still unacceptable in formal writing.

Note also that quoting is an act performed by the writer about literature, not by the writer of literature.

WRONG	Shakespeare's famous quotation "To be or not to be" . . .
RIGHT	The famous quotation from Shakespeare, "To be or not to be" . . .

RIGHT	Shakespeare's famous line "To be or not to be" . . .
BETTER	Hamlet's famous line "To be or not to be" . . .
BEST	Probably the most-quoted line by Shakespeare is Hamlet's "To be or not to be" . . .

sensuous, sensual   *Sensuous* normally pertains to the finer senses, *sensual* to the appetites. Good poetry is sensuous: it appeals through the imagination to the senses. A voluptuous woman, an attractive man, or a rich dessert may have a sensual appeal that stirs a desire for possession.

U2.   Some words and phrases to avoid are the following.

center around   A geometrical impossibility. A story may perhaps center *on* a certain feature, but to make it center *around* that feature is to make the hub surround the wheel.

just as   This phrase as a term of comparison is too precise for literary analysis because the adjective *just* means *exactly* or *identical in every possible way,* almost an impossibility when discussing literature. You should take the trouble to establish the points of similarity and dissimilarity between things that you are comparing.

lifestyle   An overused neologism, especially inappropriate for use with older literature, that is too general to mean much. One dictionary defines it as "a person's typical approach to living, including his moral attitudes, preferred entertainment, fads, fashions, etc." If you wish to define someone's moral attitudes, do so; if you try to define a person's "lifestyle," you have a monumental task of all-inclusive definition. It's easier just to avoid it.

society   The problem with this word is that it is too often used only vaguely as a substitute for some more precise idea. Any story, poem, or play that does deal with "society" will clearly indicate a *particular* society—the world of diffident middle-class English businessmen at the beginning of the twentieth century ("The Japanese Quince") or the impoverished world of rural black Louisiana in the 1960s ("Just Like a Tree"). In those cases, once one has defined the particular society and its characteristics, the term might legitimately be used. But don't use it simply to mean "people in general at that time in that place." And it is important to avoid the glib assumption that *society* makes a person do something. A person's desire to be a member of a social group may lead to actions that appear to be imposed or forced, but what makes a person conform is the desire to be or remain a member, not the fact that there are codes of behavior.

somewhat (also *rather, more or less, as it were, in a manner*) All of these terms are specifically designed to avoid or evade precision—to create a sense of vagueness. Since clarity and precision are the goals of critical analysis, these terms should be avoided. They also sound wishy-washy, while you should strive to sound firm and convinced.

upset   As an adjective to define an emotional condition, the word is just too vague. Your dictionary will tell you that its synonyms are "distressed, disturbed, agitated, perturbed, irritated," and so forth. All of those terms are more precise than *upset,* and the one that most nearly indicates your meaning should be chosen.

what the author is trying to say is   The implication of this expression is that the author *failed* to say it. You don't say "I'm trying to get to Boston" if you are already there; give the author credit for having got where he or she was going.

Others suggested by your instructor:

_____   _____

_____   _____

_____   _____

_____   _____

_____   _____

X. A SAMPLE EXPLICATION

"A Study of Reading Habits"

The first noteworthy feature of Philip Larkin's "A Study of Reading Habits" (reprinted in Thomas R. Arp, *Perrine's Literature: Structure, Sound, and Sense,* 7th ed. [Fort Worth: Harcourt, 1998] 581) is the ironic discrepancy between the formal language of its title and the colloquial, slangy, even vulgar language of the poem itself. The title by its tone implies a formal sociological research paper, possibly one that samples a cross section of a population and draws conclusions about people's reading. The poem presents, instead, the confessions of one man whose attitudes toward reading have progressively deteriorated to the point where books seem to him "a load of crap." The poem's real subject, moreover, is not the man's reading habits but the revelation of life and character they provide.

The poem is patterned in three stanzas having an identical rime scheme (*abcbac*) and the same basic meter (iambic-anapestic trimeter). The stanzaic division of the poem corresponds to the internal structure of meaning, for the three stanzas present the speaker at three stages of his life: as schoolboy, adolescent, and adult. The chronological progression is signaled in the first lines of the stanzas by the words "When," "Later," and "now." The "now" is the present out of which the adult speaks, recalling the two earlier periods.

The boy he remembers in stanza 1 was unhappy, both in his home and, even more so, at school. Perhaps small and bullied by bigger boys, probably an indifferent student, making poor grades, and scolded by teachers, he found a partial escape from his miseries through reading. The books he read--tales of action and adventure, pitting good guys against bad guys, full of physical conflict, and ending with victory for the good guy--enabled him to construct a fantasy life in which he identified with the virtuous hero and in his imagination beat up villains twice his size, thus reversing the situations of his real life.

In stanza 2 the speaker recalls his adolescence when his dreams were of sexual rather than muscular prowess. True to the prediction of "ruining [his] eyes" in stanza 1, he had to wear spectacles, which he describes hyperbolically as "inch-thick"--a further detriment to his social life. To compensate for his lack of success with girls, he envisioned himself as a Dracula-figure with cloak and fangs, enjoying a series of sexual triumphs. His reading continued to feed his fantasy life, but, instead of identifying with the virtuous hero, he identified with the glamorous, sexually ruthless villain. The poet puns on the word "ripping" (the speaker "had ripping times in the dark"), implying both the British slang meaning of "splendid" and the violence of the rapist who rips the clothes off his victim.

In stanza 3 the speaker, now a young adult, confesses that he no longer reads much. His accumulated experience of personal failure and his long familiarity with his shortcomings have made it impossible for him to identify, even in fantasy, with the strong virtuous hero or the viciously potent villain. He can no longer hide from himself the truth that he resembles more closely the weak secondary characters of the escapist tales he picks up. He recognizes himself in the undependable dude who fails the heroine, or the cowardly storekeeper who knuckles under to the bad guys. He therefore has turned to a more powerful means of escape, one that protects him from dwelling on what he knows about himself: drunkenness. His final words are memorable--so "unpoetical" in a traditional sense, so poetically effective in characterizing this speaker. "Get stewed," he tells himself. "Books are a load of crap."

It would be a serious mistake to identify the speaker of the poem, or his attitudes or his language, with the poet. Poets, writers of books themselves, do not think that "books are a load of crap." Philip Larkin, moreover, an English poet and a graduate of Oxford, was for many years until his death a university librarian (Ian Hamilton, ed., *Oxford Companion to Twentieth-Century Poetry* [Oxford: Oxford UP, 1994] 288). "A Study of Reading Habits" is both dramatic and ironic. It presents a first-person speaker who has been unable to cope with the realty of his life in any of its stages and has therefore turned toward various means of escaping it. His confessions reveal a progressive deterioration of values (from good to evil to sodden indifference) and a decline in reading tastes (from adventure stories to prurient sexual novels to none) that reflect his downward slide.

Comments

The title of this paper is enclosed in quotation marks because the writer has used the title of the poem for the title of the paper. The paper uses textual and parenthetical documentation. Line numbers for quotations from the poem are not supplied, because the poem is too short to require them: they would serve no useful purpose. Notice that in quoting from stanza 1, the writer has changed the phrase "ruining my eyes" to fit the essay's syntax, but has indicated the alteration by putting the changed word within brackets. The paper is written for an American audience; if it had been written for an English audience the writer would not have needed to explain that "ripping" is British slang or to have made it a point that the poet is English. The paper is documented for an audience using this textbook. If it were directed toward a wider audience, the writer would want to refer for his text of the poem not to a textbook or anthology but to the volume of Larkin's poetry containing this poem (*The Whitsun Weddings* [London: Faber, 1964] 31). Also, the writer would probably wish to include the poet's name in his title: Philip Larkin's "A Study of Reading Habits" (or) An Examination of Larkin's "A Study of Reading Habits."

XI. A SAMPLE ANALYSIS

The Function of the Frame Story in "Once Upon a Time"

Nadine Gordimer's "Once Upon a Time" (reprinted in Thomas R. Arp, *Perrine's Literature: Structure, Sound, and Sense,* 7th ed. [Fort Worth: Harcourt, 1998] 252) is a complex, ironic presentation of the results of fear and hatred. This "children's story," so flat in its tone, characterization, and reporting of events, proceeds by gradual steps to show a family systematically barricading itself behind various security devices, the last of which has an effect opposite of what was intended in destroying the child that the parents are trying to protect.

The tale is especially harrowing because of the tone, which is first hinted at in the title. This is an easy, casual narration that repeats such standard phrases as "living happily ever after" (253) and identifies its characters only by their functions and relationships, never exploring motivations or revealing the steps of their decision making. The deeper causes for fear are not defined in the tale. All these qualities, and others, establish the tone of fairy tales and other stories for children. In this story, however, no one lives "happily ever after," for in attempting to safeguard themselves, the parents destroy their lives.

But that tale doesn't begin until the ninth paragraph of Gordimer's story. What precedes it is the frame story of a writer who has been asked to write a story for a children's collection, who refuses to contribute, and then is awakened in the night by some noise that frightens her. Her fear first chillingly creates a burglar or murderer "moving from room to room, coming up the passage--to [her] door" (252). Then the actual cause of her waking comes to her: deep down, "three thousand feet below" her house, some rock face has fallen in the gold mine beneath (253). She is not in personal danger, then. Yet she cannot return to sleep, so she tells herself "a bedtime story" to relax her mind--and the story is of the family that grows obsessed with security and protection, the awful story of the mutilation of the little boy.

The frame story initially seems little more than an introductory explanation of how the tale came to be written, against the writer's will and purpose. Its details are unrelated to the children's tale--explicitly so, as the writer, despite her knowledge of two recent murders in her neighborhood, and the rational fears that such events arouse, has "no burglar bars, no gun under the pillow" (252), in contrast to the precautions taken in the tale. There is no fairy-tale gold mine in her life, only the knowledge of the mining of gold a half-mile beneath her. So what does this frame have to do with the tale, other than to place the reader within the literal reality of a writer's time and place, from which the imagination journeys to "once upon a time"? Is it more than an ironic contrast in subject and tone?

For answers, we need to consider the writer's time and place as parallels to those of the tale. Both are located in South Africa, both are in the present (even though the phrase "once upon a time" normally signals a long time ago, in a far-off place). The family in the tale, with their burglar bars, walls, alarms, and finally "the razor-bladed coils all round the walls of the house," are like those people in the writer's world who *do* keep guns under their pillows. Like the real people of the writer's neighborhood, their fears are focused on the black African populace who surround and outnumber them. On the one hand, in the writer's world, the fears focus on "a casual day laborer . . . dismissed without pay" who returns to strangle the watchdogs and knife the man who treated him unfairly (252); on the other hand, in the children's story, the fears focus on the hungry, out-of-work, and begging multitudes who fill and spoil the suburban streets of the fictitious family's neighborhood. In both worlds, unfairness, want, and deprivation mark the blacks, while the whites feel surrounded and threatened by them.

Why cannot the writer return to sleep after she has discovered the innocent cause of her awakening? Because the comforting natural explanation, which removes her from personal danger, is in fact more horrifying than a murderous prowler. She thinks of

> the Chopi and Tsonga migrant miners who might [be] down there, under [her] in the earth at that moment. The stope where the [rock] fall was could have been disused, dripping water from its ruptured veins; or men might now be interred there in the most profound of tombs. (253)

Two possibilities occur to her--one of no harm to men, the other of burial alive--both a consequence of the wage-slavery of "migrant miners" over whose heads (literally and figuratively) the white society lives in "uneasy strain . . . of brick, cement, wood and glass" (253). If no miner has been harmed by *this* rock fall, others have been and will be; and moreover, being killed in that subterranean world of "ruptured veins" is not the only harm that the whites have inflicted on the original inhabitants of the country they control, nor on their own sensitivities and consciences.

The frame story of "Once Upon a Time," then, foreshadows the fear, the violence, and the pain of the children's tale, and points to the ultimate cause of its terrible sacrifice of a child--the systematic maltreatment of one race by another and the brutality and self-destruction that are its result.

Comments

This analysis has as its subject an aspect of the story that can be fully developed in a limited space. It is written for our hypothetical class journal, as indicated by the way in which the writer refrains from giving a detailed summary of the tale enclosed in the frame (since the audience is known to be familiar with the story), and presents details from the frame narration as they support the writer's argument. It employs some information about the author that is common knowledge to the class (her nationality and her contemporaneity having been supplied in the introductory footnote to the story). Notice the way in which quotations are integrated into the sentence structures and the manner in which the writer's interpolated words are presented in the extended quotation.

Glossary of Terms

These definitions sometimes repeat and sometimes differ in language from those in the text. Where they differ, the intention is to give a fuller sense of the term's meaning by allowing the reader a double perspective on it. Page numbers refer to the discussions in the text, which in most but not all cases are fuller than those in the glossary. Multiple page references may indicate separate discussions in the various sections of this book—fiction, poetry, drama.

Absurd, Drama of the   A type of drama, allied to comedy, radically nonrealistic in both content and presentation, that emphasizes the absurdity, emptiness, or meaninglessness of life. 953

Accent   In this book, the same as *stress*. A syllable given more prominence in pronunciation than its neighbors is said to be accented. 735

Allegory   A narrative or description having a second meaning beneath the surface one. 647

Alliteration   The repetition at close intervals of the initial consonant sounds of accented syllables or important words (for example, *m*ap-*m*oon, *k*ill-*c*ode, *pr*each-ap*pr*ove). Important words and accented syllables beginning with vowels may also be said to alliterate with each other inasmuch as they all have the same lack of an initial consonant sound (for example, "*I*nebriate of *a*ir am *I*"). 723

Allusion   A reference, explicit or implicit, to something in previous literature or history. (The term is reserved by some writers for implicit references only, such as those in "in Just-," 684; and "On His Blindness," 685, but the distinction between the two kinds of reference is not always clear-cut.) 680

Anacrusis   In metrical verse, the omission of an unaccented syllable at the beginning of a line. 740

Anapest   A metrical foot consisting of two unaccented syllables followed by one accented syllable (for example, un-der-stand). 739

Anapestic meter   A meter in which a majority of the feet are anapests. (But see *Triple meter.*) 739

Antagonist   Any force in a story that is in conflict with the *protagonist.* An antagonist may be another person, an aspect of the physical of social environment, or a destructive element in the protagonist's own nature. See *Conflict.* 42–43

Apostrophe   A figure of speech in which someone absent or dead or something nonhuman is addressed as if it were alive and present and could reply. 624

Approximate rime   (also known as *imperfect rime, near rime, slant rime,* or *oblique rime*) A term used for words in a riming pattern that have some kind of sound correspondence but are not perfect rimes. See *Rime.* Approximate rimes occur occasionally in patterns where most of the rimes are perfect (for example, push-rush in "Leda and the Swan," 687), and sometimes are used systematically in place of perfect rime (for example, "Mr. Z," 675). 724

Artistic unity   That condition of a successful literary work whereby all its elements work together for the achievement of its central purpose. In an artistically unified work nothing is included that is irrelevant to the central purpose, nothing is omitted that is essential to it, and the parts are arranged in the most effective order for the achievement of that purpose. 47, 238–39, 314–16

Aside   A brief speech in which a character turns from the person being addressed to speak directly to the audience; a dramatic device for letting the audience know what a character is really thinking or feeling as opposed to what the character pretends to think or feel. 910

Assonance   The repetition at close intervals of the vowel sounds of accented syllables or important words (for example, h*a*t-r*a*n-*a*mber, v*ei*n-m*a*de). 723

Aubade   A poem about dawn; a morning love song; or a poem about the parting of lovers at dawn. 870

Ballad   A fairly short narrative poem written in a songlike stanza form. Examples: "Ballad of Birmingham," 572; "Ettrick," 725; "Edward," 792; "La Belle Dame sans Merci," 864. Also see *Folk ballad.*

Blank verse   Unrimed iambic pentameter. 749

Cacophony   A harsh, discordant, unpleasant-sounding choice and arrangement of sounds. 762

Caesura   See *Grammatical pause* and *Rhetorical pause.* 736

Catharsis   A term used by Aristotle to describe some sort of emotional release experienced by the audience at the end of a successful tragedy. 1080–81, 1082

Chance   The occurrence of an event that has no apparent cause in antecedent events or in predisposition of character. 48

Character   (1) Any of the persons involved in a story or play. (2) The distinguishing moral qualities and personal traits of *a character.* 76–80

> *Developing* (or *dynamic*) *character*   A *character* who during the course of a story undergoes a permanent change in some distinguishing moral qualities or personal traits or outlook. 79–80
>
> *Flat character*   A *character* whose distinguishing moral qualities or personal traits are summed up in one or two traits. 78–79
>
> *Foil character*   A minor character whose situation or actions parallel those of a major character, and thus by contrast sets off or illuminates the major character; most often the contrast is complimentary to the major character.
>
> *Round character*   A *character* whose distinguishing moral qualities or personal traits are complex and many-sided. 78–79
>
> *Static character*   A character who is the same sort of person at the end of a story as at the beginning. 79–80
>
> *Stock character*   A stereotyped character: one whose nature is familiar to us from prototypes in previous literature. 79

Chorus   A group of actors speaking or chanting in unison, often while going through the steps of an elaborate formalized dance; a characteristic device of Greek drama for conveying communal or group emotion. 957–58, 1092

Climax   The turning point or high point in a plot. 48

Coincidence   The chance concurrence of two events having a peculiar correspondence between them. 48

Comedy   A type of drama, opposed to tragedy, having usually a happy ending, and emphasizing human limitation rather than human greatness. 1079–80, 1083–85

> *Scornful comedy*   A type of comedy whose main purpose is to expose and ridicule human folly, vanity, or hypocrisy. 1083–84
>
> *Romantic comedy*   A type of comedy whose likable and sensible main characters are placed in difficulties from which they are rescued at the end of the play, either attaining their ends or having their good fortunes restored. 1084–85

Commercial fiction   Fiction written to meet the taste of a wide popular audience and relying usually on tested formulas for satisfying such taste. 6

Conflict   A clash of actions, desires, ideas, or goals in the plot of a story or drama. Conflict may exist between the main character and some other person or persons; between the main character and some external force—physical nature, society, or "fate"; or between the main character and some destructive element in his or her own nature. 42–48

Connotation   What a word suggests beyond its basic definition; a word's overtones of meaning. 595

Consonance   The repetition at close intervals of the final consonant sounds of accented syllables or important words (for example, boo*k*-pla*qu*e-thic*k*er). 723

Continuous form   That form of a poem in which the lines follow each other without formal grouping, the only breaks being dictated by units of meaning. 777

Couplet   Two successive lines, usually in the same meter, linked by rime. 782

Dactyl   A metrical foot consisting of one accented syllable followed by two unaccented syllables (for example, mér-ri-ly). 739

Dactylic meter   A meter in which a majority of the feet are dactyls. (But see *Triple meter.*) 739

Denotation   The basic definition or dictionary meaning of a word. 595

Denouement   That portion of a plot that reveals the final outcome of its conflicts or the solution of its mysteries.

Deus ex machina ("god from the machine")   The resolution of a plot by use of a highly improbable chance or coincidence (so named from the practice of some Greek dramatists of having a god descend from heaven at the last possible minute—in the theater by means of a stage machine—to rescue the protagonist from an impossible situation).47–48

Developing character   See *Character.*

Didactic poetry   Poetry having as a primary purpose to teach or preach. 798

Dilemma   A situation in which a character must choose between two courses of action, both undesirable. 43–44

Dimeter   A metrical line containing two feet. 740

Direct presentation of character   That method of characterization in which the author, by exposition or analysis, tells us directly what a character is like, or has someone else in the story do so. 77–78

Double rime   A rime in which the repeated vowel is in the second last syllable of the words involved (for example, politely-rightly-spritely); one form of *feminine rime.* 724, 731

Dramatic convention   Any dramatic device which, though it departs from reality, is implicitly accepted by author and audience as a means of representing reality. 957–58

Dramatic exposition   The presentation through dialogue of information about events that occurred before the action of a play, or that occur offstage or between the staged actions; this may also refer to the presentation of information about individual characters' backgrounds or the general situation (political, historical, etc.) in which the action takes place.

Dramatic framework   The situation, whether actual or fictional, realistic or fanciful, in which an author places his or her characters in order to express the theme. 583–84

Dramatic irony   See *Irony.*

Dramatic point of view   See *Point of view.*

Dramatization   The presentation of character or of emotion through the speech or action of characters rather than through exposition, analysis, or description by the author. See *Indirect presentation of character.* 78, 240–41

Duple meter   A meter in which a majority of the feet contain two syllables. Iambic and trochaic are both duple meters. 739

Dynamic character   See *Character.*

Editorializing   Writing that departs from the narrative or dramatic mode and instructs the reader how to think or feel about the events of a story or the behavior of a character. 241

End rime   Rimes that occur at the ends of lines. 724

End-stopped line   A line that ends with a natural speech pause, usually marked by punctuation. 763

English (or *Shakespearean) sonnet*   A sonnet riming *ababcdcdefefgg.* Its content or structure ideally parallels the rime scheme, falling into three coordinate quatrains and a concluding couplet; but it is often structured, like the Italian sonnet, into octave and sestet, the principal break in thought coming at the end of the eighth line. 782, 783–84 (Exercise 1)

Escape literature   Literature written purely for entertainment, with little or no attempt to provide insights into the true nature of human life or behavior. 3–7

Euphony   A smooth, pleasant-sounding choice and arrangement of sounds. 762

Expected rhythm   The rhythmic expectation set up by the basic meter of a poem. 747

Extended figure (also known as *sustained figure*)   A figure of speech (usually metaphor, simile, personification, or apostrophe) sustained or developed through a considerable number of lines or through a whole poem. 629, 630

Extra-metrical syllables   In metrical verse, extra unaccented syllables added at the beginnings or endings of lines; these may be either a feature of the metrical form of a poem (example, "Epitaph on an Army of Mercenaries," even-numbered lines, 752) or occur as exceptions to the form (example, "Virtue," lines 9 and 11, 740). In iambic lines, they occur at the end of the line; in trochaic, at the beginning. 740, 744–45, 753 (Question 2)

Falling action   That segment of the plot that comes between the climax and the conclusion. 48

Fantasy   A kind of fiction that pictures creatures or events beyond the boundaries of known reality. 288–90

Farce   A type of drama related to comedy but emphasizing improbable situations, violent conflicts, physical action, and coarse wit over characterization or articulated plot. 1086

Feminine rime   A rime in which the repeated accented vowel is in either the second or third last syllable of the words involved (for example, ceiling-appealing; hurrying-scurrying). 724, 731

Figurative language   Language employing figures of speech; language that cannot be taken literally or only literally. 620

Figure of speech   Broadly, any way of saying something other than the ordinary way; more narrowly (and for the purposes of this book) a way of saying one thing and meaning another. 620

First person point of view   See *Point of view.*

Fixed form   A form of poem in which the length and pattern are prescribed by previous usage or tradition, such as *sonnet, limerick, villanelle, haiku,* and so on. 780

Flat character   See *Character.*

Foil character   See *Character.*

Folk ballad   A narrative poem designed to be sung, composed by an anonymous author, and transmitted orally for years or generations before being written down. It has usually undergone modification through the process of oral transmission. 762 (Question 1)

Foot   The basic unit used in the scansion or measurement of verse. A foot usually contains one accented syllable and one or two unaccented syllables (the *spondaic foot* is a modification of this principle). 738

Form   The external pattern or shape of a poem, describable without reference to its content, as *continuous form, stanzaic form, fixed form* (and their varieties), *free verse,* and *syllabic verse.* 777. See *Structure.*

Free verse   Nonmetrical poetry in which the basic rhythmic unit is the line, and natural speech rhythms replace metrical regularity as a formal device. 736

Grammatical pause (also known as *caesura*)   A pause introduced into the reading of a line by a mark of punctuation. 736, 748

Haiku   A three-line poem, Japanese in origin, narrowly conceived of as a fixed form in which the lines contain respectively five, seven, and five syllables (in American practice this requirement is frequently dispensed with). Haiku are generally concerned with some aspect of nature and present a single image or two juxtaposed images without comment, relying on suggestion rather than on explicit statement to communicate their meaning. 785

Happy ending   An ending in which events turn out well for a sympathetic protagonist. 45–46

Heard rhythm   The actual rhythm of a metrical poem as we hear it when it is read naturally. The heard rhythm mostly conforms to but sometimes departs from or modifies the *expected rhythm.* 747

Hexameter   A metrical line containing six feet. 740

Hyperbole   See *Overstatement.*

Iamb   A metrical foot consisting of one unaccented syllable followed by one accented syllable (for example, re-hearse). 739

Iambic meter   A meter in which the majority of feet are iambs. The most common English meter. 739

Imagery   The representation through language of sense experience. 707

Indeterminate ending   An ending in which the central problem or conflict is left unresolved. 46–47

Indirect presentation of character   That method of characterization in which the author shows us a character in action, compelling us to infer what the character is like from what is said or done by the character. 77–78

Internal rime   A rime in which one or both of the rime-words occurs *within* the line. 724

Interpretive literature   Literature that provides valid insights into the nature of human life or behavior. 3–7

Irony   A situation or a use of language involving some kind of incongruity or discrepancy. 187–90, 663–68 Three kinds of irony are distinguished in this book:

Verbal irony   A figure of speech in which what is said is the opposite of what is meant. 187–88, 663

Dramatic irony   An incongruity or discrepancy between what a
character says or thinks and what the reader knows to be true
(or between what a character perceives and what the author
intends the reader to perceive). 188–89, 665

Irony of situation   A situation in which there is an incongruity
between appearance and reality, or between expectation and
fulfillment, or between the actual situation and what would
seem appropriate. 189–90, 667

Italian (or *Petrarchan*) *sonnet*   A sonnet consisting of an octave riming *abbaabba* and of a sestet using any arrangement of two or
three additional rimes, such as *cdcdcd* or *cdecde*. 781, 783–84 (Exercise 1)

Limerick   A fixed form consisting of five lines of anapestic meter, the
first two trimeter, the next two dimeter, the last line trimeter, riming *aabba;* used exclusively for humorous or nonsense verse. 780

Limited omniscient point of view   See *Point of view.*

Masculine rime (also known as *single rime*)   A rime in which the repeated accented vowel sound is in the final syllable of the words
involved (for example, dance-pants, scald-recalled). 723, 731

Melodrama   A type of drama related to tragedy but featuring sensational incidents, emphasizing plot at the expense of characterization, relying on cruder conflicts (virtuous protagonist versus
villainous antagonist), and having a happy ending in which good
triumphs over evil. 1085–86

Metaphor   A figure of speech in which an implicit comparison is
made between two things essentially unlike. It may take one of
four forms: (1) that in which the literal term and the figurative
term are *both named;* (2) that in which the literal term is *named*
and the figurative term *implied;* (3) that in which the literal term is
implied and the figurative term *named;* (4) that in which *both* the
literal and the figurative terms are *implied.* 620–23

Meter   The regular patterns of accent that underlie metrical verse;
the measurable repetition of accented and unaccented syllables in
poetry. 737

Metonymy   A figure of speech in which some significant aspect or detail of an experience is used to represent the whole experience. In
this book the single term *metonymy* is used for what are sometimes distinguished as two separate figures: *synecdoche* (the use of
the part for the whole) and *metonymy* (the use of something
closely related for the thing actually meant). 625

Metrical variations   Departures from the basic metrical pattern (see *anacrusis, substitution, extra-metrical syllables*). 740

Monometer   A metrical line containing one foot. 740

Moral   A rule of conduct of maxim for living expressed or implied as the "point" of a literary work. Compare *Theme*. 662

Motivation   The incentives or goals that, in combination with the inherent natures of characters, cause them to behave as they do. In poor fiction actions may be unmotivated, insufficiently motivated, or implausibly motivated. 78

Mystery   An unusual set of circumstances for which the reader craves an explanation; used to create *Suspense*. 43–44

Narrator   In drama a character, found in some plays, who, speaking directly to the audience, introduces the action and provides a string of commentary between the dramatic scenes. The narrator may or may not be a major character in the action itself. 958

Nonrealistic drama   Drama that, in content, presentation, or both, departs markedly from fidelity to the outward appearances of life. 955–60

Objective point of view   See *Point of view.*

Octave   (1) An eight-line stanza. (2) The first eight lines of a sonnet, especially one structured in the manner of an Italian sonnet. 781

Omniscient point of view   See *Point of view.*

Onomatopoeia   The use of words that supposedly mimic their meaning in their sound (for example, boom, click, plop). 760

Onomatopoetic language   Language employing *onomatopoeia.*

Overstatement (or *hyperbole*)   A figure of speech in which exaggeration is used in the service of truth. 660

Paradox   A statement or situation containing apparently contradictory or incompatible elements. 659

Paradoxical situation   A situation containing apparently but not actually incompatible elements. The celebration of a fifth birthday anniversary by a twenty-year-old man is paradoxical but explainable if the man was born on February 29. The Christian doctrines that Christ was born of a virgin and is both God and man are, for a Christian believer, paradoxes (that is, apparently impossible but true). 659

Paradoxical statement (or *verbal paradox*)   A figure of speech in which an apparently self-contradictory statement is nevertheless found to be true. 659

Paraphrase   A restatement of the content of a poem designed to make its *prose meaning* as clear as possible. 581–83

Pentameter   A metrical line containing five feet. 740

Personification   A figure of speech in which human attributes are given to an animal, an object, or a concept. 623

Petrarchan sonnet   See *Italian sonnet*.

Phonetic intensive   A word whose sound, by an obscure process, to some degree suggests its meaning. As differentiated from *onomatopoetic* words, the meanings of phonetic intensives do not refer explicitly to sounds. 760

Playwright   A maker of plays. 909

Plot   The sequence of incidents or events of which a story is composed. 41–49

Plot manipulation   A situation in which an author gives the plot a twist or turn unjustified by preceding action or by the characters involved. 47

Poeticizing   Writing that uses immoderately heightened or distended language to sway the reader's feelings. 241

Point of view   The angle of vision from which a story is told. 148–54
The four basic points of view are as follows:

Omniscient point of view   The author tells the story using the third person, knowing all and free to tell us anything, including what the characters are thinking or feeling and why they act as they do. 149–50

Limited omniscient point of view   The author tells the story using the third person, but is limited to a complete knowledge of one character in the story and tells us only what that one character thinks, feels, sees, or hears. 150–51

First person point of view   The story is told by one of its characters, using the first person. 151–52

Objective (or *Dramatic*) *point of view*   The author tells the story using the third person, but is limited to reporting what the characters say or do; the author does not interpret their behavior or tell us their private thoughts or feelings. 152–53

Prose   Nonmetrical language; the opposite of *Verse*.

Prose meaning   That part of a poem's *total meaning* that can be separated out and expressed through paraphrase. 691

Prose poem   Usually a short composition having the intentions of poetry but written in prose rather than verse. 737

Protagonist   The central character in a story. 42

Quality fiction   Fiction that rejects formulas in an attempt to give a fresh interpretation of life. 6

Quatrain   (1) A four-line stanza. (2) A four-line division of a sonnet marked off by its rime scheme. 782

Realistic drama   Drama that attempts, in content and in presentation, to preserve the illusion of actual, everyday life. 955–60

Refrain   A repeated word, phrase, line, or group of lines, normally at some fixed position in a poem written in stanzaic form. 725, 779

Rhetorical pause (also known as *caesura*)   A natural pause, unmarked by punctuation, introduced into the reading of a line by its phrasing or syntax. 736, 748

Rhetorical poetry   Poetry using artificially eloquent language, that is, language too high-flown for its occasion and unfaithful to the full complexity of human experience. 798

Rhythm   Any wavelike recurrence of motion or sound. 735

Rime (or *rhyme*)   The repetition of the accented vowel sound and all succeeding sounds in important or importantly positioned words (for example, old-cold, vane-reign, court-report, order-recorder). The above definition applies to *perfect rime* and assumes that the accented vowel sounds involved are preceded by differing consonant sounds. If the preceding consonant sound is the same (for example, manse-romance, style-stile), or if there is no preceding consonant sound in either word (for example, aisle-isle, alter-altar), or if the same word is repeated in the riming position (for example, hill-hill), the words are called *identical rimes*. Both *perfect rimes* and *identical rimes* are to be distinguished from *approximate rimes*. 723

Rime scheme   Any fixed pattern of rimes characterizing a whole poem or its stanzas. 778–80

Rising action   That development of plot in a story that precedes and leads up to the climax. 48

Romantic comedy   See *Comedy.*

Round character   See *Character.*

Run-on line   A line which has no natural speech pause at its end, allowing the sense to flow uninterruptedly into the succeeding line. 736

Sarcasm   Bitter or cutting speech; speech intended by its speaker to give pain to the person addressed. 663

Satire   A kind of literature that ridicules human folly or vice with the purpose of bringing about reform or of keeping others from falling into similar folly or vice. 663

Scansion   The process of measuring verse, that is, of marking accented and unaccented syllables, dividing the lines into feet, identifying the metrical pattern, and noting significant variations from that pattern. 740

Scornful comedy   See *Comedy.*

Sentimentality   Unmerited or contrived tender feeling; that quality in a story that elicits or seeks to elicit tears through an oversimplification or falsification of reality. 798

Sentimental poetry   Poetry aimed primarily at stimulating the emotions rather than at communicating experience honestly and freshly. 797

Sestet   (1) A six-line stanza. (2) The last six lines of a sonnet structured on the Italian model. 781

Setting   The context in time and place in which the action of a story occurs.

Shakespearean sonnet   See *English sonnet.*

Simile   A figure of speech in which an explicit comparison is made between two things essentially unlike. The comparison is made explicit by the use of some such word or phrase as *like, as, than, similar to, resembles,* or *seems.* 620–23

Single rime   See *Masculine rime.*

Situational irony   See *Irony.*

Soliloquy   A speech in which a character, alone on the stage, addresses himself or herself; a soliloquy is a "thinking out loud," a dramatic means of letting an audience know a character's thoughts and feelings. 910

Sonnet   A fixed form of fourteen lines, normally iambic pentameter, with a rime scheme conforming to or approximating one of two main types—the *Italian* or the *English.* 781–82

Spondee   A metrical foot consisting of two syllables equally or almost equally accented (for example, trúe–blúe). 739

Stanza   A group of lines whose metrical pattern (and usually its rime scheme as well) is repeated throughout a poem. 740, 778

Stanzaic form   The form taken by a poem when it is written in a series of units having the same number of lines and usually other characteristics in common, such as metrical pattern or rime scheme. 778

Static character   See *Character.*

Stock character   See *Character.*

Stream of consciousness   Narrative that presents the private thoughts of a character without commentary or interpretation by the author. 181

Stress   In this book, the same as *Accent.* But see 735 (footnote).

Structure   The internal organization of a poem's content. See *Form.* 777

Substitution   In metrical verse, the replacement of the expected metrical foot by a different one (for example, a trochee occurring in an iambic line). 740

Surprise   An unexpected turn in the development of a plot. 45

Surprise ending   A completely unexpected revelation or turn of plot at the conclusion of a story or play. 45

Suspense   That quality in a story that makes the reader eager to discover what happens next and how it will end. 43–45

Sustained figure   See *Extended figure*.

Syllabic verse   Verse measured by the number of syllables rather than the number of feet per line. 755 Also see *Haiku*.

Symbol   Something that means *more* than what it is; an object, person, situation, or action that in addition to its literal meaning suggests other meanings as well, a figure of speech which may be read both literally and figuratively. 182–87, 639

Synecdoche   A figure of speech in which a part is used for the whole. In this book it is subsumed under the term *Metonymy*. 625

Terza rima   An interlocking rime scheme with the pattern *aba bcb cdc*, etc. 791

Tetrameter   A metrical line containing four feet. 739

Theme   The central idea of a literary work. 102–109, 581

Tone   The writer's or speaker's attitude toward the subject, the audience, or herself or himself; the emotional coloring, or emotional meaning, of a work. 704

Total meaning   The total experience communicated by a poem. It includes all those dimensions of experience by which a poem communicates—sensuous, emotional, imaginative, and intellectual—and it can be communicated in no other words than those of the poem itself. 691

Tragedy   A type of drama, opposed to comedy, which depicts the causally related events that lead to the downfall and suffering of the protagonist, a person of unusual moral or intellectual stature or outstanding abilities. 1079–83

Trimeter   A metrical line containing three feet. 739

Triple meter   A meter in which a majority of the feet contain three syllables. (Actually, if more than 25 percent of the feet in a poem are triple, its effect is more triple than duple, and it ought perhaps to be referred to as triple meter.) Anapestic and dactylic are both triple meters. 739

Trochaic meter   A meter in which the majority of feet are trochees. 739

Trochee   A metrical foot consisting of one accented syllable followed by one unaccented syllable (for example, bar-ter). 739

Understatement   A figure of speech that consists of saying less than one means, or of saying what one means with less force than the occasion warrants. 661

Unhappy ending   An ending that turns out unhappily for a sympathetic protagonist. 45–46

Verbal irony   See *Irony.*

Verse   Metrical language; the opposite of *Prose.*

Villanelle   See 784 (Exercise 2).

Copyrights and Acknowledgments

FICTION

SHERWOOD ANDERSON "I'm a Fool." Copyright 1922 by Dial Publishing Company, renewed 1949 by Eleanor Copenhaver Anderson. Reprinted by permission of Harold Ober Associates.

MARGARET ATWOOD "When It Happens" from *Dancing Girls and Other Stories.* Copyright © 1977, 1982 by O.W. Toad, Ltd. Reprinted by permission of Simon & Schuster and by Canadian Publishers, McClelland & Stewart, Inc.

TONI CADE BAMBARA "The Lesson" from *Gorilla, My Love.* Copyright © 1972 by Toni Cade Bambara. Reprinted by permission of Random House, Inc.

ANN BEATTIE "Janus" from *Where You'll Find Me.* Copyright © 1986 by Irony & Pity, Inc. Reprinted by permission of Simon & Schuster.

ALBERT CAMUS "The Guest" from *Exile and the Kingdom,* translated by Justin O'Brien. Copyright © 1957, 1958 by Alfred A. Knopf, Inc. Reprinted by permission of the publisher.

TRUMAN CAPOTE "A Christmas Memory" from *A Christmas Memory.* Copyright © 1956 by Truman Capote. Reprinted by permission of Random House, Inc.

BENJAMIN CAPPS "The Night Old Santa Claus Came" from *Tales of the Southwest.* Copyright © 1991 by Benjamin Capps. Reprinted by permission of Doubleday, a division of Bantam Doubleday Dell Publishing Group, Inc.

RAYMOND CARVER "The Father" from *Will You Please Be Quiet, Please?* Copyright © 1991 by Tess Gallagher. Reprinted by permission of International Creative Management, Inc.

JOHN CHEEVER "The Swimmer" from *The Stories of John Cheever.* Copyright © 1964 by John Cheever. Reprinted by permission of Alfred A. Knopf, Inc.

ANTON CHEKHOV "In Exile" from *Anton Chekhov: Selected Stories,* translated by Ann Dunnigan. Translation copyright © 1960 by Ann Dunnigan. Reprinted by permission of Dutton Signet, a division of Penguin Books USA Inc.

RICHARD CONNELL "The Most Dangerous Game." Copyright 1924, renewed 1962 by Louise Fox Connell. Reprinted by permission of Brandt & Brandt.

WILLIAM FAULKNER "Mule in the Yard" from *Collected Stories of William Faulkner.* Copyright © 1934 by Random House, Inc. and renewed 1962 by William Faulkner. "Spotted Horses" from *Uncollected Stories of William Faulkner,* edited by

POETRY

JANE KENYON "The Letter" from *Let Evening Come*. Copyright 1990 by Jane Kenyon. Reprinted by permission of Graywolf Press, Saint Paul, Minnesota.

GALWAY KINNELL "Blackberry Eating" from *Mortal Acts, Mortal Words* by Galway Kinnell. Copyright © 1980 by Galway Kinnell. Reprinted by permission of Houghton Mifflin Co. All rights reserved.

ETHERIDGE KNIGHT "The warden said to me" from *Poems from Prison*. Copyright © 1968 by Broadside Press. Reprinted by permission of Broadside Press.

MAXINE KUMIN "The Sound of Night" from *Halfway*. Copyright © 1961 by Maxine Kumin. Reprinted by permission of Curtis Brown Ltd.

PHILIP LARKIN "A Study of Reading Habits" from *The Whitsun Weddings* by Philip Larkin. "Aubade" from *Collected Poems*. Reprinted by permission of Faber and Faber Limited. "Church Going" and "Toads" by Philip Larkin from *The Less Deceived*. Reprinted by permission of The Marvell Press, England and Australia.

WALTER McDONALD "Life With Father" from *Counting Survivors* by Walter McDonald. Copyright © 1995 by Walter McDonald. Reprinted by permission of the University of Pittsburgh Press.

KATHARYN HOWD MACHAN "Leda's Sister and the Geese" from *Sometime the Cow Kick Your Head: Light Year '88/9* (Cleveland: Bits Press, 1988). Reprinted by permission of the author.

ARCHIBALD MacLEISH "Ars Poetica" from *Collected Poems 1917–1982* by Archibald MacLeish. Copyright © 1985 by The Estate of Archibald MacLeish. Reprinted by permission of Houghton Mifflin Co. All rights reserved.

NAOMI LONG MADGETT "Offspring" from *Pink Ladies in the Afternoon* (Detroit: Lotus, 1972, 1990). Reprinted by permission of the author.

CLEOPATRA MATHIS "Getting Out" from *Aerial View of Louisiana* by Cleopatra Mathis. Copyright 1980 by Sheep Meadow Press and Cleopatra Mathis. Reprinted by permission of the author and Sheep Meadow Press.

MARIANNE MOORE "Nevertheless" from *Collected Poems of Marianne Moore*. Copyright 1944 by Marianne Moore, renewed 1972 by Marianne Moore. "What Are Years?" from *Collected Poems of Marianne Moore*. Copyright 1941, renewed 1969 by Marianne Moore. Reprinted by permission of Simon & Schuster Inc.

OGDEN NASH "The Turtle" from *Verses from 1929 On* by Ogden Nash. Copyright 1940 by Ogden Nash. Reprinted by permission of Little, Brown and Company.

HOWARD NEMEROV "Grace to Be Said at the Supermarket" from *Trying Conclusions: New and Selected Poems*, 1991, University of Chicago Press. Reprinted by permission of the author.

NILA NORTHSUN "what gramma said about her grandpa" by nila northSun in *New Worlds of Literature* (Norton 1989). First published by The Greenfield Review Press. Reprinted by permission of The Greenfield Review Press.

SHARON OLDS "The Victims" from *The Dead and the Living* by Sharon Olds. Copyright © 1983 by Sharon Olds. Reprinted by permission of Alfred A. Knopf, Inc.

SIMON J. ORTIZ "Speaking" appeared in *New Worlds of Literature* (Norton 1989). Reprinted by permission of the author.

WILFRED OWEN "Dulce et Decorum Est" and "Anthem for Doomed Youth" from *The Collected Poems of Wilfred Owen*. Copyright © 1963 by Chatto & Windus, Ltd. Reprinted by permission of New Directions Publishing Corp.

GRACE PALEY   "The Sad Children's Song" from *Leaning Forward.* Copyright © by Grace Paley. Reprinted by permission of Tilbury House Publishers, Gardiner, Maine.

DOROTHY PARKER   "One Perfect Rose" from *The Portable Dorothy Parker* by Dorothy Parker. Introduction by Brendan Gill. Copyright © 1929, renewed © 1957 by Dorothy Parker. Reprinted by permission of Viking Penguin, a division of Penguin Books USA Inc.

LINDA PASTAN   "The Hat Lady" from *Heroes in Disguise* by Linda Pastan. Copyright © 1991 by Linda Pastan. "after minor surgery" from *PM/AM: New and Selected Poems.* Copyright © 1981 by Linda Pastan. "To a Daughter Leaving Home" and "The Imperfect Paradise" from *The Imperfect Paradise.* Copyright © 1988 by Linda Pastan. Reprinted by permission of W. W. Norton & Company, Inc.

LAURENCE PERRINE   Excerpts from *A Limerick's Always a Verse: 200 Original Limericks* by Laurence Perrine. Copyright ©1990 by Harcourt Brace & Company. Reprinted by permission of the publisher.

MARGE PIERCY   "A Work of Artifice" from *Circles on the Water* by Marge Piercy. Copyright © 1982 by Marge Piercy. Reprinted by permission of Alfred A. Knopf, Inc.

SYLVIA PLATH   "Metaphors" from *Crossing the Water* by Sylvia Plath. Copyright © 1960 by Ted Hughes. Copyright Renewed. "Mirror" from *Crossing the Water.* Copyright © 1963 by Ted Hughes. Originally appeared in *The New Yorker.* Reprinted by permission of HarperCollins Publishers, Inc. "Metaphors" also in *Collected Poems* by Sylvia Plath, edited with an introduction by Ted Hughes, with permission of Faber & Faber Limited, London. "Spinster" from *The Colossus and Other Poems* by Sylvia Plath. Copyright © 1961 by Sylvia Plath. Reprinted by permission of Alfred A. Knopf, Inc. and Faber & Faber Limited, London.

DEBORAH POPE   "Getting Through" from *Mortal World, Poems by Deborah Pope.* Copyright © 1995 by Deborah Pope. Reprinted by permission of Louisiana State University Press.

EZRA POUND   "The River-Merchant's Wife: A Letter" from *Personae* by Ezra Pound. Copyright © 1926 by Ezra Pound. Reprinted by permission of New Directions Publishing Corp.

DUDLEY RANDALL   "Blackberry Sweet" from *New Black Poetry,* edited by Clarence Major. Copyright 1969 by International Publishers Co., Inc. Reprinted by permission of International Publishers Co., Inc. "Ballad of Birmingham" and "To the Mercy Killers" from *After the Killing* (Chicago: Third World Press, 1973). Reprinted by permission of Third World Press.

JOHN CROWE RANSOM   "Bells for John Whiteside's Daughter" from *Selected Poems* by John Crowe Ransom. Copyright 1924 by Alfred A. Knopf, Inc. and renewed 1952 by John Crowe Ransom. Reprinted by permission of the publisher.

HENRY REED   "Naming of Parts" from *A Map of Verona* by Henry Reed. Reprinted by permission of Jonathan Cape Ltd.

ALASTAIR REID   "Curiosity" from *Passwords* by Alastair Reid. Copyright © 1959 by Alastair Reid; originally published in *The New Yorker.* Reprinted by permission of the author.

CARTER REVARD   "Discovery of the New World" appeared in *New Worlds of Literature,* ed. Jerome Beaty and J. Paul Hunter. Copyright © by Carter Revard. Reprinted by permission of the author.

ADRIENNE RICH   "Living in Sin" and "Aunt Jennifer's Tigers" from *Collected Early Poems: 1950–1970* by Adrienne Rich. Copyright © 1993 by Adrienne Rich.

DRAMA

Index of Authors, Titles, and First Lines

Author's names appear in capitals, titles of selections in italics, and first lines of poems in roman type. Numbers in bold face indicate the page of the selection, and roman numbers indicate discussion of the selection.